PERSUASIVE COMMUNICATION

This updated and expanded edition of *Persuasive Communication* offers a comprehensive introduction to persuasion and real-world decision making. Drawing on empirical research from social psychology, neuroscience, cognitive science, and behavioral economics, Young reveals the thought processes of many different audiences—from army officers to CEOs—to help students better understand why audiences make the decisions they make and how to influence them.

The book covers a broad range of communication techniques, richly illustrated with compelling examples, including resumes, speeches, and slide presentations, to help students recognize persuasive methods that do, and do not, work. A detailed analysis of the emotions and biases that go into decision making arms students with perceptive insights into human behavior and helps them apply this understanding with various decision-making aids. Students will learn how to impact potential employers, clients, and other audiences essential to their success.

This book will prove fascinating to many, and especially useful for students of persuasion, rhetoric, and business communication.

Richard O. Young is a Professor of Management Communication at Carnegie Mellon University, USA.

Richard Young's book is the most insightful work I've read on "audience" in years. Typically audience analysis is taught by considering demographic data, the nature of relationships, and content relevance. These types of analyses do not penetrate what it means to "get inside the heads" of those one needs to persuade. Richard's book tackles this challenge adroitly.

Priscilla S. Rogers, *University of Michigan, USA*

Persuasive Communication exemplifies Richard Young's intellectual commitments: it draws deeply from research in cognitive psychology, it reflects the importance that rhetorical scholars give to audience analysis, and it illustrates the real-world situations that communicators in business settings will face.

Davida Charney, *University of Texas, USA*

Richard Young's new edition of *Persuasive Communication* will be the standard reference work on the subject of rhetorical choices in decision-making processes for years to come. The empirical data from evidence-based research, including original cognitive models of rational, intuitive, and emotional decision making give this second edition added value to students and practitioners in the field of Managerial Communication. It will be our required reference in all our Managerial Communication courses.

Frank Jaster, *Tulane University, USA*

Richard O. Young has written the go-to resource for anyone interested in audience-centered communication. In the revised edition, Young pulls together diverse threads of research and provides numerous real-world examples. Ultimately, this book will help students as well as seasoned professionals achieve their communication objectives with business audiences.

Ronald J. Placone, *Carnegie Mellon University, USA*

PERSUASIVE COMMUNICATION

How Audiences Decide

Second Edition

Richard O. Young

Routledge
Taylor & Francis Group

NEW YORK AND LONDON

Second edition published 2017
by Routledge
711 Third Avenue, New York, NY 10017

and by Routledge
2 Park Square, Milton Park, Abingdon, Oxon OX14 4RN

Routledge is an imprint of the Taylor & Francis Group, an informa business

First edition published by Routledge 2011

Library of Congress Cataloging in Publication Data
Names: Young, Richard O. author.
Title: Persuasive communication : how audiences decide / Richard Young.
Other titles: How audiences decide
Description: 2nd edition. | New York, NY ; Milton Park, Abingdon, Oxon : Routledge, 2016. | Previously published in 2011 under title: How audiences decide. | Includes bibliographical references and indexes.
Identifiers: LCCN 2016019727 | ISBN 9781138920361 (hbk) | ISBN 9781138920378 (pbk) | ISBN 9781315687117 (ebk)
Subjects: LCSH: Business communication—Psychological aspects.
Classification: LCC HF5718 .Y686 2016 | DDC 658.4/5—dc23
LC record available at https://lccn.loc.gov/2016019727

ISBN: 978-1-138-92036-1 (hbk)
ISBN: 978-1-138-92037-8 (pbk)
ISBN: 978-1-315-68711-7 (ebk)

Typeset in Bembo
by Apex CoVantage, LLC

Printed and bound by CPI Group (UK) Ltd, Croydon, CR0 4YY

CONTENTS

DETAILED CONTENTS

PART III
Understanding Emotional Decision Making

ACKNOWLEDGMENTS

Persuasive Communication: How Audiences Decide could not have been written without Professor Herbert Simon's groundbreaking work in human cognition or without the aid and support of my family, friends, colleagues, students, and publisher. Among the friends and colleagues who generously came to my aid, I am particularly grateful to professors Evelyn Pierce, Patricia Carpenter, Priscilla Rogers, and Sandra Collins who read and commented on early drafts of the book and who encouraged me to keep working on it. For this second edition, I also owe a tremendous debt of gratitude to professors John R. Hayes, John R. Anderson, Ron Placone, David Kaufer, Davida Charney, Julia Deems, Frank Jaster, Lili Powell, and Judy Tisdale as well as to Dr. Karen Schriver, Samuel Perl, Robert Floodeen, Jennifer Cowley, and Thomas G. Young for the many ways they supported my quest to better understand audience decision making. I am especially indebted to Dr. Cliff Parsons for his friendship and the substantive contributions he made to this book.

Perhaps my best teachers over the last 30 years have been the MBA students at the Tepper School of Business at Carnegie Mellon. I greatly appreciate all those students who collected think-aloud comments of audience members, who tested, wrote, and revised business presentations and documents, and who shared their work-related stories with me. The think-aloud comments Kirk Botula collected so many years ago opened my eyes to the significance of audience decision-making expertise. This volume also owes a special debt to Aaron Oh and his teammates, Andrew Bennett and his teammates, Kurt Ernst, Alan Michaels, and Matt Lysaught and their teammates, to Vero Anderson, Raphael Matarazzo, and Louis Zaretsky and their teammates, to Eric Schwalm, Stephen Kraus, Kalpesh Dadbhawala, Dominic Joseph, Laurie Barkman, Pradeep U. N., William Pomper, Sung-Ju Pak, Kirk Pond, Jack Deem, and Noriko Sasaki, and to several other wonderful former students whose names now escape me.

Rosemarie Lang, Carol Salerno, Phil Conley, and my copy editor Lana Arndt all put in many long hours preparing the manuscript of the second edition for publication. And thanks to my publisher Sharon Golan and her colleagues Erin Arata, Olivia Hatt, and Autumn Spalding, the manuscript made its way from acquisition to publication without a hitch.

Barbara J. O'Brien Young helped me every step of the way, listening patiently to me explain each new problem I encountered and rejoicing with me in each new insight. To her I am forever grateful.

INTRODUCTION

It's a commonly held belief that knowing your audience—your readers, listeners, viewers, and conversational partners—is the key to persuasive communication. But what does "knowing your audience" really mean? Does it mean knowing your audience's name, age, gender, and socioeconomic status?

This book shows that if you want to be persuasive the most important thing you need to know about your audience is how your audience makes decisions. And it demonstrates with numerous examples and research findings that when experienced and otherwise highly skilled professionals—CEOs, medical doctors, magazine publishers—fail to grasp how their audiences make decisions they also fail to persuade them.

Part I encompasses the first four chapters of the book and describes how audiences make rational decisions. Chapter 1 explains what audiences already know about making rational decisions. Whether you ask your audience to try out a new product, vote for a political candidate, approve a loan, take a prescribed medicine, convict a felon, acquire a new firm, or reply to an ad in the personal columns, many members of your audience will already know what type of information they need in order to make a good decision. What's more, they will expect you to provide that information to them.

Chapter 2 describes 13 major types of decisions that professionals from a wide range of fields routinely ask their audiences to make and outlines the audience's information requirements for each decision type. Chapter 3 presents a simple model of audience decision making and explains why you need to attend to each of the six cognitive processes in it. Chapter 4 reviews communication techniques that help make rational decision making easy for audiences and demonstrates that different techniques enable different cognitive processes to operate more efficiently.

If audiences were entirely logical, an understanding of how they make rational decisions would suffice. But audiences base their decisions on intuitions and emotions as well as sound reasoning. Part II consists of Chapters 5 and 6 and describes how audiences make intuitive decisions, decisions based on their subjective feelings. Chapter 5 shows that the same communication techniques that make audience decision making easy also make your messages to them more intuitively appealing. Chapter 6 explains how your audience's subjective feelings about you as a person, as opposed to the information you communicate to them, influence and bias their decisions.

Part III consists of the final chapter of the book and describes the role of emotions in audience decision making. It demonstrates that when you are able to evoke the values of your audience, their decision-making process becomes truncated and their emotions come to dominate the decisions they make. Moreover, it shows that different emotions affect audience decisions in different ways. Taken together, the three parts of the book give a complete picture of audiences as decision makers. The three parts explain how audiences make decisions with their head, gut, and heart, based on appeals to what the ancient Greeks termed *logos, ethos,* and *pathos.*

Most of the chapters of the book include *think-aloud protocols* of real audience members using real documents to make decisions. Think-aloud protocols are verbatim transcripts of people thinking aloud as they make decisions or solve problems. Think-aloud protocols have been used to investigate decision making in an ever-increasing number of areas including chess,[1] writing,[2] policy-making,[3] business,[4] law,[5] and most recently, cyber security.[6]

In this book, think-aloud protocols provide a unique window on audience decision making. They reveal the information an audience considers to be important when making a particular decision, as well as the information it considers to be irrelevant, the information it has difficulty comprehending, and much more. Exposure to think-aloud protocols of audiences has been shown to improve communication skills. College students given think-aloud protocols of audiences reading one set of documents made dramatic gains in their ability to predict problems that audiences would have with another set of documents of the same genre.[7]

The book as a whole draws on a vast research literature and summarizes relevant theories and findings from the fields of social cognition, leadership, consumer behavior, decision science, behavioral economics, psycholinguistics, sociolinguistics, affective science, cognitive science, and neuroscience. It delves into the hearts and minds of a wide array of audiences: from Wall Street analysts to viewers of the evening news, from army officers to hospital patients, from venture capitalists to grocery shoppers, from CEOs to college admissions officers, from corporate recruiters to mock jurors. It surveys a broad range of communication techniques—including those concerning speaking and writing, interviews and group meetings, leading and critical thinking, content and style, verbal and nonverbal behaviors, the use of charts and images, the construction of rational arguments and emotional appeals—and examines the empirical evidence supporting each of them.

If you agree that the key to persuasive communication is knowing your audience, if you are looking for techniques to influence the decisions your audiences make, and if you want a scientific understanding of why those techniques work, then *Persuasive Communication: How Audiences Decide* is the introduction to persuasive communication for you.

Notes

1 e.g., de Groot, A. D. (1965). *Thought and choice in chess.* The Hague, Netherlands: Mouton.
2 e.g., Flower, L. S., & Hayes, J. R. (1978). The dynamics of composing: Making plans and juggling constraints. In L. Gregg & I. Steinberg (Eds.), *Cognitive processes in writing* (pp. 31–50). Hillsdale, NJ: Lawrence Erlbaum Associates.
3 e.g., Voss, J. F., Greene, T. R., Post, T. A., & Penner, B. C. (1983). Problem solving skill in the social sciences. In G. H. Bower (Ed.), *The psychology of learning and motivation: Advances in research theory* (Vol. 17, pp. 165–213). New York: Academic Press.
4 e.g., Hall, J., & Hofer, C. W. (1993). Venture capitalists' decision criteria in new venture evaluation. *Journal of Business Venturing, 8*(1), 25–42.
5 e.g., Wright, D. B., & Hall, M. (2007). How a "reasonable doubt" instruction affects decisions of guilt. *Basic and Applied Social Psychology, 29*(1), 91–98.
6 e.g., Perl, S., & Young, R. O. (2015, June). *A cognitive study of incident handling expertise.* Presented at the Annual Forum of Incident Response and Security Teams (FIRST) Conference, Berlin, Germany.
7 e.g., Schriver, K. A. (1992). Teaching writers to anticipate readers' needs: A classroom-evaluated pedagogy. *Written Communication, 9*(2), 179–208.

PART I

Understanding Rational Decision Making

1

AUDIENCE DECISION-MAKING EXPERTISE

In June 2008, a sourcing manager for a large networking company was asked to find a new subcontractor. The subcontractor had to be capable of designing an essential hardware component for one of the firm's multimillion-dollar networking projects. Although the firm had never contracted out the design of this component before, the sourcing manager soon found three interested design firms who appeared to be good candidates for the job.

In his initial discussions with the salespeople from each design firm via email or phone, the sourcing manager explained the goals of the project and gave them the information they would need to evaluate the opportunity they were being offered, such as the forecasted demand, the timeline expectations, and the technical performance requirements. In order to expedite his selection process, the sourcing manager also sent each sales team the following questions to be answered in a crisp one-hour meeting:

- How would you describe your company?
- How complex were your past projects, and when were they completed?
- How long did it take you to complete the projects?
- Were they completed on schedule?
- What kind of issues came up, and how did you overcome them?
- What do you see as the biggest risks, and how would you mitigate them?

The VP of Sales for the first design firm and his team of technical experts spent most of their hour-long meeting presenting an overview of their company. The sourcing manager reiterated his need to get answers to the rest of his questions. So the VP requested another meeting to answer them. The manager told the VP that he did not have time for another meeting. Later, when the VP sent emails and left voicemails asking for another meeting, the sourcing manager politely declined once again.

The salespeople who represented the second design firm were equally disappointing. They spent about half their allotted time giving an overview of their company and then asked the sourcing manager to supply more details about his firm's project. The sourcing manager declined to tell them more and spent the remainder of the hour re-asking his initial questions.

After the meeting, he wondered whether he wanted to work with a company that needed him to repeat his criteria for choosing a subcontractor.

The sales team for the third design firm was different. They addressed every one of the sourcing manager's questions during their one-hour meeting with him. They willingly disclosed the issues that had come up in similar projects just as the manager had requested, giving them added credibility in the manager's eyes. In addition, the third sales team asked relevant questions about the firm's objective for pursuing this particular networking project, the firm's required pricing, and the features they desired.

It should come as no surprise that the sourcing manager recommended the third design firm to his upper management. The favorable impression made by that firm's sales team led to two significant contracts for the design firm totaling $15 million per year or $80 million over the lifetime of the project.

Although most audiences do not spell out their information requirements as clearly as the sourcing manager did for the three sales teams who presented to him, we can still learn several lessons from this true story. One of the most important lessons we can learn is that experienced audiences, like the sourcing manager, already know what information they need from other professionals in order to make the types of decisions they make routinely. What's more, experienced audiences may judge the quality of a recommendation or firm on the basis of how thoroughly, efficiently, and honestly business people and other professionals address their information needs. Chapter 1 amplifies these lessons. It describes the nature of audience expertise in decision making and what professionals in many fields need to know about it in order to be persuasive.

The audiences of professionals include all the people who read the documents professionals write, attend the presentations professionals give, and listen to what professionals have to say either in person or on the phone. Some important audiences of business executives are board members, stockholders, customers, employees, bankers, suppliers, distributors, and Wall Street analysts. Some important audiences of physicians are patients, residents, nurses, pharmacists, hospital administrators, health insurance companies, state medical boards, and government agencies. A few of the important audiences of judges are litigants, attorneys, legal academics, other judges, ideological groups, and think tanks.[1]

Audiences use the documents, presentations, and other information that professionals convey to make informed decisions. Board members use executives' strategic plans to decide whether to allow management to pursue a new strategic direction. Consumers use manufacturers' advertisements, packaging, product brochures, and warranties to decide whether to purchase a product. Bankers use entrepreneurs' proposals for credit lines to decide whether to extend credit. Undecided voters use politicians' campaign speeches to decide whether to vote for a particular candidate. Even U.S. Army personnel do not blindly obey the orders of superior officers but use their directives to make decisions, decisions that might surprise the officers who issued the orders.[2] Research finds that 78% to 85% of all the reading employees do at work is for the purpose of making decisions and taking immediate action. In contrast, only 15% of the reading students do is for that purpose—students read primarily to learn and to recall later.[3]

Sometimes audience members make decisions as individuals, and at other times they make decisions as a group, usually after much discussion and debate. For example, jurors decide as a group whether defendants are guilty or innocent, school board members decide as a group which curricula can be taught in local schools, legislators decide as a group which bills to pass into law, and faculty selection committee members decide as a group which candidates to hire. Most strategic business decisions are made by groups, as opposed to individuals.[4] In all these cases, group members interact with each other, playing the roles of both communicators and audience members. As communicators, group members make arguments to the other group members for or against alternative proposals. As audience members, group members help decide which of the proposals made to the group is best.

Understanding audiences as decision makers differs dramatically from viewing them as passive receivers or decoders of information, the conventional view unintentionally inspired by the field of information theory.[5] Understanding that many audience members are expert at making the decisions professionals want them to make differs even more profoundly from the notion that audiences are empty cups waiting to be filled with the communicator's knowledge about a topic.

Audiences gain decision-making expertise as they make a particular type of decision repeatedly. For example, consumers, a primary audience of computer manufacturers, develop expertise that helps them choose the best computer after buying and using several different computers. Board members, a primary audience of business executives, develop expertise that helps them decide which new management proposal merits their approval by attending numerous board meetings. Voters, a primary audience of politicians, develop expertise that helps them decide which political candidate most deserves their vote by reading the news and voting regularly.

With time and experience many audience members learn how to make good decisions. More specifically, they learn what information to look for in a document or presentation and what questions to pose in meetings and conversations. Of course, audiences will sometimes lack the expertise they need to make some decisions. In these cases, audience members are dependent upon others to tell them what information they need to consider in order to ensure their decisions are well informed.

This chapter shows that professionals who understand audience decision-making expertise are in a good position to give novice or inexperienced audiences the information they need to make informed decisions. The before and after examples of documents in this chapter and others show that professionals who understand audience decision-making expertise are also in a good position to select and deliver the information expert audiences will find most relevant and persuasive.

Decision Criteria of Expert Audiences

Decision Criteria: The Audience's Mental Checklist of Questions

As audience members become expert at making a particular type of decision, they develop a set of *decision criteria*. Top management teams use decision criteria, both quantitative and qualitative, to make corporate financing decisions.[6] Experienced consumers typically decide whether to purchase products based on decision criteria regarding the product's price, quality, reliability, and warranty. Similarly, experienced board members decide whether to approve management's plans based on decision criteria regarding the plan's projected profitability, strategy, action items, and proposed source of financing. Even members of the public use decision criteria regarding the economy, international relations, and the environment when asked to rate U.S. presidents.[7] As the previous examples illustrate, different types of decisions require audiences to use different decision criteria. A job applicant does not use the same decision criteria to decide whether to accept a new job that a banker uses to decide whether to call an overdue loan.

Decision criteria for any particular type of decision can be thought of as a mental checklist of questions expert audience members want answers to before they make that decision.[8] For example, experienced used car buyers want answers to questions such as "What is the car's make, model, and year?" "What is its mileage?" "What condition is the car in?" "What is the car's maintenance history?" "What accessories are included?" and "What is the asking price?" before they are willing to purchase a used car. Decision criteria such as these guide the information search of expert audience members for the relatively small amounts of specific information upon which their decisions will be based.[9]

Because expert audiences possess decision criteria, they notice when important information about any option or alternative they are considering is missing.[10] If important information about an alternative is not available, they tend to discount the value of that alternative or reject it outright.[11] For example, if an experienced used car buyer is unable to determine the mileage on a particular used car, it is unlikely she will consider purchasing it.

Because expert audiences know exactly what type of information they are looking for, they may not read a document from start to finish but may jump around in it in order to more rapidly acquire the information each decision criterion demands.[12] For example, expert business appraisers jump around in the documents they are given to more quickly locate the information they need to evaluate the worth of a company.[13] During a presentation, expert audience members may ask questions or interrupt a presenter to more quickly gain the information they require.[14]

As soon as they find the answers to their decision criteria or mental checklist of questions, expert audience members stop searching and make their decisions.[15] Although experts in corporate real estate disposition ask many short-answer questions about each property under consideration, they make their decision to dispose of a property as soon as they acquire the answers to all of their questions.[16]

The Number of Decision Criteria in Audience Decisions

Audiences' mental checklists of decision criteria do not appear to be long or complex. Even when they are given large amounts of relevant information, expert audiences rarely use more than a few criteria to make their decisions.[17]

For most decisions, expert audiences seem to seek answers to only six or seven basic questions.[18] For example, expert investors selecting stocks use six "general evaluative factor categories," or decision criteria, that include both accounting and nonaccounting information.[19] CFOs and VPs of Development use six basic criteria, or "lines of reasoning," to make acquisition decisions as they read company descriptions: the strategic fit of the candidate with the acquirer, the competitive environment of the candidate, the management expertise of the candidate, the financial condition of the candidate and terms of the deal, the operational capabilities of the candidate, and the synergies between the candidate and the acquirer.[20] The overwhelming majority (94%) of comments expert venture capitalists make when screening business plans focus on only seven factors other than the way the plan is presented: the market, the product, the management, the company, the financials, the board of directors, and the terms of the deal.[21]

Other expert audiences also rely on a finite list of criteria to make decisions. A study of the selection criteria of more than 400 top executives finds they have 6.7 requirements on average that they look for in candidates for top leadership positions. Listed in order the top seven requirements are the following: specific functional background, managerial skills, interpersonal skills, communication skills, technical knowledge, leadership skills, and team skills.[22] U.S. Army officers use a core set of six criteria to evaluate noncommissioned officers: initiative, responsibility, organizational skills, technical proficiency, assertive leadership skills, and supportive leadership skills.[23]

A study comparing the commercial lending decisions of 10 real estate banking lenders and 10 private banking lenders finds that on average, the real estate lenders spend more than 30 seconds on just seven pieces of information—the guarantor's income statement, the guarantor's balance sheet, the project's rent roll, the project's profit/loss statement, the market demographics, the project's pro forma profit/loss statement, and the market rents. Private banking lenders, on the other hand, spend more than 30 seconds on only two pieces of information—the guarantor's income statement and balance sheet. Both groups of lenders use other available pieces of information much less if at all.[24]

Consumers also use a limited number of decision criteria when deciding to purchase goods and services. Although the typical American consumer is exposed to 300 advertisements per day,[25] consumers consider only a small proportion of the available information relevant to the products and services they buy.[26] Even when they are presented with a great deal of product information, consumers usually rely upon a common, small set of criteria to make their decisions.[27]

Under time constraints audiences may use even fewer criteria when making a decision. For example, most consumers do not use information about energy efficiency when under time pressure to choose a new refrigerator even though the information is prominently displayed on each new refrigerator's door.[28] Given their busy schedules, managers sometimes opt to base their business decisions on a single financial criterion such as a discounted cash flow or cost-based calculation. However, considering multiple criteria, both financial and nonfinancial, tends to produce superior results even for relatively routine business decisions such as supplier selection and evaluation.[29]

Metrics and Tests That Operationalize Decision Criteria

Although audiences seem to seek answers to only six or seven basic questions, each question may subsume several related or follow-up questions that operationalize or better define it. Audiences operationalize and elaborate on their decision criteria via *metrics* and *tests*. Metrics and tests indicate more specifically what audience members are looking for when they ask a decision-making question.

Metrics are quantitative in nature and provide results that can be measured and compared with other quantitative data. For example, many car buyers make their purchasing decision in part on the basis of the car's reliability. Metrics indicating the reliability of the various models under consideration might include the average number of days in the shop per year, the average number of repairs per year, and the average cost of repairs per year. Metrics indicating a firm's profitability might include its net income for the year, its return on equity, its return on assets, and its economic value added, to name a few. Metrics that sales force managers use to measure the productivity of their salespeople include sales volume, number of orders, profitability of sales, and the percentage of sales quotas attained.[30]

Unlike metrics, tests are qualitative in nature. For example, to test if management has recommended a reasonable competitive strategy, board members may try to determine if the strategy builds on the firm's core competency, offers a distinct competitive advantage, and matches the management's corporate objectives.

Metrics and tests are especially helpful for making decisions about difficult-to-describe sensory attributes such as the feel of a shirt, the comfort of a mattress, the fragrance of a perfume, the taste of a wine, or the sound quality of a stereo. Lacking the appropriate metrics and tests, consumers of products with attributes like these are more prone to trust biased product advertising than their own experience trying out the products.[31] However, if consumers are provided with metrics and tests that allow them to rate the sensory attributes of the products themselves, they make better decisions. In a study that provided novice consumers of stereos with one metric and two tests of a stereo's sound quality (the number of instruments audible, the sound's clarity, and the sound's "full-bodyness"), the consumers not only discounted misleading marketing information, they placed more weight on their own ratings of the stereos' sound quality when making their purchasing decisions. Ultimately, these consumers purchased higher quality stereos than they would have purchased otherwise.[32]

The Similarity of Decision Criteria Among Audience Members

What makes knowing an audience's decision criteria so useful to professionals is the fact that different expert audience members tend to use the same decision criteria to make similar types of decisions. Knowing how expert audiences make decisions would not be very useful if every individual audience member used different criteria when making the same type of decision. But studies of experienced audience members making decisions show they are highly constrained by the type of decision they make. For example, experienced investors of any age, nationality, political party, gender, education level, or income bracket all use the same basic criteria to evaluate a business plan before writing the entrepreneur a check.[33] If they forget to evaluate the nature of the new business, the management team's experience, the projected sales, ROI, and so on, then they know from experience that they are very likely to lose their money. And this is one thing few investors care to do! Similarly, studies of jurors making decisions find that most demographic variables—including the juror's gender, age, intelligence, marital status, race, and occupation—rarely have any significant impact on the verdicts they hand down.[34]

The commonality of decision criteria among experts in a field is a robust research finding. Public school administrators use similar decision criteria to make budget decisions.[35] Computer experts use similar decision criteria and give each criterion similar weight when selecting hardware and software products.[36] Middle school principals use similar criteria when hiring new teachers and, surprisingly, are not influenced by the unique characteristics of their schools.[37] Organizational buyers in the United States and Germany use the same five criteria when choosing domestic suppliers: quality, price, firm characteristics, vendor reputation/past business, and vendor attitude.[38] Finance directors from both U.S. and UK multinational corporations making overseas financing decisions use similar decision criteria and give each criterion similar weight.[39] Consumers use similar decision criteria for deciding among brands of exercise equipment in different product categories and use them consistently.[40] Consumers also use similar decision criteria, in this case similar product attributes, when choosing among brands within other product classes.[41]

Experts in other fields also use similar criteria to make similar decisions. For example, pharmacists use the same four to six criteria when deciding whether to counsel a patient on a prescription: indication, the patient's age, drug interactions, adverse reactions, new prescription versus refill, and the number of medications currently being taken.[42] U.S. apparel manufacturers use virtually identical criteria when they decide whether to outsource production to other countries. The criteria they most commonly use include price, quality, technology access, and lead time, as well as criteria related to the specific sourcing country, such as absence of labor disputes, proximity to the market, and cultural similarity.[43] Financial analysts employed by different financial institutions use similar types and amounts of information to assess a company's earning power.[44] As one researcher noted, "[The analysts from different banks] seemed to be discussing many of the same issues and offering similar insights to one another."[45] And as a review of the literature on venture capitalists' decision making reports, among the three most complete studies reviewed[46] "the most important area of consensus is the identity of the venture capitalists' criteria."[47]

Audience Expectations Based on Decision Criteria

Expert audiences expect professionals to address their decision criteria and are more likely to be persuaded by those who do. Jurors are more likely to be persuaded by fellow jurors whose arguments address their verdict criteria than by jurors who base their arguments on other grounds.[48] Both corporate recruiters and line managers rate job applicants' résumés more highly when the résumés address the criteria they have determined to be critical for success on the job.[49] Moreover, recruiters rate job applicants more highly when the applicants come to the job interview prepared to address their decision criteria.[50] Unfortunately, job applicants are usually prepared to address only one-third to one-half of the decision criteria recruiters use to evaluate them.[51]

Expert audiences in other fields also expect professionals to address their decision criteria. Buyers are more likely to purchase products from salespeople who accurately ascertain and explain the product attributes, or decision criteria, that are important to them.[52] Like the sourcing manager in the story at the beginning of this chapter, purchasing agents rate salespeople's effectiveness more highly when salespeople accurately assess their purchasing criteria.[53] Surprisingly, a salesperson's level of motivation has a negative relationship to purchasing agents' evaluations of their effectiveness. Other attributes of salespeople such as their personality traits, job tenure, and selling experience have little if any effect on their sales performance.[54]

Wall Street analysts expect firms to disclose specific financial and nonfinancial information pertaining to their decision criteria and may penalize firms that fail to do so. As one analyst notes, "Analysts are always skeptical that if you're not giving out the information perhaps it's because you overpaid for something or there's some other reason." Another analyst observed that when firms "didn't provide us with a lot of information, it was normally a sign that they didn't have a lot of good information themselves."[55]

Effective "issue selling," or focusing a group's attention on needed change within an organization, depends on one group's ability to address another group's decision criteria. A case study of issue selling in a large chip manufacturing firm tells the story of a group composed of only 11 members that was tasked with reducing the emissions of the firm's manufacturing processes. Initially, the small group was unsuccessful at convincing the firm's 1,500-person technology group to make the needed changes. The small group finally convinced their audience to make the necessary changes when they stopped enumerating the environmental benefits of lowering emissions and addressed the larger group's technical decision criteria for changing manufacturing processes instead.[56]

One important function of management consultants is to inform clients of the decision criteria of the clients' expert audiences. A study comparing an expert management consultant to a freshly minted MBA who had just been hired by a top consulting firm asked both the expert and novice consultants to analyze two actual business plans and to give advice to the entrepreneurs who wrote them. The expert consultant based his advice on the decision criteria of venture capitalists—entrepreneurs often send their business plans to venture capitalists in hopes of raising money for their new businesses. The expert consultant first explained to the entrepreneur the problems a venture capitalist would have with her current plan. He then helped her discover how she could change her business plan to satisfy the venture capitalist's decision criteria. For example, she could find a partner who possessed the business experience she lacked. In contrast, the new MBA relied on his function area or textbook knowledge to advise his client and never mentioned venture capitalists or their decision criteria. For the expert consultant the client's business problem was identical to her rhetorical problem—how to satisfy a venture capitalist's decision criteria. For the new MBA, the client's business problems were independent of the audience. From the new MBA's perspective, his client simply needed to plan his new business "correctly."[57]

Some expert audience members put an extremely high premium on getting information that addresses their decision criteria. A study of the responses of business executives to two business communication students' memos actually found an inverse relationship between the students' level of knowledge of and skill in business communication and the executives' ratings of the two students' memos. To the researcher's surprise, the executives rated the memo composed by the high-knowledge, highly skilled business communication student as ineffective. And despite the less skilled student's poor spelling, incorrect grammar, tortured syntax, lack of knowledge about business genres, and inability to defend a point of view, the executives rated his memo as highly effective. Why? As one of the executives explained, the strength of the less skilled student's memo was that it included "sufficient information for decision making."[58]

Expert audiences also expect professionals to avoid presenting information that does not address their decision criteria. Purchasing agents react negatively to sales presentations that include information irrelevant to their decision criteria. Purchasing agents have especially negative reactions to salespeople who begin their initial sales calls with in-depth descriptions of the selling firm's organization chart.[59] Similarly, apartment seekers are more persuaded by recommendations that exclude features or benefits that are irrelevant to their decision criteria than by recommendations that include such features.[60] A think-aloud study of venture capitalists reading business plans finds "the thrust of the [venture capitalists'] protocol comments was that venture proposals should be short documents that provide the major pieces of information the venture capitalist needs to make a decision."[61]

It's important for professionals to remember that the criteria they use to make decisions probably differ from the criteria their audiences use. For example, physicians rarely use the same decision criteria to decide among possible treatments that their patients use.[62] Professionals also need to remember that arguments based on their own criteria will probably fail to persuade their audiences. Research shows that health guidelines for patients are less effective than they could be because they are usually written from a physician's perspective and tend to downplay the criteria most important to patients.[63]

Techniques for Discovering and Using Audience Decision Criteria

Two of the more commonly used techniques for teasing out experts' decision criteria and their weights, or degree of importance, are Multi-Attribute Utility Analysis[64] and the Analytical Hierarchy Process.[65] Both techniques first elicit a set of decision criteria from the experts and then determine the weights experts assign them. Decisions computed by the resulting models tend to agree with experts' actual decisions with an average convergent validity ranging from 0.70 to 0.95.[66] Not surprisingly, the models generated by the two techniques tend to yield similar decisions.[67]

Persuasive documents based on the models generated by these techniques have been empirically tested by real audience members. One study used multi-attribute utility models of renters' decision criteria to automatically generate arguments for choosing specific apartments. The arguments generated successfully persuaded real renters to choose the apartment the model recommended.[68] Another study used a multi-attribute utility model of several hundred hospital patients' decision criteria to write a brochure that persuaded many to get flu shots. Of those patients who received the model-based brochure, 64% obtained flu shots compared to only 34% of the control group who received a brochure written, as is typically done, without the benefit of the model. A second model-based brochure improved patient compliance rates to Pap smear procedures by approximately 15% over rates achieved with conventionally produced brochures.[69]

Another technique for teasing out experts' decision criteria is to ask experts to think out loud as they make decisions.[70] On the following pages, an experienced investor's think–aloud comments, or protocol, about two versions of the same business plan's executive summary illustrate the dramatic difference that addressing the audience's decision criteria can make (note: The product and its attributes, the dates and numbers, and the entrepreneur's name and background have been changed). The comments the investor made while reading the plan and "thinking aloud" were recorded, transcribed, numbered, and inserted into the text of the executive summary in bold and brackets.

As can be seen, the investor's comments about the original executive summary are quite negative. They indicate the investor is not interested in investing his money in the new business. Missing from the original plan's summary are the answers to the investor's mental checklist of questions or decision criteria.

Notice that the investor spontaneously listed his decision criteria in comments 20 through 28 after he finished reading the original executive summary. The decision criteria he lists concern the tax ramifications of the investment, the nature of the project, the amount of the investment required, the projected revenue and profit, the qualifications of the entrepreneur, and the plan for cashing out of the investment. When the investor read the revised version about a week later, he came away with a much more positive impression. Notice that the writer of the revision explicitly addressed each of the investor's decision criteria and used section headings to highlight them.

ORIGINAL EXECUTIVE SUMMARY OF A BUSINESS PLAN WITH AN INVESTOR'S COMMENTS

Smartphone MBA

January 15, 2005
Limited Partnership Interests for $350,000
Copy 12

Executive Summary

The following is a business plan for a new company to be titled *Smartphone MBA* that will develop, sell, and deliver via smartphones a line of educational modules in the form of three-minute videos each of which briefly addresses an important topic covered in the curricula of top twenty business schools. This business plan provides a description of the new service, a look at the market for subscribers and advertisers, as well as action plans for starting operations.

The target market for *Smartphone MBA* consists of three main groups of subscribers: current MBA students who are presently enrolled in an MBA program, graduated MBAs who want a quick and easy refresher, and prospective MBA students who are planning to get an MBA in the near future **[1. Current MBA students, graduated MBAs, and prospective MBA students.]** Taken together, these three groups are expected to total over 2 million potential subscribers by 2010. Currently, there are no smartphone services targeted specifically to people who are enrolled in, plan to enroll in, or have graduated from an MBA program. This creates a significant opportunity for subscription sales as well as for advertisement of a wide range of elite business and consumer goods and services.

Sales projections for *Smartphone MBA* estimate a subscriber base of 40,000 for the premier installment. **[2. What's this 40,000 for the premier installment?]** Subscription sales are expected to quadruple to 160,000 within five years. **[3. They say there are two million potential subscribers out of this group, these three categories. And they have a goal of reaching an initial subscription of 40,000 and 160,000 within five years. Okay. That's understandable.]** The management's five-year projections concerning *Smartphone MBA's* profits from subscriptions and advertisements can be found in the attachments provided at the end of this document. **[4. Management's projections? What the management of Smartphone MBA projects? That's what they're talking about. Okay.]** However, as is explained in the section titled "Scenario Analysis," no guarantees about these projections can be made. **[5. Now where in the heck's the "Scenario Analysis"? See the way they've got this organized, they say they'll start off with the Scenario Analysis. But then they begin with editorial concepts. Then they refer to the Scenario Analysis. Now you've got to go dig out the Scenario Analysis.]**

Seven interests in a limited partnership to be organized under the laws of the State of California and to be known as Smartphone MBA Company (the "Partnership") are being offered by Pallav Srisuwanporn (the "General Partner"). Purchasers of such interests shall be referred to herein as Limited Partners. The General Partner will contribute the concept and vision of the subscription service. The entire capital of the Partnership will be contributed by the Limited Partners. **[6. He doesn't have any risk in it. He has no risk at all.]** The total profit-sharing interests in the Partnership for the Limited Partners will be 15.05000%. The General Partner will reserve a 84.95000% profit-sharing interest in the Partnership. **[7. That sounds extraordinarily high for the General Partner. He doesn't have anything at risk. All he has is an idea and he's asking the limited partners to take 85% of the risk. That's outrageous! I mean this would have to be a sure thing.]**

The General Partner may raise additional capital by selling additional Limited Partnership Interests in the Partnership up to a maximum amount, including the amount hereunder, of $900,000 without the consent of any of the Limited Partners. **[8. Oh, he's only trying to raise $900,000. It's not that big a partnership, is it? It doesn't require much capital.]** The sale of these Partnership Interests shall not dilute the Partnership Interests of the Limited Partners. **[9. In essence, what's he doing? He has 85%. Okay, so he sells off interest in his 85% interest. It doesn't say anything about his background, does it? Oh, here's the Scenario Analysis on another page. Just let me jump around here a minute to see what we've got ... Educational Concepts ... This thing isn't put in the order it's listed. When I read these things I like to start off with the people involved. Is there anything in here about the background of the guy who is going to be the General Partner? (The investor then finds the General Partner's résumé in an appendix.) Oh, here he is.]** With the consent of Limited Partners holding as a group a 50% Partnership Interest in the Partnership, the General Partner may raise capital in excess of such amount by selling additional Limited Partnership Interests. **[10. What the heck does that mean? It says your Limited Partnerships start out with 15% of the partnership. This is really poorly written.]**

The purpose of the Partnership formation is to perform a test market advertisement campaign to determine if starting *Smartphone MBA* makes economic sense. For a subscription service, a greater than 3% positive response to a test market campaign is generally necessary before going to the next phase. If the response to the test marketing falls below this percentage, the plans for the service will be terminated and no remuneration to the Limited Partners will be provided. If the response is greater than 3%, the next step will be full-scale production of the educational modules. To start full-scale production will require the rental of office space, the recruitment of qualified educators, technical staff, and advertisement salespeople, the acquisition of office equipment, the selling of advertising space, the creation of relations with vendors, **[11. Etcetera, etcetera.]** and the raising of additional capital (see the section entitled "Phase One"). Purchase of servers and other equipment necessary to establish an online presence will be delayed until Phase

Two is complete. Monies from the sale of interests in the Partnership will be expended on design of the MBA modules ($11,500), legal services ($10,000), advertising expenses ($240,000), production equipment ($60,000), and other ($28,500), for a grand total of $350,000. **[12. So...you've got 350 thou' but he's raising 900.]**

No person is authorized to give any information or representation not contained in this memorandum. Any information or representation not contained herein **[13. Etcetera, etcetera.]** must not be relied upon as having been authorized by the Partnership or the General Partner. **[14. Blah, blah, blah.]**

[15. This guy wants to raise 900 thousand dollars. He's going to spend 350 thousand on this. He says if Phase One isn't successful based on the test market, that the Partnership will be disbanded. There's no mention of what happens with the difference between 900 and the 350 thousand.

16. He doesn't have anything to risk. I mean how much incentive is there for this guy? How heavily tied is he to the success of the project? What's his incentive to watch expenses?

17. This is a lousy deal.

18. Wait a minute. It says 350,000 Partnership interest, I misread this. They're going to raise 350,000 initially, and then they can sell additional Partnership Interests to bring it up to the 900,000. I see.

19. But still he has nothing at risk. One of the things I look at is what the General Partners have at risk. If they don't have anything at risk, move on. It reflects how enthusiastic he is about his idea. I mean a guy like this ought to mortgage his home.

20. I want to see "John Doe", his background in the business, what he's done. Now his background is back here, you could dig it out.

21. Telling you who their market is, is a good idea.

22. But I want to see right out front what kind of money this Srisuwanporn guy is putting up of his own.

23. I'd like to see what the tax ramifications are right up front. If you buy a 50,000 dollar unit, how much of a tax write off, if any, do you get the first year or the second year?

24. I want to know what the project is, the amount of the required investment, what the tax ramifications are, projected revenue and profit.

25. The expenses he lists aren't necessary to include. I want something on him.

26. I want to be able to look at this and say, in five years, my $50,000 will be worth $250,000 or whatever. I want to look at ventures that will potentially give me five times my investment within five years, that's an extreme example. What I would say is that I want to look at projects that will give me a 20% return on my money in four years at the very least. Today I can get 12% and 13% in a mutual fund, why should I go into a venture that doesn't double my money in four years?

27. So I want to know right off the top what the profit potential is.

28. Once you know what the profit potential is, how do you get out of this thing?

29. These are the things that would tell me how much I want to dig into it.]

**REVISED EXECUTIVE SUMMARY OF A BUSINESS PLAN
WITH AN INVESTOR'S COMMENTS**

Smartphone MBA

January 15, 2005
Seven Limited Partnership Interests for $50,000 each
Copy 12

Executive Summary

Objective: This is a brief overview of some of the critical characteristics of a unique investment opportunity. It covers the nature of the investment, who is behind the project, as well as the expected returns on the project. All of the topics covered in the summary, as well as other subjects not addressed here, are discussed in greater detail in the body of the business plan. **[1. Okay.]**

What is the venture?

We are presently offering limited partnerships in a new educational subscription service to be delivered via smartphones called *Smartphone MBA*. **[2. Right.]** An educational subscription service developed specifically for smartphone owners does not yet exist. *Smartphone MBA* will target an audience of over 2 million potential subscribers:

> **Current MBA students** – students currently enrolled in an MBA program.
> **Graduates of MBA programs** – executives who have already earned an MBA.
> **Prospective MBA students** – people interested in enrolling in an MBA program.

Who is doing this?

Pallav Srisuwanporn is the General Partner of this project as well as being the president of this subscription service. He is a thirty-year-old graduate of the Stanford Business School. His experience includes positions with the McGraw-Hill Companies, publishers of *Business Week, Aviation Week,* **[3. That's impressive.]** and other consumer and business communications. Mr. Srisuwanporn was also Vice President of Planning and Finance of Condé Nast Publications. Among the Condé Nast magazines were *Vogue, W, GQ, Brides* and others. He is currently the Senior Vice President of the Wiley Computer Publishing Division. **[4. Well, this guy ought to know what he's doing.]**

How much can I invest?

Seven limited Partnership Interests are being sold for $50,000 each. You can buy as many of the Interests as you like. Once the project is underway you will have opportunities to contribute additional capital.

What is the projected return?

Each of your limited Partnerships represents a 2.15% profit-sharing interest. All together the seven interests will receive 15.05% of the profit-share. The General Partner accounts for an 84.95% share. The projected return over the next five years is:

YEAR	NET CASHFLOW	A 2.15% SHARE
Initial Phase	-$ 4,985,000	-$107,260
2006	-$ 3,187,000	-$ 68,570
2007	$ 4,193,000	$ 90,220
2008	$12,247,000	$263,530
2009	$25,988,000	$559,200
2010	$38,132,000	$820,520

[5. They've got to be kidding. For a $50,000 investment? I'll have to look at that more closely in the plan.]

How will this affect my taxes?

A Partnership is not a taxable entity. Instead, each item of partnership income, gain, loss, deduction, or credit flows through to you and Mr. Srisuwanporn.

FOR EXAMPLE: You own a 2.15% profit-share of *Smartphone MBA*. During the initial phase you will experience a $107,260 loss from the Partnership. Since you are in the 35% tax bracket **[6. Yup, yup, yup.]** you save $37,541 in taxes because of the write off. If the projected returns continue to prove accurate you will save $24,000 the first year of business because of losses. The second year you will be entitled to a $90,220 profit which, after taxes, will leave you with $58,643. So it will continue into the coming years.

What if I want out?

This partnership is only for the serious investor who does not plan to immediately resell his share. The Interests are not freely transferable. **[7. Hmmmm.]**

Is this investment right for me?

This project is only for those who share the true spirit of the entrepreneur. Because of the lack of liquidity and the high degree of risk involved in starting *Smartphone MBA* you should only consider this project if you can afford to lose it all! To be sure if this investment could be for you, read the entire plan. **[8. Okay, I'll read this thing. It could be good.]**

Benchmarks of Expert Audiences

Benchmarks: The Comparative Information Audiences Require

Audiences not only use decision criteria to ask relevant questions about the person, product, proposal, or performance under consideration, they also use decision criteria to ask relevant questions about their alternatives, or options, as well as about relevant averages and norms. Audiences then use this comparative information to evaluate the relative benefits of the recommended alternative. For example, used car buyers would be foolish to purchase a used car immediately after

the seller addressed their decision criteria. To make a good decision, that is, a fully informed decision, the car buyers must first acquire comparative information about similar used cars and the fair
market value of that make and model as quoted in the *Blue Book*.

A common term for the comparative information audiences seek in order to evaluate the
responses to their decision criteria is *benchmark*. For example, a benchmark investors often use to
decide how well their stock portfolio is doing is the current value of the S&P 500. Investors know
something is wrong if the value of their portfolio has declined, while the value of the S&P 500 has
skyrocketed.

Some benchmarks are organization specific, such as predefined quotas and hurdle rates. Others are audience member specific, such as comparisons to one's own previous experience. The
benchmark most commonly used when audiences consider only one alternative and simply decide
whether to accept or reject it is the status quo.[71]

Ultimately, audiences need comparative data in order to make rational decisions. When making
most decisions, a value, such as the price of a car, is good or bad only relative to another value, not
in the absolute. Relative, not absolute, levels of risk and return account for the decisions investors
make.[72] When choosing among investments, investors opt for different levels of risk and return
depending on the range of investments they have to choose from.

All types of audiences use benchmarks to make decisions. Expert auditors from large international accounting firms compare their client firm's performance and practices to industry norms
before making their audit decisions.[73] When asked to evaluate their MBA program, MBA students
compare their program to other MBA programs.[74] Patients' reactions to information about risks to
their health depend on the comparative information that is available to them.[75] Not surprisingly,
patients tend to search selectively for comparative information that casts their health situation in
a favorable light.[76] Expert financial analysts use a number of benchmarks to evaluate a company's
current results, including the firm's historical results, the current value of the S&P 500, competitor
results, overall industry results, and the state of the general economy.[77]

The finding that audiences depend on benchmarks to make decisions has been especially robust
in the area of consumer decision making. Expert consumers actively seek comparative product
information from ads when choosing among brands with which they are not already familiar.[78]
Consumers choosing among noncomparable items base their choices on abstract decision criteria
such as necessity and enjoyment.[79] These more abstract criteria allow consumers to make comparisons among otherwise noncomparable alternative products, just as they would if they were
choosing among comparable products. When evaluating a new product or a brand extension,
consumers tend to rely on prototypical products from the product category or on the parent brand
category as comparative standards.[80]

Although audience members may be aware they are evaluating their options in relation to a
standard of comparison or benchmark, they are not always aware of the particular benchmark they
are actually using. Oftentimes, audiences unconsciously compare the current option to an option
they encountered earlier, even when the two options are noncomparable.[81] One study found that
tourists shopping at beachfront booths were willing to pay more for music CDs when sweaters
at a neighboring booth they just visited were high priced than when the same sweaters were low
priced.[82] This phenomenon is called *anchoring* and will be treated more fully in Chapter 5.

Audience Expectations About Benchmark Information

Audiences expect professionals to provide them with benchmark information. On the next page,
two excerpts from a board meeting of a simulated detergent manufacturing firm illustrate the
importance of benchmarks to an experienced audience.[83] MBA students comprised the top

management team of the simulated firm. In the board meeting the MBA students presented their report of last year's performance and their plans for the next year to a board of directors composed of experienced top managers. The board members' questions in bold and italics are requests for benchmark information.

The fact that the board members had to request benchmark information from the student team indicates the students were unaware of the crucial role benchmarks play in the audience's decision-making process (note: the names of the students have been changed). In the first excerpt, a board member requests benchmark information in order to evaluate the interest rate and type of loan the team secured. Given that interest rates rose the previous year, locking in the lower rate seemed to be a good decision for the team. In the second excerpt, the chairman of the board requests benchmark information about competitors' financial results. Initially the team's financial results sound outstanding. But when compared to their competitors' results, the team's results turn out to be about average.

TWO EXCERPTS FROM A PRESENTATION GIVEN BY MBA STUDENTS TO AN EXPERIENCED BOARD OF DIRECTORS

Excerpt 1: A Request for Interest Rate Benchmarks

Student VP of Finance: Just give you a quick overview of the way we went about funding our expansion. Cost of our expansion was approximately $36.6 million. We had 15 million of long-term debt that we renewed at 14% fixed rate amortized for the next five years. We wanted to finance construction [of a plant expansion] with as much internal generated funds as possible. And we had $19.2 million in cash from market securities at the end of last year. We negotiated a $20 million line of credit with the bank to help us finance the expansion and also to help with the operating expenses. As a result, using our cash and our line of credit we were able to fund the expansion, and since then the line of credit has now been reduced to $12.5 million. And if we can, we hope to continue to reduce this as fast as possible.

   Board Member: *How does the 14% fixed rate compare to what benchmark rates or government rates were at the time for the same term?*

   Student VP of Finance: The prime rate at the time was 12% with a prime plus two. And talking to people in our bank this was an average and much more favorable rate in relation to our competitors.

   Board Member: You have prime plus two fixed though for five years, not floating with the prime?

   Student VP of Finance: Right, yes. Prime was at 12% at the time that we negotiated.

   Student VP of Marketing: It is now at 19.

   Board Member: It's now 19. So the outlook for rates was that they were going to be rising.

   Student VP of Finance: Right. Inflation was running at a fairly good clip, and we thought the best thing to do was to try to lock in a rate. If you don't have any questions I would like to go over the results of the labor negotiations.

Excerpt 2: A Request for Competitive Benchmarks

Student CEO: Okay. Fine. Okay. Very quickly I want to just give you the highlights from last year. That is on July 1 we opened the new $38 million factory and warehouse. Also during the

year we submitted in our new advertising campaign, and we participated in the labor negotiations which Aditya just went through. Currently, we are producing two products for the
commercial market inside the nation. A high sudser detergent, a medium sudser, and we're
producing one product in the industrial market.

Right now, we have overall a 31% market share. And on a financial note net income
rose $6.9 million last year to $23.7 million this year. This was on an increase to retained
earnings of $22.5 million versus last year at $5.7 million. Much of this increase is due as
Bob mentioned to the additional capacity that we have with the factory, with the new
factory. It allowed us to do two things. One was to produce more goods for sale within
the commercial end of the business, and the other allows us to also get into the industrial
market.

Stock price rose from last year roughly at this time from the low 50s to almost $90 per
share right now. And earnings per share climbed from $6.96 last year to $23.68. Return on
investment for the year was 23%, and return on equity was 42%. So with that in mind, what
we would like to do is present to you our main concerns for next year.

Chairman of the Board: No. We would like to discuss that a little more. *Do you have
any comparative numbers for the competitors in our nation? What did the competitors' stock
prices do?*

Student CEO: In our nation, Team 3, Yun Wang's team is at $90 stock price and Brenda
Kelley, the third competitor, is at $110. I think it is. She's number one in the nation and in the
world right now which is at $110. We are in at $90. We are sort of in the thick of things.

Audience-Provided Benchmarks

Audiences sometimes compare recommended alternatives to personal or subjective standards or
benchmarks. A study of recruiters screening résumés for a supervisory position finds recruiters
use themselves as benchmarks: The more similar the applicant's background is to the background of the recruiter evaluating that applicant, the higher the probability the applicant will
be hired.[84] Consumers often generate a subjective reference price for a product based on its
quality, and then evaluate different brands by comparing their subjective reference price to the
actual price.[85] A study of renters' decision making gave renters descriptions of seven houses
with each house described in a separate booklet. Of all the comparisons the renters made, 71%
were comparisons to a subjective standard, the remaining 29% were comparisons among the
seven houses.[86]

When comparative information about alternatives is missing from a document or presentation,
expert audiences may supply it. Interestingly, the comparative information consumers retrieve from
their memories has a stronger effect on their decisions than comparative information provided
by external sources.[87] If consumers are unable to retrieve missing benchmark information from
their memories, they may attempt to infer it, especially when the information has high subjective
importance.[88]

In a study comparing the effects of missing information on experts and novices, expert and
novice bicycle buyers received written descriptions of bicycles in which important comparative
information such as the weight of the bicycle was missing for some of the bicycles. Although
novices were unconcerned that information was missing, experts who understood the importance of the missing benchmark information tried to guess what it would be for each bicycle

before making their decisions.[89] Similar expert/novice differences regarding missing benchmark information have been reported among other types of consumers.[90] However, even experts may not take the time necessary to infer missing benchmark information if the amount of missing information is large or if they are not confident in their ability to make the inferences accurately.[91]

Decision Schemata of Expert Audiences

Decision Schemata: The Audience's Decision-Making Framework

When experts' decision criteria and benchmarks are plotted out, they form a grid or *decision matrix*. Table 1.1 shows an example of a decision matrix for deciding on a laptop computer in 2015. The first column of the matrix lists possible decision criteria. The first row indicates the recommended laptop and benchmark, or alternative, laptops. The cells of the matrix give the values for the recommended and benchmark laptops. But do such matrix representations have any psychological reality? Do they reflect something about the underlying structure of decision-making expertise? Research suggests the answer is *yes*. Expert decision makers appear to have decision-specific knowledge structures,[92] or mental representations, stored in their long-term memories that correspond to decision matrices. It is these knowledge structures that lead experts to mentally represent each alternative they consider as values along a number of attributes or decision criteria.[93]

Cognitive scientists call such knowledge structures *schemata*.[94] Schemata are mental frameworks that reside in an expert's long-term memory and into which new information can be fitted and made sense of.[95] Other terms for schemata include *scripts*,[96] *frames*,[97] *mental models*,[98] *templates*,[99] and *knowledge representations*.[100]

Some scientists believe schemata are stored in the prefrontal cortex of the brain.[101] Other scientists find evidence for schemata being distributed over different areas of the cortex.[102] More recently, neuroscientists have demonstrated that the medial prefrontal cortex, interacting with the hippocampus, is involved in assimilating new information into existing schemata and in retrieving it later as needed for decision making.[103]

Schemata, like the decision matrix illustrated in Table 1.1, consist of slots that indicate the expert's knowledge relevant to a particular decision as well as empty slots that can be filled with situation-specific information called *slot values*.[104] In Table 1.1 the slot values for the laptop

TABLE 1.1 Decision Matrices Incorporate Both Decision Criteria and Benchmarks

DECISION CRITERIA	RECOMMENDATION Laptop under consideration	BENCHMARK 1 Comparable laptop	BENCHMARK 2 Current laptop
Year, make, and model	2015 13" Apple MacBook Air	2015 13" Apple MacBook Pro with Retina display	2014 11" Apple MacBook Air
Processor speed	1.6GHz	2.9GHz	1.3GHz
Memory	4GB SDRAM	8GB SDRAM	4GB SDRAM
Storage	256GB Flash Storage	512GB Flash Storage	128GB Flash Storage
Display quality	Very good	Excellent	Very good
Retail price	$1,200	$1,800	$1,000 (new)

under consideration are *2015 13" Apple MacBook Air, 1.6GHz, 4GB SDRAM, 256GB Flash Storage, Very Good*, and *$1,200*. Sometimes the slots in an expert's schema may already be filled with default values (e.g., an expert's default value for the retail price of the recommended laptop in Figure 1.1 might be *more than $1,000*). But when experts start to instantiate their schemata, they usually replace those default values with the actual values of the alternatives under consideration.[105]

The audience's long-term memory is largely composed of schemata,[106] and much of what we call expertise is schema driven. Expertise has been shown to be schema driven in accounting,[107] financial analysis,[108] physics,[109] algebra,[110] and medicine.[111] Expertise in making parole decisions has been shown to be schema driven.[112] Wall Street analysts' ability to value firms and their acquisitions has been shown to depend on the analysts' schemata.[113] In addition, the ability of business leaders and military officers to effectively lead their subordinates has been shown to depend on their possessing complex and highly organized schemata.[114] Similarly, the ability of cyber security analysts to effectively respond to cyber attacks has been shown to depend on the analysts possessing robust incident handling and cyber attack schemata.[115]

The knowledge experienced consumers have about evaluating brands in a product class may also be thought of as schemata.[116] A consumer's schemata for particular brands "largely determine how the consumer reacts to advertising."[117] Expert supervisors evaluate employee performance using highly differentiated performance schemata that include performance criteria relevant to specific jobs.[118] Because more experienced supervisors use more differentiated performance schemata, they are able to provide more accurate ratings of their employees than their less-experienced colleagues.[119]

Many cognitive scientists agree that schemata are critical to decision making and high-level thought. As the authors of a study of 713 product decisions conclude, "Decisions reflect the schemata employed in the decision-making process."[120] Others argue that "a rich collection of schemata constitutes an essential engine for high-level thinking in a domain."[121] John R. Anderson, a leader in the field of cognitive science, identifies both reasoning and decision making as "schema-based inference processes" that can approach the level of normative decision-making principles if people "lock into the right schema."[122] Moreover, he has since confirmed this view.[123]

Perhaps in part because of the similarities between internal schemata and decision matrices, consumers spontaneously create alternative-by-attribute decision matrices when deciding among different products and sources of credit.[124] Figure 1.1 shows the decision matrix one consumer created while comparing five different brands (labeled A through E) of do-it-yourself storage buildings along six different decision criteria (Warranty, Size, Materials, Assembly, Ease, and Price).[125] Not only did the consumer rearrange randomly presented information, she also made calculations to fill empty schema slots, re-scaled slot values that were hard to compare, and ranked each of the six attributes or decision criteria.

Decision Schemata as Guides to the Decision-Making Process

Schemata not only store important information in an organized way, they also guide the process of decision making. Ultimately, schemata guide behavior.[126] Social psychologists Susan Fiske and Shelley Taylor explain just how fundamental schemata are: "Once cued, schemas affect how quickly we perceive, what we notice, how we interpret what we notice, and what we perceive as similar and different."[127] Schemata direct attention during information search, specify which

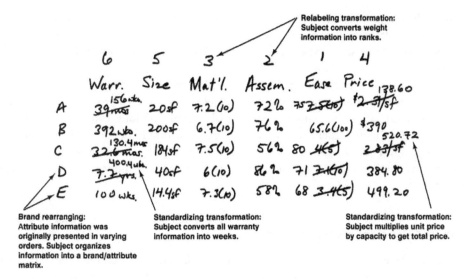

FIGURE 1.1 Decision Makers Spontaneously Create Decision Matrices

Source: Coupey (1994, p. 90)

information is relevant and which is irrelevant, code information, organize it in memory, direct the retrieval of information from memory, and specify which important information is missing.[128] Voters' schemata can affect their attention to, interpretation, and recall of political information.[129] The schemata of experienced voters lead them to give attention to and to seek information about political events that inexperienced voters tend to overlook.[130] The influence of schemata can even be retroactive. An audience member's current schema can help them retrieve memories that were formed before the schema had been acquired.[131]

Well-developed schemata provide many advantages for expert audience members. For example, voters with more highly developed political schemata are able to produce higher quality arguments about current issues than less sophisticated voters.[132] The ability of experienced physicians to recognize the significance of secondary physiological measurements[133] can be credited to their more complete schemata.[134] Schemata help experienced consumers recall product information, make accurate inferences about the product information with which they are presented, and put new information into context quickly.[135] Internal knowledge structures, or schemata, allow expert business appraisers to quickly search for and assess the information they need to evaluate the worth of a company.[136]

Limitations of Decision Schemata

The schemata of expert audiences sometimes have negative effects on the decisions they make. When activated, an expert's schemata may lead the expert to distort new information that is inconsistent with their schemata.[137] An expert's schemata may also lead them to discount schema-inconsistent information altogether.[138] In addition, an expert's schemata can limit the types of problems they perceive. For example, business executives have been found to define problems largely in terms of their functional expertise, such as marketing, finance, or operations, and not recognize business problems outside their function area.[139] Sometimes experts try to apply their schemata to decisions outside their domain of expertise. But experts' schemata are domain specific and cannot be used as the basis of expertise in a second domain even when that domain appears to be similar.[140]

Such limitations can lead experts to make biased decisions, particularly if they try to use their schemata to make nonroutine decisions or to solve ill-structured problems.[141] In such circumstances, expert audiences do not necessarily make better decisions than novices.[142] Experts' schemata can even incline them to overlook information simply because it is not formatted in the typical way. For example, expert, but nonprofessional, investors have been found to use comprehensive income information only when it is presented in the format they have come to expect.[143]

The Shared Decision Schemata of Groups

Shared schemata underpin the corporate cultures of diverse organizations[144] and guide the decision-making processes of effective groups and teams.[145] A study of 25 four- to six-person groups of business executives making hiring decisions reports that the executives in each group shared the same schema concerning the characteristics of suitable applicants, tended to search for the same information about each applicant, mentioned that same information in group discussions, and used that information to make group decisions. When group members repeated information during their discussions, they were more likely to repeat information that was schema relevant than schema irrelevant. Any information that was unshared, or known by only one group member, was more likely to be mentioned in group discussions if it were schema-relevant information than if it were schema irrelevant. Finally, the study reports that the most influential person in each group was the group member with the most complete knowledge of information relevant to the group's shared schema.[146]

Factions within a group who are initially in a minority can successfully advocate their preferred alternative by appealing to shared knowledge structures or schemata upon which all members agree.[147] Any alternative consistent with the group's shared schema is easier for the minority to defend. That alternative is also more likely to be chosen by the group as a whole, although usually after some delay.[148] The group is more likely to choose that alternative even when it is not demonstrably correct, as is often the case with jury decisions.[149] However, if group members do not share a schema, or if they possess multiple and conflicting schemata, the group will tend to choose an alternative on the basis of majority/plurality rule.[150]

Shared mental models, a type of shared schema, predict both team processes and team performance.[151] They are associated with higher team satisfaction,[152] increased within-team helping behavior,[153] reduced absenteeism,[154] and greater team effectiveness.[155] They have an even greater effect on team performance than demographic similarities among team members.[156]

The benefits of shared schemata or shared mental models arise because they enable team members to anticipate each other's information needs, communicate efficiently, and work in sync.[157] In many cases, a shared mental model about the task is necessary if a team is to complete its task successfully.[158] Furthermore, as the differences among the team members' mental models decrease, team performance increases. High-performing teams tend to have not only more widely shared mental models than low-performing teams, but also more elaborate ones.[159] Teams that fail to develop shared mental models tend to be uncoordinated and to perform poorly.[160]

Decision Schemata of Novice Audiences

Novices' Less Well-Developed Decision Schemata

Important differences have been discovered between expert and novice consumers and the way they make decisions.[161] Important differences have been discovered between many other expert and novice audiences and how they make decisions as well.[162] Interestingly, expert and novice decision makers differ not only at the cognitive level, but also at the neurological level. Neuroscientists find evidence that expertise leads to a functional reorganization of the brain.[163] When making a decision that falls within their domain of expertise, expert audience members activate different brain systems than novices activate.[164]

At the cognitive level, the most fundamental difference between expert and novice audiences is that, in contrast to experts, novice audiences come to documents, presentations, and group meetings without well-developed or appropriate schemata in mind.[165] In fact, most expert/novice differences can be attributed to "quantitative and qualitative differences in their respective stores of relevant problem schemas."[166]

Thus, novice audience members may lack the well-formed and matrix-like decision schemata they need to make a good decision. Instead of a matrix-like schema, a novice's schema may consist of a simple list of reasons for the alternative they prefer and against the alternative they dislike. If the novice has more experience, her schema may consist of a random list of pros and cons for several alternatives.[167] Unlike experts who attempt to estimate each alternative's overall value along a specific set of dimensions or decision criteria, novices try to find unique reasons for and against each alternative they consider.[168]

Not surprisingly, novice audiences employ fewer decision criteria when making a decision than experts.[169] For example, novice consumers of insurance evoke fewer decision criteria than experts when trying to choose the best insurance policy.[170] Novice consumers of newspapers search for information about fewer attributes, or decision criteria, than more knowledgeable consumers when choosing among newspapers.[171] Even when information pertinent to an expert's decision criteria is provided to them in ads (e.g., the fact that a computer has 8GB SDRAM), novice consumers may neglect to process it.[172] Unless given incentives, novices will process only the benefit information ads contain (e.g., the computer is "Great for gamers").

Even when novice audiences apply the decision criteria experts possess, they may not weight those criteria appropriately. For example, novice investors weight the decision criteria provided by financial analysts' forecasts less appropriately than expert investors.[173] Novice consumers give more weight to nonfunctional dimensions of products such as the brand name and packaging than expert consumers.[174] Because novices lack the prestored decision criteria that experts possess, they sometimes try, without much success, to create them.[175]

Novice audiences also use fewer benchmarks and make fewer comparisons than experts when making decisions. Novice consumers of insurance are less likely to make pair-wise comparisons of one policy to another than experts.[176] Novice consumers in general make fewer comparisons because they have less knowledge about alternative products, an important category of benchmarks, than expert consumers.[177] Novice financial analysts are less likely to compare a firm's financials to internal norms or benchmarks than expert analysts.[178] Even when novice audiences have access to the benchmarks that experts rely on, they may not use them. A study of consumers reading comparative and noncomparative ads in order to choose among brands finds that, unlike the expert consumers, novice consumers fail to use the comparative product information comparative ads provide.[179]

Not only do novices possess less well-developed schemata than experts, novices are also less likely than experts to agree among each other about which decision criteria should comprise their schemata.[180] In addition, novices are less likely than experts to use decision criteria consistently when making a decision.[181] For example, when screening résumés for a supervisory position, recruiters with less hiring experience are less consistent in applying their decision criteria than more experienced recruiters.[182] When selecting hardware and software products, technical novices not only agree less on decision criteria than technical experts, they also apply them less consistently.[183]

Consequences of Less Well-Developed Decision Schemata

What happens when audience members lack the appropriate schemata to make good decisions? A survey of 43 U.S. Army officers and enlisted personnel who trained new platoon leaders reveals that the root cause of many problems experienced by novice platoon leaders is their lack of well-developed schemata. Novice platoon leaders are quickly overwhelmed by incoming information and are slow to comprehend which information is important. They often fail to request and communicate schema-relevant information. Without the appropriate schemata to support their decision making, novice platoon leaders have difficulty integrating information into a coherent picture and specifying alternate courses of action (COAs).[184]

Without the experts' well-developed schemata, novice audiences are unable to make as many inferences about the messages they read,[185] to ask as many pertinent questions,[186] or to recall as much of the information they do obtain.[187] Ultimately, novices make decisions that are inferior to those of experts.[188]

When audiences lack or fail to activate the appropriate decision schema, they may rely more on intuitive forms of decision making. For example, in one study, two groups of consumers were given the same product advertisements. The first group was asked to evaluate the products advertised. The second group was asked to evaluate the entertainment value of each ad. Later, both groups were asked to describe the content of the ads. The second group took longer to verify product information, generated fewer product-related thoughts, did not generate arguments either for or against purchasing the products, and yet formed more positive attitudes toward the products than the first group. The authors conclude that the second group had not activated the appropriate schemata and thus never fully comprehended the ads' contents. Instead, the second group had relied on its subjective or intuitive feelings toward the ads to guide its evaluation of the products.[189]

Without the appropriate schema, novice audiences may also rely more on emotional forms of decision making. Given the task of prioritizing patients for psychotherapy, novice clinicians tend to base their decisions on the apparent urgency of the patient's condition, whereas expert clinicians base their decisions on well-defined suitability criteria.[190] When making buy and sell decisions, novice investors often make their decisions based on their emotional reactions to market information. Expert financial advisors from New York Stock Exchange brokerage firms, on the other hand, tend to make such decisions based on predetermined investment criteria.[191] In a study of the effects of emotions on consumer decision making, a mood manipulation affected the responses of consumers with little knowledge about automobiles to car ads. In contrast, expert consumers were unaffected by the mood manipulation and made their decisions based on the quality of the ads' contents.[192]

The differences between the schemata of expert and novice audiences can lead to big differences in the way the two groups search for information. A study of expert and novice home buyers choosing a mortgage reveals that a home-buyer's level of expertise strongly affects their search effort, search patterns, and how efficiently they eliminate inferior alterna-tives.[193] Whereas experts actively search for specific information in a top-down fashion using their domain knowledge, or schemata, to structure the search, novices examine information in the way it is presented.[194] Thus, product novices are more influenced by the way the con-tents of ads are displayed than product experts.[195] Lacking the expert's schemata, novices may only search for information that confirms their underdeveloped schemata. With somewhat more developed schemata, novices are more likely to notice information that disconfirms components of their schemata and to revise their schemata accordingly.[196] As expertise grows, audiences find fewer instances of disconfirming information and the need to revise their schemata lessens.[197]

Without a well-developed schema to guide search, novice audiences make decisions less effi-ciently than experts.[198] Novice audiences process more information than experts when making similar decisions[199] and have trouble identifying information that is irrelevant and safe to ignore.[200] For this reason, novice newspaper consumers take longer to choose between newspapers than more knowledgeable ones.[201] Expert consumers, on the other hand, are able to use search strategies that reduce their effort without compromising the quality of their decisions.[202]

The Development of Expert-Like Decision Schemata

How do novice audience members become experts? In order to acquire expertise in a domain, novices must develop expert schemata.[203] Novices begin to develop a schema of a task or deci-sion as they repeat it.[204] Novices can develop a schema after performing a task or making a decision only twice if they are able to identify what the two experiences have in common.[205] Abstract diagrams that highlight decision criteria can help novices formulate schemata,[206] as can decision matrices.[207]

Exposure to analogies can also help novices formulate schemata.[208] Novices are sometimes able to acquire a schema by comparing just two analogs to one another.[209] They may also develop a schema as a side effect of applying what they learned from solving one problem to an unsolved target problem.[210] Not surprisingly, novices' schemata become more developed and complex with additional experience.[211]

Schemata can be developed both consciously and unconsciously. Helping novice leaders con-sciously develop expert-like schemata is the focus of many leadership training programs.[212] Novices also develop more complex schemata by unconsciously combining several simpler existing sche-mata into one.[213] Interestingly, sleep appears to facilitate the development of new schemata, as well as the integration of new information into existing schemata and the disbandment of existing schemata that are no longer useful—a process critical to creative thinking.[214]

Although truly novice audience members do not possess predefined schemata to guide their decision making, they sometimes appreciate and use experts' decision criteria and benchmarks when they are made available to them. Note consumers' widespread reliance on *Consumer Reports* to make purchasing decisions. *Consumer Reports* provides novice consumers with experts' decision criteria for a variety of products and rates each product according to how well it meets the experts' criteria for that product category. Each product attribute that is rated—quality, capacity, efficiency, reliability, and so on—corresponds to one of the experts' decision criteria. *Consumer Reports* also provides consumers with benchmark information, comparing the ratings and prices of many different products within the same product cat-egory. In addition, *Consumer Reports* computes an overall score for each product using the weighted sums rule. When novice consumers are presented with decision matrices such as those provided by *Consumer Reports*, they become "instant experts."[215] As cognitive scientists have observed, the online version of *Consumer Reports* amounts to a personal decision support system.[216]

Consumer Reports is not the only source of instant expertise. Insurance policies featuring decision matrices that contrast different types of insurance help novice consumers develop the schemata they need to understand the policies and to pose the right questions about them.[217] Health care pamphlets containing decision matrices that contrast alternative medications and their possible side effects not only help patients develop the schemata they need to make more informed decisions,[218] they also increase compliance rates.[219] Fact sheets providing decision matrices for choosing among both comparable and noncomparable products significantly improve the quality of consumers' purchasing decisions.[220]

Some large organizations, including Toyota, Chevron, and the U.S. Department of Defense, routinely require project managers to develop decision matrices (also called *analytical comparisons of multiple alternatives*) and to present them to upper management prior to investing the organization's resources in any of the options.[221] Some top consulting firms routinely provide their business clients with decision matrices to support their decision making. When seeking expert advice, many clients actually prefer to receive matrix-like information about alternatives and their attributes instead of a recommendation regarding which alternative to choose.[222]

It turns out that novices are usually happy to base their decisions on whatever decision criteria are presented to them, whether or not the criteria are the experts' decision criteria.[223] Basing one's decision on another's criteria may not always be a good idea, however. One study reports that during the course of a sales interaction, salespeople often use expressions that encourage consumers to consider decision criteria not necessarily relevant to their purchasing decision (e.g., what others will think, the possibility of a missed opportunity). Thus, consumers' thoughts are diverted from more important criteria such as the price and quality of the product.[224]

The Development of Shared Decision Schemata in Groups

Groups and teams become more expert and more cohesive when members coordinate their individual schemata with those of other team members and develop shared schemata, or shared mental models, to structure their decisions and other tasks.[225] The number and complexity of teams' shared mental models relevant to their tasks increase significantly over time and are vital to the coordination of team efforts.[226]

In order to develop such shared schemata, team members must have the ability to coordinate the potentially different mental models of all the members of the team.[227] When they encounter new, nonroutine tasks, higher-performing teams use significantly different processes to develop shared mental models than those used by lower-performing teams.[228] For example, higher-performing teams may consciously coordinate divergent schemata by negotiating which decision criteria are relevant to the team's decisions.[229] They may also use employee training and leader briefings to help team members arrive at a shared mental model.[230]

Face-to-face interaction, especially at the beginning of a new project, is critical to a team's development of a shared schema or mental model. Technology-mediated interaction via video-conferencing, on the other hand, can negatively impact a team's ability to develop a shared mental model[231] as can a division of labor among team members and any other behavior that inhibits knowledge sharing.[232] But encouraging team members to take time to explain and justify their recommendations to each other helps the team integrate their divergent schemata more quickly and completely.[233]

As team members interact and acquire greater expertise in making specific types of decisions, their shared mental models change and become more refined,[234] with the more highly skilled members of the team using them much more successfully than their less skilled colleagues.[235]

Expert Audiences vs. Linear Models and Normative Rules

Linear Models: The Gold Standard of Rational Decision Making

As we have seen, expert audiences typically consider multiple decision criteria when making decisions and their decisions typically produce superior outcomes to those of novices. But do experts consistently make the best decisions possible given their decision criteria? And do experts consistently follow the rules of normative, or proper, decision making? If experts followed normative rules, such as those prescribed by multi-attribute utility theory (MAUT), they would consistently choose those alternatives that maximized their values.[236]

To answer the first question—"Do expert audiences consistently make the best decisions possible given their decision criteria?"—decision researchers use a statistical technique called *multiple regression analysis* to identify how much weight (if any) the experts should ideally give each of their decision criteria in order to choose the best alternative. The result is called a *linear model*. Linear models are usually represented as equations. For example, a linear model for deciding on the best MBA applicants might to represented as:

$$\text{Applicant value} = 0.2 \text{ (GMAT score)} + 0.3 \text{ (GPA)} + 0.4 \text{ (Communication Skills)} + 0.1 \text{ (Work Experience)}$$

But linear models can also be expressed in the form of value trees, or, like decision schemata, in the form of decision matrices.

The decisions experts make are usually inferior to those computed by linear models. Linear models are more accurate than clinical psychologists in diagnosing psychiatric patients.[237] Linear models are more accurate than medical doctors in diagnosing medical patients.[238] Linear models are better than faculty members on admissions committees at choosing the best students for graduate school.[239] Linear models are more accurate than commercial bankers in deciding which firms are most likely to go bankrupt.[240] Linear models are more accurate than expert investors in predicting stock prices.[241] In fact, hundreds of studies have consistently shown that in virtually every domain, statistical predictions produced by linear models outperform those of experts.[242]

Even *bootstrapped models*, improper linear models that use the same weights experts give their decision criteria, produce better decisions than the experts they model.[243] A bootstrapped model can be expressed in the same three ways as a linear model. Bootstrapped models are called improper because, unlike linear models, they cannot produce an optimal decision. Surprisingly, another type of improper linear model, the equal-weight additive model, which weights all of the experts' decision criteria equally, also produces better decisions than experts.[244]

The Causes of Individual Experts' Normally Inferior Performance

One reason linear and bootstrapped models outperform experts is that experts do not consistently follow the rules of normative decision making when choosing among alternatives.[245]

To apply the rules of normative decision making, an expert must first create a model, that is, identify the appropriate attributes or decision criteria, the correct weight for each, as well as the appropriate alternatives or benchmarks. Once the model has been generated, they must enter the correct attribute values, or slot values, for each alternative, multiply each attribute value by the weight for that attribute, calculate the total attribute value for each alternative, and select the alternative with the highest overall value. A meta-analysis finds that experts' lack of consistency in applying normative rules accounts for much of the advantage linear models have over them.[246]

Most experts are effective at collecting information about each of their alternatives but are less effective at weighting that information and integrating it into a final decision.[247] However, some experts, such as some experienced investors, neither collect all the available information about their alternatives nor do they fully compare the available choices. For example, experienced investors are much more likely to tally pros and cons for the handful of investments they decide to consider than to compute weighted sums from the complete set of options they have to choose among.[248] Moreover, most experts show only moderate levels of self-insight about the cognitive processes they use to arrive at their decisions.[249]

Other anomalies and biases crop up in the decision-making processes of expert audiences as well. Expert financial analysts often neglect base-rate benchmark information and focus exclusively on case-specific information when predicting stock prices.[250] Experts may make different decisions based on the way their choice was elicited.[251] For example, experts may make different decisions when asked to select instead of reject one of two alternatives.[252] They may also make different decisions when asked to evaluate one alternative at a time as opposed to all alternatives concurrently.[253]

In addition, many experts do not exclusively use compensatory choice rules—rules for deciding that involve trading off a low value on one criterion (e.g., poor gas mileage) for a high value on another (e.g., excellent safety features)—when making decisions as the normative rules of decision making dictate. Instead, experts often use noncompensatory choice rules and simply eliminate from consideration any alternative that has a low value on an important decision criterion prior to computing the remaining alternatives' overall values.[254] Of course, some experts do routinely use compensatory choice rules when making important decisions. For example, corporate recruiters regularly use compensatory choice rules when making hiring decisions.[255] *Consumer Reports* also uses a compensatory choice rule to compute an overall score for each product it evaluates.

Even when decision makers fully understand compensatory choice rules, they do not necessarily use them to make decisions. One study found that MBAs taught to use compensatory choice rules did *not* use them to make their real job decisions. However, MBAs did use compensatory choice rules to justify their already-made decisions.[256] Similarly, undergraduates taught to use compensatory choice rules did not increase their use of them. Nonetheless, they did increase their desire for their agents, for example, their doctors and advisors, to use compensatory choice rules when making decisions on their behalf.[257]

Another cause of experts' normally inferior performance is that some types of decisions are inherently difficult for human beings to make. As indicated in Table 1.2, expert audiences perform relatively well in domains that involve decisions about objects or things.[258] These domains have a high degree of predictability and provide feedback readily. Expert audiences perform less well in domains that involve decisions about human behavior which is highly unpredictable and for which feedback is less readily available.[259] In such domains, experts tend to disagree with each other and have a low degree of consensus.[260]

TABLE 1.2 The Decision Performance of Experts Depends on Their Domain

Better Performance Domains Concerning Things	Poorer Performance Domains Concerning People
Weather forecasting	Clinical psychology
Astronomy	Astrology
Aeronautics	Student admissions
Agriculture	Law
Chess	Behavioral research
Physics	Counseling
Mathematics	Human resources
Accounting	Parole granting
Actuarial statistics	Stock market investing

Source: Adapted from Shanteau (1992)

The Causes of Groups of Experts' Normally Inferior Performance

One might expect groups of experts to outperform individual experts and to match the performance of linear models. After all, a crowd's average answer to a factual question is typically more accurate than an individual's answer, given that the average of many different answers cancels out the errors of individual answers.[261] So it's a surprise to learn that groups usually make decisions that are inferior to those made by their most expert members and may perform considerably worse than even their average members on some tasks.[262]

Majorities/pluralities, not the most knowledgeable members, "win" most of the time.[263] Majority/plurality rule has been observed in a variety of group-level audience decisions, including decisions made by mock juries,[264] groups of investors,[265] groups of voters,[266] budgetary committees,[267] and teams of recruiters.[268] Even when they know the right answers to factual questions, minority members tend to succumb to majority pressure and act against their better judgment.[269]

Majority/plurality rule is particularly prevalent when a group does not share a schema for making the decision they need to make.[270] Thus, it may not enhance group performance if a minority of group members has the expertise needed to make a good decision since many group members may neither appreciate their expertise or use it. Without a shared schema, the majority of group members may assume the most confident and verbose among them is the most expert,[271] although these traits rarely correlate with accuracy.[272]

The Importance of Expert Audiences Despite Their Limitations

While acknowledging the limitations of experts to weight decision criteria appropriately and their deviations from normative decision-making processes, professionals must still understand experts and be able to convince them.

Expert audiences have the final say in most decisions and are not likely be replaced altogether by linear models any time soon. The judgments of expert audiences are perceived as fairer than the judgments of linear models.[273] Expert audiences are still indispensable for selecting, weighting, and measuring the criteria that go into linear models[274] and for discovering new decision criteria.[275] In addition, expert audiences have the ability to recognize rare but highly diagnostic cues that may not be accounted for in linear models.[276] Most importantly, expert audiences are less likely than linear models to make big mistakes.[277]

AUDIENCE DECISION-MAKING EXPERTISE: IMPLICATIONS FOR COMMUNICATORS

- The main takeaway for communicators in Chapter 1 is that expert audiences already know what information they want from professionals—the values that will populate their decision schemata. Audiences are not empty cups waiting to be filled with whatever information professionals want to give them.
- Use the information presented in the chapter to guide the selection of content for your documents, presentations, meetings, and interviews. The alternative is to select content based on subjective opinion or convention.
- Why use the information? To make your communications more persuasive, especially with expert audiences. To enable all types of audiences—experts, novices, groups, and individuals—to make more informed decisions.
- See Chapter 2 for a classification scheme that makes it easier to anticipate the audience's information requirements for any specific decision.

Notes

1 Baum, L. (2009). *Judges and their audiences: A perspective on judicial behavior.* Princeton, NJ: Princeton University Press.
2 Shattuck, L. G. (1995). Communication of intent in distributed supervisory control systems (Doctoral dissertation. The Ohio State University, 1995). *Dissertation Abstracts International, 56*(09B), 5209.
3 Mikulecky, L. (1981). *Job literacy: The relationship between school preparation and workplace actuality.* Bloomington, IN: Indiana University.

Sticht, T. G. (1977). Comprehending reading at work. In M. A. Just & P. A. Carpenter (Eds.), *Cognitive processes in comprehension* (pp. 221–246). Hillsdale, NJ: Lawrence Erlbaum.

Sticht, T. G., Fox, L. C., Hauke, R. N., & Welty-Sapf, D. (1977). *The role of reading in the navy,* NPRDC-TR-77-40. San Diego, CA: Navy Personnel Research and Development Center, September 1977. NTIS No. AD A044 228.
4 Levine, J. M., Resnick, L. B., & Higgins, E. T. (1993). Social foundations of cognition. *Annual Review of Psychology, 44,* 585–612.

Orasanu, J., & Salas, E. (1993). Team decision making in complex environments. In G. A. Klein, J. Orasanu, R. Calderwood & C. E. Zsambok (Eds.), *Decision making in action: Models and methods* (pp. 327–345). Westport, CT: Ablex Publishing.
5 Schriver, K. A. (1997, pp. 6–8). *Dynamics in document design: Creating text for readers.* New York: Wiley.
6 Tsai, W., Yang, C., Leu, J., Lee, Y., & Yang, C. (2013). An integrated group decision making support model for corporate financing decisions. *Group Decision and Negotiation, 22*(6), 1103–1127.
7 Druckman, J. N., & Holmes, J. W. (2004). Does presidential rhetoric matter? Priming and presidential approval. *Presidential Studies Quarterly, 34*(4), 755–778.

Malhotra, N., & Krosnick, J. A. (2007). Retrospective and prospective performance assessments during the 2004 election campaign: Tests of mediation and news media priming. *Political Behavior, 29*(2), 249–278.

Newman, B. (2003). Integrity and presidential approval, 1980–2000. *Public Opinion Quarterly, 67*(3), 335–367.
8 Goldstein, W. M., & Weber, E. U. (1995). Content and discontent: Indications and implications of domain specificity in preferential decision making. In J. Busemeyer, D. Medin & R. Hastie (Eds.), *Decision-making from a cognitive perspective (the psychology of learning and motivation)* (Vol. 32, pp. 83–136). San Diego, CA: Academic Press.

Hitt, M. A., & Tyler, B. B. (1991). Strategic decision models: Integrating different perspectives. *Strategic Management Journal, 12*(5), 327–351.

Wells, W. A. (1974). Venture capital decision-making (Doctoral dissertation, Carnegie Mellon University, 1974). *Dissertation Abstracts International, 35*(12A), 74–75.

9 Bouman, M. J. (1980). Application of information-processing and decision-making research. In G. R. Ungson & D. N. Braunstein (Eds.), *Decision making: An interdisciplinary inquiry* (pp. 129–167). Boston: Kent Publishing.

Brucks, M. (1985). The effects of product class knowledge on information search behavior. *Journal of Consumer Research, 12*(1), 1–16.

Johnson, E. J., & Russo, J. E. (1984). Product familiarity and learning new information. *Journal of Consumer Research, 11*(1), 542–550.

10 Kardes, F. R., & Sanbonmatsu, D. M. (1993). Direction of comparison, expected feature correlation, and the set-size effect in preference judgment. *Journal of Consumer Psychology, 2*(1), 39–54.

Sanbonmatsu, D. M., Kardes, F. R., & Herr, P. M. (1992). The role of prior knowledge and missing information in multiattribute evaluation. *Organizational Behavior and Human Decision Processes, 51*(1), 76–91.

11 Beaulieu, P. R. (1994). Commercial lenders' use of accounting information in interaction with source credibility. *Contemporary Accounting Research, 10*(2), 557–585.

Markman, A. B., & Medin, D. L. (1995). Similarity and alignment in choice. *Organizational Behavior and Human Decision Processes, 63*(2), 117–130.

12 Bouwman, M. J., Frishkoff, P. A., & Frishkoff, P. (1987). How do financial analysts make decisions? A process model of the investment screening decision. *Accounting, Organizations and Society, 12*(1), 1–29.

Johnson, E. J. (1988a). Expertise and decision under uncertainty: Performance and process. In M. T. H. Chi, R. Glaser & M. J. Farr (Eds.), *The nature of expertise* (pp. 209–228). Hillsdale, NJ: Lawrence Erlbaum Associates.

Libby, R., & Frederick, D. M. (1989, February). *Expertise and the ability to explain audit findings* (Technical Report No. 21). Ann Arbor, MI: University of Michigan Cognitive Science and Machine Intelligence Laboratory.

13 Paek, S. N. (1997). A cognitive model for selecting business appraisal methods (Doctoral dissertation, University of Nebraska, Lincoln, 1997). *Dissertation Abstracts International*, (06A), 2283.

14 Collins, A., Brown, J. S., & Larkin, K. M. (1980). Inference in text understanding. In R. J. Spiro, B. C. Bruce & W. F. Brewer (Eds.), *Theoretical issues in reading comprehension* (pp. 385–407). Hillsdale, NJ: Lawrence Erlbaum Associates.

Serfaty, D., MacMillan, J., Entin, E. E., & Entin, E. B. (1997). The decision making expertise of battle commanders. In C. E. Zsambok & G. Klein (Eds.), *Naturalistic decision making* (pp. 233–246). Mahwah, NJ: Lawrence Erlbaum Associates.

15 Nickles, K. R. (1995). Judgment-based and reasoning-based stopping rules in decision making under uncertainty (Doctoral dissertation, University of Minnesota, 1995). *Dissertation Abstracts International, 56*(03A), 1005.

Saad, G., & Russo, J. E. (1996). Stopping criteria in sequential choice. *Organizational Behavior and Human Decision Processes, 67*(3), 258–270.

16 Lipp, A., Nourse, H. O., Bostrom, R. P., & Watson, H. J. (1992). The evolution of questions in successive versions of an expert system for real estate disposition. In T. W. Lauer, E. Peacock & A. C. Graesser (Eds.), *Questions and information systems* (pp. 63–84). Hillsdale, NJ: Lawrence Erlbaum Associates.

17 Reilly, B. A., & Doherty, M. E. (1989). A note on the assessment of self-insight in judgment research. *Organizational Behavior and Human Decision Processes, 44*(1), 123–131.

Shanteau, J., & Edwards, W. (2014). Decision making by experts: Influence of five key psychologists. In E. A. Wilhelms & V. F. Reyna (Eds.), *Neuroeconomics, judgment, and decision making* (pp. 3–26). New York: Psychology Press.

18 Bhagan, S. (2009). A chief executive officer and chief information officer consensus decision-making model for information technology investments (Doctoral dissertation, University of Phoenix, 2009). *Dissertation Abstracts International: Section A, 69*, 4023.

Pfeiffer, J., Meißner, M., Brandstätter, E., Riedl, R., Decker, R., & Rothlauf, F. (2014). On the influence of context-based complexity on information search patterns: An individual perspective. *Journal of Neuroscience, Psychology, and Economics, 7*(2), 103–124.

Sonmez, M., & Moorhouse, A. (2010). Purchasing professional services: Which decision criteria? *Management Decision*, *48*(2), 189–206.

19 Kercsmar, J. (1985). Individual investors' information choice, information processing, and judgment behavior: A process-tracing study of the verbal protocols associated with stock selection (Doctoral dissertation, University of Houston, University Park, 1985). *Dissertation Abstracts International*, *46*(09A), 2740.

20 Melone, N. P. (1987). Expertise in corporate acquisitions: An investigation of the influence of specialized knowledge on strategic decision making (Doctoral dissertation, University of Minnesota, 1987). *Dissertation Abstracts International*, *48*(09A), 2388.

Melone, N. P. (1994). Reasoning in the executive suite: The influence of role/experience-based expertise on decision processes of corporate executives. *Organization Science*, *5*(3), 438–455.

21 Pfeffer, M. G. (1987). Venture capital investment and protocol analysis (Doctoral dissertation, University of North Texas, 1987). *Dissertation Abstracts International*, *49*(01A), 112.

22 Sessa, V. I., Kaiser, R., Taylor, J. K., & Campbell, R. J. (1998). *Executive selection: A research report on what works and what doesn't (Rep. No. 179)*. Greensboro, NC: Center for Creative Leadership.
Sessa, V. I. (2001). Executive promotion and selection. In M. London (Ed.), *How people evaluate others in organizations* (pp. 91–110). Hillsdale, NJ: Lawrence Erlbaum Associates.

23 Borman, W. C. (1987). Personal constructs, performance schemata, and "folk theories" of subordinate effectiveness: Explorations in an Army officer sample. *Organizational Behavior and Human Decision Processes*, *40*(3), 307–322.

24 Hardin, W. G. (1996). An investigation into the information processing heuristics of private banking and real estate banking lenders in a commercial banking environment (Doctoral dissertation, Georgia State University, 1996). *Dissertation Abstracts International*, *58*(11A), 4384.

25 Britt, S. H., Adams, S. C., & Miller, A. S. (1972). How many advertising exposures per day. *Journal of Advertising Research*, *12*(6), 3–9.

26 Russo, J. E. (1977). The value of unit price information. *Journal of Marketing Research*, *14*(2), 193–201.

Russo, J. E., Staelin, R., Nolan, C. A., Russell, G. J., & Metcalf, B. L. (1986). Nutrition information in the supermarket. *Journal of Consumer Research*, *13*(1), 48–70.

27 Alpert, M. I. (1971). Identification of determinant attributes: A comparison of methods. *Journal of Marketing Research*, *8*(2), 184–191.

Green, P. E., & Srinivasan, V. (1978). Conjoint analysis in consumer research: Issues and outlook. *Journal of Consumer Research*, *5*(2), 103–123.

28 Verplanken, B. W., & Weenig, M. W. H. (1993). Graphical energy labels and consumers' decisions about home appliances: A process tracing approach. *Journal of Economic Psychology*, *14*(4), 739–752.

29 Ho, W., Xu, X., & Dey, P. K. (2010). Multi-criteria decision making approaches for supplier evaluation and selection: A literature review. *European Journal of Operational Research*, *202*(1), 16–24.

Ngeru, J. (2013). Multi-criteria decision analysis framework in the selection of an Enterprise Integration (EI) approach that best satisfies organizational requirements (Doctoral dissertation, Morgan State University, 2013). *Dissertation Abstracts International: Section B*, *73*(11-B)(E).

30 Hawes, J. M., Jackson Jr, D. W., Schlacter, J. L., & Wolfe, W. G. (1995). Selling and sales management in action examining the bases utilized for evaluating salespeoples' performance. *Journal of Personal Selling & Sales Management*, *15*(4), 57–65.

31 Hoch, S. J., & Ha, Y. W. (1986). Consumer learning: Advertising and the ambiguity of product experience. *Journal of Consumer Research*, *13*(2), 221–233.

32 Shapiro, S., & Spence, M. T. (2002). Factors affecting encoding, retrieval, and alignment of sensory attributes in a memory-based brand choice task. *Journal of Consumer Research*, *28*(4), 603–617.

33 Ding, Z., Sun, S. L., & Au, K. (2014). Angel investors' selection criteria: A comparative institutional perspective. *Asia Pacific Journal of Management*, *31*(3), 705–731.

Hall, J., & Hofer, C. W. (1993). Venture capitalists' decision criteria in new venture evaluation. *Journal of Business Venturing*, *8*(1), 25–42.

Sandberg, W. R., Schweiger, D. M., & Hofer, C. W. (1988). The use of verbal protocols in determining venture capitalists' decision processes. *Entrepreneurship Theory and Practice*, *13*(2), 8–20.

34 Ding, Sun, & Au (2014).

Hall, J., & Hofer, C. W. (1993). Venture capitalists' decision criteria in new venture evaluation. *Journal of Business Venturing*, *8*(1), 25–42.

Sandberg, Schweiger, & Hofer (1988).

35 Smotas, P. E. (1996). An analysis of budget decision criteria and selected demographic factors of school business officials of Connecticut school districts (Doctoral dissertation, The University of Connecticut, 1996). *Dissertation Abstracts International, 58*(02A), 388.

36 Galletta, D., King, R. C., & Rateb, D. (1993). The effect of expertise on software selection. *Association for Computing Machinery, 24*(2), 7–20.

37 Woodburn, J. L. (2014). A case study analysis of middle school principals' teacher selection criteria (Doctoral dissertation, University of Maryland, College Park, 2014). *Dissertation Abstracts International: Section A, 74*(8-A)(E).

38 Van Winter, J. A. (2007). The impact of selected cultural dimensions on international services vendor selection criteria: An exploratory investigation (Doctoral dissertation, George Washington University, 2008). *Dissertation Abstracts International: Section A, 69*, 299.

39 Hooper, V. J. (1994). Multinational capital budgeting and finance decisions. In J. Pointon (Ed.), *Issues in business taxation* (pp. 211–225). Aldershot, UK: Ashgate.

40 Graonic, M. D. (1995). The effects of context and consumer knowledge on transferability of preferences (Doctoral dissertation, University of Minnesota, 1995). *Dissertation Abstracts International, 56*(07A), 2772.

41 Haines, G. H. (1974). Process models of consumer decision making. In G. D. Hughes & M. L. Ray (Eds.), *Buyer/consumer information processing* (pp. 89–107). Chapel Hill, NC: University of North Carolina Press.

Palmer, J., & Faivre, J. P. (1973). The information processing theory of consumer behavior. *European Research, 1*, 231–240.

42 Kier, K. L. (2000). A study of the adaptive decision making ability of pharmacists when patient counseling using a process-tracing technique (Doctoral dissertation, The Ohio State University, 2000). *Dissertation Abstracts International, 61*(02B), 807.

43 Jin, B., & Farr, C. A. (2010). Supplier selection criteria and perceived benefits and challenges of global sourcing apparel firms in the United States. *Family and Consumer Sciences Research Journal, 39*(1), 31–44.

44 Biggs, S. F. (1984, p. 313). Financial analysts' information search in the assessment of corporate earning power. *Accounting, Organizations and Society, 9*(3–4), 313–323.

45 Kuperman, J. C. (2000, p. 12). Financial analyst sensemaking following strategic announcements: Implications for the investor relations activities of firms (Doctoral dissertation, New York University, 2000). *Dissertation Abstracts International, 61*(05A), 1936.

46 MacMillan, I. C., Siegal, R., & Narasimha, P. N. S. (1985). Criteria used by venture capitalists to evaluate new venture proposals. *Journal of Business Venturing, 1*(1), 119–128.

Robinson Jr, R. B. (1985). Emerging strategies in the venture capital industry. *Journal of Business Venturing, 2*(1), 53–77.

Tyebjee, T. T., & Bruno, A. V. (1984). A model of venture capitalist investment activity. *Management Science, 30*(9), 1051–1066.

47 *See* n33, Sandberg et al. (1988), p. 12.

48 Warren, J., Kuhn, D., & Weinstock, M. (2010). How do jurors argue with one another? *Judgment and Decision Making, 5*(1), 64–71.

49 Brown, B. K., & Campion, M. A. (1994). Biodata phenomenology: Recruiters' perceptions and use of biographical information in resume screening. *Journal of Applied Psychology, 79*(6), 897–908.

50 Griffin, B. (2014). The ability to identify criteria: Its relationship with social understanding, preparation, and impression management in affecting predictor performance in a high-stakes selection context. *Human Performance, 27*(2), 147–164.

51 Melchers, K. G., Klehe, U. C., Richter, G. M., Kleinmann, M., König, C. J., & Lievens, F. (2009). "I know what you want to know": The impact of interviewees' ability to identify criteria on interview performance and construct-related validity. *Human Performance, 22*(4), 355–374.

Preckel, D., & Schüpbach, H. (2005). Zusammenhänge zwischen rezeptiver Selbstdarstellungskompetenz und Leistung im Assessment Center. *Zeitschrift für Personalpsychologie, 4*(4), 151–158.

52 Weitz, B. A. (1978). Relationship between salesperson performance and understanding of customer decision making. *Journal of Marketing Research, 15*(4), 501–516.

53 Frame, C. D. (1990). Salesperson impression formation accuracy: A person-perception approach (Doctoral dissertation, Indiana University, 1990). *Dissertation Abstracts International, 51*(12A), 4199.

54 Baehr, M. E., & Williams, G. B. (1968). Prediction of sales success from factorially determined dimensions of personal background data. *Journal of Applied Psychology, 52*(2), 98–103.

Ghiselli, E. E. (1969). Prediction of success of stockbrokers. *Personnel Psychology, 22*(2), 25–130. Ghiselli, E. E. (1973). The validity of aptitude tests in personnel selection. *Personnel Psychology, 26*(4), 461–477.

Tanofsky, R., Shepps, R. R., & O'Neill, P. J. (1969). Pattern analysis of biographical predictors of success as an insurance salesman. *Journal of Applied Psychology, 53*(2, Pt. 1), 136–139.

55 *See* n45, Kuperman (2000), p. 39.

56 Howard-Grenville, J. A. (2007). Developing issue-selling effectiveness over time: Issue selling as resourcing. *Organization Science, 18*(4), 560–577.

57 Young, R. O. (1989). Cognitive processes in argumentation: An exploratory study of management consulting expertise (Doctoral dissertation, Carnegie Mellon University, 1989). *Dissertation Abstracts International, 50*(08B), 3764.

58 Nicholas, S. K. (1983, p. 89). A video observational study of the writing process of college students in a non-academic situation (Doctoral dissertation, Oakland University, 1983). *Dissertation Abstracts International, 44*(03A), 684.

59 *See* n45, Kuperman (2000).

60 Carenini, G. (2001). Generating and evaluating evaluative arguments (Doctoral dissertation, University of Pittsburgh, 2001). *Dissertation Abstracts International, 62*(05B), 2377.

61 *See* n33, Hall & Hofer (1993), p. 40.

62 Berger, Z. D., Yeh, J. C., Carter, H. B., & Pollack, C. E. (2014). Characteristics and experiences of patients with localized prostate cancer who left an active surveillance program. *The Patient-Patient-Centered Outcomes Research, 7*(4), 427–436.

63 Solomon, J., Knapp, P., Raynor, D. K., & Atkin, K. (2013). Worlds apart? An exploration of prescribing and medicine-taking decisions by patients, GPs and local policy makers. *Health Policy, 112*(3), 264–272.

64 Keeney, R. L., & Raiffa, H. (1976/1993). *Decisions with multiple objectives: Preferences and value tradeoffs.* New York: Cambridge University Press.

65 Saaty, T. L. (1980). *The analytic hierarchy process.* New York: McGraw-Hill.

66 Beach, L. R., Campbell, F. L., & Townes, B. O. (1979). Subjective expected utility and the prediction of birth-planning decisions. *Organizational Behavior and Human Performance, 24*(1), 18–28.

Borcherding, K., & Rohrmann, B. (1990). An analysis of multiattribute utility models using field data. In K. Borcherding, O. I. Larichev & D. M. Messick (Eds.), *Contemporary issues in decision making* (pp. 223–241). Amsterdam: North-Holland.

Von Winterfeldt, D., & Edwards, W. (1973). *Evaluation of complex stimuli using multi-attribute utility procedures.* Ann Arbor, MI: Technical Report, Engineering Psychology Laboratory, University of Michigan.

67 Stillwell, W. G., Barron, F. H., & Edwards, W. (1983). Evaluating credit applications: A validation of multiattribute utility weight elicitation techniques. *Organizational Behavior & Human Performance, 32*(1), 87–108.

68 *See* n60, Carenini (2001).

69 Carter, W. B., Beach, L. R., & Inui, T. S. (1986). The flu shot study: Using multiattribute utility theory to design a vaccination intervention. *Organizational Behavior and Human Decision Processes, 38*(3), 378–391.

70 Ericsson, K. A. (2001). Protocol analysis in psychology. In N. Smelser & P. Baltes (Eds.), *International encyclopedia of the social and behavioral sciences* (pp. 12256–12262). Oxford, UK: Elsevier.

Ericsson, K. A. (2006). Protocol analysis and expert thought: Concurrent verbalizations of thinking during experts' performance on representative tasks. In K. A. Ericsson, N. Charness, P. Feltovich & R. Hoffman (Eds.), *The Cambridge handbook of expertise and expert performance* (pp. 223–241). Cambridge, UK: Cambridge University Press.

Ericsson, K. A., & Simon, H. A. (1993). *Protocol analysis: Verbal reports as data* (revised edition). Cambridge, MA: Bradford Books/MIT Press.

71 Kahneman, D., Knetsch, J. L., & Thaler, R. H. (1990). Experimental tests of the endowment effect and the Coase theorem. *Journal of Political Economy, 98*, 1325–1348.

Schweitzer, M. (1994). Disentangling status quo and omission effects: An experimental analysis. *Organizational Behavior and Human Decision Processes, 58*(3), 457–476.

Svenson, O. (2003). Values, affect, and processes in human decision making: A differentiation and consolidation perspective. In S. L. Schneider & J. Shanteau (Eds.), *In emerging perspectives on judgment and decision research* (pp. 287–326). Cambridge, UK: Cambridge University Press.

72 Vlaev, I., Chater, N., & Stewart, N. (2007). Financial prospect relativity: Context effects in financial decision-making under risk. *Journal of Behavioral Decision Making, 20*(3), 273–304.

73 Lauer, T. W., & Peacock, E. (1992). Question-driven information search in auditor diagnosis. In T. W. Lauer, E. Peacock & A. C. Graesser (Eds.), *Questions and information systems* (pp. 253–271). Hillsdale, NJ: Lawrence Erlbaum Associates.

74 Burgoyne, J.G. (1975). The judgment process in management students' evaluation of their learning experiences. *Human Relations*, *28*(6), 543–569.

75 Edwards, A., Elwyn, G., Covey, J., Matthews, E., & Pill, R. (2001). Presenting risk information a review of the effects of framing and other manipulations on patient outcomes. *Journal of Health Communication*, *6*(1), 61–82.

Rothman, A. J., Haddock, G., & Schwarz, N. (2001). How many partners is too many? Shaping perceptions of vulnerability. *Journal of Applied Social Psychology*, *31*(10), 2195–2214.

Klein, W. M., & Weinstein, N. D. (1997). Social comparison and unrealistic optimism about personal risk. In B. P. Buunk & F. X. Gibbons (Eds.), *Health, coping, and well-being: Perspectives from social comparison theory* (pp. 25–61). Mahwah, NJ: Erlbaum.

76 Wood, J. V., Taylor, S. E., & Lichtman, R. R. (1985a). Social comparison in adjustment to breast cancer. *Journal of Personality and Social Psychology*, *49*(5), 1169–1183.

77 Gunderson, E. A. W. (1991). Expertise in security valuation: Operationalizing the valuation process (Doctoral dissertation, The Union Institute, 1991). *Dissertation Abstracts International*, *52*(02A), 0592.

78 Lee, D. (1989a). The differential impact of comparative advertising on novice and expert consumers (Doctoral dissertation, University of Pittsburgh, 1989). *Dissertation Abstracts International*, *50*(11a), 3666.

79 Bettman, J. R., & Sujan, M. (1987). Effects of framing on evaluation of comparable and noncomparable alternatives by expert and novice consumers. *Journal of Consumer Research*, *14*(2), 141–154.

Johnson, M. D. (1986). Modeling choice strategies for noncomparable alternatives. *Marketing Science*, *5*(1), 37–54.

Johnson, M. D. (1988b). Comparability and hierarchical processing in multialternative choice. *Journal of Consumer Research*, *15*(3), 303–314.

80 Jung, K. (1996). Line extension versus new brand name introduction: Effects of new products discrepancy and relationship to an existing brand on the information process of new product evaluation (Doctoral dissertation, University of Illinois, Urbana-Champaign, 1996). *Dissertation Abstracts International*, *57*(11A), 4833.

Kim, H., & John, D. R. (2008). Consumer response to brand extensions: Construal level as a moderator of the importance of perceived fit. *Journal of Consumer Psychology*, *18*(2), 116–126.

81 Kahneman, D. (2003). Maps of bounded rationality: Psychology for behavioral economics. *American Economic Review*, *93*(5), 1449–1475.

82 Nunes, J. C., & Boatwright, P. (2004). Incidental prices and their effect on willingness to pay. *Journal of Marketing Research*, *41*(4), 457–466.

83 Stratman, J., & Young, R. O. (1986, April). *An analysis of novice managers' performances in board meetings*. Annual Conference of the Management Communication Association. Durham, NC.

84 Ruck, H. W. (1980). A cross-company study of decision policies of manager resume evaluations (Doctoral dissertation, Stevens Institute of Technology, 1980). *Dissertation Abstracts International*, *41*(08B), 3222.

85 Ordonez, L. D. (1994). Expectations in consumer decision-making: A model of reference price formation (Doctoral dissertation, University of California, Berkeley, 1994). *Dissertation Abstracts International*, *56*(05B), 2911.

86 Svenson, O. (1974). *A note on think aloud protocols obtained during the choice of a home* (Report No. 421). Stockholm: Psychology Lab, University of Stockholm.

87 Dhar, R., & Simonson, I. (1992). The effect of the focus of comparison on consumer preferences. *Journal of Marketing Research*, *29*(4), 430–440.

Ranyard, R., Charlton, J. P., & Williamson, J. (2001). The role of internal reference prices in consumers' willingness to pay judgments: Thaler's beer pricing task revisited. *Acta Psychologica*, *106*(3), 265–283.

88 Kühberger, A., & Huber, O. (1998). Decision making with mission information: A verbal protocol study. *European Journal of Cognitive Psychology*, *10*(3), 269–290.

89 *See* n10, Sanbonmatsu et al. (1992).

90 Hernandez, J. M. C., Han, X., & Kardes, F. R. (2014). Effects of the perceived diagnosticity of presented attribute and brand name information on sensitivity to missing information. *Journal of Business Research*, *67*(5), 874–881.

91 Burke, S. J. (1992). The effects of missing information and inferences on decision processing and evaluation (Doctoral dissertation, The University of Michigan, 1992). *Dissertation Abstracts International*, *53*(11A), 3997.

92 Walsh, J. P. (1995). Managerial and organizational cognition: Notes from a trip down memory lane. *Organization Science*, *6*(3), 280–321.

93 Svenson, O. (1979). Process descriptions of decision making. *Organizational Behavior and Human Performance*, *23*(1), 86–112.

Wallsten, T.S. (1980). Processes and models to describe choice and inference. In T.S. Wallsten (Ed.), *Cognitive processes in choice and decision behavior* (pp. 215–237). Hillsdale, NJ: Erlbaum.

94 Bartlett, F. C. (1932). *Remembering: A Study in experimental and social psychology.* Cambridge, UK: Cambridge University Press.

Chi, M. T. H., & Ohlsson, S. (2005). Complex declarative learning. In K. J. Holyoak & R. G. Morrison (Eds.), *The Cambridge handbook of thinking and reasoning* (pp. 371–399). Cambridge, UK: Cambridge University Press.

Rentsch, J. R., Small, E. E., & Hanges, P. J. (2008). Cognitions in organizations and teams: What is the meaning of cognitive similarity? In D. B. Smith (Ed.), *The people make the place: Dynamic linkages between individuals and organizations* (pp. 127–155). New York: Lawrence Erlbaum Associates.

95 Fiedler, K. (1982). Causal schemata: Review and criticism of research on a popular construct. *Journal of Personality and Social Psychology, 42,* 1001–1013.

96 Schank, R. C., & Abelson, R. P. (1977). *Scripts, plans, goals and understanding: An inquiry into human knowledge structures.* Oxford, UK: Lawrence Erlbaum.

97 Minsky, M. A. (1975). A framework for the representation of knowledge. In P. Winston (Ed.), *The psychology of computer vision* (pp. 211–277). New York: McGraw-Hill.

98 Johnson-Laird, P. N. (1980). Mental models in cognitive science. *Cognitive Science: A Multidisciplinary Journal, 4*(1), 71–115.

99 Gobet, F., & Simon, H. A. (1996). Templates in chess memory: A mechanism for recalling several boards. *Cognitive Psychology, 31*(1), 1–40.

100 Markman, A. B. (1999). *Knowledge representation.* Mahwah, NJ: Erlbaum.

101 Grafman, J. (1995). Similarities and distinctions among current models of prefrontal cortical functions. *Annals of the New York Academy of Sciences, 769,* 337–368.

102 Mason, R. A., & Just, M. A. (2006). Neuroimaging contributions to the understanding of discourse processes. In M. J. Traxler & M. A. Gernsbacher (Eds.), *Handbook of psycholinguistics* (2nd ed., pp. 765–800). London: Elsevier Inc.

103 Tse, D., Takeuchi, T., Kakeyama, M., Kajii, Y., Okuno, H., Tohyama, C., . . . Morris, R. G. (2011). Schema-dependent gene activation and memory encoding in neocortex. *Science, 333*(6044), 891–895.

van Kesteren, M. T., Fernández, G., Norris, D. G., & Hermans, E. J. (2010). Persistent schema-dependent hippocampal-neocortical connectivity during memory encoding and postencoding rest in humans. *Proceedings of the National Academy of Sciences, 107*(16), 7550–7555.

Wang, S. H., Tse, D., & Morris, R. G. (2012). Anterior cingulate cortex in schema assimilation and expression. *Learning & Memory, 19*(8), 315–318.

Ghosh, V. E., & Gilboa, A. (2014). What is a memory schema? A historical perspective on current neuroscience literature. *Neuropsychologia, 53,* 104–114.

104 Brewer, W. F., & Nakamura, G. V. (1984). The nature and functions of schemes. In R. S. Wyer & T. K. Srull (Eds.), *Handbook of social cognition* (Vol. 1, pp. 119–160). Hillsdale, NJ: Erlbaum.

Marshall, S. P. (1995). *Schemas in problem solving.* Cambridge, UK: Cambridge University Press.

See n97, Minsky (1975).

105 Brewer, W. F., & Tenpenny, P. L. (1996). *The role of schemata in the recall and recognition of episodic information.* Unpublished manuscript, University of Illinois at Urbana-Champaign, Champaign, IL.

106 Neisser, U. (1976). *Cognition and reality: Principles and implications of cognitive psychology.* New York: W. H. Freeman/Times Books/Henry Holt & Co.

107 Bhaskar, R. (1978). Problem solving in semantically rich domains (Doctoral dissertation, Carnegie Mellon University, 1978). *Dissertation Abstracts International, 41*(05B), 1826.

108 Bouwman, M. J., Frishkoff, P., & Frishkoff, P. A. (1995). The relevance of GAAP-based information: A case study exploring some uses and limitations. *Accounting Horizons, 9*(4), 22–47.

Olsen, R. A. (2002). Professional investors as naturalistic decision makers: Evidence and market implications. *The Journal of Psychology and Financial Markets, 3*(3), 161–167.

109 Larkin, J. H., McDermott, J., Simon, D. P., & Simon, H. A. (1980). Models of competence in solving physics problems. *Cognitive Science, 4*(4), 317–345.

110 Hinsley, D. A., Hayes, J. R., & Simon, H. A. (1977). From words to equations: Meaning and representation in algebra word problems. In M. A. Just & P. A. Carpenter (Eds.), *Cognitive processes in comprehension* (pp. 89–106). Hillsdale, NJ: Lawrence Erlbaum Associates.

111 Heller, R. F., Saltzstein, H. D., & Caspe, W. B. (1992). Heuristics in medical and non-medical decision-making. *The Quarterly Journal of Experimental Psychology A: Human Experimental Psychology, 44A*(2), 211–235.

112 Carroll, J. S. (1978). Causal attributions in expert parole decisions. *Journal of Personality and Social Psychology*, *36*(12), 1501–1511.

113 *See* n45, Kuperman (2000).

114 Connelly, M. S., Gilbert, J. A., Zaccaro, S. J., Threlfall, K. V., Marks, M. A., & Mumford, M. D. (2000). Exploring the relationship of leadership skills and knowledge to leader performance. *Leadership Quarterly*, *11*, 65–86.

Mumford, M. D., Marks, M. A., Connelly, M. S., Zaccaro, S. J., & Reiter-Palmon, R. (2000). Development of leadership skills: Experience and timing. *Leadership Quarterly, 11*, 87–114.

Wofford, J. C., Goodwin, V. L., & Whittington, J. L. (1998). A field study of a cognitive approach to understanding transformational and transactional leadership. *Leadership Quarterly, 9*, 55–84.

115 Perl, S., & Young, R. O. (2015, June). *A cognitive study of incident handling expertise.* Presented at the Annual Forum of Incident Response and Security Teams (FIRST) Conference, Berlin, Germany.

116 Rossiter, J. R., Percy, L., & Donovan, R. J. (1991). A better advertising planning grid. *Journal of Advertising Research*, *28*(1), 11–21.

Sjödin, H., & Törn, F. (2006). When communication challenges brand associations: A framework for understanding consumer responses to brand image incongruity. *Journal of Consumer Behaviour*, *5*(1), 32–42.

Boush, D. M., & Loken, B. (1991). A process-tracing study of brand extension evaluation. *Journal of Marketing Research*, *28*(1), 16–28.

117 Sentis, K., & Markus, H. (1986, p. 133). Brand personality and self. In J. C. Olson & K. Sentis (Eds.), *Advertising and consumer psychology* (Vol. 3, pp. 132–148). New York: Praeger.

See also Goodstein, R. C. (1993). Category-based applications and extensions in advertising: Motivating more extensive ad processing. *Journal of Consumer Research*, *20*(1), 87–99.

Halkias, G., & Kokkinaki, F. (2012). Cognitive and affective responses to schema-incongruent brand messages. In A. Innocenti & A. Sirigu (Eds.), *Neuroscience and the economics of decision making* (pp. 165–181). New York: Routledge.

118 Govaerts, M. J. B., Van de Wiel, M. W. J., Schuwirth, L. W. T., Van der Vleuten, C. P. M., & Muijtjens, A. M. M. (2013). Workplace-based assessment: Raters' performance theories and constructs. *Advances in Health Sciences Education*, *18*(3), 375–396.

119 Cardy, R. L., Bernardin, H., Abbott, J. G., Senderak, M. P., & Taylor, K. (1987). The effects of individual performance schemata and dimension familiarization on rating accuracy. *Journal of Occupational Psychology*, *60*(3), 197–205.

Ostroff, C., & Ilgen, D. R. (1992). Cognitive categories of raters and rating accuracy. *Journal of Business and Psychology*, *7*(1), 3–26.

120 Walsh, J. P., Henderson, C. M., & Deighton, J. (1988, p. 207). Negotiated belief structures and decision performance: An empirical investigation. *Organizational Behavior and Human Decision Processes*, *42*(2), 194–216.

121 Ritchhart, R., & Perkins, D. N. (2005, p. 790). Learning to think: The challenges of teaching thinking. In K. J. Holyoak & R. G. Morrison (Eds.), *The Cambridge handbook of thinking and reasoning* (pp. 775–802). Cambridge, UK: Cambridge University Press.

122 Anderson, J. R. (2000, p. 351). *Cognitive psychology and its implications* (5th ed.). New York: Worth Publishers.

123 Anderson, J. R. (2010, July 19). Personal communication.

124 Ranyard, R., & Williamson, J. (2005). Conversation-based process tracing methods for naturalistic decision making: Information search and verbal analysis. In H. Montgomery, R. Lipshitz & B. Brehmer (Eds.), *How professionals make decisions* (pp. 305–317). Mahwah, NJ: Lawrence Erlbaum Associates.

125 Coupey, E. (1994). Restructuring: Constructive processing of information displays in consumer choice. *Journal of Consumer Research*, *21*(1), 83–99.

126 Kumaran, D., Summerfield, J. J., Hassabis, D., & Maguire, E. A. (2009). Tracking the emergence of conceptual knowledge during human decision making. *Neuron*, *63*(6), 889–901.

Shea, N., Krug, K., & Tobler, P. N. (2008). Conceptual representations in goal-directed decision making. *Cognitive, Affective, and Behavioral Neuroscience*, *8*(4), 418–428.

127 Fiske, S. T., & Taylor, S. E. (1991, p. 122). *Social cognition* (2nd ed.). New York: McGraw-Hill.

128 Carlston, D. E., & Smith, E. R. (1996). Principles of mental representation. In E. T. Higgins & A. Kruglanski (Eds.), *Social psychology: Handbook of basic principles* (2nd ed., pp. 184–210). New York: Guilford Press.

DeWitt, M. R., Knight, J. B., Hicks, J. L., & Ball, B. H. (2012). The effects of prior knowledge on the encoding of episodic contextual details. *Psychonomic Bulletin & Review*, *19*(2), 251–257.

Preston, A. R., & Eichenbaum, H. (2013). Interplay of hippocampus and prefrontal cortex in memory. *Current Biology, 23*(17), R764–R773.

129 Haste, H., & Torney-Purta, J. (1992). *The development of political understanding: A new perspective.* San Francisco: Jossey-Bass.

Price, V., & Zaller, J. (1993). Who gets the news? Alternative measures of news reception and their implications for research. *Public Opinion Quarterly, 57,* 133–164.

Sniderman, P. M., Brody, R. A., & Tetlock, P. E. (1991). *Reasoning and choice: Explorations in political psychology.* New York: Cambridge University Press.

130 Fredin, E. S., Kosicki, G. M., & Becker, L. B. (1996). Cognitive strategies for media use during a presidential campaign. *Political Communication, 13,* 23–42.

131 Gentner, D., Loewenstein, J., Thompson, L., & Forbus, K. D. (2009). Reviving inert knowledge: Analogical abstraction supports relational retrieval of past events. *Cognitive Science, 33*(8), 1343–1382.

Kurtz, K. J., & Loewenstein, J. (2007). Converging on a new role for analogy in problem solving and retrieval: When two problems are better than one. *Memory & Cognition, 35*(2), 334–341.

132 Rhee, J. W., & Cappella, J. N. (1997). The role of political sophistication in learning from news: Measuring schema development. *Communication Research, 24,* 197–233.

133 Alberdi, E., Becher, J. C., Gilhooly, K., Hunter, J., Logie, R., Lyon, A., . . . & Reiss, J. (2001). Expertise and the interpretation of computerized physiological data: Implications for the design of computerized monitoring in neonatal intensive care. *International Journal of Human-Computer Studies, 55,* 191–216.

134 Chi, M. T. H. (2006). Two approaches to the study of expert's characteristics. In K. A. Ericsson, N. Charness, P. Feltovich & R. Hoffman (Eds.), *The Cambridge handbook of expertise and expert performance* (pp. 21–30). Cambridge, UK: Cambridge University Press.

135 *See* n104, Brewer & Nakamura (1984).

136 *See* n13, Paek (1997).

137 Endsley, M. R. (2006). Expertise and situation awareness. In K. A. Ericsson, N. Charness, P. Feltovich & R. Hoffman (Eds.), *The Cambridge handbook of expertise and expert performance* (pp. 633–651). Cambridge, UK: Cambridge University Press.

Vendetti, M. S., Wu, A., Rowshanshad, E., Knowlton, B. J., & Holyoak, K. J. (2014). When reasoning modifies memory: Schematic assimilation triggered by analogical mapping. *Journal of Experimental Psychology: Learning, Memory, and Cognition, 40*(4), 1172–1180.

138 Frensch, P. A., & Sternberg, R. J. (1989). Expertise and intelligent thinking: When is it worse to know better? In R. J. Sternberg (Ed.), *Advances in the psychology of human intelligence* (Vol. 5, pp. 157–188). Hillsdale, NJ: Lawrence Erlbaum Associates.

Staw, B. (1981). The escalation of commitment to a course of action. *Academy of Management Review, 6*(4), 577–587.

Tversky, A., & Kahneman, D. (1988). Rational choice and the framing of decisions. In D. E. Bell, H. Raiffa & A. Tversky (Eds.), *Decision making: Descriptive, normative, and prescriptive interactions* (pp. 167–192). New York: Cambridge University Press.

139 Dearborn, D. C., & Simon, H. A. (1958). Selective perception: A note on the departmental identifications of executives. *Sociometry, 21,* 140–144.

140 Barnett, S. M., & Ceci, S. J. (2002). When and where do we apply what we learn?: A taxonomy for far transfer. *Psychological Bulletin, 128*(4), 612–637.

Ericsson, K. A., & Lehmann, A. C. (1996). Expert and exceptional performance: Evidence on maximal adaptations on task constraints. *Annual Review of Psychology, 47,* 273–305.

Feltovich, P. J., Prietula, M. J., & Ericsson, K. A. (2006). Studies of expertise from psychological perspectives. In K. A. Ericsson, N. Charness, P. J. Feltovich & R. Hoffman (Eds.), *The Cambridge handbook of expertise and expert performance* (pp. 41–67). Cambridge, UK: Cambridge University Press.

141 Schwenk, C. R. (1984). Cognitive simplification process in strategic decision making. *Strategic Management Journal, 5*(2), 111–128.

142 Camerer, C. F., & Johnson, E. J. (1991). The process-performance paradox in expert judgment: How can experts know so much and predict so badly? In K. A. Ericsson & J. Smith (Eds.), *Toward a general theory of expertise: Prospects and limits* (pp. 195–217). New York: Cambridge University Press.

Chan, S. (1982). Expert judgments under uncertainty: Some evidence and suggestions. *Social Science Quarterly, 63,* 428–444.

Lichtenstein, S., Fischhoff, B., & Phillips, L. D. (1982). Calibration of probabilities: The state of the art to 1980. In D. Kahneman, P. Slovic & A. Tversky (Eds.), *Judgment under uncertainty: Heuristics and biases* (pp. 306–334). New York: Cambridge University Press.

143   Maines, L. A., & McDaniel, L. S. (2000). Effects of comprehensive-income characteristics on nonprofessional investors' judgments: The role of financial-statement presentation format. *The Accounting Review*, *75*(2), 79–207.

144   Lau, C. M., Kilbourne, L. M., & Woodman, R. W. (2003). A shared schema approach to understanding organizational culture change. In W. P. Pasmore & R. W. Woodman (Eds.). *Research in organizational change and development* (pp. 225–256). Bingley, UK: Emerald Group Publishing.

145   Rentsch, Joan R., & Hall, Rosalie J. (1994). Members of great teams think alike: A model of team effectiveness and schema similarity among team members. In M. M. Beyerlein & D. A. Johnson (Eds.), *Advances in interdisciplinary studies of work teams: Theories of self-managing work teams* (Vol. 1, pp. 223–261). Greenwich, CT: Elsevier Science/JAI Press.

146   Vaughan, S. I. (1999). Information sharing and cognitive centrality: Patterns in small decision-making groups of executives. *Dissertation Abstracts International: Section B: The Sciences and Engineering, 60*(4-B), 1919.

147   Laughlin, P. R., & Ellis, A. L. (1986). Demonstrability and social combination processes on mathematical intellective tasks. *Journal of Experimental Social Psychology, 22*(3), 177–189.

148   Crano, W. D. (2001). Social influence, social identity, and ingroup leniency. In C. K. W. De Dreu, & N. K. De Vries (Eds.), *Group consensus and minority influence: Implications for innovation* (pp. 122–143). Oxford, U. K.: Blackwell Publishers.

149   Tindale, R. S., Smith, C. M., Thomas, L. S., Filkins, J., & Sheffey, S. (1996). Shared representations and asymmetric social influence processes in small groups. In E. H. Witte & J. H. Davis (Eds.), *Understanding group behavior* (Vol. 1: *Consensual action by small groups*, pp. 81–103). Hillsdale, NJ: Lawrence Erlbaum Associates.

150   Tindale, R. S., Kameda, T., & Hinsz, V. (2003). Group decision making: Review and integration. In M. A. Hogg & J. Cooper (Eds.), *Sage handbook of social psychology* (pp. 381–403). London: Sage.

151   Cannon-Bowers, J. A., Salas, E., & Converse, S. (1993). Shared mental models in expert team decision making. In N. J. Castellan (Ed.), *Individual and group decision making: Current issues* (pp. 221–246). Hillsdale, NJ: Lawrence Erlbaum Associates.

DeChurch, L. A., & Mesmer-Magnus, J. R. (2010). The cognitive underpinnings of effective teamwork: A meta-analysis. *Journal of Applied Psychology, 95*(1), 32–53.

Giske, R., Rodahl, S. E., & Høigaard, R. (2015). Shared mental task models in elite ice hockey and handball teams: Does it exist and how does the coach intervene to make an impact? *Journal of Applied Sport Psychology, 27*(1), 20–34.

Randall, K. R., Resick, C. J., & DeChurch, L. A. (2011). Building team adaptive capacity: The roles of sensegiving and team composition. *Journal of Applied Psychology, 96*(3), 525–540.

152   Mason, C. M., & Griffin, M. A. (2003). Identifying group task satisfaction at work. *Small Group Research, 34*(4), 413–442.

153   Naumann, S. E., & Bennett, N. (2000). A case for procedural justice climate: Development and test of a multilevel model. *Academy of Management Journal, 43*(5), 881–889.

154   Colquitt, J. A., Noe, R. A., & Jackson, C. L. (2002). Justice in teams: Antecedents and consequences of procedural justice climate. *Personnel Psychology, 55*(1), 83–109.

155   Kirkman, B. L., Tesluk, P. E., & Rosen, B. (2001). Assessing the incremental validity of team consensus ratings over aggregation of individual-level data in predicting team effectiveness. *Personnel Psychology, 54*(3), 645–667.

Rentsch, J. R., & Klimoski, R. J. (2001). Why do "great minds" think alike? Antecedents of team member schema agreement. *Journal of Organizational Behavior, 22*(2), 107–120.

156   Kang, H. R., Yang, H. D., & Rowley, C. (2006). Factors in team effectiveness: Cognitive and demographic similarities of software development team members. *Human Relations, 59*(12), 1681–1710.

157   Lim, B. C., & Klein, K. J. (2006). Team mental models and team performance: A field study of the effects of team mental model similarity and accuracy. *Journal of Organizational Behavior, 27*(4), 403–418.

Mathieu, J. E., Heffner, T. S., Goodwin, G. F., Cannon-Bowers, J. A., & Salas, E. (2005). Scaling the quality of teammates' mental models: Equifinality and normative comparisons. *Journal of Organizational Behavior, 26*(1), 37–56.

Waller, M. J., Gupta, N., & Giambatista, R. C. (2004). Effects of adaptive behaviors and shared mental models on control crew performance. *Management Science, 50*(11), 1534–1544.

158   Lee, M. Y. (2008). Understanding changes in team-related and task-related mental models and their effects on team and individual performance. *Dissertation Abstracts International Section A: Humanities and Social Sciences, 69*(2-A), 491.

159   Carley, K. M. (1997). Extracting team mental models through textual analysis. *Journal of Organizational Behavior, 18*(Spec Issue), 533–558.

160 HelmReich, R. L. (1997). Managing Human Error in Aviation. *Scientific American, 277*(5), 40.

Langan-Fox, J., Anglim, J., & Wilson, J. R. (2004). Mental models, team mental models, and performance: Process, development, and future directions. *Human Factors and Ergonomics in Manufacturing, 14*(4), 331–352.

161 *See* n79, Bettman & Sujan (1987).

Maheswaran, D., & Sternthal, B. (1990). The effects of knowledge, motivation, and type of message on ad processing and product judgments. *Journal of Consumer Research, 17*(1), 66–73.

Simonson, I., Huber, J., & Payne, J. (1988). The relationship between prior brand knowledge and information acquisition order. *Journal of Consumer Research, 14*(4), 566–578.

162 Carroll, M. L. (1997). A comparative analysis and evaluation of knowledge structures between expert novice and struggling novice accounting students (Doctoral dissertation, Loyola University of Chicago, 1997). *Dissertation Abstracts International, 58*(03A), 0733.

Peskin, J. (1998). Constructing meaning when reading poetry: An expert-novice study. *Cognition and Instruction, 16*(3), 235–263.

Rouet, J. F., Favart, M., Britt, M. A., & Perfetti, C. A. (1997). Studying and using multiple documents in history: Effects of discipline expertise. *Cognition and Instruction, 15*(1), 85–106.

163 Guida, A., Gobet, F., Tardieu, H., & Nicolas, S. (2012). How chunks, long-term working memory and templates offer a cognitive explanation for neuroimaging data on expertise acquisition: A two-stage framework. *Brain and Cognition, 79*(3), 221–244.

Neumann, N., Lotze, M., & Eickhoff, S. B. (2016). Cognitive expertise: An ALE meta-analysis. Human Brain Mapping, 37(1), 262–272.

164 Campitelli, G., Gobet, F., & Parker, A. (2005). Structure and stimulus familiarity: A study of memory in chess-players with functional magnetic resonance imaging. *The Spanish Journal of Psychology, 8*(02), 238–245.

Bilalić, M., Langner, R., Erb, M., & Grodd, W. (2010). Mechanisms and neural basis of object and pattern recognition: A study with chess experts. *Journal of Experimental Psychology: General, 139*(4), 728–742.

Henson, R. (2005). What can functional neuroimaging tell the experimental psychologist? *The Quarterly Journal of Experimental Psychology Section A, 58*(2), 193–233.

165 Currie-Rubin, R. (2012). Ill-Structured problem solving of novice reading specialists and expert assessment specialists: Learning and expertise (Doctoral dissertation, Harvard University, 2013). *Dissertation Abstracts International: Section A, 74*(4-A)(E).

Govaerts, M. J. B., Van de Wiel, M. W. J., Schuwirth, L. W. T., Van der Vleuten, C. P. M., & Muijtjens, A. M. M. (2013). Workplace-based assessment: Raters' performance theories and constructs. *Advances in Health Sciences Education, 18*(3), 375–396.

166 Holyoak, K. J. (1984, p. 205). Mental models in problem solving. In J. R. Anderson & S. M. Kosslyn (Eds.), *Tutorials in learning and memory: Essays in honor of Gordon Bower* (pp. 193–218). San Francisco: Freeman.

See also Chi, M. T. H., Feltovich, P. J., & Glaser, R. (1981). Categorization and representation of physics problems by experts and novices. *Cognitive Science, 5*, 121–152.

Ericsson, K. A. (2006). The influence of experience and deliberate practice on the development of superior expert performance. In K. A. Ericsson & N. Charness (Eds.), *The Cambridge handbook of expertise and expert performance* (pp. 683–703). Cambridge: Cambridge University Press.
See n109, Larkin et al. (1980).

167 Cassie, J. R. B., & Robinson, F. G. (1982). A decision schema approach to career decision making. *International Journal of Advances in Counseling, 5*, 165–182.

168 Shafir, E., Simonson, I., & Tversky, A. (1993). Reason-based choice. *Cognition Special Issue: Reasoning and Decision Making, 49*(1–2), 11–36.

169 Andersson, P. (2004). Does experience matter in lending? A process-tracing study on experienced loan officers' and novices' decision behavior. *Journal of Economic Psychology, 25*(4), 471–492.

Mulvey, M. S., Olson, J. C., Celsi, R. L., & Walker, B. A. (1994). Exploring the relationship between means-end knowledge and involvement. *Advances in Consumer Research, 21*, 51–57.

Walker, B. A., Celsi, R. L., & Olson, J. C. (1986). Exploring the structural characteristics of consumers' knowledge. *Advances in Consumer Research, 14*(1), 17–21.

170 Kuusela, H., Spence, M. T., & Kanto, A. J. (1998). Expertise effects on prechoice decision processes and final outcomes: A protocol analysis. *European Journal of Marketing, 32*(5–6), 559–576.

171 Polansky, S. H. (1987). An information-processing analysis of the effects of product class knowledge on newspaper consumer behavior (Doctoral dissertation, The University of North Carolina, Chapel Hill, 1987). *Dissertation Abstracts International, 48*(07a), 1572.

172 *See* n161, Maheswaran & Sternthal (1990).

173 Bonner, S. E., Walther, B. R., & Young, S. M. (2003). Sophistication-related differences in investors' models of the relative accuracy of analysts' forecast revisions. *The Accounting Review, 78*(3), 679–706.

174 Park, C. W., & Lessig, V. P. (1981). Familiarity and its impact on consumer decision biases and heuristics. *Journal of Consumer Research, 8*(2), 223–230.

175 *See* n79, Bettman & Sujan (1987).

176 *See* n170, Kuusela et al. (1998).

177 Bettman, J. R., & Park, C. W. (1980). Effects of prior knowledge and experience and phase of the choice process on consumer decision processes: A protocol analysis. *Journal of Consumer Research, 7*(3), 234–248.

  See n9, Johnson & Russo (1984).

178 *See* n77, Gunderson (1991).

179 *See* n78, Lee (1989a).

180 *See* n40, Graonic (1995).

  O'Shaughnessy, J. (1987). *Why people buy.* Oxford: Oxford University Press.

181 Marks, L. J., & Olson, J. C. (1981). Toward a cognitive structure conceptualization of product familiarity. *Advances in Consumer Research, 8,* 145–150.

  McKeithen, K. B., Reitman, J. S., Rueter, H. H., & Hirtle, S. C. (1981). Knowledge organization and skill differences in computer programmers. *Cognitive Psychology, 13*(3), 307–325.

182 *See* n84, Ruck (1980).

183 *See* n36, Galletta et al. (1993).

184 Strater, L. D., Jones, D. G., & Endsley, M. R. (2001). *Analysis of infantry situation awareness training requirements.* (No. SATech 01–15). Marietta, GA: SA Technologies.

185 Lee, D. H. (1989b). Consumer inferencing behavior in processing product information: The roles of product class knowledge and information processing goal (Doctoral dissertation, Indiana University, 1989). *Dissertation Abstracts International, 51*(03A), 933.

  Lee, D. H., & Olshavsky, R. W. (1995). Conditions and consequences of spontaneous inference generation: A concurrent protocol approach. *Organizational Behavior and Human Decision Processes, 61*(2), 177–189.

186 *See* n14, Serfaty et al. (1997).

187 Alba, J. W., & Hutchinson, J. W. (1987). Dimensions of consumer expertise. *Journal of Consumer Research, 13*(4), 411–454.

  See n185, Lee (1989b).

  Srull, T. K. (1983). Organizational and retrieval processes in person memory: An examination of processing objectives, presentation format, and the possible role of self-generated retrieval cues. *Journal of Personality and Social Psychology, 44*(6), 1157–1170.

188 Shanteau, J. (1988). Psychological characteristics and strategies of expert decision makers. *Acta Psychologica, 68*(1–3), 203–215.

189 Gardner, M. P., Mitchell, A. A., & Russo, J. E. (1985). Low involvement strategies for processing advertisements. *Journal of Advertising, 14*(2), 4–13.

190 Fredelius, G., Sandell, R., & Lindqvist, C. (2002). Who should receive subsidized psychotherapy? Analysis of decision makers' think-aloud protocols. *Qualitative Health Research, 12*(5), 640–654.

191 Hollman, W. A. (2005). Buy and sell decisional analysis of financial advisors (Doctoral dissertation, Walden University, 2005). *Dissertation Abstracts International: Section A, 66,* 1103.

192 *See* n187, Srull (1983).

193 Gomez Borja, M. A. (2000). Effects of expertise and similarity of alternatives on consumer decision strategies and decision quality: A process tracing approach (Doctoral dissertation, Universidad de Castilla–La Mancha, 2000). *Dissertation Abstracts International, 62*(10A), 3479.

194 Johnson, E. J. (1981). Expertise in admissions judgment (Doctoral dissertation, Carnegie Mellon University, 1981). *Dissertation Abstracts International, 45*(06B), 1941.

195 *See* n185, Lee (1989b).

196 Roese, N. J., & Sherman, J. W. (2007). Expectancy. In A. W. Kruglanski & E. T. Higgins (Eds.), *Social psychology: Handbook of basic principles* (2nd ed., pp. 91–115). New York: The Guilford Press.

197 Karniol, R. (2003). Egocentrism versus protocentrism: The status of self in social prediction. *Psychological Review, 110*(3), 564–580.

198 *See* n9, Brucks (1985).

  Kardash, C. A., Royer, J. M., & Greene, B. A. (1988). Effects of schemata on both encoding and retrieval of information from prose. *Journal of Educational Psychology, 80*(3), 324–329.

199 *See* n12, Johnson (1988a).

  See n9, Johnson & Russo (1984).

200 Davis, J. T. (1996). Experience and auditors' selection of relevant information for preliminary control risk assessments. *Auditing, 15*(1), 16–37.

See n188, Shanteau (1988).

201 *See* n171, Polansky (1987).

202 Boyle, P. J. (1994). Expertise in a constructive product-choice process (Doctoral dissertation, Cornell University, 1994). *Dissertation Abstracts International, 55*(05a), 1323.

203 *See* n187, Alba & Hutchinson (1987).

Fredrickson, J. W. (1985). Effects of decision motive and organizational performance level on strategic decision processes. *Academy of Management Journal, 28*(4), 821–843.

Isenberg, D. J. (1986). Thinking and managing: A verbal protocol analysis of managerial problem solving. *Academy of Management Journal, 29*(4), 775–788.

204 Chase, W. G., & Simon, H. A. (1973). Perception in chess. *Cognitive Psychology, 4*(1), 55–81.

205 Martin, J. (1982). Stories and scripts in organizational settings. In A. M. Hastorf & A. M. Isen (Eds.), *Cognitive social psychology* (pp. 255–306). New York: Elsevier/North-Holland. Nelson, K. (1980, September). *Characteristics of children's scripts for familiar events.* Paper presented at the Meeting of the American Psychological Association, Montreal, Canada.

206 Beveridge, M., & Parkins, E. (1987). Visual representation in analogical problem solving. *Memory & Cognition, 15*(3), 230–237.

Gick, M. L., & Holyoak, K. J. (1983). Schema induction and analogical transfer. *Cognitive Psychology, 15*(1), 1–38.

207 Swaney, J. H., Janik, C. J., Bond, S. J., & Hayes, J. R. (1991). Editing for comprehension: Improving the process through reading protocols. In E. R. Steinberg (Ed.), *Plain language: Principles and practice* (pp. 173–203). Detroit, MI: Wayne State University Press. (Original article published in 1981 as Document Design Project Tech. Rep. No. 14, Pittsburgh, PA: Carnegie Mellon University).

208 Kotovsky, L., & Gentner, D. (1996). Comparison and categorization in the development of relational similarity. *Child Development, 67*(6), 2797–2822.

Loewenstein, J., Thompson, L., & Gentner, D. (1999). Analogical encoding facilitates knowledge transfer in negotiation. *Psychonomic Bulletin and Review, 6*(4), 586–597.

Ross, B. H., & Kennedy, P. T. (1990). Generalizing from the use of earlier examples in problem solving. *Journal of Experimental Psychology: Learning, Memory, and Cognition, 16*(1), 42–55.

209 Lowenstein, J., Thompson, L., & Gentner, D. (2003). Analogical encoding facilitates transfer in negotiation. *Psychonomic Bulletin and Review, 6*, 586–597.

See n206, Gick & Holyoak (1983).

210 Novick, L. R., & Holyoak, K. J. (1991). Mathematical problem solving by analogy. *Journal of Experimental Psychology: Learning, Memory, and Cognition, 17*(3), 398–415.

See n208, Ross & Kennedy (1990).

211 Chi, M. T. H., & Koeske, R. D. (1983). Network representation of a child's dinosaur knowledge. *Developmental Psychology, 19*(1), 29–39.

See n198, Kardash et al. (1988).

Rouse, W. B., & Morris, N. M. (1986). On looking into the black box: Prospects and limits in the search for mental models. *Psychological Bulletin, 100*(3), 349–363.

212 Brown, D. J., Scott, K. A., & Lewis, H. (2004). Information processing and leadership. In J. Antonakis, A. T. Cianciolo & R. J. Sternberg (Eds.), *The nature of leadership* (pp. 125–147). Thousand Oaks, CA: Sage.

London, M. (2002). *Leadership development: Paths to self-insight and professional growth.* Mahwah, NJ: Lawrence Erlbaum.

Smither, J. W., & Reilly, S. P. (2001). Coaching in organizations. In M. London (Ed.), *How people evaluate others in organizations* (pp. 221–252). Mahwah, NJ: Lawrence Erlbaum.

213 *See* n94, Chi & Ohlsson (2005).

Ohlsson, S., & Hemmerich, J. (1999). Articulating an explanation schema: A preliminary model and supporting data. In M. Hahn & S. Stones (Eds.), *Proceedings of the twenty first annual conference of the Cognitive Science Society* (pp. 490–495). Mahwah, NJ: Erlbaum.

Ohlsson, S., & Lehtinen, E. (1997). Abstraction and the acquisition of complex ideas. *International Journal of Educational Research, 27*, 37–48.

214 Landmann, N., Kuhn, M., Piosczyk, H., Feige, B., Baglioni, C., Spiegelhalder, K., . . . Nissen, C. (2014). The reorganisation of memory during sleep. *Sleep Medicine Reviews, 18*(6), 531–541.

215 Rosen, D. L., & Olshavsky, R. W. (1987). A protocol analysis of brand choice strategies involving recommendations. *Journal of Consumer Research, 14*(3), 440–444.

216 Yates, J. F., Veinott, E. S., & Patalano, A. L. (2003). Hard decisions, bad decisions: On decision quality and decision aiding. In S. L. Schneider & J. Shanteau (Eds.), *Emerging perspectives on judgment and decision research* (pp. 13–63). Cambridge, UK: Cambridge University Press.

217 *See* n207, Swaney et al. (1991).

218 Cameron, L. D., & Leventhal, H. (2003). *The self-regulation of health and illness behavior.* London: Routledge.

219 Whiskey, E., & Taylor, D. (2005). Evaluation of an antipsychotic information sheet for patients. *International Journal of Psychiatry in Clinical Practice, 9*(4), 264–270.

220 *See* n79, Bettman & Sujan (1987).

221 Georgiadis, D. R., Mazzuchi, T. A., & Sarkani, S. (2013). Using multi criteria decision making in analysis of alternatives for selection of enabling technology. *Systems Engineering, 16*(3), 287–303.

222 Dalal, R. S., & Bonaccio, S. (2010). What types of advice do decision-makers prefer? *Organizational Behavior and Human Decision Processes, 112*(1), 11–23.

223 Sanbonmatsu, D. M., Kardes, F. R., Houghton, D. C., Ho, E. A., & Posavac, S. S. (2003). Overestimating the importance of the given information in multiattribute consumer judgment. *Journal of Consumer Psychology, 13*(3), 289–300.

224 Whittler, T. E. (1994). Eliciting consumer choice heuristics: Sales representatives' persuasion strategies. *Journal of Personal Selling & Sales Management, 14*(4), 41–53.

225 Cannon-Bowers, J. A., & Salas, E. (2001). Reflections on shared cognition. *Journal of Organizational Behavior, 22*(2), 195–202.

Gutwin, C., & Greenberg, S. (2004). The importance of awareness for team cognition in distributed collaboration. In E. Salas & S. M. Fiore (Eds.), *Team cognition: Understanding the factors that drive process and performance* (pp. 177–201). Washington, DC: American Psychological Association.

226 Eccles, D. W., & Tenenbaum, G. (2004). Why an expert team is more than a team of experts: A social-cognitive conceptualization of team coordination and communication in sport. *Journal of Sport & Exercise Psychology, 26*(4), 542–560.

Espinosa, J. A., & Carley, K. M. (2001). *Measuring team mental models.* Paper presented at the Academy of Management Conference Organizational Communication and Information Systems Division, Washington, DC.

Kraiger, K., & Wenzel, L. H. (1997). Conceptual development and empirical evaluation of measures of shared mental models as indicators of team effectiveness. In M. T. Brannick, E. Salas & C. Prince (Eds.), *Team performance assessment and measurement: Theory, methods, and applications* (pp. 63–84). Mahwah, NJ: Lawrence Erlbaum.

227 *See* n4, Levine et al. (1993).

228 Waller, M. J., Gupta, N., & Giambatista, R. C. (2004). Effects of adaptive behaviors and shared mental models on control crew performance. *Management Science, 50*(11), 1534–1544.

229 *See* n120.

230 Murase, T., Carter, D. R., DeChurch, L. A., & Marks, M. A. (2014). Mind the gap: The role of leadership in multiteam system collective cognition. *The Leadership Quarterly, 25*(5), 972–986.

Marks, M. A., Zaccaro, S. J., & Mathieu, J. E. (2000). Performance implications of leader briefings and team-interaction training for team adaptation to novel environments. *Journal of Applied Psychology, 85*(6), 971–986.

231 Andres, H. P. (2011). Shared mental model development during technology-mediated collaboration. *International Journal of E-Collaboration, 7*(3), 14–30.

232 Jo, I. (2011). Effects of role division, interaction, and shared mental model on team performance in project-based learning environment. *Asia Pacific Education Review, 12*(2), 301–310.

Gross, N., & Kluge, A. (2014). Predictors of knowledge-sharing behavior for teams in extreme environments: An example from the steel industry. *Journal of Cognitive Engineering and Decision Making, 8*(4), 352–373.

233 Crespin, T. R. (1997). Cognitive convergence in developing groups: The role of sociocognitive elaboration. *Dissertation Abstracts International: Section B: The Sciences and Engineering, 57*(7-B), 4758.

234 McIntyre, R. M., & Salas, E. (1995). Measuring and managing for team performance: Emerging principles from complex environments. In R. A. Guzzo & E. Salas (Eds.), *Team effectiveness and decision making in organizations* (pp. 9–45). San Francisco: Jossey-Bass.

235 Mohammed, S., & Dumville, B. C. (2001). Team mental models in a team knowledge framework: Expanding theory and measurement across disciplinary boundaries. *Journal of Organizational Behavior, 22*(2), 89–106.

Smith-Jentsch, K. A., Campbell, G. E., Milanovich, D. M., & Reynolds, A. M. (2001). Measuring teamwork mental models to support training needs assessment, development, and evaluation: Two empirical studies. *Journal of Organizational Behavior, 22*(2), 179–194.

236 Einhorn, H. J., & Hogarth, R. M. (1981). Behavioral decision theory: Processes of judgment and choice. *Annual Review of Psychology, 32,* 53–88.

237 Goldberg, L. R. (1968). Simple models or simple processes? Some research on clinical judgments. *American Psychologist, 23*(7), 483–496.

238 Einhorn, H. J. (1972). Expert measurement and mechanical combination. *Organizational Behavior & Human Performance, 7*(1), 86–106.

239 Dawes, R. M. (1971). A case study of graduate admissions: Application of three principles of human decision making. *American Psychologist, 26*(2), 180–188.

240 Libby, R. (1976). Man versus model of man: Some conflicting evidence. *Organizational Behavior & Human Performance, 16*(1), 1–12.

241 Johnson, E. J., & Sathi, A. (1984). *Expertise in security analysts.* Working Paper, Graduate School of Industrial Administration, Carnegie Mellon University, Pittsburgh, PA.

Wright, W. F. (1979). Properties of judgment models in a financial setting. *Organizational Behavior & Human Performance, 23*(1), 73–85.

242 Grove, W. M., Zald, D. H., Lebow, B. S., Snitz, B. E., & Nelson, C. (2000). Clinical versus mechanical prediction: A meta-analysis. *Psychological Assessment, 12*(1), 19–30.

Tetlock, P. (2005). *Expert political judgment: How good is it? How can we know?* Princeton, NJ: Princeton University Press.

243 Camerer, C. F. (1981). General conditions for the success of bootstrapping models. *Organizational Behavior & Human Performance, 27*(3), 411–422.

Dawes, R. M., & Corrigan, B. (1974). Linear models in decision making. *Psychological Bulletin, 81*(2), 95–106.

See n241, Johnson & Sathi (1984).

244 *See* n243, Dawes & Corrigan (1974).

245 Edwards, W., & Newman, J. R. (1986). Multiattribute evaluation. In H. R. Ares & K. R. Hammond (Eds.), *Judgment and decision making: An interdisciplinary reader* (pp. 13–37). New York: Cambridge University Press.

See n64, Keeney & Raiffa (1976/1993).

Massaro, D. W., & Friedman, D. (1990). Models of integration given multiple sources of information. *Psychological Review, 97*(2), 225–252.

246 Karelaia, N., & Hogarth, R. M. (2008). Determinants of linear judgment: A meta-analysis of lens model studies. *Psychological Bulletin, 134*(3), 404–426.

247 Grove, W. M., & Meehl, P. E. (1996). Comparative efficiency of informal (subjective, impressionistic) and formal (mechanical, algorithmic) prediction procedures: The clinical–statistical controversy. *Psychology, Public Policy, and Law, 2*(2), 293–323.

See n242, Grove et al. (2000).

Kuncel, N. R., Klieger, D. M., Connelly, B. S., & Ones, D. S. (2013). Mechanical versus clinical data combination in selection and admissions decisions: A meta-analysis. *Journal of Applied Psychology, 98*(6), 1060–1072.

248 Monti, M., Boero, R., Berg, N., Gigerenzer, G., & Martignon, L. (2012). How do common investors behave? Information search and portfolio choice among bank customers and university students. *Mind & Society, 11*(2), 203–233.

249 Ow, T. T., & Morris, J. G. (2010). An experimental study of executive decision-making with implications for decision support. *Journal of Organizational Computing and Electronic Commerce, 20*(4), 370–397.

Evans, J. S. B., Clibbens, J., Cattani, A., Harris, A., & Dennis, I. (2003). Explicit and implicit processes in multicue judgment. *Memory & Cognition, 31*(4), 608–618.

Zacharakis, A. L., & Meyer, G. D. (1998). A lack of insight: Do venture capitalists really understand their own decision process? *Journal of Business Venturing, 13*(1), 57–76.

250 *See* n241, Johnson & Sathi (1984).

251 Lichtenstein, S., & Slovic, P. (1971). Reversals of preference between bids and choices in gambling decisions. *Journal of Experimental Psychology, 89*(1), 46–55.

252 Shafir, E. (1993). Choosing versus rejecting: Why some options are both better and worse than others. *Memory & Cognition, 21*(4), 546–556.

253 Hsee, C. K., Loewenstein, G. F., Blount, S., & Bazerman, M. H. (1999). Preference reversals between joint and separate evaluations of options: A review and theoretical analysis. *Psychological Bulletin, 125*(5), 576–590.

254 Russo, J. E., & Dosher, B. A. (1983). Strategies for multiattribute binary choice. *Journal of Experimental Psychology: Learning, Memory, and Cognition, 9*(4), 676–696.

255 Hanák, R., Sirota, M., & Juanchich, M. (2013). Experts use compensatory strategies more often than novices in hiring decisions. *Studia Psychologica, 55*(4), 251–263.

256 Soelberg, P. O. (1967). Unprogrammed decision making. *Industrial Management Review, 8*(2), 19–29.

257 Kahn, B. E., & Baron, J. (1995). An exploratory study of choice rules favored for high-stakes decisions. *Journal of Consumer Psychology, 4*(4), 305–328.

258 Shanteau, J. (1992). Competence in experts: The role of task characteristics. *Organizational Behavior and Human Decision Processes Special Issue: Experts and Expert Systems, 53*(2), 252–266.

259 Bolger, F., & Wright, G. (1992). Reliability and validity in expert judgment. In G. Wright & F. Bolger (Eds.), *Expertise and decision support* (pp. 47–76). New York: Plenum Press.

  Smith, J. F., & Kida, T. (1991). Heuristics and biases: Expertise and task realism in auditing. *Psychological Bulletin, 109*(3), 472–489.

260 *See* n169, Andersson (2004).

  Fritzsche, B. A., & Brannick, M. T. (2002). The importance of representative design in judgment tasks: The case of resume screening. *Journal of Occupational and Organizational Psychology, 75*(2), 163–169.

  See n115, Rossiter et al. (1991).

261 Mannes, A. E., Larrick, R. P., & Soll, J. B. (2012). The social psychology of the wisdom of crowds. In J. I. Krueger (Ed.), *Social judgment and decision making* (pp. 227–242). New York: Psychology Press.

  Surowiecki, J. (2004). *The wisdom of crowds: Why the many are smarter than the few and how collective wisdom shapes business, economies, societies and nations little.* New York: Doubleday.

262 Cosier, R. A., & Schwenk, C. R. (1990). Agreement and thinking alike: Ingredients for poor decisions. *The Executive, 4*(1), 69–74.

  Tindale, R. S. (1993). Decision errors made by individuals and groups. In N. J. Castellan (Ed.), *Individual and group decision making: Current issues* (pp. 109–124). Hillsdale, NJ: Lawrence Erlbaum Associates.

263 Gigone, D., & Hastie, R. (1997). The impact of information on small group choice. *Journal of Personality and Social Psychology, 72*(1), 132–140.

264 Kameda, T., & Sugimori, S. (1995). Procedural influence in two-step group decision making: Power of local majorities in consensus formation. *Journal of Personality and Social Psychology, 69*(5), 865–876.

265 Kameda, T., & Davis, J. H. (1990). The function of the reference point in individual and group risk decision making. *Organizational Behavior and Human Decision Processes, 46*(1), 55–76.

266 Stasser, G., & Titus, W. (1985). Pooling of unshared information in group decision making: Biased information sampling during discussion. *Journal of Personality and Social Psychology, 48*(6), 1467–1478.

267 Tindale, R. S., & Davis, J. H. (1985). Individual and group reward allocation decisions in two situational contexts: Effects of relative need and performance. *Journal of Personality and Social Psychology, 48*(5), 1148–1161.

268 Kameda, T., & Sugimori, S. (1993). Psychological entrapment in group decision making: An assigned decision rule and a groupthink phenomenon. *Journal of Personality and Social Psychology, 65*(2), 282–292.

269 Li, H., & Sakamoto, Y. (2014). Social impacts in social media: An examination of perceived truthfulness and sharing of information. *Computers in Human Behavior, 41*, 278–287.

270 *See* n147, Laughlin & Ellis (1986).

  See n149, Tindale et al. (1996).

271 Littlepage, G., Robison, W., & Reddington, K. (1997). Effects of task experience and group experience on group performance, member ability, and recognition of expertise. *Organizational Behavior and Human Decision Processes, 69*(2), 133–147.

272 Burson, K. A., Larrick, R. P., & Klayman, J. (2006). Skilled or unskilled, but still unaware of it: How perceptions of difficulty drive miscalibration in relative comparisons. *Journal of Personality and Social Psychology, 90*(1), 60–77.

273 *See* n239, Dawes (1971).

274 *See* n243, Camerer (1981).

  Sawyer, J. (1966). Measurement and prediction, clinical and statistical. *Psychological Bulletin, 66*(3), 178–200.

275 *See* n12, Johnson (1988a).

276 Meehl, P. E. (1954). *Clinical versus statistical prediction: A theoretical analysis and a review of the evidence.* Minneapolis, MN: University of Minnesota Press.

277 Shanteau, J. (1988). Psychological characteristics and strategies of expert decision makers. *Acta Psychologica, 68*(1–3), 203–215.

2

TYPES OF AUDIENCE DECISIONS

> It didn't help that the executive sent to deliver the decision [to lay off] the assembled staff started off with a glowing account of how well rival operations were doing, and that he had just returned from a wonderful trip to Cannes. The news itself was bad enough, but the brusque, even contentious manner of the executive incited something beyond the expected frustration. People became enraged—not just at the management decision, but also at the bearer of the news himself. The atmosphere became so threatening, in fact, that it looked as though the executive might have to call security to usher him safely from the room.
>
> The next day, another executive visited the same staff. He took a very different approach. He spoke from his heart about the crucial importance of journalism to the vibrancy of a society, and of the calling that had drawn them all to the field in the first place. He reminded them that no one goes into journalism to get rich—as a profession its finances have always been marginal, with job security ebbing and flowing with larger economic tides. And he invoked the passion, even the dedication, the journalists had for the service they offered. Finally, he wished them all well in getting on with their careers. When this leader finished speaking, the staff cheered.

This excerpt from *Primal Leadership* by Daniel Goleman and his colleagues illustrates the importance of understanding your audience and the type of decision you want them to make.[1] The excerpt contrasts how two executives from the British Broadcasting Corporation (BBC) informed their audience of about 200 journalists and editors of upper management's plan to shut down their news reporting division. Notice how unsympathetic and immature the first executive appears to be as he reports on the success of the other divisions at the BBC and then adds that the apparently unprofitable news reporting division is to be shut down. Giving such a report to a different audience, say the BBC's board of directors with oversight responsibility for upper management's plans, might have been totally appropriate. In order to make an informed oversight decision, most board members would appreciate the comparative information the first executive shared as well as his apparent concern for profitability. But for this audience of soon-to-be unemployed journalists, the first executive appears to have no clue to whom he is speaking or the type of decision he wants them to make:

Does he want the journalists to decide to go along with upper management's plan or to fight it? No doubt this executive was surprised by the journalists' angry response to his speech; it seems likely his speaking experience was limited to delivering similar factual reports.

Notice, on the other hand, how empathetic and leader-like the second executive appears to be. The second executive addresses the group's values, their sacrifices, and the difficulties they will face. He knows his job is not simply to report the facts but to inspire and rally the journalists' flagging spirits. To inspire the group, the second executive elicits what this text terms a rallying decision from the journalists. Chapter 2 shows us how we can be more like the second executive. We too can know what to say and when to say it, even when circumstances are most trying and difficult.

As we saw in Chapter 1, to be effective communicators, professionals must first be aware of their audiences' decision schemata. But how can professionals ever prepare for such a task when the number of individual decisions their audiences make is seemingly infinite? Physicists who want to persuade their audiences to fund new research projects are often able to interact with them directly to learn about their information requirements and concerns.[2] But many professionals do not have the time or the opportunity to interview audience members, much less to conduct a Multi-Attribute Utility Analysis, build a linear model, or conduct a think-aloud study in order to discover the decision schema of their audience. Instead, professionals need a classification scheme that makes sense of the bewildering array of audience decisions and helps them produce the numerous documents and presentations, and orchestrate the many interactions, required to elicit those decisions.

Chapter 2 proposes a scheme that classifies a large number of audience decisions, as well as the documents, presentations, and interactions designed to elicit them, into 13 major types: *oversight, compliance, staffing, employment, exonerative, rallying, investment, lending, usage, sourcing, budgetary, borrowing*, and *policy* decisions. For example, a student's decision to apply an instructor's lesson, a patient's decision to follow the doctor's orders, and a customer's decision to try a free sample after hearing a salesperson's product pitch can all be classified as usage decisions—decisions to use or try out certain products, services, or information. And all usage decisions require communicators to address similar decision criteria and thus to deliver similar types of information. Moreover, the instructor's lesson, the doctor's orders, and the salesperson's product pitch can all be classified as documents, presentations, or interactions whose communicative purpose is to elicit a usage decision. Interestingly, a growing number of scholars agree that the most productive way to classify any form of communication is according to its communicative purpose.[3]

The major benefit of such a classification scheme is that it can help professionals predict the information or content their audiences expect them to provide. In contrast, knowing the format of a document, presentation, or an interaction—such as *an email*, an *impromptu presentation*, or a *team meeting*—says little about the content the audience expects. Although letters to the editor are formatted as *letters*, they are usually exhortations advising needed change. The contents of letters to the editor are more similar to the contents of political speeches than to the contents of many other types of letters.[4]

Likewise, knowing the source of a message says little about the content audiences require. For instance, knowing that an attorney generated a particular document says little about an audience's content expectations given the many different types of documents attorneys generate. In the same way, simply identifying the audience to whom a message is directed tells practically nothing about the content required in it. For example, consumers, one of salespeople's primary audiences, are asked to make compliance, investment, usage, sourcing, staffing, exonerative, borrowing, and rallying decisions. And again, each decision type requires professionals to provide quite different types of information to their audiences.

In addition to helping professionals predict the information or content requirements of their audiences, the scheme can also be used to classify *genres*, or categories of discourse to which various documents, presentations, and interactions belong.[5] Business genres, for example, include business plans, quarterly reports, directives, job interviews, policy meetings, and standard operating procedures, as well as many other types of management documents, presentations, and interactions. Although one might reasonably assume that all documents labeled *plans* differ from all documents labeled *reports*, an understanding of decision types reveals that strategic plans and annual reports are both designed to elicit an oversight decision, and thus both require similar information. An understanding of decision types also reveals profound differences among documents and presentations that seemingly belong to the same genre. For example, not all documents or presentations called *plans* are meant to elicit an oversight decision. Some plans are meant to elicit an investment decision (e.g., many business plans), some a lending decision (e.g., some acquisition plans), some a usage decision (e.g., most medical treatment plans), and so on.

The 13 decision types this chapter describes cover a wide range of rhetorical situations professionals face. They can be used to meaningfully group dozens of genres, to address scores of different audiences, and to accomplish many different communication goals. However, some types of decisions are not included among the 13 in this classification scheme. For instance, this classification scheme does not include domain-specific decisions professionals are more likely to make themselves, as opposed to ask an audience to make, such as judicial, marketing, regulatory, financing, and technical decisions. Table 2.1 illustrates a few of the many audience decisions and the documents, presentations, or interactions designed to elicit them that are readily classified as belonging to one of the 13 major decision types described in this chapter.

One of the best-known types of decisions—policy decisions—will be discussed last in this chapter. This category includes many of the decisions world leaders, legislators, and CEOs make every day. Policy decisions are nonroutine decisions to which little routine decision-making expertise can be applied. In addition, many policy decisions are quite controversial and generate much debate. Unlike routine decisions, policy decisions sometimes require professionals to generate decision criteria and to convince their audiences to accept those criteria.[6]

The remaining 12 types of audience decisions this chapter includes can be divided into two groups of six. The first group helps audiences manage their professional relationships both within

TABLE 2.1 Many Audience Decisions Can Be Classified as One of Thirteen Types

Professional	Audience	Document, Presentation, or Interaction	Audience Decision	Decision Type
Politician	Voters	Campaign speech	Vote for candidate or not	Rallying
Applicant	Recruiters	Job interview	Hire applicant or not	Staffing
Attorney	Jurors	Defense arguments	Acquit defendant or not	Exonerative
Consultant	Clients	Project proposal	Hire consultants or not	Staffing
Executive	Directors	Strategic plan	Approve strategy or not	Oversight
Teacher	Students	Lesson	Apply instructions or not	Usage
Commander	Subordinates	Intent statement	Follow orders or not	Compliance
Salesperson	Customers	Sales pitch	Try out product or not	Usage

an organizational hierarchy and outside it. The second group helps them manage their own or their organization's financial resources.

Before we go into more detail about each of the 13 major decision types the audiences of professionals make, we should be aware of several important caveats regarding decision types and the extent to which they can help professionals predict the audience's information needs. First, even when two genres are meant to elicit the same type of decision, the decision criteria audiences use to evaluate the content in one genre will vary slightly from the decision criteria they use to evaluate the content in the other genre. For instance, strategic plans and marketing plans are both meant to elicit oversight decisions. But where board members expect strategic plans to address the corporate objective, the corporate strategy, the corporate-wide action plan, and so on, top management expects marketing plans to address the marketing department's objective, the marketing department's strategy, and the marketing department's action plan. Similarly, commercial bank loan officers require somewhat different financial information when making lending decisions about requests for credit from small privately held companies as opposed to requests from large publicly held ones.[7]

Second, audience members are free to make any type of decision they wish, no matter what type of decision a professional intends to elicit from them. For example, a supervisor might imagine her request for a productivity increase from her staff would elicit a straightforward compliance decision from them. But while considering her request, some staff members may make employment decisions instead and decide to look elsewhere for a less demanding job. Similarly, an employee might imagine his request for a salary increase would evoke a straightforward budgetary decision from his boss. But while considering the employee's request, the boss may make an oversight decision and decide to eliminate the employee's position altogether. In general, any unilateral request for change can trigger an unintended decision type.

Third, some genres, such as annual reports, are routinely used by different audiences to make different types of decisions. For example, board members and shareholders may use annual reports to make oversight decisions when casting their votes on management's recommendations. Potential investors and financial analysts may use them to make investment decisions when buying shares or recommending the purchase of a company's stock. Job applicants may use them to make employment decisions when applying for a new position. Customers may use them to make usage decisions when educating themselves about a company's new product line. Bankers may use them to make lending decisions when considering a company's creditworthiness. Some firms try to address the information needs of their annual reports' different audiences in different sections of their annual reports. Some firms only address the needs of the primary audience— their shareholders.

Finally, a few situations exist in which a professional may not care what type of decision the audience makes or even if it makes any decision at all. Some communications may be purely perfunctory. Others may be routine exchanges of information. In these cases a professional may not need to consider the type of decision the audience will make. The following sections describe the types of audience decisions professionals do need to attend to seriously.

Audience Decisions About Principal/Agent Relationships

In order to understand the first group of six decision types—oversight, compliance, staffing, employment, exonerative, and rallying decisions—we must first understand the differences between principals and their agents. *Principals* are the people to whom agents must answer. Principals of managers, for example, include their firm's shareholders, board members, and upper management. More broadly speaking, principals of managers can also be said to include their clients, customers, and creditors, or else anyone to whom they are contractually obligated. Managers themselves

TABLE 2.2 Examples of Principal/Agent Pairs

Principal	Agent
1. Stockholders	Board members
2. Employers	Employees
3. Customers	Suppliers
4. Clients	Attorneys
5. Legislators	Bureaucrats
6. Investors	Fund managers
7. Creditors	Borrowers
8. Funding agencies	Scientists

function as principals to their subordinates, suppliers, and borrowers. Principals set the terms and conditions of any principal/agent relationship. They write the employee contracts, draw up the requests for proposals, and stipulate the covenants for loans.

Agents, on the other hand, are the people who are obligated to act on behalf of principals. Agents who are unhappy with the principal/agent relationships they have entered into may decide to leave them once they have met their obligations to the principals. Employees may resign and leave an employer; credit card holders may transfer their balances to another bank; suppliers may refuse shipment to untrustworthy customers. Table 2.2 lists common principal/agent pairs as this text more broadly defines the terms.

The six decision types concerned with the management of principal/agent relationships can be further divided into three complementary pairs. The first pair, oversight and compliance decisions, execute principal/agent relationships that have already been established. For example, board members make oversight decisions when they approve or reject executives' plans and when they approve or disapprove of executives' performance. And executives make compliance decisions when they decide whether to comply with directives from their board.

The second pair, staffing and employment decisions, establish principal/agent relationships within an organization or between individuals. For example, employers make staffing decisions when they hire, fire, promote, or demote employees. And job applicants make employment decisions when they accept or reject a job offer.

The third pair, exonerative and rallying decisions, help maintain good principal/agent relationships. For example, customers make exonerative decisions when they decide whether to exonerate from blame a supplier who failed to meet a delivery deadline. And suppliers make rallying decisions when they decide whether to make an extra effort to provide high-quality service to their customers. In each of these three complementary pairs of decision types, one type is typically made by the principal in the principal/agent pair and the other type by the agent. The principal typically makes oversight, staffing, and exonerative decisions. The agent typically makes compliance, employment, and rallying decisions.

Oversight Decisions: Responses to Requests for Permission

Audiences who are the superiors of others within an organization or to whom others are contractually obligated, in other words principals, make oversight decisions about their agents' plans and performance. For example, board members, acting as principals, make oversight decisions when they decide whether to approve management's plans to pursue a new strategy; clients, acting as principals, make oversight decisions when they decide whether to allow consultants to continue working on a project that has fallen behind schedule; employers, acting as principals, make oversight decisions when they decide whether to approve an employee's creative new product proposal. U.S. presidents make oversight decisions when, as Commander in Chief, they decide whether to permit their top military officers to implement their plans for battle.

Principals make oversight decisions in order to protect the interests of the projects, organizations, or even countries for which they are responsible. Agents seek oversight decisions from principals when they attempt to gain approval for their past performance or to obtain permission to implement their plans for the future. Documents and presentations agents produce in order to elicit oversight decisions from principals include *strategic plans*, *annual reports*, *marketing plans*, *progress reports*, and *operating reviews*.

In the following letter, we see how President Abraham Lincoln approached making an important oversight decision during the American Civil War. The letter is the president's response to a 22-page plan of attack that his top general, George B. McClellan, submitted to him for approval. The general presented his plan as an alternative to a plan Lincoln himself had proposed a few days earlier. Lincoln was not persuaded by the general's plan, in part because he had been disappointed by the general's poor performance in the prior year.

In the letter, Lincoln enumerates the criteria for his oversight decision in a list of questions about the objectives, competitive strategy, implementation, and risk mitigation of the general's plan. He says he will agree to the general's plan if the general can demonstrate his plan has a better chance than Lincoln's of meeting those criteria. Although the general never addressed Lincoln's decision criteria, the President reluctantly permitted the general's plan to be implemented out of respect for his top officer.

LINCOLN'S RESPONSE TO GENERAL MCCLELLAN'S PLAN

Executive Mansion, Washington
Feb. 3, 1862

To Major General McClellan

My dear Sir:

You and I have distinct, and different plans for a movement of the Army of the Potomac—yours to be down the Chesapeake, up the Rappahannock to Urbana, and across land to the terminus of the Railroad on the York River —mine to move directly to a point on the Railroad South West of Manassas.

If you will give me satisfactory answers to the following questions, I shall gladly yield my plan to yours.

1st. Does not your plan involve a greatly larger expenditure of *time*, and *money* than mine?

2nd. Wherein is a victory *more certain* by your plan than mine?

3rd. Wherein is a victory *more valuable* by your plan than mine?

4th. In fact, would it not be *less valuable*, in this, that it would break no great line of the enemy's communications, while mine would?

5th. In case of disaster, would not a safe retreat be *more difficult* by your plan than by mine?

Yours truly,

A. LINCOLN

Much like U.S. presidents oversee the plans and performance of their top military commanders, an organization's board of directors oversees the plans and performance of its top management team.[8] When top management does not meet the performance objectives set by the board, board members may decide to replace the CEO,[9] much like Lincoln soon replaced General McClellan.

In addition to overseeing the firm's past performance, board members oversee the firm's mission, competitive strategy, and operating plans.[10] But unlike Lincoln, board members can usually trigger change in management's strategy by simply expressing their concerns about it.[11] Related oversight responsibilities of board members include setting strategic parameters, monitoring strategic coherence, and evaluating consistency among management's proposed strategies.[12] In addition, board members see themselves as responsible for overseeing the risks taken on by management, including legal, geopolitical, and reputational risks.[13]

The following list of questions subsumes many of the criteria identified previously and provides a starting point for predicting a principal's decision criteria for any particular oversight decision. The list can also serve as an outline for the documents and presentations agents produce in order to elicit oversight decisions from principals.

- What is the organization's or project's past performance?
- What are the reasons for that performance?
- What are the financial objectives for the future?
- What is the competitive strategy for meeting those objectives?
- What is the action plan for implementing the strategy?
- What are the contingency plans for mitigating risks?

In addition to agents' answers to the previous questions, principals in both for-profit and non-profit organizations may also require benchmark information about the organization's or project's historical performance, the average performance in the industry, alternative strategies and plans, as well as competing firms' and projects' financial results, strategies, and plans.[14] Research finds that most annual reports do a good job of describing the firm's past performance, explaining the reasons for the firm's past performance, and communicating the firm's objectives and plans for the future, but they rarely benchmark the firm's plans and performance against those of the competitors.[15]

Table 2.3 displays some of the think-aloud comments made by two experienced audience members (a Ph.D. in finance and a Ph.D. in business policy, both with high-level corporate experience)

TABLE 2.3 Experts' Comments That Reveal Their Decision Criteria for Making Oversight Decisions

	Expert Comments on a Strategic Plan From General Motors	Expert Comments on an Annual Report From Control Data
Past performance	10. They've listed their own and the three major competitors' vehicle sales growth, three-year average, the three-year profitability, and market share. Again it's just a listing of data with no insights. My sense of a good strategic plan is that what one begins with is this data.	5. They say they had a loss across the board. These are good years. These are very good years for the country. Control Data, I would think, would share in that.
Reasons for performance	[This expert noted in the second sentence that the plan lacks reasons that explain the firm's past financial performance.]	9. Well, at this point I still don't know what threw their earnings off. Sometimes they make phenomenal earnings, other times they don't. And other times they have phenomenal losses. So is it just that their earnings fluctuate that much even though they make that much revenue? Or is there some sort of driver involved here that's causing this? Is it correlated with something? I still don't know that yet.
Financial objectives	[This expert did not indicate whether he noted the plan's lack of financial objectives.]	59. If this were a presentation to the board of directors, I would like to see the pro forma statements, too. I'd like to see what they expect income to be over the next several years, and why they think they're going to get that. This has just been a statement of the history of the company for the last three years. Nothing with respect to the future. So again from a board member's point of view, that's lacking.
Competitive strategy	26. I am reminded that the company said it was going to move from a low cost to a differentiated position [i.e., strategy]. And that really is the crux of the issue for the company. 27. Now I realize that what is lacking in the subsequent ten sections is any focused discussion on precisely what moving to a differentiated position means.	23. Their strategy is to cut costs rather than progress their technology. Nobody wants to buy last year's computer even if it is a hundred dollars cheaper. 57. It doesn't look like these people are on the right track as far as I'm concerned. Yes, I think they should be concerned about cost, everybody should be. But tell me more about technology growth. How they plan to position themselves in the future.
Action plan	22. I think this [chart of action plans] is useful information because it's probably the important milestones in the next three or four years within the company. It would probably be useful to support this kind of chart with a little bit more discussion, since these are the actual plans that have been chosen by management.	54. I see nothing in here or very little about developing technology. This business is what strategists would call a fast-cycle business. New technology becomes obsolete very quickly. Cost cutting won't do much. They better have good R&D going on. 55. Maybe cut the dividends. Certainly don't pay dividends and special dividends especially. Instead, go to the commercial credit paper market or the credit market to raise more cash.

(Continued)

TABLE 2.3 (Continued)

	Expert Comments on a Strategic Plan From General Motors	Expert Comments on an Annual Report From Control Data
Contingency plans	30. Based on the document itself, I would *not* feel comfortable granting authority requested. 31. The document does a poor job of focusing the reader's attention on the important issues, priorities, and the major risks involved in this strategy. And those kinds of questions would be the ones I would focus on in a discussion and presentation. 32. The ability to present information in a well-organized way, either in the written form or the verbal form, in a short amount of time, say fifteen minutes (which would not be unusual at the corporate level for something like this) is sufficient to either make or break a strategic plan. I've seen it happen, and make or break the individuals involved.	[This expert did not indicate whether he noted the report's lack of contingency plans.]

as they read two documents produced by top management teams to elicit oversight decisions: a strategic plan from General Motors and the *Management's Discussion and Analysis* section of Control Data Corporation's annual report. Each expert was asked to put himself into the role of a board member of those firms and to make an oversight decision based on the information the plan or report provided. The comments reflect the decision criteria for making oversight decisions and illustrate how important it is that they be addressed fully. All of the comments each expert made are numbered in the order they were made. Comments that did not directly reflect the experts' decision criteria, such as comprehension-related comments and complaints about superfluous information, are not included here.

Both expert audience members found the information they required about each organization's past financial performance, but both noted that the reasons for that performance were lacking. The expert reading the strategic plan was glad to see an action plan was included, but complained that the strategy for positioning the firm vis-à-vis its competitors and the risks, usually included in a contingency plan, were not clearly spelled out. The expert reading the annual report complained that financial objectives for the future were not included, that the report lacked a competitive strategy for positioning the firm, and that the action plan was too vague. Neither of the expert audience members found that enough of his decision criteria were adequately addressed and, as a consequence, each withheld his approval.

On the following pages are slides that a team of MBA students presented to their board of directors—a group of five experienced top managers. The student team played the role of top management in a simulated watch manufacturing firm. The students' firm was in competition with four other simulated watch firms run by other teams of MBA students. Notice how the student team's slides address each of the board's decision criteria for oversight decisions: the firm's past performance, the reasons for that performance, the firm's financial objectives, as well as the financial objectives, competitive strategy, action plans, and contingency plans for the firm's premium "Omicron" watch (note: the slides pertaining to the firm's less expensive "Iota" watch have been omitted. Those slides follow the same outline as the slides for the "Omicron" watch). The charts in the team's slides provide many benchmarks as well. Unsurprisingly, the team's board rated their presentation as well above average.

AN MBA TEAM'S STRATEGIC PLAN SLIDES (ABRIDGED)

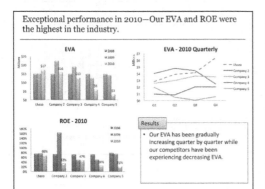

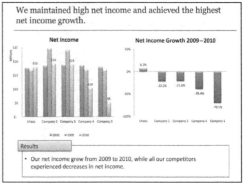

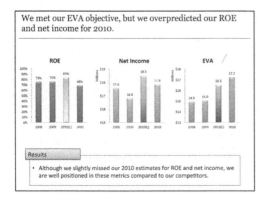

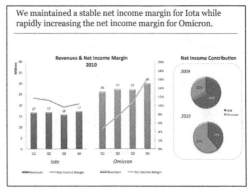

Our financial objectives for next year will greatly increase shareholder value.

Next year, Lhazo will achieve the following:
- One of the top two positions for ROE
- Highest net income margin
- One of the top two positions for EVA

To attain these goals, we are targeting 10% increases for the subsequent year:

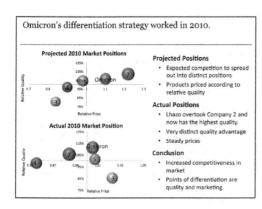

Our goals for Omicron in 2011 are to increase both margins and market shares in target countries.

Margin Goal:
Increase net income margin for Omicron by 10 percentage points in the next year.

Market Share Goals:
Achieve 26–30% market shares in target markets.

Omicron's differentiation strategy worked in 2010.

Projected Positions
- Expected competition to spread out into distinct positions
- Products priced according to relative quality

Actual Positions
- Lhazo overtook Company 2 and now has the highest quality.
- Very distinct quality advantage
- Steady prices

Conclusion
- Increased competitiveness in market
- Points of differentiation are quality and marketing.

Omicron held the second highest market share among all luxury watch brands in 2010.

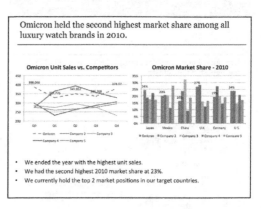

- We ended the year with the highest unit sales.
- We had the second highest 2010 market share at 23%.
- We currently hold the top 2 market positions in our target countries.

In 2011, we will maintain Omicron's differentiation strategy and increase prices to gain higher profitability.

Current Position
- Medium price (101% relative)
- High quality (111% relative)

Target Position
- Higher price (105% relative)
- Same quality (111% relative)

Results
- Higher profitability
- Cater to higher-end customers who are willing to pay for a high-quality product
- Exclusive image supported by high price, high quality, extensive marketing, and high greenness

We will accomplish our goals for Omicron through targeted marketing and price differentiation.

Target markets:
- US, UK, and Japan will continue to be Omicron's target markets
- Since high quality has been achieved, Germany is also now a target market

- Continue to invest heavily in marketing in target countries
- Increase marketing in non-target countries

- Increase relative prices in the least price sensitive markets
- Decrease relative prices in price-sensitive markets

We expect our 2011 pricing and marketing, R&D, and green decisions to result in positive NPVs.

Price & Marketing Decisions

- Our Omicron strategy of targeted marketing and price differentiation has an expected NPV of $4.54mm.

R&D/Quality Decisions

- With our factory in Germany, maintaining the lead position in quality is expected to result in an NPV of nearly $6mm for Omicron.

Green Decisions

- Maintaining slightly above average greenness for Omicron will result in $6.24mm in NPV.

Our production plan for Omicron will continue to support our strategy of differentiation.

Actions	Goals
Decrease R&D spending steadily at 10% to match overall trend, and adjust to shift in competitors' strategy	Maintain a strong lead position in relative quality among competitors
Increase production consulting from $125k to $175k per quarter	Decrease manufacturing cost at approximately 1% per quarter
Maintain a low inventory level at below 20%	Maintain inventory holding cost at $1 per unit, thereby achieving the best profit margin
Expand production capacity accordingly to support increasing demand	Avoid purchasing inventory at a premium cost and prevent stockouts

We will continue to minimize receivables, maintain a small balance sheet, and minimize the cost of capital.

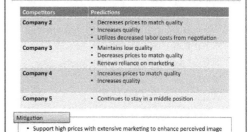

Cash Flow & Balance Sheet Monitoring

- **Receivables**
  We will maintain DSO at its current level - approximately 30 days.

Cost of Capital

- **D/E Ratio**
  Our target D/E ratio is just below 50% which will minimize the cost of capital.
- **Financing Activities**
  To achieve the targeted D/E ratio, we will use loan payments and share repurchases.

Our contingency plans for Omicron anticipate competitors' responses to our strategy.

Competitors	Predictions
Company 2	• Decreases prices to match quality • Increases quality • Utilizes decreased labor costs from negotiation
Company 3	• Maintains low quality • Decreases prices to match quality • Renews reliance on marketing
Company 4	• Increases prices to match quality • Increases quality
Company 5	• Continues to stay in a middle position

Mitigation

- Support high prices with extensive marketing to enhance perceived image
- Implement price differentiation to extract the greatest value

In summary, we are well positioned to sustain profitability and outpace the competition.

2010 Accomplishments

- Highest ROE
- Highest increase in net income
- Premium market quality leader through strategic R&D investment

2011 Outlook

- As economic conditions improve, we are well-positioned to achieve higher levels of profitability and deliver the greatest amount of shareholder value.
- Having developed a greater understanding of our competitive landscape, we are well-equipped to respond to market changes.

Compliance Decisions: Responses to Demands

Audiences who are subordinate or under obligation to another party, in other words agents, make compliance decisions in response to principals' demands. For example, employees make compliance decisions when they decide whether to take the actions management has directed them to take, customers in arrears make compliance decisions when they decide whether to pay their bills, and suppliers make compliance decisions when they decide whether to grant a dissatisfied customer's demand for a refund.

Agents make compliance decisions in order to assess the legitimacy of the demands that are made of them as well as to assess how easy those demands are to implement. Principals seek compliance decisions when they attempt to get their agents to pursue a particular course of action. Documents and presentations principals produce in order to elicit compliance decisions from their agents include *directives, orders, intent statements, contracts, standard operating procedures (SOPs), invoices, policies, promissory notes, reprimands,* and *safety warnings.*

The following list of questions provides a starting point for predicting an agent's decision criteria for any particular compliance decision. The list can also serve as an outline for the documents and presentations principals produce in order to elicit compliance decisions from their agents.

- What is the purpose of the demand?
- What is the due date?
- What are the steps for completion?
- What are the evaluation criteria (i.e., the communicator's decision criteria)?
- What are unwanted outcomes and the consequences for noncompliance?
- Whom should I contact if I have problems?

In addition to principals' answers to the previous questions, agents may also require benchmark information about prior demands made on them, other current demands, the terms and conditions of any relevant contracts, industry norms, or corporate policies, as well as applicable laws and regulations.

Of course, agents do not always comply with their principals' demands. A study of U.S. Army officers reading their commanding officers' intent statements finds that the subordinate officers took the actions their superior officers intended them to take only 34% of the time.[16] One reason the subordinate officers failed to comply is that their commanders' intent statements usually neglected to address all of their criteria for compliance decisions. A content analysis of 35 intent statements by U.S. Army commanders finds that although steps for completion were included in 92% of the statements, the purpose of the demand was stated in just 42% of them, plans for handling problems that may arise in only 37%, and unwanted outcomes were mentioned in a mere 14%.[17]

In corporations, when upper management fails to articulate the purpose behind their strategic plans, mid-level managers often fail to implement the plans as upper management intended.[18] In hazardous work situations, when safety hazard warnings fail to explain the purpose or rationale behind them, employees are more likely to ignore them.[19] Conversely, when safety warnings clearly state the rationale, consequences of noncompliance, and the necessary steps for avoiding injury, the target audience is much more likely to comply.[20]

On the following pages are two versions of the same directive from a quality manager in a large engineering firm to supervisors and shop floor foremen as well as think-aloud comments made by one of the firm's supervisors who actually received the directive (note: the names of the employees, the ISO 9001 auditor, the dates, and the firm's locations have been changed). The supervisor's comments are numbered and inserted into each version in bold and brackets. The comments illustrate how important it is for principals to address each of their agents' criteria for making a compliance decision. The comments about the original version are quite negative. Much of the information included is irrelevant to the supervisor. What is missing from the original directive are clear-cut answers to the supervisor's decision criteria. Without those answers—such as a due date, specific requirements, and a procedure for implementing those requirements—the supervisor decided to disregard the directive. When the supervisor read the revised version about a week later, he came away ready to comply. Notice that the writer of the revision explicitly addresses each of the decision criteria that are typically relevant for compliance decisions. Notice also that the writer of the revised directive replaces the vague requirements of the original with a more specific, actionable, and testable requirement—a mock quality audit to be conducted by supervisors prior to the official audit.

ORIGINAL DIRECTIVE WITH A SUPERVISOR'S COMMENTS

From:	Quality Systems
Sent:	Wednesday, September 10, 2014 1:15PM
To:	'ALL CALIFORNIA EMPLOYEES'
Subject:	GENERAL NOTICE - QUALITY SYSTEM ASSESSMENTS **[1. OK, another general notice. What's this one about?]**

Totalt Kvalitet Tjanster **[2. What the heck is that?]** (TKT), OUR ISO 9001 REGISTRAR, IS SCHEDULED TO PERFORM TWO ASSESSMENTS OF OUR QUALITY SYSTEM IN 2014. **[3. It must be a company that will audit us. Never heard of them.]** TKT will be here at our California facilities in November to continue the periodic assessments that have already been performed at our Nevada facilities over the past two years. In January, TKT will be conducting a "re-certification" assessment across the firm including our San Jose facility. The Quality Systems group of Total Quality Operations **[4. This must be a subgroup. They don't really need to distinguish because most people don't know who's in one group or the other. They don't explain why we should care.]** will coordinate the assessments. To ensure we are ready, the following activities are planned:
 - Briefings to Senior Management **[5. Not me.]**
 - Making Training and Awareness Material Available Online **[6. I think it is already.]**
 - Forming and training a team of experts from various departments to guide/escort TKT Auditors. **[7. This won't affect me.]**
In the mean time, management and supervision should ensure:
 - Procedures and work instructions are current and available and employees know how to access them. **[8. Supervision does not have time to update work instruction manuals. We have too many fires to put out. This is not a fire.]**
 - Employees know and understand our Quality Policy. **[9. Do they want us to quiz all of our employees?]**
 - Corrective actions are timely and effective. **[10. Corrective actions for what? I assume they want us to discipline employees who aren't up to snuff on the Quality Policy.]**
 - Records are properly **[11. Define *properly*.]** stored, are current, and accurately reflect required data. **[12. This says "ensure records accurately reflect required data" – how general is that? Quality records? Job records? I don't know what they mean, and therefore, I don't know what required data they're talking about.]**
 - General compliance to any of our Quality System Elements that apply to your functional area.

Quality Systems will continue to communicate with managers and supervisors to provide up-to-date information on the progress of the assessments.

Rob Morton, Manager
Quality Systems

[13. The quality policy is frankly a bunch of lofty statements like "We are dedicated to providing the highest quality, lowest cost, most dependable products available which exceed all of our customers' expectations." In real day-to-day operations, it is pretty meaningless. We all do our jobs to the best of our abilities. The only thing of real value is the standard work procedures, but that is not kept current so even its value is limited.

14. I won't take any action on this notice. I'll wait until I hear some *requirements*.]

REVISED DIRECTIVE WITH A SUPERVISOR'S COMMENTS

To: All California engineering supervisors and shop floor foremen
From: Rob Morton, Manager, Quality Systems
Date: September 10, 2014
Subject: Preparing your employees for the upcoming ISO 9001 quality audit

---

The purpose of preparing for the quality audit

We are being audited for conformance with ISO 9001 quality standards, and all employees must be able to pass it. In order to prepare, engineering supervisors and shop floor foremen will be responsible for conducting a mock quality audit with each employee who reports to them. [**1. OK, this affects me.**] If we do not pass this audit, we will lose either a significant portion or all of our current government contracts. This will result in a company-wide loss of jobs. [**2. I guess it is worth the time to make sure we pass.**]

The deadlines that you must meet

Each group's mock audit will occur October 22 through 24. The first actual quality audit will occur during the first and third weeks of November. In January, a re-certification assessment will be conducted. [**3. OK, we have the time to prepare.**]

What you must do

Supervisors and foremen will receive a packet of instructions on how to conduct the mock audit within the next ten days. The packet will include a list of typical questions that auditors may ask. [**4. Good.**] The answers to the auditor's questions should be contained in your group's standard work procedures. [**5. My work manual isn't up to date. I'll have to file the revisions.**] You should identify all employees who are unable to give good answers and ensure that they receive corrective training. [**6. This will take some time. I hope it's really that important.**]

The criteria for passing the mock audit

You must find a 95% compliance rate with ISO 9001 regulations. [**7. So we don't have to be perfect. That helps.**]

What happens if your employees are not prepared

You must send employees who fail the mock audit to quality policy training prior to November 1. Employees who fail an actual audit will be subject to disciplinary action which may include termination of employment. [**8. Not a note on their permanent record!**]

What to do if you have questions

If you have any questions concerning the upcoming audits, please contact me directly at the Quality Systems Department at x32769. [**9. This is an excellent memo! It answers all of my questions. I think I can get the employees to prepare properly for the audit.**]

Staffing Decisions: Responses to Applications

Audiences who are in the position to employ others, that is to say principals, make staffing decisions in response to applications for employment and promotion. For example, employers make staffing decisions when they decide whether to interview a job applicant for a newly opened position;

clients make staffing decisions when they decide whether to accept a consultant's proposal to start a new project; litigants make staffing decisions when they decide whether to hire an attorney to represent them.

Principals make staffing decisions in order to meet the staffing or personnel requirements of themselves or their organizations. Agents seek staffing decisions from principals when they attempt to obtain a job offer, get contracted to do a project, or get a promotion. Documents and presentations agents produce in order to elicit staffing decisions from principals include job applicants' *résumés, cover letters for résumés,* and *letters of recommendation,* current employees' *curriculum vitae* and *performance review packets,* and *consultants' project proposals, letters of engagement,* and *responses to requests for proposals (RFPs).*

When employers make staffing decisions about job applicants, they are especially concerned about the applicants having the right qualifications for the job. Consequently, corporate recruiters and line managers both rate an applicant's résumé more highly the more it reflects the qualifications the specific job requires.[21] Two of the most important qualifications for recent college graduates are their work experience and college record—together these two qualifications account for 75% of the variance in résumé ratings.[22] When it comes to hiring MBAs, the top five qualifications corporate recruiters look for in order of importance are communication skills, analytical thinking skills, the ability to work collaboratively, strategic thinking skills, and leadership skills.[23] School principals seek yet another set of qualifications when hiring new teachers: content knowledge, the ability to scaffold instruction, and the ability to build relationships, as well as enthusiasm, professionalism, and commitment to student learning.[24]

Other characteristics that increase a job applicant's chances of being hired include their apparent fit with the organization's culture, fit with the job, and interview behaviors.[25] Business executives use similar criteria when choosing managers to be their direct reports. In addition to evaluating each candidate's experience, previous contributions, and education, executives also evaluate the candidate's fit with the organization's culture, their personality's fit with the job, and their leadership style.[26] The more executives, employers, and recruiters know about the job to be filled, the more agreement there is among their staffing decisions[27] and the fewer irrelevant candidate characteristics influence those decisions.[28]

Performance evaluations reflect another type of staffing decision. The top performance criteria executives use when deciding whether to promote a manager include the manager's track record, business network, interpersonal/communication skills, knowledge base, work ethic, ability to build teams, and character.[29] Retail sales managers commonly use six criteria to evaluate the performance of their salespeople: productivity, appearance and manner, product knowledge, communication skills, attitude, and initiative.[30] Any supervisor's performance evaluations and promotion decisions will be more accurate when they base them on specific job-related performance criteria instead of generic performance criteria or holistic impressions of their employees.[31] Moreover, when a supervisor's performance criteria are vague, employee job satisfaction and performance decrease.[32]

In addition to hiring employees and evaluating their performance, managers also retain consultants for special projects and contract with corporate partners to create joint ventures. When deciding among consultants who offer training services, managers commonly use six criteria: competence to meet the firm's needs, knowledge and understanding of the organization, educational product, reputation, organizational capability, and cost.[33] Managers commonly use another six criteria to select partners for joint ventures: the partner's reputation for ethical behavior, fit with the firm's goals and objectives, market power, production capabilities, political connections, and past partnering record.[34]

Consumers make staffing decisions, without hiring permanent staff, when they choose a doctor, an attorney, a personal trainer, or other professionals who can provide them with individualized services. For example, investors make a staffing decision when choosing to subscribe to one financial analyst's reports as opposed to another's. In this instance, investors tend to prefer to use the services of analysts who have higher historical accuracy, work for large brokerage firms, forecast more frequently, and have greater experience.[35] Mental health patients make a staffing decision when they choose a therapist to counsel them. Their top criteria for choosing a therapist include the therapist's credentials, their specific expertise, as well as their personal characteristics. Mental health patients tend to give little weight to the therapist's demographic characteristics.[36]

The following list of questions subsumes many of the decision criteria used to make staffing decisions, especially those used within organizations, and provides a starting point for predicting a principal's decision criteria for any particular staffing decision. The list can also serve as an outline for the documents and presentations agents produce in order to elicit staffing decisions from principals.

- What is the applicant's or employee's knowledge of the organization's objectives?
- What is their knowledge of the requirements for the position or project?
- What is their action plan for meeting the requirements?
- How well do they fit with the organization's culture?
- What are their qualifications for the job?
- What steps for engagement do they propose?

In addition to agents' answers to the previous questions, principals may also require benchmark information about other employees,[37] the ideal applicant,[38] and other current applicants.[39] One source of benchmark information for staffing decisions is the letter of recommendation. Although employers often request letters of recommendation to help them make staffing decisions, research finds a large gap between recommenders' intentions and the effects their letters have on employers' perceptions.[40]

Table 2.4 displays some of the think-aloud comments of two real-world audience members as they made staffing decisions. The comments in the first column were made by the director of a firm's human resources (HR) department as she read the cover letter for an MBA's résumé. The comments in the second column were made by the director of another firm's management information systems (MIS) department as he read an 18-page project proposal sent to Pacific Bell from a consulting firm. Each expert was asked to make a decision based on the information provided. The comments displayed reflect the decision criteria for making staffing decisions and illustrate how important it is that professionals address them fully. All of the comments are numbered in the order they were made. Repetitive comments or those that did not directly reflect the experts' decision criteria, such as comprehension-related comments, are not included here.

Notice that both expert audience members complained that the potential hires lacked knowledge of their firms and their firms' requirements. Both experts questioned the qualifications of the potential hires as well as their fit with the firm's culture. In addition, the MIS director complained about the lack of specificity in the action plan of the consulting firm's proposal. And the HR director suggested that the MBA was wrong to expect the employer to suggest steps for engagement. Because so few criteria for staffing decisions were addressed, the first expert decided against interviewing the job applicant and the second was not interested in retaining the consulting firm.

TABLE 2.4 Experts' Comments That Reveal Their Decision Criteria for Making Staffing Decisions

	Comments on an MBA's Cover Letter by an HR Director	*Comments on a Consulting Firm's Project Proposal by an MIS Director*
Knowledge of organization's objectives	6. This letter appears to be a form letter. No indication is given that research was done on our firm. The person does not appear to be very knowledgeable.	10. There's nothing specific to what they are working off of or how much they know about Bell. 26. I feel that they had no idea about Bell in the slightest before they wrote this thing. That's deadly. They are not interested at all.
Knowledge of requirements	2. What specific job are they applying for? As the HR director at my firm, I need to be able to determine if openings are available for that position.	11. They haven't given me a clue to that they know what's going on and that they are responding to what I specifically want and what we're all about. 24. I want to see them telling me "Yes, we know you have this request for proposal. We know generally what you are trying to do." I want to see their approach build off of this base.
Proposed action plan	[Note: Entry-level managers are not ordinarily expected to provide a plan of action in their cover letters.]	17. They've been talking in general terms of what they're going to do and what we are going to get out of this. The essence of this is how are they going to do it? How long? What type of staffing? What's it going to cost? What is the involvement of Bell's general management and the other functional areas? How are the heads of marketing, finance etc. going to be involved in this and what type of effort do they have to give? Where's the structural approach in how they're going to conduct this study and what the impact is going to be in these functional areas? What is MIS's involvement? Role? Looks like MIS is on the sideline. Again no specifics.
Fit with organization's culture	3. I don't get any sense of the person, their skills, experiences, interests, etc.	28. I want to know: What are they doing in these phases? How they are going to do it? How is their staff going to be doing this? How are they going to be interfacing with MIS and user communities? 31. They're setting a tone that's so bad that it will screw up the morale of the entire MIS department. They're not working *with* me. They're just going to come in and rip the guts out of my company because they know better. They're going to run this and then hand it over and say, "Now you can run this thing."
Qualifications	4. Where are all their relevant experiences, qualifications, and achievements? 5. Some experiences have been listed, manufacturing, marketing, consulting, etc. But this is too broad, no focus.	3. I want to see a profile on the [consulting] company, sales, the types of things they have done, their types of clients, etc. They are not specific to what Bell is wanting. I want to know background but this section has nothing to do with the proposal. 39. I want to know who they are putting in charge of this project. What kind of structure they're going to have in your organization? Analysts? Principals? What level? Don't just throw me a wrath of resumes.
Steps for engagement	8. When do they plan to contact us? I hope they're not counting on us to contact them. 9. Overall, this cover letter needs a lot of work to be effective in securing an interview.	36. I come away with *no* confidence that this company knows what they are doing, or how to organize it, or how to organize the attack.

On the following pages are résumé cover letters two MBA students produced as well as two versions of a third MBA student's résumé (note: the dates, names, and addresses of the students, the firms for which they worked, the schools they attended, and the recipients of the letters have been changed). The first cover letter requests an interview for a summer internship. It not only resulted in rejection, but also provoked an angry reaction from the potential employer. Notice that it appears to be a form letter. Although the writer claims to have knowledge of the firm's objectives and requirements, he obviously does not.

The second cover letter is a request for an interview for a full-time position written by a different MBA student. It was one of several applications the student made that ultimately resulted in a job offer. Notice that the writer of the second cover letter shows real knowledge of the firm's objectives and makes the case that she can satisfy the firm's requirements. The writer also quantifies the results she has obtained for her current employer, suggesting she has an action plan ready to implement. In addition, the writer provides benchmark information about the firm that currently retains her and the schools she has attended.

The third MBA student's résumé is shown as originally composed and after it was revised. The original version of the student's resume also includes comments made by a recruiter that are numbered and inserted into it in bold and brackets. The student was hoping to land a summer internship in marketing in the high-tech industry that would allow her to travel internationally. Notice that the recruiter's think-aloud comments about the student's original résumé are generally quite negative. The recruiter is not convinced she has the education, experience, and ability to deliver the results the recruiter's high-tech marketing internship requires. In addition, the small font makes the original version difficult for the recruiter to read.

The revised résumé is much easier to read and highlights the student's interest in marketing, high-tech, and international travel. It also puts greater focus on the results she achieved in prior positions. The revised résumé made a more positive impression on recruiters and ultimately helped the student land a marketing internship in the high-tech industry and travel abroad.

UNSUCCESSFUL COVER LETTER FOR A RÉSUMÉ

2843 Congress Ave., Apt. B
Austin, TX 78704

November 20, 2013

Mr. John R. Abrams,
Chairman and CEO,
ENERglobal Corporation,
444 Fayette St.,
Houston, TX 77002

Dear Mr. Abrams:

I have become interested in your company through articles and advertisements which have appeared in several magazines. Your organization appears to be growing in a direction which parallels my interests and career goals. Through my conversations with the staff at the University Career Center and with other professionals, I have heard that your company is a dynamic and innovative one which also has a strong culture. These compliments have confirmed my initial positive impressions of your company, and I want to express my strong interest in working as a summer intern for you.

For the past academic year, I have attended our University's distinguished School of Business and expect to receive an MBA degree in May 2015.

During my first year at the Business School, I have gained an intensive education in basic managerial and quantitative skills. I am confident that these invaluable skills, in combination with my computer skills, would be beneficial to you in your assignments or projects. My interests and work at the Business School are in Finance and Information Systems. I look forward to discussing with you possible careers in your company.

I am sure that the intern you are looking for is as important to you as your firm is to me. Not only am I aware of your present needs and confident that I can fulfill them, but even more important, believe that I can be an asset for your future needs as well. I wish that you will give me an opportunity to prove my claim.

Thank you for your kind consideration of my request. If you need any additional information, please feel free to call me at (512) 521-2705. I look forward to hearing from you in the very near future.

Sincerely yours,

Evan Robbins

SUCCESSFUL COVER LETTER FOR A RÉSUMÉ

1914 Riverside Dr., Apt. #37
Paterson, NJ 07505
Phone: (973) 321-4757

October 16, 2012

Sarah Wymard
NRG Inc.
1200 Market Street
Fairfax, VA 22031

Dear Ms. Wymard:

My abilities fit the needs of NRG's energy practice. I presently provide consulting services to Edison Light's Treasury Group. My work there focuses on projects requiring expertise in both power plant engineering and corporate finance. I have four years electrical utility experience at both power plants and corporate headquarters. Three of these years were spent as an engineer working for one of the best and most innovative utilities in the U.S. at one of the most highly rated nuclear power stations in the world. My engineering and management educations are from premier schools in their fields. Finally, I greatly desire to continue a career related to electric utilities and energy generation. I sincerely believe that, when combined, these factors make me an outstanding candidate for employment at NRG.

My work with Edison Light's nuclear fuel financing is an excellent example of my unique abilities. While undertaking a review of Edison's nuclear fuel financing I found that they were not taking full advantage of the current New Jersey regulations for the recovery of nuclear fuel financing interest expense. I developed and coordinated the adoption of an accounting method which increased the recovery rate to the maximum allowed under the NJUC regulations. The changes made will reduce Edison's nuclear fuel financing costs by at least $300,000 per year. To date the present value of this and other work I have performed at Edison Light has been in excess of $2,500,000. I can safely say that my work has also saved their ratepayers approximately $8,000,000.

My desire to work with energy-related matters and my expertise in the area of electric utilities will make me a very effective NRG consultant. NRG's focus on energy consulting will in turn provide me with projects which match my interests. Therefore, I would very much appreciate the chance to interview for a position at NRG when you come to our university.

Sincerely,

Davida Wilkinson

Davida Wilkinson

ORIGINAL RÉSUMÉ WITH A RECRUITER'S COMMENTS

PATTY R. SPEAKMAN

3905 Market Street
Philadelphia, PA 19104
[1. This is killing my eyes! Nine point font is too small!]

215-687-2043
E-Mail: pspeakman@wharton.upenn.edu

EDUCATION

May 2015 UNIVERSITY OF PENNSYLVANIA   Philadelphia, PA
Master of Business Administration (MBA) **[2. So she's getting an MBA.]**
Concentrations in Marketing, Information Technology and Strategy **[3. This résumé does not exude strategy. I want more about technology and marketing here, too.]**

May 2009 CORNELL UNIVERSITY   Ithaca, NY
Bachelor of Science in Industrial and Labor Relations
GPA: 3.4/4.0 **[4. I don't care.]**
Dean's List for Academic Achievement
Fall Semester at University of Brussels, International Business Program, 2008 **[5. Does she have any other international elements?]**

EXPERIENCE

INGERSOLL-RAND COMPANY
Worldwide manufacturer of industrial equipment and machinery with sales of 12.3 billion

2010 to 2013 Project Leader
Promoted to position in Human Resources leading teams up to 10 people to restructure processes.
Developed local information system using Microsoft Access and corporate payroll software. **[6. Okay, so you can use Access. Why should I care?]** Resulted in 100% increase in reporting and administrative productivity. **[7. This I care about.]**

Restructured processes and teams resulting in 20% reduction of salaried employee headcount.
Developed outplacement services that enabled employees to terminate with dignity and minimized legal risks. **[8. I don't care.]**

Led team of marketing managers to redesign departmental structure. Increased customer focus through addition of product training and market analysis of functions.

Implemented process enhancements for in-house suppliers' order entry function resulting in a 30% increase in deliver reliability and 40% decrease in backorders. **[9. Tell me results first. Then fill in the details.]**

2010 Reengineering Team Member [10. I have an aversion to titles like this.]
Part of cross-functional team focusing on supply chain improvements.
Achieved 60% decrease in purchase order processing time through EDI technology.

Initiated new procurement and manufacturing planning processes which resulted in a 20% increase in ability to reliably meet weekly production schedules and a 90% reduction in order fulfillment cycle time. **[11. Again, tell me the results first.]**

2008 to 2010 Management Development Program Member
Selected from 100 candidates for program of project experience and management skills development.
Evaluated off the shelf product supporting information technology strategy for human resource management functions.

Guided general manager succession planning process approved by company Chairman.

Created orientation process which increased new employee productivity and effectiveness. **[12. So?]**

ADDITIONAL INFORMATION
Marketing Club: Developed Marketing Club Web Page to stimulate interest in university's marketing resources. **[13. Result?]** Management of Technology Club: Organized plant tour and benchmarking. **[14. What benchmarking? For what goal?]** Graduate Women Business Network: Planned networking conference as First Year Representative on Steering Committee.   Enjoy skiing and international budget travel.

[15. My initial impressions: One. East Coast. Two. Big company. Three. HR or Manufacturing. We're a high tech firm planning to go international. We're looking for a marketing person. Someone familiar with intellectual property issues and the application of technology, (i.e., payroll, etc.), who has process and project management experience.]

REVISED RÉSUMÉ

Patty R. Speakman

3905 Market Street   215-687-2043
Philadelphia, PA 19104   E-Mail: pspeakman@wharton.upenn.edu

Objective Marketing internship in the high technology industry.

Education

May 2015, University of Pennsylvania, Philadelphia, PA
Master of Business Administration (MBA)
- Concentrations in Marketing, Information Technology and Strategy
- Independent market research project for Nexus Corporation to develop strategy for voice command software application.
- Co-Chair of Graduate Women in Business Network. Planned first annual networking conference.
- Marketing Club webpage development team.

May 2009, Cornell University, Ithaca, NY
Bachelor of Science in Industrial and Labor Relations
- GPA: 3.4/4.0, Dean's List
- Fall Semester at University of Copenhagen, International Business Program, 2008. Studied privatization strategies of Polish and East German organizations.

Experience

Ingersoll-Rand Company, Davidson, NC
Global manufacturer of industrial equipment and machinery with sales over 12 billion

2010 to 2013 Project Leader
Promoted to position in Human Resources leading teams up to 10 people to restructure processes.
- Achieved 100% increase in reporting and administrative productivity by developing local information system using database and corporate payroll software.
- Generated 30% increase in delivery reliability and 40% decrease in backorders from in-house supplier by implementing order entry process enhancements.
- Led team of marketing managers to redesign departmental structure. Increased customer focus through addition of product training and market analysis functions.

2010 Order Fulfillment Team Member
Cross-functional team member tasked to generate supply chain improvements.
- Achieved 60% decrease in purchase order processing time through EDI implementation.
- Reduced order fulfillment cycle time by 90% and improved ability to reliably meet weekly production schedules by 20% through implementation of new procurement and manufacturing planning processes.

2008 to 2010 Management Development Program Member
One of three selected from 100 candidates for program of project experience and management skills development.
- Evaluated off the shelf product supporting information technology strategy for human resource management functions.

Interests Travel throughout Europe and Southeast Asia, skiing, soccer, and golf.

Employment Decisions: Responses to Recruiting Efforts

Employment decisions are complementary to staffing decisions and are made by agents or those who wish to become agents. Examples of employment decisions include a job-seeker's decision whether to make an application, a job applicant's decision whether to accept a job offer, and a current employee's decision whether to stay with her firm.

Agents make employment decisions in order to obtain the best job they can. Principals seek employment decisions from agents or potential agents when they recruit and interview candidates for open positions and when they make counteroffers to their own employees who are recruited by competing firms. Documents and presentations principals produce in order to elicit employment decisions from agents include *job descriptions, recruiting literature, recruiting presentations,* and *job advertisements.*

Job seekers appreciate job advertisements and other forms of recruiting literature that address their criteria for employment decisions. For example, nursing students evaluating job advertisements much prefer the "standard" job ad over testimonial job ads or minimal ads that contain only the job title and the employer's internet address.[41] Standard job ads address many of the criteria job seekers have including company information, a job description, job requirements, application procedure, salary, and conditions of employment. Although job applicants give most attention to the location of the job and compensation,[42] they rate job advertisements as more effective when the ads also include the size of the organization,[43] the job's attributes,[44] as well as the organization's staffing policy.[45] Unsurprisingly, experienced job seekers are more affected by the content in job advertisements than their stylistic features. Their less experienced counterparts, however, are more affected by irrelevant cues such as the attractiveness of the people shown in the ads.[46]

When it comes to choosing among job offers, a meta-analysis of 232 studies finds six decision criteria account for most applicants' job choice decisions: characteristics of the job, the organization, and the recruitment process, as well as recruiter behaviors, hiring expectancies, and their perceived fit with the job.[47] The primary criterion applicants use when choosing among job offers is their perceived fit with the job. Happily, this is also the criterion recruiters weight most heavily when making their staffing decisions.[48]

The following list of questions subsumes many of the criteria identified previously and provides a starting point for predicting agents' decision criteria for any particular employment decision. The list can also serve as an outline for documents and presentations principals produce in order to elicit employment decisions from their agents or potential agents.

- How does the job fit with my education, experience, and career goals?
- What are the job's responsibilities and status?
- What are the job's working conditions and the firm's culture?
- What is the job location's cost of living and quality of life?
- What is the size and reputation of the employer?
- What is the job's compensation and benefits package?

In addition to employers' answers to the previous questions, job seekers may also require benchmark information about salaries, benefits, and working conditions at competing firms and at firms in the same geographical locale. Job seekers may also seek comparative ratings of regional educational and cultural resources, as well as comparative information on job scarcity in different locales.[49]

Exonerative Decisions: Responses to Requests for Pardon

Audiences, usually acting as principals, make exonerative decisions when they decide whether to exonerate an agent from blame. For example, customers make exonerative decisions when deciding whether to continue to patronize a business that has provided poor service, jurors make exonerative decisions when deciding whether to convict a business executive accused of fraud, supervisors make exonerative decisions when deciding whether to allow a routinely late employee to keep her job.

Principals make exonerative decisions in order to ensure fair outcomes for all concerned and to avoid setting a bad precedent. Agents seek exonerative decisions from principals when they want to be, or when they want others to be, exonerated from blame. Documents and presentations agents produce in order to elicit exonerative decisions from principals include *crisis press releases, media interviews, responses to customer complaints, rate hike notices,* and *defense arguments,* as well as the more commonplace *excuses, denials*, and *apologies.*

Failure to elicit a favorable exonerative decision can be costly to an individual or an organization. When society decides a business is to blame for an unfortunate incident, the business can have a hard time attracting new customers, investors, and employees.[50] A firm's inappropriate behavior can also lead to lawsuits, sales declines, increases in the cost of capital, market share deterioration, and network partner loss.[51]

How the audience perceives an organization's response to a crisis is critical to retaining organizational legitimacy and to maintaining employee morale.[52] Nondefensive crisis responses, as opposed to defensive ones, give audience members significantly better impressions of the organization and lead to greater levels of trust.[53] When individuals or organizations face a crisis for which they truly are to blame, accepting responsibility and expressing regret affects audience perceptions of them positively and decreases the anger audience members feel.[54]

Ironically, the more a business attempts to deny responsibility for a crisis, the more the audience will judge it to be responsible.[55] Audience members are also more likely to assign blame when they can identify a particular person (for instance, a firm's CEO) as being responsible, when they believe the person should have foreseen and prevented the event, when they believe the person's actions were not justified by the situation, and when they believe the person was free to choose another course of action.[56]

Audiences are more likely to exonerate the responsible party from blame if the responsible party offers an explanation for the incident and offers help or compensation to the victims.[57] The victims themselves generally have more favorable impressions of the responsible party, experience more positive affect, and are more likely to refrain from seeking revenge when the responsible party apologizes to them for the wrongdoing.[58] From the audience's perspective, an effective apology includes expressions of remorse, acknowledgements of responsibility, promises of forbearance, and offers of reparation. However, audiences do not require all four components to be present for the apology to be effective, nor do they limit apology components to these four.[59]

The following list of questions subsumes many of the criteria identified previously and provides a starting point for predicting a principal's decision criteria for any particular exonerative decision. The list can also serve as an outline for documents and presentations agents produce in order to elicit exonerative decisions from principals.

- Who is responsible for the incident?
- What is the reason for the incident?
- Could it have been prevented?
- What has been done to relieve the victims?
- How much compensation is the responsible party prepared to offer?
- What guarantee is there that the incident will not be repeated?

In addition to agents' answers to the previous questions, principals may also require benchmark information about the individual's or the organization's prior responses to similar situations, others' responses, possible alternative responses, as well as industry best practices in similar situations.

Occasionally principals seek, or should seek, what amounts to an exonerative decision from their agents. On the following page is a notice of organizational downsizing from a manager in a health care network as well as think-aloud comments made by one of the employees, or agents, who actually received the notice (note: the dates, names of the firms, and names of the employees have been changed). The employee's comments are numbered and inserted into the notice in bold and brackets. The comments about the notice are quite negative, even hostile. What is missing from the notice are clear-cut answers to the employee's decision criteria. The employee needed answers to questions such as "Who is responsible for the decision to downsize?" (see comment 5), "What was the reason?" (see comments 5 and 7), "Could the downsizing have been prevented?"

(see comment 7), "How will the affected staff be assisted?" (see comment 12), and "What guarantee is there that more staff will not be affected or even laid off?" (see comment 13). Because the notice does not address those questions, the employee is left demoralized and resentful of those responsible.

DOWNSIZING NOTICE WITH AN EMPLOYEE'S COMMENTS

Memo [1. (Shouting) If I don't know anything else I know this is a memo.]

To: Alliance Health Plus Staff
RE Staff **[2. Is it safe to assume all us "staff" know who we are? Do the secretaries belong to the "staff"?]**
From: Bob Ruston **[3. He should initial or sign a memo of this type.]**
Date: 11/03/14
Re: Organization Changes

The purpose of this memo is to announce an organization change. **[4. Redundant ... I already know this.]** A decision has been made **[5. Who made it? Why? What was the impetus? Conversely, as a recipient who has/had no input, do I care?]** to consolidate the medical management activities provided by Reliance Enterprises with the medical management provided by Medi-Serve. Both groups have been working with physicians in our networks to improve clinical performance and the outcomes for our members. **[6. The truth is, these groups don't really know what the other does.]** By consolidating the expertise and resources of two teams, we believe that we can serve our providers more effectively. **[7. What was ineffective? Redundant service? Overlapping duties? Internal lost productivity? Again, why are we doing this?]**

The combined unit will be under the leadership of Joyce O'Brien, Director of Medi-Serve. **[8. Why Joyce? Will this new team therefore be part of M-S?]** The new team will be in place by December 1st with most transition activities complete by the end of the year. The team will include staff **[9. If you mention staff along with activities in paragraph one you don't need this sentence.]** from both RE and M-S and provide medical management services to the entire network. Once the team is in place, a communication **[10. This is a very formal and stilted way of saying this. "Memo" would have sufficed. What will this communication tell us? Once the team is in place it's a little late to tell people that they are on the team. A meeting to explain new duties would be more appropriate than a memo. The only useful purpose this could be is a general informational announcement to the rest of Alliance and to outside providers to inform them of a procedure change.]** will be issued. If you have any questions, please call Joyce at 699-3769.

The consolidation will result in the displacement **[11. Ah, now the real reason for the whole memo: job elimination. Displacement and elimination mean two different things. When will these people find out who they are, in the aforementioned "communication"?]** of several staff from RE and M-S. ALLIANCE HEALTH PLUS's practice is to work with displaced staff to try to locate other comparable positions within the company. Every effort will be made to assist those individuals who have been impacted by this decision. **[12. Who will "assist" these people?]**

[13. So, effective 12/1/14 the medical management activities and staff of RE and M-S will be combined and some of us may be looking for another job.]

Rallying Decisions: Responses to Attempts to Inspire and Lead

Audience members, acting as agents or followers and often as a group, make rallying decisions when others try to inspire or lead them. Examples of rallying decisions include the decision of exhausted employees to work harder, the decision of a disenchanted voting block to throw its weight behind a political candidate, and the decision of a losing sports team to go out and "win just one for the Gipper."

Agents make rallying decisions in order to determine if supporting a leader and her vision for the group's future is worthwhile. Principals, acting as leaders, seek rallying decisions from agents when they try to garner support for themselves, a project, or a mission by boosting follower morale. The show of support may take many forms—a donation,[60] a sacrifice of some sort, or simply a vote of confidence. Documents and presentations principals produce in order to elicit rallying decisions include introductions of new employees, participants, and speakers. They also include *commencement speeches, elegies, farewells, campaign speeches, motivational speeches, mission statements, vision statements,* and *pep talks.* It should come as no surprise that coaches' pep talks have been shown to lift the spirits of collegiate football players and to inspire them to perform at higher levels.[61]

Followers' schemata for one type of rallying decision—the decision that groups make when choosing their leaders—has generated much research interest.[62] A group will often choose as its leader the member who best fits the schema of the group, in other words the member who is most representative of it.[63] A group will also tend to rate that member as more likable, influential, and charismatic than other group members.[64] The decision criteria groups use to choose leaders from among their members also include that member's endorsement of the group's norms, goals, and aspirations, as well as the member's preferential treatment of other group members.

Followers' schemata for a second type of rallying decision—the decision they make when evaluating a leaders' charisma (i.e., the leader's ability to rally and inspire them) has also generated much research interest.[65] Charisma is an important attribute for leaders to possess. Compared to leaders who are not charismatic, charismatic leaders get higher performance ratings from their followers,[66] attract more new followers, promote greater follower identification with the group, and more effectively regulate followers' emotions and reactions to crises.[67] Charismatic leaders also motivate followers to perform better and help them feel greater job satisfaction.[68] The decision criteria followers rely on most when evaluating a leader's charisma include the leader's sensitivity to the followers' needs, the leader's sensitivity to constraints on the followers, the personal risk the leader takes on the followers' behalf, and the leader's vision for the group's future, a vision which must embody the followers' ideals and aspirations.

The following list of questions expands on the criteria identified previously and provides a starting point for predicting agents' decision criteria for any particular rallying decision. The list can also serve as an outline for the documents and presentations principals produce in order to elicit rallying decisions from their agents.

- Does the leader endorse the values our group holds dear?
- Does the leader understand the significance of the occasion to our group?
- Does the leader appreciate the sacrifices our group has already made?
- Is the leader ready to do his or her part?
- Does the leader acknowledge the difficulty of the task that lies ahead?
- What is the leader's vision for our future?

In addition to the leader's answers to these questions, followers may also require benchmark information about the group's responses to comparable challenges in the past as well as information about competing visions for their future.

Getting followers to make favorable rallying decisions requires more than rational arguments, doing so requires artistry, emotion, conviction, and a sense of history. The leader's spoken delivery of her vision can have as great an impact as the content of her vision on how effective her followers perceive her to be.[69] Not surprisingly, speeches that elicit rallying decisions—Abraham Lincoln's Gettysburg Address, Dr. Martin Luther King's "I have a dream" speech, John F. Kennedy's inaugural address, George Washington's farewell to the troops—are among the most memorable speeches ever made. Notice how Lincoln's speech evokes deep emotion as it addresses each of the six key criteria listed previously for rallying decisions. As we will see in Chapter 7, the audiences' emotions tend to influence their decisions any time a leader speaks to the values they hold dear.

LINCOLN'S GETTYSBURG ADDRESS

With the Six Criteria for Rallying Decisions
Lincoln Addressed in Brackets

Four score and seven years ago our fathers brought forth on this continent a new nation, conceived in liberty, and dedicated to the proposition that all men are created equal. **[Criterion 1. Our values: Liberty and equality.]**

Now we are engaged in a great civil war, testing whether that nation, or any nation, so conceived and so dedicated, can long endure. We are met on a great battlefield of that war. We have come to dedicate a portion of that field, as a final resting place for those who here gave their lives that that nation might live. It is altogether fitting and proper that we should do this. **[Criterion 2. The significance of the occasion: To commemorate our brave soldiers.]**

But, in a larger sense, we cannot dedicate, we cannot consecrate, we cannot hallow this ground. The brave men, living and dead, who struggled here, have consecrated it, far above our poor power to add or detract. The world will little note, nor long remember what we say here, but it can never forget what they did here. **[Criterion 3. The sacrifices already made: Our soldiers paid the ultimate price.]** It is for us the living, rather, to be dedicated here to the unfinished work which they who fought here have thus far so nobly advanced. **[Criterion 4. The president is ready to do his part to win the war.]** It is rather for us to be here dedicated to the great task remaining before us–that from these honored dead we take increased devotion to that cause for which they gave the last full measure of devotion—[**Criterion 5. The task ahead will not be easy.**] that we here highly resolve that these dead shall not have died in vain—that this nation, under God, shall have a new birth of freedom—and that government of the people, by the people, for the people, shall not perish from the earth. [**Criterion 6. Lincoln's vision for the future: A nation of free people.**]

Audience Decisions About Financial Resources

In addition to making decisions that help them manage their professional relationships, audience members also make a number of decisions that help them manage their own or their organization's financial resources. The six decision types concerned with the management of financial resources are investment, lending, usage, sourcing, budgetary, and borrowing decisions. These six types can be further divided into three complementary pairs. The first pair, investment and lending decisions, are made in an effort to use money to make money. Investment decisions are made when audiences decide whether to buy equity. Lending decisions are made when audiences decide whether to buy debt.

The second pair, usage and sourcing decisions, are made in an effort to spend money wisely. Usage decisions are made when audiences decide whether they can use a particular product, service, or piece of information. Sourcing decisions are made when audiences decide who should supply them with the product, service, or piece of information when the same product, service, or information is offered by several different providers.

The third pair, budgetary and borrowing decisions, are made in order to find money from either internal or external sources to pay for the desired product, service, or information. Budgetary decisions are made when audiences look for money generated internally to fund what they desire. Borrowing decisions are made when audiences decide whether to accept others' offers to lend them money. The principal in a principal/agent relationship generally makes all six types of decisions about financial resources.

Investment Decisions: Responses to Requests for Investment

Audiences, acting as investors, who want to choose the best investment opportunity available to them make investment decisions. For example, venture capitalists make investment decisions when they decide to buy equity in a new firm. Wall Street analysts make investment decisions when they decide to recommend a "buy," "hold," or "sell." Private investors make these decisions when they decide to purchase shares in a mutual fund. CFOs make them when they decide to acquire another firm.

Investors make investment decisions in order to earn a good return for the amount of risk they take, and in the case of one firm acquiring another, to strategically position the firm against competing firms. Once an investment decision to buy is executed, investors become owners and may be entitled to assume an oversight role in the firm's or the fund's management and operations.

Professionals seek investment decisions from audiences when they want to raise cash for their funds or businesses. Documents and presentations professionals produce in order to elicit investment decisions from potential investors include *business plans* (See the two versions of the business plan executive summary on pp. 11–15), *acquisition plans, acquisition announcements, prospectuses, tender offers, earnings reports,* and *stock research reports.*

The specific criteria used to make investment decisions depends on both the investment and the audience. Investment advisors typically recommend investments to their clients based on a number of quantifiable criteria: the investment's amount of risk, fixed return rate, time horizon, management fees, liquidity, and cost of redemption.[70] Wall Street analysts, on the other hand, not only use quantifiable criteria to make their recommendations, they also use a number of qualitative criteria such as their personal evaluations of the firm's CEO and top management, the cogency of the firm's stated goals and strategy, the firm's ability to find and exploit market niches, and its ability to produce a quality product.[71] As it turns out, such qualitative criteria explain twice as much variance in firm performance as explained by more quantitative factors.[72]

When CFOs make the investment decision to acquire another firm, their decision criteria include the strategic fit of the candidate with the acquirer, the competitive environment of the candidate, the management expertise of the candidate, the financial condition of the candidate and terms of the deal, the operational capabilities of the candidate, and the synergies between the candidate and the acquirer.[73] Similarly, when buy-side analysts evaluate a firm's acquisitions, their decision criteria include the price of the acquisition, the acquisition's financial impact on the acquirer, the likely synergies, the new management, the acquisition's fit with the acquiring firm's strategy, and the acquiring firm's implementation plan.[74]

Studies of venture capitalists (VCs) screening business plans find that VCs' decision criteria for investing in a new business include the start-up's projected revenues and profits, its market, its product, its management, and the terms of the deal.[75] Likewise, angel investors' decision criteria for investing in a new business include its projected sales and revenues, evidence of marketplace acceptance, market size, patent protection, the valuation of the venture, as well as the management's personal and professional characteristics.[76]

The decisions investors and managers make to divest themselves of their current assets reflect another type of investment decision. When managers of multinationals consider divesting one of their foreign operations, their decision criteria include not only the performance of the operation but also the market's growth, the political stability of the host country and the exchange rate volatility of the host country's currency.[77]

The following list of questions generalizes many of the investor-specific decision criteria identified previously and provides a starting point for predicting an investor's decision criteria for any particular investment decision. The list can also serve as an outline for the documents and presentations professionals produce in order to elicit investment decisions from potential investors.

- What is the nature of the investment?
- What is the price and terms of the deal?
- What is the current and future value of the investment?
- What are the risks and liabilities associated with the investment?
- What are the qualifications of the management?
- What is the management's strategy and implementation plan?

In addition to answers to the previous questions, investors may also require benchmark information about the value of "comps" (i.e., comparable publicly-traded firms), alternative investment opportunities, the investment's historical financial performance, as well as industry averages for similar investments.[78] Investment advisors often use U.S. treasury bills as benchmarks when discussing risk with their clients. Treasuries serve as the closest real-world analog to risk-free returns.[79]

Table 2.5 displays some of the think-aloud comments of two real-world audience members as they made investment decisions. The comments in the first column were made by a partner in a private equity firm as he read a plan developed by partners in another private equity firm to acquire a bankrupt textile manufacturer (note: the names of the firms and the partners have been changed). The comments in the second column were made by an experienced private investor

TABLE 2.5 Experts' Comments That Reveal Their Decision Criteria for Making Investment Decisions

	Comments on an Acquisition Plan by a Partner in a Private Equity Firm	Comments on a Financial Analyst's Stock Research Report by a Private Investor
Nature of the investment	9. The company is in bankruptcy. They [the managing partners] are buying the assets from the receiver. 27. Based on this description, it sounds like a great company for a bankrupt company. 34. I'll read through all this stuff on their products and markets because it's useful to know, but most of my questions are going to have to do with the financial information. 36. Oh that's good they have new equipment. At least they won't have to put a lot of money into new machinery. I'm sort of familiar with this type of operation since we have experience in a similar industry. 50. I want them to say up front that they are buying this company out of bankruptcy.	1. I assume the company's making some kind of chemicals. 22. I'd like to see what percentage each chemical is of their product mix. 33. I assume that most of their products are similar chemical products. Only because my father was a chemical engineer do I understand the chemical process they just talked us through. If you weren't a chemical engineer you probably wouldn't be interested, from an investment point of view.
Price/Terms of the deal	10. So, so far they have set up the partnerships with equity—1.4 million, debt—7.2 million, but they still haven't told us, oh here it is, what the transaction is. Our equity contributions are $1,470,000. So the bank doesn't make anything, but they can put this loan on their books as secure now. 48. I want to see what are the sources and uses of the transaction, the $8,670,000 on the second page. Where do we fit into the total financial picture?	4. Then they give me a bunch of data, the 52 week high and low, 20 to 50. So we're selling near high. [Note: The company's stock was currently trading at $48 per share.] That would make me wonder why we expect the stock that's more than double the price to triple within the next 12 months.
Current and future value	12. What I usually like to see is a snapshot of the company, which it doesn't appear that they have. Just the company's financials, their sales, operating income at least, those two things, at least for the last three years. Depreciation and capital expenditures . . . some things to give an idea of cash flows. They make you flip to the back to look through the numbers, which I will do now.	5. We're talking about $150 price value, that seems a little outrageous to me, but maybe these guys know something I don't. 10. They give current capitalization. And yet they said one of the reasons they recommended it was because that was changing. And they give you no idea how that's changing.

26. I don't know why they're using a sales multiple of five times instead of an operating multiple and adjusted cash flow. They don't tell you what they're adjusting cash flow for. So based on who knows why they're getting an IRR of 38.9% (which is acceptable), but who knows what it's based on. This year their margins are up to two million seven. I'm figuring you could sell it for say seven times that. That's about 17 million dollars and they're putting in 7 million in debt and 1.5 in equity. So that would make a decent return, but not 38.9% that they claimed.
43. They think they know what fair value the company has, and they think they're getting a very good price for it. But there is nothing in here that really tells me that. Nothing tells me the rationale for the price.
45. If this was any one of my partnerships, I'd be on the phone telling them this is a piece of trash.

12. Book value per share is only $5.60. And they're recommending $150 value for this company. I don't know about that.
26. They don't tell me why the current market only values it at seven times its earnings. Obviously some investors have different views.
27. Then they give me an Estimated Segment Earnings Model. If I was really knowledgeable in the industry that might interest me, but probably all I really care about is the bottom line, which is operating income, interest expense, pretax income, etc. and would probably just prefer a note that says if I want further information, contact my account representative.
50. Okay, a question that keeps coming back to my mind is that this is obviously a very cyclical industry. I take it that they're building their price estimates up to 21 P/E based on the fact that the industry is expanding. My question is, however, are investors going to buy that?

Risks and liabilities

6. Murray and Robins are the managing partners, so they have the liability, everybody else is limited
30. I'm kind of wondering at this point why they don't say anything about the bankruptcy. This gives background information, which you have to read to find out where the company is coming from. But they're leaving out the most important information of all. Why did the company go down the tubes in the last three years?

40. So the firm's profitability is very sensitive to the chlorine open market price, for which I see no future estimates. If I were these guys, I'd surely want to make sure you were in bed with Georgia Pacific. But if GP goes down. . . . I don't see any future analysis of GP's market, who is their big buyer.
41. So 50% of this company's earnings appear to be tied to one industry, the paper industry. I'm not sure what that says about the future from what they're telling me.
56. One of the things they haven't talked about is liability. When you manufacture and sell chemicals, you have to consider any liabilities, environmental suits, etc. they may face.

Management qualifications

42. The two guys who are managing partners were with the Highland Company when the Highland Company bought it, so they're familiar with the business.

[Note: No mention was made of management qualifications in the report or by the investor.]

Management strategy and action plan

51. I want them to tell me "We've had experience with this company in the past and there are two key things we need to do to turn this company around, and how we're going to do it." Something like, "We can cut costs by doing this, and we can increase sales by doing this."
52. If it's the competition that is the problem, then what are they going to do about it? They didn't talk about the future at all.

46. But I still don't see what these guys' big advantage is.
51. I don't see a good analysis of how these guys fit into the industry, and the industry's movements together.
63. One of the questions that kept coming back to my mind, is where is DuPont? Where are some of the other companies in this industry?
64. My gut reaction is, I don't understand why these guys are better than buying Dow Chemical or anybody else, and therefore I probably would not invest in them.
65. This report is very lengthy. I don't need to know or care how they make these chemicals. What I want to know is: "Is it profitable? Why is it profitable? What are their advantages?" If it's important to be technical because they have an advantage in a certain process, that's fine. But if they make it the same way everybody else does, I really don't care.

as he read a financial analyst's stock research report on a recently listed chemical manufacturer, Georgia Gulf Corporation (GGLF). Each expert was asked to play himself and to make a decision based on the information provided. The comments displayed reflect the decision criteria for making investment decisions and illustrate how important it is that professionals address them fully. In addition, the comments show how important it is that professionals are mindful of the benchmarks experts use to evaluate new investment opportunities. All of the comments are numbered in the order they were made. Comments that were repetitive or did not directly reflect the experts' decision criteria, such as comprehension-related comments, are not included here.

Both expert investors found information about the nature of the investment in the documents they read. And both investors were either satisfied with, or had no questions about, the management of the firms. However, neither investor was satisfied with the terms of the deal. Neither investor was convinced by the arguments made for the values of the firms, neither was certain he had the information needed to ascertain the risks and liabilities associated with the proposed investment, and neither was convinced the firms had sustainable competitive strategies. Thus, although both investors found several of their decision criteria addressed, neither thought the recommended investments compared favorably with other investment opportunities, and, as a consequence, decided not to part with their money.

Lending Decisions: Responses to Requests for Loans

Audiences, acting as lenders, who want to choose the best lending opportunity available to them make lending decisions. Examples of lending decisions include a commercial banker's decision to approve a new line of credit for a client company, a credit committee's decision to renegotiate the terms of an existing loan for a client in financial distress, and an investment banker's decision to underwrite a bond on behalf of a client company.

Audiences make lending decisions in order to increase the value of their portfolios while keeping risk at an optimal level. To accomplish this, they must be able to assess the risk of any specific loan and its impact on the risk level of their portfolio as a whole.

Consumers regularly seek lending decisions from potential lenders when they do not have enough cash to cover an expense. Corporations seek lending decisions when they need to raise capital or protect it but do not want to dilute the value of their shareholder's equity. Documents and presentations professionals produce in order to elicit lending decisions include consumers' *credit applications*, bankers' *internal loan recommendations*, as well as some *business plans* and *acquisition plans*.

The 5Cs credit model with its five decision criteria—*character, capacity, capital, conditions*, and *collateral*—is a widely recognized framework for making lending decisions. A study of 104 lenders finds that experienced lenders use the 5Cs model but weight accounting-related criteria more heavily and character data less heavily than novice lenders.[80]

When making residential mortgage-lending decisions, the criteria loan officers most commonly use include the borrower's profession, the borrower's employment situation, the borrower's assets and liabilities, the borrower's capacity for repayment, the loan-to-value ratio of the property, and the existence of guarantors.[81] Unsurprisingly, these criteria are highly correlated with the default risk of residential mortgages.[82] If lenders have the opportunity to meet borrowers face-to-face, they will also evaluate the borrowers' nonverbal behaviors and the narratives borrowers create to explain questionable information on their credit reports.[83]

Commercial bankers use somewhat different decision criteria when lending to new companies as opposed to existing ones. When deciding whether to lend to existing companies, commercial bankers favor objective information about the borrower's past profitability over subjective information about the management's competence.[84] But when evaluating new companies, bankers are significantly influenced by the management's personal characteristics such as the realism of their ambitions.[85]

Commercial bankers also use somewhat different decision criteria depending on the industry the borrower belongs to. Commercial bankers deciding whether to extend credit to construction project owners base their decisions on criteria that include the borrower's creditworthiness, the borrower's marketing and operating experience, the tightness of credit, and the risk at the construction site, as well as the political and economic stability of the project location.[86] Experienced real estate banking lenders make commercial loans to apartment complex developers on the basis of the developers' experience, the strength of the market, occupancy rates, and the nature of the underwriting.[87]

The following list of questions generalizes the lender-specific decision criteria identified previously and provides a starting point for predicting an expert lender's decision criteria for any particular lending decision. The list can also serve as an outline for the documents and presentations borrowers produce in order to elicit lending decisions from potential lenders.

- What is the amount and use of the loan applied for?
- What is the nature and character of the borrower?
- What is the borrower's current and future financial performance?
- What is the borrower's credit history and rating?
- Does the borrower have sufficient liquidity and collateral?
- What are the current conditions in the economy and the industry?

In addition to borrowers' answers to the previous questions, lenders may also need to consider benchmark information about the borrowers' prior loans, alternative lending opportunities, and other loans in the lender's current portfolio.

Usage Decisions: Responses to Requests to Try Out

Audiences who want to choose the best product, service, or information available to them make usage decisions. For example, consumers make usage decisions when they decide to try out a new product or when they give up their attempt to use a new product. Students make them when deciding to try out a new technique their teacher recommends. Purchasing agents make usage decisions when they beta test a new piece of equipment for their firm.

A usage decision in the commercial environment is the first half of many purchasing decisions. The other half of a purchasing decision is a sourcing decision. When making sourcing decisions, the audience decides which supplier offers them the best deal on the desired product, service, or information. Sourcing decisions will be covered in detail in the next section of this chapter.

Audiences make usage decisions for many different reasons, but usually in order to make their work more productive or their lives easier and more enjoyable. Product manufacturers and service providers seek usage decisions when they encourage their clients and customers to use their product, service, or information. Documents and presentations manufacturers and providers produce in order to elicit usage decisions include *product packages, direct mail ads, sales pitches, cut sheets, manufacturer's advertisements,* and *training manuals.*

Although specific decision criteria vary depending on the audience and the product or service, more generic criteria for usage decisions such as quality and price show up repeatedly. Purchasing agents procuring new products for their organizations routinely use seven decision criteria: product price, quality, reliability, ease of use, after-sales support, compatibility with existing equipment or practices, and salesperson responsiveness to questions or problems.[88] Women in the United States tend to choose clothing on the basis of comfort, quality, style, color, coordination with other clothing, and price.[89] Jewelry shoppers' top seven criteria for choosing a piece of precious jewelry are the quality of material, design, workmanship, durability, warranty, comfort of wearing, and price.[90] Furniture shoppers' prepurchase search criteria include the price, the quality of the materials used, cleaning instructions, guarantees, and warranties. Moreover, these criteria coincide with the information furniture shoppers expect to find on labels for all types of furniture.[91]

The following list of questions subsumes many of the user-specific decision criteria identified previously and provides a starting point for predicting an expert user's decision criteria for any particular usage decision. The list can also serve as an outline for the documents and presentations professionals produce in order to elicit usage decisions from potential users and customers.

- What are the benefits of the product, service, or information?
- How much does it cost in terms of time and money?
- What is its quality and reliability?
- How easy is it to use or implement?
- What is the reputation of its manufacturer or provider?
- How compatible is it with prior purchases or information?

When consumers have to choose between products in different product categories, say between a dishwasher and a refrigerator, they use higher-order, abstract decision criteria that are similar to the criteria listed previously.[92] Even when choosing among comparable products, consumers actually use similar higher-order constructs as decision criteria more often than they use product attributes.[93]

To make an informed decision, consumers and other prospective users may also require benchmark information about competing products, services, or information, third-party ratings of the product such as those provided by *Consumer Reports*, in addition to their own evaluations of similar products, services, or information they have already adopted.[94]

On the following two pages are two versions of a direct mail letter inviting potential clients to a financial planning seminar (note: the firm's service and its benefits, the dates, the names and address of the firm and its owners, and the names of the universities have been changed). Both versions include a description of the service provider, some of the benefits of the service, and a response form with dates and locations of the seminars. Although the original version was successful in attracting people to the seminar, the revised letter more than doubled the response rate of the original. Notice how the revision addresses several of the audience's criteria for usage decisions that were not addressed in the original including the seminar's length and the ease of using the information provided. Notice also how the revised letter highlights what was likely the audience's most important decision criterion—the cost of the seminar.

ORIGINAL DIRECT MAIL LETTER

PFA Price
Financial Associates

One Franklin Center, P.O. Box 711, Las Vegas, NV 89120   1-800-215-323-0410   FAX 215-323-0410
Bob Dawson • Frank Kirby • Robert Davidson • John Ableson, CLU,ChFC

Dear Mr. Jamison,

You are cordially invited to attend a financial planning seminar sponsored by our company in conjunction with Pauline Roberts, Esq., of the law firm of Roberts & Shaw. This is not a sales seminar, but rather is designed to educate you in available financial planning options. We, in conjunction with Roberts & Shaw, have been providing financial planning seminars over the last two years in Nevada with a favorable response.

Ms. Roberts, a graduate of the University of Hawaii Law School, who holds an LL.M. (masters degree in taxation) from San Francisco University, and who practices exclusively in the area of financial planning, will discuss the following:

- The utilization of a Financial Plan to get out of debt, save money automatically, and retain control of your credit rating.

- How to prepare for the coming Social Security Crisis.

- How to discover the best credit cards, online savings accounts, and CD rates.

We have over fifty years of experience, in providing financial planning services to over 6,000 satisfied clients, and we are committed to help families utilize the financial planning tools available to minimize taxes, maximize income and get control over their finances.

Very Truly Yours,

John Abelson

John Abelson, CLU, ChFc

Please tear off here and return

PLEASE CHECK WHICH FUTURE SEMINAR YOU WILL ATTEND

DOWNTOWN HILTON

Tuesday,	November 10, 2016	1:00 p.m._____
Tuesday,	November 10, 2016	7:00 p.m._____

There is no charge for the Seminar and your registered guests are welcome.

(Please remember to mark your calendar with the seminar date and time you have selected)

_____

"Serving the Tri-state area"

REVISED DIRECT MAIL LETTER

Learn how your family can benefit from a Financial Plan

Attend a free Financial Planning Seminar

What you'll get from this seminar
- Learn how to protect your family from the coming Social Security Crisis.
- Find out the critical differences between systematic risk and specific risk.
- Have your individual questions answered by a financial planning attorney.
- Discover how your family can get the best credit cards, online accounts, and CD rates.
- See the in-depth 60 minute, full-color slide presentation.
- Hear how other high-income families have maintained dividend income even during the economic downturn.
- Take home a complete, free packet of financial planning information.

Who should attend:
1. Married couples who want to save for their children's education.
2. Working people who want to protect their hard-earned assets.
3. Family members of elderly parents.

The 60 minute slide presentation: Informative and Entertaining
Sit back and be enlightened and entertained by the full-color Financial Planning slide presentation. You'll learn more about your financial planning options during this sixty minute presentation than you would reading a 500 page book.

Your speaker: Acclaimed author on the benefits of Financial Plans
Your speaker for this seminar is attorney Pauline Roberts. A dynamic and highly respected financial planner, Pauline is also the author of numerous articles on the benefits of Financial Plans. She holds an advanced degree in tax law and dedicates her practice to providing Financial Plans for the people of Nevada.

The sponsors: Two trusted legal and financial firms
The sponsors of the Financial Planning seminar are two of Southern Nevada's most respected legal and financial firms: The law firm of Roberts & Shaw and Price Financial Associates. They have helped more than 6000 families build their savings and take control of their finances.

What people are saying about the Pauline Robert's Seminar
"Pauline's seminar saved my family and me over $250,000!"

B.J., Las Vegas

"This seminar is probably the most profitable hour you'll ever spend."

C.P., Searchlight

- -

To reserve your seats, please return this form in the enclosed envelope to:

Price Financial Associates, One Franklin Center, Las Vegas, NV 89120

Please check the free seminar you will attend.　　　　　　Your guests are also welcome.

Tuesday, November 10, 2016 at the Downtown Hilton	☐ 1:00 p.m.	Home Phone:_____
Tuesday, November 10, 2016 at the Downtown Hilton	☐ 7:00 p.m.	Work Phone: _____

Unable to attend at the times listed? Call 1-800-215-323-8410 for times and dates of the next free seminar.

Sourcing Decisions: Responses to Offers From Vendors

Audiences who want to choose the best supplier or vendor of a product, service, or piece of information make sourcing decisions. For example, purchasing agents make sourcing decisions when they choose among competing vendors or designate a preferred supplier. Consumers make them when they decide among competing fast food restaurants. Students make them when they choose among competing MBA programs. Readers make sourcing decisions when they choose between reading an article from *The New York Times* posted online at nytimes.com and the same article posted online at msn.com.

Suppliers seek sourcing decisions when they want their clients and customers to use their firm, school, website, or store as a source of goods or services. Documents and presentations suppliers produce in order to elicit sourcing decisions include *e-commerce websites, retail advertisements, store catalogs,* and *sales presentations.*

Many criteria, such as convenience and product availability, show up repeatedly in consumer sourcing decisions.[95] When women in the United States choose a department store at which to shop, the five criteria most important to them are ease of locating merchandise, return policy, knowledgeable salespeople, quality of fitting rooms, and store location.[96] When adolescents shop for clothes, price is the most important criterion for store selection. Other criteria, such as product variety, product availability, and store display are also important but carry more weight for adolescent females than males.[97] For young adults, apparel store selection is driven by the store's layout, ambience, product availability, convenience, and promotions.[98] Online shoppers choose all types of online retailers on the basis of the site's ease of use, product offerings, and order handling, as well as the e-tailer's size and reputation.[99]

Purchasing agents for large organizations go through multiple steps when selecting suppliers for long-term contracts. They first eliminate suppliers who have a poor record of quality, delivery, service, or a consistently higher price.[100] After receiving quotes from the remaining vendors, the purchasing agents' decision criteria include the vendor's shipping costs, payment terms, and warranties. Only after the agents identify the vendors who meet these criteria does price become an important factor.

When purchasing agents decide whether to repurchase from a current supplier, the suppliers' commitment to the customer relationship, payment facilities, and product quality all have an impact on purchasing agents' repurchase intentions; the influence of price is comparatively insignificant.[101] New suppliers, on the other hand, typically need to quote a price between 5% and 8% lower than existing suppliers to get a piece of the organization's business.

The decision criteria professional retail buyers use when selecting vendors include the vendor's reputation, anticipated margin, reliability, speed of delivery, and the reputation of the products offered.[102] Surprisingly, buyers weight the vendor's production facilities and the gross margins on the vendor's merchandise more heavily than customer demand for the products.[103] For global sourcing decisions, the most commonly used supplier selection criteria include price, quality, technology access, lead time, labor relations, proximity to the market, and cultural similarity.[104]

The following list of questions generalizes the buyer-specific decision criteria identified previously and provides a starting point for predicting an expert audience's decision criteria for any particular sourcing decision. The list can also serve as an outline for the documents and presentations professionals produce in order to elicit sourcing decisions from potential buyers.

- What are the supplier's prices?
- How available and extensive is their selection?

- How convenient is their location?
- What customer service and ambiance do they provide?
- What payment terms and delivery options do they offer?
- What return policy and after-sales service do they offer?

In addition to answers to these questions, buyers may also require benchmark information about the supplier's historical price levels and performance, well as competing vendors' prices, delivery schedules, and service levels.

Budgetary Decisions: Responses to Requests for Resources

Audience members who have the power to allocate an organization's resources make budgetary decisions. Such decisions grant other professionals the right to spend the organization's money on projects, equipment, new personnel, and so on. Examples of budgetary decisions by upper management include decisions to allow middle managers to upgrade the firm's computer system, to add a requested line item to next year's budget, and to reject an employee's request for a raise.

Despite their apparent similarities, budgetary decisions differ from oversight decisions. Whereas oversight decisions focus on the organization's objectives and the strategies necessary to achieve them, budgetary decisions focus on allocating resources appropriately and keeping costs under control. Professionals seek budgetary decisions when they want funding from sources within their own organization. Documents and presentations professionals produce in order to elicit budgetary decisions from those in charge of the purse strings include *purchase proposals*, *capital projects proposals*, *staffing proposals*, *salary requests*, and *departmental budget proposals*.

Budgetary decisions are often political. Both internal and external politics play a big role in university CFOs' choice of budget decision criteria, especially in the budgetary decisions of younger CFOs and those with less seniority.[105] To a large extent, top managers are able to control the outcome of budgetary decisions by selecting the people who are included in the budget-making process.[106]

Decision criteria for budgetary decisions vary somewhat depending on the audience and the organization. A study comparing how corporate CEOs and Chief Information Officers (CIOs) allocate existing funds in their IT budgets finds that CEOs base their decisions on only three criteria: capital budgeting calculations, cost-benefit calculations, and return on investment. CIOs, on the other hand, base their decisions on the same three criteria used by CEOs as well as an additional four: the proposed expenditure's strategic and operational alignment, its risks, fit with the social subsystem, and technical benefits.[107] Unlike managers in small firms, managers in large firms tend to employ sophisticated techniques such as discounted cash flow analysis when making capital budgeting decisions[108] and use different decision criteria when budgeting for existing as opposed to new capabilities.[109]

Organizations in the health care sector use a different but parallel set of criteria when making budgetary decisions. When times are tough, state health agencies commonly use five key criteria for deciding which programs get funding: whether the program is "mission critical," the consequences of not funding the program, the availability of financing, external directives and mandates, and the magnitude of the problem the program addresses.[110] Criteria used by budgetary committees in hospitals worldwide when committing resources to health technology include clinical need, health impact, affordability, and efficiency, that is, value for the money.[111]

Audience members' schemata for budgetary decisions include, but are not limited to, decision criteria that lead expert audiences to ask the following questions.[112] The list can also serve as an outline for the documents and presentations professionals produce in order to elicit budgetary decisions from their organizations.

- What is the nature and cost of the expenditure?
- How will it impact the firm's strategy and operations?
- What are its financial benefits?
- What are the risks involved with its implementation?
- How urgent is the request?
- What are the qualifications of the requester?

Good budgetary decisions also require the audience to have access to benchmark information such as past expenses, other divisions' expenses, and competitors' expenses.

Table 2.6 displays some of the think-aloud comments of two real-world audience members as they made budgetary decisions. The comments in the first column were made by the CEO of a medium-size e-commerce firm as he read a manager's 17-page proposal to acquire a $392,515 application server. The comments in the second column were made by a manager in a large credit corporation as he read a four-page proposal one of his subordinates wrote requesting $6,240 for the purchase of an automated envelope stuffer. Each expert was asked to play himself and to make a decision based on the information provided. The comments displayed reflect the decision criteria for making budgetary decisions and illustrate how important it is that professionals address them fully. All of the comments are numbered in the order they were made. Comments the CEO made that were repetitive or did not directly reflect his decision criteria, such as format-related comments, are not included here. All of the comments made by the manager from the credit corporation are included.

Notice that the CEO voices several major complaints about the proposal to purchase a new server, all of which are related to criteria for making budgetary decisions:

(1) there is no evidence that the purchase will have a positive impact on the strategy and operations of his organization;
(2) there are unexamined risks associated with its implementation;
(3) there is no indication that the purchase is urgent or necessary; and
(4) the requester has not gotten others within the organization on board with the idea.

Notice that the manager from the credit corporation has even more basic problems with the proposal to purchase an envelope stuffer:

(1) the manager could not figure out what was being proposed or how much it would cost;
(2) he did not understand the reason for the purchase; and
(3) he was not told what the financial benefits would be.

TABLE 2.6 Experts' Comments That Reveal Their Decision Criteria for Making Budgetary Decisions

	Comments on a Purchase Proposal by an e-Business CEO	*Comments on a Purchase Proposal by a Manager in a Credit Company*
Nature and cost of the expenditure	1. Do we have to spend that much [$392,515] *up front*? Why can't we phase this in? 6. Why are you pushing JAVA? Give me some industry or company perspective on your premise. 7. This techie stuff could be rolled up into concepts that map to a business goal.	1. What exactly is it that you're proposing? 2. Are you also proposing changes to how the mail is processed? I can't tell from the information you provide just what you're getting at. 5. You indicate that there is an additional expense in reordering envelopes for the mail stuffer. Is this a big cost? I would have to know this in order to make a decision.
Impact on strategy and operations	5. I would have expected business goals or something to start with. This section on background information is not the best lead material. 9. What are the factors that were used to evaluate our options? This should be shown up front. For example, "Here are the key challenges for us. Here are the factors we used. Here's where the industry is going. Here's how we can get there." 11. You get into factors like scalability and reliability but they are buried.	3. You've provided lots of facts and figures about costs and options, but why? What problem are you trying to resolve? Your proposal just presents a lot of information, but never explains why you're providing it.
Financial benefits	2. Cost savings are *always* hard to even estimate. I would not lead with something like this.	4. By reducing the manpower required to stuff envelopes, doesn't that save money as well? How much?
Risks involved with implementation	12. How about the cultural fit and ability for our e-company to support this? How about vendor stability, market momentum? 23. Did anyone tire-kick this stuff by laying hands on it?	[Perhaps because of the small up-front cost—$6,240—this expert did not indicate whether or not he noted the proposal's lack of a risk assessment.]
Urgency of request	18. Even if it is stated that we need this *now*, how do you draw this conclusion? In other words, traffic, load, etc. Do you reference our current platforms?	[This expert did not indicate whether or not he noted the proposal's lack of urgency.]
Qualifications of requester	22. I'm not sure on the bias of the writer of this proposal. Were business unit folks consulted? At a minimum, marketing folks?	[This expert knew the requester well and did not indicate a need for further information about him.]

On the next page is a salary request from a manager in an engineering firm to his upper management (note: the dates, the position and its attributes, the names of the firm's employees, and the locations of the teams have been changed). The think–aloud comments are those of an experienced business manager who was asked to put himself into the role of a high-level manager and to make a decision based on the information provided. The expert manager's comments are numbered and inserted into the salary request memo in bold and brackets.

Notice that the expert's comments about the request are quite skeptical. What is missing from the salary request is information that addresses the audience's decision criteria about the cost of the salary increase, the manager's impact on the operation of the firm, the financial benefit the manager provides to the firm, and information that shows the manager is uniquely qualified to hold his position. In addition, critical benchmark information is missing, such as the amount of the manager's current salary, the amount of competitive salaries, and the amount of work performed this year compared to the amount performed in the previous year.

Even more interesting is the way the expert shifts from thinking about the manager's request as requiring a budgetary decision (is the request justified?) to thinking about it:

(1) as requiring a staffing decision (perhaps more managers are needed, or maybe the manager really just wants a promotion);

(2) as requiring an oversight decision (perhaps the division is inefficiently run), and finally;

(3) as requiring a policy decision (perhaps the organization needs a formal process for promotions and salary increases).

The expert's comments highlight the fact that audiences are free to make any type of decision they wish no matter what type of decision a professional intends to elicit from them and that a unilateral request for change can trigger a type of decision that the professional did not intend. The expert's comments also provide an excellent example of the critical thinking skills that top managers are able to bring to bear on business issues.

SALARY REQUEST WITH A SENIOR MANAGER'S COMMENTS

```
TO: Jennifer Junejo
FROM: Aaron Schwark
RE: Global Product Division
DATE: September 14, 2013
```

Having completed two years as manager of the global product division, I would like to discuss how the responsibilities of the division have grown during that time. The product line that I manage is highly interrelated with other products at our firm. As such, I often have to be involved in cross-functional meetings or other projects that involve individuals from several departments or teams. I have had to learn – very quickly – how to manage and work with different teams of engineers, salespeople, and marketing employees from around the world.

There are now three "teams" that I must manage or interface with every day; the first is a team of development engineers located in Kyoto, Japan, the second is a worldwide sales force, and the third is a team of production technicians located in San Diego, CA. In regards to my dealings with the software development team in Japan, although this team of engineers does not directly report to me, I have a certain level of responsibility in providing guidance so that they are using their time to work on the highest priority software issues and development requests. More and more they turn to me for advice on how to interpret given requirements, or whether or not to proceed on certain projects.

One of the more unofficial teams that I now "lead" **[1. I don't quite understand that.]** is our worldwide sales force. Even though none of these people report to me directly, I am now indirectly responsible for helping to increase their sales of my particular product. Of course, this is of mutual benefit, since the salespeople receive additional compensation and the increase in total product sales is one of the performance metrics by which I am evaluated. However in the past year, I have had to conduct many sales teleconferences with groups of salespeople from different geographical areas. These training sessions are generally requested by the regions, and not my idea. In an effort to more effectively inspire and lead these sales teams, I have begun setting up monthly or bi-monthly sales training sessions with each of the different regions.

```
I recently instituted monthly meetings with the development engineers, product
segment manager, and representatives from marketing to discuss, prioritize and
assign target development dates to new marketing or customer requirements.
During this meeting, it is my responsibility - as chair of the board - to keep
the meeting moving forward and keep the team focused. In addition, I am
increasingly involved in conference calls between sales account managers and
consultants, to help provide assistance while the two parties work through the
terms of a major contract.

I would like to request a salary adjustment which would reflect the extra
responsibility of these kinds of activities. I think a salary of $85,000 per
year would fairly reflect the work and responsibility carried by my position.
```

[2. I would look into it, but based this document I would not grant the request. There's not enough evidence.

3. This does show that we have a manager that is unhappy in the position. He believes that he has taken on more responsibility, and therefore should get paid more. That may be true, if he's contributing more to the bottom line.

4. What's wrong with this is he doesn't make a strong case. I would like to see how his responsibilities have increased, what exactly he is doing, how the sales volume's increased.

5. Quite possibly we may just need to hire additional management for the division. Or maybe this individual would not be happy working in the product division over the next year or two and is looking for more opportunity. But you can only elicit that from a face-to-face meeting.

6. There may be some inefficiency going on that I'd want to discuss.

7. The only thing this document would do would get me to talk to this person. But otherwise, the memo does not document enough what the contributions to the bottom line are, or how much more time is spent, how only he with his experience can do these kinds of jobs, etc.

8. Perhaps our company needs a more formal process for promotion and salary increase. Usually what you would have would be a set of objectives that would be agreed upon at the first of the year. So that at the end of the year, I could look at your objectives and agree that you had met them.]

Borrowing Decisions: Responses to Offers of Loans

Audiences, such as consumers and CFOs who are open to borrowing money in order to pay for expenditures, make borrowing decisions. Homeowners make borrowing decisions when they decide whether to take out a second mortgage on their home; students make borrowing decisions when they decide whether to apply for a student loan; upper management makes borrowing decisions when they accept or reject lower-management's recommendation to borrow funds for a costly new project.

Consumers, CFOs, and others make borrowing decisions for a number of reasons: to increase the value of their household or firm, to reestablish liquidity, to defer payment, or to manage their debt load. Banks and other lending agencies seek borrowing decisions from potential borrowers in order to earn interest on their capital. Documents and presentations lenders produce in order to elicit borrowing decisions from potential borrowers include *credit card offers, bond issuance proposals, line of credit proposals,* as well as *assessments of optimal capital structure and cost of capital.*

When CFOs make borrowing decisions, they are most concerned about maintaining the firm's financial flexibility and good credit rating.[113] CFOs are somewhat less concerned about transactions costs, free cash flows, tax advantages, or the perceptions of customers and suppliers. It is no coincidence that debt financing as compared to equity financing is followed by significantly worse stock performance. CFOs tend to finance new acquisitions by debt rather than by equity as a result of making overly optimistic predictions about the value of their newly acquired assets.[114]

The biggest borrowing decision many consumers make is the decision to get a mortgage. Mortgage decisions can be complex and risky even for sophisticated borrowers[115] since the terms of mortgage loan products vary widely.[116] For example, mortgage offers can differ in terms of fixed interest vs. adjustable interest rates; maturity (e.g. 5, 15, or 30 years); finance charges and fees (e.g., an interest rate with points charged upfront vs. a higher rate with no points); payment structures (e.g., a 5/1 ARM, in which the borrower pays a fixed rate for the first five years after which it adjusts annually); and other options (e.g., interest-only, in which the loan balance does not decline with additional payments).[117]

Decisions about student loans also require consumers to possess borrowing savvy. Some students borrow too little and, as a result, underinvest in their education. Carefully calculating the return on their college investment can help students determine the appropriate amount of debt. When making a borrowing decision about a particular academic program at a particular school, financial advisors recommend that students use criteria such as their anticipated earnings in the future labor market, the likelihood of their completing the program, the costs of the program, as well as the cost of any debt they will incur.[118]

The following list of questions generalizes the borrower-specific decision criteria identified previously and provides a starting point for predicting an expert audience's decision criteria for any particular borrowing decision. The list can also serve as an outline for the documents and presentations lenders produce in order to elicit borrowing decisions from potential borrowers.

- What are the loan's interest rates and terms of repayment?
- What are its fees and transaction costs?
- What method of computing interest does it use?
- What are its restrictive covenants and penalties?
- What are its tax advantages?
- What effect will it have on my credit rating?

In addition to lenders' answers to the previous questions, borrowers may also require benchmark information about the offers of competing lenders as well as the terms and conditions of other funding sources. When CFOs issue debt, they seek benchmark information about the debt levels of other firms in the industry, the potential costs of bankruptcy, the relative risk of other sources of funds, and the relative cost of other sources of funds.[119]

On the following page is a student's revision of a complex, multipage introduction to a student loan application form. The original version was so full of information irrelevant to a borrower's decision criteria that even experienced financial aid officers found it difficult to use. Information that addressed the borrower's decision criteria was especially hard to locate in the original version due its organization under vague headings such as "General Information." The revised version, on the other hand, directly addresses several of the student borrower's important decision criteria, omits background information irrelevant to a borrowing decision, and uses descriptive headings that speed information search.

REVISED FIRST PAGE OF A LOAN APPLICATION FORM

DO YOU NEED HELP PAYING FOR COLLEGE?

If you are a student looking for financial assistance for college,
you may be interested in our Supplemental Student Loan.

Who Is Eligible?

To be eligible, you must be a U.S. Citizen or a permanent resident of the United States. You also must be enrolling or currently enrolled either full-time or part-time (at least 20 hours per week) at a college or university in our state. You must not be in default on any prior student loans.

What Schools Are Eligible?

You can obtain a loan from us to meet the costs of education at practically any accredited two or four-year college, university, graduate or professional school located in our state. You can call us at 1-800-GET-LOAN if you need to inquire about the eligibility of the school you wish to attend.

Is the Supplemental Loan Right for Me?

There are several different loan programs available to college students. You should first consider both the Guaranteed Student Loan (or GSL) and a PLUS Loan before applying for our Supplemental Loan. Both the GSL and PLUS are less expensive loans than our Supplemental Loan. You can get information about GSL and PLUS loans from any bank in your community.

How Much Can I Borrow?

You can borrow a maximum of $10,000 for a single academic year. If you are borrowing a GSL or PLUS loan then these loans will be counted against the $10,000. For example, if it is your sophomore year as an undergraduate and you borrow $2,500 under GSL and $4,000 under PLUS, the maximum supplemental loan you can borrow this year is $3,500 ($10,000 - $6,500). You can borrow for as many academic years as you require.

What Are the Charges and Interest Rates?

We charge a fee of 5% of your total loan. This fee will cover the costs of processing your loan. It allows us to guarantee your loan in the event you default. Your fixed interest rate will be 9.5% per year.

What Is the Repayment Schedule?

You have ten years over which to pay back your loan. We will begin to charge you interest on the loan as soon as you receive your loan check. You are required to make monthly payments of both interest and principal.

How Much Will My Payments Be?

Since you repay your loan over ten years, your monthly payments should not be a financial burden. If you borrowed $10,000 your payments would be $130 per month. We require you to make payments of at least $50 per month. So if your loan was small, you may completely repay it in less than ten years.

How and When Should I Apply?

STEP 1: Fill out the attached Eligibility Application right now. It will take you only thirty minutes to fill out and will provide us with enough information to determine your eligibility. If you mail the completed application to us today, we will notify you about your approval by mail within thirty days. Just call us at 1-800-GET-LOAN if you have any questions about the Eligibility Application.

STEP 2: Once your eligibility has been approved, we will send you the Loan Request Form. This form asks for more detailed information about you and your credit history. This information will allow us to fully process the loan. You will need a copy of your most recent Federal Tax Return in order to fill in some sections of the Loan Request Form.

It is important to APPLY EARLY! It generally takes 30 days from the time we receive your fully completed Loan Request Form to the time you receive your loan check. By applying early you will be certain to have the money by the time classes begin.

How Do I Receive My Loan Check?

We will send your loan check directly to you. By law we cannot issue the check more than ten days before classes begin.

Audience Decisions About Organizational Policies

Audience members, acting as policy makers, make policy decisions when they decide whether to adopt a new policy—a new rule, regulation, or set of criteria for making a decision or evaluating behavior within an organization.[120] University policy committees make policy decisions when they decide on new criteria that professors must meet for promotion. Employers make policy decisions when they decide on new rules and regulations to add to their employee handbooks. State legislators make policy decisions when they decide on new laws citizens must abide by. U.S. presidents make policy decisions when they decide whether to sign or veto a piece of legislation.

Policy decisions are nonroutine decisions, out of the ordinary. Yet they are the type of decisions that world leaders, legislators, and CEOs must make every day. The need for a policy decision can arise any time a group or organization experiences a question or controversy about what policy or rules to follow. Should we sell guns in our stores? Should our firm do business in countries that abuse human rights? Should our nation cap carbon emissions? Should we ever launch a preemptive attack on another country?

Because policy decisions are nonroutine, the group or organization will likely have no shared schemata for making them. Thus, professionals who seek policy decisions from others must often develop a set of decision criteria for addressing the issue and convince their audience to accept their criteria before they can successfully argue for the policy option they prefer.[121] Once agreement on the decision criteria has been reached, a new policy can be chosen.

The Influence of Group Affiliations on Policy Decisions

Policy decisions are often made by committees or by a leader who has asked for advice from subordinates or consultants.[122] When policy decisions are made by committees, the committee members act both as communicators and as the audience. As communicators, committee members make arguments for or against alternative policies in order to garner support for the policy they prefer. As audience members, they act as policy makers who decide which of the proposed policies is best.

Unlike other types of decisions that rely primarily on audience decision-making expertise, the departmental affiliations and special interests of audience members often have a significant impact on the decision criteria they use to make policy decisions.[123] The membership of a policy-making group often mirrors the structure of the organization to which the group belongs, with each member arguing for the decision criteria and proposals that promote the interests and views of his or her own department.[124] If a department or other stakeholder in the decision has no representative in the group, the policy alternative they would have recommended and the decision criteria they would have used to evaluate alternative proposals will likely be overlooked.[125] Thus, organization leaders are able to exert a great deal of influence over policy decisions simply by deciding which departments should or should not be represented at a particular policy meeting.[126]

Table 2.7 categorizes the statements made by Dutch cabinet members as they met to decide their government's policy about Indonesia's bid for independence in 1948.[127] The numbers in the table indicate the percentage of statements made by each Dutch minister that related to one of the six types of decision criteria discussed in the meeting. The table illustrates that the types of decision criteria the group used to make its decision reflected the departmental affiliations of the ministers present. The percentages in bold show that each departmental minister's focus was on the decision criteria most relevant to his own department. Had the Minister of Justice been included in the meeting, we would expect to see more discussion of legal or law-related decision criteria. The table also shows that the prime minister, whose power depended on domestic politics, was the group member most focused on decision criteria related to domestic politics.

TABLE 2.7 The Departmental Affiliation of Group Members Often Determines Which Criteria Will Be Used to Make a Policy Decision

(Numbers indicate percentage of statements made by each minister about each type of decision criterion)

Department of Minister	Types of Decision Criteria Used					
	Foreign Affairs-Related Criteria	Defense-Related Criteria	Finance-Related Criteria	Overseas Territories-Related Criteria	Law-Related Criteria	Domestic Politics-Related Criteria
Foreign Affairs	**39**	15	12	28	0	6
Defense	10	**57**	8	24	0	1
Finance	18	13	**54**	2	0	13
Overseas Territories	32	6	3	**48**	1	10
Prime Minister	34	6	4	40	0	16

Source: Adapted from Gallhofer and Saris (1996, p. 211)

The Influence of External Groups on Policy Decisions

Sometimes it's important for a group or an organization to take into account the decision criteria of external groups who have a stake in the group's policy decision. In fact, successful policy development in organizations often depends on managers being able to clarify and incorporate the criteria of multiple audiences or *stakeholders*.[128]

Table 2.8 lists decision criteria that the Federal Bureau of Reclamation found to be most important to community interest groups who contested the Bureau's decision to build a new dam, to be named the Orme Dam, at a location near Phoenix, Arizona.[129] Residents and business people from the area were concerned a dam at that location would not be adequate to control flooding or prevent property damage; the League of Women Voters thought a dam at that site would not afford suitable recreational opportunities for families; developers believed a dam located there would limit their access to clean water; environmental groups claimed a dam at that site would destroy wetlands and wildlife; and tribal representatives pointed out that a dam located there would force tribe members from their homes.

Initially, the Bureau neglected to solicit either the decision criteria of the interest groups or their ratings of alternative dam sites. The Bureau did so only after being forced to delay construction of the Orme Dam for more than 10 years due to protests from local citizens. The numbers in the table indicate the average approval rating on a scale of 1 to 100 that the groups as a whole gave each alternative dam for each decision criterion. Although as far as the Bureau was concerned, all three dams met its two decision criteria—flood control and water storage—the community's ratings show it much preferred the Waddell Dam to the Orme Dam. After the community ratings were published, even those public interest groups and politicians who had originally supported the Orme Dam chose to support construction of the Waddell Dam instead.

Taking a stakeholder, or audience-based, approach to policy formation also makes sense in the business world. High-performing companies tend to be run by managers who consider the criteria of all of the companies' major stakeholders—customers, employees, suppliers, investors—when making important business decisions.[130] Studies of top management decision making show that taking a stakeholder, audience-based approach is correlated with higher 10-year rates of return,[131] sales growth and market share,[132] talent retention,[133] CEO salaries, bonuses, and stock options,[134] and share price.[135]

TABLE 2.8 Allowing Stakeholders to Determine Decision Criteria and to Rate Alternatives on the Basis of Them Can Resolve Conflicts
(Numbers indicate average approval rating on a 100-point scale)

Community's Decision Criteria	Build No Dam	Build Orme Dam	Build Cliff Dam	Build Waddell Dam
Control flooding in valley	57	33	68	71
Control flooding in city	52	39	72	75
Promote recreation	62	26	68	72
Increase water supply	58	34	70	72
Protect environment	75	17	70	72
Respect tribal property	80	16	70	74
Overall Approval Rating	**64**	**28**	**70**	**73**

Source: Adapted from Brown (1988, p. 335)

Organizational Decision Criteria for Policy Decisions

The following list of questions provides a starting point for predicting the decision criteria of policy makers in many for-profit and nonprofit organizations. Each question tests the proposed new policy against the organization's established goals. The first question tests the policy against the mission and values, or high-level goals, of the organization as a whole. The remaining questions test the policy against the goals of the departments that make up many organizations—that is, the finance department, the strategy and marketing departments, various departments that deal with operations, the legal department, and the public relations department. For a new policy to meet the goals of the PR department, it may have to meet the goals of external stakeholders in the policy decision as well.

- Is the policy consistent with the organization's mission and values?
- Is the policy consistent with the organization's financial objectives?
- Is the policy consistent with the organization's strategy?
- Is the policy consistent with the organization's operational capabilities?
- Is the policy consistent with the organization's legal and ethical obligations?
- Will the policy generate positive PR for the organization?

In addition to answers to the previous questions, policy makers may also require benchmark information about the outcomes of other, prior policies, of competitors' policies, as well as the outcomes of the organization's current policy.

Note that professionals may need to develop different sets of questions to address the decision criteria of different types of groups and organizations. For example, decision criteria for U.S. foreign policy decisions typically include criteria related to the policy's diplomatic, military, political, and economic implications for the country.[136] As we have seen, the decision criteria used by the Dutch ministers differ from those used by the community groups with an interest in the Orme Dam, and the decision criteria of both groups differ from those used by businesses. Moreover, as we saw in the Dutch case, different department heads within the same organization focus on different decision criteria while evaluating the same set of policy options. And as we saw in the Orme Dam case, allowing external stakeholders to have a say in an organization's policy decision can dramatically affect the decision criteria and the choice of the best alternative.

TYPES OF AUDIENCE DECISIONS: IMPLICATIONS FOR COMMUNICATORS

- The main takeaway for communicators in Chapter 2 is that audiences use variations on a small number of decision schemata to make most of the decisions that professionals want them to make. Thus, the audience's information requirements are often predictable.
- Use the information presented in the chapter to more quickly ascertain the content that is appropriate for your communications. The alternative is to start from scratch when planning the content of your documents, presentations, meetings, or interviews.
- Why use the information? To save yourself time. To improve your accuracy in predicting the information your audience requires. To persuade your audience.
- To apply the information presented in the chapter: (1) Determine the type of decision you want your audience to make; (2) Address the decision criteria and provide the benchmarks for that type of decision; (3) Add or subtract decision criteria and other information depending on the needs and preferences of your specific audience.

Notes

1 Goleman, D., Boyatzis, R. E., & McKee, A. (2002, p. 4). *Primal leadership: Learning to lead with emotional intelligence*. Cambridge, MA: Harvard Business School Press.

2 Blakeslee, A. M. (2001). *Interacting with audiences: Social influences on the production of scientific writing*. Mahwah, NJ: Lawrence Erlbaum Associates.

3 Askehave, I., & Swales, J. M. (2001). Genre identification and communicative purpose: A problem and a possible solution. *Applied Linguistics, 22*(2), 195–212.

Bhatia, V. K. (1997). Introduction: Genre analysis and world Englishes. *World Englishes, 16*(3), 313–319.

Johns, A. M. (1997). *Text, role and context: Developing academic literacies*. Cambridge, UK: Cambridge University Press.

Nickerson, C. (1999). The use of English in electronic mail in a multinational corporation. In F. Bargiela-Chiappini & C. Nickerson (Eds.), *Writing business: Genres, media and discourses* (pp. 35–56). Harlow, UK: Longman.

Swales, J. (1990). *Genre analysis: English in academic and research settings*. New York: Cambridge University Press.

4 Martin, J. R. (1985). Process and text: Two aspects of semiosis. In J. Benson & W. Greaves (Eds.), *Systemic perspectives on discourse* (Vol. I: *Selected Theoretical Papers from the 9th International Systemic Workshop*, pp. 248–274). Norwood, NJ: Ablex.

5 Berkenkotter, C., & Huckin, T. N. (1995, p. 13). *Genre knowledge in disciplinary communication: Cognition, culture, power*. Hillsdale, NJ: Lawrence Erlbaum Associates.

6 Beasley, R. (1998). Collective interpretations: How problem representations aggregate in foreign policy groups. In D. Sylvan & J. Voss (Eds.), *Problem representation in foreign policy decision making* (pp. 80–115). New York: Cambridge University Press.

7 Campbell, J. E. (1981). An empirical investigation of the impact on the decision processes of loan officers of separate accounting standards for smaller and/or closely held companies (Doctoral dissertation, The University of Tennessee, 1981). *Dissertation Abstracts International, 42*(09A), 4050.

Campbell, J. E. (1984). An application of protocol analysis to the "Little GAAP" controversy. *Accounting, Organizations and Society, 9*(3–4), 329–343.

8 Goold, M. (1996). The (limited) role of the board. *Long Range Planning, 29*(4), 572–575.

Helmer, H. W. (1996). A director's role in strategy: There has been no clear consensus on how a board should involve itself in strategy formulation. *Directors and Boards, 20*, 22–25.

Parker, L. D. (2008). Boardroom operational and financial control: An insider view. *British Journal of Management, 19*(1), 65–88.

9 Puffer, S. M., & Weintrop, J. B. (1991). Corporate performance and CEO turnover: The role of performance expectations. *Administrative Science Quarterly, 36*(1), 1–19.

10 Dulewicz, V., & Herbert, P. (1999). The priorities and performance of boards in UK public companies. *Corporate Governance: An International Review*, 7(2), 178–189.

11 Hendry, K. P., Kiel, G. C., & Nicholson, G. (2010). How boards strategise: A strategy as practice view. *Long Range Planning, 43*(1), 33–56.

12 Stiles, P. (2001). The impact of the board on strategy: An empirical examination. *Journal of Management Studies, 38*(5), 627–650.

13 Nicholson, G., & Newton, C. (2010). The role of the board of directors: Perceptions of managerial elites. *Journal of Management & Organization, 16*(2), 204–218.

14 Stratman, J., & Young, R. O. (1986, April). An Analysis of Novice Managers' Performances in Board Meetings. Annual Conference of the Management Communication Association, Durham, NC.

15 Chandler, R. C. (1988). Organizational communication to corporate constituents: The role of the company annual report (Doctoral dissertation, University of Kansas, 1988). *Dissertation Abstracts International, 49*(11a), 3200.

16 Shattuck, L. G. (1995). Communication of intent in distributed supervisory control systems (Doctoral dissertation, The Ohio State University, 1995). *Dissertation Abstracts International, 56*(09B), 5209.

17 Klein, G. A. (1994). A script for the commander's intent statement. In A. H. Levis & I. S. Levis (Eds.), *Science of command and control: Part III: Coping with change* (pp. 75–86). Fairfax, VA: AFCEA International Press.

18 Kellermanns, F. W., Walter, J., Lechner, C., & Floyd, S. W. (2005). The lack of consensus about strategic consensus: Advancing theory and research. *Journal of Management, 31*(5), 719–737.

19 Will, K. E., Decina, L. E., Maple, E. L., & Perkins, A. M. (2015). Examining the relative effectiveness of different message framing strategies for child passenger safety: Recommendations for increased comprehension and compliance. *Accident Analysis & Prevention, 79*, 170–181.

20 Laughery, K. R., & Page-Smith, K. R. (2006). Explicit information in warnings. In M. S. Wogalter (Ed.), *Handbook of warnings* (pp. 419–428). Mahwah, NJ: Lawrence Erlbaum.

21 Brown, B. K., & Campion, M. A. (1994). Biodata phenomenology: Recruiters' perceptions and use of biographical information in resume screening. *Journal of Applied Psychology, 79*(6), 897–908.

22 Ruck, H. W. (1980). A cross-company study of decision policies of manager resume evaluations (Doctoral dissertation, Stevens Institute of Technology, 1980). *Dissertation Abstracts International, 41*(08B), 3222.

23 Otani, A. (2015, January 5). These are the skills you need if you want to be headhunted. *Bloomberg Businessweek*. Retrieved December 31, 2015 from http://www.bloomberg.com/news/articles/2015–01–05/the-job-skills-that-recruiters-wish-you-had

24 Woodburn, J. L. (2014). A case study analysis of middle school principals' teacher selection criteria (Doctoral dissertation, University of Maryland, College Park, 2014). *Dissertation Abstracts International: Section A, 74*(8-A)(E).

25 Kwok, L., Adams, C. R., & Feng, D. (2012). A comparison of graduating seniors who receive job offers and those who do not according to hospitality recruiters' selection criteria. *International Journal of Hospitality Management, 31*(2), 500–510.

26 Whitmore, R. C. (2014). The use of heuristics by senior executives when selecting senior-level executive direct reports (Doctoral dissertation, Fielding Graduate University, 2014). *Dissertation Abstracts International: Section A, 74*(11-A)(E).

27 Langdale, J. A., & Weitz, J. (1973). Estimating the influence of job information on interviewer agreement. *Journal of Applied Psychology, 57*(1), 23–27.

28 Wiener, Y., & Schneiderman, M. L. (1974). Use of job information as a criterion in employment decisions of interviewers. *Journal of Applied Psychology, 59*(6), 699–704.

29 Longenecker, C. O., & Fink, L. S. (2008). Key criteria in twenty-first century management promotional decisions. *Career Development International, 13*(3), 241–251.

30 Hawes, J. M., Jackson Jr, D. W., Schlacter, J. L., & Wolfe, W. G. (1995). Selling and sales management in action examining the bases utilized for evaluating salespeoples' performance. *Journal of Personal Selling & Sales Management, 15*(4), 57–65.

31 Rojon, C., McDowall, A., & Saunders, M. N. (2015). The relationships between traditional selection assessments and workplace performance criteria specificity: A comparative meta-analysis. *Human Performance, 28*(1), 1–25.

32 Behrman, D. N., Bigoness, W. J., & Perreault Jr, W. D. (1981). Sources of job related ambiguity and their consequences upon salespersons' job satisfaction and performance. *Management Science*, *27*(11), 1246–1260.

Dubinsky, A. J., & Skinner, S. J. (1984). Impact of job characteristics on retail salespeople's reactions to their jobs. *Journal of Retailing*, *60*(2), 35–62.

33 Roy, J. P., & Oliver, C. (2009). International joint venture partner selection: The role of the host-country legal environment. *Journal of International Business Studies*, *40*(5), 779–801.

34 Sonmez, M., & Moorhouse, A. (2010). Purchasing professional services: Which decision criteria? *Management Decision*, *48*(2), 189–206.

35 Brown, L. D. (2001). Predicting individual analyst earnings forecast accuracy. *Financial Analysts Journal*, *57*(6), 44–49.

Clement, M. B., & Tse, S. Y. (2003). Do investors respond to analysts' forecast revisions as if forecast accuracy is all that matters? *The Accounting Review*, *78*(1), 227–249.

Jacob, J., Lys, T., & Neale, M. (1999). Expertise in forecasting performance of security analysts. *Journal of Accounting and Economics*, *28*(1), 27–50.

36 Lipscomb, T. J., Shelley, K., & Root, T. (2010). Selection criteria for choosing mental health service providers: A pilot study. *Health Marketing Quarterly*, *27*(4), 321–333.

37 Martin, S. L. (1987). An attributional analysis of differences in rating type in a performance evaluation context: A use of verbal protocol analysis (Doctoral dissertation, The Ohio State University, 1987). *Dissertation Abstracts International*, *49*(02B), 0562.

38 Webster, E. D. (Ed.). (1964). *Decision-making in the employment interview*. Montreal, Canada: McGill University.

39 Highhouse, S., & Gallo, A. (1997). Order effects in personnel decision making. *Human Performance*, *10*(1), 31–46.

40 Doyle, A. E. (1990). Readers' and writers' genre expectations in letters of recommendation: Two case studies (Doctoral dissertation, University of Illinois, Chicago, 1990). *Dissertation Abstracts International*, *52*(01A), 0209.

41 Van Rooy, L., Hendriks, B., Van Meurs, F., & Korzilius, H. (2006). Job advertisements in the Dutch mental health care sector: Preferences of potential applicants. In S. Carliner, J. P. Verckens & C. De Waile (Eds.), *Information and document design: Varieties on recent research* (pp. 61–84). The Netherlands: John Benjamins.

42 Barber, A. E., & Roehling, M. V. (1993). Job postings and the decision to interview: A verbal protocol analysis. *Journal of Applied Psychology*, *78*(5), 845–856.

43 *Ibid*.

44 Winter, P. A. (1996). Applicant evaluations of formal position advertisements: The influence of sex, job message content, and information order. *Journal of Personnel Evaluation in Education*, *10*, 105–116.

Yuce, P., & Highhouse, S. (1998). Effects of attribute set size and pay ambiguity on reactions to "help wanted" advertisements. *Journal of Organizational Behavior*, *19*(4), 337–352.

45 Highhouse, S., Stierwalt, S. L., Bachchiochi, P., Elder, A. E., & Fisher, G. (1999). Effects of advertised human resource management practices on attraction of African American applicants. *Personnel Psychology*, *52*(2), 425–442.

Breaugh, J. A., & Starke, M. (2000). Research on employee recruitment: So many studies, so many remaining questions. *Journal of Management*, *26*(3), 405–434.

46 Walker, H. J., Feild, H. S., Giles, W. F., & Bernerth, J. B. (2008). The interactive effects of job advertisement characteristics and applicant experience on reactions to recruitment messages. *Journal of Occupational and Organizational Psychology*, *81*(4), 619–638.

47 Uggerslev, K. L., Fassina, N. E., & Kraichy, D. (2012). Recruiting through the stages: A meta-analytic test of predictors of applicant attraction at different stages of the recruiting process. *Personnel Psychology*, *65*(3), 597–660.

48 Kristof-Brown, A. L. (2000). Perceived applicant fit: Distinguishing between recruiters' perceptions of person-job and person-organization fit. *Personnel Psychology*, *53*(3), 643–671.

49 Highhouse, S., Beadle, D., Gallo, A., & Miller, L. (1998). Get' em while they last! Effects of scarcity information in job advertisements. *Journal of Applied Social Psychology*, *28*(9), 779–795.

50 Fombrun, C. (1996). *Reputation*. New York: John Wiley & Sons Ltd.

51 Baucus, M. S., & Baucus, D. A. (1997). Paying the piper: An empirical examination of longer-term financial consequences of illegal corporate behavior. *Academy of Management Journal*, *40*(1), 129–151.

Sullivan, B. N., Haunschild, P., & Page, K. (2007). Organizations non gratae? The impact of unethical corporate acts on interorganizational networks. *Organization Science*, *18*(1), 55–70.

Karpoff, J. M., Lee, D. S., & Martin, G. S. (2008). The cost to firms of cooking the books. *Journal of Financial and Quantitative Analysis*, *43*(03), 581–611.

52 Blewitt, J. C. (2015). A time of crisis is a time of opportunity for organizations: A strategic examination of managerial response and stakeholder perception (Doctoral dissertation, Saint Louis University, 2015). *Dissertation Abstracts International: Section A, 75*(10-A)(E).

St. James, W. D. (2009). Relationships between airline employee morale, motivation, and leadership (Doctoral dissertation, University of Phoenix, 2009). *Dissertation Abstracts International: Section A, 69*, 4796.

53 De Blasio, A., & Veale, R. (2009). Why say sorry? Influencing consumer perceptions post organizational crises. *Australasian Marketing Journal (AMJ), 17*(2), 75–83.

54 Kim, P. H., Ferrin, D. L., Cooper, C. D., & Dirks, K. T. (2004). Removing the shadow of suspicion: The effects of apology versus denial for repairing competence-versus integrity-based trust violations. *Journal of Applied Psychology, 89*(1), 104–118.

Lewick, R., & Bunker, B. B. (1996). Developing and maintaining trust in work relationships. In R. M. Kramer & T. R. Tyler (Eds.), *Trust in Organizations: Frontiers of Theory and Reach* (pp. 114–139). Thousand Oaks, CA: Sage.

Pace, K. M., Fediuk, T. A., & Botero, I. C. (2010). The acceptance of responsibility and expressions of regret in organizational apologies after a transgression. *Corporate Communications: An International Journal, 15*(4), 410–427.

55 Lee, B. K. (2005). Hong Kong consumers' evaluation in an airline crash: A path model analysis. *Journal of Public Relations Research, 17*(4), 363–391.

56 Shaver, K. G. (1975). *An introduction to attribution processes.* Cambridge, MA: Winthrop Publishing.

Shaver, K. G. (1985). *The attribution of blame: Causality, responsibility, and blame-worthiness.* New York: Springer-Verlag.

Shaver, K. G., & Drown, D. (1986). On causality, responsibility, and self-blame: A theoretical note. *Journal of Personality and Social Psychology, 50*(4), 697–702.

57 Bragger, J., Evans, D., Kutcher, G., Sumner, K., & Fritzky, E. (2015). Factors affecting perceptions of procedural fairness of downsizing: A policy capturing approach. *Human Resource Development Quarterly, 26*(2), 127–154.

Coombs, T., & Schmidt, L. (2000). An empirical analysis of image restoration: Texaco's racism crisis. *Journal of Public Relations Research, 12*(2), 163–178.

58 Ohbuchi, K. I., Kameda, M., & Agarie, N. (1989). Apology as aggression control: Its role in mediating appraisal of and response to harm. *Journal of Personality and Social Psychology, 56*(2), 219–227.

59 Bentley, J. M. (2015). Shifting identification: A theory of apologies and pseudo-apologies. *Public Relations Review, 41*(1), 22–29.

60 Schkade, D. A., & Payne, J. W. (1994). How people respond to contingent valuation questions: A verbal protocol analysis of willingness to pay for an environmental regulation. *Journal of Environmental Economics and Management, 26*(1), 88–109.

61 Gonzalez, S., Metzler, J., & Newton, M. (2011). The influence of a simulated "Pep Talk" on athlete inspiration, situational motivation, and emotion. *International Journal of Sports Science and Coaching, 6*(3), 445–460.

62 Hogg, M. A. (2001). A social identity theory of leadership. *Personality and Social Psychology Review, 5*, 184–200.

Hogg, M. A., & Hardie, E. A. (1991). Social attraction, personal attraction and self-categorization: A field study. *Personality and Social Psychology Bulletin, 17*, 175–180.

Hogg, M. A., & Terry, O. J. (2000). Social identity and self-categorization processes in organizational contexts. *Academy of Management Review, 25*, 121–140.

63 Fielding, K. S., & Hogg, M. A. (1997). Social identity, self-categorization, and leadership: A field study of small interactive groups. *Group Dynamics: Theory, Research, and Practice, 1*, 39–51.

64 Hogg, M. A., & Hains, S. C. (1998). Friendship and group identification: A new look at the role of cohesiveness in group think. *European Journal of Social Psychology, 28*, 323–341.

Platow, M. J., van Knippenberg, D., Haslam, S. A., van Knippenberg, B., & Spears, R. (2001). *A special gift we bestow on you for being representative of us: Considering leader charisma from a self-categorization perspective.* Unpublished manuscript, La Trobe University, Melbourne, Victoria, Australia.

van Knippenberg, D., Lossie, N., & Wilke, H. (1994). In-group prototypicality and persuasion: Determinants of heuristic and systematic message processing. *British Journal of Social Psychology, 33*, 289–300.

65 Conger, J. A., & Kanungo, R. N. (Eds.). (1988). *Charismatic leadership: The elusive factor in organizational effectiveness.* San Francisco: Jossey-Bass.

Conger, J. A., & Kanungo, R. N. (1998). *Charismatic leadership in organizations.* Thousand Oaks, CA: Sage.

Conger, J. A., Kanungo, R. N., Menon, S. T., & Mathur, P. (1997). Measuring charisma: Dimensionality and validity of the Conger-Kanungo scale of charismatic leadership. *Canadian Journal of Administrative Sciences, 14*(3), 290–302.

66 Shamir, B., House, R., & Arthur, M. B. (1993). The motivational effects of charismatic leadership: A self-concept based theory. *Organization Science, 4*(4), 577–594.

67 Halevy, N., Berson, Y., & Galinsky, A. D. (2011). The mainstream is not electable: When vision triumphs over representativeness in leader emergence and effectiveness. *Personality and Social Psychology Bulletin, 37*(7), 893–904.

68 Agle, B. R., & Sonnenfeld, J. A. (1994). Charismatic chief executive officers: Are they more effective? An empirical test of charismatic leadership theory. *Academy of Management Proceedings, 1994*(1), 2–6.

Yammarino, F. J., & Bass, B. M. (1990). Long-term forecasting of transformational leadership and its effects among naval officers. In K. E. Clark & M. B. Clark (Eds.), *Measures of leadership* (pp. 151–170). West Orange, NJ: Leadership Library of America.

Zaccaro, Stephen J. (2001). *The nature of executive leadership: A conceptual and empirical analysis of success.* Washington, DC: American Psychological Association.

69 Awamleh, R., & Gardner, W. L. (1999). Perceptions of leader charisma and effectiveness: The effects of vision content, delivery, and organizational performance. *Leadership Quarterly, 10,* 345–373.

70 Monti, M., Boero, R., Berg, N., Gigerenzer, G., & Martignon, L. (2012). How do common investors behave? Information search and portfolio choice among bank customers and university students. *Mind & Society, 11*(2), 203–233.

71 Frishkoff, P., Frishkoff, P. A., & Bouwman, M. J. (1984). Use of accounting data in screening by financial analysts. *Journal of Accounting, Auditing & Finance, 8*(1), 44–53.

Sambharya, R. B. (2011). Security analysts' earnings forecasts as a measure of firm performance: An empirical exploration of its domain. *Management Decision, 49*(7), 1160–1181.

72 Hansen, G. S., & Wernerfelt, B. (1989). Determinants of firm performance: The relative importance of economic and organizational factors. *Strategic Management Journal, 10*(5), 399–411.

73 Melone, N. P. (1994). Reasoning in the executive suite: The influence of role/experience-based expertise on decision processes of corporate executives. *Organization Science, 5*(3), 438–455.

74 Kuperman, J. C. (2000, p. 12). Financial analyst sensemaking following strategic announcements: Implications for the investor relations activities of firms (Doctoral dissertation, New York University, 2000). *Dissertation Abstracts International, 61*(05A), 1936.

75 Hall, J., & Hofer, C. W. (1993). Venture capitalists' decision criteria in new venture evaluation. *Journal of Business Venturing, 8*(1), 25–42.

Pfeffer, M. G. (1987). Venture capital investment and protocol analysis (Doctoral dissertation, University of North Texas, 1987). *Dissertation Abstracts International, 49*(01A), 112.

Zacharakis, A. L., & Meyer, G. D. (2000). The potential of actuarial decision models: Can they improve the venture capital investment decision? *Journal of Business Venturing, 15*(4), 323–346.

76 Ding, Z., Sun, S. L., & Au, K. (2014). Angel investors' selection criteria: A comparative institutional perspective. *Asia Pacific Journal of Management, 31*(3), 705–731.

Haines Jr, G. H., Madill, J. J. & Riding, A. L. (2003). Informal investment in Canada: Financing small business growth. *Journal of Small Business & Entrepreneurship, 16*(3–4), 13–40.

Mason, C., & Stark, M. (2004). What do investors look for in a business plan? A comparison of the investment criteria of bankers, venture capitalists and business angels. *International Small Business Journal, 22*(3), 227–248.

77 Berry, H. (2013). When do firms divest foreign operations? *Organization Science, 24*(1), 246–261.

78 Clarkson, G. P. (1962). *Portfolio selection: A simulation of trust investment.* Englewood Cliffs, NJ: Prentice Hall.

Gunderson, E. A. W. (1991). Expertise in security valuation: Operationalizing the valuation process (Doctoral dissertation, The Union Institute, 1991). *Dissertation Abstracts International, 52*(02A), 0592.

79 *See* n70, Monti et al. (2012).

80 Beaulieu, P. R. (1994). Commercial lenders' use of accounting information in interaction with source credibility. *Contemporary Accounting Research, 10*(2), 557–585.

81 Ferreira, F. A., Santos, S. P., Marques, C. S., & Ferreira, J. (2014). Assessing credit risk of mortgage lending using MACBETH: A methodological framework. *Management Decision, 52*(2), 182–206.

82 Gau, G. W. (1978). A taxonomic model for the risk-rating of residential mortgages. *Journal of Business, 51*(4), 687–706.

83 Moulton, L. (2007). Divining value with relational proxies: How moneylenders balance risk and trust in the quest for good borrowers. *Sociological Forum, 22*(3), 300–330.

84 Bruns, V., & Fletcher, M. (2008). Banks' risk assessment of Swedish SMEs. *Venture Capital, 10*(2), 171–194.

Trönnberg, C. C., & Hemlin, S. (2014). Lending decision making in banks: A critical incident study of loan officers. *European Management Journal, 32*(2), 362–372.

85 Hedelin, L., & Sjöberg, L. (1993). *Riskbedömning-bankmäns bedömning av nyföretagares personliga egenskaper.* [Risk assessments: Loan officers' assessment of new entrepreneurs' personal characteristics]. Stockholm: NUTEK.

86 Al-Dughaither, K. A. (1996). International construction financing strategies: Influential factors and decision-making (Doctoral dissertation, Carnegie Mellon University, 1996). *Dissertation Abstracts International, 57*(11a), 4857.

87 Hardin, W. G. (1996). An investigation into the information processing heuristics of private banking and real estate banking lenders in a commercial banking environment (Doctoral dissertation, Georgia State University, 1996). *Dissertation Abstracts International, 58*(11A), 4384.

88 Weitz, B. A. (1978). Relationship between salesperson performance and understanding of customer decision making. *Journal of Marketing Research, 15*(4), 501–516.

89 Hsu, H. J., & Burns, L. D. (2002). Clothing evaluative criteria: A cross-national comparison of Taiwanese and United States consumers. *Clothing and Textiles Research Journal, 20*(4), 246–252.

90 Jamal, A., & Goode, M. (2001). Consumers' product evaluation: A study of the primary evaluative criteria in the precious jewellery market in the UK. *Journal of Consumer Behaviour, 1*(2), 140–155.

91 Labuschagne, A., van Zyl, S., van der Merwe, D., & Kruger, A. (2012). Consumers' expectations of furniture labels during their pre-purchase information search: An explication of proposed furniture labelling specifications. *International Journal of Consumer Studies, 36*(4), 451–459.

92 Graonic, M. D. (1995). The effects of context and consumer knowledge on transferability of preferences (Doctoral dissertation, University of Minnesota, 1995). *Dissertation Abstracts International, 56*(07A), 2772.

93 Walker, B. A., Celsi, R. L., & Olson, J. C. (1986). Exploring the structural characteristics of consumers' knowledge. *Advances in Consumer Research, 14*(1), 17–21.

94 Jung, K. (1996). Line extension versus new brand name introduction: Effects of new products discrepancy and relationship to an existing brand on the information process of new product evaluation (Doctoral dissertation, University of Illinois, Urbana-Champaign, 1996). *Dissertation Abstracts International, 57*(11A), 4833.

Lee, D. (1989a). The differential impact of comparative advertising on novice and expert consumers (Doctoral dissertation, University of Pittsburgh, 1989). *Dissertation Abstracts International, 50*(11a), 3666.

Rothman, A. J., Haddock, G., & Schwarz, N. (2001). How many partners is too many? Shaping perceptions of vulnerability. *Journal of Applied Social Psychology, 31*(10), 2195–2214.

95 Mader, F. H. (1988). The influence of multi stop decision making on store choice (Doctoral dissertation, University of Georgia, 1988). *Dissertation Abstracts International, 49*(11A), 3430.

96 Williams, J. M. (1990). Women's preferences for and satisfaction with the convenience services offered by a department store (Doctoral dissertation, Texas Woman's University, 1990). *Dissertation Abstracts International, 51*(06B), 2848.

97 Chen-Yu, J. H., & Seock, Y. K. (2002). Adolescents' clothing purchase motivations, information sources, and store selection criteria: A comparison of male/female and impulse/nonimpulse shoppers. *Family and Consumer Sciences Research Journal, 31*(1), 50–77.

98 Narang, R. (2011). Examining the role of various psychographic characteristics in apparel store selection: A study on Indian youth. *Young Consumers, 12*(2), 133–144.

99 Konradt, U., Wandke, H., Balazs, B., & Christophersen, T. (2003). Usability in online shops: Scale construction, validation and the influence on the buyers' intention and decision. *Behaviour & Information Technology, 22*(3), 165–174.

100 Vyas, N. M. (1981). Observation of industrial purchasing decisions on supplier choices for long-term contracts in naturalistic settings (Doctoral dissertation, University of South Carolina, 1981). *Dissertation Abstracts International, 42*(05A), 2275.

Ho, W., Xu, X., & Dey, P. K. (2010). Multi-criteria decision making approaches for supplier evaluation and selection: A literature review. *European Journal of Operational Research, 202*(1), 16–24.

101 Gill, D., & Ramaseshan, B. (2007). Influences on supplier repurchase selection of UK importers. *Marketing Intelligence & Planning, 25*(6), 597–611.

102 Hirschman, E. C., & Mazursky, D. (1982). *A trans-organizational investigation of retail buyers' criteria and information sources.* Working Paper No. 82–8, New York: University Institute of Retail Management.

103 Hirschman, E. C. (1981). An exploratory comparison of decision criteria used by retailers. In W. R. Darden & R. F. Lusch (Eds.), *Proceedings of 1981 workshop in retail patronage theory* (pp. 1–5). Norman, OK: University of Oklahoma.

104 Jin, B., & Farr, C. A. (2010). Supplier selection criteria and perceived benefits and challenges of global sourcing apparel firms in the United States. *Family and Consumer Sciences Research Journal, 39*(1), 31–44.

105 Taggart, B. M. (1993). An analysis of budget decision criteria and selected demographic factors of chief fiscal officers in higher education (Doctoral dissertation, The University of Connecticut, 1993). *Dissertation Abstracts International, 54*(10A), 3674.

106 Markus, D. W. (1983). The budgeting process: Decision makers' perceptions of constraints (Doctoral dissertation, Northwestern University, 1983). *Dissertation Abstracts International, 44*(09A), 2642.

107 Bhagan, S. (2009). A chief executive officer and chief information officer consensus decision-making model for information technology investments (Doctoral dissertation, University of Phoenix, 2009). *Dissertation Abstracts International: Section A, 69*, 4023.

108 Bennouna, K., Meredith, G. G., & Marchant, T. (2010). Improved capital budgeting decision making: Evidence from Canada. *Management Decision, 48*(2), 225–247.

109 Maritan, C. A. (2001). Capital investment as investing in organizational capabilities: An empirically grounded process model. *Academy of Management Journal, 44*(3), 513–531.

110 Leider, J. P., Resnick, B., Kass, N., Sellers, K., Young, J., Bernet, P., & Jarris, P. (2014). Budget-and priority-setting criteria at state health agencies in Times of Austerity: A mixed-methods study. *American Journal of Public Health, 104*(6), 1092–1099.

111 Stafinski, T., Menon, D., Philippon, D. J., & McCabe, C. (2011). Health technology funding decision-making processes around the world. *Pharmacoeconomics, 29*(6), 475–495.

112 Smotas, P. E. (1996). An analysis of budget decision criteria and selected demographic factors of school business officials of Connecticut school districts (Doctoral dissertation, The University of Connecticut, 1996). *Dissertation Abstracts International, 58*(02A), 388.

113 Graham, J. R., & Harvey, C. R. (2001). The theory and practice of corporate finance: Evidence from the field. *Journal of Financial Economics, 60*(2–3), 187–243.

114 Gombola, M., & Marciukaityte, D. (2007). Managerial overoptimism and the choice between debt and equity financing. *The Journal of Behavioral Finance, 8*(4), 225–235.

115 Green, R. K. (2008). Imperfect information and the housing finance crisis: A descriptive overview. *Journal of Housing Economics, 17*(4), 262–271.

116 Kwon, K., & Lee, J. (2009). The effects of reference point, knowledge, and risk propensity on the evaluation of financial products. *Journal of Business Research, 62*(7), 719–725.

117 Perry, V. G., & Lee, J. D. (2012). Shopping for a home vs. a loan: The role of cognitive resource depletion. *International Journal of Consumer Studies, 36*(5), 580–587.

118 Oreopoulos, P., & Petronijevic, U. (2013). *Making college worth it: A review of research on the returns to higher education* (No. w19053). National Bureau of Economic Research.

119 *See* n113, Graham & Harvey (2001).

120 Pfeffer, J. (1981). *Power in organizations* (Vol. 33). Marshfield, MA: Pitman.

Uhlmann, E. L., & Cohen, G. L. (2005). Constructed criteria redefining merit to justify discrimination. *Psychological Science, 16*(6), 474–480.

121 Beasley, R. (1998). Collective interpretations: How problem representations aggregate in foreign policy groups. In D. A. Sylvan & J. F. Voss (Eds.), *Problem representation in foreign policy decision making* (pp. 80–115). Cambridge: Cambridge University Press.

122 Hill, P. H. (1984). Decisions involving the corporate environment. In W. Swap (Ed.), *Group decision making* (pp. 251–279). Beverly Hills, CA: Sage.

Sniezek, J. A., & Buckley, T. (1995). Cueing and cognitive conflict in Judge-Advisor decision making. *Organizational Behavior and Human Decision Processes, 62*(2), 159–174.

123 Bonham, G. M., Shapiro, M. J., & Heradstveit, D. (1988). Group cognition: Using an oil policy game to validate a computer simulation. *Simulations & Games, 19*(4), 379–407.

Gallhofer, I. N., & Saris, W. E. (1996). *Foreign policy decision-making: A qualitative and quantitative analysis of policy argumentation.* Westport, CT: Praeger.

124 Downs, A. (1994). *Inside bureaucracy.* Prospect Heights, IL: Waveland.

Drezner, D. W. (2000). Ideas, bureaucratic politics, and the crafting of foreign policy. *American Journal of Political Science, 44*(4), 733–749.

Hermann, C. F., Geva, N., & Bragg, B. (2001, July). *Group dynamics in conflict management strategies: An experimental analysis of the effects on foreign policy decision making.* Hong Kong: Hong Kong Convention of International Studies.

125 Brown, C. A. (1988). The central Arizona water control study: A case for multiobjective planning and public involvement. *Water Resources Bulletin, 20*(3), 331–337.

126 *See* n106, Markus (1983).

127 *See* n123, Gallhofer & Saris (1996).

128 Doren, R. F., Trexler, J. C., Gottlieb, A. D., & Harwell, M. C. (2009). Ecological indicators for system-wide assessment of the greater everglades ecosystem restoration program. *Ecological Indicators, 9*(6), S2–S16.

Frundt, H. J. (2010). Sustaining Labor-Environmental Coalitions: Banana Allies in Costa Rica. *Latin American Politics and Society, 52*(3), 99–129.

Jovanovic, S., & Wood, R. V. (2006). Communication ethics and ethical culture: A study of the ethics initiative in Denver city government. *Journal of Applied Communication Research, 34*(4), 386–405.

129 *See* n125, Brown (1988).

130 Kotter, J., & Heskett, J. 1992. *Corporate culture and performance.* New York: Free Press.

131 Preston, L. E., & Sapienza, H. J. (1991). Stakeholder management and corporate performance. *Journal of Behavioral Economics, 19*(4), 361–375.

132 Greenley, G. E., & Foxall, G. R. (1997). Multiple stakeholder orientation in UK companies and the implications for company performance. *Journal of Management Studies, 34*(2), 259–284.

133 Greening, D. W., & Turban, D. B. (2000). Corporate social performance as a competitive advantage in attracting a quality workforce. *Business & Society, 39*(3), 254–280.

134 Arora, A., & Alam, P. (2005). CEO Compensation and Stakeholders' Claims★. *Contemporary Accounting Research, 22*(3), 519–547.

135 Hillman, A. J., & Keim, G. D. (2001). Shareholder value, stakeholder management, and social issues: What's the bottom line? *Strategic Management Journal, 22*(2), 125–139.

Sisodia, R., Sheth, J., & Wolfe, D. B. (2007). *Firms of Endeavor: The pursuit of purpose and profit.* Upper Saddle River, NJ: FT Press.

136 Mintz, A., Geva, N., Redd, S. B., & Carnes, A. (1997). The effect of dynamic and static choice sets on political decision making: An analysis of using the decision board platform. *American Political Science Review, 91*(3), 553–566.

3

COGNITIVE PROCESSES IN AUDIENCE DECISION MAKING

VP of R&D starting his presentation to his firm's board of directors: Okay. In as far as our middle sudser market goes, there is really not a better product that we can copy in our nation. We're looking around the world to see if there isn't one we can copy that, come in and it has great productivity or whatever then we can use that [*sic*]. Otherwise, we have to either improve on one of the product characteristics, meaning washing power and gentleness, or else try and bring the cost down and compete on that basis. The retail high sudsers, again the competitors meaning Team 2 and Team 3, both have very good products. Our improvement research has brought our 7.5 product in washing power from a 1.5 to a 4.5 as indicated here [in the slide presentation].

    Chairman of the Board: Would we be fair in assuming that what you're telling us is that we can spend our research bucks to get an expected result?

    VP of R&D: In using which kind of research?

    Chairman of the Board: I don't care. I mean do you have some recommendations and some ideas there on how you would like to spend the money to achieve some product improvement?

    VP of R&D: Yes.

    Chairman of the Board: Okay. Well from a policy-setting point of view, does the board have any more questions on that subject? Okay. Let's move on to the next subject on the list then.[1]

What prompted the chairman's abrupt remarks to the VP of R&D, remarks excerpted from a board meeting of a simulated detergent manufacturing firm run by MBA students and overseen by a board of experienced business people? In essence, the VP had failed to activate the appropriate schema in the mind of the chairman. Had the VP activated the right schema before diving into product characteristics and competitor positions by first explaining what he would be recommending and why, the chairman might have been able to follow the VP's line of reasoning and to have made a decision about the VP's recommendation. Without knowing what the VP wanted him to do with the information being delivered, the chairman became more and more frustrated with every additional, and seemingly meaningless, detail.

Chapter 3 explores the thought processes, or cognitive processes, such as schema activation, that audiences must go through if they are to make informed decisions. Professionals who understand their audience's cognitive processes are in a better position to choose the best style, format, illustrations, and organization for their documents, presentations, and interactions.

The chapter presents a model of audience decision making that consists of six fundamental cognitive processes. Four processes—*perception, attention, sentence-level comprehension*, and *schema activation*—have been studied in the context of a wide variety of reading and listening tasks. The other two processes—*information acquisition* and *information integration*—have been studied primarily in the context of decision making. All six processes come into play any time an audience reads a persuasive document or listens to a persuasive presentation in order to make a decision.

Figure 3.1 shows the model in the form of a flow chart. The flow chart is, of course, an over-simplification of a much more complex, recursive, and parallel process most of which takes place below the level of conscious awareness.[2] In the first step of the model, perception, the audience perceives, that is sees or hears, the information being presented. The audience gets frustrated if that information is illegible or inaudible. In the second step, attention, the audience pays attention to the information long enough to take the third step unless something more interesting grabs and keeps its attention. In the third step, sentence-level comprehension, the audience begins to comprehend the meaning of the information presented sentence by sentence. If the information is hard to comprehend, the audience may re-read it, paraphrase it, ask a question, or just give up. As soon as the audience starts to comprehend the first sentence it reads or hears, it tries to take the fourth step.

In step four of the model, schema activation, represented as gray diamonds and boxes, the audience seeks to activate the appropriate decision schema for interpreting the information it has received and for making a decision. Is someone asking the audience to approve a plan? To purchase a product? To hire a new employee? The model suggests the audience is forced to put its decision-making process on hold until it is successful at finding an answer to that question. Having to put his decision-making process on hold in this way was the source of the chairman's frustration with the VP in the episode recounted previously. Once the audience understands the decision the professional wants it to make, it decides whether it is willing and able to make that decision. At that point, it activates the appropriate schema and takes the fifth step.

In the fifth step, information acquisition, the audience's activated decision schema guides its search for information relevant to making a good decision. Initially, the audience searches for the slot values of the recommendation and the benchmarks relevant to the first or most important decision criterion in its schema. For example, if a salesperson recommends a customer buy a particular laptop, the customer's first decision criterion would likely be price. The customer would then want to know the price of the recommended laptop (say $999) as well as the prices of comparable laptops (which might be $1,499 and $1,599).

In step six of the model, information integration, the audience integrates the two sets of slot values by comparing the slot value of the recommendation to the slot values of the benchmarks. If the slot value of the recommendation is preferable to the values of the benchmarks, for example, if the price of the recommended laptop is less than the prices of comparable laptops, then the audience will continue the decision-making process and search for the slot values relevant to the second decision criterion in its schema. However, if the slot value of the recommendation is not preferable to the values of the benchmarks, it will likely stop the decision-making process and reject the recommendation. If the audience cannot find one or more of the slot values, then it may ask the professional to provide those values, or it may simply not make the decision the professional desires.

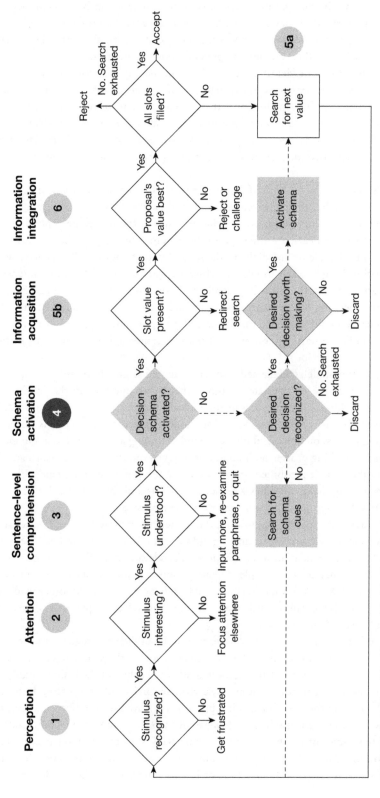

FIGURE 3.1 A Cognitive Process Model of Audience Decision Making

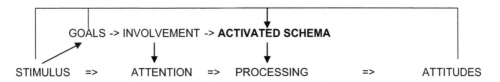

FIGURE 3.2 A Cognitive Process Model of Consumers Reading Ads

Source: Adapted from Mitchell (1981)

Most of the basic steps of the model have been proposed previously by other students of decision making. For example, one team of cognitive scientists proposes a cognitive process model of decision making that includes four basic steps:

(1) the perception of data;
(2) the activation of relevant knowledge in long-term memory;
(3) the making of inferences about the data based on the activated knowledge; and
(4) a search for more data.[3]

The four steps in their model correspond to the processes of perception, schema activation, information integration, and information acquisition in the model presented in this text.

Figure 3.2 depicts a cognitive process model of audience decision making that Andrew Mitchell, an authority in the field of consumer research, developed to represent consumers reading advertisements.[4] The model highlights the role experts' schemata play in making purchasing decisions. In the model, schema activation depends on the consumer's level of expertise and involvement. The model predicts that expert consumers who are involved in the decision-making task will activate a decision schema specific to the product category of the advertised brand and use it to compare the values of the advertised brand against the values of other brands in the product category. It predicts that novice consumers—those who lack the appropriate schema and do not know which attributes (i.e., decision criteria) to use to evaluate a brand—will weight most heavily whatever attributes are prominent in the advertisement.[5]

Like the two models of decision making just described, the model of audience decision making presented in Chapter 3, and most of the research cited in explanation of it, takes an information-processing approach to the analysis of decision making. One of the hallmarks of the information-processing approach is that it explains tasks by first breaking them into elementary cognitive processes.[6] The information-processing approach is most forcefully articulated by computer scientist Allen Newell and Nobel laureate Herbert Simon in their seminal text, *Human Problem Solving*.[7] Despite the challenges put forward by competing theories, the information-processing approach "has become dominant in cognitive psychology."[8] The information-processing approach has also become dominant in fields outside cognitive psychology that investigate the decision making of professionals, including the study of decision making in the field of accounting.[9]

The information-processing approach is now the leading theory for explaining group as well as individual decision making. Groups can be understood as information-processing systems that encode, store, and retrieve information much like individuals.[10] Information processing at the

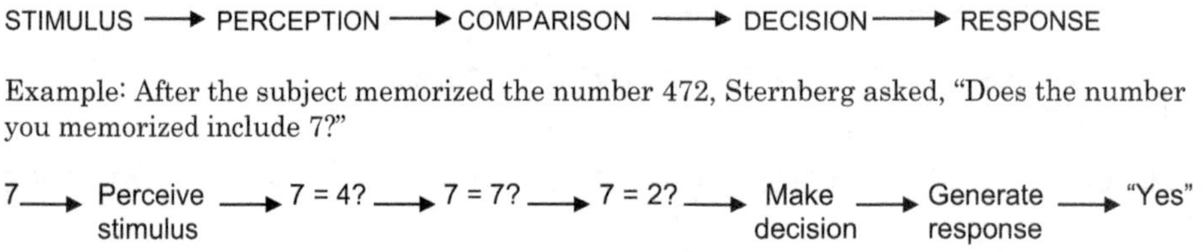

STIMULUS ⟶ PERCEPTION ⟶ COMPARISON ⟶ DECISION ⟶ RESPONSE

Example: After the subject memorized the number 472, Sternberg asked, "Does the number you memorized include 7?"

7 ⟶ Perceive ⟶ 7 = 4? ⟶ 7 = 7? ⟶ 7 = 2? ⟶ Make ⟶ Generate ⟶ "Yes"
　　　stimulus　　　　　　　　　　　　　　　decision　　response

FIGURE 3.3 Sternberg's Information-Processing Model of a Simple Decision

group level is "the degree to which information, ideas, or cognitive processes are shared or are being shared among the group members."[11]

The information-processing approach is also the leading theoretical approach to the emerging field of team cognition and decision making.[12] Much like a single individual, a team makes decisions on the basis of internalized cognitive processes rather than automatically accepting any new information presented to it.[13]

Figure 3.3 represents a famous early model of a simple decision-making task developed by psychologist Saul Sternberg that inspired many cognitive scientists to adopt the information-processing approach.[14] The model predicts that people go through four elementary steps when deciding whether a particular one-digit number (e.g., 7) is a part of a multiple-digit number (e.g., 472) they had memorized earlier. First they perceive the one-digit number, then they compare it to each digit in the multiple-digit number they had memorized, then they make their decision, and finally they generate a response.

Tests of the model showed that people take each step in the model in sequence and independently of the other steps. If the one-digit number were made to look blurry and hard to perceive, only the time subjects took to complete the perception step was affected. If a digit were added to the memorized multiple-digit number, subjects took an additional 38 milliseconds to complete the comparison step but took no additional time to complete the other steps. If subjects had been biased to decide yes or no before they saw the one-digit number, only the time taken to complete the decision-making step was affected.

Outside the laboratory, audiences are less likely to take each subsequent step in the decision-making process than the step before it. For example, the decision to comply with warning labels and signs has been shown to be impeded because people rarely perceive the warnings in the first place.[15] Only 24% of the swimmers at a high school pool they regularly used recalled seeing the conspicuous "NO DIVING" sign next to it. Only 20% of the students in a home economics class recalled seeing any information on an iron they regularly used for two weeks despite the fact the iron was clearly labeled with a hazard warning.[16]

Even if audience members do perceive information, they may not attend to and comprehend it. In another study of warning labels, although 88% of the consumers in the study recalled seeing the warning on the product, only 46% read even a portion of the warning.[17] Moreover, only 27% made the decision to comply with the warning. Prior steps in the decision-making process can influence subsequent steps in other ways as well. For example, faster recognition of letters and words predicts better comprehension skills, whereas increases in comprehension do not predict increases in word recognition.[18]

The information-processing approach has several other important characteristics. It focuses on the mental behaviors of individuals and views people as active, goal-oriented information processors, not as passive blank slates to be written upon. It acknowledges, for example, that audiences of presenters are far from passive even while they are sitting quietly, listening to a presentation. As audiences listen to presentations, they construct goals, evaluate information, express affective reactions, make inferences, interpret information, monitor and activate comprehension repair strategies, attend to information selectively, integrate information, and ask questions.[19] We saw the same type of active information processing during reading by the expert audience members who commented on the sample documents and presentations presented in Chapters 1 and 2.

Another important characteristic of the information-processing approach is that it is content oriented. It views content as "a substantial determinant of human behavior."[20] And the approach views expertise as dependent upon content-specific, schema-based, prior knowledge.[21] Thus, the information-processing approach to decision making differs from the content-free economic theories of decision making. Unlike economic theories of decision making, it does not use the concepts of probability and utility to explain decision behavior. And because it recognizes that human working memory is of limited capacity,[22] it typically characterizes decision making as an act of "satisficing" not of optimization.[23]

The sections that follow explain in detail each of the six major cognitive processes that comprise this text's model of audience decision making—perception, attention, sentence-level comprehension, schema activation, information acquisition, and information integration. In addition, each section identifies the brain regions activated during processing. The sections also compare and contrast the ways that audiences process text, speech, pictures, and graphs in each step toward their final decision.

Perception

To perceive information, audiences must be able both to register and to recognize sensory stimuli. Patients with visual agnosia are intelligent and have good eyesight but are not able to recognize the objects they see.[24] Similarly, some patients with an injury to their left frontal lobe are intelligent and have good hearing but cannot recognize the words they hear.[25] Thus, neither group is able to perceive normally what their senses register. Perception in reading and listening involves both sensing and recognizing letters, phonemes, and complete words. Perception of documents and presentation slides can also involve sensing and recognizing charts, graphs, and images. An audience's perception of a document or presentation will be impaired to the extent that the words and illustrations in it are illegible, inaudible, or not recognizable to them.

Readers' Perception of Text

How do readers perceive the information professionals present to them? Research shows that readers perceive only bits and pieces of information at a time. Readers perceive text in documents and slide presentations letter by letter, word by word, line by line, left to right. The perception of written text involves two overlapping and parallel subprocesses: *word encoding* and *lexical access*.[26]

The first subprocess, word encoding, inputs the visual features of the individual letters in a word and registers their position. As readers recognize the visual features and positions of the individual letters in a word, they construct a mental representation of the visual form of the whole word and automatically map the letters onto the sounds they represent.[27] The second subprocess, lexical access, inputs the encoded sound of the word, and if the word is in the reader's mental dictionary, outputs the word's meaning.[28] If the word's meaning is ambiguous, readers must access all its meanings before they can determine the intended meaning of the word.[29]

Brain Regions Activated. Neuroscientists find that readers' encoding of written words takes place in three regions of the brain's left hemisphere: the Visual Word Form Area (or fusiform gyrus) located in the lower left temporal and occipital lobes,[30] Wernicke's area also located in the left temporal lobe, and Broca's area located in the left frontal lobe (see Figure 3.4).[31] Neurological disorders associated with these three regions include dyslexia, fluent aphasia, and expressive aphasia.

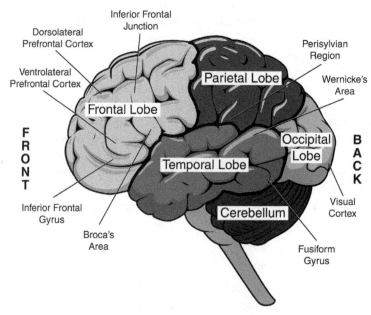

FIGURE 3.4 Lateral View of the Brain's Left Hemisphere

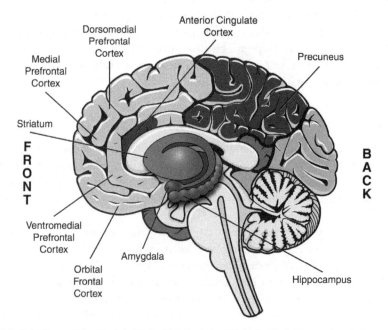

FIGURE 3.5 Medial View of the Brain's Right Hemisphere With the Left Hemisphere's Striatum, Amygdala, and Hippocampus Superimposed

Lexical access of both written and spoken words also takes place in three regions of the brain's left hemisphere: the front and rear regions of the left temporal lobe, and the area at the junction of the left temporal and parietal lobes.[32] Disorders associated with these three regions include primary progressive aphasia and semantic dementia.

When perceiving written words, readers can recognize only those letters or words that appear in a very small area of their retinas called the *fovea*, the area in which they have maximum visual acuity. In fact, they can recognize only five to six letters on either side of the letter upon which their eyes focus or *fixate*.[33] Readers cannot recognize words on lines either above or below the one on which they are fixating.[34] Readers' ability to recognize printed letters and numbers depends on their ability to perceive each letter's or number's distinct visual features. They will confuse two letters only when the letters have many visual features in common, for example, *C* and *G*.[35] However, readers can recognize any letter more accurately if it is in the context of a word rather than standing alone.[36]

The amount of time readers spend fixating on any word is very brief. The average fixation time per word is about 250 milliseconds, or one-quarter of a second.[37] The more letters in the word, the more fixations made on the word, and the longer the duration of the fixations.[38] Readers fixate on each word an average of 30 additional milliseconds for each additional letter in it.[39]

As one would expect, readers' fixation times on words are longer when the letters in the word are hard to perceive.[40] Readers' fixation times are also longer if the word is unfamiliar to them.[41] They are longer on words that are not predictable from the preceding context.[42] In addition, readers' fixation times are longer if the word is ambiguous or has multiple meanings.[43] Readers' fixation times on pronouns are longer the farther the pronoun is from its antecedent.[44] Fixation times are also longer if the antecedent violates a gender stereotype, for example a truck driver referred to as *she*.[45]

Readers fixate on most of the words in each sentence,[46] but take longer fixating on the more important words. For example, they may spend over 1,500 milliseconds on a content word that introduces the topic of a new paragraph, but they will spend much less time on it when they encounter that same word a second time. Moreover, readers tend to fixate longer on the final word in both clauses and sentences.[47]

A series of studies that tracked the eye movements of students reading 15 short expository passages from *Newsweek* and *Time* magazines finds that readers' eyes focus directly on over 80% of the content words but skip about 40% of the function words such as *the* and *a*.[48] When a passage is difficult to comprehend, readers fixate on a larger percentage of words in the passage. But when words in the passage are highly predictable due to their context, readers are much more likely to skip over them.[49]

Readers' fixations account for more than 90% of the readers' total reading time. Eye movements in small jumps or *saccades* account for the other 10%. Most saccades take only about 25 to 45 milliseconds, during which time a reader's vision is blurred. Readers who recognize that they do not understand a sentence make regressive eye movements, or saccades to re-read previously read words by returning to the point at which they began an incorrect syntactic analysis of the sentence.[50] Readers of expository texts also re-read headings in order to more thoroughly integrate text information with the topic signaled by the heading.[51] In addition, re-reading headings serves to enhance recall.[52]

Figure 3.6 displays one reader's eye fixations and saccades detected by an eye-tracking device as she read an online newspaper.[53] Notice the reader made most fixations, represented as angles in the black lines, on headlines, photographs, and the first sentences of news stories. Such a pattern is typical of audiences skilled at getting their news from either online or print newspapers.

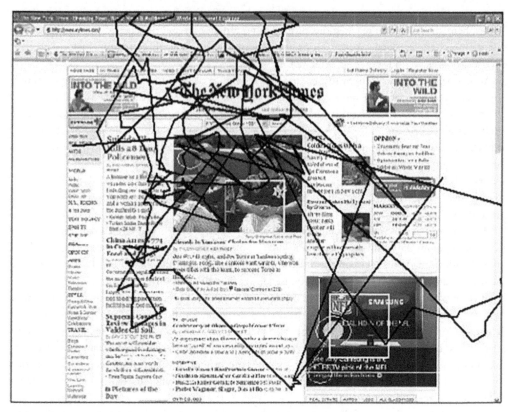

FIGURE 3.6 A Reader's Eye-Fixation Pattern Reading an Online Newspaper

Source: Gibbs and Bernas (2009, p. 158)

Listeners' Perception of Speech

Much like the way reading audiences perceive text, listening audiences perceive speech sound by sound and word by word in the order it is spoken. But there are significant differences between speech and text that cause speech perception to be more complex than text perception. Speech is not presented as discrete units the way printed letters and words are. Instead it is presented as a continuous stream of sound. Speech sounds—the consonants and vowels that form the words of a language—overlap each other as they are spoken in a process called *coarticulation*.[54] To make speech perception even more complex, different speakers, unlike different writers, produce the same words in different ways[55] and at different speaking rates.[56]

Brain Regions Activated. Listeners' encoding of spoken words takes place in three regions of the brain: the temporal voice areas located at the top of the temporal lobes of the left and right hemispheres[57] and Broca's area located in the left frontal lobe (see Figure 3.4, p. 108).[58] Disorders associated with these three regions include voice agnosia and autism.

When listening to speech, listeners must map the acoustic signals they perceive onto speech sounds or phonemes. Through a process of elimination, they are able to recognize the word being spoken even before the speaker has finished saying it.[59] As listeners hear each successive sound in a word, for example "elephant," they narrow down the list of possible words they might be hearing. They activate approximately 1,000 words that start with the "e" sound as soon as they perceive the "e" sound in elephant. They quickly narrow that list to about 100 words that start with "el" once they perceive the "l" sound. By the time they perceive the "f" sound, there is only one word left on their list of possible words.[60] In addition, contextual cues from the activated schema and from the current sentence being spoken can also constrain the number of words the listener activates.[61]

Once listeners recognize the word, for 200 to 400 milliseconds they activate all possible meanings of the word, even those meanings that do not fit into the context of the sentence.[62] Although listeners typically recognize the words in clearly spoken sentences, they either fail to recognize the words in unclear speech or initially misrecognize them and then correctly recognize them as more context is provided.[63]

Viewers' Perception of Images and Graphs

Many people imagine viewers perceive pictures all at once or *holistically*. However, research shows that audiences perceive images in much the same way they read text—by fixating on one visual feature then jumping to another part of the picture and fixating on it. Each fixation during image viewing averages about 300 milliseconds, but the duration of individual fixations can vary widely. The pattern of viewers' fixations and saccades is not random. For example, when viewers look at images of faces, they primarily fixate on the eyes, the mouth, and general shape of the face—the features most critical to face recognition (see Figure 3.7).[64]

Brain Regions Activated. Different regions of the brain are activated depending on what the viewer is perceiving. For example, object recognition takes place in the visual cortex located in the occipital lobe of both hemispheres (see Figure 3.4, p. 108). Scene perception takes place in the parahippocampal place area located inside the middle region of the temporal lobe beneath the hippocampus (see Figure 3.5, p. 108).[65] Face recognition activates the fusiform face area located in the lower temporal and occipital lobes of both hemispheres.[66] Disorders associated with these three regions include visual agnosia, topographical disorientation, Alzheimer's disease, and schizophrenia.

The longer viewers are exposed to images, the more accurately they recognize and recall the images they have seen. For example, magazine readers were able to recognize only 50% of the illustrations in a magazine when the illustrations were presented at a 500-millisecond exposure

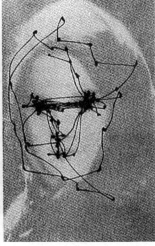

FIGURE 3.7 A Viewer's Eye-Fixation Pattern Looking at a Photograph

Source: Yarbus (1967, p. 179)

rate, but they were able to recognize 93% at a two-second exposure rate.[67] Recognition of more complex pictures requires even longer exposure rates.[68] Such longer exposure rates increase image recognition and recall independently of the viewer's opportunity to verbally label the picture.[69] After a one-year delay, just two exposures enabled the viewers in one study to recognize 72% of the images they viewed.[70] However, more than two exposures do not add significantly to viewers' recognition rates.[71]

Audiences perceive graphs in much the same way they perceive pictures—by fixating many times on the graph's different regions and elements. In an eye-tracking study of viewers interpreting line graphs, viewers perceived the graphs by making numerous fixations on different regions of them.[72] In addition to fixating on the trend lines, viewers frequently fixated on the variable names, variable values, and the X and Y axes. In other words, audiences viewing a chart or graph repeatedly fixate on those elements that are most relevant to evaluating its content. The viewers in the study also spent a large portion of their time fixating on the graphs' captions and legends as well as on the values of the variables. Not surprisingly, the viewers made more fixations when viewing complex graphs as opposed to simple ones.

In a follow-up eye-tracking study, for relatively simple graphs, such as the line graph in Figure 3.8, viewers averaged 29 fixations and spent an average of 33 seconds viewing each graph. For the more complex graphs in the study, viewers averaged 40.5 fixations and spent an average of 40.6 seconds viewing each graph.[73]

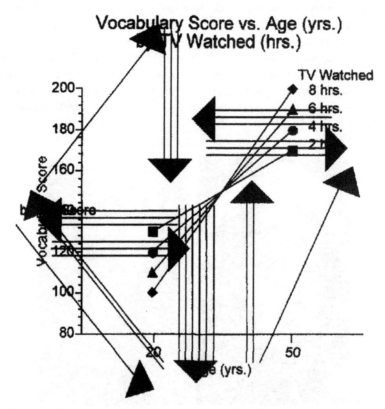

FIGURE 3.8 A Viewer's Eye-Fixation Pattern Interpreting a Line Chart

Source: Carpenter and Shah (1998, p. 86)

Attention

Audiences sense and perceive much more information peripherally than they are able to attend to, focus on, and consciously evaluate. Their attention acts as a bottleneck that enhances the processing of the stimulus attended to and weakens the processing of all other perceived stimuli. Studies find that attention plays an important role in audience decision making. For example, consumers' attention to advertising controls a substantial portion of the variability in their purchasing decisions.[74] Surprisingly, consumers' attention to product photos, as measured by pupil dilation,[75] is more highly correlated with sales of those products than traditional verbal measures of consumers' attitudes.[76]

Stimulus-Driven Attention

There are two types of attention: *task driven* and *stimulus driven*. An audience's attention is task driven when the audience intentionally searches for a specific piece of information. For example, readers' attention is task driven when they search a newspaper ad for the price of an item. Listeners' attention is task driven when they interrupt a speaker to ask a question. In task-driven attention, the audience's task guides and controls perception. Even the simple task of reading causes readers to shift their attention to the next word in a sentence before they have been able to fixate on it.[77] Task-driven attention is also called *search*. We treat search more fully later in this chapter in the section on information acquisition.

An audience's attention is stimulus driven when they peripherally perceive a stimulus, such as a loud noise or a flashing advertisement on a web page, and divert their attention to it. Certain types of stimuli are more attention getting than others. For example, information that has clear and direct implications for personal outcomes is more attention getting and has a greater impact on audience judgments than information that is not personally relevant.[78] Compared to typical and familiar advertisements, ads that are novel and original also attract more attention, as indicated by an increase in ad readers' eye fixations.[79]

The audience's present goals also make certain stimuli more attention getting to them.[80] For example, in a study of consumers reading almost 8,000 newspaper ads, nearly twice as many prospective customers recalled seeing the target ad as nonprospective customers, although none of the readers were intentionally searching for ads.[81] A later eye-tracking study showed that in 98% of the cases in which prospective customers opened to a page with a target ad, they fixated on the ad at least once.[82] For nonprospects, the figure was 77%. Of the prospects who noticed the ad, 38% read it. Only 14% of nonprospects read the ad.[83] Although attention is a factor in all cognitive processes, our model depicts stimulus-driven attention occurring immediately after the audience senses and perceives stimuli.

Brain Regions Activated. Separate brain areas are involved in stimulus-driven and task-driven attention. Stimulus-driven attention, or attentional capture, involves activation of the area at the front of the inferior frontal junction (IFJ) of the right hemisphere (see Figure 3.4, p. 108). The right IFJ is located in the middle region of the right hemisphere's frontal lobe. Areas in the parietal lobe may also be involved in stimulus-driven attention. Task-driven attention, on the other hand, involves an area at the top of the right IFJ, an area in the left IFJ, as well as areas in the parietal lobe.[84] Disorders associated with all of these regions include deficits in executive functions that are typical of early stage dementia.

Constraints on Auditory Attention

In most cases audiences can recall very little about stimuli they do not attend to, even when those stimuli are perfectly audible or visible.[85] In two seminal studies of auditory attention,[86] listeners were given special headphones to wear that allowed them to hear two different conversations spoken into each ear simultaneously. Listeners had to selectively attend to one conversation and tune out the other. The only thing listeners could remember about the conversation they tuned out was whether the speakers were male or female. Listeners were not able to tell which language was spoken or to remember any words. In a follow-up study, listeners not only had to listen to two conversations simultaneously and selectively attend to one conversation, they also had to listen for a target word in both conversations.[87] Although listeners recognized the target word when it was spoken in the conversation they attended to, they did not recognize it when it was spoken in the unattended-to second conversation.

Nonetheless, listeners may perceive a fraction of the words they do not attend to. Listeners who are asked if they recall target words from an unattended conversation immediately after each target word is spoken are able to recall the target words 25% of the time.[88] Although listeners can perceive two simultaneous messages simultaneously, they can only attend to one message at a time. Thus, an unattended-to message delivered simultaneously can still divert a listener's attention to it, especially if it is loud, important to the listener, or relevant to the message the listener was attending to.[89]

Constraints on Visual Attention

Viewers' visual attention works very much like listeners' auditory attention. When viewers attend to one set of simultaneously presented images, their processing of the other set drops off. In one experiment, viewers watched a video that showed a set of objects in silhouette moving from left to right and another set moving from right to left at the same time. The objects were large, easy to see, easy to identify, and were semitransparent so they could be seen even while they passed through each other. When viewers were asked to attend to objects moving left to right, they were able to recognize all those objects easily. The same was true for viewers asked to attend to objects moving right to left. However, the first group of viewers could not remember anything about the objects that moved right to left. Neither could the second group remember anything about the objects that moved from left to right.[90]

Readers can perceive unattended written words but do not consciously remember them. In a study that demonstrated the interplay between perception and attention, scientists gave mild shocks to readers as they showed them different words. The scientists then presented those same words to the readers, but out of the focus of their attention. Although the readers did not attend to the words or consciously recognize them, it was clear they still perceived the words because they gave galvanic skin responses when the words were presented to them a second time.[91] In a similar way, nonfocal information in print ads can influence consumers' evaluations of brand names even when consumers do not attend to or consciously recognize that information.[92]

One situation exists in which audience members can attend to two stimuli at the same time, and that is when the two stimuli are presented in different perceptual modes. Audiences who are presented with visual and auditory information in rapid succession are able to begin processing the auditory information about 60 milliseconds before they finish processing the visual information.[93] Similarly, audiences can identify one visual and one auditory stimulus even when the two stimuli are presented simultaneously.[94] Consequently, students in online geometry courses learn more when audio, as opposed to on-screen text, is used to describe the geometric diagrams displayed on their computer screens.[95] However, attending to two stimuli simultaneously presented in two different modalities is difficult for anyone if both stimuli consist of verbal information. For example, for most audience members simultaneously reading a newspaper and listening to the news on TV requires extraordinary effort.[96]

Finally, it is important to note that not all of the information an audience attends to during reading or listening comes from sensory inputs such as the written words in a professional's document or the spoken words of a presentation. Audience members can also attend to information coming from nonsensory sources. For example, audiences may access information from their own long-term memories to use in decision making as when something a professional says reminds them of an important concept. When consumers retrieve comparative product information from their memories, the information actually has a stronger effect on their decisions than comparative product information provided to them by external sources.[97] In addition to recalling information, the audience may also generate information during the decision-making process, such as when they evaluate and make inferences about the information they have seen or heard.[98]

Sentence-Level Comprehension

The Sentence Comprehension Process

An audience's process for comprehending sentences involves three overlapping and parallel subprocesses: *syntactic analysis*, *semantic analysis*, and the construction of a *referential representation* or mental image of the meaning of each sentence.[99]

The first subprocess, syntactic analysis, inputs individual words from the sentence whose meanings have already been accessed during perception and outputs the grammatical role each word plays in that sentence. For instance, in the sentence "The board promoted the CFO," *The board* would be recognized (albeit not consciously) as a determiner and noun that constitute the subject of the verb, *promoted* would be recognized as the verb, and *the CFO* recognized as a determiner and noun that constitute the object noun phrase. In a study that demonstrates the importance of syntactic analysis to sentence comprehension, readers were presented with sentences to read either one phrase, or syntactic unit, at a time or one randomly divided segment of a sentence at a time. Readers had significantly better comprehension of the sentences when they read them one phrase at time.[100]

The second subprocess, semantic analysis, inputs the syntax of the sentence as well as the meaning of the verb. It outputs the conceptual relationships, or case roles, of the words and phrases in the sentence.[101] For instance, in the sentence "The board promoted the CFO," *The board* would be recognized as the agent, *promoted* as the action, and *the CFO* as the object of the action. In essence, semantic analysis determines who is doing what to whom. Readers can sometimes bypass the syntactic analysis process if semantic cues are sufficient to provide them with the meaning of the sentence.[102]

The third subprocess, the construction of a referential representation, inputs the syntax and semantics of the sentence and outputs a mental image of the actual or imaginary objects and actions referred to in the sentence. The same sentence may have only one syntactic and semantic representation but several different referential representations. As cognitive scientists Marcel Just and Patricia Carpenter explain, the sentence "He flew to Cairo," could have three different referential representations depending on how the person who is referred to flew: on a jet; in an antique biplane; or on a magic carpet.[103] When a sentence contains a pronoun, referential processing identifies any antecedent words to which the pronoun refers as well.

Brain Regions Activated. Syntactic analysis of both spoken and written sentences takes place in two regions of the brain's left hemisphere: Broca's area in the left frontal lobe and a region of the left temporal lobe (see Figure 3.4, p. 108).[104] Structural disconnection of these two regions is associated with syntactic impairments. Semantic analysis of both spoken and written sentences also takes place in Broca's area as well as the area immediately above it. The more complex the sentence, the more these regions are activated.[105] During semantic analysis of verb information, including analysis of the verb's argument structure and thematic role, the perisylvian region at the juncture of the temporal and parietal lobes in the left hemisphere is also activated.[106] Damage to these regions results in impaired sentence processing.[107]

Unlike syntactic and semantic analyses that take place in regions of the left hemisphere, referential analysis recruits right hemispheric regions. Specifically, referential analysis of spoken and written sentences recruits the right fusiform gyrus located in the lower portion of the right temporal and occipital lobes,[108] as well as a region in the right frontal lobe.[109] Williams syndrome is one neurological disorder commonly associated with the right fusiform gyrus. Its symptoms include below-normal IQ, inability to orient oneself in space, as well as other deficits in visuospatial functioning.

Readers' Comprehension

Almost all of a reader's comprehension subprocesses concern the word they are fixating on and its relationship to the text that preceded it. For example, readers must spend a relatively long time fixating on pronouns in order to assign a referent to them.[110] As readers fixate on each successive word in a sentence, they try to integrate it with what they already know.[111] Thus, readers begin to interpret a sentence even before they come to the main verb in it. When readers come to the end of a sentence, they have to pause longer because they cannot process some syntactic information until they have finished reading the whole sentence.[112]

Readers use a number of strategies to ensure their interpretation of each sentence is correct. As they read each new word in a sentence, they check its meaning against their current representation of the sentence and revise their representation when necessary.[113] If readers have trouble interpreting the meaning of a sentence because it is ambiguous, they slow down and fixate on the each word in the sentence for a significantly longer duration.[114] Then, just as they do for ambiguous words, readers process all possible meanings of the ambiguous sentence.[115]

Readers can clearly remember the specific words in a sentence only while they are processing that sentence's meaning.[116] Consequently, they often cannot recall the form or style in which a sentence was presented. Instead, they only remember the meaning of the sentence.[117] In one study, readers were asked to read sentences written either in the active or passive voice, to wait a few minutes, and then to decide whether a test sentence was in the same voice as a previously read sentence. None of the readers could accurately recall the voice in which the original sentence had been written.[118]

Oftentimes when readers encounter a sentence that is difficult to comprehend, they will paraphrase it or try to put it into their own words. Sometimes readers translate individual sentences into scenarios, or story-like paraphrases.[119] For example, the investor who read the executive summary of *Smartphone MBA*'s business plan in Chapter 1 translated the following sentences into a scenario in comment 3.

> Sales projections for *Smartphone MBA* estimate a subscriber base of 40,000 for the premier installment. **[2. What's this 40,000 for the premier installment?]** Subscription sales are expected to quadruple to 160,000 within five years. **[3. They say there are two million**

potential subscribers out of this group, these three categories. And they have a goal of reaching an initial subscription of 40,000 and 160,000 within five years. Okay. That's understandable.]

When the reading process is going smoothly, readers are usually unaware of it. But when something makes comprehension difficult, they often become aware of their process and may comment on it.[120] For example, as the investor continued reading the executive summary of *Smartphone MBA*'s business plan, he made a comment about the difficulty of comprehending the following sentence.

With the consent of Limited Partners holding as a group a 50% Partnership Interest in the Partnership, the General Partner may raise capital in excess of such amount by selling additional Limited Partnership Interests. **[13. What the heck does that mean? It says your Limited Partnerships start out with 15% of the partnership. This is really poorly written.]**

Listeners' Comprehension

In contrast to the way readers comprehend written sentences, listeners' comprehension of spoken sentences depends on how the sentences are spoken, not just on their content and structure. One classic study of face-to-face communication concluded that only 7% of the meaning of a spoken message is communicated verbally. Because the meaning of a spoken message depends in large part on the emotion the speaker communicates, the remaining 93% of the meaning is communicated by the speaker's tone of voice and facial expression.[121] For a listener, a sarcastic versus an enthusiastic tone of voice can convey more meaning than the words in a sentence. Chapter 6 explores the process listeners go through as they infer a speaker's emotions.

Listeners base much of their syntactic analysis of spoken sentences on sentence *prosody*—the way the speaker rhythmically groups and accentuates the words in the sentences she speaks. Listeners prefer a syntactic analysis of a sentence that is consistent with sentence prosody and base much of their semantic analysis on sentence prosody as well.[122] They actively listen for the words speakers accentuate[123] because they realize that accented words are cues to the meaning of the speakers' messages.[124]

Brain Regions Activated. Neuroscientists find that when listeners process sentence prosody regions of the right temporal lobe[125] and also a region in the right frontal lobe are activated (see Figure 3.4, p. 108).[126] Damage to the regions in the right temporal lobe causes defects in a listener's ability to interpret prosody[127] as well as difficulties in interpreting others' nonverbal communication.

The following repeated sentence[128] shows how different placements of a vocal accent can change the meaning of a sentence entirely. The accented word in examples 1 through 5 is in bold and italicized. A final rise in intonation is added to the italicized word in example 6. One possible meaning of each of the six sentences is suggested in parentheses.

(1) ***He's*** giving this money to Tyler. (*He* is the one giving the money; nobody else.)
(2) He's ***giving*** this money to Tyler. (He is *giving*, not lending, the money.)
(3) He's giving ***this*** money to Tyler. (The money is *this* particular money.)
(4) He's giving this ***money*** to Tyler. (*Cash* is being exchanged, not a check.)
(5) He's giving this money to ***Tyler***. (The recipient is *Tyler*, not Evan or Ethan.)
(6) He's giving this money to ***Tyler?*** (Why is he giving the money to *Tyler* and not to me?)

Similar to reading audiences, listening audiences usually forget the specific words uttered in a spoken sentence almost immediately after they have heard it. In one study of listeners' sentence comprehension, people listened to sentences and then had to distinguish between the original sentence and a close paraphrase of it. Listeners' memory for the exact wording of the sentence decayed rapidly, but their memory for the sentence's meaning persisted much longer.[129] In a subsequent study, although the listeners remembered verbatim the words in the clause they were currently processing, they forgot the exact words and word order of prior clauses as soon as each sentence was spoken.[130]

Interestingly, listeners do tend to remember the exact wording of any message that has an emotional impact on them, as challenges or insults often do.[131] The exact wording of poems, song lyrics, and important phrases are also more likely to be remembered. In addition, listeners are often able to remember the exact wording of a sentence if they are requested to do so. In a study of auditory recall, two groups of listeners listened to recorded instructions. The first group was told to remember the sentences in the instructions verbatim; the second group was not. Then both groups' memory of the style and content of the sentences was tested. The first group remembered the sentences in the instructions verbatim—both style and content. The second group remembered each sentence's meaning but little of its exact wording.[132]

Viewers' Comprehension

When audiences comprehend images they spontaneously assign verbal labels to them (e.g., "That is a picture of a young mother holding her baby").[133] Older children and adults automatically assign a verbal label to all except the most complex and novel images.[134] Although audiences normally extract meaning from a verbal message and forget the style in which it was presented, they typically remember the exact picture they saw as well as its meaning. Asked to look at a set of 10,000 pictures, viewers were later able to identify 83% of the pictures they had seen.[135] In a study of advertisement recall, consumers were presented 600 magazine ads all containing text and pictures. Consumers recognized 96.7% of the pictures immediately after viewing them, 99.7% after a two-hour delay, 92% after three days, 87% after seven days, and 57.7% after 120 days. Consumers had an 11.8% error rate in distinguishing read versus unread sentences in the ads, but only a 1.5% error rate in distinguishing viewed versus not-viewed pictures.[136]

Graph comprehension is a combination of text and image comprehension. The time needed for graph comprehension is similar to that needed to read and understand a paragraph of moderate length.[137] But before an audience can comprehend a graph, they must first translate its visual features into the concepts those features represent.[138] One theory of graph comprehension proposes that after viewers encode the visual features in a graph, they then interpret the meanings of those features as quantitative concepts. For example, viewers may recognize that a straight line in a graph represents a linear relationship. Only then do they identify what each feature of the graph refers to. Additional graph comprehension processes include keeping track of multiple comparisons, performing calculations, and mentally translating from one scale to another.[139]

More recent experimental studies of graph comprehension indicate that viewers first activate a mental model or schema of a graph when trying to interpret its meaning. Then they map its graphic elements onto the schema's conceptual entities and its spatial relations onto the schema's semantic relations.[140] Errors that viewers make when interpreting graphs primarily result from inadequate schemata rather than inaccurate perceptual processes. In one study of graph comprehension, all of the viewers accurately reproduced from memory the graphs they had seen, but because many of them lacked the knowledge or schemata needed to interpret the quantitative information depicted by the graphs, they were unable to grasp their meaning.[141]

Schema Activation

Schema Activation in Decision Making and Discourse Comprehension

Schema activation is at the heart of information processing in general and of decision making and discourse, or text-level, comprehension in particular. Some cognitive scientists assert that the whole activity of "information processing may be seen as consisting of schema formation or activation, of the integration of input with these schemas, and of the updating or revision of these schemas to accommodate new input."[142] Moreover, they say, "information processing cannot be carried out without them." Others see schema activation at the heart of the decision-making process.[143] After an extensive review of the research on both decision making and reasoning, cognitive scientist John R. Anderson confirms that decision making and reasoning are not the application of the content-free rules of logic, syllogistic reasoning, or statistics as they are commonly thought to be, but are essentially schema-based processes.[144]

Brain Regions Activated. Neuroscientists find that schemata develop gradually as networks of neurons in the medial prefrontal cortex (mPFC) of both brain hemispheres (see Figure 3.5, p. 108). Once schemata are developed and activated, they can be updated with new information very rapidly via an interaction between the mPFC and the hippocampus, a structure located inside the middle region of both temporal lobes.[145] In one fMRI study, beginning second-year biology and education students were scanned as they read new information that was either related or unrelated to schemata they had acquired in their first-year courses. The extent of schema-related activation in each student's mPFC predicted their subsequent performance in their second-year courses.[146]

Damage to the lower portion of the mPFC, the ventromedial prefrontal cortex (vmPFC), can make it difficult for patients to keep inappropriate schemata from being activated and can result in confabulation.[147] In fMRI studies of multi-attribute decision making, that is, the type of decision making described in our model, schema-related activation, with a selective boosting of decision-relevant attributes, has also been observed in the dorsolateral prefrontal cortex (dlPFC), an area at the top of the prefrontal cortex (see Figure 3.4, p. 108).[148] Damage to the dlPFC causes dramatic impairments to decision making, especially to multi-attribute decision making.[149]

In addition to giving audiences a framework for decision making, schemata provide them with the interpretive framework for comprehending written discourse,[150] spoken dialog,[151] and graphical displays.[152] Cognitive scientists Michelene Chi and Stellan Ohlsson find that "Comprehension as normally understood results in the construction of a specific instance of a schema or the accretion of schema-relevant facts. New information is *assimilated* to existing schemas."[153] Neuroscientists find that unlike sentence-level comprehension, which is primarily a left hemisphere activity, discourse comprehension routinely involves both hemispheres of the brain.[154]

Much of what we know about the cognitive processes involved in schema activation comes from research on audiences reading texts in order to comprehend them. Studies demonstrate that comprehending the meaning of texts as opposed to comprehending individual sentences depends upon schema-level processing. One prominent model of reader comprehension consists of processes that first activate an appropriate schema after which "the schema slots are filled in with the information from the passage."[155] Other research demonstrates that schemata strongly influence not only what readers comprehend when reading a text[156] but also what they remember from it.[157]

Many different types of schemata are activated in the discourse comprehension process. One type of schema, often called a *script*, provides a framework for understanding events. In an effort to discover the script for dining at a restaurant, 32 people were interviewed separately and asked about the major steps involved in dining out. The restaurant script of all 32 contained the same six steps: sitting down, looking at the menu, ordering, eating, paying the bill, and leaving.[158] Other schemata provide frameworks for understanding specific genres such as fairy tales or biographies. If expert

Slot name	Slot value
Name	Flywheel
Goals	To store energy
Principles	Faster spinning stores up more energy
Physical properties	Made of fiberglass and rubber
Physical movements	Spinning
Made by	Humans
Used by	Humans
Exemplars	Car engine flywheels

Flywheels are one of the oldest mechanical devices known to man. Every internal-combustion engine contains a small flywheel that **converts the jerky motion** of the pistons **into the smooth flow of energy** that powers the drive shaft. The greater the mass of a flywheel and **the faster it spins, the more energy can be stored in it.** But its maximum spinning speed is limited by the strength of the material it is made from. If it spins too fast for its mass, any flywheel will fly apart. One type of flywheel **consists of** round sandwiches of **fiberglass and rubber** providing the maximum possible storage of energy when the wheel is confined in a small space **as in an automobile**. Another type, the "superflywheel," consists of a series of rimless spokes. This flywheel stores the maximum energy when space is unlimited.

FIGURE 3.9 A Mechanism Schema Filled With Slot Values From the Passage Following It

Source: Adapted from Thibadeau, Just, and Carpenter (1982)

readers are told they will read a particular genre, they will activate a schema of that genre that will guide their interpretation of the text.[159]

Other types of schemata are used to comprehend objects. Figure 3.9 is a depiction of a schema for comprehending a mechanism, in this case a flywheel.[160] The slots in the mechanism schema have been filled in or *instantiated* with information from the expository passage following it. This schema enabled a computer model of a human reader to comprehend the expository passage and to answer questions about it.

Depending upon which schema a reader activates, the same text can be comprehended in different ways.[161] In a fascinating study of schema effects on reader recall, cognitive scientists asked one group of readers to assume the role of thieves and another group to assume the role of prospective home buyers. The scientists hypothesized the two groups would activate two different schemata. They then asked both groups to read a brief story about a very expensive house. The "thieves" recalled the valuable items described in the story that could be stolen from the house. The "home buyers," on the other hand, remembered information related to the quality of the house.[162]

In a study of schema effects on viewer recall, viewers watched a video of two men walking around in a room talking about drug use, the police, and theft. Before watching the video, viewers had been primed with one of three schema-inducing ideas: two burglars; two students waiting for a friend; or two friends attempting to conceal illegal drugs. Viewers primed with the two-burglars schema recalled more theft-relevant objects and comments from the video than those in the other two conditions. However, the two students and two friends conditions did not produce significant results.[163]

The Schema Activation Process

How do audiences activate the appropriate schemata? When readers begin reading a passage, they hypothesize that the grammatical subject of the first or second sentence in the passage is its topic. They then activate a schema for the topic of that grammatical subject.[164] In one study, readers were asked to think aloud and guess the theme of a short technical passage as they read it. The results showed that readers hypothesized the theme of the passage immediately after reading the initial sentence. Readers revised their hypothesis later if subsequent sentences did not fit the theme they had hypothesized.[165]

A study of students listening to algebra word problems found that early verbal cues led them to activate one of several possible schemata for the word problems they heard.[166] Half of the students in the study categorized problems after hearing less than one-fifth of the problem stated. Viewers, on the other hand, activate multiple schemata simultaneously until one schema emerges as the dominant one.[167] For example, when trying to categorize atypical targets such as males with very long hair or females with very short hair, viewers simultaneously activate schemata for both male and female genders.[168]

Other schemata can be internally activated by the audience's own goals for reading or listening or by the schemata already activated in their minds.[169] If readers believe a sentence states the main theme of a text, and is thereby capable of activating the appropriate schema, they will read it more slowly than other sentences.[170] Surprisingly, readers spend more time reading sentences that introduce new topics even when paragraph boundaries are not indicated.[171] However, readers take just as long to read the first sentence of a text whether it is a topic sentence or, contrary to the typical reader's hypothesis, merely a supporting detail.[172]

Consequences of Faulty Schema Activation

If the audience is unable to activate the appropriate schema for a document or presentation, their comprehension suffers.[173] The reason a schema is not activated may be that the audience does not possess the appropriate schema, or it may be that the wording of the text or presentation is ineffective in activating it.[174] In an intriguing experiment, cognitive scientists John Bransford and Marcia Johnson asked readers to read the following paragraph. Interestingly, readers could not make sense of the paragraph as a whole although each separate sentence was easy for them to comprehend.

> The procedure is actually quite simple. First you arrange things into different groups. Of course, one pile may be sufficient depending on how much there is to do. If you have to go somewhere else due to a lack of facilities that is the next step, otherwise you are pretty well set. It is important not to overdo things. That is, it is better to do a few things at once than too many. In the short run this may not seem important but complications can easily arise. A mistake can be expensive as well. At first the whole procedure will seem complicated. Soon, however, it will become just another facet of life. It is difficult to foresee any end to the necessity for this task in the immediate future, but then, one never can tell. After the procedure is completed one arranges the materials into different groups again. Then they can be put into their appropriate places. Eventually, they will be used once more and the whole cycle will have to be repeated.

However, if readers were allowed to read the paragraph's title, "Washing Clothes," before they read the paragraph, then they had no difficulty understanding it. Those readers also recalled more information from the paragraph than the readers who read the paragraph without its schema-activating title.[175]

Audiences can, of course, activate the wrong schema. The study cited earlier of students listening to algebra word problems and classifying them into problem types found that fully one-half of them activated the wrong schema as they heard the first part of each problem.[176] For instance, some students activated the schema for a triangle problem when they should have activated the schema for a distance, time, rate problem. Activating the wrong schema caused several students to mishear the rest of the information in the word problem as they tried to make the information they heard conform to the wrong schema or problem type.

Even activating the right schema can sometimes lead to problems. After researchers identified the elements of readers' restaurant script or schema, they asked the readers to read stories about dining in restaurants and then to recall the stories they read. Readers erroneously recalled and recognized statements that were not in the stories but that were part of their restaurant schema.[177]

Information Acquisition

Information acquisition is another name for search. It is the process by which audiences search for the information that can fill the slots of their activated schema.[178] Because the audience's activated schema directs their search, information acquisition is a form of task-driven, as opposed to stimulus-driven, attention.

The information-acquisition process enables audiences to attend to the information that is relevant to their activated schema by filtering out information that is irrelevant to it.[179] Information relevant to any unactivated schemata is also filtered out. Apparently, audiences acquire information for only one schema at a time when comprehending texts or making decisions.[180] For example, audiences cannot simultaneously encode information about a home from the perspective of a home buyer and a burglar, even though both schemata are equally available to them and equally well known.

The interest that audiences have in acquiring new information is determined by their activated schema. New information per se is neither more interesting nor less interesting than information with which the audience is already familiar.[181] But audience members do find new information interesting and easy to recall when it fills slots in their activated schema.[182] For example, teachers who first developed a schema for categorizing students' learning strategies later showed higher levels of interest in acquiring more information about students' strategies and achieved better educational outcomes than teachers who received the same factual information but no schema-inducing framework.[183]

In our model information acquisition starts after schema activation. It has two steps: (1) filling in schema slots with information that has already been comprehended and identified as relevant to the schema; and (2) searching for the information that will fill the next schema slot.

Brain Regions Activated. Information acquisition, or task-driven attention, involves activation of the area at the top front of the right inferior frontal junction (IFJ), located in the middle region of the right frontal lobe,[184] and may involve activation of the left IFJ as well (see Figure 3.4, p. 108).[185] Disorders associated with these regions include deficits in executive functions that are typical of early stage dementia.

The Process of Filling Schema Slots

The time it takes to fill a schema slot with a slot value, as opposed to search for a slot value, varies with the slot's importance. A series of studies of readers reading 15 expository texts showed that readers fixate longer on words that fill important schema slots than on words that fill less important ones.[186] For example, readers spent more time per word when reading about the purpose of flywheels than when reading about the physical properties of flywheels. Similarly, readers of narratives take more time to read a sentence if the information in the sentence plays a significant role in the story than if it plays a minor one.[187] Readers also remember words longer when the words fill important schema slots.[188]

The order in which readers search for information to fill the slots of a schema reveals the slots' relative importance to the reader's goals for a particular task.[189] Readers can fill a slot quite easily if the slot value is already labeled in the text (e.g., "Exemplars include . . ."). When readers cannot locate slot values in a text, they may fill empty schema slots with default values stored in their memories.[190]

Targeted vs. General Search

There are two types of task-driven search: *targeted search* and *general search*. When conducting a targeted search, the audience tries to quickly locate a particular piece of information that will fill a specific empty schema slot. When conducting a general search, the audience reads or listens to longer passages hoping to find information that will fill several empty schema slots. An example of a targeted search is a consumer's scanning document headings, indexes, and directories for a keyword such as *price* in order to fill the "price slot" in her purchasing schema. Examples of audiences conducting a general search include a trainee reading a potentially helpful chapter from a training manual line by line or a nurse listening to a drug representative's sales presentation without interrupting.

Listeners necessarily conduct general searches unless they interrupt the speaker to request specific information. Readers may conduct either type of search of the same document. A survey of 201 instruction-manual users reports that only 15% of the users read the manual word for word, cover to cover. The majority conducted either general or targeted searches. Forty-six percent scanned the manuals for the major points and 35% used the manuals to find specific instructions. The remaining 4% of those surveyed never read them at all.[191]

Viewers of images, like readers, may also conduct either type of search. In his classic eye-tracking experiment, psychologist Alfred Yarbus selected a painting, "An Unexpected Visitor," by the Russian artist Ilya Repin, and asked different questions of viewers while recording their eye movements and fixations. In the general search condition, viewers were allowed to view the painting as they chose. In targeted search conditions, viewers were asked about the economic status, age, activities, clothing, locations, and relationships of the people in the picture. The locus of the viewers' eye fixations varied widely according to the question Yarbus asked.[192]

Figure 3.10 depicts some of the experiment's results. It shows the painting and seven recordings of eye movements made by the same viewer. Each recording lasted three minutes. The first recording (1) was of general search or free examination. The remaining six recordings were of targeted search. Before making each of those remaining recordings, Yarbus asked the viewer to perform a specific task: in the second recording (2) to estimate the economic status of the family; in (3) to give the ages of the people; in (4) to guess what the family had been doing before the "unexpected visitor" arrived; in (5) to remember the clothes the people wore; in (6) to remember the position of the people and objects in the room; and in (7) to estimate how long the "unexpected visitor" had been away.[193] As we can see, each task required the viewer to search for answers in different parts of the painting. More recently, neuroscientists find that brain activation patterns change just as markedly as eye-fixation patterns when viewers are asked to answer different questions while viewing the same scene.[194]

Targeted search of images is also associated with audience expertise. The greater the audience's expertise, the more targeted and efficient their search for information can be. For example, the pattern of eye movements expert radiologists produce as they make a diagnosis from an X-ray is far more efficient than that of novices.[195] Experts not only search images more efficiently than novices, they also search for different image elements. An eye-tracking study of art experts and novices finds qualitative differences in the searches they conduct as they look at paintings.[196] Novices, untrained in art, focus their attention on elements that indicate how accurately the paintings depict "objective" reality. In contrast, art experts focus on elements that indicate the composition, balance, and symmetry of the paintings.

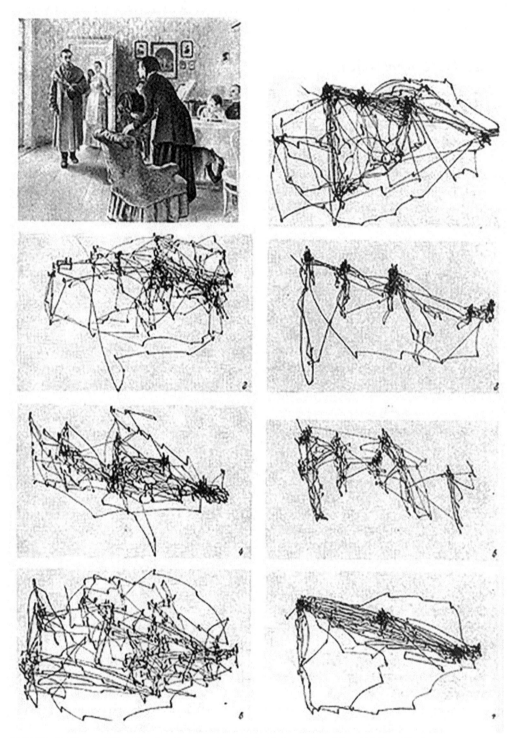

FIGURE 3.10 Viewers' Eye-Fixation Patterns Reveal the Information They Wish to Find

Source: Yarbus (1967, p. 174)

Viewers of graphs, like readers and viewers of images, may conduct either type of search. Graph viewers will conduct a general search if they are simply asked to describe a graph's meaning. In a study that asked viewers to describe the meaning of a line graph, viewers first read the title, inspected the graph, and then began to slowly identify the graph's variables and referents. After conducting this type of general search, one of the viewers in the study described the line graph as follows:

> This is vocabulary score vs. age by TV watched in hours. And it shows that vocabulary scores increase with age very dramatically for someone who watches a lot of TV and not so dramatically for someone who watches a little TV.[197]

More often, the information an audience extracts from a graph depends on their reason for looking at the graph.[198] According to one schema-driven model of graph comprehension, viewers first pose a question about the variables in a graph. For example, the question, "What was the average per capita income in France in 2014?" could be answered if the graph contained three variables: *per capita income*, *France*, and *2014*. Viewers next search the graph's legend and axes for the variables in their question. In the last step viewers identify the relevant value, for example, the amount of income people in France made on average in 2014, or $42,732. In this model graph viewers do not try to comprehend everything about the graph as they would in a general search. Instead they target their search of the elements in the graph to get the answer to their particular question.[199]

Attribute-Based vs. Alternative-Based Search

When audiences conduct a targeted search within a text or table in order to make a decision, they use one of two basic search patterns. One search pattern is termed *attribute-based* search. Such a search pattern could also be called "criterion-based" search since attributes are one type of decision criterion. The other search pattern is *alternative-based* search.[200] This search pattern could also be called "benchmark-based" search since alternatives are one type of benchmark.

Brain Regions Activated. Both attribute-based and alternative-based searches are coordinated by the ventromedial prefrontal cortex (vmPFC) of both hemispheres (see Figure 3.5, p. 108).[201] Unlike healthy individuals who normally conduct attribute-based searches, people with damage to the vmPFC routinely use alternative-based search when faced with a multi-attribute decision.[202]

Our model of decision making depicts search as attribute based. Attribute-based search is illustrated in the following passage in which a renter thinks aloud as she decides which apartment to rent, A or B. Notice how she first compares both apartments with respect to the cost to rent each of them. Then she compares both apartments with respect to the noise level of each:[203]

> OK, we have an A and a B.
> First, look at the rent for both of them.
> The rent for A is $170 and the rent for B is $140.
> $170 is a little steep, but it might have a low noise level.
> So we'll check A's noise level.
> A's noise level is low.
> We'll go to B's noise level.
> It's high.
> Gee, I can't really very well study with a lot of noise.
> So I'll ask myself the question, "Is it worth spending that extra $30 a month,
> to be able to study in my apartment?"

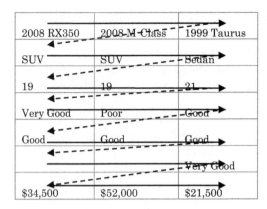

FIGURE 3.11 An Attribute-Based Search

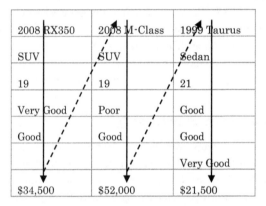

FIGURE 3.12 An Alternative-Based Search

When conducting an attribute-based search, audience members compare the first alternative's value for the first decision criterion, in this case apartment A's cost, to the corresponding values of the other alternatives, in this case apartment B's cost, before moving on to compare the first alternative's value for the second criterion, in this case apartment A's noise level, to the corresponding values of the other alternatives. Conversely, when conducting an alternative-based search, audience members input all of the attribute values of one alternative (e.g., apartment A's cost and noise level) before moving on to input all of the attribute values of the next alternative (e.g., apartment B's cost and noise level).

Figures 3.11 and 3.12 illustrate the difference between the two search patterns if an audience member were to scan the cells of a decision matrix to decide among three used cars—a 2008 Lexus RX350, a 2008 Mercedes M-Class, and a 1999 Ford Taurus—described by six attributes: body type, miles per gallon, reliability, safety record, depreciation rate, and retail price.

The Audience's Preference for Attribute-Based Search

Audiences show a marked preference for conducting attribute-based searches. In a study of expert decision making, an experienced trust investment officer from a large commercial bank was asked to think aloud as he chose equity stocks for a client portfolio. The study revealed that the investment officer made an attribute-based search of his investment options. Before choosing to invest in a firm (Firm A), the investment officer first compared Firm A's current value for an important attribute to the values of the other firms in the client's portfolio for the same attribute. Next he compared Firm A's value for that attribute to the values of other firms in the industry as well as to mean growth rates and expected growth rates for that attribute. Then the investment officer compared Firm A's current value for a second important attribute to the values of the other firms in the client's portfolio, and so on.[204]

Other expert audiences also show a preference for making attribute-based searches.[205] In a study of expert auditors, seven senior auditors thought aloud as they planned an audit of a company's internal control procedures. The auditors were presented with the company's financial statements, background information about the company, and flow charts of the company's internal control procedures. Most of the auditors' time was spent making one of two types of attribute-based comparisons: (1) the auditors compared two line-item amounts across years to determine if there was a significant change from one year to the next; and (2) they compared the information in the company's financial statements to their conceptions of the information a prototypical firm would disclose in its financial statements.[206]

In the case of executive selection, one study finds that higher level executives first activate "their schema of what it takes to perform well in a particular position."[207] They then conduct an attribute-based search comparing each candidate to the ideal candidate one attribute at a time. When the comparison process is finished, the executives select the candidate who best matches the ideal.

Most searches conducted by consumers as they make decisions are attribute based. A think-aloud study of consumer decision making finds that out of 80 searches, 57 (or about 71%) were by attribute, 15 by alternative or brand, and 8 used some other search pattern.[208] A subsequent study agrees that consumers use attribute-based search 71% of the time.[209] Another study that tracked consumers' eye movements as they decided among six used cars (alternatives) that were described in terms of three decision criteria (attributes) also finds that consumers rely most heavily on attribute-based search.[210] Consumers' eye fixations consisted of comparing pairs of alternatives one attribute at a time. Even when consumers search by asking questions instead of reading about various products, they typically use attribute-based search, with approximately 75% of their questions being attribute based.[211]

Audiences use attribute-based search in a variety of circumstances. In field studies of consumer decision making, attribute-based search strategies are the ones most frequently observed.[212] When either alternative-based or attribute-based strategies can be used, audiences overwhelming use attribute-based strategies.[213] Under time pressure, audiences' search patterns become increasingly attribute based.[214] Audiences' search patterns also become more attribute based as the amount of information about the alternatives increases[215] and when they have to trade off one attribute value against another.[216]

Even when audiences initially read and search by alternative, they may have to search their notes or their memories a second time by attribute in order to make the comparisons their decision requires. In a study of new home buyers, the buyers thought aloud as they decided among seven houses that were described in seven separate booklets. In their initial reading of the booklets, buyers conducted alternative-based searches. They read all about one house before reading anything about another. But they conducted more attribute-based searches when reviewing the information in the booklets a second time.[217] An eye-tracking study of judges choosing among scholarship applicants who were described by three attributes came to a similar conclusion. Although the judges read the information by alternative, they processed the information by attribute. Even when information was structured to bias processing by alternative, half of the judges still processed that information by attribute.[218]

Audiences also tend to recall information that is relevant to their decisions in an attribute-based way. In a study of consumer recall, consumers read about three brands of color televisions: Sanyo, Philco, and Sharp. Then after a short delay, the consumers were asked to choose one of the brands. Consumers recalled product attributes and made attribute-based choices. Consumers did not recall their overall evaluations of the three brands or use them to make alternative-based choices.[219] As this study illustrates, when consumers make a decision based on memory, they conduct an attribute-based search of their memories, which determines their comparison process and ultimately their choice of brands.[220]

Constraints on the Search Process

Audiences rarely have time to conduct a thorough search and fill all of the slots in their activated schema. Consequently, audiences tend to search for the values of the most important decision criteria or attributes first. In a study of consumer decision making, consumers chose products from three product categories: CD players, clock radios, and compact refrigerators. Each product category was represented by a set of 20 attributes. The later the consumers accessed an attribute's value, the less weight they gave it when they made their decisions.[221]

As the number of attributes presented to consumers increases, the proportion of the attribute values they search for decreases.[222] When audiences face severe time pressure, they may search for only one or two of the most important attribute values[223] and fail to use other important attribute values when making their choice.[224] Whether under time pressure or not, audiences tend to consider only a small set of alternatives when making decisions.[225] For many product categories consumers consider only two to eight brands on average.[226] As time pressure increases audiences stop searching for positive information and instead search for negative information about each alternative in an effort to eliminate inferior alternatives as quickly as possible.[227]

Even with ample time, the audience will often end its information-acquisition process long before they have processed all of the relevant information available to them due to the limited capacity of working memory.[228] As we have seen, consumers usually process only a small proportion of the information relevant to deciding among products and services,[229] especially when the products or services are not highly important to them.[230] Reviews of studies of consumers using information display boards (a form of decision matrix) to make purchasing decisions confirm that as the number of alternatives and attributes displayed on the boards increases, the proportion of the available information used decreases.[231]

Information Integration

As audience members acquire the information they need to fill their schema slots, they begin to compare and integrate that information in order to arrive at a decision. The information integration process has two major stages: the *valuation stage*, or the assignment of attribute values to each alternative, and the *integration stage*, or the application of a choice rule for comparing and deciding among alternatives. During the valuation stage, audience members compute missing attribute values and convert the values of non-comparable alternatives into a common currency. During the integration stage, audience members combine attribute values using either a compensatory or noncompensatory choice rule.[232]

Brain Regions Activated. Neuroscientists find that the valuation stage involves the ventromedial prefrontal cortex (vmPFC) of both brain hemispheres (see Figure 3.5, p. 108). If no attribute values are provided to the audience, the vmPFC will automatically compute them. Simply asking consumers to consider one attribute of the alternatives presented to them—such as the healthiness of an apple, an orange, and a candy bar—increases vmPFC activity for the attribute and the weight the consumers give the attribute, and in this case, the healthiness of their choices.[233] When consumers decide among different types of alternatives—such as food, clothing, and money—the vmPFC transforms attribute information about each alternative into a common currency in which all the options can be compared and evaluated.[234] Patients who suffer from bilateral lesions of the vmPFC have great difficulty making decisions, especially when choosing among alternatives with uncertain outcomes.

In the integration stage, the vmPFC passes on the values it computes to two other brain regions for comparison: the dorsomedial prefrontal cortex and an area in the parietal lobe (see Figures 3.4 and 3.5, p. 108).[235] A third region involved in the information integration process is the right dorsolateral prefrontal cortex (dlPFC). Repetitive transcranial magnetic stimulation applied to the right dlPFC diminishes the activation of that area and also that of the vmPFC and consistently changes the choices people make.[236] Damage to these two regions causes dramatic impairments to decision making, especially to multi-attribute decision making.[237]

The Conversion of Cardinal Numbers Into Ordinal Numbers and Scale Values

When audiences make decisions they generally do not mentally represent the values that fill the slots in their schemata as cardinal numbers (e.g., a price of $5,367,892.00) but represent them as ordinal numbers (e.g., "third highest priced") or scale values instead.[238] The think-aloud study described earlier of a bank's trust investment officer making investment decisions for clients found that the trust officer tended to convert the cardinal numbers in the financial reports into scale values before comparing them. The study's author then incorporated this finding into a computer model he developed and simulated the trust officer's investment decisions by first converting numerical data for each attribute or decision criterion into a three-value scale: *Below, equal to,* or *above.*[239]

Research finds that hospital patients also spontaneously transform numerical information about the risks of medical procedures into scale values.[240] Consumers make similar transformations when deciding among products and assign a scale value to each attribute of the recommended product during the valuation stage of the information integration process.[241]

Compensatory vs. Noncompensatory Choice Rules

Many different choice rules for integrating values have been observed.[242] The two basic types of choice rules audiences use to integrate attribute values are called *compensatory choice rules* and *noncompensatory choice rules.* When audiences use compensatory rules, they make trade-offs and accept a low value on one attribute or decision criterion in order to get a high value on another attribute. For example, a car buyer may accept fewer miles per gallon in order to get an increase in safety. Such rules require the same attributes be examined for each alternative. Examples of compensatory rules include the *weighted additive rule* and *the equal weight rule*, both of which rely on alternative-based search.

When audiences use the weighted additive rule, they evaluate each alternative one at a time. For each attribute or decision criterion of the alternative under consideration, they multiply the attribute's weight by the attribute's value. Next they add all of that alternative's weighted attribute values together in order to produce an overall value for that alternative. They repeat the process for each alternative. Then they compare the overall values of all the alternatives and choose the alternative with the highest overall value. Audiences go through a similar process when they use the equal weight rule. The difference is that they do not weight the relative importance of each attribute. Instead, they produce an overall value for each alternative by adding the unweighted values for each attribute of that alternative.

Unlike compensatory choice rules, noncompensatory rules do not allow trade-offs among attributes. Examples of noncompensatory rules include the *elimination-by-aspects rule* and the *lexicographic rule*, two rules that rely on attribute-based search and two rules that are suggested by our model of audience decision making. When audiences use the elimination-by-aspects rule, they first rank all the attributes or decision criteria according to their importance.[243] Then they compare each alternative's value for the top-ranked attribute to some minimally satisfactory value and eliminate any alternative from further consideration whose value is less than the satisfactory value. For example, if safety were the most important feature to a new car buyer, then the buyer would immediately eliminate any car with a poor safety record. Next the audience eliminates alternatives that do not have satisfactory values for the second-ranked attribute. The audience continues this process of elimination until only one alternative remains. Many financial analysts report that they rely on the elimination-by-aspects rule when making multi-attribute investment decisions.[244]

When audiences use the lexicographic rule, they also rank each attribute or decision criterion in terms of its importance. They then compare the values of the alternatives on the highest ranked attribute and choose the alternative with the highest value on that attribute, regardless of the values the alternatives have on other attributes. If, for example, miles-per-gallon were the highest ranked attribute or decision criterion for a new car buyer, and if the new Toyota Prius had the best gas mileage of all the cars under consideration, then the buyer would chose the Prius without examining other attributes. Such noncompensatory choice rules can minimize cognitive effort without severely decreasing the accuracy of the audience's decision. For example, in one experiment a simple noncompensatory rule increased the error rate from 8% to only 14% over that of the compensatory expected-value rule.[245] But the time saving was dramatic. Audience members took about two minutes to apply the expected-value rule but only 15 seconds to use the noncompensatory rule.

Constraints on the Use of Compensatory Choice Rules

Can professionals predict which choice rule their audience will use? As we have seen, consumers show a strong preference to use choice rules that rely on attribute-based search and comparisons.[246] Choice rules that rely on attribute-based search include noncompensatory rules such as the elimination-by-aspects rule and the lexicographic rule, as well as compensatory rules such as the *additive-difference rule* and the *majority-of-confirming-dimensions rule*.

When audiences choose between just two alternatives, they typically use an attribute-based compensatory choice rule.[247] However, as the number of alternatives they have to consider increases, their use of compensatory choice rules decreases. For example, physicians asked to choose among three anti-infective drugs used a compensatory choice rule. But they used a noncompensatory choice rule when asked to choose among six anti-infective drugs.[248]

If from the outset the audience has a large number of alternatives to choose among, they will typically use a noncompensatory choice rule such as the elimination-by-aspects rule.[249] Venture capitalists use the elimination-by-aspects rule to screen the many business plans that come across their desks.[250] Investors use the elimination-by-aspects rule to pick stocks.[251] Industrial buyers use similar noncompensatory rules to choose among large numbers of potential suppliers.[252]

Sometimes, when faced with a large number of alternatives, audience members start with a noncompensatory choice rule in order to quickly reduce the number of alternatives under consideration and then switch to a compensatory rule.[253] Consumers use such a two-phase choice strategy, particularly when choosing among six or more alternative brands.[254] Consumers eliminate the unacceptable alternatives in the first phase and then compare the remaining alternatives in more detail in the second phase. In a study of consumers choosing among a number of brands of typewriters, consumers first eliminated any alternative with a low value for an important criterion or attribute and then computed the total values for the remaining alternatives.[255] In a study of experienced consumers choosing among multiple brands of microwave ovens, consumers started with a noncompensatory evaluation of the microwaves, comparing each microwave to benchmark standards. Only after eliminating failing alternatives did they compare the remaining microwaves to each other using a compensatory choice rule.[256]

Audiences sometimes use noncompensatory choice rules even when the number of alternatives is small, especially when the decision they are making is not important to them. For example, consumers choosing stores at which to shop use simple noncompensatory choice rules to plan shopping trips for unimportant items.[257] They only use the more complex compensatory choice rules to plan shopping trips for important items.

Audiences may also use noncompensatory choice rules when faced with a large number of attributes.[258] In such cases, they often rely on a two-phase strategy similar to the two-phase strategy for deciding among multiple alternatives described previously. First they eliminate less important attributes. Then they use a compensatory choice rule to compare their alternatives along the remaining attributes.[259] A two-phase strategy can work in the other direction as well. When incomparable scaling of attribute values across alternatives makes comparisons difficult, for example, when the price of similar foreign products is quoted in different currencies, audiences may switch from compensatory to noncompensatory choice rules.[260]

COGNITIVE PROCESSES IN AUDIENCE DECISION MAKING: IMPLICATIONS FOR COMMUNICATORS

- The main takeaway for communicators in Chapter 3 is that in order for audiences to arrive at a rational decision, they must first be able to complete a specific set of cognitive processes. The audience's decision-making process is not a black box. It is predictable and subject to many information-processing constraints.

- Use the information presented in the chapter to make stylistic and organizational choices that aid audience decision making, to diagnose problems with ineffective communications, and to handle communication issues with new media adaptively.

- Why use the information? To help your audience make decisions faster and more efficiently. To reduce the risk that your audience will discard your information because it seems unclear or disorganized to them.

- To apply the information presented in the chapter, (1) identify likely problems when editing or planning communications; (2) determine which cognitive process is affected by each problem; and (3) refer to the section of Chapter 4 dealing with proven techniques for aiding that particular process.

Notes

1 Stratman, J., & Young, R. O. (1986, April). *An analysis of novice managers' performances in board meetings.* Annual Conference of the Management Communication Association. Durham, NC.

2 Velmans, M. (1991). Is human information processing conscious? *Behavioral and Brain Sciences, 14*(4), 651–726.

3 Feltovich, P. J., Prietula, M. J., & Ericsson, K. A. (2006). Studies of expertise from psychological perspectives. In K. A. Ericsson, N. Charness, P. J. Feltovich & R. Hoffman (Eds.), *The Cambridge handbook of expertise and expert performance* (pp. 41–67). Cambridge, UK: Cambridge University Press.

4 Mitchell, A. A. (1981). The dimensions of advertising involvement. *Advances in Consumer Research, 8,* 25–30.

5 Wright, P., & Rip, P. D. (1980). Product class advertising effects on first-time buyers' decision strategies. *Journal of Consumer Research, 7*(2), 176–188.

6 Payne, J. W., & Bettman, J. R. (2004). Walking with the scarecrow: The information-processing approach to decision research. In D. J. Koehler & N. Harvey (Eds.), *Blackwell handbook of judgment and decision making* (pp. 110–132). Oxford, UK: Blackwell Publishing.

Johnson, E. J., & Weber, E. U. (2009). Mindful judgment and decision making. *Annual Review of Psychology, 60,* 53–85.

7 Newell, A., & Simon, H. A. (1972). *Human problem solving.* Englewood Cliffs, NJ: Prentice Hall.

8 Anderson, J. R. (2004, p. 11). *Cognitive psychology and its implications* (6th ed.). New York: Worth Publishers.

Levine, J. M., & Smith, E. R. (2013). Group cognition: Collective information search and distribution. In D. E. Carlston (Ed.), *The Oxford handbook of social cognition* (pp. 616–633). New York: Oxford University Press.

9 Kotchetova, N., & Salterio, S. (2004). Judgment and decision-making accounting research: A quest to improve the production, certification, and use of accounting information. In D. J. Koehler & N. Harvey (Eds.), *Blackwell handbook of judgment and decision making* (pp. 547–566). Oxford, UK: Blackwell Publishing.

10 Brauner, E., & Scholl, W. (2000). Editorial: The information processing approach as a perspective for groups research. *Group Processes and Intergroup Relations, 3*(2), 115–122.

Hinsz, V. B., Tindale, R. S., & Vollrath, D. A. (1997). The emerging conceptualization of groups as information processes. *Psychological Bulletin, 121*(1), 43–64.

Larson, J. R., & Christensen, C. (1993). Groups as problem-solving units: Toward a new meaning of social cognition. *British Journal of Social Psychology, 32*(1), 5–30.

11 *See* n10, Hinsz et al. (1997), p. 43.

12 Albers, M. (2002). Complex problem solving and content analysis. In M. Albers & B. Mazur (Eds.), *Content and complexity: Information design in software development and documentation* (pp. 285–305). Hillsdale, NJ: Erlbaum.

Cooke, N. J., Salas, E., Kiekel, P. A., & Bell, B. (2004). Advances in measuring team cognition. In E. Salas & S. M. Fiore (Eds.), *Team cognition: Understanding the factors that drive process and performance* (pp. 83–106). Washington, DC: American Psychological Association.

Gibson, C. B. (2001). From knowledge accumulation to accommodation: Cycles of collective cognition in work groups. *Journal of Organizational Behavior, 22*(2), 121–134.

13 MacMillan, J., Entin, E. E., & Serfaty, D. (2004). Communication overhead: The hidden cost of team cognition. In E. Salas & S. M. Fiore (Eds.), *Team cognition: Understanding the factors that drive process and performance* (pp. 61–82). Washington, DC: American Psychological Association.

14 Sternberg, S. (1966). High-speed scanning in human memory. *Science, 153*(3736), 652–654.

15 deTurck, M. A., & Goldhaber, G. M. (1991). A developmental analysis of warning signs: The case of familiarity and gender. *Journal of Products Liability, 13,* 65–78.

16 Goldhaber, G. M., & deTurck, M. A. (1988). Effects of product warnings on adolescents in an education context. *Product Safety & Liability Reporter, 16,* 949–955.

17 Friedman, K. (1988). The effect of adding symbols to written warning labels on user behavior and recall. *Human Factors, 30,* 507–515.

18 Lesgold, A. M., & Resnick, L. (1982). How reading difficulties develop: Perspectives from a longitudinal study. In J. Das, R. Mulcahey & A. Wall (Eds.), *Theory and research in learning disabilities* (pp. 155–187). New York: Plenum Press.

19 Stein, S. K. (1999). Uncovering listening strategies: Protocol analysis as a means to investigate student listening in the basic communication course (Doctoral dissertation, University of Maryland, College Park, 1999). *Dissertation Abstracts International, 61*(01A), 28.

20 *See* n7, Newell & Simon (1972), p. 11.
21 Anderson, J. R. (2000). *Cognitive psychology and its implications* (5th ed.). New York: Worth Publishers.

   See n3, Feltovich et al. (2006).

   Glaser, R., & Chi, M. T. H. (1988). Overview. In M. T. H. Chi, R. Glaser & M. J. Farr (Eds.), *The nature of expertise* (pp. xv–xxviii). Hillsdale, NJ: Erlbaum.
22 Miller, G. A. (1956). The magical number seven, plus or minus two: Some limits on our capacity for processing information. *Psychological Review, 63*(2), 81–97.
23 Simon, H. A. (1955). A behavioral model of rational choice. *Quarterly Journal of Economics, 69*, 99–118.

   Simon, H. A. (1956). Rational choice and the structure of the environment. *Psychological Review, 63*(2), 129–138.
24 Ratcliff, G., & Newcombe, F. (1982). Object recognition: Some deductions from the clinical evidence. In A. W. Ellis (Ed.), *Normality and pathology in cognitive functions* (pp. 147–171). London: Academic Press.
25 Goldstein, M. N. (1974). Auditory agnosia for speech ("pure word deafness"): A historical review with current implications. *Brain and Language, 1*, 195–204.
26 Just, M. A., & Carpenter, P. A. (1987). *The psychology of reading and language comprehension*. Boston: Allyn and Bacon.
27 Rayner, K. (1998). Eye movements in reading and information processing: 20 years of research. *Psychological Bulletin, 124*(3), 372–422.

   Van Orden, G. C. (1987). A rows is a rose: Spelling, sound, and reading. *Memory & Cognition, 15*(3), 181–198.
28 *See* n26, Just & Carpenter (1987).
29 Cairns, H. S., & Kamerman, J. (1975). Lexical information processing during sentence comprehension. *Journal of Verbal Learning & Verbal Behavior, 14*(2), 170–179.

   Warren, R. E., Warren, N. T., Green, J. P., & Bresnick, J. H. (1978). Multiple semantic encoding of homophones and homographs in contexts biasing dominant or subordinate meanings. *Memory & Cognition, 6*(4), 364–371.
30 McCandliss, B. D., Cohen, L., & Dehaene, S. (2003). The visual word form area: Expertise for reading in the fusiform gyrus. *Trends in Cognitive Sciences, 7*(7), 293–299.
31 Cavina-Pratesi, C., Large, M. E., & Milner, A. D. (2015). Visual processing of words in a patient with visual form agnosia: A behavioural and fMRI study. *Cortex, 64*, 29–46.

   Wallentin, M., Michaelsen, J. L. D., Rynne, I., & Nielsen, R. H. (2014). Lateralized task shift effects in Broca's and Wernicke's regions and in visual word form area are selective for conceptual content and reflect trial history. *NeuroImage, 101*, 276–288.
32 Fujimaki, N., Hayakawa, T., Ihara, A., Wei, Q., Munetsuna, S., Terazono, Y., . . . Murata, T. (2009). Early neural activation for lexico-semantic access in the left anterior temporal area analyzed by an fMRI-assisted MEG multidipole method. *NeuroImage, 44*(3), 1093–1102.

   Gesierich, B., Jovicich, J., Riello, M., Adriani, M., Monti, A., Brentari, V., . . . Gorno-Tempini, M. L. (2012). Distinct neural substrates for semantic knowledge and naming in the temporoparietal network. *Cerebral Cortex, 22*(10), 2217–2226.

   Race, D. S., Tsapkini, K., Crinion, J., Newhart, M., Davis, C., Gomez, Y., . . . Faria, A. V. (2013). An area essential for linking word meanings to word forms: Evidence from primary progressive aphasia. *Brain and Language, 127*(2), 167–176.
33 Pollatsek, A., & Rayner, K. (1990). Eye movements and lexical access in reading. In D. A. Balota, G. B. Flores d'Arcais & K. Rayner (Eds.), *Comprehension processes in reading* (pp. 143–163). Hillsdale, NJ: Lawrence Erlbaum Associates.
34 Pollatsek, A., Raney, G. E., LaGasse, L., & Rayner, K. (1993). The use of information below fixation in reading and in visual search. *Canadian Journal of Psychology, 47*(2), 179–200.
35 Kinney, G. G., Marsetta, M., & Showman, D. J. (1966). Studies of display symbol legibility, Part XII, the legibility of alphanumeric symbols for digitalized television: ESD-TR-66–117. MTR-206. *Tech Doc Rep U S Air Force Syst Command Electron Syst Div*, 1–33.
36 Nelson, D. L., Wheeler, J., & Engel, J. (1970). Stimulus meaningfulness and similarity, recall direction and rate of recall test. *Psychonomic Science, 20*(6), 346–347.

   Reicher, G. M. (1969). Perceptual recognition as a function of meaningfulness of stimulus material. *Journal of Experimental Psychology, 81*(2), 275–280.
37 Just, M. A., & Carpenter, P. A. (1980). A theory of reading: From eye fixations to comprehension. *Psychological Review, 87*(4), 329–354.

38 McDonald, S. A. (2006). Parafoveal preview benefit in reading is only obtained from the saccade goal. *Vision Research, 46*(26), 4416–4424.

39 *See* n26, Just & Carpenter (1987).

40 Rayner, K., Reichle, E. D., Stroud, M. J., Williams, C. C., & Pollatsek, A. (2006). The effect of word frequency, word predictability, and font difficulty on the eye movements of young and elderly readers. *Psychology and Aging, 21*(3), 448–465.

Reingold, E., & Rayner, K. (2006). Examining the word identification stages identified by the E-Z reader model. *Psychological Science, 17*(9), 742–746.

41 Calvo, M. G., & Meseguer, E. (2002). Eye movements and processing stages in reading: Relative contribution of visual, lexical and contextual factors. *Spanish Journal of Psychology, 5*(1), 66–77.

Liversedge, S. P., Rayner, K., White, S. J., Vergilino-Perez, D., Findlay, J. M., & Kentridge, R. W. (2004). Eye movements when reading disappearing text: Is there a gap effect in reading? *Vision Research, 44*(10), 1013–1024.

42 Ashby, J., Rayner, K., & Clifton, C. (2005). Eye movements of highly skilled and average readers: Differential effects of frequency and predictability. *Quarterly Journal of Experimental Psychology, 58A*(6), 1065–1086.

Drieghe, D., Rayner, K., & Pollatsek, A. (2005). Eye movements and word skipping during reading revisited. *Journal of Experimental Psychology: Human Perception and Performance, 31*(5), 954–969.

Ehrlich, S. F., & Rayner, K. (1981). Contextual effects on word perception and eye movements during reading. *Journal of Verbal Learning and Verbal Behavior, 20*(6), 641–655.

43 Binder, K. S. (2003). Sentential and discourse topic effects on lexical ambiguity processing: An eye-movement examination. *Memory & Cognition, 31*(5), 690–702.

Rayner, K., & Duffy, S. A. (1986). Lexical complexity and fixation times in reading: Effects of word frequency, verb complexity, and lexical ambiguity. *Memory and Cognition, 14*(3), 191–201.

Sereno, S. C., O'Donnell, P., & Rayner, K. (2006). Eye movements and lexical ambiguity resolution: Investigating the subordinate bias effect. *Journal of Experimental Psychology: Human Perception and Performance, 32*(2), 335–350.

44 Garrod, S., Freudenthal, S., & Boyle, E. (1994). The role of different types of anaphor in the on-line resolution of sentences in a discourse. *Journal of Memory and Language, 33*(1), 39–68.

O'Brien, E. J., Raney, G. E., Albrecht, J., & Rayner, K. (1997). Processes involved in the resolution of explicit anaphors. *Discourse Processes, 23*, 1–24.

45 Duffy, S., & Keir, J. A. (2004). Violating stereotypes: Eye movements and comprehension processes when text conflicts with world knowledge. *Memory and Cognition, 32*(4), 551–559.

Sturt, P. (2003). The time course of the application of binding constraints in reference resolution. *Journal of Memory and Language, 48*(3), 542–562.

Sturt, P., & Lombardo, V. (2005). Processing coordinated structures: Incrementality and connectedness. *Cognitive Science, 29*(2), 291–305.

46 *See* n37, Just & Carpenter (1980).

47 Rayner, K., Kambe, G., & Duffy, S. A. (2000). Clause wrap-up effects on eye movements during reading. *Quarterly Journal of Experimental Psychology, 53A*(4), 1061–1080.

48 Carpenter, P. A., & Just, M. A. (1981). Cognitive processes in reading: Models based on readers' eye fixations. In A. M. Lesgold & C. A. Perfetti (Eds.), *Interactive processes in reading* (pp. 177–213). Hillsdale, NJ: Erlbaum.

Carpenter, P. A., & Just, M. A. (1983). What your eyes do while your mind is reading. In K. Rayner (Ed.), *Eye movements in reading: Perceptual and language processes* (pp. 275–307). New York: Academic Press.

Just, M. A., & Carpenter, P. A. (1984). Using eye fixations to study reading comprehension. In D. E. Kieras & M. A. Just (Eds.), *New methods in reading comprehension research* (pp. 151–182). Hillsdale, NJ: Erlbaum.

49 Gautier, V., O'Regan, J. K., & LaGargasson, I. F. (2000). "The skipping" revisited in French programming saccades to skip the article "les". *Vision Research, 40*, 2517–2531.

Rayner, K., & Well, A. D. (1996). Effects of contextual constraint on eye movements in reading: A further examination. *Psychonomic Bulletin & Review, 3*(4), 504–509.

50 Frazier, L., & Rayner, K. (1982). Making and correcting errors during sentence comprehension: Eye movements in the analysis of structurally ambiguous sentences. *Cognitive Psychology, 14*(2), 178–121.

Meseguer, E., Carreiras, M., & Clifton, C. (2002). Overt reanalysis strategies and eye movements during the reading of mild garden path sentences. *Memory & Cognition, 30*(4), 551–561.

51 Hyönä, J., Lorch Jr, R. F., & Kaakinen, J. K. (2002). Individual differences in reading to summarize expository text: Evidence from eye fixation patterns. *Journal of Educational Psychology, 94*(1), 44–55.

Hyönä, J., & Lorch Jr, R. F. (2004). Effects of topic headings on text processing: Evidence from adult readers' eye fixation patterns. *Learning and Instruction, 14*(2), 131–152.

Hyönä, J., & Nurminen, A. M. (2006). Do adult readers know how they read? Evidence from eye movement patterns and verbal reports. *British Journal of Psychology, 97*(1), 31–50.

52 Cauchard, F., Eyrolle, H., Cellier, J. M., & Hyönä, J. (2010). Vertical perceptual span and the processing of visual signals in reading. *International Journal of Psychology, 45*(1), 40–47.

53 Gibbs, W. J., and Bernas, R. S. (2009). Visual attention in newspaper versus TV-oriented news websites. *Journal of Usability Studies, 4*(4), 147–165.

54 Liberman, A. M., Cooper, F. S., Shankweiler, D. P., & Studdert-Kennedy, M. (1967). Perception of the speech code. *Psychological Review, 74*(6), 431–461.

55 Nearey, T. M. (1989). Static, dynamic, and relational properties in vowel perception. *Journal of the Acoustical Society of America, 85*(5), 2088–2113.

56 Miller, J. L. (1981). Effects of speaking rate on segmental distinctions. In P. D. Eimas & J. L. Miller (Eds.), *Perspectives on the study of speech* (pp. 39–74). Hillsdale, NJ: Erlbaum.

57 Ahrens, M., Hasan, B. A., Giordano, B. L., & Belin, P. (2014). Gender differences in the temporal voice areas. *Frontiers in Neuroscience, 8,* 228.

Belin, P., Zatorre, R. J., Lafaille, P., Ahad, P., & Pike, B. (2000). Voice-selective areas in human auditory cortex. *Nature, 403,* 309–312.

Strelnikov, K., Massida, Z., Rouger, J., Belin, P., & Barone, P. (2011). Effects of vocoding and intelligibility on the cerebral response to speech. *BMC Neuroscience, 12*(1), 122.

58 Sugimori, E., Mitchell, K. J., Raye, C. L., Greene, E. J., & Johnson, M. K. (2014). Brain mechanisms underlying reality monitoring for heard and imagined words. *Psychological Science, 25*(2), 403–413.

See also Service, E. (2009). From auditory traces to language learning: Behavioural and neurophysiological evidence. In A. C. Thorn & M. A. Page (Eds.), *Interactions between short-term and long-term memory in the verbal domain* (pp. 277–299). New York: Psychology Press.

Zhuang, J., Tyler, L. K., Randall, B., Stamatakis, E. A., & Marslen-Wilson, W. D. (2014). Optimally efficient neural systems for processing spoken language. *Cerebral Cortex, 24*(4), 908–918.

59 Marslen-Wilson, W. D. (1987). Parallel processing in spoken word recognition. *Cognition, 25,* 71–102.

60 Clark, H. H. (1999). Psycholinguistics. In R. A. Wilson & F. C. Keil (Eds.), *MIT encyclopedia of the cognitive sciences* (pp. 688–689). Cambridge, MA: MIT Press.

61 Boudewyn, M. A., Long, D. L., & Swaab, T. Y. (2015). Graded expectations: Predictive processing and the adjustment of expectations during spoken language comprehension. *Cognitive, Affective, & Behavioral Neuroscience, 15*(3), 607–624.

62 McQueen, J. M., Cutler, A., Briscoe, T., & Norris, D. (1995). Models of continuous speech recognition and the contents of the vocabulary. *Language and Cognitive Processes, 10*(3–4), 309–331.

Swinney, D. A. (1979). Lexical access during sentence comprehension: (Re)consideration of context effects. *Journal of Verbal Learning & Verbal Behavior, 18*(6), 645–659.

63 Bard, E. G., Shillcock, R. C., & Altmann, G. T. M. (1988). The recognition of words after their acoustic offsets in spontaneous speech: Effects of subsequent context. *Perception and Psychophysics, 44*(5), 395–408.

64 Yarbus, A. L. (1967). *Eye movements and vision.* Translated from Russian by Basil Haigh. New York: Plenum Press.

65 Stevens, W. D., Kahn, I., Wig, G. S., & Schacter, D. L. (2012). Hemispheric asymmetry of visual scene processing in the human brain: Evidence from repetition priming and intrinsic activity. *Cerebral Cortex, 22*(8), 1935–1949.

66 Kanwisher, N., McDermott, J., & Chun, M. M. (1997). The fusiform face area: A module in human extrastriate cortex specialized for face perception. *The Journal of Neuroscience, 17*(11), 4302–4311.

McCarthy, G., Puce, A., Gore, J. C., Allison, T., (1997). Face-specific processing in the human fusiform gyrus. *Journal of Cognitive Neuroscience, 9*(5), 604–609.

67 Potter, M. C., & Levy, E. I. (1969). Recognition memory for a rapid sequence of pictures. *Journal of Experimental Psychology, 81*(1), 10–15.

68 Fleming, M. L., & Sheikhian, M. (1972). Influence of pictorial attributes on recognition memory. *AV Communication Review, 20*(4), 423–441.

69 Intraub, H. (1979). The role of implicit naming in pictorial encoding. *Journal of Experimental Psychology: Human Learning and Memory, 5*(2), 78–87.

70 Nickerson, R. S. (1968). On long-term recognition memory for pictorial material. *Psychonomic Science, 11*(2), 58.

71 Robinson, J. S. (1969). Familiar patterns are no easier to see than novel ones. *American Journal of Psychology, 82*(4), 513–522.

72 Shah, P. (1995). Cognitive processes in graph comprehension (Doctoral dissertation, Carnegie Mellon University, 1995). *Dissertation Abstracts International, 57*(03B), 2191.

73 Carpenter, P. A., & Shah, P. (1998). A model of the perceptual and conceptual processes in graph comprehension. *Journal of Experimental Psychology: Applied, 4*(2), 75–100.

74 Bettman, J. R. (1979). *An information processing theory of consumer choice.* Reading, MA: Addison Wesley.

75 Beatty, J., & Kahneman, D. (1966). Pupillary changes in two memory tasks. *Psychonomic Science, 5*(10), 371–372.

Hess, E. H., & Polt, J. M. (1964). Pupil size in relation to mental activity during simple problem-solving. *Science, 143*(3611), 1190–1192.

Kahneman, D., & Beatty, J. (1966). Pupil diameter and load on memory. *Science, 154*(3756), 1583–1585.

Kahneman, D., & Beatty, J. (1967). Pupillary responses in a pitch-discrimination task. *Perception & Psychophysics, 2*(3), 101–105.

76 Krugman, H. E. (1964). Some applications of pupil measurement. *Journal of Marketing Research, 1,* 15–19.

77 Hoffman, J. E., & Subramaniam, B. (1995). The role of visual attention in saccadic eye movements. *Perception & Psychophysics, 57*(6), 787–795.

Kowler, E., Anderson, E., Dosher, B., & Blaser, E. (1995). The role of attention in the programming of saccades. *Vision Research, 35*(13), 1897–1916.

78 Sivacek, J., & Crano, W. D. (1982). Vested interest as a moderator of attitude-behavior consistency. *Journal of Personality and Social Psychology, 43*(2), 210–221.

Wingenfeld, K., Mensebach, C., Driessen, M., Bullig, R., Hartje, W., & Beblo, T. (2006). Attention bias towards personally relevant stimuli: The individual emotional Stroop task. *Psychological Reports, 99*(3), 781–793.

79 Pieters, R., Warlop, L., & Wedel, M. (2002). Breaking through the clutter: Benefits of advertisement originality and familiarity for brand attention and memory. *Management Science, 48*(6), 765–781.

80 Bruner, J. S. (1957). On perceptual readiness. *Psychological Review, 64*(2), 123–152.
Kahneman, D. (1973). *Attention and effort.* Englewood Cliffs, NJ: Prentice Hall.

81 Newspaper Advertising Bureau. (1964). *A study of the opportunity for exposure to national newspaper advertising.* New York: Author.

82 Newspaper Advertising Bureau. (1987). *An eye camera study of ads.* New York: Author.

83 Tolley, B. S., & Bogart, L. (1994). How readers process newspaper advertising. In E. M. Clark, T. C. Brock & D. W. Stewart (Eds.), *Attention, attitude, and affect in response to advertising* (pp. 69–77). Hillsdale, NJ: Lawrence Erlbaum Associates.

84 Kim, H. (2014). Involvement of the dorsal and ventral attention networks in oddball stimulus processing: A meta-analysis. *Human Brain Mapping, 35*(5), 2265–2284.

Talsma, D., Senkowski, D., Soto-Faraco, S., & Woldorff, M. G. (2010). The multifaceted interplay between attention and multisensory integration. *Trends in Cognitive Sciences, 14*(9), 400–410.

Woolgar, A., Williams, M. A., & Rich, A. N. (2015). Attention enhances multi-voxel representation of novel objects in frontal, parietal and visual cortices. *NeuroImage, 109,* 429–437.

85 Wolford, G., & Morrison, F. (1980). Processing of unattended visual information. *Memory & Cognition, 8*(6), 521–527.

86 Cherry, E. C. (1953). Some experiments on the recognition of speech, with one and with two ears. *Journal of the Acoustical Society of America, 25,* 975–979.

Moray, N. (1959). Attention in dichotic listening: Affective cues and the influence of instructions. *The Quarterly Journal of Experimental Psychology, 11,* 56–60.

87 Treisman, A. M., & Geffen, G. (1967). Selective attention: Perception or response? *The Quarterly Journal of Experimental Psychology, 19*(1), 1–17.

88 Glucksberg, S., & Cowen Jr, G. N. (1970). Memory for nonattended auditory material. *Cognitive Psychology, 1*(2), 149–156.

89 *See* n21, Anderson (2000), p. 81.

90 Rock, I. (1977, June). *Form perception as process of description.* Presented at the 10th Symposium of the Center for Visual Science, Rochester, NY.

91 Corteen, R. S., & Dunn, D. (1974). Shock-associated words in a nonattended message: A test for momentary awareness. *Journal of Experimental Psychology, 102*(6), 1143–1144.

92 Janiszewski, C. (1988). Preconscious processing effects: The independence of attitude formation and conscious thought. *Journal of Consumer Research*, *15*(2), 199–209.

Janiszewski, C. (1990). The influence of nonattended material on the processing of advertising claims. *Journal of Marketing Research*, *27*(3), 263–278.

93 Karlin, L., & Kestenbaum, R. (1968). Effects of the number of alternatives on the psychological refractory period. *Quarterly Journal of Experimental Psychology*, *20*, 167–178.

94 Treisman, A. M., & Davies, A. (1973). Divided attention to ear and eye. In S. Kornblum (Ed.), *Attention and performance IV* (pp. 101–117). London: Academic Press.

95 Jeung, H. J., Chandler, P., & Sweller, J. (1997). The role of visual indicators in dual sensory mode instruction. *Educational Psychology*, *17*(3), 329–345.

96 Sternberg, R. J. (1999, p. 98). *Cognitive Psychology* (2nd ed.). New York: Harcourt Brace College Publishers.

97 Dhar, R., & Simonson, I. (1992). The effect of the focus of comparison on consumer preferences. *Journal of Marketing Research*, *29*(4), 430–440.

98 Holland, J. H., Holyoak, K., Nisbett, R. E., & Thagard, P. R. (1986). *Induction: Processes of inference, learning, and discovery*. Cambridge, MA: MIT Press.

Payne, J. W., Bettman, J. R., & Johnson, E. J. (1993). *The adaptive decision maker*. New York: Cambridge University Press.

99 *See* n26, Just & Carpenter (1987).

100 Graf, R., & Torrey, J. W. (1966). Perception of phrase structure in written language. *Proceedings of the Annual Convention of the American Psychological Association*, 83–84.

101 Fillmore, C. J. (1968). The case for case. In E. Bach & R. T. Harms (Eds.), *Universals of linguistic theory* (pp. 1–88). New York, NY: Holt, Rinehart, and Winston.

Schank, R. C. (1975). *Conceptual information processing*. Amsterdam: North-Holland.

102 Bever, T. (1970). The cognitive basis for linguistic structures. In J. R. Hayes (Ed.), *Cognition and the development of language* (pp. 279–362). New York: Wiley.

103 *See* n26, Just & Carpenter (1987), p. 196.

104 Goucha, T., & Friederici, A. D. (2015). The language skeleton after dissecting meaning: A functional segregation within Broca's Area. *NeuroImage*, *114*, 294–302.

Sakai, K. L., Noguchi, Y., Takeuchi, T., & Watanabe, E. (2002). Selective priming of syntactic processing by event-related transcranial magnetic stimulation of Broca's area. *Neuron*, *35*(6), 1177–1182.

105 Friederici, A. D. (2009). Pathways to language: Fiber tracts in the human brain. *Trends in Cognitive Sciences*, *13*(4), 175–181.

Magnusdottir, S., Fillmore, P., den Ouden, D. B., Hjaltason, H., Rorden, C., Kjartansson, O., . . . Fridriksson, J. (2013). Damage to left anterior temporal cortex predicts impairment of complex syntactic processing: A lesion-symptom mapping study. *Human Brain Mapping*, *34*(10), 2715–2723.

Tyler, L. K., Wright, P., Randall, B., Marslen-Wilson, W. D., & Stamatakis, E. A. (2010). Reorganization of syntactic processing following left-hemisphere brain damage: Does right-hemisphere activity preserve function? *Brain*, *133*(11), 3396–3408.

106 Gernsacher, M. A., & Kaschak, M. P. (2003). Neuroimaging studies of language production and comprehension. *Annual Review of Psychology*, *54*, 91–114.

Rodd, J. M., Vitello, S., Woollams, A. M., & Adank, P. (2015). Localising semantic and syntactic processing in spoken and written language comprehension: An activation likelihood estimation meta-analysis. *Brain and Language*, *141*, 89–102.

107 Okada, R., Okuda, T., Nakano, N., Nishimatsu, K., Fukushima, H., Onoda, M., . . . Kato, A. (2013). Brain areas associated with sentence processing: A functional MRI study and a lesion study. *Journal of Neurolinguistics*, *26*(4), 470–478.

108 Marconi, D., Manenti, R., Catricala, E., Della Rosa, P. A., Siri, S., & Cappa, S. F. (2013). The neural substrates of inferential and referential semantic processing. *Cortex*, *49*(8), 2055–2066.

109 Menenti, L., Petersson, K. M., Scheeringa, R., & Hagoort, P. (2009). When elephants fly: Differential sensitivity of right and left inferior frontal gyri to discourse and world knowledge. *Journal of Cognitive Neuroscience*, *21*(12), 2358–2368.

110 Carpenter, P. A., & Just, M. A. (1977). Reading comprehension as the eyes see it. In M. A. Just & P. A. Carpenter (Eds.), *Cognitive processes in comprehension* (pp. 109–139). Hillsdale, NJ: Erlbaum.

Ehrlich, K., & Rayner, K. (1983). Pronoun assignment and semantic integration during reading: Eye movements and immediacy of processing. *Journal of Verbal Learning & Verbal Behavior*, *22*(1), 75–87.

See n26, Just & Carpenter (1987).

111 *See* n26, Just & Carpenter (1987).

Mason, R. A., & Just, M. A. (2006). Neuroimaging contributions to the understanding of discourse processes. In M. J. Traxler & M. A. Gernsbacher (Eds.), *Handbook of psycholinguistics* (2nd ed., pp. 765–800). London: Elsevier Inc.

112 Aaronson, D., & Scarborough, H. S. (1977). Performance theories for sentence coding: Some quantitative models. *Journal of Verbal Learning & Verbal Behavior, 16*(3), 277–303.

113 See n26, Just & Carpenter (1987).

114 Rayner, K., & Frazier, L. (1987). Parsing temporarily ambiguous complements. *The Quarterly Journal of Experimental Psychology A: Human Experimental Psychology, 39*(4, Pt. A), 657–673.

115 Foss, D. J., & Jenkins, C. M. (1973). Some effects of context on the comprehension of ambiguous sentences. *Journal of Verbal Learning & Verbal Behavior, 12*(5), 577–589.

Holmes, V. M., Arwas, R., & Garrett, M. F. (1977). Prior context and the perception of lexically ambiguous sentences. *Memory & Cognition, 5*(1), 103–110.

116 Caplan, D. (1972). Clause boundaries and recognition latencies for words in sentences. *Perception & Psychophysics, 12*(1, Pt. B), 73–76.

117 Bransford, J. D., Barclay, J. R., & Franks, J. J. (1972). Sentence memory: A constructive versus interpretive approach. *Cognitive Psychology, 3*(2), 193–209.

118 Anderson, J. R. (1974). Verbatim and propositional representation of sentences in immediate and long-term memory. *Journal of Verbal Learning & Verbal Behavior, 13*(2), 149–162.

119 Flower, L. S., Hayes, J. R., & Swarts, H. (1983). Revising functional documents: The scenario principle. In P. V. Anderson, R. J. Brockmann & C. R. Miller (Eds.), *New essays in technical and scientific communication* (pp. 41–58). New York: Baywood Press.

120 Daneman, M., & Carpenter, P. A. (1983). Individual differences in integrating information between and within sentences. *Journal of Experimental Psychology: Learning, Memory, and Cognition, 9*(4), 561–584.

121 Mehrabian, A., & Ferris, S. R. (1967). Inference of attitudes from nonverbal communication in two channels. *Journal of Consulting Psychology, 31*(3), 248–252.

122 Nespor, M., & Vogel, I. (1983). Prosodic structure above the word. In A. Cutler & D. R. Ladd (Eds.), *Prosody: Models and measurements* (pp. 123–140). Heidelberg: Springer.

123 Cutler, A. (1982). Prosody and sentence perception in English. In J. Mehler, E. C. T. Walker & M. F. Garrett (Eds.), *Perspectives on mental representation: Experimental and theoretical studies of cognitive processes and capacities* (pp. 201–216). Hillsdale, NJ: Erlbaum.

Sedivy, J., Tanehaus, M., Spivey-Knowlton, M., Eberhard, K., & Carlson, G. (1995). Using intonationally marked presuppositional information in on-line language processing: Evidence from eye movements to a visual model. In J. D. Moore & J. F. Lehman (Eds.), *Proceedings of the Seventeenth Annual Conference of the Cognitive Science Society* (pp. 375–380). Hillsdale, NJ: Erlbaum.

124 Bolinger, D. L. (1978). Intonation across languages. In J. H. Greenberg, C. A. Ferguson & E. A. Moravcsik (Eds.), *Universals of human language, vol. 2: Phonology* (pp. 471–524). Palo Alto, CA: Stanford University Press.

Ladd, D. R. (1996). *Intonational phonology*. Cambridge, UK: Cambridge University Press.

125 Bornkessel-Schlesewsky, I. D., & Friederici, A. D. (2007). Neuroimaging studies of sentence and discourse comprehension. In G. Gaskell (Ed.), *The Oxford handbook of psycholinguistics* (pp. 407–424). New York: Oxford University Press.

Wildgruber, D., Ethofer, T., Grandjean, D., & Kreifelts, B. (2009). A cerebral network model of speech prosody comprehension. *International Journal of Speech-Language Pathology, 11*(4), 277–281.

126 Belyk, M., & Brown, S. (2014). Perception of affective and linguistic prosody: An ALE meta-analysis of neuroimaging studies. *Social Cognitive and Affective Neuroscience, 9*(9), 1395–1403.

127 Alba-Ferrara, L., Ellison, A., & Mitchell, R. L. C. (2012). Decoding emotional prosody: Resolving differences in functional neuroanatomy from fMRI and lesion studies using TMS. *Brain Stimulation, 5*(3), 347–353.

128 Adapted from Knapp, M. L. (1978). *Nonverbal communication in human interaction* (2nd ed.). New York: Holt, Rinehart and Winston.

129 Sachs, J. S. (1967). Recognition of semantic, syntactic and lexical changes in sentences. *Psychonomic Bulletin, 1*(2), 17–18.

130 Jarvella, R. J. (1971). Syntactic processing of connected speech. *Journal of Verbal Learning & Verbal Behavior, 10*(4), 409–416.

131 Keenan, J. M., MacWhinney, B., & Mayhew, D. (1977). Pragmatics in memory: A study of natural conversion. *Journal of Verbal Learning & Verbal Behavior, 16*(5), 549–560.

132 Wanner, H. E. (1968). On remembering, forgetting, and understanding sentences. A study of the deep structure hypothesis (Doctoral dissertation, Harvard University, 1968). *American Doctoral Dissertations, X1968,* 0158.

133 Kunen, S., Green, D., & Waterman, D. (1979). Spread of encoding effects within the nonverbal visual domain. *Journal of Experimental Psychology: Human Learning and Memory, 5*(6), 574–584.

134 Pezdek, K., & Evans, G. W. (1979). Visual and verbal memory for objects and their spatial locations. *Journal of Experimental Psychology: Human Learning and Memory, 5*(4), 360–373.

135 Standing, L. (1973). Learning 10,000 pictures. *The Quarterly Journal of Experimental Psychology, 25*(2), 207–222.

136 Shepard, R. N. (1967). Recognition memory for words, sentences, and pictures. *Journal of Verbal Learning & Verbal Behavior, 6*(1), 156–163.

137 *See* n72, Shah (1995).

138 Kosslyn, S. M. (1989). Understanding charts and graphs. *Applied Cognitive Psychology, 3*(3), 185–225.

139 Pinker, S. (1990). A theory of graph comprehension. In R. Freedle (Ed.), *Artificial intelligence and the future of testing* (pp. 73–126). Hillsdale, NJ: Lawrence Erlbaum Associates.

140 Schnotz, W., & Bannert, M. (2003). Construction and interference in learning from multiple representation. *Learning and Instruction, 13*(2), 141–156.

Schnotz, W., & Baadte, C. (2015). Surface and deep structures in graphics comprehension. *Memory & Cognition, 43*(4), 605–618.

141 *See* n72, Shah (1995).

142 Markus, H., & Zajonc, R. B. (1985, p. 150). The cognitive perspective in social psychology. In G. Lindzey & E. Aronson (Eds.), *The handbook of social psychology* (3rd ed., Vol. 1, pp. 137–230). New York: Knopf.

143 *See* n3, Feltovich et al. (2006).

Goldstein, W. M., & Weber, E. U. (1995). Content and discontent: Indications and implications of domain specificity in preferential decision making. In J. Busemeyer, D. Medin & R. Hastie (Eds.), *Decision-making from a cognitive perspective (the psychology of learning and motivation)* (Vol. 32, pp. 83–136). San Diego, CA: Academic Press.

144 *See* n21, Anderson (2000), p. 351.

145 Kumaran, D., Summerfield, J. J., Hassabis, D., & Maguire, E. A. (2009). Tracking the emergence of conceptual knowledge during human decision making. *Neuron, 63*(6), 889–901.

Qiu, J., Li, H., Chen, A., & Zhang, Q. (2008). The neural basis of analogical reasoning: An event-related potential study. *Neuropsychologia, 46*(12), 3006–3013.

Tse, D., Langston, R. F., Kakeyama, M., Bethus, I., Spooner, P. A., Wood, E. R., . . . Morris, R. G. (2007). Schemas and memory consolidation. *Science, 316*(5821), 76–82.

146 van Kesteren, M. T., Rijpkema, M., Ruiter, D. J., Morris, R. G., & Fernández, G. (2014). Building on prior knowledge: Schema-dependent encoding processes relate to academic performance. *Journal of Cognitive Neuroscience, 26*(10), 2250–2261.

147 Gilboa, A., & Moscovitch, M. (2002). The cognitive neuroscience of confabulation: A review and a model. In A. D. Baddeley, M. D. Kopelman & B. A. Wilson (Eds.), *Handbook of memory disorders* (2nd ed., pp. 315–342). Hoboken, NJ: John Wiley & Sons Ltd.

Ghosh, V. E., Moscovitch, M., Colella, B. M., & Gilboa, A. (2014). Schema representation in patients with ventromedial PFC lesions. *The Journal of Neuroscience, 34*(36), 12057–12070.

148 Khader, P. H., Pachur, T., Meier, S., Bien, S., Jost, K., & Rösler, F. (2011). Memory-based decision-making with heuristics: Evidence for a controlled activation of memory representations. *Journal of Cognitive Neuroscience, 23*(11), 3540–3554.

149 Fellows, L. K. (2006). Deciding how to decide: Ventromedial frontal lobe damage affects information acquisition in multi-attribute decision making. *Brain, 129*(4), 944–952.

Rudebeck, P. H., Bannerman, D. M., & Rushworth, M. F. S. (2008). The contribution of distinct subregions of the ventromedial frontal cortex to emotion, social behavior, and decision making. *Cognitive, Affective, & Behavioral Neuroscience, 8*(4), 485–497.

150 Kintsch, W., & Kintsch, E. H. (1978). The role of schemata in text comprehension. *International Journal of Psycholinguistics, 5*(2), 17–29.

Rumelhart, D. E., & Ortony, A. (1976). The representation of knowledge in memory. In R. C. Anderson, R. J. Spiro & W. E. Montague (Eds.), *Semantic factors in cognition* (pp. 99–136). Hillsdale, NJ: Erlbaum.

Schank, R. C., & Abelson, R. P. (1977). *Scripts, plans, goals and understanding: An inquiry into human knowledge structures.* Oxford, UK: Lawrence Erlbaum.

151 Stokes, A. F., Kemper, K., & Kite, K. (1997). Aeronautical decision making, cue recognition, and expertise under time pressure. In C. E. Zsambok & G. Klein (Eds.), *Naturalistic decision making* (pp. 183–196). Mahwah, NJ: Erlbaum.

152 Randel, J. M., Pugh, H. L., & Reed, S. K. (1996). Differences in expert and novice situation awareness in naturalistic decision making. *International Journal of Human-Computer Studies, 45*(5), 579–597.

153 Chi, M. T. H., & Ohlsson, S. (2005, p. 377). Complex declarative learning. In K. J. Holyoak & R. G. Morrison (Eds.), *The Cambridge handbook of thinking and reasoning* (pp. 371–399). Cambridge, UK: Cambridge University Press.

154 Blake, M. L., Tompkins, C. A., Scharp, V. L., Meigh, K. M., & Wambaugh, J. (2015). Contextual Constraint Treatment for coarse coding deficit in adults with right hemisphere brain damage: Generalisation to narrative discourse comprehension. *Neuropsychological Rehabilitation, 25*(1), 15–52.

Gouldthorp, B. (2015). Hemispheric differences in the processing of contextual information during language comprehension. *Laterality: Asymmetries of Body, Brain and Cognition, 20*(3), 348–370.

Long, D. L., & Baynes, K. (2002). Discourse representation in the two cerebral hemispheres. *Journal of Cognitive Neuroscience, 14*(2), 228–242.

155 *See* n26, Just & Carpenter (1987), p. 254.

156 Spilich, G. J., Vesonder, G. T., Chiesi, H. L., & Voss, J. F. (1979). Text processing of domain-related information for individuals with high and low domain knowledge. *Journal of Verbal Learning & Verbal Behavior, 18*(3), 275–290.

Sticht, T. G., Armijo, L., Weitzman, R., Koffman, N., Roberson, K., Chang, F., & Moracco, J. (1986). *Progress report.* Monterey, CA: U.S. Naval Postgraduate School.

157 Bower, G. H., Black, J. B., & Turner, T. J. (1979). Scripts in memory for text. *Cognitive Psychology, 11*(2), 177–220.

Kintsch, W., & van Dijk, T. A. (1978). Toward a model of text comprehension and production. *Psychological Review, 85*(5), 363–394.

Weldon, D. E., & Malpass, R. S. (1981). Effects of attitudinal, cognitive, and situational variables on recall of biased communications. *Journal of Personality and Social Psychology, 40*(1), 39–52.

158 *See* n157, Bower et al. (1979).

159 McDaniel, M. A., & Einstein, G. O. (1989). Material-appropriate processing: A contextualist approach to reading and studying strategies. *Educational Psychology Review, 1*(2), 113–145.

Zwaan, R. A., & Brown, C. M. (1996). The influence of language proficiency and comprehension skill on situation-model construction. *Discourse Processes, 21*(3), 289–327.

160 Thibadeau, R., Just, M. A., & Carpenter, P. A. (1982). A model of the time course and content of reading. *Cognitive Science, 6*, 157–203.

161 Anderson, R. C., Reynolds, R. E., Schallert, D. L., & Goetz, E. T. (1977). Frameworks for comprehending discourse. *American Educational Research Journal, 14*(4), 367–381.

Spiro, R. J. (1977). Remembering information from text: The "state of schema" approach. In R. C. Anderson, R. J. Spiro & W. E. Montague (Eds.), *Schooling and the acquisition of knowledge* (pp. 137–165). Hillsdale, NJ: Erlbaum.

162 Anderson, R. C., & Pichert, J. W. (1978). Recall of previously unrecallable information following a shift in perspective. *Journal of Verbal Learning & Verbal Behavior, 17*(1), 1–12.

163 Zadny, J., & Gerard, H. B. (1974). Attributed intentions and informational selectivity. *Journal of Experimental Social Psychology, 10*(1), 34–52.

164 *See* n26, Just & Carpenter (1987).

165 Kieras, D. E., & Bovair, S. (1981, November). *Strategies for abstracting main ideas from simple technical prose.* Technical report. Tucson, AZ: Arizona University of Tucson Department of Psychology.

166 Hinsley, D. A., Hayes, J. R., & Simon, H. A. (1977). From words to equations: Meaning and representation in algebra word problems. In M. A. Just & P. A. Carpenter (Eds.), *Cognitive processes in comprehension* (pp. 89–106). Hillsdale, NJ: Lawrence Erlbaum Associates.

167 Macrae, C. N., & Martin, D. (2007). A boy primed Sue: Feature-based processing and person construal. *European Journal of Social Psychology, 37*(5), 793–805.

Martin, D., & Macrae, C. N. (2007). A face with a cue: Exploring the inevitability of person categorization. *European Journal of Social Psychology, 37*(5), 806–816.

168 Freeman, J. B., Ambady, N., Rule, N. O., & Johnson, K. L. (2008). Will a category cue attract you? Motor output reveals dynamic competition across person construal. *Journal of Experimental Psychology: General, 137*(4), 673–690.

169 *See* n142, Markus & Zajonc (1985).

170 Hyönä, J. (1995). An eye movement analysis of topic-shift effect during repeated reading. *Journal of Experimental Psychology: Learning, Memory, and Cognition, 21*(5), 1365–1373.

See n37, Just & Carpenter (1980).

171 Hyönä, J. (1994). Processing of topic shifts by adults and children. *Reading Research Quarterly, 29*(1), 76–90.

172 Budd, D., Whitney, P., & Turley, K. J. (1995). Individual differences in working memory strategies for reading expository text. *Memory and Cognition, 23*(6), 735–748.

173 Dooling, D. J., & Mullet, R. L. (1973). Locus of thematic effects in retention of prose. *Journal of Experimental Psychology, 97*(3), 404–406.

Swaney, J. H., Janik, C. J., Bond, S. J., & Hayes, J. R. (1991). Editing for comprehension: Improving the process through reading protocols. In E. R. Steinberg (Ed.), *Plain language: Principles and practice* (pp. 173–203). Detroit, MI: Wayne State University Press. (Original article published in 1981 as Document Design Project Tech. Rep. No. 14, Pittsburgh, PA: Carnegie Mellon University).

174 *See* n162, Anderson & Pichert (1978).

Pichert, J. W., & Anderson, R. C. (1977). Taking different perspectives on a story. *Journal of Educational Psychology, 69*(4), 309–315.

See n161, Spiro (1977).

175 Bransford, J. D., & Johnson, M. K. (1973, p. 400). Considerations of some problems of comprehension. In W. G. Chase (Ed.), *Visual information processing* (pp. 383–438). Oxford, UK: Academic.

176 *See* n166, Hinsley et al. (1977).

177 *See* n157, Bower et al. (1979).

178 Abelson, R. P., & Levi, A. (1985, p. 273). Decision making and decision theory. In G. Lindzey & E. Aronson (Eds.), *The handbook of social psychology* (3rd ed., Vol. 1, pp. 231–309). New York: Knopf.

179 Baluch, F., & Itti, L. (2011). Mechanisms of top-down attention. *Trends in Neurosciences, 34*(4), 210–224.

180 Malt, B. C., Ross, B. H., & Murphy, G. L. (1995). Predicting features for members of natural categories when categorization is uncertain. *Journal of Experimental Psychology: Learning, Memory, and Cognition, 21*, 646–661.

181 Teigen, K. H. (1985). The novel and the familiar: Sources of interest in verbal information. *Current Psychology, 4*(3), 224–238.

Teigen, K. H. (1987). Intrinsic interest and the novelty-familiarity interaction. *Scandinavian Journal of Psychology, 28*(3), 199–210.

182 Yarlas, A. S. (1999). Learning as a predictor of interest: The knowledge-schema theory of cognitive interest (Doctoral dissertation, University of California, 1999). *Dissertation Abstracts International: Section B, 59*, 5130.

183 Ohst, A., Fondu, B. M., Glogger, I., Nückles, M., & Renkl, A. (2014). Preparing learners with partly incorrect intuitive prior knowledge for learning. *Frontiers in Psychology, 5*, 664.

See also Kumaran, D. (2013). Schema-driven facilitation of new hierarchy learning in the transitive inference paradigm. *Learning & Memory, 20*(7), 388–394.

184 Sebastian, A., Jung, P., Neuhoff, J., Wibral, M., Fox, P. T., Lieb, K., . . . Mobascher, A. (2015). Dissociable attentional and inhibitory networks of dorsal and ventral areas of the right inferior frontal cortex: A combined task-specific and coordinate-based meta-analytic fmri study. *Brain Structure & Function*, 1–7, doi:10.1007/s00429–015–0994-y.

185 *See* n84, Kim (2014); Talsma et al. (2010).

186 *See* n48, Carpenter & Just (1981).

See n37, Just & Carpenter (1980).

See n160, Thibadeau et al. (1982).

187 Cirilo, R. K., & Foss, D. J. (1980). Text structure and reading time for sentences. *Journal of Verbal Learning and Verbal Behavior, 19*(1), 96–109.

188 *See* n160, Thibadeau et al. (1982).

189 *See* n48, Carpenter & Just (1981).

See n37, Just & Carpenter (1980).

See n160, Thibadeau et al. (1982).

190 *See* n160, Thibadeau et al. (1982).

191 Schriver, K. A. (1997, p. 213). *Dynamics in document design: Creating text for readers.* New York: Wiley.

192 *See* n64, Yarbus (1967).

193 *See* n64, Yarbus (1967).

194 Prostko, A. L. (2014). Effects of social and non-social interpretations of complex images on human eye movement and brain activation (Doctoral dissertation, West Virginia University, 2014). *Dissertation Abstracts International: Section B, 74*(7-B)(E).

195 Nodine, C. F., & Kundel, H. L. (1987). Perception and display in diagnostic imaging. *RadioGraphs, 7*, 1241–1250.

196 Nodine, C. F., Locher, P. J., & Krupinski, E. A. (1993). The role of formal art training on perception and aesthetic judgment of art compositions. *Leonardo, 26,* 219–227.

197 *See* n72, Shah (1995), p. 61.

198 Carswell, C. M., & Wickens, C. D. (1987). Information integration and the object display: An interaction of task demands and display superiority. *Ergonomics, 30*(3), 511–527.

199 Lohse, G. L. (1993). A cognitive model for understanding graphical perception. *Human-Computer Interaction, 8,* 353–388.

200 Tversky, A. (1969). Intransitivity of preferences. *Psychological Review, 76*(1), 31–48.

201 Taber-Thomas, B. C. (2012). A model of the neural basis of predecisional processes: The fronto-limbic information acquisition network (Doctoral dissertation, University of Iowa, 2012). *Dissertation Abstracts International: Section B, 73,* 2717.

202 *See* n149, Fellows (2006).

203 Payne, J. W. (1976, p. 378). Task complexity and contingent processing in decision making: An information search and protocol analysis. *Organizational Behavior & Human Performance, 16*(2), 366–387.

204 Clarkson, G. P. (1962). *Portfolio selection: A simulation of trust investment.* Englewood Cliffs, NJ: Prentice Hall.

205 Dai, J., & Busemeyer, J. R. (2014). A probabilistic, dynamic, and attribute-wise model of intertemporal choice. *Journal of Experimental Psychology: General, 143*(4), 1489–1514.

   Ziebarth, G. E. (2012). Information search and selection of heuristics in multi-attribute choice tasks (Doctoral dissertation, University of South Dakota, 2012). *Dissertation Abstracts International: Section B, 72,* 7078.

206 Selling, T. I. (1982). Cognitive processes in information system choice (Doctoral dissertation, The Ohio State University, 1982). *Dissertation Abstracts International, 43*(08A), 2713.

207 Sessa, V. I. (2001, p. 99). Executive promotion and selection. In M. London (Ed.), *How people evaluate others in organizations* (pp. 91–110). Hillsdale, NJ: Lawrence Erlbaum Associates.

208 Russo, J. E. (1971). The multi-alternative choice process as tracked by recording eye fixations (Doctoral dissertation, University of Michigan, 1971). *Dissertation Abstracts International, 32*(03B), 1882.

209 Capon, N., & Burke, M. (1977). Information seeking in consumer durable purchases. In B. A. Greenberg & D. N. Bellenger (Eds.), *Contemporary marketing thought, 1977 educator's proceedings* (pp. 110–115). Chicago: American Marketing Association.

210 Russo, J. E., & Rosen, L. D. (1975). An eye fixation analysis of multialternative choice. *Memory & Cognition, 3*(3), 267–276.

211 Ranyard, R., & Williamson, J. (2005). Conversation-based process tracing methods for naturalistic decision making: Information search and verbal analysis. In H. Montgomery, R. Lipshitz & B. Brehmer (Eds.), *How professionals make decisions* (pp. 305–317). Mahwah, NJ: Lawrence Erlbaum Associates.

212 Aschenbrenner, K. M. (1978). Single-peaked risk preferences and their dependability on the gambles' presentation mode. *Journal of Experimental Psychology: Human Perception and Performance, 4*(3), 513–520.

   Svenson, O. (1979). Process descriptions of decision making. *Organizational Behavior and Human Performance, 23*(1), 86–112.

213 Russo, J. E., & Dosher, B. A. (1983). Strategies for multiattribute binary choice. *Journal of Experimental Psychology: Learning, Memory, and Cognition, 9*(4), 676–696.

214 Payne, J. W., Bettman, J. R., & Johnson, E. J. (1988). Adaptive strategy selection in decision making. *Journal of Experimental Psychology: Learning, Memory, and Cognition, 14*(3), 534–552.

215 Cook, G. J. (1987). An analysis of information search strategies for decision making (Doctoral dissertation, Arizona State University, 1987). *Dissertation Abstracts International, 48*(02A), 0430.

   See n203, Payne (1976).

   Payne, J. W., & Braunstein, M. L. (1978). Risky choice: An examination of information acquisition behavior. *Memory & Cognition, 6*(5), 554–561.

216 Pfeiffer, J., Meißner, M., Brandstätter, E., Riedl, R., Decker, R., & Rothlauf, F. (2014). On the influence of context-based complexity on information search patterns: An individual perspective. *Journal of Neuroscience, Psychology, and Economics, 7*(2), 103–124.

217 Svenson, O. (1974). *A note on think aloud protocols obtained during the choice of a home* (Report No. 421). Stockholm: Psychology Lab, University of Stockholm.

218 *See* n213, Russo & Dosher (1983).

219 Lynch, J. G., Marmorstein, H., & Weigold, M. F. (1988). Choices from sets including remembered brands: Use of recalled attributes and prior overall evaluations. *Journal of Consumer Research, 15*(2), 169–184.

220 Biehal, G., & Chakravarti, D. (1982). Information-presentation format and learning goals as determinants of consumers' memory retrieval and choice processes. *Journal of Consumer Research, 8*(4), 431–441.

   Biehal, G., & Chakravarti, D. (1983). Information accessibility as a moderator of consumer choice. *Journal of Consumer Research, 10*(1), 1–14.

221 Jacoby, J., Morrin, M., Jaccard, J., Gurhan, Z., Kuss, A., & Maheswaran, D. (2002). Mapping attitude formation as a function of information input: Online processing models of attitude formation. *Journal of Consumer Psychology, 12*(1), 21–34.

222 Jacoby, J., Speller, D. E., & Berning, C. K. (1974a). Brand choice behavior as a function of information load: Replication and extension. *Journal of Consumer Research, 1*(1), 33–42.

Jacoby, J., Speller, D. E., & Kohn, C. A. (1974b). Brand choice behavior as a function of information load. *Journal of Marketing Research, 11*(1), 63–69.

223 *See* n214, Payne et al. (1988).

224 Wallsten, T. S. (1980). Processes and models to describe choice and inference. In T. S. Wallsten (Ed.), *Cognitive processes in choice and decision behavior* (pp. 215–237). Hillsdale, NJ: Erlbaum.

225 Hauser, J. R., & Wernerfelt, B. (1990). An evaluation cost model of consideration sets. *Journal of Consumer Research, 16*, 393–408.

Kardes, F. R., Kalyanaram, G., Chandrashekaran, M., & Dornof, R. J. (1993). Brand retrieval, consideration set composition, consumer choice, and the pioneering advantage. *Journal of Consumer Research, 20*(1), 62–75.

Nedungadi, P. (1990). Recall and consumer consideration sets: Influencing choice without altering brand evaluations. *Journal of Consumer Research, 17*(3), 263–276.

226 *See* n225. Hauser & Wernerfelt (1990).

227 *See* n214, Payne et al. (1988).

Svenson, O., & Edland, A. (1987). Change of preferences under time pressure: Choices and judgements. *Scandinavian Journal of Psychology, 28*(4), 322–330.

Wallsten, T. S., & Barton, C. (1982). Processing probabilistic multidimensional information for decisions. *Journal of Experimental Psychology: Learning, Memory, and Cognition, 8*(5), 361–384.

228 *See* n22, Miller (1956).

229 Russo, J. E. (1977). The value of unit price information. *Journal of Marketing Research, 14*(2), 193–201.

Russo, J. E., Staelin, R., Nolan, C. A., Russell, G. J., & Metcalf, B. L. (1986). Nutrition information in the supermarket. *Journal of Consumer Research, 13*(1), 48–70.

230 Batra, R., & Ray, M. L. (1986). Situational effects of advertising repetition: The moderating influence of motivation, ability, and opportunity to respond. *Journal of Consumer Research, 12*(4), 432–445.

Park, C. W., & Young, S. M. (1986). Consumer response to television commercials: The impact of involvement and background music on brand attitude formation. *Journal of Marketing Research, 23*(1), 11–24.

Yalch, R. F., & Elmore-Yalch, R. (1984). The effect of numbers on the route to persuasion. *Journal of Consumer Research, 11*(1), 522–527.

231 *See* n212.

232 Anderson, N. H. (1974). Cognitive algebra: Integration theory applied to social attribution. In L. Berkowitz (Ed.), *Advances in experimental social psychology* (Vol. 7, pp. 1–101). New York: Academic Press.

Anderson, N. H. (1981). *Foundations of information theory.* New York: Academic Press.

Anderson, N. H. (1989). Functional memory and on-line attribution. In J. N. Bassili (Ed.), *On-line cognition in person perception* (pp. 175–220). Hillsdale, NJ: Erlbaum.

233 Hare, T. A., Malmaud, J., & Rangel, A. (2011). Focusing attention on the health aspects of foods changes value signals in vmPFC and improves dietary choice. *The Journal of Neuroscience, 31*(30), 11077–11087.

234 Platt, M., & Plassmann, H. (2014). Multistage valuation signals and common neural currencies. In P. W. Glimcher & E. Fehr (Eds.), *Neuroeconomics: Decision making and the brain* (2nd ed., pp. 237–258). New Yok, NY: Academic Press.

235 Hare, T. A., Camerer, C. F., & Rangel, A. (2009). Self-control in decision-making involves modulation of the vmPFC valuation system. *Science, 324*(5927), 646–648.

Kahnt, T., Heinzle, J., Park, S. Q., & Haynes, J. D. (2011). Decoding different roles for vmPFC and dlPFC in multi-attribute decision making. *NeuroImage, 56*(2), 709–715.

Clithero, J. A., & Rangel, A. (2014). Informatic parcellation of the network involved in the computation of subjective value. *Social Cognitive and Affective neuroscience, 9*(9), 1289–1302.

236 Baumgartner, T., Knoch, D., Hotz, P., Eisenegger, C., & Fehr, E. (2011). Dorsolateral and ventromedial prefrontal cortex orchestrate normative choice. *Nature Neuroscience, 14*(11), 1468–1474.

237 *See* n149.

238 *See* n178, Abelson & Levi (1985).

239 *See* n204, Clarkson (1962).

240 Bottorff, J. L., Ratner, P. A., Johnson, J. L., Lovato, C. Y., & Joab, S. A. (1998). Communicating cancer risk information: The challenges of uncertainty. *Patient Education and Counseling, 33*(1), 67–81.

241 *See* n232.

242 *See* n98, Payne et al. (1993).

Tversky, A. (1972). Elimination by aspects: A theory of choice. *Psychological Review, 79*(4), 281–299.

See n224, Wallsten (1980).

243 *See* n242, Tversky (1972).

Tversky, A., & Sattath, S. (1979). Preference trees. *Psychological Review, 86*(6), 542–573.

244 Olsen, R. A. (2002). Professional investors as naturalistic decision makers: Evidence and market implications. *The Journal of Psychology and Financial Markets, 3*(3), 161–167.

245 Johnson, E. J. (1979). *Deciding how to decide: The effort of making a decision.* Unpublished manuscript, University of Chicago, Chicago, IL.

246 Russo, J. E., & Dosher, B. A. (1980). *Cognitive effort and strategy selection in binary choice.* Chicago, IL: Center for Decision Research, Graduate School of Business, University of Chicago.

247 *See* n203, Payne (1976).

248 Chinburapa, V. (1991). Physician prescribing decisions: The effects of situational involvement and task complexity on information acquisition and decision making (Doctoral dissertation, The University of Arizona, 1991). *Dissertation Abstracts International, 52*(04B), 1975.

249 Johnson, E. J., Meyer, R. J., & Ghose, S. (1989). When choice models fail: Compensatory models in negatively correlated environments. *Journal of Marketing Research, 26*(3), 255–270.

Klayman, J. (1985). Children's decision strategies and their adaptation to task characteristics. *Organizational Behavior and Human Decision Processes, 35*(2), 179–201.

Onken, J., Hastie, R., & Revelle, W. (1985). Individual differences in the use of simplification strategies in a complex decision-making task. *Journal of Experimental Psychology: Human Perception and Performance, 11*(1), 14–27.

250 Pfeffer, M. G. (1987). Venture capital investment and protocol analysis (Doctoral dissertation, University of North Texas, 1987). *Dissertation Abstracts International, 49*(01A), 112.

251 Kercsmar, J. (1985). Individual investors' information choice, information processing, and judgment behavior: A process-tracing study of the verbal protocols associated with stock selection (Doctoral dissertation, University of Houston, University Park, 1985). *Dissertation Abstracts International, 46*(09A), 2740.

252 LeBlanc, R. P. (1981). Organizational purchase decision making: Information-processing strategies and evoked sets of qualified suppliers (Doctoral dissertation, The University of Arizona, 1981). *Dissertation Abstracts International, 42*(02A), 0830.

253 Biehal, G., & Chakravarti, D. (1986). Consumers' use of memory and external information in choice: Macro and micro perspectives. *Journal of Consumer Research, 12*(4), 382–405.

254 Lussier, D. A., & Olshavsky, R. W. (1979). Task complexity and contingent processing in brand choice. *Journal of Consumer Research, 6*(2), 154–165.

See n217, Svenson (1974).

255 *See* n254, Lussier & Olshavsky (1979).

256 Bettman, J. R., & Park, C. W. (1980). Effects of prior knowledge and experience and phase of the choice process on consumer decision processes: A protocol analysis. *Journal of Consumer Research, 7*(3), 234–248.

257 Peterson, K. (1984). An investigation of consumer patronage/shopping decision-making behavior using an information processing approach (Doctoral dissertation, The University of Wisconsin, Madison, 1984). *Dissertation Abstracts International, 45.*

258 Biggs, S. F., Bedard, J. C., Gaber, B. G., & Linsmeier, T. J. (1985). The effects of task size and similarity on the decision behavior of bank loan officers. *Management Science, 31*(8), 970–987.

Sundström, G. A. (1987). Information search and decision making: The effects of information displays. *Acta Psychologica, 65*(2), 165–179.

259 *See* n254, Lussier & Olshavsky (1979).

van Raaij, W. F. (1976). *Direct monitoring of consumer information processing by eye movement recorder.* Unpublished paper, Tilburg University, Tilburg, Netherlands.

260 Wright, P. (1974). *The use of phased, noncompensatory strategies in decisions between multi-attribute products* (Research Paper 223). Stanford, CA: Graduate School of Business, Stanford University.

4

AIDS TO AUDIENCE DECISION MAKING

On August 5, 1977, New York State became the first state in the United States to enact a general-purpose plain English law. The impetus for the new law was a plain English loan agreement form introduced earlier that same year by Citibank (then First National City Bank). Understandably, the bank's attorneys and upper management were initially skeptical of the new form, as shown on p. 147. But when the bank finally approved it, TV and the national press saw its introduction as a major event. A bill was soon on the governor's desk requiring all consumer contracts in New York to be modeled on the new Citibank form. Within a few months, the plain English bill was signed into law.

What effect did the new loan agreement form have on the bank and its customers? Both benefited. A survey of more than 100 borrowers found that they believed the original version, as shown on p. 146, contained too much information, had too much small print, was formatted in a confusing way, and was hard to read. In contrast, the borrowers said the revised form was written in a more specific and precise style, that it gave a good breakdown of information, and that it was easy to read.

The survey also showed the borrowers believed that banks using the two versions would be radically different. In addition, four out of five borrowers surveyed expressed positive feelings about borrowing from a bank using the new form. They also expressed interest in using the bank's other services.[1]

ORIGINAL CITIBANK LOAN AGREEMENT FORM

FIRST NATIONAL CITY BANK

Personal Finance Department ●New York	PROCEEDS TO BORROWER	(1) $ _____
APPLICATION	PROPERTY INS.PREMIUM	(2) $ _____
NUMBER_____	FILING FEE	(3) $ _____
ANNUAL PER-	AMOUNT FINANCED (1) ♦ (2) ♦ (3)	(4) $ _____
CENTAGE RATE_____ %	PREPAID FINANCE CHARGE	(5) $ _____
	GROUP CREDIT LIFE INS.PREMIUM	(6) $ _____
$_____	FINANCE CHARGE (5) ♦ (6)	(7) $ _____
TOTAL OF PAYMENTS (4) ♦ (7)		

FOR THE VALUE RECEIVED, the undersigned (jointly and severally) hereby promises(s) to pay to FIRST NATIONAL CITY BANK (the "Bank") at it office at 399 Park Avenue, New York, New York 10022 (i) THE SUM OF

_____ ($_____) (TOTAL OF PAYMENTS) ( ) IN _____ EQUAL CONSECUTIVE MONTHLY INSTALLMENTS OF $_____ EACH ON THE SAME DAY OF EACH MONTH, COMMENCING _____DAYS FROM THE DATE THE LOAN IS MADE; OR ( ) IN _____ EQUAL CONSECUTIVE WEEKLY INSTALLMENTS OF $ _____ EACH ON THE SAME DAY OF EACH WEEK, COMMENCING NOT EARLIER THAN 5 DAYS NOR LATER THAN 45 DAYS FROM THE DATE THE LOAN IS MADE; OR ( ) IN _____ EQUAL CONSECUTIVE BI-WEEKLY INSTALLMENTS OF $_____ EACH, COMMENCING NOT EARLIER THAN 10 AYS NOR LATER THAN 45 DAYS FROM THE DATE THE LOAN IS MADE, AND ON THE SAME DAY OF EACH SECOND WEEK THEREAFTER; OR ( ) IN _____ EQUAL CONSECUTIVE SEMI-MONTHLY INSTALLMENTS OF $_____ EACH, COMMENCING NOT EARLIER THAN 10 DAYS NOT LATER THAN 45 DAYS FROM THE DATE THE LOAN IS MADE, AND ON THE SAME DAY OF EACH SEMI-MONTHLY PERIOD THEREAFTER, (ii) A FINE COMPUTED AT THE RATE OF 5 CENTS PER $1 ON ANY INSTALMENT WHICH HAS BECOME DUE AND REMAINED UNPAID FOR A PERIOD IN EXCESS OF 10 DAYS, PROVIDED (A) IF THE PROCEEDS TO THE BORROWER ARE $10,000 OR LESS, NO SUCH FINE SHALL EXCEED $5 AND THE AGGREGATE OF ALL SUCH FINES SHALL NOT EXCEED THE LESSER OF 2% OF THE AMOUNT OF THIS NOTE OR $25, OR (B) IF THE ANNUAL PERCENTAGE RATE STATED ABOVE IS 7.50% OR LESS, THE LIMITATIONS PROVIDED IN (A) SHALL NOT APPLY AND NO SUCH FINE SHALL EXCEED $25 AND THE AGGREGATE OF ALL SUCH FINES SHALL NOT EXCEED 2% OF THE AMOUNT OF THIS NOTE, AND SUCH FINE(S) SHALL BE DEEMED LIQUIDATED DAMAGES OCCASIONED BY THE LATE PAYMENT(S); (iii) IN THE EVENT OF THIS NOTE MATURING, SUBJECT TO AN ALLOWANCE FOR UNEARNED INTEREST ATTRIBUTABLE TO THE MATURED AMOUNTINTEREST AT A RATE EQUAL TO 1% PER MONTH AND (iv) THIS NOTE IS REFERRED TO AN ATTORNEY FOR COLLECTION, A SUM EQUAL TO ALL COSTS AND EXPENSES THEREOF, INCLUDING AN ATTORNEYS FEE EQUAL TO 15% OF THE AMOUNT OWNING ON THIS NOTE AT THE TIME OF SUCH REFERENCE, FOR SUCH NECESSARY COURT COSTS. THIS ACCEPTANCE BY THE BANK OF ANY PAYMENT(S) EVEN IF MARKED PAYMENT IN FULL OR SIMILAR WORDING, OR IF MADE AFTER ANY DEFAULT HEREUNDER, SHALL NOT OPERATE TO EXTEND THE TIME OF PAYMENT OF OR TO WAIVE ANY AMOUNT(S) THEN REMAINING UNPAID OR CONSTITUTE A WAIVER OF ANY RIGHTS OF THE BANK HEREUNDER.

IN THE EVENT THIS NOTE IS PREPAID IN FULL OR REFINANCED, THE BORROWER SHALL RECEIVE A REFUND OF THE UNEARNED PORTION OF THE PREPAID FINANCE CHARGE COMPUTED IN ACCORDANCE WITH THE RULE OF 78 (THE "SUM OF THE DIGITS" METHOD), PROVIDED THAT THE BANK MAY RETAIN A MINIMUM FINANCE CHARGE OF $10, WHETHER OR NOT EARNED, AND EXCEPT IN THE CASE OF A REFINANCING, NO REFUND SHALL BE MADE IF IT AMOUNTS TO LESS THAN $1. IN ADDITION, UPON ANY SUCH PREPAYMENT OR REFINANCING, THE BORROWER SHALL RECEIVE A REFUND OF THE CHARGE, IF ANY, FOR GROUP CREDIT LIFE INSURANCE INCLUDED IN THE LOAN EQUAL TO THE UNEARNED PORTION OF THE PREMIUM PAID OR PAYABLE BY THE HOLDER OF THE OBLIGATION (COMPUTED IN ACCORDANCE WITH THE RULE OF 78), PROVIDED THAT NO REFUND SHALL BE MADE OF AMOUNTS LESS THAN $1.

AS COLLATERAL SECURITY FOR THE PAYMENT OF THE INDEBTEDNESS OF THE UNDERSIGNED HEREUNDER AND ALL OTHER INDEBTEDNESS OR LIABILITIES OF THE UNDERSIGNED TO THE BANK, WHETHER JOINT, SEVERAL, ABSOLUTE, CONTINGENT, SECURED, UNSECURED, MATURED OR UNMATURED, UNDER ANY PRESENT OR FUTURE NOTE OR CONTRACT OR AGREEMENT WITH THE BANK (ALL SUCH INDEBTEDNESS AND LIABILITIES BEING HEREINAFTER COLLECTIVELY CALLED THE "OBLIGATIONS"), THE BANK SHALL HAVE, AND IS HEREBY GRANTED, A SECURITY INTEREST AND/OR RIGHT OF SET-OFF IN AND TO (a) ALL MONIES, SECURITIES AND OTHER PROPERTY OF THE UNDERSIGNED NOW OR HEREAFTER ON DEPOSIT WITH OR OTHERWISE HELD BY OR TO THE POSSESSION OR UNDER THE CONTROL OF THE BANK, WHETHER HELD FOR SAFEKEEPING, COLLECTION, TRANSMISSION OR OTHERWISE OR AS CUSTODIAN, INCLUDING THE PROCEEDS THEREOF, AND ANY AND ALL CLAIMS OF THE UNDERSIGNED AGAINST THE BANK, WHETHER NOW OR HEREAFTER EXISTING, AND (b) THE FOLLOWING DESCRIBED PERSONAL PROPERTY (ALL MONIES, SECURITIES, PROPERTY, PROCEEDS, CLAIMS AND PERSONAL PROPERTY BEING HEREINAFTER COLLECTIVELY CALLED THE "COLLATERAL"); ( ) MOTOR VEHICLE ( ) BOAT ( ) STOCKS, ( ) BONDS, ( ) SAVINGS, and/or_____

SEE CUSTOMER'S COPY OF SECURITY AGREEMENT(S) OR COLLATERAL RECEIPT(S) RELATIVE TO THIS LOAN FOR FULL DESCRIPTION.

IF THIS NOTE IS SECURED BY A MOTOR VEHICLE, BOAT OR AIRCRAFT, PROPERTY INSURANCE ON THE COLLATERAL IS REQUIRED, AND THE BORROWER MAY OBTAIN THE SAME THROUGH A PERSON OF HIS OWN CHOICE.

IF THIS NOTE IS NOT FULLY SECURED BY THE COLLATERAL MENTIONED ABOVE, AS FURTHER SECURITY FOR THE PAYMENT OF THIS NOTE, THE BANK HAS TAKEN AN ASSIGNMENT OF 10% OF THE UNDERSIGNED BORROWER'S WAGES IN ACCORDANCE WITH THE WAGE ASSIGNMENT ATTACHED TO THIS NOTE.

In the event of default in the payment of this or any other Obligation or the performance or observance of any term or covenant contained herein or in any note or other contract or agreement evidencing or relating to any Obligation or any Collateral on the Borrower's part to be performed or observed; or the undersigned Borrower shall die; or any of the undersigned become insolvent or make an assignment for the benefit of creditors; or a petition shall be filed by or against any of the undersigned under any provision of the Bankruptcy Act; or any money, securities or property of the undersigned now or hereafter on deposit with or in the possession or under the control of the Bank shall be attached or become subject to distraint proceedings or any order or process of any court; or the Bank shall deem itself to be insecure, then and in any such event, the Bank shall have the right (at its option), without demand or notice of any kind, to declare all or any part of the Obligations to be immediately due and payable, whereupon such Obligations shall become and be immediately due and payable, and the Bank shall have the right to exercise all the rights and remedies available to a secured upon default under the Uniform Commercial Code (the "Code".) in effect in New York at the time, and such other rights and as may otherwise be provided by the law. Each of the undersigned agrees (for the purpose of the "code") that written notice of any proposed sale of, or of the Bank's election to retain, Collateral mailed to the undersigned Borrower (who is hereby appointed agent of each of the undersigned for such purpose) by first class mail, postage prepaid, at the address of the undersigned Borrower indicated below three business days prior to such sale or election shall be deemed reasonable notification thereof. The remedies of the Bank hereunder are cumulative and may be exercised concurrently or separately. If any provision of this paragraph shall conflict with any remedial provision contained in any security agreement or Collateral receipt covering any Collateral, the provision of such security agreement of Collateral, the provision of such security agreement or collateral receipt shall control.

Acceptance by the Bank of payments in shall not constitute a waiver of or otherwise affect any acceleration of payment hereunder or other right or remedy exercisable hereunder. No failure or delay on the part of the Bank in exercising, and no failure to file or otherwise perfect or enforce the Bank's security interest in or with respect to any Collateral, shall operate as a waiver of any right or remedy hereunder or release any of the undersigned, and the Obligation of the undersigned may be extended or waived by the Bank contract or other agreement evidencing or relating to any Obligation or any Collateral may be amended and any Collateral exchanged surrendered or otherwise dealt with in accordance with any agreement relative thereto, all without affecting the liability of any of the undersigned. In any litigation (whether or not arising out of or relating to any Obligation or Collateral or other matter connected herewith) in which the Bank and any of the undersigned may be adverse parties, the Bank and each such undersigned hereby waives their respective right to demand trial by jury and, additionally, each such undersigned waives his right to interpose in any such litigation any counterclaim of any nature or description which he may have against the Bank. In addition, the Bank shall not be deemed to have obtained knowledge of any fact or notice with respect to any matter relating to this note or any Collateral unless contained in a written mailed, postage prepaid, or personally delivered to the Personal Finance Department of the Bank at its address set forth above. Each of the undersigned, by his signature hereto, hereby waives presentation for payment, demand, notice of non-payment, protest and notice of protest with respect to the indebtedness evidenced by this note, and each such undersigned hereby agrees that this note shall be deemed to have been made under and shall be construed in accordance with the laws of the State of New York. Each of the undersigned hereby authorizes the Bank to date this note as of the day the loan evidenced hereby is made to correct patent errors herein and, at its option, to cause the signatures of one or more co-makers to be added without notice of any prior obligor.

RECEIPT OF A COPY OF THIS NOTE, APPROPRIATELY FILLED IN, IS HEREBY ACKNOWLEDGED BY THE BORROWER

	FULL SIGNATURE	COMPLETE ADDRESS
BORROWER	_____	_____
WIFE OR HUSBAND OF BORROWER AS CO-MAKER	_____	_____
CO-MAKER	_____	_____
CO-MAKER	_____	_____

REVISED CITIBANK LOAN AGREEMENT FORM

Consumer Loan Note   Date _____ , 19 ____

(In this note, the words I, me, mine and my mean each and all of those who signed it. The words you, your and yours mean First National City Bank.)

Terms of Repayment To repay my loan, I promise to pay you _____Dollars ($_____). I'll pay this sum at one of your branches in _____uninterrupted _____ installments of $_____each. Payments will be due _____, starting from the date the loan is made.

Here's the breakdown of my payments:

1. Amount of the Loan $ _____
2. Property Insurance Premium $ _____
3. Filing Fee for
   Security Interest $ _____
4. Amount Financed (1+2+3) $ _____
5. Finance Charge $ _____
6. Total of Payments (4+5) $ _____

Annual Percentage Rate _____%

Prepayment of Whole Note Even though I needn't pay more that the fixed installments, I have the right to prepay the whole outstanding amount of this note at any time. If I do, or if this loan is refinanced - that is, replaced by a new note you will refund the unearned finance charge, figured by the rule of 78 - a commonly used formula for figuring rebates on installment loans. However, you can change a minimum finance charge of $10.

Late Charge If I fall more than 10 days behind in paying an installment, I promise to pay a late charge of 5% of the overdue installment, but no more the $5. However, the sum total of late charges on all installments can't be more than 2% of the total of payments or $25, whichever is less.

Security To protect you if I default on this or any other debt to you, I give you what is known as a security interest in my O Motor Vehicle and/or_____ (see the Security Agreement I have given you for a full description of this property), O Stocks, O Bonds, O Savings Account (more fully described in the receipt you gave me today) and any account or other property of mine coming into your possession.

Insurance I understand I must maintain property insurance on the property covered by the Security Agreement for its full insurable value, but I can buy this insurance through a person of my choosing.

Default I'll be in default:
1. If I don't pay an installment on time; or
2. If any other creditor tries by legal process to take any money of mine in your possession.

You can then demand immediate repayment of the balance of this note, minus the part of the finance charge which hasn't been earned figured by the rule of 78. You will also have other legal rights, for instance, the right to repossess, sell and apply security to the payments under this note and any other debts I may then owe you.

Irregular Payments You can accept late payments or partial payments, even though marked "payment in full", without losing any of your rights under this notice.

Delay in Enforcement You can delay enforcing any of your rights under this note without losing them.

Collection Costs If I'm in default under this note and you demand full payment, I agree to pay you interest on the unpaid balance at the rate of 1% per month, after an allowance for the unearned finance charge. If you have to sue me, I also agree to pay your attorney's fees equal to 15% of the amount due, and court costs. But if I defend and the court decides I am right, I understand that you will pay my reasonable attorney's fees and the court costs.

Comakers If I'm signing this note as a comaker, I agree to be equally responsible with the borrower, although you may sue either of us. You don't have to notify me that this note hasn't been paid. You can change the terms of payment and release any security without notifying or releasing me from responsibility on this note.

Copy Received The borrower acknowledges receipt of a completely filled-in copy of this note.

Signatures   Addresses

Borrower:_____   _____

Comaker: _____   _____

Comaker _____   _____

Comaker:_____   _____

Hot Line If something should happen and you can't pay on time, please call us immediately at (212) 559-3061.

Personal Finance Department
First National City Bank

Citibank's experience with the new loan agreement form illustrates just a few of the benefits to be gained when professionals are able to increase the speed and accuracy of the decisions they ask their audiences to make. To realize similar benefits, professionals must make it easy for their audiences to complete each of the six cognitive processes required in audience decision making—perception, attention, sentence-level comprehension, schema activation, information acquisition, and information integration.

Chapter 4 describes many of the stylistic choices available to professionals and explains how each choice either helps or hinders one or more of the cognitive processes involved in audience decision making. For example, an advertiser's choice of typeface, type size, and background color can determine how easily reading audiences perceive the words on a page. Similarly, a politician's speaking rate, volume, and prosody can determine how easily listening audiences perceive the words being spoken.

In addition to influencing the speed and accuracy of audience decision making, stylistic choices can affect how intuitively appealing and persuasive a document, presentation, or even a point made during a meeting is to an audience. The intuitive appeal of stylistic choices is the subject of Chapter 5. Other stylistic choices can affect the way the audience views the writer or speaker. Is she polite or impolite, confident or uncertain, friendly or aloof, credible or untrustworthy? Chapter 6 explores these choices.

Then there are those stylistic choices that appear to have little or no effect on audience decision making. For example, a study of employee responses to their managers' directives finds no correlation between the directives' organizational plans (inductive or deductive) and the likelihood that employees take the actions their managers request.[2] Likewise, a study of customer responses to sales letters finds no correlation between either the letters' formats (block, marginal message, or hanging indention) or the color of the letterheads (white, pink, yellow, blue, or green) and the number of orders customers place.[3] Similarly, a study comparing emailed versions of persuasive messages to printed versions finds no difference in the effects of email or print on the behaviors and perceptions of the message recipients.[4]

Aids to Perception

The first of the six cognitive processes required in audience decision making is perception. Professionals aid audience decision making when the words they write are easy for their readers to see, when the words they speak are easy for their listeners to hear and recognize, and when the elements of the graphs and charts they present are easy for their viewers to discern.

Legible Characters

Readers' perception of the text in a document or on a presentation slide depends first of all on the legibility of each letter or character of type in it. The legibility of each character of type depends on its print quality, type size, case, and typeface, as well as its contrast with the background. Poor print quality increases the amount of time it takes the audience to recognize letters and words.[5] The medium also influences legibility. For example, the legibility of text in e-books is inferior to that in paper books. Compared to audiences reading paper books, audiences reading e-books fixate longer, make more saccades, blink more, and suffer more from eye fatigue.[6]

High Contrast Between Type and Background

The greatest legibility is achieved when there is maximum contrast between the color of the type and the color of the background the type is printed or projected on.[7] Reading times are slower for color combinations with less tonal contrast between type and background (e.g., black type on a dark blue background) due to the reader's need to increase their eye-fixation frequency and pause duration. When the tonal shade of the background color is greater than 10%, readers have trouble discerning black type on it.[8]

Reversing the color of type (i.e., placing light-colored type against a dark background) can affect legibility, too. When the color of the type is reversed, as it is in many slide shows, the dark background makes the light type appear thinner than it actually is.[9] If the type color is reversed over long passages, reading speed may be reduced by up to 15%.[10]

Eleven-Point Type Size for Documents, 24 for Slides

The size of the type also affects how easily the audience can perceive letters and words. The most legible type size for a variety of typefaces, or fonts, in documents ranges from 9 points to 12 points.[11] Audiences read fastest when type sizes are between 9 and 12 points and tend to rate 11-point type as most legible.[12]

Slightly smaller type sizes may also be legible in some situations. For example, a study of newspaper print finds little difference in legibility for type sizes between 7.5 and 9 points.[13] Similarly, a study of instructional texts finds that type as small as 8 points is still legible for many readers.[14] Most studies agree that type sizes below 6 points are very hard to read.[15] However, one study finds the range of type sizes over which it is possible to read text at maximum speed extends all the way from 4 to 40 points as long as the reader is at the standard distance of 16 inches from the page.[16]

Twenty-four points is often the minimum type size recommended for the typical slide presentation. However, type as small as 16 points on slides may be legible to many viewers depending on the size of the screen and their distance from it.

Lower-Case Letters

Both headings and text are less legible when typed in all upper-case letters than when typed in both upper- and lower-case letters.[17] Because the outline of a capital letter is not as distinctive as the outline of a lower-case letter, reading speed is optimal when both upper- and lower-case letters are used and the use of all caps is avoided.[18] Words and phrases in all capital letters, such as those in Figure 4.1, take about 12% longer to read.[19] Headlines in all caps take between 13% and 20% longer to read.[20]

Italic type can also slow readers down.[21] Continuous prose in italic type takes readers about 5% longer to read than continuous prose in nonitalic type.[22]

Legible Typeface

Typeface, or font, can also affect legibility. A series of 11 studies of the effects of typography in which more than 11,000 readers took part finds readers prefer the most legible typefaces and their preferences for typefaces are highly correlated with reading speed.[23] Serif typefaces with their

BOTH HEADINGS AND TEXT ARE LESS LEGIBLE WHEN TYPED IN ALL UPPER-CASE LETTERS THAN WHEN TYPED IN BOTH UPPER AND LOWERCASE LETTERS.[17] BECAUSE THE OUTLINE OF A CAPITAL LETTER IS NOT AS DISTINCTIVE AS THE OUTLINE OF A LOWER-CASE LETTER, READING SPEED IS OPTIMAL WHEN BOTH UPPER-CASE AND LOWER-CASE LETTERS ARE USED AND THE USE OF ALL CAPS IS AVOIDED.[18] WORDS AND PHRASES IN ALL CAPITAL LETTERS TAKE ABOUT 12% LONGER TO READ.[19] HEADLINES IN ALL CAPS TAKE BETWEEN 13% AND 20% LONGER TO READ.[20]

FIGURE 4.1 A Paragraph in All Caps

curved or straight serifs added to the ends of letters (e.g., the word "APPLE" shown here in a serif typeface) and the more block-like sans serif typefaces (e.g., the word "**APPLE**" shown here in a sans serif typeface) are equally preferred by readers.[24]

Serif typefaces may be easier to read in continuous text than sans serif typefaces.[25] In other reading situations serif and sans serif typefaces are likely to be read equally quickly.[26] In a study comparing reader responses to serif and sans serif typefaces, adult readers read an instruction manual, tax form instructions, a business letter, and a short story all typeset both in serif and sans serif typefaces. Readers had no significant preference for sans serif versus serif typefaces overall. However, when readers read the highly segmented prose of the manual, much like the highly segmented bullet points of slide presentations, they preferred sans serif typefaces. When readers read the long continuous prose of the short story, they preferred serif typefaces. [27]

One reason readers in the study preferred serif typefaces for the short story may be that serif typefaces tend to evoke more emotion than sans serif typefaces. Readers asked to read satirical articles from *The New York Times* printed in serif typeface Times New Roman found the articles both funnier and angrier than when they read the same articles printed in sans serif Arial.[28]

No matter which typeface is chosen, consistent use of the same typeface increases reading speed,[29] as does the use of any standard typeface with letters of uniform proportions.[30]

Ten to 12 Words per Line

The number of words on each line affects the overall legibility of a page or a presentation slide. In documents, 10 to 12 words per line is optimal.[31] For most type sizes, that amounts to about 50 to 70 characters per line. A line length of 50 to 70 characters is also easiest for the eye to scan.[32] Keeping lines to 50 to 70 characters may mean typing two or more columns to a page. When lines of type are shorter or longer than 50 to 70 characters, readers decrease their normal rate of reading,[33] which for most adults is between 150 and 250 words per minute.

For internet articles displayed on computer screens, a medium line length of 55 characters per line supports faster reading than shorter lines and also produces the highest level of comprehension.[34] On presentation slides with type sizes no smaller than 24 points, bulleted lines of type will typically contain 55 characters or fewer.

Some Space Between Lines

Reading audiences read faster when text has 1 to 4 points of *leading*, or space between the lines, than when the type is *set solid*—when no space is inserted between the lines.[35] For a 10-point type size,

Reading audiences read faster when text has 1 to 4 points of *leading*, or space between the lines, than when the type is *set solid*—when no space is inserted between the lines.[35] For a 10-point type size, a space of 3 points is preferred. Type that is set solid has a dense appearance, like the type in many contracts and credit card agreements. Although readers dislike type that is set solid,[36] they also dislike type with too much space between the lines. However, an added blank line between paragraphs or between bullet points on slides and a blank space between columns of type can actually increase legibility.[37]

FIGURE 4.2 A Paragraph Set Solid

a space of 3 points is preferred. Type that is set solid has a dense appearance (see Figure 4.2), like the type in many contracts and credit card agreements. Although readers dislike type that is set solid,[36] they also dislike type with too much space between the lines. However, an added blank line between paragraphs or between bullet points on slides and a blank space between columns of type can actually increase legibility.[37]

Unjustified Right Margins

Text with unjustified right margins, or ragged edges, in documents or on presentation slides can be more legible than right-justified text that forms a straight margin down the right-hand side. In a study conducted at NASA, 61% of the readers surveyed preferred unjustified right margins to justified margins when reading technical reports.[38] A study of text presented online finds that unjustified right margins can increase online reading speed by 10%.[39] However, several other studies of adult readers find that justified and unjustified texts are read at similar speeds and with the same level of comprehension.[40]

Short, Familiar Words

Whether spoken or written, some words are more easily perceived and recognized than others. Easily perceived and recognized words include short words, high-frequency words, personal pronouns, concrete words, and words that are easy to pronounce.[41] Long, difficult to understand, and less frequently used words take longer to recognize[42] and are harder to remember.[43]

Semantic variables can also influence word recognition. For example, animate nouns such as *investors* are easier to process and recall than inanimate nouns such as *investments*.[44] A review of the psycholinguistic research concludes that the key to word difficulty in isolation lies not in word frequency but in the semantic variables of animateness, affirmativeness, and concreteness.[45]

Visible Speakers

Listeners' perception of speech involves sensing and recognizing both phonemes and complete words. Speakers who allow listeners to see their faces make it easier for listeners to recognize their words, especially in a noisy room.[46] Familiarity with a speaker's face also facilitates speech recognition, even for audience members with no hearing deficits.[47] In addition, when listeners are able to see a speaker's head movements, which are strongly correlated with the pitch and amplitude, or loudness, of the speaker's voice, they can more easily recognize the speaker's words and syllables.[48]

Appropriate Prosody, Intonation, and Articulation

A speaker's articulation, intonation, and prosody all impact the listener's ability to perceive and recognize the speaker's words. Appropriate prosody and intonation help listeners segment the continuous stream of sounds coming from the speaker into distinct and intelligible words.[49] Inappropriate prosody, on the other hand, can seriously impair word recognition[50] as can disfluent speech that includes frequent filler words, repetitions, false starts, and word fragments.[51] Almost any disruption to fluent speech can make it difficult for listeners to resume processing the speaker's words. However, silent pauses between words can actually help listeners recognize subsequent words.[52]

Listeners' perception of speech will also be impaired when phonemes and words are inaudible, garbled, or unfamiliar. Retention of the speaker's message can be affected as well. A test of listeners' memory for a message that contained six high-quality arguments supporting a recommended position finds that lowering the perceptibility of the message with a poor-quality audio recording reliably lowers message retention.[53]

Easy-to-Discern Graphic Elements

Viewers' perception of graphs involves both sensing and recognizing the graphic elements in them. Perceptual research indicates that small solid symbols such as triangles, squares, and circles often become difficult to perceive when clustered together in the same line graph.[54] On the other hand, distinctively shaped symbols such as a solid triangle, an "x," a solid circle, and an empty square are easy to discriminate.

The use of different colors, or color coding, can help viewers more rapidly discriminate elements of some graphs.[55] Color coding graphic elements provides the perceptual cues viewers need to recognize the different elements within a graph and to search the graph efficiently.[56] By making the different elements of maps more visually distinct, color coding improves map comprehension.[57] However, for people who suffer from color blindness, differences among color-coded items can be impossible to discern. In the United States, about 7% of the male population and 0.4% of the female population have trouble distinguishing red from green. Fortunately, black-and-white graphs with highly differentiated symbols are almost as easy for viewers with normal vision to discern as graphs that use color.[58]

Aids to Attention

The second of the six cognitive processes required in audience decision making is attention. Professionals aid audience decision making when they make text, speech, or graphics easy for their audiences to attend to.

Titles and Section Headings

Titles and section headings can attract attention both to themselves and to the sections of text they precede. They can affect what information in a document or slide presentation is attended to and how that information gets organized in the reader's memory.[59] In addition, differences in the size of section headings provide the most visible cue to the hierarchical organization of topics within a text.[60]

A large sample study of magazine advertising inserts finds that titles and section headings are often the only verbal elements of ad inserts to be attended to and read. About half of the consumers who received the ad inserts did not read them at all. Of the 50% who read an insert, most read only the insert's headlines.[61] A study of employees reading documents related to their work finds that employees normally fail to identify or recall any topics that are not reflected in the documents' section headings.[62]

Informative section headings are especially likely to increase readers' attention to and recall of information in a document.[63] In a test of the effects of informative section headings, consumers received four warranties for new TVs written in plain English that had no section headings and four warranties that included informative section headings. The section headings used were: "Who was covered? What was covered? What was not covered? What the manufacturer will do and for how long. What you must do. How to get warranty service." Although there was no difference in the time it took the consumers to read the warranties or in their comprehension of them, 90% of the consumers indicated that the warranties with informative section headings motivated them to pay attention to and use the information in the warranties.[64]

A study of print ads investigated the effects of incorporating consumers' decision criteria into the ads' headlines. After finding that scent was a decision criterion consumers used to select cooking oils, the study's author tested an ad headline for a fictitious brand of oil that read "Pleasantly Scented Cooper's Cooking Oil." The presence of a decision criterion for the product class in the ad's headline facilitated recall of that criterion and inhibited recall of other decision criteria for both expert and novice consumers of cooking oils. The author concludes that the format, rather than the content, of an ad directs attention and determines the decision criteria, or product attributes, consumers will recall later.[65]

Typographic Cues

Typographic cues can attract readers' attention as long as they are not overused.[66] For example, selective use of big print draws attention to keywords. It also enhances recall.[67] Printing warnings in bigger, bolder type than the other text in owner's manuals draws readers' attention to the warnings and leads to improved memory for them.[68]

In most contexts, boldface type attracts attention even more than upper-case type.[69] Used correctly, boldface is not only an effective attention-getting technique, it can also help readers comprehend information and follow directions more accurately.[70] Information in boldface is processed longer and recalled better than information in ordinary type.[71] Moreover, a normal level of boldface can be read as quickly as ordinary type.[72] Like boldface, italic type increases readers' attention to the text and the depth to which they process it.[73]

Selective color coding can also draw readers' attention to important ideas.[74] Color coding warnings increases their noticeability as well as the likelihood they will be read.[75] Color coding graphs can both increase attention to graphic elements and aid the audience's comprehension and recall by making key parts of the graphs perceptually salient.[76]

As a general rule, readers pay attention to contrast among typographic elements.[77] The use of too many different highlighting techniques can be confusing and can impair readers' understanding of the text.[78] When typographic cues are overdone, they may even have the opposite effect as was intended. For example, the extensive use of italic in continuous prose may make nonitalicized words more attention getting than the italicized words.[79]

Prominent Size and Placement

Size affects audience attention. For example, readers give more attention to larger magazine ads than to smaller ones.[80] Viewers give more attention to larger images than to smaller images. Larger images in ads also increase ad recognition.[81] When scanning the design elements of a product's packaging, consumers start by attending to the largest element of the package design and end by attending to the smallest.[82]

Placement also affects audience attention. Readers' attention to magazine ads increases when the ad is placed either on a right-hand page, on the cover of the magazine, or on one of the first few pages of the magazine.[83] Readers of expository texts spend more time reading text that is placed earlier in the document, earlier on each page, and earlier in each paragraph.[84] Consumers searching online usually give more attention to search results that appear at the top of the page than to those showing up beneath them.[85] Consumers exposed to product warnings are more likely to notice, read, and comply with warnings placed on the front of a product than warnings placed on the product's back or side or inside the owner's manual.[86] Similarly, warnings placed before instructions for carrying out a task are more likely to be noticed and read than warnings located after the instructions.[87]

In addition to being more attention getting, a well-designed document in terms of the size and placement of the elements within it can aid the comprehension of poorly motivated readers.[88] Attention-getting devices such as enumerated lists make readers more aware of the organization of the text and provide a retrieval plan that supports better recall of key ideas.[89] Ultimately, layouts and formats can affect the persuasive appeal of texts. A study of consumers reading different versions of product warning labels demonstrates that different formats have varying effects on consumers' intentions to take precautions.[90]

White Space

Audiences find documents and slides to be more visually appealing and attention getting if they incorporate white space. Documents with ample white space attract and hold readers' attention longer than those with little white space.[91] In addition, readers rate documents that use ample white space more highly. Newspaper readers rate news stories with wide margins as more appealing than the same stories with narrow margins and thus little white space.[92] Similarly, teachers rate instructional materials that use white space to separate sections more highly than instructional materials that do not.[93] For audience members with language difficulties, increasing the amount of white space in a document can even boost their comprehension of it.[94]

Personally Relevant Information

Whether presented in written or spoken form, some information is more attention getting than other information. Personally relevant information is especially attention getting[95] and has a greater impact on the audience's decisions than information that lacks personal relevance.[96] Neuroscientists find that personally relevant information activates more neurons in the brain than information that is less personally relevant. It is also linked to memories of a larger variety of experiences.[97]

Simply addressing the audience directly as *you* versus *one* can enhance personal relevance, increase audience attention, and improve their message processing.[98] Addressing the audience directly can also increase the persuasiveness of a message. In a test of differently worded pesticide warning labels, the version that used personal pronouns (e.g., statements beginning "You should . . . ") resulted in the highest levels of compliance.[99]

Information relevant to the audience's current goals and intentions is attention getting as well.[100] For example, information about food is attention getting to audiences who are hungry, and information about entertainment is attention getting to audiences who are bored.[101]

Concrete Words

The use of concrete words aids attention and makes the message more memorable. A study comparing abstract to concrete wording (e.g., *familiarization period* vs. *practice time*) tested readers' ability to recall four texts that described either a familiar or an unfamiliar topic and that were written either in a concrete or an abstract style. Each of the four texts contained the same number of sentences with the same sentence lengths and scored the same when rated for cohesion and readability. Readers recalled texts about familiar topics better when they were written in a concrete as opposed to an abstract style. What's more, readers recalled texts about unfamiliar topics written in a concrete style just as well as they recalled texts about familiar topics written in an abstract style.[102]

Sentences using concrete words are easy to visualize. In a test of the impact of high-imagery concrete verbs on students' recall, *Time/Life* editors revised a section of a history textbook, replacing less vivid verbs such as *increased* with high-imagery attention-getting verbs such as *skyrocketed*. The editors also added high-imagery anecdotes and quotations from other sources. Students' recall of the information in the textbook jumped by 40%.[103] Concrete wording, with its high-imagery value, is more memorable than abstract wording because it permits pictorial as well as verbal coding of the words in the text.[104] Moreover, audiences can read high-imagery sentences 30% faster on average[105] and can comprehend them more easily as well.[106]

Explicit Language

Explicit language is specific, detailed, clearly stated, and leaves little or nothing to the imagination. Like concrete wording, explicit language captures the audience's attention and aids their comprehension. Explicit language is also more persuasive than vague language. Recruitment literature using explicit language not only helps job seekers better comprehend their fit with an organization, it positively affects their intention to apply.[107]

Recently, explicit language has emerged as an important factor in warning effectiveness.[108] For example, the following two warnings both contain information about a health hazard, its consequence, and instructions for avoiding it. But which warning would be more effective in preventing a factory's employees from inhaling vapors that could lead to severe and permanent lung damage?

Warning A

Hazardous Environment
Potential Health Effects
Use Appropriate Precautions

Warning B

Toxic Chemical Vapors
Can Result in Severe Lung Damage
Always Wear a Respirator in This Area

Warning A is vague and generic. It is not explicit about what the specific safety problem is, its consequences, or what to do about it. Warning B, on the other hand, clearly specifies the hazard, the consequence, and the appropriate action to take.

Spoken vs. Written Messages

In most cases, spoken information is more attention getting, memorable, and persuasive than printed information. For example, employees are more likely to attend to and comply with voice warnings.[109] Job seekers are more likely to attend to spoken testimonials on recruitment websites than to print testimonials presented via photographs and text on the same websites.[110] They also find spoken testimonials to be more credible.

In a test of audience recall, TV commercials were compared to specially matched print advertisements that used an image from the commercial as the pictorial component of the ad and the verbatim audio script of the commercial as the ad copy. Audience recall was 81% for the TV ads versus 56% for the print ads. Recall of the main message point was 75% for the TV ads versus 39% for the print ads. The study's authors hypothesized that the superior performance of the TV commercials was due to the fact that they were more attention getting.[111]

Even attention-getting TV commercials are susceptible to "wear out" and are likely to be ignored when they are repeated too often.[112] Similarly, professors' lectures are likely to be ignored if the students listening to them already possess too much prior knowledge about the lecturer's topic.[113]

The Linguistic Style of the Powerful

The linguistic style in which a message is written or spoken can influence the amount of attention the audience gives it. In an often-cited study of speech styles, sociologist Bonnie Erickson and three colleagues first identified the linguistic cues that indicate the social status and power of speakers. They found the "powerless" style includes frequent use of linguistic features such as intensifiers (e.g., *very, really*), hedges (e.g., *probably, I think*), hesitation forms (e.g., *uh, and uh*), and questioning intonations, whereas the "powerful" style is marked by less frequent use of these features. The researchers then asked 152 undergraduates to listen to or read the testimony of a witness who used either a powerful or a powerless style to deliver the same substantive evidence. Both the listeners and readers of the testimony delivered in the powerful style paid greater attention to it than the listeners or readers of the testimony delivered in the powerless style.[114]

Expressive Nonverbal Behaviors

Certain types of nonverbal behaviors are also more attention getting than others. Vocal variety—including variations in tempo, pitch, intensity, and tone quality—increases listeners' attention to speech and improves their comprehension of the speaker's message.[115] Words spoken clearly and with feeling are also more likely to be persuasive than those spoken in a monotone.[116]

Faster speech is more attention getting as well. A test of listeners' attention varied a broadcast ad announcer's speech rate as he made an announcement. Increases in his speech rate led listeners to attend to the announcement more carefully and thereby enhanced their processing of it.[117] Other studies confirm that listeners pay more attention to and better comprehend messages that are delivered at rates 25% or 50% faster than normal conversational rates, which range from 100 to 150 words per minute.[118] However, more complex and difficult information must be spoken at a slower pace in order to avoid harming comprehension.

Expressive movements and gestures can also be attention getting. In a comparison of expressive and unexpressive nonverbal styles, undergraduates watched a video of a graduate student speaking against a ban on fraternities and sororities at a nearby college. The graduate student delivered her arguments either in an expressive or unexpressive nonverbal style. When the graduate student spoke using an expressive nonverbal style, she maintained constant eye contact with her audience, made appropriate hand and head gestures, made many facial expressions, and varied her tone of voice.

When she spoke using an unexpressive style, she made little eye contact, no hand or head gestures, few facial expressions, and spoke in a monotone voice.[119]

Undergraduates who watched the expressive nonverbal delivery reported they tried harder to attend to the speaker's arguments than students who watched the unexpressive delivery. In addition, the undergraduates who watched the expressive nonverbal delivery were better able to discriminate the strong arguments she made from the weak ones.

Relevant Images

Audience members are more likely to attend to and prefer documents and slide presentations that include relevant images and graphic elements in addition to text.[120] If documents or slide presentations contain no visually appealing images or graphics, some audience members may not attend to them at all.[121]

In a large-scale study of consumers' attention to ads, 300 adults were exposed to a total of 1,070 magazine ads. Consumers paid more attention to ads that had more photos and fewer words.[122] Other studies report similar findings. When online search results include images of the products consumers search for, consumers evaluate more products, review each product more carefully, and pay more attention to the accompanying text.[123] When cigarette warning labels include a graphic image of the health-related risks of smoking, consumers nearly triple the viewing time they would otherwise give the warnings.[124] Graphic images increase consumers' recall of warnings as well.[125]

Although any image is likely to be attention getting, some images are more attention getting than others. For example, viewers pay more attention to color than to black-and-white photographs and also rate color photographs as more attractive and recall more information from them.[126] Charts and graphs that effectively use contrast and color are also more attention getting than those that do not.[127]

Despite their many benefits, images must be chosen with some discretion. Clip art and other embellishments to slide presentations can actually reduce viewers' comprehension.[128] Merely decorative images in documents or slide presentations distract readers and viewers from the content,[129] and unlike relevant images, impair their memory for the important messages.[130] Vivid images aid message recall only when they are congruent with the message content. When vivid but incongruent images are added to a message, the audience's attention to the message is substantially reduced.[131]

Audience members may purposefully ignore otherwise attention-getting images when performing some tasks. For many tasks that computer users have to perform, the attention-getting quality of graphic elements on the screen does not predict their eye fixations.[132] For example, when job seekers search company websites for relevant information, they tend to focus less on the sites' graphic images and more on the site's text and hyperlinks.[133] Experts in a domain, as well as novices with a high initial interest in a domain, are especially likely to ignore images and to find them both distracting and redundant.[134]

Aids to viewers' attention to other people are treated separately in Chapter 6. Emotionally charged images that attract viewers' attention are explored in Chapter 7.

Aids to Sentence-Level Comprehension

Comprehension as defined in this section refers to the audience's comprehension of individual sentences as opposed to their comprehension of discourse—groups of sentences in paragraphs, whole documents, or presentations. Discourse comprehension depends on schema activation, the topic of the next section. As Chapter 3 explains, sentence comprehension involves three major subprocesses: syntactic analysis, semantic analysis, and referential representation.[135] Aids to each of these three subprocesses make sentence comprehension easier.

Short Words and Sentences

Aids to the first sentence-comprehension subprocess, syntactic analysis, make it easier for the audience to determine the grammatical role each word plays in a sentence. Because a rough measure of syntactic complexity is sentence length, longer sentences tend to be more difficult to comprehend than shorter ones.[136] Syntactic analysis becomes even more difficult when the individual words in a sentence are long, complex in meaning, or infrequently used.[137] Thus, two aids to sentence comprehension would appear to be the use of short sentences and easily understood short words.

Readability formulas implicitly advocate keeping words and sentences short as an aid to reading comprehension. The formulas use sentence length and word length to estimate the difficulty or ease of comprehending prose passages. Readability formulas are based on studies that show syntactic complexity and vocabulary difficulty account for a large proportion of the variance in reading comprehension.[138] Other studies show that sentence length and word length also determine reading speed.[139]

Three popular readability formulas are the Flesch readability formula,[140] the FOG index readability formula,[141] and the Dale-Chall readability formula (see Table 4.1).[142] All three formulas use word and sentence length as proxies for word familiarity and sentence complexity. The Flesch formula assigns passages of prose a reading ease score, 100 being the easiest and 0 being the most difficult. The FOG index and the Dale-Chall formula both assign passages a reading grade level from 1 to 12, 1 indicating that the passage could be understood by the typical first grader.

Other readability formulas such as the Flesch-Kincaid readability formula,[143] the New Dale-Chall readability formula,[144] Lexile,[145] and Degrees of Reading Power (DRP)[146] also use word and sentence length as proxies for word familiarity and sentence complexity.[147] Although not a perfect measure of reading difficulty, the New Dale-Chall formula may be the most valid of the popular traditional readability formulas.[148] The formulas that Lexile and DRP use to compute reading difficulty are not publically released, but their scores for texts are highly correlated with Flesch-Kincaid readability scores.[149]

Despite the fact that ideas expressed in short words and sentences are usually easier to comprehend than ideas expressed in longer words and sentences, it is debatable whether readability formulas are useful guidelines for revising difficult-to-comprehend sentences and discourse.[150] On the one hand, shortening long sentences has been shown to aid readers' understanding of written prose.[151] On the other hand, a number of studies show that improving readability as measured by readability formulas does not reliably affect readers' comprehension or recall of material.[152]

TABLE 4.1 How Three Readability Formulas Calculate Reading Ease

The Flesch readability formula calculates reading ease as follows: Reading ease =
206.835 – .846(number of syllables per 100 words) – 1.015(average number of words per sentence)

The FOG index is very similar: Reading grade =
.4(average number of words per sentence + percentage of words of more than two syllables)

In the Dale-Chall formula, word familiarity replaces syllable length: Reading grade =
.16(percentage of uncommon words) + .05(average number of words per sentence)

In one study, four texts were revised using a "writing to the formulas" approach. Readers given the revised texts did not find them easier to comprehend than the originals. When the four texts were revised a second time, changes that did make the texts easier to comprehend ran counter to what the formulas would suggest.[153] Similarly, a test of revised jury instructions showed that revised instructions that simply improved readability scores resulted in no greater comprehension than the original instructions.[154] A similar study tested car owners' comprehension of three versions of an automobile recall letter. The original version of the recall letter scored "difficult" on the Flesch scale. A revision of the recall letter lowered the score to "fairly easy." Car owners who read the revised letter did not have significantly better comprehension than those who read the original version.[155] For readability-based revisions to improve comprehension, the revisions must lower reading difficulty scores significantly. For formulas that calculate a grade level, the grade level must be lowered by at least 6.5 grades to have an impact on readers' comprehension.[156]

Simple Sentence Structure

One reason for the seemingly contradictory findings about readability formulas is that sentence length is only a rough measure of syntactic complexity.[157] Another cause of syntactic problems is the placement of phrases and clauses within a sentence. For example, sentences with subordinate clauses placed in the middle of them are more difficult to understand than sentences with clauses placed at the beginning.[158] Sentences with phrases added either to the beginning or middle are more difficult to comprehend than sentences with phrases added to the end.[159] And sentences with more embedded propositions take longer to read than less syntactically complex sentences of equal length.[160]

In addition to being imperfect measures of syntactic complexity, readability formulas do not measure other factors that also affect the audience's comprehension of a text. These factors include the text's organization and cohesiveness, the reader's prior knowledge of the topic, and how well the purpose of the text matches the purpose of the reader. In fact, readability formulas cannot distinguish a meaningful sequence of sentences from a sequence of randomly selected sentences. Even complete nonsense or scrambled sentences can score as very readable.[161]

Parallel Sentence Structure

Another aid to syntactic analysis in particular and to sentence comprehension in general is the use of *parallelism*, or the repetition of the syntax of a clause or sentence in the clause or sentence that immediately follows it. As illustrated in Table 4.2, parallelism is a technique job applicants often use when listing their accomplishments in their résumés. Notice how each bulleted sentence starts with an active verb in the past tense. Of course, job applicants are not the only ones

TABLE 4.2 Examples of Sentences Written in Parallel From an MBA's Résumé

- Achieved 100% increase in reporting and administrative productivity by developing local information system using database and corporate payroll software.
- Generated 30% increase in delivery reliability and 40% decrease in backorders from in-house supplier by implementing order entry process enhancements.
- Led team of marketing managers to redesign departmental structure. Increased customer focus through addition of product training and market analysis functions.

to use parallelism. Abraham Lincoln used parallelism to great persuasive effect in the Gettysburg Address (see pp. 73–74).

Sentences and clauses in parallel can be read and comprehended more quickly than those that are not.[162] In a study of readers reading parallel sentences, 72 undergraduates were timed as they read each sentence in a set of 60 sentences. Each sentence consisted of two clauses that either were or were not parallel. Each sentence also varied according to style (e.g., active voice versus passive voice, animate object versus inanimate object). For each style of sentence tested, the undergraduates read the second clause consistently faster when the first clause was parallel to it.[163] A similar study of readers reading parallel clauses in compound sentences demonstrates that when syntactic structures are the same in both clauses, recall is enhanced regardless of the particular syntactic form tested.[164]

Active Voice in Most Cases

Aids to the second subprocess in sentence comprehension, semantic analysis, make it easier for the audience to grasp the conceptual relationships, or case roles, among the words in a sentence such as the agent, object, instrument, or location.[165] In other words, they make it easier to determine who did what to whom. Semantic analysis is typically easier for audiences when sentences are written in the active voice than when they are written in the passive voice.[166]

Active voice sentence:	*Our firm made a profit.*
Passive voice sentence:	*A profit was made by our firm.*

In most cases, audiences not only find active sentences easier to comprehend than passive ones, they also find them easier to recognize and recall.[167] Passive sentences are especially difficult to understand when they give sentences the wrong focus.[168] For example, the passive sentence in the previous box would present even more difficulties to audiences in the context of a paragraph about "our firm" since its grammatical subject makes the focus of the sentence "a profit" as opposed to "our firm."

Sentences in which the verb expresses the action and the subject identifies the actor (as is the case for most but not all active sentences) are more concrete and easier for audiences visualize than other types of sentences. Thus, semantic analysis goes more smoothly when the action of a sentence is expressed as an active verb rather than as a nominalized verb[169] or as part of a multiple-word noun string.[170]

Action as a nominalized verb:	Our *expectation* was that we would get invited.
Actor as subject, action as verb:	*We expected* to get invited.
Action in a noun string:	*Event admittance tag distribution* took place yesterday.
Actor as subject, action as verb:	Yesterday, *someone distributed* tags that admit people to the event.

A think-aloud study of professionals reading hard-to-comprehend government regulations found that they spontaneously translated the abstract, passive-nominal sentences in regulations into concrete, active-verbal sentences in order to better comprehend their meaning. When the regulations were revised by making similar transformations, readers' comprehension increased.[171] The following before and after paragraphs illustrate this type of revision based on semantic analysis.[172]

Original Paragraph Written in an Abstract, Passive-Nominal Style

The Protocol Familiarization Period may be employed to run additional preliminary tests of the performance of the device. These tests may evaluate linearity, recovery, or any other feature not addressed in this document. The purpose of such preliminary acceptability tests should be the early discovery of any serious problems with the device. If such problems are encountered, the manufacturer should be contacted to determine the cause of error. No final judgment as to the acceptability of the device should be made from such limited tests.

Revised Paragraph Written in a Concrete, Active-Verbal Style

While practicing the experiment, you can also test other features of the equipment, such as linearity or recovery. Use these tests to see if there are any serious problems with the equipment. If you find any problems, contact the manufacturer to find out what is causing the problem. Don't decide if the equipment is acceptable solely on the basis of these limited, preliminary tests.

Passive Voice in Some Cases

When the object of the action is the intended focus of a sentence or paragraph, audiences find passive sentences easier to comprehend and recall than active sentences.[173] As illustrated in the following two pairs of sentences, passive sentences are more accurately comprehended than active ones when the preceding sentence contains the antecedent for the subject of the passive sentence.[174] In the first pair, both sentences are written in the active voice. In the second pair, an active voice sentence is followed by a sentence in the passive voice, yet sentence pairs like this are more quickly comprehended.

The batter hit the ball over the short stop. The left fielder caught it.
The batter hit the ball over the short stop. It was caught by the left fielder.

Sentences in the Affirmative

Avoiding the use of negative words in sentences (e.g., *not, none*) simplifies semantic processing and aids sentence comprehension. The use of negative words, on the other hand, makes sentence comprehension more difficult.[175] Negative words slow down reading speed[176] because a sentence must first be understood in the affirmative before negations can be integrated into the sentence meaning.[177] In a study of the effects of negative sentences on sentence comprehension, readers received cards with symbols on them and were asked to verify true and false affirmative and negative sentences about each card. Readers took longer to verify negative sentences than affirmative ones and longer to identify false sentences than sentences that were true.[178]

Easy-to-Identify Referents

The third subprocess in sentence comprehension is referential representation. This process identifies the references that words in a sentence make to the external world (e.g., understanding that the words *majority whip* refer to a member of Congress and not to an instrument for flogging the rest of us). The process also identifies the antecedents or referents of pronouns.

Referential representation is aided by making referents easy to identify. Readers take less time to identify the referent of a pronoun when the referent has been mentioned recently in the text.[179] Each sentence that comes between a pronoun and its antecedent increases the time the audience needs to assign a referent to it.[180] Each sentence that comes between a pronoun and its antecedent also increases the number of errors audiences make when they try to choose the correct referent.[181]

The likelihood that the audience will choose the correct referent can be increased by putting the word *the* in front of a repeated noun phrase.[182] It can also be increased by the use of a synonym. When a synonym is used in one sentence to refer to an object mentioned in the prior sentence (e.g., *jet* to refer to *airplane*), the time the audience needs to comprehend the sentence containing the synonym is no greater than if the same word had been used in it.[183] Repeating the referent instead of using a pronoun can actually slow down the comprehension process in some cases.[184] For example, after reading the sentence "Bill bought a car," readers take longer to comprehend the sentence "Bill drove it home" than to comprehend the sentence "He drove it home."

Repetition of Concepts Within Paragraphs

An additional aid to referential representation in particular and to comprehension in general is the repetition of concepts within a paragraph. The number of new ideas introduced in a paragraph creates more comprehension problems for audiences than either sentence length or word length.[185] Repeated concepts in a paragraph make it easier for readers to integrate their referential representations of the individual sentences in it into a coherent whole.[186] Repeated concepts can also decrease the time it takes to read a text.[187] Thus, readers take longer to read sentences in paragraphs that introduce many new concepts than to read sentences in which a few concepts reoccur repeatedly.[188]

Reading rate and recall both increase if the number of new ideas in a paragraph is lowered by including examples and paraphrases in the paragraph[189] or by restricting all the sentences in it to the amplification of just one or two main points.

Fluent Speech

Most aids to sentence comprehension are equally helpful to both readers and listeners. Other aids, such as fluent speech, are specifically helpful to listeners. Disfluent speech impairs sentence comprehension in a similar fashion as incorrect punctuation.[190] Fluent speech, with appropriate intonation and pauses, on the other hand, helps listeners correctly comprehend the meaning of the speaker's sentences.[191]

Interestingly, filler words, such as *uh* and *um* so often found in disfluent speech, can sometimes facilitate comprehension and recall because they usually signal that the speaker is about to change topics and say something new.[192] However, listeners generally infer that speakers who use filler words are less honest and less comfortable with the topic under discussion than those speakers who can avoid them.[193]

Congruent Nonverbal Behaviors

Hand gestures that are congruent with the meaning of the speaker's message can enhance listeners' comprehension of the message.[194] For example, listeners better understand speakers' answers to their questions about the size and relative position of objects when speakers gesture while verbally describing the objects.[195] Hand gestures can also aid listeners' comprehension in a deeper, less literal way. Spontaneous hand gestures produced along with speech often signal the syntactic subject of the speaker's sentence, the topic the speaker is focused on, and the elements of the schema the speaker has activated.[196]

Hand gestures can play an important role in listeners' comprehension and memory especially when the speaker's message is somewhat ambiguous. Emblematic gestures, such as the OK sign or extending two fingers to signal *two,* are particularly helpful in aiding memory for verbal information. One study found that listeners recalled 34% of a message when the speaker accompanied it with emblematic gestures, 11% when the speaker accompanied it with emphasizing gestures, and only 5% when the speaker did not make any gestures.[197]

Other congruent nonverbal behaviors, such as head nodding, eye movements, and lip and facial movements, can also improve listeners' comprehension of the speaker's message.[198] However, some types of information may be equally well understood even when listeners cannot see the speakers' nonverbal behaviors. Apparently, college students who listen to audio recordings of lectures can comprehend just as much of the lectures as those who attend the actual lectures.[199]

Pictorial Illustrations

In addition to capturing attention and promoting recall,[200] pictorial illustrations (e.g., photos, drawings, and video clips) in documents and presentations can aid sentence comprehension.[201] Pictures on warning labels, for example, both capture attention[202] and increase readers' comprehension of the warnings.[203] Whether pictorial illustrations of events and activities are static pictures, such as still photographs, or video footage, they can often enhance comprehension equally well.[204]

Pictorial illustrations are more likely to aid sentence comprehension when they provide visual referents to the words in the sentences audiences read or hear. Thus, related words and pictures presented together enhance comprehension and recall more than the same words and pictures presented separately.[205] A study of the effects of pictorial illustrations on learning finds that students given instructional materials combining text and pictures learn significantly more than those given the same materials without illustrations.[206] Moreover, a review of 46 experimental studies finds that in 81% of the studies, readers' comprehension was better for text and pictures than text alone. Readers with poor reading skills performed 44% better on average with text and illustrations than with text alone. More skilled readers performed 23% better.[207]

Pictorial illustrations will not enhance comprehension if they are irrelevant to the accompanying sentences[208] or if they are placed too far from the sentences to which they refer.[209] Neither will pictures enhance comprehension if their implications are redundant with the implications of the information presented verbally.[210] A study that compared seven different versions of a users' manual for a new telephone system found that the "words only" version enabled consumers to follow the instructions most quickly and accurately. Consumers actually had more difficulty following the instructions when pictures of the steps accompanied verbal descriptions of those same steps.[211] In a similar way, pictures of products can interfere with consumers' attempts to integrate verbal descriptions of the products' attributes and, as a result, negatively impact consumers' evaluations of the products pictured.[212]

The effects of pictorial illustrations on comprehension also depend on characteristics of the pictures themselves, such as the perspective from which they are taken.[213] When text and pictures intended to work together are poorly written, poorly visualized, contradictory, or not complementary, the audience's comprehension will suffer.[214] Comprehension will also suffer when the sentence or caption to which the picture refers captures the audience's attention before the picture captures their attention, particularly if the sentence or caption is high in visual imagery.[215]

The effects of pictorial illustrations on comprehension also depend on characteristics of the audience. In some cases, pictures only have a positive effect when the audience has little initial interest in the information presented.[216] In other cases, only novices in a domain will benefit from the addition of pictorial illustrations—experts may find pictures distracting.[217]

Graphs

Quantitative information is often easier for audiences to comprehend when it is presented in a graphic as opposed to a tabular or sentence format,[218] especially for those audiences with high graph literacy.[219] Health care consumers, for example, find risk/benefit information easier to comprehend and more helpful to their decision making when it is presented in a graphic format as opposed to either sentences or tables.[220] However, even a well-designed graph that highlights task-relevant information will have little effect on comprehension if the viewer lacks the domain expertise to interpret it.[221]

Viewers can comprehend most graphs more quickly if the plot lines, bars, pie segments, and other depictions of the data in them are labeled.[222] The use of legends or keys instead of labels makes graph comprehension more difficult and poses special demands on viewers' working memory.[223] Other impediments to graph comprehension include the use of arbitrary symbols such as stars, ships, castles, trees,[224] or faces.[225] Positioning graphs at the end of a document instead of in proximity to their mention can also decrease the audience's comprehension of them.[226]

Although the use of an attention-getting third dimension in charts and graphs does not necessarily reduce the viewer's accuracy or speed of making comparisons,[227] in general, two-dimensional graphs support viewer comprehension better than three-dimensional ones.[228]

Aids to Schema Activation

In order to fully comprehend and use the information in a paragraph, document, graph, image, or presentation, the audience must first activate the appropriate schema. Audiences must activate the appropriate schema regardless of the communicator's purpose—whether it is to inform, instruct, entertain, or persuade the audience to make a decision. Any contextual information—such as a title, section heading, or introductory paragraph—can help audiences activate the right schema. The right graph or picture can also activate the appropriate schema and portray the "big picture" at what seems like a single glance.[229]

Titles

Titles not only attract attention, they also activate readers' schemata and in doing so make text easier to comprehend and recall.[230] In a seminal study of titles and schema activation (described in detail on p. 121), readers were asked to make sense of an untitled paragraph. Although all the words and individual sentences were understandable, the paragraph as a whole seemed nonsensical to the readers until they were provided with its title "Washing Clothes." The title activated the appropriate schema for interpreting the various activities involved in washing clothes that were described in the paragraph.[231]

By activating the appropriate schema, titles help readers comprehend intersentence coherence within paragraphs and longer passages.[232] When a title indicates the text is about a topic for which the readers already possess the relevant background knowledge or schema, readers will even "remember" reading content that is not actually present in the text.[233]

By activating one schema as opposed to another, titles influence what information is recalled[234] and how that information is interpreted.[235] In other words, titles "frame" the information that follows them. In one experiment, readers were given paragraphs that could be interpreted in two different ways depending on the title that introduced them. For example, the same paragraph could be interpreted as being about "the worries of a baseball team manager" or "the worries of a glassware factory manager." The title that introduced the paragraph determined how readers comprehended it by making one schema more accessible to them than the other.[236]

Section Headings

Like good titles, good section headings not only attract attention, they also aid comprehension and recall by activating the appropriate schema.[237] Informative section headings help readers understand the prose content that immediately follows them.[238] Section headings also help readers identify the topics and organization of a text as they read.[239] In addition, section headings enable readers to more accurately summarize a text after they read it.[240] In a study of the effects of section headings, students were asked to read texts both with and without section headings. Students who read the texts with section headings had significantly higher scores on both comprehension and recall than those who read the same texts without the headings.[241]

Informative section headings in either statement or question form (e.g., "The Management Team Is Respected Industry Wide" versus "How Qualified Is the Management Team?") can help audiences recall and retrieve information from both familiar and unfamiliar texts.[242] But vague section headings can mislead readers. A study of government regulations found that the section headings of the original regulations were uninformative nouns and phrases: "Definitions," "General Policy," "Requirements," "Procedure," and "Use of Advance Payment Funds." When the uninformative headings were replaced with more informative ones (e.g., "Setting Up the Bank Account"), readers performed significantly better both in predicting what information would follow each heading and in matching headings with the appropriate text.[243]

Topic Sentences

Topic sentences are another aid to schema activation and comprehension. Starting a paragraph with a topic sentence improves both reading speed and accuracy of recall, it also enhances the reader's ability to identify the main point of the paragraph.[244] Systematically grouping sentences by topic produces better recall than arranging sentences randomly.[245] Hierarchically structuring major points before minor points makes prose easier to recall as well.[246]

An Introductory Decision Matrix

Novice audience members who have never made a particular type of decision before need to be educated about the appropriate schema before they can activate it.[247] A think-aloud study of novices reading revisions of a policy for automobile liability insurance found that the novices had difficulty comprehending the first revision even though it solved all of the lexical and structural problems in the original policy. The novices often raised the wrong questions about the revised policy. For example, they asked why the policy did not mention deductibles and their own injuries and damages. The researchers concluded that the novices lacked the appropriate schema for understanding the different types of car insurance.

To provide the needed schema, the researchers started the final revision of the policy with a matrix that described and contrasted different types of car insurance. Although the final revision was four times as long as the original policy, it took the novices only half the time to read. In addition, the final revision had a comprehension error rate of 22% versus an error rate of 40% for the original. Moreover, the final revision evoked no complaints from the novices, whereas the original prompted many.[248]

Initial Contextual Information

Any initial contextual information—titles, section headings, topic sentences, agendas, outlines, as well as previews that combine graphics and text—can enhance comprehension and recall of documents and presentations.[249] Starting a document or presentation with an overview of its purpose can also enhance comprehension and recall. Such overviews aid comprehension because they enable the audience to activate the appropriate schema.[250] Placing recommendations and conclusions at the beginning of documents and presentations, also known as placing the "Bottom Line Up Front" or BLUF, serves a similar function and is standard practice for many U.S. military personnel.

For contextual information to have a positive effect, it must be presented first, before the rest of the message is delivered. In a test of the sequencing of contextual information, 48 undergraduates were asked to listen to two ambiguous passages about familiar topics. Half of the listeners received the contextual information required to activate the appropriate schema either just before or just after hearing the passages. The other half received either no contextual information or inappropriate contextual information about the passages. Listeners who were given the appropriate contextual information prior to hearing the passages had significantly higher recall of the material than the other groups. Listeners given inappropriate contextual information recalled even less material than those given no contextual information.[251] A similar study finds that readers who are given a title at the end of a message show no better recall than those who are not exposed to a title at all.[252]

It is important to note that introductory contextual information may fail to increase comprehension and recall if it is inconsistent with the audience's existing schemata.[253] A study of medical patients reading health care pamphlets found that conflicts between the pamphlets' introductory statements and the patients' existing schemata hindered patients' comprehension of the information in the pamphlets.[254] The study's authors recommend relating new information in health care pamphlets to patients' current schemata.

Genre Labels

When documents and presentations are introduced with a genre label such as *strategic plan*, *medical report*, or *sales pitch*, audience members may activate a genre schema that influences their understanding and recall of the information they subsequently read or hear.[255] As linguist Ronald Langacker explains,

> Our knowledge of a given genre consists in a set of schemas abstracted from encountered instances. Each schema represents a recurring commonality in regard to some facet of their structure: their global organization, more local structural properties, typical content, specific expressions employed, matters of style and register, etc.[256]

In a study of a genre schema's effect on recall, one group of college students received instruction in the schema of scientific journal articles, a genre with which they were initially unfamiliar. A second group received no schema instruction. The group that received instruction in the schema of the genre recalled five times as much information from a scientific article they subsequently read as the second group.[257]

Different genre labels can lead to different understandings of the same information. A test of the effects of genre labels on comprehension found consistent differences in readers' interpretations of stories when they were told the story was an autobiography versus a work of fiction.[258] A similar study found differences in the audience's interpretations of stories that were labeled either as spy stories or travelogues.[259] Depending on the genre schema activated, even the same sentence can serve very different functions. For example, in a news report, the statement "The Bellagio hotel in Las Vegas cost $1.2 billion to build" functions to describe the amount of money it costs to build the hotel. In an ad, the same sentence provides a reason for the audience to visit it.[260]

The two mailings on the following pages from a city's Chamber of Commerce illustrate the importance of genre labels and genre-specific textual features in eliciting the desired decision (note: the dates, the numbers, and the names and addresses of the Chamber and Chamber member have been changed). Although both mailings had the same purpose, to collect dues from Chamber members, their effectiveness varied significantly. The number of Chamber members who paid their dues on time more than doubled when the revised letter was sent out in place of the original. The Chamber member's think-aloud comments about the original mailing indicate he was making a budgetary decision rather than the compliance decision the Chamber wanted from him. He saw the mailing as more of a request for a donation than as a financial obligation that must be paid on time.

The revised mailing is titled with the label of the genre of the mailing—*Invoice*. In addition, the revised mailing includes textual features that are characteristic of that genre: It uses an invoice format as opposed to a letter format; it is addressed to a specific person in the accounts payable department who is responsible for paying the bills; and it demands, rather than requests, payment of the amount due.

ORIGINAL MAILING WITH A CHAMBER MEMBER'S COMMENTS

Titusville Chamber of Commerce
100 Main Street, Titusville, NC 27401

May 15, 2015

Nanolinc, Inc.
445 Technology Drive
Titusville, NC 27401

Dear Chamber Member, **[1. This letter's sent to a Chamber member. It has my address on it, but it doesn't have my name.]**

Your membership in the Chamber of Commerce is set to expire at the end of this month. Please detach the lower portion of this billing and submit it with your annual dues payment of $1,250.00 to:
[2. It sounds like, reading this letter … I feel it's very … It's not personalized.]

Titusville Chamber of Commerce
100 Main Street
Titusville, NC 27401

We appreciate your continued support. **[3. So I have continued to pay. 4. It doesn't create any urgency for me to pay this bill. 5. So I feel that I don't have to pay this right away. I can probably hold on to it for a little while with no repercussions and maybe pay it next quarter instead of this lump sum hitting on this quarter. So I think I'll hold on to this until, oh, until the third quarter at least. And then I'll pay my dues for the Chamber.]**

- -

Please find enclosed $1,250.00. This amount is payment in full of the dues for:

Nanolinc, Inc.
445 Technology Drive
Titusville, NC 27401

REVISED MAILING

INVOICE

Invoice No: 100066

Date: May 15, 2015

From: **Titusville Chamber of Commerce**

100 Main Street

Titusville, NC 27401

Phone (336) 437-4500

Fax (336) 437-4503

To: Ms. Judy Hamric

Accounts Payable

Nanolinc, Inc.

445 Technology Drive

Titusville, NC 27401

Your Chamber membership is set to expire on May 30, 2015.

Length of membership renewal............   One year

TOTAL AMOUNT DUE................... $1,250.00

Plus additional contributions.............. $

Amount of payment........................ $

Please make checks payable to the Titusville Chamber of Commerce. Or try our new "Pay by Phone" service using a major credit card.

Questions about this statement? Call (336) 437-4500

Thank you for your continued support

Captions for Images

Similar to the way titles and headings aid text comprehension by activating the appropriate schema, captions can aid the activation of schemata needed for comprehending pictures and graphs. For this reason, students reading science textbooks with captioned illustrations can outperform those reading the same textbooks with illustrations that lack captions.[261] Captioned pictures are especially effective at capturing readers' attention. When a caption about health risks accompanies graphic imagery on cigarette packets, readers cannot easily divert their attention away from the packets' warning labels.[262]

Captions can also dramatically increase viewers' recall. In an innovative study of the importance of captions to image recall, viewers were invited to look at two sets of line drawings of unintelligible objects called "droodles." A droodle is a hard-to-interpret drawing that has a funny meaning.[263] One set of drawings included explanatory captions for each drawing, the other set did not. Viewers recalled 70% of the captioned drawings, but only 51% of the drawings without captions. The authors conclude that a good memory for drawings and pictures depends on the audience's ability to interpret their meaning.[264] The two droodles in Figure 4.3 lack captions. Can you guess what is depicted in them?

The strategic use of captions can change how viewers interpret the pictures and charts they see.[265] For example, a chart depicting a sharp rise in a firm's stock price may have a dramatically different effect on investors than normal if its caption reads "Short-term gains have already happened." In case you're still wondering, Droodle A is "A duck playing a trombone in a telephone booth." B is "An early bird who caught a very strong worm."

Aids to Information Acquisition

After the appropriate schema for making a decision has been activated, audience members begin the information-acquisition process and start searching for the information their schema requires. Section headings, global organizations, and formats that are schema based, or *task based*, can aid the audience's information-acquisition process.

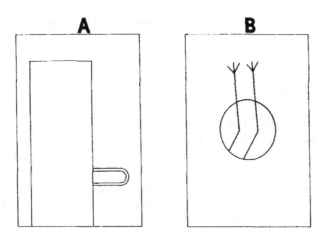

FIGURE 4.3 How easy are these drawings to comprehend without captions?

Source: Bower, Karlin, and Dueck (1975, p. 217)

Task-Based Section Headings

Task-based section headings reflect the structure and content of the audience's schema for performing a task such as operating a computer, comprehending the gist of a story, or deciding which insurance policy to buy. When instruction manuals lack task-based headings, users have difficulty locating the specific help they need. Their comprehension is negatively affected as well.[266] But when headings address the key questions or criteria from the audience's activated schema, readers can quickly locate the information they need to complete their task. [267] For an example, see the "Revised Executive Summary of a Business Plan with an Investor's Comments" on pp. 14–15.

Task-Based Formats

Audiences prefer information to be expressed in a format that helps them complete their task as efficiently as possible. Consequently, audiences sometimes prefer information to be expressed in prose as opposed to chart form, as was the case for the experienced board member who commented on the strategic plan for GM in Chapter 2:

> **19. I'm on Section 9 looking at the McKinsey Nine Box Grid: Business Strengths, Industry Attractiveness. They indicate that they are moving from a low industry attractiveness today, to what they feel will be midpoint in the future with average business strengths. This kind of summary to me is not worth the paper it's written on. It could be stated in a sentence. You don't have to use a chart.**

At other times audiences prefer charts to prose, as was the case for the experienced investor who commented on the financial analyst's report on Georgia Gulf in Chapter 2:

> *Salt* supplied from Georgia Gulf's leased salt domes in Louisiana, is split into *chlorine, caustic soda, and sodium chlorate.* Annual merchant-sales capacity for these products is 118,000 tons, 501,000 tons, and 27,000 tons, respectively. **[28. I'd prefer that they told me what it was for each product, like 118,000 tons of chlorine, rather than otherwise.]** The average prices of these commodities, which are collectively *Inorganic Chemicals* are estimated at $140 per ton, $95 per ton, and $335 per ton. **[29. Again, they should just chart this for me. It would be much easier to see.]**

The best format for presenting any information—whether as a diagram, list of bullet points, paragraph, table, or chart—varies with the purpose of the information and the task that the audience is asked to perform.[268] For example, graphs are a better format for helping the audience interpret trends than tables.[269] The best graph for any particular task is one that represents task information most explicitly.[270] Because line graphs explicitly display trends and continuous data,[271] viewers are more accurate in retrieving $x–y$ trend information from line graphs than from other types of graphs.[272]

Even expert performance can be enhanced with task-based formats. Expert plant operators perform at significantly higher levels when they monitor plant processes using task-based displays instead of traditional schematic displays.[273] Experienced intelligence analysts come to less biased conclusions when they use task-based graphical layouts to weigh evidence than when they attempt to weigh evidence presented as text.[274]

If the audience needs to perform a task that requires them to act in a particular way, a live or video demonstration may be most helpful. For example, student teachers learn more about interacting with students by watching video examples of experienced teachers in the classroom than by reading narrative texts that describe teacher–student interactions.[275] Similarly, medical students learn more from video presentations of a patient's case than from text narratives of the same case.[276] Viewers of on-screen instructions find animated demonstrations of procedures that involve motion to be clearer and easier to follow than static graphics.[277] However, static graphics inserted into video animations can increase viewers' comprehension and recall of more complex procedures.[278]

When their task is to choose among many different products, consumers prefer visual depictions to verbal descriptions of products regardless of the number of products they are choosing among. Consumers prefer visual depictions even when there is no natural visual representation of the product category (e.g., mutual funds) and even when verbal descriptions facilitate greater product differentiation (e.g., differentiating among nail polishes in a similar color). For large choice sets of unfamiliar products, visual depictions help consumers scan the alternatives faster. However, visual depictions may also lead them to make less thorough product comparisons and may even decrease the likelihood they make any choice at all.[279]

Task-Based Organization

Similar to task-based section headings and formats, a task-based organization of the contents of a document or presentation can help the audience locate the information it needs when it needs it. Users find training manuals easier to follow when the contents of the manuals reflect the structure of the task they are trying to perform.[280] Manuals and other forms of instructions that use a task-based organization are both faster to use and require fewer examples and elaborations to be effective.[281]

When the audience's task is to comprehend and recall, an organizational structure that adheres to the appropriate genre schema promotes efficient information acquisition. For example, newspaper readers find newspaper articles easier to comprehend when the articles adhere to the "newspaper schema"—headlines, leads, major events, consequences, commentaries, and evaluations.[282] College students read history texts faster when the texts follow the standard organizational sequence of goal-attempt-outcome as compared to a reordered sequence.[283] In a study of story recall, one group of readers read a story written in the conventional way and another group read the same story with its sentences presented in a scrambled order. Readers who read the story in its original order, an order that conformed to their story schema, recalled 85% of the facts in it. Those who read the story in the scrambled order recalled only 32% of the facts in it.[284]

A task-based organization will be less effective if the layout of the document or presentation slides does not make that organization clear. Audiences make inferences about the intended reading sequence and organization of a text based on its layout on the page or presentation slide. Unfortunately, the audience's inferences about the intended reading sequence do not always match the intended reading sequence of the writer.[285] A study of science textbooks, for example, found their page layouts often made it difficult for students to determine the order in which the information was intended to be read. Students' actual reading order was quite different from the order the textbook writers intended.[286] Readers can more easily see the organization of a text when the layout keeps the number of different line lengths to a minimum.[287] Readers can also make more accurate

TABLE 4.3 Expert Audiences Expect Information to Be Presented in a Specific Order

Expert investor reading the original *Smartphone MBA* business plan
9. When I read these things I like to start off with the people involved. Is there anything in here about the background of the guy who is going to be the General Partner? <The investor then finds the General Partner's résumé in an appendix.> Oh, here he is.

Partner in a private equity firm reading the acquisition plan for a textile manufacturer

12. What I usually like to see is a snapshot of the company, which it doesn't appear that they have. Just the company's financials, their sales, operating income at least, those two things, at least for the last three years. Depreciation and capital expenditures . . . some things to give an idea of cash flows. They make you flip to the back to look through the numbers, which I will do now. <The expert now turns to read Schedule A in the appendix.>

Experienced board member reading the strategic plan from General Motors

10. Under "Most Relevant Competitors," they've listed their own and the three major competitors' vehicle sales growth, three-year average, the three-year profitability, and market share. Again it's just a listing of data with no insights. My sense of a good strategic plan is that what one begins with is this data. One does not present data like this as a summary.

decisions when the layout of a text makes the more important pieces of information in it more attention getting.[288]

The think-aloud remarks in Table 4.3, made by three experts whose comments we saw in Chapters 1 and 2, reveal the importance of task-based organization. All three experts express their frustration with the organization of the documents they are reading. Notice that the investor and the partner in the private equity firm do not wait until they run across the information they expect to be delivered, but immediately start thumbing through the long documents they have been given until they discover it.

Many documents and presentations are topic based as opposed to task based. Topic-based documents and presentations are organized around the concepts the communicator thinks are important instead of the sequence in which the audience needs information to be presented. Topic-based documents and presentations create problems for audiences who try to use them to perform specific tasks such as make a decision or follow a set of instructions. In a study of readers' difficulties with topic-based organization, three experts read a topic-based federal regulation about eligibility for Small Business Association grants and thought aloud as they read. It so happened that one of the experts tried to use the information in the regulation to determine her own business's eligibility for a grant. During the experiment she actively searched for the information she needed. The other two experts simply followed the organization of the regulation as they read and interpreted it. The expert who actively searched for information that would help her decide if she were eligible for a grant made many more negative comments about the organization of the regulation and about the difficulty of her search process than the other two experts. In fact, 50 of her 200 comments were complaints about the organization of the regulation.[289]

The two versions of the instructions on the following pages illustrate the difference between topic-based and task-based organization. Both versions describe the five steps soldiers must take if they are to respond quickly and effectively to chemical, biological, or radioactive attacks. However, one would expect the effectiveness of the two versions to vary considerably if soldiers were to use them to respond to an actual attack.

A careful reading of the original, topic-based instructions on p. 173 reveals that the first step is not mentioned until Sentence 10, toward the end of the long, 14-sentence paragraph. The final step is mentioned in Sentence 2 near the beginning. The second step is spread throughout the paragraph in Sentences 1, 3, 8, 9, 12, 13, and 14. The student revision on pp. 173–174 reorganizes the five steps in a task-based manner. It adds a section heading to each step. The revision also uses other techniques mentioned in this chapter—11 point and larger type sizes, moderate line length, a captioned image, ample white space, personally relevant information, explicit language, short words and sentences, active voice, parallel sentence construction, and a schema-activating title—all of which make it easier for the reader to perceive, attend to, comprehend, and ultimately follow the instructions.

TOPIC-BASED INSTRUCTIONS
(Source: Kern et al. 1977)

CBR: THE LOCAL ALARM

The local alarm (warning) is given by any person recognizing or suspecting the presence of a CBR hazard. Unit SOPs must provide for the rapid transmission of the warning to all elements of the unit and to adjacent units. Brevity codes should be used where feasible. Suspicion of the presence of a chemical hazard is reported to the unit commander for confirmation. It is important to avoid false alarms and to prevent unnecessary transmission of alarms to unaffected areas. Consistent with the mission and circumstances of the unit, the alarm will be given by use of any device that produces an audible sound that cannot be easily confused with other sounds encountered in combat. Examples of suitable devices for local alarms are empty shell cases, bells, metal triangles, vehicle horns, and iron pipes or rails. As a supplement to the audible (sound) alarms or to replace them when the tactical situation does not permit their use, certain visual signals are used to give emergency warning of a CBR hazard or attack. These visual signals consist of donning the protective mask and protective equipment, followed by an agitated action to call attention to this fact. In the event of a chemical agent attack, there is a danger of breathing in the agent if the vocal warning is given before masking. The individual suspecting or recognizing this attack will mask first and then give the alarm. The vocal alarm for chemical agent attack will be "SPRAY" for a spray attack and "GAS" for an attack delivered by other means. The vocal warning is intended for those individuals in the immediate vicinity of the person recognizing the attack. The vocal alarm does not take the place of the sound alarm or the visual signal to alert a unit of a chemical attack.

TASK-BASED INSTRUCTIONS

CBR: Chemical, Biological, Radioactive

What to do in a CBR attack

"Fast action can save your life!"

Step 1: Protect yourself

Put on your gas mask. Make sure there are no gaps between your face and mask. If needed, put on other protective gear.

Step 2: Alert your neighbors

If the enemy sprays chemicals, shout "Spray!" For other attacks, shout "Gas!" Make sure the soldiers near you start to put on their masks.

If the soldiers near you don't hear you, signal to them by waving your arms and pointing to your mask.

Step 3: Alert your entire unit

Alert the rest of your unit by banging on empty cases, ringing bells, or honking horns. Make sure all unit members start to put on their masks.

Step 4: Alert your unit commander

Run to your unit commander. Wave your arms and point to your mask. Make sure your commander sees you and nods.

Step 5: If your commander gives the "OK," alert units nearby

If your unit commander decides you are under a CBR attack, follow their instructions for alerting neighboring units.

Attribute-Based Organization for Decision Making

When the audience's task is to make a decision, as opposed to follow instructions or comprehend a story, the best organization for a document, presentation, or meeting is one that promotes attribute-based processing and addresses each decision criterion in the audience's decision schema one by one. For an example, see "An MBA Team's Strategic Plan Slides" on pp. 55–57.

Information that is organized to promote attribute-based processing makes the audience's task of comparing different alternatives cognitively easier[290] and less prone to error.[291] It also helps consumers make difficult trade-offs among alternative products.[292] When product information is displayed to facilitate attribute-based, processing consumers tend to choose on the basis of product quality. When the same information is displayed to facilitate alternative-based processing, consumers' choices tend to be driven by price.[293] Ultimately, information that is organized to promote attribute-based processing helps audiences make more accurate decisions more efficiently.[294]

When audience members are allowed to choose an information-acquisition strategy, the better decision makers among them tend to acquire and process information by attribute.[295] For example, better performing financial analysts generally engage in more "between-stock" attribute-based search when choosing stocks. They select one attribute, such as earnings per share, and check its value for all stocks they are considering before moving on to check the values of all those stocks for the next attribute, such as long-term debt. Poorer performing analysts engage in more "within-stock" alternative-based search. They first select one stock and check its value on all attributes of interest, such as earnings per share, long-term debt, 52-week high, etc. Then they form an overall, holistic judgment of that particular stock before moving on to do the same for the other stocks.[296]

Although attribute-based processing affords many advantages, most audience members, especially those who are novices, generally acquire and process information in the order in which they receive it.[297] When criteria for deciding among several alternatives are displayed simultaneously, audiences tend to process by attribute. But when alternatives are displayed sequentially (as they are in newspaper advertisements for competing brands), audiences tend to process by alternative.[298]

Audiences process information in the order it is presented to reduce the cognitive effort involved in decision making.[299] A study of the eye movements of consumers reading product packages finds that package formats make processing by alternative easier. In that study, fully 50% of the consumers' eye transitions were by brand (i.e., using alternative-based processing) and only 17% by attribute.[300] Unfortunately, alternative-based organization, as found in package formats and point-of-purchase displays, hinders the ability of consumers to make product comparisons and negatively affects their ability to choose the best product.[301]

Decision Matrices

One format that facilitates attribute-based decision making is the matrix format.[302] Although matrices are usually displayed as tables, both documents and presentations can reflect the matrix format and promote attribute-based processing if they address each decision criterion in the expert audience's schema one by one.

Note that all of the revised documents and effective presentation slides reproduced in this book, to a greater or lesser extent, reflect a decision matrix in verbal form. When done right, the decision criteria from the audience's schema become the document's or slide presentation's outline. Keywords from the audience's decision criteria are incorporated in section headings or slide titles. Paragraphs, charts, and bullet points answer the audience's questions about each criterion and provide benchmark information for evaluating the recommended alternative.

Consumers almost always process by attribute when information about unfamiliar brands is displayed in a matrix format.[303] They also make better decisions when they do. When pricing information for competing brands is displayed in a matrix format in grocery stores, the average consumers saves about 2% more than when they view the same pricing information displayed on separate tags for each item.[304]

The matrix format outperforms other formats in terms of reducing the time it takes audiences to make a good decision. In a test of the matrix format, 60 MBA students were asked to choose the best loan application from different sets of eight loan applications. Each set of applications described four relevant attributes or criteria and presented them in six different ways: organized either as a matrix or as a list, with values expressed in either verbal or numeric form, and arranged in either a sorted or random sequence. The matrix versus list organization strongly influenced the MBAs' information-acquisition process and provided the largest benefit in terms of the time required to make a good decision.[305]

Another benefit of the matrix format is that it promotes rational as opposed to intuitive or emotional decision making. When evaluating options separately, audience members tend to prefer the most emotionally vivid option.[306] But when audience members compare options simultaneously in a matrix format, they are more likely to engage in logical, deliberate processing and thus to make more rational decisions.[307] They are also more likely to become aware that relevant information is missing and to correct any evaluation errors they previously made.[308]

Switching the format from a sequential one to a simultaneous overview of all the relevant information, as the matrix format provides, also reduces the confirmation bias.[309] When audience members access attributes about each alternative in a sequence, the current best alternative distorts their view of the next attribute. Simultaneous presentation of all attribute values for multiple alternatives, on the other hand, reduces such distortion.[310] Unfortunately, the matrix format does not eliminate all bias from audience decisions. In fact, product comparison matrices actually create one particular bias: Consumers have a bias for products presented in the far right-hand column of such matrices and perceive products presented in columns to the left more negatively.[311]

Aids to Group Information Acquisition and Critical Thinking

Access to more and better information for decision making is the *raison d'être* of most groups, yet group members rarely discuss any relevant information that is not already known by the group as a whole.[312] Surprisingly, groups will often ignore the expertise of their most knowledgeable members.[313] Thus, groups seldom realize the knowledge gains and improved decision quality they hope for.[314]

Information acquisition and decision making can be more effective when the group is small (four as opposed to eight group members) and the amount of information possessed in common by its members is minimal.[315] If given enough time, groups usually overcome their tendency to discuss commonly shared information and start to discuss more information that initially is known only by single individuals within the group.[316] Under time pressure, groups place much more emphasis on information that all members share and consequently focus on fewer alternatives.[317]

Groups whose members propose different alternatives and have more disagreements communicate more unshared information.[318] They also produce better decisions than groups whose members all prefer the same alternative at the outset.[319] A study of groups of managers and employees shows that real dissent is effective in preventing the confirmation bias, a bias that inhibits group discussion of unshared information.[320] Dissent is most effective when the dissenting minority provides more schema-relevant information than the majority and when they forcefully advocate their position.[321]

A number of structured group interventions have been designed to improve group information acquisition and thus enhance the quality and creativity of group decisions, but few of them have proven to be effective. Contrived dissent, encouraged by techniques such as "Dialectical Inquiry" and the "Devil's Advocate Approach," appears to have little or no effect on decision quality or group commitment to the decision.[322] Brainstorming has been shown to have questionable effectiveness.[323] Simply brainstorming ideas in a group can actually decrease creativity and productivity.[324] What's more, people working in brainstorming groups tend to perform at the level of the least productive group member.[325] Groups using the "Stepladder Technique," a technique in which one member at a time is allowed to join the group discussion, also fail to perform better than unstructured groups.[326]

One structured technique—the "Multi-Attribute Utility Decision Decomposition Technique"—has been shown to enhance efficient sharing of relevant information among group members and to improve decision quality.[327] This method, based on the widely used multi-attribute utility model,[328] helps group members identify and weight decision criteria, identify alternatives, assign a preference score to each alternative for each decision criteria, and determine the alternative with the highest overall score. An almost identical technique called "Frame of Reference Training" has also proven to be highly effective.[329] Essentially, these two techniques help group members construct a common decision matrix or shared schema and use it to determine the best alternative. Unlike group brainstorming, testing multiple options against decision criteria in a decision matrix improves group creativity and the quality of ideas generated.[330]

Information acquisition in groups, or the sharing of relevant, previously unshared information during group discussions, can also be promoted by:

- Publicly designating each group member as an expert in a distinct area.[331] Including participants with the necessary expertise can actually impair group performance unless the group is encouraged to make good use of that expertise.[332] When participants are personally identified and their expertise made known to the rest of the group, more critical information possessed by only one group member will be shared with the group at large.[333] Team decision making and performance also improve when all members of the team understand "who knows what."[334]

- Meeting face-to-face at the beginning of an engagement.[335] The more a dispersed group relies on electronic technologies for communication, the more challenging it is for them to identify who knows what.[336]
- Instructing the group to explicitly state its objectives[337] and framing the group's task as a problem to be solved.[338] Groups given a problem/solution frame pay more attention to decision criteria that are critical for identifying the best alternative.[339]
- Asking group members to keep a record of their discussions. Group performance improves when one of the group members keeps a record of the information discussed by the group.[340] Group members are unlikely to recall any new information not previously shared by all unless it is written down.[341]
- Encouraging group members to think critically,[342] to listen actively,[343] and to speak up when they notice errors or missing information.[344] Critical thinking skills can help group members correct erroneous intuitive decisions[345] and are positively correlated with better decision making and decisiveness.[346] Studies of top management teams solving strategy problems show their critical thinking skills are positively correlated with superior firm performance.[347] Moreover, critical thinking skills can even compensate for a lack of domain expertise in many tasks.[348]
- Eliciting and legitimizing dissenting views[349] and encouraging group leaders to refrain from promoting their preferred solutions.[350] Encouraging the expression of opposing viewpoints promotes critical thinking, information search, creative thinking, and leads teams to make better decisions.[351] Asking group members to examine the other side's arguments can bring out contradictory evidence overlooked in their own holistic assessments.[352]
- Making group members aware of the need to look for unshared information[353] and having the leader repeat information that is unshared.[354] More unshared information also becomes available when group members rank order decision alternatives rather than simply choose one.[355]
- Requiring group members to evaluate and justify their decisions and their decision-making process.[356] Holding the group accountable not so much for the outcome, as for the process by which they generate their decisions, leads to better decisions.[357]

Aids to Information Integration

As audience members acquire enough information to start making comparisons among alternatives, they begin to integrate that information. The information integration process is aided when documents and presentations contain only highly relevant information in limited amounts. Too much information can actually decrease the accuracy of the audience's decision. Too much information can decrease the audience's confidence in their decision as well.[358]

A Limited Number of Alternatives

Audiences find integrating or combining information to be easier when they are not given too many alternatives to choose among. A study of prospective home buyers choosing among different houses varied the number of alternative houses from 5 to 25.[359] Buyers reported experiencing information overload and made significantly fewer optimal choices when the number of alternative houses reached 10.

In a study that varied choice rules as well as the number of alternatives, audience members were asked to use either the lexicographic, conjunctive, or averaging choice rule to decide among either 2, 6, or 10 alternatives. Across all three choice rules audiences made fairly accurate decisions when deciding between 2 alternatives but they were much less accurate when deciding among 6 or 10 alternatives.[360]

Having to choose among many different alternatives is not only difficult for audience members, it also depletes the cognitive resources they need to make subsequent decisions. When home buyers have to evaluate many different properties, they subsequently devote less attention to choosing a mortgage and are more likely to select higher risk, adjustable-rate mortgage products than when they have only a few properties to evaluate.[361] Information overload may also explain the effectiveness of sequential influence tactics such as the "Foot-in-the-Door" technique. Responding to an initial request of a "Foot-in-the-Door" technique depletes the audience's cognitive resources and makes it more difficult for them to refuse subsequent requests.[362] Having too many alternatives or benchmarks to compare can even impair experts' ability to make good decisions. For example, the accuracy of bankers' bankruptcy predictions decreases when they have to compare more than two years of benchmark data along five or more attributes.[363]

In some cases, however, experts prefer to have a large number of alternatives to choose among. Expert audience members with predefined attribute preferences are more likely to prefer a larger number of alternatives to choose among than novices without such preferences.[364] Unlike novice investors, expert investors are actually less likely to invest when given just a few investments from which to choose.[365]

A Slightly Larger Number of Attributes

Decision quality may also decrease as the number of attributes or decision criteria increases.[366] The study of prospective home buyers described in the previous section not only varied the number of alternative houses but also varied the number of attributes that described each house from 5 to 25. Buyers reported experiencing information overload and made significantly fewer optimal choices when the number of house attributes reached 15. The author concludes that when buyers face too many alternatives or attributes, they can no longer make all of the comparisons necessary to rank the alternatives accurately.[367]

A meta-analysis of bankers making bankruptcy predictions finds that even a moderate increase in the number of attributes, e.g. an increase from five to six or seven, can hinder decision quality.[368] Similarly, when attribute information about products increases, consumers make poorer quality decisions and are more likely to choose on the basis of the products' popularity.[369]

Two studies of consumers choosing among various brands of laundry detergents, rice, and prepared dinners come to a somewhat different conclusion. Although consumers' accuracy decreased as the number of alternatives they considered in a product category increased, in these studies consumers' accuracy increased as they considered more attributes about each alternative. How many attributes or decision criteria are too many depends in part on the amount of time the audience has available for decision making.[370]

The Complete Set of Slot Values for Each Alternative

Although audiences tend to use whatever comparative information is made available to them, they make few additional comparisons on their own.[371] A study of consumers reading ads finds that 75% of those who read comparative ads made comparisons among products whereas only 10% of those who read noncomparative ads did so.[372]

Alignable differences, for example the price of one item versus the price of another, drive the comparison process.[373] Consequently, comparative ads tend to be more effective than noncomparative ads only when they allow different products to be compared along the same attributes.[374] However, a noncomparative ad can change consumers' attitudes if it enables them to compare information they previously acquired about a product's attributes with new and different information about those same attributes.[375] For example, weight-conscious consumers would likely change their minds about a soft drink they thought had 250 calories per serving if they read an ad stating that each serving had only 90 calories instead.

Audiences tend to discount or ignore any comparative information they have to memorize, infer, or transform.[376] When audience members are aware that comparative information about an alternative's attributes is missing, they often treat that missing information as a reason to reject that option. Thus, they are more inclined to reject alternatives about which they know less than to reject options about which they know more.[377] When comparison shopping, consumers tend to interpret missing attribute values in a way that supports the purchase of the option that is superior on the common attributes.[378] At other times, audience members make decisions without making the necessary comparisons because they are not aware that comparative information is missing.[379] For more on how missing slot values bias audience decisions, see Chapter 5 pp. 238–239.

Slot Values for Each Alternative in Numeric Form

Although audiences mentally convert cardinal numbers into ordinal numbers or scale values prior to making comparisons, they integrate or combine information more accurately and efficiently when comparative information is expressed in numeric rather than verbal form.[380] When expert recruiters screen résumé profiles—résumés with numeric ratings of each résumé element—as opposed to actual résumés, their judgments are more predictable and there is higher agreement among them. Résumé profiles simplify the recruiters' task by having third-party raters substitute numeric values (e.g., 2.0 on a 4-point scale) for the verbal descriptions in the actual résumés (e.g., "Career Objective: To pursue a career in which I can use my marketing and management skills to actively participate as a team member"). Real-world résumé screening, on the other hand, involves the more complex task of first determining attribute values before combining those values into judgments.[381]

When consumers are given numeric values for product attributes, they make more attribute-based comparisons than when they are given qualitative information about those attributes.[382] Conversely, when attribute values are represented as words instead of numbers, consumers make more alternative-based comparisons and use more noncompensatory choice rules to integrate the information they find.[383] Numeric information helps audience members make better trade-offs. It also encourages them to demand multicriteria arguments to aid their decision-making process. Without numeric information, audience members are often swayed by overly simplistic arguments when faced with conflicts of choice.[384]

Although audiences prefer to receive information about probabilities in numeric form, they prefer to use words (e.g., *doubtful, likely*) to express probabilities to others.[385] Occasionally, words or a combination of numbers and words may prove optimal for decision making. For example, consumers who were asked to choose between two health maintenance organizations (HMOs) on the basis of a bar chart gave the numerical ratings (48% versus 56%) more weight when the qualitative verbal scale, Poor, Fair, Good, Excellent, was added to the chart (see Figure 4.4).[386]

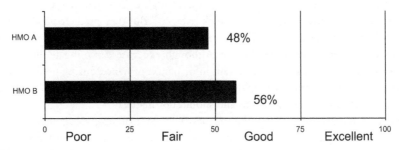

FIGURE 4.4 Consumers' Overall Satisfaction With Two HMOs

Source: Adapted from Finucane et al. (2003)

Easy-to-Compare Slot Values

Audiences will integrate information more accurately and efficiently when comparable slot values for each alternative are expressed in comparable ways, for example when the values for several international currencies are all expressed in U.S. dollars.[387] Comparable scaling (e.g., Good, Very Good, Excellent) of slot values is another way to improve the accuracy of the audience's information-integration process. Noncomparable scaling (e.g., Good, B+, ★★★★★) across alternatives tends to decrease the audience's use of more normative compensatory choice rules.[388]

The Right Graph for the Comparison

The best graph for any particular task is one that minimizes the number of steps needed for making the intended comparison.[389] For example, bar charts are better than pie charts when viewers need to compare quantities because bar charts display quantities as lengths on a common scale, whereas pie charts display quantities as areas of a circle or slices and require viewers to mentally rotate the slices before making a comparison.[390] By the same token, pie charts are better than bar charts when viewers need to make accurate part/whole judgments because pie charts give viewers a better sense of the size of the whole at a glance.[391]

For a graph to be effective, it must also activate the appropriate schema for interpreting the data in it.[392] Viewers may misinterpret the meaning of a graph if its graphic elements do not map onto their schema as expected. For example, viewers expect the dependent variable in a line graph to be plotted on the y axis, such that a steeper slope implies a faster rate of change. When a line graph violates this expectation, graph viewers tend to misinterpret the meaning of the slopes.[393]

The Elimination of Irrelevant and Inconsistent Information

Irrelevant information can have a dilutive effect on the audience's information–integration process.[394] Irrelevant information mixed with relevant information on complex charts and graphs impairs viewers' ability to interpret them correctly.[395] Visuals and text that are topically related to a teacher's lesson but irrelevant to the learning goal decrease student learning.[396] Such irrelevant but "seductive" details interfere with learning by priming inappropriate schemata which students then use to organize the relevant information in the lesson.[397]

Another reason irrelevant information has a dilutive effect on audience decisions is that audiences often use a weighted averaging rule to make their predictions and other judgments. Thus, when audience members receive irrelevant information mixed with information that is relevant, their predictions become more regressive and less based on the relevant information presented to them.[398] For example, when college students were asked to predict another student's grade point average (GPA), they predicted the student would earn a high GPA when they were given only relevant information about the student's good work habits.[399] But they predicted a lower GPA when the relevant information about the student's work habits was presented along with irrelevant information about the student's age, hair color, etc. Although expertise can mitigate dilution effects,[400] it does not always do so. For example, irrelevant information provided during performance reviews distorts supervisors' assessments of employee performance even when supervisors recognize the information is irrelevant to the assessment and should not matter.[401]

Irrelevant information also dilutes the persuasive impact of strong arguments in much the same way that weak arguments dilute the persuasive impact of strong arguments[402] and mildly favorable information dilutes the persuasive impact of highly favorable information.[403] Irrelevant information added to highly relevant and factual policy arguments, for example, reduces the

TABLE 4.4 Expert Audiences Are Frustrated by Unnecessary Information

Expert investor reading the original *Smartphone MBA* business plan

11. Etcetera, etcetera.
13. Etcetera, etcetera.
14. Blah, blah, blah.

Expert investor reading the financial analyst's report on Georgia Gulf

48. Etcetera. I'm skimming it, because that's what I would have done three pages ago.

65. This report is very lengthy. I don't need to know or care how they make these chemicals. What I want to know is: "Is it profitable? Why is it profitable? What are their advantages?" If it's important to be technical because they have an advantage in a certain process, that's fine. But if they make it the same way everybody else does, I really don't care.

Experienced board member reading the strategic plan from General Motors

5. This environmental scan chart in Section 2 is something that I've not seen before. I'm looking at x's. I'm looking at the words "Market, Economics, Technical and Social." It's ranked from negative to positive on an attractiveness scale. Models like this don't impress me, because in my opinion, they are examples of a lot of information with no knowledge. I've seen all this data, now what do I do with it?
28. The data in Sections 4 and 5 is superfluous and backup, as is the data in Section 6, and the data in Sections 7 and 8. As I said before, Section 9 is not useful to me.

persuasiveness of those arguments.[404] Irrelevant information added to product benefits information reduces consumers' beliefs about the product's benefits even when consumers acknowledge the irrelevance of the information.[405]

In group decision making, nondiagnostic, or irrelevant, information produces a dilutive effect on group decisions similar to its effect on individual decisions.[406] Even explicit instructions to discriminate between relevant and irrelevant information do not reduce the dilution effect. Rather, the dilution effect disappears only when the group actively removes irrelevant pieces of information from view before making a judgment.[407]

The think-aloud remarks in Table 4.4, made by three experts whose comments we also saw in Chapters 1 and 2, reveal the importance of eliminating irrelevant information from business documents. All three experts express their frustration with the contents of the documents they are reading. Indeed, many think-aloud studies show that the presence of irrelevant information in business documents is pervasive and a chief complaint of expert audiences. Notice that the experienced board member dismisses as irrelevant Sections 2, 4, 5, 6, 7, 8, and 9 of the GM strategic plan, a plan that consisted of only 11 sections to begin with.

Inconsistent information can also have an adverse effect on the audience's information integration process. Inconsistent information takes longer to integrate because of the extra time the audience needs to notice and interpret the inconsistency.[408] Inconsistent information also annoys and confuses audience members, as was the case with the experienced board member who read the strategic plan from GM:

> **15. They say they have a bad service record. Well, that's related to saying that they have low-quality products. But above they say their strength is high-quality products. So I'm thoroughly confused.**

The following two versions of the beginning of an MBA team's strategic plan illustrate the importance of using techniques that can aid the audience's information-acquisition and information-integration processes. The revision provides side-by-side comparisons, or benchmarks, for each quantity it mentions. Thus, the audience can see immediately which important metrics have improved or will improve, and by how much, and will be less likely to ask for or search for that information. The revision adds a heading to the first paragraph that allows an audience who might be searching the plan for the 2015 financial results to quickly find them. The vague qualitative terms used in the original—*increase significantly* and *maintaining strong earnings*—have been replaced with specific numbers. In addition, the revised version includes comparative values for 2015's net income, earnings per share, and ROE, slot values missing in the original.

TABLE 4.5 Headings and Comparative Numbers Aid Information Acquisition and Integration

Original First Paragraphs of an MBA Team's Strategic Plan	*Revised First Paragraphs of an MBA Team's Strategic Plan*
Coming off an outstanding year that saw our stock price increase significantly, Chronos Watch Company is poised to maintain earnings levels again in 2016. Chronos, the world's second largest producer of watches, posted a net income of $3.0M and had an average earnings per share of $2.98, generating a net return on equity of 9%. These results handily beat our peer group average of $2.54 EPS and 7% ROE.	**Financial Results for 2015** 2015 was an outstanding year for Chronos Watch Company. Since last year, our stock price increased from ***$83 per share to $107*** and our net income rose from ***$2.7M*** to $3.0M. Today, Chronos Watch Company is the world's second largest producer of watches. Although our average earnings per share ***dropped from $3.40*** to $2.98 and our ROE ***dropped from 12%*** to 9%, our results handily beat our peer group average of $2.54 EPS and 7% ROE.
Objectives For 2016, Chronos's executive management has set certain concrete goals. In addition to maintaining strong earnings, Chronos expects to: • Generate a Return on Equity of 15% • Reduce Debt to Equity Ratio to from 32% to 12%	**Financial Objectives for 2016** For the year 2016, our executive management has set the following goals: • Increase net income from ***$3 M to $4 M*** • Increase return on equity from ***9%*** to 15% • Reduce debt to equity from 32% to 12%

AIDS TO AUDIENCE DECISION MAKING: IMPLICATIONS FOR COMMUNICATORS

- The main takeaway for communicators in Chapter 4 is that all six of the cognitive processes audiences use to make decisions can be enhanced by a set of process-specific stylistic techniques. Thus, stylistic techniques are useful not only for enhancing audience comprehension, but also for enhancing the other major cognitive processes that make informed decision making possible.
- Use the information presented in the chapter to choose specific stylistic techniques that make it easy for your audience to complete each step in the decision-making process.
- Why use the information? To save yourself time. To improve your accuracy in predicting the techniques and organizational structures that will aid audience decision making. To combat "groupthink."
- To apply a technique presented in the chapter, refer to the appropriate chapter section for an example.

Notes

1 Felsenfeld, C. (1991). The plain English experience in New York. In E. R. Steinberg (Ed.), *Plain language: Principles and practice* (pp. 13–18). Detroit, MI: Wayne State University Press.

Felsenfeld, C., & Siegel, A. (1981). *Writing contracts in plain English*. St. Paul, MN: West Publishing Co.

2 Krajewski, L. A. (1979). Effectiveness of the inductive and the deductive organizational plans in a special request letter (Doctoral dissertation, Arizona State University, 1979). *Dissertation Abstracts International, 40*(08A), 4368.

3 Wakefield, D. S. (1961). A test to determine the relative effectiveness of different styles, colors, and return order solicitation methods in sales letters (Doctoral dissertation, The University of Tennessee, 1961). *Dissertation Abstracts International, 22*(10), 3453.

4 Hill, K., & Monk, A. F. (2000). Electronic mail versus printed text: The effects on recipients. *Interacting with Computers, 13*(2) 253–263.

5 Becker, C. A., & Killion, T. H. (1977). Interaction of visual and cognitive effects in word recognition. *Journal of Experimental Psychology: Human Perception and Performance, 3*(3), 389–401.

   Stanners, R. F., Jastrzembski, J. E., & Westbrook, A. (1975). Frequency and visual quality in a word-nonword classification task. *Journal of Verbal Learning & Verbal Behavior, 14*(3), 259–264.

6 Kim, J.Y., Min, S. N., Subramaniyam, M., & Cho, Y. J. (2014). Legibility difference between e-books and paper books by using an eye tracker. *Ergonomics, 57*(7), 1102–1108.

7 Shieh, K. K., & Lai, Y. K. (2008). Effects of ambient illumination, luminance contrast, and stimulus type on subjective preference of VDT target and background color combinations. *Perceptual and Motor Skills, 107*(2), 336–352.

8 Wheildon, C. (1995). *Type and layout.* Berkeley, CA: Strathmoor Press.

9 Rehe, R. F. (1974). *Typography: How to make it legible.* Carmel, IN: Design Research International.

10 Holmes, G. (1931). The relative legibility of black and white print. *Journal of Applied Psychology, 15*(3), 248–251.

   Taylor, C. D. (1934). The relative legibility of black and white print. *Journal of Educational Psychology, 25*(8), 561–578.

11 Poulton, E. C. (1955). Letter differentiation and rate of comprehension of reading. *Journal of Applied Psychology, 49*, 358–362.

12 Tinker, M. A. (1965). *Bases for effective reading.* Minneapolis, MN: University of Minnesota Press.

13 Davenport, J. S., & Smith, S. A. (1963). Effects of hyphenation, justified, and type size on readability. *Journalism Quarterly, 42*, 382–388.

14 Hartley, J. (1978). *Designing instructional text.* New York: Nichols Publishing Company.

15 Poulton, E. C. (1967). Skimming (scanning) news items printed in 8-point and 9-point letters. *Ergonomics, 10*(6), 713–716.

16 Legge, G. E., & Bigelow, C. A. (2011). Does print size matter for reading? A review of findings from vision science and typography. *Journal of Vision, 11*(5), 1–22.

17 Coles, P., & Foster, J. J. (1975). Typographic cuing as an aid to learning from typewritten text. *Programmed Learning and Educational Technology, 12*, 102–108.

   Rickards, E. C., & August, G. J. (1975). Generative underlining strategies in prose recall. *Journal of Educational Psychology, 67*(6), 860–865.

   See n12, Tinker (1965).

18 Just, M. A., & Carpenter, P. A. (1987). *The psychology of reading and language comprehension.* Boston: Allyn and Bacon.

   See n17, Rickards & August (1975).

   Salcedo, R. N., Reed, H., Evans, J. F., & Kong, A. C. (1972). A broader look at legibility. *Journalism Quarterly, 49*, 285–289.

   Although see White, S. J., & Liversedge, S. P. (2006). Linguistic and nonlinguistic influences on the eyes' landing positions during reading. *The Quarterly Journal of Experimental Psychology, 59*(4), 760–782.

19 *See* n12, Tinker (1965).

20 Breland, K., & Breland, M. K. (1944). Legibility of newspaper headlines printed in capitals and in lower case. *Journal of Applied Psychology, 28*(2), 117–120.

   Foster, J. J., & Bruce, M. (1982). Reading upper and lower case on Viewdata. *Applied Ergonomics, 13*(2), 145–149.

21 Tinker, M. A., & Paterson, D. G. (1928). Influence of type form on speed of reading. *Journal Of Applied Psychology, 12*(4), 359–368.

22 *See* n12, Tinker (1965).

23 Tinker, M. A., & Paterson, D. G. (1942). Reader preferences and typography. *Journal of Applied Psychology, 26*(1), 38–40.

24 Hartley, J., & Rooum, D. (1983). Sir Cyril Burt and typography: A re-evaluation. *British Journal of Psychology, 74*(2), 203–212.

   Tinker, M. A. (1963). *Legibility of print.* Ames, IA: Iowa State University Press.

25 Hvistendahl, J. K., & Kahl, M. R. (1975). Roman v. sans serif body type: Readability and reader preference. *News Research Bulletin, 2,* 3–11.

Robinson, D. O., Abbamonte, M., & Evans, S. H. (1971). Why serifs are important: The perception of small print. *Visible Language, 4,* 353–359.
See n8, Wheildon (1995).

26 Arditi, A., & Cho, J. (2005). Serifs and font legibility. *Vision Research, 45*(23), 2926–2933.

Gould, J. D., Alfaro, L., Finn, R., Haupt, B., & Minuto, A. (1987). Reading from CRT displays can be as fast as reading from paper. *Human Factors, 29*(5), 497–517.

See n24.

27 Schriver et al. as described in Schriver, K. A. (1997, pp. 288–303). *Dynamics in document design: Creating text for readers.* New York: Wiley.

28 Juni, S., & Gross, J. S. (2008). Emotional and persuasive perception of fonts. *Perceptual and Motor Skills, 106*(1), 35–42.

29 Sanocki, T. (1987). Visual knowledge underlying letter perception: Font-specific, schematic tuning. *Journal of Experimental Psychology: Human Perception and Performance, 13*(2), 267–278.

Gauthier, I., Wong, A. C., Hayward, W. G., & Cheung, O. S. (2006). Font tuning associated with expertise in letter perception. *Perception, 35*(4), 541–559.

Walker, P. (2008). Font tuning: A review and new experimental evidence. *Visual Cognition, 16*(8), 1022–1058.

30 Sanocki, T., & Dyson, M. C. (2012). Letter processing and font information during reading: Beyond distinctiveness, where vision meets design. *Attention, Perception, & Psychophysics, 74*(1), 132–145.

31 See n24, Tinker (1963).

32 See n12, Tinker (1965).

33 Paterson, D. G., & Tinker, M. A. (1942). Influence of line width on eye movements for six-point type. *Journal of Educational Psychology, 33*(7), 552–555.

34 Dyson, M. C. (2004). How physical text layout affects reading from screen. *Behaviour & Information Technology, 23*(6), 377–393.

Dyson, M. C., & Haselgrove, M. (2001). The influence of reading speed and line length on the effectiveness of reading from screen. *International Journal of Human-Computer Studies, 54*(4), 585–612.

35 Becker, D., Heinrich, J., van Sichowsky, R., & Wendt, D. (1970). Reader preferences for typeface and leading. *Journal of Typographic Research, 1,* 61–66.

36 See n24, Tinker (1963).

Mackey, M. A., & Metz, M. (2009). Ease of reading of mandatory information on Canadian food product labels. *International Journal of Consumer Studies, 33*(4), 369–381.

37 Smith, J. M., & McCombs, E. (1971). The graphics of prose. *Visible Language, 4*(Autumn), 365–369.

38 Pinelli, T. E., Glassman, M., & Cordle, V. M. (1982). *Survey of reader preferences concerning the format of NASA technical reports* (NASA TM-No 84502). Washington, DC: National Aeronautics and Space Administration.

39 Trollip, S. R., & Sales, G. (1986). Readability of computer-generated fill-justified text. *Human Factors, 28*(2), 159–163.

40 Gregory, M., & Poulton, E. C. (1970). Even versus uneven right-hand margins and the rate of comprehension in reading. *Ergonomics, 13*(4), 427–434.

Hartley, J., & Mills, R. (1973). Unjustified experiments in typographical research and instructional design. *British Journal of Educational Technology, 4,* 120–131.

41 Dahan, D., Magnuson, J. S., & Tanenhaus, M. K. (2001). Time course of frequency effects in spoken-word recognition: Evidence from eye movements. *Cognitive Psychology, 42*(4), 317–367.

Redish, J. C. (1980). Readability. In D. Felker (Ed.), *Document design: A review of the relevant research* (pp. 69–93). Washington, DC: American Institutes for Research.

Scarborough, D. L., Gerard, L., & Cortese, C. (1979). Accessing lexical memory: The transfer of word repetition effects across task and modality. *Memory & Cognition, 7*(1), 3–12.

42 Gibson, E. J., Bishop, C., Schiff, W., & Smith, J. (1964). Comparison of meaningfulness and pronounceability as grouping principles in the perception and retention of verbal material. *Journal of Experimental Psychology, 67*(2), 173–182.

Reicher, G. M. (1969). Perceptual recognition as a function of meaningfulness of stimulus material. *Journal of Experimental Psychology, 81*(2), 275–280.

Wheeler, D. D. (1970). Processes in word recognition. *Cognitive Psychology, 1,* 59–85.

43 Anderson, R. C. (1974). Concretization and sentence learning. *Journal of Educational Psychology, 66*(2), 179–183.

Jorgensen, C. C., & Kintsch, W. (1973). The role of imagery in the evaluation of sentences. *Cognitive Psychology, 4*(1), 110–116.

44 Rohrman, N. L. (1970). More on the recall of nominalizations. *Journal of Verbal Learning & Verbal Behavior, 9*(5), 534–536.

45 Holland, V. M. (1981). *Psycholinguistic alternatives to readability formulas* (Document Design Project Tech. Rep. No. 12). Washington, DC: American Institutes for Research.

46 Reisberg, D., Mclean, J., & Goldfield, A. (1987). Easy to hear but hard to understand: A lip-reading advantage with intact auditory stimuli. In B. Dodd & R. Campbell (Eds.), *Hearing by eye: The psychology of lip-reading* (pp. 97–114). New York: Lawrence Erlbaum.

47 Nygaard, L. C. (2005). Perceptual integration of linguistic and nonlinguistic properties of speech. In D. Pisoni & R. Remez (Eds.), *Handbook of speech perception* (pp. 390–414). Oxford, UK: Wiley-Blackwell.

Rosenblum, L. D. (2008). Speech perception as a multimodal phenomenon. *Current Directions in Psychological Science, 17*(6), 405–409.

48 Munhall, K. G., Jones, J. A., Callan, D. E., Kuratate, T., & Vatikiotis-Bateson, E. (2004). Visual prosody and speech intelligibility head movement improves auditory speech perception. *Psychological Science, 15*(2), 133–137.

49 Cutler, A., & Norris, D. (1988). The role of strong syllables in segmentation for lexical access. *Journal of Experimental Psychology: Human Perception and Performance, 14*(1), 113–121.

Otake, T., & Cutler, A. (Eds.). (1996). *Phonological structure and language processing: Cross-linguistic studies.* Berlin: Mouton.

50 Cohen, H., Douaire, J., & Elsabbagh, M. (2001). The role of prosody in discourse processing. *Brain and Cognition, 46*(1), 73–82.

51 Fox Tree, J. E. (1995). The effects of false starts and repetitions on the processing of subsequent words in spontaneous speech. *Journal of Memory and Language, 34*(6), 709–738.

Goldwater, S., Jurafsky, D., & Manning, C. D. (2010). Which words are hard to recognize? Prosodic, lexical, and disfluency factors that increase speech recognition error rates. *Speech Communication, 52*(3), 181–200.

52 MacGregor, L. J., Corley, M., & Donaldson, D. I. (2009). Not all disfluencies are equal: The effects of disfluent repetitions on language comprehension. *Brain and Language, 111*(1), 36–45.

MacGregor, L. J., Corley, M., & Donaldson, D. I. (2010). Listening to the sound of silence: Disfluent silent pauses in speech have consequences for listeners. *Neuropsychologia, 48*(14), 3982–3992.

53 Eagly, A. H. (1974). Comprehensibility of persuasive arguments as a determinant of opinion change. *Journal of Personality and Social Psychology, 29*(6), 758–773.

54 Chen, L. (1982). Topological structure in visual perception. *Science, 218*(4573), 699–700.

Cleveland, W. S., & McGill, R. (1984). Graphical perception: Theory, experimentation, and application to the development of graphical methods. *Journal of the American Statistical Association, 77*, 541–547.

Kosslyn, S. M. (1994). *Elements of graph design.* New York: W. H. Freeman.

55 Lewandowsky, S., & Spence, I. (1989). Discriminating strata in scatterplots. *Journal of the American Statistical Association, 84*, 682–688.

56 Levie, W. H. (1973). Pictorial research: An overview. *Viewpoints, 49*(2), 37–45.

Yamani, Y., & McCarley, J. S. (2010). Visual search asymmetries within color-coded and intensity-coded displays. *Journal of Experimental Psychology: Applied, 16*(2), 124–132.

57 Yeh, M., & Wickens, C. D. (2001). Attentional filtering in the design of electronic map displays: A comparison of color coding, intensity coding, and decluttering techniques. *Human Factors: The Journal of the Human Factors and Ergonomics Society, 43*(4), 543–562.

58 Schutz, H. G. (1961). An evaluation of methods for presentation of graphic multiple trends: Experiment III. *Human Factors, 3*(2), 108–119.

59 Cauchard, F., Eyrolle, H., Cellier, J. M., & Hyönä, J. (2010). Vertical perceptual span and the processing of visual signals in reading. *International Journal of Psychology, 45*(1), 40–47.

Hyönä, J., & Lorch Jr, R. F. (2004). Effects of topic headings on text processing: Evidence from adult readers' eye fixation patterns. *Learning and Instruction, 14*(2), 131–152.

Lagerwerf, L., Cornelis, L., de Geus, J., & Jansen, P. (2008). Advance organizers in advisory reports selective reading, recall, and perception. *Written Communication, 25*(1), 53–75.

60 Williams, T. R., & Spyridakis, J. H. (1992). Visual discriminability of headings in text. *Professional Communication, IEEE Transactions On, 35*(2), 64–70.

61 *See* n8, Wheildon (1995).

62 Eyrolle, H., Virbel, J., & Lemarié, J. (2008). Impact of incomplete correspondence between document titles and texts on users' representations: A cognitive and linguistic analysis based on 25 technical documents. *Applied Ergonomics, 39*(2), 241–246.

63 Sanchez, R. P., Lorch, E. P., & Lorch Jr, R. F. (2001). Effects of headings on text processing strategies. *Contemporary Educational Psychology, 26*(3), 418–428.

Surber, J. R., & Schroeder, M. (2007). Effect of prior domain knowledge and headings on processing of informative text. *Contemporary Educational Psychology, 32*(3), 485–498.

64 Charrow, V. R., & Redish, J. (1980). *A study of standardized headings for warranties* (Document Design Project Technical Report No. 6). Washington, DC: American Institutes for Research.

65 Gardner, M. P. (1981). An information processing approach to examining advertising effects (Doctoral dissertation, Carnegie Mellon University, 1981). *Dissertation Abstracts International, 43*(05A), 1662.

66 Spyridakis, J. H. (1989a). Signaling effects: Part I. *Journal of Technical Writing and Communication, 19*(1), 227–239.

Spyridakis, J. H. (1989b). Signaling effects: Part II. *Journal of Technical Writing and Communication, 19*(4), 395–415.

67 Barlow, T., & Wogalter, M. S. (1993). Alcoholic beverage warnings in magazine and television advertisements. *Journal of Consumer Research, 20*(1), 147–156.

68 Young, S. L., & Wogalter, M. S. (1990). Comprehension and memory of instruction manual warnings: Conspicuous print and pictorial icons. *Human Factors: The Journal of the Human Factors and Ergonomics Society, 32*(6), 637–649.

69 *See* n17, Coles & Foster (1975).

Foster, J. J., & Coles, P. (1977). An experimental study of typographic cueing in printed text. *Ergonomics, 20*(1), 57–66.

70 Poulton, E. C., & Brown, C. H. (1968). Rate of comprehension of an existing teleprinter output and of possible alternatives. *Journal of Applied Psychology, 52*(1, Pt. 1), 16–21.

See n18, Salcedo et al. (1972).

71 Lorch Jr, R. F. (1989). Text-signaling devices and their effects on reading and memory processes. *Educational Psychology Review, 1*(3), 209–234.

72 *See* n12, Tinker (1965).

Bernard, J. B., Kumar, G., Junge, J., & Chung, S. T. (2013). The effect of letter-stroke boldness on reading speed in central and peripheral vision. *Vision Research, 84*, 33–42.

73 Sanford, A. J., Sanford, A. J., Molle, J., & Emmott, C. (2006). Shallow processing and attention capture in written and spoken discourse. *Discourse Processes, 42*(2), 109–130.

74 Anderson, R. C. (1967). Educational psychology. *Annual Review of Psychology, 18*, 129–164.

Briggs, L., Campeau, P., Gagne, R., & May, M. (1966). *Instructional media: A procedure for the design of multi-media instruction: A critical review of research and suggestions for future research.* Pittsburgh, PA: American Institutes for Research.

Crouse, J., & Idstein, P. (1972). Effects of encoding cues on prose learning. *Journal of Educational Psychology, 63*(4), 309–313.

75 Braun, C. C., Mine, P. B., & Silver, N. C. (1995). The influence of color on warning label perceptions. *International Journal of Industrial Ergonomics, 15*(3), 179–187.

76 Keller, T., Gerjets, P., Scheiter, K., & Garsoffky, B. (2006). Information visualizations for knowledge acquisition: The impact of dimensionality and color coding. *Computers in Human Behavior, 22*(1), 43–65.

Ozcelik, E., Karakus, T., Kursun, E., & Cagiltay, K. (2009). An eye-tracking study of how color coding affects multimedia learning. *Computers & Education, 53*(2), 445–453.

77 Spencer, H., Reynolds, L., & Coe, B. (1974). Typographic coding in lists and bibliographies. *Applied Ergonomics, 5*(3), 136–141.

78 Glynn, S. M., & Di Vesta, F. J. (1979). Control of prose processing via instructional and typographical cues. *Journal of Educational Psychology, 71*(5), 595–603.

Hershberger, W. A., & Terry, D. F. (1965). Typographical cuing in conventional and programed texts. *Journal of Applied Psychology, 49*(1), 55–60.

79 Glynn, S. M., Britton, B. K., & Tillman, M. H. (1985). Typographical cues in text: Management of the reader's attention. In D. H. Jonassen (Ed.), *Technology of text: Principles for structuring, designing, and displaying text* (Vol. 2, pp. 192–209). Englewood Cliffs, NJ: Educational Technology Publications.

80 Diamond, D. S. (1968). A quantitative approach to magazine advertisement format selection. *Journal of Marketing Research, 5*(4), 376–386.

81 Hendon, D. W. (1973). How mechanical factors affect ad perception. *Journal of Advertising Research, 13*(4), 39–46.

Holbrook, M. B., & Lehmann, D. R. (1980). Form versus content in predicting Starch scores. *Journal of Advertising Research, 20*(4), 53–62.

82 Rebollar, R., Lidón, I., Martín, J., & Puebla, M. (2015). The identification of viewing patterns of chocolate snack packages using eye-tracking techniques. *Food Quality and Preference, 39*, 251–258.

83 *See* n81, Hendon (1973).

84 Duggan, G. B., & Payne, S. J. (2009). Text skimming: The process and effectiveness of foraging through text under time pressure. *Journal of Experimental Psychology: Applied, 15*(3), 228–242.

85 Pan, B., Zhang, L., & Law, R. (2013). The complex matter of online hotel choice. *Cornell Hospitality Quarterly, 54*(1), 74–83.

86 Laughery, K. R., Young, S. L., Vaubel, K. P., & Brelsford Jr, J. W. (1993). The noticeability of warnings on alcoholic beverage containers. *Journal of Public Policy & Marketing, 12*(1), 38–56.

87 Wogalter, M. S., Godfrey, S. S., Fontenelle, G. A., Desaulniers, D. R., Rothstein, P. R., & Laughery, K. R. (1987). Effectiveness of warnings. *Human Factors: The Journal of the Human Factors and Ergonomics Society, 29*(5), 599–612.

Wogalter, M. S., Barlow, T., & Murphy, S. A. (1995). Compliance to owner's manual warnings: Influence of familiarity and the placement of a supplemental directive. *Ergonomics, 38*(6), 1081–1091.

88 McLaughlin, G. H. (1966). Comparing styles of presenting technical information. *Ergonomics, 9*(3), 257–259.

89 Lorch Jr, R. F. (1985). Effects on recall of signals to text organization. *Bulletin of the Psychonomic Society, 23*(4), 374–376.

Lorch Jr, R. F., & Chen, A. H. (1986). Effects of number signals on reading and recall. *Journal of Educational Psychology, 78*(4), 263–270.

90 Viscusi, W. K., Magat, W. A., & Huber, J. (1986). Informational regulation of consumer health risks: An empirical evaluation of hazard warnings. *The RAND Journal of Economics, 17*(3), 351–365.

91 Strong Jr, E. K. (1926). Value of white space in advertising. *Journal of Applied Psychology, 10*(1), 107–116.

92 *See* n37, Smith & McCombs (1971).

93 Drew, C. J., Altman, R., & Dykes, M. K. (1971). Evaluation of instructional materials as a function of material complexity and teacher manual format (Working Paper No. 10). Unpublished manuscript, Texas University, 1971 (ERIC Document Reproduction Service No. ED 079916).

94 Brennan, A., Worrall, L., & McKenna, K. (2005). The relationship between specific features of aphasia-friendly written material and comprehension of written material for people with aphasia: An exploratory study. *Aphasiology, 19*(8), 693–711.

95 Wingenfeld, K., Mensebach, C., Driessen, M., Bullig, R., Hartje, W., & Beblo, T. (2006). Attention bias towards personally relevant stimuli: The individual emotional Stroop task. *Psychological Reports, 99*(3), 781–793.

96 Scannell, L., & Gifford, R. (2013). Personally relevant climate change the role of place attachment and local versus global message framing in engagement. *Environment and Behavior, 45*(1), 60–85.

Sivacek, J., & Crano, W. D. (1982). Vested interest as a moderator of attitude-behavior consistency. *Journal of Personality and Social Psychology, 43*(2), 210–221.

97 Viskontas, I. V., Quiroga, R. Q., & Fried, I. (2009). Human medial temporal lobe neurons respond preferentially to personally relevant images. *Proceedings of the National Academy of Sciences, 106*(50), 21329–21334.

98 Burnkrant, R. E., & Unnava, H. R. (1989). Self-referencing: A strategy for increasing processing of message content. *Personality and Social Psychology Bulletin, 15*(4), 628–638.

99 Edworthy, J., Hellier, E., Morley, N., Grey, C., Aldrich, K., & Lee, A. (2004). Linguistic and location effects in compliance with pesticide warning labels for amateur and professional users. *Human Factors: The Journal of the Human Factors and Ergonomics Society, 46*(1), 11–31.

100 Bruner, J. S. (1957). On perceptual readiness. *Psychological Review, 64*(2), 123–152.

Tversky, A., & Kahneman, D. (1973). Availability: A heuristic for judging frequency and probability. *Cognitive Psychology, 5*(2), 207–232.

101 Klinger, E. (1975). Consequences of commitment to and disengagement from incentives. *Psychological Review, 82*(1), 1–25.

102 Sadoski, M., Goetz, E. T., & Avila, E. (1995). Concreteness effects in text recall: Dual coding or context availability? *Reading Research Quarterly, 30*(2), 278–288.

103 Graves, M. F., & Slater, W. H. (1986). Could textbooks be better written and would it make a difference? *American Educator, 10*(1), 36–42.

104 Sadoski, M., & Paivio, A. (2001). *Imagery and text: A dual coding theory of reading and writing*. Mahwah, NJ: Erlbaum.

105 *See* n43, Jorgensen & Kintsch (1973).

106 Holyoak, K. J. (1974). The role of imagery in the evaluation of sentences: Imagery or semantic factors. *Journal of Verbal Learning & Verbal Behavior, 13*(2), 163–166.

107 Roberson, Q. M., Collins, C. J., & Oreg, S. (2005). The effects of recruitment message specificity on applicant attraction to organizations. *Journal of Business and Psychology, 19*(3), 319–339.

Breaugh, J. A., & Starke, M. (2000). Research on employee recruitment: So many studies, so many remaining questions. *Journal of management, 26*(3), 405–434.

108 Laughery, K. R., & Page-Smith, K. R. (2006). Explicit information in warnings. In M. S. Wogalter (Ed.), *Handbook of warnings* (pp. 419–428). Mahwah, NJ: Lawrence Erlbaum.

109 Walker, H. J., Feild, H. S., Giles, W. F., Armenakis, A. A., & Bernerth, J. B. (2009). Displaying employee testimonials on recruitment web sites: Effects of communication media, employee race, and job seeker race on organizational attraction and information credibility. *Journal of Applied Psychology, 94*(5), 1354–1364.

110 Conzola, V. C., & Wogalter, M. S. (1999). Using voice and print directives and warnings to supplement product manual instructions. *International Journal of Industrial Ergonomics, 23*(5), 549–556.

111 Grass, R. C., & Wallace, W. H. (1974). Advertising communications: Print vs. TV. *Journal of Advertising Research, 14*(5), 19–23.

112 Calder, B. J., & Sternthal, B. (1980). Television commercial wearout: An information processing view. *Journal of Marketing Research, 17*(2), 173–186.

Craig, C. S., Sternthal, B., & Leavitt, C. (1976). Advertising wearout: An experimental analysis. *Journal of Marketing Research, 13*(4), 365–372.

113 Nicosia, G. E. (1988). College students' listening comprehension strategies in a lecture situation (Doctoral dissertation, New York University, 1988). *Dissertation Abstracts International, 49*(05A), 0998.

114 Erickson, B., Lind, E. A., Johnson, B. C., & O'Barr, W. M. (1978). Speech style and impression formation in a court setting: The effects of "powerful" and "powerless" speech. *Journal of Experimental Social Psychology, 14*(3), 266–279.

115 Burgoon, J. K., Buller, D., & Woodall, G. (1989). *Nonverbal communication: The unspoken dialogue*. New York: Harper & Row.

116 *See* n.53, Eagly (1974).

Holtgraves, T., & Lasky, B. (1999). Linguistic power and persuasion. *Journal of Language and Social Psychology, 18*(2), 196–205.

117 Chattopadhyay, A., Dahl, D. W., Ritchie, R. J. B., & Shahin, K. N. (2003). Hearing voices: The impact of announcer speech characteristics on consumer response to broadcast advertising. *Journal of Consumer Psychology, 13*(3), 198–204.

118 Duker, S. (1974). *Time compressed speech: An anthology and bibliography* (Vol. 3). Metuchen, NJ: Scarecrow Press.

LaBarbera, P. A., & MacLachlan, J. M. (1979). Response latency in telephone interviews. *Journal of Advertising Research, 19*(3), 49–55.

119 Hrubes, D. A. (2001). The role of nonverbal behavior in persuasion (Doctoral dissertation, University of Massachusetts, Amherst, 2001). *Dissertation Abstracts International, 62*(9–B), 4274.

120 Atman, C. J., & Puerzer, R. (1995). *Reader preference and comprehension of risk diagrams* (Tech Rep. No 95–8). Pittsburgh, PA: University of Pittsburgh, Department of Industrial Engineering.

See also Moreno, R., & Valdez, A. (2007). Immediate and delayed effects of using a classroom case exemplar in teacher education: The role of presentation format. *Journal of Educational Psychology, 99*(1), 194–206.

Park, S., & Lim, J. (2007). Promoting positive emotion in multimedia learning using visual illustrations. *Journal of Educational Multimedia and Hypermedia, 16*(2), 141–162.

121 Redish, J. C. (1993). Understanding readers. In C. M. Barnum & S. Carliner (Eds.), *Techniques for technical communicators* (pp. 14–41). New York: Macmillan.

Schriver, K. A., Hayes, J. R., & Steffy Cronin, A. (1996). *"Just say no to drugs" and other unwelcome advice: Explorin creation and interpretation of drug education literature* (Final Rep.). Berkeley, CA, and Pittsburgh, PA: University of Califorina at Berkeley and Carnegie Mellon University, National Center for the Study of Writing and Literacy.

Wright, P., Creighton, P., & Threlfall, S. M. (1982). Some factors determining when instructions will be read. *Ergonomics, 25*(3), 225–237.

122 *See* n80, Diamond (1968).

123 Pan, B., Zhang, L., & Law, R. (2013). The complex matter of online hotel choice. *Cornell Hospitality Quarterly*, *54*(1), 74–83.

124 Peterson, E. B., Thomsen, S., Lindsay, G., & John, K. (2010). Adolescents' attention to traditional and graphic tobacco warning labels: An eye-tracking approach. *Journal of Drug Education*, *40*(3), 227–244.

125 Strasser, A. A., Tang, K. Z., Romer, D., Jepson, C., & Cappella, J. N. (2012). Graphic warning labels in cigarette advertisements: Recall and viewing patterns. *American Journal of Preventive Medicine*, *43*(1), 41–47.

126 Katzman, N., & Nyenhuis, J. (1972). Color vs. black-and-white effects on learning, opinion, and attention. *AV Communication Review*, *20*(1), 16–28.

127 *See* n54, Kosslyn (1994).

128 Levasseur, D. G., & Kanan Sawyer, J. (2006). Pedagogy meets PowerPoint: A research review of the effects of computer-generated slides in the classroom. *The Review of Communication*, *6*(1–2), 101–123.

129 Peeck, J. (1987). The role of illustrations in processing and remembering illustrated text. In D. M. Willows & H. A. Houghton (Eds.), *The psychology of illustration: Basic research* (Vol. 1, pp. 115–151). New York: Springer-Verlag.

130 Levin, J. R., Anglin, G. J., & Carney, R. N. (1987). On empirically validating functions of pictures in prose. In D. M. Willows & H. A. Houghton (Eds.), *The psychology of illustration: Basic research* (Vol. 1, pp. 51–85). New York: Springer-Verlag.

131 Smith, S. M., & Shaffer, D. R. (2000). Vividness can undermine or enhance message processing: The moderating role of vividness congruency. *Personality and Social Psychology Bulletin*, *26*(7), 769–779.

132 Foulsham, T., & Underwood, G. (2007). How does the purpose of inspection influence the potency of visual salience in scene perception? *Perception*, *36*(8), 1123–1138.

Henderson, J. M., Brockmole, J. R., Castelhano, M. S., & Mack, M. (2007). Visual saliency does not account for eye movements during visual search in real-world scenes. In R. van Gompel, M. H. Fischer, W. S. Murray & R. L. Hill (Eds.), *Eye movements: A window on mind and brain* (pp. 537–562). Oxford, UK: Elsevier.

Underwood, G., & Foulsham, T. (2006). Visual saliency and semantic incongruency influence eye movements when inspecting pictures. *The Quarterly Journal of Experimental Psychology*, *59*(11), 1931–1949.

133 Allen, D. G., Biggane, J. E., Pitts, M., Otondo, R., & Van Scotter, J. (2013). Reactions to recruitment web sites: Visual and verbal attention, attraction, and intentions to pursue employment. *Journal of Business and Psychology*, *28*(3), 263–285.

134 Durik, A. M., & Harackiewicz, J. M. (2007). Different strokes for different folks: How individual interest moderates the effects of situational factors on task interest. *Journal of Educational Psychology*, *99*(3), 597–610.

Mayer, R. E. (2009). *Multimedia learning*. Cambridge: Cambridge University Press.

135 *See* n18, Just & Carpenter (1987).

136 *See* n41, Redish (1980).

137 Clark, H. H. (1969). Linguistic processes in deductive reasoning. *Psychological Review*, *76*(4), 387–404.

Clark, H. H., & Chase, W. G. (1972). On the process of comparing sentences against pictures. *Cognitive Psychology*, *3*(3), 472–517.

Just, M. A., & Clark, H. H. (1973). Drawing inferences from the presuppositions and implications of affirmative and negative sentences. *Journal of Verbal Learning & Verbal Behavior*, *12*(1), 21–31.

138 Chall, J. S. (1958). *Readability: An appraisal of research and application*. Columbus, OH: Ohio State University. Reprinted 1974. Epping, UK: Bowker Publishing Company.

Klare, G. M. (1963). *The measurement of readability*. Ames, IA: Iowa State University Press.

Klare, G. R. (1984). Readability. In P. D. Pearson, R. Barr, M. Kamil & P. Mosenthal (Eds.), *Handbook of reading research* (pp. 681–744). New York: Longman.

139 *See* n18, Just & Carpenter (1987).

Rayner, K. (1998). Eye movements in reading and information processing: 20 years of research. *Psychological Bulletin*, *124*(3), 372–422.

140 Flesch, R. (1948). A new readability yardstick. *Journal of Applied Psychology*, *32*(3), 221–233.

141 Gunning, R. (1964). *How to take the fog out of writing*. Chicago: Dartnell.

142 Dale, E., & Chall, J. S. (1948). A formula for predicting readability. *Educational Research Bulletin*, *27*, 11–20, 37–54.

143 Kincaid, J. P., Fishburne Jr, R. P., Rogers, R. L., & Chissom, B. S. (1975). *Derivation of new readability formulas (automated readability index, fog count and flesch reading ease formula) for Navy enlisted personnel* (No. RBR-8-75). Millington, TN: Naval Technical Training Command.

144 Chall, J.S., & Dale, E. (1995). *Readability revisited: The new Dale-Chall readability formula.* Northhampton, MA: Brookline Books.

145 Smith, D., Stenner, A. J., Horabin, I., & Smith, M. (1989). *The Lexile scale in theory and practice: Final report.* Washington, DC: MetaMetrics. (ERIC document reproduction service number ED 307 577).

146 Koslin, B. I., Zeno, S., & Koslin, S. (1987). *The DRP: An effective measure in reading.* New York: College Entrance Examination Board.

147 Benjamin, R.G. (2012). Reconstructing readability: Recent developments and recommendations in the analysis of text difficulty. *Educational Psychology Review, 24*(1), 63–88.

148 DuBay, W.H. (2004). The principles of readability. *Online Submission.* (ERIC document reproduction service number ED 490 073).

149 Graesser, A. C., & McNamara, D.S. (2011). Computational analyses of multilevel discourse comprehension. *Topics in Cognitive Science, 3*(2), 371–398.

150 Duffy, T. M., & Kabance, P. (1982). Testing a readable writing approach to text revision. *Journal of Educational Psychology, 74*(5), 733–748.

151 Coleman, E. B. (1962). Improving comprehensibility by shortening sentences. *Journal of Applied Psychology, 46*(2), 131–134.

152 *See* n138, Klare (1963), p. 14.

Schriver, K. A. (2000). Readability formulas in the new millennium: What's the use? *ACM Journal of Computer Documentation (JCD), 24*(3), 138–140.

153 Davison, A., & Kantor, R. N. (1982). On the failure of readability formulas to define readable texts: A case study from adaptations. *Reading Research Quarterly, 17*(2), 187–209.

154 Charrow, R., & Charrow, V.R. (1979). Making legal language understandable: Psycholinguistic study of jury instructions. *Columbia Law Review, 79,* 1306–1374.

155 Charrow, V.R. (1988). Readability vs. comprehensibility: A case study in improving a real document. In A. Davison & G. M. Green (Eds.), *Linguistic complexity and text comprehension: Readability issues reconsidered* (pp. 85–114). Hillsdale, NJ: Lawrence Erlbaum Associates.

156 Klare, G. R. (1976). A second look at the validity of readability formulas. *Journal of Reading Behavior, 8*(2), 129–152.

157 Bever, T. (1970). The cognitive basis for linguistic structures. In J. R. Hayes (Ed.), *Cognition and the development of language* (pp. 279–362). New York: Wiley.

Fodor, J. A., Bever, T. G., & Garrett, M. F. (1974). *The psychology of language: An introduction to psycholinguistics and generative grammar.* New York: McGraw-Hill.

158 Clark, H. H., & Clark, E. V. (1968). Semantic distinctions and memory for complex sentences. *The Quarterly Journal of Experimental Psychology, 20*(2), 129–138.

Schwartz, D., Sparkman, J. P., & Deese, J. (1970). The process of understanding and judgments of comprehensibility. *Journal of Verbal Learning & Verbal Behavior, 9*(1), 87–93.

Stolz, W. S. (1967). A study of the ability to decode grammatically novel sentences. *Journal of Verbal Learning & Verbal Behavior, 6*(6), 867–873.

159 *See* n157, Fodor et al. (1974).

Hakes, D. T., & Cairns, H. S. (1970). Sentence comprehension and relative pronouns. *Perception & Psychophysics, 8*(1), 5–8.

Larkin, W., & Burns, D. (1977). Sentence comprehension and memory for embedded structure. *Memory & Cognition, 5*(1), 17–22.

160 Kintsch, W., & Keenan, J. (1973). Reading rate and retention as a function of the number of propositions in the base structure of sentences. *Cognitive Psychology, 5*(3), 257–274.

161 *See* n138, Klare (1963), p. 162.

162 Sturt, P., Keller, F., & Dubey, A. (2010). Syntactic priming in comprehension: Parallelism effects with and without coordination. *Journal of Memory and Language, 62*(4), 333–351.

163 Frazier, L., Taft, L., Roeper, T., Clifton, C., & Ehrlich, K. (1984). Parallel structure: A source of facilitation in sentence comprehension. *Memory & Cognition, 12*(5), 421–430.

164 Kamil, M. L. (1972). Memory of repeated words and parallel structure in compound sentences. *Journal of Verbal Learning & Verbal Behavior, 11*(5), 634–643.

165 Fillmore, C. J. (1968). The case for case. In E. Bach & R. T. Harms (Eds.), *Universals of linguistic theory* (pp. 1–88). New York: Holt, Rinehart, and Winston.

166 Gough, P. B. (1966). The verification of sentences: The effects of delay of evidence and sentence length. *Journal of Verbal Learning and Verbal Behavior, 5*(5), 492–496.

Savin, H. B., & Perchonock, E. (1965). Grammatical structure and the immediate recall of English sentences. *Journal of Verbal Learning and Verbal Behavior, 4*(5), 348–353.

Slobin, D. I. (1966). Grammatical transformations and sentence comprehension in childhood and adult-hood. *Journal of Verbal Learning and Verbal Behavior, 5*(3), 219–277.

167 Bradley, S. D., & Meeds, R. (2002). Surface-structure transformations and advertising slogans: The case for moderate syntactic complexity. *Psychology & Marketing, 19*(7–8), 595–619.

Kulhavy, R. W., & Heinen, J. R. (1977). Recognition memory for paraphrases. *Journal of General Psychology, 96*(2), 223–230.

Layton, P., & Simpson, A. J. (1975). Surface and deep structure in sentence comprehension. *Journal of Verbal Learning & Verbal Behavior, 14*(6), 658–664.

168 Johnson-Laird, P. N. (1968). The choice of the passive voice in a communicative task. *British Journal of Psychology, 59*(1), 7–15.

Turner, E. A., & Rommetveit, R. (1968). Focus of attention in recall of active and passive sentences. *Journal of Verbal Learning & Verbal Behavior, 7*(2), 543–548.

169 Coleman, E. B. (1964). The comprehensibility of several grammatical transformations. *Journal of Applied Psychology, 48*(3), 186–190.

170 Gleitman, L. R., & Gleitman, H. (1970). *Phrase and paraphrase: Some innovative uses of language.* New York: W. W. Norton & Company.

171 Flower, L. S., Hayes, J. R., & Swarts, H. (1983). Revising functional documents: The scenario principle. In P. V. Anderson, R. J. Brockmann & C. R. Miller (Eds.), *New essays in technical and scientific communication* (pp. 41–58). New York: Baywood Press.

172 Felker, D. B., Redish, J. C., & Peterson, J. (1985, pp. 53–54). Training authors of informative documents. In T. Duffy & R. Walker (Eds.), *Designing usable texts* (pp. 43–61). New York: Academic Press.

173 *See* n154, Charrow & Charrow (1979).

Hupet, M., & Le Bouedec, B. (1975). Definiteness and voice in the interpretation of active and passive sentences. *The Quarterly Journal of Experimental Psychology, 27*(2), 323–330.

See n168, Johnson-Laird (1968).

174 Glucksberg, S., Trabasso, T., & Wald, J. (1973). Linguistic structures and mental operations. *Cognitive Psychology, 5*(3), 338–370.

Olson, D. R., & Filby, N. (1972). On the comprehension of active and passive sentences. *Cognitive Psychology, 3*(3), 361–381.

175 Jacoby, J., Nelson, M. C., & Hoyer, W. D. (1982). Corrective advertising and affirmative disclosure statements: Their potential for confusing and misleading the consumer. *Journal of Marketing, 46*(1), 61–72.

Ratner, N. B., & Gleason, J. B. (1993). An introduction to psycholinguistics: What do language users know? In J. B. Gleason & N. B. Ratner (Eds.), *Psycholingulstics* (pp. 1–40). Fort Worth, TX: Harcourt Brace.

Sherman, M. A. (1976). Adjectival negation and the comprehension of multiply negated sentences. *Journal of Verbal Learning & Verbal Behavior, 15*(2), 143–157.

176 Kaup, B., Lüdtke, J., & Zwaan, R. A. (2006). Processing negated sentences with contradictory predicates: Is a door that is not open mentally closed? *Journal of Pragmatics, 38*(7), 1033–1050.

177 Hasson, U., & Glucksberg, S. (2006). Does understanding negation entail affirmation? An examination of negated metaphors. *Journal of Pragmatics, 38*(7), 1015–1032.

Lüdtke, J., Friedrich, C. K., De Filippis, M., & Kaup, B. (2008). Event-related potential correlates of negation in a sentence–picture verification paradigm. *Journal of Cognitive Neuroscience, 20*(8), 1355–1370.

178 *See* n137, Clark & Chase (1972).

179 Ehrlich, K., & Rayner, K. (1983). Pronoun assignment and semantic integration during reading: Eye movements and immediacy of processing. *Journal of Verbal Learning & Verbal Behavior, 22*(1), 75–87.

180 Clark, H. H., & Sengul, C. J. (1979). In search of referents for nouns and pronouns. *Memory & Cognition, 7*(1), 35–41.

181 Daneman, M., & Carpenter, P. A. (1980). Individual differences in working memory and reading. *Journal of Verbal Learning & Verbal Behavior, 19*(4), 450–466.

182 de Villiers, P. A. (1974). Imagery and theme in recall of connected discourse. *Journal of Experimental Psychology, 103*(2), 263–268.

183 Yekovich, F. R., & Walker, C. H. (1978). Identifying and using referents in sentence comprehension. *Journal of Verbal Learning & Verbal Behavior, 17*(3), 265–277.

184 Gordon, P. C., & Chan, D. (1995). Pronouns, passives, and discourse coherence. *Journal of Memory and Language, 34*(2), 216–231.

185 Fajardo, I., Ávila, V., Ferrer, A., Tavares, G., Gómez, M., & Hernández, A. (2014). Easy-to-read texts for students with intellectual disability: Linguistic factors affecting comprehension. *Journal of Applied Research in Intellectual Disabilities, 27*(3), 212–225.

Kintsch, W., & Kozminsky, E. (1977). Summarizing stories after reading and listening. *Journal of Educational Psychology, 69*(5), 491–499.

Kintsch, W., & Vipond, D. (1979). Reading comprehension and readability in education practice and psychological theory. In L. G. Nilsson (Ed.), *Perspectives on memory research: Essays in honor of Uppsala University's 500th anniversary* (pp. 329–365). Hillsdale, NJ: Erlbaum.

186 Huang, Y. T., & Gordon, P. C. (2011). Distinguishing the time course of lexical and discourse processes through context, coreference, and quantified expressions. *Journal of Experimental Psychology: Learning, Memory, and Cognition, 37*(4), 966–978.

See n18, Just & Carpenter (1987).

187 Benatar, A., & Clifton, C. (2014). Newness, givenness and discourse updating: Evidence from eye movements. *Journal of Memory and Language, 71*(1), 1–16.

Goetz, E. T., & Armbruster, B. B. (1980). Psychological correlates of text structure. In R. J. Spiro, B. C. Bruce & W. F. Brewer (Eds.), *Theoretical issues in reading comprehension: Perspectives from cognitive psychology, artificial intelligence, linguistics, and education* (pp. 201–220). Hillsdale, NJ: Erlbaum.

188 Manelis, L., & Yekovich, F. R. (1976). Repetitions of propositional arguments in sentences. *Journal of Verbal Learning & Verbal Behavior, 15*(3), 301–312.

189 Wright, P. (1968). Reading to learn. *Chemistry in Britain, 4,* 445–450.

Frase, L. T., & Fisher, D. (1976). *Rating technical documents,* Case 25952, Memorandum for File. Piscataway, NJ: Bell Laboratories.

190 Cohen, H., Douaire, J., & Elsabbagh, M. (2001). The role of prosody in discourse processing. *Brain and Cognition, 46*(1), 73–82.

191 Giraud, S., & Thérouanne, P. (2010, March). *Role of lexico-syntactic and prosodic cues in spoken comprehension of enumeration in sighted and blind adults.* Presented at Multidisciplinary Approaches to Discourse Conference, Moissac, France.

Lemarié, J., Eyrolle, H., & Cellier, J. M. (2006). Visual signals in text comprehension: How to restore them when oralizing a text via a speech synthesis? *Computers in Human Behavior, 22*(6), 1096–1115.

Mautone, P. D., & Mayer, R. E. (2001). Signaling as a cognitive guide in multimedia learning. *Journal of Educational Psychology, 93*(2), 377–389.

192 Arnold, J. E., Fagnano, M., & Tanenhaus, M. K. (2003). Disfluencies signal theee, um, new information. *Journal of Psycholinguistic Research, 32*(1), 25–36.

Barr, D. J., & Seyfeddinipur, M. (2010). The role of fillers in listener attributions for speaker disfluency. *Language and Cognitive Processes, 25*(4), 441–455.

Fraundorf, S. H., & Watson, D. G. (2011). The disfluent discourse: Effects of filled pauses on recall. *Journal of Memory and Language, 65*(2), 161–175.

193 Fox Tree, J. E. (2002). Interpreting pauses and ums at turn exchanges. *Discourse Processes, 34*(1), 37–55.

194 Driskell, J. E., & Radtke, P. H. (2003). The effect of gesture on speech production and comprehension. *Human Factors: The Journal of the Human Factors and Ergonomics Society, 45*(3), 445–454.

Holler, J., Schubotz, L., Kelly, S., Hagoort, P., Schuetze, M., & Özyürek, A. (2014). Social eye gaze modulates processing of speech and co-speech gesture. *Cognition, 133*(3), 692–697.

Hostetter, A. B. (2011). When do gestures communicate? A meta-analysis. *Psychological Bulletin, 137*(2), 297–315.

195 Beattie, G., & Shovelton, H. (1999). Mapping the range of information contained in the iconic hand gestures that accompany spontaneous speech. *Journal of Language and Social Psychology, 18*(4), 438–462.

196 Chui, K. (2012). Cross-linguistic comparison of representations of motion in language and gesture. *Gesture, 12*(1), 40–61.

Parrill, F. (2008). Subjects in the hands of speakers: An experimental study of syntactic subject and speech-gesture integration. *Cognitive Linguistics, 19*(2), 283–299.

197 Woodall, W. G., & Folger, J. P. (1981). Encoding specificity and nonverbal cue context: An expansion of episodic memory research. *Communication Monographs, 48*(1), 39–53.

Woodall, W. G., & Folger, J. P. (1985). Nonverbal cue context and episodic memory: On the availability and endurance of nonverbal behaviors as retrieval cues. *Communication Monographs, 52*(4), 319–333.

198 Rogers, W. T. (1978). The contribution of kinesic illustrators toward the comprehension of verbal behavior within utterances. *Human Communication Research, 5*(1), 54–62.

199 Popham, W. J. (1961). Tape recorded lectures in the college classroom. *Audiovisual Communication Review, 9*(2), 109–118.

Menne, J., Klingensmith, J., & Nord, D. (1969). Use of taped lectures to replace class attendance. *AV Communication Review, 17*, 47–51.

200 Houts, P. S., Doak, C. C., Doak, L. G., & Loscalzo, M. J. (2006). The role of pictures in improving health communication: A review of research on attention, comprehension, recall, and adherence. *Patient Education and Counseling, 61*(2), 173–190.

201 Glenberg, A. M., & Langston, W. E. (1992). Comprehension of illustrated text: Pictures help to build mental models. *Journal of Memory and Language, 31*(2), 129–151.

Larkin, J. H., & Simon, H. A. (1987). Why a diagram is (sometimes) worth ten thousand words. *Cognitive Science: A Multidisciplinary Journal, 11*(1), 65–100.

Mayer, R. E., & Gallini, J. K. (1990). When is an illustration worth ten thousand words? *Journal of Educational Psychology, 82*(4), 715–726.

202 Davies, S., Haines, H., Norris, B., & Wilson, J. R. (1998). Safety pictograms: Are they getting the message across? *Applied Ergonomics, 29*(1), 15–23.

203 Boersema, T., & Zwaga, H. J. (1989, October). Selecting comprehensible warning symbols for swimming pool slides. In *Proceedings of the Human Factors and Ergonomics Society Annual Meeting* (Vol. 33, No. 15, pp. 994–998). Thousand Oaks, CA: Sage.

204 Findahl, O. (1971). *The effects of visual illustrations upon perception and retention of news programmes.* Stockholm, Sweden: Swedish Broadcasting Corporation, Audience and Program Research Department.

Findahl, O., & Hoijer, B. (1976). *Fragments of reality: An experiment with news and TV visuals.* Stockholm, Sweden: Swedish Broadcasting Corporation, Audience and Program Research Department.

Gunter, B. (1987, p. 248). *Poor reception: Misunderstanding and forgetting broadcast news.* Hillsdale, NJ: Lawrence Erlbaum Associates.

205 Carney, R. N., & Levin, J. R. (2002). Pictorial illustrations still improve students' learning from text. *Educational Psychology Review, 14*(1), 5–26.

Hegarty, M., & Just, M. A. (1993). Constructing mental models of machines from text and diagrams. *Journal of Memory and Language, 32*(6), 717–742.

Mayer, R. E., & Sims, V. K. (1994). For whom is a picture worth a thousand words? Extensions of a dual-coding theory of multimedia learning. *Journal of Educational Psychology, 86*(3), 389–401.

206 *See* n134, Mayer (2009).

207 Levie, W. H., & Lentz, R. (1982). Effects of text illustrations: A review of research. *Educational Communication & Technology Journal, 30*(4), 195–232.

208 Duchastel, P. C. (1979). *A functional approach to illustrations in text* (Occasional Paper 2). Bryn Mawr, PA: The American College.

Duchastel, P. C. (1980). *Research on illustrations in instructional texts* (Occasional Paper 3). Bryn Mawr, PA: The American College.

Macdonald-Ross, M. (1978). Graphics in texts. In L. S. Shulman (Ed.), *Review of research in education* (Vol. 5, pp. 49–85). Itasca, IL: F. E. Peacock Publishers.

209 Clark, R. C., & Mayer, R. E. (2011). *E-learning and the science of instruction: Proven guidelines for consumers and designers of multimedia learning.* Hoboken, NJ: John Wiley & Sons Ltd.

Holsanova, J., Holmberg, N., & Holmqvist, K. (2009). Reading information graphics: The role of spatial contiguity and dual attentional guidance. *Applied Cognitive Psychology, 23*(9), 1215–1226.

Sweller, J., Chandler, P., Tierney, P., & Cooper, M. (1990). Cognitive load as a factor in the structuring of technical material. *Journal of Experimental Psychology: General, 119*(2), 176–192.

210 Costley, C. L., & Brucks, M. (1992). Selective recall and information use in consumer preferences. *Journal of Consumer Research, 18*(4), 464–474.

211 Westendorp, P. (1995, June). *Testing pictures, texts, and animations for procedural instructions.* Paper presented at the Conference on Verbal Communications in Professional Settings, Utrecht, Netherlands.

212 Adaval, R., & Wyer, R. S. (1998). The role of narratives in consumer information processing. *Journal of Consumer Psychology, 7*(3), 207–245.

Adaval, R., Isbell, L. M., & Wyer, R. S. (2007). The impact of pictures on narrative-and list-based impression formation: A process interference model. *Journal of Experimental Social Psychology, 43*(3), 352–364.

213 Meyers-Levy, J., & Peracchio, L. A. (1992). Getting an angle in advertising: The effect of camera angle on product evaluations. *Journal of Marketing Research, 29*(4), 454–461.

214 Benson, P. J. (1994). Problems in picturing text (Doctoral dissertation, Carnegie Mellon University, 1994). *Dissertation Abstracts International, 55*(11A), 3357.

See n204, Gunter (1987).

See n130, Levin et al. (1987).

215 Glass, A. L., Eddy, J. K., & Schwanenflugel, P. J. (1980). The verification of high and low imagery sentences. *Journal of Experimental Psychology: Human Learning and Memory*, *6*(6), 692–704.

216 Miniard, P. W., Bhatla, S., Lord, K. R., Dickson, P. R., & Unnava, H. R. (1991). Picture-based persuasion processes and the moderating role of involvement. *Journal of Consumer Research*, *18*(1), 92–107.

217 Canham, M., & Hegarty, M. (2010). Effects of knowledge and display design on comprehension of complex graphics. *Learning and Instruction*, *20*(2), 155–166.

Kalyuga, S., & Renkl, A. (2010). Expertise reversal effect and its instructional implications: Introduction to the special issue. *Instructional Science*, *38*(3), 209–215.

See n201, Mayer & Gallini (1990).

218 Stone, E. R., Yates, J. F., & Parker, A. M. (1997). Effects of numerical and graphical displays on professed risk-taking behavior. *Journal of Experimental Psychology: Applied*, *3*(4), 243–256.

219 Gaissmaier, W., Wegwarth, O., Skopec, D., Müller, A. S., Broschinski, S., & Politi, M. C. (2012). Numbers can be worth a thousand pictures: Individual differences in understanding graphical and numerical representations of health-related information. *Health Psychology*, *31*(3), 286–296.

220 Tait, A. R., Voepel-Lewis, T., Zikmund-Fisher, B. J., & Fagerlin, A. (2010). The effect of format on parents' understanding of the risks and benefits of clinical research: A comparison between text, tables, and graphics. *Journal of Health Communication*, *15*(5), 487–501.

221 Cook, M., Wiebe, E. N., & Carter, G. (2008). The influence of prior knowledge on viewing and interpreting graphics with macroscopic and molecular representations. *Science Education*, *92*(5), 848–867.

Hegarty, M., Canham, M. S., & Fabrikant, S. I. (2010). Thinking about the weather: How display salience and knowledge affect performance in a graphic inference task. *Journal of Experimental Psychology: Learning, Memory, and Cognition*, *36*(1), 37–53.

222 Milroy, R., & Poulton, E. C. (1978). Labelling graphs for improved reading speed. *Ergonomics*, *21*(1), 55–61.

223 Shah, P., & Hoeffner, J. (2002). Review of graph comprehension research: Implications for instruction. *Educational Psychology Review, 14,* 47–69.

224 Fienberg, S. E. (1979). Graphical methods in statistics. *The American Statistician*, *33*, 165–178.

Kleiner, B., & Hartigan, J. A. (1981). Representing points in many dimensions by trees and castles. *Journal of the American Statistical Association*, *76*, 499–512.

225 Chernoff, H. (1973). Using faces to represent points in k-dimensional space graphically. *Journal of the American Statistical Association*, *68*, 361–368.

226 Winn, W. (1991). Learning from maps and diagrams. *Educational Psychology Review*, *3*(3), 211–247.

227 Spence, I. (1990). Visual psychophysics of simple graphical elements. *Journal of Experimental Psychology: Human Perception and Performance*, *16*(4), 683–692.

228 Fischer, M. H. (2000). Do irrelevant depth cues affect the comprehension of bar graphs? *Applied Cognitive Psychology*, *14*(2), 151–162.

Keller, T., Gerjets, P., Scheiter, K., & Garsoffky, B. (2006). Information visualizations for knowledge acquisition: The impact of dimensionality and color coding. *Computers in Human Behavior*, *22*(1), 43–65.

229 Holliday, W. G. (1975). The effects of verbal and adjunct pictorial-verbal information in science instruction. *Journal of Research in Science Teaching*, *12*, 77–83.

Holliday, W. G., Brunner, L. L., & Donais, E. L. (1977). Differential cognitive and affective responses for flow diagrams in science. *Journal of Research in Science Teaching*, *14*, 129–138.

Holliday, W. G., & Harvey, D. A. (1976). Adjunct labeled drawings in teaching physics to junior high school students. *Journal of Research in Science Teaching*, *13*, 37–43.

230 Bransford, J. D., & Johnson, M. K. (1973). Considerations of some problems of comprehension. In W. G. Chase (Ed.), *Visual information processing* (pp. 383–438). Oxford, UK: Academic.

Smith, E. E., & Swinney, D. A. (1992). The role of schemas in reading text: A real-time examination. *Discourse Processes*, *15*(3), 303–316.

von Hippel, W., Jonides, I., Hilton, J. L., & Narayan, S. (1993). Inhibitory effect of schematic processing on perceptual encoding. *Journal of Personality and Social Psychology*, *64*(6), 921–935.

231 Bransford & Johnson (1973).

232 Anderson, R. C., Spiro, R. J., & Anderson, M. C. (1978). Schemata as scaffolding for the representation of information in connected discourse. *American Educational Research Journal*, *15*(3), 433–440.

Dansereau. D. F., Brooks, L. W., Spurlin, J. E., & Holley, C. D. (1982). *Headings and outlines as processing aids for scientific text* (National Institute of Education, Final Report, NIE-G-79–0157). Fort Worth, TX: Texas Christian University.

233 Dooling, D. J., & Lachman, R. (1971). Effects of comprehension on retention of prose. *Journal of Experimental Psychology, 88*(2), 216–222.

Dooling, D. J., & Mullet, R. L. (1973). Locus of thematic effects in retention of prose. *Journal of Experimental Psychology, 97*(3), 404–406.

Sulin, R. A., & Dooling, D. J. (1974). Intrusion of a thematic idea in retention of prose. *Journal of Experimental Psychology, 103*(2), 255–262.

234 Kozminsky, E. (1977). Altering comprehension: The effect of biasing titles on text comprehension. *Memory & Cognition, 5*(4), 482–490.

235 Lemarié, J., Lorch Jr, R. F., & Péry-Woodley, M. P. (2012). Understanding how headings influence text processing. *Discours, 10,* 2–22.

236 Schallert, D. L. (1976, p. 622). Improving memory for prose: The relationship between depth of processing and context. *Journal of Verbal Learning & Verbal Behavior, 15*(6), 621–632.

237 Bransford, J. D., & McCarrell, N. S. (1974). A sketch of a cognitive approach to comprehension. In W. Weimer & D. Palermo (Eds.), *Cognition and the symbolic processes* (pp. 189–229). Hillsdale, NJ: Erlbaum.

Krug, D., George, B., Hannon, S. A., & Glover, J. A. (1989). The effect of outlines and headings on readers' recall of text. *Contemporary Educational Psychology, 14*(2), 111–123.

Smith-Jackson, T. L., & Wogalter, M. S. (2007). Application of a mental models approach to MSDS design. *Theoretical Issues in Ergonomics Science, 8*(4), 303–319.

238 *See* n233, Dooling & Mullet (1973).

Sjogren, D., & Timpson, W. (1979). Frameworks for comprehending discourse: A replication study. *American Educational Research Journal, 16*(4), 341–346.

239 *See* n59, Cauchard et al. (2010).

240 *See* n59, Hyönä & Lorch (2004).

Lorch Jr, R. F., Lorch, E. P., Ritchey, K., McGovern, L., & Coleman, D. (2001). Effects of headings on text summarization. *Contemporary Educational Psychology, 26*(2), 171–191.

Ritchey, K., Schuster, J., & Allen, J. (2008). How the relationship between text and headings influences readers' memory. *Contemporary Educational Psychology, 33*(4), 859–874.

241 *See* n232, Dansereau et al. (1982).

242 Hartley, J., & Trueman, M. (1982, March). *Headings in text: Issues and data.* Paper presented at Annual Meeting of American Educational Research Association, New York.

243 Swarts, H., Flower, L., & Hayes, J. R. (1980). *How headings in documents can mislead readers* (Document Design Project Tech. Rep. No. 9). Pittsburgh, PA: Carnegie Mellon University, Communications Design Center.

244 Bridge, C. A., Belmore, S. M., Moskow, S. P., Cohen, S. S., & Matthews, P. D. (1984). Topicalization and memory for main ideas in prose. *Journal of Literacy Research, 16*(1), 61–80.

Kieras, D. E. (1978). Good and bad structure in simple paragraphs: Effects on apparent theme, reading time, and recall. *Journal of Verbal Learning & Verbal Behavior, 17*(1), 13–28.

Kintsch, W. (1979). On modeling comprehension. *Educational Psychologist, 14,* 3–14.

Kintsch, W., & van Dijk, T. A. (1978). Toward a model of text comprehension and production. *Psychological Review, 85*(5), 363–394.

245 Myers, J. L., Pezdek, K., & Coulson, D. (1973). Effect of prose organization upon free recall. *Journal of Educational Psychology, 65*(3), 313–320.

Perlmutter, J., & Royer, J. M. (1973). Organization of prose materials: Stimulus, storage, and retrieval. *Canadian Journal of Psychology/Revue Canadienne de Psychologie, 27*(2), 200–209.

246 Gardner, E. T., & Schumacher, G. M. (1977). Effects of contextual organization on prose retention. *Journal of Educational Psychology, 69*(2), 146–151.

Lorch Jr, R. F., & Lorch, E. P. (1995). Effects of organizational signals on text-processing strategies. *Journal of Educational Psychology, 87*(4), 537–544.

Meyer, B. J., & McConkie, G. W. (1973). What is recalled after hearing a passage? *Journal of Educational Psychology, 65*(1), 109–117.

247 Cameron, L. D., & Leventhal, H. (2003). *The self-regulation of health and illness behaviour.* New York: Psychology Press.

248 Swaney, J. H., Janik, C. J., Bond, S. J., & Hayes, J. R. (1991). Editing for comprehension: Improving the process through reading protocols. In E. R. Steinberg (Ed.), *Plain language: Principles and practice* (pp. 173–203). Detroit, MI: Wayne State University Press. (Original article published in 1981 as Document Design Project Tech. Rep. No. 14, Pittsburgh, PA: Carnegie Mellon University).

249 Dupont, V., & Bestgen, Y. (2002). Structure and topic information in expository text overviews. *Document design*, *3*(1), 2–12.

Lorch Jr, R. F., Chen, H. T., & Lemarié, J. (2012). Communicating headings and preview sentences in text and speech. *Journal of Experimental Psychology: Applied*, *18*(3), 265–276.

Nesbit, J. C., & Adescope, O. O. (2006). Learning with concept and knowledge maps: A meta-analysis. *Review of Educational Research, 76*, 413–448.

250 Hartley, J., & Davies, I. (1976). Preinstructional strategies: The role of pretests, behavioral objectives, overviews, and advance organizers. *Review of Educational Research*, *46*, 239–265.

Luiten, J., Ames, W., & Ackerson, G. (1980). A meta-analysis of the effects of advance organizers on learning and retention. *American Educational Research Journal*, *17*(2), 211–218.

251 Townsend, M. A. (1980). Schema activation in memory for prose. *Journal of Reading Behavior*, *12*(1), 49–53.

252 *See* n233, Dooling & Mullet (1973).

253 Morris, C. D., Stein, B. S., & Bransford, J. D. (1979). Prerequisites for the utilization of knowledge in the recall of prose passages. *Journal of Experimental Psychology: Human Learning and Memory*, *5*(3), 253–261.

254 Reid, J. C., Kardash, C. M., Robinson, R. D., & Scholes, R. (1994). Comprehension in patient literature: The importance of text and reader characteristics. *Health Communication Special Issue: Communicating With Patients About Their Medications*, *6*(4), 327–335.

255 Mehrabian, A., & Ferris, S. R. (1967). Material-appropriate processing: A contextualist approach to reading and studying strategies. *Educational Psychology Review*, *1*(2), 113–145.

Zwaan, R. A., & Brown, C. M. (1996). The influence of language proficiency and comprehension skill on situation-model construction. *Discourse Processes*, *21*(3), 289–327.

256 Langacker, R. W. (2008, p. 478). *Cognitive grammar: A basic introduction.* New York: Oxford University Press.

257 Samuels, S. J., Tennyson, R., Sax, M., Patricia, M., Schermer, N., & Hajovy, H. (1988). Adults' use of text structure in the recall of a scientific journal article. *The Journal of Educational Research*, *81*(3), 171–174.

258 Feldman, C., & Kalmar, D. (1996). Autobiography and fiction as modes of thought. In D. Olson & N. Torrance (Eds.), *Modes of thought: Explorations in culture and cognition* (pp. 106–122). Cambridge, UK: Cambridge University Press.

259 Kalmar, D. A. (1996). The effect of perspective on recall and interpretation of stories: An extension of Anderson and Pichert (Doctoral dissertation, Yale University, 1996), *Dissertation Abstracts International*, *57*(06B), 4064.

260 Kricorian, K. T. (2000). The judgment and memory effects of the activation of general knowledge structures related to persuasion and information (Doctoral dissertation, Stanford University, 2000). *Dissertation Abstracts International*, *61*(09A), 3662.

261 Mason, L., Pluchino, P., Tornatora, M. C., & Ariasi, N. (2013). An eye-tracking study of learning from science text with concrete and abstract illustrations. *The Journal of Experimental Education*, *81*(3), 356–384.

262 Brown, K. G., Reidy, J. G., Weighall, A. R., & Arden, M. A. (2013). Graphic imagery is not sufficient for increased attention to cigarette warnings: The role of text captions. *Addiction*, *108*(4), 820–825.

263 Price, R. (1972). *Droodles.* Los Angeles: Price/Stern/Sloan.

264 Bower, G. H., Karlin, M. B., & Dueck, A. (1975). Comprehension and memory for pictures. *Memory & Cognition*, *3*(2), 216–220.

265 *See* n231, Bransford & Johnson (1972).

266 *See* n36, Mackey & Metz (2009).

267 *See* n243, Swarts et al. (1980).

See also n59, Cauchard et al. (2010).

Goldman, S. R., & Durán, R. P. (1988). Answering questions from oceanography texts: Learner, task, and text characteristics. *Discourse Processes*, *11*(4), 373–412.

268 Kern, R. P., Sticht, T. G., Welty, D., & Hauke, R. N. (1977). *Guidebook for the development of Army training literature.* Arlington, VA: U.S. Army Research Institute for the Behavioral and Social Sciences.

Wright, P., & Reid, F. (1973). Written information: Some alternatives to prose for expressing the outcomes of complex contingencies. *Journal of Applied Psychology*, *57*(2), 160–166.

269 Wright, P. (1977). Decision making as a factor in the ease of using numerical tables. *Ergonomics*, *20*(1), 91–96.

270 Carswell, C. M., & Wickens, C. D. (1987). Information integration and the object display: An interaction of task demands and display superiority. *Ergonomics*, *30*(3), 511–527.

271 Kosslyn, S. M. (2006). *Graph design for the eye and mind.* New York: Oxford University Press.

Shah, P., Mayer, R. E., & Hegarty, M. (1999). Graphs as aids to knowledge construction: Signaling techniques for guiding the process of graph comprehension. *Journal of Educational Psychology, 91*(4), 690–702.

272 *See* n270, Carswell & Wickens (1987).

273 Tharanathan, A., Bullemer, P., Laberge, J., Reising, D. V., & Mclain, R. (2012). Impact of functional and schematic overview displays on console operators' situation awareness. *Journal of Cognitive Engineering and Decision Making, 6*(2), 141–164.

274 Cook, M. B., & Smallman, H. S. (2008). Human factors of the confirmation bias in intelligence analysis: Decision support from graphical evidence landscapes. *Human Factors: The Journal of the Human Factors and Ergonomics Society, 50*(5), 745–754.

275 Moreno, R., & Ortegano-Layne, L. (2008). Do classroom exemplars promote the application of principles in teacher education? A comparison of videos, animations, and narratives. *Educational Technology Research and Development, 56*(4), 449–465.

276 Kamin, C., O'Sullivan, P., Deterding, R., & Younger, M. (2003). A comparison of critical thinking in groups of third-year medical students in text, video, and virtual PBL case modalities. *Academic Medicine, 78*(2), 204–211.

277 Ayres, P., Marcus, N., Chan, C., & Qian, N. (2009). Learning hand manipulative tasks: When instructional animations are superior to equivalent static representations. *Computers in Human Behavior, 25*(2), 348–353.

de Souza, J. M. B., & Dyson, M. (2008). Are animated demonstrations the clearest and most comfortable way to communicate on-screen instructions? *Information Design Journal, 16*(2), 107–124.

Höffler, T. N., & Leutner, D. (2007). Instructional animation versus static pictures: A meta-analysis. *Learning and Instruction, 17*(6), 722–738.

278 Arguel, A., & Jamet, E. (2009). Using video and static pictures to improve learning of procedural contents. *Computers in Human Behavior, 25*(2), 354–359.

279 Townsend, C., & Kahn, B. E. (2014). The "visual preference heuristic": The influence of visual versus verbal depiction on assortment processing, perceived variety, and choice overload. *Journal of Consumer Research, 40*(5), 993–1015.

280 *See* n268, Kern et al. (1977).

281 Dunbar, G. (2010). Task-based nutrition labelling. *Appetite, 55*(3), 431–435.

Huckin, T. N., & Olsen, L. A. (1991). *Technical writing and professional communication for nonnative speakers of English.* New York: McGraw-Hill.

282 Kintsch, W., & Yarborough, J. (1982). The role of rhetorical structure in text comprehension. *Journal of Educational Psychology, 74*(2), 828–834.

283 Vauras, M., Hyönä, J., & Niemi, P. (1992). Comprehending coherent and incoherent texts: Evidence from eye movement patterns and recall performance. *Journal of Research in Reading, 15*(1), 39–54.

284 Thorndyke, P. W. (1977). Cognitive structures in comprehension and memory of narrative discourse. *Cognitive Psychology, 9*(1), 77–110.

285 Schriver, K. A. (1997, pp. 316–320). *Dynamics in document design: Creating text for readers.* New York: Wiley.

286 Goldsmith, E. (1987). The analysis of illustration in theory and practice. In H. A. Houghton & D. M. Willows (Eds.), *The psychology of illustration: Instructional issues* (Vol. 2, pp. 53–85). New York: Springer-Verlag.

287 Bonsiepe, G. (1968). A method of quantifying order in typographic design. *Journal of Typographic Research, 3*, 203–220.

288 MacGregor, D., & Slovic, P. (1986). Graphic representation of judgmental information. *Human-Computer Interaction, 2*(3), 179–200.

289 *See* n171, Flower et al. (1983).

290 Russo, J. E., & Dosher, B. A. (1983). Strategies for multiattribute binay choice. *Journal of Experimental Psychology: Learning, Memory, and Cognition, 9*(4), 676–696.

291 Jarvenpaa, S. L. (1989). The effect of task demands and graphical format on information processing strategies and decision making performance. *Management Science, 35*(3), 285–303.

292 Jang, J. M., & Yoon, S. O. (2015). The effect of attribute-based and alternative-based processing on consumer choice in context. *Marketing Letters*, 1–14.

293 Pizzi, G., Scarpi, D., & Marzocchi, G. L. (2014). Showing a tree to sell the forest: The impact of attribute- and alternative-based information presentation on consumers' choices. *Journal of Economic Psychology, 42*, 41–51.

294 Payne, J. W., Bettman, J. R., & Johnson, E. J. (1988). Adaptive strategy selection in decision making. *Journal of Experimental Psychology: Learning, Memory, and Cognition, 14*(3), 534–552.

295 Capon, N., & Burke, M. (1977). Information seeking in consumer durable purchases. In B. A. Greenberg & D. N. Bellenger (Eds.), *Contemporary marketing thought, 1977 educator's proceedings* (pp. 110–115). Chicago: American Marketing Association.

Olshavsky, R. W., & Acito, F. (1980). The impact of data collection procedure on choice rule. *Advances in Consumer Research, 7,* 729–732.

296 Jacoby, J., Kuss, A., Mazursky, D., & Troutman, T. (1985). Effectiveness of security analyst information accessing strategies: A computer interactive assessment. *Computers in Human Behavior, 1*(1), 95–113.

297 Slovic, P. (1972). *From Shakespeare to Simon: Speculations—and some evidence—about man's ability to process information,* ORI research monograph, (Vol. 12). Eugene, OR: Oregon Research Institute.

298 *See* n291, Jarvenpaa (1989).

299 Todd, P., & Benbasat, I. (1991). An experimental investigation of the impact of computer based decision aids on decision making strategies. *Information Systems Research, 2*(2), 87–115.

300 van Raaij, W. F. (1976). *Direct monitoring of consumer information processing by eye movement recorder.* Unpublished paper, Tilburg University, Tilburg, Netherlands.

301 Bettman, J. R., & Kakkar, P. (1977). Effects of information presentation format on consumer information acquisition strategies. *Journal of Consumer Research, 3*(4), 233–240.

302 Shi, S. W., Wedel, M., & Pieters, F. (2013). Information acquisition during online decision making: A model-based exploration using eye-tracking data. *Management Science, 59*(5), 1009–1026.

303 *See* n301, Bettman & Kakkar (1977).

304 Russo, J. E. (1977). The value of unit price information. *Journal of Marketing Research, 14*(2), 193–201.

Russo, J. E., Krieser, G., & Miyashita, S. (1975). An effective display of unit price information. *Journal of Marketing, 39,* 11–19.

305 Schkade, D. A., & Kleinmuntz, D. N. (1994). Information displays and choice processes: Differential effects of organization, form, and sequence. *Organizational Behavior and Human Decision Processes, 57*(3), 319–337.

306 Slovic, P., Finucane, M., Peters, E., & MacGregor, D. G. (2002). Rational actors or rational fools: Implications of the affect heuristic for behavioral economics. *The Journal of Socio-Economics, 31*(4), 329–342.

307 Bazerman, M. H., Tenbrunsel, A. E., & Wade-Benzoni, K. (1998). Negotiating with yourself and losing: Making decisions with competing internal preferences. *Academy of Management Review, 23*(2), 225–241.

308 Muthukrishnan, A. V., & Ramaswami, S. (1999). Contextual effects on the revision of evaluative judgments: An extension of the omission-detection framework. *Journal of Consumer Research, 26*(1), 70–84.

309 Carlson, C. A., Gronlund, S. D., & Clark, S. E. (2008). Lineup composition, suspect position and the sequential lineup advantage. *Journal of Experimental Psychology: Applied, 14*(2), 118–128.

Jonas, E., Schulz-Hardt, S., Frey, D., & Thelen, N. (2001). Confirmation bias in sequential information search after preliminary decisions: An expansion of dissonance theoretical research on selective exposure to information. *Journal of Personality and Social Psychology, 80*(4), 557–571.

310 Russo, J. E. (2015). The predecisional distortion of information. In E. A. Wilhelms & V. F. Reyna (Eds.), *Neuroeconomics, judgment, and decision making* (pp. 91–110). New York: Psychology Press.

311 Choi, J., & Myer, D. W. (2012). The effect of product positioning in a comparison table on consumers' evaluation of a sponsor. *Marketing Letters, 23*(1), 367–380.

312 Argote, L., Ingram, P., Levine, J. M., & Moreland, R. L. (2000). Knowledge transfer in organizations: Learning from the experience of others. *Organizational Behavior and Human Decision Processes, 82*(1), 1–8.

Dahlin, K. B., Weingart, L. R., & Hinds, P. J. (2005). Team diversity and information use. *Academy of Management Journal, 48*(6), 1107–1123.

Thomas-Hunt, M. C., Ogden, T. Y., & Neale, M. A. (2003). Who's really sharing? Effects of social and expert status on knowledge exchange within groups. *Management Science, 49*(4), 464–477.

313 Cosier, R. A., & Schwenk, C. R. (1990). Agreement and thinking alike: Ingredients for poor decisions. *Academy of Management Executive, 4*(1), 69–74.

314 Mojzisch, A., & Schulz-Hardt, S. (2005). Information sampling in group decision making: Sampling biases and their consequences. In K. Fiedler & P. Juslin (Eds.), *Information sampling and adaptive cognition* (pp. 299–326). Cambridge, UK: Cambridge University Press.

Stasser, G., & Birchmeier, Z. (2003). Group creativity and collective choice. In P. B. Paulus & B. A. Nijstad (Eds.), *Group creativity: Innovation through collaboration* (pp. 85–109). New York: Oxford University Press.

315 Cruz, M. G., Boster, F. J., & Rodríguez, J. I. (1997). The impact of group size and proportion of shared information on the exchange and integration of information in groups. *Communication Research, 24*(3), 291–313.

316 Larson, J. R., Foster-Fishman, P. G., & Keys, C. B. (1994). Discussion of shared and unshared information in decision-making groups. *Journal of Personality and Social Psychology, 67*(3), 446–461.

317 Karau, S. J., & Kelly, J. R. (1992). The effects of time scarcity and time abundance on group performance quality and interaction process. *Journal of Experimental Social Psychology, 28*(6), 542–571.

Kelly, J. R., & Karau, S. J. (1999). Group decision making: The effects of initial preferences and time pressure. *Personality and Social Psychology Bulletin, 25*(11), 1342–1354.

318 Brodbeck, F. C., Kerschreiter, R., Mojzisch, A., Frey, D., & Schulz-Hardt, S. (2002). The dissemination of critical, unshared information in decision-making groups: The effects of pre-discussion dissent. *European Journal of Social Psychology, 32*(1), 35–56.

Choi, H. S., & Levine, J. M. (2004). Minority influence in work teams: The impact of newcomers. *Journal of Experimental Social Psychology, 40*(2), 273–280.

319 Klocke, U. (2007). How to improve decision making in small groups: Effects of dissent and training interventions. *Small Group Research, 38*(3), 437–468.

Schulz-Hardt, S., Brodbeck, F. C., Mojzisch, A., Kerschreiter, R., & Frey, D. (2006). Group decision making in hidden profile situations: Dissent as a facilitator for decision quality. *Journal of Personality and Social Psychology, 91*(6), 1080–1093.

320 Schulz-Hardt, S., Jochims, M., & Frey, D. (2002). Productive conflict in group decision making: Genuine and contrived dissent as strategies to counteract biased information seeking. *Organizational Behavior and Human Decision Processes, 88*(2), 563–586.

321 Stasser, G., & Vaughan, S. I. (1996). Models of participation during face-to-face unstructured discussion. In E. H. Witte & J. H. Davis (Eds.), *Understanding group behavior, vol. 1: Consensual action by small groups* (pp. 165–192). Hillsdale, NJ: Lawrence Erlbaum.

322 Greitemeyer, T., Schulz-Hardt, S., Brodbeck, F. C., & Frey, D. (2006). Information sampling and group decision making: The effects of an advocacy decision procedure and task experience. *Journal of Experimental Psychology: Applied, 12*(1), 31–42.

Robertson, D. W. (2006). A comparison of three group decision-making strategies and their effects on the group decision-making process. *Dissertation Abstracts International Section A: Humanities and Social Sciences, 66*(10-A), 3722.

See n320, Schulz-Hardt et al. (2002).

323 Diehl, M., & Stroebe, W. (1987). Productivity loss in brainstorming groups: Toward the solution of a riddle. *Journal of Personality and Social Psychology, 53*(3), 497–509.

324 Mullen, B., Johnson, C., & Salas, E. (1991). Productivity loss in brainstorming groups: A meta-analytic integration. *Basic and Applied Social Psychology, 12*(1), 3–23.

Rietzschel, E. F., Nijstad, B. A., & Stroebe, W. (2006). Productivity is not enough: A comparison of interactive and nominal brainstorming groups on idea generation and selection. *Journal of Experimental Social Psychology, 42*(2), 244–251.

325 Camacho, L. M., & Paulus, P. B. (1995). The role of social anxiousness in group brainstorming. *Journal of Personality and Social Psychology, 68*(6), 1071–1080.

326 Winquist, J. R., & Franz, T. M. (2008). Does the Stepladder technique improve group decision making? A series of failed replications. *Group Dynamics: Theory, Research, and Practice, 12*(4), 255–267.

327 Eils, L. C., & John, R. S. (1980). A criterion validation of multiattribute utility analysis and of group communication strategy. *Organizational Behavior & Human Performance, 25*(2), 268–288.

Sainfort, F. C., Gustafson, D. H., Bosworth, K., & Hawkins, R. P. (1990). Decision support systems effectiveness: Conceptual framework and empirical evaluation. *Organizational Behavior and Human Decision Processes, 45*(2), 232–252.

Timmermans, D., & Vlek, C. (1996). Effects on decision quality of supporting multi-attribute evaluation in groups. *Organizational Behavior and Human Decision Processes, 68*(2), 158–170.

328 Von Winterfeldt, D., & Edwards, W. (1986). *Decision analysis and behavioral research.* Cambridge, UK: Cambridge University Press.

329 Sulsky, L. M., & Kline, T. J. (2007). Understanding frame-of-reference training success: A social learning theory perspective. *International Journal of Training and Development, 11*(2), 121–131.

Woehr, D. J. (1994). Understanding frame-of-reference training: The impact of training on the recall of performance information. *Journal of Applied Psychology, 79*(4), 525–534.

330 Barlow, C. M. (2000). Deliberate insight in team creativity. *The Journal of Creative Behavior, 34*(2), 101–117.

331 Stewart, D. D., & Stasser, G. (1995). Expert role assignment and information sampling during collective recall and decision making. *Journal of Personality and Social Psychology, 69*(4), 619–628.

van Ginkel, W. P., & van Knippenberg, D. (2009). Knowledge about the distribution of information and group decision making: When and why does it work? *Organizational Behavior and Human Decision Processes, 108*(2), 218–229.

332 Woolley, A. W., Gerbasi, M. E., Chabris, C. F., Kosslyn, S. M., & Hackman, J. R. (2008). Bringing in the experts how team composition and collaborative planning jointly shape analytic effectiveness. *Small Group Research, 39*(3), 352–371.

333 Gruenfeld, D. H., Mannix, E. A., Williams, K. Y., & Neale, M. A. (1996). Group composition and decision making: How member familiarity and information distribution affect process and performance. *Organizational Behavior and Human Decision Processes, 67*(1), 1–15.

Stasser, G., Stewart, D. D., & Wittenbaum, G. M. (1995). Expert roles and information exchange during discussion: The importance of knowing who knows what. *Journal of Experimental Social Psychology, 31*(3), 244–265.

334 Faraj, S., & Sproull, L. (2000). Coordinating expertise in software development teams. *Management Science, 46*(12), 1554–1568.

See n331, van Ginkel & van Knippenberg (2009).

335 De Meyer, A. (1991). Tech talk: How managers are stimulating global R&D communication. *MIT Sloan Management Review, 32*(3), 49–59.

Robey, D., Khoo, H. M., & Powers, C. (2000). Situated learning in cross-functional virtual teams. *Technical Communication, 47*(1), 51–66.

336 Nemiro, J., Beyerlein, M., Bradley, L., & Beyerlein, S. (2008). The challenges of virtual teaming. In J. Nemiro, M. M. Beyerlein, L. Bradley & S. Beyerlein (Eds.), *The handbook of high-performance virtual teams: A toolkit for collaborating across boundaries* (pp. 1–27). San Francisco, CA: Jossey-Bass.

337 Hackman, J. R. (1987). The design of work teams. In J. Lorsch (Ed.), *Handbook of organizational behavior* (pp. 315–342). Englewood Cliffs, NJ: Prentice Hall.

Quigley, N. R., Tesluk, P. E., Locke, E. A., & Bartol, K. M. (2007). A multilevel investigation of the motivational mechanisms underlying knowledge sharing and performance. *Organization Science, 18*(1), 71–88.

Schippers, M. C., Den Hartog, D. N., Koopman, P. L., & van Knippenberg, D. (2008). The role of transformational leadership in enhancing team reflexivity. *Human Relations, 61*(11), 1593–1616.

338 Stasser, G., & Stewart, D. (1992). Discovery of hidden profiles by decision-making groups: Solving a problem versus making a judgment. *Journal of Personality and Social Psychology, 63*(3), 426–434.

339 Stewart, D. D., & Stasser, G. (1998). The sampling of critical, unshared information in decision-making groups: The role of an informed minority. *European Journal of Social Psychology, 28*(1), 95–113.

340 Parks, C. D., & Cowlin, R. A. (1996). Acceptance of uncommon information into group discussion when that information is or is not demonstrable. *Organizational Behavior and Human Decision Processes, 66*(3), 307–315.

Sheffey, S., Tindale, R. S., & Scott, L. A. (1989). *Information sharing and group decision-making.* Presented at the Midwestern Psychological Association Annual Convention, Chicago, IL.

341 Gigone, D., & Hastie, R. (1993). The common knowledge effect: Information sharing and group judgment. *Journal of Personality and Social Psychology, 65*(5), 959.

342 Okhuysen, G. A., & Eisenhardt, K. M. (2002). Integrating knowledge in groups: How formal interventions enable flexibility. *Organization Science, 13*(4), 370–386.

Postmes, T., Spears, R., & Cihangir, S. (2001). Quality of decision making and group norms. *Journal of Personality and Social Psychology, 80*(6), 918–930.

343 Van den Bossche, P., Gijselaers, W. H., Segers, M., & Kirschner, P. A. (2006). Social and cognitive factors driving teamwork in collaborative learning environments team learning beliefs and behaviors. *Small Group Research, 37*(5), 490–521.

344 Edmondson, A. C. (1996). Learning from mistakes is easier said than done: Group and organizational influences on the detection and correction of human error. *Journal of Applied Behavioural Sciences, 32*(1), 5–32.

Edmondson, A. C. (2003). Speaking up in the operating room: How team leaders promote learning in interdisciplinary action teams. *Journal of Management Studies, 40*(6), 1419–1452.

345 Kelley, C. M., & Jacoby, L. L. (1996). Adult egocentrism: Subjective experience versus analytic bases for judgment. *Journal of Memory and Language, 35*(2), 157–175.

346 Berardi-Coletta, B., Buyer, L. S., Dominowski, R. L., & Rellinger, E. R. (1995). Metacognition and problem solving: A process-oriented approach. *Journal of Experimental Psychology: Learning, Memory, and Cognition, 21*(1), 205–223.

Pliske, R. M., Crandall, B., & Klein, G. (2004). Competence in weather forecasting. In J. Shanteau, P. Johnson & K. Smith (Eds.), *Psychological investigations of competence in decision making* (pp. 40–70). Cambridge: Cambridge University Press.

Symes, B. A., & Stewart, J. B. (1999). The relationship between metacognition and vocational indecision. *Canadian Journal of Counselling, 33*(3), 195–211.

347 Boyd, B. K. (1991). Strategic planning and financial performance: A meta-analytic review. *Journal of Management Studies, 28*(4), 353–374.

Miller, C. C., & Cardinal, L. B. (1994). Strategic planning and firm performance: A synthesis of more than two decades of research. *Academy of Management Journal, 37*(6), 1649–1665.

Simons, T., Hope-Pelled, L., & Smith, K. A. (1999). Making use of difference: Diversity, debate, and decision comprehensiveness in top management teams. *Academy of Management Journal, 42*(6), 662–673.

348 Swanson, H. L. (1990). Influence of metacognitive knowledge and aptitude on problem solving. *Journal of Educational Psychology, 82*(2), 306–314.

Slife, B. D., Weiss, J., & Bell, T. (1985). Separability of metacognition and cognition: Problem solving in learning disabled and regular students. *Journal of Educational Psychology, 77*(4), 437–445.

349 *See* n319, Schulz-Hardt et al. (2006).

350 Ahlfinger, N. R., & Esser, J. K. (2001). Testing the groupthink model: Effects of promotional leadership and conformity predisposition. *Social Behavior and Personality: An International Journal, 29*(1), 31–41.

351 Moscovici, S. (1980). Toward a theory of conversion behavior. *Advances in Experimental Social Psychology, 13*, 209–239.

Nemeth, C., & Rogers, J. (1996). Dissent and the search for information. *British Journal of Social Psychology, 35*(1), 67–76.

Van Dyne, L., & Saavedra, R. (1996). A naturalistic minority influence experiment: Effects on divergent thinking, conflict and originality in work-groups. *British Journal of Social Psychology, 35*(1), 151–167.

352 Schum, D. A., & Martin, A. W. (1993). Formal and empirical research on cascaded inference in jurisprudence. In R. Hastie (Ed.), *Inside the juror: The psychology of juror decision making* (pp. 136–174). New York: Cambridge University Press.

353 Schittekatte, M. (1996). Facilitating information exchange in small decision-making groups. *European Journal of Social Psychology, 26*(4), 537–556.

354 Larson Jr, J. R., Christensen, C., Franz, T. M., & Abbott, A. S. (1998). Diagnosing groups: The pooling, management, and impact of shared and unshared case information in team-based medical decision making. *Journal of Personality and Social Psychology, 75*(1), 93–108.

355 Hollingshead, A. B. (1996). The rank-order effect in group decision making. *Organizational Behavior and Human Decision Processes, 68*(3), 181–193.

356 Hoch, S. J. (1985). Counterfactual reasoning and accuracy in predicting personal events. *Journal of Experimental Psychology: Learning, Memory, and Cognition, 11*(4), 719–731.

Koriat, A., Lichtenstein, S., & Fischhoff, B. (1980). Reasons for confidence. *Journal of Experimental Psychology: Human Learning and Memory, 6*(2), 107–118.
Berardi-Coletta et al. (1995)

357 Scholten, L., Van Knippenberg, D., Nijstad, B. A., & De Dreu, C. K. (2007). Motivated information processing and group decision-making: Effects of process accountability on information processing and decision quality. *Journal of Experimental Social Psychology, 43*(4), 539–552.

358 Heuer, L., & Penrod, S. D. (1994). Trial complexity: A field investigation of its meaning and its effect. *Law and Human Behavior, 18*(1), 29–51.

359 Malhotra, N. K. (1982). Information load and consumer decision making. *Journal of Consumer Research, 8*(4), 419–430.

360 Wright, P. (1975). Consumer choice strategies: Simplifying vs. optimizing. *Journal of Marketing Research, 12*(1), 60–67.

361 Perry, V. G., & Lee, J. D. (2012). Shopping for a home vs. a loan: The role of cognitive resource depletion. *International Journal of Consumer Studies, 36*(5), 580–587.

362 Fennis, B. M., & Janssen, L. (2010). Mindlessness revisited: Sequential request techniques foster compliance by draining self-control resources. *Current Psychology, 29*(3), 235–246.

363 Hwang, M. I., & Lin, J. W. (1999). Information dimension, information overload and decision quality. *Journal of Information Science, 25*(3), 213–218.

364 Chernev, A. (2003). Product assortment and individual decision processes. *Journal of Personality and Social Psychology, 85*(1), 151–162.

See also Scheibehenne, B., Greifeneder, R., & Todd, P. M. (2010). Can there ever be too many options? A meta-analytic review of choice overload. *Journal of Consumer Research, 37*(3), 409–425.

365 Kida, T., Moreno, K. K., & Smith, J. F. (2010). Investment decision making: Do experienced decision makers fall prey to the paradox of choice? *The Journal of Behavioral Finance, 11*(1), 21–30.

366 Keller, K. L., & Staelin, R. (1987). Effects of quality and quantity of information on decision effectiveness. *Journal of Consumer Research, 14*(2), 200–213.

Lee, B. K., & Lee, W. N. (2004). The effect of information overload on consumer choice quality in an on-line environment. *Psychology & Marketing, 21*(3), 159–183.

Sundstrom, G. A. (1987). Information search and decision making: The effects of information displays. *Acta Psychologica, 65*(2), 165–179.

367 *See* n359, Malhotra (1982).

368 *See* n363, Hwang & Lin (1999).

369 Sasaki, T., Becker, D. V., Janssen, M. A., & Neel, R. (2011). Does greater product information actually inform consumer decisions? The relationship between product information quantity and diversity of consumer decisions. *Journal of Economic Psychology, 32*(3), 391–398.

370 Jacoby, J., Speller, D. E., & Kohn, C. A. (1974b). Brand choice behavior as a function of information load. *Journal of Marketing Research, 11*(1), 63–69.

Jacoby, J., Speller, D. E., & Berning, C. K. (1974a). Brand choice behavior as a function of information load: Replication and extension. *Journal Of Consumer Research, 1*(1), 33–42.

371 Sheluga, D. A., & Jacoby, J. (1978). Do comparative claims encourage comparison shopping? In J. Leigh & C. R. Martin (Eds.), *Current issues and research in advertising* (pp. 23–37). Ann Arbor, MI: University of Michigan Press.

372 Walker. B. A.. Swasy, J. L., & Rethans, A. J. (1985). The impact of comparative advertising research. *Advances in Consumer Research, 13*, 121–125.

373 Lindemann, P. G., & Markman, A. B. (1996, July). Alignability and attribute importance in choice. In Garrison W. Cottrell (Ed.), *Proceedings of the 18th Annual Conference of the Cognitive Science Society* (pp. 358–363). San Diego, CA: Lawrence Erlbaum Associates.

Markman, A. B., & Medin, D. L. (1995). Similarity and alignment in choice. *Organizational Behavior and Human Decision Processes, 63*(2), 117–130.

374 Zhang, S., Kardes, F. R., & Cronley, M. L. (2002). Comparative advertising: Effects of structural alignability on target brand evaluations. *Journal of Consumer Psychology, 12*(4), 303–311.

375 Pham, M. T., & Muthukrishnan, A. V. (2002). Search and alignment in judgment revision: Implications for brand positioning. *Journal of Marketing Research, 39*(1), 18–30.

376 *See* n297, Slovic (1972).

377 Potter, R. E., & Beach, L. R. (1998). Imperfect information in prechoice screening of options. In L. R. Beach & L. R. Beach (Eds.), *Image theory: Theoretical and empirical foundations* (pp. 73–86). Mahwah, NJ: Lawrence Erlbaum Associates.

378 Kivetz, R., & Simonson, I. (2000). The effects of incomplete information on consumer choice. *Journal of Marketing Research, 37*(4), 427–448.

379 Fischhoff, B., Slovic, P., & Lichtenstein, S. (1978). Fault trees: Sensitivity of estimated failure probabilities to problem representation. *Journal of Experimental Psychology: Human Perception and Performance, 4*(2), 330–344.

380 *See* n305, Schkade & Kleinmuntz (1994).

381 Fritzsche, B. A., & Brannick, M. T. (2002). The importance of representative design in judgment tasks: The case of resume screening. *Journal of Occupational and Organizational Psychology, 75*(2), 163–169.

382 Huber, O. (1980). The influence of some task variables on cognitive operations in an information-processing decision model. *Acta Psychologica, 45*(1–3), 187–196.

383 Stone, D. N., & Schkade, D. A. (1991). Numeric and linguistic information representation in multiattribute choice. *Organizational Behavior and Human Decision Processes, 49*(1), 42–59.

384 Hogarth, R. M., & Kunreuther, H. (1995). Decision making under ignorance: Arguing with yourself. *Journal of Risk and Uncertainty, 10*(1), 15–36.

385 Budescu, D. V., Weinberg, S., & Wallsten, T. S. (1988). Decisions based on numerically and verbally expressed uncertainties. *Journal of Experimental Psychology: Human Perception and Performance, 14*(2), 281–294.

Erev, I., & Cohen, B. L. (1990). Verbal versus numerical probabilities: Efficiency, biases, and the preference paradox. *Organizational Behavior and Human Decision Processes, 45*(1), 1–18.

Wallsten, T. S. (1990). The costs and benefits of vague information. In R. Hogarth (Ed.), *Insights in decision making: A tribute to Hillel J. Einhorn* (pp. 28–43). Chicago: University of Chicago Press.

386 Peters, reported in Finucane, M. L., Peters, E., & Slovic, P. (2003). Judgment and decision making: The dance of affect and reason. In S. L. Schneider & J. Shanteau (Eds.), *Emerging perspectives on judgment and decision research* (pp. 327–364). New York: Cambridge University Press.

387 Helgeson, J. G., & Ursic, M. L. (1993). Information load, cost/benefit assessment and decision strategy variability. *Journal of the Academy of Marketing Science, 21*(1), 13–20.

388 Wright, P. (1974). *The use of phased, noncompensatory strategies in decisions between multi-attribute products.* Research Paper 223. Stanford, CA: Graduate School of Business, Stanford University.

389 Simkin, D. K., & Hastie, R. (1986). An information processing analysis of graph perception. *Journal of the American Statistical Association, 82,* 454–465.

390 Shah, P., & Hoeffner, J. (2002). Review of graph comprehension research: Implications for instruction. *Educational Psychology Review, 14*(1), 47–69.

391 Hollands, J. G., & Spence, I. (2001). The discrimination of graphical elements. *Applied Cognitive Psychology, 15*(4), 413–431.

392 Schnotz, W., & Baadte, C. (2015). Surface and deep structures in graphics comprehension. *Memory & Cognition, 43*(4), 605–618.

393 Gattis, M., & Holyoak, K. J. (1996). Mapping conceptual to spatial relations in visual reasoning. *Journal of Experimental Psychology: Learning, Memory, and Cognition, 22*(1), 231–239.

394 Gaeth, G. J., & Shanteau, J. (1984). Reducing the influence of irrelevant information on experienced decision makers. *Organizational Behavior & Human Performance, 33*(2), 263–282.

Labella, C., & Koehler, D. J. (2004). Dilution and confirmation of probability judgments based on non-diagnostic evidence. *Memory & Cognition, 32*(7), 1076–1089.

Waller, W. S., & Zimbelman, M. F. (2003). A cognitive footprint in archival data: Generalizing the dilution effect from laboratory to field settings. *Organizational Behavior and Human Decision Processes, 91*(2), 254–268.

395 *See* n217, Canham & Hagarty (2010).

396 Harp, S. F., & Mayer, R. E. (1998). How seductive details do their damage: A theory of cognitive interest in science learning. *Journal of Educational Psychology, 90*(3), 414–434.

397 *Ibid.*

398 Nisbett, R. E., Zukier, H., & Lemley, R. E. (1981). The dilution effect: Nondiagnostic information weakens the implications of diagnostic information. *Cognitive Psychology, 13*(2), 248–277.

399 Tetlock, P. E., Lerner, J. S., & Boettger, R. (1996). The dilution effect: Judgmental bias, conversational convention. or a bit of both? *European Journal of Social Psychology, 26,* 915–934.

400 Bamber, E. M., Tubbs, R. M., Gaeth, G., & Ramsey, R. J. (1991). *Characteristics of audit experience in belief revision.* Presented at USC Audit Judgment Symposium. Los Angeles, CA: University of Southern California.

Baranski, J. V., & Petrusic, W. M. (2010). Aggregating conclusive and inconclusive information: Data and a model based on the assessment of threat. *Journal of Behavioral Decision Making, 23*(4), 383–403.

401 Chinander, K. R., & Schweitzer, M. E. (2003). The input bias: The misuse of input information in judgments of outcomes. *Organizational Behavior and Human Decision Processes, 91*(2), 243–253.

402 Friedrich, J., Fetherstonhaugh, D., Casey, S., & Gallagher, D. (1996). Argument integration and attitude change: Suppression effects in the integration of one-sided arguments that vary in persuasiveness. *Personality and Social Psychology Bulletin, 22*(2), 179–191.

Martire, K. A., Kemp, R. I., Watkins, I., Sayle, M. A., & Newell, B. R. (2013). The expression and interpretation of uncertain forensic science evidence: Verbal equivalence, evidence strength, and the weak evidence effect. *Law and Human Behavior, 37*(3), 197–207.

403 Weaver, K., Garcia, S. M., & Schwarz, N. (2012). The presenter's paradox. *Journal of Consumer Research, 39*(3), 445–460.

404 de Vries, G., Terwel, B. W., & Ellemers, N. (2014). Spare the details, share the relevance: The dilution effect in communications about carbon dioxide capture and storage. *Journal of Environmental Psychology, 38,* 116–123.

405 Meyvis, T., & Janiszewski, C. (2002). Consumers' beliefs about product benefits: The effect of obviously irrelevant product information. *Journal of Consumer Research, 28*(4), 618–635.

406 Young II, G. R., Price, K. H., & Claybrook, C. (2001). Small group predictions on an uncertain outcome: The effect of nondiagnostic information. *Theory and Decision, 50*(2), 149–167.

407 Kemmelmeier, M. (2004). Separating the wheat from the chaff: Does discriminating between diagnostic and nondiagnostic information eliminate the dilution effect? *Journal of Behavioral Decision Making, 17*(3), 231–243.

408 Greeno, J. G., & Noreen, D. L. (1974). Time to read semantically related sentences. *Memory & Cognition, 2*(1-A), 117–120.

PART II

Understanding Intuitive Decision Making

5

HEURISTICS AND BIASES IN AUDIENCE DECISION MAKING

In May 2000, the president and CEO of Heinz (now Kraft Heinz) picked out his brightest young marketing executives and challenged each of them to propose a project that would significantly increase ketchup sales in the United States without spending any additional dollars. Only the best proposal would get the CEO's approval to proceed.

One of the young execs chosen to propose a project to the CEO, although somewhat quiet and reserved, was a whiz at the numbers. After several months of grueling data collection and statistical analysis, the young exec made his presentation to the boss. It contained hundreds of complex charts and numbers to back up his claim: By optimizing marketing and promotion spend in each city, Heinz could regain lost market share from its competitors.

To the young exec's chagrin, when he concluded his presentation the CEO told him he had no idea what he was talking about but that he would give him a chance to try again. The CEO attended other, more engaging, presentations, but none of the proposals sold him.

Soon the young exec came back to present to the CEO and other top executives in one final effort. This time, before he began, he first gave each person in the room a fleece jacket with a big red rocket logo on it. He then announced the *Red Rocket Project*—optimization of marketing spend would make Heinz ketchup sales take off!

This presentation was all visual, just exciting images that illustrated the exec's key points. When he finished, the whole room was buzzing with questions, and the exec had a backup chart for each. The Red Rocket Project was a go. It soon exceeded sales expectations. Wall Street analysts loved it. And the Heinz brand was re-energized.

Why didn't the CEO approve the young executive's proposal after hearing his first presentation? Unlike his first presentation, the second was both easier for the CEO to understand and was framed by an easily visualized name—*The Red Rocket Project*, a compelling vision the CEO could get excited about.

Audiences, even expert ones like the CEO in the story, do not always make decisions in a cold, rational, and calculating fashion, weighing each alternative's pros and cons. Instead, audiences often make decisions intuitively and revise their intuitive decisions only if they are motivated to do so. Think of the millions of consumers who have been influenced to drink Coca-Cola by slogans such as *Coke is it!* and *Taste the feeling.*

When audiences make decisions primarily on the basis on their intuitions, the form or style of a message can have a greater persuasive impact on them than its content or substance. Consequently, persuasive documents and presentations must not only appeal to them on a rational level, they must also appeal to the audience on an intuitive level if only to ensure that competing proposals are not more persuasive for purely subjective reasons. Chapter 5 explores intuitive decision making and the techniques, such as framing, that appeal to audiences on the intuitive level.

Some of the many differences between the rational mode of decision making and the intuitive mode are highlighted in Table 5.1, adapted from a paper by Nobel laureate Daniel Kahneman and his colleague Shane Frederick.[1] Whereas rational decisions are based on objective experience and information, intuitive decisions are based on subjective experience or the feelings of the decision maker. Unlike the rational mode, which is used consciously and only if believed to be necessary, the intuitive mode operates automatically at all times. The rational mode of decision making is a slow and deliberate process that requires effort to make the necessary comparisons, calculations, and trade-offs. The intuitive mode, on the other hand, is fast and effortless, and the decisions it comes up with are not based on comparisons or calculations but on holistic impressions.

The rational mode requires abstract and quantitative information for its comparisons and calculations. It makes sense of the information it inputs using rules and deductive reasoning. The intuitive mode, in contrast, responds best to concrete and attention-getting stimuli, a photograph of a shiny red sports car, for example. It interprets the information it inputs by making associations with situations from the past that produced similar responses. In the rational mode information-acquisition and information-integration processes are carried out in a serial sequence, one comparison at a time. In the intuitive mode audiences carry out those processes beneath conscious awareness in a parallel manner that allows them to recognize different configurations or patterns of information immediately.[2]

Brain Regions Activated. In his review of the neuroscience research, social psychologist Matthew Lieberman concludes that rational-mode processing activates lateral and medial regions of both the frontal and parietal lobes, as well as medial regions of the temporal lobe (see Figures 3.4 and 3.5, p. 108). These regions have been linked to executive control and explicit learning.

TABLE 5.1 A Comparison of Intuitive and Rational Cognitive Processes

	Intuitive Mode	*Rational Mode*
Focus of awareness	Subjective experience	Objective experience
When activated	At all times	As needed
How activated	Automatically	Consciously
Speed	Rapid	Slow
Output	Holistic impression	Effortful trade-offs
Stimuli	Concrete and attention getting	Abstract and quantitative
Comprehension	Associative, Similarity based	Deductive, Rule based
Information acquisition	Parallel	Serial
Information integration	Configural	Feature by feature

Source: Adapted from Kahneman and Frederick (2002)

In contrast, intuitive-mode processing activates the amygdala, the ventromedial prefrontal cortex (vmPFC), and lateral regions of the temporal lobe. These regions have been linked to associative learning and thus to the implicit processes of the intuitive mode.[3] Although a component of intuitive-mode processing, the vmPFC is also essential to many aspects of rational-mode processing, especially to the information acquisition and integration steps in our model of audience decision making.

When audiences make intuitive decisions, they are said to be using shortcuts to decision making or *heuristics*. For example, when audiences decide that a person must be a librarian simply because the person is dressed like a librarian, they are said to be using the *representativeness* heuristic. The person's appearance is representative or stereotypical of a librarian's. When audiences decide that a house must be worth about $250,000 just because the first price they encounter is $250,000, they are said to be using the *anchoring* heuristic. The first price anchors or fixes the audience's estimate of the value at $250,000.

Any information may be used either heuristically or nonheuristically. Deciding someone is a librarian based on their appearance alone exemplifies using information about their appearance heuristically. Deciding someone is a librarian based on their appearance as well as all of the other relevant information available exemplifies using the same information in a nonheuristic way.

Although each individual heuristic describes a different rule by which the intuitive mode operates, all heuristics derive their persuasive power or intuitive appeal from the subjective ease of using them, or how *fluently* the information is processed. Decisions based on processing information heuristically *feel* right simply because they are easy and effortless to make. When audiences use heuristics to make decisions, they give more weight to and have more confidence in information that is easy to process, even when that information is irrelevant to the decision. Audiences also tend to associate positive emotions with, and like, information that is easy to process.[4] Consequently, the easier information is to process, the more it will be liked,[5] and the more heavily it will be weighted. At the same time, audiences may dislike and give little or no weight to relevant information that is hard to process.

Heuristics serve the audience well in many situations and may lead them to make satisfactory decisions based on what amounts to informed guesses. In some cases, the audience's subjective feelings are the most relevant information for decision making, as is the case with judgments of liking.[6] More often, according to normative theory at least, the audience's subjective experiences of processing information, or feelings, should have no bearing on their decisions at all.

The use of heuristics can lead audiences to systematically distort the steps normative theory prescribes and thus to make biased decisions. For example, when audiences use the representativeness heuristic to make decisions they simultaneously neglect to consider other relevant information such as base-rate information (the odds of something being true) or information about the size of the sample studied (four doctors or 4,000?)—information needed to make a rational and statistically meaningful decision.

The audience's use of heuristics and their susceptibility to the resulting biases are predictable. Most audience members will use the same heuristic when processing the same information and their decisions will deviate from normative theory in the same way.[7] For example, the moment the prices of securities reach their peak is the time most unsophisticated investors buy them. Instead of buying low and selling high, most inexperienced investors use the information about high stock prices heuristically and proceed to buy high, only to sell low when prices hit bottom.

Fortunately for the professional, the same aids to audience decision making—such as those described in Chapter 4—that make it easy for the audience to process a professional's documents and presentations also bias the audience, usually in the professional's favor. When audiences use information heuristically, they choose the alternative presented in the style or format that:

- is easiest to perceive;[8]
- is most attention getting;[9]
- is easiest to comprehend;[10]
- makes activating a schema easy;[11]
- makes acquiring information easy;[12]
- makes integrating information easy.[13]

Such stylistic techniques do not bias all audience members equally. Expert audience members are less likely than novices to rely on heuristics and thus are less susceptible to bias when performing realistic tasks in their domain of expertise.[14] For example, medical residents are less susceptible to the sunk-cost bias, less likely to "throw good money after bad," when making medical decisions than when making nonmedical decisions.[15] Similarly, accountants are less susceptible to bias when making accounting than nonaccounting decisions.[16] Experienced bank loan officers rely on heuristics only rarely when making commercial loan decisions, less often than they themselves believe.[17] Nonetheless, some experts appear to rely on heuristics routinely. For example, research indicates that federal judges routinely use heuristics such as anchoring, framing, and representativeness in making their judicial decisions.[18]

Whereas expertise tends to mitigate the audience's use of heuristics and their susceptibility to bias, being part of a group often accentuates heuristic use and susceptibility to bias.[19] For example, groups tend to accentuate the bias of individual audience members to neglect base-rate information.[20] Groups also display a more pronounced optimism bias[21] and show more unrealistic overconfidence than individual members of the group.[22]

Groups amplify other biases as well. Groups are persuaded by sunk-cost arguments even when only a minority of group members mentions them as a reason for their decision.[23] Positive/negative framing effects (e.g., arguing for a medical procedure in terms of lives saved versus lives lost) at the group level tend to be stronger than those at the individual level.[24] For example, groups given the "lives lost" version of the Asian disease problem[25] choose the riskier alternative even when a majority of the members initially favor the less risky alternative.[26] Groups also amplify, rather than weaken, reliance on the representativeness heuristic.[27] Thus, they amplify the tendency of individuals to use stereotypes when making evaluations.[28]

Groups are just as susceptible as individuals to other biases. Groups are just as susceptible as individuals to anchoring-related biases.[29] Groups are just as susceptible as individuals to the confirmation bias. For example, groups of managers prefer information that confirms the majority's initial decision over information that contradicts it.[30] Groups are equally susceptible to the conjunctive fallacy: Instead of calculating the correct response, they simply exchange information concerning their individual judgments and endorse the judgment of a single, oftentimes incorrect, group member.[31]

Some biased information processing is unique to groups. Groups may be prone to take courses of action about which all members secretly disagree.[32] A group bias termed *pluralistic ignorance* is caused by group members' tendency to underestimate the extent to which other group members share their concerns.[33] For example, outside board members are often reluctant to express their concerns about the management of underperforming firms and do not realize other board members have similar concerns. Groups are also prone to polarize the predispositions of individual members toward risk. Group polarization results in decisions that are either too risky or too conservative.[34] When the pressure on members to conform overrides their need to produce a good decision, a bias psychologist Irving Janis termed *groupthink*,[35] groups tend to produce poorly reasoned decisions. More recently, groupthink has been attributed to a shared schema or shared mental model.[36]

Note that the heuristics described in this chapter are all associated with the audience's ease of processing information, or what is called *processing fluency*.[37] They should not be confused with the heuristics cues identified in the dual-mode persuasion literature, cues that provide audiences with substantive information such as whether the communicator is an expert or a novice, is attractive or unattractive, or has high status or low status.[38] Dual-mode heuristic cues, as described in Chapter 6, do not make information easier to process. Instead, they provide additional information upon which an unmotivated or distracted audience may base its decisions.

Note too that dual-mode persuasion theory predicts even strong arguments in a message will not be persuasive unless the audience is highly motivated to think about them. More recently, studies show that strong arguments that are easy to process will be persuasive even if the audience is not highly motivated to think about them. When the difficulty of processing arguments and the use of dual-mode heuristic cues is controlled for, the previously found interactions with the audience's motivation and attention levels disappear.[39]

Dual-mode persuasion theory also predicts that more deliberative thought leads to fewer biases. Yet more thought can lead to the use of more heuristics[40] and is rarely a successful antidote against biases.[41] Ironically, the more motivated audience members are to deliberate about a choice, the bigger the framing effects[42] and the greater the biasing effects of the representativeness heuristic.[43]

Perception-Related Heuristics and Biases

The Perceptual Fluency Heuristic

Anything that impacts the speed and accuracy of perception can affect perceptual fluency, or the ease with which audiences perceive stimuli.[44] For example, stimuli, such as words and pictures, presented for long durations are usually easier for audiences to perceive than stimuli presented for short durations. Perceiving stimuli that have high clarity is easier for the audience than perceiving stimuli with low clarity. Perceiving familiar stimuli is easier for them than perceiving novel stimuli. Perceiving foreground stimuli or figures that contrast with their backgrounds is also easier.[45] In addition, certain attributes of stimuli—such as simplicity, prototypicality, symmetry, balance, as well as proportions such as the golden section—may facilitate the audience's perceptual processing and as a result give the stimuli more aesthetic appeal.[46]

Audiences use the perceptual fluency heuristic when their subjective experience of easily perceiving information leads them to prefer that information more, weight it more heavily, assume it is more true, or find it more persuasive than equally relevant or more relevant information that is difficult to perceive.[47] Although anything that aids perceptual processing can lead to perceptual fluency, audiences rarely attribute the experience of perceptual fluency to its true cause. For example, audience members who have seen a particular stimulus before are likely to mistakenly believe they viewed it for a longer time period or that it possessed a higher clarity than it actually did.[48]

Figure 5.1 uses a simple flow chart to represent how the perceptual fluency heuristic can lead to perceptual biases. Similar flow charts could represent how heuristics related to each of the other five cognitive processes in our model also lead to process-related biases. For perception, irrelevant stimuli that are familiar, highly audible, highly legible, or otherwise easy to perceive lead the audience to experience positive subjective feelings about those stimuli, such as liking and certainty. The audience's positive subjective feelings, in turn, lead them to give the irrelevant stimuli undue value and weight and to place unwarranted confidence in them. On the other hand, relevant stimuli that are less familiar, less audible, less legible, or otherwise difficult to perceive lead the audience to experience negative subjective feelings about them, such as disliking and uncertainty. The audience's negative subjective feelings, in turn, lead the audience to unduly discount the relevant stimuli.

The intuitive-mode processes take place every time one of the six major cognitive processes in decision making has been completed. The information on which the intuitive processes act is not content information (i.e., what is perceived, attended to, comprehended, etc.) but is processing information (i.e., the ease or difficulty with which something is perceived, attended to, comprehended, and so on).

Brain Regions Activated. Intuitive-mode processes are a form of *metacognition*,[49] which is the subjective experience people have of their cognitive processes.[50] Typically, the only time audience members become consciously aware of an intuitive process is when processing becomes difficult. When that happens, the metacognitive experience of disfluency may activate rational-mode processes.[51] Neuroscientists find that disfluency, or the subjective difficulty of processing information, triggers the anterior cingulate cortex (ACC), a brain region located below the dorsomedial prefrontal cortex (see Figure 3.5, p. 108).[52] The ACC acts as an alarm that activates areas in the frontal lobe responsible for rational-mode thinking.[53]

Legibility Effects: The Intuitive Appeal of Easy-to-See Messages

Audience members are more likely to believe highly legible messages than less legible ones. For instance, they are more likely to judge a statement to be true when it is shown in colors that are easy to read against the background color. In a study of legibility effects, readers were asked to quickly

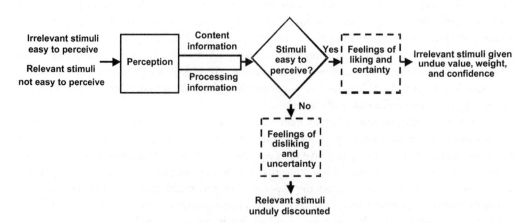

FIGURE 5.1 Intuitive Processes Leading to Perceptual Biases

decide if statements such as "Osorno is a city in Chile" were true. Some of the statements were printed in colors that were easy to read against the background color and others in colors that were hard to read. Readers were more likely to judge a statement as true when it was printed in a color that made reading it easy.[54]

Legibility effects have shown up in other studies of decision making as well. Consumers who read descriptions of two digital cameras were much more likely to decide to purchase a camera when the descriptions were printed in an easy-to-read font than when they were printed in a font that was difficult to read.[55] Teachers who read student essays written in more legible as opposed to less legible handwriting evaluated the content of the more legible essays more positively.[56] Readers who read descriptions of increasing or decreasing trends in an easy-to-read font were more likely to predict the trend would continue into the future.[57]

Readers also experience contrast effects when they encounter a less legible document before reading a more legible one. For example, consumers who read an ad after first reading a movie review written in a difficult-to-read font felt the ad was easier to process and gave the advertised product higher-than-normal ratings.[58]

Visibility Effects: The Intuitive Appeal of Easy-to-See Images

Audiences are more persuaded by easy-to-see images than hard-to-see images. Larger easy-to-see pictures of an advertised product produce stronger persuasion effects than identical but smaller, hard-to-see ones.[59] The visibility of an image even affects the persuasiveness of the verbal information associated with it. In a study of visibility effects, readers were presented with either strong or weak arguments and either a high- or low-quality image of the person who wrote the arguments (a sharp color photograph of the writer versus a degraded copy of the same photo). Readers who received the sharp color photograph of the writer mistakenly judged weak arguments to be as persuasive as strong ones. But those who received the hard-to-see photo correctly judged the weak arguments to be less persuasive.[60]

Viewers also prefer images that are prototypical, symmetrical, and simple.[61] Why? Because those attributes make images easy to process.[62] Readers prefer documents with a symmetrical layout for similar reasons. Readers find documents with a symmetrical layout to be more visually appealing and personally relevant than the same documents with an asymmetrical layout. In addition, readers are more likely to be persuaded by the arguments in them.[63]

Audiences also have stronger emotional responses to easy-to-process images than to hard-to-process ones.[64] When images are presented on big, easy-to-see screens, audiences become more aroused by the images and like them better.[65]

Audibility Effects: The Appeal of Easy-to-Hear Messages

Sound-related variables can influence the persuasive impact of messages. In a study of the persuasive effects of sound quality, audience members listened to a message that contained six high-quality arguments supporting a recommended position. Lowering message perceptibility with a poor-quality audio recording significantly lessened the listeners' agreement with the recommended position.[66] Conversely, enhancing the audio fidelity of a message can increase both audience attention and liking.[67] The fluency of a speaker also has a persuasive impact on the audience. When speakers are able to avoid disfluent filler words such as "uh" and "um," the audience is more likely to believe them.[68]

Euphonious Sound Effects: The Appeal of Melodious Messages

Words and sentences that sound good are more persuasive than those that do not. For example, audiences are more likely to decide a statement is true when it is expressed in a rhyming form. Made-up sayings expressed in a rhyming form, such as "woes unite foes," are more likely to be judged as true than the same sayings expressed in a nonrhyming form, for instance "woes unite enemies."[69] Audiences are more likely to judge a rhyming statement to be true simply because it is easier to process.[70]

Political scientists find that candidates have a better chance of being elected when their names are euphonious, as was true in the case of a LaRouche, Illinois election in which a candidate with the surname of Fairchild defeated a candidate with the less euphonious-sounding surname of Sangmeister.[71] In general, audiences judge easy-to-pronounce names more positively than difficult-to-pronounce ones. This may explain in part why attorneys with easy-to-pronounce surnames tend to occupy higher status positions in law firms[72] and why easy-to-pronounce, fluently named stocks perform better than disfluently named ones.[73]

Repetition Effects: The Appeal of the Familiar

Audience members prefer stimuli they have encountered before and recognize as familiar.[74] One of the best-known perceptual biases and one of the first to be identified is the *mere-exposure effect*.[75] Mere or repeated exposure to a stimulus without any reinforcement leads to more fluent perceptual processing and a gradual increase in liking.[76]

For example, songs with repetitive lyrics are processed more fluently and thus adopted more broadly and quickly than songs without much repetition. The more repetitive the lyrics, the greater the odds of debuting in the Top 40 and the less time it takes to reach #1.[77] Numbers in a sequence that are repetitive, in the sense that they are multiples of one another, are processed more fluently. This so-called *numeracy effect* can lead consumers to choose deals that offer less value for the money but feature a combination of numbers that are easier to process.[78] Familiarity with a risky option can lower an investor's perceptions of risk and create the *home bias effect* in investing—the tendency of investors to invest more money than is prudent into stocks of their home country or into stock of the company they work for.[79] Repeated exposure to news coverage of a given issue leads audience members to rate the issue as more important.[80] Repeated exposure to the source of persuasive arguments, even subliminal or supraliminal exposure, leads audiences to be more persuaded by the arguments.[81]

Other equally fascinating examples of repetition effects have been identified as well. Names that the audience has been exposed to repeatedly seem more famous than other names.[82] Hearing the same question asked repeatedly leads audiences to increase their confidence in the answer they hear.[83] Asking audiences to repeatedly express an attitude leads them to maintain that attitude with increased certainty.[84] And when the audience has already formulated a response to a piece of information, repeated exposure to it can accentuate their response.[85] Thus, repeating information that the audience judges to be negative can make that information seem even more negative to them.[86]

Perhaps the most significant finding is that the more often any message is repeated to an audience, the more likely the audience is to judge it as true.[87] A classic study of how rumors spread during World War II shows that the best predictor of whether an audience will believe a rumor is the number of times they have heard the rumor repeated.[88] Similarly, the number of times the audience is exposed to advertisements, trivia statements, or even foreign words predicts how likely they are to believe them.[89] Even when repeated statements are explicitly identified as false, audiences are more likely to judge them as true.[90]

Attention-Related Heuristics and Biases

The Vividness and Salience Heuristics

Audiences often neglect to use important information in decision making and instead use less important information when the less important information is presented in a more attention-getting way.[91] One reason stimuli attract attention is that they are vivid. Stimuli that are vivid, such as many graphs and images, are intrinsically attention getting. So it is not surprising that venture capitalists often cite the use of graphs as an important characteristic of a good business plan.[92]

When audiences such as venture capitalists allow the vividness of a stimulus to influence their decisions, they can be said to be using the vividness heuristic. Audiences use the vividness heuristic when their subjective experience of selectively attending to vivid information leads them to prefer it more, weight it more heavily, be more confident in it, or find it more persuasive than equally relevant or more relevant but pallid information that is not attention getting.[93]

Another reason stimuli attract attention is because they are salient, that is to say, because they are different from the norm.[94] Any unexpected or surprising stimulus is salient.[95] Audiences use the salience heuristic when their subjective experience of having their attention attracted to salient information leads them to prefer it or find it more persuasive than nonsalient information. The salience heuristic is this text's term for the heuristic sometimes called the *surprise heuristic*.[96] The surprise heuristic explains surprise in terms of salience: the extent to which a stimulus stands out from the norm and attracts attention relative to other stimuli in its environment.

Vivid Language Effects: The Persuasive Impact of Concrete Words

Audiences are more likely to be persuaded by vivid writing and speaking styles than by pallid ones. Messages presented in a vivid style—with concrete words and easily visualized phrases—are more persuasive than the same messages presented in a bland or abstract way.[97] For example, people are willing to pay more for airline travel insurance covering death from "terrorist acts" than for the more pallid but more comprehensive insurance covering death from "all possible causes."[98] Vivid concrete claims in print ads produce more definite intentions to buy the advertised product than abstract claims.[99] Vivid health and fear appeals are more persuasive than pallid ones.[100]

In a study of mock jurors deciding a drunk-driving case, half of the mock jurors read vivid (i.e., concrete and image-provoking) prosecution arguments and pallid (i.e., abstract and bland) defense arguments. The other jurors read pallid prosecution arguments and vivid defense arguments. Initially, the decisions of the two groups were the same, but after a 48-hour delay, the jurors who read the vivid prosecution arguments judged the defendant as more likely to be guilty. On the other hand, the jurors who read the vivid defense arguments judged the defendant as more likely to be innocent.[101] In a similar study mock jurors in a civil trial watched video recordings of witnesses testifying about the concrete foundation of a recently constructed building. Witnesses described the foundation using either vivid phrases such as "a spider web of cracks" and "a jagged slab" or pallid phrases such as "a network of cracks" and "a rough slab." Mock jurors' verdicts and damage awards favored the side with the vivid testimonies.[102]

Vivid Image Effects: The Persuasive Impact of Images

Vivid pictures and graphics can have a bigger persuasive impact than words or numbers.[103] For example, trends in employees' performance displayed in a graphic format have a greater impact on managers' evaluations of employees than the same information expressed in a table.[104]

Vivid pictures can also enhance the persuasive appeal of verbal information.[105] In a study of print ads, one group of consumers was shown a version of a print ad for facial tissues that used a vivid color photograph of a fluffy kitten to communicate the product's softness. Another group was shown either a version of the ad that verbally described the attribute of softness or one that included color photographs conceptually irrelevant to the product's softness. Consumers developed stronger beliefs about the softness of the brand of tissue, as well as more favorable attitudes toward the brand, when they saw the ad with the vivid color photo of the kitten.[106]

Compared to ads without images of the advertised product, ads that include images of the product also produce more definite consumer intentions to buy.[107] Compared to warning labels without pictures, warnings labels with images increase compliance.[108] For instance, cigarette warning labels that include a graphic image of the negative effects of smoking dramatically lower consumer intentions to smoke.[109]

Vivid Modality Effects: The Power of Speech, Video, and Live Performance

Even more persuasive than written words or static images, are spoken words and moving images. Messages presented in the more vivid video or audio modality have a significantly stronger persuasive impact than the same messages presented in the less vivid written modality.[110] In addition, the more sophisticated the presentation technology the more likely it is to bias audience decisions. In a study that compared the effects of the written word to an animated slide show, both experts and novices in the domain of football were asked to rate the likely success of a new football recruit. The participants were given either a "low-tech" typed summary of the recruit's statistics, a "moderate tech" printed handout of the stats in PowerPoint charts, or a "high-tech" animated slide show of the stats in PowerPoint charts. For both novice and expert judges, the greater the technological sophistication of the presentation, the more highly they rated the projected success of the new football recruit.[111]

Live performances can also have a persuasive impact. In fact, the vivid visual cues in live performances can have an even greater impact on the audience than the content the audience is evaluating. For example, venture capitalists and other investors often neglect the content of entrepreneurs' pitches and instead overweight the vivid visual elements of the entrepreneurs' performance when making investment decisions. When watching presentations by CEOs, financial analysts tend to respond to the visual elements of the CEOs' performance in a way that leads them to make less accurate forecasts of the firms' future earnings.[112] Job applicants are more likely to accept an offer after a brief face-to-face meeting with a recruiter than after reading detailed recruiting literature.[113]

Surprisingly, professional musicians primarily use visual criteria to judge musical performances, even though they report that sound is the most important criterion in their evaluations. Music ensembles that win international recognition are those that display more convincing visible leadership and attention-getting group dynamics. Sound-only recordings actually inhibit a judge's ability to identify the winning group.[114]

The first six slides of two slide presentations on the following pages illustrate the persuasive impact of information presented in a vivid, attention-getting style. A team of MBA students who tried to make the business case that an electric utility they dubbed "Southern Company" should build new nuclear reactors produced the first slide presentation. A second team opposed to Southern Company building new reactors developed the second slide presentation. Even without reading the bullet points of either slide presentation, guessing which team won the debate is not difficult. Although both teams addressed the audience's decision criteria and used many facts and figures to support their claims, notice that only the second team incorporated vivid charts, graphs, and photographs into their slide deck. And notice that only the second team began each slide with a title that made a vivid claim.

SLIDES FROM A PRESENTATION THAT WAS RATIONALLY APPEALING

Nuclear Energy:
The future of Southern Company

Financial Rewards

- Nuclear Energy is Cheaper to Produce
  - Two New Reactors at Plant Vogtle
    - Construction costs expected to be $4B for two reactors (2000 MW capacity)
    - Production capacity costs $540m less than coal, $970m less than gas, by 2015
    - Rate case for $51m in nuclear studies looks positive
    - Expected NPV of approximately $2.5B using 8% IRR relative to coal
  - Government Encouraging New Nuclear
    - 1.8¢ per kWh tax credit will mean $350m per year starting in 2015
    - U.S. DOE expects 30% growth in demand in Southern's market by 2020
  - Fossil Fuel Costs are Expected to Continue Rise
    - Natural gas has seen large volatilities, making projections risky
    - Both coal and gas are subject to natural disasters, shipping, and politics
    - Uranium fuel costs declined relative to fossil fuels
    - New nuclear technology continuing to improve

Technology Advancements

- In the last two decades, technology advancements have:
  - Decreased Capital Cost
    - Advanced reactor designs have fewer valves, fewer pumps, and less pipe
    - Pebble-Bed Modular Reactor (PBMR) design, which virtually eliminates the risk of a meltdown and the need for a containment building
    - PBMR does not need safety backup and off-site emergency support
  - Decreased Recurring Cost
    - Capacity utilization of 90% vs 71% with Coal Plants
    - 30 times the energy from uranium than existing reactors
    - A Fast Reactor produces enough plutonium to make up for the uranium-235 used
  - Reduced Waste Produced
    - Fast reactor is capable of destroying the major source of long-life radiotoxicity in spent fuel

---

Quote

"Today, there are 103 nuclear reactors quietly delivering just 20 percent of America's electricity. Eighty percent of the people living within 10 miles of these plants approve of them (that's not including the nuclear workers). Although I don't live near a nuclear plant, I am now squarely in their camp."

Patrick Moore, co-founder of Greenpeace, 4/16/06

Environmental Impact

- Nuclear power creates no green house gases
- Nuclear waste is controlled by plant and Department of Energy (DOE)
- Fossil fuel plants release unmanaged waste such as smoke stake waste
- A typical coal plant produces 100,000 tons of sulphur dioxide, 75,000 tons of nitrogen oxides, and 5,000 tons of fly ash
- A nuclear plant produces 0 tons of each type

Environmental Cost

- Nuclear waste is currently stored locally at each plant
- Nuclear waste can be stored locally for 100+ years
- Cost of disposal is unknown as the US and other countries have not finalized disposal plans

SLIDES FROM A PRESENTATION THAT WAS INTUITIVELY APPEALING

The Case Against Nuclear Power

Prepared for:
Southern Company
Board of Directors
June 20, 2006

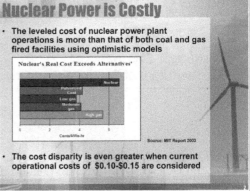

Nuclear Power is Costly

- The leveled cost of nuclear power plant operations is more than that of both coal and gas fired facilities using optimistic models

- The cost disparity is even greater when current operational costs of $0.10-$0.15 are considered

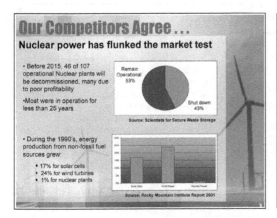

Our Competitors Agree ...

Nuclear power has flunked the market test

- Before 2015, 46 of 107 operational Nuclear plants will be decommissioned, many due to poor profitability
- Most were in operation for less than 25 years

- During the 1990's, energy production from non-fossil fuel sources grew:
  - 17% for solar cells
  - 24% for wind turbines
  - 1% for nuclear plants

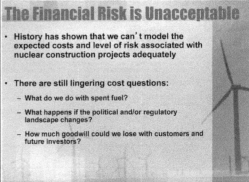

The Financial Risk is Unacceptable

- History has shown that we can't model the expected costs and level of risk associated with nuclear construction projects adequately

- There are still lingering cost questions:
  - What do we do with spent fuel?
  - What happens if the political and/or regulatory landscape changes?
  - How much goodwill could we lose with customers and future investors?

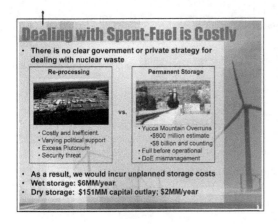

Dealing with Spent-Fuel is Costly

- There is no clear government or private strategy for dealing with nuclear waste

Re-processing	Permanent Storage

• Costly and Inefficient.
 • Varying political support
 • Excess Plutonium
 • Security threat
	• Yucca Mountain Overruns
	   •$800 million estimate
	   •$8 billion and counting
	 • Full before operational
	 • DoE mismanagement

- As a result, we would incur unplanned storage costs
- Wet storage: $6MM/year
- Dry storage: $151MM capital outlay; $2MM/year

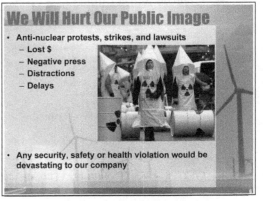

We Will Hurt Our Public Image

- Anti-nuclear protests, strikes, and lawsuits
  - Lost $
  - Negative press
  - Distractions
  - Delays

- Any security, safety or health violation would be devastating to our company

The Negativity Bias: The Impact of Negative Information

As politicians know, negative campaign ads work. One negative fact about their opponent can outweigh 10 positive attributes. Although audiences will not judge a person's character on the basis of one socially desirable behavior, they will judge a person on the basis of one behavior they deem socially undesirable.[115] In fact, one negative adjective describing a person can contribute more to an audience's overall impression of that person than many positive adjectives.[116] Similarly, one piece of negative information about a firm can have a greater impact on a job seeker's intentions to apply for a job there than many pieces of positive information about it.[117]

The reason negative information has such a powerful persuasive impact is that it is salient: Audiences pay attention to negative information because they tend to take positive information for granted.[118] Thus, the salience of negative information leads audiences to weight it more heavily than positive information and creates a bias called the *negativity bias*.[119] Although making alternatives with positive attributes more salient biases the audience to favor them, making alternatives with negative attributes more salient has the opposite effect.[120]

Outlier Effects: The Impact of Unusual Behaviors and Events

Unusual behaviors and events are more salient and attention getting than routine ones and have a greater persuasive impact on audience decisions. Audiences remember unusual events and behaviors better than ones that are routine and thus give them more weight when predicting future events and behaviors.[121] For example, if someone sees a person giving an unusually generous tip, she will remember that event and use it to predict the size of the person's future tips.[122]

In addition, audiences will be more persuaded by information related to unusual events than by information about events they consider to be normal. For example, when the audience thinks getting a flu shot is normal, they are more persuaded by information about the negative consequences of not getting vaccinated.[123] When the audience views not getting a flu shot as normal, they are more persuaded by information about the positive consequences of getting vaccinated.

Explicit Language Effects: The Impact of Specificity

Explicit language, with its many specific details, is conceptually salient and captures attention. For this reason, audiences are more likely to be persuaded by explicit language than by vague or implicit language. A study of verbal claims in advertisements found that explicit verbal claims led consumers to have more favorable attitudes toward the advertised brands than implicit claims. For example, explicit claims such as "Affordably priced at $7.99 per six pack" and "Winner of 5 out of 5 taste tests in the US against all major American beers and leading imports" led them to form very favorable opinions. Implicit claims, on the other hand, such as "Affordably priced" and "Great taste" had little impact on the consumers' attitudes.[124]

Explicit language has been shown to affect other audience decisions as well. Giving employees a specific date for receiving a future payment increases their patience and reduces the likelihood they will discount the future value of the payments.[125] Providing consumers with specific versus vague product cost savings in comparative ads leads them to infer that the advertised brand offers cost savings on its services as well.[126] A study of mock jurors finds that when the testimony of the prosecution's eyewitness is highly detailed and explicit, mock jurors are more likely to find the defendant guilty than when their testimony leaves a lot to the imagination.[127]

Immediacy Effects: The Impact of Recent Trends and Events

Recent trends and events are more salient and attention getting than those that happened in the distant past or those that may happen in the distant future. The salience of the present leads audiences to overreact to recent trends and events and to make predictions that are insufficiently regressive to the mean. For example, the recent performance trends of NBA basketball players predict club owners' compensation decisions over and above the players' performance means.[128] Investors often assume a firm's future earnings will be directly predictable from its recent earnings. Although securities with good performance typically receive extremely high valuations, these valuations, on average, return to the mean.[129]

Even experts can make insufficiently regressive predictions and overreact to recent trends. In a study of sales forecasting, professional retail buyers were asked to examine one week's worth of actual sales data from two department stores and then make sales forecasts for the following week. Although the actual sales from the first week regressed to the mean by the second week, the forecasts of the professional buyers failed to.[130] A study of financial analysts' forecasts that matched analysts' earnings forecasts for one- and two-year time horizons with actual stock returns and accounting numbers finds similar results. In every case, the analysts' forecasts failed to regress to the mean and were too extreme. The actual changes to earnings per share (EPS) averaged only 65% of the forecasted one-year changes and only 46% of the forecasted two-year earnings.[131] A strong overreaction to recent trends in analysts' EPS forecasts has also been found in subsequent studies.[132]

The temporal salience of the present leads all types of audiences to weight short-term benefits more heavily than potentially higher long-term costs. This particular bias is termed *discounting the future*.[133]

Physical Salience Effects: The Persuasive Impact of Standing Out

People, words, and objects that stand out physically are more salient and attention getting to the audience than those that appear in the background. Simply inserting a pause between the initial presentation of an online banner ad and the introduction of the product's brand name makes the product name stand out from the ad's background, increasing its salience, thus increasing its processing fluency, which ultimately increases consumers' preference for the product.[134]

A person may be salient, and as a consequence more persuasive, if she is well lit and others are dimly lit, if she is moving and others are seated, if she is speaking and others are silent, if she is casually dressed and others are dressed in suits, and if she is seated in the middle of a group rather than at the extremes.[135] Leaders, in particular, have greater influence on their followers when they are physically close as opposed to distant from them.[136]

A study of salience created by camera effects finds that the camera angle used to video confessions and courtroom testimony can have a persuasive impact on jurors' decisions. When the camera focused solely on the accused, mock jurors perceived the suspect to be more culpable and recommended more severe sentences than when the camera focused equally on the prosecutor and suspect.[137] A similar study varied the salience of a group's leader by changing the camera angles used in filming the group. Viewers were more likely to attribute the level of the group's performance to the leader when the camera angle made the leader stand out.[138]

Other studies find that group members who are physically salient are more likely to be chosen as group leaders. For example, group members who sit at the head of the table or who are able to have face-to-face contact with other members of the group are more likely to be chosen as leaders.[139] In a now classic experiment, managerial psychologist Harold Leavitt created different types of communication networks that allowed members of five-person groups to converse with one another. In groups with highly centralized networks, networks in which only one group member could directly communicate with every other group member, the member in the central, and thus most salient, position was chosen to be the group leader in 100% of the groups. In the less centralized networks in which no one group member was more salient than any other, group members in every position had an equal chance to be chosen as their group's leader.[140]

Comprehension-Related Heuristics and Biases

The easier a message is for an audience to comprehend the more likely it is to persuade them. Thus, any communication technique that makes comprehension easy will also promote heuristic processing. For example, listeners are more persuaded by spoken messages that are easy to comprehend—well organized and delivered fluently—than by either a well-organized message delivered nonfluently or by a randomly ordered message delivered fluently.[141] When the comprehensibility of product information is manipulated—by varying information exposure time and the audience's relevant prior knowledge—consumers find the same product information to be more persuasive when it is easy to comprehend than when comprehension is difficult.[142]

The Representativeness and Causality Heuristics

Two well-studied heuristics that are related to ease of comprehension and that are often contrasted with normative rules for decision making are the representativeness heuristic and the causality heuristic.

The representativeness heuristic may be the most basic and widely used of all the heuristics.[143] Audiences use the representativeness heuristic when their subjective experience of easily categorizing or stereotyping a stimulus based on descriptive, anecdotal, or otherwise easy-to-understand information leads them to give little or no weight to equally relevant or more relevant quantitative, statistical, or otherwise hard-to-comprehend information about the stimulus.[144] For example, recruiters of MBAs use the representativeness heuristic any time they base their hiring decisions on the extent to which the MBAs "look like" or "act like" successful managers.[145]

Audiences use the causality heuristic when their subjective experience of easily comprehending explanations or predictions of events presented in the form of stories leads them to give little or no weight to equally relevant or more relevant explanations or predictions presented in a quantitative, statistical, or otherwise hard-to-comprehend way.[146] Audiences automatically comprehend sequences of events in terms of stories, or causal schemata, even when they realize no causal relationship exists between the events.[147] The ease or fluency of causal thinking makes decisions based on stories very compelling. It also inhibits the audience from revising its causal schemata except in rare instances.[148]

Base-Rate Neglect: The Intuitive Appeal of Anecdotal Evidence

One of the most studied biases related to the representativeness heuristic is base-rate neglect. In this bias, audiences overlook relevant but difficult-to-comprehend statistical information and base their decision on the extent to which easy-to-comprehend anecdotal or descriptive information fits a stereotype instead.

In a landmark series of experiments that explored base-rate neglect, Nobel laureate Daniel Kahneman and his colleague Amos Tversky told one group of college students that a person had been chosen at random from a set of 100 people consisting of 70 engineers and 30 lawyers.[149]

They told a second group that the individual had been chosen from a set of 30 engineers and 70 lawyers. Both groups were able to determine the correct probability that the person chosen would be an engineer. The first group estimated a 70% probability and the second group estimated a 30% probability. Then the researchers told both groups that another person, Jack, was chosen at random from the same set of 100 people. In addition, the researchers gave both groups the following description of Jack:

> Jack is a 45-year-old man. He is married and has four children. He is generally conservative, careful, and ambitious. He shows no interest in political and social issues and spends most of his free time on his many hobbies, which include home carpentry, sailing, and mathematical puzzles.

This time, both groups estimated that there was a 90% probability that Jack was an engineer. If the second group had used the base-rate information of 30%, as Bayes Theorem demands, their probability estimate should have been much lower. Thus, the second group neglected the base-rate information and based its estimate solely on the description that seemed representative, or was stereotypical, of an engineer.

In a follow-up experiment, Kahneman and Tversky told one group that there was a 70% probability that a randomly chosen person, Dick, was an engineer and told another group that there was a 30% probability that Dick was an engineer. But in this experiment they gave the two groups a description that provided no diagnostic information about Dick's profession:

> Dick is a 30-year-old man. He is married with no children. A man of high ability and high motivation, he promises to be quite successful in his field. He is well liked by his colleagues.

According to Bayes' theorem the two groups should not modify their original probability estimates of 70% and 30% since the description was not informative. However, both groups now estimated a 50% probability that Dick was an engineer. In this study both groups neglected the base-rate information and based their estimates solely on the extent to which the description seemed representative of an engineer. A number of other studies have since confirmed that audiences tend to ignore base rates when they receive less valid, but easier-to-comprehend, anecdotal evidence.[150]

Audiences are susceptible to base-rate neglect in many different decision-making tasks,[151] especially those involving person perception.[152] For example, a large proportion of actual voting behavior reflects how much voters think the candidate "looks like" a competent leader.[153] Audiences making staffing decisions are also susceptible to base-rate neglect. A study of performance appraisal decisions finds that appraisers give much more weight to supervisors' subjective verbal descriptions of employees' performance than to objective statistical data about the employees' performance.[154] In this study, supervisors' subjective assessments accounted for 68% of the variance in the performance appraisal ratings.

Investor behavior often reflects base-rate neglect as well. For example, investors tend to predict the future value of a company's stock will go up after they read a description of the company that "sounds good," since a good stock price will then seem to be most representative.[155] But if they read a description that makes the company sound mediocre, a mediocre stock value will appear most representative, and investors will tend to predict the stock price will drop. In both these cases investors are predicting future stock values solely on the basis of company descriptions without questioning the reliability of the evidence or its statistical relevance to future profit. Likewise, when making health care decisions, patients do not think about numerical probabilities when estimating risk, but instead focus on descriptive information regarding their physical symptoms and exposure to bodily harm. Attempts to promote healthy behaviors by providing consumers with probabilistic information are generally unsuccessful.[156]

Sample-Size Insensitivity: The Intuitive Appeal of Examples

A second bias related to the representativeness heuristic is insensitivity to sample size. Although sample size is fundamental to statistics, consideration of sample size is rarely a part of the audience's intuitive decision-making process.[157] Advertisers' statements such as "Four out of five dentists surveyed recommend sugarless gum for their patients who chew gum" persuade many consumers despite the fact that the survey results are statistically meaningless without mention of the number of dentists surveyed. Even when audiences receive information about a sample's typicality, they will often fail to use it.[158]

Instead of basing their decisions on the appropriately sized sample, audiences tend to overgeneralize from a single, easy-to-comprehend but unrepresentative example.[159] TV viewers often base their perceptions of newsworthy events on a single example provided to them by the media.[160] The person or event featured in the news story supposedly exemplifies a whole category. Even when viewers are presented with accurate information, frequent exposure to such exemplars can lead them to make biased decisions.[161]

A single example can have a stronger impact on audience decision making than statistics.[162] For example, mock jurors in a simulated capital sentencing hearing were more persuaded by a psychologist who gave his personal clinical assessment of the dangerousness of the defendant than by a psychologist who presented a statistically accurate actuarial assessment.[163] In a study that presented the same information in a statistical and nonstatistical format, one group of high school teachers read information about a new science curriculum that was in the form of a case study written by a single teacher who had used the curriculum. The same information was given to another group but in the form of a statistical summary of the findings of 12 teachers who had used the curriculum. The high school teachers found the case study to be much more persuasive than the statistical summary.[164]

Audiences are especially likely to disregard sample size when they encounter extreme examples.[165] Audiences are also likely to disregard sample size when they encounter well-known examples. For example, audiences weight identifiable victims more heavily than statistical victims.[166] As behavioral economists George Loewenstein and Jane Mather have observed, when Rock Hudson and Magic Johnson were diagnosed with AIDS, the public's concern for the disease skyrocketed.[167]

Surprisingly, experts, even expert statisticians, regularly fail to take sample size into account.[168] A study of senior auditors planning an audit of a company's internal control procedures finds that auditors do not use the optimal sample size even when given all of the necessary information. Neither do they use the sample-size selection methodology the American Institute of Certified Public Accountants (AICPA) prescribes, nor do they notice sample-size errors.[169]

The Causality Bias: The Appeal of Narratives and Stories

Audiences give the same information more weight when it is presented to them in chronological order as an easy-to-comprehend narrative or story than when it is presented as a hard-to-comprehend random list of facts. In a study comparing two versions of a travel brochure, one group of consumers read a version of the brochure that described a vacation using a narrative form. Another group read a version that described the vacation in a list form. Consumers who read the narrative version evaluated the vacation much more positively than those who read the list of facts.[170]

A good narrative can outweigh good arguments. In a study of mock jurors, jurors were most likely to convict the defendant (78% chose guilty) when the prosecution presented its evidence in the chronological order of a narrative and the defense presented its evidence in random order as given by the witnesses. Jurors were least likely to convict when the prosecution presented evidence in random order and the defense presented it in chronological order (31% chose guilty). When attorneys on both sides of the case presented evidence in chronological order or both presented in random order, jurors chose to convict in 59% and 63% of the cases respectively.[171] Consumers who immerse themselves in the narrative of an ad decrease their tendency to counter-argue the ad's implications and are persuaded by the ad independently of the quality of its arguments.[172]

A good narrative can also outweigh statistics. In a study of the effect of stories on policy decisions, audience members were given written statistical data and a verbal story and then asked to make policy decisions. Although the statistical data influenced the audience's decisions when it was used to refute a current organizational policy, stories still tended to have a greater impact on the audience's policy decisions.[173] For moderately involved audience members, stories used to support arguments are at least as persuasive as statistics.[174] In addition to activating causal schemata, narratives and stories heighten the audience's emotional reactions to claims, while statistical evidence heightens the audience's rational reactions to them.[175]

Readability Effects: The Appeal of Simple Words and Sentences

Audiences find information presented in readable, easy-to-comprehend words and sentences to be more persuasive than the same information presented in a less readable way. A study of graduate school applications finds that admissions officers rate applicants as more intelligent and are more likely to admit them when their essays use simple, easy-to-process words, as opposed to complicated words.[176]

In a study of the effects of syntactic complexity in advertisements on consumers' attitudes toward the products advertised, consumers were more persuaded by strong arguments in ads than by weak ones only when the sentences in the ads were syntactically simple.[177] When the sentences were syntactically complex, consumers' attitudes were not affected by the arguments' strength. Semantic complexity affects consumers' attitudes as well. Because the semantics of active voice sentences usually makes them easier to comprehend, consumers perceive print ads written in the active voice to be more believable, appealing, and attractive than similar ads written in the passive voice.[178]

Written Modality Effects: The Power of the Written Word

Communication modality—written, audio, or video—affects the persuasiveness of difficult-to-comprehend messages. Both attitude change and retention of persuasive arguments are greater when complex messages are presented in written form. A study that compared a traditional recruitment website composed of words and pictures to a recruitment website featuring an interactive virtual world finds that users who viewed the traditional site recalled more factual information about the organization. The interactive recruitment website, on the other hand, actually distracted job seekers from reading the information that would have persuaded them to apply.[179]

Because complex messages are often too difficult for an audience to comprehend unless they are written out, audiences are less persuaded by complex messages delivered in an audio or a video mode than by those put into writing. The audience's comprehension of simple messages is the same regardless of the modality. However, due to the attention-getting attributes of video, attitude change for simple messages is greatest when they are presented in video format and least when they are written.[180]

Schema Activation-Related Heuristics and Biases

The Schema Accessibility Heuristic

Before making a decision, audience members spontaneously activate a schema to guide their search for information. The schema they activate affects both their decision-making process and its outcome.[181] The schema directs their attention toward information that is relevant to it and away from information that is not. Yet at a conscious level, audience members remain unaware their attention is being directed selectively. Instead, they believe they are considering all the evidence in an open-minded way.[182]

Audiences evoke what this text terms the schema accessibility heuristic when they base their search for information on the schema that is easiest for them to access. Easy-to-access schemata include those that are frequently activated and recently used.[183] For expert decision makers, the most accessible schemata are usually the most relevant ones.[184] This is not the case for novices.

However, both experts and novices are susceptible to activating irrelevant or slanted schemata based on contextual cues or "frames."[185] Voters are susceptible to activating schemata that frame issues to the advantage of one politician or the other when they hear catchphrases such as "law and order," "forced busing," and "right-wing conspiracy."[186] TV news viewers are susceptible to activating schemata based on the newscasters' framing of the day's events.[187] The media can frame the news in ways that prime viewers to activate particular schemata regarding their beliefs about equality, freedom, gender, race, patriotism, international concerns, and the economy and thus lead them to attend to particular aspects of an issue and to formulate particular opinions about it.[188]

Relying on an easily accessible schema can be appropriate in many situations,[189] even when it is at the expense of statistical information. For example, a study of medical residents at a major New York City teaching hospital finds that only first-year residents use base-rate information to make their diagnoses. Experienced residents disregard base-rate information about the patient group and yet are more likely to make the correct diagnosis of an individual patient. The study's authors conclude that experienced residents develop a schema that allows them to make decisions based on the symptoms presented by the individual patient.[190] Nonetheless, relying on an easily accessible schema can also be a source of bias as the following sections indicate.

Framing Effects: The Power of Spin

Framing effects occur when two sets of information that apparently have the same meaning but use different wording activate different schemata and thus lead to different decisions.[191] Marketers know that consumers are especially susceptible to framing effects. Consumers are generally more willing to pay premiums to avoid losses when the label "insurance" is used to explain those payments.[192] Consumers prefer ground beef described as 75% lean to ground beef described as 25% fat.[193] How many consumers would want to eat a hamburger if the product in the burger called "lean, finely textured meat" were labeled "pink slime" instead? Not many, it turns out.[194]

Audiences other than consumers are also affected by framing. For example, voters tend to allocate more police to a community with a 3.7% crime rate as opposed to one described as 96.3% "crime free."[195] Doctors are more likely to recommend a procedure that saves 10 out of 100 lives than one that allows 90 out of 100 to die.[196] Pollsters routinely find that wording a survey question in a particular way can frame an issue and that differently worded survey questions can produce contrary results.[197]

Changes in message frames influence both the process and outcome of a wide range of business and economic decisions. Superficial differences in the naming of financial products with identical returns lead investors to make different investment decisions.[198] Managers evaluate the same employee more favorably when their performance is framed positively—"The employee was present 97% of the time"—than when it is framed negatively—"The employee was absent 3% of the time."[199] Tax cuts framed as a "bonus" are more likely to be spent than tax cuts framed as a "rebate."[200] Merely renaming the prisoner's dilemma game the "Community Game" leads to twice as much cooperation among student negotiators as renaming it the "Wall Street Game."[201]

Which frame makes the thing described sound more appealing?	
"Our burgers are 25% fat"	"Our burgers are 75% lean"
Wall Street bailout	Economic rescue
Capitalism	Free enterprise
Treated wastewater	Recycled water
High-risk loans	Subprime loans
Socialized medicine	National health care

In politics, opposing sides on an issue often compete to frame the issue in the audience's mind. Framing an issue can result in a contest over the issue's scope, who is responsible for it, who is affected by it, and which values are relevant to it.[202] The success of a particular policy option often depends upon the number and influence of people who subscribe to the way it is framed.[203] Altering how social policies are framed (e.g., naming a policy affirmative action vs. equal rights) alters how citizens value and/or discount those policies.[204]

For politicians, framing is a strategic choice.[205] They recognize that framing a debate takes them a long way toward winning it.[206] In August 1990, Representative Lee Hamilton, chairman of the House Foreign Affairs Middle East Subcommittee, spoke to Congress about the best way to frame the Persian Gulf War, saying that "The United States must not go it alone. We must frame this confrontation as a confrontation between the international community, on the one hand, and Iraq, on the other."[207] Political psychologist Drew Westen makes the case that Republicans have regularly won the hearts and minds of U.S. voters because they have been better at framing issues than Democrats:

> [Republicans] have kept government off our backs, torn down that wall, saved the flag, left no child behind, protected life, kept our marriages sacred, restored integrity to the Oval Office, spread democracy to the Middle East, and fought an unrelenting war on terror . . . I have it on good authority (i.e., off the record) that leading conservatives have chortled with joy (usually accompanied by astonishment) as they watched their Democratic counterparts campaign by reciting their best facts and figures, as if they were trying to prevail in a high school debate tournament.[208]

Across a variety of political scenarios, moral policy frames, such as those Westen attributes to Republicans, elicit more audience support than more pragmatic or economic frames.[209]

Films, TV news shows, newspapers, and magazines also frame issues and use specific techniques to do so.[210] Framing techniques used in the design of newspapers, such as page placement, influence the degree of concern readers express about current issues.[211] Framing techniques also influence the level of readership for specific news stories.[212] Elements of news stories that newspapers manipulate in order to frame them include news story headlines, subheads, photos, photo captions, sources and quotes, and concluding paragraphs.[213] Misleading newspaper headlines that emphasize minor details rather than the article's main point routinely bias readers' comprehension in ways that make it difficult for them to correct their initial misconceptions.[214]

The formats of different graphs can also affect how audiences interpret and use the same information.[215] For example, audiences interpret the same data differently depending on whether it is presented in pie charts, bar graphs, or line graphs.[216] They also interpret the same information differently depending on which variables are assigned to the *x*- and *y*-axes.[217]

In addition, excluding information from a message frame affects how people interpret the message.[218] A study of the effects of message framing on newspaper readers compared the selective publication of UPI photos of an antiwar protest by *The New York Times* with the more extensive publication of UPI photos by *The National Guardian*. The photos *The Times* editors chose to omit, or to leave outside the frame, made a significant difference in how readers interpreted the protest.[219]

Despite the dramatic effects of frames on decision making, audiences "are normally unaware of alternative frames and of their potential effects on the relative attractiveness of options."[220] One reason audiences usually fail to recognize that differently framed decision problems are similar to each other is that the surface characteristics of the frames distract them.[221] Even when two competing frames are presented one after the other, as they are in debates, audience members rarely choose between them. Instead, they simply adopt the position most consistent with their preexisting values.[222] Audiences with high levels of statistical sophistication also fail to recognize the impact of frames on their decisions.[223] For example, experienced physicians are just as likely as their patients to fail to recognize how framing a treatment either in terms of mortality rates or survival rates affects their decision about it.[224]

Nonetheless, it is sometimes possible for the audience to recognize and reject message frames. For example, TV audiences will sometimes reject the media's frames and access frames from other sources to make sense of the news.[225] A study of older adults (aged 65 to 89) asked to choose a treatment for lung cancer described either in terms of mortality rates or survival rates finds they are less susceptible to framing effects than younger adults (aged 18 to 24). The reason? Older adults rely more on their own experience as opposed to the data presented to them to make their decisions.[226]

Framing is most effective when the framed message recommends behaviors that are congruent with the frame. Thus, consumers are more likely to take action and make purchases when product ads are positively framed (e.g., "Save money!") versus negatively framed (e.g., "Stop wasting money!"). One study asked 390 women who either owned or were thinking about buying a video camera to read positively and negatively framed ads and to make purchase decisions. Women who read the positively framed advertising were much more likely to decide to purchase the advertised camera than those who read the negatively framed ads.[227]

Depending on the behavior recommended, either a positively or negatively framed message might be more congruent with it. In the health care field, for example, messages that are positively framed and stress benefits, also called *gain-framed* messages (e.g., "Enjoy a healthy life style"), are most effective when they encourage preventative behaviors such as regular physical exercise,[228] smoking cessation,[229] and using sunscreen to prevent skin cancer.[230] Negatively framed messages that emphasize potential problems, also called *loss-framed* messages (e.g., "Stay out of the hospital"), are most effective when they encourage detection behaviors such as HIV screening,[231] breast self-examination,[232] and mammography use.[233]

Brain Regions Activated. Frame-congruent choices, such as those described above, are emotionally satisfying. Neuroscientists find that amygdala activation, which is associated with an increased emotional response to information, is greater when subjects make frame-congruent choices than when they make frame-incongruent ones (see Figure 3.5, p. 108).[234] By contrast, frame-incongruent choices generate feelings of internal conflict. Neuroscientists find that frame-incongruent messages produce greater activation in the anterior cingulate cortex (ACC). The ACC is connected both to the amygdala and to the frontal and parietal lobes. ACC activity during frame-incongruent choices reflects the detection of a conflict between the responses of the emotional and rational systems. Any such conflict makes audiences less susceptible to framing effects. Activity in the orbital frontal cortex and the medial prefrontal cortex predicts reduced susceptibility to framing effects altogether.[235]

Framing Effects: The Power of Analogy

Analogies can serve as powerful decision frames: They can constrain the set of alternatives the audience considers and can influence the audience's evaluations of those alternatives.[236] Analogies have been shown to influence the decisions of many different audiences, including consumers,[237] voters,[238] mock jurors,[239] and investors.[240]

Analogies work by activating a well-understood schema in one domain that can organize attribute information about a little-understood target in another domain.[241] For example, what most audiences already know about the structure of the solar system—it has a number of small planets that revolve around a large central star—can be used to explain the structure of the atom—atoms have a number of small electrons that spin around a relatively large central nucleus.

Different analogies provide different frames and lead to different decisions. For example, consumers who read an ad that made an analogy between a personal digital assistant (PDA) and a librarian formed a more favorable impression of the PDA than consumers who read an ad that made an analogy between the PDA and a secretary.[242] Similarly, consumers who read an ad that made an analogy between a digital camera and a film-based camera had a greater intention to buy the digital camera than those who read a similar ad that made an analogy between a digital camera and a scanner.[243]

Analogies can lead audiences to make biased predictions if some feature of the current situation that has no diagnostic significance has triggered the analogy. For example, football scouts sometimes make irrelevant analogies with pro football stars when judging the talent of rookies. Football scouts tend to choose rookies who win awards named after a star football player rather than rookies who win equally prestigious but differently named awards.[244]

Analogies are often used to frame the terms of political debates[245] despite their tendency to undermine the role of accurate information in determining causes and effects. For example, many U.S. policy makers used two analogies extensively to decide on military strategy during the pre-Vietnam era: (1) Vietnam will be another Korean War, and (2) the U.S. experience in Vietnam will be like the French experience in Vietnam in the 1950s.[246] Other policy makers used the French analogy to argue against the appropriateness of the Korean analogy. They conducted this argument by comparing the two analogies to each other.[247]

Later, in the 1960s, policy makers used the "domino theory" analogy to frame the debate about Vietnam.[248] The success of this analogy played an important role in the decision of the United States to enter into the Vietnam War.[249] Interestingly, the policy makers themselves never fully recognized the role of the analogy in framing the debate about Vietnam.[250]

The Self-Serving Bias: The Power of Roles

When presented with identical information, different audience members activate different schemata depending on their role in the situation. The particular schema they activate tends to be the one that best promotes their perceived self-interest. For example, Democrats typically support a program if it is referred to as a Democratic program and reject the same program if it is referred to as a Republican program; the converse is true of Republicans.[251] Similarly, when audience members are asked to take the role of someone personally affected by a policy, they tend to make a different decision about the policy than when they are asked to take the role of the policy maker.[252]

Psychologists call this tendency the self-serving bias.[253] The bias is not caused by a desire to be unfair, but by a human inability to interpret information in an unbiased manner.[254] Furthermore, audiences tend to confuse what is beneficial to them personally with what is fair or moral. Consider the following two scenarios. Does your answer change depending on your role in it?

SCENARIO 1: AN ACROSS-THE-BOARD RAISE TO EMPLOYEES

Imagine you are an employee. Do you think a 10% raise is a good idea?

Imagine you are the business owner. Do you think a 10% raise is a good idea?

SCENARIO 2: DAMAGES FOR A CAR ACCIDENT

Imagine you were in a car accident. The judge determined it was *their* fault. Should the other driver pay for all of the damages and receive a fine?

Imagine you were in a car accident. The judge determined it was *your* fault. Should you pay for all of the damages and receive a fine?

Even professional tax accountants, who are trained to be unbiased, tend to interpret judicial cases in a way that is consistent with their client's preferences.[255] As a consequence, many recommendations made by tax accountants tend to be overly aggressive and cannot be justified when challenged by the IRS.

The self-serving bias is perhaps best known for leading people to take more responsibility for their successes than for their failures[256] and to take more credit than they deserve.[257] A content analysis of one year's annual reports from Fortune 500 companies found that CEOs whose firms had a net loss for the year took responsibility for the loss in fewer than 11% of the cases. In about 89% of the cases, the CEOs blamed external factors such as the economy, the competition, government regulations, or their employees. Conversely, CEOs whose firms had a net profit for the year took credit for their firm's profitability in fully 90% of the cases.[258]

The self-serving bias is not the only bias triggered by the schemata that roles activate. Other biases can be triggered by the schemata activated by the role a speaker assumes in relation to her audience. For example, a child advocating a protection-themed message such as nuclear disarmament activates a "protector" schema in adult audience members and is more persuasive than an expert advocating the same message. An expert, on the other hand, activates an "unknowing public" schema in audience members and is more persuasive than a child when advocating for a technical issue such as a tenth planet.[259]

Priming Effects: The Power of Subtle Influences

In addition to being activated by framing techniques and the role the audience or speaker plays in a situation, schemata and their components can be primed—brought to mind or activated—in a number of different and sometimes subtle ways. For example, the mere presence of a TV can prime a schema consistent with television content and evoke audience perceptions of violence and crime.[260] Words related to the elderly stereotype (e.g., *traditional, retired*) prime young people to walk more slowly than normal. The concept of rudeness primes listeners to interrupt speakers more quickly and more frequently than the concept of politeness.[261] A heart shape on donation boxes primes people who encounter the boxes to contribute more to humanitarian projects than a round or square shape.[262] Reading one passage of text primes readers to prefer related passages; viewing one product primes consumers to prefer similar products.[263]

Background designs and templates in presentation slides can serve as another subtle prime. In a study of website design, the background design of an e-commerce website was manipulated to prime either product quality attributes (e.g., safety for cars, comfort for couches) or price. The prime affected the choices of both novices and experts in the product class.[264] Note, too, how the background template of the intuitively appealing slide presentation shown earlier in this chapter (p. 218) primes a preference for the wind-generated power alternative, whereas the background template of the more purely rational slide presentation with its symbol of the atom (p. 217) may unintentionally prime fears of radioactive fallout.

Priming can have a powerful effect on consumers' decisions. Priming the schema for a product category can change consumers' choices.[265] A study of background music played in a store selling both German and French wines found that background music from a wine's country of origin increased sales of wines from that country.[266] Priming a product attribute can increase the weight consumers give that attribute.[267] Questions that prime intentions, such as "Do you intend to buy a personal computer in the next six months?" influence purchase decisions by making consumers' attitudes about products in the category more accessible to them.[268] Remarkably, the effect can last up to a year.[269]

Priming can also determine how heavily voters will weight the criteria they use to evaluate public officials.[270] For example, if last week's news stories focused on environmental issues, then voters will weight environmental criteria more heavily in their evaluation of public officials. On the other hand, if last week's news stories focused on defense issues, then voters will weight defense criteria more heavily.

Priming can even determine whether voters support politically conservative or liberal policies. In a two-part study, college students were primed to view success in life as dependent either on one's personal merit or on good fortune. In Study 1, the students were asked to explain their academic success by focusing either on the role of hard work, self-discipline, and wise decision-making (the personal merit prime) or on the role of chance, opportunity, and help from others (the good fortune prime). In Study 2, questionnaire items served as the personal merit versus good fortune primes. In both studies, students given the good fortune prime subsequently indicated more support for liberal policies than those given the personal merit prime. Why? Because the personal merit prime activated a conservative political schema, whereas the good fortune prime activated a liberal one.[271]

Priming also makes it easier for audiences to form certain kinds of impressions of other people.[272] In a study of the priming effects of pretrial publicity, mock jurors were asked to render verdicts both before and after viewing an edited video recording of an actual trial. Jurors' verdicts were significantly affected by pretrial publicity, especially negative pretrial publicity about the defendant's character, even when they heard the trial evidence prior to viewing the publicity.[273]

A follow-up study finds that jury deliberation fails to diminish the influence pretrial publicity has on jurors' verdicts.[274]

Most audiences are highly susceptible to priming because they are easily influenced to interpret events with the communicator's schema.[275] In court cases, the opening statements made by prosecution and defense attorneys prime competing schemata in the minds of the jurors.[276] In this situation, the longer opening statement tends to win the competition because it primes jurors with a more complete schema for making sense of the case.

Primacy Effects: The Power of Being First to Frame an Issue

The schema the audience activates first will unduly influence its decision. For example, shortly before World War II began, Americans were asked if they should be allowed to join the German army. Only 23% answered yes when the question was presented first. However, 34% answered yes when the question was presented after two questions that asked if Americans should be allowed to join the French and the British armies.[277] The first presentation order apparently activated a "loyalty and treason" schema. Americans should not help the enemy. The second presentation order, on the other hand, activated a "freedom of choice" schema. Americans should be free to fight in any army they choose.[278]

Information Acquisition–Related Heuristics and Biases

The Anchoring and Availability Heuristics

Once an audience has activated a schema, it can then search for the value or information that belongs in each slot of the schema. For example, the schema home buyers activate to decide whether to purchase a new house likely includes a slot for the monetary value of the house. When audiences allow a value that is easily acquired from an external source (e.g., a seller's asking price of $320,000) to unduly influence, or anchor, their estimate of the real slot value (e.g., the price that an appraiser might calculate after investigating the current housing market), they are said to be using the anchoring heuristic.[279]

In addition to filling empty schema slots with values based on information that is easy to acquire from external sources, the audience may also fill those slots with information that is easy to imagine or to retrieve from their memories. When audiences allow a value they can easily retrieve from their memories or imaginations (e.g., the price of the last house they purchased) to unduly influence their estimate of the actual slot value, they are said to be using the availability heuristic.[280] Information is easy for the audience to retrieve from memory if they paid close attention to it when it was presented to them, if they fully comprehended it, and if they have been exposed to it frequently.[281]

Insufficient Adjustment: The Power of Easily Acquired Information

When easily acquired external information anchors an audience's estimate of a schema slot value, the audience rarely changes or adjusts the anchor's value sufficiently.[282] For example, managers often use an employee's salary of the past year as an anchor to determine the employee's salary for the upcoming year and rarely adjust the anchor sufficiently to account for the employee's more recent performance.[283] Different anchors can yield different decisions about the same issue. For example, in mock negotiations between buyers and sellers, a buyer's initial offer can act as an anchor that has a dramatic effect on the final selling price, with very low initial offers leading sellers to sell at lower-than-normal prices.[284] Similarly, a low minimum repayment amount printed on a credit card statement can act as an anchor that influences the credit card customer to repay less than they otherwise would, and as a consequence, to pay much more in interest.[285]

All types of audience decisions are susceptible to the insufficient-adjustment bias. When consumers evaluate two or more items bundled together, the value of the most important item anchors their overall evaluation of the entire bundle.[286] When mock jurors are instructed to consider the harshest verdict first, the jurors anchor on that verdict and render significantly harsher verdicts.[287] A study of the insufficient adjustment bias in investment decisions asked 499 investors to read two versions of a print ad for a mid-cap mutual fund. Except for the names of the two funds, *Euro Star 100 Fund™* and *Euro Star 500 Fund™*, both versions of the ad were identical. Both versions presented the same product information and the same risk-return profile. Incredibly, investors anchored on the first value they read—the number in the fund's name—to determine the fund's expected return. On average, investors who read the ad for the *Euro Star 100 Fund™* said they expected a return of 11.8%. Those who read the same ad for the *Euro Star 500 Fund™* expected a 22.6% return.[288]

Experts as well as novices make insufficient adjustment to the anchor. For example, professional real estate agents make insufficient adjustment to the anchor when they predict various values regarding houses for sale. In one study, agents were allowed to take up to 20 minutes to inspect a house before they were asked for their predictions. Agents also received one of two versions of a 10-page handout of the statistics on the house and other houses in the area. The two versions of the handout were identical except for the asking price—the first version had an asking price of $119,900; the second had an asking price of $149,900. Those agents who received the $119,900 asking price on average predicted that the appraisal value of the house would be $114,204, that the listing price would be $117,745, that the purchase price would be $111,454, and that the seller would accept an offer no lower than $111,136. On the other hand, agents who received the asking price of $149,900 on average predicted an appraisal value of $128,754, a listing price of $130,981, a purchase price of $127,318, and a lowest offer price of $123,818. Thus, the value of the asking price changed all the average predicted values by 11 to 14%.[289]

Even financial experts are not immune to anchoring effects. Auditors from global accounting firms insufficiently adjust the anchor when asked to estimate the incidence of fraud.[290] Fund managers anchor on the current value of the Dow Jones Industrial Average when asked to determine what the value of the Dow would be if dividends were included in its calculation.[291] Their highest guesses only double or triple the current value even in quarters when the actual value is more than 70 times greater than the Dow's current value.[292] When valuing firms, financial analysts tend to anchor on the firm's current market price and then add or subtract 5% of the price instead of calculating the firm's value using the well-accepted discounted cash flow valuation method.[293]

The most common anchor that audiences use to judge other people is themselves.[294] For example, when asked questions such as, "How does your driving ability compare to that of your peers?" audiences tend to anchor on their own abilities and then adjust for the skills of their peers.[295] Audiences also anchor on their first impressions of others. Personal traits mentioned early in impression formation tasks receive more weight than traits mentioned later. Thus, audiences tend to rate a person described as "intelligent, slender, and suspicious" more positively than they rate a person described as "suspicious, slender, and intelligent."[296] Invariably, when audiences try to adjust their initial impressions, they adjust too little and infer more about a person's character than is warranted.[297]

Anchors acquired from external sources can bias both the external search for further information and the retrieval of additional information from memory.[298] However, some easily acquired values will not serve to anchor the audience's estimates. Audiences will not use a value as an anchor if it is expressed on a different scale than the value the audience is trying to estimate. For example, an audience would not use a value expressed as a percentage as an anchor to estimate a value expressed in dollars.[299]

The audience's tendency to anchor on whatever information is presented often makes them insensitive to missing attribute information, an effect called *omission neglect*. Insensitivity to missing attributes and their values occurs because missing information is not salient,[300] and its implications are difficult to comprehend.[301] For novice consumers, one consequence of omission neglect is that it leads them to make decisions based solely on the attributes and attribute values presented to them.[302] Moreover, the presented attributes and values actually interfere with their ability to identify missing attributes.[303] Even when consumers do identify missing attributes, they typically adjust insufficiently for the implications of those attributes and their values.[304]

The Recall Bias: The Power of Easily Recalled Information

Audiences often make decisions based upon the subjective ease with which they can retrieve schema slot values from their memories. For example, the easier it is for voters to retrieve arguments either for or against an issue, the more confident they are that those arguments are valid,[305] and the more likely they are to be persuaded by them.[306] Decisions about risk,[307] stereotypes,[308] interpersonal closeness,[309] and consumer products[310] are all influenced by ease of recall.

Conversely, the more difficult it is for the audience to recall information about something, the less they like it and the less confident they are in it. British students who were asked to retrieve eight positive attribute values regarding Tony Blair, the Prime Minister of the United Kingdom at the time, tended to have a more negative attitude about him than students who were asked to retrieve only two positive attribute values.[311] German investors liked mutual funds less after they listed many of the funds' advantages than after they listed just a few.[312] And American men inferred that they were at less risk of heart disease after they recalled many risk-increasing behaviors than after they recalled only two or three such behaviors.[313] Interestingly, feelings of power make audience members even more likely to base their decisions on the subjective ease with which information comes to mind.[314]

The Imagination Bias: The Power of Easily Imagined Information

Audiences may make decisions based upon the subjective ease with which they can imagine information that fills schema slots.[315] Voters who were asked to imagine the outcome of a presidential election later rated it more probable that the candidate they had imagined winning would actually win than voters who had not been asked to imagine the election's outcome.[316] Audiences who were asked to imagine experiencing a disease judged themselves as more likely to catch the disease.[317] Audiences asked to imagine winning a contest or being arrested for a crime decided it was more probable that those events could happen to them. Homeowners asked to imagine enjoying the benefits of a subscription to cable TV were later more likely to subscribe.[318] Moreover, followers find leaders who infuse their speeches with words such as *dream* and *imagine* to be more persuasive than leaders leave them out.[319]

Like the recall bias, the imagination bias also works in reverse. People asked to form a mental image of a resort rated the resort more highly when given a verbal description that made the image easy to construct, but decreased their ratings when given numerical data on the resort that were not image evoking.[320] Similarly, readers asked to imagine taking a vacation trip increased their evaluations of the trip when it was described in an easy-to-visualize narrative. But they lowered their evaluations when the trip was described in an unordered list of attributes.[321]

Undue Optimism: The Appeal of Best Case Scenarios

Because positive information is more accessible and easier to bring to mind than negative information,[322] audiences tend to fill empty schema slots about future outcomes with positive information. The audience's bias toward a positive future leads them to overestimate the likelihood they will contribute to charity, vote in an upcoming election, or have a long-lasting romantic relationship.[323] Similarly, college students' undue optimism leads them to overpredict their performance on examinations[324] and to underpredict the amount of time it will take them to complete class assignments.[325] Perhaps the undue optimism bias explains why many remain unconvinced by arguments against risky pursuits such as playing the lottery and day trading, and unfazed by arguments for quite reasonable pursuits such as saving money and exercising more.

The Confirmation Bias: The Power of Previously Acquired Information

The confirmation bias leads audiences to distort newly acquired ambiguous or even contradictory information that fills schema slots so as to make it consistent with information they acquired earlier.[326] For example, recruiters tend to unconsciously distort the new information they acquire about applicants during job interviews in a way that confirms their pre-interview impressions.[327] In one study, 64 mock recruiters were asked to read résumés of job applicants for a sales position and then to observe and evaluate video recordings of the job applicants' interviews. Mock recruiters who had read more favorable résumés rated the same applicants as giving better answers to their questions, as displaying more sales-consistent traits, and as making more persuasive statements during the interviews than recruiters who had read less favorable résumés.[328] Another study finds that both mock recruiters' and actual recruiters' pre-interview impressions of job applicants' résumés significantly influence the questions they ask the applicants during job interviews—the stronger the résumé, the easier the interview questions.[329]

The confirmation bias has also been found to influence juror decision making. Because jurors hear the prosecution's evidence before they hear the defendant's testimony, they are more likely to accept the prosecution's evidence, even if it is later discredited, and to become more critical of the defendant's testimony.[330] Defense attorneys can counteract this tendency by having their strongest witnesses testify first. Ordering witness testimony from strongest to weakest leads jurors to hand down the fewest number of guilty verdicts.[331]

In addition to first impressions, prior decisions can also lead to the confirmation bias. For example, one study revealed that nine out of 10 voters who watched televised U.S. presidential debates believed their preferred candidate won the debate.[332] Another study asked people who either strongly supported or opposed the death penalty to read two contradictory reports. The first report presented evidence that the death penalty was a deterrent to crime, whereas the second report presented evidence to the contrary. Members of both groups claimed the report favoring their opinion was "better conducted" and "more convincing" than the other report. Surprisingly, each group became even more convinced of the correctness of their initial opinion after reading the report that contradicted their opinion.[333] A similar study finds that the more misinformed voters are about a policy, the more confident they are in their opinions about it, and the more resistant they are to changing their opinions, even when presented with factual information to the contrary.[334]

Experts as well as novices are susceptible to the confirmation bias. Like the mock recruiters mentioned previously, seasoned managers' preinterview evaluations of job applicants influence their postinterview evaluations of the applicants' qualifications.[335] Moreover, managers with favorable preinterview impressions are more likely to attribute good interview performances to the applicants' qualifications for the job and to attribute poor performances to external factors. Political scientists rarely change their theories even when events prove their predictions wrong. Instead, they tend to keep their theories and discount the evidence.[336] Rather than change their initial diagnoses, medical doctors tend to distort important diagnostic cues.[337] And when police detectives uncover evidence that disconfirms their initial suspicion against a suspect, they often rate it as less reliable and generate more arguments to question it.[338]

The Confirmation Bias in Groups

The confirmation bias not only affects the information acquisition process of individuals, it also affects information acquisition in group discussions. Group members tend to discuss and repeat information, or schema slot values, that confirms their prior preferences and decisions.[339] In addition, they perceive information that supports the alternative they prefer as being more valuable, more credible, and more relevant than information that opposes it.[340]

Even if group members are not motivated to advocate the alternative they personally prefer, they are more likely to mention information that is consistent with it.[341] Once the group makes a decision, group members begin to prefer information that supports their choice.[342] Groups that cannot agree on the best alternative are less confident about the correctness of the group's decision and less committed to implementing it.

The Common Knowledge Effect in Groups

One reason people meet in groups is to allow group members to share information relevant to making a decision, in other words, to share and acquire information that fills their schema slots. Yet groups typically fail to make better decisions than individual decision makers. In a seminal study of the common knowledge effect, social psychologists Daniel Gigone and Reid Hastie asked 40, three-person groups to determine the grades received by 32 students in an introductory psychology class.[343] Each group of three was given information about six attributes or decision criteria relevant to the students' grades—their aptitude test scores, high-school grade point averages, attendance, enjoyment of the course, overall workload, and self-rated anxiety. For each student a group evaluated, all three group members always received information about the same two attributes, information about two other attributes was always shared by two of the group members, and information about the remaining two attributes was always given to only one group member, with the specific group members receiving a particular unshared cue varying across cases. Thus, each group member always received four items of information about each case. If the three group members pooled their information, information about all six attributes would be available to them.

Surprisingly, the groups consistently failed to discuss all the information that was unshared or to use it to make their decisions. Even though the groups were in possession of more information than any of the individuals, placing people in groups did not result in better judgments than would have been obtained by simply averaging their individual judgments together. Moreover, group weighting of information was a linear function of its degree of sharedness or common knowledge.

The likelihood that a piece of information, or slot value, will be recalled by a group is also a function of the number of group members who share that information[344] as is the likelihood that it will be repeated after it is first mentioned.[345] Why? Because shared information is easier to remember, easier to understand, is seen as more accurate and trustworthy, and leads group members to perceive themselves as more competent when they discuss it.[346]

When, as in the study described previously, no single group member possesses all of the information relevant to making the decision, or the values filling all the schema slots, but the group as a whole does—a situation called the *hidden profile condition*—groups rarely discover the best alternative.[347] Instead, groups typically choose the alternative that is supported by the information all group members hold in common. In one study only 18% of groups in a hidden profile condition chose the best alternative. In contrast, when all the relevant information was known by every group member, 83% of groups selected the best alternative.[348]

Information Integration–Related Heuristics and Biases

Heuristic Choice Rules

Audience members often have great difficulty accurately combining or integrating the slot values they acquire for their schemata. A computer given the same information will always do as well or better than people at information integration tasks.[349] One reason for the difference between computers and people is that people attend to the values of only a few of the important attributes or decision criteria and fail to combine those attribute values with the values of other attributes.[350]

Because of the difficulties inherent in integrating information, audiences will usually prefer easy-to-choose options over difficult-to-choose ones.[351] Audience members who must combine the pros and cons of many alternatives described by many attributes may even make a decision contrary to the one they would have made had the information been easier to integrate.[352] Because of the difficulties inherent in the information integration process, consumers are willing to pay more for products if the effort required to choose among them is reduced.[353]

The use of heuristic choice rules enables audiences to simplify or avoid outright the information integration process.[354] We have already examined several heuristic choice rules in Chapter 3. For example, the *elimination-by-aspects rule* and the *lexicographic rule* are heuristic choice rules because they are noncompensatory, that is to say, they allow the audience to side-step making difficult trade-offs.[355] The *equal weight rule*, although a compensatory choice rule, is a heuristic choice rule because audiences who use it automatically assign an equal weight to all attributes. In contrast, the *weighted additive rule* is a compensatory choice rule that is a normative or nonheuristic rule. It demands that the audience weight every attribute or decision criteria independently and consider every value of every alternative for every attribute.

Another way audiences can simplify the information integration process is by deciding on the basis of a single "if-then," or configural, heuristic choice rule. For example, a recruiter might have the rule that if a job applicant does not give her a firm handshake, then she will not hire them. Experts often use such "if-then" rules to make decisions.[356] For example, magistrates in the United Kingdom tend to rely on "if-then" heuristic choice rules based on the prosecutor's recommendation or the age of the defendant when reaching an exonerative decision.[357]

Like other heuristic choice rules, "if-then" heuristic choice rules allow the audience to bypass making trade-offs and avoid the difficult weighting and combination processes that are involved in normative information integration.[358] Although the audience's heuristic use of "if-then" choice rules can occasionally yield nearly optimal choices,[359] choices made on this basis are usually inaccurate. When audiences formulate such rules from their experience, they tend to overgeneralize from a very small sample.

Audiences can avoid the difficulties of the information integration process altogether if they simply choose the same alternative they chose the last time they had to make a similar decision. Audiences rely on the habitual choice heuristic when they retrieve prior evaluations of their current options from memory and then choose the option they had previously evaluated most highly.[360]

Trade-Off Avoidance: The Impact of a Dominant Attribute

In many situations each alternative under consideration has both positive and negative slot values for different attributes or decision criteria. For example, a higher quality product usually comes with higher cost. But most people tend to avoid making such trade-offs.[361]

In a seminal study of trade-off avoidance, consumers were asked to identify pairs of alternatives that had equal value for them.[362] For example, consumers said Gift Package A, which contains $10 in cash and a book of coupons worth $32, had the same value to them as Gift Package B, which contains twice the cash but a coupon book worth significantly less.

	Gift Package A	Gift Package B
Cash	$10	$20
Coupon book worth	$32	$18

A week later, the consumers were asked to choose between the two alternatives. They were also asked which decision criterion—cash or coupons—they considered more important. Eighty-eight percent of the consumers chose the alternative that had a higher value for the criterion the participant considered more important. Similar results obtain for many different decisions, including choices among college applicants, auto tires, baseball players, and routes to work. A likely explanation is that avoiding trade-offs makes it easier for people to justify their choices both to themselves and others.

A similar explanation may account for the tendency of policy makers to neglect mentioning trade-offs and to avoid arguing the pros and cons of their policy proposals. Instead they tend to justify their proposals with one-sided arguments to which a simple noncompensatory choice rule can be applied.[363]

The Mere Quantity Effect: The Impact of a Seemingly Dominant Alternative

Audiences can avoid many of the difficulties of the information integration process if they simply choose the alternative that is agreed on by the most people. In a study of the persuasiveness of multiple sources, audience members weighted descriptions of other people's personality traits more heavily when the descriptions were presented by multiple sources than when they were presented by a single source.[364] Another study finds that three speakers conveying three arguments are more persuasive than one speaker conveying the same three arguments.[365] For audiences who lack the information or expertise to make an informed decision themselves, the greater the number of their advisors and the fewer the differences among their advisors' proposals, the greater the persuasive effect.[366]

Audiences can also avoid many of the difficulties of information integration if they simply choose the alternative that is supported by the most arguments. The more arguments that are presented for a position the more likely the audience will be persuaded to adopt it.[367] For example, increasing the number of arguments supporting the guilt of a defendant significantly increases mock jurors' tendency to render guilty verdicts.[368] Likewise, increasing the number of not-guilty arguments increases jurors' tendency to judge the defendant innocent. Moreover, mock jurors are more likely to be persuaded by the number of supporting arguments made during jury deliberations than by the number of jurors who initially support a verdict.[369]

When audiences make no concerted effort to evaluate the quality of the arguments presented or lack the expertise to do so, they are even likely to judge a large number of irrelevant arguments to be more persuasive than a smaller number of highly relevant ones.[370] Perhaps this tendency explains why merit raise decisions made by university committees can be predicted by simply counting the number of activities faculty members list in their annual reports.[371]

The Common Dimension Effect: The Impact of Direct Comparisons

Audiences find comparing alternatives that have slot values for the same attributes (i.e., for the same decision criteria or dimensions) easier than comparing alternatives that have unique attributes or missing slot values. For this reason, the audience will often eliminate alternatives with unique attributes or missing slot values from consideration or else weight those attributes less heavily, a tendency called the *common dimension effect.*[372]

When the audience is given the slot value of each attribute or decision criterion for all of the alternatives under consideration, it only needs to know the relative utility of each attribute. For example, when the audience is told that one computer has 16GB SDRAM (a type of random access memory) and another has 8GB SDRAM, it can see that the first computer has a higher value for the attribute of SD RAM than the second, even if it does not know the meaning of SD RAM. But if the audience is not given the values for some attributes or criteria, it needs to know the absolute level of utility of each attribute. Thus, if the audience knows only that one computer has 16GB SDRAM, then it must know the absolute worth of that value in order to evaluate it.[373]

Because of the difficulties involved in calculating a value's absolute worth, if the audience finds some alternatives are missing values for some attributes, they will tend to weight those attributes less heavily.[374] In a study illustrating this effect, judges were asked to evaluate the grade point averages of two students, each of whom was described by two test scores. One of the test scores came from a test both students took and the other came from a test only one of the students took. Judges systematically gave more weight to the scores from the test taken by both students.[375]

Audiences are susceptible to the common dimension effect even when information is presented to them in paragraph form as opposed to tabular or matrix form. Paragraph form makes finding the common attributes or decision criteria of alternatives more difficult than a matrix format. In a study of the common dimension effect in paragraphs, readers were presented with pairs of paragraph that described videogames and asked to choose the game they thought would sell best and to justify their decision. Each pair of games had two attributes in common and two unique attributes. Despite the difficulties caused by the paragraph format, readers still tended to ignore the slot values of the unique attributes and to make and justify their decisions based on the different slot values each game had on the two common attributes.[376]

In a follow-up study, college students were shown descriptions of colleges written in paragraph form. The students were asked to think aloud as they decided which college they would recommend to a younger brother or sister. They were also asked to rate the importance of all the attributes or decision criteria mentioned in the paragraphs. When making their decisions, the students discounted the slot values of the unique attributes despite claiming they believed that information to be important.[377]

When a format makes it too difficult for audiences to compare alternatives along a common dimension or decision criterion, they may discount that dimension regardless of its importance to them. An unusual format, recommended by National Academy of Sciences in 1996, displayed automobile safety information in a way that made it hard for consumers to compare the safety levels of new vehicles. As a result, consumers did not give safety data the weight it deserved. Instead, consumers gave undue weight to less relevant but easier-to-compare information such as a car's color and style. Consumers make better decisions when displays of safety information use meaningful symbols such as letter grades or stars that make comparing safety ratings easy.[378]

Some consumers have developed strategies for avoiding the common dimension effect. When making choices between comparable products (e.g., two toasters), consumers can easily compare slot values for the concrete attributes of the products, for example, the number of settings on each toaster. But some products have few concrete attributes in common (e.g., a toaster and a smoke detector). To choose among noncomparable products such as these, many consumers have learned to rise to a higher level of abstraction where they can identify different slot values on common dimensions.[379] For example, consumers might compare their *need* for a toaster versus their *need* for a smoke detector.

The Asymmetric Dominance Effect: The Impact of a Third Option

Audiences find it easier to make trade-offs between two equally desirable alternatives if given a third alternative whose slot values are clearly inferior to one alternative but not to the other. The presence of a third alternative gives audiences a compelling reason to choose one alternative over the other and is known as the *asymmetric dominance effect*.[380] For example, when students were given a choice between $6.00 in cash and a nice pen, 64% chose the money and 36% chose the pen.[381] But when students were given a choice between $6.00, a nice pen, and a cheap pen, only 52% chose the money. Forty-six percent chose the nice pen and the remaining 2% chose the cheap pen. Because comparing two pens is easier than comparing a pen to cash, an additional 10% of the students chose the nice pen.

The Limited Options Bias: The Appeal of Yes or No Choices

Providing audiences with too many alternatives, and thus with too many schema slot values to integrate easily, can stop them from making a decision. For example, employees' participation in 401(k) plans dramatically drops as the number of funds their employer allows them to choose from increases.[382] Experienced physicians are less likely to prescribe a new medication if they are asked to choose between two medications than if they are asked whether to prescribe a single medication.[383]

In an often-cited study of consumer decision making, grocery store shoppers were offered the opportunity to taste any of six jams at one booth, or any of 24 jams at another. At the six-jam booth, 40% of shoppers stopped to taste and 30% who tasted purchased a jam. At the 24-jam booth, 60% stopped to taste but only 3% who tasted purchased.[384] Similar effects have been shown for other types of products,[385] for loan offers,[386] and for retirement plans.[387] When, under large choice set conditions, the audience does make a decision, it tends to select predefined default options.[388] The audience also exhibits more disappointment and regret.[389]

A study of the persuasive impact of single versus multiple options examined the responses of 57,000 potential borrowers to a lender's mailing that offered them large, short-term loans. The offer letter gave either an example of one possible loan—its size, term, and monthly payments—or examples of four different loans. Borrowers were more likely to apply for a loan when they were presented with only one example. The one-example description had the same positive effect on loan acceptance as dropping the monthly interest rate by two percentage points.[390]

The First Good Option Bias: The Appeal of a Quick Fix

People often prefer the first option with favorable attributes that is presented to them. In one study, audience members were given information about six attributes of two alternatives. Positive information that favored one of two alternatives was presented either as the first or fourth attribute out of the six. In 70% of their choices, audience members chose the alternative whose positive attribute was presented as the first attribute despite the fact that the totality of the information was net neutral.[391] Similar effects have been identified outside the laboratory. For example, in the poll booth, the order of candidates' names on a ballot is sufficient to determine the outcomes of many elections.[392]

The Status Quo Bias: The Appeal of Past Decisions

The status quo bias circumvents the need to search for schema slot values and to integrate that new information. In this bias keeping things the way they are, doing things the way they have always been done, is the favorite option.[393] Marketing professors refer to this bias as *brand loyalty*.[394] In many purchase situations, brand loyalty is the best predictor of consumers' future purchases.[395]

The status quo option is often chosen even when the audience is given clear reasons to deviate from it.[396] Under time pressure, audiences may even decide against their own explicitly formed intentions to choose something other than the status quo.[397] Of course, audience members may have good reasons for maintaining the status quo. For example, untried alternatives necessarily involve more risk, the costs can be high to switch to a different alternative (e.g., switching from a Mac to a PC), and the audience may have based previous choices on good reasons they can no longer remember. Not choosing but maintaining the status quo also minimizes the negative emotions that the decision-making process sometimes creates.[398]

HEURISTICS AND BIASES IN AUDIENCE DECISION MAKING: IMPLICATIONS FOR COMMUNICATORS

- The main takeaway for communicators in Chapter 5 is that audiences are unconsciously biased by techniques that make each of the decision-making processes easy for them to complete. Audiences do not base their decisions exclusively on facts and reason.
- Use the information presented in the chapter to identify techniques that make processing easy. Do not expect the facts you present to speak for themselves.
- Why use the information? To enhance the intuitive appeal of your communications. To compete successfully with other skilled communicators.
- To apply a technique that makes processing easy, refer to the section describing the appropriate process. Also, refer to the techniques described in Chapter 4 for additional ways to make the audience's decision-making process easy.

Notes

1 Kahneman, D., & Frederick, S. (2002). Representativeness revisited: Attribute substitution in intuitive judgment. In T. Gilovich, D. Griffin & D. Kahneman (Eds.), *Heuristics and biases: The psychology of intuitive judgment* (pp. 49–81). New York: Cambridge University Press.

2 Cobos, P. L., Almaraz, J., & Garcia-Madruga, J. A. (2003). An associative framework for probability judgment: An application to biases. *Journal of Experimental Psychology: Learning, Memory, and Cognition, 29*(1), 80–96.

Lieberman, M. D., Gaunt, R., Gilbert, D. T., & Trope, Y. (2002). Reflection and reflexion: A social cognitive neuroscience approach to attributional inference. In M. P. Zanna (Ed.), *Advances in experimental social psychology* (Vol. 34, pp. 199–249). San Diego, CA: Academic Press.

Whittlesea, B. W. (1997). Production, evaluation, and preservation of experiences: Constructive processing in remembering and performance tasks. In D. L. Medin (Ed.), *The psychology of learning and motivation: Advances in research and theory* (Vol. 37, pp. 211–264). San Diego, CA: Academic Press.

3 Lieberman, M. D. (2007). Social cognitive neuroscience: A review of core processes. *Annual Review of Psychology, 58*, 259–289.

4 Garcia-Marques, T., & Mackie, D. M. (2000). The positive feeling of familiarity: Mood as an information processing regulation mechanism. In H. Bless & J. Forgas (Eds.), *The message within: The role of subjective experience in social cognition and behavior* (pp. 240–261). Philadelphia: Psychology Press.

Ramachandran, V. S., & Hirstein, W. (1999). The science of art: A neurological theory of aesthetic experience. *Journal of Consciousness Studies, 6*(6–7), 15–51.

Schwarz, N. (2004). Meta-cognitive experiences in consumer judgment and decision making. *Journal of Consumer Psychology, 14*(4), 332–348.

5 Lee, A. Y., & Aaker, J. L. (2004). Bringing the frame into focus: The influence of regulatory fit on processing fluency and persuasion. *Journal of Personality and Social Psychology, 86*(2), 205–218.

6 Schwarz, N., & Clore, G. L. (1996). Feelings and phenomenal experiences. In E. T. Higgins & A. W. Kruglanski (Eds.), *Social psychology: Handbook of basic principles* (pp. 433–465). New York: Guilford Press.

Winkielman, P., & Cacioppo, J. T. (2001). Mind at ease puts a smile on the face: Psychophysiological evidence that processing facilitation elicits positive affect. *Journal of Personality and Social Psychology, 81*(6), 989–1000.

7 Kahneman, D., & Tversky, A. (1982). On the study of statistical intuitions. *Cognition, 11*(2), 123–141.

Tversky, A., & Kahneman, D. (1974). Judgment under uncertainty: Heuristics and biases. *Science, 185*(4157), 1124–1131.

8 Gigerenzer, G., & Goldstein, D. G. (1996). Reasoning the fast and frugal way: Models of bounded rationality. *Psychological Review, 103*(4), 650–669.

Schwarz, N., & Vaughn, L. A. (2002). The availability heuristic revisited: Ease of recall and content of recall as distinct sources of information. In T. Gilovich, D. Griffin & D. Kahneman (Eds.), *Heuristics and biases: The psychology of intuitive judgment* (pp. 103–119). New York: Cambridge University Press.

Tversky, A., & Kahneman, D. (1973). Availability: A heuristic for judging frequency and probability. *Cognitive Psychology, 5*(2), 207–232.

9 Kahneman, D., & Miller, D. T. (1986). Norm theory: Comparing reality to its alternatives. *Psychological Review, 93*(2), 136–153.

Kahneman, D., & Varey, C. A. (1990). Propensities and counterfactuals: The loser that almost won. *Journal of Personality and Social Psychology, 59*(6), 1101–1110.

10 Fiske, S. T., Lin, M., & Neuberg, S. L. (1999). The continuum model: Ten years later. In S. Chaiken & Y. Trope (Eds.), *Dual-process theories in social psychology* (pp. 231–254). New York: Guilford Press.

See n9, Kahneman & Varey (1990).

Tversky, A., & Kahneman, D. (1983). Extensional versus intuitive reasoning: The conjunction fallacy in probability judgment. *Psychological Review, 90*(4), 293–315.

11 Shah, D. V., Domke, D., & Wackman, D. B. (2001). The effects of value-framing on political judgment and reasoning. In S. D. Reese, O. H. Gandy & A. E. Grant (Eds.), *Framing public life: Perspectives on media and our understanding of the social world* (pp. 227–243). Mahwah, NJ: Lawrence Erlbaum Associates.

Simon, H. A., & Hayes, J. R. (1976). The understanding process: Problem isomorphs. *Cognitive Psychology, 8*(2), 165–190.

Tversky, A., & Kahneman, D. (1981). The framing of decisions and the psychology of choice. *Science, 211*(4481), 453–458.

Tversky, A., & Kahneman, D. (1988). Rational choice and the framing of decisions. In D. E. Bell, H. Raiffa & A. Tversky (Eds.), *Decision making: Descriptive, normative, and prescriptive interactions* (pp. 167–192). New York: Cambridge University Press.

12 *See* n7.

13 Camerer, C. F., & Johnson, E. J. (1991). The process-performance paradox in expert judgment: How can experts know so much and predict so badly? In K. A. Ericsson & J. Smith (Eds.), *Toward a general theory of expertise: Prospects and limits* (pp. 195–217). New York: Cambridge University Press.

Frederick, S. (2002). Automated choice heuristics. In T. Gilovich, D. Griffin & D. Kahneman (Eds.), *Heuristics and biases: The psychology of intuitive judgment* (pp. 548–558). New York: Cambridge University Press.

14 Cohen, M. S. (1993). The naturalistic basis of decision biases. In G. A. Klein, J. Orasanu, R. Calderwood & C. E. Zsambok (Eds.), *Decision making in action: Models and methods* (pp. 51–99). Norwood, NJ: Ablex.

Keren, G. (1987). Facing uncertainty in the game of bridge: A calibration study. *Organizational Behavior and Human Decision Processes, 39*(1), 98–114.

Shanteau, J. (1989). Cognitive heuristics and biases in behavioral auditing: Review, comments, and observations. *Accounting, Organizations and Society, 14*(1–2), 165–177.

15 Bornstein, B. H., Emler, A. C., & Chapman, G. B. (1999). Rationality in medical treatment decisions: Is there a sunk-cost effect? *Social Sciences & Medicine, 49*(2), 215–222.

16 Smith, J. F., & Kida, T. (1991). Heuristics and biases: Expertise and task realism in auditing. *Psychological Bulletin, 109*(3), 472–489.

17 Khatri, N., & Ng, H. A. (2000). The role of intuition in strategic decision making. *Human Relations, 53*(1), 57–86.

Trönnberg, C. C., & Hemlin, S. (2014). Lending decision making in banks: A critical incident study of loan officers. *European Management Journal, 32*(2), 362–372.

18 Guthrie, C., Rachlinski, J. J., & Wistrich, A. J. (2001). Inside the judicial mind. *Cornell Law Review, 86*, 777–830.

Rachlinski, J. J., Guthrie, C., & Wistrich, A. J. (2006). Inside the bankruptcy Judge's mind. *Boston University Law Review, 86*, 1227–1265.

19 Castellan, N. J. (Ed.). (1993). *Individual and group decision making: Current issues.* Hillsdale, NJ: Lawrence Erlbaum.

Kerr, N. L., MacCoun, R. J., & Kramer, G. P. (1996). "When are N heads better (or worse) than one?": Biased judgment in individuals versus groups. In E. H. Witte & J. H. Davis (Eds.), *Understanding group behavior, vol. 1: Consensual action by small groups* (pp. 105–136). Hillsdale, NJ: Lawrence Erlbaum.

20 Hinsz, V. B., Tindale, R. S., & Nagao, D. H. (2008). Accentuation of information processes and biases in group judgments integrating base-rate and case-specific information. *Journal of Experimental Social Psychology, 44*(1), 116–126.

21 Buehler, R., Messervey, D., & Griffin, D. (2005). Collaborative planning and prediction: Does group discussion affect optimistic biases in time estimation? *Organizational Behavior and Human Decision Processes, 97*(1), 47–63.

Buehler, R., Griffin, D., & Peetz, J. (2010). The planning fallacy: Cognitive, motivational, and social origins. *Advances in Experimental Social Psychology, 43*, 1–62.

22 Sniezek, J. A., & Henry, R. A. (1989). Accuracy and confidence in group judgment. *Organizational Behavior and Human Decision Processes, 43*(1), 1–28.

23 Smith, C. M., Tindale, R. S., & Steiner, L. (1998). Investment decisions by individuals and groups in "sunk cost" situations: The potential impact of shared representations. *Group Processes & Intergroup Relations, 1*(2), 175–189.

24 Cheng, P. Y., & Chiou, W. B. (2008). Framing effects in group investment decision making: The role of group polarization. *Psychological Reports, 102*(1), 283–292.

Paese, P. W., Bieser, M., & Tubbs, M. E. (1993). Framing effects and choice shifts in group decision making. *Organizational Behavior and Human Decision Processes, 56*(1), 149–165.

25 *See* n11, Tversky & Kahneman (1981).

26 Tindale, R. S., Sheffey, S., & Scott, L. A. (1993). Framing and group decision-making: Do cognitive changes parallel preference changes? *Organizational Behavior and Human Decision Processes, 55*(3), 470–485.

27 Stasser, G., & Dietz-Uhler, B. (2002). Collective choice, judgment, and problem solving. In M. A. Hogg & S. Tindale (Eds.), *Blackwell handbook of social psychology: Group processes*, (Vol. 3, pp. 31–55). Hoboken, NJ: Wiley-Blackwell.

28 Friedkin, N. E. (1999). Choice shift and group polarization. *American Sociological Review, 64*(6), 856–875.

Zuber, J. A., Crott, H. W., & Werner, J. (1992). Choice shift and group polarization: An analysis of the status of arguments and social decision schemes. *Journal of Personality and Social Psychology, 62*(1), 50–61.

29 Whyte, G., & Sebenius, J. K. (1997). The effect of multiple anchors on anchoring in individual and group judgment. *Organizational Behavior and Human Decision Processes*, *69*(1), 75–85.

30 Schulz-Hardt, S., Frey, D., Luthgens, C., & Moscovici, S. (2000). Biased information search in group decision making. *Journal of Personality and Social Psychology*, *78*(4), 655–669.

31 Tindale, R. S., Heath, L., Edwards, J., Posavac, E. J., Bryant, F. B., Suarez-Balcazar, Y., . . . Myers, J. (1998). *Theory and research on small groups*. New York: Plenum Press.

32 Harvey, J. B. (1974). The Abilene paradox and other meditations on management. *Organizational Dynamics*, *3*(1), 63–80.

33 Westphal, J. D., & Bednar, M. K. (2005). Pluralistic ignorance in corporate boards and firms' strategic persistence in response to low firm performance. *Administrative Science Quarterly*, *50*(2), 262–298.

34 Bazerman, M. H. (1994). *Judgment in managerial decision making* (3rd ed.). New York: John Wiley & Sons Ltd.

35 Janis, I. L. (1972). *Victims of groupthink: A psychological study of foreign-policy decisions and fiascoes*. Oxford, UK: Houghton Mifflin.

36 Fischhoff, B., & Johnson, S. (1997). The possibility of distributed decision making. In Z. Shapira (Ed.), *Organizational decision making* (pp. 217–237). New York: Cambridge University Press.

37 Benjamin, A. S., & Bjork, R. A. (1996). Retrieval fluency as a metacognitive index. In L. Reder (Ed.), *Metacognition and implicit memory* (pp. 309–338). Mahwah, NJ: Erlbaum.

Johnston, W. A., & Hawley, K. J. (1994). Perceptual inhibition of expected inputs: The key that opens closed minds. *Psychonomic Bulletin and Review*, *1*, 56–72.

Whittlesea, B. W., & Williams, L. D. (2001). The discrepancy-attribution hypothesis: II. expectation, uncertainty, surprise and feelings of familiarity. *Journal of Experimental Psychology: Learning, Memory, and Cognition*, *27*(1), 14–33.

38 Chaiken, S., Liberman, A., & Eagly, A. H. (1989). Heuristic and systematic information processing within and beyond the persuasion context. In J. S. Uleman & J. A. Bargh (Eds.), *Unintended thought* (pp. 212–252). New York: Guilford Press.

Petty, R. E., & Cacioppo, J. T. (1986). *Communication and persuasion: Central and peripheral routes to attitude change*. New York: Springer-Verlag.

39 Kruglanski, A. W., & Sleeth-Keppler, D. (2007). The principles of social judgment. In A. W. Kruglanski & E. T. Higgins (Eds.), *Social psychology: Handbook of basic principles* (2nd ed., pp. 116–137). New York: The Guilford Press.

Pierro, A., Mannetti, L., Erb, H. P., Spiegel, S., & Kruglanski, A. W. (2005). Informational length and order of presentation as determinants of persuasion. *Journal of Experimental Social Psychology*, *41*(5), 458–469.

Pierro, A., Mannetti, L., Kruglanski, A. W., & Sleeth-Keppler, D. (2004). Relevance override: On the reduced impact of "cues" under high motivation conditions of persuasion studies. *Journal of Personality and Social Psychology*, *86*(2), 251–264.

40 LeBoeuf, R. A., & Shafir, E. (2003). Deep thoughts and shallow frames: On the susceptibility to framing effects. *Journal of Behavioral Decision Making*, *16*(2), 77–92.

41 Dijksterhuis, A. P. (2010). Automaticity and the unconscious. In S. T. Fiske, D. T. Gilbert & G. Lindzey (Eds.), *Handbook of social psychology* (5th ed., Vol. 1, pp. 228–267). Hoboken, NJ: John Wiley & Sons Ltd.

42 Igou, E. R., & Bless, H. (2007). On undesirable consequences of thinking: Framing effects as a function of substantive processing. *Journal of Behavioral Decision Making*, *20*(2), 125–142.

43 Pelham, B. W., & Neter, E. (1995). The effect of motivation of judgment depends on the difficulty of the judgment. *Journal of Personality and Social Psychology*, *68*(4), 581–594.

44 Jacoby, L. L., Kelley, C. M., & Dywan, J. (1989a). Memory attributions. In H. L. Roediger & F. I. M. Craik (Eds.), *Varieties of memory and consciousness: Essays in honour of Endel Tulving* (pp. 391–422). Hillsdale, NJ: Lawrence Erlbaum Associates.

45 Winkielman, P., Schwarz, N., Reber, R., & Fazendeiro, T. A. (2003b). Cognitive and affective consequences of visual fluency: When seeing is easy on the mind. In L. M. Scott & R. Batra (Eds.), *Persuasive imagery: A consumer response perspective* (pp. 75–89). Mahwah, NJ: Lawrence Erlbaum Associates.

46 Halberstadt, J., & Rhodes, G. (2000). The attractiveness of nonface averages: Implications for an evolutionary explanation of the attractiveness of average faces. *Psychological Science*, *11*(4), 285–289.

Langlois, J. H., & Roggman, L. A. (1990). Attractive faces are only average. *Psychological Science*, *1*(2), 115–121.

Reber, R., Schwarz, N., & Winkielman, P. (2004). Processing fluency and aesthetic pleasure: Is beauty in the perceiver's processing experience? *Personality and Social Psychology Review*, *8*(4), 364–382.

47 *See* n4, Ramachandran & Hirstein (1999).

48 Whittlesea, B. W., Jacoby, L. L., & Girard, K. (1990). Illusions of immediate memory: Evidence of an attributional basis for feelings of familiarity and perceptual quality. *Journal of Memory and Language, 29*(6), 716–732.

Witherspoon, D., & Allan, L. G. (1985). The effect of a prior presentation on temporal judgments in a perceptual identification task. *Memory & Cognition, 13*(2), 101–111.

49 Koriat, A., & Levy-Sadot, R. (1999). Processes underlying metacognitive judgments: Information-based and experience-based monitoring of one's own knowledge. In S. Chaiken & Y. Trope (Eds.), *Dual-process theories in social psychology* (pp. 483–502). New York: Guilford Press.

Petty, R. E., Brinol, P., Tormala, A. L., & Wegener, D. (2007, p. 258). The role of metacognition in social judgment. In A. W. Kruglanski & E. T. Higgins (Eds.), *Social psychology: Handbook of basic principles* (2nd ed., pp. 254–284). New York: The Guilford Press.

50 Flavell, J. H. (1979). Metacognition and cognitive monitoring: A new area of cognitive-developmental inquiry. *American Psychologist, 34*(10), 906–911.

51 Alter, A. L., Oppenheimer, D. M., Epley, N., & Eyre, R. N. (2007). Overcoming intuition: Metacognitive difficulty activates analytic reasoning. *Journal of Experimental Psychology: General, 136*(4), 569–576.

Dreisbach, G., & Fischer, R. (2011). If it's hard to read . . . try harder! Processing fluency as signal for effort adjustments. *Psychological Research, 75*(5), 376–383.

Hernandez, I., & Preston, J. L. (2013). Disfluency disrupts the confirmation bias. *Journal of Experimental Social Psychology, 49*(1), 178–182.

52 Boksman, K., Théberge, J., Williamson, P., Drost, D. J., Malla, A., Densmore, M., . . . Neufeld, R. W. (2005). A 4.0-T fMRI study of brain connectivity during word fluency in first-episode schizophrenia. *Schizophrenia Research, 75*(2), 247–263.

53 *See* n51, Alter et al. (2007).

De Neys, W., Vartanian, O., & Goel, V. (2008). Smarter than we think when our brains detect that we are biased. *Psychological Science, 19*(5), 483–489.

54 Reber, R., & Schwarz, N. (1999). Effects of perceptual fluency on judgments of truth. *Consciousness and Cognition: An International Journal, 8*(3), 338–342.

See also Norwick, R., & Epley, N. (2003, February). *Experiential determinants of confidence.* Poster presented at the Society for Personality and Social Psychology, Los Angeles, California.

Werth, L., & Strack, F. (2003). An inferential approach to the knew-it-all-along effect. *Memory, 11*(4–5), 411–419.

55 Novemsky, N., Dhar, R., Schwarz, N., & Simonson, I. (2007). Preference fluency in choice. *Journal of Marketing Research, 44*(3), 347–356.

56 Greifeneder, R., Alt, A., Bottenberg, K., Seele, T., Zelt, S., & Wagener, D. (2010). On writing legibly processing fluency systematically biases evaluations of handwritten material. *Social Psychological and Personality Science, 1*(3), 230–237.

57 Huang, J. Y., Song, H., & Bargh, J. A. (2011). Smooth trajectories travel farther into the future: Perceptual fluency effects on prediction of trend continuation. *Journal of Experimental Social Psychology, 47*(2), 506–508.

58 Shen, H., Jiang, Y., & Adaval, R. (2010). Contrast and assimilation effects of processing fluency. *Journal of Consumer Research, 36*(5), 876–889.

59 Rossiter, J. R., & Percy, L. (1980). Attitude change through visual imagery in advertising. *Journal of Advertising, 9*(2), 10–17.

60 Pallak, S. R. (1983). Salience of a communicator's physical attractiveness and persuasion: A heuristic versus systematic processing interpretation. *Social Cognition, 2*(2), 158–170.

61 Rhodes, G., Halberstadt, J., & Brajkovich, G. (2001). Generalization of mere exposure effects to averaged composite faces. *Social Cognition, 19*(1), 57–70.

Winkielman, P., Halberstadt, J., Fazendeiro, T., & Catty, S. (2006). Prototypes are attractive because they are easy on the mind. *Psychological Science, 17*(9), 799–806.

62 *See* n46, Reber et al. (2004).

63 Middlewood, B. L., & Gasper, K. (2014). Making information matter: Symmetrically appealing layouts promote issue relevance, which facilitates action and attention to argument quality. *Journal of Experimental Social Psychology, 53*, 100–106.

64 *See* n6, Winkielman & Cacioppo (2001).

65 Detenber, B., & Reeves, B. (1996). A bio-information theory of emotion: Motion and image size effects on viewers. *Journal of Communication, 46*(3), 66–84.

66 Eagly, A. H. (1974). Comprehensibility of persuasive arguments as a determinant of opinion change. *Journal of Personality and Social Psychology, 29*(6), 758–773.

67 Reeves, B., Detenber, B., & Steuer, J. (1993, May). *New televisions: The effects of big pictures and big sound on viewer responses to the screen.* Paper presented to the Information Systems Division of the International Communication Association, Chicago.

68 Brennan, S. E., & Williams, M. (1995). The feeling of Another's Knowing: Prosody and filled pauses as cues to listeners about the metacognitive states of speakers. *Journal of Memory and Language, 34*(3), 383–398.

69 McGlone, M. S., & Tofighbakhsh, J. (2000). Birds of a feather flock conjointly? Rhyme as reason in aphorisms. *Psychological Science, 11*(5), 424–428.

70 *See* n46, Reber et al. (2004).

71 O'Sullivan, C. S., Chen, A., Mohapatra, S., Sigelman, L., & Lewis, E. (1988). Voting in ignorance: The politics of smooth-sounding names. *Journal of Applied Social Psychology, 18*(13), 1094–1106.

Smith, G. W. (1998b). The political impact of name sounds. *Communication Monographs, 65*(2), 154–172.

72 Laham, S. M., Koval, P., & Alter, A. L. (2012). The name-pronunciation effect: Why people like Mr. Smith more than Mr. Colquhoun. *Journal of Experimental Social Psychology, 48*(3), 752–756.

73 Alter, A. L., & Oppenheimer, D. M. (2006). Predicting short-term stock fluctuations by using processing fluency. *Proceedings of the National Academy of Sciences, 103*(24), 9369–9372.

74 Fang, X., Singh, S., & Ahluwalia, R. (2007). An examination of different explanations for the mere exposure effect. *Journal of Consumer Research, 34*(1), 97–103.

Newell, B. R., & Shanks, D. R. (2007). Recognising what you like: Examining the relation between the mere-exposure effect and recognition. *European Journal of Cognitive Psychology, 19*(1), 103–118.

Szpunar, K. K., Schellenberg, E. G., & Pliner, P. (2004). Liking and memory for musical stimuli as a function of exposure. *Journal of Experimental Psychology: Learning, Memory, and Cognition, 30*(2), 370–381.

75 Zajonc, R. B. (1968). Attitudinal effects of mere exposure. *Journal of Personality and Social Psychology, 9*(2, Pt.2), 1–27.

76 Albarracín, D., & Vargas, P. (2010). Attitudes and persuasion: From biology to social responses to persuasive intent. In D. Albarracin & P. Vargas (Eds.), *Handbook of social psychology* (5th ed., Vol. 1, pp. 394–427). Hoboken, NJ: John Wiley & Sons Ltd.

Harmon-Jones, E., & Allen, J. J. B. (2001). The role of affect in the mere exposure effect: Evidence from psychophysiological and individual differences approaches. *Personality and Social Psychology Bulletin, 27*(7), 889–898.

Monahan, J. L., Murphy, S. T., & Zajonc, R. B. (2000). Subliminal mere exposure: Specific, general, and diffuse effects. *Psychological Science, 11*(6), 462–466.

77 Nunes, J. C., Ordanini, A., & Valsesia, F. (2015). The power of repetition: Repetitive lyrics in a song increase processing fluency and drive market success. *Journal of Consumer Psychology, 25*(2), 187–199.

78 Coulter, K. S., & Roggeveen, A. L. (2014). Price number relationships and deal processing fluency: The effects of approximation sequences and number multiples. *Journal of Marketing Research, 51*(1), 69–82.

79 Weber, E. U., Siebenmorgen, N., & Weber, M. (2005). Communicating asset risk: How name recognition and the format of historic volatility information affect risk perception and investment decisions. *Risk Analysis, 25*(3), 597–609.

80 Cook, F. L., Tyler, T. R., Goetz, E. G., Gordon, M. T., Protess, D., Leff, D. R., & Molotch, H. L. (1983). Media and agenda setting: Effects on the public, interest group leaders, policy makers, and policy. *Public Opinion Quarterly, 47*(1), 16–35.

Leff, D. R., Protess, D. L., & Brooks, S. C. (1986). Crusading journalism: Changing public attitudes and policy-making agendas. *Public Opinion Quarterly, 50*(3), 300–315.

81 Weisbuch, M., Mackie, D. M., & Garcia-Marques, T. (2003). Prior source exposure and persuasion: Further evidence for misattributional processes. *Personality and Social Psychology Bulletin, 29*(6), 691–700.

82 Jacoby, L. L., Woloshyn, V., & Kelley, C. M. (1989b). Becoming famous without being recognized: Unconscious influences of memory produced by dividing attention. *Journal of Experimental Psychology: General, 118*(2), 115–125.

83 Hastie, R., Landsman, R., & Loftus, E. F. (1978). Eyewitness testimony: The dangers of guessing. *Jurimetrics Journal, 19*, 1–8.

84 Holland, R. W., Verplanken, B., & van Knippenberg, A. (2003). From repetition to conviction: Attitude accessibility as a determinant of attitude certainty. *Journal of Experimental Social Psychology, 39*(6), 594–601.

85 Brickman, P., Redfield, J., Harrison, A. A., & Crandall, R. (1972). Drive and predisposition as factors in the attitudinal effects of mere exposure. *Journal of Experimental Social Psychology, 8*(1), 31–44.

86 Cacioppo, J. T., & Petty, R. E. (1989). Effects of message repetition on argument processing, recall, and persuasion. *Basic and Applied Social Psychology, 10*(1), 3–12.

87 Fazio, L. K., Brashier, N. M., Payne, B. K., & Marsh, E. J. (2015). Knowledge does not protect against illusory truth. *Journal of Experimental Psychology: General, 144*(5), 993–1002.

88 Allport, F. H., & Lepkin, M. (1945). Wartime rumors of waste and special privilege: Why some people believe them. *The Journal of Abnormal and Social Psychology, 40*(1), 3–36.

89 Brown, A. S., & Nix, L. A. (1996). Turning lies into truths: Referential validation of falsehoods. *Journal of Experimental Psychology: Learning, Memory, and Cognition, 22*(5), 1088–1100.

Gilbert, D. T., Krull, D. S., & Malone, P. S. (1990). Unbelieving the unbelievable: Some problems in the rejection of false information. *Journal of Personality and Social Psychology, 59*(4), 601–613.

Hawkins, S. A., & Hoch, S. J. (1992). Low-involvement learning: Memory without evaluation. *Journal of Consumer Research, 19*(2), 212–225.

90 Skurnik, I., Yoon, C., Park, D. C., & Schwarz, N. (2005). How warnings about false claims become recommendations. *Journal of Consumer Research, 31*(4), 713–724.

91 MacGregor, D., & Slovic, P. (1986). Graphic representation of judgmental information. *Human-Computer Interaction, 2*(3), 179–200.

92 Hall, J., & Hofer, C. W. (1993). Venture capitalists' decision criteria in new venture evaluation. *Journal of Business Venturing, 8*(1), 25–42.

93 Clark, N. K., & Rutter, D. R. (1985). Social categorization, visual cues, and social judgements. *European Journal of Social Psychology, 15*(1), 105–119.

Herr, P. M., Kardes, F. R., & Kim, J. (1991). Effects of word-of-mouth and product-attribute information on persuasion: An accessibility-diagnosticity perspective. *Journal of Consumer Research, 17*(4), 454–462.

94 McArthur, L. Z., & Ginsberg, E. (1981). Causal attribution to salient stimuli: An investigation of visual fixation mediators. *Personality and Social Psychology Bulletin, 7*(4), 547–553.

Nesdale, A. R., & Dharmalingam, S. (1986). Category salience, stereotyping and person memory. *Australian Journal of Psychology, 38*(2), 145–151.

Oakes, P., & Turner, J. C. (1986). Distinctiveness and the salience of social category memberships: Is there an automatic perceptual bias towards novelty? *European Journal of Social Psychology, 16*(4), 325–344.

95 Hastie, R., & Kumar, P. A. (1979). Person memory: Personality traits as organizing principles in memory for behaviors. *Journal of Personality and Social Psychology, 37*(1), 25–38.

96 *See* n9, Kahneman & Miller (1986).

97 Meyerowitz, B., & Chaiken, S. (1987). The effect of message framing on breast self-examination attitudes, intentions, and behavior. *Journal of Personality and Social Psychology, 52*(3), 500–510.

98 Johnson, E. J., & Tversky, A. (1983). Affect, generalization, and the perception of risk. *Journal of Personality and Social Psychology, 45*(1), 20–31.

99 Rossiter, J. R., & Percy, L. (1978). Visual imaging ability as a mediator of advertising response. *Advances in Consumer Research, 5*(1), 621–629.

100 *See* n97, Meyerowitz & Chaiken (1987).

Robberson, M. R., & Rogers, R. W. (1988). Beyond fear appeals: Negative and positive persuasive appeals to health and self-esteem. *Journal of Applied Social Psychology, 18*(3, Pt. 1), 277–287.

Sherer, M., & Rogers, R. W. (1984). The role of vivid information in fear appeals and attitude change. *Journal of Research in Personality, 18*(3), 321–334.

101 Reyes, R. M., Thompson, W. C., & Bower, G. H. (1980). Judgmental biases resulting from differing availabilities of arguments. *Journal of Personality and Social Psychology, 39*(1), 2–12.

102 Wilson, M. G., Northcraft, G. B., & Neale, M. A. (1989a). Information competition and vividness effects in on-line judgments. *Organizational Behavior and Human Decision Processes, 44*(1), 132–139.

103 Kisielius, J., & Sternthal, B. (1984). Detecting and explaining vividness effects in attitudinal judgments. *Journal of Marketing Research, 21*(1), 54–64.

Smith, S. M., & Shaffer, D. R. (2000). Vividness can undermine or enhance message processing: The moderating role of vividness congruency. *Personality and Social Psychology Bulletin, 26*(7), 769–779.

104 Reb, J., & Cropanzano, R. (2007). Evaluating dynamic performance: The influence of salient Gestalt characteristics on performance ratings. *Journal of Applied Psychology, 92*(2), 490–499.

105 Nisbett, R. E., Borgida, E., Crandall, R., & Reed, H. (1982). Popular induction: Information is not necessarily informative. In D. Kahneman, P. Slovic & A. Tversky (Eds.), *Judgments under uncertainty: Heuristics and biases* (pp. 101–116). New York: Cambridge University Press.

106 Mitchell, A. A., & Olson, J. C. (1981). Are product attribute beliefs the only mediator of advertising effects on brand attitude? *Journal of Marketing Research, 18*(3), 318–332.

107 *See* n99, Rossiter & Percy (1978).

108 Jaynes, L. S., & Boles, D. B. (1990, October). The effect of symbols on warning compliance. In *Proceedings of the human factors and ergonomics society annual meeting* (Vol. 34, No. 14, pp. 984–987). Thousand Oaks, CA: Sage.

Wogalter, M. S., Sojourner, R. J., & Brelsford, J. W. (1997). Comprehension and retention of safety pictorials. *Ergonomics, 40*(5), 531–542.

109 White, V., Webster, B., & Wakefield, M. (2008). Do graphic health warning labels have an impact on adolescents' smoking-related beliefs and behaviours? *Addiction, 103*(9), 1562–1571.

110 Chaiken, S., & Eagly, A. H. (1976). Communication modality as a determinant of message persuasiveness and message comprehensibility. *Journal of Personality and Social Psychology, 34*(4), 605–614.

111 Guadagno, R. E., Muscanell, N. L., Sundie, J. M., Hardison, T. A., & Cialdini, R. B. (2013). The opinion-changing power of computer-based multimedia presentations. *Psychology of Popular Media Culture, 2*(2), 110–116.

112 Tsay, C. J. (2013). Sight over sound in the judgment of music performance. *Proceedings of the National Academy of Sciences, 110*(36), 14580–14585.

113 Allen, D. G., Van Scotter, J. R., & Otondo, R. F. (2004). Recruitment communication media: Impact on prehire outcomes. *Personnel Psychology, 57*(1), 143–171.

114 Tsay, C. J. (2014). The vision heuristic: Judging music ensembles by sight alone. *Organizational Behavior and Human Decision Processes, 124*(1), 24–33.

115 Reeder, G. D., & Brewer, M. B. (1979). A schematic model of dispositional attribution in interpersonal perception. *Psychological Review, 86*(1), 61–79.

116 Anderson, N. H. (1965). Averaging versus adding as a stimulus-combination rule in impression formation. *Journal of Experimental Psychology, 70*(4), 394–400.

Hamilton, D. L., & Zanna, M. P. (1972). Differential weighting of favorable and unfavorable attributes in impressions of personality. *Journal of Experimental Research in Personality, 6*(2–3), 204–212.

Hodges, B. H. (1974). Effect of valence on relative weighting in impression formation. *Journal of Personality and Social Psychology, 30*(3), 378–381.

117 Kanar, A. M., Collins, C. J., & Bell, B. S. (2010). A comparison of the effects of positive and negative information on job seekers' organizational attraction and attribute recall. *Human Performance, 23*(3), 193–212.

118 Fiske, S. T. (1980). Attention and weight in person perception: The impact of negative and extreme behavior. *Journal of Personality and Social Psychology, 38*(6), 889–906.

119 Kanouse, D. E., & Hanson Jr, L. R. (1972). Negativity in evaluations. In E. E. Jones, D. E. Kanouse, H. H. Kelley, R. E. Nisbett, S. Valins & B. Weiner (Eds.), *Attribution: Perceiving the causes of behavior* (pp. 47–62). Morristown, NJ: General Learning Press.

120 Armel, K. C., Beaumel, A., & Rangel, A. (2008). Biasing simple choices by manipulating relative visual attention. *Judgment and Decision Making, 3*(5), 396–403.

Milosavljevic, M., Navalpakkam, V., Koch, C., & Rangel, A. (2012). Relative visual saliency differences induce sizable bias in consumer choice. *Journal of Consumer Psychology, 22*(1), 67–74.

Shimojo, S., Simion, C., Shimojo, E., & Scheier, C. (2003). Gaze bias both reflects and influences preference. *Nature Neuroscience, 6*(12), 1317–1322.

121 Pryor, J. B., & Kriss, M. (1977). The cognitive dynamics of salience in the attribution process. *Journal of Personality and Social Psychology, 35*(1), 49–55.

Taylor, S. E., & Fiske, S. T. (1975). Point of view and perceptions of causality. *Journal of Personality and Social Psychology, 32*(3), 439–445.

122 Kahneman, D., & Tversky, A. (1973). On the psychology of prediction. *Psychological Review, 80*(4), 237–251.

123 Blanton, H., Stuart, A. E., & VandenEijnden, R. J. (2001). An introduction to deviance-regulation theory: The effect of behavioral norms on message framing. *Personality and Social Psychology Bulletin, 27*(7), 848–858.

124 *See* n59, Rossiter & Percy (1980).

125 Read, D., Frederick, S., Orsel, B., & Rahman, J. (2005). Four score and seven years from now: The date/delay effect in temporal discounting. *Management Science, 51*(9), 1326–1335.

126 Pechmann, C. (1996). Do consumers overgeneralize one-sided comparative price claims, and are more stringent regulations needed? *Journal of Marketing Research, 33*(2), 150–162.

127 Bell, B. E., & Loftus, E. F. (1988). Degree of detail of eyewitness testimony and mock juror judgments. *Journal of Applied Social Psychology, 18*(14), 1171–1192.

Bell, B. E., & Loftus, E. F. (1989). Trivial persuasion in the courtroom: The power of (a few) minor details. *Journal of Personality and Social Psychology, 56*(5), 669–679.

128 Barnes, C. M., Reb, J., & Ang, D. (2012). More than just the mean: Moving to a dynamic view of performance-based compensation. *Journal of Applied Psychology, 97*(3), 711–718.

129 Shleifer, A. (2000). *Inefficient markets: An introduction to behavioral finance.* New York: Oxford University Press.

130 Cox, A. D., & Summers, J. O. (1987). Heuristics and biases in the intuitive projection of retail sales. *Journal of Marketing Research, 24*(3), 290–297.

131 De Bondt, W. F. M., & Thaler, R. H. (1990). Do security analysis overreact? *The American Economic Review, 80*(2), 52–57.

132 Amir, E., & Ganzach, Y. (1998). Overreaction and underreaction in analysts' forecasts. *Journal of Economic Behavior & Organization, 37*(3), 333–347.

Capstaff, J., Paudyal, K., & Rees, W. (2001). A comparative analysis of earnings forecasts in Europe. *Journal of Business Finance & Accounting, 28*(5–6), 531–562.

133 Hirshleifer, S. (1970). *Investment, interest and capital.* Englewood Cliffs, NJ: Prentice Hall.

134 Mantonakis, A. (2012). A brief pause between a tagline and brand increases brand name recognition and preference. *Applied Cognitive Psychology, 26*(1), 61–69.

135 Fiske, S. T., & Taylor, S. E. (1991). *Social cognition* (2nd ed.). New York: McGraw-Hill.

McArthur, L. Z., & Post, D. L. (1977). Figural emphasis and person perception. *Journal of Experimental Social Psychology, 13*(6), 520–535.

Raghubir, P., & Valenzuela, A. (2006). Center-of-inattention: Position biases in decision-making. *Organizational Behavior and Human Decision Processes, 99*(1), 66–80.

136 Howell, J. M., & Hall-Merenda, K. E. (1999). The ties that bind: The impact of leader-member exchange, transformational and transactional leadership, and distance on predicting follower performance. *Journal of Applied Psychology, 84*, 680–694.

137 Lassiter, G. D. (2002). Illusory causation in the courtroom. *Current Directions in Psychological Research, 11*(6), 204–208.

138 Phillips, J. S., & Lord, R. G. (1981). Causal attributions and perceptions of leadership. *Organizational Behavior and Human Performance, 28*, 143–163.

139 Howells, L. T., & Becker, S. W. (1962). Seating arrangement and leadership emergence. *Journal of Abnormal and Social Psychology, 64*, 148–150.

Sommer, R. (1961). Leadership and group geography. *Sociometry, 24*, 99–110.

140 Leavitt, H. J. (1951). Some effects of certain communication patterns on group performance. *Journal of Abnormal and Social Psychology, 46*, 38–50.

141 McCroskey, J. C., & Mehrley, R. S. (1969). The effects of disorganization and nonfluency on attitude change and source credibility. *Speech Monographs, 36*, 13–21.

142 Ratneshwar, S., & Chaiken, S. (1991). Comprehension's role in persuasion: The case of its moderating effect on the persuasive impact of source cues. *Journal of Consumer Research, 18*(1), 52–62.

143 *See* n135, Fiske & Taylor (1991), p. 384.

144 Bar-Hillel, M., & Fischhoff, B. (1981). When do base rates affect predictions? *Journal of Personality and Social Psychology, 41*(4), 671–680.
See n122, Kahneman & Tversky (1973).

Kirsch, M. P. (1985). The effect of information quality and type of data on information integration strategies. (Master of Arts thesis, Michigan State University, 1985). *Masters Abstracts International, 24*(04), 0422.

145 Griffin, D., & Tversky, A. (1992). The weighing of evidence and the determinants of confidence. *Cognitive Psychology, 24*(3), 411–435.

146 Ajzen, I. (1977). Intuitive theories of events and the effects of base-rate information on prediction. *Journal of Personality and Social Psychology, 35*(5), 303–314.

Tversky, A., & Kahneman, D. (1980). Causal schemata in judgments under uncertainty. In M. Fishbein (Ed.), *Progress in social psychology* (pp. 49–72). Hillsdale, NJ: Erlbaum.

147 Michotte, A. (1963). *The perception of causality.* Oxford, UK: Basic Books.

148 *See* n146, Tversky & Kahneman (1980).

149 *See* n122, Kahneman & Tversky (1973).

150 *See* n144, Bar-Hillel & Fischhoff (1981).

Manis, M., Dovalina, I., Avis, N. E., & Cardoze, S. (1980). Base rates can affect individual predictions. *Journal of Personality and Social Psychology, 38*(2), 231–248.

151 Hogarth, R. M. (1980). *Judgment and choice.* New York: Wiley.

Nisbett, R. E., & Ross, L. (1980). *Human inference: Strategies and shortcomings of social judgment.* Englewood Cliffs, NJ: Prentice Hall.

152 Locksley, A., Borgida, E., Brekke, N., & Hepburn, C. (1980). Sex stereotypes and social judgment. *Journal of Personality and Social Psychology, 39*(5), 821–831.

Locksley, A., Hepburn, C., & Ortiz, V. (1982). Social stereotypes and judgments of individuals: An instance of the base-rate fallacy. *Journal of Experimental Social Psychology, 18*(1), 23–42.

153 Martin, D. S. (1978). Person perception and real-life electoral behaviour. *Australian Journal of Psychology, 30*(3), 255–262.

154 *See* n144, Kirsch (1985).

155 Shefrin, H., & Statman, M. (1995). Making sense of beta, size, and book-to-market. *Journal of Portfolio Management, 21*(2), 26–34.

Solt, M., & Statman, M. (1989). Good companies, bad stocks. *Journal of Portfolio Management, 15*(4), 39–44.

156 French, D. P., & Hevey, D. (2008). What do people think about when answering questionnaires to assess unrealistic optimism about skin cancer? A think aloud study. *Psychology, Health and Medicine, 13*(1), 63–74.

157 *See* n7, Tversky & Kahneman (1974).

158 Hamill, R., Wilson, T. D., & Nisbett, R. E. (1980). Insensitivity to sample bias: Generalizing from atypical cases. *Journal of Personality and Social Psychology, 39*(4), 578–589.

159 *See* n151, Nisbett & Ross (1980).

See n7, Tversky & Kahneman (1974).

160 Gibson, R., & Zillmann, D. (1994). Exaggerated versus representative exemplification in news reports: Perception of issues and personal consequences. *Communication Research, 21*(5), 603–624.

Zillmann, D., Gibson, R., Sundar, S. S., & Perkins, J. W. (1996). Effects of exemplification in news reports on the perception of social issues. *Journalism & Mass Communication Quarterly, 73*, 427–444.

161 Sotirovic, M. (2001). Media use and perceptions of welfare. *Journal of Communication, 51*(4), 750–774.

Zillmann, D. (2002). Exemplification theory of media influence. In J. Bryant & D. Zillmann (Eds.), *Media effects: Advances in theory and research* (pp. 19–42). Mahwah, NJ: Lawrence Erlbaum.

162 Feldman, M. S., & March, J. G. (1981). Information in organizations as signal and symbol. *Administrative Science Quarterly, 26*(2), 171–186.

See n151, Nisbett & Ross (1980).

Kogut, T., & Ritov, I. (2005). The "identified victim" effect: An identified group, or just a single individual? *Journal of Behavioral Decision Making, 18*(3), 157–167.

163 Krauss, D. A., & Sales, B. D. (2001). The effects of clinical and scientific expert testimony on juror decision making in capital sentencing. *Psychology, Public Policy, and Law, 7*(2), 267–310.

164 Koballa, T. R. (1986). Persuading teachers to reexamine the innovative elementary science programs of yesterday: The effect of anecdotal versus data-summary communications. *Journal of Research in Science Teaching, 23*(6), 437–449.

165 Rothbart, M., Fulero, S., Jensen, C., Howard, J., & Birrel, B. (1978). From individual to group impressions: Availability heuristics in stereotype formation. *Journal of Experimental Social Psychology, 14*(3), 237–255.

166 Schelling, T. C. (1984). *Choice and consequence.* Cambridge, MA: Harvard University Press.

167 Loewenstein, G., & Mather, J. (1990). Dynamic processes in risk perception. *Journal of Risk and Uncertainty, 3*, 155–175.

168 Tversky, A., & Kahneman, D. (1971). Belief in the law of small numbers. *Psychological Bulletin, 76*(2), 105–110.

169 Selling, T. I. (1982). Cognitive processes in information system choice (Doctoral dissertation, The Ohio State University, 1982). *Dissertation Abstracts International, 43*(08A), 2713.

170 Adaval, R., & Wyer, R. S. (1998). The role of narratives in consumer information processing. *Journal of Consumer Psychology, 7*(3), 207–245.

171 Pennington, N., & Hastie, R. (1992). Explaining the evidence: Tests of the story model for juror decision making. *Journal of Personality and Social Psychology, 62*(2), 189–206.

172 Escalas, J. E. (2007). Self-referencing and persuasion: Narrative transportation versus analytical elaboration. *Journal of Consumer Research, 33*(4), 421–429.

Escalas, J. E., & Luce, M. F. (2004). Understanding the effects of process-focused versus outcome-focused thought in response to advertising. *Journal of Consumer Research, 31*(2), 274–285.

173 Martin, J., & Powers, M. E. (1979, September). *If case examples provide no proof, why underutilize statistical information?* Paper presented at the American Psychological Association, New York.

Martin, J., & Powers, M. E. (1980, May). *Skepticism and the true believer: The effects of case and/or baserate information on belief and commitment.* Paper presented at the Western Psychological Association Meetings, Honolulu, HI.

174 Baesler, E. J. (1997). Persuasive effects of story and statistical evidence. *Argumentation and Advocacy, 33*, 170–175.

Baesler, E. J., & Burgoon, J. K. (1994). The temporal effects of story and statistical evidence on belief change. *Communication Research, 21*(5), 582–602.

Kazoleas, D. C. (1993). A comparison of the persuasive effectiveness of qualitative versus quantitative evidence: A test of explanatory hypotheses. *Communication Quarterly, 41*, 40–50.

175 Kopfman, J. E., Smith, S. W., Ah Yun, J. K., & Hodges, A. (1998). Affective and cognitive reactions to narrative versus statistical evidence organ donation messages. *Journal of Applied Communication Research*, *26*(3), 279–300.

176 Oppenheimer, D. M. (2004). Spontaneous discounting of availability in frequency judgment tasks. *Psychological Science*, *15*(2), 100–105.

Oppenheimer, D. M. (2006). Consequences of erudite vernacular utilized irrespective of necessity: Problems with using long words needlessly. *Applied Cognitive Psychology*, *20*(2), 139–156.

177 Lowrey, T. M. (1998). The effects of syntactic complexity on advertising persuasiveness. *Journal of Consumer Psychology*, *7*(2), 187–206.

See also n39.

178 Motes, W. H., Hilton, C. B., & Fielden, J. S. (1992). Language, sentence, and structural variations in print advertising. *Journal of Advertising Research*, *32*, 63–77.

179 Badger, J. M., Kaminsky, S. E., & Behrend, T. S. (2014). Media richness and information acquisition in internet recruitment. *Journal of Managerial Psychology*, *29*(7), 866–883.

180 *See* n110, Chaiken & Eagly (1976).

181 *See* n11, Simon & Hayes (1976).

182 Bilalić, M., McLeod, P., & Gobet, F. (2010). The mechanism of the einstellung (set) effect a pervasive source of cognitive bias. *Current Directions in Psychological Science*, *19*(2), 111–115.

See also Russo, J. E., Carlson, K. A., & Meloy, M. G. (2006). Choosing an inferior alternative. *Psychological Science*, *17*(10), 899–904.

Russo, J. E., & Yong, K. (2011). The distortion of information to support an emerging evaluation of risk. *Journal of Econometrics*, *162*(1), 132–139.

183 Andersen, S. M., Glassman, N. S., Chen, S., & Cole, S. W. (1995). Transference in social perception: The role of chronic accessibility in significant-other representations. *Journal of Personality and Social Psychology*, *69*(1), 41–57.

See n11, Shah et al. (2001).

184 Fazio, R. H. (1989). On the power and functionality of attitudes: The role of attitude accessibility. In A. R. Pratkanis, S. J. Breckler & A. G. Greenwald (Eds.), *Attitude structure and function* (pp. 153–179). Hillsdale, NJ: Lawrence Erlbaum Associates.

Higgins, E. T., & King, G. (1981). Accessibility of social constructs: Information-processing consequences of individual and contextual variability. In N. Cantor & J. Kihlstrom (Eds.), *Personality, cognition, and social interaction* (pp. 69–121). Hillsdale, NJ: Lawrence Erlbaum Associates.

Krosnick, J. A. (1988). The role of attitude importance in social evaluation: A study of policy preferences, presidential candidate evaluations, and voting behavior. *Journal of Personality and Social Psychology*, *55*(2), 196–210.

185 Pan, Z., & Kosicki, G. M. (2001). Framing as a strategic action in public deliberation. In S. D. Reese, O. H. Gandy & A. E. Grant (Eds.), *Framing public life: Perspectives on media and our understanding of the social world* (pp. 35–65). Mahwah, NJ: Lawrence Erlbaum Associates.

Tourangeau, R., & Rasinski, K. A. (1988). Cognitive processes underlying context effects in attitude measurement. *Psychological Bulletin*, *103*(3), 299–314.

See n11, Tversky & Kahneman (1988).

186 Newman, B. I., & Perloff, R. M. (2004). Political marketing: Theory, research, applications. In L. L. Kaid (Ed.), *Handbook of political communication research* (pp. 17–43). Mahwah, NJ: Lawrence Erlbaum Associates.

187 Fredin, E. S. (2001). Frame breaking and creativity: A frame database for hypermedia news. In S. D. Reese, O. H. Gandy & A. E. Grant (Eds.), *Framing public life: Perspectives on media and our understanding of the social world* (pp. 269–293). Mahwah, NJ: Lawrence Erlbaum Associates.

188 Deli Carpini, M. X. (2004). Mediating democratic engagement: The impact of communications on citizens' involvement in political and civil life. In L. L. Kaid (Ed.), *Handbook of political communication research* (pp. 395–434). Mahwah, NJ: Lawrence Erlbaum Associates.

Gilens, M. (1999). *Why Americans hate welfare: Race, media, and the politics of antipoverty policy*. Chicago: University of Chicago Press.

Iyengar, S. (1991). *Is anyone responsible: How television frames political issues*. Chicago: University of Chicago Press.

189 *See* n151, Nisbett & Ross (1980).

190 Heller, R. F., Saltzstein, H. D., & Caspe, W. B. (1992). Heuristics in medical and non-medical decision-making. *The Quarterly Journal of Experimental Psychology A: Human Experimental Psychology*, *44A*(2), 211–235.

191 Maule, J., & Villejoubert, G. (2007). What lies beneath: Reframing framing effects. *Thinking & Reasoning,* *13*(1), 25–44.

See n185, Pan & Kosicki (2001).

See n11, Simon & Hayes (1976).

192 Hershey, J. C., & Schoemaker, P. J. (1980). Prospect theory's reflection hypothesis: A critical examination. *Organizational Behavior & Human Performance, 25*(3), 395–418.

193 Levin, I. P. (1987). Associative effects of information framing. *Bulletin of the Psychonomic Society, 25*(2), 85–86.

Braun, K. A., Gacth, G. J., & Levin, I. P. (1997). Framing effects with differential impact: The role of attribute salience. *Advances in Consumer Research, 24,* 405–411.

Jasper, J. D., Goel, R., Einarson, A., Gallo, M., and Koren, G. (2001). Effects of framing on teratogenic risk perception in pregnant women. *The Lancet, 358*(9289): 1237–1238.

194 Avila, J. (2012, March 7). 70 Percent of Ground Beef at Supermarkets Contains "Pink Slime." *ABC News.*

195 Quattrone, G. A., & Tversky, A. (1988). Contrasting rational and psychological analyses of political choice. *American Political Science Review, 82,* 719–736.

196 McNeil, B. J., Pauker, S. G., Cox Jr, H. C., & Tversky, A. (1982). On the elicitation of preferences for alternative therapies. *New England Journal of Medicine, 306,* 1259–1262.

197 Tumulty, K. (1990, September 3). Abortion polls yield contradictory results. *Austin American Statesman,* A29.

198 Monti, M., Boero, R., Berg, N., Gigerenzer, G., & Martignon, L. (2012). How do common investors behave? Information search and portfolio choice among bank customers and university students. *Mind & Society, 11*(2), 203–233.

199 Wong, K. F. E., & Kwong, J. Y. (2005). Comparing two tiny giants or two huge dwarfs? Preference reversals owing to number size framing. *Organizational Behavior and Human Decision Processes, 98*(1), 54–65.

200 Epley, N., Mak, D., & Idson, L. C. (2006). Bonus or rebate? The impact of income framing on spending and saving. *Journal of Behavioral Decision Making, 19*(3), 213–227.

201 Liberman, V., Samuels, S. M., & Ross, L. (2004). The name of the game: Predictive power of reputations versus situational labels in determining prisoner's dilemma game moves. *Personality and Social Psychology Bulletin, 30*(9), 1175–1185.

202 Cobb, R. W., & Elder, C. D. (1983). *Participation in American politics: The dynamics of agenda building.* Baltimore: Johns Hopkins University Press.

Hilgartner. S., & Bosk, C. L. (1988). The rise and fall of social problems: A public arenas model. *American Journal of Sociology, 94,* 53–78.

203 Gamson, W. A., & Modigliani, A. (1989). Media discourse and public opinion on nuclear power: A constructionist approach. *American Journal of Sociology, 95*(1), 1–37.

Snow, D. A., & Benford, R. D.(1988). Ideology, frame resonance, and participant mobilization. In B. Klandermans, H. Kriesi & S. Tarrow (Eds.), *From structure to action: Comparing social movement research across countries* (pp. 197–217). Greenwich, CT: JAI Press.

204 Plumm, K. M., Borhart, H., & Weatherly, J. N. (2012). Choose your words wisely: Delay discounting of differently titled social policy issues. *Behavior and Social Issues, 21,* 26–48.

205 Ryan, C. (1991). *Prime time activism: Media strategies for grass roots organizing.* Boston: South End Press.

206 Tankard, J. W. (2001). The empirical approach to the study of media framing. In S. D. Reese, O. H. Gandy & A. E. Grant (Eds.), *Framing public life: Perspectives on media and our understanding of the social world* (pp. 95–106). Mahwah, NJ: Lawrence Erlbaum Associates.

207 Keen, J. (1990, August 21). How long will U.S. stay in the gulf? *USA Today,* pp. 1A, 2A.

208 Westen, D. (2007, p. 36). *The political brain: The role of emotion in deciding the fate of the nation.* New York: Public Affairs.

209 Van Zant, A. B., & Moore, D. A. (2015). Leaders' use of moral justifications increases policy support. *Psychological Science, 26*(6), 934–943.

210 Neuman, R., Just, M., & Crigler, A. (1992). *Common knowledge: News and the construction of political meaning.* Chicago: University of Chicago Press.

211 Ghanem, S. (1997). Filling in the tapestry: The second level of agenda setting. In M. McCombs, D. L Shaw & D. Weaver (Eds.), *Communication and democracy* (pp. 3–15). Mahwah, NJ: Lawrence Erlbaum Associates.

212 McCombs, M., & Mauro, J. (1977). Predicting newspaper readership from content characteristics. *Journalism Quarterly, 54*(1), 3–49.

213 Tankard, J., Hendrickson, L., Silberman, J., Bliss, K., & Ghanem, S. (1991, August). *Media frames: Approaches to conceptualization and measurement.* Paper presented to the Association for Education in Journalism and Mass Communication, Boston.

214 Ecker, U. K., Lewandowsky, S., Chang, E. P., & Pillai, R. (2014). The effects of subtle misinformation in news headlines. *Journal of Experimental Psychology: Applied, 20*(4), 323–335.

215 Larkin, J. H., & Simon, H. A. (1987). Why a diagram is (sometimes) worth ten thousand words. *Cognitive Science, 11*(1), 65–100.

Zhang, J., & Norman, D. A. (1994). Representations in distributed cognitive tasks. *Cognitive Science, 18*(1), 87–122.

Zhang, J. (1997). The nature of external representations in problem solving. *Cognitive Science, 21*(2), 179–217.

216 Shah, P., Mayer, R. E., & Hegarty, M. (1999). Graphs as aids to knowledge construction: Signaling techniques for guiding the process of graph comprehension. *Journal of Educational Psychology, 91*(4), 690–702.

217 Gattis, M., & Holyoak, K. J. (1996). Mapping conceptual to spatial relations in visual reasoning. *Journal of Experimental Psychology: Learning, Memory, and Cognition, 22*(1), 231–239.

Peebles, D., & Cheng, P. C. H. (2003). Modeling the effect of task and graphical representation on response latency in a graph reading task. *Human Factors: The Journal of the Human Factors and Ergonomics Society, 45*(1), 28–46.

218 *See* n11, Tversky & Kahneman (1981).

219 Gitlin, T. (1980). *The whole world is watching.* Berkeley, CA: University of California Press.

220 *See* n11, Tversky & Kahneman (1981), p. 457.

221 Kahneman, D., & Tversky, A. (1984). Choices, values, and frames. *American Psychologist, 39*(4), 341–350.

See n11, Tversky & Kahneman (1981).

222 Sniderman, P. M., & Theriault, S. M. (2004). The structure of political argument and the logic of issue framing. In W. E. Saris & P. M. Sniderman (Eds.), *Studies in public opinion: Attitudes, nonattitudes, measurement error and change.* Princeton, NJ: Princeton University Press.

223 Levin, I. P., Schnittjer, S. K., & Thee, S. L. (1988). Information framing effects in social and personal decisions. *Journal of Experimental Social Psychology, 24*(6), 520–529.

Neale, M. A., Huber, V. L., & Northcraft, G. B. (1987). The framing of negotiations: Contextual versus task frames. *Organizational Behavior and Human Decision Processes, 39*(2), 228–241.

Slovic, P., Fischhoff, B., & Lichtenstein, S. (1982). Facts versus fears: Understanding perceived risk. In D. Kahneman, P. Slovic & A. Tversky (Eds.), *Judgment under uncertainty: Heuristics and biases* (pp. 463–489). New York: Cambridge University Press.

224 *See* n196, McNeil et al. (1982).

225 Gamson, W. A. (1992). *Talking politics.* New York: Cambridge University Press.

See n210, Neuman et al. (1992).

226 Woodhead, E. L., Lynch, E. B., & Edelstein, B. A. (2011). Decisional strategy determines whether frame influences treatment preferences for medical decisions. *Psychology and aging, 26*(2), 285–294.

227 Smith, G. E. (1996). Framing in advertising and the moderating impact of consumer education. *Journal of Advertising Research, 36*(5), 49–64.

228 *See* n100, Robberson & Rogers (1988).

229 Schneider, T. R., Salovey, P., Pallonen, U., Mundorf, N., Smith, N. F., & Steward, W. (2001b). Visual and auditory message framing effects on tobacco smoking. *Journal of Applied Social Psychology, 31*(4), 667–682.

230 Detweiler, J. B., Bedell, B. T., Salovey, P., Pronin, E., & Rothman, A. J. (1999). Message framing and sunscreen use: Gain-framed messages motivate beach-goers. *Health Psychology, 18*(2), 189–196.

231 Kalichman, S. C., & Coley, B. (1995). Context framing to enhance HIV-antibody-testing messages targeted to African American women. *Health Psychology, 14*(3), 247–254.

232 *See* n97, Meyerowitz & Chaiken (1987).

233 Schneider, T. R., Salovey, P., Apanovirch, A. M., Pizarro, J., McCarthy, D., Zullo, J., & Rothman, A. J. (2001a). The effects of message framing and ethnic targeting on mammography use among low-income women. *Health Psychology, 20*(4), 256–266.

Apanovitch, A. M., McCarthy, D., & Salovey, P. (2003). Using message framing to motivate HIV testing among low-income, ethnic minority women. *Health Psychology, 22*(1), 60–67.

234 de Martino, B., Kumaran, D., Seymour, B., & Dolan, R. J. (2006). Frames, biases, and rational decision-making in the human brain. *Science, 313*(5787), 684–687.

235 Roiser, J. P., de Martino, B., Tan, G. C., Kumaran, D., Seymour, B., Wood, N. W., & Dolan, R. J. (2009). A genetically mediated bias in decision making driven by failure of amygdala control. *The Journal of Neuroscience, 29*(18), 5985–5991.

236 Markman, A. B., & Moreau, C. P. (2001). Analogy and analogical comparison in choice. In D. Gentner, K. J. Holyoak & B. N. Kokinov (Eds.), *The analogical mind: Perspectives from cognitive science* (pp. 363–399). Cambridge, MA: The MIT Press.

Sopory, P., & Dillard, J. P. (2002). The persuasive effects of metaphor: A meta-analysis. *Human Communication Research, 28*(3), 382–419.

237 Gregan-Paxton, J., & Roedder, J. D. (1997). Consumer learning by analogy: A model of internal knowledge transfer. *Journal of Consumer Research, 24*(3), 266–284.

238 Blanchette, I., & Dunbar, K. (2000). How analogies are generated: The roles of structural and superficial similarity. *Memory & Cognition, 28*(1), 108–124.

239 Holyoak, K. J., & Simon, D. (1999). Bidirectional reasoning in decision making by constraint satisfaction. *Journal of Experimental Psychology: General, 128*(1), 3–31.

Holyoak, K. J., & Thagard, P. (1995). *Mental leaps: Analogy in creative thought.* Cambridge, MA: The MIT Press.

240 Gregan-Paxton, J., & Cote, J. (2000). How do investors make predictions? Insights from analogical reasoning research. *Journal of Behavioral Decision Making, 13*(3), 307–327.

241 Chi, M. T. H., & Ohlsson, S. (2005). Complex declarative learning. In K. J. Holyoak & R. G. Morrison (Eds.), *The Cambridge handbook of thinking and reasoning* (pp. 371–399). Cambridge, UK: Cambridge University Press.

Gentner, D., & Forbus, K. D. (1991). MAC/FAC: A model of similarity-based access and mapping. In K. J. Hammond & D. Gentner (Eds.), *Proceedings of the thirteenth annual conference of the cognitive science society* (pp. 504–509). Hillsdale, NJ: Erlbaum.

Holland, J. H., Holyoak, K. J., Nisbett, R. E., & Thagard, P. R. (1993). Deductive reasoning. In A. I. Goldman (Ed.), *Readings in philosophy and cognitive science* (pp. 23–41). Cambridge, MA: The MIT Press.

242 Azar, P. G. (1994). Learning new-to-the-world products (cognitive processing, analogy) (Doctoral dissertation, Northwestern University, 1994). *Dissertation Abstracts International, 56*(03A), 1028.

243 Moreau, C. P., Markman, A. B., & Lehmann, D. R. (2001). What is it? Categorization flexibility and consumers' responses to really new products. *Journal of Consumer Research, 27*(4), 489–498.

244 Gilovich, T. (1981). Seeing the past in the present: The effect of associations to familiar events on judgments and decisions. *Journal of Personality and Social Psychology, 40*(5), 797–808.

245 *See* n238, Blanchette & Dunbar (2000).

Blanchette, I., & Dunbar, K. (2002). Representational change and analogy: How analogical L inferences alter target representations. *Journal of Experimental Psychology: Learning, Memory, and Cognition, 28*(4), 672–685.

246 May, E. R. (1973). *"Lessons" of the past.* New York: Oxford University Press.

247 Khong, Y. F. (1992). *Analogies at war.* Princeton, NJ: Princeton University Press.

248 Glad, B., & Taber, C. S. (1990). Images, learning, and the decision to use force: The domino theory of the United States. In B. Glad (Ed.), *Psychological dimensions of war* (pp. 56–81). Thousand Oaks, CA: Sage.

249 *See* n247, Khong (1992).

250 Shimko, K. L. (1994). Metaphors and foreign policy decision making. *Political Psychology, 15*(4), 655–671.

251 Druckman, J. N. (2001b). Using credible advice to overcome framing effects. *Journal of Law, Economics & Organization, 17*, 62–82.

252 Bizer, G. Y., & Krosnick, J. A. (2001). Exploring the structure of strength-related attitude features: The relation between attitude importance and attitude accessibility. *Journal of Personality and Social Psychology, 81*(4), 566–586.

Wagenaar, W. A., Keren, G., & Lichtenstein, S. (1988). Islanders and hostages: Deep and surface structures of decision problems. *Acta Psychologica, 67*, 175–189.

253 Messick, D. M., & Sentis, K. P. (1985). Estimating social and nonsocial utility functions from ordinal data. *European Journal of Social Psychology, 15*(4), 389–399.

254 Diekmann, K. A., Samuels, S. M., Ross, L., & Bazerman, M. H. (1997). Self-interest and fairness in problems of resource allocation: Allocators versus recipients. *Journal of Personality and Social Psychology, 72*(5), 1061–1074.

255 Cloyd, C. B., & Spilker, B. (1999). The influence of client preferences on tax professionals' search for judicial precedents, subsequent judgments, and recommendations. *The Accounting Review, 74*, 299–322.

256 Arkin, R. M., Appelman, A. J., & Burger, J. M. (1980). Social anxiety, self-presentation, and the self-serving bias in causal attribution. *Journal of Personality and Social Psychology, 38*(1), 23–35.

Arkin, R. M., Cooper, H. M., & Kolditz, T. A. (1980). A statistical review of the literature concerning the self-serving attribution bias in interpersonal influence situations. *Journal of Personality, 48*(4), 435–448.

Riess, M., Rosenfeld, P., Melburg, V., & Tedeschi, J. T. (1981). Self-serving attributions: Biased private perceptions and distorted public descriptions. *Journal of Personality and Social Psychology, 41*(2), 224–231.

257 Ross, M., & Sicoly, F. (1979). Egocentric biases in availability and attribution. *Journal of Personality and Social Psychology, 37*(3), 322–336.

258 Chandler, R. C. (1988). Organizational communication to corporate constituents: The role of the company annual report (Doctoral dissertation, University of Kansas, 1988). *Dissertation Abstracts International, 49*(11a), 3200.

259 Pratkanis, A. R., & Gliner, M. D. (2004). And when shall a little child lead them? Evidence for an altercasting theory of source credibility. *Current Psychology, 23*(4), 279–304.

260 Shrum, L. J., Wyer Jr, R. S., & O'Guinn, T. C. (1998). The effects of television consumption on social perceptions: The use of priming procedures to investigate psychological processes. *Journal of Consumer Research, 24*(4), 447–458.

261 Bargh, J. A., Chen, M., & Burrows, L. (1996). Automaticity of social behavior: Direct effects of trait construct and stereotype activation on action. *Journal of Personality and Social Psychology, 71*(2), 230–244.

262 Guéguen, N., Jacob, C., & Charles-Sire, V. (2011). Helping with all your heart: The effect of cardioids cue on compliance to a request for humanitarian aid. *Social Marketing Quarterly, 17*(4), 2–11.

263 Day, S. B., & Gentner, D. (2007). Nonintentional analogical inference in text comprehension. *Memory & Cognition, 35*(1), 39–49.

Labroo, A. A., Dhar, R., & Schwarz, N. (2008). Of frog wines and frowning watches: Semantic priming, perceptual fluency, and brand evaluation. *Journal of Consumer Research, 34*(6), 819–831.

264 Mandel, N., & Johnson, E. J. (2002). When web pages influence choice: Effects of visual primes on experts and novices. *Journal of Consumer Research, 29*(2), 235–245.

265 Herr, P. M. (1989). Priming price-prior knowledge and context effects. *Journal of Consumer Research, 16*(1), 67–75.

266 North, A. C., Hargreaves, D. J., & McKendrick, J. (1997). In-store music affects product choice. *Nature, 390*(6656), 132.

North, A. C., Hargreaves, D. J., & McKendrick, J. (1999). Research reports: The influence of in-store music on wine selections. *Journal of Applied Psychology, 84*(2), 271–276.

267 Yi, Y. J. (1990). The effects of contextual priming in print advertisements. *Journal of Consumer Research, 17*(2), 215–222.

268 Morwitz, V. G., Johnson, E., & Schmittlein, D. (1993). Does measuring intent change behavior. *Journal of Consumer Research, 20*(1), 46–61.

Morwitz, V. G., & Fitzsimons, G. J. (2004). The mere-measurement effect: Why does measuring intentions change actual behavior? *Journal of Consumer Psychology, 14*(1–2), 64–74.

269 Dholakia, U. M., & Morwitz, V. G. (2002). The scope and persistence of mere-measurement effects: Evidence from a field study of customer satisfaction measurement. *Journal of Consumer Research, 29*(2), 159–167.

270 Iyengar, S., & Kinder, D. R. (1987). *News that matters: Television and American opinion.* Chicago: University of Chicago Press.

271 Bryan, C. J., Dweck, C. S., Ross, L., Kay, A. C., & Mislavsky, N. O. (2009). Political mindset: Effects of schema priming on liberal-conservative political positions. *Journal of Experimental Social Psychology, 45*(4), 890–895.

272 Gill, M. J., Swann, W. B., & Silvera, D. H. (1998). On the genesis of confidence. *Journal of Personality and Social Psychology, 75*(5), 1101–1114.

273 Penrod, S., & Otto, A. L. (1992, September). *Pretrial publicity and juror decision making: Assessing the magnitude and source of prejudicial effects.* Paper presented at the Third European Conference on Law and Psychology, Oxford, UK.

274 Otto, A. L., Penrod, S. D., & Dexter, H. R. (1994). The biasing impact of pretrial publicity on juror judgments. *Law and Human Behavior, 18*(4), 453–469.

275 *See* n187, Fredin (2001).

276 Pyszczynski, T. A., & Wrightsman, L. S. (1981). The effects of opening statements on mock jurors' verdicts in a simulated criminal trial. *Journal of Applied Social Psychology, 11*(4), 301–313.

277 Rugg, D., & Cantril, H. (1944). The wording of questions. In H. Cantril (Ed.), *Gauging public opinion* (pp. 23–50). Princeton, NJ: Princeton University Press.

278 Markus, H., & Zajonc, R. B. (1985). The cognitive perspective in social psychology. In G. Lindzey & E. Aronson (Eds.), *The handbook of social psychology* (3rd ed., Vol. 1, pp. 137–230). New York: Knopf.

279 Fischhoff, B., & MacGregor, D. (1980). *Judged lethality.* Decision Research Report 80–4. Eugene, OR: Decision Research.

See n7, Tversky & Kahneman (1974).

280 *See* n278, Markus & Zajonc (1985).

See n8, Tversky & Kahneman (1973).

281 *See* n151, Nisbett & Ross (1980).

282 Critcher, C. R., & Gilovich, T. (2008). Incidental environmental anchors. *Journal of Behavioral Decision Making, 21*(3), 241–251.

Mussweiler, T., & Englich, B. (2005). Subliminal anchoring: Judgmental consequences and underlying mechanisms. *Organizational Behavior and Human Decision Processes, 98*(2), 133–143.

Thorsteinson, T. J., Breier, J., Atwell, A., Hamilton, C., & Privette, M. (2008). Anchoring effects on performance judgments. *Organizational Behavior and Human Decision Processes, 107*(1), 29–40.

283 Slovic, P., & Lichtenstein, S. (1971). Comparison of Bayesian and regression approaches to the study of information processing in judgment. *Organizational Behavior & Human Performance, 6*(6), 649–744.

284 Ritov, I. (1996). Anchoring in simulated competitive market negotiation. *Organizational Behavior and Human Decision Processes, 67*(1), 16–25.

285 Navarro-Martinez, D., Salisbury, L. C., Lemon, K. N., Stewart, N., Matthews, W. J., & Harris, A. J. (2011). Minimum required payment and supplemental information disclosure effects on consumer debt repayment decisions. *Journal of Marketing Research, 48*(SPL), S60–S77.

Stewart, N. (2009). The cost of anchoring on credit-card minimum repayments. *Psychological Science, 20*(1), 39–41.

286 Yadav, M. S. (1994). How buyers evaluate product bundles: A model of anchoring and adjustment. *Journal of Consumer Research, 21*(2), 342–353.

287 Greenberg, J., Williams, K. D., & O'Brien, M. K. (1986). Considering the harshest verdict first: Biasing effects on mock juror verdicts. *Personality and Social Psychology Bulletin, 12*(1), 41–50.

288 Jordan, J., & Kaas, K. P. (2002). Advertising in the mutual fund business: The role of judgmental heuristics in private investors' evaluation of risk and return. *Journal of Financial Services Marketing, 7*(2), 129–140.

289 Northcraft, G. B., & Neale, M. A. (1987). Experts, amateurs, and real estate: An anchoring-and-adjustment perspective on property pricing decisions. *Organizational Behavior and Human Decision, 39*(1), 84–97.

290 Joyce, E. J., & Biddle, G. C. (1981). Anchoring and adjustment in probabilistic inference in auditing. *Journal of Accounting Research, 19,* 120–145.

291 Montier, J. (2002). *Behavioural finance: Insights into irrational minds and markets.* Hoboken: Wiley.

292 Statman, M., & Fisher, K. (1998). *The DJIA crossed 652,230 (in 1998).* Working Paper, Santa Clara University, Santa Clara, CA.

293 *See* n291, Montier, J. (2002).

294 Fong, G. T., & Markus, H. (1982). Self-schemas and judgments about others. *Social Cognition, 1*(3), 191–204.

Markus, H., & Smith, J. (1981). The influence of self-schemas on the perception of others. In N. Cantor & J. F. Kihlstrom (Eds.), *Personality, cognition, and social interaction* (pp. 233–262). Hillsdale, NJ: Erlbaum.

295 Kruger, J. (1999). Lake Wobegon be gone! The "below-average effect" and the egocentric nature of comparative ability judgments. *Journal of Personality & Social Psychology, 77*(2), 221–232.

296 *See* n116, Anderson (1965).

Asch, S. E. (1946). Forming impressions of personality. *The Journal of Abnormal and Social Psychology, 41*(3), 258–290.

297 Gilbert, D. T. (2002). Inferential correction. In T. Gilovich, D. Griffin, & D. Kahneman (Eds.), *Heuristics and biases: The psychology of intuitive judgment* (pp. 167–184). New York: Cambridge University Press.

298 Chapman, G. B., & Johnson, E. J. (1999). Anchoring, activation, and the construction of values. *Organizational Behavior and Human Decision Processes, 79*(2), 115–153.

Jacowitz, K. E., & Kahneman, D. (1995). Measures of anchoring in estimation tasks. *Personality and Social Psychology Bulletin, 21*(11), 1161–1166.

Mussweiler, T., & Strack, F. (2000). The use of category and exemplar knowledge in the solution of anchoring tasks. *Journal of Personality and Social Psychology, 78*(6), 1038–1052.

299 Kahneman, D., & Knetsch, J. (1993). *Anchoring or shallow inferences: The effect of format.* Unpublished manuscript, University of California, Berkeley.

300 Sanbonmatsu, D. M., Kardes, F. R., Posavac, S. S., & Houghton, D. C. (1997). Contextual influences on judgment based on limited information. *Organizational Behavior and Human Decision Processes, 69*(3), 251–264.

301 Bechkoff, J., Krishnan, V., Niculescu, M., Kohne, M. L., Palmatier, R. W., & Kardes, F. R. (2009). The role of Omission Neglect in response to non-gains and non-losses in gasoline price fluctuations. *Journal of Applied Social Psychology, 39*(5), 1191–1200.

Rozin, P., Fischler, C., & Shields-Argelès, C. (2009). Additivity dominance: Additives are more potent and more often lexicalized across languages than are "subtractives". *Judgment and Decision Making, 4*(5), 475–478.

302 Sanbonmatsu, D. M., Kardes, F. R., Houghton, D. C., Ho, E. A., & Posavac, S. S. (2003). Overestimating the importance of the given information in multiattribute consumer judgment. *Journal of Consumer Psychology, 13*(3), 289–300.

303 Kardes, F. R., Posavac, S. S., Silvera, D., Cronley, M. L., Sanbonmatsu, D. M., Schertzer, S., . . . Chandrashekaran, M. (2006). Debiasing omission neglect. *Journal of Business Research, 59*(6), 786–792.

Silvera, D. H., Kardes, F. R., Harvey, N., Cronley, M. L., & Houghton, D. C. (2005). Contextual influences on Omission Neglect in the fault tree paradigm. *Journal of Consumer Psychology, 15*(2), 117–126.

304 Pfeiffer, B. E. (2008). Omission detection and inferential adjustment (Doctoral dissertation, University of Cincinnati, 2008). *Dissertation Abstracts International, 69*(08A), 3232.

305 Tormala, Z. L., Petty, R. E., & Brinol, P. (2002). Ease of retrieval effects in persuasion: The roles of elaboration and thought-confidence. *Personality and Social Psychology Bulletin, 28*(12), 1700–1712.

306 Wänke, M., & Bless, H. (2000). The effects of subjective ease of retrieval on attitudinal judgments: The moderating role of processing motivation. In H. Bless & J. P. Forgas (Eds.), *The message within: The role of subjective experience in social cognition and behavior* (pp. 143–161). New York: Psychology Press.

307 Grayson, C., & Schwarz, N. (1999). Beliefs influence information processing strategies: Declarative and experiential information in risk assessment. *Social Cognition, 17*(1), 1–18.

308 Dijksterhuis, A., Macrae, C. N., & Haddock, G. (1999). When recollective experiences matter: Subjective ease of retrieval and stereotyping. *Personality and Social Psychology Bulletin, 25*(6), 766–774.

309 Broemer, P. (2001). Ease of recall moderates the impact of relationship-related goals on judgments of interpersonal closeness. *Journal of Experimental Social Psychology, 37*(3), 261–266.

310 Menon, G., & Raghubir, P. (2003). Ease-of-retrieval as an automatic input in judgments: A mere-accessibility framework? *Journal of Consumer Research, 30*(2), 230–243.

Raghubir, P., & Menon, G. (2005). When and why is ease of retrieval informative? *Memory & Cognition, 33*(5), 821–832.

Wånke, M., Bohner, G., & Jurkowitsch, A. (1997). There are many reasons to drive a BMW: Does imagined ease of argument generation influence attitudes? *Journal of Consumer Research, 24*(2), 170–178.

311 Haddock, G. (2002). It's easy to like or dislike Tony Blair: Accessibility experiences and the favourability of attitude judgments. *British Journal of Psychology, 93*(2), 257–267.

312 Florack, A., & Zoabi, H. (2003). Risk behavior in share transactions: When investors think about reasons. *Zeitschrift für Sozialpsychologie, 34*(2), 65–78.

313 Rotliman, A., & Schwarz, N. (1998). Constructing perceptions of vulnerability: Personal relevance and the use of experiential information in health judgments. *Personality and Social Psychology Bulletin, 28*(10), 1053–1064.

Raghubir, P., & Menon, G. (1998). AIDS and me, never the twain shall meet: The effects of information accessibility on judgments of risk and advertising effectiveness. *Journal of Consumer Research, 25*(1), 52–63.

314 Weick, M., & Guinote, A. (2008). When subjective experiences matter: Power increases reliance on the ease of retrieval. *Journal of Personality and Social Psychology, 94*(6), 956–970.

315 *See* n4, Schwarz (2004).

316 Carroll, J. S. (1978). Causal attributions in expert parole decisions. *Journal of Personality and Social Psychology, 36*(12), 1501–1511.

317 Sherman, S. J., Cialdini, R. B., Schwartzman, D. F., & Reynolds, K. D. (1985). Imagining can heighten or lower the perceived likelihood of contracting a disease: The mediating effect of ease of imagery. *Personality and Social Psychology Bulletin, 11*(1), 118–127.

318 Gregory, W. L., Cialdini, R. B., & Carpenter, K. M. (1982). Self-relevant scenarios as mediators of likelihood estimates and compliance: Does imagining make it so? *Journal of Personality and Social Psychology, 43*(1), 89–99.

319 Emrich, C. G., Brower, H. H., Feldman, J. M., & Garland, H. (2001). Images in words: Presidential rhetoric, charisma, and greatness. *Administrative Science Quarterly, 46*, 527–557.

320 Petrova, P. K., & Cialdini, R. B. (2005). Fluency of consumption imagery and the backfire effects of imagery appeals. *Journal of Consumer Research, 32*(3), 442–452.

321 *See* n70, Adaval & Wyer (1998).

322 Sanna, L. J., & Schwarz, N. (2004). Integrating temporal biases: The interplay of focal thoughts and accessibility experiences. *Psychological Science, 15*(7), 474–481.

323 Epley, N., & Dunning, D. (2000). Feeling "holier than thou": Are self-serving assessments produced by errors in self-or social prediction? *Journal of Personality and Social Psychology, 79*(6), 861–875.

Epley, N., & Dunning, D. (2004). *The mixed blessing of self-knowledge in behavioral prediction.* Unpublished manuscript, Cornell University, Ithaca, New York.

Sherman, S. J. (1980). On the self-erasing nature of errors of prediction. *Journal of Personality and Social Psychology, 39*(2), 211–221.

324 Gilovich, T., Kerr, M., & Medvec, V. H. (1993). The effect of temporal perspective on subjective confidence. *Journal of Personality and Social Psychology, 64,* 552–560.

325 Newby-Clark, I. R., Ross, M., Buehler, R., Koehler, D. J., & Griffin, D. (2000). People focus on optimistic and disregard pessimistic scenarios while predicting their task completion times. *Journal of Experimental Psychology: Applied, 6*(3), 171–182.

326 Greitemeyer, T., & Schulz-Hardt, S. (2003). Preference-consistent evaluation of information in the hidden profile paradigm: Beyond group-level explanations for the dominance of shared information in group decisions. *Journal of Personality and Social Psychology, 84*(2), 322–339.

Klayman, J., & Ha, Y. (1987). Confirmation, disconfirmation, and information in hypothesis testing. *Psychological Review, 94*(2), 211–228.

Russo, J. E., Medvec, V. H., & Meloy, M. G. (1996). The distortion of information during decisions. *Organizational Behavior and Human Decision Processes, 66*(1), 102–110.

327 Smith, D. M., Neuberg, S. L., Judice, T. N., & Biesanz, J. C. (1997). Target complicity in the confirmation and disconfirmation of erroneous perceiver expectations: Immediate and longer term implications. *Journal of Personality and Social Psychology, 73*(5), 974–991.

328 Macan, T. H., & Dipboye, R. L. (1994). The effects of the application on processing of information from the employment interview. *Journal of Applied Social Psychology, 24*(14), 1291–1314.

329 Binning, J. F., Goldstein, M. A., Garcia, M. F., & Scattaregia, J. H. (1988). Effects of preinterview impressions on questioning strategies in same-and opposite-sex employment interviews. *Journal of Applied Psychology, 73*(1), 30–37.

Dougherty, T. W., Turban, D. B., & Callender, J. C. (1994). Confirming first impressions in the employment interview: A field study of interviewer behavior. *Journal of Applied Psychology, 79*(5), 659–665.

Macan, T. H., & Dipboye, R. L. (1988). The effects of interviewers' initial impressions on information gathering. *Organizational Behavior and Human Decision Processes, 42*(3), 364–387.

330 Saunders, D. M., Vidmar, N., & Hewitt, E. C. (1983). Eyewitness testimony and the discrediting effect. In S. M. A. Lloyd-Bostock & B. R. Clifford (Eds.), *Evaluating witness evidence* (pp. 57–78). New York: Wiley.

331 Pennington, D. C. (1982). Witnesses and their testimony: Effects of ordering on juror verdicts. *Journal of Applied Social Psychology, 12*(4), 318–333.

332 Kinder, D. R., & Sears, D. O. (1985). Public opinion and political action. In G. Lindzey & E. Aronson (Eds.), *The handbook of social psychology* (3rd ed., Vol. 2, pp. 659–743). New York: Knopf.

See also Moskowitz, D., & Stroh, P. (1996). Expectation-driven assessments of political candidates. *Political Psychology, 17*(4), 695–712.

333 Lord, C. G., Ross, L., & Lepper, M. R. (1979). Biased assimilation and attitude polarization: The effects of prior theories on subsequently considered evidence. *Journal of Personality and Social Psychology, 37*(11), 2098–2109.

334 Kuklinski, J. H., Quirk, P. J., Jerit, J., Schwieder, D., & Rich, R. E. (2000). Misinformation and the currency of democratic citizenship. *Journal of Politics, 62,* 790–816.

335 Phillips, A. P., & Dipboye, R. L. (1989). Correlational tests of predictions from a process model of the interview. *Journal of Applied Psychology, 74*(1), 41–52.

336 Tetlock, P. (2005). *Expert political judgment: How good is it? How can we know?* Princeton, NJ: Princeton University Press.

337 Kostopoulou, O., Mousoulis, C., & Delaney, B. C. (2009). Information search and information distortion in the diagnosis of an ambiguous presentation. *Judgment and Decision Making, 4*(5), 408–418.

338 Ask, K., Rebelius, A., & Granhag, P. A. (2008). The "elasticity" of criminal evidence: A moderator of investigator bias. *Applied Cognitive Psychology, 22*(9), 1245–1259.

339 Dennis, A. R. (1996). Information exchange and use in small group decision making. *Small Group Research, 27*(4), 532–550.

Schulz-Hardt, S., Brodbeck, F. C., Mojzisch, A., Kerschreiter, R., & Frey, D. (2006). Group decision making in hidden profile situations: Dissent as a facilitator for decision quality. *Journal of Personality and Social Psychology, 91*(6), 1080–1093.

340 Van Swol, L. M. (2007). Perceived importance of information: The effects of mentioning information, shared information bias, ownership bias, reiteration, and confirmation bias. *Group Processes & Intergroup Relations, 10*(2), 239–256.

341 Kerschreiter, R., Schulz-Hardt, S., Faulmuller, N., Mojzisch, A., & Frey, D. (2004). *Psychological explanations for the dominance of shared and preference-consistent information in group discussions: Mutual enhancement or rational-decision making?* Working Paper, Ludwig Maximilians University Munich, Munich, Germany.

342 *See* n30, Schulz-Hardt et al. (2000).

343 Gigone, D., & Hastie, R. (1993). The common knowledge effect: Information sharing and group judgment. *Journal of Personality and Social Psychology, 65*(5), 959–974.

344 Brodbeck, F. C., Kerschreiter, R., Mojzisch, A., & Schulz-Hardt, S. (2007). Group decision making under conditions of distributed knowledge: The information asymmetries model. *Academy of Management Review, 32*(2), 459–479.

Mesmer-Magnus, J. R., & DeChurch, L. A. (2009). Information sharing and team performance: A meta-analysis. *Journal of Applied Psychology, 94*(2), 535.

Tindale, R. S., & Sheffey, S. (2002). Shared information, cognitive load, and group memory. *Group Processes & Intergroup Relations, 5*(1), 5–18.

345 Stasser, G., Taylor, L. A., & Hanna, C. (1989). Information sampling in structured and unstructured discussions of three-and six-person groups. *Journal of Personality and Social Psychology, 57*(1), 67.

346 Greitemeyer, T., & Schulz-Hardt, S. (2003). Preference-consistent evaluation of information in the hidden profile paradigm: Beyond group-level explanations for the dominance of shared information in group decisions. *Journal of Personality and Social Psychology, 84*(2), 322.

Larson, J. R., & Harmon, V. M. (2007). Recalling shared vs. unshared information mentioned during group discussion: Toward understanding differential repetition rates. *Group processes & Intergroup Relations, 10*(3), 311–322.

Wittenbaum, G. M., & Bowman, J. M. (2004). A social validation explanation for mutual enhancement. *Journal of Experimental Social Psychology, 40*(2), 169–184.

347 Lam, S. S., & Schaubroeck, J. (2000). The role of locus of control in reactions to being promoted and to being passed over: A quasi experiment. *Academy of Management Journal, 43*(1), 66–78.

See n339, Schulz-Hardt et al. (2006).

Van Swol, L. M., Savadori, L., & Sniezek, J. A. (2003). Factors that may affect the difficulty of uncovering hidden profiles. *Group Processes & Intergroup Relations, 6*(3), 285–304.

348 Stasser, G., & Titus, W. (1985). Pooling of unshared information in group decision making: Biased information sampling during discussion. *Journal of Personality and Social Psychology, 48*(6), 1467–1478.

349 Dawes, R. M., Faust, D., & Meehl, P. E. (1989). Clinical versus actuarial judgment. *Science, 243*(4899), 1668–1674.

350 Dawes, R. M. (1976). Shallow psychology. In J. S. Carroll & J. W. Payne (Eds.), *Cognition and social behavior* (pp. 3–12). Hillsdale, NJ: Lawrence Erlbaum Associates.

Dawes, R. M. (1980). You can't systematize human judgment: Dyslexia. In R. A. Shweder (Ed.), *New directions for methodology of social and behavioral science* (Vol. 4, pp. 67–78). San Francisco: Jossey-Bass.

351 Iyengar, S. S., & Lepper, M. R. (2000). When choice is demotivating: Can one desire too much of a good thing? *Journal of Personality and Social Psychology, 79*(6), 995–1006.

352 Hsee, C. K. (1996). The evaluability hypothesis: An explanation for preference reversals between joint and separate evaluations of alternatives. *Organizational Behavior and Human Decision Processes, 67*(3), 247–257.

353 Garbarino, E. C., & Edell, J. A. (1997). Cognitive effort, affect, and choice. *Journal of Consumer Research, 24*(2), 147–158.

354 Payne, J. W., Bettman, J. R., & Johnson, E. J. (1993). *The adaptive decision maker.* New York: Cambridge University Press.

Tversky, A. (1972). Elimination by aspects: A theory of choice. *Psychological Review, 79*(4), 281–299.

355 *See* n354, Tversky (1972).

356 Johnson, E. J. (1988a). Expertise and decision under uncertainty: Performance and process. In M. T. H. Chi, R. Glaser & M. J. Farr (Eds.), *The nature of expertise* (pp. 209–228). Hillsdale, NJ: Lawrence Erlbaum Associates.

357 Dhami, M. K., & Ayton, P. (2001). Bailing and jailing the fast and frugal way. *Journal of Behavioral Decision Making, 14*(2), 141–168.

358 *See* n13, Camerer & Johnson (1991).

359 Johnson, E. J., & Payne, J. W. (1985). Effort and accuracy in choice. *Management Science, 31*, 394–414.

360 Hartman, R. S., Doane, M. J., & Woo, C. K. (1991). Consumer rationality and the status quo. *The Quarterly Journal of Economics, 106*(1), 141–162.

361 Axelrod, R. (1976). *The structure of decision.* Princeton, NJ: Princeton University Press.

Jervis, R. (1976). *Perception and misperception in international relations.* Princeton, NJ: Princeton University Press.

362 Slovic, P. (1975). Choice between equally valued alternatives. *Journal of Experimental Psychology: Human Perception and Performance*, 1(3), 280–287.

363 Gallhofer, I. N., & Saris, W. E. (1996). *Foreign policy decision-making: A qualitative and quantitative analysis of policy argumentation*. Westport, CT: Praeger.

364 Himmelfarb, S. (1972). Integration and attribution theories in personality impression formation. *Journal of Personality and Social Psychology*, 23(3), 309–313.

365 Harkins, S. G., & Petty, R. E. (1981). Effects of source magnification of cognitive effort on attitudes: An information-processing view. *Journal of Personality and Social Psychology*, 40(3), 401–413.

See also Lee, K. M. (2004). The multiple source effect and synthesized speech. *Human Communication Research*, 30(2), 182–207.

366 Budescu, D. V., & Rantilla, A. K. (2000). Confidence in aggregation of expert opinions. *Acta Psychologica*, 104(3), 371–398.

367 Chaiken, S. (1980). Heuristic versus systematic information processing and the use of source versus message cues in persuasion. *Journal of Personality and Social Psychology*, 39(5), 752–766.

Eagly, A. H., & Warren, R. (1976). Intelligence, comprehension, and opinion change. *Journal of Personality*, 44(2), 226–242.

Maddux, J. E., & Rogers, R. W. (1980). Effects of source expertness, physical attractiveness, and supporting arguments on persuasion: A case of brains over beauty. *Journal of Personality and Social Psychology*, 39(2), 235–244.

368 Calder, B. J., Insko, C. A., & Yandell, B. (1974). The relation of cognitive and memorial processes to persuasion in a simulated jury trial. *Journal of Applied Social Psychology*, 4(1), 62–93.

Insko, C. A., Lind, E. A., & LaTour, S. (1976). Persuasion, recall, and thoughts. *Representative Research in Social Psychology*, 7(1), 66–78.

369 Stasser, G., Stella, N., Hanna, C., & Colella, A. (1984). The majority effect in jury deliberations: Number of supporters versus number of supporting arguments. *Law & Psychology Review*, 8, 115–127.

370 Petty, R. E., & Cacioppo, J. T. (1984). The effects of involvement on responses to argument quantity and quality: Central and peripheral routes to persuasion. *Journal of Personality and Social Psychology*, 46(1), 69–81.

Wood, W., Kallgren, C. A., & Preisler, R. M. (1985b). Access to attitude-relevant information in memory as a determinant of persuasion: The role of message attributes. *Journal of Experimental Social Psychology*, 21(1), 73–85.

371 Barclay, L. A., & York, K. M. (2003). Clear logic and fuzzy guidance: A policy capturing study of merit raise decisions. *Public Personnel Management*, 32(2), 287–299.

372 Hsee, C. K. (1998). Less is better: When low-value options are valued more highly than high-value options. *Journal of Behavioral Decision Making*, 11(2), 107–121.

Körner, C., Gertzen, H., Bettinger, C., & Albert, D. (2007). Comparative judgments with missing information: A regression and process tracing analysis. *Acta Psychologica*, 125(1), 66–84.

See n236, Markman & Moreau (2001).

373 *See* n236, Markman & Moreau (2001).

374 Yates, J. F., Jagacinski, C. M., & Faber, M. D. (1978). Evaluation of partially described multiattribute options. *Organizational Behavior & Human Performance*, 21(2), 240–251.

375 Slovic, P., & MacPhillamy, D. (1974). Dimensional commensurability and cue utilization in comparative judgment. *Organizational Behavior & Human Performance*, 11(2), 172–194.

376 Markman, A. B., & Medin, D. L. (1995). Similarity and alignment in choice. *Organizational Behavior and Human Decision Processes*, 63(2), 117–130.

377 Lindemann, P. G., & Markman, A. B. (1996, July). *Alignability and attribute importance in choice*. Paper presented at the Eighteenth Annual Meeting of the Cognitive Science Society, San Diego, California.

378 Finucane, M. L., Peters, E., & Slovic, P. (2003). Judgment and decision making: The dance of affect and reason. In S. L. Schneider & J. Shanteau (Eds.), *Emerging perspectives on judgment and decision research* (pp. 327–364). New York: Cambridge University Press.

379 Johnson, M. D. (1986). Modeling choice strategies for noncomparable alternatives. *Marketing Science*, 5(1), 37–54.

Johnson, M. D. (1988b). Comparability and hierarchical processing in multialternative choice. *Journal of Consumer Research*, 15(3), 303–314.

380 Huber, J., Payne, J. W., & Puto, C. (1982). Adding asymmetrically dominated alternatives: Violations of regularity and the similarity hypothesis. *Journal of Consumer Research*, 9(1), 90–98.

Tversky, A., & Shafir, E. (1992). Choice under conflict: The dynamics of deferred decision. *Psychological Science*, 3(6), 358–361.

381 Shafir, E., Simonson, I., & Tversky, A. (1993). Reason-based choice. *Cognition Special Issue: Reasoning and Decision Making, 49*(1–2), 11–36.

382 Huberman, G., Iyengar, S. S., & Jiang, W. (2007). Defined contribution pension plans: Determinants of participation and contribution rates. *Journal of Financial Services Research, 31*(1), 1–32.

383 Redelmeier, D. A., & Shafir, E. (1995). Medical decision making in situations that offer multiple alternatives. *Journal of the American Medical Association, 273,* 302–305.

384 Boatwright, P., & Nunes, J. C. (2001). Reducing assortment: An attribute-based approach. *Journal of Marketing, 65*(3), 50–63.

385 *Ibid.*

386 Bertrand, M., & Morse, A. (2011). Information disclosure, cognitive biases, and payday borrowing. *The Journal of Finance, 66*(6), 1865–1893.

387 Iyengar, S. S., Huberman, G., & Jiang, W. (2004). How much choice is too much? Contributions to 401 (k) retirement plans. In O. S. Mitchell & S. P. Utkus (Eds.), *Pension design and structure: New lessons from behavioral finance* (pp. 83–95). New York: Oxford University Press.

388 Tversky, A., & Shafir, E. (1992). Choice under conflict: The dynamics of deferred decision. *Psychological Science, 3*(6), 358–361.

389 *See* n351, Iyengar & Lepper (2000).

390 Bertrand, M., Karlan, D., Mullainathan, S., Shafir, E., & Zinman, J. (2005). *What's psychology worth? A field experiment in the consumer credit market.* Working Paper No. 11892, Cambridge, MA: National Bureau of Economic Research.

391 Carlson, K. A., Meloy, M. G., & Russo, J. E. (2006). Leader-driven primacy: Using attribute order to affect consumer choice. *Journal of Consumer Research, 32*(4), 513–518.

392 Krosnick, J. A., Miller, J. M., & Tichy, M. P. (2004). An unrecognized need for ballot reform: The effects of candidate name order on election outcomes. In A. N. Crigler, M. R. Just & E. J. McCaffery (Eds.), *Rethinking the vote: The politics and prospects of American election reform.* (pp. 51–73). New York: Oxford University Press.

393 Samuelson, W., & Zeckhauser, R. (1988). Status quo bias in decision making. *Journal of Risk and Uncertainty, 1,* 7–59.

394 Fader, P. S., & Lattin, J. M. (1993). Accounting for heterogeneity and nonstationarity in a cross-sectional model of consumer purchase behavior. *Marketing Science, 12*(3), 304–317.

395 Guidagni, P. M., & Little, J. D. C. (1983). A logit model of brand choice calibrated on scanner data. *Marketing Science, 2,* 203–238.

396 Betsch, T., Haberstroh, S., Glöckner, A., Haar, T., & Fiedler, K. (2001). The effects of routine strength on adaptation and information search in recurrent decision making. *Organizational Behavior and Human Decision Processes, 84*(1), 23–53.

397 Betsch, T., Haberstroh, S., Molter, B., & Glöckner, A. (2004). Oops, I did it again—Relapse errors in routinized decision making. *Organizational Behavior and Human Decision Processes, 93*(1), 62–74.

398 Luce, M. F. (1998). Choosing to avoid: Coping with negatively emotion-laden consumer decisions. *Journal of Consumer Research, 24*(4), 409–433.

Nowlis, S. M., Kahn, B. E., & Dhar, R. (2002). Coping with ambivalence: The effect of removing a neutral option on consumer attitude and preference judgments. *Journal of Consumer Research, 29*(3), 319–334

6

PERSON PERCEPTION IN AUDIENCE DECISION MAKING

On September 26, 1960, 70 million Americans saw the first televised presidential debate. The debate was between then-vice president Richard Nixon and soon-to-be-president John F. Kennedy. Richard Nixon, just out of the hospital, looked pale and uncomfortable. Kennedy, fresh from a vacation, looked tanned and relaxed. Nixon's light gray suit blended in with the light gray background of the black-and-white TV image. But Kennedy's black suit made him stand out.

According to the polls, radio listeners thought Nixon won the debate. But the TV audience who saw as well as heard the two candidates gave the victory to Kennedy.

How could such an important issue be decided by personal appearance and the color of a suit? Yet there is little doubt that person perception—the mental activity of evaluating other people—played an essential role in Kennedy's victory over Nixon in the televised debates.[1] Experimental studies have since verified that evaluations of political candidates by debate viewers and listeners differ significantly.[2]

Skill in person perception enables audiences to recognize a professional's emotions, comprehend their character traits, and judge how well they fit an occupational role—such as executive, accountant, physician, or professor. Person perception is typically based on direct observation of a professional's verbal behaviors (the words they write or speak), their nonverbal behaviors (their eye contact, facial expressions, tone of voice, and so on), and their appearance. Recruiters engage in this type of person perception when they interview job applicants. In fact, any number of audiences engage in this type of person perception when they listen to presentations, read reports and proposals, and talk with professionals one on one. Person perception can also be based on verbal descriptions of professionals and their behaviors.

In addition, the concept of person perception can be broadened to include not only the activity of evaluating individual professionals but also the activity of evaluating groups of professionals, organizations, and even brands. Just as audiences ascribe human personality traits to themselves and other individuals,[3] they also ascribe human traits to organizations[4] and product brands.[5] For example, consumers generally perceive the Coca-Cola brand as having a personality that is all-American.[6] They perceive the Pepsi brand as young and exciting.[7]

The two versions of Citibank's loan agreement form on pp. 146–147 illustrate how audiences may ascribe personality traits to organizations on the basis of the documents they produce. After the revised loan agreement was completed, the bank surveyed more than 100 borrowers and asked them to evaluate the two versions of the form. In addition to preferring the revised form, the borrowers inferred that the traits of banks using the two forms would be radically different. The borrowers said a bank using the old form would not be customer oriented. Conversely, they said a bank using the new form would be trustworthy, sensitive to the customer, modern, and efficient.

Audiences incorporate their judgments of professionals and organizations into many types of decisions that Chapter 2 reviews, including investment decisions, staffing decisions, sourcing decisions, and employment decisions. For example, most financial analysts would be reluctant to recommend investing in a firm whose CEO they judged to be incompetent. Most recruiters would not want to hire a job applicant they judged to be unlikable. Most consumers would be reluctant to purchase a product from a supplier they deemed unreliable. And most job seekers would not bother to apply to an organization they perceived to be unethical or hidebound.[8]

If a professional or organization is the source of information for an audience, the audience will also incorporate its judgment of the professional or organization into its evaluation of the information they receive. Audiences tend to discount any information they receive from sources they perceive to be biased or dishonest regardless of the type of decision they are asked to make.

The Impact of Person Perception on Decision Making

Person Perception and Voters' Decisions

One of the most widely known research findings from the person perception literature is that the personal characteristics of a political candidate have a greater relative impact on voters' decisions than the candidate's stand on the issues or their party affiliation.[9] In U.S. presidential elections, up to 60% of the variance in voters' preference for the Democratic or Republican candidate can be accounted for by voters' perceptions of the two candidates' personality traits.[10]

Voters' perceptions of candidates' personalities may be based on very little information. In a study of the impact of candidates' photographs on voters, university students cast hypothetical votes for 11 candidates solely on the basis of the candidates' election photos. The students' voting behavior reflected their judgments of the candidates' competence more than other traits. Interestingly, the distribution of the students' votes was significantly correlated with the distribution of votes cast in the actual election.[11]

Person Perception and Recruiters' Decisions

The impact of person perception is especially evident in recruiters' hiring decisions, with their perceptions of applicants' nonverbal behaviors playing a significant role. A study of recruiters making hiring decisions finds that recruiters' evaluations of job applicants' nonverbal behaviors account for more than 80% of the rating variance.[12]

Other studies confirm that recruiters weight applicants' nonverbal behaviors heavily. In one study, 52 recruiters reviewed video recordings of one of two versions of an applicant's mock job interview. The applicant's verbal responses were identical in both versions but their nonverbal behaviors were systematically varied. In the first version the applicant showed minimal eye contact, low energy, lack of affect, low voice modulation, and a lack of speech fluency. In the second version the applicant engaged in the opposite behaviors. All 26 recruiters who saw the first version of the interview said they would not have invited the candidate back for a second interview. Conversely, 23 of the 26 recruiters who saw the second version said they would have invited the candidate back.[13] A follow-up study of actual job interviews found that no job candidates who had inhibited nonverbal behaviors (such as minimal eye contact, low energy, lack of affect, low voice modulation, and lack of speech fluency) during a first interview were invited back for a second one.[14]

Person Perception and Job Applicants' Decisions

Just as recruiters' staffing decisions are affected by their impressions of job applicants, job applicants' employment decisions are significantly affected by their perceptions of recruiters.[15] In a study of 237 college students who had been interviewed for jobs, students described their reactions to recruiters and indicated their subsequent decisions. The students' perceptions of the recruiters' personalities and their manner of delivery, as well as the adequacy of information the recruiters provided, significantly influenced the students' evaluations of the recruiting firms and the likelihood they would accept a job offer from them.[16] In a study of online recruitment, students viewed videos on recruitment websites featuring either cheerful recruiters providing feeling-inducing information or formal recruiters providing fact-laden information. Sixty-two percent of the students decided to apply for jobs at organizations whose recruitment websites featured cheerful recruiters.[17]

Person Perception and Financial Analysts' Decisions

Financial analysts' investment decisions are significantly affected by their perception of the firm's management. In a nationwide survey of 268 top financial analysts, 42% of the analysts surveyed reported their personal evaluation of top management is worth more than 60% of their total valuation of the company's price/earnings multiple. An additional 34% said their personal appraisal of management is worth more than 33% of their total valuation.[18]

Person Perception and the Decisions of Speakers' Audiences

Audience perceptions of the source of information can also impact their decisions. For example, consumers' perceptions of the spokespeople who advertise products influence their purchase decisions.[19] The reputation and enthusiasm of the employees who propose new projects are the among the six most frequently mentioned criteria senior managers use to select new projects to commercialize, mentioned more often than profitability.[20]

The audience's initial impressions of a speaker's credibility and likeability play an especially important role in the speaker's ability to persuade them.[21] The more positive the audience's perceptions of the speaker, the more persuaded they are by the speaker's message.[22] Sometimes the audience's impression of a speaker is the main determinant of the audience's decision, especially when their interest in the speaker's message is low.[23] For this reason, the nonverbal behaviors of spokespeople in TV ads are often more highly correlated with an ad's persuasiveness than its verbal content.[24] The audience's perception of the speaker also becomes a major determinant of the decision when they are distracted from paying attention to the speaker's message.[25]

Role Schemata of Expert Audiences

There is widespread agreement among social psychologists that social knowledge and expertise are held in schemata.[26] One type of schema—role schemata—embodies much of the expertise audiences use in person perception.[27] Audiences possess role schemata for different professionals such as doctors, lawyers, and managers, as well as role schemata for leaders, job applicants, and speakers.

Role schemata play a critical role in person perception and audience decision making. Audiences depend on role schemata more than perceived personality traits to make sense of others.[28] They also use role schemata more than personality traits to cue their memories of their acquaintances.[29] For example, it is easier for audience members to think of all the lawyers they know than to recollect all the introverts they know.

Decision Criteria in Role Schemata

Like decision schemata, role schemata are organized by decision criteria. An experiment with 104 undergraduates explored the organization of their role schemata for political candidates. Students' information about political candidates appeared to be organized by attributes, or decision criteria (e.g., experience, personality traits, emotional characteristics, etc.), particularly among those students who were more politically expert. Political novices, lacking organized attribute information, tended to make decisions about candidates based on their intuitive impressions of the candidates.[30] Other studies find that when the audience is asked to form an impression of a person or to make a prediction about a person's future behavior, they organize what they know about the person's current behaviors almost completely by trait categories[31] within a schema that seldom reflects any actual behavioral details.[32]

Benchmarks in Role Schemata

Like decision schemata, role schemata include benchmarks. Audiences often judge a professional's attributes against group-specific standards and expectations.[33] Audiences also use themselves as a point of comparison when evaluating others.[34] When audiences evaluate another's leadership skills and potential, they use their images of prototypical leaders as benchmarks.[35]

Recruiters use several types of benchmarks when evaluating job applicants during employment interviews. Recruiters compare the actual applicants to their image of the ideal applicant.[36] Recruiters base their image of the ideal applicant on applicants from the past, on their analysis of the job, on their general impressions of good employees, and on their own image of themselves.[37] Recruiters also compare applicants to the other applicants who have recently applied for the position.[38] A study of 120 recruiters and 180 managers who watched video recordings of four applicants interviewing for a management trainee position found that the performance of earlier applicants influenced the evaluator's assessment of subsequent applicants.[39] Similarly, a study of candidates interviewing for medical school found that the performance of the two most recent candidates influenced the evaluator's assessment of the candidate they were currently evaluating.[40]

Audiences may also use one person in a conversation as a benchmark with which to evaluate the other person in the conversation. In a study of viewers' perceptions of interviewees, researchers presented nine videos portraying different interviewer/interviewee nonverbal behaviors to nine groups of 25 viewers each. The viewers' perceptions of the interviewees were influenced by their perceptions of the interviewers. Aggressive interviewers caused the viewers to evaluate interviewees more positively. Obliging interviewers caused the viewers to evaluate interviewees more negatively.[41]

When audiences receive new benchmark information during a person perception task, their judgments may exhibit the "change-of-standard effect." In the change-of-standard effect, the new benchmark information changes the audience's initial impression of the person they are evaluating as well as what the audience remembers about them.[42] For example, an audience might initially decide a judge is harsh when comparing her to lenient judges and then mistakenly remember her as very harsh when later comparing her to moderately harsh judges.

Audience Expectations About Professionals Playing Their Roles

Audiences may penalize professionals whose traits do not fit their role schemata. A study of wholesale drug salespeople and retail pharmacist buyers demonstrates that buyer loyalty to a given supplier is negatively related to the degree to which a salesperson's actual behaviors differ from the buyer's role expectation of them.[43] Salespeople who are uncertain about the best way to fulfill their customers' role expectations suffer from what is called *role ambiguity*. The greater the salesperson's role ambiguity, the poorer their sales performance.[44]

When audiences are asked to evaluate an individual's leadership abilities, they automatically draw on their leader schemata.[45] Audiences make leadership judgments by activating a leader schema and matching the attributes of the individual they are evaluating against the attributes in their leader schema.[46] The better the match, the more favorable the audience's leadership perceptions.[47]

Audiences also perceive leaders who behave in ways that match their leader schemata to be more effective than those whose behaviors do not match.[48] A manager who fails to conform to her employees' schemata for a good business leader will not be perceived as a leader in her organization.[49] In one leadership study, audience members watched videos of groups in which a target person's behavior varied on two dimensions: prototypicality of leadership behavior and frequency of leadership behavior. Both dimensions significantly affected the audience's leadership ratings of the target person.[50] Even more important to business professionals is the finding that managers who fail to conform to their employees' leader schemata tend to be less effective as managers.[51]

Types of Role Schemata

Occupation Schemata: How Audiences Evaluate Professionals

Audiences have role schemata for all types of professionals: for managers, teachers, engineers, politicians, as well as for those involved in other more specialized occupations.[52] For example, industry analysts have a clear role schema for investor-relations representatives that is very different from their role schema for senior managers.[53]

As might be expected, recruiters have a highly differentiated and reliable understanding of the personality traits and emotional characteristics specific occupations require.[54] For example, recruiters expect a good applicant for an advertising position to be thrill seeking, impulsive, changeable, attention seeking, and fun loving. Conversely, they expect a good applicant for an accounting position to be meek, definiteness seeking, and orderly. And they expect applicants for supervisory and coaching positions to be dominant, ambitious, aggressive, and persistent. Interestingly, recruiters' expectations are a good match with applicants' self-reported measures of personality and vocational interests.[55]

Leader Schemata: How Audiences Evaluate Leaders

Decision criteria in leader schemata are widely shared by people of all ages and backgrounds.[56] Even as early as first grade, children can clearly differentiate leaders from nonleaders and can articulate the criteria they use to distinguish them.[57] Studies of group decision making also indicate there is substantial agreement among group members about which member of the group is its leader and which members are not.[58]

Decision criteria in leader schemata are composed of the personality traits and emotional characteristics that audiences believe leaders should possess. A study of undergraduates' schemata for effective leaders finds five traits to be most important: dedication, intelligence, sensitivity, charisma, and strength.[59] Another study of leader schemata identifies a somewhat different set of traits: intelligence, understanding, friendliness, energy, honesty, and helpfulness.[60] A meta-analysis of research on leader schemata finds that three traits—intelligence, assertiveness, and dominance—are significantly related to audience perceptions of leadership.[61] The three traits that actually predict effective leadership appear to be intelligence, extroversion and conscientiousness.[62]

Audiences also have well-developed role schemata for leaders that are specific to different occupations and professions.[63] Priming different leader schemata with the appropriate labels, for instance *business leader* versus *political leader*, significantly affects how the audience will perceive the target individual.[64] In the political world, voters possess schemata with decision criteria comprised of traits appropriate for political leaders.[65] Traits in U.S. voters' schemata for the ideal president include honesty, courage, charisma, and warmth.[66]

In the business world, employees possess schemata with decision criteria consisting of traits appropriate for business leaders.[67] Employees view traits such as strict, conservative, manipulative, and unemotional, as inappropriate and atypical of effective business leaders.[68] Some authors use the phrase *implicit leadership theories* (ILTs) to describe employees' schemata for business leaders. They find that employees' ILTs consist of employees' assumptions about the skills, abilities, and traits of an ideal business leader. Employees' ILTs are relatively constant across individuals and types of businesses. Stored in memory, they are activated when employees interact with their upper management.[69]

Managers also possess schemata comprised of traits appropriate for business leaders. A cross-cultural study of 15,022 middle managers from 60 different countries asked managers to rate the degree to which 112 different leadership traits either impede or facilitate effective leadership. Middle managers from almost every country rated five traits as characteristic of outstanding business leaders—charismatic, team oriented, participative, humane, and autonomous. Middle managers from all 60 countries agreed that one trait, being self-protective, inhibits leaders.[70]

Audiences use physical appearance as a visual cue to identify leaders and other dominant individuals. Research demonstrates that an individual's physical attractiveness is positively related to the audience's perception of their dominance.[71] Audiences also associate a mature physical appearance with leadership and dominance. Both men and women with mature facial features impress others as competent, dominant, and shrewd. Whereas people with less mature features impress others as submissive, shy, and naïve.[72] Large eyes, for example, signal low dominance to many audience members.[73]

Audience responses to physical appearance can have a real impact on aspiring leaders and the organizations they serve. Perceptions of physical attractiveness predict a man's leadership position in groups.[74] Physical height—a feature closely associated with social dominance[75]—is highly correlated with greater income and occupational success.[76] Audience assessments of West Point cadets' dominance-related traits, based solely on the cadets' photos, reliably predict the cadets' future rank in the military.[77] Audience inferences about CEOs' power-related traits, based solely on the CEOs' photos, reliably predict company profits.[78] In one study of the effects of physical appearance on leadership judgments, participants viewed photos of pairs of political candidates who ran against each other in previous elections for the U.S. House and Senate. Participants only saw faces of candidates they did not recognize. Their task was to judge which person in each pair looked more competent. The candidate judged to have the more competent-looking face won the actual election in two-thirds of the trials.[79]

Audiences also use nonverbal behaviors as visual cues to identify leaders and other dominant individuals.[80] Employees can accurately predict a professional's organizational status based on nonverbal behaviors depicted in photographs—downward head tilt for women, formal dress and forward lean for men.[81] Audiences perceive those who maintain a closer interaction distance and who touch others, especially when the touch is nonreciprocal, to have higher status and to be more leader-like.[82] Audiences perceive those with more youthful gaits to be more powerful, regardless of their gender or age.[83] Audiences also perceive out-stretched arms as indicating dominance typical of leaders.[84] In fact, audiences tend to perceive any expansive gesture, such as pointing at others or gesturing to direct others, as dominant.[85]

In a study of the leadership perceptions of top managers, 26 senior managers watched video recorded interviews of 22 mid-level managers from the same industry and rated each one's leadership potential. The study revealed that the senior managers' ratings of mid-level managers were significantly correlated with the mid-level managers' scores on five nonverbal visual dimensions: physical attractiveness, amount of smiling, amount of gaze in the direction of the interviewer, amount of hand movement, and the extent to which the mid-level manager leaned toward, instead of away from, the interviewer.[86]

Eye contact plays an especially important role in the audience's identification of leaders. In one study, 120 students watched videos in which an interviewee maintained eye contact with an interviewer for either 15, 30, or 50 seconds. The results demonstrated that students perceived the interviewee to be more powerful as her eye contact increased.[87] Another study of job applicants' eye contact in interviews finds that it is especially important for high-status applicants to maintain eye contact with the recruiter during their interviews.[88] It is also important for presenters to maintain good eye contact. Audience perceptions of a speaker's status and power are associated with a high degree of eye contact while speaking.[89]

Facial displays of emotions also help the audience identify leaders. Audiences infer that people with happy faces are both high in dominance and high in likeability, that people with angry faces are high in dominance but low in likeability, and that people with fearful faces are low in dominance.[90] Moreover, a leader's facial expression of fear or evasion tends to undermine support for the leader and can disturb their followers.[91]

In addition to using nonverbal visual cues, audiences also use a number of nonverbal vocal cues to identify leaders. For example, audiences associate short response latencies, or pauses, as well as loudness with dominance.[92] Speakers with lower-pitched voices are also perceived to be more dominant, more competent, but less warm than those with childlike voices.[93] Speakers who vary the pitch of their voice come across as more leader-like—dynamic, extroverted, benevolent, and competent—than those who speak in a monotone.[94] Longer talking time generally communicates leadership as well,[95] although the quality of what is said also matters.[96]

To a large extent, vocal cues determine whether a leader will be perceived as charismatic. Voters rate political leaders as more charismatic when they vary their pitch and amplitude, or loudness, and speak at a faster pace than normal.[97] Followers also rate leaders as more charismatic when the leaders' speeches combine visionary content with expressive vocal delivery.[98]

The study of 26 senior managers described previously also found that the senior managers' leadership ratings of mid-level managers were significantly correlated with the mid-level managers' scores on five nonverbal vocal dimensions: lower pitch, variable as opposed to monotone pitch, faster speech rate, fewer and shorter pauses, and minimal variability in amplitude. In addition, the mid-level manager's scores on the visual dimensions were significantly correlated with their scores on the vocal dimensions. In other words, the senior managers perceived that mid-level managers who looked like leaders also sounded like leaders.[99]

Powerful language plays an important role in audience perceptions of effective leaders as well.[100] Audiences rate both male and female speakers who use a powerful speech style higher on traits of assertiveness, politeness, and warmth than speakers who use a powerless speech style.[101] Powerless speech styles are associated with the frequent use of verbal behaviors such as intensifiers (e.g., "really big"), and hedges (e.g., "I think").[102] Conversely, the speech styles of powerful and high-status individuals rarely display those verbal behaviors. Audiences are also more likely to view others as powerful when they use abstract as opposed to concrete language. Audiences tend to believe that abstract language reflects not only the ability to think more abstractly but also a willingness to make decisions.[103]

A number of other verbal behaviors also lead audiences to view the speaker as dominant and leader-like. In a study of dominance perception, audience members first watched videos of pairs of people engaged in conversations. Then they were asked to rate the dominance of each individual in each pair. The audience gave higher dominance ratings to those who initiated new topics of conversation and to those who made many forceful requests.[104]

Audience leadership judgments also rely on verbal cues to emotions. For example, the prevalence of positive emotion words is correlated with audience perceptions of leader-like dominance.[105] In addition, audiences find leaders who pepper their speeches with inclusive personal pronouns such as *we, our,* and *us* to be more charismatic, persuasive, and able to elicit more positive emotions.[106] Note how often Lincoln used *we, our,* and *us* in the Gettysburg Address. And to what effect.

Applicant Schemata: How Recruiters Evaluate Job Applicants

Just as employees have implicit leadership theories (ILTs) or schemata for identifying good business leaders, corporate recruiters have implicit followership theories (IFTs) or schemata for identifying good job applicants,[107] and they tend to agree on the personality traits and emotional characteristics good job applicants should possess.[108] The personality traits and emotional characteristics recruiters look for in job applicants include conscientiousness, achievement striving, and self-discipline,[109] as well as industriousness, reliability, cooperativeness, and enthusiasm.[110]

When making hiring decisions, experienced corporate recruiters weight applicants' personality traits and emotional characteristics more heavily than the applicants' knowledge, skills, and abilities.[111] Surprisingly, job applicants' emotional characteristics turn out to be a good predictor of their future success. One study found that 15 years after graduation, highly cheerful undergraduates from a number of universities were averaging almost $114,000 more per year (in today's dollars) than their less cheerful counterparts.[112]

Recruiters' evaluations of an applicant's personality traits and emotional characteristics are affected by the nonverbal visual cues that job applicants display during job interviews—cues such as eye contact, body orientation, smiling, and hand gestures.[113] High levels of eye contact, gesturing, nodding, and smiling are all related to more favorable evaluations of applicants.[114] In fact, any time applicants exhibit highly expressive nonverbal behaviors, recruiters' ratings of them tend to increase.[115] Physical attractiveness also impacts employment suitability ratings across positions. However, the weight recruiters give to attractiveness is greatest for positions that require high customer contact.[116]

An analysis of actual job interviews concludes that recruiters' impressions of an applicant's personality are based in large part on the applicant's nonverbal facial behaviors, including direct eye contact and smiling, which in turn are associated with the recruiters' hiring decisions.[117] Behaviors such as avoidance glances and neutral facial expressions are typical of unsuccessful applicants.[118]

Interestingly, the nonverbal visual cues recruiters observe in job applicants are correlated with supervisors' subsequent ratings of the applicants' performance on the job.[119] Supervisors' ratings of applicants' on-the-job performance are significantly correlated with the applicant's physical attractiveness in the interview and with the amount of time the applicant gazes at the interviewer.[120] Moreover, interviewers' and supervisors' ratings are both significantly correlated with a composite score of the applicant's physical attractiveness, amount of gaze, amount of smiling, amount of hand movement, posture, body orientation, and dress characteristics.

In addition to visual cues, a number of vocal cues influence recruiters' perceptions of job applicants. An analysis of the relative importance of verbal and nonverbal behaviors to hiring decisions reveals that an applicant's speech fluency and voice level are among the top seven predictors of a job offer.[121] In a study of the effect of accents on applicants' chances for success, judges were asked to rate the suitability for employment of people whose speech varied on different phonological variables such as postvocalic *r*. The judges rated speakers of the standard dialect as much more competent and suitable for employment than speakers of nonstandard dialects.[122]

Verbal cues are another strong predictor of perceived competence[123] and of a job offer.[124] Judges' perceptions of applicants' competence are inversely related to the percentage of self-referent words (e.g., *I, me, mine*) applicants use.[125] Applicants who use a high proportion of self-referent words are generally perceived to be relatively shy and incompetent.[126] The use of *we*, on the other hand, is viewed much more favorably. For example, the use of *we* in college applicants' essays is a strong predictor of college admissions decisions.[127]

In addition to the use of self-referent words, other verbal behaviors, such as an applicant's willingness to make bold statements, affect the audience's perceptions of an applicant's competence.[128] Negations and negative emotion words, on the other hand, are negatively related to audience perceptions of an applicant's competence.[129]

Speaker Schemata: How Audiences Evaluate Speakers

Audiences want to be informed by those whom they perceive to be both competent and trustworthy, that is to say, credible. Unless the audience perceives the source of information to be credible, any attempt by the source to frame an issue will fail.[130] Moreover, when audience members distrust a speaker, they automatically make semantic associations that are incongruent with the speaker's message even as the speaker speaks.[131]

Audiences use a number of nonverbal visual cues to identify credible speakers. For example, audiences perceive speakers who smile as more credible than speakers who do not.[132] Audiences view speakers who make more eye contact to be more credible as well.[133] Audiences also view confident speakers as more credible. In a study of mock jurors evaluating the credibility of eyewitness identification of defendants, only the confidence displayed by the eyewitnesses affected juror judgments of their credibility.[134]

Studies of people telling lies confirm the commonly accepted belief that people behave differently when they are lying.[135] When people lie, they blink more, fidget more, tap more, and scratch themselves more than when they speak truthfully. When people lie, they tend to avoid the audience's gaze unless they are being purposefully manipulative. Although deceptive people do behave differently, audiences still have difficulty identifying them. For example, consumers have great difficulty discriminating truthful from deceptive salespeople.[136]

Audiences also use a number of vocal cues to identify credible sources of information. For example, speech rate and fluency correlate with audience perceptions of truthfulness.[137] Audiences perceive fast-talking speakers as more credible than slow-talking ones.[138] Audiences find speakers who talk with a faster than average speech rate to be more persuasive as well.[139]

On the other hand, audiences perceive speakers who frequently use hesitation forms and questioning intonations to be less credible than other speakers.[140] The more problems a speaker has speaking fluently—problems such as a repetitive use of filler words, the use of long pauses and response latencies, or the unnecessary repetition of words or sounds—the lower audiences rate that speaker's competence and expertise.[141]

Studies of people lying confirm many of the audience's preconceptions about vocal cues to lying.[142] When people lie, they typically speak less fluently, hesitate more, make more grammatical errors, and vocalize more "ums" and "ers." However, increased latency of response and a slower rate of speech do not reliably discriminate between deceptive speakers and honest ones.

In addition to nonverbal cues, verbal cues can influence the audience's perceptions of a speaker's credibility. Audiences give higher credibility ratings to speakers who document their evidence.[143] They give higher credibility ratings to speakers whose message is clear.[144] Unequivocal claims (e.g., "Apple's stock price will fall" vs. "I think Apple's stock price may fall") can also enhance perceived source credibility, but only when the source of information backs them up with high-quality arguments.[145] With low-quality arguments, unequivocal claims decrease the audience's perception of source credibility.

Audiences perceive any speaker who frequently uses intensifiers and hedges to be less credible than other speakers.[146] Speakers who elaborate unnecessarily may also be perceived as less credible. In a study of defendants' credibility, mock jurors read courtroom testimony in which the defendant provided more information than the prosecutor requested. For example, at one point when the prosecutor asked the defendant if he were an insured driver, the defendant replied, "Yes, I've never lost my insurance because of speeding tickets." The jurors judged the defendant to be guilty more often than other defendants who simply answered yes or no.[147]

Ironically, speakers or writers who deny an assertion the audience initially believes to be false often lead the audience to conclude the assertion must be true. For example, claiming that one is not arrogant can boomerang and increase audience perceptions of arrogance.[148] When a group of voters was asked to read a newspaper report that denied President Ronald Reagan was an alcoholic—a statement most of them initially believed was false—the group came to believe Reagan was an alcoholic to a greater extent than those who did not read the report. Conversely, voters who read a newspaper report that affirmed a statement they initially believed to be true (e.g., Republican congressmen belong to elitist country clubs) came to believe that statement less.[149]

Cognitive Processes in Person Perception

This section presents a model of person perception that describes how audiences evaluate the professionals who communicate with them. Social psychological processes, such as person perception, rest on and involve more rudimentary psychological processes such as attention, perception, memory, etc.[150] The model, as illustrated in Figure 6.1, consists of six basic cognitive processes—*perception, attention, trait/emotion comprehension, schema activation, information acquisition,* and *information integration.*

The processes described in this model of person perception are essentially the same cognitive processes as described in Chapter 3. However, the model of person perception differs from the model of audience decision making in several ways. First the model allows for the input of professionals' nonverbal behaviors in addition to the input of the verbal information they convey. Next, the model assumes audience perceptions of professionals' nonverbal behaviors are automatic and occur in parallel with their perceptions of verbal information.[151]

Finally, the model characterizes the verbal information conveyed by professionals as verbal behaviors as opposed to information about a topic. To grasp this distinction, suppose a salesman at a Toyota dealership excitedly tells a customer, "The new Toyota Prius gets 60 miles per gallon in the city compared to 36 mpg for the Ford Hybrid Escape!" If the customer uses the salesman's sentence to compare the two cars, the customer would be characterizing the sentence as information about the topic of the two cars' fuel efficiency. On the other hand, if the customer uses the sentence to infer the salesman's personality traits, emotions, and competency as a salesperson, then the customer would be characterizing the sentence as a set of verbal behaviors (e.g., the sentence has specific quantifiable facts; it uses correct grammar, and was spoken with feeling). Thus, instead of thinking that the Prius is more economical than the Escape, the customer might infer that the salesman is knowledgeable, articulate, and enthusiastic. Moreover, the customer may begin to believe that this salesman is good at his job.

Perception of Professionals' Trait-Related Behaviors

Audiences spontaneously infer a professional's personality traits—extraversion, neuroticism, conscientiousness, agreeableness, openness—when they perceive the professional's nonverbal behaviors.[152] For example, audiences spontaneously infer a person is highly extroverted if the person has a stylish haircut, wears fashionable clothing, has a friendly expression, displays frequent and rapid body movements, and walks in a relaxed manner.[153] Audiences spontaneously infer a person is intelligent if they see them formally dressed.[154] When college students see an instructor who is dressed informally, they infer the instructor is less intelligent but more friendly than instructors who dress in more formal attire.[155]

Audiences also spontaneously infer a professional's traits based on observations of verbal cues such as word choice.[156] An individual's word choice plays an especially significant role in audience perceptions of traits such as dominance, competence, trustworthiness, cooperativeness,[157] and intelligence.[158]

The audience's spontaneous inferences about others' traits are preconscious and automatic.[159] When given a written description of another person's verbal and nonverbal behaviors, readers spontaneously infer the other person's traits yet they are typically unaware they do so.[160] In fact, most audience members are not aware of how the trait inferences they make arise. For example, although loan officers' assessments of loan applicants' traits can be traced to specific observable cues in the applicants' behavior, most loan officers regard their assessments as arising from intuitions or gut feelings.[161]

Brain Regions Activated. Neuroscientists find that four brain regions are activated during such spontaneous forms of person perception. These regions include the amygdala, the ventromedial prefrontal cortex (vmPFC), lateral regions of the temporal lobe, and the ventral striatum, a region at the lower front of the striatum that functions as part of the reward system (see Figures 3.4 and 3.5, p. 108).[162]

The nonverbal cues that trigger spontaneous trait inferences about others are most often valid.[163] For example, the nonverbal visual cues audiences use to infer extraversion and aloofness are valid indicators of those traits.[164] People who wear glasses do tend to be more introverted and less open to experience just as most audiences assume.[165] "Baby-faced" men are indeed more introverted and less assertive than those with more mature-appearing facial features.[166] People who make less eye contact do tend to be shy and socially anxious.[167] People who maintain greater interpersonal

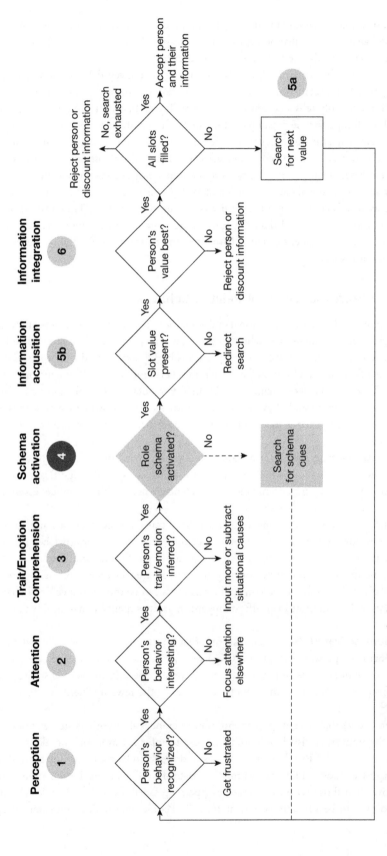

FIGURE 6.1 A Cognitive Process Model of Person Perception

distance also tend to be shy and socially anxious.[168] The ways in which people dress and move have also been shown to be valid indicators of traits such as extraversion, openness, and even intelligence.[169]

Nonverbal vocal cues such as tone of voice are additional valid indicators of the speaker's actual traits.[170] Speakers who speak in a very loud voice do indeed tend to be extroverts.[171] Speakers with shorter response latencies are more likely to be extroverts as well.[172]

Thus, the audience's spontaneous inferences about the personality traits of others are usually quite accurate.[173] Based on their observation of another's body movements alone, viewers can make accurate inferences regarding the person's extraversion, warmth, and trustworthiness.[174] Based on their observation of nonverbal vocal cues alone, listeners can accurately determine a speaker's personality traits.[175] Another reason that the audience's judgments about others' personality traits are usually accurate is that people tend to be consistent in their behavior patterns across situations, both in their verbal[176] and nonverbal style.

In a study demonstrating the consistency of a person's nonverbal style across situations,[177] viewers watched videos of 164 college students in three meetings with another student of the opposite sex and then rated the degree to which the students engaged in each of 62 different nonverbal behaviors. In the first two meetings, the students were strangers to each other and were given no prescribed topic of conversation. In the third meeting, the two students from the second meeting met again and were asked to debate the issue of capital punishment. The viewers ascertained that a large number of the students' nonverbal behaviors were consistent across all three situations. The eight most consistent nonverbal behaviors follow in order of their degree of consistency:

1. Speaks in a loud voice
2. Behaves in a fearful or timid manner
3. Expressive in face, voice, or gestures
4. Speaks quickly
5. Engages in constant eye contact
6. Has high enthusiasm and energy
7. Is reserved and unexpressive
8. Is unconventional in appearance

Given their ability to make accurate trait inferences, it's not surprising that audience members tend to agree with each other when asked to judge the personality traits of others.[178] For example, judges of college applicants' essays show substantial agreement in the personality traits they attribute to the applicants who wrote them.[179] Audience members tend to agree on the personality traits of others even when they base their judgments on their first impressions alone.[180] Consensus among audience members has even been observed cross-culturally, suggesting that audience perceptions of personality traits may have a universal basis.[181]

Audience members' spontaneous inferences about others' personality traits are not only remarkably accurate, they are also remarkably fast.[182] A mere 100 millisecond exposure to an unfamiliar face is sufficient for audience members to draw inferences about the person's likeability, trustworthiness, competence, and aggressiveness that are similar to those generated under longer viewing times.[183] For threat judgments, a 39 millisecond exposure to an unfamiliar face is sufficient.[184]

In a now classic series of experiments, social psychologists Nalini Ambady and Robert Rosenthal asked college students to watch three 10-second video clips, or "thin slices," of unfamiliar professors and then rate the professors' teaching effectiveness. Even with the sound turned off, the students had no trouble rating the professors on the basis of their nonverbal behaviors alone. Students also gave the professors similar ratings after viewing silent video clips just five seconds and two seconds long. Surprisingly, the students' ratings were highly correlated with ratings made by the professors' actual students after a full semester of classes.[185] Similar experiments with thin-slice exposures to others' nonverbal behaviors find that audience members can also make accurate inferences about trial outcomes,[186] employees' status within a company,[187] and conversing partners' IQs.[188]

In addition to making fast and accurate inferences about others' personality traits, audience members are also accurate when making other types of inferences based on nonverbal behaviors. For example, listeners can reliably predict a manager's job performance based solely on the manager's tone of voice.[189] From nonverbal vocal cues alone, listeners can determine not only a speaker's gender,[190] age,[191] socioeconomic background,[192] ethnic group,[193] and place of origin,[194] but also their status in small groups.[195]

Perception of Professionals' Emotion-Related Behaviors

For the audience to comprehend which emotion a professional is experiencing, they must first be able to see, hear, and recognize that professional's verbal and nonverbal behaviors. Even the direction of a speaker's eye gaze is an important nonverbal visual cue to their emotions. Direct eye gaze enhances the audience's perception of both anger and joy whereas averted eye gaze enhances their perception of fear and sadness.[196] An often cited study finds that audience perceptions of a speaker's emotions are determined 55% by nonverbal visual cues, 38% by nonverbal vocal cues, and only 7% by the verbal content of the speaker's message.[197]

One of the most important nonverbal visual cues to others' emotions is their facial expression of emotion (see Figure 6.2). There is widespread cross-cultural agreement about the emotions certain facial expressions communicate.[198] A review of 25 studies involving participants from more than 35 cultures worldwide finds that people in different cultures exhibit similar prototypical facial displays of anger, contempt, disgust, fear, pride, sadness, surprise, and happiness when in comparable situations.[199]

The specific emotions an audience can infer on the basis of another's facial expressions include happiness, anger, sadness, fear, disgust, contempt, and surprise.[200] A series of electromyograph (EMG) studies of viewers looking at photographs of happy and sad facial expressions demonstrated that audiences can infer emotions from facial expressions automatically. Viewers smile slightly when looking at happy faces and frown slightly when looking at angry faces even when the photographs of the faces are presented to them subliminally.[201]

Although perceiving another's emotions can be done automatically, it does take some effort. An eye-fixation study finds that viewers who are asked to identify another's emotion make significantly more fixations on faces that express emotion than on faces expressing no emotion. On average, viewers in the study made 11 fixations on faces that showed emotion versus 6.5 fixations on neutral

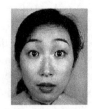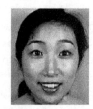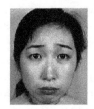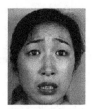

FIGURE 6.2 Audiences Scan Others' Facial Expressions to Infer Their Emotions

Source: The Japanese Female Facial Expression (JAFFE) Database. Lyons, Akamatsu, Kamachi, and Gyoba (1998 , p. 203)

faces. Moreover, the more fixations the viewers made, the more accurate their identification of the other's emotions.[202] To identify different emotions, viewers must fixate on different parts of the face.[203] Identifying anger, fear, and sadness requires viewers to scan the top half of the face. Identifying disgust and happiness requires them to scan the bottom half. However, viewers can accurately identify surprise by scanning either the top or bottom half of the face.

Audiences are remarkably fast at identifying the emotions of other people on the basis of their facial expressions. It typically takes audiences only 12 to 25 milliseconds.[204] Audiences can identify another's facial expressions of emotions most rapidly when their facial expression is emotionally congruent with their body posture.[205]

Audiences are also remarkably accurate at identifying the emotions of other people on the basis of their facial expressions.[206] Audiences recognize the facial expressions associated with joy and disgust with close to 100% accuracy.[207] Their accuracy is due to the fact that smiling for joy and nose wrinkling for disgust are highly specific expressions for those emotions. Audiences are also quite accurate at judging others' emotions even when they observe their facial expressions only briefly.[208] However, audiences can more accurately recognize another's emotions when they see a video of them making facial expressions as opposed to viewing a static photograph of their face.[209]

Brain Regions Activated. Neuroscientists find that emotional faces elicit increased activity in the viewer's amygdala. Emotional faces also increase activity in core regions of the face-processing system such as the fusiform face area located in the lower temporal and occipital lobes of both hemispheres (see Figures 3.4 and 3.5, p. 108).[210] The amygdala is especially attuned to recognizing facial expressions that signal danger or fear.[211] The brain region attuned to recognizing facial expressions of disgust, on the other hand, is the insular cortex, located beneath the juncture of the frontal, temporal, and parietal lobes.[212]

Audiences can also make accurate judgments of others' emotions on the basis of their bodily postures. A study of audience members' attributions of six emotions (anger, disgust, fear, happiness, sadness, and surprise) to static body postures finds that although audience members often confuse postures that indicate happiness and surprise, they rarely confuse postures indicating the other four emotions.[213]

When the audience can see a person move, their ability to recognize the person's emotions is significantly enhanced.[214] Even the motion of isolated body parts, such as the manner in which a person moves her arm while drinking a beverage, waving goodbye, or lifting a chair, can be sufficient to enable viewers to infer the emotional state of the person.[215] When observing another's movements, viewers infer anger or elation from faster, more energetic, and spatially expansive movements. They infer contempt, sadness, and boredom from movements that are slower and constricted.[216]

Brain Regions Activated. Neuroscientists find that emotionally expressive body postures and movements evoke an elevated response in the viewer's core body perception system located in the temporal and occipital lobes.[217] Observation of such postures also increases activity in the amygdala (see Figures 3.4 and 3.5, p. 108).[218]

In addition to using nonverbal visual cues to infer others' emotions, audiences also infer emotions on the basis of nonverbal vocal cues. In an analysis of how listeners evaluate emotional speech, 12 professional theater actors vocally expressed 14 different emotions. The analysis revealed that listeners judged each emotion expressed by the actors, such as rage, panic, and elation, to have a distinct acoustic profile. Listeners inferred anger when the actors spoke in a high and varied pitch that also varied in intensity. Listeners inferred sadness when the actors spoke quietly. Listeners inferred fear when the actors spoke quietly but in a sustained high pitch. And listeners inferred boredom when the actors spoke quietly and slowly in a low pitched voice.[219]

Other tests of the role vocal attributes play in emotion perception find that variations in speed and pitch tend to have the strongest influence on audience impressions. Audiences interpret moderate pitch variations in a speaker's voice as an indication of sadness, disgust, and boredom. They interpret a rising pitch and extreme pitch variations as indications of happiness, interest, and fear.[220]

Interestingly, members of one culture can recognize the vocal expressions of emotions made by members of other cultures.[221] In a cross-cultural study of emotion perception, listeners from different countries all associated a slow speaking rate and minimal pitch variation with sadness. In contrast, they associated a fast speaking rate and greater pitch variation with anger and fear, and a moderate speaking rate but greater pitch variation with happiness.[222] In another cross-cultural study, people from nine countries, eight European and one Asian, listened to language-free speech samples in which vocal cues expressed emotions. The listeners had an average accuracy of 66% across all emotions and countries, with the emotion of anger being recognized most accurately and joy least.[223] Apparently, speakers across the globe vocally express most emotions in similar ways.[224]

When listening to speech in their native language, listeners can recognize vocally expressed emotion with accuracy rates that approach 70% for anger, fear, sadness, happiness, and tenderness.[225] Listeners generally recognize the emotions of sadness and anger best, followed by fear.[226] Listeners can even tell whether their conversational partner on the telephone is smiling.[227] However, native listeners' recognition of vocal expressions of disgust is rarely above the level of chance.

Brain Regions Activated. Neuroscientists find that emotional prosody, as expressed in the voices of emotional speakers, activates a region of the right temporal lobe, whereas nonemotional prosody does not (see Figure 3.4, p. 108).[228]

Although audiences are able to infer emotions on the basis of the speaker's tone of voice alone, they are more accurate at inferring emotions when they can see the speaker's facial expressions as they speak.[229] In a study of multichannel cues to emotions, one group of students watched a video of speakers shown from the shoulders up who expressed anger, sadness, happiness, fear, and indifference. A second group watched the same video with the audio off. A third group listened to the video's audio track without watching the visual portion. The speakers read sentences whose content was emotionally neutral, such as "Please pass the salt" and "John, there is a man at the door." As expected, the students were most accurate at identifying the speakers' emotions when they could both see and hear the speakers. Yet the students were only slightly less accurate when they could see but not hear the speakers. When students heard the audio but could not see the speakers, their accuracy at identifying the speakers' emotions decreased significantly.[230]

When both facial and vocal cues are available but incongruent, audiences will tend to base their evaluations of the speaker's emotions predominantly on facial cues.[231] Even so, audiences are fastest and most accurate at identifying a speaker's emotions when the speaker speaks in a tone of voice that is emotionally congruent with their facial expression.[232]

In addition to nonverbal cues, audiences use verbal cues to infer speakers' emotions. One verbal cue that indicates emotional arousal is a low frequency of unique words (i.e., a smaller vocabulary). Greater numbers of unique words tend to indicate that speakers are experiencing only a low level of arousal.[233] Another verbal behavior that indicates the speaker is emotionally aroused is a decrease in speaking fluency.

If the audience perceives that a speaker's facial expressions are emotionally inconsistent with their verbal message, the audience will make inferences based either on the speaker's facial expressions or on the speaker's verbal message, but not on both together.[234] In those situations, perceptions of facial expressions usually dominate the verbal message.[235] When sentencing a defendant, for example, mock jurors are more influenced by the defendant's facial expressions of remorse than by their verbal statements of remorse.[236]

Audiences also use verbal cues to infer the emotions of writers, as the story of the following email reprimand illustrates. Verbal behaviors indicating upset and anger in a CEO's email to his managers—profanity, threats, insults, sarcasm, and ultimatums—caused a stir on Wall Street after an offended manager posted the CEO's email on one of Yahoo's online investor message boards. "We are getting less than 40 hours of work from a large number of our K C-based EMPLOYEES," the CEO's email began.

> The parking lot is sparsely used at 8 a.m.; likewise at 5 p.m. As managers—you either do not know what your EMPLOYEES are doing; or you do not CARE. You have created expectations on the work effort which allowed this to happen inside Cerner, creating a very unhealthy environment. In either case, you have a problem and you will fix it or I will replace you. NEVER in my career have I allowed a team which worked for me to think they had a 40-hour job. I have allowed YOU to create a culture which is permitting this. NO LONGER.

After listing the ways employees would be punished if the company parking lot were not full between 7:30 a.m. and 6:30 p.m. and exclaiming that "what you are doing, as managers, with this company makes me SICK," the email ended with "You have two weeks. Tick, tock."[237]

Almost immediately after the CEO's email was posted, the company's stock price plummeted 22%. A few days later, the CEO apologized to his staff in a follow-up email as well as in an article in the local newspaper, but his efforts were not enough. The company's stock hit bottom three weeks after an article about the email appeared on the front page of the business section of *The New York Times*.

Attention to Professionals and Their Behaviors

Compared with objects, human beings capture a disproportionate amount of the audience's attention.[238] Professionals attract more attention than other people within the audience's view when they are better lit, dressed differently, or walking while others are sitting.[239] A professional also attracts more attention from audience members when she sits down directly opposite them.[240] In addition, unusual vocal behaviors such as an unusual pitch or a foreign accent can be attention getting. Audiences detect more typical behaviors in other people only if they attend to them carefully.[241]

When audience members are able to see a person speaking, they devote as much as 96% of their total viewing time attending to their face.[242] The default location of audience members' eye fixations is the bridge of the speaker's nose or the eye area.[243] A speaker's gaze triggers automatic shifts in the viewer's visual attention. When a speaker averts her gaze, audience members tend to follow the direction of her eyes to ensure they are attending to the same object or person, a phenomenon referred to as *joint attention*.[244]

Since audience members spend 96% of their viewing time looking at the speaker's face, they only occasionally fixate on the speaker's gestures.[245] In fact, audiences directly fixate on only 7% of all arm and hand gestures. However, audience members' peripheral vision is sufficient to allow them to perceive the speaker's gestures and to make sense of them even while they are fixating on the speaker's face.[246]

Audiences selectively attend to one speaker versus another depending on their current goal. For example, if two people are talking and one is a subordinate and the other a prospective client, the audience will attend to the person who is more important to them at the moment.[247] Audiences also selectively attend to those with power over them,[248] especially to leaders.[249] In addition, they will tend to ignore those who cannot help them achieve their goals.[250]

When attending to others during social interactions, audience members spontaneously imitate their nonverbal behaviors.[251] In conversation, people appear to imitate each other's accents, vocal tone, and vocal speed.[252] Audiences also spontaneously mimic others' postures, gestures, and mannerisms.[253] During social interactions, spontaneous imitation is actually the default behavior. Not engaging in imitation requires additional mental processing and tends to cause the audience stress. Interestingly, a conversational partner who is "anti-mimicked" during a social interaction will show signs of ego-depletion relative to one who is mimicked.[254]

Brain Regions Activated. Neuroscientists find that spontaneous imitation of another's nonverbal behaviors is associated with activation of the brain's *mirror system,* which is located in areas of the frontal and parietal lobes of both hemispheres (see Figure 3.4, p. 108).[255]

Unusual verbal and typographic behaviors can attract attention, too. The following email presents a CEO's quarterly report to his employees and one of his employee's think-aloud comments about it (note: the dates, firm's products, product names, and the employee's name have been changed). The CEO's use of all capital letters, block text, unusual words, unusual spacing and punctuation, and awkward phrasing stood out to the employee. These errors and unusual practices caught the employee's attention more than the report's verbal content about the firm's progress that quarter. Although the firm might have been on the right track financially, the CEO's verbal behaviors led the employee to infer that the firm's top management may be incompetent.

QUARTERLY REPORT FROM A CEO WITH AN EMPLOYEE'S COMMENTS

```
Sent: Monday, April 18, 2016 7:35 AM
Subject: 1st quarter results
```

JUST WANT TO TAKE A FEW MINUTES TO UPDATE YOU ON OUR FIRST QUARTER RESULTS. **[1. Why are you writing in all capital letters?]** WE FINISHED THE QUARTER WITH ALL OUR WIND TURBINES ON MRP II EXCEPT x5000's WHICH WERE MISSED DUE TO LATE PARTS FROM OUR OEM. I RECENTLY VISITED OUR OEM AND HAVE BEEN ASSURED THAT THEY WILL BE BACK ON PLAN BY 5/16. TIME WILL TELL FOR THEY HAVE NOT BEEN VERY RELIABLE IN THE PAST. WE HIT OUR INVENTORY TURNS GOAL OF 16.2 WHICH WAS A GREAT ACCOMPLISHMENT. **[2. One single paragraph jumping from one point to the next.]** WE ARE BEATING ALL OUR EH&S GOALS AND I DO NOT TAKE THIS FOR GRANTED. I KNOW IT TAKES A LOT OF WORK TO MAINTAIN A SAFE WORK ENVIRONMENT. WE HAVE HAD SOME BUMPS AND LUMPS ALONG THE WAY **[3. "bumps and lumps" doesn't sound like the proper choice of words. Did someone actually get hurt or is he referring to negative business results?]** BUT ALL OUR .NEW **[4. Extra space and/or punctuation.]** WIND TURBINE PROGRAMS ARE IN PRETTY GOOD SHAPE. WE WILL START ASSEMBLING THE FIRST PRODUCTION HS7000 ON MONDAY AND I HAVE BEEN ASSURED BY ASHISH AND HIS FOLKS THAT THE TURBINE WILL BE ASSEMBLED AND TESTED WITHIN THE NEXT DAYS. THIS HAS BEEN A SUPER EFFORT ON BEHALF OF A LOT OF HIS FOLKS WHO HAVE PUT IN HUNDREDS OF OVERTIME HOURS TO MAKE THIS HAPPEN. WE HAD SOME UNPLANNED COST ROLL IN ON US THAT PUTS OUR FINANCIAL PLAN AT RISK FOR THE YEAR IF WE DO NOT TAKE IMMEDIATE ACTION. HOWEVER, WE HAVE PUT IN PLACE A COST ASSURANCE PLAN TO GET US BACK ON PLAN AND I WILL ENSURE THAT YOU ALL UNDERSTAND THIS PLAN, FOR WITHOUT YOUR HELP AND COOPERATION WE WILL FAIL. **[5. This sentence regarding the cost assurance plan sounds very awkward and leaves me confused as to the CEO's intentions.]**

AGAIN, WE HAVE HAD A VERY GOOD FIRST QUARTER. THANK YOU, AND I WANT YOU TO KNOW THAT I APPRECIATE YOUR EFFORTS EVERY DAY. **[6. This doesn't make me feel confident about management's ability to lead.]**

Comprehension of Professionals' Traits and Emotions

How audiences infer a person's traits or comprehend a person's character from observations of their behaviors is a central concern of the field of person perception as well as the field that grew out of it—social cognition.[256] As we have seen, audiences quickly and spontaneously encode perceived behaviors in terms of trait categories, such as friendliness, dominance, competence, and intelligence.[257] Audiences also quickly and spontaneously encode perceived behaviors in terms of specific emotions, such as fear, anger, and happiness.[258]

Although spontaneous, the ability to comprehend another's traits is a learned skill and requires more than simply perceiving their behaviors. As developmental psychologists have observed, young children do not explain others' behaviors in terms of their traits. Instead, they explain behaviors in terms of the concrete situations that others are involved in.[259]

Just as the ability to comprehend another person's traits is a learned skill, the ability to comprehend another's emotions is a learned skill as well and requires more than simply perceiving another's behaviors. In a study of emotion comprehension, children aged 5 to 14 years watched videos of speakers who were either happy, angry, sad, or emotionally neutral. Chronological age was a significant predictor of a child's ability to infer a speaker's emotions, with older children doing better than younger ones. Verbal intelligence is another significant predictor of a child's ability to infer another's emotions.[260]

The process of comprehending another's traits sometimes includes more than one step. If the audience is not preoccupied with other tasks, it may use situational information to modify or correct initial trait inferences. In a study of how audiences comprehend speakers' traits, two groups listened to a speaker read either a proabortion or an antiabortion speech. Both groups received the same situational information: The speaker had not written the speech but had been assigned to read a speech written by another person. One group simply listened to the speaker. The other group listened to the speaker knowing that later they would be asked to write and read aloud a speech of their own. The first group who simply listened discounted the speech's verbal content when inferring the speaker's traits. They took into account the fact that the speaker had been assigned to read a speech she had not written. In contrast, the preoccupied group inferred the speaker's traits based on the speech's verbal content and neglected to adjust their initial impressions to account for the situational information they had been given.[261] Once audience members develop an understanding of someone's personality traits, they are usually reluctant to revise it.[262]

Just as they do in trait comprehension, audiences may also take into account situational variables when trying to comprehend another's emotions. In a study of emotion comprehension, audience members viewed ambiguous or unambiguous facial reactions of target individuals to emotional situations. When the audience tried to identify ambiguous facial expressions, the emotional situation to which the target individual was reacting had a significant influence on the audience's inferences about the target's emotions.[263]

Brain Regions Activated. Neuroscientists find that a different set of brain regions are activated when audience members engage in controlled, as opposed to purely spontaneous, forms of person perception. When audience members take into account situational information and revise the spontaneous inferences they have made about others, the lateral, medial, and dorsomedial prefrontal cortex, as well as the lateral parietal lobe, precuneus, and medial temporal lobe are all activated (see Figures 3.4 and 3.5, p. 108).[264]

Activation of Role Schemata

One of the primary reasons audiences infer the traits of professionals is to determine how well they fit a particular occupational or leadership role. Does my new doctor exhibit the traits I expect in a good doctor? Does our team's new coach display the enthusiasm a good coach requires? To make decisions of this nature, the audience must first activate a role schema.

Particular role schemata may be activated through either a bottom-up or a top-down process. Bottom-up activation may result from the audience's perception of physical cues to the person's role such as their clothing (e.g., a clerical collar, a lab coat, or a chef's hat), their tools (e.g., a stethoscope, a dust mop, or a pitchfork), or the vehicle they drive (e.g., an ambulance, a delivery van, or a backhoe).[265] Top-down activation of a role schema might result from any one of several causes, including the recency of the schema's prior activation or priming,[266] its frequency of activation,[267] or the audience's goal or purpose for observing the individual.[268]

Situational information can also activate role schemata. In a study of leadership schemata, two groups of mock recruiters selected job candidates to manage either in a crisis or in a tranquil situation. Both groups received the same information about the candidates. But the recruiters who expected the candidates they interviewed to manage in a crisis had a greater false recall of leadership behaviors compared to the recruiters who expected the candidates to manage when everything was going smoothly. The study argues that crisis scenarios activate recruiters' leadership schemata.[269] The activation of voters' leadership schemata may explain why presidential approval ratings consistently increase after government-issued warnings of impending terrorist attacks.[270]

In another study of the effects of role schema activation on audience perceptions, some viewers were led to believe they would see a trial and other viewers to believe they would watch a social interaction. Viewers who expected to watch a trial inferred that the target individual was a defendant and decided the target was more responsible for a crime than viewers who thought they had seen a social interaction.[271]

Acquisition of Information About Behaviors, Traits, and Emotions

Audiences actively search for information about professionals' behaviors, traits, and emotions once they have activated a role schema. The activated role schema guides the audience to attend to the behaviors, traits, and emotions that are relevant to that role. In a study of how different role schemata lead viewers to observe different behaviors, two groups of viewers watched videos of couples interacting with each other in ways that were rated as ambiguous in terms of their degree of intimacy. One group of viewers was told they would see a couple just becoming acquainted. The other group was told they would observe a married couple. The two groups of viewers, primed with different role schemata, observed different nonverbal behaviors and made different types of inferences when making judgments about the couple.[272]

Depending on the role schema that has been activated, viewers also infer different meaningful breaks in the same sequence of actions or interactions. In a study of perceived breakpoints, two groups of viewers watched a video of an interaction between one large and two small geometric figures that represented people of different sizes. The two groups were asked to press a button each time they perceived a meaningful break in the action such as when the figures moved toward each other, stopped moving, or grasped each other. One group of viewers was told the large figure was a rapist (rapist role) attacking the two smaller figures (victim role). The other group was told the large figure was a "guardian of treasure" (guard role) and that the two smaller figures were burglars (thief role). The first group identified breaks in the action that were substantially different from the ones the second group identified.[273] A review of the breakpoint research concludes that audiences are able to search for different features of others' ongoing nonverbal behaviors just as they are able to search for different verbal information in documents.[274]

Audiences will assume that the default slot values of their activated role schema are correct unless they have access to more accurate individuating information about the person they are observing.[275] When audiences have little individuating information about the person, they will fill the empty slots in their schema with information that is true of the stereotype.[276]

Moreover, when stereotypical information is made available to them, audiences seek less individuating information about target individuals. In one study, 346 undergraduates were allowed to request information describing several target individuals so they could form impressions of them. The target individuals were identified either by occupations associated with a stereotype (e.g., a librarian) or by nondescriptive labels (e.g., "Person 1"). When targets were identified by occupations associated with a stereotype, the students requested very little information about them.[277]

An activated role schema also affects audience recall. Audience members who are told about a person's occupation before meeting them remember information about the person that is consistent with the person's occupation better than information that is inconsistent with it.[278] In a study of the effects of role schemata activated after the audience had observed an individual, viewers first watched a video of a conversation between a woman and her husband. Then half of the viewers were told she was a waitress, and the other half the woman was a librarian. In the video, she exhibited an equal number of prototypical waitress and librarian behaviors. After learning the woman's occupation, the viewers recalled behaviors that were consistent with the primed role schema more accurately than behaviors that did not fit the stereotype.[279]

In another study of the effects of role schemata on recall, mock recruiters read a list of traits describing a job applicant. The mock recruiters were then asked to decide if the applicant was suitable for a particular occupation, thus activating a particular role schema. The mock recruiters recalled applicant traits from the list that were relevant to the activated role schema better than irrelevant traits.[280] In a similar study, students watched another student registering for college classes. Then the students were told that the other student was either a chemistry, music, or psychology major. The students recalled significantly more facts about the other student that were consistent with the other student's supposed major than facts that were inconsistent with it.[281]

Once a role schema is activated, audiences may even confuse a person's actual behavior with the schema's default behaviors. A test of viewers' memories of prototypical leadership behaviors finds that viewers have difficulty distinguishing between schema-consistent behaviors that were present in a target leader and those that were not.[282] When audiences encounter behaviors that are inconsistent with the default behaviors of their activated role schema, they take longer both to encode and to acquire them.[283]

Integration of Information About Behaviors, Traits, and Emotions

Once the audience acquires information about a professional's behaviors, traits, and emotions that is relevant to their activated role schema, how does the audience combine that information to arrive at an overall impression of or attitude toward the person? A think-aloud study of voters deciding between two political candidates found that the voters rarely produced overall evaluative statements about the two candidates. Instead, they first conducted an attribute-based search and compared the two candidates on the basis of a few traits or attributes. Then they used a noncompensatory choice rule called the *majority-of-confirming-dimensions rule* and chose the candidate with the highest number of favorable comparisons. Only if this comparison resulted in a tie did voters decide on the basis of political party stereotypes. Interestingly, this model of voter decision making appears to be highly predictive of voter choice.[284]

When the audience's task is to evaluate a single individual, as opposed to decide among different individuals, the two rules audiences most frequently use are the weighted and unweighted averaging rules.[285] Both rules are compensatory and rely on alternative-based search. And both have much in common with the normative weighted additive choice rule.

In his seminal study of information integration, social psychologist Norman Anderson asked participants to read paragraphs about several U.S. presidents and then to rate each president's statesmanship and accomplishments on a scale that that ranged from 0 to 10. For each president readers received two paragraphs that were either positive, neutral, or negative toward that president. Readers who read two positive paragraphs about a president formed a very positive impression of him. Readers who received both a neutral and a positive paragraph formed a moderately positive impression. And readers who received two negative paragraphs formed an extremely negative impression. Professor Anderson found that all readers, even those who were exposed to conflicting messages about a president, formed an impression that corresponded to the unweighted average value of the two messages.[286]

Audiences use the weighted and unweighted averaging rules to evaluate others in a wide range of situations. In a study of personnel selection, personnel managers read verbal descriptions of job applicants' personality traits. Each trait was described in terms of one of four scale values (low, below average, above average, and high). The results showed that the personnel managers used the weighted averaging rule to judge each of the applicants.[287] In a study of health care decisions, parents read verbal descriptions of pediatricians and were asked to evaluate them. Each pediatrician was described in terms of the doctor's ability to handle children and the quality of her staff's manners. Each of these attributes varied across four scale values (low, below average, above average, and high). In this case, the parents evaluated each pediatrician using the unweighted averaging rule.[288]

Audiences also use averaging rules to integrate visual information about other people with verbal information about them. In a study of visual/verbal information integration, female college students looked at photographs of male college students, read descriptions of the male students' personal characteristics, and then evaluated the male students' dating desirability. The study showed that the female students used the weighted averaging rule to integrate the male students' physical attractiveness with the verbal descriptions of their personal characteristics.[289] A study of juror decision making comes to a similar conclusion: Jurors decide the guilt or innocence of defendants by combining relevant verbal information with the defendants' nonverbal behaviors using the weighted averaging rule.[290]

What types of information do audiences tend to weight more heavily when integrating information about the people they perceive? Research shows that audiences tend to give more weight to information that is inconsistent with the other information they have about the individual.[291] It also shows that they weight negative information more heavily than positive information.[292] Recruiters weight negative information about job applicants more heavily[293] because they believe that negative behaviors, as well as extreme ones, are particularly diagnostic of job applicants' personality traits.[294]

When making some types of decisions, audience members must also be able to integrate quantitative information with their subjective impressions of others. For example, when loan officers make lending decisions, they have to integrate "hard" financial data about the loan applicant's credit worthiness with their "soft" intuitions about the loan applicant's credibility.[295] Interestingly, loan officers regard their intuitions as more valid indicators of the worthiness of a loan application than the relevant financial indicators.

Biases in Person Perception

The Attractiveness Bias: The Persuasive Appeal of Good Looks

Audiences are more likely to be biased toward and persuaded by attractive professionals than by unattractive ones.[296] For example, attractive product endorsers in advertisements are more persuasive than less attractive endorsers.[297] Somewhat alarmingly, attractive professionals are equally persuasive whether or not their messages include supportive argumentation.[298] Even when no explicit evaluation of them or their message is required, attractive professionals elicit feelings of positivity from audience members.[299]

Attractive professionals are more persuasive in a variety of situations and media. Attractive professionals tend to be more persuasive as salespeople,[300] as survey solicitors,[301] and as attitude change agents.[302] In the courtroom, physically attractive surrogates who read the depositions of expert witnesses unable to appear in court are more persuasive than less attractive surrogates.[303] In a study of fundraisers for the American Heart Association, attractive fundraisers generated nearly twice as many donations as less attractive ones.[304] When emotionally charged advertisements are attributed to attractive endorsers, customers tend to like the product more and express more intentions to buy.[305] A large-scale study of a lender's direct mail solicitation to potential borrowers that offered them substantial, short-term loans finds that adding a photograph of an attractive smiling woman has the same positive effect on both male and female borrowers' acceptance of a loan offer as dropping the monthly interest rate by 25%.[306]

Audiences also tend to attribute more desirable personal traits to physically attractive professionals.[307] Attractive people are deemed to be more sociable, altruistic, and intelligent than their less attractive counterparts.[308] Voters attribute more desirable personal traits to physically attractive political candidates than to less attractive opposing candidates.[309] Although they are unaware of the role physical appearance plays in their hiring decisions, students conducting mock job interviews are more likely to hire well-groomed but less qualified job applicants than better qualified but poorly groomed applicants.[310] Mock jurors are less likely to find attractive defendants guilty, unless they used their good looks to commit the crime.[311] Indeed, actual courtroom evidence shows that physical attractiveness is one of the greatest advantages a defendant can have.[312] On the job, heightened attractiveness is related to better employment prospects,[313] more advantageous work evaluations,[314] and increased earning potential.[315]

Expertise has the power to mitigate the effects of the attractiveness bias. In contrast to the way students playing recruiters make hiring decisions, a study of experienced personnel managers finds they make hiring decisions exclusively on the basis of recommendations and experience. None of the personnel managers in the study showed significant effects for irrelevant attributes such as the applicants' gender, age, or physical attractiveness.[316]

The Status Bias: The Persuasive Appeal of High Status

Audiences who believe a professional has high status are more likely to comply with the professional's requests. For example, audiences are more likely to comply with the requests of speakers who are well dressed—suits and ties for men, dress clothes for women—than with the requests of speakers who are poorly dressed.[317] Speakers who wear more formal and higher-status clothing are especially effective at gaining compliance from lower-status listeners.[318]

Speakers who have a high-status speaking style are also more persuasive.[319] Movie theater audiences are more likely to comply with a request made over the public address system when the announcer uses a standard speaking style versus a colloquial, lower-status style.[320] Consumers sometimes make purchasing decisions on the basis of a salesperson's speaking style alone.[321] Audience attitudes about the status of a speakers' speaking style also play a role in medical encounters,[322] legal settings,[323] employment contexts,[324] offers of help,[325] and housing discrimination hearings.[326]

Audience evaluations of professionals' speaking styles are based in part on the social class the professionals' linguistic behaviors activate.[327] Sociolinguists have demonstrated the existence of social class differences for several linguistic variables, including syntax,[328] lexical choice,[329] and intonation.[330] Sociolinguists have also shown that audiences use such linguistic cues not only to determine a speaker's social class[331] but also to determine the validity of their arguments. In a study of the effects of regional dialects, 250 people from two dialect areas listened to arguments spoken in the standard dialect and in regional dialects of lesser prestige. The listeners' perceptions of argument quality varied directly with the prestige of the speaker's accent.[332] Moreover, standard English speakers are evaluated more favorably than nonstandard speakers, even when information about their social class is held constant.[333]

Surprisingly, if listeners are led to believe a professional has high status, they will perceive her speaking style to be more like the standard style than if they believe she is of lower status.[334] Standard speech is not intrinsically more appealing than nonstandard speech, however. Listeners cannot discriminate among unfamiliar foreign speaking styles on the basis of aesthetic criteria. Instead, listeners' evaluations of familiar speaking styles reflect the levels of status and prestige of those who speak that way.[335]

The Confidence Bias: The Persuasive Appeal of Confidence

Professionals' confidence in their recommendations, regardless of their recommendations' actual validity, is one of the primary determinants of audiences' decisions.[336] Audiences weight the recommendations of confident speakers more heavily and are more confident when adopting them. Confident group members have more influence on group decisions than group members who are tentative and uncertain.[337]

Linguistic style is one cue audiences use to assess a professional's confidence. Audiences are more persuaded by speakers who express confidence by speaking in a powerful style than by those who speak in a style that indicates powerlessness.[338] As we have seen, the frequent use of intensifiers (e.g., "really big"), hedges (e.g., "I think"), hesitation forms (e.g., "and, uh"), and questioning intonations characterizes the powerless speaking style. Conversely, the speaking styles of powerful and confident individuals rarely display those behaviors. In juror decision making, witnesses who speak in a confident or powerful speech style obtain more favorable jury decisions.[339] In employment interviews, job candidates who speak in a confident or powerful speech style are deemed to be more employable.[340] When audiences read written transcriptions of spoken messages that were delivered in a confident, powerful speech style, however, the persuasive effects of the powerful speech style are greatly diminished.[341]

Provocative statements are another cue audiences use to assess the confidence of a professional. For example, clients perceive consultants who take an extreme position (e.g., asserting that a stock will double in value in the next month) to be more confident than those who take a more moderate position. Clients also find them to be more persuasive.[342]

Speakers who combine high status with a powerful speaking style are especially persuasive. For example, witnesses who have a high occupational status and who use a powerful speech style have a greater influence on mock jurors than low-status witnesses who use a powerless speech style.[343] Similarly, in group discussions, group members are more persuaded by subject-matter experts who combine high status with a powerful speech style.[344]

The Likeability Bias: The Persuasive Appeal of Friendliness

Audiences are more likely to be biased toward and persuaded by likable professionals than by unlikable ones.[345] For example, more likable job candidates tend to be rated more highly by recruiters.[346] More likable employees tend to be rated more highly on performance appraisals by their supervisors.[347] More likable surgeons are less likely to be sued by their patients for malpractice than their equally skilled but less agreeable counterparts.[348] Much of the reason for the difference in their patients' reactions appears to be determined by the surgeon's tone of voice.[349]

In all walks of life, likable, friendly professionals tend to be more persuasive. For example, well-liked U.S. presidents are more effective in swaying public opinion than less-liked presidents.[350] In fact, less-liked presidents sometimes sway opinion in the opposite direction of the positions they advocate.[351] Solicitors who first give prospective donors a friendly handshake before requesting a donation are more effective at raising money for charities than less friendly solicitors do not first shake hands.[352] Other friendly nonverbal behaviors displayed by donation solicitors such as smiling[353] and eye contact[354] also produce more donations.

Audiences tend to like those who are expressive nonverbally more than those who are less expressive.[355] An audience's rating of another's likeability is highly influenced by nonverbal cues such as smiling, hand gestures, body posture, and eye contact.[356] It comes as no surprise that job applicants who smile more often in mock job interviews are rated as much more likable.[357]

Studies of audiences considering a wide range of requests find that increased compliance is associated with increased requester likeability. And increased likeability, in turn, is associated with increased gaze, conversational proximity, touch, open body orientation, smiling, nodding, and gesturing.[358] Salespeople who use high levels of gaze and expressive body movements influence customers more than salespeople who are less expressive[359] as do salespeople who display happy versus negative emotions.[360] Gazing at listeners while making a request is an especially effective way to increase their compliance.[361]

However, there are some limits to the persuasive power of likeability. For example, expert audiences appear to be less biased by likeability than novices.[362] And a speaker's likeability exerts greater influence in video or audio recordings of their messages than in written transcripts of them.[363]

The Similarity Bias: The Persuasive Appeal of Similarity

Audiences are more likely to be biased toward and persuaded by professionals they perceive to be similar to themselves than by those they perceive to be dissimilar. For example, consumers who perceive a salesperson as similar to themselves are more likely to make the purchases the salesperson recommends.[364] Listeners who hear a speaker's arguments spoken in their own regional dialect are more likely to be persuaded by them than when they hear those same arguments are spoken in the standard dialect.[365] A study of the effects of similar dress finds that well-dressed solicitors are more successful in gaining compliance in airports where people are typically better dressed than in bus stops where people are typically less well dressed. Conversely, casually dressed solicitors are more successful at bus stops.[366] Audiences also tend to like others more when they perceive them to be similar to themselves.[367]

Similarity biases a wide range of audience decisions. Mock jurors are less likely to convict when they and the defendant have similar backgrounds, ethnicity, and beliefs.[368] Recruiters give higher ratings to job applicants who have similar attitudes and characteristics.[369] Similarities between a recruiter and a job applicant on demographic characteristics,[370] attitudes,[371] and experience[372] also affect the likelihood that the applicant will be offered a job.

Studies of group decision making find that as a group becomes more tight knit, the group's evaluation of their leader's effectiveness comes to depend less on the leader's fit with a generic leader schema and more on the degree to which the leader is perceived to be prototypical of, or similar to, the specific group's membership.[373] Perhaps this bias explains why U.S. presidents who put greater emphasis on their similarity to their followers are rated as more charismatic.[374]

Audiences also like more and are more persuaded by professionals who exhibit nonverbal behaviors similar to their own.[375] For example, people like conversational partners who mimic their smiling behaviors more than partners who do not.[376] A conversational partner's similar posture can also lead to increased rapport.[377] Mimicking the audience's behavior without their awareness causes them to be more helpful,[378] and in service situations, to provide bigger tips.[379] In a negotiation, vocal mirroring occurring within the first five minutes of the negotiation is highly predictive of the negotiated outcome, with more mirroring leading to better outcomes for the negotiator doing the mirroring.[380]

The Salience Bias: The Persuasive Appeal of Standing Out

Attention-getting or salient professionals are more persuasive than those who do not attract attention. Members of group discussions see attention-getting or salient group members as intrinsically persuasive. They may credit them with setting the tone of the meeting, deciding on topics to be covered, or guiding the discussion.[381] When a speaker gains attention and becomes salient by delivering an unexpected message—for example, when a member of the Republican party advocates a liberal policy—the persuasiveness of their message is amplified.[382]

In addition to being more persuaded by salient individuals, participants in meetings tend to view salient individuals as representing the group to which they belong. For example, a lone marketer in a meeting of accountants is likely to be seen as presenting the "marketing" perspective. Audiences will also exaggerate their evaluations of salient people. When a person is salient, audiences tend to evaluate the person's positive attributes more positively and to evaluate their negative attributes more negatively than when the person does not attract as much attention.[383]

Cognitive Centrality: The Power of Knowing What Others Know

Group members who possess more information shared by other group members (for a discussion of shared information, see Chapter 5, pp. 235–236), or who are more cognitively central, tend to be more persuasive in group decision making than those who possess less shared information.[384] A study of persuasive minority members finds that when the person in the minority in a three-person group possesses the most shared information, the other group members agree with their position 67% of the time.[385] When the person in the minority possesses the least amount of shared information, the other group members agree with their position only 42% of the time. Groups also tend to agree with the minority position when the person in the minority repeats more shared information than is repeated by those in the majority.[386]

Group members who possess more shared information tend to participate more in group discussions, get more reactions from other group members, and agree more with the group's decision than those who possess mostly unshared information that only they possess.[387] Group members who communicate more shared information are also viewed more favorably by the other members of the group.[388]

One reason shared information enhances a group member's influence is that other group members perceive shared information (i.e., the information they too possess) to be more credible and more valuable than unshared information.[389] Group members also evaluate information that can be corroborated by other group members more favorably whether or not they personally can corroborate it.[390] However, there is an important exception to the rule. Group members with more unshared information can be highly influential if their unshared information is relevant to the group's shared schema.[391]

PERSON PERCEPTION IN AUDIENCE DECISION MAKING: IMPLICATIONS FOR COMMUNICATORS

- The main takeaway for communicators in Chapter 6 is that audience decisions are based in part on audience perceptions of how well the professionals who communicate with them play their roles. Audience decisions are also biased by additional communicator attributes such as likeability and similarity. Who you are perceived to be can be as important as what you say and how you say it.
- Use the information presented in the chapter to adjust your behaviors and appearance to meet audience role expectations and to bias audiences in your favor. Do not expect audiences to adjust their biases to suit your personal style.
- Why use the information? To enhance the persuasiveness of your communications. To enhance audience perceptions of you as a leader.
- To become competent at the behaviors presented in the chapter, practice them and ask the audience for feedback.

Notes

1 Kraus, S. (1996). Winners of the first 1960 televised debate between Kennedy and Nixon. *Journal of Communication, 46,* 78–96.

2 McKinnon, L. M., & Tedesco, J. C. (1999). The influence of medium and media commentary on presidential debate effects. In L. L. Kaid & D. G. Bystrom (Eds.), *The electronic election: Perspectives on the 1996 campaign communication* (pp. 191–206). Mahwah, NJ: Lawrence Erlbaum.

McKinnon, L. M., Tedesco, J. C., & Kaid, L. L. (1993). The third 1992 presidential debate: Channel and commentary effects. *Argumentation and Advocacy, 30,* 106–118.

Patterson, M. L., Churchill, M. E., Burger, G. K., & Powell, J. L. (1992). Verbal and nonverbal modality effects on impressions of political candidates: Analysis from the 1984 presidential debates. *Communication Monographs, 59*(3), 231–242.

3 Hogan, R. (1991). Personality and personality measurement. In M. D. Dunnette & L. M. Hough (Eds.), *Handbook of industrial and organizational psychology* (2nd ed., Vol. 2, pp. 873–919). Palo Alto, CA: Consulting Psychologists Press.

Shamir, B. (1991). Meaning, self and motivation in organizations. *Organization Studies, 12*(3), 405–424.

Watson, D. (1989). Strangers' ratings of the five robust personality factors: Evidence of a surprising convergence with self-report. *Journal of Personality and Social Psychology, 57*(1), 120–128.

4 Slaughter, J. E., Zickar, M. J., Highhouse, S., & Mohr, D. C. (2004). Personality trait inferences about organizations: development of a measure and assessment of construct validity. *Journal of Applied Psychology, 89*(1), 85.

5 Aaker, J. L. (1997). Dimensions of brand personality. *Journal of Marketing Research*, *34*(3), 347–356.

Siguaw, J. A., Mattila, A., & Austin, J. R. (1999). The brand-personality scale. *The Cornell Hotel and Restaurant Administration Quarterly*, *40*(3), 48–5.

6 Pendergrast, M. (1993). *For God, country and Coca-Cola*. New York: Macmillan.

7 Plummer, J. T. (1985, February). Brand personality: A strategic concept for multinational advertising. In *Marketing Educators' Conference* (pp. 1–31). New York: Young & Rubicam.

8 Slaughter, J. E., & Greguras, G. J. (2009). Initial attraction to organizations: The influence of trait inferences. *International Journal of Selection and Assessment*, *17*(1), 1–18.

9 Abelson, R. P., Kinder, D. R., Peters, M. D., & Fiske, S. T. (1982). Affective and semantic components in political person perception. *Journal of Personality and Social Psychology*, *42*(4), 619–630.

Kinder, D. R., & Abelson, R. P. (1981, August). *Appraising presidential candidates: Personality and affect in the 1980 campaign*. Paper presented at the 1981 annual meeting of the American Political Science Association, New York.

Popkin, S., Gonnan, J. W., Phillips, C., & Smith, J. A. (1976). What have you done for me lately? Toward an investment theory of voting. *The American Political Science Review*, *70*, 779–805.

10 Glass, D. P. (1985). Evaluating presidential candidates: Who focuses on their personal attributes? *Public Opinion Quarterly*, *49*(4), 517–534.

11 Martin, D. S. (1978). Person perception and real-life electoral behaviour. *Australian Journal of Psychology*, *30*(3), 255–262.

12 Young, D. M., & Beier, E. G. (1977). The role of applicant nonverbal communication in the employment interview. *Journal of Employment Counseling*, *14*(4), 154–165.

13 McGovern, T. V., & Tinsley, H. E. (1978). Interviewer evaluations of interviewee nonverbal behavior. *Journal of Vocational Behavior*, *13*(2), 163–171.

14 McGovern, T. V., Jones, B. W., & Morris, S. E. (1979). Comparison of professional versus student ratings of job interviewee behavior. *Journal of Counseling Psychology*, *26*(2), 176–179.

15 Macan, T. H., & Dipboye, R. L. (1990). The relationship of interviewers' preinterview impressions to selection and recruitment outcomes. *Personnel Psychology*, *43*(4), 745–768.

Uggerslev, K. L., Fassina, N. E., & Kraichy, D. (2012). Recruiting through the stages: A meta-analytic test of predictors of applicant attraction at different stages of the recruiting process. *Personnel Psychology*, *65*(3), 597–660.

16 Schmitt, N., & Coyle, B. W. (1976). Applicant decisions in the employment interview. *Journal of Applied Psychology*, *61*(2), 184–192.

17 Kraichy, D., & Chapman, D. S. (2014). Tailoring web-based recruiting messages: Individual differences in the persuasiveness of affective and cognitive messages. *Journal of Business and Psychology*, *29*(2), 253–268.

18 Pincus, T. H. (1986). A crisis parachute: Helping stock prices have a soft landing. *The Journal of Business Strategy*, *6*(4), 32–38.

19 Haley, R. I., Richardson, J., & Baldwin, B. M. (1984). The effects of nonverbal communications in television advertising. *Journal of Advertising Research*, *24*(4), 11–18.

20 Albar, F. M. (2014). An investigation of fast and frugal heuristics for new product project selection (Doctoral dissertation, Portland State University, 2013). *Dissertation Abstracts International: Section B*, *74*(10-B)(E).

21 Chaiken, S., & Eagly, A. H. (1983). Communication modality as a determinant of persuasion: The role of communicator salience. *Journal of Personality and Social Psychology*, *45*(2), 241–256.

22 Carli, L. L., LaFleur, S. J., & Loeber, C. C. (1995). Nonverbal behavior, gender, and influence. *Journal of Personality and Social Psychology*, *68*(6), 1030–1041.

23 Chaiken, S. (1980). Heuristic versus systematic information processing and the use of source versus message cues in persuasion. *Journal of Personality and Social Psychology*, *39*(5), 752–766.

Petty, R. E., Cacioppo, J. T., & Schumann, D. (1983). Central & peripheral routes to advertising effectiveness: The moderating role of involvement. *Journal of Consumer Research*, *10*(2), 135–146.

24 Haley, R. I. (1985). *Developing effective communication strategy: A benefit segmentation approach*. New York: Ronald Press.

25 Kiesler, S. B., & Mathog, R. B. (1968). Distraction hypothesis in attitude change: Effects of effectiveness. *Psychological Reports*, *23*(3, Pt. 2), 1123–1133.

26 Carlston, D. E., & Smith, E. R. (1996). Principles of mental representation. In E. T. Higgins & A. Kruglanski (Eds.), *Social psychology: Handbook of basic principles* (2nd ed., pp. 184–210). New York: Guilford Press.

Klimoski, R. J., & Donahue, L. M. (2001). Person perception in organizations: An overview of the field. In M. London (Ed.), *How people evaluate others in organizations* (pp. 5–43). Mahwah, NJ: Lawrence Erlbaum Associates.

Smith, E. (1998a). Mental representations and memory. In D. Gilbert, S. Fiske & G. Lindzey (Eds.), *The handbook of social psychology* (4th ed., pp. 391–445). New York: McGraw-Hill.

27 Pennington, D. C. (2000). *Social cognition.* New York: Psychology Press.

28 Andersen, S. M., & Klatzky, R. L. (1987). Traits and social stereotypes: Levels of categorization in person perception. *Journal of Personality and Social Psychology, 53*(2), 235–246.

29 Bond, C. F., & Brockett, D. R. (1987). A social context-personality index theory of memory for acquaintances. *Journal of Personality and Social Psychology, 52*(6), 1110–1121.

Bond, C. F., & Sedikides, C. (1988). The recapitulation hypothesis in person retrieval. *Journal of Experimental Social Psychology, 24*(3), 195–221.

30 McGraw, K. M., & Steenbergen, M. R. (1995). Pictures in the head: Memory representations of political candidates. In M. Lodge & K. M. McGraw (Eds.), *Political judgment: Structure and process* (pp. 15–41). Ann Arbor, MI: The University of Michigan Press.

31 Jeffrey, K. M., & Mischel, W. (1979). Effects of purpose on the organization and recall of information in person perception. *Journal of Personality, 47,* 397–419.

32 Markus, H., & Zajonc, R. B. (1985). The cognitive perspective in social psychology. In G. Lindzey & E. Aronson (Eds.), *The handbook of social psychology* (3rd ed., Vol. 1, pp. 137–230). New York: Knopf.

For an opposing view, *see* n29, Bond & Brockett (1987).

33 Biernat, M., Manis, M., & Nelson, T. F. (1991). Stereotypes and standards of judgment. *Journal of Personality and Social Psychology, 60*(4), 485–499.

Hogg, M. A. (2001). A social identity theory of leadership. *Personality and Social Psychology Review, 5,* 184–200.

Hogg, M. A., & Terry, O. J. (2000). Social identity and self-categorization processes in organizational contexts. *Academy of Management Review, 25,* 121–140.

34 Dunning, D. (1999). A newer look: Motivated social cognition and the schematic representation of social concepts. *Psychological Inquiry, 10*(1), 1–11.

35 Lord, R. G. (1985). Accuracy in behavioral measurement: An alternative definition based on raters' cognitive schema and signal detection theory. *Journal of Applied Psychology, 70*(1), 66–71.

Lord, R. G., Foti, R. J., & Phillips, J. S. (1982). A theory of leadership categorization. In H. G. Hunt, U. Sekaran & C. Schriescheim (Eds.), *Leadership: Beyond establishment views* (pp. 104–121). Carbondale, IL: Southern Illinois University Press.

36 Bolster, B. I., & Springbett, B. M. (1961). The reaction of interviewers to favorable and unfavorable information. *Journal of Applied Psychology, 45*(2), 97–103.

Hakel, M. D., Hollmann, T. D., & Dunnette, M. D. (1970). Accuracy of interviewers, certified public accountants, and students in identifying the interests of accountants. *Journal of Applied Psychology, 54*(2), 115–119.

37 Webster, E. D. (Ed.). (1964). *Decision-making in the employment interview.* Montreal, Canada: McGill University.

38 Highhouse, S., & Gallo, A. (1997). Order effects in personnel decision making. *Human Performance, 10*(1), 31–46.

39 Schuh, A. J. (1978). Contrast effect in the interview. *Bulletin of the Psychonomic Society, 11*(3), 195–196.

40 Kopelman, M. D. (1975). The contrast effect in the selection interview. *British Journal of Educational Psychology, 45*(3), 333–336.

41 Kepplinger, H. M., Brosius, H. B., & Heine, N. (1990). Contrast effects of nonverbal behavior in television interviews. *Communications, 15*(1–2), 121–134.

42 Clark, L. F., Martin, L. L., & Henry, S. M. (1993). Instantiation, interference, and the change of standard effect: Context functions in reconstructive memory. *Journal of Personality and Social Psychology, 64*(3), 336–346.

Higgins, E. T., & Lurie, L. (1983). Context, categorization, and recall: The "change-of-standard" effect. *Cognitive Psychology, 15*(4), 525–547.

Higgins, E. T., & Stangor, C. A. (1988). "Change-of-standard" perspective on the relations among context, judgment, and memory. *Journal of Personality and Social Psychology, 54*(2), 181–192.

43 Tosi, H. (1971). Organization stress as a moderator of the relationship between influence and role response. *Academy of Management Journal, 14,* 7–20.

44 Bagozzi, R. P. (1978). Salesforce performance and satisfaction as a function of individual difference, interpersonal, and situational factors. *Journal of Marketing Research, 15*(4), 517–531.

Futrell, C. M., Swan, J. S., & Todd, J. T. (1976). Job performance related to management control systems for pharmaceutical salesmen. *Journal of Marketing Research, 13,* 25–33.

Walker, O. C., Churchill, G. A., & Ford, N. M. (1975). Organizational determinants of the industrial salesman's role conflict and ambiguity. *Journal of Marketing, 39*(1), 32–39.

45 Calder, B. J. (1977). An attribution theory of leadership. In B. M. Staw & G. R. Salancik (Eds.), *New directions in organizational behavior* (pp. 179–204). Chicago: St. Claire Press.

Eden, D., & Leviatan, U. (1975). Implicit leadership theory as a determinant of the factor structure underlying supervisory behavior scales. *Journal of Applied Psychology, 60*(6), 736–741.

Lord, R. G., & Maher, K. J. (1991). *Leadership and information processing: Linking perceptions and performance.* Cambridge, MA: Unwin Hyman.

46 Bartol, K. M., & Butterfield, D. A. (1976). Sex effects in evaluating leaders. *Journal of Applied Psychology, 61*(4), 446–454.

Hogg, M. A. (2007). Social psychology of leadership. In A. W. Kruglanski & E. Tory Higgins (Eds.), *Social psychology: Handbook of basic principles* (2nd ed., pp. 716–733). New York: The Guilford Press.

See n35, Lord (1985).

47 Cronshaw, S. F., & Lord, R. G. (1987). Effects of categorization, attribution, and encoding processes on leadership perceptions. *Journal of Applied Psychology, 72*(1), 97–106.

Fraser, S. L., & Lord, R. G. (1988). Stimulus prototypicality and general leadership impressions: Their role in leadership and behavioral ratings. *Journal of Psychology: Interdisciplinary and Applied, 122*(3), 291–303.

Lord, R. G., Foti, R. J., & de Vader, C. L. (1984). A test of leadership categorization theory: Internal structure, information processing, and leadership perceptions. *Organizational Behavior & Human Performance, 34*(3), 343–378.

48 Hains, S. C., Hogg, M. A., & Duck, J. M. (1997). Self-categorization and leadership: Effects of group prototypicality and leader stereotypicality. *Personality and Social Psychology Bulletin, 23*(10), 1087–1099.

49 House, R. J., & Aditya, R. M. (1997). The social scientific study of leadership: Quo vadis? *Journal of Management, 23*, 409–473.

50 Maurer, T. J., & Lord, R. G. (1988). *August IP variables in leadership perception: Is cognitive demand a moderator?* Paper presented at the Annual Conference of the American Psychological Association (Div. 14), Atlanta, Georgia.

51 Epitropaki, O., & Martin, R. (2004). Implicit leadership theories in applied settings: Factor structure, generalizability, and stability over time. *Journal of Applied Psychology, 89*(2), 293–310.

52 Fiske, S. T., & Taylor, S. E. (1991). *Social cognition* (2nd ed.). New York: McGraw-Hill.

53 Kuperman, J. C. (2000). Financial analyst sensemaking following strategic announcements: Implications for the investor relations activities of firms (Doctoral dissertation, New York University, 2000). *Dissertation Abstracts International, 61*(05A), 1936.

54 Jackson, D. N., Peacock, A. C., & Holden, R. R. (1982). Professional interviewers' trait inferential structures for diverse occupational groups. *Organizational Behavior & Human Performance, 29*(1), 1–20.

55 Siess, T. F., & Jackson, D. N. (1970). Vocational interests and personality: An empirical integration. *Journal of Counseling Psychology, 17*(1), 27–35.

56 Lord, R. G., Brown, D. J., Harvey, J. L., & Hall, R. J. (2001). Contextual constraints on prototype generation and their multilevel consequences for leadership perceptions. *The Leadership Quarterly, 12*(3), 311–338.

Lord, R. G., & Hall, R. (2003). Identity, leadership categorization, and leadership schema. In D. van Knippenberg & M. A. Hogg (Eds.), *Leadership and power: Identity processes in groups and organizations* (pp. 49–64). Thousand Oaks, CA: Sage.

Weiss, H. M., & Adler, S. (1981). Cognitive complexity and the structure of implicit leadership theories. *Journal of Applied Psychology, 66*(1), 69–78.

57 Matthews, A. M., Lord, R. G., & Walker, J. B. (1990). *The development of leadership perceptions in children,* Unpublished manuscript. University of Akron, Akron, OH.

58 Livi, S., Kenny, D. A., Albright, L., & Pierro, A. (2008). A social relations analysis of leadership. *Leadership Quarterly, 19*(2), 235–248.

59 Offermann, L. R., Kennedy, J. K., & Wirtz, P. W. (1994). Implicit leadership theories: Content, structure, and generalizability. *Leadership Quarterly, 5*(1), 43–58.

60 Winn, A. R. (1984). A cognitive social information processing approach to leadership perceptions (Doctoral dissertation, University of South Carolina, 1984). *Dissertation Abstracts International, 46*(02A), 0464.

61 Lord, R. G., de Vader, C. L., & Alliger, G. M. (1986). A meta-analysis of the relation between personality traits and leadership perceptions: An application of validity generalization procedures. *Journal of Applied Psychology, 71*(3), 402–410.

62 Judge, T. A., Bono, J. E., Ilies, R., & Gerhardt, M. W. (2002). Personality and leadership: A qualitative and quantitative review. *Journal of Applied Psychology, 87*(4), 765.

63 *See* n45, Lord & Maher (1991).

Rush, M. C., & Russell, J. E. (1988). Leader prototypes and prototype-contingent consensus in leader behavior descriptions. *Journal of Experimental Social Psychology, 24*(1), 88–104.

Sande, G. N., Ellard, J. H., & Ross, M. (1986). Effect of arbitrarily assigned status labels on self-perceptions and social perceptions: The mere position effect. *Journal of Personality and Social Psychology, 50*(4), 684–689.

64 Foti, R. J., Fraser, S. L., & Lord, R. G. (1982). Effects of leadership labels and prototypes on perceptions of political leaders. *Journal of Applied Psychology, 67*(3), 326–333.

65 Fiske, S. T., & Kinder, D. R. (1981). Involvement, expertise, and schema use: Evidence from political cognition. In N. Cantor & J. Kihlstrom (Eds.), *Personality, cognition, and social interaction* (pp. 171–190). Hillsdale, NJ: Lawrence Erlbaum Associates.

66 Kinder, D. R., Peters, M. D., Abelson, R. P., & Fiske, S. T. (1980). Presidential prototypes. *Political Behavior, 2*, 315–338.

67 *See* n59,Offermann et al. (1994).

68 Gerstner, C. R., & Day, D. V. (1994). Cross-cultural comparison of leadership prototypes. *The Leadership Quarterly, 5*(2), 121–134.

69 Kenney, R. A., Schwartz-Kenney, B. M., & Blascovich, J. (1996). Implicit leadership theories: Defining leaders described as worthy of influence. *Personality and Social Psychology Bulletin, 22*(11), 1128–1143.

See also Epitropaki, O., & Martin, R. (2004). Implicit leadership theories in applied settings: Factor structure, generalizability, and stability over time. *Journal of Applied Psychology, 89*(2), 293–310.

70 Den Hartog, D. N., House, R. J., Hanges, P. J., Ruiz-Quintanilla, S. A., & Dorfman, P. W. (1999). Culture specific and cross-cultural generalizable implicit leadership theories: Are attributes of charismatic/transformational leadership universally endorsed? *Leadership Quarterly, 10,* 219–256.

71 Cunningham, M. R., Barbee, A. P., & Pike, C. L. (1990). What do women want? Facialmetric assessment of multiple motives in the perception of male facial physical attractiveness. *Journal of Personality and Social Psychology, 59*(1), 61–72.

72 Berry, D. S. (1991b). Attractive faces are not all created equal: Joint effects of facial babyishness and attractiveness on social perception. *Personality and Social Psychology Bulletin, 17*(5), 523–531.

73 Keating, C. F., & Doyle, J. (2002). The faces of desirable mates and dates contain mixed social status cues. *Journal of Experimental Social Psychology, 38*(4), 414–424.

74 Anderson, C., John, O. P., Keltner, D., & Kring, A. M. (2001). Who attains social status? Effects of personality and physical attractiveness in social groups. *Journal of Personality and Social Psychology, 81*(1), 116–132.

75 Young, T. J., & French, L. A. (1998). Heights of US presidents: A trend analysis for 1948–1996. *Perceptual and Motor Skills, 87*(1), 321–322.

76 Judge, T. A., & Cable, D. M. (2004). The effect of physical height on workplace success and income: Preliminary test of a theoretical model. *Journal of Applied Psychology, 89*(3), 428–441.

77 Mueller, U., & Mazur, A. (1996). Facial dominance of West Point cadets as a predictor of later military rank. *Social Forces, 74*(3), 823–850.

78 Rule, N. O., & Ambady, N. (2008). The face of success inferences from chief executive officers' appearance predict company profits. *Psychological Science, 19*(2), 109–111.

79 Todorov, A., Mandisodza, A. N., Goren, A., & Hall, C. C. (2005). Inferences of competence from faces predict election outcomes. *Science, 308*(5728), 1623–1626.

80 Fiske, S. T. (2010). Interpersonal stratification: Status, power, and subordination. In S. T. Fiske, D. T. Gilbert & G. Lindzey (Eds.), *Handbook of social psychology* (5th ed., Vol. 1, pp. 941–982). Hoboken, NJ: John Wiley & Sons Ltd.

81 Hall, J. A., Coats, E. J., & LeBeau, L. S. (2005). Nonverbal behavior and the vertical dimension of social relations: A meta-analysis. *Psychological Bulletin, 131*(6), 898–924.

Mast, M. S., & Hall, J. A. (2004). Who is the boss and who is not? Accuracy of judging status. *Journal of Nonverbal Behavior, 28*(3), 145–165.

82 Henley, N. M. (1995). Body politics revisited: What do we know today? In P. J. Kalbfleisch & M. J. Cody (Eds.), *Gender, power, and communication in human relationships* (pp. 27–61). Hillsdale, NJ: Lawrence Erlbaum Associates.

Leary, M. R. (1990). Self-presentation processes in leadership emergence and effectiveness. In R. A. Giacalone & P. Rosenfeld (Eds.), *Impression management in the organization* (pp. 363–374). Hillsdale, NJ: Lawrence Erlbaum Associates.

83 Montepare, J. M., & Zebrowitz-McArthur, L. (1988). Impressions of people created by age-related qualities of their gaits. *Journal of Personality and Social Psychology, 55*(4), 547–556.

84 Tiedens, L. Z., & Fragale, A. R. (2003). Power moves: Complementarity in dominant and submissive nonverbal behavior. *Journal of Personality and Social Psychology, 84*(3), 558–568.

85 Andersen, P. A., & Bowman, L. L. (1999). Positions of power: Nonverbal influence in organizational communication. In L. K. Guerrero, J. A. DeVito & M. L. Hecht (Eds.), *The nonverbal communication reader: Classic and contemporary readings* (pp. 317–334). Prospect Heights, IL: Waveland.

86 de Groot, T., & Motowidlo, S. J. (1999). Why visual and vocal interview cues can affect interviewers' judgments and predict job performance. *Journal of Applied Psychology, 84*(6), 986–993.

87 Brooks, C. I., Church, M. A., & Fraser, L. (1986). Effects of duration of eye contact on judgments of personality characteristics. *Journal of Social Psychology, 126*(1), 71–78.

88 Tessler, R., & Sushelsky, L. (1978). Effects of eye contact and social status on the perception of a job applicant in an employment interviewing situation. *Journal of Vocational Behavior, 13*(3), 338–347.

89 Dovidio, J. F., & Ellyson, S. L. (1982). Decoding visual dominance: Attributions of power based on relative percentages of looking while speaking and looking while listening. *Social Psychology Quarterly, 45*(2), 106–113.

90 Hess, U., Blairy, S., & Kleck, R. E. (1997). The intensity of emotional facial expressions and decoding accuracy. *Journal of Nonverbal Behavior, 21*(4), 241–257.

Knutson, B. (1996). Facial expressions of emotion influence interpersonal trait inferences. *Journal of Nonverbal Behavior, 20*, 165–182.

Montepare, J. M., & Dobish, H. (2003). The contribution of emotion perceptions and their overgeneralizations to trait impressions. *Journal of Nonverbal Behavior, 27*(4), 237–254.

91 Chance, M. R. A. (1976). The organization of attention in groups. In M. von Cranach (Ed.), *Methods of inference from animal to human behavior* (pp. 213–235). The Hague, Netherlands: Mouton.

92 Burgoon, J. K. (1994). Nonverbal signals. In M. L. Knapp & G. R. Miller (Eds.), *Handbook of interpersonal communication* (2nd ed., pp. 229–285). Thousand Oaks, CA: Sage.

93 Montepare, J. M., & Zebrowitz-McArthur, L. (1987). Perceptions of adults with childlike voices in two cultures. *Journal of Experimental Social Psychology, 23*(4), 331–349.

94 Brown, B. L., Strong, W. J., & Rencher, A. C. (1973). Perceptions of personality from speech: Effects of manipulations of acoustical parameters. *Journal of the Acoustical Society of America, 54*(1), 29–35.

Greene, M. C. L., & Mathieson, L. (1989). *The voice and its disorders*. London: Whurr.

Scherer, K. R. (1979a). Personality markers in speech. In K. R. Scherer & H. Giles (Eds.), *Social markers in speech* (pp. 58–79). Cambridge, MA: Cambridge University Press.

95 Mast, M. S. (2002). Dominance as expressed and inferred through speaking time. *Human Communication Research, 28*(3), 420–450.

96 Jones, E. E., & Kelly, J. R. (2007). Contributions to a group discussion and perceptions of leadership: Does quantity always count more than quality? *Group Dynamics: Theory, Research, and Practice, 11*(1), 15.

97 Rosenberg, A., & Hirschberg, J. (2009). Charisma perception from text and speech. *Speech Communication, 51*(7), 640–655.

98 Johnson, S. K., & Dipboye, R. L. (2008). Effects of charismatic content and delivery on follower task performance the moderating role of task charisma conduciveness. *Group & Organization Management, 33*(1), 77–106.

99 *See* n86, de Groot & Motowildo (1999).

100 Fiske, S. T. (2010). Interpersonal stratification: Status, power, and subordination. In S. T. Fiske, D. T. Gilbert, & G. Lindzey (Eds.), *Handbook of social psychology* (5th ed., Vol. 2, pp. 941–982). Hoboken, NJ: Wiley & Sons.

101 Newcombe, N., & Arnkoff, D. B. (1979). Effects of speech style and sex of speaker on person perception. *Journal of Personality and Social Psychology, 37*(8), 1293–1303.

102 Erickson, B., Lind, E. A., Johnson, B. C., & O'Barr, W. M. (1978). Speech style and impression formation in a court setting: The effects of "powerful" and "powerless" speech. *Journal of Experimental Social Psychology, 14*(3), 266–279.

Blankenship, K. L., & Holtgraves, T. (2005). The role of different markers of linguistic powerlessness in persuasion. *Journal of Language and Social Psychology, 24*(1), 3–24.

103 Wakslak, C. J., Smith, P. K., & Han, A. (2014). Using abstract language signals power. *Journal of Personality and Social Psychology, 107*(1), 41–55.

104 Wish, M., D'Andrade, R. G., & Goodnow, J. E. (1980). Dimensions of interpersonal communication: Correspondences between structures for speech acts and bipolar scales. *Journal of Personality and Social Psychology, 39*(5), 848–860.

105 Berry, D. S., Pennebaker, J. W., Mueller, J. S., & Hiller, W. S. (1997). Linguistic bases of social perception. *Personality and Social Psychology Bulletin, 23*(5), 526–537.

106 *See* n97, Rosenberg & Hirschberg (2009).

Seyranian, V. (2014). Social identity framing communication strategies for mobilizing social change. *The Leadership Quarterly, 25*(3), 468–486.

107 Sy, T. (2010). What do you think of followers? Examining the content, structure, and consequences of implicit followership theories. *Organizational Behavior and Human Decision Processes, 113*(2), 73–84.

108   Hakel, M. D., & Schuh, A. J. (1971). Job applicant attributes judged important across seven diverse occupations. *Personnel Psychology*, *24*(1), 45–52.

Keenan, A. (1976). Interviewers' evaluation of applicant characteristics: Differences between personnel and non-personnel managers. *Journal of Occupational Psychology*, *49*(4), 223–230.

Shaw, E. A. (1972). Commonality of applicant stereotypes among recruiters. *Personnel Psychology*, *25*(3), 421–432.

109   Thomason, S. J., Weeks, M., Bernardin, H. J., & Kane, J. (2011). The differential focus of supervisors and peers in evaluations of managerial potential. *International Journal of Selection and Assessment*, *19*(1), 82–97.

110   Carsten, M. K., Uhl-Bien, M., West, B. J., Patera, J. L., & McGregor, R. (2010). Exploring social constructions of followership: A qualitative study. *The Leadership Quarterly*, *21*(3), 543–562.

111   Moy, J. W., & Lam, K. F. (2004). Selection criteria and the impact of personality on getting hired. *Personnel Review*, *33*(5), 521–535.

112   Diener, E., Nickerson, C., Lucas, R. E., & Sandvik, E. (2002). Dispositional affect and job outcomes. *Social Indicators Research*, *59*(3), 229–259.

113   Gifford, R., Ng, C. F., & Wilkinson, M. (1985). Nonverbal cues in the employment interview: Links between applicant qualities and interviewer judgments. *Journal of Applied Psychology*, *70*(4), 729–736.

Kinicki, A. J., & Lockwood, C. A. (1985). The interview process: An examination of factors recruiters use in evaluating job applicants. *Journal of Vocational Behavior*, *26*(2), 117–125.

Raza, S. M., & Carpenter, B. N. (1987). A model of hiring decisions in real employment interviews. *Journal of Applied Psychology*, *72*(4), 596–603.

114   *See* n113, Gifford et al. (1985).

Imada, A. S., & Hakel, M. D. (1977). Influence of nonverbal communication and rater proximity on impressions and decisions in simulated employment interviews. *Journal of Applied Psychology*, *62*(3), 295–300.

Parsons, C. K., & Liden, R. C. (1984). Interviewer perceptions of applicant qualifications: A multivariate field study of demographic characteristics and nonverbal cues. *Journal of Applied Psychology*, *69*(4), 557–568.

115   Rasmussen, K. G. (1984). Nonverbal behavior, verbal behavior, resumé credentials, and selection interview outcomes. *Journal of Applied Psychology*, *69*(4), 551–556.

116   Tews, M. J., Stafford, K., & Zhu, J. (2009). Beauty revisited: The impact of attractiveness, ability, and personality in the assessment of employment suitability. *International Journal of Selection and Assessment*, *17*(1), 92–100.

117   Anderson, N. H., & Shackleton, V. J. (1990). Decision making in the graduate selection interview: A field study. *Journal of Occupational Psychology*, *63*(1), 63–76.

118   Forbes, R. J., & Jackson, P. R. (1980). Non-verbal behaviour and the outcome of selection interviews. *Journal of Occupational Psychology*, *53*(1), 65–72.

Harris, M. M. (1989). Reconsidering the employment interview: A review of recent literature and suggestions for future research. *Personnel Psychology*, *42*(4), 691–726.

119   Burnett, J. R. (1993). Utilization and validity of nonverbal cues in the structured interview (Doctoral dissertation, University of Florida, 1993). *Dissertation Abstracts International*, *55*(07A), 2041.

Motowidlo, S. J., & Burnett, J. R. (1995). Aural and visual sources of validity in structured employment interviews. *Organizational Behavior and Human Decision Processes*, *61*(3), 239–249.

120   *See* n119, Burnett (1993).

121   Hollandsworth, J. G., Kazelskis, R., Stevens, J., & Dressel, M. E. (1979). Relative contributions of verbal, articulative, and nonverbal communication to employment decisions in the job interview setting. *Personnel Psychology*, *32*(2), 359–367.

122   Labov, W. (1966). *The social stratification of English in New York City*. Washington, DC: Center for Applied Linguistics.

123   Borkenau, P., & Liebler, A. (1992a). The cross-modal consistency of personality: Inferring strangers' traits from visual or acoustic information. *Journal of Research in Personality*, *26*(2), 183–204.

Feingold, A. (1992). Good-looking people are not what we think. *Psychological Bulletin*, *111*(2), 304–341.

124   *See* n121, Hollandsworth et al. (1979).

125   *See* n105, Berry et al. (1997).

126   Ickes, W. (1982). A basic paradigm for the study of personality, roles, and social behavior. In W. Ickes & E. S. Knowles (Eds.), *Personality, roles, and social behavior* (pp. 305–341). New York: Springer-Verlag.

127   Hatch, J. A., Hill, C. A., & Hayes, J. R. (1993). When the messenger is the message: Readers' impressions of writers. *Written Communication*, *10*(4), 569–598.

128 Yates, J. F., Price, P. C., Lee, J. W., & Ramirez, J. (1996). Good probabilistic forecasters: The "consumer's" perspective. *International Journal of Forecasting, 12*, 41–56.

129 *See* n105, Berry et al. (1997).

130 Druckman, J. N. (2001a). On the limits of framing effects: Who can frame? *Journal of Politics, 63*, 1041–1066.

131 Schul, Y., Mayo, R., & Burnstein, E. (2004). Encoding under trust and distrust: The spontaneous activation of incongruent cognitions. *Journal of Personality and Social Psychology, 86*(5), 668–679.

132 LaFrance, M., & Hecht, M. A. (1995). Why smiles generate leniency. *Personality and Social Psychology Bulletin, 21*(3), 207–214.

133 Argyle, M., & Cook, M. (1976). *Gaze and mutual gaze.* Oxford, UK: Cambridge University Press.

134 Cutler, B. L., Penrod, S. D., & Dexter, H. R. (1990). Juror sensitivity to eyewitness identification evidence. *Law and Human Behavior, 14*(2), 185–191.

135 DePaulo, B. M., Stone, J. I., & Lassiter, G. D. (1985). Deceiving and detecting deceit. In B. R. Schlenker (Ed.), *The self and social life* (pp. 323–370). New York: McGraw-Hill.

   Zuckerman, M., DePaulo, B. M., & Rosenthal, R. (1981). Verbal and nonverbal communication of deception. In L. Berkowitz (Ed.), *Advances in experimental social psychology* (Vol. 14, pp. 1–59). New York: Academic Press.

136 DePaulo, P. J., & DePaulo, B. M. (1989). Can deception by salespersons and customers be detected through nonverbal behavioral cues? *Journal of Applied Social Psychology, 19*(18, Pt. 2), 1552–1577.

137 *See* n135, Zuckerman et al. (1981).

138 Brown, B. L. (1980). Effects of speech rate on personality attributions and competency evaluations. In H. Giles, W. P. Robinson & P. M. Smith (Eds.), *Language: Social psychological perspectives* (pp. 116–133). Oxford, UK: Pergamon Press.

   Miller, N., Maruyama, G., Beaber, R. J., & Valone, K. (1976). Speed of speech and persuasion. *Journal of Personality and Social Psychology, 34*(4), 615–624.

   Woodall, W. G., & Burgoon, J. K. (1983). Talking fast and changing attitudes: A critique and clarification. *Journal of Nonverbal Behavior, 8*(2), 126–142.

139 *See* n138, Miller et al. (1976).

   Smith, S. M., & Shaffer, D. R. (1995). Speed of speech and persuasion: Evidence for multiple effects. *Personality and Social Psychology Bulletin, 21*(10), 1051–1060.

140 *See* n102, Erickson et al. (1978).

141 Burgoon, J. K., Birk, T., & Pfau, M. (1990). Nonverbal behaviors, persuasion, and credibility. *Human Communication Research, 17*(1), 140–169.

   Engstrom, E. (1994). Effects of nonfluencies on speaker's credibility in newscast settings. *Perceptual and Motor Skills, 78*(3, Pt. 1), 739–743.

   Scherer, K. R. (1978). Personality inference from voice quality: The loud voice of extroversion. *European Journal of Social Psychology, 8*(4), 467–487.

142 *See* n135.

143 Fleshier, H., Ilardo, J., & Demoretcky, J. (1974). The influence of field dependence, speaker credibility set, and message documentation on evaluations of speaker and message credibility. *Southern Speech Communication Journal, 39*, 389–402.

144 Hamilton, M. A., & Hunter, J. E. (1998). The effect of language intensity on receiver evaluations of message, source, and topic. In M. Allen & R. W. Preiss (Eds.), *Persuasion: Advances through meta-analysis* (pp. 99–138). Cresskill, NJ: Hampton.

145 Hamilton, M. A. (1998). Message variables that mediate and moderate the effect of equivocal language on source credibility. *Journal of Language and Social Psychology, 17*(1), 109–143.

   Hamilton, M. A., & Mineo, P. J. (1998). A framework for understanding equivocation. *Journal of Language and Social Psychology, 17*(1), 3–35.

146 *See* n102, Erickson et al. (1978).

   Hosman, L. A., & Siltanen, S. A. (1994). The attributional and evaluative consequences of powerful and powerless speech styles: An examination of the "control over others" and "control of self" explanations. *Language & Communication, 14*(3), 287–298.

147 Holtgraves, T., & Grayer, A. R. (1994). I am not a crook: Effects of denials on perceptions of a defendant's guilt, personality, and motives. *Journal of Applied Social Psychology, 24*(23), 2132–2150.

148 El-Alayli, A., Myers, C. J., Petersen, T. L., & Lystad, A. L. (2008). "I don't mean to sound arrogant, but . . .": The effects of using disclaimers on person perception. *Personality and Social Psychology Bulletin, 34*(1), 130–143.

149 Gruenfeld, D. H., & Wyer, R. S. (1992). Semantics and pragmatics of social influence: How affirmations and denials affect beliefs in referent propositions. *Journal of Personality and Social Psychology, 62*(1), 38–49.

150 Blascovich, J., & Seery, M. D. (2007, p. 27). Visceral and somatic indexes of social psychological constructs: History, principles, propositions, and case studies. In A. Kruglanski & E. T. Higgins (Eds.), *Social psychology: Handbook of basic principles* (2nd ed., pp. 19–38). New York: Guilford.

151 Langton, S. R. H., & Bruce, V. (2000). You must see the point: Automatic processing of cues to the direction of social attention. *Journal of Experimental Psychology: Human Perception and Performance, 26*(2), 747–757.

Langton, S. R. H., O'Malley, C., & Bruce, V. (1996). Actions speak no louder than words: Symmetrical cross-modal interference effects in the processing of verbal and gestural information. *Journal of Experimental Psychology: Human Perception and Performance, 22*(6), 1357–1375.

152 Fiedler, K., & Schenck, W. (2001). Spontaneous inferences from pictorially presented behaviors. *Personality and Social Psychological Bulletin, 27*, 1533–1546.

153 Borkenau, P., & Liebler, A. (1992b). Trait inferences: Sources of validity at zero acquaintance. *Journal of Personality and Social Psychology, 62*(4), 645–657.

154 Behling, D. U., & Williams, E. A. (1991). Influence of dress on perceptions of intelligence and expectations of scholastic achievement. *Clothing and Textiles Research Journal, 9*(4), 1–7.

155 Davis, M. A. (1992). Age and dress of professors: Influence on students' first impressions of teaching effectiveness (Doctoral dissertation, Virginia Polytechnic Institute and State University, 1992). *Dissertation Abstracts International, 53*(02B), 0806.

Workman, J. E., Johnson, K. K., & Hadeler, B. (1993). The influence of clothing on students' interpretative and extended inferences about a teaching assistant. *College Student Journal, 27*(1), 119–128.

156 Gifford, R., & Hine, D. W. (1994). The role of verbal behavior in the encoding and decoding of interpersonal dispositions. *Journal of Research in Personality, 28*(2), 115–132.

See n126, Ickes (1982).

See n101, Newcombe & Arnkoff (1979).

157 *See* n105, Berry et al. (1997).

See n126, Ickes (1982).

See n101, Newcombe & Arnkoff (1979).

158 Borkenau, P., & Liebler, A. (1993). Convergence of stranger ratings of personality and intelligence with self-ratings, partner ratings, and measured intelligence. *Journal of Personality and Social Psychology, 65*(3), 546–553.

159 Todorov, A., & Uleman, J. S. (2003). The efficiency of binding spontaneous trait inferences to actors' faces. *Journal of Experimental Social Psychology, 39*(6), 549–562.

Wigboldus, D. H., Dijksterhuis, A., & Van Knippenberg, A. (2003). When stereotypes get in the way: Stereotypes obstruct stereotype-inconsistent trait inferences. *Journal of Personality and Social Psychology, 84*(3), 470–484.

160 Uleman, J. S. (1999). Spontaneous versus intentional inferences in impression formation. In S. Chaiken & Y. Trope (Eds.), *Dual-process theories in social psychology* (pp. 141–160). New York: Guilford Press.

Uleman, J. S., Newman, L. S., & Moskowitz, G. B. (1996). People as flexible interpreters: Evidence and issues from spontaneous trait inference. In M. P. Zanna (Ed.), *Advances in experimental social psychology* (Vol. 28, pp. 179–211). San Diego, CA: Academic Press.

Winter, L., & Uleman, J. S. (1984). When are social judgments made? Evidence for the spontaneousness of trait inferences. *Journal of Personality and Social Psychology, 47*(2), 237–252.

161 Lipshitz, R., & Shulimovitz, N. (2007). Intuition and emotion in bank loan officers' credit decisions. *Journal of Cognitive Engineering and Decision Making, 1*(2), 212–233.

162 Lieberman, M. D. (2007). Social cognitive neuroscience: A review of core processes. *Annual Review of Psychology, 58*, 259–289.

163 Funder, D. C., & Sneed, C. D. (1993). Behavioral manifestations of personality: An ecological approach to judgmental accuracy. *Journal of Personality and Social Psychology, 64*(3), 479–490.

164 *See* n156, Gifford & Hine (1994).

165 Borkenau, P. (1991). Evidence of a correlation between wearing glasses and personality. *Personality and Individual Differences, 12*(11), 1125–1128.

166 Berry, D. S., & Brownlow, S. (1989). Were the physiognomists right? Personality correlates of facial babyishness. *Personality and Social Psychology Bulletin, 15*(2), 266–279.

Berry, D. S., & Landry, J. C. (1997). Facial maturity and daily social interaction. *Journal of Personality and Social Psychology, 72*(3), 570–580.

Bond, C. F., Berry, D. S., & Omar, A. (1994). The kernel of truth in judgments of deceptiveness. *Basic and Applied Social Psychology, 15*(4), 523–534.

167 Asendorpf, J.B. (1987). Videotape reconstruction of emotions and cognitions related to shyness. *Journal of Personality and Social Psychology, 53*(3), 542–549.

Daly, S. (1978). Behavioural correlates of social anxiety. *British Journal of Social & Clinical Psychology, 17*(2), 117–120.

168 Patterson, M.L., & Ritts, V. (1997). Social and communicative anxiety: A review and meta-analysis. In B.R. Burleson & A.W. Kunkel (Eds.), *Communication yearbook 20* (pp. 263–303). Thousand Oaks, CA: Sage Publications.

Pilkonis, P.A. (1977). The behavioral consequences of shyness. *Journal of Personality, 45*(4), 596–611.

169 Borkenau, P., & Liebler, A. (1995). Observable attributes as manifestations and cues of personality and intelligence. *Journal of Personality, 63*(1), 1–25.

170 Berry, D.S. (1990). Vocal attractiveness and vocal babyishness: Effects on stranger, self, and friend impressions. *Journal of Nonverbal Behavior, 14*(3), 141–153.

Berry, D.S. (1991a). Accuracy in social perception: Contributions of facial and vocal information. *Journal of Personality and Social Psychology, 61*(2), 298–307.

171 *See* n141, Scherer (1978).

172 Ramsey, R. (1966). Personality and speech. *Journal of Personality and Social Psychology, 4*, 116–118.

173 Albright, L., & Forziati, C. (1995). Cross-situational consistency and perceptual accuracy in leadership. *Personality and Social Psychology Bulletin, 21*(12), 1269–1276.

See n153, Borkenau & Liebler (1992b).

Moskowitz, D.S. (1982). Coherence and cross-situational generality in personality: A new analysis of old problems. *Journal of Personality and Social Psychology, 43*(4), 754–768.

174 Heberlein, A.S., Adolphs, R., Tranel, D., & Damasio, H. (2004). Cortical regions for judgments of emotions and personality traits from point-light walkers. *Journal of Cognitive Neuroscience, 16*(7), 1143–1158.

Heberlein, A.S., & Saxe, R.R. (2005). Dissociation between emotion and personality judgments: Convergent evidence from functional neuroimaging. *NeuroImage, 28*(4), 770–777.

175 Scherer, K.R., & Scherer, U. (1981). Speech behavior and personality. In J. Darby (Ed.), *Speech evaluation in psychiatry* (pp. 115–135). New York: Grune & Stratton.

176 Fast, L.A., & Funder, D.C. (2008). Personality as manifest in word use: Correlations with self-report, acquaintance report, and behavior. *Journal of Personality and Social Psychology, 94*(2), 334–346.

Mehl, M.R., Gosling, S.D., & Pennebaker, J.W. (2006). Personality in its natural habitat: Manifestations and implicit folk theories of personality in daily life. *Journal of Personality and Social Psychology, 90*(5), 862–877.

Oberlander, J., & Gill, A.J. (2006). Language with character: A stratified corpus comparison of individual differences in e-mail communication. *Discourse Processes, 42*(3), 239–270.

177 Funder, D.C., & Colvin, C.R. (1991). Explorations in behavioral consistency: Properties of persons, situations, and behaviors. *Journal of Personality and Social Psychology, 60*(5), 773–794.

178 *Ibid.* Also *see* n123, Borkenau & Liebler (1992a).

179 *See* n127, Hatch et al. (1993).

180 Berry, D.S., & Finch Wero, J.L. (1993). Accuracy in face perception: A view from ecological psychology. *Journal of Personality Special Issue: Viewpoints on Personality: Consensus, Self-other Agreement, and Accuracy in Personality Judgment, 61*(4), 497–520.

Kenny, D.A., Horner, C., Kashy, D.A., & Chu, L.C. (1992). Consensus at zero acquaintance: Replication, behavioral cues, and stability. *Journal of Personality and Social Psychology, 62*(1), 88–97.

Watson, D. (1989). Strangers' ratings of the five robust personality factors: Evidence of a surprising convergence with self-report. *Journal of Personality and Social Psychology, 57*(1), 120–128.

181 Albright, L., Malloy, T.E., Dong, Q., Kenny, D.A., Fang, X., Winquist, L., & Yu, D. (1997). Cross-cultural consensus in personality judgments. *Journal of Personality and Social Psychology, 72*(3), 558–569.

182 Ambady, N., Bernieri, F.J., & Richeson, J.A. (2000). Toward a histology of social behavior: Judgmental accuracy from thin slices of the behavioral stream. In M.P. Zanna (Ed.), *Advances in experimental social psychology* (Vol. 32, pp. 201–271). San Diego, CA: Academic Press.

Ambady, N., & Rosenthal, R. (1992). Thin slices of expressive behavior as predictors of interpersonal consequences: A meta-analysis. *Psychological Bulletin, 111*(2), 256–274.

Gray, H.M., & Ambady, N. (2006). Methods for the study of nonverbal communication. In V. Manusov & M.L. Patterson (Eds.), *The SAGE handbook of nonverbal communication* (pp. 41–58). Thousand Oaks, CA: Sage.

183 Willis, J., & Todorov, A. (2006). First impressions making up your mind after a 100-ms exposure to a face. *Psychological Science, 17*(7), 592–598.

184 Bar, M., Neta, M., & Linz, H. (2006). Very first impressions. *Emotion, 6*(2), 269–278.

185 Ambady, N., & Rosenthal, R. (1993). Half a minute: Predicting teacher evaluations from thin slices of nonverbal behavior and physical attractiveness. *Journal of Personality and Social Psychology, 64*(3), 431–441.

186 Blanck, P. D., Rosenthal, R., & Cordell, L. H. (1985). The appearance of justice: Judges' verbal and nonverbal behavior in criminal jury trials. *Stanford Law Review, 38,* 89–164.

187 Hall, J. A., & Friedman, G. B. (1999). Status, gender, and nonverbal behavior: A study of structured interactions between employees of a company. *Personality and Social Psychology Bulletin, 25*(9), 1082–1091.

188 Murphy, N. A., Hall, J. A., & Colvin, C. R. (2003). Accurate intelligence assessments in social interactions: Mediators and gender effects. *Journal of Personality, 71*(3), 465–493.

189 Ambady, N., Krabbenhoft, M. A., & Hogan, D. (2006). The 30-sec sale: Using thin-slice judgments to evaluate sales effectiveness. *Journal of Consumer Psychology, 16*(1), 4–13.

Hecht, M. A., & LaFrance, M. (1995). How (fast) can i help you? Tone of voice and telephone operator efficiency in interactions. *Journal of Applied Social Psychology, 25*(23), 2086–2098.

190 Smith, P. M. (1979). Sex markers in speech. In K. R. Scherer & H. Giles (Eds.), *Social markers in speech* (pp. 109–146). Cambridge, UK: Cambridge University Press.

Smith, P. M. (1980). Judging masculine and feminine social identities from content-controlled speech. In H. Giles, W. P. Robinson & P. M. Smith (Eds.), *Language: Social psychological perspectives* (pp. 121–126). Oxford, UK: Pergamon.

191 Helfrich, H. (1979). Age markers in speech. In K. R. Scherer & H. Giles (Eds.), *Social markers in speech* (pp. 63–107). Cambridge, UK: Cambridge University Press.

192 Robinson, W. P. (1979). Speech markers and social class. In K. R. Scherer & H. Giles (Eds.), *Social markers in speech* (pp. 211–249). Cambridge, UK: Cambridge University Press.

193 Giles, H. (1973). Communicative effectiveness as a function of accented speech. *Speech Monographs, 40*(4), 330–331.

194 Tannen, D. (1984). *Conversational style: Analyzing talk among friends.* Norwood, NJ: Ablex.

195 Scherer, K. R. (1979b). Voice and speech correlates of perceived social influence. In H. Giles & R. St. Clair (Eds.), *The social psychology of language* (pp. 88–120). London: Blackwell.

196 Adams Jr, R. B., & Kleck, R. E. (2005). Effects of direct and averted gaze on the perception of facially communicated emotion. *Emotion, 5*(1), 3–11.

197 Mehrabian, A., & Ferris, S. R. (1967). Inference of attitudes from nonverbal communication in two channels. *Journal of Consulting Psychology, 31*(3), 248–252.

198 Ekman, P., Friesen, W. V., O'Sullivan, M., Chan, A., Diacoyanni-Tarlatzis, I., Heider, K., . . . Tzavaras, A. (1987). Universals and cultural differences in the judgments of facial expressions of emotion. *Journal of Personality and Social Psychology, 53*(4), 712–717.

Elfenbein, H. A., & Ambady, N. (2002). On the universality and cultural specificity of emotion recognition: A meta-analysis. *Psychological Bulletin, 128*(2), 203–235.

199 Matsumoto, D., Yoo, S. H., & Fontaine, J. (2008). Mapping expressive differences around the world the relationship between emotional display rules and individualism versus collectivism. *Journal of Cross-Cultural Psychology, 39*(1), 55–74.

200 Fridlund, A. J., Ekman, P., & Oster, H. (1987). Facial expressions of emotion. In A. W. Siegman & S. Feldstein (Eds.), *Nonverbal behavior and communication* (2nd ed., pp. 143–223). Hillsdale, NJ: Lawrence Erlbaum Associates.

Izard, C. E. (1994). Innate and universal facial expressions: Evidence from developmental and cross-cultural research. *Psychological Bulletin, 115*(2), 288–299.

201 Dimberg, U. (1997). Psychophysiological reactions to facial expressions. In U. Segerstrale & P. Molnar (Eds.), *Nonverbal communication: Where nature meets culture* (pp. 47–60). Mahwah, NJ: Lawrence Erlbaum.

Dimberg, U., Thunberg, M., & Elmehed, K. (2000). Unconscious facial reactions to emotional facial expressions. *Psychological Science, 11*(1), 86–89.

202 Wong, B., Cronin-Golomb, A., & Neargarder, S. (2005). Patterns of visual scanning as predictors of emotion identification in normal aging. *Neuropsychology, 19*(6), 739–749.

203 Calder, A. J., Young, A. W., Keane, J., & Dean, M. (2000). Configural information in facial expression perception. *Journal of Experimental Psychology: Human Perception and Performance, 26*(2), 527–551.

Ekman, P. (1982). *Emotion in the human face* (2nd ed.). Cambridge, UK: Cambridge University Press.

204 McAndrew, F. T. (1986). A cross-cultural study of recognition thresholds for facial expressions of emotion. *Journal of Cross-Cultural Psychology, 17*(2), 211–224.

205 Meeren, H. K., van Heijnsbergen, C. C., & de Gelder, B. (2005). Rapid perceptual integration of facial expression and emotional body language. *Proceedings of the National Academy of Sciences of the United States of America, 102*(45), 16518–16523.

Van den Stock, J., Righart, R., & De Gelder, B. (2007). Body expressions influence recognition of emotions in the face and voice. *Emotion, 7*(3), 487–494.

206 *See* n198, Elfenbein & Ambady (2002).

Tracy, J. L., & Robins, R. W. (2008). The automaticity of emotion recognition. *Emotion, 8*(1), 81–95.

207 Ekman, P., & Friesen, W. V. (1978). *Facial action coding system: A technique for the measurement of facial movement.* Palo Alto, CA: Consulting Psychologists Press.

208 Albright, L., Kenny, D. A., & Malloy, T. E. (1988). Consensus in personality judgments at zero acquaintance. *Journal of Personality and Social Psychology, 55*(3), 387–395.

See n182, Ambady & Rosenthal (1992).

See n180, Watson (1989).

209 Wehrle, T., Kaiser, S., Schmidt, S., & Scherer, K. R. (2000). Studying the dynamics of emotional expression using synthesized facial muscle movements. *Journal of Personality and Social Psychology, 78*(1), 105–119.

210 Vuilleumier, P., & Pourtois, G. (2007). Distributed and interactive brain mechanisms during emotion face perception: Evidence from functional neuroimaging. *Neuropsychologia, 45*(1), 174–194.

211 Adolphs, R., Gosselin, F., Buchanan, T. W., Tranel, D., Schyns, P., & Damasio, A. R. (2005). A mechanism for impaired fear recognition after amygdala damage. *Nature, 433*(7021), 68–72.

212 Calder, A. J., Keane, J., Manes, F., Antoun, N., & Young, A. W. (2000). Impaired recognition and experience of disgust following brain injury. *Nature Neuroscience, 3*(11), 1077–1078.

213 Coulson, M. (2004a). Attributing emotion to static body postures: Recognition accuracy, confusions, and viewpoint dependence. *Journal of Nonverbal Behavior, 28*(2), 117–139.

Coulson, M. (2004b). Erratum for attributing emotion to static body postures: Recognition accuracy, confusions, and viewpoint dependence. *Journal of Nonverbal Behavior Special Issue: Interpersonal Sensitivity, 28*(4), 297.

214 Atkinson, A. P., Dittrich, W. H., Gemmell, A. J., & Young, A. W. (2004). Emotion perception from dynamic and static body expressions in point-light and full-light displays. *Perception-London, 33*(6), 717–746.

Chouchourelou, A., Matsuka, T., Harber, K., & Shiffrar, M. (2006). The visual analysis of emotional actions. *Social Neuroscience,, 1*(1), 63–74.

Clarke, T. J., Bradshaw, M. F., Field, D. T., Hampson, S. E., & Rose, D. (2005). The perception of emotion from body movement in point-light displays of interpersonal dialogue. *Perception-London, 34*(10), 1171–1180.

215 Pollick, F. E., Paterson, H. M., Bruderlin, A., & Sanford, A. J., (2001). Perceiving affect from arm movement. *Cognition, 82*(2), B51–B61.

216 Camras, L. A., Sullivan, J., & Michel, G. (1993). Do infants express discrete emotions? Adult judgments of facial, vocal, and body actions. *Journal of Nonverbal Behavior, 17*(3), 171–186.

Montepare, J., Koff, E., Zaitchik, D., & Albert, M. (1999). The use of body movements and gestures as cues to emotions in younger and older adults. *Journal of Nonverbal Behavior, 23*(2), 133–152.

Wallbott, H. G. (1998). Bodily expression of emotion. *European Journal of Social Psychology, 28*(6), 879–896.

217 Gallagher, H. L., & Frith, C. D. (2004). Dissociable neural pathways for the perception and recognition of expressive and instrumental gestures. *Neuropsychologia, 42*(13), 1725–1736.

Grezes, J., Pichon, S., & De Gelder, B. (2007). Perceiving fear in dynamic body expressions. *NeuroImage, 35*(2), 959–967.

218 Peelen, M. V., Atkinson, A. P., Andersson, F., & Vuilleumier, P. (2007). Emotional modulation of body-selective visual areas. *Social Cognitive and Affective Neuroscience, 2*(4), 274–283.

Grezes, J., Pichon, S., & De Gelder, B. (2007). Perceiving fear in dynamic body expressions. *NeuroImage, 35*(2), 959–967.

219 Banse, R., & Scherer, K. R. (1996). Acoustic profiles in vocal emotion expression. *Journal of Personality and Social Psychology, 70*(3), 614–636.

220 Scherer, K. R. (1974). Acoustic concomitants of emotional dimensions: Judging affects from synthesized tone sequences. In S. Weitz (Ed.), *Nonverbal communication* (pp. 105–111). New York: Oxford University Press.

Scherer, K. R., & Oshinsky, J. (1977). Cue utilization in emotion attribution from auditory stimuli. *Motivation and Emotion, 1*(4), 331–346.

221 Frick, R. W. (1985). Communicating emotion: The role of prosodic features. *Psychological Bulletin, 97*(3), 412–429.

van Bezooijen, R., Otto, S. A., & Heenan, T. A. (1983). Recognition of vocal expressions of emotion: A three-nation study to identify universal characteristics. *Journal of Cross-Cultural Psychology, 14*(4), 387–406.

222 Breitenstein, C., Van Lancker, D., & Daum, I. (2001). The contribution of speech rate and pitch variation to the perception of vocal emotions in a German and an American sample. *Cognition & Emotion, 15*(1), 57–79.

223 Scherer, K. R., Banse, R., & Wallbott, H. G. (2001). Emotion inferences from vocal expression correlate across languages and cultures. *Journal of Cross-Cultural Psychology, 32*(1), 76–92.

224 Wallbott, H. G., & Scherer, K. R. (1986b). How universal and specific is emotional experience? Evidence from 27 countries on five continents. *Social Science Information, 25*(4), 763–795.

225 Juslin, P. N., & Laukka, P. (2003). Communication of emotions in vocal expression and music performance: Different channels, same code? *Psychological Bulletin, 129*(5), 770–814.

Sauter, D. A., & Scott, S. K. (2007). More than one kind of happiness: Can we recognize vocal expressions of different positive states? *Motivation and Emotion, 31*(3), 192–199.

226 Scherer, K. R., Johnstone, T., & Klasmeyer, G. (2003). Vocal expression of emotion. In R. J. Davidson, K. R. Scherer & H. H. Goldsmith (Eds.), *Handbook of affective sciences* (pp. 433–456). New York: Oxford University Press.

227 Tartter, V. C. (1980). Happy talk: Perceptual and acoustic effects of smiling on speech. *Perception and Psychophysics, 27*, 24–27.

228 Beaucousin, V., Lacheret, A., Turbelin, M. R., Morel, M., Mazoyer, B., & Tzourio-Mazoyer, N. (2007). FMRI study of emotional speech comprehension. *Cerebral Cortex, 17*(2), 339–352.

Wiethoff, S., Wildgruber, D., Kreifelts, B., Becker, H., Herbert, C., Grodd, W., & Ethofer, T. (2008). Cerebral processing of emotional prosody—influence of acoustic parameters and arousal. *NeuroImage, 39*(2), 885–893.

229 Argyle, M., Alkema, F., & Gilmour, R. (1971). The communication of friendly and hostile attitudes by verbal and nonverbal signals. *European Journal of Social Psychology, 1*(3), 385–402.

Bugental, D. E., Kaswan, J. W., & Love, L. R. (1970). Perception of contradictory meanings conveyed by verbal and nonverbal channels. *Journal of Personality and Social Psychology, 16*(4), 647–655.

DePaulo, B. M., Rosenthal, R., Eisenstat, R. A., Rogers, P. L., & Finkelstein, S. (1978). Decoding discrepant nonverbal cues. *Journal of Personality and Social Psychology, 36*(3), 313–323.

230 Burns, K. L., & Beier, E. G. (1973). Significance of vocal and visual channels in the decoding of emotional meaning. *Journal of Communication, 23*(1), 118–130.

231 Graham, J. A., Ricci-Bitti, P., & Argyle, M. (1975). A cross-cultural study of the communication of emotion by facial & gestural cues. *Journal of Human Movement Studies, 1*(2), 68–77.

Hess, U., Kappas, A., & Scherer, K. R. (1988). Multichannel communication of emotion: Synthetic signal production. In K. R. Scherer (Ed.), *Facets of emotion: Recent research* (pp. 161–182). Hillsdale, NJ: Lawrence Erlbaum Associates.

Wallbott, H. G., & Scherer, K. R. (1986a). Cues and channels in emotion recognition. *Journal of Personality and Social Psychology, 51*(4), 690–699.

232 Pell, M. D. (2005). Prosody-face interactions in emotional processing as revealed by the facial affect decision task. *Journal of Nonverbal Behavior, 29*(4), 193–215.

Schirmer, A., & Kotz, S. A. (2003). ERP evidence for a sex-specific Stroop effect in emotional speech. *Journal of Cognitive Neuroscience, 15*(8), 1135–1148.

233 Sherblom, J., & Van Rheenen, D. D. (1984). Spoken language indices of uncertainty. *Human Communication Research, 11*(2), 221–230.

234 Shapiro, J. G. (1968). Variability in the communication of affect. *Journal of Social Psychology, 76*(2), 181–188.

235 Leathers, D. (1979). The impact of multichannel message inconsistency on verbal and nonverbal decoding behaviors. *Communication Monographs, 46*, 88–100.

236 Corwin, E. P., Cramer, R. J., Griffin, D. A., & Brodsky, S. L. (2012). Defendant remorse, need for affect, and juror sentencing decisions. *Journal of the American Academy of Psychiatry and the Law Online, 40*(1), 41–49.

237 Wong, E. (2001, April 5). A stinging office memo boomerangs: Chief executive is criticized after upbraiding workers by e-mail. *New York Times,* p. C1.

238 Downing, P. E., Bray, D., Rogers, J., & Childs, C. (2004). Bodies capture attention when nothing is expected. *Cognition, 93*(1), B27–B38.

239 McArthur, L. Z., & Ginsberg, E. (1981). Causal attribution to salient stimuli: An investigation of visual fixation mediators. *Personality and Social Psychology Bulletin, 7*(4), 547–553.

240 Taylor, S. E., & Fiske, S. T. (1975). Point of view and perceptions of causality. *Journal of Personality and Social Psychology*, *32*(3), 439–445.

241 Ickes, W., Stinson, L., Bissonnette, V., & Garcia, S. (1990). Naturalistic social cognition: Empathic accuracy in mixed-sex dyads. *Journal of Personality and Social Psychology*, *59*(4), 730–742.

242 Kendon, A. (1990). *Conducting interaction: Patterns of behavior in focused encounters*. New York: Cambridge University Press.

Fletcher-Watson, S., Findlay, J. M., Leekam, S. R., & Benson, V. (2008). Rapid detection of person information in a naturalistic scene. *Perception*, *37*(4), 571–583.

243 Gullberg, M., & Holmqvist, K. (1999). Keeping an eye on gestures: Visual perception of gestures in face-to-face communication. *Pragmatics & Cognition*, *7*(1), 35–63.

Gullberg, M., & Holmqvist, K. (2006). What speakers do and what addressees look at: Visual attention to gestures in human interaction live and on video. *Pragmatics & Cognition*, *14*(1), 53–82.

244 Driver IV, J., Davis, G., Ricciardelli, P., Kidd, P., Maxwell, E., & Baron-Cohen, S. (1999). Gaze perception triggers reflexive visuospatial orienting. *Visual Cognition*, *6*(5), 509–540.

245 Beattie, G., Webster, K., & Ross, J. (2010). The fixation and processing of the iconic gestures that accompany talk. *Journal of Language and Social Psychology*, *29*(2), 194–213.

246 *See* n243, Gullberg & Holmqvist (1999).

247 Neuberg, S. L., & Fiske, S. T. (1987). Motivational influences on impression formation: Outcome dependency, accuracy-driven attention, and individuating processes. *Journal of Personality and Social Psychology*, *53*(3), 431–444.

Ruscher, J. B., & Fiske, S. T. (1990). Interpersonal competition can cause individuating processes. *Journal of Personality and Social Psychology*, *58*(5), 832–843.

248 Erber, R., & Fiske, S. T. (1984). Outcome dependency and attention to inconsistent information. *Journal of Personality and Social Psychology*, *47*(4), 709–726.

See n247, Ruscher & Fiske (1990).

249 Fiske, S. T., & Depret, E. (1996). Control, interdependence and power: Understanding social cognition in its social context. In W. Stroebe & M. Hewstone (Eds.), *European review of social psychology* (Vol. 7, pp. 31–61). New York: Wiley.

250 Rodin, M. J. (1987). Who is memorable to whom: A study of cognitive disregard. *Social Cognition*, *5*(2), 144–165.

251 Chartrand, T. L., & Bargh, J. A. (1999). The chameleon effect: The perception–behavior link and social interaction. *Journal of Personality and Social Psychology*, *76*(6), 893.

252 Neumann, R., & Strack, F. (2000). "Mood contagion": The automatic transfer of mood between persons. *Journal of Personality and Social Psychology*, *79*(2), 211–223.

253 Bernieri, F. J. (1988). Coordinated movement and rapport in teacher–student interactions. *Journal of Nonverbal Behavior*, *12*(2), 120–138.

Bernieri, F. J., Reznick, J. S., & Rosenthal, R. (1988). Synchrony, pseudosynchrony, and dissynchrony: Measuring the entrainment process in mother-infant interactions. *Journal of Personality and Social Psychology*, *54*(2), 243–253.

254 Finkel, E. J., Campbell, W. K., Brunell, A. B., Dalton, A. N., Scarbeck, S. J., & Chartrand, T. L. (2006). High-maintenance interaction: Inefficient social coordination impairs self-regulation. *Journal of Personality and Social Psychology*, *91*(3), 456–475.

255 de C Hamilton, A. F., Wolpert, D. M., Frith, U., & Grafton, S. T. (2006). Where does your own action influence your perception of another person's action in the brain? *NeuroImage*, *29*(2), 524–535.

Urgesi, C., Moro, V., Candid, M., & Aglioti, S. M. (2006). Mapping implied body actions in the human motor system. *The Journal of Neuroscience*, *26*(30), 7942–7949.

256 *See* n52, Fiske & Taylor (1991).

257 Gilbert, D. T. (1989). Thinking lightly about others: Automatic components of the social inference process. In J. S. Uleman & J. A. Bargh (Eds.), *Unintended thought* (pp. 189–211). New York: Guilford Press.

See n160, Uleman et al. (1996).

258 *See* n208, Albright et al. (1988).

See n182, Ambady & Rosenthal (1992).

See n201, Dimberg et al. (2000).

259 Kassin, S. M., & Pryor, J. B. (1985). The development of attribution processes. In J. Pryor & J. Day (Eds.), *The development of social cognition* (pp. 3–34). New York: Springer-Verlag.

Rholes, W. S., Jones, M., & Wade, C. (1988). Children's understanding of personal dispositions and its relationship to behavior. *Journal of Experimental Child Psychology*, *45*(1), 1–17.

White, P. A. (1988). Causal processing: Origins and development. *Psychological Bulletin, 104*(1), 36–52.

260 Egan, G. J., Brown, R. T., Goonan, L., Goonan, B. T., & Celano, M. (1998). The development of decoding of emotions in children with externalizing behavioral disturbances and their normally developing peers. *Archives of Clinical Neuropsychology, 13*(4), 383–396.

261 Gilbert, D. T., Pelham, B. W., & Krull, D. S. (1988). On cognitive busyness: When person perceivers meet persons perceived. *Journal of Personality and Social Psychology, 54*(5), 733–740.

262 Rapp, D. N., & Kendeou, P. (2009). Noticing and revising discrepancies as texts unfold. *Discourse Processes, 46*(1), 1–24.

263 Trope, Y. (1986). Identification and inferential processes in dispositional attribution. *Psychological Review, 93*(3), 239–257.

264 *See* n162, Lieberman (2007).

265 *See* n52, Fiske & Taylor (1991).

Higgins, E. T., & Bargh, J. A. (1987). Social cognition and social perception. *Annual Review of Psychology, 38*, 369–425.

See n35, Lord (1985).

266 *See* n265, Higgins & Bargh (1987).

Johnston, W. A., & Dark, V. J. (1986). Selective attention. *Annual Review of Psychology, 37*, 43–75.

Srull, T. K., & Wyer, R. S. (1979). The role of category accessibility in the interpretation of information about persons: Some determinants and implications. *Journal of Personality and Social Psychology, 37*(10), 1660–1672.

267 *See* n52, Fiske & Taylor (1991).

Wyer, R. S., & Carlston, D. E. (1979). *Social cognition, inference, and attribution*. Hillsdale, NJ: Lawrence Erlbaum Associates.

268 Cohen, C. E. (1981a). Goals and schemata in person perception: Making sense from the stream of behavior. In N. Cantor & J. F. Kihlstrom (Eds.), *Personality, cognition and social interaction* (pp. 45–68). Hillsdale, NJ: Lawrence Erlbaum Associates.

Ebbesen, E. B. (1980). Cognitive processes in understanding ongoing behavior. In R. Hastie, T. M. Ostrom, C. B. Ebbesen, R. S. Wyer, D. L. Hamilton & E. L. Carlston (Eds.), *Person memory: The cognitive basis of social perception* (pp. 179–225). Hillsdale, NJ: Lawrence Erlbaum Associates.

269 Emrich, C. G. (1999). Context effects in leadership perception. *Personality and Social Psychology Bulletin, 25*(8), 991–1006.

270 Willer, R. (2004). The effects of government-issued terror warnings on presidential approval ratings. *Current Research in Social Psychology, 10*(1), 1–12.

271 Eisen, S. V., & McArthur, L. Z. (1979). Evaluating and sentencing a defendant as a function of his salience and the perceiver's set. *Personality and Social Psychology Bulletin, 5*(1), 48–52.

272 Smith, S. W. (1986). A social-cognitive approach to the nature of input processes in reception of nonverbal messages (Doctoral dissertation, University of Southern California, 1986). *Dissertation Abstracts International, 47*(07A), 2372.

273 Massad, C. M., Hubbard, M., & Newtson, D. (1979). Selective perception of events. *Journal of Experimental Social Psychology, 15*(6), 513–532.

274 *See* n268, Ebbesen (1980).

275 Baron, R. M., Albright, L., & Mallory, T. E. (1995). Effects of behavioral and social class information on social judgment. *Personality and Social Psychology Bulletin, 21*(4), 308–315.

276 Duffy, S. A., & Keir, J. A. (2004). Violating stereotypes: Eye movements and comprehension processes when text conflicts with world knowledge. *Memory & Cognition, 32*(4), 551–559.

277 Hattrup, K., & Ford, J. K. (1995). The roles of information characteristics and accountability in moderating stereotype-driven processes during social decision making. *Organizational Behavior and Human Decision Processes, 63*(1), 73–86.

278 Cohen, C. E. (1976). Cognitive basis of stereotyping: An information processing approach to social perception (Doctoral dissertation, University of California, San Diego, 1976). *Dissertation Abstracts International, 38*(01B), 0412.

279 Cohen, C. E. (1981b). Person categories and social perception: Testing some boundaries of the processing effect of prior knowledge. *Journal of Personality and Social Psychology, 40*(3), 441–452.

280 Lingle, J. H., Geva, N., Ostrom, T. M., Leippe, M. R., & Baumgardner, M. H. (1979). Thematic effects of person judgments on impression organization. *Journal of Personality and Social Psychology, 37*(5), 674–687.

281 Zadny, J., & Gerard, H. B. (1974). Attributed intentions and informational selectivity. *Journal of Experimental Social Psychology, 10*(1), 34–52.

282 Phillips, J.S., & Lord, R.G. (1982). Schematic information processing and perceptions of leadership in problem-solving groups. *Journal of Applied Psychology, 67*(4), 486–492.

283 Belmore, S.M. (1987). Determinants of attention during impression formation. *Journal of Experimental Psychology: Learning, Memory, and Cognition, 13*(3), 480–489.

Fiske, S.T., & Neuberg, S.L. (1990). A continuum of impression formation, from category-based to individuating processes: Influences of information and motivation on attention and interpretation. In M.P. Zanna (Ed.), *Advances in experimental social psychology* (Vol. 23, pp. 1–74). New York: Academic Press.

Jamieson, D.W., & Zanna, M.P. (1989). Need for structure in attitude formation and expression. In A.R. Pratkanis, S.J. Breckler, & A.G. Greenwald (Eds.), *Attitude structure and function* (pp. 383–406). Hillsdale, NJ: Lawrence Erlbaum Associates.

284 Herstein, J.A. (1981). Keeping the voter's limits in mind: A cognitive process analysis of decision making in voting. *Journal of Personality and Social Psychology, 40*(5), 843–861.

285 Anderson, N.H. (1981). *Foundations of information theory.* New York: Academic Press.

286 Anderson, N.H. (1973). Information integration theory applied to attitudes about U.S. presidents. *Journal of Educational Psychology, 64*(1), 1–8.

287 Nagy, G. (1981). How are personnel selections made? An analysis of decision strategies in a simulated personnel selection task (Doctoral dissertation, Kansas State University, 1981). *Dissertation Abstracts International, 42*(07B), 3022.

288 Troutman, C.M., & Shanteau, J. (1976). Do consumers evaluate products by adding or averaging attribute information? *Journal of Consumer Research, 3*(2), 101–106.

289 Nagy, G. (1975). *Female dating strategies as a function of physical attractiveness and other social characteristics of males.* Unpublished thesis, Kansas State University, Manhattan, Kansas.

290 Kaplan, M.F., & Kemmerick, G.D. (1974). Juror judgment as information integration: Combining evidential and non-evidential information. *Journal of Personality and Social Psychology, 30*(4), 493–499.

291 Hamilton, D.L., & Zanna, M.P. (1972). Differential weighting of favorable and unfavorable attributes in impressions of personality. *Journal of Experimental Research in Personality, 6*(2–3), 204–212.

Hodges, B.H. (1974). Effect of valence on relative weighting in impression formation. *Journal of Personality and Social Psychology, 30*(3), 378–381.

292 Fiske, S.T. (1980). Attention and weight in person perception: The impact of negative and extreme behavior. *Journal of Personality and Social Psychology, 38*(6), 889–906.

See n291, Hodges (1974).

Kanouse, D.E., & Hanson Jr, L.R. (1972). Negativity in evaluations. In E.E. Jones, D.E. Kanouse, H.H. Kelley, R.E. Nisbett, S. Valins & B. Weiner (Eds.), *Attribution: Perceiving the causes of behavior* (pp. 47–62). Morristown, NJ: General Learning Press.

293 Hollman, T.D. (1972). Employment interviewers' errors in processing positive and negative information. *Journal of Applied Psychology, 56*, 130–134.

294 Skowronski, J.J., & Carlston, D.E. (1987). Social judgment and social memory: The role of cue diagnosticity in negativity, positivity, and extremity biases. *Journal of Personality and Social Psychology, 52*(4), 689–699.

Skowronski, J.J., & Carlston, D.E. (1989). Negativity and extremity biases in impression formation: A review of explanations. *Psychological Bulletin, 105*(1), 131–142.

295 *See* n161, Lipshitz & Shulimovitz (2007).

296 Messner, M., Reinhard, M.A., & Sporer, S.L. (2008). Compliance through direct persuasive appeals: The moderating role of communicator's attractiveness in interpersonal persuasion. *Social Influence, 3*(2), 67–83.

Mills, J., & Harvey, J. (1972). Opinion change as a function of when information about the communicator is received and whether he is attractive or expert. *Journal of Personality and Social Psychology, 21*(1), 52–55.

297 Petty, R.E., & Cacioppo, J.T. (1980). Effects of issue involvement on attitudes in an advertising context. In G. Gorn & M. Goldberg (Eds.), *Proceedings of the division 23 program* (pp. 75–79). Montreal, Canada: Division 23 of the American Psychological Association (09A), 2921.

298 Norman, R. (1976). When what is said is important: A comparison of expert and attractive sources. *Journal of Experimental Social Psychology, 12*(3), 294–300.

299 Olson, I.R., & Marshuetz, C. (2005). Facial attractiveness is appraised in a glance. *Emotion, 5*(4), 498–502.

van Leeuwen, M.L., & Neil Macrae, C. (2004). Is beautiful always good? Implicit benefits of facial attractiveness. *Social Cognition, 22*(6), 637–649.

300 Reingen, P. H., & Kernan, J. B. (1993). Social perception and interpersonal influence: Some consequences of the physical attractiveness stereotype in a personal selling setting. *Journal of Consumer Psychology, 2*(1), 25–38.

301 Gueguen, N., Legoherel, P., & Jacob, C. (2003). Solicitation of participation in an investigation by e-mail: Effect of the social presence of the physical attraction of the petitioner on the response rate. *Canadian Journal of Behavioural Science, 35*(2), 84–96.

302 Chaiken, S. (1979). Communicator physical attractiveness and persuasion. *Journal of Personality and Social Psychology, 37*(8), 1387.

303 Kassin, S. M. (1983). Deposition testimony and the surrogate witness: Evidence for a "messenger effect" in persuasion. *Personality and Social Psychology Bulletin, 9*(2), 281–288.

304 *See* n300, Reingen & Kernan (1993).

See also Landry, C. E., Lange, A., List, J. A., Price, M. K., & Rupp, N. G. (2006). Toward an understanding of the economics of charity: Evidence from a field experiment. *Quarterly Journal of Economics, 121*(2), 747–782.

305 Pallak, S. R., Murroni, E., & Koch, J. (1983). Communicator attractiveness and expertise, emotional versus rational appeals, and persuasion: A heuristic versus systematic processing interpretation. *Social Cognition, 2*(2), 122–141.

306 Bertrand, M., Karlin, D., Mullainathan, S., Shafir, E., & Zinman, J. (2010). What's advertising content worth? Evidence from a consumer credit marketing field experiment. *Quarterly Journal of Economics, 125*(1), 263–306.

307 Cunningham, M. R. (1986). Measuring the physical in physical attractiveness: Quasi-experiments on the sociobiology of female facial beauty. *Journal of Personality and Social Psychology, 50*(5), 925–935.

See n71, Cunningham et al. (1990).

308 Griffin, A. M., & Langlois, J. H. (2006). Stereotype directionality and attractiveness stereotyping: Is beauty good or is ugly bad? *Social Cognition, 24*(2), 187.

309 Budesheim, T. L., & DePaola, S. J. (1994). Beauty or the beast? The effects of appearance, personality, and issue information on evaluations of political candidates. *Personality and Social Psychology Bulletin, 20*(4), 339–348.

310 Mack, D., & Rainey, D. (1990). Female applicants' grooming and personnel selection. *Journal of Social Behavior and Personality, 5*(5), 399–407.

311 Sigall, H., & Ostrove, N. (1975). Beautiful but dangerous: Effects of offender attractiveness and nature of the crime on juridic judgment. *Journal of Personality and Social Psychology, 31*(3), 410–414.

312 Mazzella, R., & Feingold, A. (1994). The effects of physical attractiveness, race, socioeconomic status, and gender of defendants and victims on judgments of mock jurors: A meta-analysis. *Journal of Applied Social Psychology, 24*(5), 1315–1344.

313 Dubois, M., & Pansu, P. (2004). Facial attractiveness, applicants' qualifications, and judges' expertise about decisions in pre-selective recruitment. *Psychological Reports, 95*(3f), 1129–1134.

314 Hamermesh, D. S., & Parker, A. (2005). Beauty in the classroom: Instructors' pulchritude and putative pedagogical productivity. *Economics of Education Review, 24*(4), 369–376.

315 Frieze, I. H., Olson, J. E., & Russell, J. (1991). Attractiveness and income for men and women in management. *Journal of Applied Social Psychology, 21*(13), 1039–1057.

316 *See* n287, Nagy (1981).

317 Levine, L. R., Bluni, T. D., & Hochman, S. H. (1998). Attire and charitable behavior. *Psychological Reports, 83*(1), 15–18.

Pascual, A., Guéguen, N., Pujos, S., & Felonneau, M. L. (2013). Foot-in-the-door and problematic requests: A field experiment. *Social Influence, 8*(1), 46–53.

318 Segrin, C. (1993). The effects of nonverbal behavior on outcomes of compliance gaining attempts. *Communication Studies, 44*, 169–187.

319 *See* n102, Blankenship & Holtgraves (2005).

320 Bourhis, R. Y., & Giles, H. (1976). The language of co-operation in Wales: A field study. *Language Sciences, 42*, 13–16.

321 Sparks, J. R., & Areni, C. S. (2002). The effects of sales presentation quality and initial perceptions on persuasion: A multiple role perspective. *Journal of Business Research, 55*(6), 517–528.

322 Fielding, G., & Evered, C. (1978). An exploratory experimental study of the influence of patients' social background upon diagnostic process and outcome. *Psychiatria Clinica, 11*(2), 61–86.

323 Seggre, I. (1983). Attribution of guilt as a function of ethnic accent and type of crime. *Journal of Multilingual and Multicultural Development, 4*, 197–206.

324 Kalin, R., & Rayko, D. (1980). The social significance of speech in the job interview. In R. N. St. Clair & H. Giles (Eds.), *The social and psychological contexts of language* (pp. 39–50). Hillsdale, NJ: Lawrence Erlbaum Associates.

325 Gaertner, S., & Bickman, L. (1971). Effects of race on the elicitation of helping behavior: The wrong number technique. *Journal of Personality and Social Psychology, 20*(2), 218–222.

326 Purnell, T., Idsardi, W., & Baugh, J. (1999). Perceptual and phonetic experiments on American English dialect identification. *Journal of Language and Social Psychology, 18*(1), 10–30.

327 Pennebaker, J. W., & King, L. A. (1999). Linguistic styles: Language use as an individual difference. *Journal of Personality and Social Psychology, 77*(6), 1296–1312.

328 Lavandera, B. (1978). Where does the sociolinguistic variable stop? *Language in Society, 7*, 171–182.

329 Sankoff, D., Thibault, P., & Berube, H. (1978). Semantic field variability. In D. Sankoff (Ed.), *Linguistic variation: Models and methods* (pp. 23–44). New York: Academic Press.

330 Guy, G. R., & Vonwiller, J. (1984). The meaning of an intonation in Australian English. *Australian Journal of Linguistics, 4*(1), 1–17.

331 Labov, W. (1972). *Sociolinguistic patterns.* Oxford, UK: University Pennsylvania Press.

Campbell-Kibler, K. (2007). Accent, (ING), and the social logic of listener perceptions. *American Speech, 82*(1), 32–64.

332 Giles, H. (1973). Communicative effectiveness as a function of accented speech. *Speech Monographs, 40*(4), 330–331.

333 Giles, H., & Sassoon, C. (1983). The effect of speaker's accent, social class background and message style on British listeners' social judgements. *Language & Communication, 3*(3), 305–313.

334 Thakerar, J. N., & Giles, H. (1981). They are—so they spoke: Noncontent speech stereotypes. *Language & Communication, 1*(2–3), 255–261.

335 Giles, H., & Niedzielski, N. (1998). German sounds awful, but Italian is beautiful. In L. Bauer & P. Trudgill (Eds.), *Language myths* (pp. 85–93). Harmondsworth, UK: Penguin.

336 Salvadori, L., van Swol, L. M., & Sniezek, J. A. (2001). Information sampling and confidence within groups and Judge advisor systems. *Communication Research, 28*(6), 737–771.

Thomas, J. P., & McFadyen, R. G. (1995). The confidence heuristic: A game-theoretic analysis. *Journal of Economic Psychology, 16*(1), 97–113.

Van Swol, L. M. & Sniezek, J. A. (2002). *Trust me, I'm and expert: Trust and confidence and acceptance of expert advice.* Paper presented at the 8th Conference on Behavioral Decision Research in Management (BDRM), Chicago.

337 Schulz-Hardt, S., Jochims, M., & Frey, D. (2002). Productive conflict in group decision making: Genuine and contrived dissent as strategies to counteract biased information seeking. *Organizational Behavior and Human Decision Processes, 88*(2), 563–586.

338 *See* n102, Blankenship & Holtgraves (2005).

Burrell, N. A., & Koper, R. J. (1998). The efficacy of powerful/powerless language on attitudes and source credibility. In M. Allen & R. W. Preiss (Eds.), *Persuasion: Advances through metaanalysis* (pp. 203–215). Cresskill, NJ: Hampton.

Holtgraves, T., & Lasky, B. (1999). Linguistic power and persuasion. *Journal of Language and Social Psychology, 18*(2), 196–205.

339 Hahn, R. W., & Clayton, S. D. (1996). The effects of attorney presentation style, attorney gender, and juror gender on juror decisions. *Law and Human Behavior, 20*(5), 533–554.

340 Parton, S. R., Siltanen, S. A., Hosman, L. A., & Langenderfer, J. (2002). Employment interview outcomes and speech style effects. *Journal of Language and Social Psychology, 21*(2), 144–161.

341 Sparks, J. R., Areni, C. S., & Cox, K. C. (1998). An investigation of the effects of language style and communication modality on persuasion. *Communication Monographs, 65*(2), 108–125.

342 Price, P. C., & Stone, E. R. (2004). Intuitive evaluation of likelihood judgment producers: Evidence for a confidence heuristic. *Journal of Behavioral Decision Making, 17*(1), 39–57.

See n128, Yates et al. (1996).

343 Jules, S. J., & McQuiston, D. E. (2013). Speech style and occupational status affect assessments of eyewitness testimony. *Journal of Applied Social Psychology, 43*(4), 741–748.

344 Loyd, D. L., Phillips, K. W., Whitson, J., & Thomas-Hunt, M. C. (2010). Expertise in your midst: How congruence between status and speech style affects reactions to unique knowledge. *Group Processes & Intergroup Relations, 13*(3), 379–395.

345 Berscheid, E., & Reis, H. T. (1998). Attraction and close relationships. In D. T. Gilbert, S. T. Fiske & G. Lindzey (Eds.), *The handbook of social psychology* (4th ed., Vol. 2, pp. 193–281). New York: McGraw-Hill.

346 Keenan, A. (1977). Some relationships between interviewers' personal feelings about candidates and their general evaluation of them. *Journal of Occupational Psychology, 50*(4), 275–283.

347 Cardy, R. L., & Dobbins, G. H. (1986). Affect and appraisal accuracy: Liking as an integral dimension in evaluating performance. *Journal of Applied Psychology, 71*(4), 672–678.

348 Levinson, W., Roter, D. L., Mullooly, J. P., Dull, V. T., & Frankel, R. M. (1997). Physician-patient communication: The relationship with malpractice claims among primary care physicians and surgeons. *Journal of the American Medical Association, 277*(7), 553–559.

349 Ambady, N., Laplante, D., Nguyen, T., Rosenthal, R., Chaumeton, N., & Levinson, W. (2002). Surgeons' tone of voice: A clue to malpractice history. *Surgery, 132*(1), 5–9.

350 Kernell, S. (1993). *Going public: New strategies of presidential leadership* (2nd ed.). Washington, DC: CQ Press.

Mondak, J. J. (1993). Source cues and policy approval: The cognitive dynamics of public support for the Reagan agenda. *American Journal of Political Science, 37*(1), 186–212.

351 Sigelman, L., & Sigelman, C. K. (1981). Presidential leadership of public opinion: From "Benevolent Leader" to kiss of death? *Experimental Study of Politics, 7*(3), 1–22.

352 Guéguen, N. (2013). Handshaking and compliance with a request: A door-to-door setting. *Social Behavior and Personality: An International Journal, 41*(10), 1585–1588.

353 Solomon, H., Zener-Solomon, L., Arnone, M., Maur, B., Reda, R., & Roth, E. (1981). Anonymity and helping. *The Journal of Social Psychology, 113*(1), 37–43.

354 Kleinke, C. L. (1980). Interaction between gaze and legitimacy of request on compliance in a field setting. *Journal of Nonverbal Behavior, 5*(1), 3–12.

355 *Ibid.*

356 Hart, A. J., & Morry, M. M. (1997). Trait inferences based on racial and behavioral cues. *Basic and Applied Social Psychology, 19*(1), 33–48.

Hrubes, D. A. (2001). The role of nonverbal behavior in persuasion (Doctoral dissertation, University of Massachusetts, Amherst, 2001). *Dissertation Abstracts International, 62*(9–B), 4274.

Mason, M. F., Tatkow, E. P., & Macrae, C. N. (2005). The look of love gaze shifts and person perception. *Psychological Science, 16*(3), 236–239.

357 Levine, S. P. (1998). Implicit self-presentational goals and nonverbal behavior. *Dissertation Abstracts International: Section B: The Sciences and Engineering, 59*(10-B), 5621.

358 Baron, R. A., & Bell, P. A. (1976). Physical distance and helping: Some unexpected benefits of "crowding in" on others. *Journal of Applied Social Psychology, 6*(2), 95–104.

Edinger, J. A., & Patterson, M. L. (1983). Nonverbal involvement and social control. *Psychological Bulletin, 93*(1), 30–56.

See n354, Kleinke (1980).

359 Sommers, M. S., Greeno, D. W., & Boag, D. (1989). The role of nonverbal communication in service provision and representation. *Service Industries Journal, 9*(4), 162–173.

360 Englis, B. G., & Reid, D. (1990). Salesperson expressions of emotions influence personal selling outcomes. *Proceedings of the Society for Consumer Psychology,* 79–83.

361 *See* n318, Segrin (1993).

362 Wood, W., & Kallgren, C. A. (1988). Communicator attributes and persuasion: Recipients' access to attitude-relevant information in memory. *Personality and Social Psychology Bulletin, 14*(1), 172–182.

363 Andreoli, V., & Worchel, S. (1978). Effects of media, communicator, and message position on attitude change. *Public Opinion Quarterly, 42,* 59–70.

See n21, Chaiken & Eagly (1983).

364 Matthews, H. L., Wilson, D. T., & Monoky Jr, J. F. (1972). Bargaining behavior in a buyer-seller dyad. *Journal of Marketing Research, 9*(1), 103–105.

Woodside, A. G., & Davenport, W. J. (1974). The effect of salesmen similarity and expertise on consumer purchasing behavior. *Journal of Marketing Research, 11*(2), 198–202.

365 *See* n332, Giles (1973).

366 Hensley, W. E. (1981). The effects of attire, location, and sex on aiding behavior: A similarity explanation. *Journal of Nonverbal Behavior, 6,* 3–11.

367 Carli, L. L., Ganley, R., & Pierce-Otay, A. (1991). Similarity and satisfaction in roommate relationships. *Personality and Social Psychology Bulletin, 17*(4), 419–426.

Hill, C. T., & Stull, D. E. (1981). Sex differences in effects of social and value similarity in same-sex friendship. *Journal of Personality and Social Psychology, 41*(3), 488–502.

368 Kerr, N. L., Hymes, R. W., Anderson, A. B., & Weathers, J. E. (1995). Defendant-juror similarity and mock juror judgments. *Law and Human Behavior, 19*(6), 545–567.

Stephan, C. W., & Stephan, W. G. (1986). Habla Ingles? The effects of language translation on simulated juror decisions. *Journal of Applied Social Psychology, 16*(7), 577–589.

369 Graves, L. M., & Powell, G. N. (1988). An investigation of sex discrimination in recruiters' evaluations of actual applicants. *Journal of Applied Psychology, 73*(1), 20–29.

Peters, L. H., & Terborg, J. R. (1975). The effects of temporal placement of unfavorable information and of attitude similarity on personnel selection decisions. *Organizational Behavior and Human Performance, 13*(2), 279–293.

Schmitt, N. (1976). Social and situational determinants of interview decisions: Implications for the employment interview. *Personnel Psychology, 29*(1), 79–101.

370 Frank, L. L., & Hackman, J. R. (1975). Effects of interviewer-interviewee similarity on interviewer objectivity in college admissions interviews. *Journal of Applied Psychology, 60*(3), 356–360.

371 Berscheid, E. (1985). Interpersonal attraction. In G. Lindzey & E. Aronson (Eds.), *Handbook of social psychology* (3rd ed., Vol. 2, pp. 413–484). New York: Random House.

372 Wade, K. J., & Kinicki, A. J. (1997). Subjective applicant qualifications and interpersonal attraction as mediators within a process model of interview selection decisions. *Journal of Vocational Behavior, 50*(1), 23–40.

373 *See* n46, Hogg (2007).

Hogg, M. A., & van Knippenberg, D. (2003). Social identity and leadership processes in groups. In M. P. Zanna (Ed.), *Advances in experimental social psychology* (Vol. 35, pp. 1–52). San Diego, CA: Academic Press.

374 Seyranian, V., & Bligh, M. C. (2008). Presidential charismatic leadership: Exploring the rhetoric of social change. *The Leadership Quarterly, 19*(1), 54–76.

375 Bailenson, J. N., & Yee, N. (2005). Digital chameleons: Automatic assimilation of nonverbal gestures in immersive virtual environments. *Psychological Science, 16*, 814–819.

Bates, J. E. (1975). Effects of a child's imitation versus nonimitation on adults' verbal and nonverbal positivity. *Journal of Personality and Social Psychology, 31*(5), 840–851.

Manusov, V. (1993). "It depends on your perspective": Effects of stance and beliefs about intent on person perception. *Western Journal of Communication, 57*(1), 27–41.

376 Cappella, J. N. (1993). The facial feedback hypothesis in human interaction: Review and speculation. *Journal of Language and Social Psychology Special Issue: Emotional Communication, Culture, and Power, 12*, 13–29.

377 Scheflen, A. (1964). The significance of posture in communication systems. *Psychiatry, 27*, 316–331.

378 van Baaren, R. B., Holland, R. W., Kawakami, K., & van Knippenberg, A. (2004). Mimicry and prosocial behavior. *Psychological Science, 15*, 71–74.

379 van Baaren, R. B., Holland, R. W., Steenaert, B., & van Knippenberg, A. (2003). Mimicry for money: Behavioral consequences of imitation. *Journal of Experimental Social Psychology, 39*, 393–398.

380 Curhan, J. R., & Pentland, A. (2007). Thin slices of negotiation: Predicting outcomes from conversational dynamics within the first 5 minutes. *Journal of Applied Psychology, 92*(3), 802–811.

381 McArthur, L. Z. (1981). What grabs you? The role of attention in impression formation and causal attribution. In E. T. Higgins, C. P. Herman & M. P. Zanna (Eds.), *Social cognition: The Ontario Symposium* (Vol. 1, pp. 201–246). Hillsdale, NJ: Lawrence Erlbaum Associates.

Taylor, S. E., & Fiske, S. T. (1978). Salience, attention, and attribution: Top of the head phenomena. In L. Berkowitz (Ed.), *Advances in experimental social psychology* (Vol. 11, pp. 249–288). New York: Academic Press.

382 Erb, H. P., Bohner, G., Rank, S., & Einwiller, S. (2002). Processing minority and majority communications: The role of conflict with prior attitudes. *Personality and Social Psychology Bulletin, 28*(9), 1172–1182.

383 Taylor, S. E. (1981). A categorization approach to stereotyping. In D. L. Hamilton (Ed.), *Cognitive processes in stereotyping and intergroup behavior* (pp. 88–114). Hillsdale: Lawrence Erlbaum Associates.

384 Vaughan, S. I. (1999). Information sharing and cognitive centrality: Patterns in small decision-making groups of executives. *Dissertation Abstracts International: Section B: The Sciences and Engineering, 60*(4-B), 1919.

385 Kameda, T., Ohtsubo, Y., & Takezawa, M. (1997). Centrality in sociocognitive networks and social influence: An illustration in a group decision-making context. *Journal of Personality and Social Psychology, 73*(2), 296–309.

386 Van Swol, L. M., & Seinfeld, E. (2006). Differences between minority, majority, and unanimous group members in the communication of information. *Human Communication Research, 32*(2), 178–197.

387 Sargis, E. G., & Larson Jr, J. R. (2002). Informational centrality and member participation during group decision making. *Group Processes & Intergroup Relations, 5*(4), 333–347.

Schittekatte, M., & Van Hiel, A. (1996). Effects of partially shared information and awareness of unshared information on information sampling. *Small Group Research*, 27(3), 431–449.

388 Wittenbaum, G. M., Hubbell, A. P., & Zuckerman, C. (1999). Mutual enhancement: Toward an understanding of the collective preference for shared information. *Journal of Personality and Social Psychology*, 77(5), 967–978.

389 Kerschreiter, R., Schulz-Hardt, S., Faulmuller, N., Mojzisch, A., & Frey, D. (2004). *Psychological explanations for the dominance of shared and preference-consistent information in group discussions: Mutual enhancement or rational-decision making?* Working Paper, Ludwig Maximilians University of Munich, Munich, Germany.

390 Mojzisch, A., Schulz-Hardt, S., Kerschreiter, R., Brodbeck, F. C., & Frey, D. (2004). *Social validation as an explanation for the dominance of shared information in group decisions: A critical test and extension.* Working Paper, Dresden: University of Technology.

391 Larson, J. R., Sargis, E. G., Elstein, A. S., & Schwartz, A. (2002). Holding shared versus unshared information: Its impact on perceived member influence in decision-making groups. *Basic and Applied Social Psychology*, 24(2), 145–155.

PART III

Understanding Emotional Decision Making

7

EMOTIONS IN AUDIENCE DECISION MAKING

On October 3, 2000, then-vice president Al Gore and soon-to-be-president George W. Bush engaged in the first of three televised presidential debates. Minutes into the first debate, Gore and Bush exchanged views on Medicare coverage.

GORE: Under the Governor's plan, if you kept the same fee for service that you have now under Medicare, your premiums would go up by between 18% and 47%, and that is the study of the Congressional plan that he's modeled his proposal on by the Medicare actuaries. Let me give you one quick example. There is a man here tonight named George McKinney from Milwaukee. He's 70 years old, has high blood pressure, his wife has heart trouble. They have an income of $25,000 a year. They can't pay for their prescription drugs. They're some of the ones that go to Canada regularly in order to get their prescription drugs. Under my plan, half of their costs would be paid right away. Under Governor Bush's plan, they would get not one penny for four to five years and then they would be forced to go into an HMO or to an insurance company and ask them for coverage, but there would be no limit on the premiums or the deductibles or any of the terms and conditions.

BUSH: I cannot let this go by, the old-style Washington politics, if we're going to scare you in the voting booth. Under my plan the man gets immediate help with prescription drugs. It's called Immediate Helping Hand. Instead of squabbling and finger pointing, he gets immediate help. Let me say something.

MODERATOR: Your

GORE: They get $25,000 a year income; that makes them ineligible.

BUSH: Look, this is a man who has great numbers. He talks about numbers. I'm beginning to think not only did he invent the Internet, but he invented the calculator. It's fuzzy math.[1]

Political psychologist Drew Westen uses the exchange between the two candidates to illustrate the difference between a highly logical and reasonable appeal to voters and an appeal based on emotions.[2] Whereas Vice President Gore spoke in a cold and humorless manner, then-governor Bush delivered his remarks in a friendly, affable style. Whereas Gore framed his Medicare plan in the language of an economist, Bush framed his plan so as to achieve maximum emotional resonance with the voting public, calling it the "Immediate Helping Hand."

> Instead of getting voters to *feel* the difference between his concern for the welfare of seniors struggling to pay their medical bills and Bush's, Gore went to a level of numerical precision— premised on a model of expected utility, giving them every number they needed to make the appropriate calculations—that played right into Bush's strategy of portraying Gore as an emotionless policy wonk, "not a regular guy, like us."
>
> (Westen 2007, p. 33)

The ability to make an emotional connection with an audience is an essential leadership skill. The extent to which U.S. presidents' speeches evoke emotions is directly related to the public's perception of each president's charisma and greatness.[3] Indeed, the hallmark of truly great speeches and the leaders who deliver them is their ability to stir the audience's emotions. However, many professionals overestimate their ability to elicit the emotions they intend. For example, audiences often interpret professionals' emails intended to be funny as being sarcastic and insulting instead.[4]

Obviously, emotions play an important role in audience decision making, but what are emotions? Emotions are comprised of:

(1) thoughts and feelings;
(2) physical responses in the brain and body;
(3) facial, vocal, and postural expressions; and
(4) action tendencies or readiness for certain behaviors.[5]

Audience members acquire emotions early in life. By age six months, children have acquired the emotions of surprise, interest, joy, anger, sadness, fear, and disgust. By age two, they have acquired envy and empathy. By age three, embarrassment, pride, shame, and guilt.[6]

Psychologically, emotions alter the audience's attention, change the way they process information, and activate associative memories.[7] Physiologically, emotions produce a bodily state in audience members that is optimal for an effective response to the perceived situation. Emotions alter the audience's skeletomuscular system, their autonomic nervous system, and their endocrine system—the hormonal system that affects audience members' reflexes, as well as their cardiovascular, electrodermal, gastrointestinal, and thyroid activity.[8] Thus, when audiences encounter emotion-evoking information, their bodies respond. For example, threateningly worded and emotion-evoking emailed reprimands, like the one from the CEO quoted in Chapter 6 (p. 277), significantly increase the diastolic blood pressure of the employees reading them.[9] Emotions not only change blood pressure levels in audience members, they can even change the number of immune and antibody cells in their blood.[10]

Emotions, although similar to moods, do not last as long. Whereas audiences may experience moods for days, their emotions last only minutes or hours.[11]

The emotions audience members experience allow them to evaluate stimuli, to sort out which stimuli are good and which are bad, and to decide which stimuli should be approached and which should be avoided.[12] Emotions also function to prepare audience members to respond to stimuli in particular ways that cognitive scientists refer to as "action tendencies."[13] And since emotions are usually accompanied by expressive postures, gestures, and facial and vocal expressions, emotions also serve to communicate the audience's feeling states to others.[14] Short-circuiting the audience's rational processing of information is another primary function of emotions.[15]

In addition, emotions serve to enhance the audience's memory. Audiences are more likely to remember emotional stimuli than neutral stimuli.[16] In a study of emotional words in messages, adults of different ages read sentences that were written either to stir emotions (e.g., "There was a raging fire in the forest") or to be emotionally neutral (e.g., "There was a dirt road in the forest"). Both younger and older adults showed enhanced memory for the emotional words in the sentences they read.[17]

Audiences are also likely to remember emotional stimuli more vividly.[18] Many studies show that audiences have enhanced "flashbulb memories" of emotionally salient public events.[19] At the same time audiences may have difficulty intentionally forgetting emotional stimuli. Although audiences can intentionally forget neutral photographs, they find it hard to forget either emotionally negative or positive photographs.[20]

The Impact of Emotions on Decision Making

Emotional Decisions vs. Rational Decisions

Emotions are often better predictors of audience behavior than reason.[21] When emotions and reason are consistent with one another, both exert equal influence on the audience's attitudes and behaviors.[22] However, when emotions and reason are at odds, the audience's emotions have a greater influence on them than reason.

Surprisingly, when audience decisions are based on emotions, individual audience members may agree more with other members of the audience than when their decisions are based on reason.[23] The consensual nature of audience members' emotional responses may explain why jurors often agree strongly on how they feel about legal cases yet disagree just as strongly on the amount of punitive damages to award.[24]

Unlike rational decisions, the emotional decisions audiences make are insensitive to quantity. For example, audiences donate less to save pandas when they see the number of pandas to be saved represented as dots as opposed to seeing a photograph of a single panda.[25] Emotional decisions are insensitive to probabilities as well.[26] Contrary to the assumptions of economic theory, research participants are unwilling to pay more to avoid a high probability of receiving an electric shock than to avoid a low probability of receiving the same shock.[27]

Up to 50% of consumer purchase decisions can be classified as emotional or impulse purchases.[28] And almost 90% of consumers make impulsive, emotion-based purchases at least occasionally.[29] What's more, they do so across a broad range of product offerings in a variety of price ranges.[30]

Emotions can even determine decisions that require substantial rational thought and deliberation from the audience.[31] For example, emotions play a critical role in determining voters' decisions during U.S. presidential elections.[32] Sociologist Amitai Etzioni goes so far as to assert that "the majority of choices people make, including economic ones, are completely or largely based on normative-affective [i.e., emotional] considerations."[33]

In some situations, audiences are especially likely to make emotional as opposed to rational decisions. For example, a consumer's decisions are more likely to be based on emotional considerations when the consumer is looking for a particular experience such as having fun as opposed to accomplishing a pragmatic goal such as buying groceries.[34] Thus, a consumer's decision to buy a vacation package is more likely to be based on emotions than is their decision to buy a mobile phone plan.[35] Consumers' evaluations of certain product attributes such as styling are also more likely to be based on emotions than their evaluations of other types of product attributes such as cost.[36] Sometimes audiences rely more on emotion than reason simply because they lack the motivation, ability, or opportunity to process all the information required for making a totally rational decision.[37]

An ad's ability to evoke emotions often determines the purchase intentions of its audience. In a study of ad formats, consumers read four versions of an ad for a hypothetical brand of facial tissues and were asked to decide if they wanted to purchase the product. One version contained only an emotionally neutral verbal claim about the product. Two versions contained the same verbal claim together with a headline and two different, but emotionally positive, photographs. The fourth version contained the same verbal claim as well as a headline and an emotionally neutral photograph. The two versions containing the emotionally positive photographs elicited the most positive emotions. Moreover, the more positive a consumer's emotional reaction to a version of the ad, the greater their intention to purchase the product.[38] Related studies of advertising confirm that when rational responses to the product are statistically controlled for, consumers' emotional reactions to ads account for a significant amount of the variance in their attitudes toward the brand,[39] especially toward new brands.[40]

Jurors' verdicts are influenced by their emotional reactions to pre-trial publicity. In one study, mock jurors read either factual news reports describing the defendant's previous convictions and the discovery of incriminating evidence or emotional pretrial publicity that identified the defendant as a suspect in a hit-and-run killing of a child. The emotional pretrial publicity produced a 20% higher conviction rate than the factual pretrial publicity, despite judicial instructions to discount the pretrial publicity altogether.[41]

The Positive Impact of Emotions on Decision Making

The impact of emotions on audience decision making is mostly positive. Emotions help the audience recognize the personal significance of the information they use to make judgments and decisions,[42] and to recognize the desirability of different alternatives as well.[43] Emotions also help the audience recognize the moral and aesthetic values implicated by their decisions.[44]

Surprisingly, audience decisions based on emotions are sometimes more accurate than decisions based on analytic reasoning. In a study that compared novices to experts, the ratings of consumers who were asked how much they liked the taste of various brands of jam corresponded better with ratings of gustatory experts than ratings of consumers who were asked to rationally justify their preferences.[45] In a follow-up study, consumers who were asked to choose the poster they liked most ended up liking the poster they chose more than consumers who were asked to analyze each poster along several attributes or decision criteria before making their final choice.[46]

Emotions also provide the audience with the motivation necessary to implement their decisions.[47] Traditional decision theory assumes that once an audience member chooses an appropriate course of action she will automatically take it. But many studies of decision making have shown that although audience members may decide to do what is best, they do not necessarily do what is best.[48] Emotions provide the audience with the motivation to follow through.

The Negative Impact of Emotions

Emotions are well known for their negative effects on audience decision making. Emotions can cause audience members to reverse a prior rational decision, such as a decision to diet, to stop drinking, or to hold a stock that is dropping in value.[49] Emotions can cause the audience to scrutinize information either too much or too little.[50] Emotions can cut short rational processing and cause audiences to jump to unwarranted conclusions.[51]

Thus, emotions can potentially override rational deliberations and can even cause audience members to behave self-destructively.[52] Intense emotions create a sense of urgency that can lead audience members to respond only to emotion-related cues and unconscious processes[53] and to engage in automatic and dangerous behaviors.[54] Sometimes intense emotions also lead audience members to be unreasonably harsh with others. In the courtroom, emotionally arousing testimony and/or evidence can inhibit rational decision making and lead jurors to render excessively severe sentencing judgments.[55]

Emotions can distort the audience's judgment about the consequences of their decisions.[56] For example, negative emotions can cause investors to be excessively risk-averse and to choose safer investments such as bonds over higher-performing stocks.[57] Conversely, positive emotions can make audiences less sensitive to possible risks. For example, cigarette advertising designed to increase the positive emotions associated with smoking can suppress the audience's perception of the risks involved with smoking.[58] Positive emotions have even been shown to lead foreign exchange traders to take unwarranted risks and to lose money unnecessarily.[59] Positive emotions can lead consumers to pay twice as much to insure a beloved antique clock as to insure a similar clock of equal value but to which they have no emotional attachment, all despite the fact that the insurance pays $100 in both cases.[60] Positive emotions can also make consumers more likely to buy a warranty on a newly purchased used car when the car is a beautiful convertible than when it is an ordinary-looking station wagon even though the expected repair expenses and the cost of the warranty are the same.[61]

Emotions can even hamper the audience's ability to reason logically about logic problems. In a classic study of emotion versus reason, participants read 20 syllogisms that dealt with emotionally charged topics and 20 that dealt with emotionally neutral topics. Participants were then asked to determine if the syllogisms were valid and to state whether they agreed with their conclusions. Interestingly, the participants were much more accurate judging the validity of the syllogisms dealing with emotionally neutral topics than judging the emotionally charged ones.[62]

The Impact of Emotional Deficits

Ironically, the ability to experience emotions is essential to rational decision making. In spite of otherwise normal intellectual abilities, patients with damage to the ventromedial prefrontal cortex (vmPFC) are unable to experience emotions and, consequently, have great difficulty making rational decisions (see Figure 3.5, p. 108).[63] These patients often make decisions against their best interests and repeat prior decisions that led to negative consequences.[64] The decisions they make often result in financial losses, losses in social standing, and losses of family and friends.

Other symptoms of the emotional deficits caused by damage to the vmPFC include indecisiveness, inability to prioritize, inability to plan future activity, inappropriate social manners, disregard of risks, and lack of concern for others.[65] Yet vmPFC patients possess all of their other faculties, including normal intelligence, comprehension, memory, and attention.[66]

In his book *Descartes' Error*, neuroscientist Antonio Damasio described one of his patients with vmPFC damage who, when asked to decide which of two days he would prefer to come for his next appointment, spent almost a half-hour enumerating reasons for and against each of the two dates: previous engagements, proximity to other engagements, possible meteorological conditions. The patient even went through "a tiresome cost-benefit analysis, an endless outlining and fruitless comparison of options and possible consequences." The same patient showed no emotional reactions to grisly pictures, although he described them as "disgusting." Despite the fact the patient had an intellectual understanding of emotional states, he had no emotional experiences, and as a consequence, had great difficulty making even the simplest of decisions.[67]

The Antecedents of Emotional Decision Making

Audience Goals and Values

At the cognitive level, the antecedents of the audience's emotions are their personal goals and values.[68] Audience goals tend to be specific and short term, like the goal to exercise five times a week; audience values, such as freedom, security, and honesty, are more abstract and slower to change. Because emotions are evaluations of stimuli as they relate to a person's goals and values, audience members would not experience emotions without them.[69]

Negative emotions result from threats to the audience's goals and values. Positive emotions result from attainment of their goals and values.[70] The strength of an audience member's emotional response to a situation is determined both by how relevant that situation is to their goals and values, and by how invested they are in those goals and values.[71] Table 7.1 indicates the values of Americans in different age groups. Although all three age groups rank freedom and self-respect among their top five values, 20-year-olds tend to value freedom and happiness most highly. Older people tend to value family security and world peace most highly.[72] In the political realm, the audience's values predict a broad range of policy preferences.[73] An audience member's commitment to the value of equality, for example, predicts their attitudes toward many social policies, including welfare programs and government provision of jobs.[74]

Different Goals and Values, Different Emotions

Different audience members can have different emotional reactions to the same stimulus.[75] The Greek philosopher Epictetus said much the same thing almost 2,000 years ago when he observed that people are not disturbed by things but rather by their view of them. An old story illustrates this point. It describes "three persons of much the same age and temperament" traveling in the same carriage who were told of the sudden death of another. The first person was not affected; the second started to cry; the third smiled. Why? The first person had never heard of the deceased. The second person was the sister of the deceased. The third person was a long-time rival of the

TABLE 7.1 Top Five Values of Three Age Groups

Rank	20-year-olds	30-year-olds	60-year-olds
1	Freedom	Family security	World peace
2	Happiness	World peace	Family security
3	Wisdom	Freedom	Freedom
4	Self-respect	Self-respect	National security
5	Love	Wisdom	Self-respect

Source: Adapted from Rokeach (1973)

deceased. Thus each person had a different emotional reaction to the same event because each valued the deceased differently.

The fact that different audience members have different goals and values appears to explain many individual differences in consumer behavior and media exposure.[76] For example, a cross-cultural study finds that consumers in France purchase expensive bottles of wine because of their desire for social interaction, whereas consumers in the United States purchase the same wines in order to prove themselves to others.[77] Thus, an ad that motivates consumers in Boston is unlikely to be effective with consumers in Paris. Likewise, because different citizens have different values that come into play when they decide whether to recycle, recycling campaigns focused on a single value tend to have only limited success.[78]

The Link Between Decision Criteria and Goals and Values

The audience's decision criteria determine which of their goals and values are implicated when they make a decision.[79] For instance, when deciding between two cars, the criterion or attribute of safety may implicate the value of personal survival, whereas the criterion of styling may implicate the value of personal expression. In addition, there is a direct connection between the goals and values that product attributes implicate and consumer purchases and preferences.[80] Consumers are motivated to buy a product to the extent they are able to link the product's attributes to their own goals and values.[81]

The values consumers link to products are often better predictors of their product preferences than the products' attributes.[82] The values consumers link to products correlate not only with their initial purchase intentions, but also with their product and/or service evaluations and with their repeat purchases as well.[83]

Much like consumers responding to products that implicate their goals and values, subordinates respond more positively to leaders who endorse their goals and values.[84] Business leaders who frame messages in terms of their subordinates' goals and values, as opposed to their own, increase their employees' motivation, commitment, and satisfaction.[85]

Decision criteria or attributes with implications for the audience's more highly valued goals trigger more emotion.[86] Although economic attributes such as price may be highly important to consumers, economic attributes do not have as much potential to elicit emotion as other attributes such as safety features.[87] Decision criteria or attributes with implications for the audience's more highly valued goals are also higher in "trade-off difficulty."[88] For instance, new parents who purchase an automobile may be very reluctant to accept losses on the attribute of safety for gains on the attribute of fuel efficiency. Similarly, voters are rarely willing to trade off a positive evaluation of a candidate on an economic issue for a negative evaluation of the same candidate on a highly valued ethical issue.[89]

Cognitive and Physiological Processes in Emotional Decision Making

Unlike rational decision making, emotional decision making includes physiological as well as cognitive processes. Emotional decision making starts as soon as the audience perceives an emotionally significant stimulus or recognizes an emotionally significant attribute of a stimulus. Only those stimuli or attributes of a stimulus that are relevant to the audience's goals and values can be said to be emotionally significant. As we have seen, the stimulus itself does not trigger an emotion or the decisions based on it, instead an emotion is triggered when the stimulus implicates one of the audience's goals or values.[90]

The model of emotional decision making proposed here and shown in Figure 7.1 builds on this understanding of emotionally significant stimuli. The model also presents an account of emotions

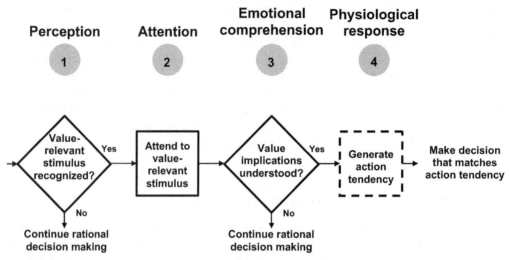

FIGURE 7.1 A Cognitive Process Model of Emotional Decision Making

as "interrupt mechanisms."[91] As soon as an audience member perceives a stimulus that has emotional significance to them, the stimulus captures their attention, demands fast comprehension of its implications, and evokes an emotional response that includes a tendency to take a particular type of physical action such as embracing, attacking, or withdrawing from the stimulus. The emotional response interrupts and overrides the more deliberate and rational decision-making process of making comparisons and trade-offs and leads the audience to make a decision congruent with the emotion's action tendency.

Perception of Emotionally Significant Stimuli

Audiences perceive emotionally significant images very rapidly.[92] Although audiences need 240 milliseconds to recognize a neutral picture, they can perceive a negative picture within 105 milliseconds and a positive picture within 180 milliseconds.[93] Even abstract images are perceived more quickly if an emotion is associated with them.[94]

Audiences are especially fast at perceiving emotional facial expressions. Audience responses to positive versus negative facial expressions are distinguishable within just 80 to 160 milliseconds after the faces are presented.[95] Even in tasks for which the emotional expression on a face is irrelevant, audience members respond to emotional faces more rapidly than neutral ones.[96] Audience responses to threatening faces are most rapid. Audiences can detect threatening faces faster and more accurately than friendly faces even when only one facial feature, such as the eyebrows, the mouth, or the eyes, conveys the threat.[97]

Audiences are also quick to perceive emotionally significant words. When presented a series of words very rapidly, about one every 100 milliseconds, readers are more likely to recognize the emotionally significant words in a series than the neutral ones.[98]

Some audience members can perceive emotionally significant stimuli even when the stimuli are outside the focus of their attention.[99] In a study of gender differences, men and women who had been induced to attend to something else overheard syllables spoken either in an emotional or a neutral way. Although both sexes detected non-emotional acoustic changes in the speaker's voice, only the women in the study detected changes in the speaker's emotional tone.[100]

However, neither male nor female readers can perceive emotionally significant written words unless they fixate on them. An eye-tracking study found no evidence of semantic processing of either emotional words (sex-related, threat-related, or curse words) or neutral words that were outside readers' foveal vision but within their peripheral vision. In addition, the study found that readers' pupil size did not increase when they were presented with emotional words peripherally, again indicating a lack of emotional response.[101]

Attention to Emotionally Significant Stimuli

Audiences selectively attend to emotionally significant stimuli. When a neutral and an emotionally significant picture are simultaneously projected into viewers' eyes, viewers give the emotionally significant picture preferential processing.[102] Viewers are also more likely to fixate first on either pleasant or unpleasant emotional images than on neutral ones.[103]

Emotionally significant stimuli capture the audience's attention[104] even when the emotional stimuli are presented simultaneously with a number of different neutral stimuli that should otherwise distract them.[105] For example, fear-relevant stimuli (e.g., a picture of a snake or a spider) "pop out" of visual displays regardless of the number of neutral objects in the display.[106] An angry face among many neutral faces also yields a pop-out effect.[107] Interestingly, the number of neutral images in a display does not influence the time takes to detect a fear-relevant stimulus within that display.[108]

In addition to quickly popping out, emotionally significant stimuli capture the audience's attention for longer periods of time. Viewers explore emotionally significant pictures longer and more extensively than neutral ones.[109] Readers maintain their attention longer on any location where an emotionally significant word has been presented.[110] Emotionally significant messages also elicit sustained attention and processing from the audience.[111] In a study of spoken messages, audience members listened to neutral, pleasant, and unpleasant verbal messages that each lasted two minutes. Changes in the diameter of their pupils before, during, and after each message was spoken were monitored continuously. Dilation of the audience members' pupils indicated they spent more time attending to and processing the pleasant and unpleasant messages than the neutral ones.[112]

Pupil size also increases when audiences view images that have an emotional significance to them.[113] For example, in one study, male viewers showed the greatest change in pupil size in response to a picture of a nude female. Female viewers, on the other hand, showed the greatest change in response to a picture of a mother holding a young child. In a similar study, viewers examined a series of pictures related to different emotionally significant themes (e.g., disease). The size of the viewers' pupils differed for each theme presented.[114]

Another indicator that an emotionally significant stimulus has captured the audience's attention is the *orienting response*.[115] The orienting response is associated with the emotion of surprise. When audience members are surprised, they stop whatever behavior they were engaged in and give their full attention to the stimulus.[116] The orienting response also elicits anticipation and a readiness to respond physically.[117] Although the orienting response to an intensely emotional stimulus is automatic, it can be overridden if the stimulus is only a mildly emotional one.[118]

The audience's attentional biases are strongest for stimuli that are most closely related to their goals and values.[119] For example, expert bird watchers display a selective attentional bias toward bird-related words.[120] Smokers, but not nonsmokers, maintain their gaze longer on smoking-related pictures than on pictures unrelated to smoking. The longer smokers fixate on smoking-related pictures, the more positively they rate them and the greater their urge to smoke.[121]

Another attentional bias is termed the "weapon-focus" effect.[122] In this bias, the audience's attention to and memory for neutral information in scenes is substantially reduced by the presence of emotionally significant stimuli.[123] Thus, when shown scenes of crimes taking place, audience members spend a disproportionate amount of time looking at the weapon in the scenes (e.g., a gun). Both the unusualness and the threat of the weapon decrease the audience's attention to peripheral information.[124] Moreover, the amount of time audience members spend looking at the weapon is inversely related to their ability to remember peripheral information in the scene, such as the face of the criminal.[125]

A review of the weapon focus literature concludes that the presence of any emotionally significant element in a scene makes it less likely audience members will remember neutral elements. Instead, they are more likely to remember those same neutral elements if they occur in a scene without an emotional component.[126] Emotionally significant stimuli also degrade attention to and memory for neutral stimuli presented immediately before the emotional stimuli.[127] For example, reading audiences are more likely to forget words that appear just before emotionally significant words than to forget other words in the text.[128]

Comprehension or "Appraisal" of Emotionally Significant Stimuli

According to appraisal theory—the dominant psychological explanation of emotions—each distinct emotion the audience experiences is elicited by a distinct appraisal, or understanding, of a situation.[129] According to this theory, a change in an audience member's emotions, say from anger to shame after the being called on by a speaker, is caused by a change in their appraisal of the situation, in this case from blaming the speaker for calling on them to blaming themselves for being unable to answer the speaker's question.[130] Table 7.2 indicates the appraisals audiences are thought to make for several of the core emotions.

The appraisal process usually proceeds effortlessly, beneath the conscious awareness of audience members, and generates emotions automatically.[131] Surprisingly, conscious awareness is not necessary for most cognitive processes, including perception, comprehension, learning, memory, or even the control of action.[132]

A small number of appraisal dimensions—such as valence, certainty, and agency—account for most of the different emotions that audiences experience.[133] A review of the appraisal literature

TABLE 7.2 Each Emotion Is the Result of a Distinct Appraisal

Appraisal of a Stimulus	The Resulting Emotion
My expectation is violated.	Surprise
Something I value is available to me.	Happiness
Something I value may become available to me.	Hope
Something I value is no longer available to me.	Sadness
Something I value may be taken from me.	Fear
Something I value has been taken from me by someone.	Anger
Something I value is available because of me.	Pride
Something I value has been defiled.	Disgust
Something I value has been defiled by me.	Shame

finds substantial agreement among appraisal theorists on the appraisal dimensions that differenti-ate the various emotions. The five dimensions appraisal theorists have commonly proposed are unexpectedness, valence (positive or negative), certainty (certain or uncertain), agency (caused by another, oneself, or no one), and norm violation (committed by another or oneself).[134]

Cross-cultural studies demonstrate that audiences in the United States, much of Western Europe, and parts of Africa, Asia, and South Asia make similar appraisals when experiencing similar emo-tions.[135] In one study, almost 1,000 people in the United States, Japan, and the People's Republic of China were asked to recall emotional situations and to describe how they had appraised them.[136] The study found few differences from one country to another in terms of the appraisal dimensions associated with each emotion. For example, in all of the cultures studied, anger involved moderately negative valence and fairly high other-agency, whereas fear involved both negative valence and uncertainty.

The Sequence of Emotional Appraisals

Emotionally significant stimuli appear to be appraised one dimension at a time in a fixed sequence with the audience member's emotional experience changing each time a new dimension is appraised.[137]

The first appraisal audiences make is that of unexpectedness—something in their environ-ment unexpectedly changes and attracts their attention.[138] The appraisal of unexpectedness also serves a purely rational function: It indicates to the audience that they need to update or change a schema they have activated.[139] Once the audience recognizes something unexpected has occurred, they generally display the orienting response, at which point they stop any ongoing activities and become ready to make additional appraisals.[140] Together with the orienting response, audiences also display the emotion of surprise, with the degree of unexpectedness determining the intensity of the surprise felt.[141]

The second appraisal audiences make is that of valence, positive or negative, which can also be thought of as like or dislike.[142] Liking encourages approach; disliking or aversion leads to avoid-ance.[143] Valence appraisals occur quickly, sometimes so quickly that they cannot be distinguished from the experience of attention.[144] Occasionally the same stimulus that is conducive for one of the audience's goals or values is obstructive for another. When this happens, the audience experi-ences mixed emotions and emotional conflict.[145] For example, an employee might be both happy and somewhat sad to learn that a respected and well-liked supervisor is at last able to retire from the workforce. Although the audience can simultaneously experience low levels of bad feelings with low levels of pleasant feelings, they cannot experience both strong positive and strong negative emotions at the same time.[146]

The third appraisal audiences make is that of certainty. Anger, disgust, and happiness are associ-ated with the appraisal of certainty—something either positive or negative has definitely happened. Hope, fear, and worry are associated with the appraisal of uncertainty—something either positive or negative may possibly happen.[147]

The attribution of agency, determining who caused an event, is the fourth appraisal in the sequence. The attribution of agency is especially important in distinguishing among the negative emotions.[148] Anger is evoked when the audience understands someone else to be the cause of the problem or agent and sadness when the cause or agent is thought to be the circumstances (e.g., an unavoidable accident).

The last appraisal audiences make is that of norm violation. Societies depend upon their mem-bers to abide by shared rules or norms of acceptable behavior. Violations of norms lead audiences to experience contempt or disgust when judging the behavior of others and guilt or shame when judging themselves.[149] The emotions associated with one's own norm violations are among the last to appear developmentally.[150] Although children experience surprise, joy, anger, sadness, and fear by the age of six months, they do not experience embarrassment, shame, or guilt until age three.[151]

Figure 7.2 represents the audience's appraisal sequence as a decision tree. Each branch on the tree represents an appraisal in the appraisal sequence. An audience member either likes or dislikes a surprising stimulus. If she likes it and it seems the stimulus is sure to happen, happiness results. If she likes it but the stimulus may not happen, hope results. Happiness may transform into gratitude if someone else is responsible for the stimulus. Happiness may transform into pride if her own efforts are responsible for the stimulus. The appraisal of a disliked stimulus is parallel to that of a liked stimulus except that a disliked stimulus may also be appraised for a norm violation.

In an innovative study designed to elicit a wide range of emotional reactions, a high-speed camera captured participants' facial expressions as they played an interactive videogame. Analysis of the players' facial expressions supports the idea of a fixed emotional appraisal sequence. For example, whenever players encountered an event that made it difficult for them to score, they would rapidly raise their eyebrows, indicating the appraisal of unexpectedness, and then follow that behavior with an immediate frown, indicating the appraisal of negative valence.[152]

Figure 7.3 depicts the sequence of facial reactions of three players to three videogame events. The three events elicited either fear, disappointment, or anger. The first sequence shows a player's facial expressions after seeing a threatening videogame "enemy" suddenly appear. The player's initial neutral expression is followed by an expression of surprise, then dislike, and finally fear. The second sequence shows a player's facial expressions after she found out the game would become much more difficult to play than she had realized. Her initial neutral expression is followed by an expression of surprise, then dislike, and finally sadness or disappointment. The third sequence shows a player's facial expressions after she was told her video assistant would no longer be there to help her. Her initial expression of surprise/dislike is followed by an expression of regret and then anger.[153]

Brain Regions Activated. The audience's appraisal sequence has recently been explored by neuroscientists. They find that the presentation of an emotionally significant stimulus initially activates

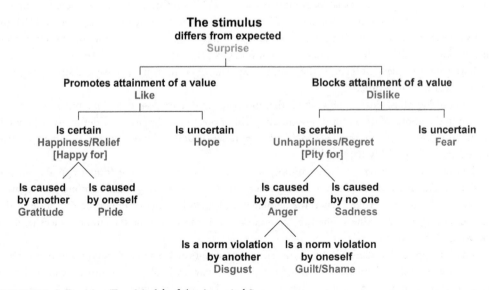

FIGURE 7.2 A Decision Tree Model of the Appraisal Sequence

(A) Response to a frightening event

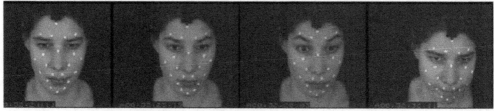

(B) Response to a disappointing event

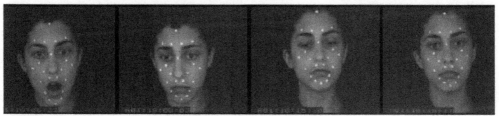

(C) Response to an angering event

FIGURE 7.3 High-Speed Photography Captures the Sequence of Emotional Appraisals

Source: Kaiser, Wehrle, and Schmidt (1998, p. 86)

the dorsal anterior cingulate cortex (ACC), or upper portion of the ACC (see Figure 3.5, p. 108). Activation of the dorsal ACC is commonly associated with the orienting response and surprise.[154] Within 200 milliseconds of the presentation of the stimulus, the amygdala is automatically activated.[155] At that point, even before the stimulus is identified, automatic appraisal processes in the amygdala provide an estimate of the stimulus's positive or negative valence.[156] Subsequently, each basic emotion is associated with a consistent pattern of brain activation that differs significantly from those of other emotions. For example, fear is primarily associated with activity in the left amygdala and insular cortex, a brain region located beneath the juncture of the frontal, temporal, and parietal lobes. Anger is primarily associated with activity in the left inferior frontal gyrus. Disgust with activity in right inferior frontal gyrus. Sadness with activity in the left medial prefrontal cortex. And happiness is primarily associated with activity in the upper region of the right temporal lobe.[157]

Physiological Responses to Emotional Appraisals

Emotional appraisals elicit bodily responses in audience members' autonomic nervous systems, their immune systems, their cardiovascular systems, and their digestive systems.[158] They elicit changes in the audience's facial expressions, somatic muscular tonus, tone of voice, and hormone levels.[159]

Different emotional appraisals lead to different physiological changes. For example, the appraisal of negatively valenced pictures decelerates viewers' heart rates, whereas the appraisal of positively valenced pictures produces a large peak in heart rate acceleration.[160]

The audience's physiological responses to emotional appraisals also evoke specific action tendencies in them.[161] In an early account of action tendencies, psychologist Robert Plutchik proposed that anger evokes the action tendency to destroy; fear to protect; sadness to reintegrate; joy to reproduce; and disgust to reject.[162] Somewhat later, psychologist Richard Lazarus proposed a similar set of action tendencies for each emotion.[163] Table 7.3 shows the overall agreement among five prominent theorists about the action tendencies associated with eight different emotions.

Action tendencies, such as those illustrated in Figure 7.4, play an influential role in audience decision making. For example, sadness amplifies the audience's commitment to hold on to their possessions, whereas disgust triggers an impulse to get rid of them.[164] Consumers who experience regret after failing to receive good service have a different action tendency than consumers who are angry about poor service. Consumers who experience regret switch to another service provider, whereas consumers who are angry actively engage in negative word-of-mouth.[165]

TABLE 7.3 Researchers Are in Basic Agreement About Action Tendencies

	Plutchik (1980)	*Frijda (1986)*	*Lazarus (1991)*	*Roseman (2001)*
Surprise	Stop	Interrupt		Interrupt
Joy	Reproduce	Activate	Expand	Act
Fear	Protect	Avoid	Escape	Prevent
Anger	Destroy	Attack	Attack	Attack
Sadness	Reintegrate	Deactivate	Withdraw	Inaction
Disgust	Reject	Reject	Eject	Expel
Shame		Submit	Hide	Withdraw
Pride		Dominate	Expand	Dominate

Anger → Attack   Joy → Possess   Sadness→ Withdraw   Pride→ Dominate

FIGURE 7.4 Emotional Appraisals Trigger Action Tendencies

When news stories are framed to evoke different emotions, the decisions audience members make after reading them are congruent with the action tendencies of the emotions evoked.[166] For example, a news story about a social issue framed to evoke anger led readers to prefer policies that punished the wrong doers. Conversely, a news story about the same issue framed to evoke sadness led other readers to prefer policies that helped the victims.[167]

In another framing study, pictures and audio clips from news stories about the 9/11 terrorist attacks were combined to evoke either anger or fear in a nationwide sample of 973 Americans.[168] The anger-evoking pictures and clips, showing groups in other countries celebrating the attacks, increased audience support for punitive policy measures to deal with terrorism, including the deportation of foreigners who lack valid visas. On the other hand, the fear-evoking pictures and clips, warning of anthrax and bioterrorism, increased audience support for precautionary policy measures such as strengthening ties with America's Middle-Eastern allies.

When audience members change their emotional appraisals of events, they change their action tendencies and the decisions they make about those events as well. If an audience member simply tries to suppress her anger and disgust about an unfair offer, she will be unable to change the action tendency to reject the offer. However, if she reinterprets her emotional response to an unfair offer (e.g., by concluding that the real cause of her upset was her bad day at the office), she will change the action tendency to reject the offer and change the decision she makes as well.[169]

Brain Regions Activated. Neuroscientists find that such emotional reappraisals increase activation of the frontal lobe which reduces amygdala activation in a top-down manner (see Figures 3.4 and 3.5, p. 108).[170]

The Inhibition of Information Acquisition and Integration

Because emotional appraisals automatically trigger an action tendency in response to a situation (e.g., attack, escape, dominate), they can simultaneously inhibit the process of information acquisition or search and lead audiences to inadequately scrutinize information.[171] Consequently, emotional decisions often entail no deliberation at all—the "right" choice appears to be "self-evident."[172]

Emotional appraisals also inhibit the audience's information integration process. Whereas trade-offs among decision criteria are common in rational decision making (e.g., to get better quality you may have to pay more), emotional appraisals inhibit trade-offs.[173] As we have seen, product attributes with implications for consumers' highly valued goals trigger more emotion and are higher in trade-off difficulty than product attributes with few emotionally relevant implications.

Emotional appraisals inhibit trade-offs in voter decision making as well. In a study of framing effects, one group of voters read news stories about the positions of political candidates on health care issues whose arguments were framed in emotional, value-laden terms. Another group of voters read similar news stories about the positions of candidates whose arguments were framed in neutral, economic terms. Then both groups were asked to vote for a candidate. Voters who read the health care arguments framed in emotional, value-laden terms were more likely to use a noncompensatory decision strategy and thus avoid making trade-offs than voters who read the health care arguments framed in neutral, economic terms. Forty-one percent of the voters who read the emotionally framed arguments used a noncompensatory strategy when making their decisions compared to only 16% of the voters who read the economically framed arguments.[174]

Emotional Appeals and Intensifiers

Emotional Appeals

When audiences encounter emotional appeals, they may find themselves making decisions based on their emotions as opposed to reason. Emotional appeals may be presented as either words or images and consist of photographs, videos, or verbal messages.[175] Successful emotional appeals elicit real emotions from their audiences. For example, a sentence such as "Animal research causes unnecessary suffering to animals" can be used as an emotional appeal that elicits a real emotional response in readers.[176] Similarly, television commercials can make emotional appeals that elicit real emotional responses in viewers.[177] Emotional appeals can either produce the same emotional response, such as a feeling of anger while listening to an angry speaker's call for revenge, or a different but complementary emotional response, such as a feeling of pity when hearing an emotional plea for help.[178]

Emotional appeals that are able to elicit emotions can have a significant impact on audience decision making. For example, fear-arousing product warning labels have been found to significantly affect users' safety behavior.[179] Fear-arousing health warnings influence patients to heed their doctor's advice.[180] Appeals to other negative emotions can impact audience decisions as well. A study of emotional appeals made during an anti-littering campaign in Oklahoma City found that the campaign succeeded because it was able to attach the negative emotions of shame and embarrassment to littering.[181] Appeals to positive emotions can also be effective. Leaders who make inspirational appeals are more likely to get the support of their followers.[182] In a study of group decision making, members of policy-making groups rated inspirational appeals as persuasive as rational appeals and more persuasive than pressure tactics, ingratiation, exchange tactics, or other persuasive techniques.[183]

Ads that feature emotional appeals can make a big impact on consumers' decisions. Cigarette ads designed to increase the positive emotions associated with smoking decrease consumers' perceptions of risk.[184] The joy some television commercials elicit increases consumers' intentions to purchase the products advertised.[185] A study of the effectiveness of TV commercials for frequently purchased products finds that emotional ads are much more likely to increase sales than neutral ones,[186] with ads that elicit positive emotions being the most likely to produce a significant sales increase. Consumers' emotional responses to ads are also important predictors of their attitudes toward the advertised brand.[187]

U.S. consumers routinely encounter ads designed to appeal to pride, fear, joy, sadness, guilt, love, anger, and pity.[188] The most studied emotional appeal is the appeal to fear, although there is increasing interest in other emotional appeals including appeals to happiness,[189] sadness,[190] pride,[191] disgust,[192] shame,[193] and guilt.[194] Advertisers commonly use appeals to fear to promote products such as insurance, toothpaste, deodorants, mouthwash, and detergents. Fear appeals promoting these types of products make social threats and are more effective in persuading potential consumers than fear appeals that make physical threats.[195] Public service announcements also use appeals to fear to discourage smoking, drinking and driving, and participation in unsafe sex. As fear appeals increase in fearfulness, they tend to become increasingly persuasive.[196]

A fear appeal is more effective when the audience feels vulnerable to the threat it warns of.[197] A fear appeal is also more effective when the audience believes it can help them avoid the threat's negative consequences.[198] For example, earthquake preparedness messages are more effective when they describe an earthquake's threat and explain how to avoid an earthquake's dangers,[199] giving specific instructions on when, where, and how to take action.[200] The most effective fear appeals present such instructions immediately after presenting the threat.[201]

Although increasing the fearfulness of a threat usually makes a fear appeal more persuasive, this is not always the case. If the audience does not believe it can cope effectively with the threat, then increasing the threat's fearfulness tends to produce a boomerang effect.[202]

Are emotional appeals always a hindrance to rational decision making? Political scientist Ted Brader finds that it is the most knowledgeable citizens, not the uniformed ones, who are the most responsive to emotional appeals in political ads.[203] In *The Place of Emotion in Argument*, rhetorician Douglas Walton contends that emotional appeals can play a legitimate role as persuasive arguments since emotions are indicative of one's most fundamental values. But Walton also warns of four types of emotional appeals that are often used fallaciously. The first type is *Argumentum ad baculum*, an appeal to fear. The Michelin tire slogan, "Because so much is riding on your tires," appeals to fear for the safety of one's family. But it says nothing to prove that Michelin tires are any safer than other brands. The second type, *Argumentum ad misericordiam*, is an appeal to pity. Advertisements requesting donations to support medical research often include photographs of extremely ill children and their personal stories in order to elicit the reader's sympathy. However, the ads typically lack any information about the trustworthiness of the source of the ad, the truth of their claims, or the percentage of contributions used for research.[204]

The third type of emotional appeal often used fallaciously is *Argumentum ad populum*, an appeal to popular values or pride. Politicians appeal to popular values when they say the flag must be honored and law and order restored. However, those same politicians may neglect to prove a problem existed in the first place. The final type of emotional appeal Walton identifies as typically fallacious is *Argumentum ad hominem*, an attack against the person that is often an appeal to anger. For example, some politicians disparage their rivals as Ivy League "elitists" although they themselves are graduates of Ivy League schools.

Despite the possibility of using emotional appeals to support fallacious reasoning, many of the most memorable speeches throughout history have made strong appeals to specific emotions. We have already read the Gettysburg Address by Abraham Lincoln. Lincoln's speech is an appeal to the emotion of gratitude: Gratitude triggers the action tendency to repay the debt that is owed. Lincoln called on his audience at the memorial service in Gettysburg, Pennsylvania to repay the debt they owed the fallen soldiers by finishing the task the soldiers had begun. Another famous speech, the "I have a dream" speech by Dr. Martin Luther King, delivered on August 28, 1963, is an appeal to the emotion of hope. Hope triggers the action tendency to prepare or to make happen.[205] King wanted his audience to take the action necessary to turn his dream of freedom for all into a reality.

On the following pages, four other famous speeches are reproduced in part or in their entirety. The first two speeches are fictional and are excerpted from Shakespeare's *Julius Caesar*, Act III, Scene 2: The Forum. In the first speech Brutus makes a rational argument—an appeal to reason— to the crowd of onlookers. He asks them to understand that his decision to assassinate Caesar was difficult for him but was made with their best interests in mind. The crowd gives Brutus their approval. Moments later Brutus invites Antony to speak and then leaves the stage. By the time Antony finishes speaking, the same audience that had applauded Brutus for ridding Rome of a tyrant is now ready to kill him for betraying and murdering their beloved leader.

Unlike the speech Brutus gave, Antony's speech is an emotional appeal. Notice how Shakespeare, the master communicator, depicts the crowd's process of emotional decision making in sequence. Shakespeare's Antony first surprises and shocks the crowd by unexpectedly throwing off the garment that covered the dead Caesar and revealing Caesar's bloody body with its gaping knife wounds. The crowd's surprise turns to pity as they grieve for their now-beloved leader. Pity quickly turns to anger and anger to the action tendency of attack, and this is exactly what Antony wants his audience in Rome to do—to attack and kill Brutus. Audiences comprehend emotions faster and more accurately when information about others' emotional appraisals is provided to them not in random order but in sequence—unexpectedness, valence, certainty, agency, and norm violation[206]—just as Shakespeare does so brilliantly.

The last two speeches are the actual words of two great American leaders. The "D-day order" speech by Dwight D. Eisenhower, delivered on June 6, 1944, is an appeal to the emotion of pride.

Pride triggers the action tendency to dominate,[207] and domination of the Nazis through total victory was Eisenhower's goal. In stark contrast to Eisenhower's speech, the "Surrender" speech, by Chief Joseph of the Nez Perce, to the U.S. Army in 1877, translated by a scout and transcribed by an artist for *Harper's Weekly* magazine,[208] is an appeal to the emotion of sadness. Sadness triggers the action tendency to withdraw.[209] His own robes riddled with bullet holes, his people killed or starving, Chief Joseph was convinced that further resistance was futile. It was time for him and his warriors to withdraw from the stage of history.

A RATIONAL ARGUMENT

BRUTUS
Romans, countrymen, and lovers! hear me for my cause, and be silent, that you may hear: Believe me for mine honor, and have respect to mine honor, that you may believe: Censure me in your wisdom, and awake your senses, that you may the better judge. If there be any in this assembly, any dear friend of Caesar's, to him I say, that Brutus' love to Caesar was no less than his. If then that friend demand why Brutus rose against Caesar, this is my answer: Not that I loved Caesar less, but that I loved Rome more. Had you rather Caesar were living and die all slaves, than that Caesar were dead, to live all free men? As Caesar loved me, I weep for him; as he was fortunate, I rejoice at it; as he was valiant, I honor him: but, as he was ambitious, I slew him. There is tears for his love; joy for his fortune; honor for his valor; and death for his ambition. Who is here so base that would be a bondman? If any, speak; for him have I offended. Who is here so rude that would not be a Roman? If any, speak; for him have I offended. Who is here so vile that will not love his country? If any, speak; for him have I offended. I pause for a reply.

ALL None, Brutus, none.

BRUTUS
Then none have I offended. I have done no more to Caesar than you shall do to Brutus. The question of his death is enrolled in the Capitol; his glory not extenuated, wherein he was worthy, nor his offences enforced, for which he suffered death.

Enter ANTONY and others, with CAESAR's body

Here comes his body, mourned by Mark Antony: who, though he had no hand in his death, shall receive the benefit of his dying, a place in the commonwealth; as which of you shall not? With this I depart,--that, as I slew my best lover for the good of Rome, I have the same dagger for myself, when it shall please my country to need my death.

ALL Live, Brutus! live, live!

AN APPEAL TO ANGER

ANTONY
If you have tears, prepare to shed them now. You all do know this mantle: I remember the first time ever Caesar put it on; 'Twas on a summer's evening, in his tent, that day he overcame the Nervii: Look, in this place ran Cassius' dagger through: See what a rent the envious Casca made: Through this the well-beloved Brutus stabb'd; and as he pluck'd his cursed steel away, mark how the blood of Caesar follow'd it, as rushing out of doors, to be resolved if Brutus so unkindly knock'd, or no; for Brutus, as you know, was Caesar's angel: Judge, O you gods, how dearly Caesar lov'd him. This was the most unkindest cut of all; for when the noble Caesar saw him stab, ingratitude, more strong than traitors' arms, quite vanquish'd him: then burst his mighty heart; and, in his mantle muffling up his face, even at the base of Pompey's statue, which all the while ran blood, great Caesar fell. O, what a fall was there, my countrymen! Then I, and you, and all of us fell down, whilst bloody treason flourish'd over us. O, now you weep; and, I perceive, you feel the dint of pity: these are gracious drops. Kind souls, what, weep you when you but behold our Caesar's vesture wounded? Look you here, here is himself, marr'd, as you see, with traitors.

FIRST CITIZEN O piteous spectacle!

SECOND CITIZEN O noble Caesar!

THIRD CITIZEN O woeful day!

FOURTH CITIZEN O traitors, villains!

FIRST CITIZEN O most bloody sight!

SECOND CITIZEN We will be revenged.

ALL Revenge! About! Seek! Burn! Fire! Kill! Slay! Let not a traitor live!

AN APPEAL TO PRIDE

D-Day Order Speech by Dwight D. Eisenhower

You will bring about the destruction of the German war machine, the elimination of Nazi tyranny over the oppressed peoples of Europe, and security for ourselves in a free world. Your task will not be an easy one. Your enemy is well trained, well equipped, and battle-hardened. He will fight savagely.

But this is the year 1944. Much has happened since the Nazi triumphs of 1940–41. The United Nations have inflicted upon the Germans great defeat in open battle man to man. Our air offensive has seriously reduced their strength in the air and their capacity to wage war on the ground. Our home fronts have given us an overwhelming superiority in weapons and munitions of war and placed at our disposal great reserves of trained fighting men. The tide has turned.

The free men of the world are marching together to victory. I have full confidence in your courage, devotion to duty, and skill in battle. We will accept nothing less than full victory. Good luck, and let us all beseech the blessings of Almighty God upon this great and noble undertaking.

AN APPEAL TO SADNESS

Surrender Speech by Chief Joseph of the Nez Perce

Tell General Howard I know his heart. What he told me before, I have it in my heart. I am tired of fighting. Our chiefs are killed; Looking Glass is dead, Ta-Hool-Hool-Shute is dead. The old men are all dead. It is the young men who say yes or no. He who led on the young men is dead.

It is cold, and we have no blankets; the little children are freezing to death. My people, some of them, have run away to the hills, and have no blankets, no food. No one knows where they are—perhaps freezing to death. I want to have time to look for my children, and see how many of them I can find. Maybe I shall find them among the dead.

Hear me, my chiefs! I am tired; my heart is sick and sad. From where the sun now stands I will fight no more forever.

Emotionally Charged Words and Images

Attorneys, politicians, and advertisers routinely use emotionally charged words and images to intensify the effects of their emotional appeals. An audience member's emotional reaction to the emotionally charged term "child abusers" predicts how they will judge a particular child abuser better than their rational beliefs about the group of child abusers as a whole.[210] In the courtroom, emotionally charged words are highly damaging to defendants even when the words have no evidentiary value.[211] Unfortunately, any attempt to stifle the negative emotions jurors feel when they hear testimony using emotive language usually results in the jurors being even more biased by the testimony. When used in skin cancer warnings, emotionally charged words such as *deadly problems*, *ugly wrinkles*, *extreme risk* have been shown to lead adults to reduce their sun exposure and to practice solar protection for both themselves and their children.[212]

CEOs use emotionally charged words to appeal to the emotions of their audiences as well. When new CEOs use emotionally charged words in their initial letters to their shareholders, financial analysts who read the letters tend to make more favorable earnings forecasts. The typical new CEO letter to shareholders uses negatively charged words to describe the past and positively charged ones such as "faith," "challenge," and "inspiration" to describe the CEO's vision of the future and how it will be achieved. The more emotional language the new CEOs uses, the more inclined analysts are to issue favorable recommendations.[213]

Emotionally charged images also have a significant impact on the emotions and the decisions of audiences who see them. A study of the effects of live testimony and video re-creations of a crime on mock jurors' decisions finds that jurors who either viewed live testimony or who viewed live testimony and then watched video re-creations had stronger emotional reactions to the evidence than jurors who simply read a transcript of the trial.[214] Moreover, mock jurors who view gruesome videos have lower thresholds to convict than those who do not view the videos but instead hear a verbal description of the evidence.[215] Another study presented two groups of mock jurors with the same transcript of a murder trial but showed autopsy photographs to only one of the two groups.[216] Although the transcript described the victim's wounds verbally, the group exposed to the autopsy photographs was twice as likely to find the defendant guilty.

In addition, the sentences mock jurors hand down are more extreme when the jurors are presented with vivid photographic evidence. Mock jurors who view extremely gruesome photographic evidence are more likely to decide on the death sentence.[217] Mock jurors who view photographs of a victim's injury award a greater proportion of the requested damages.[218] Moreover, when the victim's injuries are severe and the defendant is clearly to blame, mock jurors who view color photographs of the injured party give higher monetary awards than those who view either black-and-white photographs or no photographs at all.[219]

Audiences also respond strongly to a combination of emotionally charged words and images. A study of investor decision making found that emotionally charged verbal and pictorial elements in an ad for a mutual fund decreased the amount of risk both expert and novice investors perceived. However, the emotional elements of the ad had a greater effect on the novices than on the experts.[220]

One of the most famous examples of the use of emotionally charged words and images in a political campaign is the "Daisy" ad (see Figure 7.5), created by advertising guru Tony Schwartz

FIGURE 7.5 A Visual Appeal to Fear: President Johnson's "Daisy" ad juxtaposed images of a little girl and a nuclear explosion

Source: courtesy of Democratic National Committee

and aired on U.S. TV on September 7, 1964. Its purpose was to promote President Lyndon Johnson's campaign for reelection. The "Daisy" ad begins by showing a little girl slowly counting each petal she picks off a daisy. When the little girl reaches the count of "nine," a threatening male voice begins the countdown of a missile launch, at which point the little girl looks up toward the sky. As the girl looks to the sky, the camera zooms in on her eyes. Next, a nuclear bomb is shown exploding while President Johnson can be heard to say, "These are the stakes! To make a world in which all of God's children can live, or to go into the dark. We must either love each other, or we must die." Another speaker then says, "Vote for President Johnson on November 3. The stakes are too high for you to stay home." Because so many complained that President Johnson's campaign used the ad to frighten voters into believing his opponent, Republican Barry Goldwater, would start a nuclear war, his campaign never aired the "Daisy" ad again.

Narratives and Metaphors as Emotional Intensifiers

The written word can evoke a number of different emotions in audiences.[221] Writing in narrative or story form is especially likely to evoke the audience's emotions. A study of readers reading 4,000-word stories finds they are aware of having about five emotions per story.[222] Narrative poems, such as Coleridge's "The Rime of the Ancient Mariner," are effective at arousing readers' emotions as well.[223]

Although readers tend to respond emotionally to narrative forms of writing, they typically respond with little emotion to the style of writing newspaper reporters commonly use.[224] Readers also respond with less emotion to logical arguments than to arguments presented as narratives.[225] Consequently, the persuasive impact of emotional appeals is stronger when they are communicated in the form of narratives and stories or when narratives and stories are included in the appeals along with facts.[226] In one study of fear appeals, including personal stories about victims' injuries resulted in a 19% improvement in compliance with safety regulations.[227]

In addition to responding emotionally to narratives, audiences also respond emotionally to metaphors. Metaphors can persuade audience members to change their attitudes toward various social and political issues.[228] Furthermore, it is the ability of metaphors to evoke specific emotions that accounts for a significant part of their persuasiveness.[229] Metaphors are particularly influential when introduced early in a persuasive communication.[230]

Politicians routinely use metaphors to evoke emotions and to persuade. U.S. presidents whom voters rate as charismatic used nearly twice as many metaphors in their inaugural addresses (adjusted for speech length) as presidents voters rate as noncharismatic. Moreover, the passages in inaugural addresses that voters rate as most inspirational are those that contain metaphors.[231]

During the three-day debate in the U.S. Senate in 1991 over the Persian Gulf War, both Republicans and Democrats often used metaphors to bolster their positions. For example, one Republican senator used the following metaphorical description of Saddam Hussein as a glutton to evoke the negative emotional response of disgust:

> Saddam Hussein is like a glutton—a geopolitical glutton. He is sitting down at a big banquet table, overflowing with goodies. And let me tell you—like every glutton, he is going to have them all. Kuwait is just the appetizer—He is gobbling it up—but it is not going to satisfy him. After a noisy belch or two, he is going to reach across the table for the next morsel. What is it going to be? Saudi Arabia? . . . He is going to keep grabbing and gobbling, . . . It is time to let this grisly glutton know the free lunch is over. It is time for him to pay the bill.[232]

Believability as an Emotional Intensifier

Only when audiences believe an event is real can the event elicit their emotions.[233] Unreal events can elicit emotions only if "the stimulating fantasy succeeds in inducing a sense of reality in the reader or viewer."[234] In an empirical test of this concept, a research team manipulated the believability of three emotional ads. The audience's emotional responses to all three ads showed significant differences due to the believability manipulation.[235]

In another test of the effects of believability, viewers watched a gruesome anthropological film that showed a "subincision" procedure adolescent boys in New Guinea must undergo. One group of viewers watched a silent film version of the excruciatingly painful procedure. A second group first received a written statement that said the procedure was actually painless before they watched the same silent version of the film. A third group watched the same film with a soundtrack added and heard a narrator claim the procedure was painless. The second and third groups responded with less emotion, as measured by changes in their electrodermal activity, than the first group, an indication that reducing the believability of a film reduces its emotional impact.[236]

Brain Regions Activated. In an fMRI study of believability effects, audience members looked at two sets of pictures that depicted needles going through the skin of a person's hand. For the second set, the audience was told the "hand had already been numbed for a biopsy." The bottom-up visual inputs from both sets of images activated pain regions in the brain: the dorsal, or upper, anterior cingulate cortex (ACC), the upper portion of the insular cortex, a brain region located beneath the juncture of the frontal, temporal, and parietal lobes, as well as a region near the front of the parietal lobe (see Figures 3.4 and 3.5, p. 108). But the top-down cognitive appraisal that the hand was actually numb in the second set of pictures activated regions involved in inferring another's thoughts and feelings (the medial prefrontal cortex, the dorsomedial prefrontal cortex, the ventro-medial prefrontal cortex [vmPFC], and the precuneus) as well as a region involved in self-control (the right ventrolateral prefrontal cortex). These regions typically play a role in contextualizing empathic responses to others.[237]

Temporal and Physical Proximity as Emotional Intensifiers

As an emotionally significant event draws nearer in time, the emotions the event evokes, such as fear or happiness, tend to intensify even when the audience's evaluations of the event's probability or likely outcomes stay the same.[238] For example, when researchers told subjects they would receive an electric shock at a specific time, they found that the subjects' levels of fear as measured by their heart rates, galvanic skin conductance, and reports of anxiety all increased as the moment approached.[239]

In another study of the effects of temporal proximity, 49 students were offered one dollar each to tell a joke in front of the class the next week. Only nine students accepted the offer. When the next week came, all 49 students were given a chance to change their minds. Six of the nine students who had previously accepted the offer to tell a joke decided not to do so. None of the students who had initially declined the offer decided to tell a joke at the last minute.[240]

Physical proximity can have an effect on emotions similar to the effect of temporal proximity. Physical proximity and sensory contact can lead to impulsive behavior, behavior that grocery store checkout lanes are ready to take advantage of.[241]

Emotional Contagion

The emotions of speakers who are nonverbally expressive typically spread spontaneously throughout the audience—a phenomenon known as *emotional contagion*.[242] Emotional contagion most often occurs below the level of conscious awareness and is based on automatic cognitive processes and physiological responses.[243] Audiences experience emotional contagion when speakers use their facial expressions,[244] gestures, and bodily postures to communicate their emotions.[245]

Most displays of emotions, including most facial expressions of emotions,[246] elicit either the same or complementary emotions from the viewer.[247] For example, photographs of angry faces tend to evoke the complementary emotion of fear, even when viewers do not consciously perceive the faces.[248] Facial expressions of distress and shame evoke the complementary emotions of compassion and sympathy.[249] Beginning as early as age eight months, displays of distress, including facial expressions indicating distress, evoke the child's readiness to help.[250] Facial expressions of sympathy produce increased liking and, when relevant, more forgiveness.[251] Facial expressions of embarrassment often evoke amusement.[252] A study that collected both fMRI and pupillometry data on viewers finds evidence for "pupillary contagion." When viewers are presented with photos of sad faces with different pupil sizes, their own pupil size mirrors those shown in the photos.[253]

Leaders have a special ability to elicit emotions from their audiences.[254] Even brief, televised clips of politicians' nonverbal displays of emotions are capable of eliciting noticeable emotional reactions from voters[255] and can influence their attitudes toward the leader independent of the leader's verbal message.[256] Moreover, the different emotions political candidates elicit have different effects on voters' attitudes toward the candidates and the issues on the national agenda.[257]

Not surprisingly, some emotional displays by leaders elicit stronger emotional responses than others. In one study, voters watched video recordings of national leaders who displayed either happiness and reassurance, anger and threat, or fear and evasion at different levels of consistency and intensity. Leaders who displayed emotions in a consistent and intense manner elicited much stronger emotional responses than those whose emotional displays were inconsistent or weak. Uncommitted voters were especially susceptible to influence by emotional appeals and the leaders' nonverbal displays of emotion.[258]

Professionals can also elicit emotions in their audiences through their tone of voice. In a study that measured the effect of a speaker's tone of voice on her audience, audience members listened to a speech that was delivered in either a slightly happy or a slightly sad voice and then rated their own mood. Not only was the audience's mood affected by the speaker's tone of voice, but when asked to repeat the message they heard, audience members spontaneously and unconsciously mimicked the speaker's tone.[259]

Emotional contagion can influence the decisions audience members make. In a study of emotional contagion in pairs of consumers, one consumer in several of the pairs was primed to be especially happy just before they inspected a new product with their partner. Partners who inspected the product with a consumer primed to be happy (and who was not allowed to speak) liked the product more than partners inspecting the product with a consumer in a neutral mood. When a translucent screen was used to block the partner's exposure to the happy consumer's nonverbal behaviors, no attitude change occurred.[260] In another study of the effects of emotional contagion on decision making, solicitors displayed either sadness, anger, or no emotion as they requested donations for charities from prospective donors. When the solicitors displayed sadness, donors gave more than when the solicitors displayed anger or no emotion.[261]

Groups as well as individuals are susceptible to emotional contagion. A study of teams of nurses and accountants finds that team members' moods are shared even after controlling for shared work problems.[262] A study of professional cricket teams finds similar results even after controlling for each team's status in the league.[263] Emotional contagion has also been found to occur in a variety of automotive, information technology, and creative advertising work groups.[264]

Emotional contagion in groups can have a significant influence on group processes and outcomes.[265] A study of senior management teams finds that a group's emotions affect both individual attitudes and team dynamics.[266] Groups experiencing positive emotional contagion show improved cooperation, decreased conflict, and increased perceived performance.[267] Conversely, groups experiencing negative group emotions are less likely to cooperate and more likely to miss work.[268]

Biases in Emotional Decision Making

The Effects of Incidental Moods and Emotions on Audience Decisions

Moods and emotions triggered by events pertinent to a decision, *or integral* moods and emotions, generally have a stronger influence on audience decisions than *incidental* moods and emotions, or ones triggered by unrelated events.[269] For example, the integral fear an investor feels after a sudden drop in stock prices will generally have a stronger effect on her investment decisions than the incidental fear she feels after being startled by a sudden loud noise. But because people cannot distinguish clearly between the integral emotion actually elicited by an event and the incidental ones they happen to be experiencing for other, unrelated reasons, incidental moods and emotions can influence their decisions as well. For example, traders in the financial markets trade differently when the music they listen to changes their mood. When the music puts them into a good mood, traders tend to be overconfident and make less profitable trades than normal. When the music puts them into a bad mood, on the other hand, they tend to be more conservative and to make more profitable decisions.[270]

A wide range of events unrelated to the decision to be made have been shown to affect audience emotions and influence their decisions, events such as the weather, receiving a small gift, and reminiscing about a happy or sad past experience.[271] Even the upbeat or depressed color of the paper on which information is printed can trigger a shift in mood and influence the audience's decision.[272]

Once a mood or emotion is triggered, it and its action tendency will linger after the triggering event has passed if the audience does not take the emotion-relieving action.[273] In such cases the action tendencies triggered by one situation bias the audience's assessment of unrelated situations.[274] In a study of the effects of incidental emotions on audience decision making, one group of viewers watched a film in which a violent criminal was punished and a second group watched another film in which the criminal evaded punishment due to a legal technicality. Both groups reported equivalent levels of anger in response to the crime. Soon afterward, the two groups were asked to read a legal case about a different crime and to recommend an appropriate punishment for the perpetrator. Because the incidental anger felt by the second group went unrelieved, the second group handed down harsher sentences.[275]

Other studies confirm that incidental moods and emotions can bias the audience's action tendencies. Readers whose anger was first aroused by a story about toxic waste dumping were later more likely to decide to punish the perpetrator of an unrelated incident than to help the victims of that incident.[276] In a study that first primed either anger or fear in two groups of participants, each group was subsequently asked how they might reduce the problem of drunk driving. Sixty-five percent of the fear-primed group proposed safety or protection-oriented solutions, whereas 64% of the anger-primed group proposed punishment or blame-oriented solutions.[277]

Incidental moods and emotions can also bias cognitive processes such as perception,[278] attention,[279] and recall[280] in a way that leads the audience to make decisions congruent with their emotional state.[281] A study that compared viewers who were and were not clinically depressed tracked viewers' eye movements while they looked at a series of pictures depicting both happy and sad events. Viewers who were not clinically depressed fixated on happy regions of the pictures significantly sooner, more often, and longer than they fixated on sad regions. Viewers who were depressed fixated more on the sad regions.[282]

Although the audience's incidental moods and emotions enable them to quickly recognize congruent emotions in others,[283] they can also bias the audience's perception of others.[284] One partner in a relationship will often misinterpret the other partner's emotional state as congruent with her own. Likewise, happy people tend to see others as happy, and sad people will often see others as sad.[285] In a study of the effects of exercise on person perception, one group of people was put into a positive mood by exercising immediately before viewing another person. A second group did not exercise prior to viewing the person. The group of exercisers associated the person's positive verbal and nonverbal communication with more intense positive emotions than the nonexercisers. For instance, whereas the nonexercisers saw the person expressing contentment, the exercisers saw the person expressing joy.[286] In a another study, one group of people evaluated a person while they were working in an unpleasantly hot and crowded room. Another group evaluated the same person while they were working in a pleasant, uncrowded room. Interestingly, the two groups made significantly different but mood-congruent evaluations.[287]

Incidental moods and emotions typically bias the decisions of novice audience members more than those of experts. In a study that compared automotive experts and novices, partcipants were first put into a positive, neutral, or negative mood and then asked to read an ad for a new car. After 48 hours both experts and novices were asked to rate the car. In contrast to the experts' ratings, the novices' ratings were strongly affected by the mood they were in when they read the ad.[288]

Surprisingly, incidental moods and emotions can sometimes bias experts and novices in opposing ways. For example, when political novices are put into a positive mood, they show typical mood congruency effects and make more favorable judgments of candidates. Conversely, when political experts are put into a positive mood, they show a contrast effect and make less favorable judgments.[289] In a similar way, new and seasoned employees react differently to polite directives from their supervisors. Politeness increases compliance for new employees but decreases it for those with experience.[290]

Audience members are rarely aware of how their incidental moods and emotions affect their decisions,[291] yet the consequences of those moods and emotions can be far reaching.[292] The power of incidental moods and emotions to bias decision making can be decreased if audiences become aware that irrelevant situational factors are influencing their judgments.[293] A de-biasing study asked readers to read a sad story and then to estimate how satisfactory their lives were. Readers asked to reflect on the cause of their sad feelings prior to making their estimates reported more satisfaction with their lives.[294] Usually, people are completely unaware that a mood or an emotion triggered by one situation has influenced their judgment in another situation.[295]

The power of incidental moods and emotions to bias audience decision making also decreases when audiences are held accountable for their decisions. For example, the tendency of happy audiences to base their impressions of others on stereotypes decreases when they are held accountable for their decisions regarding them.[296] The tendency of angry jurors to demand more severe punishment in unrelated legal cases also decreases when they are held accountable for their decisions.[297]

Being polite to the audience can reduce the biasing effects of incidental moods and emotions. One study induced a positive or negative mood in an audience and then made an unexpected request to them either in a polite or impolite manner. The audience's response to the impolite request was significantly more mood congruent than their response to the polite request; audience members in both positive and negative moods responded positively to the polite request.[298] Not surprisingly, audiences also view senders of polite messages more positively than senders of impolite ones.[299]

The Effects of Incidental Happiness

Each specific incidental emotion produces a number of predictable effects. Audiences put into happy moods, such as employees at an office party or viewers of a funny TV commercial, tend to overestimate the frequency of positive events and to underestimate the likelihood of negative outcomes and events.[300] Thus, they tend to make optimistic judgments and risk-seeking decisions. For example, audiences who read upbeat newspaper articles subsequently are willing to take more risks than audiences who read sad articles.[301] However, happy audience members are less likely to take risks when the stakes are high and the potential for loss is genuine.[302]

Audiences put into happy moods also tend to make more positive evaluations of other people and situations. For example, audiences put into happy moods make significantly more positive than negative evaluations of strangers, whereas those in bad moods are unlikely to allow their feelings to influence their evaluations.[303] Consumers put into happy moods rate various products, brands, and ads more positively.[304] In one study, consumers who viewed subliminally presented photos of happy faces not only drank more, they also paid more for their drinks. Whereas, consumers who viewed subliminally presented angry faces both drank less and paid less.[305] In a large random-sample interview of the U.S. population, researchers found that interviewees who felt good at the time of their interview gave more positive responses than interviewees in a bad mood.[306]

Audiences put into happy moods generally agree more with persuasive messages than audiences in other moods,[307] and are much more compliant than those put into angry moods.[308] When an ad for a product puts consumers in a happy mood, they tend to adopt a positive attitude toward the advertised brand.[309] When the music and images in a political campaign ad put voters in a happy mood, voters feel greater certainty about their prior choice of candidates. As a consequence, happy campaign ads both rally a candidate's supporters and harden their opposition.[310]

In most cases, audiences put into happy moods process persuasive messages without much rational thought or deliberation.[311] A study of the effects of readers' incidental moods finds that readers in a neutral mood are more persuaded by strong arguments than weak ones, as they should be if their decision-making process were rational. But readers put into happy moods are equally persuaded by both strong and weak arguments.[312] Inducing happy moods can even cause audiences to perceive weak arguments to be more persuasive than strong ones. The use of humor in an ad produces more positive attitudes among consumers when the ad uses weak arguments, and fewer positive attitudes when the ad uses strong arguments.[313] Audiences in a happy mood are also more likely to perceive novel arguments as familiar, which may contribute to their acceptance of them as true.[314]

In special cases, audiences put into happy moods will process persuasive messages in a rational and deliberate way. For example, audiences put into happy moods are more influenced by strong arguments than sad audiences when both groups believe the message causes happiness.[315] Compared with unhappy audience members, audiences put into happy moods show less confusion, less redundancy, and are better able to integrate task-relevant information when making decisions.[316] If happy audiences are asked to make a decision that is interesting or important, they will make the effort to process relevant information rationally and systematically.[317] And as long as the decisions to be made are interesting or important, audiences put into happy moods also make good decisions faster.[318] For example, happy consumers make purchasing decisions that are just as rational as those made by consumers in neutral moods, but they make their decisions more quickly.[319]

The Effects of Incidental Sadness

Audiences put into sad or depressed moods, such as the recently unemployed or viewers watching distressing events on the evening news, tend to make pessimistic judgments and decisions.[320] Thus, they tend to overestimate the frequency of sad events and underestimate the likelihood of positive events.[321] Audiences who are induced to feel sad are also more likely to expect future events to result from uncontrollable situational forces.[322] Incidental sadness affects the audience's risk/reward preference as well. For example, job applicants put into a sad mood prefer job opportunities that offer both high risk and high reward.[323]

Audiences put into sad moods generally agree with persuasive messages that emphasize saddening problems or outcomes. They have more favorable views of a message if it argues that failing to adopt a position is likely to make bad things happen than if it argues that adopting the position will make good things happen.[324] In a study of the effects of incidental moods on persuasion, readers who were in a neutral mood or who were put into a sad mood read one of two equally strong arguments for a proposed tax increase. One argument justified the proposed tax increase by claiming it would help address saddening problems (e.g., the plight of senior citizens). The other justified the increase by claiming it would address angering problems (e.g., long traffic delays). The saddening reasons, but not the angering ones, persuaded readers in a sad mood. In addition, the sadder a reader felt, the more positively she responded to the tax proposal justified by the saddening reasons. Neither type of argument persuaded readers in a neutral mood to support a tax increase.[325]

In many cases, audiences put into sad moods will process persuasive messages in a rational and deliberate way despite their mood.[326] One study asked students to read either strong or weak arguments for a proposed final examination before graduation. Students put into sad moods were persuaded only by the strong arguments, whereas students put into happy moods were moderately persuaded by both strong and weak arguments.[327]

The Effects of Incidental Anger

Audiences put into angry moods, such as listeners to politically oriented talk radio, tend to make optimistic judgments and risk-seeking decisions just as happy people do.[328] But unlike happy people, audiences put into angry moods overestimate the frequency of angering events.[329] Angry audiences also believe that negative events caused by human agents are more likely to occur than sad ones where no one is to blame.[330] Consequently, audiences put into angry moods are more likely to quickly attribute blame to others, to perceive another's ambiguous behavior as hostile, and to punish others for their mistakes.[331] As compared with mock jurors in neutral moods, mock jurors who are angry are more likely to ignore evidence that would exonerate the defendant.[332] As compared with voters who are sad, angry voters are more likely to support vengeful policies and reject policies that are conciliatory.[333]

Audiences put into angry moods are less likely to comply with persuasive messages.[334] They do tend to agree, however, with persuasive messages that emphasize angering problems. In one study of incidental mood effects, researchers first hypnotized newspaper readers to feel either anger or disgust and then asked them to read one of two reviews of a local restaurant. One review consisted of several positive comments as well as several negative comments that were associated with anger (e.g., an extremely careless waiter). The other review consisted of several positive comments as well as several negative comments that were associated with disgust (e.g., a view of the garbage). Readers put into an angry mood formed the most negative attitudes toward the restaurant after they read the review with the angry comments.[335] In a similar study, readers were put into an angry or sad mood and then asked to read arguments for a proposed tax increase. Readers in angry moods were more persuaded by arguments that described the angering consequences of inaction.[336]

Audiences put into angry moods tend to process persuasive messages without much rational thought or deliberation.[337] For example, mock jurors who are put into an angry mood are more likely than sad ones to convict a defendant on the basis of an ethnic stereotype.[338] Yet because audience members in an angry mood preferentially attend to arguments hostile to their own positions,[339] they are less likely to engage the confirmation bias. When voters put into an angry mood were given the opportunity to read more about a U.S. presidential election, they were more likely to choose to read information that disconfirmed their position than voters put into sad or neutral moods. They were also more likely to change their position after reading the disconfirming information.[340]

The Effects of Incidental Fear

Audiences put into fearful moods, such as employees who have received a threatening reprimand, tend to make pessimistic judgments about future events much as sad people do. They also tend to make relatively pessimistic risk assessments and risk-averse choices.[341] In a study of the influence of incidental fear on recruiters' hiring decisions, recruiters put into a fearful mood perceived their hiring decision as being more risky than recruiters put into an angry mood. The angry recruiters tended to be optimistic about the applicants' ability to satisfy the job requirements. In contrast, the fearful recruiters were pessimistic about the applicants' ability and were reluctant to give them high ratings.[342] Interestingly, job applicants put into fearful moods are also more risk averse. They avoid taking big risks when choosing among job offers even when the potential reward is great.[343]

Despite its drawbacks, incidental fear can actually aid audience decision making. Audiences put into fearful moods tend to process persuasive messages in a rational and systematic way.[344] Incidental fear can also break the audience out of their habitual decision-making routines[345] and stimulate a reassessment of their previous preferences. For example, voters watching political campaign ads feel less certain about their choice of candidates when the music and images in the ads put them in a fearful mood. Campaign ads that induce a fearful mood motivate voters, especially knowledgeable ones, to search for more information about the other candidates.[346]

EMOTIONS IN AUDIENCE DECISION MAKING: IMPLICATIONS FOR COMMUNICATORS

- The main takeaway for communicators in Chapter 7 is that each different emotion an audience experiences will affect its decision in an emotion-specific way.
- Use the information presented in the chapter to anticipate the effects of your audience's current moods and emotions on their decisions and to make appeals that affect your audience's decisions in specific ways.
- Why use the information? To increase the chances of the audience making the decision you desire. To enhance audience perceptions of you as a leader.
- If you need to improve your ability to recognize others' emotions, refer to the section on emotions in Chapter 6. You can then determine the effect of that emotion on decision making. If you need to evoke a different emotion from your audience, refer to the section in this chapter on emotional appeals and intensifiers.

Notes

1 Gore, A., & Bush, G. W. (2000). *The first Gore–Bush presidential debate.* Retrieved November 9, 2009 from www.debates.org/pages/trans2000a.html.
2 Westen, D. (2007, p. 33). *The political brain: The role of emotion in deciding the fate of the nation.* New York: Public Affairs.

3 Emrich, C. G., Brower, H. H., Feldman, J. M., & Garland, H. (2001). Images in words: Presidential rhetoric, charisma, and greatness. *Administrative Science Quarterly, 46*, 527–557.

4 Kruger, J., Epley, N., Parker, J., & Ng, Z. (2005). Egocentrism over e-mail: Can we communicate as well as we think? *Journal of Personality and Social Psychology, 89*(6), 925–936.

5 Oatley, K., & Jenkins, J. M. (1996). *Understanding emotions.* Malden, MA: Blackwell Publishing.

Roseman, I. J. (1994, July). *The discrete emotions form a coherent set: A theory of emotional responses.* Paper presented at the Sixth Annual Convention of the American Psychological Society, Washington, DC.

Smith, C. A., & Lazarus, R. S. (1990). Emotion and adaptation. In L. A. Pervin (Ed.), *Handbook of personality: Theory and research* (pp. 609–637). New York: Guilford Press.

6 Lewis, M. (1999). The role of the self in cognition and emotion. In T. Dalgleish & M. J. Power (Eds.), *Handbook of cognition and emotion* (pp. 125–142). New York: John Wiley & Sons Ltd.

Mascolo, M. F., & Fischer, K. W. (1995). Developmental transformations in appraisals for pride, shame, and guilt. In J. P. Tangney & K. W. Fischer (Eds.), *Self-conscious emotions: The psychology of shame, guilt, embarrassment, and pride* (pp. 64–113). New York: Guilford Press.

Sroufe, L. A. (1995). *Emotional development: The organization of emotional life in the early years.* Cambridge, UK: Cambridge University Press.

7 Levenson, R. W. (2003). Blood, sweat, and fears: The autonomic architecture of emotion. In P. Ekman, J. J. Campos, R. J. Davidson & F. B. M. de Waal (Eds.), *Emotions inside out: 130 years after Darwin's* The expression of the emotions in man and animals (pp. 348–366). New York: New York University Press.

8 Cacioppo, J. T., Tassinary, L. G., & Berntson, G. G. (2000). *Handbook of psychophysiology* (2nd ed.). New York: Cambridge University Press.

9 Taylor, H., Fieldman, G., & Lahlou, S. (2005). The impact of a threatening e-mail reprimand on the recipient's blood pressure. *Journal of Managerial Psychology, 20*(1) 43–50.

10 Maier, S. F., & Watkins, L. R. (1998). Cytokines for psychologists: Implications of bidirectional immune-to-brain communication for understanding behavior, mood, and cognition. *Psychological Review, 105*(1), 83–107.

11 *See* n5, Oatley & Jenkins (1996).

Rosenberg, E. L. (1998). Levels of analysis and the organization of affect. *Review of General Psychology Special Issue: New Directions in Research in Emotion, 2*(3), 247–270.

12 Lang, P. J., Bradley, M. M., & Cuthbert, B. N. (1990). Emotion, attention, and the startle reflex. *Psychological Review, 97*(3), 377–395.

13 Frijda, N. H. (1986). *The emotions.* New York: Cambridge University Press.

Plutchik, R. (1980). *Emotion: A psychoevolutionary synthesis.* New York: Harper & Row.

See n5, Smith & Lazarus (1990).

14 Ekman, P. (1971). Universals and cultural differences in facial expressions of emotion. In J. K. Cole (Ed.), *Nebraska symposium on motivation* (pp. 207–283). Lincoln, NE: University of Nebraska Press.

Scherer, K. R. (1986). Vocal affect expression: A review and a model for future research. *Psychological Bulletin, 99*(2), 143–165.

15 Levenson, R. W. (1994). Human emotion: A functional view. In P. Ekman & R. J. Davidson (Eds.), *The nature of emotion: Fundamental questions* (pp. 123–126). New York: Oxford University Press.

Simon, H. A. (1967). Motivational and emotional controls of cognition. *Psychological Review, 74*(1), 29–39.

16 Brown, R., & Kulik, J. (1977). Flashbulb memories. *Cognition, 5*(1), 73–99.

Buchanan, T. W., & Adolphs, R. (2002). The role of the human amygdala in emotional modulation of long-term declarative memory. In S. C. Moore & M. Oaksford (Eds.), *Emotional cognition: From brain to behaviour* (pp. 9–34). Amsterdam, Netherlands: John Benjamins Publishing Company.

Hamann, S. (2001). Cognitive and neural mechanisms of emotional memory. *Trends in Cognitive Sciences, 5*(9), 394–400.

17 Kensinger, E. A., Piguet, O., Krendl, A. C., & Corkin, S. (2005). Memory for contextual details: Effects of emotion and aging. *Psychology and Aging, 20*(2), 241–250.

18 Heuer, F., & Reisberg, D. (1990). Vivid memories of emotional events: The accuracy of remembered minutiae. *Memory & Cognition, 18*(5), 496–506.

Kensinger, E. A., & Corkin, S. (2003). Memory enhancement for emotional words: Are emotional words more vividly remembered than neutral words? *Memory & Cognition, 31*(8), 1169–1180.

Ochsner, K. N. (2000). Are affective events richly recollected or simply familiar? The experience and process of recognizing feelings past. *Journal of Experimental Psychology: General, 129*(2), 242–261.

19 Cohen, G., Conway, M. A., & Maylor, E. A. (1994). Flashbulb memories in older adults. *Psychology and Aging, 9*(3), 454–463.

Davidson, P. S. R., & Glisky, E. L. (2002). Is flashbulb memory a special instance of source memory? Evidence from older adults. *Memory, 10*(2), 99–111.

20 Ochsner, K. N., & Sanchez, H. (2001). *The relation between the regulation and recollection of affective experience.* Unpublished manuscript. Department of Psychology, Stanford University, Stanford, CA.

21 Breckler, S. J., & Wiggins, E. C. (1989). Affect versus evaluation in the structure of attitudes. *Journal of Experimental Social Psychology, 25*(3), 253–271.

22 Lavine, H., Thomsen, C. J., Zanna, M. P., & Borgida, E. (1998). On the primacy of affect in the determination of attitudes and behavior: The moderating role of affective-cognitive ambivalence. *Journal of Experimental Social Psychology, 34*(4), 398–421.

23 Pham, M. T., Cohen, J. B., Pracejus, J. W., & Hughes, G. D. (2001). Affect monitoring and the primacy of feelings in judgment. *Journal of Consumer Research, 28*(2), 167–188.

24 Kahneman, D., Schkade, D., & Sunstein, C. R. (1998). Shared outrage and erratic awards: The psychology of punitive damages. *Journal of Risk and Uncertainty, 16*(1), 49–86.

25 Hsee, C. K., & Rottenstreich, Y. (2004). Music, pandas, and muggers: On the affective psychology of value. *Journal of Experimental Psychology: General, 133*(1), 23–30.

26 Loewenstein, G., Weber, E. U., Hsee, C. K., & Welch, E. (2001). Risk as feelings. *Psychological Bulletin, 127*(2), 267–286.

27 Rottenstreich, Y., & Hsee, C. K. (2001). Money, kisses, and electric shocks: On the affective psychology of risk. *Psychological Science, 12*(3), 185–190.

28 Bellenger, D. N., Robertson, D. H., & Hirschman, E. C. (1978). Impulse buying varies by product. *Journal of Advertising Research, 18*(6), 15–18.

Cobb, C. J., & Hoyer, W. D. (1986). Planned versus impulse purchase behavior. *Journal of Retailing, 62*(4), 384–409.

Han, Y. K., Morgan, G. A., Kotsiopulos, A., & Kang-Park, J. (1991). Impulse buying behavior of apparel purchasers. *Clothing and Textile Research Journal, 9*(3), 15–21.

29 Welles, G. (1986). We're in the habit of impulsive buying. *USA Today*, May 21, p. 1.

30 *See* n28, Cobb & Hoyer (1986).

Rook, D. W. (1987). The buying impulse. *Journal of Consumer Research, 14*(2), 189–199.

Rook, D. W., & Fisher, R. J. (1995). Trait and normative aspects of impulsive buying behavior. *Journal of Consumer Research, 22*(3), 305–13.

31 Loewenstein, G., & Lerner, J. S. (2003). The role of affect in decision making. In R. J. Davidson, K. R. Scherer & H. H. Goldsmith (Eds.), *Handbook of affective sciences* (pp. 619–642). New York: Oxford University Press.

32 Abelson, R. P., Kinder, D. R., Peters, M. D., & Fiske, S. T. (1982). Affective and semantic components in political person perception. *Journal of Personality and Social Psychology, 42*(4), 619–630.

33 Etzioni, A. (1992, p. 90). Normative-affective factors: Toward a new decision-making model. In M. Zey (Ed.), *Decision making: Alternatives to rational choice models* (pp. 89–111). Thousand Oaks, CA: Sage.

34 Pham, M. T. (1998). Representativeness, relevance, and the use of feelings in decision making. *Journal of Consumer Research, 25*(2), 144–159.

35 Adaval, R. (2001). Sometimes it just feels right: The differential weighting of affect-consistent and affect-inconsistent product information. *Journal of Consumer Research, 28*(1), 1–17.

Yeung, C. W., & Wyer, R. S. (2004). Affect, appraisal, and consumer judgment. *Journal of Consumer Research, 31*(2), 412–424.

36 Wyer, R. S., Clore, G. L., & Isbell, L. M. (1999). Affect and information processing. In M. P. Zanna (Ed.), *Advances in experimental social psychology* (Vol. 31, pp. 1–77). San Diego, CA: Academic Press.

37 Albarracín, D., & Wyer Jr, R. S. (2001). Elaborative and nonelaborative processing of a behavior-related communication. *Personality and Social Psychology Bulletin, 27*(6), 691–705.

Miniard, P. W., Bhatla, S., Lord, K. R., Dickson, P. R., & Unnava, H. R. (1991). Picture-based persuasion processes and the moderating role of involvement. *Journal of Consumer Research, 18*(1), 92–107.

38 Mitchell, A. A., & Olson, J. C. (1981). Are product attribute beliefs the only mediator of advertising effects on brand attitude? *Journal of Marketing Research, 18*(3), 318–332.

39 Moore, D. L., & Hutchinson, J. W. (1983). The effects of ad affect on advertising effectiveness. *Advances in Consumer Research, 10*, 526–531.

Park, C. W., & Young, S. M. (1986). Consumer response to television commercials: The impact of involvement and background music on brand attitude formation. *Journal of Marketing Research, 23*(1), 11–24.

40 Edell, J. A., & Burke, M. C. (1986). The relative impact of prior brand attitude and attitude toward the ad on brand attitude after ad exposure. In J. C. Olson & K. Sentis (Eds.), *Advertising and consumer psychology* (Vol. 3, pp. 93–107). New York: Praeger.

Stayman, D. M., & Aaker, D. A. (1987). *Repetition and affective response: Differences in specific feeling responses and the mediating role of attitude toward the ad.* Working Paper, Austin: University of Texas.

41 Kramer, G. P., Kerr, N. L., & Carroll, J. (1990). Pretrial publicity, judicial remedies, and jury bias. *Law and Human Behavior, 14*(5), 409–438.

42 Isen, A. M., & Means, B. (1983). The influence of positive affect on decision-making strategy. *Social Cognition, 2*(1), 18–31.

Schwarz, N., & Clore, G. L. (1983). Mood, misattribution, and judgments of well-being: Informative and directive functions of affective states. *Journal of Personality and Social Psychology, 45*(3), 513–523.

43 Keltner, D., & Kring, A. M. (1998). Emotion, social function, and psychopathology. *Review of General Psychology Special Issue: New Directions in Research on Emotion, 2*(3), 320–342.

Lerner, J. S., & Keltner, D. (2000). Beyond valence: Toward a model of emotion-specific influences on judgement and choice. *Cognition & Emotion Special Issue: Emotion, Cognition, and Decision Making, 14*(4), 473–493.

See n15., Bornstein et. al (1999).

44 Forgas, J. P. (1995). Mood and judgment: The affect infusion model (AIM). *Psychological Bulletin, 117*(1), 39–66.

Isen, A. M. (1993). Positive affect and decision making. In M. Lewis & J. M. Haviland (Eds.), *Handbook of emotions* (pp. 261–277). New York: Guilford Press.

See n43, Lerner & Keltner (2000).

45 Wilson, T. D., Kraft, D., & Dunn, D. S. (1989b). The disruptive effects of explaining attitudes: The moderating effect of knowledge about the attitude object. *Journal of Experimental Social Psychology, 25*(5), 379–400.

Wilson, T. D., & Schooler, J. W. (1991). Thinking too much: Introspection can reduce the quality of preferences and decisions. *Journal of Personality and Social Psychology, 60*(2), 181–192.

46 Wilson, T. D., Lisle, D. J., Schooler, J. W., Hodges, S. D., Klaaren, K. J., & LaFleur, S. J. (1993). Introspecting about reasons can reduce post-choice satisfaction. *Personality and Social Psychology Bulletin, 19*(3), 331–339.

47 Frijda, N. H. (1988). The laws of emotion. *American Psychologist, 43*(5), 349–358.

Frijda, N. H., & Mesquita, B. (1994). The social roles and functions of emotions. In S. Kitayama & H. R. Markus (Eds.), *Emotion and culture: Empirical studies of mutual influence* (pp. 51–87). Washington, DC: American Psychological Association.
Keltner, D., & Gross, J. J. (1999). Functional accounts of emotions. *Cognition & Emotion Special Issue: Functional Accounts of Emotion, 13*(5), 467–480.

48 Loewenstein, G. (1996). Out of control: Visceral influences on behavior. *Organizational Behavior and Human Decision Processes, 65*(3), 272–292.

Metcalfe, J., & Mischel, W. (1999). A hot/cool-system analysis of delay of gratification: Dynamics of willpower. *Psychological Review, 106*(1), 3–19.

Mischel, W., Cantor, N., & Feldman, S. (1996). Principles of self-regulation: The nature of willpower and self-control. In E. T. Higgins & A. W. Kruglanski (Eds.), *Social psychology: Handbook of basic principles* (pp. 329–360). New York: Guilford Press.

49 Sjöberg, L. (1980). Volitional problems in carrying through a difficult decision. *Acta Psychologica, 45*(1–3), 123–132.

50 Bless, H., Clore, G. L., Schwarz, N., Golisano, V., Rabe, C., & Wölk, M. (1996). Mood and the use of scripts: Does a happy mood really lead to mindlessness? *Journal of Personality and Social Psychology, 71*(4), 665–679.

Bodenhausen, G. V., Kramer, G. P., & Süsser, K. (1994a). Happiness and stereotypic thinking in social judgment. *Journal of Personality and Social Psychology, 66*(4), 621–632.

Bodenhausen, G. V., Sheppard, L. A., & Kramer, G. P. (1994b). Negative affect and social judgment: The differential impact of anger and sadness. *European Journal of Social Psychology Special Issue: Affect in Social Judgments and Cognition, 24*(1), 45–62.

51 *See* n33, Etzioni (1992).

52 Bazerman, M. H., Tenbrunsel, A. E., & Wade-Benzoni, K. (2005). *Negotiating with yourself and losing: Making decisions with competing internal preferences.* Northampton, MA: Edward Elgar Publishing.

See n48, Loewenstein (1996).

53 Wallace, J. F., Newman, J. P., & Bachorowski, J. A. (1991). Failures of response modulation: Impulsive behavior in anxious and impulsive individuals. *Journal of Research in Personality, 25*(1), 23–44.

54 Wallace, J. F., & Newman, J. P. (1997). Neuroticism and the attentional mediation of dysregulatory psychopathology. *Cognitive Therapy and Research, 21*(2), 135–156.

55 Myers, B., & Greene, E. (2004). The prejudicial nature of victim impact statements: Implications for capital sentencing policy. *Psychology, Public Policy, and Law, 10*(4), 492–515.

56 Goldberg, J. H., Lerner, J. S., & Tetlock, P. E. (1999). Rage and reason: The psychology of the intuitive prosecutor. *European Journal of Social Psychology, 29*(5–6), 781–795.

Lerner, J. S., & Keltner, D. (2001). Fear, anger, and risk. *Journal of Personality and Social Psychology, 81*(1), 146–159.

See n26, Loewenstein et al. (2001).

57 *See* n26, Loewenstein et al. (2001).

58 Finucane, M. L., Alhakami, A., Slovic, P., & Johnson, S. M. (2000). The affect heuristic in judgments of risks and benefits. *Journal of Behavioral Decision Making, 13*(1), 1–17.

59 Au, K., Chan, F., Wang, D., & Vertinsky, I. (2003). Mood in foreign exchange trading: Cognitive processes and performance. *Organizational Behavior and Human Decision Processes, 91*(2), 322–338.

60 Hsee, C. K., & Kunreuther, H. (2000). The affection effect in insurance decisions. *Journal of Risk and Uncertainty, 20*(2), 141–159.

61 Hsee, C. K., & Menon, S. (1999). *Affection effect in consumer choices.* Unpublished study, University of Chicago, Chicago, IL.

62 Lefford, A. (1946). The influence of emotional subject matter on logical reasoning. *Journal of General Psychology, 34*, 127–151.

63 Bechara, A., Damasio, H., Tranel, D., & Anderson, S. W. (1998). Dissociation of working memory from decision making within the human prefrontal cortex. *Journal of Neuroscience, 18*(1), 428–437.

Damasio, A. R., Tranel, D., & Damasio, H. (1990). Individuals with sociopathic behavior caused by frontal damage fail to respond autonomically to social stimuli. *Behavioural Brain Research, 41*(2), 81–94.

Eslinger, P. J., & Damasio, A. R. (1985). Severe disturbance of higher cognition after bilateral frontal lobe ablation: Patient EVR. *Neurology, 35*(12), 1731–1741.

64 Bechara, A. (2003). Risky business: Emotion, decision-making, and addiction. *Journal of Gambling Studies, 19*(1), 23–51.

65 Bechara, A., Damasio, A. R., Damasio, H., & Anderson, S. W. (1994). Insensitivity to future consequences following damage to human prefrontal cortex. *Cognition, 50*(1–3), 7–15.

Bechara, A., Damasio, H., Damasio, A. R., & Lee, G. P. (1999). Different contributions of the human amygdala and ventromedial prefrontal cortex to decision-making. *Journal of Neuroscience, 19*(13), 5473–5481.

Damasio, A. R. (1994). *Descartes' error: Emotion, reason, and the human brain.* New York: G. P. Putnam.

66 Anderson, S. W., Bechara, A., Damasio, H., Tranel, D., & Damasio, A. R. (1999). Impairment of social and moral behavior related to early damage in human prefrontal cortex. *Nature Neuroscience, 2*(11), 1032–1037.

Anderson, S. W., Damasio, H., Jones, R. D., & Tranel, D. (1991). Wisconsin card sorting test performance as a measure of frontal lobe damage. *Journal of Clinical and Experimental Neuropsychology, 13*(6), 909–922.

See n63, Bechara et al. (1998).

67 *See* n65, Damasio (1994), p. 193.

68 Clore, G. L., & Isbell, L. M. (2001). Emotion as virtue and vice. In J. H. Kuklinski (Ed.), *Citizens and politics: Perspectives from political psychology* (pp. 103–123). New York: Cambridge University Press.

Ellsworth, P. C., & Scherer, K. R. (2003). Appraisal processes in emotion. In R. J. Davidson, K. R. Scherer & H. H. Goldsmith (Eds.), *Handbook of affective sciences* (pp. 572–595). New York: Oxford University Press.

Smith, C. A., & Kirby, L. D. (2001). Toward delivering on the promise of appraisal theory. In K. R. Scherer, A. Schorr & T. Johnstone (Eds.), *Appraisal processes in emotion: Theory, methods, research* (pp. 121–138). New York: Oxford University Press.

69 Lazarus, R. S. (1999). *Stress and emotion: A new synthesis.* New York: Springer Publishing Co.

See n5, Smith & Lazarus (1990).

Smith, C. A., & Pope, L. K. (1992). Appraisal and emotion: The interactional contributions of dispositional and situational factors. In M. S. Clark (Ed.), *Emotion and social behavior* (pp. 32–62). Thousand Oaks, CA: Sage.

70 Carver, C. S., & Scheier, M. F. (1990). Origins and functions of positive and negative affect: A control-process view. *Psychological Review, 97*(1), 19–35.

71 Griner, L. A., & Smith, C. A. (2000). Contributions of motivational orientation to appraisal and emotion. *Personality and Social Psychology Bulletin, 26*(6), 727–740.

Ross, M., & Conway, M. (1986). Remembering one's own past: The construction of personal histories. In R. M. Sorrentino & E. T. Higgins (Eds.), *Handbook of motivation and cognition: Foundations of social behavior* (pp. 122–144). New York: Guilford Press.

Singer, J. A., & Salovey, P. (1996). Motivated memory: Self-defining memories, goals, and affect regulation. In L. L. Martin & A. Tesser (Eds.), *Striving and feeling: Interactions among goals, affect, and self-regulation* (pp. 229–250). Hillsdale, NJ: Lawrence Erlbaum Associates.

See n69, Smith & Pope (1992).

72 Rokeach, M. (1973). *The nature of human values.* New York: Free Press.

73 Hurwitz, J., & Peffley, M. (1987). How are foreign policy attitudes structured? A hierarchical model. *American Political Science Review, 81*(04), 1099–1120.

74 Feldman, S. (1988). Structure and consistency in public opinion: The role of core beliefs and values. *American Journal of Political Science, 32*(2), 416–440.

75 Shaver, P., Hazan, C., & Bradshaw, D. (1988). Love as attachment. In R. J. Sternberg & M. L. Barnes (Eds.), *The psychology of love* (pp. 68–99). New Haven, CT: Yale University Press.

Smith, C. A., & Ellsworth, P. C. (1987). Patterns of appraisal and emotion related to taking an exam. *Journal of Personality and Social Psychology, 52*(3), 475–488.

See n69, Smith & Pope (1992).

76 Kahle, L. R., Beatty, S. E., & Homer, P. M. (1986). Alternative measurement approaches to consumer values: The list of values (LOV) and values and life style (VALS). *Journal of Consumer Research, 13*(3), 405–409.

Kamakura, W. A., & Novak, T. P. (1992). Value-system segmentation: Exploring the meaning of LOV. *Journal of Consumer Research, 19*(1), 119–132.

Richins, M. L. (1994). Special possessions and the expression of material values. *Journal of Consumer Research, 21*(3), 522–533.

77 Overby, J. W., Gardial, S. F., & Woodruff, R. B. (2004). French versus American consumers' attachment of value to a product in a common consumption context: A cross-national comparison. *Journal of the Academy of Marketing Science, 32*(4), 437–460.

78 Smeesters, D., Warlop, L., Vanden Abeele, P., & Ratneshwar, S. (1999). *Exploring the recycling dilemma: Consumer motivation and experiences in mandatory garbage recycling programs.* Research report no. 9924, Department of Applied Economics, Catholic University of Leuven, Belgium.

79 Luce, M. F. (1998). Choosing to avoid: Coping with negatively emotion-laden consumer decisions. *Journal of Consumer Research, 24*(4), 409–433.

Luce, M. F., Bettman, J. R., & Payne, J. W. (2000). Minimizing negative emotion as a decision goal: Investigating emotional trade-off difficulty. In S. Ratneshwar, D. G. Mick & C. Huffman (Eds.), *The why of consumption: Contemporary perspectives on consumer motives, goals, and desires* (pp. 59–80). London and New York: Routledge.

80 Bagozzi, R. P., & Dholakia, U. (1999). Goal setting and goal striving in consumer behavior. *Journal of Marketing Special Issue: Fundamental Issues and Directions for Marketing, 63,* 19–32.

Huffman, C., Ratneshwar, S., & Mick, D. G. (2000). Consumer goal structures and goal-determination processes: An integrative framework. In S. Ratneshwar, D. G. Mick & C. Huffman (Eds.), *The why of consumption: Contemporary perspectives on consumer motives, goals, and desires* (pp. 9–35). London and New York: Routledge.

Walker, B. A., & Olson, J. C. (1997). The activated self in consumer behavior: A cognitive structure perspective. In R. W. Belk (Ed.), *Research in consumer behavior* (pp. 135–171). Greenwich, CT: JAI Press.

81 Grunert, K. G., & Bech-Larsen, T. (2005). Explaining choice option attractiveness by beliefs elicited by the laddering method. *Journal of Economic Psychology, 26*(2), 223–241.

82 *Ibid.* See also Perkins, W. S., & Reynolds, T. J. (1988). The explanatory power of values in preference judgments: Validation of the means-end perspective. *Advances in Consumer Research, 15,* 122–126).

83 Cronin Jr, J. J., Brady, M. K., & Hult, G. T. M. (2000). Assessing the effects of quality, value, and customer satisfaction on consumer behavioral intentions in service environments. *Journal of Retailing, 76*(2), 193–218.

Patterson, P. G., & Spreng, R. A. (1997). Modeling the relationship between perceived value, satisfaction and repurchase intentions in a business-to-business, services context: An empirical examination. *International Journal of Service Industry Management, 8*(5), 415–432.

84 Conger, J. A., & Kanungo, R. N. (1998). *Charismatic leadership in organizations.* Thousand Oaks, CA: Sage.

Shamir, B., House, R., & Arthur, M. B. (1993). The motivational effects of charismatic leadership: A self-concept based theory. *Organization Science, 4*(4), 577–594.

Sheldon, K. M., & Elliot, A. J. (1999). Goal striving, need satisfaction, and longitudinal well-being: The self-concordance model. *Journal of Personality and Social Psychology, 76*(3), 482–497.

85 Bono, J. E., & Judge, T. A. (2003). Self-concordance at work: Toward understanding the motivational effects of transformational leaders. *Academy of Management Journal, 46*(5), 554–571.

86 *See* n79, Luce (1998).

87 *See* n79, Luce et al. (2000).

88 *See* n79, Luce (1998).

89 Shah, D. V., Domke, D., & Wackman, D. B. (1996). "To thine own self be true": Values, framing, and voter decision-making strategies. *Communication Research, 23*(5), 509–560.

90 Derryberry, D., & Tucker, D. M. (1992). Neural mechanisms of emotion. *Journal of Consulting and Clinical Psychology, 60*(3), 329–338.

91 *See* n15, Simon (1967).

92 Lundqvist, D., & Öhman, A. (2005). Caught by the evil eye: Nonconscious information processing, emotion, and attention to facial stimuli. In L. F. Barrett, P. M. Niedenthal & P. Winkielman (Eds.), *Emotion and consciousness* (pp. 97–122). New York: Guilford Press.

Öhman, A., Esteves, F., & Soares, J. J. F. (1995). Preparedness and preattentive associative learning: Electrodermal conditioning to masked stimuli. *Journal of Psychophysiology, 9*(2), 99–108.

Schupp, H. T., Junghöfer, M., Weike, A. I., & Hamm, A. O. (2003). Emotional facilitation of sensory processing in the visual cortex. *Psychological Science, 14*(1), 7–13.

93 Carretié, L., Hinojosa, J. A., Martín-Loeches, M., Mercado, F., & Tapia, M. (2004). Automatic attention to emotional stimuli: Neural correlates. *Human Brain Mapping, 22*(4), 290–299.

94 Batty, M. J., Cave, K. R., & Pauli, P. (2005). Abstract stimuli associated with threat through conditioning cannot be detected preattentively. *Emotion, 5*(4), 418–430.

95 Pizzagalli, D., Regard, M., & Lehmann, D. (1999). Rapid emotional face processing in the human right and left brain hemispheres: An ERP study. *NeuroReport: For Rapid Communication of Neuroscience Research, 10*(13), 2691–2698.

96 Eger, E., Jedynak, A., Iwaki, T., & Skrandies, W. (2003). Rapid extraction of emotional expression: Evidence from evoked potential fields during brief presentation of face stimuli. *Neuropsychologia, 41*(7), 808–817.

Sato, W., Kochiyama, T., Yoshikawa, S., & Matsumura, M. (2001). Emotional processing boosts early visual processing of the face: ERP recording and its decomposition by independent component analysis. *NeuroReport, 12*(4), 709–714.

97 *See* n92, Lundqvist & Öhman (2005).

98 Anderson, A. K., & Phelps, E. A. (2001). Lesions of the human amygdala impair enhanced perception of emotionally salient events. *Nature, 411*(6835), 305–309.

99 Compton, R. J. (2003). The interface between emotion and attention: A review of evidence from psychology and neuroscience. *Behavioral and Cognitive Neuroscience Reviews, 2*(2), 115–129.

Vuilleumier, P., Armony, J. L., Clarke, K., Husain, M., Driver, J., & Dolan, R. J. (2002). Neural response to emotional faces with and without awareness: Event-related fMRI in a parietal patient with visual extinction and spatial neglect. *Neuropsychologia, 40*(12), 2156–2166.

White, M. (1996). Anger recognition is independent of spatial attention. *New Zealand Journal of Psychology, 25*(1), 30–35.

100 Schirmer, A., Striano, T., & Friederici, A. D. (2005). Sex differences in the preattentive processing of vocal emotional expressions. *NeuroReport: For Rapid Communication of Neuroscience Research, 16*(6), 635–639.

101 Hyönä, J., & Häikiö, T. (2005). Is emotional content obtained from parafoveal words during reading? An eye movement analysis. *Scandinavian Journal of Psychology, 46*(6), 475–483.

102 Alpers, G. W., Ruhleder, M., Walz, N., Mühlberger, A., & Pauli, P. (2005). Binocular rivalry between emotional and neutral stimuli: A validation using fear conditioning and EEG. *International Journal of Psychophysiology Special Issue: Neurobiology of Fear and Disgust, 57*(1), 25–32.

103 Calvo, M. G., & Lang, P. J. (2004). Gaze patterns when looking at emotional pictures: Motivationally biased attention. *Motivation and Emotion, 28*(3), 221–243.

104 *See* n17, Kensinger et al. (2005).

Mackintosh, B., & Mathews, A. (2003). Don't look now: Attentional avoidance of emotionally valenced cues. *Cognition & Emotion, 17*(4), 623–646.

Stormark, K. M., Nordby, H., & Hugdahl, K. (1995). Attentional shifts to emotionally charged cues: Behavioural and ERP data. *Cognition & Emotion, 9*(5), 507–523.

105 *See* n102, Alpers et al. (2005).

See n103, Calvo & Lang (2004).

106 Hansen, C. H., & Hansen, R. D. (1988). Finding the face in the crowd: An anger superiority effect. *Journal of Personality and Social Psychology, 54*(6), 917–924.

107 Eastwood, J. D., Smilek, D., & Merikle, P. M. (2001). Differential attentional guidance by unattended faces expressing positive and negative emotion. *Perception & Psychophysics, 63*(6), 1004–1013.

108 Öhman, A., Flykt, A., & Esteves, F. (2001). Emotion drives attention: Detecting the snake in the grass. *Journal of Experimental Psychology: General, 130*(3), 466–478.

109 Quirk, S. W., & Strauss, M. E. (2001). Visual exploration of emotion eliciting images by patients with schizophrenia. *Journal of Nervous and Mental Disease, 189*(11), 757–765.

110 *See* n104, Stormark et al. (1995).

111 *See* n101, Hyönä & Häikiö (2005).

112 White, G. L., & Maltzman, I. (1978). Pupillary activity while listening to verbal passages. *Journal of Research in Personality, 12*(3), 361–369.

113 Hess, E. H., & Polt, J. M. (1960). Pupil size as related to interest value of visual stimuli. *Science, 132*, 349–350.

114 Metalis, S. A., & Hess, E. H. (1982). Pupillary response/semantic differential scale relationships. *Journal of Research in Personality, 16*(2), 201–216.

115 Öhman, A., & Wiens, S. (2003). On the automaticity of autonomic responses in emotion: An evolutionary perspective. In R. J. Davidson, K. R. Scherer & H. H. Goldsmith (Eds.), *Handbook of affective sciences* (pp. 256–275). New York: Oxford University Press.

116 Öhman, A. (1979). The orienting response, attention, and learning: An information-processing perspective. In H. D. Kimmel, E. H. van Gist & J. F. Orlebeke (Eds.), *The orienting reflex in humans* (pp. 443–472). Hillsdale, NJ: Lawrence Erlbaum Associates.

117 Jennings, J. R. (1992). Is it important that the mind is in a body? Inhibition and the heart. *Psychophysiology, 29*(4), 369–383.

Öhman, A., Hamm, A., & Hugdahl, K. (2000). Cognition and the autonomic nervous system: Orienting, anticipation, and conditioning. In J. T. Cacioppo, L. G. Tassinary & G. G. Berntson (Eds.), *Handbook of psychophysiology* (2nd ed., pp. 533–575). New York: Cambridge University Press.

118 *See* n104, Mackintosh & Mathews (2003).

119 MacLeod, C., & Rutherford, E. M. (1992). Anxiety and the selective processing of emotional information: Mediating roles of awareness, trait and state variables, and personal relevance of stimulus materials. *Behaviour Research and Therapy, 30*(5), 479–491.

Mathews, A., & Klug, F. (1993). Emotionality and interference with color-naming in anxiety. *Behaviour Research and Therapy, 31*(1), 57–62.

120 Dalgleish, T. (1995). Performance on the emotional Stroop task in groups of anxious, expert, and control subjects: A comparison of computer and card presentation formats. *Cognition & Emotion, 9*(4), 341–362.

121 Mogg, K., Bradley, B. P., Field, M., & De Houwer, J. (2003). Eye movements to smoking-related pictures in smokers: Relationship between attentional biases and implicit and explicit measures of stimulus valence. *Addiction, 98*(6), 825–836.

122 Loftus, E. F. (1979). *Eyewitness testimony.* Cambridge, MA: Harvard University Press.

123 *See* n98, Anderson & Phelps (2001).

See n17, Kensinger et al. (2005).

Libkuman, T. M., Stabler, C. L., & Otani, H. (2004). Arousal, valence, and memory for detail. *Memory, 12*(2), 237–247.

124 Hope, L., & Wright, D. (2007). Beyond unusual? Examining the role of attention in the weapon focus effect. *Applied Cognitive Psychology, 21*(7), 951–961.

125 Loftus, E. F., Loftus, G. R., & Messo, J. (1987). Some facts about "weapon focus." *Law and Human Behavior, 11*(1), 55–62.

126 *See* n16, Buchanan & Adolphs (2002).

127 Loftus, E. F., & Burns, T. E. (1982). Mental shock can produce retrograde amnesia. *Memory & Cognition, 10*(4), 318–323.

Strange, B. A., Hurleman, R., & Dolan, R. J. (2003). An emotion-induced retrograde amnesia in humans is amygdala- and beta-adrenergic-dependent. *Proceedings of the National Academy of Sciences, USA, 100*(3), 13626–13631.

128 *See* n127, Strange et al. (2003).

129 Arnold, M. B. (1960). *Emotion and personality.* New York: Columbia University Press.

Lazarus, R. S. (1991). *Emotion and adaptation.* New York: Oxford University Press.

Ortony, A., Clore, G. L., & Collins, A. (1988). *The cognitive structure of emotions.* New York: Cambridge University Press.

130 Roseman, I. J. (1984). Cognitive determinants of emotion: A structural theory. *Review of Personality & Social Psychology*, 5, 11–36.

See n5, Smith & Lazarus (1990).

131 See n129, Arnold (1960).

Lazarus, R. S. (1968). Emotions and adaptation: Conceptual and empirical relations. *Nebraska Symposium on Motivation*, 16, 175–266.

Scherer, K. R. (1987). Toward a dynamic theory of emotion: The component process model of affective states. *Geneva Studies in Emotion and Communication*, 1(1), 1–98.

132 Velmans, M. (1991). Is human information processing conscious? *Behavioral and Brain Sciences*, 14(4), 651–726.

133 Izard, C. E. (1977). *Human emotions*. New York: Plenum Press. Tomkins, S. S. (1962). *Affect, imagery, consciousness: Vol. I. The positive affects*. New York: Springer Publishing Co.

134 Smith, C. A., & Kirby, L. D. (2000). Consequences require antecedents: Toward a process model of emotion elicitation. In J. P. Forgas (Ed.), *Feeling and thinking: The role of affect in social cognition* (pp. 83–106). New York: Cambridge University Press.

135 Roseman, I. J., Dhawan, N., Rettek, S. I., Naidu, R. K., & Thapa, K. (1995). Cultural differences and cross-cultural similarities in appraisals and emotional responses. *Journal of Cross-Cultural Psychology*, 26(1), 23–48.

136 Mauro, R., Sato, K., & Tucker, J. (1992). The role of appraisal in human emotions: A cross-cultural study. *Journal of Personality and Social Psychology*, 62(2), 301–317.

137 Aue, T., Flykt, A., & Scherer, K. R. (2007). First evidence for differential and sequential efferent effects of stimulus relevance and goal conduciveness appraisal. *Biological Psychology*, 74(3), 347–357.

Lanctôt, N., & Hess, U. (2007). The timing of appraisals. *Emotion*, 7(1), 207–212.

Scherer, K. R. (1984). Emotion as a multicomponent process: A model and some cross-cultural data. *Review of Personality & Social Psychology*, 5, 37–63.

138 Delplanque, S., Grandjean, D., Chrea, C., Coppin, G., Aymard, L., Cayeux, I., . . . Scherer, K. R. (2009). Sequential unfolding of novelty and pleasantness appraisals of odors: Evidence from facial electromyography and autonomic reactions. *Emotion*, 9(3), 316–328.

See n68, Ellsworth & Scherer (2003).

139 Meyer, W. U., Reisenzein, R., & Schützwohl, A. (1997). Toward a process analysis of emotions: The case of surprise. *Motivation and Emotion*, 21(3), 251–274.

O'Reilly, J. X., Schüffelgen, U., Cuell, S. F., Behrens, T. J., Mars, R. B., & Rushworth, M. S. (2013). Dissociable effects of surprise and model update in parietal and anterior cingulate cortex. PNAS Proceedings Of The National Academy Of Sciences Of The United States Of America, 110(38), E3660-E3669.

140 Ellsworth, P. C. (1994). Levels of thought and levels of emotion. In P. Ekman & R. J. Davidson (Eds.), *The nature of emotion: Fundamental questions* (pp. 192–196). New York: Oxford University Press.

Kagan, J. (1991). A conceptual analysis of the affects. *Journal of the American Psychoanalytic Association*, 39(Suppl.), 109–129.

Posner, M. I., & Rothbart, M. K. (2007). Research on attention networks as a model for the integration of psychological science. *Annual Review of Psychology*, 58, 1–23.

141 Reisenzein, R. (2000). The subjective experience of surprise. In H. Bless & J. P. Forgas (Eds.), *The message within: The role of subjective experience in social cognition and behavior* (pp. 262–282). Philadelphia: Psychology Press.

142 See n68, Ellsworth & Scherer (2003).

143 Schneirla, T. C. (1959). An evolutionary and developmental theory of biphasic processes underlying approach and withdrawal. In M. R. Jones (Ed.), *Nebraska symposium on motivation* (pp. 1–42). Lincoln, NE: University of Nebraska Press.

144 See n68, Ellsworth & Scherer (2003).

145 Weigert, A. J. (1991). *Mixed emotions: Certain steps toward understanding ambivalence*. New York: State University of New York Press.

146 Diener, E., & Iran-Nejad, A. (1986). The relationship in experience between various types of affect. *Journal of Personality and Social Psychology*, 50(5), 1031–1038.

147 See n130, Roseman (1984).

See n137, Scherer (1984).

Smith, C. A., & Ellsworth, P. C. (1985). Patterns of cognitive appraisal in emotion. *Journal of Personality and Social Psychology*, 48(4), 813–838.

148 Ellsworth, P. C., & Smith, C. A. (1988). From appraisal to emotion: Differences among unpleasant feelings. *Motivation and Emotion, 12*(3), 271–302.

149 *See* n68, Ellsworth & Scherer (2003).

150 Scherer, K. R. (1982). Emotion as a process: Function, origin and regulation. *Social Science Information, 21*(4–5), 555–570.

151 *See* n6, Lewis (1999).

152 Kaiser, S., & Wehrle, T. (2001). Facial expressions as indicators of appraisal processes. In K. R. Scherer, A. Schorr & T. Johnstone (Eds.), *Appraisal processes in emotion: Theory, methods, research* (pp. 285–300). New York: Oxford University Press.

153 Kaiser, S., Wehrle, T., & Schmidt, S. (1998). Emotional episodes, facial expressions, and reported feelings in human-computer interactions. In A. H. Fischer (Ed.), *Proceedings of the xth conference of the international society for research on emotions* (pp. 82–86). Würzburg: ISRE Publications.

154 Hayden, B. Y., Heilbronner, S. R., Pearson, J. M., & Platt, M. L. (2011). Surprise signals in anterior cingulate cortex: Neuronal encoding of unsigned reward prediction errors driving adjustment in behavior. *The Journal of Neuroscience, 31*(11), 4178–4187.

Williams, L. M., Brammer, M. J., Skerrett, D., Lagopolous, J., Rennie, C., Kozek, K., . . . Gordon, E. (2000). The neural correlates of orienting: An integration of fMRI and skin conductance orienting. *NeuroReport, 11*(13), 3011–3015.

155 Krolak-Salmon, P., Hénaff, M. A., Vighetto, A., Bertrand, O., & Mauguière, F. (2004). Early amygdala reaction to fear spreading in occipital, temporal, and frontal cortex: A depth electrode ERP study in human. *Neuron, 42*(4), 665–676.

156 Schwartz, C. E., Wright, C. I., Shin, L. M., Kagan, J., Whalen, P. J., McMullin, K. G., & Rauch, S. L. (2003). Differential amygdalar response to novel versus newly familiar neutral faces: A functional MRI probe developed for studying inhibited temperament. *Biological Psychiatry, 53*(10), 854–862.

157 Vytal, K., & Hamann, S. (2010). Neuroimaging support for discrete neural correlates of basic emotions: A voxel-based meta-analysis. *Journal of Cognitive Neuroscience, 22*(12), 2864–2885.

158 *See* n8, Cacioppo et al. (2000).

159 *See* n10, Maier & Watkins (1998).

160 Hamm, A. O., Schupp, H. T., & Weike, A. I. (2003). Motivational organization of emotions: Autonomic changes, cortical responses, and reflex modulation. In R. J. Davidson, K. R. Scherer, & H. H. Goldsmith (Eds.), *Handbook of affective sciences* (pp. 187–211). New York: Oxford University Press.

161 *See* n47, Frijda & Mesquita (1994).

Roseman, I. J. (1996). Why these appraisals? Anchoring appraisal models to research on emotional behavior and related response systems. In N. H. Frijda (Ed.), *Proceedings of the ninth international conference of the international society for research on emotions* (pp. 106–110). Toronto, Canada: International Society for Research on Emotions.

Smith, C. A. (1989). Dimensions of appraisal and physiological response in emotion. *Journal of Personality and Social Psychology, 56*(3), 339–353.

162 *See* n13, Plutchik (1980).

163 *See* n129, Lazarus (1991).

164 Lerner, J. S., Small, D. A., & Loewenstein, G. (2004). Heart strings and purse strings: Carryover effects of emotions on economic transactions. *Psychological Science, 15*(5), 337–341.

165 Zeelenberg, M., & Pieters, R. (1999). Comparing service delivery to what might have been: Behavioral responses to regret and disappointment. *Journal of Service Research, 2*, 86–97.

166 Zebel, S., Zimmermann, A., Tendayi Viki, G., & Doosje, B. (2008). Dehumanization and guilt as distinct but related predictors of support for reparation policies. *Political Psychology, 29*(2), 193–219.

167 Kühne, R., & Schemer, C. (2015). The emotional effects of news frames on information processing and opinion formation. *Communication Research, 42*(3), 387–407.

168 Lerner, J. S., Gonzalez, R. M., Small, D. A., & Fischhoff, B. (2003). Effects of fear and anger on perceived risks of terrorism: A national field experiment. *Psychological Science, 14*(2), 144–150.

169 van't Wout, M., Chang, L. J., & Sanfey, A. G. (2010). The influence of emotion regulation on social interactive decision-making. *Emotion, 10*(6), 815–821.

170 Ochsner, K. N., & Gross, J. J. (2005). The cognitive control of emotion. *Trends in Cognitive Sciences, 9*(5), 242–249.

Taylor, J. G., & Fragopanagos, N. F. (2005). The interaction of attention and emotion. *Neural Networks, 18*(4), 353–369.

171 *See* n50, Bless et al. (1996).

Nolen-Hoeksema, S., & Morrow, J. (1993). Effects of rumination and distraction on naturally occurring depressed mood. *Cognition & Emotion, 7*(6), 561–570.

Nolen-Hoeksema, S., Morrow, J., & Fredrickson, B. L. (1993). Response styles and the duration of episodes of depressed mood. *Journal of Abnormal Psychology, 102*(1), 20–28.

172　*See* n33, Etzioni (1992).

See n31, Loewenstein & Lerner (2003).

Medvec, V. H., Madey, S. F., & Gilovich, T. (1995). When less is more: Counterfactual thinking and satisfaction among Olympic medalists. *Journal of Personality and Social Psychology, 69*(4), 603–610.

173　*See* n79, Luce (1998).

Luce, M. F., Bettman J. R., & Payne J. W. (1997). Choice processing in emotionally difficult decisions. *Journal of Experimental Psychology: Learning, Memory, and Cognition, 23*(2), 384–405.

174　*See* n89, Shah et al. (1996).

175　Bowers, J. W., Metts, S. M., & Duncanson, W. T. (1985). Emotion and interpersonal communication. In M. L. Knapp & G. R. Miller (Eds.), *Handbook of interpersonal communication* (pp. 500–550). Beverly Hills, CA: Sage.

176　Rosselli, F., Skelly, J. J., & Mackie, D. M. (1995). Processing rational and emotional messages: The cognitive and affective mediation of persuasion. *Journal of Experimental Social Psychology, 31*(2), 163–190.

177　Englis, B. G. (1991). Consumer Emotional Reactions to Television Advertising and Their Effects on Message Recall. In S. J. Agres, J. A. Edell, & T. M. Dubitsky (Eds.), *Emotion in advertising: Theoretical and practical explorations* (pp. 231–253). Westport, CN: Greenwood Press.

178　Andersen, P. A., & Guerrero, L. K. (1998). Principles of communication and emotion in social interaction. In P. A. Andersen & L. K. Guerrero (Eds.), *Handbook of communication and emotion: Research, Theory, Applications, and Contexts* (pp. 49–96). San Diego, CA: Academic Press.

Miller, K. I., Stiff, J. B., & Ellis, B. H. (1988). Communication and empathy as precursors to burnout among human service workers. *Communication Monographs, 55*(3), 250–265.

Stiff, J. B., Dillard, J. P., Somera, L., Kim, H., & Sleight, C. (1988). Empathy, communication, and prosocial behavior. *Communication Monographs, 55*(2), 198–213.

179　Cox, E. P., III, Wogalter, M. S., Stokes, S. L., & Murff, E. J. T. (1997). Do product warnings increase safe behavior? A meta-analysis. *Journal of Public Policy, 16*, 195–204.

180　Das, E. H., de Wit, J. F., & Stroebe, W. (2003). Fear appeals motivate acceptance of action recommendations: Evidence for a positive bias in the processing of persuasive messages. *Personality and Social Psychology Bulletin, 29*(5), 650–664.

De Hoog, N., Stroebe, W., & de Wit, J. F. (2005). The impact of fear appeals on processing and acceptance of health messages. *Personality and Social Psychology Bulletin, 31*(1), 24–33.

181　Grasmick, H. G., Bursik, R. J., & Kinsey, K. A. (1991). Shame and embarrassment as deterrents to noncompliance with the law – The case of an antilittering campaign. *Environment and Behavior, 23*, 233–251.

182　Yukl, G. A., & Falbe, C. M. (1990). Influence tactics and objectives in upward, downward, and lateral influence attempts. *Journal of Applied Psychology, 75*(2), 132–140.

Yukl, G. A., & Tracey, J. B. (1992). Consequences of influence tactics used with subordinates, peers, and the boss. *Journal of Applied Psychology, 77*, 525–535.

183　Jensen, J. L. (2007). Getting one's way in policy debates: Influence tactics used in group decision-making settings. *Public Administration Review, 67*(2), 216–227.

184　*See* n58, Finucane et al. (2000).

185　Holbrook, M. B. (1986). Emotion in the consumption experience: Toward a new model of the human consumer. In R. A. Peterson, W. D. Hoyer & W. R. Wilson (Eds.), *The role of affect in consumer behavior: Emerging theories and applications* (pp. 17–52). Lexington, MA: Lexington Books.

186　MacInnis, D. J., Rao, A. G., & Weiss, A. M. (2002). Assessing when increased media weight of real-world advertisements helps sales. *Journal of Marketing Research, 39*(4), 391–407.

187　Holbrook, M. B., & Batra, R. (1987). Assessing the role of emotions as mediators of consumer responses to advertising. *Journal of Consumer Research, 14*(3), 404–420.

188　Chang, M. J., & Gruner, C. R. (1981). Audience reaction to self-disparaging humor. *Southern Speech Communication Journal, 46*, 419–426.

Lulofs, R. S. (1991). Persuasion: Contexts, people, and messages. Scottsdale, AZ: Gorsuch-Scarisbrick.

Moog, C. (1991). Are they selling her lips? Advertising and identity. New York: Morrow & Co.

189　Brader, T. (2006). *Campaigning for hearts and minds: How emotional appeals in political ads work.* Chicago, IL: University of Chicago Press.

190 Roozen, I. (2013). The impact of emotional appeal and the media context on the effectiveness of commercials for not-for-profit and for-profit brands. *Journal of Marketing Communications, 19*(3), 198–214.

191 Aaker, J. L., & Williams, P. (1998). Empathy versus pride: The influence of emotional appeals across cultures. *Journal of Consumer Research, 25*(3), 241–261.

Kemp, E., Kennett-Hensel, P. A., & Kees, J. (2013). Pulling on the heartstrings: Examining the effects of emotions and gender in persuasive appeals. *Journal of Advertising, 42*(1), 69–79.

192 Nabi, R. L. (1998). The effect of disgust-eliciting visuals on attitudes toward animal experimentation. *Communication Quarterly, 46*, 472–484.

193 Grasmick, H. G., Bursik, R. J., & Kinsey, K. A. (1991). Shame and embarrassment as deterrents to noncompliance with the law the case of an antilittering campaign. *Environment and Behavior, 23*(2), 233–251.

194 Boudewyns, V., Turner, M. M., & Paquin, R. S. (2013). Shame-free guilt appeals: Testing the emotional and cognitive effects of shame and guilt appeals. *Psychology & Marketing, 30*(9), 811–825.

Duhachek, A., Agrawal, N., & Han, D. (2012). Guilt versus shame: Coping, fluency, and framing in the effectiveness of responsible drinking messages. *Journal of Marketing Research, 49*(6), 928–941.

van Leeuwen, E., van Dijk, W., & Kaynak, Ü. (2013). Of saints and sinners: How appeals to collective pride and guilt affect outgroup helping. *Group Processes & Intergroup Relations, 16*(6), 781–796.

195 Evans, R., Rozelle, R., Lasater, T., Dembroski, T., & Allen, B. (1970). Fear arousal, persuasion and actual vs. implied behavioral change. *Journal of Personality and Social Psychology, 16*(2), 220–227.

196 Boster, E. J., & Mongeau, P. (1984). Fear-arousing persuasive messages. In R. N. Bostrom & B. H. Westley (Eds.), *Communication yearbook, 8* (pp. 330–375). Newbury Park, CA: Sage.

Mongeau, P. A. (1998). Another look at fear-arousing persuasive appeals. In M. Allen & R. W. Preiss (Eds.), *Persuasion: Advances through meta-analysis* (pp. 53–68). Cresskill, NJ: Hampton Press.

Witte, K., & Allen, M. (2000). A meta-analysis of fear appeals: Implications for effective public health campaigns. *Health Education and Behavior, 27*(5), 591–615.

197 Das, E. H., De Wit, J. B., & Stroebe, W. (2003). Fear appeals motivate acceptance of action recommendations: Evidence for a positive bias in the processing of persuasive messages. *Personality and Social Psychology Bulletin, 29*(5), 650–664.

198 Petty, R. E., DeSteno, D., & Rucker, D. D. (2001). The role of affect in attitude change. In J. P. Forgas (Ed.), *Handbook of affect and social cognition* (pp. 212–233). Mahwah, NJ: Lawrence Erlbaum Associates.

199 Johnson, L. (1994). Educating about risk: Designing more effective disaster preparedness messages (earthquakes) (Doctoral dissertation, University of Washington, 1994). *Dissertation Abstracts International, 56*(04A), 1184.

200 Weinstein, N. D., Lyon, J. E., Sandman, P. M., & Cuite, C. L. (1998). Experimental evidence for stages of health behavior change: The precaution adoption process model applied to home radon testing. *Health Psychology, 17*(5), 445–453.

Witte, K., & Allen, M. (2000). A meta-analysis of fear appeals: Implications for effective public health campaigns. *Health Education & Behavior, 27*(5), 591–615.

201 Leventhal, H., & Singer, R. P. (1966). Affect arousal and positioning of recommendations in persuasive communications. *Journal of Personality and Social Psychology, 4*(2), 137–146.

Skilbeck, C., Tulips, J., & Ley, P. (1977). The effects of fear arousal, fear position, fear exposure, and sidedness on compliance with dietary instructions. *European Journal of Social Psychology, 7*(2), 221–239.

202 Ditto, P. H., & Lopez, D. F. (1992). Motivated skepticism: Use of differential decision criteria for preferred and nonpreferred conclusions. *Journal of Personality and Social Psychology, 63*(4), 568–584.

Mulilis, J. P., & Lippa, R. (1990). Behavioral change in earthquake preparedness due to negative threat appeals: A test of protection motivation theory. *Journal of Applied Social Psychology, 20*(8, Pt. 1), 619–638.

Witte, K., & Allen, M. (1996, November). *When do scare tactics work? A meta-analysis of fear appeals.* Paper presented at the Annual Meeting of the Speech Communication Association, San Diego, California.

203 *See* n189, Roozen (2013).

204 Walton, D. N. (1992). *The place of emotion in argument.* University Park, PA: Pennsylvania State University Press.

205 Roseman, I. J. (2001). A model of appraisal in emotion system: Integrating theory, research, and applications. In K. R. Scherer, A. Schorr & T. Johnstone (Eds.), *Appraisal processes in emotion: Theory, methods, research* (pp. 68–91). New York: Oxford University Press.

206 Scherer, K. R. (1999). On the sequential nature of appraisal processes: Indirect evidence from a recognition task. *Cognition and Emotion, 13*(6), 763–793.

207 *See* n13, Frijda (1986).

See n205, Roseman (2001).

208 Safire, W. (2004). *Lend me your ears: Great speeches in history.* New York: Norton.

209 *See* n129, Lazarus (1991).

210 Jussim, L., Nelson, T. E., Manis, M., & Soffin, S. (1995). Prejudice, stereotypes, and labeling effects: Sources of bias in person perception. *Journal of Personality and Social Psychology, 68*(2), 228–246.

211 Edwards, K., & Bryan, T. S. (1997). Judgmental biases produced by instructions to disregard: The (paradoxical) case of emotional information. *Personality and Social Psychology Bulletin, 23*(8), 849–864.

212 Buller, D. B., Burgoon, M., Hall, J. R., Levine, N., Taylor, A. M., Beach, B., . . . Melcher, C. (2000). Long-term effects of language intensity in preventive messages on planned family solar protection. *Health Communication, 12*(3), 261–275.

213 Fanelli, A., Misangyi, V. F., & Tosi, H. L. (2009). In charisma we trust: The effects of CEO charismatic visions on securities analysts. *Organization Science, 20*(6), 1011–1033.

214 Fishfader, V. L., Howells, G. N., Katz, R. C., & Teresi, P. S. (1996). Evidential and extralegal factors in juror decisions: Presentation mode, retention, and level of emotionality. *Law and Human Behavior, 20*(5), 565–572.

215 Kassin, S. M., & Garfield, D. A. (1991). Blood and guts: General and trial-specific effects of videotaped crime scenes on mock jurors. *Journal of Applied Social Psychology, 21*(18), 1459–1472.

216 Douglas, K. S., Lyon, D. R., & Ogloff, J. R. P. (1997). The impact of graphic photographic evidence on mock jurors' decisions in a murder trial: Probative or prejudicial? *Law and Human Behavior, 21*(5), 485–501.

217 Nemeth, R. J. (2002). The impact of gruesome evidence on mock juror decision making: The role of evidence characteristics and emotional response (Doctoral dissertation, Louisiana State University, 2002). *Dissertation Abstracts International, 63*(11B), 5546.

218 Oliver, E., & Griffitt, W. (1976). Emotional arousal and "objective" judgment. *Bulletin of the Psychonomic Society, 8*(5), 399–400.

219 Whalen, D. H., & Blanchard, F. A. (1982). Effects of photographic evidence on mock juror judgement. *Journal of Applied Social Psychology, 12*(1), 30–41.

220 Jordan, J., & Kaas, K. P. (2002). Advertising in the mutual fund business: The role of judgmental heuristics in private investors' evaluation of risk and return. *Journal of Financial Services Marketing, 7*(2), 129–140.

221 Van den Oetelaar, S., Tellegen, S., & Wober, M. (1997). Affective response to reading: A comparison of reading in the United Kingdom and the Netherlands. In S. Totosy de Zepetnek & I. Sywenky (Eds.), *The systemic and empirical approach to literature and culture as theory and application* (pp. 505–513). Siegen: LUMIS.

222 Larsen, S. F., & Seilman, U. (1988). Personal meanings while reading literature. *Text, 8,* 411–429.

223 Sikora, S., Miall, D. S., & Kuiken, D. (1998). *Enactment versus interpretation: A phenomenological study of readers' responses to Coleridge's "The rime of the ancient mariner."* Paper presented at the Sixth Biennial Conference of the International Society for the Empirical Study of Literature. Utrecht, The Netherlands.

224 Donohew, L. (1981). Arousal and affective responses to writing styles. *Journal of Applied Communication Research, 9,* 109–119.

Donohew, L. (1982). Newswriting styles: What arouses the readers? *Newspaper Research Journal, 3,* 3–6.

225 Kopfman, J. E., Smith, S. W., Ah Yun, J. K., & Hodges, A. (1994, November). *Affective and cognitive reactions to narrative versus logical argument organ donation strategies.* Paper presented at the Speech Communication Association Annual Convention, New Orleans, LA.

226 *See* n199, Weinstein et al. (1998).

227 Ricketts, M., Shanteau, J., McSpadden, B., & Fernandez-Medina, K. M. (2010). Using stories to battle unintentional injuries: Narratives in safety and health communication. *Social Science & Medicine, 70*(9), 1441–1449.

228 Bosman, J. (1987). Persuasive effects of political metaphors. *Metaphor & Symbolic Activity, 2*(2), 97–113.

Read, S. J., Cesa, I. L., Jones, D. K., & Collins, N. L. (1990). When is the federal budget like a baby? Metaphor in political rhetoric. *Metaphor & Symbolic Activity, 5*(3), 125–149.

229 Gibbs Jr, R. W., Leggitt, J. S., & Turner, E. A. (2002). What's special about figurative language in emotional communication? In S. R. Fussell (Ed.), *The verbal communication of emotions: Interdisciplinary perspectives* (pp. 125–149). Mahwah, NJ: Lawrence Erlbaum Associates.

230 Sopory, P., & Dillard, J. P. (2002). The persuasive effects of metaphor: A meta-analysis. *Human Communication Research, 28*(3), 382–419.

231 Mio, J. S., Riggio, R. E., Levin, S., & Reese, R. (2005). Presidential leadership and charisma: The effects of metaphor. *The Leadership Quarterly, 16*(2), 287–294.

232 Voss, J. F., Kennet, J., Wiley, J., & Schooler, T. Y. (1992, p. 205). Experts at debate: The use of metaphor in the U.S. Senate debate on the Gulf Crisis. *Metaphor & Symbolic Activity Special Issue: Expertise and Metaphor, 7*(3–4), 197–214.

233 *See* n47, Frijda (1988).

234 *See* n129, Ortony et al. (1988), p. 61.

235 *See* n40, Stayman & Aaker (1987).

236 Lazarus, R. S., & Alfert, E. (1964). Short-circuiting of threat by experimentally altering cognitive appraisal. *The Journal of Abnormal and Social Psychology*, *69*(2), 195–205.

237 Lamm, C., Nusbaum, H. C., Meltzoff, A. N., & Decety, J. (2007). What are you feeling? Using functional magnetic resonance imaging to assess the modulation of sensory and affective responses during empathy for pain. *PLoS One*, *2*(12), e1292-e1292.

238 Breznitz, S. (Ed.). (1983). *The denial of stress*. New York: International Universities Press. Loewenstein, G. (1987). Anticipation and the valuation of delayed consumption. *Economic Journal*, *97*(387), 666–684.

Roth, W. T., Breivik, G., Jorgensen, P. E., & Hofmann, S. (1996). Activation in novice and expert parachutists while jumping. *Psychophysiology*, *33*(1), 63–72.

239 Breznitz, S. (1971). A study of worrying. *British Journal of Social & Clinical Psychology*, *10*(3), 271–279. Monat, A. (1976). Temporal uncertainty, anticipation time, and cognitive coping under threat. *Journal of Human Stress*, *2*(2), 32–43.

240 VanBoven, L., Loewenstein, G., Welch, E., & Dunning, D. (2001). *The illusion of courage: Underestimating social risk aversion in self and others*. Working Paper, Department of Social and Decision Sciences, Carnegie Mellon University, Pittsburgh, PA.

241 Hoch, S. J., & Loewenstein, G. F. (1991). Time-inconsistent preferences and consumer self-control. *Journal of Consumer Research*, *17*(4), 492–507.

242 Friedman, H. S., & Riggio, R. E. (1981). Effect of individual differences in nonverbal expressiveness on transmission of emotion. *Journal of Nonverbal Behavior*, *6*(2), 96–104.

Sullins, E. S. (1991). Emotional contagion revisited: Effects of social comparison and expressive style on mood convergence. *Personality and Social Psychology Bulletin*, *17*(2), 166–174.

243 Hatfield, E., Cacioppo, J. T., & Rapson, R. L. (1994). *Emotional contagion*. New York: Cambridge University Press.

Neumann, R., & Strack, F. (2000). "Mood contagion": The automatic transfer of mood between persons. *Journal of Personality and Social Psychology*, *79*(2), 211–223.

244 Englis, B. G. (1990). Consumer emotional reactions to television advertising and their effects on message recall. In S. J. Agres, J. A. Edell & T. M. Dubitsky (Eds.), *Emotion in advertising: Theoretical and practical explorations* (pp. 231–253). New York: Quorum Books.

Friedman, H. S., DiMatteo, M. R., & Mertz, T. I. (1980a). Nonverbal communication on television news: The facial expressions of broadcasters during coverage of a presidential election campaign. *Personality and Social Psychology Bulletin*, *6*(3), 427–435.

245 Haley, R. I., Richardson, J., & Baldwin, B. M. (1984). The effects of nonverbal communications in television advertising. *Journal of Advertising Research*, *24*(4), 11–18.

246 Dimberg, U., & Öhman, A. (1996). Behold the wrath: Psychophysiological responses to facial stimuli. *Motivation and Emotion Special Issue: Facial Expression and Emotion—The Legacy of John T. Lanzetta*, *20*(2, Pt. 1), 149–182.

See n43, Keltner & Kring (1998).

247 Eibl-Eibesfeldt, I. (1989). *Human ethology (foundations of human behavior)*. Hawthorne, NY: Aldine de Gruyter.

248 Esteves, F., Dimberg, U., & Öhman, A. (1994). Automatically elicited fear: Conditioned skin conductance responses to masked facial expressions. *Cognition & Emotion*, *8*(5), 393–413.

Öhman, A., & Dimberg, U. (1978). Facial expressions as conditioned stimuli for electrodermal responses: A case of "preparedness"? *Journal of Personality and Social Psychology*, *36*(11), 1251–1258.

249 Batson, C. D., & Shaw, L. L. (1991). Evidence for altruism: Toward a pluralism of prosocial motives. *Psychological Inquiry*, *2*(2), 107–122.

Keltner, D., Young, R. C., & Buswell, B. N. (1997). Appeasement in human emotion, social practice, and personality. *Aggressive Behavior Special Issue: Appeasement and Reconciliation*, *23*(5), 359–374.

250 Eisenberg, N., Fabes, R. A., Miller, P. A., Fultz, J., Shell, R., Mathy, R. M., & Reno, R. R. (1989). Relation of sympathy and distress to prosocial behavior: A multi-method study. *Journal of Personality and Social Psychology*, *57*(1), 55–66.

Zahn-Waxler, C., Radke-Yarrow, M., Wagner, E., & Chapman, M. (1992). Development of concern for others. *Developmental Psychology*, *28*(1), 126–136.

251 Keltner, D., & Buswell, B. N. (1997). Embarrassment: Its distinct form and appeasement functions. *Psychological Bulletin*, *122*(3), 250–270.

252 *See* n249, Keltner et al. (1997).

253 Harrison, N. A., Singer, T., Rotshtein, P., Dolan, R. J., & Critchley, H. D. (2006). Pupillary contagion: Central mechanisms engaged in sadness processing. *Social Cognitive and Affective Neuroscience*, *1*(1), 5–17.

254 Cherulnik, P. D., Donley, D. A., Wiewel, T. S. R., & Miller, S. R. (2001). Charisma is contagious: The effects of leader's charisma on observers' affect. *Journal of Applied Social Psychology, 31*, 2149–2159.

Johnson, S. K. (2009). Do you feel what I feel? Mood contagion and leadership outcomes. *The Leadership Quarterly, 20*(5), 814–827.

Lewis, K. M. (2000). When leaders display emotion: How followers respond to negative emotional expression of male and female leaders. *Journal of Organizational Behavior, 21*, 221–234.

255 McHugo, G. J., Lanzetta, J. T., Sullivan, D. G., Masters, R. D., & Englis, B. G. (1985). Emotional reactions to the expressive displays of a political leader. *Journal of Personality and Social Psychology, 49*(6), 1513–1529.

256 Lanzetta, J. T., Sullivan, D. G., Masters, R. D., & McHugo, G. J. (1985). Viewers' emotional and cognitive responses to televised images of political leaders. In S. Kraus & R. Perloff (Eds.), *Mass media and political thought* (pp. 85–116). Beverly Hills, CA: Sage.

Masters, R. D., & Sullivan, D. G. (1993). Nonverbal behavior and leadership: Emotion and cognition in political information processing. In S. Iyengar & W. J. McGuire (Eds.), *Explorations in political psychology* (pp. 150–182). Durham, NC: Duke University Press.

257 Englis, B. G. (1994). The role of affect in political advertising: Voter emotional responses to the nonverbal behavior of politicians. In E. M. Clark, T. C. Brock & D. W. Stewart (Eds.), *Attention, attitude, and affect in response to advertising* (pp. 223–247). Hillsdale, NJ: Lawrence Erlbaum Associates.

Sullivan, D. G., Masters, R. D., Lanzetta, J. T., Englis, B. G., & McHugo, G. J. (1984). *The effect of President Reagan's facial displays on observers' attitudes, impressions, and feelings about him.* Paper presented at the 1984 Annual Meeting of the American Political Science Association, Washington, DC.

258 Sullivan, D. G., & Masters, R. D. (1988). Happy warriors': Leaders' facial displays, viewers' emotions, and political support. *American Journal of Political Science, 32*, 345–368.

259 See n243, Neumann & Strack (2000).

260 Howard, D. J., & Gengler, C. (2001). Emotional contagion effects on product attitudes. *Journal of Consumer Research, 28*(2), 189–201.

Ramanathan, S., & McGill, A. L. (2007). Consuming with others: Social influences on moment-to-moment and retrospective evaluations of an experience. *Journal of Consumer Research, 34*(4), 506–524.

Tanner, R. J., Ferraro, R., Chartrand, T. L., Bettman, J. R., & van Baaren, R. (2008). Of chameleons and consumption: The impact of mimicry on choice and preferences. *Journal of Consumer Research, 34*(6), 754–766.

261 van Doorn, E. A., van Kleef, G. A., & van der Pligt, J. (2015). How emotional expressions shape prosocial behavior: Interpersonal effects of anger and disappointment on compliance with requests. *Motivation and Emotion, 39*(1), 128–141.

262 Totterdell, P., Kellett, S., Teuchmann, K., & Briner, R. B. (1998). Evidence of mood linkage in work groups. *Journal of Personality and Social Psychology, 74*(6), 1504–1515.

263 Totterdell, P. (2000). Catching moods and hitting runs: Mood linkage and subjective performance in professional sport teams. *Journal of Applied Psychology, 85*(6), 848–859.

264 Bartel, C. A., & Saavedra, R. (2000). The collective construction of work group moods. *Administrative Science Quarterly, 45*(2), 197–231.

265 George, J. M. (1989). Mood and absence. *Journal of Applied Psychology, 74*(2), 317–324.

George, J. M. (1990). Personality, affect, and behavior in groups. *Journal of Applied Psychology, 75*(2), 107–116.

George, J. M., & Brief, A. P. (1992). Feeling good-doing good: A conceptual analysis of the mood at work-organizational spontaneity relationship. *Psychological Bulletin, 112*(2), 310–329.

266 Barsade, S. G., Ward, A. J., Turner, J. D. F., & Sonnenfeld, J. A. (2000). To your heart's content: A model of affective diversity in top management teams. *Administrative Science Quarterly, 45*(4), 802–836.

267 Barsade, S. G. (2002). The ripple effects: Emotional contagion and its influence on group behavior. *Administrative Science Quarterly, 47*(4), 644–675.

268 See n265, George (1990).

269 Raghunathan, R., Pham, M. T., & Corfman, K. P. (2006). Informational properties of anxiety and sadness, and displaced coping. *Journal of Consumer Research, 32*(4), 596–601.

270 See n59, Au et al. (2003).

See also Chang, S. C., Chen, S. S., Chou, R. K., & Lin, Y. H. (2008). Weather and intraday patterns in stock returns and trading activity. *Journal of Banking & Finance, 32*(9), 1754–1766.

271 Schwarz, N., & Clore, G. L. (1996). Feelings and phenomenal experiences. In A. Kruglanski & E. T. Higgins (Eds.), *Social psychology: Handbook of basic principles* (2nd ed., pp. 385–407). New York, NY: Guilford Press.

Schwarz, N., & Clore, G. L. (2003). Mood as information: 20 years later. *Psychological Inquiry*, *14*(3–4), 296–303.

272 Sinclair, R. C., Soldat, A. S., & Mark, M. M. (1998). Affective cues and processing strategy: Color-coded examination forms influence performance. *Teaching of Psychology*, *25*(2), 130–132.

Soldat, A. S., Sinclair, R. C., & Mark, M. M. (1997). Color as an environmental processing cue: External affective cues can directly affect processing strategy without affecting mood. *Social Cognition*, *15*(1), 55–71.

273 Fredrickson, B. L., & Levenson, R. W. (1998). Positive emotions speed recovery from the cardiovascular sequelae of negative emotions. *Cognition & Emotion*, *12*(2), 191–220.

274 Keltner, D., Ellsworth, P. C., & Edwards, K. (1993a). Beyond simple pessimism: Effects of sadness and anger on social perception. *Journal of Personality and Social Psychology*, *64*(5), 740–752.

See n43, Lerner & Keltner (2000).

See n56, Lerner & Keltner (2001).

Raghunathan, R., & Pham, M. T. (1999). All negative moods are not equal: Motivational influences of anxiety and sadness on decision making. *Organizational Behavior and Human Decision Processes*, *79*(1), 56–77.

275 *See* n56, Goldberg et al. (1999).

276 Gault, B. A., & Sabini, J. (2000, Study 4). The roles of empathy, anger, and gender in predicting attitudes toward punitive, reparative, and preventative public policies. *Cognition & Emotion Special Issue: Emotion, Cognition, and Decision Making*, *14*(4), 495–520.

277 Nabi, R. L. (2003). Exploring the framing effects of emotion do discrete emotions differentially influence information accessibility, information seeking, and policy preference? *Communication Research*, *30*(2), 224–247.

278 Niedenthal, P. M., Setterlund, M. B., & Jones, D. E. (1994). Emotional organization of perceptual memory. In P. M. Niedenthal & S. Kitayama (Eds.), *The heart's eye: Emotional influences in perception and attention* (pp. 87–113). San Diego, CA: Academic Press.

Niedenthal, P. M., Halberstadt, J. B., Margolin, J., & Innes-Ker, Å. H. (2000). Emotional state and the detection of change in facial expression of emotion. *European Journal of Social Psychology*, *30*(2), 211–222.

279 Derryberry, D., & Tucker, D. M. (1994). Motivating the focus of attention. In P. M. Niedenthal & S. Kitayama (Eds.), *The heart's eye: Emotional influences in perception and attention* (pp. 167–196). San Diego, CA: Academic Press.

Niedenthal, P. M., & Kitayama, S. (Eds.). (1994). *The heart's eye: Emotional influences in perception and attention*. San Diego, CA: Academic Press.

Niedenthal, P. M., & Setterlund, M. B. (1994). Emotion congruence in perception. *Personality and Social Psychology Bulletin*, *20*(4), 401–411.

280 Isen, A. M. (1987). Positive affect, cognitive processes, and social behavior. In L. Berkowitz (Ed.), *Advances in experimental social psychology* (Vol. 20, pp. 203–253). San Diego, CA: Academic Press.

Niedenthal, P. M., Halberstadt, J. B., & Innes-Ker, Å. H. (1999). Emotional response categorization. *Psychological Review*, *106*(2), 337–361.

281 Fiedler, K. (2000). Toward an integrative account of affect and cognition phenomena using the BIAS computer algorithm. In J. P. Forgas (Ed.), *Feeling and thinking: The role of affect in social cognition* (pp. 223–252). New York, NY: Cambridge University Press.

Niedenthal, P. M. (2008). Emotion concepts. In M. Lewis, J. M. Haviland-Jones, & L. Feldman Barrett (Eds.), *Handbook of emotions* (Vol. 3, pp. 587–600). New York, NY: Guilford Press.

Schwarz, N., & Bless, H. (1991). Happy and mindless, but sad and smart? The impact of affective states on analytic reasoning. In J. P. Forgas (Ed.), *Emotion and social judgments* (pp. 55–71). Elmsford, NY: Pergamon Press.

282 Matthews, G. R., & Antes, J. R. (1992). Visual attention and depression: Cognitive biases in the eye fixations of the dysphoric and the nondepressed. *Cognitive Therapy and Research*, *16*(3), 359–371.

See also Gotlib, I. H., McLachlan, A. L., & Katz, A. N. (1988). Biases in visual attention in depressed and nondepressed individuals. *Cognition & Emotion Special Issue: Information Processing and the Emotional Disorders*, *2*(3), 185–200.

283 *See* n278, Niedenthal et al. (2000).

284 Forgas, J. P. (1992). On mood and peculiar people: Affect and person typicality in impression formation. *Journal of Personality and Social Psychology*, *62*(5), 863–875.

Hirt, E. R., Levine, G. M., McDonald, H. E., Melton, R. J., & Martin, L. L. (1997). The role of mood in quantitative and qualitative aspects of performance: Single or multiple mechanisms? *Journal of Experimental Social Psychology*, *33*(6), 602–629.

Martin, L. L., Abend, T., Sedikides, C., & Green, J. D. (1997). How would it feel if. . .? Mood as input to a role fulfillment evaluation process. *Journal of Personality and Social Psychology, 73*(2), 242–253.

285 Metha, P., & Clark, M. S. (1994). Toward understanding emotions in intimate relationships. In A. I. Weber & J. H. Harvey (Eds.), *Perspectives on close relationships* (pp. 88–109). Boston: Allyn and Bacon.

286 Clark, M. S., Milberg, S., & Erber, R. (1984). Effects of arousal on judgments of others' emotions. *Journal of Personality and Social Psychology, 46*(3), 551–560.

287 Griffit, W., & Veitch, R. (1971). Hot and crowded: Influence of population density and temperature on interpersonal affective behavior. *Journal of Personality and Social Psychology, 17*(1), 92–98.

288 Srull, T. K. (1990). Individual responses to advertising: Mood and its effects from an information process-ing perspective. In S. J. Agres, J. A. Edell & T. M. Dubitsky (Eds.), *Emotion in advertising: Theoretical and practical explorations* (pp. 35–51). New York: Quorum Books.

289 Ottati, V. C., & Isbell, L. M. (1996). Effects on mood during exposure to target information on subse-quently reported judgments: An on-line model of misattribution and correction. *Journal of Personality and Social Psychology, 71*(1), 39–53.

290 Miller, C. A., Wu, P., & Ott, T. (2012). Politeness in teams: Implications for directive compliance behavior and associated attitudes. *Journal of Cognitive Engineering and Decision Making, 6*(2), 214–242.

291 *See* n163 Lerner et al. (2004).

292 Andrade, E. B., & Ariely, D. (2009). The enduring impact of transient emotions on decision making. *Organizational Behavior and Human Decision Processes, 109*(1), 1–8.

293 Keltner, D., Locke, K. D., & Audrain, P. C. (1993b). The influence of attributions on the relevance of negative feelings to personal satisfaction. *Personality and Social Psychology Bulletin, 19*(1), 21–29.

See n42, Schwarz & Clore (1983).

294 *See* n293, Keltner et al. (1993b).

295 Johnson, E. J., & Tversky, A. (1983). Affect, generalization, and the perception of risk. *Journal of Personal-ity and Social Psychology, 45*(1), 20–31.

Lerner, J. S., Goldberg, J. H., & Tetlock, P. E. (1998). Sober second thought: The effects of accountability, anger, and authoritarianism on attributions of responsibility. *Personality and Social Psychology Bulletin, 24*, 563–574.

Wilson, T. D., & Brekke, N. (1994). Mental contamination and mental correction: Unwanted influences on judgments and evaluations. *Psychological Bulletin, 116*(1), 117–142.

296 *See* n50, Bodenhausen et al. (1994a, Study 4).

297 *See* n295, Lerner et al. (1998).

298 Forgas, J. P. (1998). Asking nicely? The effects of mood on responding to more or less polite requests. *Per-sonality and Social Psychology Bulletin, 24*(2), 173–185.

299 Jessmer, S., & Anderson, D. (2001). The effect of politeness and grammar on user perceptions of electronic mail. *North American Journal of Psychology, 3*(2), 331–346.

300 Mayer, J. D., Gaschke, Y. N., Braverman, D. L., & Evans, T. W. (1992). Mood-congruent judgment is a general effect. *Journal of Personality and Social Psychology, 63*(1), 119–132.

Mayer, J. D., & Hanson, E. (1995). Mood-congruent judgment over time. *Personality and Social Psychology Bulletin, 21*(3), 237–244.

Wright, W. F., & Bower, G. H. (1992). Mood effects on subjective probability assessment. *Organizational Behavior and Human Decision Processes, 52*(2), 276–291.

301 *See* n295, Johnson & Tversky (1983).

302 Isen, A. M., & Geva, N. (1987). The influence of positive affect on acceptable level of risk: The person with a large canoe has a large worry. *Organizational Behavior and Human Decision Processes, 39*(2), 145–154.

Isen, A. M., Nygren, T. E., & Ashby, F. G. (1988). Influence of positive affect on the subjective utility of gains and losses: It is just not worth the risk. *Journal of Personality and Social Psychology, 55*(5), 710–717.

Isen, A. M., & Patrick, R. (1983). The effect of positive feelings on risk taking: When the chips are down. *Organizational Behavior & Human Performance, 31*(2), 194–202.

303 Forgas, J. P., & Bower, G. H. (1987). Mood effects on person-perception judgments. *Journal of Personality and Social Psychology, 53*(1), 53–60.

304 Ger, G. (1989). Nature of effects of affect on judgment: Theoretical and methodological issues. In P. Caf-ferata & A. M. Tybout (Eds.), *Cognitive and affective responses to advertising* (pp. 263–275). Lexington, MA: Lexington Books.

305 Winkielman, P., Berridge, K. C., & Wilbarger, J. L. (2005). Unconscious affective reactions to masked happy versus angry faces influence consumption behavior and judgments of value. *Personality and Social Psychology Bulletin, 31*(1), 121–135.

306 *See* n300, Mayer et al. (1992).

307 McGuire, W. J. (1985). Attitudes and attitude change. In G. Lindsey & E. Aronson (Eds.), *Handbook of social psychology* (3rd ed., Vol. 2, pp. 233–346). New York: Random House.

Petty, R. E., Gleicher, F., & Baker, S. M. (1991). Multiple roles for affect in persuasion. In J. P. Forgas (Ed.), *Emotion and social judgments* (pp. 181–200). Elmsford, NY: Pergamon Press.

308 Krugman, H. E. (1983). Television program interest and commercial interruption. *Journal of Advertising Research*, *23*(1), 21–23.

Laird, J. D. (1974). Self-attribution of emotion: The effects of expressive behavior on the quality of emotional experience. *Journal of Personality and Social Psychology*, *29*(4), 475–486.

Wells, G. L., & Petty, R. E. (1980). The effects of overt head movements on persuasion: Compatibility and incompatibility of responses. *Basic and Applied Social Psychology*, *1*(3), 219–230.

309 Allen, C. T., & Madden, T. J. (1983). *Examining the link between attitude towards an ad and brand attitude: A classical conditioning approach*. Presented at the Fourteenth Annual Conference of the Association for Consumer Research, Chicago, IL.

Lutz, R. I., MacKenzie, S. B., & Belch, G. F. (1983). Attitude toward the ad as a mediator of advertising effectiveness: Determinants and consequences. *Advances in Consumer Research*, *10*(1), 532–539.

See n38, Mitchell & Olson (1981).

310 *See* n189, Roozen (2013).

311 Bless, H., Bohner, G., Schwarz, N., & Strack, F. (1990). Mood and persuasion: A cognitive response analysis. *Personality and Social Psychology Bulletin*, *16*(2), 331–345.

Bohner, G., Crow, K., Erb, H. P., & Schwarz, N. (1992). Affect and persuasion: Mood effects on the processing of message content and context cues and on subsequent behaviour. *European Journal of Social Psychology Special Issue: Positiveegative Asymmetry in Affect and Evaluations: II*, *22*(6), 511–530.

Kuykendall, D., & Keating, J. P. (1990). Mood and persuasion: Evidence for the differential influence of positive and negative states. *Psychology & Marketing*, *7*(1), 1–9.

312 Worth, L. T., & Mackie, D. M. (1987). Cognitive mediation of positive affect in persuasion. *Social Cognition*, *5*(1), 76–94.

313 Cline, T. W., & Kellaris, J. J. (1999). The joint impact of humor and argument strength in a print advertising context: A case for weaker arguments. *Psychology & Marketing*, *16*(1), 69–86.

314 Garcia-Marques, T., & Mackie, D. M. (2001). The feeling of familiarity as a regulator of persuasive processing. *Social Cognition*, *19*(1), 9–34.

315 Wegener, D. T., Petty, R. E., & Smith, S. M. (1995). Positive mood can increase or decrease message scrutiny: The hedonic contingency view of mood and message processing. *Journal of Personality and Social Psychology*, *69*(1), 5–15.

316 Isen, A. M. (2000). Some perspectives on positive affect and self regulation. *Psychological Inquiry*, *11*(3), 184–187.

317 *See* n50, Bodenhausen et al. (1994a).

Estrada, C. A., Isen, A. M., & Young, M. J. (1997). Positive affect facilitates integration of information and decreases anchoring in reasoning among physicians. *Organizational Behavior and Human Decision Processes*, *72*(1), 117–135.

318 Isen, A. M., Rosenzweig, A. S., & Young, M. J. (1991). The influence of positive affect on clinical problem solving. *Medical Decision Making*, *11*(3), 221–227.

319 *See* n42, Isen & Means (1983).

320 *See* n300, Mayer & Hanson (1995).

See n300, Wright & Bower (1992).

321 DeSteno, D., Petty, R. E., Wegener, D. T., & Rucker, D. D. (2000). Beyond valence in the perception of likelihood: The role of emotion specificity. *Journal of Personality and Social Psychology*, *78*(3), 397–416.

Nygren, T. E., Isen, A. M., Taylor, P. J., & Dulin, J. (1996). The influence of positive affect on the decision rule in risk situations: Focus on outcome (and especially avoidance of loss) rather than probability. *Organizational Behavior and Human Decision Processes*, *66*(1), 59–72.

322 *See* n274, Keltner et al. (1993a).

323 *See* n274, Raghunatham & Pham (1999).

324 Wegener, D. T., Petty, R. E., & Klein, D. J. (1994). Effects of mood on high elaboration attitude change: The mediating role of likelihood judgments. *European Journal of Social Psychology Special Issue: Affect in Social Judgments and Cognition*, *24*(1), 25–43.

325 DeSteno, D., Petty, R. E., Rucker, D. D., Wegener, D. T., & Braverman, J. (2004). Discrete emotions and persuasion: The role of emotion-induced expectancies. *Journal of Personality and Social Psychology*, *86*(1), 43–56.

326 *See* n311, Bohner et al. (1992).

See n298, Forgas (1998).

See n271, Schwarz & Clore (1996).

327 Petty, R. E., & Cacioppo, J. T. (1986). *Communication and persuasion: Central and peripheral routes to attitude change.* New York: Springer-Verlag.

328 Leith, K. P., & Baumeister, R. F. (1996). Why do bad moods increase self-defeating behavior? Emotion, risk tasking, and self-regulation. *Journal of Personality and Social Psychology, 71*(6), 1250–1267.

329 *See* n43, Lerner & Keltner (2000).

See n56, Lerner & Keltner (2001).

330 *See* n274, Keltner et al. (1993a).

331 *See* n56, Goldberg et al. (1999).

See n295, Lerner et al. (1998).

Quigley, B. M., & Tedeschi, J. T. (1996). Mediating effects of blame attributions on feelings of anger. *Personality and Social Psychology Bulletin, 22*(12), 1280–1288.

332 *See* n295, Lerner et al. (1998).

333 *See* n168, van't Wout et al. (2010).

334 *See* n307, McGuire (1985).

Petty, R. E., Cacioppo, J. T., & Kasmer, J. A. (1988). The role of affect in the elaboration likelihood model of persuasion. In L. Donohew, H. E. Sypher & E. T. Higgins (Eds.), *Communication, social cognition, and affect* (pp. 117–146). Hillsdale, NJ: Lawrence Erlbaum Associates.

335 Calder, B. J., & Gruder, C. L. (1989). Emotional advertising appeals. In P. Cafferata & A. Tybout (Eds.), *Cognitive and affective responses to advertising* (pp. 277–286). Lexington, MA: D.C. Heath and Company.

336 *See* n325, DeSteno et al. (2004).

337 Bodenhausen, G. V. (1993). Emotions, arousal, and stereotypic judgments: A heuristic model of affect and stereotyping. In D. M. Mackie & D. L. Hamilton (Eds.), *Affect, cognition, and stereotyping: Interactive processes in group perception* (pp. 13–37). San Diego, CA: Academic Press.

Tiedens, L. Z., & Linton, S. (2001). Judgment under emotional certainty and uncertainty: The effects of specific emotions on information processing. *Journal of Personality and Social Psychology, 81*(6), 973–988.

338 *See* n50, Bodenhausen et al. (1994b).

339 Smith, P., & Waterman, M. (2003). Processing bias for aggression words in forensic and nonforensic samples. *Cognition & Emotion, 17*(5), 681–701.

Smith, P., & Waterman, M. (2004). Processing bias for sexual material: The emotional stroop and sexual offenders. *Sexual Abuse: A Journal of Research and Treatment, 16*(2), 163–171.

340 Young, M. J., Tiedens, L. Z., Jung, H., & Tsai, M. H. (2011). Mad enough to see the other side: Anger and the search for disconfirming information. *Cognition and Emotion, 25*(1), 10–21.

341 *See* n43, Lerner & Keltner (2000).

See n56, Lerner & Keltner (2001).

See n168, van't Wout et al. (2010).

342 Tsai, M. H., & Young, M. J. (2010). Anger, fear, and escalation of commitment. *Cognition and Emotion, 24*(6), 962–973.

343 Raghunathan, R. (2000). What do you do when you are angry, anxious or blue? Motivational influence of negative affective states on consumer decision-making (Doctoral dissertation, New York University, 2000). *Dissertation Abstracts International, 61*(09A), 3664.

See n274, Raghunatham & Pham (1999).

344 Nabi, R. L. (2002). Anger, fear, uncertainty, and attitudes: A test of the cognitive-functional model. *Communication Monographs, 69*(3), 204–216.

345 Gray, J. A. (1987). *The psychology of fear and stress* (2nd ed.). New York: Cambridge University Press.

Gray, J. A. (1994). Three fundamental emotion systems. In P. Ekman & R. J. Davidson (Eds.), *The nature of emotion* (pp. 243–247). New York: Oxford University Press.

346 *See* n189, Roozen (2013).

CONCLUSION

This book paints a different picture of audiences than the one many of us hold in our imaginations, and by doing so redefines our roles as communicators. In the first part of the book, we see that audiences are not empty cups waiting to be filled with whatever information we would like to pour into them but are instead highly selective and highly critical decision makers. Experienced audiences already know what type of information they need from us even before they sit down to read our documents or listen to our presentations. No matter how logical, reasonable, correct, and factual our communications may be, if we fail to anticipate the information needs of our audiences, we will fail to persuade them. Thus, the job of selecting persuasive content for our documents, presentations, and meetings is less subjective than we first imagined. It is highly constrained by the audience's information requirements.

Not only is our job as communicators less subjective than we thought, it is also less formidable. A large number of our audiences' individual decisions can be viewed as instances of one of 13 major decision types. Identify the type of decision that you desire your audience to make, and you can more readily ascertain the type of information your audience will expect from you.

Perhaps the book's biggest challenge to our image of audiences is its model of the cognitive processes that underlie audience decision making. As Chapter 3 makes clear, real-world decision making does not correspond to the abstract rules of logic, syllogistic reasoning, or statistics of the classroom.[1] Nor does it correspond to preferences among formal gambles as decision researchers have often assumed. Instead, decision making is a content-specific and schema-based process. Remarkably, it is only within the last several years that decision researchers have come to appreciate the vital roles that context and basic psychological processes such as attention, comprehension, memory, and emotion play in determining decision strategies.[2] And as we review communication techniques in light of our model, we soon realize that, far from being arbitrary rules or mere conventions, each communication technique directly impacts one or more of the cognitive processes involved in audience decision making.

In the second part of the book, we see that despite our audiences' insistence on being given just the right information for making rational decisions, even the most sophisticated and statistically savvy audience can be swayed as much by our style of writing or speaking as by the facts and figures we present. This section disabuses us of any notion we may have had that facts and figures speak for themselves. It also makes clear that who we are sometimes speaks louder that what we say. When we fail to play our professional roles appropriately, we risk losing out to other communicators who behave in ways that meet the audience's expectations.

In the final section of the book, we come to understand that our audiences' emotions need not be viewed as antithetical to rational decision making. Instead, this section invites us to view the audience's emotions as essential to rationality and to admit that emotions quickly focus the audience's attention on the things that matter most to them. Taken together, the book's three sections present a 360° view of audience decision making, a view that offers us our best chance to be persuasive.

In addition to helping us become more persuasive, there is another equally important reason why we as professionals need to know, as precisely as possible, how our audiences make decisions—so that we can help them make good ones. Bad decisions can be very costly for those audiences who depend on our documents and presentations for critical information. Investors who make bad investment decisions can go bankrupt. Borrowers who make bad borrowing decisions can find themselves facing onerous payment schedules as well as exorbitant fees and interest rates. Medical patients who fail to make the necessary usage decisions can jeopardize their own and others' physical safety. Currently, relatively few documents and presentations are designed in such a way as to help their audiences make good decisions. Even the best documents and presentations typically contain a great deal of information that is superfluous to the audience's decision. And although the language they use is typically grammatically correct and may even be easy to comprehend, most will lack much of the information that the audience needs to make a good decision. Oftentimes professionals do not realize that their audiences read documents and listen to presentations in order to make decisions. Many times professionals themselves do not know how to make a good decision of the type their audience needs to make.

Evidence suggests that the average professional may be no better at anticipating the information needs of an audience than is the average undergraduate student. For example, in what was intended to be a study of the differences between expert and novice business writers, a researcher gave executives and undergraduates a business case and asked both groups to write and then revise a report to the client in the case.[3] Contrary to the researcher's expectations, the executives made neither more nor better points in their reports than the undergraduates did. The executives' performance in the study is less surprising when we consider the state of audience awareness in the field of decision support systems—a computer science field ostensibly dedicated to supporting good decisions in audiences. Incredibly, system designers "are rarely told what the key decisions are that the system must help the operator make" or how the operator will make them.[4]

Clearly the time has come for professionals in every field to form an accurate picture of audience decision making. To do so promises high returns to any professional, organization, or student of communication who can put the lessons of this book into practice—returns in the form of greater trust, respect, and long-term success.

Notes

1 Anderson, J.R. (2000, p. 351). *Cognitive psychology and its implications* (5th ed.). New York: Worth Publishers.
2 Schneider, S.L., & Shanteau, J. (2003, pp. 1–2). Introduction: Where to decision making? In S. Schneider & J. Shanteau (Eds.), *Emerging perspectives on judgment and decision research* (pp. 1–10). Cambridge, UK: Cambridge University Press.
3 Garay, M.S. (1988). Writers making points: A case study of executives and college students revising their own reports (Doctoral dissertation, Carnegie Mellon University, 1988). *Dissertation Abstracts International, 49*(12A), 3645.
4 Klein, G.A. (1998, p. 107). *Sources of power: How people make decisions.* Cambridge, MA: MIT Press.

REFERENCES

Aaker, J. L. (1997). Dimensions of brand personality. *Journal of Marketing Research, 34*(3), 347–356.

Aaker, J. L., & Williams, P. (1998). Empathy versus pride: The influence of emotional appeals across cultures. *Journal of Consumer Research, 25*(3), 241–261.

Aaronson, D., & Scarborough, H. S. (1977). Performance theories for sentence coding: Some quantitative models. *Journal of Verbal Learning & Verbal Behavior, 16*(3), 277–303.

Abelson, R. P., Kinder, D. R., Peters, M. D., & Fiske, S. T. (1982). Affective and semantic components in political person perception. *Journal of Personality and Social Psychology, 42*(4), 619–630.

Abelson, R. P., & Levi, A. (1985). Decision making and decision theory. In G. Lindzey & E. Aronson (Eds.), *The handbook of social psychology* (3rd ed., Vol. 1, pp. 231–309). New York: Knopf.

Adams, R. B., Jr., & Kleck, R. E. (2005). Effects of direct and averted gaze on the perception of facially communicated emotion. *Emotion, 5*(1), 3–11.

Adaval, R. (2001). Sometimes it just feels right: The differential weighting of affect-consistent and affect-inconsistent product information. *Journal of Consumer Research, 28*(1), 1–17.

Adaval, R., Isbell, L. M., & Wyer, R. S. (2007). The impact of pictures on narrative-and list-based impression formation: A process interference model. *Journal of Experimental Social Psychology, 43*(3), 352–364.

Adaval, R., & Wyer, R. S. (1998). The role of narratives in consumer information processing. *Journal of Consumer Psychology, 7*(3), 207–245.

Adolphs, R., Gosselin, F., Buchanan, T. W., Tranel, D., Schyns, P., & Damasio, A. R. (2005). A mechanism for impaired fear recognition after amygdala damage. *Nature, 433*(7021), 68–72.

Agle, B. R., & Sonnenfeld, J. A. (1994). Charismatic chief executive officers: Are they more effective? An empirical test of charismatic leadership theory. *Academy of Management Proceedings, 1994*(1), 2–6.

Ahlfinger, N. R., & Esser, J. K. (2001). Testing the groupthink model: Effects of promotional leadership and conformity predisposition. *Social Behavior and Personality: An International Journal, 29*(1), 31–41.

Ahrens, M., Hasan, B. A., Giordano, B. L., & Belin, P. (2014). Gender differences in the temporal voice areas. *Frontiers in Neuroscience, 8*, 228.

Ajzen, I. (1977). Intuitive theories of events and the effects of base-rate information on prediction. *Journal of Personality and Social Psychology, 35*(5), 303–314.

Alba, J. W., & Hutchinson, J. W. (1987). Dimensions of consumer expertise. *Journal of Consumer Research, 13*(4), 411–454.

Alba-Ferrara, L., Ellison, A., & Mitchell, R. L. C. (2012). Decoding emotional prosody: Resolving differences in functional neuroanatomy from fMRI and lesion studies using TMS. *Brain Stimulation, 5*(3), 347–353.

Albar, F. M. (2014). An investigation of fast and frugal heuristics for new product project selection (Doctoral dissertation, Portland State University, 2013). *Dissertation Abstracts International: Section B, 74*(10-B)(E).

Albarracín, D., & Vargas, P. (2010). Attitudes and persuasion: From biology to social responses to persuasive intent. In D. Albarracin & P. Vargas (Eds.), *Handbook of social psychology* (5th ed., Vol. 1, pp. 394–427). Hoboken, NJ: John Wiley & Sons.

Albarracín, D., & Wyer, R. S., Jr. (2001). Elaborative and nonelaborative processing of a behavior-related communication. *Personality and Social Psychology Bulletin, 27*(6), 691–705.

Alberdi, E., Becher, J. C., Gilhooly, K., Hunter, J., Logie, R., Lyon, A., . . . & Reiss, J. (2001). Expertise and the interpretation of computerized physiological data: Implications for the design of computerized monitoring in neonatal intensive care. *International Journal of Human-Computer Studies, 55*, 191–216.

Albers, M. (2002). Complex problem solving and content analysis. In M. Albers & B. Mazur (Eds.), *Content and complexity: Information design in software development and documentation* (pp. 285–305). Hillsdale, NJ: Erlbaum.

Albright, L., & Forziati, C. (1995). Cross-situational consistency and perceptual accuracy in leadership. *Personality and Social Psychology Bulletin, 21*(12), 1269–1276.

Albright, L., Kenny, D. A., & Malloy, T. E. (1988). Consensus in personality judgments at zero acquaintance. *Journal of Personality and Social Psychology, 55*(3), 387–395.

Albright, L., Malloy, T. E., Dong, Q., Kenny, D. A., Fang, X., Winquist, L., & Yu, D. (1997). Cross-cultural consensus in personality judgments. *Journal of Personality and Social Psychology, 72*(3), 558–569.

Al-Dughaither, K. A. (1996). International construction financing strategies: Influential factors and decision-making (Doctoral dissertation, Carnegie Mellon University, 1996). *Dissertation Abstracts International, 57*(11a), 4857.

Allen, C. T., & Madden, T. J. (1983). *Examining the link between attitude towards an ad and brand attitude: A classical conditioning approach*. Presented at the Fourteenth Annual Conference of the Association for Consumer Research. Chicago, IL.

Allen, D. G., Biggane, J. E., Pitts, M., Otondo, R., & Van Scotter, J. (2013). Reactions to recruitment web sites: Visual and verbal attention, attraction, and intentions to pursue employment. *Journal of Business and Psychology, 28*(3), 263–285.

Allen, D. G., Van Scotter, J. R., & Otondo, R. F. (2004). Recruitment communication media: Impact on prehire outcomes. *Personnel Psychology, 57*(1), 143–171.

Allen, K. (1970). Some effects of advance organizers and level of question on the learning and retention of written social studies materials. *Journal of Educational Psychology, 61*(5), 333–339.

Allport, F. H., & Lepkin, M. (1945). Wartime rumors of waste and special privilege: Why some people believe them. *The Journal of Abnormal and Social Psychology, 40*(1), 3–36.

Alpers, G. W., Ruhleder, M., Walz, N., Mühlberger, A., & Pauli, P. (2005). Binocular rivalry between emotional and neutral stimuli: A validation using fear conditioning and EEG. *International Journal of Psychophysiology Special Issue: Neurobiology of Fear and Disgust, 57*(1), 25–32.

Alpert, M. I. (1971). Identification of determinant attributes: A comparison of methods. *Journal of Marketing Research, 8*(2), 184–191.

Alter, A. L., & Oppenheimer, D. M. (2006). Predicting short-term stock fluctuations by using processing fluency. *Proceedings of the National Academy of Sciences, 103*(24), 9369–9372.

Alter, A. L., Oppenheimer, D. M., Epley, N., & Eyre, R. N. (2007). Overcoming intuition: Metacognitive difficulty activates analytic reasoning. *Journal of Experimental Psychology: General, 136*(4), 569–576.

Ambady, N., Bernieri, F. J., & Richeson, J. A. (2000). Toward a histology of social behavior: Judgmental accuracy from thin slices of the behavioral stream. In M. P. Zanna (Ed.), *Advances in experimental social psychology* (Vol. 32, pp. 201–271). San Diego, CA: Academic Press.

Ambady, N., Krabbenhoft, M. A., & Hogan, D. (2006). The 30-sec sale: Using thin-slice judgments to evaluate sales effectiveness. *Journal of Consumer Psychology, 16*(1), 4–13.

Ambady, N., Laplante, D., Nguyen, T., Rosenthal, R., Chaumeton, N., & Levinson, W. (2002). Surgeons' tone of voice: A clue to malpractice history. *Surgery, 132*(1), 5–9.

Ambady, N., & Rosenthal, R. (1992). Thin slices of expressive behavior as predictors of interpersonal consequences: A meta-analysis. *Psychological Bulletin, 111*(2), 256–274.

Ambady, N., & Rosenthal, R. (1993). Half a minute: Predicting teacher evaluations from thin slices of nonverbal behavior and physical attractiveness. *Journal of Personality and Social Psychology, 64*(3), 431–441.

Amir, E., & Ganzach, Y. (1998). Overreaction and underreaction in analysts' forecasts. *Journal of Economic Behavior & Organization, 37*(3), 333–347.

Andersen, P. A., & Bowman, L. L. (1999). Positions of power: Nonverbal influence in organizational communication. In L. K. Guerrero, J. A. DeVito & M. L. Hecht (Eds.), *The nonverbal communication reader: Classic and contemporary readings* (pp. 317–334). Prospect Heights, IL: Waveland.

Andersen, P. A., & Guerrero, L. K. (1998). Principles of communication and emotion in social interaction. In P. A. Andersen & L. K. Guerrero (Eds.), *Handbook of communication and emotion: Research, theory, applications, and contexts* (pp. 49–96). San Diego, CA: Academic Press.

Andersen, S. M., Glassman, N. S., Chen, S., & Cole, S. W. (1995). Transference in social perception: The role of chronic accessibility in significant-other representations. *Journal of Personality and Social Psychology, 69*(1), 41–57.

Andersen, S. M., & Klatzky, R. L. (1987). Traits and social stereotypes: Levels of categorization in person perception. *Journal of Personality and Social Psychology, 53*(2), 235–246.

Anderson, A. K., & Phelps, E. A. (2001). Lesions of the human amygdala impair enhanced perception of emotionally salient events. *Nature, 411*(6835), 305–309.

Anderson, C., John, O. P., Keltner, D., & Kring, A. M. (2001). Who attains social status? Effects of personality and physical attractiveness in social groups. *Journal of Personality and Social Psychology, 81*(1), 116–132.

Anderson, J. R. (1974). Verbatim and propositional representation of sentences in immediate and long-term memory. *Journal of Verbal Learning & Verbal Behavior, 13*(2), 149–162.

Anderson, J. R. (2000). *Cognitive psychology and its implications* (5th ed.). New York: Worth Publishers.

Anderson, J. R. (2004). *Cognitive psychology and its implications* (6th ed.). New York: Worth Publishers.

Anderson, N. H. (1965). Averaging versus adding as a stimulus-combination rule in impression formation. *Journal of Experimental Psychology, 70*(4), 394–400.

Anderson, N. H. (1968). A simple model of information integration. In R. B. Abelson, E. Aronson, W. J. McGuire, T. M. Newcomb, M. J. Rosenberg & P. H. Tannenbaum (Eds.), *Theories of cognitive consistency: A sourcebook* (pp. 731–743). Chicago: Rand McNally.

Anderson, N. H. (1973). Information integration theory applied to attitudes about U.S. presidents. *Journal of Educational Psychology, 64*(1), 1–8.

Anderson, N. H. (1974). Cognitive algebra: Integration theory applied to social attribution. In L. Berkowitz (Ed.), *Advances in experimental social psychology* (Vol. 7, pp. 1–101). New York: Academic Press.

Anderson, N. H. (1981). *Foundations of information theory.* New York: Academic Press.

Anderson, N. H. (1989). Functional memory and on-line attribution. In J. N. Bassili (Ed.), *On-line cognition in person perception* (pp. 175–220). Hillsdale, NJ: Erlbaum.

Anderson, N. H., & Shackleton, V. J. (1990). Decision making in the graduate selection interview: A field study. *Journal of Occupational Psychology, 63*(1), 63–76.

Anderson, R. C. (1967). Educational psychology. *Annual Review of Psychology, 18*, 129–164.

Anderson, R. C. (1974). Concretization and sentence learning. *Journal of Educational Psychology, 66*(2), 179–183.

Anderson, R. C., & Pichert, J. W. (1978). Recall of previously unrecallable information following a shift in perspective. *Journal of Verbal Learning & Verbal Behavior, 17*(1), 1–12.

Anderson, R. C., Reynolds, R. E., Schallert, D. L., & Goetz, E. T. (1977). Frameworks for comprehending discourse. *American Educational Research Journal, 14*(4), 367–381.

Anderson, R. C., Spiro, R. J., & Anderson, M. C. (1978). Schemata as scaffolding for the representation of information in connected discourse. *American Educational Research Journal, 15*(3), 433–440.

Anderson, S. W., Bechara, A., Damasio, H., Tranel, D., & Damasio, A. R. (1999). Impairment of social and moral behavior related to early damage in human prefrontal cortex. *Nature Neuroscience, 2*(11), 1032–1037.

Anderson, S. W., Damasio, H., Jones, R. D., & Tranel, D. (1991). Wisconsin card sorting test performance as a measure of frontal lobe damage. *Journal of Clinical and Experimental Neuropsychology, 13*(6), 909–922.

Andersson, P. (2004). Does experience matter in lending? A process-tracing study on experienced loan officers' and novices' decision behavior. *Journal of Economic Psychology, 25*(4), 471–492.

Andrade, E. B., & Ariely, D. (2009). The enduring impact of transient emotions on decision making. *Organizational Behavior and Human Decision Processes, 109*(1), 1–8.

Andreoli, V., & Worchel, S. (1978). Effects of media, communicator, and message position on attitude change. *Public Opinion Quarterly, 42*, 59–70.

Andres, H. P. (2011). Shared mental model development during technology-mediated collaboration. *International Journal of e-Collaboration, 7*(3), 14–30.

Apanovitch, A. M., McCarthy, D., & Salovey, P. (2003). Using message framing to motivate HIV testing among low-income, ethnic minority women. *Health Psychology, 22*(1), 60–67.

Arditi, A., & Cho, J. (2005). Serifs and font legibility. *Vision Research, 45*(23), 2926–2933.

Argote, L., Ingram, P., Levine, J. M., & Moreland, R. L. (2000). Knowledge transfer in organizations: Learning from the experience of others. *Organizational Behavior and Human Decision Processes, 82*(1), 1–8.

Arguel, A., & Jamet, E. (2009). Using video and static pictures to improve learning of procedural contents. *Computers in Human Behavior, 25*(2), 354–359.

Argyle, M., Alkema, F., & Gilmour, R. (1971). The communication of friendly and hostile attitudes by verbal and nonverbal signals. *European Journal of Social Psychology, 1*(3), 385–402.

Argyle, M., & Cook, M. (1976). *Gaze and mutual gaze.* Oxford, UK: Cambridge University Press.

Arkin, R. M., Appelman, A. J., & Burger, J. M. (1980). Social anxiety, self-presentation, and the self-serving bias in causal attribution. *Journal of Personality and Social Psychology, 38*(1), 23–35.

Arkin, R. M., Cooper, H. M., & Kolditz, T. A. (1980). A statistical review of the literature concerning the self-serving attribution bias in interpersonal influence situations. *Journal of Personality, 48*(4), 435–448.

Armel, K. C., Beaumel, A., & Rangel, A. (2008). Biasing simple choices by manipulating relative visual attention. *Judgment and Decision Making, 3*(5), 396–403.

Arnold, J. E., Fagnano, M., & Tanenhaus, M. K. (2003). Disfluencies signal theee, um, new information. *Journal of Psycholinguistic Research, 32*(1), 25–36.

Arnold, M. B. (1960). *Emotion and personality*. New York: Columbia University Press.

Arora, A., & Alam, P. (2005). CEO compensation and stakeholders' claims. *Contemporary Accounting Research, 22*(3), 519–547.

Asch, S. E. (1946). Forming impressions of personality. *The Journal of Abnormal and Social Psychology, 41*(3), 258–290.

Aschenbrenner, K. M. (1978). Single-peaked risk preferences and their dependability on the gambles' presentation mode. *Journal of Experimental Psychology: Human Perception and Performance, 4*(3), 513–520.

Asendorpf, J. B. (1987). Videotape reconstruction of emotions and cognitions related to shyness. *Journal of Personality and Social Psychology, 53*(3), 542–549.

Ashby, J., Rayner, K., & Clifton, C. (2005). Eye movements of highly skilled and average readers: Differential effects of frequency and predictability. *Quarterly Journal of Experimental Psychology, 58A*(6), 1065–1086.

Ask, K., Rebelius, A., & Granhag, P. A. (2008). The "elasticity" of criminal evidence: A moderator of investigator bias. *Applied Cognitive Psychology, 22*(9), 1245–1259.

Askehave, I., & Swales, J. M. (2001). Genre identification and communicative purpose: A problem and a possible solution. *Applied Linguistics, 22*(2), 195–212.

Atkinson, A. P., Dittrich, W. H., Gemmell, A. J., & Young, A. W. (2004). Emotion perception from dynamic and static body expressions in point-light and full-light displays. *Perception-London, 33*(6), 717–746.

Atman, C. J., & Puerzer, R. (1995). *Reader preference and comprehension of risk diagrams* (Tech Rep. No 95–8). Pittsburgh, PA: University of Pittsburgh, Department of Industrial Engineering.

Au, K., Chan, F., Wang, D., & Vertinsky, I. (2003). Mood in foreign exchange trading: Cognitive processes and performance. *Organizational Behavior and Human Decision Processes, 91*(2), 322–338.

Aue, T., Flykt, A., & Scherer, K. R. (2007). First evidence for differential and sequential efferent effects of stimulus relevance and goal conduciveness appraisal. *Biological Psychology, 74*(3), 347–357.

Ausubel, D., & Fitzgerald, D. (1961). The role of discriminability in meaningful verbal learning and retention. *Journal of Educational Psychology, 52*(5), 266–274.

Ausubel, D., & Fitzgerald, D. (1962). Organizer, general background and antecedent learning variables in sequential verbal learning. *Journal of Educational Psychology, 53*(6), 243–249.

Avila, J. (2012, March 7). 70 percent of ground beef at supermarkets contains 'pink slime.' *ABC News.*

Awamleh, R., & Gardner, W. L. (1999). Perceptions of leader charisma and effectiveness: The effects of vision content, delivery, and organizational performance. *Leadership Quarterly, 10,* 345–373.

Axelrod, R. (1976). *The structure of decision*. Princeton, NJ: Princeton University Press.

Ayres, P., Marcus, N., Chan, C., & Qian, N. (2009). Learning hand manipulative tasks: When instructional animations are superior to equivalent static representations. *Computers in Human Behavior, 25*(2), 348–353.

Azar, P. G. (1994). Learning new-to-the-world products (cognitive processing, analogy) (Doctoral dissertation, Northwestern University, 1994). *Dissertation Abstracts International, 56*(03A), 1028.

Bachher, J. S. (1994). Decision making criteria used by Canadian equity investors to evaluate early stage technology based companies (Doctoral dissertation, University of Waterloo, 1994). *Dissertation Abstracts International, 33*(04), 1119.

Badger, J. M., Kaminsky, S. E., & Behrend, T. S. (2014). Media richness and information acquisition in internet recruitment. *Journal of Managerial Psychology, 29*(7), 866–883.

Baehr, M. E., & Williams, G. B. (1968). Prediction of sales success from factorially determined dimensions of personal background data. *Journal of Applied Psychology, 52*(2), 98–103.

Baesler, E. J. (1997). Persuasive effects of story and statistical evidence. *Argumentation and Advocacy, 33,* 170–175.

Baesler, E. J., & Burgoon, J. K. (1994). The temporal effects of story and statistical evidence on belief change. *Communication Research, 21*(5), 582–602.

Bagozzi, R. P. (1978). Salesforce performance and satisfaction as a function of individual difference, interpersonal, and situational factors. *Journal of Marketing Research, 15*(4), 517–531.

Bagozzi, R. P., & Dholakia, U. (1999). Goal setting and goal striving in consumer behavior. *Journal of Marketing Special Issue: Fundamental Issues and Directions for Marketing, 63,* 19–32.

Bailenson, J. N., & Yee, N. (2005). Digital chameleons: Automatic assimilation of nonverbal gestures in immersive virtual environments. *Psychological Science, 16,* 814–819.

Baluch, F., & Itti, L. (2011). Mechanisms of top-down attention. *Trends in Neurosciences, 34*(4), 210–224.

Bamber, E. M., Tubbs, R. M., Gaeth, G., & Ramsey, R. J. (1991). *Characteristics of audit experience in belief revision.* Paper presented at USC Audit Judgment Symposium. Los Angeles, CA: University of Southern California.

Banse, R., & Scherer, K. R. (1996). Acoustic profiles in vocal emotion expression. *Journal of Personality and Social Psychology, 70*(3), 614–636.

Bar, M., Neta, M., & Linz, H. (2006). Very first impressions. *Emotion, 6*(2), 269–278.

Baranski, J. V., & Petrusic, W. M. (2010). Aggregating conclusive and inconclusive information: Data and a model based on the assessment of threat. *Journal of Behavioral Decision Making, 23*(4), 383–403.

Barber, A. E., & Roehling, M. V. (1993). Job postings and the decision to interview: A verbal protocol analysis. *Journal of Applied Psychology, 78*(5), 845–856.

Barclay, L. A., & York, K. M. (2003). Clear logic and fuzzy guidance: A policy capturing study of merit raise decisions. *Public Personnel Management, 32*(2), 287–299.

Bard, E. G., Shillcock, R. C., & Altmann, G. T. M. (1988). The recognition of words after their acoustic offsets in spontaneous speech: Effects of subsequent context. *Perception and Psychophysics, 44*(5), 395–408.

Bargh, J. A., Chen, M., & Burrows, L. (1996). Automaticity of social behavior: Direct effects of trait construct and stereotype activation on action. *Journal of Personality and Social Psychology, 71*(2), 230–244.

Bar-Hillel, M., & Fischhoff, B. (1981). When do base rates affect predictions? *Journal of Personality and Social Psychology, 41*(4), 671–680.

Barlow, C. M. (2000). Deliberate insight in team creativity. *The Journal of Creative Behavior, 34*(2), 101–117.

Barlow, T., & Wogalter, M. S. (1993). Alcoholic beverage warnings in magazine and television advertisements. *Journal of Consumer Research, 20*(1), 147–156.

Barnes, C. M., Reb, J., & Ang, D. (2012). More than just the mean: Moving to a dynamic view of performance-based compensation. *Journal of Applied Psychology, 97*(3), 711–718.

Barnett, S. M., & Ceci, S. J. (2002). When and where do we apply what we learn?: A taxonomy for far transfer. *Psychological Bulletin, 128*(4), 612–637.

Baron, R. A., & Bell, P. A. (1976). Physical distance and helping: Some unexpected benefits of "crowding in" on others. *Journal of Applied Social Psychology, 6*(2), 95–104.

Baron, R. M., Albright, L., & Mallory, T. E. (1995). Effects of behavioral and social class information on social judgment. *Personality and Social Psychology Bulletin, 21*(4), 308–315.

Barr, D. J., & Seyfeddinipur, M. (2010). The role of fillers in listener attributions for speaker disfluency. *Language and Cognitive Processes, 25*(4), 441–455.

Barsade, S. G. (2002). The ripple effects: Emotional contagion and its influence on group behavior. *Administrative Science Quarterly, 47*(4), 644–675.

Barsade, S. G., Ward, A. J., Turner, J. D. F., & Sonnenfeld, J. A. (2000). To your heart's content: A model of affective diversity in top management teams. *Administrative Science Quarterly, 45*(4), 802–836.

Bartel, C. A., & Saavedra, R. (2000). The collective construction of work group moods. *Administrative Science Quarterly, 45*(2), 197–231.

Bartlett, F. C. (1932). *Remembering: A study in experimental and social psychology*. Cambridge, UK: Cambridge University Press.

Bartol, K. M., & Butterfield, D. A. (1976). Sex effects in evaluating leaders. *Journal of Applied Psychology, 61*(4), 446–454.

Basso, M. R., Schefft, B. K., Ris, M. D., & Dember, W. N. (1996). Mood and global-local visual processing. *Journal of the International Neuropsychological Society, 2*(3), 249–255.

Bates, J. E. (1975). Effects of a child's imitation versus nonimitation on adults' verbal and nonverbal positivity. *Journal of Personality and Social Psychology, 31*(5), 840–851.

Batra, R., & Ray, M. L. (1986). Situational effects of advertising repetition: The moderating influence of motivation, ability, and opportunity to respond. *Journal of Consumer Research, 12*(4), 432–445.

Batson, C. D., & Shaw, L. L. (1991). Evidence for altruism: Toward a pluralism of prosocial motives. *Psychological Inquiry, 2*(2), 107–122.

Batty, M. J., Cave, K. R., & Pauli, P. (2005). Abstract stimuli associated with threat through conditioning cannot be detected preattentively. *Emotion, 5*(4), 418–430.

Baucus, M. S., & Baucus, D. A. (1997). Paying the piper: An empirical examination of longer-term financial consequences of illegal corporate behavior. *Academy of Management Journal, 40*(1), 129–151.

Baum, L. (2009). *Judges and their audiences: A perspective on judicial behavior*. Princeton, NJ: Princeton University Press.

Baumgartner, T., Knoch, D., Hotz, P., Eisenegger, C., & Fehr, E. (2011). Dorsolateral and ventromedial prefrontal cortex orchestrate normative choice. *Nature Neuroscience, 14*(11), 1468–1474.

Bazerman, M. H. (1994). *Judgment in managerial decision making* (3rd ed.). New York: J. Wiley.

Bazerman, M. H., Tenbrunsel, A. E., & Wade-Benzoni, K. (1998). Negotiating with yourself and losing: Making decisions with competing internal preferences. *Academy of Management Review, 23*(2), 225–241.

Bazerman, M. H., Tenbrunsel, A. E., & Wade-Benzoni, K. (2005). *Negotiating with yourself and losing: Making decisions with competing internal preferences*. Northampton, MA: Edward Elgar Publishing.

Beach, L. R., Campbell, F. L., & Townes, B. O. (1979). Subjective expected utility and the prediction of birth-planning decisions. *Organizational Behavior and Human Performance, 24*(1), 18–28.

Beasley, R. (1998). Collective interpretations: How problem representations aggregate in foreign policy groups. In D. Sylvan & J. Voss (Eds.), *Problem representation in foreign policy decision making* (pp. 80–115). New York: Cambridge University Press.

Beattie, G., & Shovelton, H. (1999). Mapping the range of information contained in the iconic hand gestures that accompany spontaneous speech. *Journal of Language and Social Psychology, 18*(4), 438–462.

Beattie, G., Webster, K., & Ross, J. (2010). The fixation and processing of the iconic gestures that accompany talk. *Journal of Language and Social Psychology, 29*(2), 194–213.

Beatty, J., & Kahneman, D. (1966). Pupillary changes in two memory tasks. *Psychonomic Science, 5*(10), 371–372.

Beaucousin, V., Lacheret, A., Turbelin, M. R., Morel, M., Mazoyer, B., & Tzourio-Mazoyer, N. (2007). FMRI study of emotional speech comprehension. *Cerebral Cortex, 17*(2), 339–352.

Beaulieu, P. R. (1994). Commercial lenders' use of accounting information in interaction with source credibility. *Contemporary Accounting Research, 10*(2), 557–585.

Bechara, A. (2003). Risky business: Emotion, decision-making, and addiction. *Journal of Gambling Studies, 19*(1), 23–51.

Bechara, A., Damasio, A. R., Damasio, H., & Anderson, S. W. (1994). Insensitivity to future consequences following damage to human prefrontal cortex. *Cognition, 50*(1–3), 7–15.

Bechara, A., Damasio, H., Damasio, A. R., & Lee, G. P. (1999). Different contributions of the human amygdala and ventromedial prefrontal cortex to decision-making. *Journal of Neuroscience, 19*(13), 5473–5481.

Bechara, A., Damasio, H., Tranel, D., & Anderson, S. W. (1998). Dissociation of working memory from decision making within the human prefrontal cortex. *Journal of Neuroscience, 18*(1), 428–437.

Bechkoff, J., Krishnan, V., Niculescu, M., Kohne, M. L., Palmatier, R. W., & Kardes, F. R. (2009). The role of omission neglect in response to non-gains and non-losses in gasoline price fluctuations. *Journal of Applied Social Psychology, 39*(5), 1191–1200.

Becker, C. A., & Killion, T. H. (1977). Interaction of visual and cognitive effects in word recognition. *Journal of Experimental Psychology: Human Perception and Performance, 3*(3), 389–401.

Becker, D., Heinrich, J., van Sichowsky, R., & Wendt, D. (1970). Reader preferences for typeface and leading. *Journal of Typographic Research, 1*, 61–66.

Becker, S. A. (1998). Individual differences in juror reasoning: General intelligence, social intelligence, and the story model (Doctoral dissertation, Fairleigh Dickinson University, 1998). *Dissertation Abstracts International, 59*(08B), 4533.

Behling, D. U., & Williams, E. A. (1991). Influence of dress on perceptions of intelligence and expectations of scholastic achievement. *Clothing and Textiles Research Journal, 9*(4), 1–7.

Behrman, D. N., Bigoness, W. J., & Perreault, W. D., Jr. (1981). Sources of job related ambiguity and their consequences upon salespersons' job satisfaction and performance. *Management Science, 27*(11), 1246–1260.

Belin, P., Zatorre, R. J., Lafaille, P., Ahad, P., & Pike, B. (2000). Voice-selective areas in human auditory cortex. *Nature, 403*, 309–312.

Bell, B. E., & Loftus, E. F. (1988). Degree of detail of eyewitness testimony and mock juror judgments. *Journal of Applied Social Psychology, 18*(14), 1171–1192.

Bell, B. E., & Loftus, E. F. (1989). Trivial persuasion in the courtroom: The power of (a few) minor details. *Journal of Personality and Social Psychology, 56*(5), 669–679.

Bellenger, D. N., Robertson, D. H., & Hirschman, E. C. (1978). Impulse buying varies by product. *Journal of Advertising Research, 18*, 15–18.

Belmore, S. M. (1987). Determinants of attention during impression formation. *Journal of Experimental Psychology: Learning, Memory, and Cognition, 13*(3), 480–489.

Belyk, M., & Brown, S. (2014). Perception of affective and linguistic prosody: An ALE meta-analysis of neuroimaging studies. *Social Cognitive and Affective Neuroscience, 9*(9), 1395–1403.

Benatar, A., & Clifton, C. (2014). Newness, givenness and discourse updating: Evidence from eye movements. *Journal of Memory and Language, 71*(1), 1–16.

Benjamin, A. S., & Bjork, R. A. (1996). Retrieval fluency as a metacognitive index. In L. Reder (Ed.), *Metacognition and implicit memory* (pp. 309–338). Mahwah, NJ: Erlbaum.

Benjamin, R. G. (2012). Reconstructing readability: Recent developments and recommendations in the analysis of text difficulty. *Educational Psychology Review, 24*(1), 63–88.

Bennouna, K., Meredith, G. G., & Marchant, T. (2010). Improved capital budgeting decision making: Evidence from Canada. *Management Decision, 48*(2), 225–247.

Benson, P. J. (1994). Problems in picturing text (Doctoral dissertation, Carnegie Mellon University, 1994). *Dissertation Abstracts International, 55*(11A), 3357.

Bentley, J. M. (2015). Shifting identification: A theory of apologies and pseudo-apologies. *Public Relations Review, 41*(1), 22–29.

Berardi-Coletta, B., Buyer, L. S., Dominowski, R. L., & Rellinger, E. R. (1995). Metacognition and problem solving: A process-oriented approach. *Journal of Experimental Psychology: Learning, Memory, and Cognition, 21*(1), 205–223.

Berger, Z. D., Yeh, J. C., Carter, H. B., & Pollack, C. E. (2014). Characteristics and experiences of patients with localized prostate cancer who left an active surveillance program. *The Patient-Patient-Centered Outcomes Research, 7*(4), 427–436.

Berkenkotter, C., & Huckin, T. N. (1995). *Genre knowledge in disciplinary communication: Cognition, culture, power.* Hillsdale, NJ: Lawrence Erlbaum Associates.

Bernard, J. B., Kumar, G., Junge, J., & Chung, S. T. (2013). The effect of letter-stroke boldness on reading speed in central and peripheral vision. *Vision Research, 84*, 33–42.

Bernieri, F. J. (1988). Coordinated movement and rapport in teacher-student interactions. *Journal of Nonverbal Behavior, 12*(2), 120–138.

Bernieri, F. J., Reznick, J. S., & Rosenthal, R. (1988). Synchrony, pseudosynchrony, and dissynchrony: Measuring the entrainment process in mother-infant interactions. *Journal of Personality and Social Psychology, 54*(2), 243–253.

Berry, D. S. (1990). Vocal attractiveness and vocal babyishness: Effects on stranger, self, and friend impressions. *Journal of Nonverbal Behavior, 14*(3), 141–153.

Berry, D. S. (1991a). Accuracy in social perception: Contributions of facial and vocal information. *Journal of Personality and Social Psychology, 61*(2), 298–307.

Berry, D. S. (1991b). Attractive faces are not all created equal: Joint effects of facial babyishness and attractiveness on social perception. *Personality and Social Psychology Bulletin, 17*(5), 523–531.

Berry, D. S., & Brownlow, S. (1989). Were the physiognomists right? Personality correlates of facial babyishness. *Personality and Social Psychology Bulletin, 15*(2), 266–279.

Berry, D. S., & Finch Wero, J. L. (1993). Accuracy in face perception: A view from ecological psychology. *Journal of Personality Special Issue: Viewpoints on Personality: Consensus, Self-Other Agreement, and Accuracy in Personality Judgment, 61*(4), 497–520.

Berry, D. S., & Landry, J. C. (1997). Facial maturity and daily social interaction. *Journal of Personality and Social Psychology, 72*(3), 570–580.

Berry, D. S., Pennebaker, J. W., Mueller, J. S., & Hiller, W. S. (1997). Linguistic bases of social perception. *Personality and Social Psychology Bulletin, 23*(5), 526–537.

Berry, H. (2013). When do firms divest foreign operations? *Organization Science, 24*(1), 246–261.

Berscheid, E. (1985). Interpersonal attraction. In G. Lindzey & E. Aronson (Eds.), *Handbook of social psychology* (3rd ed., Vol. 2, pp. 413–484). New York: Random House.

Berscheid, E., & Reis, H. T. (1998). Attraction and close relationships. In D. T. Gilbert, S. T. Fiske & G. Lindzey (Eds.), *The handbook of social psychology* (4th ed., Vol. 2, pp. 193–281). New York: McGraw-Hill.

Bertrand, M., Karlin, D., Mullainathan, S., Shafir, E., & Zinman, J. (2010). What's advertising content worth? Evidence from a consumer credit marketing field experiment. *Quarterly Journal of Economics, 125*(1), 263–306.

Bertrand, M., & Morse, A. (2011). Information disclosure, cognitive biases, and payday borrowing. *The Journal of Finance, 66*(6), 1865–1893.

Betsch, T., Haberstroh, S., Glöckner, A., Haar, T., & Fiedler, K. (2001). The effects of routine strength on adaptation and information search in recurrent decision making. *Organizational Behavior and Human Decision Processes, 84*(1), 23–53.

Betsch, T., Haberstroh, S., Molter, B., & Glöckner, A. (2004). Oops, I did it again—Relapse errors in routinized decision making. *Organizational Behavior and Human Decision Processes, 93*(1), 62–74.

Bettman, J. R. (1979). *An information processing theory of consumer choice*. Reading, MA: Addison Wesley.

Bettman, J. R., & Kakkar, P. (1977). Effects of information presentation format on consumer information acquisition strategies. *Journal of Consumer Research, 3*(4), 233–240.

Bettman, J. R., & Park, C. W. (1980). Effects of prior knowledge and experience and phase of the choice process on consumer decision processes: A protocol analysis. *Journal of Consumer Research, 7*(3), 234–248.

Bettman, J. R., & Sujan, M. (1987). Effects of framing on evaluation of comparable and noncomparable alternatives by expert and novice consumers. *Journal of Consumer Research, 14*(2), 141–154.

Bever, T. (1970). The cognitive basis for linguistic structures. In J. R. Hayes (Ed.), *Cognition and the development of language* (pp. 279–362). New York: Wiley.

Beveridge, M., & Parkins, E. (1987). Visual representation in analogical problem solving. *Memory & Cognition, 15*(3), 230–237.

Bhagan, S. (2009). A chief executive officer and chief information officer consensus decision-making model for information technology investments (Doctoral dissertation, University of Phoenix, 2009). *Dissertation Abstracts International: Section A, 69*, 4023.

Bhaskar, R. (1978). Problem solving in semantically rich domains (Doctoral dissertation, Carnegie Mellon University, 1978). *Dissertation Abstracts International, 41*(05B), 1826.

Bhatia, V. K. (1997). Introduction: Genre analysis and world Englishes. *World Englishes, 16*(3), 313–319.

Bickman, L. (1974). The social power of a uniform. *Journal of Applied Social Psychology, 4*(1), 47–61.

Biederman, I., Glass, A. L., & Stacy, E. W. (1973). Searching for objects in real-world scenes. *Journal of Experimental Psychology, 97*(1), 22–27.

Biehal, G., & Chakravarti, D. (1982). Information-presentation format and learning goals as determinants of consumers' memory retrieval and choice processes. *Journal of Consumer Research, 8*(4), 431–441.

Biehal, G., & Chakravarti, D. (1983). Information accessibility as a moderator of consumer choice. *Journal of Consumer Research, 10*(1), 1–14.

Biehal, G., & Chakravarti, D. (1986). Consumers' use of memory and external information in choice: Macro and micro perspectives. *Journal of Consumer Research*, *12*(4), 382–405.

Biernat, M., Manis, M., & Nelson, T. F. (1991). Stereotypes and standards of judgment. *Journal of Personality and Social Psychology*, *60*(4), 485–499.

Biggs, S. F. (1984). Financial analysts' information search in the assessment of corporate earning power. *Accounting, Organizations and Society*, *9*(3–4), 313–323.

Biggs, S. F., Bedard, J. C., Gaber, B. G., & Linsmeier, T. J. (1985). The effects of task size and similarity on the decision behavior of bank loan officers. *Management Science*, *31*(8), 970–987.

Bilalić, M., Langner, R., Erb, M., & Grodd, W. (2010). Mechanisms and neural basis of object and pattern recognition: A study with chess experts. *Journal of Experimental Psychology: General*, *139*(4), 728–742.

Bilalić, M., McLeod, P., & Gobet, F. (2010). The mechanism of the Einstellung (set) effect: A pervasive source of cognitive bias. *Current Directions in Psychological Science*, *19*(2), 111–115.

Binder, K. S. (2003). Sentential and discourse topic effects on lexical ambiguity processing: An eye-movement examination. *Memory & Cognition*, *31*(5), 690–702.

Binning, J. F., Goldstein, M. A., Garcia, M. F., & Scattaregia, J. H. (1988). Effects of preinterview impressions on questioning strategies in same-and opposite-sex employment interviews. *Journal of Applied Psychology*, *73*(1), 30–37.

Blake, M. L., Tompkins, C. A., Scharp, V. L., Meigh, K. M., & Wambaugh, J. (2015). Contextual constraint treatment for coarse coding deficit in adults with right hemisphere brain damage: Generalisation to narrative discourse comprehension. *Neuropsychological Rehabilitation*, *25*(1), 15–52.

Blakeslee, A. M. (2001). *Interacting with audiences: Social influences on the production of scientific writing*. Mahwah, NJ: Lawrence Erlbaum Associates.

Blanchette, I., & Dunbar, K. (2000). How analogies are generated: The roles of structural and superficial similarity. *Memory & Cognition*, *28*(1), 108–124.

Blanchette, I., & Dunbar, K. (2002). Representational change and analogy: How analogical L inferences alter target representations. *Journal of Experimental Psychology: Learning, Memory, and Cognition*, *28*(4), 672–685.

Blanck, P. D., Rosenthal, R., & Cordell, L. H. (1985). The appearance of justice: Judges' verbal and nonverbal behavior in criminal jury trials. *Stanford Law Review*, *38*, 89–164.

Blankenship, K. L., & Holtgraves, T. (2005). The role of different markers of linguistic powerlessness in persuasion. *Journal of Language and Social Psychology*, *24*(1), 3–24.

Blanton, H., Stuart, A. E., & VandenEijnden, R. J. (2001). An introduction to deviance-regulation theory: The effect of behavioral norms on message framing. *Personality and Social Psychology Bulletin*, *27*(7), 848–858.

Blascovich, J., & Seery, M. D. (2007). Visceral and somatic indexes of social psychological constructs: History, principles, propositions, and case studies. In A. Kruglanski & E. T. Higgins (Eds.), *Social psychology: Handbook of basic principles* (2nd ed., pp. 19–38). New York: Guilford Press.

Bless, H., Bohner, G., Schwarz, N., & Strack, F. (1990). Mood and persuasion: A cognitive response analysis. *Personality and Social Psychology Bulletin*, *16*(2), 331–345.

Bless, H., Clore, G. L., Schwarz, N., Golisano, V., Rabe, C., & Wölk, M. (1996). Mood and the use of scripts: Does a happy mood really lead to mindlessness? *Journal of Personality and Social Psychology*, *71*(4), 665–679.

Blewitt, J. C. (2015). A time of crisis is a time of opportunity for organizations: A strategic examination of managerial response and stakeholder perception (Doctoral dissertation, Saint Louis University, 2015). *Dissertation Abstracts International: Section A*, *75*(10-A)(E).

Boatwright, P., & Nunes, J. C. (2001). Reducing assortment: An attribute-based approach. *Journal of Marketing*, *65*(3), 50–63.

Bodenhausen, G. V. (1993). Emotions, arousal, and stereotypic judgments: A heuristic model of affect and stereotyping. In D. M. Mackie & D. L. Hamilton (Eds.), *Affect, cognition, and stereotyping: Interactive processes in group perception* (pp. 13–37). San Diego, CA: Academic Press.

Bodenhausen, G. V., Kramer, G. P., & Süsser, K. (1994a). Happiness and stereotypic thinking in social judgment. *Journal of Personality and Social Psychology*, *66*(4), 621–632.

Bodenhausen, G. V., Sheppard, L. A., & Kramer, G. P. (1994b). Negative affect and social judgment: The differential impact of anger and sadness. *European Journal of Social Psychology Special Issue: Affect in Social Judgments and Cognition*, *24*(1), 45–62.

Boersema, T., & Zwaga, H. J. (1989, October). Selecting comprehensible warning symbols for swimming pool slides. In *Proceedings of the human factors and ergonomics society annual meeting* (Vol. 33, No. 15, pp. 994–998). Thousand Oaks, CA: Sage.

Bohner, G., Crow, K., Erb, H. P., & Schwarz, N. (1992). Affect and persuasion: Mood effects on the processing of message content and context cues and on subsequent behaviour. *European Journal of Social Psychology Special Issue: Positiveegative Asymmetry in Affect and Evaluations: II*, *22*(6), 511–530.

Bojko, A. (2006). Using eye tracking to compare web page designs: A case study. *Journal of Usability Studies*, *1*(3), 112–120.

Boksman, K., Théberge, J., Williamson, P., Drost, D. J., Malla, A., Densmore, M., . . . & Neufeld, R. W. (2005). A 4.0-T fMRI study of brain connectivity during word fluency in first-episode schizophrenia. *Schizophrenia Research, 75*(2), 247–263.

Bolger, F., & Wright, G. (1992). Reliability and validity in expert judgment. In G. Wright & F. Bolger (Eds.), *Expertise and decision support* (pp. 47–76). New York: Plenum Press.

Bolinger, D. L. (1978). Intonation across languages. In J. H. Greenberg, C. A. Ferguson & E. A. Moravcsik (Eds.), *Universals of human language, Vol. 2: Phonology* (pp. 471–524). Palo Alto, CA: Stanford University Press.

Bolster, B. I., & Springbett, B. M. (1961). The reaction of interviewers to favorable and unfavorable information. *Journal of Applied Psychology, 45*(2), 97–103.

Bond, C. F., Berry, D. S., & Omar, A. (1994). The kernel of truth in judgments of deceptiveness. *Basic and Applied Social Psychology, 15*(4), 523–534.

Bond, C. F., & Brockett, D. R. (1987). A social context-personality index theory of memory for acquaintances. *Journal of Personality and Social Psychology, 52*(6), 1110–1121.

Bond, C. F., & Sedikides, C. (1988). The recapitulation hypothesis in person retrieval. *Journal of Experimental Social Psychology, 24*(3), 195–221.

Bonham, G. M., Shapiro, M. J., & Heradstveit, D. (1988). Group cognition: Using an oil policy game to validate a computer simulation. *Simulations & Games, 19*(4), 379–407.

Bonner, S. E., Walther, B. R., & Young, S. M. (2003). Sophistication-related differences in investors' models of the relative accuracy of analysts' forecast revisions. *The Accounting Review, 78*(3), 679–706.

Bono, J. E., & Judge, T. A. (2003). Self-concordance at work: Toward understanding the motivational effects of transformational leaders. *Academy of Management Journal, 46*(5), 554–571.

Bonsiepe, G. (1968). A method of quantifying order in typographic design. *Journal of Typographic Research, 3,* 203–220.

Borcherding, K., & Rohrmann, B. (1990). An analysis of multiattribute utility models using field data. In K. Borcherding, O. I. Larichev & D. M. Messick (Eds.), *Contemporary issues in decision making* (pp. 223–241). Amsterdam: North-Holland.

Borkenau, P. (1991). Evidence of a correlation between wearing glasses and personality. *Personality and Individual Differences, 12*(11), 1125–1128.

Borkenau, P., & Liebler, A. (1992a). The cross-modal consistency of personality: Inferring strangers' traits from visual or acoustic information. *Journal of Research in Personality, 26*(2), 183–204.

Borkenau, P., & Liebler, A. (1992b). Trait inferences: Sources of validity at zero acquaintance. *Journal of Personality and Social Psychology, 62*(4), 645–657.

Borkenau, P., & Liebler, A. (1993). Convergence of stranger ratings of personality and intelligence with self-ratings, partner ratings, and measured intelligence. *Journal of Personality and Social Psychology, 65*(3), 546–553.

Borkenau, P., & Liebler, A. (1995). Observable attributes as manifestations and cues of personality and intelligence. *Journal of Personality, 63*(1), 1–25.

Borman, W. C. (1987). Personal constructs, performance schemata, and "folk theories" of subordinate effectiveness: Explorations in an Army officer sample. *Organizational Behavior and Human Decision Processes, 40*(3), 307–322.

Bornkessel-Schlesewsky, I. D., & Friederici, A. D. (2007). Neuroimaging studies of sentence and discourse comprehension. In G. Gaskell (Ed.), *The Oxford handbook of psycholinguistics* (pp. 407–424). New York, NY: Oxford University Press.

Bornstein, B. H., Emler, A. C., & Chapman, G. B. (1999). Rationality in medical treatment decisions: Is there a sunk-cost effect? *Social Sciences & Medicine, 49*(2), 215–222.

Bornstein, R. F. (1989). Exposure and affect: Overview and meta-analysis of research, 1968–1987. *Psychological Bulletin, 106*(2), 265–289.

Bornstein, R. F., & D'Agostino, P. R. (1994). The attribution and discounting of perceptual fluency: Preliminary tests of a perceptual fluency. *Social Cognition, 12*(2), 103–128.

Bosman, J. (1987). Persuasive effects of political metaphors. *Metaphor & Symbolic Activity, 2*(2), 97–113.

Boster, E. J., & Mongeau, P. (1984). Fear-arousing persuasive messages. In R. N. Bostrom & B. H. Westley (Eds.), *Communication yearbook, 8* (pp. 330–375). Newbury Park, CA: Sage.

Bottorff, J. L., Ratner, P. A., Johnson, J. L., Lovato, C. Y., & Joab, S. A. (1998). Communicating cancer risk information: The challenges of uncertainty. *Patient Education and Counseling, 33*(1), 67–81.

Boudewyn, M. A., Long, D. L., & Swaab, T. Y. (2015). Graded expectations: Predictive processing and the adjustment of expectations during spoken language comprehension. *Cognitive, Affective, & Behavioral Neuroscience, 15*(3), 607–624.

Boudewyns, V., Turner, M. M., & Paquin, R. S. (2013). Shame-free guilt appeals: Testing the emotional and cognitive effects of shame and guilt appeals. *Psychology & Marketing, 30*(9), 811–825.

Bouman, M. J. (1980). Application of information-processing and decision-making research, I. In G. R. Ungson & D. N. Braunstein (Eds.), *Decision making: An interdisciplinary inquiry* (pp. 129–167). Boston: Kent Publishing.

Bourhis, R. Y., & Giles, H. (1976). The language of co-operation in Wales: A field study. *Language Sciences, 42*, 13–16.

Boush, D. M., & Loken, B. (1991). A process-tracing study of brand extension evaluation. *Journal of Marketing Research, 28*(1), 16–28.

Bouwman, M. J., Frishkoff, P., & Frishkoff, P. A. (1995). The relevance of GAAP-based information: A case study exploring some uses and limitations. *Accounting Horizons, 9*(4), 22–47.

Bouwman, M. J., Frishkoff, P. A., & Frishkoff, P. (1987). How do financial analysts make decisions? A process model of the investment screening decision. *Accounting, Organizations and Society, 12*(1), 1–29.

Bower, G. H., Black, J. B., & Turner, T. J. (1979). Scripts in memory for text. *Cognitive Psychology, 11*(2), 177–220.

Bower, G. H., Karlin, M. B., & Dueck, A. (1975). Comprehension and memory for pictures. *Memory & Cognition, 3*(2), 216–220.

Bowers, J. W., Metts, S. M., & Duncanson, W. T. (1985). Emotion and interpersonal communication. In M. L. Knapp & G. R. Miller (Eds.), *Handbook of interpersonal communication* (pp. 500–550). Beverly Hills, CA: Sage.

Boyd, B. K. (1991). Strategic planning and financial performance: A meta-analytic review. *Journal of Management Studies, 28*(4), 353–374.

Boyle, P. J. (1994). Expertise in a constructive product-choice process (Doctoral dissertation, Cornell University, 1994). *Dissertation Abstracts International, 55*(05a), 1323.

Brader, T. (2006). *Campaigning for hearts and minds: How emotional appeals in political ads work.* Chicago, IL: University of Chicago Press.

Bradley, S. D., & Meeds, R. (2002). Surface-structure transformations and advertising slogans: The case for moderate syntactic complexity. *Psychology & Marketing, 19*(7–8), 595–619.

Bragger, J., Evans, D., Kutcher, G., Sumner, K., & Fritzky, E. (2015). Factors affecting perceptions of procedural fairness of downsizing: A policy capturing approach. *Human Resource Development Quarterly, 26*(2), 127–154.

Bransford, J. D., Barclay, J. R., & Franks, J. J. (1972). Sentence memory: A constructive versus interpretive approach. *Cognitive Psychology, 3*(2), 193–209.

Bransford, J. D., & Johnson, M. K. (1972). Contextual prerequisites for understanding: Some investigations of comprehension and recall. *Journal of Verbal Learning & Verbal Behavior, 11*(6), 717–726.

Bransford, J. D., & Johnson, M. K. (1973). Considerations of some problems of comprehension. In W. G. Chase (Ed.), *Visual information processing* (pp. 383–438). Oxford, UK: Academic.

Bransford, J. D., & McCarrell, N. (1972, October). *A sketch of a cognitive approach to comprehension: Some thoughts about understanding what it means to comprehend.* Paper presented at the Conference on Cognition and the Symbolic Processes. Pennsylvania State University.

Bransford, J. D., & McCarrell, N. S. (1974). A sketch of a cognitive approach to comprehension. In W. Weimer & D. Palermo (Eds.), *Cognition and the symbolic processes* (pp. 189–229). Hillsdale, NJ: Erlbaum.

Braun, C. C., Mine, P. B., & Silver, N. C. (1995). The influence of color on warning label perceptions. *International Journal of Industrial Ergonomics, 15*(3), 179–187.

Braun, K. A., Gacth, G. J., & Levin, I. P. (1997). Framing effects with differential impact: The role of attribute salience. *Advances in Consumer Research, 24*, 405–411.

Brauner, E., & Scholl, W. (2000). Editorial: The information processing approach as a perspective for groups research. *Group Processes and Intergroup Relations, 3*(2), 115–122.

Breaugh, J. A., & Starke, M. (2000). Research on employee recruitment: So many studies, so many remaining questions. *Journal of Management, 26*(3), 405–434.

Breckler, S. J., & Wiggins, E. C. (1989). Affect versus evaluation in the structure of attitudes. *Journal of Experimental Social Psychology, 25*(3), 253–271.

Breitenstein, C., Van Lancker, D., & Daum, I. (2001). The contribution of speech rate and pitch variation to the perception of vocal emotions in a German and an American sample. *Cognition & Emotion, 15*(1), 57–79.

Breland, K., & Breland, M. K. (1944). Legibility of newspaper headlines printed in capitals and in lower case. *Journal of Applied Psychology, 28*(2), 117–120.

Brennan, A., Worrall, L., & McKenna, K. (2005). The relationship between specific features of aphasia-friendly written material and comprehension of written material for people with aphasia: An exploratory study. *Aphasiology, 19*(8), 693–711.

Brennan, S. E., & Williams, M. (1995). The feeling of another's knowing: Prosody and filled pauses as cues to listeners about the metacognitive states of speakers. *Journal of Memory and Language, 34*(3), 383–398.

Brewer, W. F., & Nakamura, G. V. (1984). The nature and functions of schemes. In R. S. Wyer & T. K. Srull (Eds.), *Handbook of social cognition* (Vol. 1, pp. 119–160). Hillsdale, NJ: Erlbaum.

Brewer, W. F., & Tenpenny, P. L. (1996). The role of schemata in the recall and recognition of episodic information. Unpublished manuscript, University of Illinois at Urbana-Champaign, Champaign, IL.

Breznitz, S. (1971). A study of worrying. *British Journal of Social & Clinical Psychology, 10*(3), 271–279.

Breznitz, S. (Ed.). (1983). *The denial of stress.* New York: International Universities Press.

Brickman, P., Redfield, J., Harrison, A. A., & Crandall, R. (1972). Drive and predisposition as factors in the attitudinal effects of mere exposure. *Journal of Experimental Social Psychology, 8*(1), 31–44.

Bridge, C. A., Belmore, S. M., Moskow, S. P., Cohen, S. S., & Matthews, P. D. (1984). Topicalization and memory for main ideas in prose. *Journal of Literacy Research, 16*(1), 61–80.

Briggs, L., Campeau, P., Gagne, R., & May, M. (1966). *Instructional media: A procedure for the design of multi-media instruction: A critical review of research and suggestions for future research.* Pittsburgh, PA: American Institutes for Research.

Britt, S. H., Adams, S. C., & Miller, A. S. (1972). How many advertising exposures per day. *Journal of Advertising Research, 12*(6), 3–9.

Brodbeck, F. C., Kerschreiter, R., Mojzisch, A., & Schulz-Hardt, S. (2007). Group decision making under conditions of distributed knowledge: The information asymmetries model. *Academy of Management Review, 32*(2), 459–479.

Broemer, P. (2001). Ease of recall moderates the impact of relationship-related goals on judgments of interpersonal closeness. *Journal of Experimental Social Psychology, 37*(3), 261–266.

Brooks, C. I., Church, M. A., & Fraser, L. (1986). Effects of duration of eye contact on judgments of personality characteristics. *Journal of Social Psychology, 126*(1), 71–78.

Brown, A. S., & Nix, L. A. (1996). Turning lies into truths: Referential validation of falsehoods. *Journal of Experimental Psychology: Learning, Memory, and Cognition, 22*(5), 1088–1100.

Brown, B. K., & Campion, M. A. (1994). Biodata phenomenology: Recruiters' perceptions and use of biographical information in resume screening. *Journal of Applied Psychology, 79*(6), 897–908.

Brown, B. L. (1980). Effects of speech rate on personality attributions and competency evaluations. In H. Giles, W. P. Robinson & P. M. Smith (Eds.), *Language: Social psychological perspectives* (pp. 116–133). Oxford, UK: Pergamon Press.

Brown, B. L., Strong, W. J., & Rencher, A. C. (1973). Perceptions of personality from speech: Effects of manipulations of acoustical parameters. *Journal of the Acoustical Society of America, 54*(1), 29–35.

Brown, C. A. (1988). The central Arizona water control study: A case for multiobjective planning and public involvement. *Water Resources Bulletin, 20*(3), 331–337.

Brown, D. J., Scott, K. A., & Lewis, H. (2004). Information processing and leadership. In J. Antonakis, A. T. Cianciolo & R. J. Sternberg (Eds.), *The nature of leadership* (pp. 125–147). Thousand Oaks, CA: Sage.

Brown, K. G., Reidy, J. G., Weighall, A. R., & Arden, M. A. (2013). Graphic imagery is not sufficient for increased attention to cigarette warnings: The role of text captions. *Addiction, 108*(4), 820–825.

Brown, L. D. (2001). Predicting individual analyst earnings forecast accuracy. *Financial Analysts Journal, 57*(6), 44–49.

Brown, R., & Kulik, J. (1977). Flashbulb memories. *Cognition, 5*(1), 73–99.

Brucks, M. (1985). The effects of product class knowledge on information search behavior. *Journal of Consumer Research, 12*(1), 1–16.

Bruner, J. S. (1957). On perceptual readiness. *Psychological Review, 64*(2), 123–152.

Bruns, V., & Fletcher, M. (2008). Banks' risk assessment of Swedish SMEs. *Venture Capital, 10*(2), 171–194.

Bryan, C. J., Dweck, C. S., Ross, L., Kay, A. C., & Mislavsky, N. O. (2009). Political mindset: Effects of schema priming on liberal-conservative political positions. *Journal of Experimental Social Psychology, 45*(4), 890–895.

Buchanan, T. W., & Adolphs, R. (2002). The role of the human amygdala in emotional modulation of long-term declarative memory. In S. C. Moore & M. Oaksford (Eds.), *Emotional cognition: From brain to behaviour* (pp. 9–34). Amsterdam, Netherlands: John Benjamins Publishing Company.

Budd, D., Whitney, P., & Turley, K. J. (1995). Individual differences in working memory strategies for reading expository text. *Memory and Cognition, 23*(6), 735–748.

Budescu, D. V., & Rantilla, A. K. (2000). Confidence in aggregation of expert opinions. *Acta Psychologica, 104*(3), 371–398.

Budescu, D. V., Weinberg, S., & Wallsten, T. S. (1988). Decisions based on numerically and verbally expressed uncertainties. *Journal of Experimental Psychology: Human Perception and Performance, 14*(2), 281–294.

Budesheim, T. L., & DePaola, S. J. (1994). Beauty or the beast? The effects of appearance, personality, and issue information on evaluations of political candidates. *Personality and Social Psychology Bulletin, 20*(4), 339–348.

Buehler, R., Griffin, D., & Peetz, J. (2010). The planning fallacy: Cognitive, motivational, and social origins. *Advances in Experimental Social Psychology, 43*, 1–62.

Buehler, R., Messervey, D., & Griffin, D. (2005). Collaborative planning and prediction: Does group discussion affect optimistic biases in time estimation? *Organizational Behavior and Human Decision Processes, 97*(1), 47–63.

Bugental, D. E., Kaswan, J. W., & Love, L. R. (1970). Perception of contradictory meanings conveyed by verbal and nonverbal channels. *Journal of Personality and Social Psychology, 16*(4), 647–655.

Buller, D. B., Burgoon, M., Hall, J. R., Levine, N., Taylor, A. M., Beach, B., . . . & Melcher, C. (2000). Long-term effects of language intensity in preventive messages on planned family solar protection. *Health Communication, 12*(3), 261–275.

Burgoon, J. K. (1994). Nonverbal signals. In M. L. Knapp & G. R. Miller (Eds.), *Handbook of interpersonal communication* (2nd ed., pp. 229–285). Thousand Oaks, CA: Sage.

Burgoon, J. K., Birk, T., & Pfau, M. (1990). Nonverbal behaviors, persuasion, and credibility. *Human Communication Research, 17*(1), 140–169.

Burgoon, J. K., Buller, D., & Woodall, G. (1989). *Nonverbal communication: The unspoken dialogue.* New York: Harper & Row.

Burgoyne, J. G. (1975). The judgment process in management students' evaluation of their learning experiences. *Human Relations, 28*(6), 543–569.

Burke, S. J. (1992). The effects of missing information and inferences on decision processing and evaluation (Doctoral dissertation, The University of Michigan, 1992). *Dissertation Abstracts International, 53*(11A), 3997.

Burnett, J. R. (1993). Utilization and validity of nonverbal cues in the structured interview (Doctoral dissertation, University of Florida, 1993). *Dissertation Abstracts International, 55*(07A), 2041.

Burnkrant, R. E., & Unnava, H. R. (1989). Self-referencing: A strategy for increasing processing of message content. *Personality and Social Psychology Bulletin, 15*(4), 628–638.

Burns, K. L., & Beier, E. G. (1973). Significance of vocal and visual channels in the decoding of emotional meaning. *Journal of Communication, 23*(1), 118–130.

Burrell, N. A., & Koper, R. J. (1998). The efficacy of powerful/powerless language on attitudes and source credibility. In M. Allen & R. W. Preiss (Eds.), *Persuasion: Advances through meta-analysis* (pp. 203–215). Cresskill, NJ: Hampton.

Burson, K. A., Larrick, R. P., & Klayman, J. (2006). Skilled or unskilled, but still unaware of it: How perceptions of difficulty drive miscalibration in relative comparisons. *Journal of Personality and Social Psychology, 90*(1), 60–77.

Cacioppo, J. T., & Petty, R. E. (1989). Effects of message repetition on argument processing, recall, and persuasion. *Basic and Applied Social Psychology, 10*(1), 3–12.

Cacioppo, J. T., Tassinary, L. G., & Berntson, G. G. (2000). *Handbook of psychophysiology* (2nd ed.). New York: Cambridge University Press.

Cairns, H. S., & Kamerman, J. (1975). Lexical information processing during sentence comprehension. *Journal of Verbal Learning & Verbal Behavior, 14*(2), 170–179.

Calder, A. J., Keane, J., Manes, F., Antoun, N., & Young, A. W. (2000). Impaired recognition and experience of disgust following brain injury. *Nature Neuroscience, 3*(11), 1077–1078.

Calder, A. J., Young, A. W., Keane, J., & Dean, M. (2000). Configural information in facial expression perception. *Journal of Experimental Psychology: Human Perception and Performance, 26*(2), 527–551.

Calder, B. J. (1977). An attribution theory of leadership. In B. M. Staw & G. R. Salancik (Eds.), *New directions in organizational behavior* (pp. 179–204). Chicago: St. Claire Press.

Calder, B. J., & Gruder, C. L. (1989). Emotional advertising appeals. In P. Cafferata & A. Tybout (Eds.), *Cognitive and affective responses to advertising* (pp. 277–286). Lexington, MA: D.C. Heath and Company.

Calder, B. J., Insko, C. A., & Yandell, B. (1974). The relation of cognitive and memorial processes to persuasion in a simulated jury trial. *Journal of Applied Social Psychology, 4*(1), 62–93.

Calder, B. J., & Sternthal, B. (1980). Television commercial wearout: An information processing view. *Journal of Marketing Research, 17*(2), 173–186.

Calvo, M. G., & Lang, P. J. (2004). Gaze patterns when looking at emotional pictures: Motivationally biased attention. *Motivation and Emotion, 28*(3), 221–243.

Calvo, M. G., & Meseguer, E. (2002). Eye movements and processing stages in reading: Relative contribution of visual, lexical and contextual factors. *Spanish Journal of Psychology, 5*(1), 66–77.

Camacho, L. M., & Paulus, P. B. (1995). The role of social anxiousness in group brainstorming. *Journal of Personality and Social Psychology, 68*(6), 1071–1080.

Camerer, C. F. (1981). General conditions for the success of bootstrapping models. *Organizational Behavior & Human Performance, 27*(3), 411–422.

Camerer, C. F., & Johnson, E. J. (1991). The process-performance paradox in expert judgment: How can experts know so much and predict so badly? In K. A. Ericsson & J. Smith (Eds.), *Toward a general theory of expertise: Prospects and limits* (pp. 195–217). New York: Cambridge University Press.

Cameron, L. D., & Leventhal, H. (2003). *The self-regulation of health and illness behaviour.* New York, NY: Psychology Press.

Campbell, J. E. (1981). An empirical investigation of the impact on the decision processes of loan officers of separate accounting standards for smaller and/or closely held companies (Doctoral dissertation, The University of Tennessee, 1981). *Dissertation Abstracts International, 42*(09A), 4050.

Campbell, J. E. (1984). An application of protocol analysis to the "little GAAP" controversy. *Accounting, Organizations and Society, 9*(3, 4), 329–343.

Campbell-Kibler, K. (2007). Accent, (ING), and the social logic of listener perceptions. *American Speech, 82*(1), 32–64.

Campitelli, G., Gobet, F., & Parker, A. (2005). Structure and stimulus familiarity: A study of memory in chess-players with functional magnetic resonance imaging. *The Spanish Journal of Psychology, 8*(02), 238–245.

Camras, L. A., Sullivan, J., & Michel, G. (1993). Do infants express discrete emotions? Adult judgments of facial, vocal, and body actions. *Journal of Nonverbal Behavior, 17*(3), 171–186.

Canham, M., & Hegarty, M. (2010). Effects of knowledge and display design on comprehension of complex graphics. *Learning and Instruction, 20*(2), 155–166.

Cannon-Bowers, J. A., & Salas, E. (2001). Reflections on shared cognition. *Journal of Organizational Behavior, 22*(2), 195–202.

Cannon-Bowers, J. A., Salas, E., & Converse, S. (1993). Shared mental models in expert team decision making. In N. J. Castellan (Ed.), *Individual and group decision making: Current issues* (pp. 221–246). Hillsdale, NJ: Lawrence Erlbaum Associates.

Caplan, D. (1972). Clause boundaries and recognition latencies for words in sentences. *Perception & Psychophysics, 12*(1, Pt. B), 73–76.

Capon, N., & Burke, M. (1977). Information seeking in consumer durable purchases. In B. A. Greenberg & D. N. Bellenger (Eds.), *Contemporary marketing thought, 1977 educator's proceedings* (pp. 110–115). Chicago: American Marketing Association.

Cappella, J. N. (1993). The facial feedback hypothesis in human interaction: Review and speculation. *Journal of Language and Social Psychology Special Issue: Emotional Communication, Culture, and Power, 12*, 13–29.

Capstaff, J., Paudyal, K., & Rees, W. (2001). A comparative analysis of earnings forecasts in Europe. *Journal of Business Finance & Accounting, 28*(5–6), 531–562.

Cardy, R. L., Bernardin, H., Abbott, J. G., Senderak, M. P., & Taylor, K. (1987). The effects of individual performance schemata and dimension familiarization on rating accuracy. *Journal of Occupational Psychology, 60*(3), 197–205.

Cardy, R. L., & Dobbins, G. H. (1986). Affect and appraisal accuracy: Liking as an integral dimension in evaluating performance. *Journal of Applied Psychology, 71*(4), 672–678.

Carenini, G. (2001). Generating and evaluating evaluative arguments (Doctoral dissertation, University of Pittsburgh, 2001). *Dissertation Abstracts International, 62*(05B), 2377.

Carley, K. M. (1997). Extracting team mental models through textual analysis. *Journal of Organizational Behavior, 18*(Spec Issue), 533–558.

Carli, L. L., Ganley, R., & Pierce-Otay, A. (1991). Similarity and satisfaction in roommate relationships. *Personality and Social Psychology Bulletin, 17*(4), 419–426.

Carli, L. L., LaFleur, S. J., & Loeber, C. C. (1995). Nonverbal behavior, gender, and influence. *Journal of Personality and Social Psychology, 68*(6), 1030–1041.

Carlson, C. A., Gronlund, S. D., & Clark, S. E. (2008). Lineup composition, suspect position and the sequential lineup advantage. *Journal of Experimental Psychology: Applied, 14*(2), 118–128.

Carlson, K. A., Meloy, M. G., & Russo, J. E. (2006). Leader-driven primacy: Using attribute order to affect consumer choice. *Journal of Consumer Research, 32*(4), 513–518.

Carlston, D. E., & Smith, E. R. (1996). Principles of mental representation. In E. T. Higgins & A. Kruglanski (Eds.), *Social psychology: Handbook of basic principles* (2nd ed., pp. 184–210). New York: Guilford Press.

Carney, R. N., & Levin, J. R. (2002). Pictorial illustrations still improve students' learning from text. *Educational Psychology Review, 14*(1), 5–26.

Carpenter, P. A., & Just, M. A. (1977). Reading comprehension as the eyes see it. In M. A. Just & P. A. Carpenter (Eds.), *Cognitive processes in comprehension* (pp. 109–139). Hillsdale, NJ: Erlbaum.

Carpenter, P. A., & Just, M. A. (1981). Cognitive processes in reading: Models based on readers' eye fixations. In A. M. Lesgold & C. A. Perfetti (Eds.), *Interactive processes in reading* (pp. 177–213). Hillsdale, NJ: Erlbaum.

Carpenter, P. A., & Just, M. A. (1983). What your eyes do while your mind is reading. In K. Rayner (Ed.), *Eye movements in reading: Perceptual and language processes* (pp. 275–307). New York: Academic Press.

Carpenter, P. A., & Shah, P. (1998). A model of the perceptual and conceptual processes in graph comprehension. *Journal of Experimental Psychology: Applied, 4*(2), 75–100.

Carretié, L., Hinojosa, J. A., Martín-Loeches, M., Mercado, F., & Tapia, M. (2004). Automatic attention to emotional stimuli: Neural correlates. *Human Brain Mapping, 22*(4), 290–299.

Carroll, J. S. (1978). Causal attributions in expert parole decisions. *Journal of Personality and Social Psychology, 36*(12), 1501–1511.

Carroll, M. L. (1997). A comparative analysis and evaluation of knowledge structures between expert novice and struggling novice accounting students (Doctoral dissertation, Loyola University of Chicago, 1997). *Dissertation Abstracts International, 58*(03A), 0733.

Carsten, M. K., Uhl-Bien, M., West, B. J., Patera, J. L., & McGregor, R. (2010). Exploring social constructions of followership: A qualitative study. *The Leadership Quarterly, 21*(3), 543–562.

Carswell, C. M., & Wickens, C. D. (1987). Information integration and the object display: An interaction of task demands and display superiority. *Ergonomics, 30*(3), 511–527.

Carter, W. B., Beach, L. R., & Inui, T. S. (1986). The flu shot study: Using multiattribute utility theory to design a vaccination intervention. *Organizational Behavior and Human Decision Processes, 38*(3), 378–391.

Carver, C. S., & Scheier, M. F. (1990). Origins and functions of positive and negative affect: A control-process view. *Psychological Review, 97*(1), 19–35.

Cassie, J. R. B., & Robinson, F. G. (1982). A decision schema approach to career decision making. *International Journal of Advances in Counseling, 5*, 165–182.

Castellan, N. J. (Ed.). (1993). *Individual and group decision making: Current issues.* Hillsdale, NJ: Lawrence Erlbaum.

Cauchard, F., Eyrolle, H., Cellier, J. M., & Hyönä, J. (2010). Vertical perceptual span and the processing of visual signals in reading. *International Journal of Psychology, 45*(1), 40–47.

Cauchard, F., Eyrolle, H., Cellier, J. M., & Hyönä, J. (2010). Visual signals vertically extend the perceptual span in searching a text: A gaze-contingent window study. *Discourse Processes, 47*(8), 617–640.

Cavina-Pratesi, C., Large, M. E., & Milner, A. D. (2015). Visual processing of words in a patient with visual form agnosia: A behavioural and fMRI study. *Cortex, 64*, 29–46.

Chaiken, S. (1979). Communicator physical attractiveness and persuasion. *Journal of Personality and Social Psychology, 37*(8), 1387.

Chaiken, S. (1980). Heuristic versus systematic information processing and the use of source versus message cues in persuasion. *Journal of Personality and Social Psychology, 39*(5), 752–766.

Chaiken, S., & Eagly, A. H. (1976). Communication modality as a determinant of message persuasiveness and message comprehensibility. *Journal of Personality and Social Psychology, 34*(4), 605–614.

Chaiken, S., & Eagly, A. H. (1983). Communication modality as a determinant of persuasion: The role of communicator salience. *Journal of Personality and Social Psychology, 45*(2), 241–256.

Chaiken, S., Liberman, A., & Eagly, A. H. (1989). Heuristic and systematic information processing within and beyond the persuasion context. In J. S. Uleman & J. A. Bargh (Eds.), *Unintended thought* (pp. 212–252). New York: Guilford Press.

Chall, J. S. (1958). *Readability: An appraisal of research and application.* Columbus, OH: Ohio State University. Reprinted 1974. Epping, UK: Bowker Publishing Company.

Chall, J. S., & Dale, E. (1995). *Readability revisited: The new Dale-Chall readability formula.* Northampton, MA: Brookline Books.

Chan, S. (1982). Expert judgments under uncertainty: Some evidence and suggestions. *Social Science Quarterly, 63*, 428–444.

Chance, M. R. A. (1976). The organization of attention in groups. In M. von Cranach (Ed.), *Methods of inference from animal to human behavior* (pp. 213–235). The Hague, Netherlands: Mouton.

Chandler, R. C. (1988). Organizational communication to corporate constituents: The role of the company annual report (Doctoral dissertation, University of Kansas, 1988). *Dissertation Abstracts International, 49*(11A), 3200.

Chang, M. J., & Gruner, C. R. (1981). Audience reaction to self-disparaging humor. *Southern Speech Communication Journal, 46*, 419–426.

Chang, S. C., Chen, S. S., Chou, R. K., & Lin, Y. H. (2008). Weather and intraday patterns in stock returns and trading activity. *Journal of Banking & Finance, 32*(9), 1754–1766.

Chapman, G. B., & Johnson, E. J. (1999). Anchoring, activation, and the construction of values. *Organizational Behavior and Human Decision Processes, 79*(2), 115–153.

Charrow, R., & Charrow, V. R. (1979). Making legal language understandable: Psycholinguistic study of jury instructions. *Columbia Law Review, 79*, 1306–1374.

Charrow, V. R. (1988). Readability vs. comprehensibility: A case study in improving a real document. In A. Davison & G. M. Green (Eds.), *Linguistic complexity and text comprehension: Readability issues reconsidered* (pp. 85–114). Hillsdale, NJ: Lawrence Erlbaum Associates.

Charrow, V. R., & Redish, J. (1980). *A study of standardized headings for warranties* (Document Design Project Technical Report No. 6). Washington, DC: American Institutes for Research.

Chartrand, T. L., & Bargh, J. A. (1999). The chameleon effect: The perception–behavior link and social interaction. *Journal of Personality and Social Psychology, 76*(6), 893.

Chase, W. G., & Simon, H. A. (1973). Perception in chess. *Cognitive Psychology, 4*(1), 55–81.

Chattopadhyay, A., Dahl, D. W., Ritchie, R. J. B., & Shahin, K. N. (2003). Hearing voices: The impact of announcer speech characteristics on consumer response to broadcast advertising. *Journal of Consumer Psychology, 13*(3), 198–204.

Chen, L. (1982). Topological structure in visual perception. *Science, 218*(4573), 699–700.

Cheng, P. Y., & Chiou, W. B. (2008). Framing effects in group investment decision making: The role of group polarization. *Psychological Reports, 102*(1), 283–292.

Chen-Yu, J. H., & Seock, Y. K. (2002). Adolescents' clothing purchase motivations, information sources, and store selection criteria: A comparison of male/female and impulse/nonimpulse shoppers. *Family and Consumer Sciences Research Journal, 31*(1), 50–77.

Chernev, A. (2003). Product assortment and individual decision processes. *Journal of Personality and Social Psychology, 85*(1), 151–162.

Chernoff, H. (1973). Using faces to represent points in k-dimensional space graphically. *Journal of the American Statistical Association, 68*, 361–368.

Cherry, E. C. (1953). Some experiments on the recognition of speech, with one and with two ears. *Journal of the Acoustical Society of America, 25*, 975–979.

Cherulnik, P. D., Donley, D. A., Wiewel, T. S. R., & Miller, S. R. (2001). Charisma is contagious: The effects of leader's charisma on observers' affect. *Journal of Applied Social Psychology, 31*, 2149–2159.

Chi, M. T. H. (2006). Two approaches to the study of expert's characteristics. In K. A. Ericsson, N. Charness, P. Feltovich & R. Hoffman (Eds.), *The Cambridge handbook of expertise and expert performance* (pp. 21–30). Cambridge, UK: Cambridge University Press.

Chi, M. T. H., Feltovich, P. J., & Glaser, R. (1981). Categorization and representation of physics problems by experts and novices. *Cognitive Science, 5*, 121–152.

Chi, M. T. H., & Koeske, R. D. (1983). Network representation of a child's dinosaur knowledge. *Developmental Psychology, 19*(1), 29–39.

Chi, M. T. H., & Ohlsson, S. (2005). Complex declarative learning. In K. J. Holyoak & R. G. Morrison (Eds.), *The Cambridge handbook of thinking and reasoning* (pp. 371–399). Cambridge, UK: Cambridge University Press.

Chinander, K. R., & Schweitzer, M. E. (2003). The input bias: The misuse of input information in judgments of outcomes. *Organizational Behavior and Human Decision Processes, 91*(2), 243–253.

Chinburapa, V. (1991). Physician prescribing decisions: The effects of situational involvement and task complexity on information acquisition and decision making (Doctoral dissertation, The University of Arizona, 1991). *Dissertation Abstracts International, 52*(04B), 1975.

Choi, J., & Myer, D. W. (2012). The effect of product positioning in a comparison table on consumers' evaluation of a sponsor. *Marketing Letters, 23*(1), 367–380.

Chouchourelou, A., Matsuka, T., Harber, K., & Shiffrar, M. (2006). The visual analysis of emotional actions. *Social Neuroscience, 1*(1), 63–74.

Chui, K. (2012). Cross-linguistic comparison of representations of motion in language and gesture. *Gesture, 12*(1), 40–61.

Cirilo, R. K., & Foss, D. J. (1980). Text structure and reading time for sentences. *Journal of Verbal Learning and Verbal Behavior, 19*(1), 96–109.

Citibank (1974). First National City Bank promissory note (PBR 668 REV.9–74). In C. Felsenfeld & A. Siegel (Eds.), *Writing contracts in plain English* (1981 ed., p. 3). St. Paul, MN: West Publishing Co.

Citibank (1977). Consumer loan note. In C. Felsenfeld & A. Siegel (Eds.), *Writing contracts in plain English* (1981 ed., p. 241). St. Paul, MN: West Publishing Co.

Clark, H. H. (1969). Linguistic processes in deductive reasoning. *Psychological Review, 76*(4), 387–404.

Clark, H. H. (1999). Psycholinguistics. In R. A. Wilson & F. C. Keil (Eds.), *MIT encyclopedia of the cognitive sciences* (pp. 688–689). Cambridge, MA: The MIT Press.

Clark, H. H., & Chase, W. G. (1972). On the process of comparing sentences against pictures. *Cognitive Psychology, 3*(3), 472–517.

Clark, H. H., & Clark, E. V. (1968). Semantic distinctions and memory for complex sentences. *The Quarterly Journal of Experimental Psychology, 20*(2), 129–138.

Clark, H. H., & Sengul, C. J. (1979). In search of referents for nouns and pronouns. *Memory & Cognition, 7*(1), 35–41.

Clark, L. F., Martin, L. L., & Henry, S. M. (1993). Instantiation, interference, and the change of standard effect: Context functions in reconstructive memory. *Journal of Personality and Social Psychology, 64*(3), 336–346.

Clark, M. S., Milberg, S., & Erber, R. (1984). Effects of arousal on judgments of others' emotions. *Journal of Personality and Social Psychology, 46*(3), 551–560.

Clark, N. K., & Rutter, D. R. (1985). Social categorization, visual cues, and social judgements. *European Journal of Social Psychology, 15*(1), 105–119.

Clark, R. C., & Mayer, R. E. (2011). *E-learning and the science of instruction: Proven guidelines for consumers and designers of multimedia learning.* Hoboken, NJ: John Wiley & Sons.

Clarke, T. J., Bradshaw, M. F., Field, D. T., Hampson, S. E., & Rose, D. (2005). The perception of emotion from body movement in point-light displays of interpersonal dialogue. *Perception-London, 34*(10), 1171–1180.

Clarkson, G. P. (1962). *Portfolio selection: A simulation of trust investment.* Englewood Cliffs, NJ: Prentice Hall.

Clement, M. B., & Tse, S. Y. (2003). Do investors respond to analysts' forecast revisions as if forecast accuracy is all that matters? *The Accounting Review, 78*(1), 227–249.

Cleveland, W. S., & McGill, R. (1984). Graphical perception: Theory, experimentation, and application to the development of graphical methods. *Journal of the American Statistical Association, 77*, 541–547.

Cline, T. W., & Kellaris, J. J. (1999). The joint impact of humor and argument strength in a print advertising context: A case for weaker arguments. *Psychology & Marketing, 16*(1), 69–86.

Clithero, J. A., & Rangel, A. (2014). Informatic parcellation of the network involved in the computation of subjective value. *Social Cognitive and Affective Neuroscience, 9*(9), 1289–1302.

Clore, G. L., & Isbell, L. M. (2001). Emotion as virtue and vice. In J. H. Kuklinski (Ed.), *Citizens and politics: Perspectives from political psychology* (pp. 103–123). New York: Cambridge University Press.

Clore, G. L., & Ortony, A. (1988). The semantics of the affective lexicon. In V. Hamilton, G. H. Bower & N. H. Frijda (Eds.), *Cognitive perspectives on emotion and motivation* (pp. 367–397). New York: Kluwer Academic/Plenum Publishers.

Cloyd, C. B., & Spilker, B. (1999). The influence of client preferences on tax professionals' search for judicial precedents, subsequent judgments, and recommendations. *The Accounting Review, 74*, 299–322.

Cobb, C. J., & Hoyer, W. D. (1986). Planned versus impulse purchase behavior. *Journal of Retailing, 62*(4), 384–409.

Cobb, R. W., & Elder, C. D. (1983). *Participation in American politics: The dynamics of agenda building.* Baltimore: Johns Hopkins University Press.

Cobos, P. L., Almaraz, J., & Garcia-Madruga, J. A. (2003). An associative framework for probability judgment: An application to biases. *Journal of Experimental Psychology: Learning, Memory, and Cognition, 29*(1), 80–96.

Cohen, C. E. (1976). Cognitive basis of stereotyping: An information processing approach to social perception (Doctoral dissertation, University of California, San Diego, 1976). *Dissertation Abstracts International, 38*(01B), 0412.

Cohen, C. E. (1981a). Goals and schemata in person perception: Making sense from the stream of behavior. In N. Cantor & J. F. Kihlstrom (Eds.), *Personality, cognition and social interaction* (pp. 45–68). Hillsdale, NJ: Lawrence Erlbaum Associates.

Cohen, C. E. (1981b). Person categories and social perception: Testing some boundaries of the processing effect of prior knowledge. *Journal of Personality and Social Psychology, 40*(3), 441–452.

Cohen, G., Conway, M. A., & Maylor, E. A. (1994). Flashbulb memories in older adults. *Psychology and Aging, 9*(3), 454–463.

Cohen, H., Douaire, J., & Elsabbagh, M. (2001). The role of prosody in discourse processing. *Brain and Cognition, 46*(1), 73–82.

Cohen, M. S. (1993). The naturalistic basis of decision biases. In G. A. Klein, J. Orasanu, R. Calderwood & C. E. Zsambok (Eds.), *Decision making in action: Models and methods* (pp. 51–99). Norwood, NJ: Ablex.

Coleman, E. B. (1962). Improving comprehensibility by shortening sentences. *Journal of Applied Psychology, 46*(2), 131–134.

Coleman, E. B. (1964). The comprehensibility of several grammatical transformations. *Journal of Applied Psychology, 48*(3), 186–190.

Coles, P., & Foster, J. J. (1975). Typographic cuing as an aid to learning from typewritten text. *Programmed Learning and Educational Technology, 12*, 102–108.

Colin, W. (1995). *Type & layout: How typography and design can get your message across, or get in the way.* Berkeley, CA: Strathmoor Press.

Collins, A., Brown, J. S., & Larkin, K. M. (1980). Inference in text understanding. In R. J. Spiro, B. C. Bruce & W. F. Brewer (Eds.), *Theoretical issues in reading comprehension* (pp. 385–407). Hillsdale, NJ: Lawrence Erlbaum Associates.

Colquitt, J. A., Noe, R. A., & Jackson, C. L. (2002). Justice in teams: Antecedents and consequences of procedural justice climate. *Personnel Psychology, 55*(1), 83–109.

Compton, R. J. (2003). The interface between emotion and attention: A review of evidence from psychology and neuroscience. *Behavioral and Cognitive Neuroscience Reviews, 2*(2), 115–129.

Conger, J. A. (1991). Inspiring others: The language of leadership. *The Executive, 5*(1), 31–45.

Conger, J. A., & Kanungo, R. N. (1998). *Charismatic leadership in organizations.* Thousand Oaks, CA: Sage.

Conger, J. A., & Kanungo, R. N. (Eds.). (1988). *Charismatic leadership: The elusive factor in organizational effectiveness.* San Francisco: Jossey-Bass.

Conger, J. A., Kanungo, R. N., Menon, S. T., & Mathur, P. (1997). Measuring charisma: Dimensionality and validity of the Conger-Kanungo scale of charismatic leadership. *Canadian Journal of Administrative Sciences, 14*(3), 290–302.

Connelly, M. S., Gilbert, J. A., Zaccaro, S. J., Threlfall, K. V., Marks, M. A., & Mumford, M. D. (2000). Exploring the relationship of leadership skills and knowledge to leader performance. *Leadership Quarterly, 11*, 65–86.

Consumer Reports (2009). *Smart phone ratings for AT&T smart phones.* Retrieved December 16, 2009 from www.consumerreports.org/cro/electronics-computers/phones-mobile-devices/cell-phones-services/smart-phone-ratings/ratings-overview.htm.

Control Data Corporation (1986). *Control data (annual report).* Control Data Corporation Records, Annual and Quarterly Reports (CBI 80). Minneapolis: Charles Babbage Institute, University of Minnesota.

Conway, M., & Giannopoulos, C. (1993). Dysphoria and decision making: Limited information use for evaluations of multiattribute targets. *Journal of Personality and Social Psychology, 64*(4), 613–623.

Conzola, V. C., & Wogalter, M. S. (1999). Using voice and print directives and warnings to supplement product manual instructions. *International Journal of Industrial Ergonomics, 23*(5), 549–556.

Cook, F. L., Tyler, T. R., Goetz, E. G., Gordon, M. T., Protess, D., Leff, D. R., & Molotch, H. L. (1983). Media and agenda setting: Effects on the public, interest group leaders, policy makers, and policy. *Public Opinion Quarterly, 47*(1), 16–35.

Cook, G. J. (1987). An analysis of information search strategies for decision making (Doctoral dissertation, Arizona State University, 1987). *Dissertation Abstracts International, 48*(02A), 0430.

Cook, M., Wiebe, E. N., & Carter, G. (2008). The influence of prior knowledge on viewing and interpreting graphics with macroscopic and molecular representations. *Science Education, 92*(5), 848–867.

Cook, M. B., & Smallman, H. S. (2008). Human factors of the confirmation bias in intelligence analysis: Decision support from graphical evidence landscapes. *Human Factors: The Journal of the Human Factors and Ergonomics Society, 50*(5), 745–754.

Cooke, N. J., Salas, E., Kiekel, P. A., & Bell, B. (2004). Advances in measuring team cognition. In E. Salas & S. M. Fiore (Eds.), *Team cognition: Understanding the factors that drive process and performance* (pp. 83–106). Washington, DC: American Psychological Association.

Coombs, T., & Schmidt, L. (2000). An empirical analysis of image restoration: Texaco's racism crisis. *Journal of Public Relations Research, 12*(2), 163–178.

Corteen, R. S., & Dunn, D. (1974). Shock-associated words in a nonattended message: A test for momentary awareness. *Journal of Experimental Psychology, 102*(6), 1143–1144.

Corwin, E. P., Cramer, R. J., Griffin, D. A., & Brodsky, S. L. (2012). Defendant remorse, need for affect, and juror sentencing decisions. *Journal of the American Academy of Psychiatry and the Law Online, 40*(1), 41–49.

Cosier, R. A., & Schwenk, C. R. (1990). Agreement and thinking alike: Ingredients for poor decisions. *Academy of Management Executive, 4*(1), 69–74.

Costley, C. L., & Brucks, M. (1992). Selective recall and information use in consumer preferences. *Journal of Consumer Research, 18*(4), 464–474.

Coulson, M. (2004a). Attributing emotion to static body postures: Recognition accuracy, confusions, and viewpoint dependence. *Journal of Nonverbal Behavior, 28*(2), 117–139.

Coulson, M. (2004b). Erratum for attributing emotion to static body postures: Recognition accuracy, confusions, and viewpoint dependence. *Journal of Nonverbal Behavior Special Issue: Interpersonal Sensitivity, 28*(4), 297.

Coulter, K. S., & Roggeveen, A. L. (2014). Price number relationships and deal processing fluency: The effects of approximation sequences and number multiples. *Journal of Marketing Research, 51*(1), 69–82.

Coulter, R. H., & Pinto, M. B. (1995). Guilt appeals in advertising: What are their effects? *Journal of Applied Psychology, 80*(6), 697–705.

Coupey, E. (1994). Restructuring: Constructive processing of information displays in consumer choice. *Journal of Consumer Research, 21*(1), 83–99.

Cox, A. D., & Summers, J. O. (1987). Heuristics and biases in the intuitive projection of retail sales. *Journal of Marketing Research, 24*(3), 290–297.

Cox, E. P., III, Wogalter, M. S., Stokes, S. L., & Murff, E. J. T. (1997). Do product warnings increase safe behavior? A meta-analysis. *Journal of Public Policy, 16*, 195–204.

Craig, C. S., Sternthal, B., & Leavitt, C. (1976). Advertising wearout: An experimental analysis. *Journal of Marketing Research, 13*(4), 365–372.

Crano, W. D. (2001). Social influence, social identity, and ingroup leniency. In C. K. W. De Dreu & N. K. De Vries (Eds.), *Group consensus and minority influence: Implications for innovation* (pp. 122–143). Oxford, UK: Blackwell Publishers.

Crespin, T. R. (1997). Cognitive convergence in developing groups: The role of sociocognitive elaboration. *Dissertation Abstracts International: Section B: The Sciences and Engineering, 57*(7-B), 4758.

Critcher, C. R., & Gilovich, T. (2008). Incidental environmental anchors. *Journal of Behavioral Decision Making, 21*(3), 241–251.

Cronin, J. J., Jr., Brady, M. K., & Hult, G. T. M. (2000). Assessing the effects of quality, value, and customer satisfaction on consumer behavioral intentions in service environments. *Journal of Retailing, 76*(2), 193–218.

Cronshaw, S. F., & Lord, R. G. (1987). Effects of categorization, attribution, and encoding processes on leadership perceptions. *Journal of Applied Psychology, 72*(1), 97–106.

Crouse, J., & Idstein, P. (1972). Effects of encoding cues on prose learning. *Journal of Educational Psychology, 63*(4), 309–313.

Cruz, M. G., Boster, F. J., & Rodríguez, J. I. (1997). The impact of group size and proportion of shared information on the exchange and integration of information in groups. *Communication Research, 24*(3), 291–313.

Cunningham, M. R. (1986). Measuring the physical in physical attractiveness: Quasi-experiments on the sociobiology of female facial beauty. *Journal of Personality and Social Psychology, 50*(5), 925–935.

Cunningham, M. R., Barbee, A. P., & Pike, C. L. (1990). What do women want? Facialmetric assessment of multiple motives in the perception of male facial physical attractiveness. *Journal of Personality and Social Psychology, 59*(1), 61–72.

Curhan, J. R., & Pentland, A. (2007). Thin slices of negotiation: Predicting outcomes from conversational dynamics within the first 5 minutes. *Journal of Applied Psychology, 92*(3), 802–811.

Currie-Rubin, R. (2012). Ill-structured problem solving of novice reading specialists and expert assessment specialists: Learning and expertise (Doctoral dissertation, Harvard University, 2013). *Dissertation Abstracts International: Section A, 74*(4-A)(E).

Cutler, A. (1982). Prosody and sentence perception in English. In J. Mehler, E. C. T. Walker & M. F. Garrett (Eds.), *Perspectives on mental representation: Experimental and theoretical studies of cognitive processes and capacities* (pp. 201–216). Hillsdale, NJ: Erlbaum.

Cutler, A., & Norris, D. (1988). The role of strong syllables in segmentation for lexical access. *Journal of Experimental Psychology: Human Perception and Performance, 14*(1), 113–121.

Cutler, B. L., Penrod, S. D., & Dexter, H. R. (1990). Juror sensitivity to eyewitness identification evidence. *Law and Human Behavior, 14*(2), 185–191.

Dahan, D., Magnuson, J. S., & Tanenhaus, M. K. (2001). Time course of frequency effects in spoken-word recognition: Evidence from eye movements. *Cognitive Psychology, 42*(4), 317–367.

Dahlin, K. B., Weingart, L. R., & Hinds, P. J. (2005). Team diversity and information use. *Academy of Management Journal, 48*(6), 1107–1123.

Dai, J., & Busemeyer, J. R. (2014). A probabilistic, dynamic, and attribute-wise model of intertemporal choice. *Journal of Experimental Psychology: General, 143*(4), 1489–1514.

Dalal, R. S., & Bonaccio, S. (2010). What types of advice do decision-makers prefer? *Organizational Behavior and Human Decision Processes, 112*(1), 11–23.

Dale, E., & Chall, J. S. (1948). A formula for predicting readability. *Educational Research Bulletin, 27*, 11–20, 37–54.

Dalgleish, T. (1995). Performance on the emotional stroop task in groups of anxious, expert, and control subjects: A comparison of computer and card presentation formats. *Cognition & Emotion, 9*(4), 341–362.

Daly, S. (1978). Behavioural correlates of social anxiety. *British Journal of Social & Clinical Psychology, 17*(2), 117–120.

Damasio, A. R. (1994). *Descartes' error: Emotion, reason, and the human brain.* New York: G. P. Putnam.

Damasio, A. R., Tranel, D., & Damasio, H. (1990). Individuals with sociopathic behavior caused by frontal damage fail to respond autonomically to social stimuli. *Behavioural Brain Research, 41*(2), 81–94.

Daneman, M., & Carpenter, P. A. (1980). Individual differences in working memory and reading. *Journal of Verbal Learning & Verbal Behavior, 19*(4), 450–466.

Daneman, M., & Carpenter, P. A. (1983). Individual differences in integrating information between and within sentences. *Journal of Experimental Psychology: Learning, Memory, and Cognition, 9*(4), 561–584.

Dansereau, D. F., Brooks, L. W., Spurlin, J. E., & Holley, C. D. (1982). *Headings and outlines as processing aids for scientific text* (National Institute of Education, Final Report, NIE-G-79–0157). Fort Worth, TX: Texas Christian University.

Das, E. H., de Wit, J. F., & Stroebe, W. (2003). Fear appeals motivate acceptance of action recommendations: Evidence for a positive bias in the processing of persuasive messages. *Personality and Social Psychology Bulletin, 29*(5), 650–664.

Davenport, J. S., & Smith, S. A. (1963). Effects of hyphenation, justified, and type size on readability. *Journalism Quarterly, 42*, 382–388.

Davidson, P. S. R., & Glisky, E. L. (2002). Is flashbulb memory a special instance of source memory? Evidence from older adults. *Memory, 10*(2), 99–111.

Davies, S., Haines, H., Norris, B., & Wilson, J. R. (1998). Safety pictograms: Are they getting the message across? *Applied Ergonomics, 29*(1), 15–23.

Davis, J. T. (1996). Experience and auditors' selection of relevant information for preliminary control risk assessments. *Auditing, 15*(1), 16–37.

Davis, M. A. (1992). Age and dress of professors: Influence on students' first impressions of teaching effectiveness (Doctoral dissertation, Virginia Polytechnic Institute and State University, 1992). *Dissertation Abstracts International, 53*(02B), 0806.

Davison, A., & Kantor, R. N. (1982). On the failure of readability formulas to define readable texts: A case study from adaptations. *Reading Research Quarterly, 17*(2), 187–209.

Dawes, R. M. (1971). A case study of graduate admissions: Application of three principles of human decision making. *American Psychologist, 26*(2), 180–188.

Dawes, R. M. (1976). Shallow psychology. In J. S. Carroll & J. W. Payne (Eds.), *Cognition and social behavior* (pp. 3–12). Hillsdale, NJ: Lawrence Erlbaum Associates.

Dawes, R. M. (1980). You can't systematize human judgment: Dyslexia. In R. A. Shweder (Ed.), *New directions for methodology of social and behavioral science* (Vol. 4, pp. 67–78). San Francisco: Jossey-Bass.

Dawes, R. M., & Corrigan, B. (1974). Linear models in decision making. *Psychological Bulletin, 81*(2), 95–106.

Dawes, R. M., Faust, D., & Meehl, P. E. (1989). Clinical versus actuarial judgment. *Science, 243*(4899), 1668–1674.

Day, S. B., & Gentner, D. (2007). Nonintentional analogical inference in text comprehension. *Memory & Cognition, 35*(1), 39–49.

Dearborn, D. C., & Simon, H. A. (1958). Selective perception: A note on the departmental identifications of executives. *Sociometry, 21*, 140–144.

De Blasio, A., & Veale, R. (2009). Why say sorry? Influencing consumer perceptions post organizational crises. *Australasian Marketing Journal, 17*(2), 75–83.

De Bondt, W. F. M., & Thaler, R. H. (1990). Do security analysis overreact? *The American Economic Review, 80*(2), 52–57.

de C. Hamilton, A. F., Wolpert, D. M., Frith, U., & Grafton, S. T. (2006). Where does your own action influence your perception of another person's action in the brain? *NeuroImage, 29*(2), 524–535.

DeChurch, L. A., & Mesmer-Magnus, J. R. (2010). The cognitive underpinnings of effective teamwork: A meta-analysis. *Journal of Applied Psychology, 95*(1), 32–53.

de Groot, A. D. (1965). *Thought and choice in chess.* The Hague, Netherlands: Mouton.

DeGroot, T., & Motowidlo, S. J. (1999). Why visual and vocal interview cues can affect interviewers' judgments and predict job performance. *Journal of Applied Psychology, 84*(6), 986–993.

De Hoog, N., Stroebe, W., & de Wit, J. F. (2005). The impact of fear appeals on processing and acceptance of health messages. *Personality and Social Psychology Bulletin, 31*(1), 24–33.

Deli Carpini, M. X. (2004). Mediating democratic engagement: The impact of communications on citizens' involvement in political and civil life. In L. L. Kaid (Ed.), *Handbook of political communication research* (pp. 395–434). Mahwah, NJ: Lawrence Erlbaum Associates.

Delplanque, S., Grandjean, D., Chrea, C., Coppin, G., Aymard, L., Cayeux, I., . . . & Scherer, K. R. (2009). Sequential unfolding of novelty and pleasantness appraisals of odors: Evidence from facial electromyography and autonomic reactions. *Emotion, 9*(3), 316–328.

de Martino, B., Kumaran, D., Seymour, B., & Dolan, R. J. (2006). Frames, biases, and rational decision-making in the human brain. *Science, 313*(5787), 684–687.

De Meyer, A. (1991). Tech talk: How managers are stimulating global R&D communication. *MIT Sloan Management Review, 32*(3), 49–59.

De Neys, W., Vartanian, O., & Goel, V. (2008). Smarter than we think when our brains detect that we are biased. *Psychological Science, 19*(5), 483–489.

Den Hartog, D. N., House, R. J., Hanges, P. J., Ruiz-Quintanilla, S. A., & Dorfman, P. W. (1999). Culture specific and cross-cultural generalizable implicit leadership theories: Are attributes of charismatic/transformational leadership universally endorsed? *Leadership Quarterly, 10*, 219–256.

Dennis, A. R. (1996). Information exchange and use in small group decision making. *Small Group Research, 27*(4), 532–550.

DePaulo, B. M., Rosenthal, R., Eisenstat, R. A., Rogers, P. L., & Finkelstein, S. (1978). Decoding discrepant nonverbal cues. *Journal of Personality and Social Psychology, 36*(3), 313–323.

DePaulo, B. M., Stone, J. I., & Lassiter, G. D. (1985). Deceiving and detecting deceit. In B. R. Schlenker (Ed.), *The self and social life* (pp. 323–370). New York: McGraw-Hill.

DePaulo, P. J., & DePaulo, B. M. (1989). Can deception by salespersons and customers be detected through nonverbal behavioral cues? *Journal of Applied Social Psychology, 19*(18, Pt. 2), 1552–1577.

Derryberry, D., & Tucker, D. M. (1992). Neural mechanisms of emotion. *Journal of Consulting and Clinical Psychology, 60*(3), 329–338.

Derryberry, D., & Tucker, D. M. (1994). Motivating the focus of attention. In P. M. Niedenthal & S. Kitayama (Eds.), *The heart's eye: Emotional influences in perception and attention* (pp. 167–196). San Diego, CA: Academic Press.

de Souza, J. M. B., & Dyson, M. (2008). Are animated demonstrations the clearest and most comfortable way to communicate on-screen instructions? *Information Design Journal, 16*(2), 107–124.

DeSteno, D., Petty, R. E., Rucker, D. D., Wegener, D. T., & Braverman, J. (2004). Discrete emotions and persuasion: The role of emotion-induced expectancies. *Journal of Personality and Social Psychology, 86*(1), 43–56.

DeSteno, D., Petty, R. E., Wegener, D. T., & Rucker, D. D. (2000). Beyond valence in the perception of likelihood: The role of emotion specificity. *Journal of Personality and Social Psychology, 78*(3), 397–416.

Detenber, B., & Reeves, B. (1996). A bio-information theory of emotion: Motion and image size effects on viewers. *Journal of Communication, 46*(3), 66–84.

deTurck, M. A., & Goldhaber, G. M. (1991). A developmental analysis of warning signs: The case of familiarity and gender. *Journal of Products Liability, 13*, 65–78.

Detweiler, J. B., Bedell, B. T., Salovey, P., Pronin, E., & Rothman, A. J. (1999). Message framing and sunscreen use: Gain-framed messages motivate beach-goers. *Health Psychology, 18*(2), 189–196.

de Villiers, P. A. (1974). Imagery and theme in recall of connected discourse. *Journal of Experimental Psychology, 103*(2), 263–268.

de Vries, G., Terwel, B. W., & Ellemers, N. (2014). Spare the details, share the relevance: The dilution effect in communications about carbon dioxide capture and storage. *Journal of Environmental Psychology, 38*, 116–123.

DeWitt, M. R., Knight, J. B., Hicks, J. L., & Ball, B. H. (2012). The effects of prior knowledge on the encoding of episodic contextual details. *Psychonomic Bulletin & Review, 19*(2), 251–257.

Dhami, M. K., & Ayton, P. (2001). Bailing and jailing the fast and frugal way. *Journal of Behavioral Decision Making, 14*(2), 141–168.

Dhar, R., & Simonson, I. (1992). The effect of the focus of comparison on consumer preferences. *Journal of Marketing Research, 29*(4), 430–440.

Dholakia, U. M., & Morwitz, V. G. (2002). The scope and persistence of mere-measurement effects: Evidence from a field study of customer satisfaction measurement. *Journal of Consumer Research, 29*(2), 159–167.

Diamond, D. S. (1968). A quantitative approach to magazine advertisement format selection. *Journal of Marketing Research, 5*(4), 376–386.

Diehl, M., & Stroebe, W. (1987). Productivity loss in brainstorming groups: Toward the solution of a riddle. *Journal of Personality and Social Psychology, 53*(3), 497–509.

Diekmann, K. A., Samuels, S. M., Ross, L., & Bazerman, M. H. (1997). Self-interest and fairness in problems of resource allocation: Allocators versus recipients. *Journal of Personality and Social Psychology, 72*(5), 1061–1074.

Diener, E., & Iran-Nejad, A. (1986). The relationship in experience between various types of affect. *Journal of Personality and Social Psychology, 50*(5), 1031–1038.

Diener, E., Nickerson, C., Lucas, R. E., & Sandvik, E. (2002). Dispositional affect and job outcomes. *Social Indicators Research, 59*(3), 229–259.

Dijksterhuis, A. P. (2010). Automaticity and the unconscious. In S. T. Fiske, D. T. Gilbert & G. Lindzey (Eds.), *Handbook of social psychology* (5th ed., Vol. 1, pp. 228–267). Hoboken, NJ: John Wiley & Sons.

Dijksterhuis, A., Macrae, C. N., & Haddock, G. (1999). When recollective experiences matter: Subjective ease of retrieval and stereotyping. *Personality and Social Psychology Bulletin, 25*(6), 766–774.

Dimberg, U. (1997). Psychophysiological reactions to facial expressions. In U. Segerstrale & P. Molnar (Eds.), *Nonverbal communication: Where nature meets culture* (pp. 47–60). Mahwah, NJ: Lawrence Erlbaum.

Dimberg, U., & Öhman, A. (1996). Behold the wrath: Psychophysiological responses to facial stimuli. *Motivation and Emotion Special Issue: Facial Expression and Emotion—The Legacy of John T. Lanzetta, 20*(2, Pt. 1), 149–182.

Dimberg, U., Thunberg, M., & Elmehed, K. (2000). Unconscious facial reactions to emotional facial expressions. *Psychological Science, 11*(1), 86–89.

Ding, Z., Sun, S. L., & Au, K. (2014). Angel investors' selection criteria: A comparative institutional perspective. *Asia Pacific Journal of Management, 31*(3), 705–731.

Ditto, P. H., & Lopez, D. F. (1992). Motivated skepticism: Use of differential decision criteria for preferred and nonpreferred conclusions. *Journal of Personality and Social Psychology, 63*(4), 568–584.

Donohew, L. (1981). Arousal and affective responses to writing styles. *Journal of Applied Communication Research, 9*, 109–119.

Donohew, L. (1982). Newswriting styles: What arouses the readers? *Newspaper Research Journal, 3*, 3–6.

Dooling, D. J., & Lachman, R. (1971). Effects of comprehension on retention of prose. *Journal of Experimental Psychology, 88*(2), 216–222.

Dooling, D. J., & Mullet, R. L. (1973). Locus of thematic effects in retention of prose. *Journal of Experimental Psychology, 97*(3), 404–406.

Doren, R. F., Trexler, J. C., Gottlieb, A. D., & Harwell, M. C. (2009). Ecological indicators for system-wide assessment of the greater everglades ecosystem restoration program. *Ecological Indicators, 9*(6), S2–S16.

Dougherty, T. W., Turban, D. B., & Callender, J. C. (1994). Confirming first impressions in the employment interview: A field study of interviewer behavior. *Journal of Applied Psychology, 79*(5), 659–665.

Douglas, K. S., Lyon, D. R., & Ogloff, J. R. P. (1997). The impact of graphic photographic evidence on mock jurors' decisions in a murder trial: Probative or prejudicial? *Law and Human Behavior, 21*(5), 485–501.

Dovidio, J. F., & Ellyson, S. L. (1982). Decoding visual dominance: Attributions of power based on relative percentages of looking while speaking and looking while listening. *Social Psychology Quarterly, 45*(2), 106–113.

Downing, P. E., Bray, D., Rogers, J., & Childs, C. (2004). Bodies capture attention when nothing is expected. *Cognition, 93*(1), B27–B38.

Downs, A. (1994). *Inside bureaucracy.* Prospect Heights, IL: Waveland.

Doyle, A. E. (1990). Readers' and writers' genre expectations in letters of recommendation: Two case studies (Doctoral dissertation, University of Illinois at Chicago, 1990). *Dissertation Abstracts International, 52*(01A), 0209.

Dreisbach, G., & Fischer, R. (2011). If it's hard to read… try harder! Processing fluency as signal for effort adjustments. *Psychological Research, 75*(5), 376–383.

Drew, C. J., Altman, R., & Dykes, M. K. (1971). Evaluation of instructional materials as a function of material complexity and teacher manual format (Working Paper No. 10). Unpublished manuscript, Texas University, 1971 (ERIC Document Reproduction Service No. ED 079916).

Drezner, D. W. (2000). Ideas, bureaucratic politics, and the crafting of foreign policy. *American Journal of Political Science, 44*(4), 733–749.

Drieghe, D., Rayner, K., & Pollatsek, A. (2005). Eye movements and word skipping during reading revisited. *Journal of Experimental Psychology: Human Perception and Performance, 31*(5), 954–969.

Driskell, J. E., & Radtke, P. H. (2003). The effect of gesture on speech production and comprehension. *Human Factors: The Journal of the Human Factors and Ergonomics Society, 45*(3), 445–454.

Driver, J., IV, Davis, G., Ricciardelli, P., Kidd, P., Maxwell, E., & Baron-Cohen, S. (1999). Gaze perception triggers reflexive visuospatial orienting. *Visual Cognition, 6*(5), 509–540.

Druckman, J. N. (2001a). On the limits of framing effects: Who can frame? *Journal of Politics, 63,* 1041–1066.

Druckman, J. N. (2001b). Using credible advice to overcome framing effects. *Journal of Law, Economics, & Organization, 17,* 62–82.

Druckman, J. N., & Holmes, J. W. (2004). Does presidential rhetoric matter? Priming and presidential approval. *Presidential Studies Quarterly, 34*(4), 755–778.

DuBay, W. H. (2004). *The principles of readability.* Costa Mesa, CA: Impact Information. (ERIC Document Reproduction Service Number ED 490 073).

Dubinsky, A. J., & Skinner, S. J. (1984). Impact of job characteristics on retail salespeople's reactions to their jobs. *Journal of Retailing, 60*(2), 35–62.

Dubois, M., & Pansu, P. (2004). Facial attractiveness, applicants' qualifications, and judges' expertise about decisions in pre-selective recruitment. *Psychological Reports, 95*(3f), 1129–1134.

Duchastel, P. C. (1979). *A functional approach to illustrations in text* (Occasional Paper 2). Bryn Mawr, PA: The American College.

Duchastel, P. C. (1980). *Research on illustrations in instructional texts* (Occasional Paper 3). Bryn Mawr, PA: The American College.

Duffy, S. A., & Keir, J. A. (2004). Violating stereotypes: Eye movements and comprehension processes when text conflicts with world knowledge. *Memory and Cognition, 32*(4), 551–559.

Duffy, T. M., & Kabance, P. (1982). Testing a readable writing approach to text revision. *Journal of Educational Psychology, 74*(5), 733–748.

Duggan, G. B., & Payne, S. J. (2009). Text skimming: The process and effectiveness of foraging through text under time pressure. *Journal of Experimental Psychology: Applied, 15*(3), 228–242.

Duhachek, A., Agrawal, N., & Han, D. (2012). Guilt versus shame: Coping, fluency, and framing in the effectiveness of responsible drinking messages. *Journal of Marketing Research, 49*(6), 928–941.

Duker, S. (1974). *Time compressed speech: An anthology and bibliography* (Vol. 3). Metuchen, NJ: Scarecrow Press.

Dulewicz, V., & Herbert, P. (1999). The priorities and performance of boards in UK public companies. *Corporate Governance: An International Review, 7*(2), 178–189.

Dunbar, G. (2010). Task-based nutrition labelling. *Appetite, 55*(3), 431–435.

Dunning, D. (1999). A newer look: Motivated social cognition and the schematic representation of social concepts. *Psychological Inquiry, 10*(1), 1–11.

Dupont, V., & Bestgen, Y. (2002). Structure and topic information in expository text overviews. *Document Design, 3*(1), 2–12.

Durik, A. M., & Harackiewicz, J. M. (2007). Different strokes for different folks: How individual interest moderates the effects of situational factors on task interest. *Journal of Educational Psychology, 99*(3), 597–610.

Dyson, M. C. (2004). How physical text layout affects reading from screen. *Behaviour & Information Technology*, *23*(6), 377–393.

Dyson, M. C., & Haselgrove, M. (2001). The influence of reading speed and line length on the effectiveness of reading from screen. *International Journal of Human-Computer Studies*, *54*(4), 585–612.

Eagly, A. H. (1974). Comprehensibility of persuasive arguments as a determinant of opinion change. *Journal of Personality and Social Psychology*, *29*(6), 758–773.

Eagly, A. H., & Warren, R. (1976). Intelligence, comprehension, and opinion change. *Journal of Personality*, *44*(2), 226–242.

Eastwood, J. D., Smilek, D., & Merikle, P. M. (2001). Differential attentional guidance by unattended faces expressing positive and negative emotion. *Perception & Psychophysics*, *63*(6), 1004–1013.

Ebbesen, E. B. (1980). Cognitive processes in understanding ongoing behavior. In R. Hastie, T. M. Ostrom, C. B. Ebbesen, R. S. Wyer, D. L. Hamilton & E. L. Carlston (Eds.), *Person memory: The cognitive basis of social perception* (pp. 179–225). Hillsdale, NJ: Lawrence Erlbaum Associates.

Eccles, D. W., & Tenenbaum, G. (2004). Why an expert team is more than a team of experts: A social-cognitive conceptualization of team coordination and communication in sport. *Journal of Sport & Exercise Psychology*, *26*(4), 542–560.

Ecker, U. K., Lewandowsky, S., Chang, E. P., & Pillai, R. (2014). The effects of subtle misinformation in news headlines. *Journal of Experimental Psychology: Applied*, *20*(4), 323–335.

Edell, J. A., & Burke, M. C. (1986). The relative impact of prior brand attitude and attitude toward the ad on brand attitude after ad exposure. In J. C. Olson & K. Sentis (Eds.), *Advertising and consumer psychology* (Vol. 3, pp. 93–107). New York: Praeger.

Eden, D., & Leviatan, U. (1975). Implicit leadership theory as a determinant of the factor structure underlying supervisory behavior scales. *Journal of Applied Psychology*, *60*(6), 736–741.

Edinger, J. A., & Patterson, M. L. (1983). Nonverbal involvement and social control. *Psychological Bulletin*, *93*(1), 30–56.

Edmondson, A. C. (1996). Learning from mistakes is easier said than done: Group and organizational influences on the detection and correction of human error. *Journal of Applied Behavioural Sciences*, *32*(1), 5–32.

Edmondson, A. C. (2003). Speaking up in the operating room: How team leaders promote learning in interdisciplinary action teams. *Journal of Management Studies*, *40*(6), 1419–1452.

Edwards, A., Elwyn, G., Covey, J., Matthews, E., & Pill, R. (2001). Presenting risk information a review of the effects of framing and other manipulations on patient outcomes. *Journal of Health Communication*, *6*(1), 61–82.

Edwards, K., & Bryan, T. S. (1997). Judgmental biases produced by instructions to disregard: The (paradoxical) case of emotional information. *Personality and Social Psychology Bulletin*, *23*(8), 849–864.

Edwards, W., & Newman, J. R. (1986). Multiattribute evaluation. In H. R. Arkes & K. R. Hammond (Eds.), *Judgment and decision making: An interdisciplinary reader* (pp. 13–37). New York: Cambridge University Press.

Edworthy, J., Hellier, E., Morley, N., Grey, C., Aldrich, K., & Lee, A. (2004). Linguistic and location effects in compliance with pesticide warning labels for amateur and professional users. *Human Factors: The Journal of the Human Factors and Ergonomics Society*, *46*(1), 11–31.

Egan, G. J., Brown, R. T., Goonan, L., Goonan, B. T., & Celano, M. (1998). The development of decoding of emotions in children with externalizing behavioral disturbances and their normally developing peers. *Archives of Clinical Neuropsychology*, *13*(4), 383–396.

Eger, E., Jedynak, A., Iwaki, T., & Skrandies, W. (2003). Rapid extraction of emotional expression: Evidence from evoked potential fields during brief presentation of face stimuli. *Neuropsychologia*, *41*(7), 808–817.

Ehrlich, K., & Rayner, K. (1983). Pronoun assignment and semantic integration during reading: Eye movements and immediacy of processing. *Journal of Verbal Learning & Verbal Behavior*, *22*(1), 75–87.

Ehrlich, S. F., & Rayner, K. (1981). Contextual effects on word perception and eye movements during reading. *Journal of Verbal Learning and Verbal Behavior*, *20*(6), 641–655.

Eils, L. C., & John, R. S. (1980). A criterion validation of multiattribute utility analysis and of group communication strategy. *Organizational Behavior & Human Performance*, *25*(2), 268–288.

Einhorn, H. J. (1972). Expert measurement and mechanical combination. *Organizational Behavior & Human Performance*, *7*(1), 86–106.

Einhorn, H. J., & Hogarth, R. M. (1981). Behavioral decision theory: Processes of judgment and choice. *Annual Review of Psychology*, *32*, 53–88.

Eisen, S. V., & McArthur, L. Z. (1979). Evaluating and sentencing a defendant as a function of his salience and the perceiver's set. *Personality and Social Psychology Bulletin*, *5*(1), 48–52.

Eisenberg, N., Fabes, R. A., Miller, P. A., Fultz, J., Shell, R., Mathy, R. M., & Reno, R. R. (1989). Relation of sympathy and distress to prosocial behavior: A multi-method study. *Journal of Personality and Social Psychology*, *57*(1), 55–66.

Ekman, P. (1971). Universals and cultural differences in facial expressions of emotion. In J. K. Cole (Ed.), *Nebraska symposium on motivation* (pp. 207–283). Lincoln, NE: University of Nebraska Press.

Ekman, P. (1982). *Emotion in the human face* (2nd ed.). Cambridge, UK: Cambridge University Press.

Ekman, P., & Friesen, W. V. (1978). *Facial action coding system: A technique for the measurement of facial movement.* Palo Alto, CA: Consulting Psychologists Press.

Ekman, P., Friesen, W. V., O'Sullivan, M., Chan, A., Diacoyanni-Tarlatzis, I., Heider, K., . . . & Tzavaras, A. (1987). Universals and cultural differences in the judgments of facial expressions of emotion. *Journal of Personality and Social Psychology, 53*(4), 712–717.

El-Alayli, A., Myers, C. J., Petersen, T. L., & Lystad, A. L. (2008). "I don't mean to sound arrogant, but . . ." The effects of using disclaimers on person perception. *Personality and Social Psychology Bulletin, 34*(1), 130–143.

Elfenbein, H. A., & Ambady, N. (2002). On the universality and cultural specificity of emotion recognition: A meta-analysis. *Psychological Bulletin, 128*(2), 203–235.

Ellsworth, P. C. (1994). Levels of thought and levels of emotion. In P. Ekman & R. J. Davidson (Eds.), *The nature of emotion: Fundamental questions* (pp. 192–196). New York: Oxford University Press.

Ellsworth, P. C., & Scherer, K. R. (2003). Appraisal processes in emotion. In R. J. Davidson, K. R. Scherer & H. H. Goldsmith (Eds.), *Handbook of affective sciences* (pp. 572–595). New York: Oxford University Press.

Ellsworth, P. C., & Smith, C. A. (1988). From appraisal to emotion: Differences among unpleasant feelings. *Motivation and Emotion, 12*(3), 271–302.

Emrich, C. G. (1999). Context effects in leadership perception. *Personality and Social Psychology Bulletin, 25*(8), 991–1006.

Emrich, C. G., Brower, H. H., Feldman, J. M., & Garland, H. (2001). Images in words: Presidential rhetoric, charisma, and greatness. *Administrative Science Quarterly, 46,* 527–557.

Endsley, M. R. (2006). Expertise and situation awareness. In K. A. Ericsson, N. Charness, P. Feltovich & R. Hoffman (Eds.), *The Cambridge handbook of expertise and expert performance* (pp. 633–651). Cambridge, UK: Cambridge University Press.

Englis, B. G. (1991). Consumer emotional reactions to television advertising and their effects on message recall. In S. J. Agres, J. A. Edell & T. M. Dubitsky (Eds.), *Emotion in advertising: Theoretical and practical explorations* (pp. 231–253). Westport, CN: Greenwood Press.

Englis, B. G. (1990). Consumer emotional reactions to television advertising and their effects on message recall. In S. J. Agres, J. A. Edell & T. M. Dubitsky (Eds.), *Emotion in advertising: Theoretical and practical explorations* (pp. 231–253). New York: Quorum Books.

Englis, B. G. (1994). The role of affect in political advertising: Voter emotional responses to the nonverbal behavior of politicians. In E. M. Clark, T. C. Brock & D. W. Stewart (Eds.), *Attention, attitude, and affect in response to advertising* (pp. 223–247). Hillsdale, NJ: Lawrence Erlbaum Associates.

Englis, B. G., & Reid, D. (1990). Salesperson expressions of emotions influence personal selling outcomes. *Proceedings of the Society for Consumer Psychology,* 79–83.

Engstrom, E. (1994). Effects of nonfluencies on speaker's credibility in newscast settings. *Perceptual and Motor Skills, 78*(3, Pt. 1), 739–743.

Epitropaki, O., & Martin, R. (2004). Implicit leadership theories in applied settings: Factor structure, generalizability, and stability over time. *Journal of Applied Psychology, 89*(2), 293–310.

Epley, N., & Dunning, D. (2000). Feeling "holier than thou": Are self-serving assessments produced by errors in self-or social prediction? *Journal of Personality and Social Psychology, 79*(6), 861–875.

Epley, N., & Dunning, D. (2004). The mixed blessing of self-knowledge in behavioral prediction. Unpublished manuscript, Cornell University, Ithaca, NY.

Epley, N., Mak, D., & Idson, L. C. (2006). Bonus or rebate? The impact of income framing on spending and saving. *Journal of Behavioral Decision Making, 19*(3), 213–227.

Erb, H. P., Bohner, G., Rank, S., & Einwiller, S. (2002). Processing minority and majority communications: The role of conflict with prior attitudes. *Personality and Social Psychology Bulletin, 28*(9), 1172–1182.

Erber, R., & Fiske, S. T. (1984). Outcome dependency and attention to inconsistent information. *Journal of Personality and Social Psychology, 47*(4), 709–726.

Erev, I., & Cohen, B. L. (1990). Verbal versus numerical probabilities: Efficiency, biases, and the preference paradox. *Organizational Behavior and Human Decision Processes, 45*(1), 1–18.

Erickson, B., Lind, E. A., Johnson, B. C., & O'Barr, W. M. (1978). Speech style and impression formation in a court setting: The effects of "powerful" and "powerless" speech. *Journal of Experimental Social Psychology, 14*(3), 266–279.

Ericsson, K. A. (2001). Protocol analysis in psychology. In N. Smelser & P. Baltes (Eds.), *International encyclopedia of the social and behavioral sciences* (pp. 12256–12262). Oxford, UK: Elsevier.

Ericsson, K. A. (2006a). Protocol analysis and expert thought: Concurrent verbalizations of thinking during experts' performance on representative tasks. In K. A. Ericsson, N. Charness, P. Feltovich & R. Hoffman

(Eds.), *The Cambridge handbook of expertise and expert performance* (pp. 223–241). Cambridge, UK: Cambridge University Press.

Ericsson, K. A. (2006b). The influence of experience and deliberate practice on the development of superior expert performance. In K. A. Ericsson & N. Charness (Eds.), *The Cambridge handbook of expertise and expert performance* (pp. 683–703). Cambridge: Cambridge University Press.

Ericsson, K. A., & Lehmann, A. C. (1996). Expert and exceptional performance: Evidence on maximal adaptations on task constraints. *Annual Review of Psychology, 47*, 273–305.

Ericsson, K. A., & Simon, H. A. (1993). *Protocol analysis: Verbal reports as data* (revised edition). Cambridge, MA: Bradford Books/MIT Press.

Escalas, J. E. (2007). Self-referencing and persuasion: Narrative transportation versus analytical elaboration. *Journal of Consumer Research, 33*(4), 421–429.

Escalas, J. E., & Luce, M. F. (2004). Understanding the effects of process-focused versus outcome-focused thought in response to advertising. *Journal of Consumer Research, 31*(2), 274–285.

Eslinger, P. J., & Damasio, A. R. (1985). Severe disturbance of higher cognition after bilateral frontal lobe ablation: Patient EVR. *Neurology, 35*(12), 1731–1741.

Espinosa, J. A., & Carley, K. M. (2001). *Measuring team mental models.* Paper presented at the Academy of Management Conference Organizational Communication and Information Systems Division, Washington, DC.

Esteves, F., Dimberg, U., & Öhman, A. (1994). Automatically elicited fear: Conditioned skin conductance responses to masked facial expressions. *Cognition & Emotion, 8*(5), 393–413.

Estrada, C. A., Isen, A. M., & Young, M. J. (1997). Positive affect facilitates integration of information and decreases anchoring in reasoning among physicians. *Organizational Behavior and Human Decision Processes, 72*(1), 117–135.

Etzioni, A. (1992). Normative-affective factors: Toward a new decision-making model. In M. Zey (Ed.), *Decision making: Alternatives to rational choice models* (pp. 89–111). Thousand Oaks, CA: Sage.

Evans, J. S. B., Clibbens, J., Cattani, A., Harris, A., & Dennis, I. (2003). Explicit and implicit processes in multicue judgment. *Memory & Cognition, 31*(4), 608–618.

Evans, R., Rozelle, R., Lasater, T., Dembroski, T., & Allen, B. (1970). Fear arousal, persuasion and actual vs. implied behavioral change. *Journal of Personality and Social Psychology, 16*(2), 220–227.

Eyrolle, H., Virbel, J., & Lemarié, J. (2008). Impact of incomplete correspondence between document titles and texts on users' representations: A cognitive and linguistic analysis based on 25 technical documents. *Applied Ergonomics, 39*(2), 241–246.

Fader, P. S., & Lattin, J. M. (1993). Accounting for heterogeneity and nonstationarity in a cross-sectional model of consumer purchase behavior. *Marketing Science, 12*(3), 304–317.

Fajardo, I., Ávila, V., Ferrer, A., Tavares, G., Gómez, M., & Hernández, A. (2014). Easy-to-read texts for students with intellectual disability: Linguistic factors affecting comprehension. *Journal of Applied Research in Intellectual Disabilities, 27*(3), 212–225.

Fanelli, A., Misangyi, V. F., & Tosi, H. L. (2009). In charisma we trust: The effects of CEO charismatic visions on securities nalysts. *Organization Science, 20*(6), 1011–1033.

Fang, X., Singh, S., & Ahluwalia, R. (2007). An examination of different explanations for the mere exposure effect. *Journal of Consumer Research, 34*(1), 97–103.

Faraj, S., & Sproull, L. (2000). Coordinating expertise in software development teams. *Management Science, 46*(12), 1554–1568.

Fast, L. A., & Funder, D. C. (2008). Personality as manifest in word use: Correlations with self-report, acquaintance report, and behavior. *Journal of Personality and Social Psychology, 94*(2), 334–346.

Fazio, L. K., Brashier, N. M., Payne, B. K., & Marsh, E. J. (2015). Knowledge does not protect against illusory truth. *Journal of Experimental Psychology: General, 144*(5), 993–1002.

Fazio, R. H. (1989). On the power and functionality of attitudes: The role of attitude accessibility. In A. R. Pratkanis, S. J. Breckler & A. G. Greenwald (Eds.), *Attitude structure and function* (pp. 153–179). Hillsdale, NJ: Lawrence Erlbaum Associates.

Feingold, A. (1992). Good-looking people are not what we think. *Psychological Bulletin, 111*(2), 304–341.

Feldman, C., & Kalmar, D. (1996). Autobiography and fiction as modes of thought. In D. Olson & N. Torrance (Eds.), *Modes of thought: Explorations in culture and cognition* (pp. 106–122). Cambridge, UK: Cambridge University Press.

Feldman, M. S., & March, J. G. (1981). Information in organizations as signal and symbol. *Administrative Science Quarterly, 26*(2), 171–186.

Feldman, S. (1988). Structure and consistency in public opinion: The role of core beliefs and values. *American Journal of Political Science, 32*(2), 416–440.

Felker, D. B., Redish, J. C., & Peterson, J. (1985). Training authors of informative documents. In T. Duffy & R. Walker (Eds.), *Designing usable texts* (pp. 43–61). New York: Academic Press.

Fellows, L. K. (2006). Deciding how to decide: Ventromedial frontal lobe damage affects information acquisition in multi-attribute decision making. *Brain, 129*(4), 944–952.

Felsenfeld, C. (1991). The plain English experience in New York. In E. R. Steinberg (Ed.), *Plain language: Principles and practice* (pp. 13–18). Detroit, MI: Wayne State University Press.

Felsenfeld, C., & Siegel, A. (1981). *Writing contracts in plain English*. St. Paul, MN: West Publishing Co.

Feltovich, P. J., Prietula, M. J., & Ericsson, K. A. (2006). Studies of expertise from psychological perspectives. In K. A. Ericsson, N. Charness, P. J. Feltovich & R. Hoffman (Eds.), *The Cambridge handbook of expertise and expert performance* (pp. 41–67). Cambridge, UK: Cambridge University Press.

Fennis, B. M., & Janssen, L. (2010). Mindlessness revisited: Sequential request techniques foster compliance by draining self-control resources. *Current Psychology, 29*(3), 235–246.

Ferreira, F. A., Santos, S. P., Marques, C. S., & Ferreira, J. (2014). Assessing credit risk of mortgage lending using MACBETH: A methodological framework. *Management Decision, 52*(2), 182–206.

Fiedler, K. (1982). Causal schemata: Review and criticism of research on a popular construct. *Journal of Personality and Social Psychology, 42*, 1001–1013.

Fiedler, K. (2000). Toward an integrative account of affect and cognition phenomena using the BIAS computer algorithm. In J. P. Forgas (Ed.), *Feeling and thinking: The role of affect in social cognition* (pp. 223–252). New York, NY: Cambridge University Press.

Fiedler, K., & Schenck, W. (2001). Spontaneous inferences from pictorially presented behaviors. *Personality and Social Psychological Bulletin, 27*, 1533–1546.

Fielding, G., & Evered, C. (1978). An exploratory experimental study of the influence of patients' social background upon diagnostic process and outcome. *Psychiatria Clinica, 11*(2), 61–86.

Fielding, K. S., & Hogg, M. A. (1997). Social identity, self-categorization, and leadership: A field study of small interactive groups. *Group Dynamics: Theory, Research, and Practice, 1*, 39–51.

Fienberg, S. E. (1979). Graphical methods in statistics. *The American Statistician, 33*, 165–178.

Fillmore, C. J. (1968). The case for case. In E. Bach & R. T. Harms (Eds.), *Universals of linguistic theory* (pp. 1–88). New York, NY: Holt, Rinehart, and Winston.

Findahl, O. (1971). *The effects of visual illustrations upon perception and retention of news programmes*. Stockholm, Sweden: Swedish Broadcasting Corporation, Audience and Program Research Department.

Findahl, O., & Hoijer, B. (1976). *Fragments of reality: An experiment with news and TV visuals*. Stockholm, Sweden: Swedish Broadcasting Corporation, Audience and Program Research Department.

Finkel, E. J., Campbell, W. K., Brunell, A. B., Dalton, A. N., Scarbeck, S. J., & Chartrand, T. L. (2006). High-maintenance interaction: Inefficient social coordination impairs self-regulation. *Journal of Personality and Social Psychology, 91*(3), 456–475.

Finucane, M. L., Alhakami, A., Slovic, P., & Johnson, S. M. (2000). The affect heuristic in judgments of risks and benefits. *Journal of Behavioral Decision Making, 13*(1), 1–17.

Finucane, M. L., Peters, E., & Slovic, P. (2003). Judgment and decision making: The dance of affect and reason. In S. L. Schneider & J. Shanteau (Eds.), *Emerging perspectives on judgment and decision research* (pp. 327–364). New York: Cambridge University Press.

Fischer, M. H. (2000). Do irrelevant depth cues affect the comprehension of bar graphs? *Applied Cognitive Psychology, 14*(2), 151–162.

Fischhoff, B., & Johnson, S. (1997). The possibility of distributed decision making. In Z. Shapira (Ed.), *Organizational decision making* (pp. 217–237). New York: Cambridge University Press.

Fischhoff, B., & MacGregor, D. (1980). *Judged lethality*. Decision Research Report 80–4. Eugene, OR: Decision Research.

Fischhoff, B., Slovic, P., & Lichtenstein, S. (1978). Fault trees: Sensitivity of estimated failure probabilities to problem representation. *Journal of Experimental Psychology: Human Perception and Performance, 4*(2), 330–344.

Fishfader, V. L., Howells, G. N., Katz, R. C., & Teresi, P. S. (1996). Evidential and extralegal factors in juror decisions: Presentation mode, retention, and level of emotionality. *Law and Human Behavior, 20*(5), 565–572.

Fiske, S. T. (1980). Attention and weight in person perception: The impact of negative and extreme behavior. *Journal of Personality and Social Psychology, 38*(6), 889–906.

Fiske, S. T. (2010). Interpersonal stratification: Status, power, and subordination. In S. T. Fiske, D. T. Gilbert & G. Lindzey (Eds.), *Handbook of social psychology* (5th ed., Vol. 1, pp. 941–982). Hoboken, NJ: John Wiley & Sons.

Fiske, S. T., & Depret, E. (1996). Control, interdependence and power: Understanding social cognition in its social context. In W. Stroebe & M. Hewstone (Eds.), *European review of social psychology* (Vol. 7, pp. 31–61). New York: Wiley.

Fiske, S. T., & Kinder, D. R. (1981). Involvement, expertise, and schema use: Evidence from political cognition. In N. Cantor & J. Kihlstrom (Eds.), *Personality, cognition, and social interaction* (pp. 171–190). Hillsdale, NJ: Lawrence Erlbaum Associates.

Fiske, S. T., Lin, M., & Neuberg, S. L. (1999). The continuum model: Ten years later. In S. Chaiken & Y. Trope (Eds.), *Dual-process theories in social psychology* (pp. 231–254). New York: Guilford Press.

Fiske, S. T., & Neuberg, S. L. (1990). A continuum of impression formation, from category-based to individuating processes: Influences of information and motivation on attention and interpretation. In M. P. Zanna (Ed.), *Advances in experimental social psychology* (Vol. 23, pp. 1–74). New York: Academic Press.

Fiske, S. T., & Taylor, S. E. (1991). *Social cognition* (2nd ed.). New York: McGraw-Hill.

Flavell, J. H. (1979). Metacognition and cognitive monitoring: A new area of cognitive-developmental inquiry. *American Psychologist, 34*(10), 906–911.

Fleming, M. L., & Sheikhian, M. (1972). Influence of pictorial attributes on recognition memory. *AV Communication Review, 20*(4), 423–441.

Flesch, R. (1948). A new readability yardstick. *Journal of Applied Psychology, 32*(3), 221–233.

Fleshier, H., Ilardo, J., & Demoretcky, J. (1974). The influence of field dependence, speaker credibility set, and message documentation on evaluations of speaker and message credibility. *Southern Speech Communication Journal, 39*, 389–402.

Fletcher-Watson, S., Findlay, J. M., Leekam, S. R., & Benson, V. (2008). Rapid detection of person information in a naturalistic scene. *Perception, 37*(4), 571–583.

Florack, A., & Zoabi, H. (2003). Risk behavior in share transactions: When investors think about reasons. *Zeitschrift für Sozialpsychologie, 34*(2), 65–78.

Flower, L. S., & Hayes, J. R. (1978). The dynamics of composing: Making plans and juggling constraints. In L. Gregg & I. Steinberg (Eds.), *Cognitive processes in writing* (pp. 31–50). Hillsdale, NJ: Lawrence Erlbaum Associates.

Flower, L. S., Hayes, J. R., & Swarts, H. (1983). Revising functional documents: The scenario principle. In P. V. Anderson, R. J. Brockmann & C. R. Miller (Eds.), *New essays in technical and scientific communication* (pp. 41–58). New York: Baywood Press.

Fodor, J. A., Bever, T. G., & Garrett, M. F. (1974). *The psychology of language: An introduction to psycholinguistics and generative grammar.* New York: McGraw-Hill.

Fombrun, C. (1996). *Reputation.* New York, NY: John Wiley & Sons.

Fong, G. T., & Markus, H. (1982). Self-schemas and judgments about others. *Social Cognition, 1*(3), 191–204.

Forbes, R. J., & Jackson, P. R. (1980). Non-verbal behaviour and the outcome of selection interviews. *Journal of Occupational Psychology, 53*(1), 65–72.

Forgas, J. P. (1992). On mood and peculiar people: Affect and person typicality in impression formation. *Journal of Personality and Social Psychology, 62*(5), 863–875.

Forgas, J. P. (1995). Mood and judgment: The affect infusion model (AIM). *Psychological Bulletin, 117*(1), 39–66.

Forgas, J. P. (1998). Asking nicely? The effects of mood on responding to more or less polite requests. *Personality and Social Psychology Bulletin, 24*(2), 173–185.

Forgas, J. P., & Bower, G. H. (1987). Mood effects on person-perception judgments. *Journal of Personality and Social Psychology, 53*(1), 53–60.

Foss, D. J., & Jenkins, C. M. (1973). Some effects of context on the comprehension of ambiguous sentences. *Journal of Verbal Learning & Verbal Behavior, 12*(5), 577–589.

Foster, J. J., & Bruce, M. (1982). Reading upper and lower case on viewdata. *Applied Ergonomics, 13*(2), 145–149.

Foster, J. J., & Coles, P. (1977). An experimental study of typographic cueing in printed text. *Ergonomics, 20*(1), 57–66.

Foti, R. J., Fraser, S. L., & Lord, R. G. (1982). Effects of leadership labels and prototypes on perceptions of political leaders. *Journal of Applied Psychology, 67*(3), 326–333.

Foulsham, T., & Underwood, G. (2007). How does the purpose of inspection influence the potency of visual salience in scene perception? *Perception, 36*(8), 1123–1138.

Fox Tree, J. E. (1995). The effects of false starts and repetitions on the processing of subsequent words in spontaneous speech. *Journal of Memory and Language, 34*(6), 709–738.

Fox Tree, J. E. (2002). Interpreting pauses and ums at turn exchanges. *Discourse Processes, 34*(1), 37–55.

Frame, C. D. (1990). Salesperson impression formation accuracy: A person-perception approach (Doctoral dissertation, Indiana University, 1990). *Dissertation Abstracts International, 51*(12A), 4199.

Frank, L. L., & Hackman, J. R. (1975). Effects of interviewer-interviewee similarity on interviewer objectivity in college admissions interviews. *Journal of Applied Psychology, 60*(3), 356–360.

Frase, L. T., & Fisher, D. (1976). *Rating technical documents.* Case 25952, Memorandum for File. Piscataway, NJ: Bell Laboratories.

Fraser, S. L., & Lord, R. G. (1988). Stimulus prototypicality and general leadership impressions: Their role in leadership and behavioral ratings. *Journal of Psychology: Interdisciplinary and Applied, 122*(3), 291–303.

Fraundorf, S. H., & Watson, D. G. (2011). The disfluent discourse: Effects of filled pauses on recall. *Journal of Memory and Language, 65*(2), 161–175.

Frazier, L., & Rayner, K. (1982). Making and correcting errors during sentence comprehension: Eye movements in the analysis of structurally ambiguous sentences. *Cognitive Psychology, 14*(2), 178–121.

Frazier, L., Taft, L., Roeper, T., Clifton, C., & Ehrlich, K. (1984). Parallel structure: A source of facilitation in sentence comprehension. *Memory & Cognition, 12*(5), 421–430.

Fredelius, G., Sandell, R., & Lindqvist, C. (2002). Who should receive subsidized psychotherapy? Analysis of decision makers' think-aloud protocols. *Qualitative Health Research, 12*(5), 640–654.

Frederick, S. (2002). Automated choice heuristics. In T. Gilovich, D. Griffin & D. Kahneman (Eds.), *Heuristics and biases: The psychology of intuitive judgment* (pp. 548–558). New York: Cambridge University Press.

Fredin, E. S. (2001). Frame breaking and creativity: A frame database for hypermedia news. In S. D. Reese, O. H. Gandy & A. E. Grant (Eds.), *Framing public life: Perspectives on media and our understanding of the social world* (pp. 269–293). Mahwah, NJ: Lawrence Erlbaum Associates.

Fredin, E. S., Kosicki, G. M., & Becker, L. B. (1996). Cognitive strategies for media use during a presidential campaign. *Political Communication, 13*, 23–42.

Fredrickson, B. L., & Levenson, R. W. (1998). Positive emotions speed recovery from the cardiovascular sequelae of negative emotions. *Cognition & Emotion, 12*(2), 191–220.

Fredrickson, J. W. (1985). Effects of decision motive and organizational performance level on strategic decision processes. *Academy of Management Journal, 28*(4), 821–843.

French, D. P., & Hevey, D. (2008). What do people think about when answering questionnaires to assess unrealistic optimism about skin cancer? A think aloud study. *Psychology, Health and Medicine, 13*(1), 63–74.

Frensch, P. A., & Sternberg, R. J. (1989). Expertise and intelligent thinking: When is it worse to know better? In R. J. Sternberg (Ed.), *Advances in the psychology of human intelligence* (Vol. 5, pp. 157–188). Hillsdale, NJ: Lawrence Erlbaum Associates.

Frick, R. W. (1985). Communicating emotion: The role of prosodic features. *Psychological Bulletin, 97*(3), 412–429.

Fridlund, A. J., Ekman, P., & Oster, H. (1987). Facial expressions of emotion. In A. W. Siegman & S. Feldstein (Eds.), *Nonverbal behavior and communication* (2nd ed., pp. 143–223). Hillsdale, NJ: Lawrence Erlbaum Associates.

Friederici, A. D. (2009). Pathways to language: Fiber tracts in the human brain. *Trends in Cognitive Sciences, 13*(4), 175–181.

Friedkin, N. E. (1999). Choice shift and group polarization. *American Sociological Review, 64*(6), 856–875.

Friedman, H. S., DiMatteo, M. R., & Mertz, T. I. (1980a). Nonverbal communication on television news: The facial expressions of broadcasters during coverage of a presidential election campaign. *Personality and Social Psychology Bulletin, 6*(3), 427–435.

Friedman, H. S., DiMatteo, M. R., & Taranta, A. (1980b). A study of the relationship between individual differences in nonverbal expressiveness and factors of personality and social interaction. *Journal of Research in Personality, 14*, 351–364.

Friedman, H. S., & Riggio, R. E. (1981). Effect of individual differences in nonverbal expressiveness on transmission of emotion. *Journal of Nonverbal Behavior, 6*(2), 96–104.

Friedman, K. (1988). The effect of adding symbols to written warning labels on user behavior and recall. *Human Factors, 30*, 507–515.

Friedrich, J., Fetherstonhaugh, D., Casey, S., & Gallagher, D. (1996). Argument integration and attitude change: Suppression effects in the integration of one-sided arguments that vary in persuasiveness. *Personality and Social Psychology Bulletin, 22*(2), 179–191.

Frieze, I. H., Olson, J. E., & Russell, J. (1991). Attractiveness and income for men and women in management. *Journal of Applied Social Psychology, 21*(13), 1039–1057.

Frijda, N. H. (1986). *The emotions.* New York: Cambridge University Press.

Frijda, N. H. (1988). The laws of emotion. *American Psychologist, 43*(5), 349–358.

Frijda, N. H., & Mesquita, B. (1994). The social roles and functions of emotions. In S. Kitayama & H. R. Markus (Eds.), *Emotion and culture: Empirical studies of mutual influence* (pp. 51–87). Washington, DC: American Psychological Association.

Fritzsche, B. A., & Brannick, M. T. (2002). The importance of representative design in judgment tasks: The case of resume screening. *Journal of Occupational and Organizational Psychology, 75*(2), 163–169.

Frundt, H. J. (2010). Sustaining labor-environmental coalitions: Banana allies in Costa Rica. *Latin American Politics and Society, 52*(3), 99–129.

Fujimaki, N., Hayakawa, T., Ihara, A., Wei, Q., Munetsuna, S., Terazono, Y., . . . & Murata, T. (2009). Early neural activation for lexico-semantic access in the left anterior temporal area analyzed by an fMRI-assisted MEG multidipole method. *Neuroimage, 44*(3), 1093–1102.

Funder, D. C., & Colvin, C. R. (1991). Explorations in behavioral consistency: Properties of persons, situations, and behaviors. *Journal of Personality and Social Psychology, 60*(5), 773–794.

Funder, D. C., & Sneed, C. D. (1993). Behavioral manifestations of personality: An ecological approach to judgmental accuracy. *Journal of Personality and Social Psychology, 64*(3), 479–490.

Futrell, C. M., Swan, J. S., & Todd, J. T. (1976). Job performance related to management control systems for pharmaceutical salesmen. *Journal of Marketing Research, 13*, 25–33.

Gaertner, S., & Bickman, L. (1971). Effects of race on the elicitation of helping behavior: The wrong number technique. *Journal of Personality and Social Psychology, 20*(2), 218–222.

Gaeth, G. J., & Shanteau, J. (1984). Reducing the influence of irrelevant information on experienced decision makers. *Organizational Behavior & Human Performance, 33*(2), 263–282.

Gaissmaier, W., Wegwarth, O., Skopec, D., Müller, A. S., Broschinski, S., & Politi, M. C. (2012). Numbers can be worth a thousand pictures: Individual differences in understanding graphical and numerical representations of health-related information. *Health Psychology, 31*(3), 286–296.

Gallagher, H. L., & Frith, C. D. (2004). Dissociable neural pathways for the perception and recognition of expressive and instrumental gestures. *Neuropsychologia, 42*(13), 1725–1736.

Galletta, D., King, R. C., & Rateb, D. (1993). The effect of expertise on software selection. *Association for Computing Machinery, 24*(2), 7–20.

Gallhofer, I. N., & Saris, W. E. (1996). *Foreign policy decision-making: A qualitative and quantitative analysis of policy argumentation*. Westport, CT: Praeger.

Gamson, W. A. (1992). *Talking politics*. New York: Cambridge University Press.

Gamson, W. A., & Modigliani, A. (1989). Media discourse and public opinion on nuclear power: A constructionist approach. *American Journal of Sociology, 95*(1), 1–37.

Garay, M. S. (1988). Writers making points: A case study of executives and college students revising their own reports (Doctoral dissertation, Carnegie Mellon University, 1988). *Dissertation Abstracts International, 49*(12A), 3645.

Garbarino, E. C., & Edell, J. A. (1997). Cognitive effort, affect, and choice. *Journal of Consumer Research, 24*(2), 147–158.

Garcia-Marques, T., & Mackie, D. M. (2000). The positive feeling of familiarity: Mood as an information processing regulation mechanism. In H. Bless & J. Forgas (Eds.), *The message within: The role of subjective experience in social cognition and behavior* (pp. 240–261). Philadelphia: Psychology Press.

Garcia-Marques, T., & Mackie, D. M. (2001). The feeling of familiarity as a regulator of persuasive processing. *Social Cognition, 19*(1), 9–34.

Gardner, E. T., & Schumacher, G. M. (1977). Effects of contextual organization on prose retention. *Journal of Educational Psychology, 69*(2), 146–151.

Gardner, M. P., Mitchell, A. A., & Russo, J. E. (1985). Low involvement strategies for processing advertisements. *Journal of Advertising, 14*(2), 4–13.

Garrod, S., Freudenthal, S., & Boyle, E. (1994). The role of different types of anaphor in the on-line resolution of sentences in a discourse. *Journal of Memory and Language, 33*(1), 39–68.

Gattis, M., & Holyoak, K. J. (1996a). Mapping conceptual to spatial relations in visual reasoning. *Journal of Experimental Psychology: Learning, Memory, and Cognition, 22*(1), 231–239.

Gattis, M., & Holyoak, K. J. (1996b). Mapping strategy determines whether frame influences treatment preferences for medical decisions. *Psychology and Aging, 26*(2), 285–294.

Gau, G. W. (1978). A taxonomic model for the risk-rating of residential mortgages. *Journal of Business, 51*(4), 687–706.

Gault, B. A., & Sabini, J. (2000). The roles of empathy, anger, and gender in predicting attitudes toward punitive, reparative, and preventative public policies. *Cognition & Emotion Special Issue: Emotion, Cognition, and Decision Making, 14*(4), 495–520.

Gauthier, I., Wong, A. C., Hayward, W. G., & Cheung, O. S. (2006). Font tuning associated with expertise in letter perception. *Perception, 35*(4), 541–559.

Gautier, V., O'Regan, J. K., & LaGargasson, I. F. (2000). "The skipping" revisited in French programming saccades to skip the article "les". *Vision Research, 40*, 2517–2531.

Gentner, D., & Forbus, K. D. (1991). MAC/FAC: A model of similarity-based access and mapping. In K. J. Hammond & D. Gentner (Eds.), *Proceedings of the thirteenth annual conference of the cognitive science society* (pp. 504–509). Hillsdale, NJ: Erlbaum.

Gentner, D., Loewenstein, J., Thompson, L., & Forbus, K. D. (2009). Reviving inert knowledge: Analogical abstraction supports relational retrieval of past events. *Cognitive Science, 33*(8), 1343–1382.

George, J. M. (1989). Mood and absence. *Journal of Applied Psychology, 74*(2), 317–324.

George, J. M. (1990). Personality, affect, and behavior in groups. *Journal of Applied Psychology, 75*(2), 107–116.

George, J. M., & Brief, A. P. (1992). Feeling good-doing good: A conceptual analysis of the mood at work-organizational spontaneity relationship. *Psychological Bulletin, 112*(2), 310–329.

Georgiadis, D. R., Mazzuchi, T. A., & Sarkani, S. (2013). Using multi criteria decision making in analysis of alternatives for selection of enabling technology. *Systems Engineering, 16*(3), 287–303.

Ger, G. (1989). Nature of effects of affect on judgment: Theoretical and methodological issues. In P. Cafferata & A. M. Tybout (Eds.), *Cognitive and affective responses to advertising* (pp. 263–275). Lexington, MA: Lexington Books.

Gernsacher, M. A., & Kaschak, M. P. (2003). Neuroimaging studies of language production and comprehension. *Annual Review of Psychology, 54*, 91–114.

Gerstner, C. R., & Day, D. V. (1994). Cross-cultural comparison of leadership prototypes. *The Leadership Quarterly, 5*(2), 121–134.

Gesierich, B., Jovicich, J., Riello, M., Adriani, M., Monti, A., Brentari, V., . . . & Gorno-Tempini, M. L. (2012). Distinct neural substrates for semantic knowledge and naming in the temporoparietal network. *Cerebral Cortex, 22*(10), 2217–2226.

Ghanem, S. (1997). Filling in the tapestry: The second level of agenda setting. In M. McCombs, D. L. Shaw & D. Weaver (Eds.), *Communication and democracy* (pp. 3–15). Mahwah, NJ: Lawrence Erlbaum Associates.

Ghiselli, E. E. (1969). Prediction of success of stockbrokers. *Personnel Psychology, 22*(2), 25–130.

Ghiselli, E. E. (1973). The validity of aptitude tests in personnel selection. *Personnel Psychology, 26*(4), 461–477.

Ghosh, V. E., & Gilboa, A. (2014). What is a memory schema? A historical perspective on current neuroscience literature. *Neuropsychologia, 53*, 104–114.

Ghosh, V. E., Moscovitch, M., Colella, B. M., & Gilboa, A. (2014). Schema representation in patients with ventromedial PFC lesions. *The Journal of Neuroscience, 34*(36), 12057–12070.

Gibbs, R. W., Jr., Leggitt, J. S., & Turner, E. A. (2002). What's special about figurative language in emotional communication? In S. R. Fussell (Ed.), *The verbal communication of emotions: Interdisciplinary perspectives* (pp. 125–149). Mahwah, NJ: Lawrence Erlbaum Associates.

Gibbs, W. J., & Bernas, R. S. (2009). Visual attention in newspaper versus TV-oriented news websites. *Journal of Usability Studies, 4*(4), 147–165.

Gibson, C. B. (2001). From knowledge accumulation to accommodation: Cycles of collective cognition in work groups. *Journal of Organizational Behavior, 22*(2), 121–134.

Gibson, E. J., Bishop, C., Schiff, W., & Smith, J. (1964). Comparison of meaningfulness and pronounceability as grouping principles in the perception and retention of verbal material. *Journal of Experimental Psychology, 67*(2), 173–182.

Gibson, R., & Zillmann, D. (1994). Exaggerated versus representative exemplification in news reports: Perception of issues and personal consequences. *Communication Research, 21*(5), 603–624.

Gick, M. L., & Holyoak, K. J. (1983). Schema induction and analogical transfer. *Cognitive Psychology, 15*(1), 1–38.

Gifford, R., & Hine, D. W. (1994). The role of verbal behavior in the encoding and decoding of interpersonal dispositions. *Journal of Research in Personality, 28*(2), 115–132.

Gifford, R., Ng, C. F., & Wilkinson, M. (1985). Nonverbal cues in the employment interview: Links between applicant qualities and interviewer judgments. *Journal of Applied Psychology, 70*(4), 729–736.

Gigerenzer, G., & Goldstein, D. G. (1996). Reasoning the fast and frugal way: Models of bounded rationality. *Psychological Review, 103*(4), 650–669.

Gigone, D., & Hastie, R. (1993). The common knowledge effect: Information sharing and group judgment. *Journal of Personality and Social Psychology, 65*(5), 959–974.

Gigone, D., & Hastie, R. (1997). The impact of information on small group choice. *Journal of Personality and Social Psychology, 72*(1), 132–140.

Gilbert, D. T. (1989). Thinking lightly about others: Automatic components of the social inference process. In J. S. Uleman & J. A. Bargh (Eds.), *Unintended thought* (pp. 189–211). New York: Guilford Press.

Gilbert, D. T. (2002). Inferential correction. In T. Gilovich, D. Griffin & D. Kahneman (Eds.), *Heuristics and biases: The psychology of intuitive judgment* (pp. 167–184). New York: Cambridge University Press.

Gilbert, D. T., Krull, D. S., & Malone, P. S. (1990). Unbelieving the unbelievable: Some problems in the rejection of false information. *Journal of Personality and Social Psychology, 59*(4), 601–613.

Gilbert, D. T., Pelham, B. W., & Krull, D. S. (1988). On cognitive busyness: When person perceivers meet persons perceived. *Journal of Personality and Social Psychology, 54*(5), 733–740.

Gilboa, A., & Moscovitch, M. (2002). The cognitive neuroscience of confabulation: A review and a model. In A. D. Baddeley, M. D. Kopelman & B. A. Wilson (Eds.), *Handbook of memory disorders* (2nd ed., pp. 315–342). Hoboken, NJ: John Wiley & Sons.

Gilens, M. (1999). *Why Americans hate welfare: Race, media, and the politics of antipoverty policy.* Chicago: University of Chicago Press.

Giles, H. (1973). Communicative effectiveness as a function of accented speech. *Speech Monographs, 40*(4), 330–331.

Giles, H. (1979). Ethnicity markers in speech. In K. R. Scherer & H. Giles (Eds.), *Social markers in speech* (pp. 251–289). Cambridge, UK: Cambridge University Press.

Giles, H., & Niedzielski, N. (1998). German sounds awful, but Italian is beautiful. In L. Bauer & P. Trudgill (Eds.), *Language myths* (pp. 85–93). Harmondsworth, UK: Penguin.

Giles, H., & Sassoon, C. (1983). The effect of speaker's accent, social class background and message style on British listeners' social judgements. *Language & Communication, 3*(3), 305–313.

Gill, D., & Ramaseshan, B. (2007). Influences on supplier repurchase selection of UK importers. *Marketing Intelligence & Planning, 25*(6), 597–611.

Gill, M. J., Swann, W. B., & Silvera, D. H. (1998). On the genesis of confidence. *Journal of Personality and Social Psychology, 75*(5), 1101–1114.

Gilovich, T. (1981). Seeing the past in the present: The effect of associations to familiar events on judgments and decisions. *Journal of Personality and Social Psychology, 40*(5), 797–808.

Gilovich, T., Kerr, M., & Medvec, V. H. (1993). The effect of temporal perspective on subjective confidence. *Journal of Personality and Social Psychology, 64*, 552–560.

Giraud, S., & Thérouanne, P. (2010, March). *Role of lexico-syntactic and prosodic cues in spoken comprehension of enumeration in sighted and blind adults.* Presented at the Multidisciplinary Approaches to Discourse Conference, Moissac, France.

Giske, R., Rodahl, S. E., & Høigaard, R. (2015). Shared mental task models in elite ice hockey and handball teams: Does it exist and how does the coach intervene to make an impact? *Journal of Applied Sport Psychology, 27*(1), 20–34.

Gitlin, T. (1980). *The whole world is watching.* Berkeley, CA: University of California Press.

Glad, B., & Taber, C. S. (1990). Images, learning, and the decision to use force: The domino theory of the United States. In B. Glad (Ed.), *Psychological dimensions of war* (pp. 56–81). Thousand Oaks, CA: Sage.

Glass, A. L., Eddy, J. K., & Schwanenflugel, P. J. (1980). The verification of high and low imagery sentences. *Journal of Experimental Psychology: Human Learning and Memory, 6*(6), 692–704.

Gleitman, L. R., & Gleitman, H. (1970). *Phrase and paraphrase: Some innovative uses of language.* New York: W. W. Norton & Company.

Glenberg, A. M., & Langston, W. E. (1992). Comprehension of illustrated text: Pictures help to build mental models. *Journal of Memory and Language, 31*(2), 129–151.

Glucksberg, S., & Cowen, G. N., Jr. (1970). Memory for nonattended auditory material. *Cognitive Psychology, 1*(2), 149–156.

Glucksberg, S., Trabasso, T., & Wald, J. (1973). Linguistic structures and mental operations. *Cognitive Psychology, 5*(3), 338–370.

Glynn, S. M., Britton, B. K., & Tillman, M. H. (1985). Typographical cues in text: Management of the reader's attention. In D. H. Jonassen (Ed.), *Technology of text: Principles for structuring, designing, and displaying text* (Vol. 2, pp. 192–209). Englewood Cliffs, NJ: Educational Technology Publications.

Glynn, S. M., & Di Vesta, F. J. (1979). Control of prose processing via instructional and typographical cues. *Journal of Educational Psychology, 71*(5), 595–603.

Gobet, F., & Simon, H. A. (1996). Templates in chess memory: A mechanism for recalling several boards. *Cognitive Psychology, 31*(1), 1–40.

Goetz, E. T., & Armbruster, B. B. (1980). Psychological correlates of text structure. In R. J. Spiro, B. C. Bruce & W. F. Brewer (Eds.), *Theoretical issues in reading comprehension: Perspectives from cognitive psychology, artificial intelligence, linguistics, and education* (pp. 201–220). Hillsdale, NJ: Erlbaum.

Goldberg, J. H., Lerner, J. S., & Tetlock, P. E. (1999). Rage and reason: The psychology of the intuitive prosecutor. *European Journal of Social Psychology, 29*(5–6), 781–795.

Goldberg, L. R. (1968). Simple models or simple processes? Some research on clinical judgments. *American Psychologist, 23*(7), 483–496.

Goldhaber, G. M., & deTurck, M. A. (1988). Effects of product warnings on adolescents in an education context. *Product Safety & Liability Reporter, 16*, 949–955.

Goldman, S. R., & Durán, R. P. (1988). Answering questions from oceanography texts: Learner, task, and text characteristics. *Discourse Processes, 11*(4), 373–412.

Goldsmith, E. (1987). The analysis of illustration in theory and practice. In H. A. Houghton & D. M. Willows (Eds.), *The psychology of illustration: Instructional issues* (Vol. 2, pp. 53–85). New York: Springer-Verlag.

Goldstein, M. N. (1974). Auditory agnosia for speech ("pure word deafness"): A historical review with current implications. *Brain and Language, 1*, 195–204.

Goldstein, W. M., & Weber, E. U. (1995). Content and discontent: Indications and implications of domain specificity in preferential decision making. In J. Busemeyer, D. Medin & R. Hastie (Eds.), *Decision-making from a cognitive perspective (the psychology of learning and motivation* (Vol. 32, pp. 83–136). San Diego, CA: Academic Press.

Goldwater, S., Jurafsky, D., & Manning, C. D. (2010). Which words are hard to recognize? Prosodic, lexical, and disfluency factors that increase speech recognition error rates. *Speech Communication, 52*(3), 181–200.

Goleman, D., Boyatzis, R. E., & McKee, A. (2002). *Primal leadership: Learning to lead with emotional intelligence.* Cambridge, MA: Harvard Business School Press.

Gombola, M., & Marciukaityte, D. (2007). Managerial overoptimism and the choice between debt and equity financing. *The Journal of Behavioral Finance, 8*(4), 225–235.

Gomez Borja, M. A. (2000). Effects of expertise and similarity of alternatives on consumer decision strategies and decision quality: A process tracing approach (Doctoral dissertation, Universidad de Castilla–La Mancha, 2000). *Dissertation Abstracts International, 62*(10A), 3479.

Gonzalez, S., Metzler, J., & Newton, M. (2011). The influence of a simulated 'pep talk' on athlete inspiration, situational motivation, and emotion. *International Journal of Sports Science and Coaching, 6*(3), 445–460.

Goodman, J., Loftus, E. F., & Greene, E. (1990). Matters of money: Voir dire in civil cases. *Forensic Reports, 3*, 303–329.

Goodstein, R. C. (1993). Category-based applications and extensions in advertising: Motivating more extensive ad processing. *Journal of Consumer Research, 20*(1), 87–99.

Goold, M. (1996). The (limited) role of the board. *Long Range Planning, 29*(4), 572–575.

Gordon, P. C., & Chan, D. (1995). Pronouns, passives, and discourse coherence. *Journal of Memory and Language, 34*(2), 216–231.

Gore, A., & Bush, G. W. (2000). *The first Gore–Bush presidential debate.* Retrieved November 9, 2009 from www.debates.org/pages/trans2000a.html.

Gotlib, I. H., McLachlan, A. L., & Katz, A. N. (1988). Biases in visual attention in depressed and nondepressed individuals. *Cognition & Emotion Special Issue: Information Processing and the Emotional Disorders, 2*(3), 185–200.

Goucha, T., & Friederici, A. D. (2015). The language skeleton after dissecting meaning: A functional segregation within Broca's area. *NeuroImage, 114*, 294–302.

Gough, P. B. (1966). The verification of sentences: The effects of delay of evidence and sentence length. *Journal of Verbal Learning and Verbal Behavior, 5*(5), 492–496.

Gould, J. D., Alfaro, L., Finn, R., Haupt, B., & Minuto, A. (1987). Reading from CRT displays can be as fast as reading from paper. *Human Factors, 29*(5), 497–517.

Gouldthorp, B. (2015). Hemispheric differences in the processing of contextual information during language comprehension. *Laterality: Asymmetries of Body, Brain and Cognition, 20*(3), 348–370.

Govaerts, M. J. B., Van de Wiel, M. W. J., Schuwirth, L. W. T., Van der Vleuten, C. P. M., & Muijtjens, A. M. M. (2013). Workplace-based assessment: Raters' performance theories and constructs. *Advances in Health Sciences Education, 18*(3), 375–396.

Graesser, A. C., & McNamara, D. S. (2011). Computational analyses of multilevel discourse comprehension. *Topics in Cognitive Science, 3*(2), 371–398.

Graf, R., & Torrey, J. W. (1966). Perception of phrase structure in written language. *Proceedings of the Annual Convention of the American Psychological Association*, 83–84.

Grafman, J. (1995). Similarities and distinctions among current models of prefrontal cortical functions. *Annals of the New York Academy of Sciences, 769*, 337–368.

Graham, J. A., Ricci-Bitti, P., & Argyle, M. (1975). A cross-cultural study of the communication of emotion by facial & gestural cues. *Journal of Human Movement Studies, 1*(2), 68–77.

Graham, J. R., & Harvey, C. R. (2001). The theory and practice of corporate finance: Evidence from the field. *Journal of Financial Economics, 60*(2, 3), 187–243.

Graonic, M. D. (1995). The effects of context and consumer knowledge on transferability of preferences (Doctoral dissertation, University of Minnesota, 1995). *Dissertation Abstracts International, 56*(07A), 2772.

Grass, R. C., & Wallace, W. H. (1974). Advertising communications: Print vs. TV. *Journal of Advertising Research, 14*(5), 19–23.

Graves, L. M., & Powell, G. N. (1988). An investigation of sex discrimination in recruiters' evaluations of actual applicants. *Journal of Applied Psychology, 73*(1), 20–29.

Graves, M. F., & Slater, W. H. (1986). Could textbooks be better written and would it make a difference? *American Educator, 10*(1), 36–42.

Gray, H. M., & Ambady, N. (2006). Methods for the study of nonverbal communication. In V. Manusov & M. L. Patterson (Eds.), *The SAGE handbook of nonverbal communication* (pp. 41–58). Thousand Oaks, CA: Sage.

Gray, J. A. (1987). *The psychology of fear and stress* (2nd ed.). New York, NY: Cambridge University Press.

Gray, J. A. (1994). Three fundamental emotion systems. In P. Ekman & R. J. Davidson (Eds.), *The nature of emotion* (pp. 243–247). New York, NY: Oxford University Press.

Grayson, C., & Schwarz, N. (1999). Beliefs influence information processing strategies: Declarative and experiential information in risk assessment. *Social Cognition, 17*(1), 1–18.

Green, P. E., & Srinivasan, V. (1978). Conjoint analysis in consumer research: Issues and outlook. *Journal of Consumer Research, 5*(2), 103–123.

Green, R. K. (2008). Imperfect information and the housing finance crisis: A descriptive overview. *Journal of Housing Economics, 17*(4), 262–271.

Greenberg, J., Williams, K. D., & O'Brien, M. K. (1986). Considering the harshest verdict first: Biasing effects on mock juror verdicts. *Personality and Social Psychology Bulletin, 12*(1), 41–50.

Greene, M. C. L., & Mathieson, L. (1989). *The voice and its disorders*. London: Whurr.

Greening, D. W., & Turban, D. B. (2000). Corporate social performance as a competitive advantage in attracting a quality workforce. *Business & Society, 39*(3), 254–280.

Greenley, G. E., & Foxall, G. R. (1997). Multiple stakeholder orientation in UK companies and the implications for company performance. *Journal of Management Studies, 34*(2), 259–284.

Greeno, J. G., & Noreen, D. L. (1974). Time to read semantically related sentences. *Memory & Cognition, 2*(1-A), 117–120.

Gregan-Paxton, J., & Cote, J. (2000). How do investors make predictions? Insights from analogical reasoning research. *Journal of Behavioral Decision Making, 13*(3), 307–327.

Gregan-Paxton, J., & Roedder, J. D. (1997). Consumer learning by analogy: A model of internal knowledge transfer. *Journal of Consumer Research, 24*(3), 266–284.

Gregory, M., & Poulton, E. C. (1970). Even versus uneven right-hand margins and the rate of comprehension in reading. *Ergonomics, 13*(4), 427–434.

Gregory, W. L., Cialdini, R. B., & Carpenter, K. M. (1982). Self-relevant scenarios as mediators of likelihood estimates and compliance: Does imagining make it so? *Journal of Personality and Social Psychology, 43*(1), 89–99.

Greifeneder, R., Alt, A., Bottenberg, K., Seele, T., Zelt, S., & Wagener, D. (2010). On writing legibly processing fluency systematically biases evaluations of handwritten material. *Social Psychological and Personality Science, 1*(3), 230–237.

Greitemeyer, T., & Schulz-Hardt, S. (2003). Preference-consistent evaluation of information in the hidden profile paradigm: Beyond group-level explanations for the dominance of shared information in group decisions. *Journal of Personality and Social Psychology, 84*(2), 322–339.

Greitemeyer, T., Schulz-Hardt, S., Brodbeck, F. C., & Frey, D. (2006). Information sampling and group decision making: The effects of an advocacy decision procedure and task experience. *Journal of Experimental Psychology: Applied, 12*(1), 31–42.

Grezes, J., Pichon, S., & De Gelder, B. (2007). Perceiving fear in dynamic body expressions. *Neuroimage, 35*(2), 959–967.

Griffin, A. M., & Langlois, J. H. (2006). Stereotype directionality and attractiveness stereotyping: Is beauty good or is ugly bad? *Social Cognition, 24*(2), 187.

Griffin, B. (2014). The ability to identify criteria: Its relationship with social understanding, preparation, and impression management in affecting predictor performance in a high-stakes selection context. *Human Performance, 27*(2), 147–164.

Griffin, D., & Tversky, A. (1992). The weighing of evidence and the determinants of confidence. *Cognitive Psychology, 24*(3), 411–435.

Griffit, W., & Veitch, R. (1971). Hot and crowded: Influence of population density and temperature on interpersonal affective behavior. *Journal of Personality and Social Psychology, 17*(1), 92–98.

Griner, L. A., & Smith, C. A. (2000). Contributions of motivational orientation to appraisal and emotion. *Personality and Social Psychology Bulletin, 26*(6), 727–740.

Gross, N., & Kluge, A. (2014). Predictors of knowledge-sharing behavior for teams in extreme environments: An example from the steel industry. *Journal of Cognitive Engineering and Decision Making, 8*(4), 352–373.

Grove, W. M., & Meehl, P. E. (1996). Comparative efficiency of informal (subjective, impressionistic) and formal (mechanical, algorithmic) prediction procedures: The clinical–statistical controversy. *Psychology, Public Policy, and Law, 2*(2), 293–323.

Grove, W. M., Zald, D. H., Lebow, B. S., Snitz, B. E., & Nelson, C. (2000). Clinical versus mechanical prediction: A meta-analysis. *Psychological Assessment, 12*(1), 19–30.

Gruenfeld, D. H., Mannix, E. A., Williams, K. Y., & Neale, M. A. (1996). Group composition and decision making: How member familiarity and information distribution affect process and performance. *Organizational Behavior and Human Decision Processes, 67*(1), 1–15.

Gruenfeld, D. H., & Wyer, R. S. (1992). Semantics and pragmatics of social influence: How affirmations and denials affect beliefs in referent propositions. *Journal of Personality and Social Psychology, 62*(1), 38–49.

Grunert, K. G., & Bech-Larsen, T. (2005). Explaining choice option attractiveness by beliefs elicited by the laddering method. *Journal of Economic Psychology, 26*(2), 223–241.

Guadagno, R. E., Muscanell, N. L., Sundie, J. M., Hardison, T. A., & Cialdini, R. B. (2013). The opinion-changing power of computer-based multimedia presentations. *Psychology of Popular Media Culture, 2*(2), 110–116.

Guéguen, N. (2013). Handshaking and compliance with a request: A door-to-door setting. *Social Behavior and Personality: An International Journal, 41*(10), 1585–1588.

Guéguen, N., Jacob, C., & Charles-Sire, V. (2011). Helping with all your heart: The effect of cardioids cue on compliance to a request for humanitarian aid. *Social Marketing Quarterly, 17*(4), 2–11.

Guéguen, N., Legoherel, P., & Jacob, C. (2003). Solicitation of participation in an investigation by e-mail: Effect of the social presence of the physical attraction of the petitioner on the response rate. *Canadian Journal of Behavioural Science, 35*(2), 84–96.

Guida, A., Gobet, F., Tardieu, H., & Nicolas, S. (2012). How chunks, long-term working memory and templates offer a cognitive explanation for neuroimaging data on expertise acquisition: A two-stage framework. *Brain and Cognition, 79*(3), 221–244.

Guidagni, P. M., & Little, J. D. C. (1983). A logit model of brand choice calibrated on scanner data. *Marketing Science, 2*, 203–238.

Gullberg, M., & Holmqvist, K. (1999). Keeping an eye on gestures: Visual perception of gestures in face-to-face communication. *Pragmatics & Cognition, 7*(1), 35–63.

Gullberg, M., & Holmqvist, K. (2006). What speakers do and what addressees look at: Visual attention to gestures in human interaction live and on video. *Pragmatics & Cognition, 14*(1), 53–82.

Gunderson, E. A. W. (1991). Expertise in security valuation: Operationalizing the valuation process (Doctoral dissertation, The Union Institute, 1991). *Dissertation Abstracts International, 52*(02A), 0592.

Gunning, R. (1964). *How to take the fog out of writing.* Chicago: Dartnell.

Gunter, B. (1987). *Poor reception: Misunderstanding and forgetting broadcast news.* Hillsdale, NJ: Lawrence Erlbaum Associates.

Guthrie, C., Rachlinski, J. J., & Wistrich, A. J. (2001). Inside the judicial mind. *Cornell Law Review, 86*, 777–830.

Gutwin, C., & Greenberg, S. (2004). The importance of awareness for team cognition in distributed collaboration. In E. Salas & S. M. Fiore (Eds.), *Team cognition: Understanding the factors that drive process and performance* (pp. 177–201). Washington, DC: American Psychological Association.

Guy, G. R., & Vonwiller, J. (1984). The meaning of an intonation in Australian English. *Australian Journal of Linguistics, 4*(1), 1–17.

Hackman, J. R. (1987). The design of work teams. In J. Lorsch (Ed.), *Handbook of organizational behavior* (pp. 315–342). Englewood Cliffs, NJ: Prentice-Hall.

Haddock, G. (2002). It's easy to like or dislike Tony Blair: Accessibility experiences and the favourability of attitude judgments. *British Journal of Psychology, 93*(2), 257–267.

Hahn, R. W., & Clayton, S. D. (1996). The effects of attorney presentation style, attorney gender, and juror gender on juror decisions. *Law and Human Behavior, 20*(5), 533–554.

Haines, G. H. (1974). Process models of consumer decision making. In G. D. Hughes & M. L. Ray (Eds.), *Buyer/consumer information processing* (pp. 89–107). Chapel Hill, NC: University of North Carolina Press.

Haines, G. H., Jr., Madill, J. J., & Riding, A. L. (2003). Informal investment in Canada: Financing small business growth. *Journal of Small Business & Entrepreneurship, 16*(3–4), 13–40.

Hains, S. C., Hogg, M. A., & Duck, J. M. (1997). Self-categorization and leadership: Effects of group prototypicality and leader stereotypicality. *Personality and Social Psychology Bulletin, 23*(10), 1087–1099.

Hakel, M. D., Hollmann, T. D., & Dunnette, M. D. (1970). Accuracy of interviewers, certified public accountants, and students in identifying the interests of accountants. *Journal of Applied Psychology, 54*(2), 115–119.

Hakel, M. D., & Schuh, A. J. (1971). Job applicant attributes judged important across seven diverse occupations. *Personnel Psychology, 24*(1), 45–52.

Hakes, D. T., & Cairns, H. S. (1970). Sentence comprehension and relative pronouns. *Perception & Psychophysics, 8*(1), 5–8.

Halberstadt, J., & Rhodes, G. (2000). The attractiveness of nonface averages: Implications for an evolutionary explanation of the attractiveness of average faces. *Psychological Science, 11*(4), 285–289.

Halevy, N., Berson, Y., & Galinsky, A. D. (2011). The mainstream is not electable: When vision triumphs over representativeness in leader emergence and effectiveness. *Personality and Social Psychology Bulletin, 37*(7), 893–904.

Haley, R. I. (1985). *Developing effective communication strategy: A benefit segmentation approach.* New York: Ronald Press.

Haley, R. I., Richardson, J., & Baldwin, B. M. (1984). The effects of nonverbal communications in television advertising. *Journal of Advertising Research, 24*(4), 11–18.

Halkias, G., & Kokkinaki, F. (2012). Cognitive and affective responses to schema-incongruent brand messages. In A. Innocenti & A. Sirigu (Eds.), *Neuroscience and the economics of decision making* (pp. 165–181). New York, NY: Routledge.

Hall, J., & Hofer, C. W. (1993). Venture capitalists' decision criteria in new venture evaluation. *Journal of Business Venturing, 8*(1), 25–42.

Hall, J. A., Coats, E. J., & LeBeau, L. S. (2005). Nonverbal behavior and the vertical dimension of social relations: A meta-analysis. *Psychological Bulletin, 131*(6), 898–924.

Hall, J. A., & Friedman, G. B. (1999). Status, gender, and nonverbal behavior: A study of structured interactions between employees of a company. *Personality and Social Psychology Bulletin, 25*(9), 1082–1091.

Hamann, S. (2001). Cognitive and neural mechanisms of emotional memory. *Trends in Cognitive Sciences*, *5*(9), 394–400.

Hamermesh, D. S., & Parker, A. (2005). Beauty in the classroom: Instructors' pulchritude and putative pedagogical productivity. *Economics of Education Review*, *24*(4), 369–376.

Hamill, R., Wilson, T. D., & Nisbett, R. E. (1980). Insensitivity to sample bias: Generalizing from atypical cases. *Journal of Personality and Social Psychology*, *39*(4), 578–589.

Hamilton, D. L., & Zanna, M. P. (1972). Differential weighting of favorable and unfavorable attributes in impressions of personality. *Journal of Experimental Research in Personality*, *6*(2–3), 204–212.

Hamilton, M. A. (1998). Message variables that mediate and moderate the effect of equivocal language on source credibility. *Journal of Language and Social Psychology*, *17*(1), 109–143.

Hamilton, M. A., & Hunter, J. E. (1998). The effect of language intensity on receiver evaluations of message, source, and topic. In M. Allen & R. W. Preiss (Eds.), *Persuasion: Advances through meta-analysis* (pp. 99–138). Cresskill, NJ: Hampton.

Hamilton, M. A., & Mineo, P. J. (1998). A framework for understanding equivocation. *Journal of Language and Social Psychology*, *17*(1), 3–35.

Hamm, A. O., Schupp, H. T., & Weike, A. I. (2003). Motivational organization of emotions: Autonomic changes, cortical responses, and reflex modulation. In R. J. Davidson, K. R. Scherer & H. H. Goldsmith (Eds.), *Handbook of affective sciences* (pp. 187–211). New York, NY: Oxford University Press.

Han, Y. K., Morgan, G. A., Kotsiopulos, A., & Kang-Park, J. (1991). Impulse buying behavior of apparel purchasers. *Clothing and Textile Research Journal*, *9*(3), 15–21.

Hanák, R., Sirota, M., & Juanchich, M. (2013). Experts use compensatory strategies more often than novices in hiring decisions. *Studia Psychologica*, *55*(4), 251–263.

Hansen, C. H., & Hansen, R. D. (1988). Finding the face in the crowd: An anger superiority effect. *Journal of Personality and Social Psychology*, *54*(6), 917–924.

Hansen, G. S., & Wernerfelt, B. (1989). Determinants of firm performance: The relative importance of economic and organizational factors. *Strategic Management Journal*, *10*(5), 399–411.

Hardin, W. G. (1996). An investigation into the information processing heuristics of private banking and real estate banking lenders in a commercial banking environment (Doctoral dissertation, Georgia State University, 1996). *Dissertation Abstracts International*, *58*(11A), 4384.

Hare, T. A., Camerer, C. F., & Rangel, A. (2009). Self-control in decision-making involves modulation of the vmPFC valuation system. *Science*, *324*(5927), 646–648.

Hare, T. A., Malmaud, J., & Rangel, A. (2011). Focusing attention on the health aspects of foods changes value signals in vmPFC and improves dietary choice. *The Journal of Neuroscience*, *31*(30), 11077–11087.

Harkins, S. G., & Petty, R. E. (1981). Effects of source magnification of cognitive effort on attitudes: An information-processing view. *Journal of Personality and Social Psychology*, *40*(3), 401–413.

Harmon-Jones, E., & Allen, J. J. B. (2001). The role of affect in the mere exposure effect: Evidence from psychophysiological and individual differences approaches. *Personality and Social Psychology Bulletin*, *27*(7), 889–898.

Harp, S. F., & Mayer, R. E. (1998). How seductive details do their damage: A theory of cognitive interest in science learning. *Journal of Educational Psychology*, *90*(3), 414–434.

Harris, M. M. (1989). Reconsidering the employment interview: A review of recent literature and suggestions for future research. *Personnel Psychology*, *42*(4), 691–726.

Harrison, N. A., Singer, T., Rotshtein, P., Dolan, R. J., & Critchley, H. D. (2006). Pupillary contagion: Central mechanisms engaged in sadness processing. *Social Cognitive and Affective Neuroscience*, *1*(1), 5–17.

Hart, A. J., & Morry, M. M. (1997). Trait inferences based on racial and behavioral cues. *Basic and Applied Social Psychology*, *19*(1), 33–48.

Hartley, J. (1978). *Designing instructional text*. New York: Nichols Publishing Company.

Hartley, J., & Davies, I. (1976). Preinstructional strategies: The role of pretests, behavioral objectives, overviews, and advance organizers. *Review of Educational Research*, *46*, 239–265.

Hartley, J., & Mills, R. (1973). Unjustified experiments in typographical research and instructional design. *British Journal of Educational Technology*, *4*, 120–131.

Hartley, J., & Rooum, D. (1983). Sir Cyril Burt and typography: A re-evaluation. *British Journal of Psychology*, *74*(2), 203–212.

Hartley, J., & Trueman, M. (1982, March). *Headings in text: Issues and data*. Paper presented at the Annual Meeting of American Educational Research Association, New York.

Hartman, R. S., Doane, M. J., & Woo, C. K. (1991). Consumer rationality and the status quo. *The Quarterly Journal of Economics*, *106*(1), 141–162.

Harvey, J. B. (1974). The Abilene paradox and other meditations on management. *Organizational Dynamics*, *3*(1), 63–80.

Hasson, U., & Glucksberg, S. (2006). Does understanding negation entail affirmation? An examination of negated metaphors. *Journal of Pragmatics*, *38*(7), 1015–1032.

Haste, H., & Torney-Purta, J. (1992). *The development of political understanding: A new perspective*. San Francisco: Jossey-Bass.

Hastie, R., & Kumar, P. A. (1979). Person memory: Personality traits as organizing principles in memory for behaviors. *Journal of Personality and Social Psychology, 37*(1), 25–38.

Hastie, R., Landsman, R., & Loftus, E. F. (1978). Eyewitness testimony: The dangers of guessing. *Jurimetrics Journal, 19*, 1–8.

Hatch, J. A., Hill, C. A., & Hayes, J. R. (1993). When the messenger is the message: Readers' impressions of writers. *Written Communication, 10*(4), 569–598.

Hatfield, E., Cacioppo, J. T., & Rapson, R. L. (1994). *Emotional contagion*. New York: Cambridge University Press.

Hattrup, K., & Ford, J. K. (1995). The roles of information characteristics and accountability in moderating stereotype-driven processes during social decision making. *Organizational Behavior and Human Decision Processes, 63*(1), 73–86.

Hauser, J. R., & Wernerfelt, B. (1990). An evaluation cost model of consideration sets. *Journal of Consumer Research, 16*, 393–408.

Hawes, J. M., Jackson, D. W., Jr., Schlacter, J. L., & Wolfe, W. G. (1995). Selling and sales management in action examining the bases utilized for evaluating salespeoples' performance. *Journal of Personal Selling & Sales Management, 15*(4), 57–65.

Hawkins, S. A., & Hoch, S. J. (1992). Low-involvement learning: Memory without evaluation. *Journal of Consumer Research, 19*(2), 212–225.

Hayden, B. Y., Heilbronner, S. R., Pearson, J. M., & Platt, M. L. (2011). Surprise signals in anterior cingulate cortex: Neuronal encoding of unsigned reward prediction errors driving adjustment in behavior. *The Journal of Neuroscience, 31*(11), 4178–4187.

Heberlein, A. S., Adolphs, R., Tranel, D., & Damasio, H. (2004). Cortical regions for judgments of emotions and personality traits from point-light walkers. *Journal of Cognitive Neuroscience, 16*(7), 1143–1158.

Heberlein, A. S., & Saxe, R. R. (2005). Dissociation between emotion and personality judgments: Convergent evidence from functional neuroimaging. *Neuroimage, 28*(4), 770–777.

Hecht, M. A., & LaFrance, M. (1995). How (fast) can I help you? Tone of voice and telephone operator efficiency in interactions. *Journal of Applied Social Psychology, 25*(23), 2086–2098.

Hedelin, L., & Sjöberg, L. (1993). *Riskbedömning-bankmäns bedömning av nyföretagares personliga egenskaper*. [Risk assessments: Loan officers' assessment of new entrepreneurs' personal characteristics]. Stockholm: NUTEK.

Hegarty, M., Canham, M. S., & Fabrikant, S. I. (2010). Thinking about the weather: How display salience and knowledge affect performance in a graphic inference task. *Journal of Experimental Psychology: Learning, Memory, and Cognition, 36*(1), 37–53.

Hegarty, M., & Just, M. A. (1993). Constructing mental models of machines from text and diagrams. *Journal of Memory and Language, 32*(6), 717–742.

Helfrich, H. (1979). Age markers in speech. In K. R. Scherer & H. Giles (Eds.), *Social markers in speech* (pp. 63–107). Cambridge, UK: Cambridge University Press.

Helgeson, J. G., & Ursic, M. L. (1993). Information load, cost/benefit assessment and decision strategy variability. *Journal of the Academy of Marketing Science, 21*(1), 13–20.

Heller, R. F., Saltzstein, H. D., & Caspe, W. B. (1992). Heuristics in medical and non-medical decision-making. *The Quarterly Journal of Experimental Psychology A: Human Experimental Psychology, 44A*(2), 211–235.

Helmer, H. W. (1996). A director's role in strategy: There has been no clear consensus on how a board should involve itself in strategy formulation. *Directors and Boards, 20*, 22–25.

HelmReich, R. L. (1997). Managing human error in aviation. *Scientific American, 277*(5), 40.

Henderson, J. M., Brockmole, J. R., Castelhano, M. S., & Mack, M. (2007). Visual saliency does not account for eye movements during visual search in real-world scenes. In R. van Gompel, M. H. Fischer, W. S. Murray & R. L. Hill (Eds.), *Eye movements: A window on mind and brain* (pp. 537–562). Oxford, UK: Elsevier.

Hendon, D. W. (1973). How mechanical factors affect ad perception. *Journal of Advertising Research, 13*(4), 39–46.

Hendry, K. P., Kiel, G. C., & Nicholson, G. (2010). How boards strategise: A strategy as practice view. *Long Range Planning, 43*(1), 33–56.

Henley, N. M. (1995). Body politics revisited: What do we know today? In P. J. Kalbfleisch & M. J. Cody (Eds.), *Gender, power, and communication in human relationships* (pp. 27–61). Hillsdale, NJ: Lawrence Erlbaum Associates.

Hensley, W. E. (1981). The effects of attire, location, and sex on aiding behavior: A similarity explanation. *Journal of Nonverbal Behavior, 6*, 3–11.

Henson, R. (2005). What can functional neuroimaging tell the experimental psychologist? *The Quarterly Journal of Experimental Psychology Section A, 58*(2), 193–233.

Hermann, C. F., Geva, N., & Bragg, B. (2001, July). *Group dynamics in conflict management strategies: An experimental analysis of the effects on foreign policy decision making*. Hong Kong: Hong Kong Convention of International Studies.

Hernandez, I., & Preston, J. L. (2013). Disfluency disrupts the confirmation bias. *Journal of Experimental Social Psychology*, *49*(1), 178–182.

Hernandez, J. M. C., Han, X., & Kardes, F. R. (2014). Effects of the perceived diagnosticity of presented attribute and brand name information on sensitivity to missing information. *Journal of Business Research*, *67*(5), 874–881.

Herr, P. M. (1989). Priming price-prior knowledge and context effects. *Journal of Consumer Research*, *16*(1), 67–75.

Herr, P. M., Kardes, F. R., & Kim, J. (1991). Effects of word-of-mouth and product-attribute information on persuasion: An accessibility-diagnosticity perspective. *Journal of Consumer Research*, *17*(4), 454–462.

Hershberger, W. A., & Terry, D. F. (1965). Typographical cuing in conventional and programed texts. *Journal of Applied Psychology*, *49*(1), 55–60.

Hershey, J. C., & Schoemaker, P. J. (1980). Prospect theory's reflection hypothesis: A critical examination. *Organizational Behavior & Human Performance*, *25*(3), 395–418.

Herstein, J. A. (1981). Keeping the voter's limits in mind: A cognitive process analysis of decision making in voting. *Journal of Personality and Social Psychology*, *40*(5), 843–861.

Hess, E. H., & Polt, J. M. (1960). Pupil size as related to interest value of visual stimuli. *Science*, *132*, 349–350.

Hess, E. H., & Polt, J. M. (1964). Pupil size in relation to mental activity during simple problem-solving. *Science*, *143*(3611), 1190–1192.

Hess, U., Blairy, S., & Kleck, R. E. (1997). The intensity of emotional facial expressions and decoding accuracy. *Journal of Nonverbal Behavior*, *21*(4), 241–257.

Hess, U., Kappas, A., & Scherer, K. R. (1988). Multichannel communication of emotion: Synthetic signal production. In K. R. Scherer (Ed.), *Facets of emotion: Recent research* (pp. 161–182). Hillsdale, NJ: Lawrence Erlbaum Associates.

Heuer, F., & Reisberg, D. (1990). Vivid memories of emotional events: The accuracy of remembered minutiae. *Memory & Cognition*, *18*(5), 496–506.

Heuer, L., & Penrod, S. D. (1994). Trial complexity: A field investigation of its meaning and its effect. *Law and Human Behavior*, *18*(1), 29–51.

Higgins, E. T., & Bargh, J. A. (1987). Social cognition and social perception. *Annual Review of Psychology*, *38*, 369–425.

Higgins, E. T., & King, G. (1981). Accessibility of social constructs: Information-processing consequences of individual and contextual variability. In N. Cantor & J. Kihlstrom (Eds.), *Personality, cognition, and social interaction* (pp. 69–121). Hillsdale, NJ: Lawrence Erlbaum Associates.

Higgins, E. T., & Lurie, L. (1983). Context, categorization, and recall: The "change-of-standard" effect. *Cognitive Psychology*, *15*(4), 525–547.

Higgins, E. T., & Stangor, C. A. (1988). "Change-of-standard" perspective on the relations among context, judgment, and memory. *Journal of Personality and Social Psychology*, *54*(2), 181–192.

Highhouse, S., Beadle, D., Gallo, A., & Miller, L. (1998). Get' em while they last! Effects of scarcity information in job advertisements. *Journal of Applied Social Psychology*, *28*(9), 779–795.

Highhouse, S., & Gallo, A. (1997). Order effects in personnel decision making. *Human Performance*, *10*(1), 31–46.

Highhouse, S., Stierwalt, S. L., Bachchiochi, P., Elder, A. E., & Fisher, G. (1999). Effects of advertised human resource management practices on attraction of African American applicants. *Personnel Psychology*, *52*(2), 425–442.

Hilgartner, S., & Bosk, C. L. (1988). The rise and fall of social problems: A public arenas model. *American Journal of Sociology*, *94*, 53–78.

Hill, C. T., & Stull, D. E. (1981). Sex differences in effects of social and value similarity in same-sex friendship. *Journal of Personality and Social Psychology*, *41*(3), 488–502.

Hill, K., & Monk, A. F. (2000). Electronic mail versus printed text: The effects on recipients. *Interacting with Computers*, *13*(2), 253–263.

Hill, P. H. (1984). Decisions involving the corporate environment. In W. Swap (Ed.), *Group decision making* (pp. 251–279). Beverly Hills, CA: Sage.

Hillman, A. J., & Keim, G. D. (2001). Shareholder value, stakeholder management, and social issues: What's the bottom line? *Strategic Management Journal*, *22*(2), 125–139.

Himmelfarb, S. (1972). Integration and attribution theories in personality impression formation. *Journal of Personality and Social Psychology*, *23*(3), 309–313.

Hinsley, D. A., Hayes, J. R., & Simon, H. A. (1977). From words to equations: Meaning and representation in algebra word problems. In M. A. Just & P. A. Carpenter (Eds.), *Cognitive processes in comprehension* (pp. 89–106). Hillsdale, NJ: Lawrence Erlbaum Associates.

Hinsz, V. B., Tindale, R. S., & Nagao, D. H. (2008). Accentuation of information processes and biases in group judgments integrating base-rate and case-specific information. *Journal of Experimental Social Psychology*, *44*(1), 116–126.

Hinsz, V. B., Tindale, R. S., & Vollrath, D. A. (1997). The emerging conceptualization of groups as information processes. *Psychological Bulletin, 121*(1), 43–64.

Hirschman, E. C. (1981). An exploratory comparison of decision criteria used by retailers. In W. R. Darden & R. F. Lusch (Eds.), *Proceedings of 1981 workshop in retail patronage theory* (pp. 1–5). Norman, OK: University of Oklahoma.

Hirschman, E. C., & Mazursky, D. (1982). *A trans-organizational investigation of retail buyers' criteria and information sources.* Working Paper No. 82–8. New York, NY: New York University Institute of Retail Management.

Hirshleifer, S. (1970). *Investment, interest and capital.* Englewood Cliffs, NJ: Prentice-Hall.

Hirt, E. R., Levine, G. M., McDonald, H. E., Melton, R. J., & Martin, L. L. (1997). The role of mood in quantitative and qualitative aspects of performance: Single or multiple mechanisms? *Journal of Experimental Social Psychology, 33*(6), 602–629.

Hitt, M. A., & Tyler, B. B. (1991). Strategic decision models: Integrating different perspectives. *Strategic Management Journal, 12*(5), 327–351.

Ho, W., Xu, X., & Dey, P. K. (2010). Multi-criteria decision making approaches for supplier evaluation and selection: A literature review. *European Journal of Operational Research, 202*(1), 16–24.

Hoch, S. J. (1985). Counterfactual reasoning and accuracy in predicting personal events. *Journal of Experimental Psychology: Learning, Memory, and Cognition, 11*(4), 719–731.

Hoch, S. J., & Ha, Y. W. (1986). Consumer learning: Advertising and the ambiguity of product experience. *Journal of Consumer Research, 13*(2), 221–233.

Hoch, S. J., & Loewenstein, G. F. (1991). Time-inconsistent preferences and consumer self-control. *Journal of Consumer Research, 17*(4), 492–507.

Hodges, B. H. (1974). Effect of valence on relative weighting in impression formation. *Journal of Personality and Social Psychology, 30*(3), 378–381.

Höffler, T. N., & Leutner, D. (2007). Instructional animation versus static pictures: A meta-analysis. *Learning and Instruction, 17*(6), 722–738.

Hoffman, J. E., & Subramaniam, B. (1995). The role of visual attention in saccadic eye movements. *Perception & Psychophysics, 57*(6), 787–795.

Hogan, R. (1991). Personality and personality measurement. In M. D. Dunnette & L. M. Hough (Eds.), *Handbook of industrial and organizational psychology* (2nd ed., Vol. 2, pp. 873–919). Palo Alto, CA: Consulting Psychologists Press.

Hogarth, R. M. (1980). *Judgment and choice.* New York: Wiley.

Hogarth, R. M., & Kunreuther, H. (1995). Decision making under ignorance: Arguing with yourself. *Journal of Risk and Uncertainty, 10*(1), 15–36.

Hogg, M. A. (1992). *The social psychology of group cohesiveness: From attraction to social identity.* Hemel Hempstead, UK: Harvester Wheatsheaf.

Hogg, M. A. (2001). A social identity theory of leadership. *Personality and Social Psychology Review, 5*, 184–200.

Hogg, M. A. (2007). Social psychology of leadership. In A. W. Kruglanski & E. Tory Higgins (Eds.), *Social psychology: Handbook of basic principles* (2nd ed., pp. 716–733). New York: The Guilford Press.

Hogg, M. A., & Hains, S. C. (1998). Friendship and group identification: A new look at the role of cohesiveness in group think. *European Journal of Social Psychology, 28*, 323–341.

Hogg, M. A., & Hardie, E. A. (1991). Social attraction, personal attraction and self-categorization: A field study. *Personality and Social Psychology Bulletin, 17*, 175–180.

Hogg, M. A., & Terry, O. J. (2000). Social identity and self-categorization processes in organizational contexts. *Academy of Management Review, 25*, 121–140.

Hogg, M. A., & van Knippenberg, D. (2003). Social identity and leadership processes in groups. In M. P. Zanna (Ed.), *Advances in experimental social psychology* (Vol. 35, pp. 1–52). San Diego, CA: Academic Press.

Holbrook, M. B. (1986). Emotion in the consumption experience: Toward a new model of the human consumer. In R. A. Peterson, W. D. Hoyer & W. R. Wilson (Eds.), *The role of affect in consumer behavior: Emerging theories and applications* (pp. 17–52). Lexington, MA: Lexington Books.

Holbrook, M. B., & Batra, R. (1987). Assessing the role of emotions as mediators of consumer responses to advertising. *Journal of Consumer Research, 14*(3), 404–420.

Holbrook, M. B., & Lehmann, D. R. (1980). Form versus content in predicting starch scores. *Journal of Advertising Research, 20*(4), 53–62.

Holland, J. H., Holyoak, K., Nisbett, R. E., & Thagard, P. R. (1986). *Induction: Processes of inference, learning, and discovery.* Cambridge, MA: The MIT Press.

Holland, J. H., Holyoak, K. J., Nisbett, R. E., & Thagard, P. R. (1993). Deductive reasoning. In A. I. Goldman (Ed.), *Readings in philosophy and cognitive science* (pp. 23–41). Cambridge, MA: The MIT Press.

Holland, R. W., Verplanken, B., & van Knippenberg, A. (2003). From repetition to conviction: Attitude accessibility as a determinant of attitude certainty. *Journal of Experimental Social Psychology, 39*(6), 594–601.

Holland, V. M. (1981). *Psycholinguistic alternatives to readability formulas* (Document Design Project Tech. Rep. No. 12). Washington, DC: American Institutes for Research.

Hollands, J. G., & Spence, I. (2001). The discrimination of graphical elements. *Applied Cognitive Psychology*, *15*(4), 413–431.

Hollandsworth, J. G., Kazelskis, R., Stevens, J., & Dressel, M. E. (1979). Relative contributions of verbal, articulative, and nonverbal communication to employment decisions in the job interview setting. *Personnel Psychology*, *32*(2), 359–367.

Holler, J., Schubotz, L., Kelly, S., Hagoort, P., Schuetze, M., & Özyürek, A. (2014). Social eye gaze modulates processing of speech and co-speech gesture. *Cognition*, *133*(3), 692–697.

Holliday, W. G. (1975). The effects of verbal and adjunct pictorial-verbal information in science instruction. *Journal of Research in Science Teaching*, *12*, 77–83.

Holliday, W. G., Brunner, L. L., & Donais, E. L. (1977). Differential cognitive and affective responses for flow diagrams in science. *Journal of Research in Science Teaching*, *14*, 129–138.

Holliday, W. G., & Harvey, D. A. (1976). Adjunct labeled drawings in teaching physics to junior high school students. *Journal of Research in Science Teaching*, *13*, 37–43.

Hollingshead, A. B. (1996). The rank-order effect in group decision making. *Organizational Behavior and Human Decision Processes*, *68*(3), 181–193.

Hollman, T. D. (1972). Employment interviewers' errors in processing positive and negative information. *Journal of Applied Psychology*, *56*, 130–134.

Hollman, W. A. (2005). Buy and sell decisional analysis of financial advisors (Doctoral dissertation, Walden University, 2005). *Dissertation Abstracts International: Section A*, *66*, 1103.

Holmes, G. (1931). The relative legibility of black and white print. *Journal of Applied Psychology*, *15*(3), 248–251.

Holmes, V. M., Arwas, R., & Garrett, M. F. (1977). Prior context and the perception of lexically ambiguous sentences. *Memory & Cognition*, *5*(1), 103–110.

Holsanova, J., Holmberg, N., & Holmqvist, K. (2009). Reading information graphics: The role of spatial contiguity and dual attentional guidance. *Applied Cognitive Psychology*, *23*(9), 1215–1226.

Holtgraves, T., & Grayer, A. R. (1994). I am not a crook: Effects of denials on perceptions of a defendant's guilt, personality, and motives. *Journal of Applied Social Psychology*, *24*(23), 2132–2150.

Holtgraves, T., & Lasky, B. (1999). Linguistic power and persuasion. *Journal of Language and Social Psychology*, *18*(2), 196–205.

Holyoak, K. J. (1974). The role of imagery in the evaluation of sentences: Imagery or semantic factors. *Journal of Verbal Learning & Verbal Behavior*, *13*(2), 163–166.

Holyoak, K. J. (1984). Mental models in problem solving. In J. R. Anderson & S. M. Kosslyn (Eds.), *Tutorials in learning and memory: Essays in honor of Gordon Bower* (pp. 193–218). San Francisco: Freeman.

Holyoak, K. J., & Simon, D. (1999). Bidirectional reasoning in decision making by constraint satisfaction. *Journal of Experimental Psychology: General*, *128*(1), 3–31.

Holyoak, K. J., & Thagard, P. (1995). *Mental leaps: Analogy in creative thought*. Cambridge, MA: The MIT Press.

Hooper, V. J. (1994). Multinational capital budgeting and finance decisions. In J. Pointon (Ed.), *Issues in business taxation* (pp. 211–225). Aldershot, UK: Ashgate.

Hope, L., & Wright, D. (2007). Beyond unusual? Examining the role of attention in the weapon focus effect. *Applied Cognitive Psychology*, *21*(7), 951–961.

Hosman, L. A., & Siltanen, S. A. (1994). The attributional and evaluative consequences of powerful and powerless speech styles: An examination of the "control over others" and "control of self" explanations. *Language & Communication*, *14*(3), 287–298.

Hostetter, A. B. (2011). When do gestures communicate? A meta-analysis. *Psychological Bulletin*, *137*(2), 297–315.

House, R. J., & Aditya, R. M. (1997). The social scientific study of leadership: Quo vadis? *Journal of Management*, *23*, 409–473.

Houts, P. S., Doak, C. C., Doak, L. G., & Loscalzo, M. J. (2006). The role of pictures in improving health communication: A review of research on attention, comprehension, recall, and adherence. *Patient Education and Counseling*, *61*(2), 173–190.

Howard, D. J., & Gengler, C. (2001). Emotional contagion effects on product attitudes. *Journal of Consumer Research*, *28*(2), 189–201.

Howard-Grenville, J. A. (2007). Developing issue-selling effectiveness over time: Issue selling as resourcing. *Organization Science*, *18*(4), 560–577.

Howell, J. M., & Hall-Merenda, K. E. (1999). The ties that bind: The impact of leader-member exchange, transformational and transactional leadership, and distance on predicting follower performance. *Journal of Applied Psychology*, *84*, 680–694.

Howells, L. T., & Becker, S. W. (1962). Seating arrangement and leadership emergence. *Journal of Abnormal and Social Psychology*, *64*, 148–150.

Hrubes, D. A. (2001). The role of nonverbal behavior in persuasion (Doctoral dissertation, University of Massachusetts—Amherst, 2001). *Dissertation Abstracts International, 62*(9–B), 4274.

Hsee, C. K. (1996). The evaluability hypothesis: An explanation for preference reversals between joint and separate evaluations of alternatives. *Organizational Behavior and Human Decision Processes, 67*(3), 247–257.

Hsee, C. K. (1998). Less is better: When low-value options are valued more highly than high-value options. *Journal of Behavioral Decision Making, 11*(2), 107–121.

Hsee, C. K., & Kunreuther, H. (2000). The affection effect in insurance decisions. *Journal of Risk and Uncertainty, 20*, 141–159.

Hsee, C. K., Loewenstein, G. F., Blount, S., & Bazerman, M. H. (1999). Preference reversals between joint and separate evaluations of options: A review and theoretical analysis. *Psychological Bulletin, 125*(5), 576–590.

Hsee, C. K., & Menon, S. (1999). *Affection effect in consumer choices.* Unpublished study, University of Chicago, Chicago, IL.

Hsee, C. K., & Rottenstreich, Y. (2004). Music, pandas, and muggers: On the affective psychology of value. *Journal of Experimental Psychology: General, 133*(1), 23–30.

Hsu, H. J., & Burns, L. D. (2002). Clothing evaluative criteria: A cross-national comparison of Taiwanese and United States consumers. *Clothing and Textiles Research Journal, 20*(4), 246–252.

Huang, J. Y., Song, H., & Bargh, J. A. (2011). Smooth trajectories travel farther into the future: Perceptual fluency effects on prediction of trend continuation. *Journal of Experimental Social Psychology, 47*(2), 506–508.

Huang, Y. T., & Gordon, P. C. (2011). Distinguishing the time course of lexical and discourse processes through context, coreference, and quantified expressions. *Journal of Experimental Psychology: Learning, Memory, and Cognition, 37*(4), 966–978.

Huber, J., Payne, J. W., & Puto, C. (1982). Adding asymmetrically dominated alternatives: Violations of regularity and the similarity hypothesis. *Journal of Consumer Research, 9*(1), 90–98.

Huber, O. (1980). The influence of some task variables on cognitive operations in an information-processing decision model. *Acta Psychologica, 45*(1–3), 187–196.

Huberman, G., Iyengar, S. S., & Jiang, W. (2007). Defined contribution pension plans: Determinants of participation and contribution rates. *Journal of Financial Services Research, 31*(1), 1–32.

Huckin, T. N., & Olsen, L. A. (1991). *Technical writing and professional communication for nonnative speakers of English.* New York, NY: McGraw-Hill.

Huffman, C., Ratneshwar, S., & Mick, D. G. (2000). Consumer goal structures and goal-determination processes: An integrative framework. In S. Ratneshwar, D. G. Mick & C. Huffman (Eds.), *The why of consumption: Contemporary perspectives on consumer motives, goals, and desires* (pp. 9–35). London and New York: Routledge.

Hupet, M., & Le Bouedec, B. (1975). Definiteness and voice in the interpretation of active and passive sentences. *The Quarterly Journal of Experimental Psychology, 27*(2), 323–330.

Hurwitz, J., & Peffley, M. (1987). How are foreign policy attitudes structured? A hierarchical model. *American Political Science Review, 81*(4), 1099–1120.

Hvistendahl, J. K., & Kahl, M. R. (1975). Roman v. sans serif body type: Readability and reader preference. *News Research Bulletin, 2*, 3–11.

Hwang, M. I., & Lin, J. W. (1999). Information dimension, information overload and decision quality. *Journal of Information Science, 25*(3), 213–218.

Hyönä, J. (1994). Processing of topic shifts by adults and children. *Reading Research Quarterly, 29*(1), 76–90.

Hyönä, J. (1995). An eye movement analysis of topic-shift effect during repeated reading. *Journal of Experimental Psychology: Learning, Memory, and Cognition, 21*(5), 1365–1373.

Hyönä, J., & Häikiö, T. (2005). Is emotional content obtained from parafoveal words during reading? An eye movement analysis. *Scandinavian Journal of Psychology, 46*(6), 475–483.

Hyönä, J., & Lorch, R. F., Jr. (2004). Effects of topic headings on text processing: Evidence from adult readers' eye fixation patterns. *Learning and Instruction, 14*(2), 131–152.

Hyönä, J., Lorch, R. F., Jr., & Kaakinen, J. K. (2002). Individual differences in reading to summarize expository text: Evidence from eye fixation patterns. *Journal of Educational Psychology, 94*(1), 44–55.

Hyönä, J., & Nurminen, A. M. (2006). Do adult readers know how they read? Evidence from eye movement patterns and verbal reports. *British Journal of Psychology, 97*(1), 31–50.

Ickes, W. (1982). A basic paradigm for the study of personality, roles, and social behavior. In W. Ickes & E. S. Knowles (Eds.), *Personality, roles, and social behavior* (pp. 305–341). New York: Springer-Verlag.

Ickes, W., Stinson, L., Bissonnette, V., & Garcia, S. (1990). Naturalistic social cognition: Empathic accuracy in mixed-sex dyads. *Journal of Personality and Social Psychology, 59*(4), 730–742.

Igou, E. R., & Bless, H. (2007). On undesirable consequences of thinking: Framing effects as a function of substantive processing. *Journal of Behavioral Decision Making, 20*(2), 125–142.

Imada, A. S., & Hakel, M. D. (1977). Influence of nonverbal communication and rater proximity on impressions and decisions in simulated employment interviews. *Journal of Applied Psychology, 62*(3), 295–300.

Insko, C. A., Lind, E. A., & LaTour, S. (1976). Persuasion, recall, and thoughts. *Representative Research in Social Psychology*, 7(1), 66–78.

Intraub, H. (1979). The role of implicit naming in pictorial encoding. *Journal of Experimental Psychology: Human Learning and Memory*, 5(2), 78–87.

Isen, A. M. (1987). Positive affect, cognitive processes, and social behavior. In L. Berkowitz (Ed.), *Advances in experimental social psychology* (Vol. 20, pp. 203–253). San Diego, CA: Academic Press.

Isen, A. M. (1993). Positive affect and decision making. In M. Lewis & J. M. Haviland (Eds.), *Handbook of emotions* (pp. 261–277). New York: Guilford Press.

Isen, A. M. (1999). Positive affect. In T. Dalgleish & M. J. Power (Eds.), *Handbook of cognition and emotion* (pp. 521–539). New York: John Wiley & Sons.

Isen, A. M. (2000). Some perspectives on positive affect and self-regulation. *Psychological Inquiry*, 11(3), 184–187.

Isen, A. M., & Geva, N. (1987). The influence of positive affect on acceptable level of risk: The person with a large canoe has a large worry. *Organizational Behavior and Human Decision Processes*, 39(2), 145–154.

Isen, A. M., & Means, B. (1983). The influence of positive affect on decision-making strategy. *Social Cognition*, 2(1), 18–31.

Isen, A. M., Nygren, T. E., & Ashby, F. G. (1988). Influence of positive affect on the subjective utility of gains and losses: It is just not worth the risk. *Journal of Personality and Social Psychology*, 55(5), 710–717.

Isen, A. M., & Patrick, R. (1983). The effect of positive feelings on risk taking: When the chips are down. *Organizational Behavior & Human Performance*, 31(2), 194–202.

Isen, A. M., Rosenzweig, A. S., & Young, M. J. (1991). The influence of positive affect on clinical problem solving. *Medical Decision Making*, 11, 221–227.

Isenberg, D. J. (1986). Thinking and managing: A verbal protocol analysis of managerial problem solving. *Academy of Management Journal*, 29(4), 775–788.

Iyengar, S. (1991). *Is anyone responsible: How television frames political issues.* Chicago: University of Chicago Press.

Iyengar, S., & Kinder, D. R. (1987). *News that matters: Television and American opinion.* Chicago: University of Chicago Press.

Iyengar, S. S., Huberman, G., & Jiang, W. (2004). How much choice is too much? Contributions to 401 (k) retirement plans. In O. S. Mitchell & S. P. Utkus (Eds.), *Pension design and structure: New lessons from behavioral finance* (pp. 83–95). New York, NY: Oxford University Press.

Iyengar, S. S., & Lepper, M. R. (2000). When choice is demotivating: Can one desire too much of a good thing? *Journal of Personality and Social Psychology*, 79(6), 995–1006.

Izard, C. E. (1977). *Human emotions.* New York: Plenum Press.

Izard, C. E. (1994). Innate and universal facial expressions: Evidence from developmental and cross-cultural research. *Psychological Bulletin*, 115(2), 288–299.

Jackson, D. N., Peacock, A. C., & Holden, R. R. (1982). Professional interviewers' trait inferential structures for diverse occupational groups. *Organizational Behavior & Human Performance*, 29(1), 1–20.

Jacob, J., Lys, T., & Neale, M. (1999). Expertise in forecasting performance of security analysts. *Journal of Accounting and Economics*, 28(1), 27–50.

Jacoby, J., Kuss, A., Mazursky, D., & Troutman, T. (1985). Effectiveness of security analyst information accessing strategies: A computer interactive assessment. *Computers in Human Behavior*, 1(1), 95–113.

Jacoby, J., Morrin, M., Jaccard, J., Gurhan, Z., Kuss, A., & Maheswaran, D. (2002). Mapping attitude formation as a function of information input: Online processing models of attitude formation. *Journal of Consumer Psychology*, 12(1), 21–34.

Jacoby, J., Nelson, M. C., & Hoyer, W. D. (1982). Corrective advertising and affirmative disclosure statements: Their potential for confusing and misleading the consumer. *Journal of Marketing*, 46(1), 61–72.

Jacoby, J., Speller, D. E., & Berning, C. K. (1974a). Brand choice behavior as a function of information load: Replication and extension. *Journal of Consumer Research*, 1(1), 33–42.

Jacoby, J., Speller, D. E., & Kohn, C. A. (1974b). Brand choice behavior as a function of information load. *Journal of Marketing Research*, 11(1), 63–69.

Jacoby, L. L., Kelley, C. M., & Dywan, J. (1989a). Memory attributions. In H. L. Roediger & F. I. M. Craik (Eds.), *Varieties of memory and consciousness: Essays in honour of endel tulving* (pp. 391–422). Hillsdale, NJ: Lawrence Erlbaum Associates.

Jacoby, L. L., Woloshyn, V., & Kelley, C. M. (1989b). Becoming famous without being recognized: Unconscious influences of memory produced by dividing attention. *Journal of Experimental Psychology: General*, 118(2), 115–125.

Jacowitz, K. E., & Kahneman, D. (1995). Measures of anchoring in estimation tasks. *Personality and Social Psychology Bulletin*, 21(11), 1161–1166.

Jamal, A., & Goode, M. (2001). Consumers' product evaluation: A study of the primary evaluative criteria in the precious jewellery market in the UK. *Journal of Consumer Behaviour*, 1(2), 140–155.

Jamieson, D. W., & Zanna, M. P. (1989). Need for structure in attitude formation and expression. In A. R. Pratkanis, S. J. Breckler & A. G. Greenwald (Eds.), *Attitude structure and function* (pp. 383–406). Hillsdale, NJ: Lawrence Erlbaum Associates.

Jang, J. M., & Yoon, S. O. (2015). The effect of attribute-based and alternative-based processing on consumer choice in context. *Marketing Letters*, 1–14.

Janis, I. L. (1972). *Victims of groupthink: A psychological study of foreign-policy decisions and fiascoes.* Oxford, UK: Houghton Mifflin.

Janiszewski, C. (1988). Preconscious processing effects: The independence of attitude formation and conscious thought. *Journal of Consumer Research, 15*(2), 199–209.

Janiszewski, C. (1990). The influence of nonattended material on the processing of advertising claims. *Journal of Marketing Research, 27*(3), 263–278.

Jarvella, R. J. (1971). Syntactic processing of connected speech. *Journal of Verbal Learning & Verbal Behavior, 10*(4), 409–416.

Jarvenpaa, S. L. (1989). The effect of task demands and graphical format on information processing strategies and decision making performance. *Management Science, 35*(3), 285–303.

Jasper, J. D., Goel, R., Einarson, A., Gallo, M., & Koren, G. (2001). Effects of framing on teratogenic risk perception in pregnant women. *The Lancet, 358*(9289), 1237–1238.

Jaynes, L. S., & Boles, D. B. (1990, October). The effect of symbols on warning compliance. In *Proceedings of the human factors and ergonomics society annual meeting* (Vol. 34, No. 14, pp. 984–987). Thousand Oaks, CA: Sage.

Jeffrey, K. M., & Mischel, W. (1979). Effects of purpose on the organization and recall of information in person perception. *Journal of Personality, 47*, 397–419.

Jennings, J. R. (1992). Is it important that the mind is in a body? Inhibition and the heart. *Psychophysiology, 29*(4), 369–383.

Jensen, J. L. (2007). Getting one's way in policy debates: Influence tactics used in group decision-making settings. *Public Administration Review, 67*(2), 216–227.

Jervis, R. (1976). *Perception and misperception in international relations.* Princeton, NJ: Princeton University Press.

Jessmer, S., & Anderson, D. (2001). The effect of politeness and grammar on user perceptions of electronic mail. *North American Journal of Psychology, 3*(2) 331–346.

Jeung, H. J., Chandler, P., & Sweller, J. (1997). The role of visual indicators in dual sensory mode instruction. *Educational Psychology, 17*(3), 329–345.

Jin, B., & Farr, C. A. (2010). Supplier selection criteria and perceived benefits and challenges of global sourcing apparel firms in the United States. *Family and Consumer Sciences Research Journal, 39*(1), 31–44.

Jo, I. (2011). Effects of role division, interaction, and shared mental model on team performance in project-based learning environment. *Asia Pacific Education Review, 12*(2), 301–310.

Johns, A. M. (1997). *Text, role and context: Developing academic literacies.* Cambridge, UK: Cambridge University Press.

Johnson, E. J. (1979). Deciding how to decide: The effort of making a decision. Unpublished manuscript, University of Chicago, Chicago IL.

Johnson, E. J. (1981). Expertise in admissions judgment (Doctoral dissertation, Carnegie Mellon University, 1981). *Dissertation Abstracts International, 45*(06B), 1941.

Johnson, E. J. (1988a). Expertise and decision under uncertainty: Performance and process. In M. T. H. Chi, R. Glaser & M. J. Farr (Eds.), *The nature of expertise* (pp. 209–228). Hillsdale, NJ: Lawrence Erlbaum Associates.

Johnson, E. J., Meyer, R. J., & Ghose, S. (1989). When choice models fail: Compensatory models in negatively correlated environments. *Journal of Marketing Research, 26*(3), 255–270.

Johnson, E. J., & Payne, J. W. (1985). Effort and accuracy in choice. *Management Science, 31*, 394–414.

Johnson, E. J., & Russo, J. E. (1978). The organization of product information in memory identified by recall times. *Advances in Consumer Research, 5*(1), 79–86.

Johnson, E. J., & Russo, J. E. (1984). Product familiarity and learning new information. *Journal of Consumer Research, 11*(1), 542–550.

Johnson, E. J., & Sathi, A. (1984). *Expertise in security analysts.* Working paper. Pittsburgh, PA: Graduate School of Industrial Administration, Carnegie Mellon University.

Johnson, E. J., & Tversky, A. (1983). Affect, generalization, and the perception of risk. *Journal of Personality and Social Psychology, 45*(1), 20–31.

Johnson, E. J., & Weber, E. U. (2009). Mindful judgment and decision making. *Annual Review of Psychology, 60*, 53–85.

Johnson, L. (1994). Educating about risk: Designing more effective disaster preparedness messages (earthquakes) (Doctoral dissertation, University of Washington, 1994). *Dissertation Abstracts International, 56*(04A), 1184.

Johnson, M. D. (1986). Modeling choice strategies for noncomparable alternatives. *Marketing Science, 5*(1), 37–54.

Johnson, M. D. (1988b). Comparability and hierarchical processing in multialternative choice. *Journal of Consumer Research, 15*(3), 303–314.

Johnson, S. K., & Dipboye, R. L. (2008). Effects of charismatic content and delivery on follower task performance: The moderating role of task charisma conduciveness. *Group & Organization Management, 33*(1), 77–106.

Johnson-Laird, P. N. (1968). The choice of the passive voice in a communicative task. *British Journal of Psychology, 59*(1), 7–15.

Johnson-Laird, P. N. (1980). Mental models in cognitive science. *Cognitive Science: A Multidisciplinary Journal, 4*(1), 71–115.

Johnston, W. A., & Dark, V. J. (1986). Selective attention. *Annual Review of Psychology, 37,* 43–75.

Johnston, W. A., & Hawley, K. J. (1994). Perceptual inhibition of expected inputs: The key that opens closed minds. *Psychonomic Bulletin and Review, 1,* 56–72.

Jonas, E., Schulz-Hardt, S., Frey, D., & Thelen, N. (2001). Confirmation bias in sequential information search after preliminary decisions: An expansion of dissonance theoretical research on selective exposure to information. *Journal of Personality and Social Psychology, 80*(4), 557–571.

Jones, E. E., & Kelly, J. R. (2007). Contributions to a group discussion and perceptions of leadership: Does quantity always count more than quality? *Group Dynamics: Theory, Research, and Practice, 11*(1), 15.

Jordan, J., & Kaas, K. P. (2002). Advertising in the mutual fund business: The role of judgmental heuristics in private investors' evaluation of risk and return. *Journal of Financial Services Marketing, 7*(2), 129–140.

Jorgensen, C. C., & Kintsch, W. (1973). The role of imagery in the evaluation of sentences. *Cognitive Psychology, 4*(1), 110–116.

Jovanovic, S., & Wood, R. V. (2006). Communication ethics and ethical culture: A study of the ethics initiative in Denver city government. *Journal of Applied Communication Research, 34*(4), 386–405.

Joyce, E. J., & Biddle, G. C. (1981). Anchoring and adjustment in probabilistic inference in auditing. *Journal of Accounting Research, 19,* 120–145.

Judge, T. A., Bono, J. E., Ilies, R., & Gerhardt, M. W. (2002). Personality and leadership: A qualitative and quantitative review. *Journal of Applied Psychology, 87*(4), 765.

Judge, T. A., & Cable, D. M. (2004). The effect of physical height on workplace success and income: Preliminary test of a theoretical model. *Journal of Applied Psychology, 89*(3), 428–441.

Jules, S. J., & McQuiston, D. E. (2013). Speech style and occupational status affect assessments of eyewitness testimony. *Journal of Applied Social Psychology, 43*(4), 741–748.

Jung, K. (1996). Line extension versus new brand name introduction: Effects of new products discrepancy and relationship to an existing brand on the information process of new product evaluation (Doctoral dissertation, University of Illinois at Urbana-Champaign, 1996). *Dissertation Abstracts International, 57*(11A), 4833.

Juni, S., & Gross, J. S. (2008). Emotional and persuasive perception of fonts. *Perceptual and Motor Skills, 106*(1), 35–42.

Juslin, P. N., & Laukka, P. (2003). Communication of emotions in vocal expression and music performance: Different channels, same code? *Psychological Bulletin, 129*(5), 770–814.

Jussim, L., Nelson, T. E., Manis, M., & Soffin, S. (1995). Prejudice, stereotypes, and labeling effects: Sources of bias in person perception. *Journal of Personality and Social Psychology, 68*(2), 228–246.

Just, M. A., & Carpenter, P. A. (1980). A theory of reading: From eye fixations to comprehension. *Psychological Review, 87*(4), 329–354.

Just, M. A., & Carpenter, P. A. (1984). Using eye fixations to study reading comprehension. In D. E. Kieras & M. A. Just (Eds.), *New methods in reading comprehension research* (pp. 151–182). Hillsdale, NJ: Erlbaum.

Just, M. A., & Carpenter, P. A. (1987). *The psychology of reading and language comprehension.* Boston: Allyn and Bacon.

Just, M. A., & Clark, H. H. (1973). Drawing inferences from the presuppositions and implications of affirmative and negative sentences. *Journal of Verbal Learning & Verbal Behavior, 12*(1), 21–31.

Kagan, J. (1991). A conceptual analysis of the affects. *Journal of the American Psychoanalytic Association, 39*(Suppl.), 109–129.

Kahle, L. R., Beatty, S. E., & Homer, P. M. (1986). Alternative measurement approaches to consumer values: The list of values (LOV) and values and life style (VALS). *Journal of Consumer Research, 13*(3), 405–409.

Kahn, B. E., & Baron, J. (1995). An exploratory study of choice rules favored for high-stakes decisions. *Journal of Consumer Psychology, 4*(4), 305–328.

Kahneman, D. (1973). *Attention and effort.* Englewood Cliffs, NJ: Prentice Hall.

Kahneman, D. (2003). Maps of bounded rationality: Psychology for behavioral economics. *American Economic Review, 93*(5), 1449–1475.

Kahneman, D., & Beatty, J. (1966). Pupil diameter and load on memory. *Science, 154*(3756), 1583–1585.

Kahneman, D., & Beatty, J. (1967). Pupillary responses in a pitch-discrimination task. *Perception & Psychophysics, 2*(3), 101–105.

Kahneman, D., & Frederick, S. (2002). Representativeness revisited: Attribute substitution in intuitive judgment. In T. Gilovich, D. Griffin & D. Kahneman (Eds.), *Heuristics and biases: The psychology of intuitive judgment* (pp. 49–81). New York: Cambridge University Press.

Kahneman, D., & Knetsch, J. (1993). Anchoring or shallow inferences: The effect of format. Unpublished manuscript, University of California, Berkeley.

Kahneman, D., Knetsch, J. L., & Thaler, R. H. (1990). Experimental tests of the endowment effect and the Coase theorem. *Journal of Political Economy, 98*, 1325–1348.

Kahneman, D., & Miller, D. T. (1986). Norm theory: Comparing reality to its alternatives. *Psychological Review, 93*(2), 136–153.

Kahneman, D., Schkade, D., & Sunstein, C. R. (1998). Shared outrage and erratic awards: The psychology of punitive damages. *Journal of Risk and Uncertainty, 16*(1), 49–86.

Kahneman, D., & Tversky, A. (1973). On the psychology of prediction. *Psychological Review, 80*(4), 237–251.

Kahneman, D., & Tversky, A. (1982). On the study of statistical intuitions. *Cognition, 11*(2), 123–141.

Kahneman, D., & Tversky, A. (1984). Choices, values, and frames. *American Psychologist, 39*(4), 341–350.

Kahneman, D., & Varey, C. A. (1990). Propensities and counterfactuals: The loser that almost won. *Journal of Personality and Social Psychology, 59*(6), 1101–1110.

Kahnt, T., Heinzle, J., Park, S. Q., & Haynes, J. D. (2011). Decoding different roles for vmPFC and dlPFC in multi-attribute decision making. *Neuroimage, 56*(2), 709–715.

Kaiser, S., & Wehrle, T. (2001). Facial expressions as indicators of appraisal processes. In K. R. Scherer, A. Schorr & T. Johnstone (Eds.), *Appraisal processes in emotion: Theory, methods, research* (pp. 285–300). New York: Oxford University Press.

Kaiser, S., Wehrle, T., & Schmidt, S. (1998). Emotional episodes, facial expressions, and reported feelings in human-computer interactions. In A. H. Fischer (Ed.), *Proceedings of the Xth conference of the international society for research on emotions* (pp. 82–86). Würzburg: ISRE Publications.

Kalichman, S. C., & Coley, B. (1995). Context framing to enhance HIV-antibody-testing messages targeted to African American women. *Health Psychology, 14*(3), 247–254.

Kalin, R., & Rayko, D. (1980). The social significance of speech in the job interview. In R. N. St. Clair & H. Giles (Eds.), *The social and psychological contexts of language* (pp. 39–50). Hillsdale, NJ: Lawrence Erlbaum Associates.

Kalmar, D. A. (1996). The effect of perspective on recall and interpretation of stories: An extension of Anderson and Pichert (Doctoral dissertation, Yale University, 1996). *Dissertation Abstracts International, 57*(06B), 4064.

Kalyuga, S., & Renkl, A. (2010). Expertise reversal effect and its instructional implications: Introduction to the special issue. *Instructional Science, 38*(3), 209–215.

Kamakura, W. A., & Novak, T. P. (1992). Value-system segmentation: Exploring the meaning of LOV. *Journal of Consumer Research, 19*(1), 119–132.

Kameda, T., & Davis, J. H. (1990). The function of the reference point in individual and group risk decision making. *Organizational Behavior and Human Decision Processes, 46*(1), 55–76.

Kameda, T., Ohtsubo, Y., & Takezawa, M. (1997). Centrality in sociocognitive networks and social influence: An illustration in a group decision-making context. *Journal of Personality and Social Psychology, 73*(2), 296–309.

Kameda, T., & Sugimori, S. (1993). Psychological entrapment in group decision making: An assigned decision rule and a groupthink phenomenon. *Journal of Personality and Social Psychology, 65*(2), 282–292.

Kameda, T., & Sugimori, S. (1995). Procedural influence in two-step group decision making: Power of local majorities in consensus formation. *Journal of Personality and Social Psychology, 69*(5), 865–876.

Kamil, M. L. (1972). Memory of repeated words and parallel structure in compound sentences. *Journal of Verbal Learning & Verbal Behavior, 11*(5), 634–643.

Kamin, C., O'Sullivan, P., Deterding, R., & Younger, M. (2003). A comparison of critical thinking in groups of third-year medical students in text, video, and virtual PBL case modalities. *Academic Medicine, 78*(2), 204–211.

Kanar, A. M., Collins, C. J., & Bell, B. S. (2010). A comparison of the effects of positive and negative information on job seekers' organizational attraction and attribute recall. *Human Performance, 23*(3), 193–212.

Kang, H. R., Yang, H. D., & Rowley, C. (2006). Factors in team effectiveness: Cognitive and demographic similarities of software development team members. *Human Relations, 59*(12), 1681–1710.

Kanouse, D. E., & Hanson, L. R., Jr. (1972). Negativity in evaluations. In E. E. Jones, D. E. Kanouse, H. H. Kelley, R. E. Nisbett, S. Valins & B. Weiner (Eds.), *Attribution: Perceiving the causes of behavior* (pp. 47–62). Morristown, NJ: General Learning Press.

Kanwisher, N., McDermott, J., & Chun, M. M. (1997). The fusiform face area: A module in human extrastriate cortex specialized for face perception. *The Journal of Neuroscience, 17*(11), 4302–4311.

Kaplan, M. F., & Kemmerick, G. D. (1974). Juror judgment as information integration: Combining evidential and non-evidential information. *Journal of Personality and Social Psychology, 30*(4), 493–499.

Karau, S. J., & Kelly, J. R. (1992). The effects of time scarcity and time abundance on group performance quality and interaction process. *Journal of Experimental Social Psychology, 28*(6), 542–571.

Kardash, C. A., Royer, J. M., & Greene, B. A. (1988). Effects of schemata on both encoding and retrieval of information from prose. *Journal of Educational Psychology, 80*(3), 324–329.

Kardes, F. R., Kalyanaram, G., Chandrashekaran, M., & Dornof, R. J. (1993). Brand retrieval, consideration set composition, consumer choice, and the pioneering advantage. *Journal of Consumer Research, 20*(1), 62–75.

Kardes, F. R., Posavac, S. S., Silvera, D., Cronley, M. L., Sanbonmatsu, D. M., Schertzer, S., Miller, F., Herr, P. M., & Chandrashekaran, M. (2006). Debiasing omission neglect. *Journal of Business Research, 59*(6), 786–792.

Kardes, F. R., & Sanbonmatsu, D. M. (1993). Direction of comparison, expected feature correlation, and the set-size effect in preference judgment. *Journal of Consumer Psychology, 2*(1), 39–54.

Karelaia, N., & Hogarth, R. M. (2008). Determinants of linear judgment: A meta-analysis of lens model studies. *Psychological Bulletin, 134*(3), 404–426.

Karlin, L., & Kestenbaum, R. (1968). Effects of the number of alternatives on the psychological refractory period. *Quarterly Journal of Experimental Psychology, 20*, 167–178.

Karniol, R. (2003). Egocentrism versus protocentrism: The status of self in social prediction. *Psychological Review, 110*(3), 564–580.

Karpoff, J. M., Lee, D. S., & Martin, G. S. (2008). The cost to firms of cooking the books. *Journal of Financial and Quantitative Analysis, 43*(3), 581–611.

Kassin, S. M. (1983). Deposition testimony and the surrogate witness: Evidence for a "messenger effect" in persuasion. *Personality and Social Psychology Bulletin, 9*(2), 281–288.

Kassin, S. M., & Garfield, D. A. (1991). Blood and guts: General and trial-specific effects of videotaped crime scenes on mock jurors. *Journal of Applied Social Psychology, 21*(18), 1459–1472.

Kassin, S. M., & Pryor, J. B. (1985). The development of attribution processes. In J. Pryor & J. Day (Eds.), *The development of social cognition* (pp. 3–34). New York: Springer-Verlag.

Katzman, N., & Nyenhuis, J. (1972). Color vs. black-and-white effects on learning, opinion, and attention. *AV Communication Review, 20*(1), 16–28.

Kaup, B., Lüdtke, J., & Zwaan, R. A. (2006). Processing negated sentences with contradictory predicates: Is a door that is not open mentally closed? *Journal of Pragmatics, 38*(7), 1033–1050.

Kazoleas, D. C. (1993). A comparison of the persuasive effectiveness of qualitative versus quantitative evidence: A test of explanatory hypotheses. *Communication Quarterly, 41*, 40–50.

Keating, C. F., & Doyle, J. (2002). The faces of desirable mates and dates contain mixed social status cues. *Journal of Experimental Social Psychology, 38*(4), 414–424.

Keen, J. (1990, August 21). How long will U.S. stay in the gulf? *USA Today*, pp. IA, 2A.

Keenan, A. (1976). Interviewers' evaluation of applicant characteristics: Differences between personnel and non-personnel managers. *Journal of Occupational Psychology, 49*(4), 223–230.

Keenan, A. (1977). Some relationships between interviewers' personal feelings about candidates and their general evaluation of them. *Journal of Occupational Psychology, 50*(4), 275–283.

Keenan, J. M., MacWhinney, B., & Mayhew, D. (1977). Pragmatics in memory: A study of natural conversion. *Journal of Verbal Learning & Verbal Behavior, 16*(5), 549–560.

Keeney, R. L., & Raiffa, H. (1976/1993). *Decisions with multiple objectives: Preferences and value tradeoffs.* New York: Cambridge University Press.

Keller, K. L., & Staelin, R. (1987). Effects of quality and quantity of information on decision effectiveness. *Journal of Consumer Research, 14*(2), 200–213.

Keller, T., Gerjets, P., Scheiter, K., & Garsoffky, B. (2006). Information visualizations for knowledge acquisition: The impact of dimensionality and color coding. *Computers in Human Behavior, 22*(1), 43–65.

Kellermanns, F. W., Walter, J., Lechner, C., & Floyd, S. W. (2005). The lack of consensus about strategic consensus: Advancing theory and research. *Journal of Management, 31*(5), 719–737.

Kelley, C. M., & Jacoby, L. L. (1996). Adult egocentrism: Subjective experience versus analytic bases for judgment. *Journal of Memory and Language, 35*(2), 157–175.

Kelly, J. R., & Karau, S. J. (1999). Group decision making: The effects of initial preferences and time pressure. *Personality and Social Psychology Bulletin, 25*(11), 1342–1354.

Keltner, D., & Buswell, B. N. (1997). Embarrassment: Its distinct form and appeasement functions. *Psychological Bulletin, 122*(3), 250–270.

Keltner, D., Ellsworth, P. C., & Edwards, K. (1993a). Beyond simple pessimism: Effects of sadness and anger on social perception. *Journal of Personality and Social Psychology, 64*(5), 740–752.

Keltner, D., & Gross, J. J. (1999). Functional accounts of emotions. *Cognition & Emotion Special Issue: Functional Accounts of Emotion, 13*(5), 467–480.

Keltner, D., & Kring, A. M. (1998). Emotion, social function, and psychopathology. *Review of General Psychology Special Issue: New Directions in Research on Emotion, 2*(3), 320–342.

Keltner, D., Locke, K. D., & Audrain, P. C. (1993b). The influence of attributions on the relevance of negative feelings to personal satisfaction. *Personality and Social Psychology Bulletin, 19*(1), 21–29.

Keltner, D., Young, R. C., & Buswell, B. N. (1997). Appeasement in human emotion, social practice, and personality. *Aggressive Behavior Special Issue: Appeasement and Reconciliation, 23*(5), 359–374.

Kemmelmeier, M. (2004). Separating the wheat from the chaff: Does discriminating between diagnostic and nondiagnostic information eliminate the dilution effect? *Journal of Behavioral Decision Making, 17*(3), 231–243.

Kemp, E., Kennett-Hensel, P. A., & Kees, J. (2013). Pulling on the heartstrings: Examining the effects of emotions and gender in persuasive appeals. *Journal of Advertising, 42*(1), 69–79.

Kendon, A. (1990). *Conducting interaction: Patterns of behavior in focused encounters.* New York: Cambridge University Press.

Kenney, R. A., Schwartz-Kenney, B. M., & Blascovich, J. (1996). Implicit leadership theories: Defining leaders described as worthy of influence. *Personality and Social Psychology Bulletin, 22*(11), 1128–1143.

Kenny, D. A., Horner, C., Kashy, D. A., & Chu, L. C. (1992). Consensus at zero acquaintance: Replication, behavioral cues, and stability. *Journal of Personality and Social Psychology, 62*(1), 88–97.

Kensinger, E. A., & Corkin, S. (2003). Memory enhancement for emotional words: Are emotional words more vividly remembered than neutral words? *Memory & Cognition, 31*(8), 1169–1180.

Kensinger, E. A., Piguet, O., Krendl, A. C., & Corkin, S. (2005). Memory for contextual details: Effects of emotion and aging. *Psychology and Aging, 20*(2), 241–250.

Kepplinger, H. M., Brosius, H. B., & Heine, N. (1990). Contrast effects of nonverbal behavior in television interviews. *Communications, 15*(1–2), 121–134.

Kercsmar, J. (1985). Individual investors' information choice, information processing, and judgment behavior: A process-tracing study of the verbal protocols associated with stock selection (Doctoral dissertation, University of Houston-University Park, 1985). *Dissertation Abstracts International, 46*(9A), 2740.

Keren, G. (1987). Facing uncertainty in the game of bridge: A calibration study. *Organizational Behavior and Human Decision Processes, 39*(1), 98–114.

Kern, R. P., Sticht, T. G., Welty, D., & Hauke, R. N. (1977). *Guidebook for the development of army training literature.* Arlington, VA: U.S. Army Research Institute for the Behavioral and Social Sciences.

Kernell, S. (1993). *Going public: New strategies of presidential leadership* (2nd ed.). Washington, DC: CQ Press.

Kerr, N. L., Hymes, R. W., Anderson, A. B., & Weathers, J. E. (1995). Defendant-juror similarity and mock juror judgments. *Law and Human Behavior, 19*(6), 545–567.

Kerr, N. L., MacCoun, R. J., & Kramer, G. P. (1996). When are N heads better (or worse) than one? Biased judgment in individuals versus groups. In E. H. Witte & J. H. Davis (Eds.), *Understanding group behavior, Vol. 1: Consensual action by small groups* (pp. 105–136). Hillsdale, NJ: Lawrence Erlbaum.

Kerschreiter, R., Schulz-Hardt, S., Faulmuller, N., Mojzisch, A., & Frey, D. (2004). *Psychological explanations for the dominance of shared and preference-consistent information in group discussions: Mutual enhancement or rational-decision making?* Working paper, Ludwig Maximilians University of Munich. Munich, Germany.

Khader, P. H., Pachur, T., Meier, S., Bien, S., Jost, K., & Rösler, F. (2011). Memory-based decision-making with heuristics: Evidence for a controlled activation of memory representations. *Journal of Cognitive Neuroscience, 23*(11), 3540–3554.

Khatri, N., & Ng, H. A. (2000). The role of intuition in strategic decision making. *Human Relations, 53*(1), 57–86.

Khong, Y. F. (1992). *Analogies at war.* Princeton, NJ: Princeton University Press.

Kida, T., Moreno, K. K., & Smith, J. F. (2010). Investment decision making: Do experienced decision makers fall prey to the paradox of choice? *The Journal of Behavioral Finance, 11*(1), 21–30.

Kier, K. L. (2000). A study of the adaptive decision making ability of pharmacists when patient counseling using a process-tracing technique (Doctoral dissertation, The Ohio State University, 2000). *Dissertation Abstracts International, 61*(2B), 807.

Kieras, D. E. (1978). Good and bad structure in simple paragraphs: Effects on apparent theme, reading time, and recall. *Journal of Verbal Learning & Verbal Behavior, 17*(1), 13–28.

Kieras, D. E., & Bovair, S. (1981, November). *Strategies for abstracting main ideas from simple technical prose.* Technical report, Arizona University of Tucson Department of Psychology. Tucson, AZ.

Kiesler, S. B., & Mathog, R. B. (1968). Distraction hypothesis in attitude change: Effects of effectiveness. *Psychological Reports, 23*(3, Pt. 2), 1123–1133.

Kim, H. (2014). Involvement of the dorsal and ventral attention networks in oddball stimulus processing: A meta-analysis. *Human Brain Mapping, 35*(5), 2265–2284.

Kim, H., & John, D. R. (2008). Consumer response to brand extensions: Construal level as a moderator of the importance of perceived fit. *Journal of Consumer Psychology, 18*(2), 116–126.

Kim, J. Y., Min, S. N., Subramaniyam, M., & Cho, Y. J. (2014). Legibility difference between e-books and paper books by using an eye tracker. *Ergonomics, 57*(7), 1102–1108.

Kim, P. H., Ferrin, D. L., Cooper, C. D., & Dirks, K. T. (2004). Removing the shadow of suspicion: The effects of apology versus denial for repairing competence-versus integrity-based trust violations. *Journal of Applied Psychology, 89*(1), 104–118.

Kincaid, J. P., Fishburne, R. P., Jr., Rogers, R. L., & Chissom, B. S. (1975). *Derivation of new readability formulas (automated readability index, fog count and flesch reading ease formula) for Navy enlisted personnel* (No. RBR-8–75). Millington, TN: Naval Technical Training Command.

Kinder, D. R., & Abelson, R. P. (1981, August). *Appraising presidential candidates: Personality and affect in the 1980 campaign.* Paper presented at the 1981 annual meeting of the American Political Science Association, New York.

Kinder, D. R., Peters, M. D., Abelson, R. P., & Fiske, S. T. (1980). Presidential prototypes. *Political Behavior, 2,* 315–338.

Kinder, D. R., & Sears, D. O. (1985). Public opinion and political action. In G. Lindzey & E. Aronson (Eds.), *The handbook of social psychology* (3rd ed., Vol. 2, pp. 659–743). New York: Knopf.

Kinicki, A. J., & Lockwood, C. A. (1985). The interview process: An examination of factors recruiters use in evaluating job applicants. *Journal of Vocational Behavior, 26*(2), 117–125.

Kinney, G. G., Marsetta, M., & Showman, D. J. (1966). *Studies of display symbol legibility. Part XII. The legibility of alphanumeric symbols for digitalized television.* ESD-TR-66–117. MTR-206. Tech Doc Rep U S Air Force Syst Command Electron Syst Div. 1–33.

Kintsch, W. (1979). On modeling comprehension. *Educational Psychologist, 14,* 3–14.

Kintsch, W., & Keenan, J. (1973). Reading rate and retention as a function of the number of propositions in the base structure of sentences. *Cognitive Psychology, 5*(3), 257–274.

Kintsch, W., & Kintsch, E. H. (1978). The role of schemata in text comprehension. *International Journal of Psycholinguistics, 5*(2), 17–29.

Kintsch, W., & Kozminsky, E. (1977). Summarizing stories after reading and listening. *Journal of Educational Psychology, 69*(5), 491–499.

Kintsch, W., & van Dijk, T. A. (1978). Toward a model of text comprehension and production. *Psychological Review, 85*(5), 363–394.

Kintsch, W., & Vipond, D. (1979). Reading comprehension and readability in education practice and psychological theory. In L. G. Nilsson (Ed.), *Perspectives on memory research: Essays in honor of Uppsala University's 500th anniversary* (pp. 329–365). Hillsdale, NJ: Erlbaum.

Kintsch, W., & Yarborough, J. (1982). The role of rhetorical structure in text comprehension. *Journal of Educational Psychology, 74*(2), 828–834.

Kirkman, B. L., Tesluk, P. E., & Rosen, B. (2001). Assessing the incremental validity of team consensus ratings over aggregation of individual-level data in predicting team effectiveness. *Personnel Psychology, 54*(3), 645–667.

Kirsch, M. P. (1985). The effect of information quality and type of data on information integration strategies (Master of Arts thesis, Michigan State University, 1985). *Masters Abstracts International, 2*(4), 422.

Kisielius, J., & Sternthal, B. (1984). Detecting and explaining vividness effects in attitudinal judgments. *Journal of Marketing Research, 21*(1), 54–64.

Kivetz, R., & Simonson, I. (2000). The effects of incomplete information on consumer choice. *Journal of Marketing Research, 37*(4), 427–448.

Klare, G. M. (1963). *The measurement of readability.* Ames, IA: Iowa State University Press.

Klare, G. R. (1976). A second look at the validity of readability formulas. *Journal of Reading Behavior, 8*(2), 129–152.

Klare, G. R. (1984). Readability. In P. D. Pearson, R. Barr, M. Kamil, & P. Mosenthal (Eds.), *Handbook of reading research* (pp. 681–744). New York: Longman.

Klayman, J. (1985). Children's decision strategies and their adaptation to task characteristics. *Organizational Behavior and Human Decision Processes, 35*(2), 179–201.

Klayman, J., & Ha, Y. (1987). Confirmation, disconfirmation, and information in hypothesis testing. *Psychological Review, 94*(2), 211–228.

Klein, G. A. (1994). A script for the commander's intent statement. In A. H. Levis & I. S. Levis (Eds.), *Science of command and control: Part III: Coping with change* (pp. 75–86). Fairfax, VA: AFCEA International Press.

Klein, G. A. (1998). *Sources of power: How people make decisions.* Cambridge, MA: The MIT Press.

Klein, W. M., & Weinstein, N. D. (1997). Social comparison and unrealistic optimism about personal risk. In B. P. Buunk & F. X. Gibbons (Eds.), *Health, coping; and well-being: Perspectives from social comparison theory* (pp. 25–61). Mahwah, NJ: Erlbaum.

Kleiner, B., & Hartigan, J. A. (1981). Representing points in many dimensions by trees and castles. *Journal of the American Statistical Association, 76,* 499–512.

Kleinke, C. L. (1977). Effects of dress on compliance to requests in a field setting. *Journal of Social Psychology, 101*(2), 223–224.

Kleinke, C. L. (1980). Interaction between gaze and legitimacy of request on compliance in a field setting. *Journal of Nonverbal Behavior, 5*(1), 3–12.

Klimoski, R. J., & Donahue, L. M. (2001). Person perception in organizations: An overview of the field. In M. London (Ed.), *How people evaluate others in organizations* (pp. 5–43). Mahwah, NJ: Lawrence Erlbaum Associates.

Klinger, E. (1975). Consequences of commitment to and disengagement from incentives. *Psychological Review, 82*(1), 1–25.

Klocke, U. (2007). How to improve decision making in small groups: Effects of dissent and training interventions. *Small Group Research, 38*(3), 437–468.

Knapp, M. L. (1978). *Nonverbal communication in human interaction* (2nd ed.). New York: Holt, Rinehart and Winston.

Knutson, B. (1996). Facial expressions of emotion influence interpersonal trait inferences. *Journal of Nonverbal Behavior, 20,* 165–182.

Koballa, T. R. (1986). Persuading teachers to reexamine the innovative elementary science programs of yesterday: The effect of anecdotal versus data-summary communications. *Journal of Research in Science Teaching, 23*(6), 437–449.

Kogut, T., & Ritov, I. (2005). The "identified victim" effect: An identified group, or just a single individual? *Journal of Behavioral Decision Making, 18*(3), 157–167.

Konradt, U., Wandke, H., Balazs, B., & Christophersen, T. (2003). Usability in online shops: Scale construction, validation and the influence on the buyers' intention and decision. *Behaviour & Information Technology, 22*(3), 165–174.

Kopelman, M. D. (1975). The contrast effect in the selection interview. *British Journal of Educational Psychology, 45*(3), 333–336.

Kopfman, J. E., Smith, S. W., Ah Yun, J. K., & Hodges, A. (1994, November). *Affective and cognitive reactions to narrative versus logical argument organ donation strategies.* Paper presented at the Speech Communication Association Annual Convention, New Orleans, LA.

Kopfman, J. E., Smith, S. W., Ah Yun, J. K., & Hodges, A. (1998). Affective and cognitive reactions to narrative versus statistical evidence organ donation messages. *Journal of Applied Communication Research, 26*(3), 279–300.

Koriat, A., & Levy-Sadot, R. (1999). Processes underlying metacognitive judgments: Information-based and experience-based monitoring of one's own knowledge. In S. Chaiken & Y. Trope (Eds.), *Dual-process theories in social psychology* (pp. 483–502). New York: Guilford Press.

Koriat, A., Lichtenstein, S., & Fischhoff, B. (1980). Reasons for confidence. *Journal of Experimental Psychology: Human Learning and Memory, 6*(2), 107–118.

Körner, C., Gertzen, H., Bettinger, C., & Albert, D. (2007). Comparative judgments with missing information: A regression and process tracing analysis. *Acta Psychologica, 125*(1), 66–84.

Koslin, B. I., Zeno, S., & Koslin, S. (1987). *The DRP: An effective measure in reading.* New York, NY: College Entrance Examination Board.

Kosslyn, S. M. (1989). Understanding charts and graphs. *Applied Cognitive Psychology, 3*(3), 185–225.

Kosslyn, S. M. (1994). *Elements of graph design.* New York: W. H. Freeman.

Kosslyn, S. M. (2006). *Graph design for the eye and mind.* New York, NY: Oxford University Press.

Kostopoulou, O., Mousoulis, C., & Delaney, B. C. (2009). Information search and information distortion in the diagnosis of an ambiguous presentation. *Judgment and Decision Making, 4*(5), 408–418.

Kotchetova, N., & Salterio, S. (2004). Judgment and decision-making accounting research: A quest to improve the production, certification, and use of accounting information. In D. J. Koehler & N. Harvey (Eds.), *Blackwell handbook of judgment and decision making* (pp. 547–566). Oxford, UK: Blackwell Publishing.

Kotovsky, L., & Gentner, D. (1996). Comparison and categorization in the development of relational similarity. *Child Development, 67*(6), 2797–2822.

Kotter, J., & Heskett, J. (1992). *Corporate culture and performance.* New York: Free Press.

Kowler, E., Anderson, E., Dosher, B., & Blaser, E. (1995). The role of attention in the programming of saccades. *Vision Research, 35*(13), 1897–1916.

Kozminsky, E. (1977). Altering comprehension: The effect of biasing titles on text comprehension. *Memory & Cognition, 5*(4), 482–490.

Kraichy, D., & Chapman, D. S. (2014). Tailoring web-based recruiting messages: Individual differences in the persuasiveness of affective and cognitive messages. *Journal of Business and Psychology, 29*(2), 253–268.

Kraiger, K., & Wenzel, L. H. (1997). Conceptual development and empirical evaluation of measures of shared mental models as indicators of team effectiveness. In M. T. Brannick, E. Salas, & C. Prince (Eds.), *Team performance assessment and measurement: Theory, methods, and applications* (pp. 63–84). Mahwah, NJ: Lawrence Erlbaum.

Krajewski, L. A. (1979). Effectiveness of the inductive and the deductive organizational plans in a special request letter (Doctoral dissertation, Arizona State University, 1979). *Dissertation Abstracts International, 40*(8A), 4368.

Kramer, G. P., Kerr, N. L., & Carroll, J. (1990). Pretrial publicity, judicial remedies, and jury bias. *Law and Human Behavior, 14*(5), 409–438.

Kraus, S. (1996). Winners of the first 1960 televised debate between Kennedy and Nixon. *Journal of Communication, 46,* 78–96.

Krauss, D. A., & Sales, B. D. (2001). The effects of clinical and scientific expert testimony on juror decision making in capital sentencing. *Psychology, Public Policy, and Law, 7*(2), 267–310.

Kricorian, K. T. (2000). The judgment and memory effects of the activation of general knowledge structures related to persuasion and information (Doctoral dissertation, Stanford University, 2000). *Dissertation Abstracts International, 61*(9A), 3662.

Kristof-Brown, A. L. (2000). Perceived applicant fit: Distinguishing between recruiters' perceptions of person-job and person-organization fit. *Personnel Psychology, 53*(3), 643–671.

Krolak-Salmon, P., Hénaff, M. A., Vighetto, A., Bertrand, O., & Mauguière, F. (2004). Early amygdala reaction to fear spreading in occipital, temporal, and frontal cortex: A depth electrode ERP study in human. *Neuron, 42*(4), 665–676.

Krosnick, J. A. (1988). The role of attitude importance in social evaluation: A study of policy preferences, presidential candidate evaluations, and voting behavior. *Journal of Personality and Social Psychology, 55*(2), 196–210.

Krosnick, J. A., Miller, J. M., & Tichy, M. P. (2004). An unrecognized need for ballot reform: The effects of candidate name order on election outcomes. In A. N. Crigler, M. R. Just, & E. J. McCaffery (Eds.), *Rethinking the vote: The politics and prospects of American election reform.* (pp. 51–73). New York, NY: Oxford University Press.

Krug, D., George, B., Hannon, S. A., & Glover, J. A. (1989). The effect of outlines and headings on readers' recall of text. *Contemporary Educational Psychology, 14*(2), 111–123.

Kruger, J. (1999). Lake Wobegon be gone! The "below-average effect" and the egocentric nature of comparative ability judgments. *Journal of Personality & Social Psychology, 77*(2), 221–232.

Kruger, J., Epley, N., Parker, J., & Ng, Z. (2005). Egocentrism over e-mail: Can we communicate as well as we think? *Journal of Personality and Social Psychology, 89*(6), 925–936.

Kruglanski, A. W., & Sleeth-Keppler, D. (2007). The principles of social judgment. In A. W. Kruglanski & E. T. Higgins (Eds.), *Social psychology: Handbook of basic principles* (2nd ed., pp. 116–137). New York: The Guilford Press.

Krugman, H. E. (1964). Some applications of pupil measurement. *Journal of Marketing Research, 1*, 15–19.

Krugman, H. E. (1983). Television program interest and commercial interruption. *Journal of Advertising Research, 23*(1), 21–23.

Kühberger, A., & Huber, O. (1998). Decision making with mission information: A verbal protocol study. *European Journal of Cognitive Psychology, 10*(3), 269–290.

Kühne, R., & Schemer, C. (2015). The emotional effects of news frames on information processing and opinion formation. *Communication Research, 42*(3), 387–407.

Kuklinski, J. H., Quirk, P. J., Jerit, J., Schwieder, D., & Rich, R. E. (2000). Misinformation and the currency of democratic citizenship. *Journal of Politics, 62*, 790–816.

Kulhavy, R. W., & Heinen, J. R. (1977). Recognition memory for paraphrases. *Journal of General Psychology, 96*(2), 223–230.

Kumaran, D. (2013). Schema-driven facilitation of new hierarchy learning in the transitive inference paradigm. *Learning & Memory, 20*(7), 388–394.

Kumaran, D., Summerfield, J. J., Hassabis, D., & Maguire, E. A. (2009). Tracking the emergence of conceptual knowledge during human decision making. *Neuron, 63*(6), 889–901.

Kuncel, N. R., Klieger, D. M., Connelly, B. S., & Ones, D. S. (2013). Mechanical versus clinical data combination in selection and admissions decisions: A meta-analysis. *Journal of Applied Psychology, 98*(6), 1060–1072.

Kunen, S., Green, D., & Waterman, D. (1979). Spread of encoding effects within the nonverbal visual domain. *Journal of Experimental Psychology: Human Learning and Memory, 5*(6), 574–584.

Kuperman, J. C. (2000). Financial analyst sensemaking following strategic announcements: Implications for the investor relations activities of firms (Doctoral dissertation, New York University, 2000). *Dissertation Abstracts International, 61*(5A), 1936.

Kurtz, K. J., & Loewenstein, J. (2007). Converging on a new role for analogy in problem solving and retrieval: When two problems are better than one. *Memory & Cognition, 35*(2), 334–341.

Kuusela, H., Spence, M. T., & Kanto, A. J. (1998). Expertise effects on prechoice decision processes and final outcomes: A protocol analysis. *European Journal of Marketing, 32*(5–6), 559–576.

Kuykendall, D., & Keating, J. P. (1990). Mood and persuasion: Evidence for the differential influence of positive and negative states. *Psychology & Marketing, 7*(1), 1–9.

Kwok, L., Adams, C. R., & Feng, D. (2012). A comparison of graduating seniors who receive job offers and those who do not according to hospitality recruiters' selection criteria. *International Journal of Hospitality Management, 31*(2), 500–510.

Kwon, K., & Lee, J. (2009). The effects of reference point, knowledge, and risk propensity on the evaluation of financial products. *Journal of Business Research, 62*(7), 719–725.

LaBarbera, P. A., & MacLachlan, J. M. (1979). Response latency in telephone interviews. *Journal of Advertising Research, 19*(3), 49–55.

Labella, C., & Koehler, D. J. (2004). Dilution and confirmation of probability judgments based on nondiagnostic evidence. *Memory & Cognition, 32*(7), 1076–1089.

Labov, W. (1966). *The social stratification of English in New York City.* Washington, DC: Center for Applied Linguistics.

Labov, W. (1972). *Sociolinguistic patterns.* Oxford, UK: University Pennsylvania Press.

Labroo, A. A., Dhar, R., & Schwarz, N. (2008). Of frog wines and frowning watches: Semantic priming, perceptual fluency, and brand evaluation. *Journal of Consumer Research, 34*(6), 819–831.

Labuschagne, A., van Zyl, S., van der Merwe, D., & Kruger, A. (2012). Consumers' expectations of furniture labels during their pre-purchase information search: An explication of proposed furniture labelling specifications. *International Journal of Consumer Studies, 36*(4), 451–459.

Ladd, D. R. (1996). *Intonational phonology.* Cambridge, UK: Cambridge University Press.

LaFrance, M., & Hecht, M. A. (1995). Why smiles generate leniency. *Personality and Social Psychology Bulletin, 21*(3), 207–214.

Lagerwerf, L., Cornelis, L., de Geus, J., & Jansen, P. (2008). Advance organizers in advisory reports selective reading, recall, and perception. *Written Communication, 25*(1), 53–75.

Laham, S. M., Koval, P., & Alter, A. L. (2012). The name-pronunciation effect: Why people like Mr. Smith more than Mr. Colquhoun. *Journal of Experimental Social Psychology, 48*(3), 752–756.

Laird, J. D. (1974). Self-attribution of emotion: The effects of expressive behavior on the quality of emotional experience. *Journal of Personality and Social Psychology, 29*(4), 475–486.

Lam, S. S., & Schaubroeck, J. (2000). The role of locus of control in reactions to being promoted and to being passed over: A quasi experiment. *Academy of Management Journal, 43*(1), 66–78.

Lamm, C., Nusbaum, H. C., Meltzoff, A. N., & Decety, J. (2007). What are you feeling? Using functional magnetic resonance imaging to assess the modulation of sensory and affective responses during empathy for pain. *PLoS One, 2*(12), e1292–e1292.

Lanctôt, N., & Hess, U. (2007). The timing of appraisals. *Emotion, 7*(1), 207–212.

Landmann, N., Kuhn, M., Piosczyk, H., Feige, B., Baglioni, C., Spiegelhalder, K., Frasea, L., Riemanna, D., Sterrb, A., & Nissen, C. (2014). The reorganisation of memory during sleep. *Sleep Medicine Reviews, 18*(6), 531–541.

Landry, C. E., Lange, A., List, J. A., Price, M. K., & Rupp, N. G. (2006). Toward an understanding of the economics of charity: Evidence from a field experiment. *Quarterly Journal of Economics, 121*(2), 747–782.

Lang, P. J., Bradley, M. M., & Cuthbert, B. N. (1990). Emotion, attention, and the startle reflex. *Psychological Review, 97*(3), 377–395.

Langacker, R. W. (2008). *Cognitive grammar: A basic introduction* (p. 478). New York, NY: Oxford University Press.

Langan-Fox, J., Anglim, J., & Wilson, J. R. (2004). Mental models, team mental models, and performance: Process, development, and future directions. *Human Factors and Ergonomics in Manufacturing, 14*(4), 331–352.

Langdale, J. A., & Weitz, J. (1973). Estimating the influence of job information on interviewer agreement. *Journal of Applied Psychology, 57*(1), 23–27.

Langlois, J. H., & Roggman, L. A. (1990). Attractive faces are only average. *Psychological Science, 1*(2), 115–121.

Langton, S. R. H., & Bruce, V. (2000). You must see the point: Automatic processing of cues to the direction of social attention. *Journal of Experimental Psychology: Human Perception and Performance, 26*(2), 747–757.

Langton, S. R. H., O'Malley, C., & Bruce, V. (1996). Actions speak no louder than words: Symmetrical cross-modal interference effects in the processing of verbal and gestural information. *Journal of Experimental Psychology: Human Perception and Performance, 22*(6), 1357–1375.

Lanzetta, J. T., Sullivan, D. G., Masters, R. D., & McHugo, G. J. (1985). Viewers' emotional and cognitive responses to televised images of political leaders. In S. Kraus & R. Perloff (Eds.), *Mass media and political thought* (pp. 85–116). Beverly Hills, CA: Sage.

Larkin, J. H., McDermott, J., Simon, D. P., & Simon, H. A. (1980). Models of competence in solving physics problems. *Cognitive Science, 4*(4), 317–345.

Larkin, J. H., & Simon, H. A. (1987). Why a diagram is (sometimes) worth ten thousand words. *Cognitive Science: A Multidisciplinary Journal, 11*(1), 65–100.

Larkin, W., & Burns, D. (1977). Sentence comprehension and memory for embedded structure. *Memory & Cognition, 5*(1), 17–22.

Larsen, S. F., & Seilman, U. (1988). Personal meanings while reading literature. *Text, 8*, 411–429.

Larson, J. R., & Christensen, C. (1993). Groups as problem-solving units: Toward a new meaning of social cognition. *British Journal of Social Psychology, 32*(1), 5–30.

Larson, J. R., Jr., Christensen, C., Franz, T. M., & Abbott, A. S. (1998). Diagnosing groups: The pooling, management, and impact of shared and unshared case information in team-based medical decision making. *Journal of Personality and Social Psychology, 75*(1), 93–108.

Larson, J. R., Foster-Fishman, P. G., & Keys, C. B. (1994). Discussion of shared and unshared information in decision-making groups. *Journal of Personality and Social Psychology, 67*(3), 446–461.

Larson, J. R., & Harmon, V. M. (2007). Recalling shared vs. unshared information mentioned during group discussion: Toward understanding differential repetition rates. *Group Processes & Intergroup Relations, 10*(3), 311–322.

Larson, J. R., Sargis, E. G., Elstein, A. S., & Schwartz, A. (2002). Holding shared versus unshared information: Its impact on perceived member influence in decision-making groups. *Basic and Applied Social Psychology, 24*(2), 145–155.

Lassiter, G. D. (2002). Illusory causation in the courtroom. *Current Directions in Psychological Research, 11*(6), 204–208.

Lau, C. M., Kilbourne, L. M., & Woodman, R. W. (2003). A shared schema approach to understanding organizational culture change. In W. P. Pasmore & R. W. Woodman (Eds.), *Research in organizational change and development* (pp. 225–256). Bingley, UK: Emerald Group Publishing.

Lauer, T. W., & Peacock, E. (1992). Question-driven information search in auditor diagnosis. In T. W. Lauer, E. Peacock, & A. C. Graesser (Eds.), *Questions and information systems* (pp. 253–271). Hillsdale, NJ: Lawrence Erlbaum Associates.

Laughery, K. R., & Page-Smith, K. R. (2006). Explicit information in warnings. In M. S. Wogalter (Ed.), *Handbook of warnings* (pp. 419–428). Mahwah, NJ: Lawrence Erlbaum.

Laughery, K. R., Young, S. L., Vaubel, K. P., & Brelsford, J. W., Jr. (1993). The noticeability of warnings on alcoholic beverage containers. *Journal of Public Policy & Marketing, 12*(1), 38–56.

Laughlin, P. R., & Ellis, A. L. (1986). Demonstrability and social combination processes on mathematical intellective tasks. *Journal of Experimental Social Psychology, 22*(3), 177–189.

Lavandera, B. (1978). Where does the sociolinguistic variable stop? *Language in Society, 7,* 171–182.

Lavine, H., Thomsen, C. J., Zanna, M. P., & Borgida, E. (1998). On the primacy of affect in the determination of attitudes and behavior: The moderating role of affective-cognitive ambivalence. *Journal of Experimental Social Psychology, 34*(4), 398–421.

Layton, P., & Simpson, A. J. (1975). Surface and deep structure in sentence comprehension. *Journal of Verbal Learning & Verbal Behavior, 14*(6), 658–664.

Lazarus, R. S. (1968). Emotions and adaptation: Conceptual and empirical relations. *Nebraska Symposium on Motivation, 16,* 175–266.

Lazarus, R. S. (1991). *Emotion and adaptation.* New York: Oxford University Press.

Lazarus, R. S. (1999). *Stress and emotion: A new synthesis.* New York: Springer Publishing Co.

Lazarus, R. S., & Alfert, E. (1964). Short-circuiting of threat by experimentally altering cognitive appraisal. *The Journal of Abnormal and Social Psychology, 69*(2), 195–205.

Leary, M. R. (1990). Self-presentation processes in leadership emergence and effectiveness. In R. A. Giacalone & P. Rosenfeld (Eds.), *Impression management in the organization* (pp. 363–374). Hillsdale, NJ: Lawrence Erlbaum Associates.

Leathers, D. (1979). The impact of multichannel message inconsistency on verbal and nonverbal decoding behaviors. *Communication Monographs, 46,* 88–100.

Leavitt, H. J. (1951). Some effects of certain communication patterns on group performance. *Journal of Abnormal and Social Psychology, 46,* 38–50.

LeBlanc, R. P. (1981). Organizational purchase decision making: Information-processing strategies and evoked sets of qualified suppliers (Doctoral dissertation, The University of Arizona, 1981). *Dissertation Abstracts International, 42*(2A), 830.

LeBoeuf, R. A., & Shafir, E. (2003). Deep thoughts and shallow frames: On the susceptibility to framing effects. *Journal of Behavioral Decision Making, 16*(2), 77–92.

Lee, A. Y., & Aaker, J. L. (2004). Bringing the frame into focus: The influence of regulatory fit on processing fluency and persuasion. *Journal of Personality and Social Psychology, 86*(2), 205–218.

Lee, B. K. (2005). Hong Kong consumers' evaluation in an airline crash: A path model analysis. *Journal of Public Relations Research, 17*(4), 363–391.

Lee, B. K., & Lee, W. N. (2004). The effect of information overload on consumer choice quality in an on-line environment. *Psychology & Marketing, 21*(3), 159–183.

Lee, D. (1989a). The differential impact of comparative advertising on novice and expert consumers (Doctoral dissertation, University of Pittsburgh, 1989). *Dissertation Abstracts International, 50*(11a), 3666.

Lee, D. H. (1989b). Consumer inferencing behavior in processing product information: The roles of product class knowledge and information processing goal (Doctoral dissertation, Indiana University, 1989). *Dissertation Abstracts International, 51*(3A), 933.

Lee, D. H., & Olshavsky, R. W. (1995). Conditions and consequences of spontaneous inference generation: A concurrent protocol approach. *Organizational Behavior and Human Decision Processes, 61*(2), 177–189.

Lee, K. M. (2004). The multiple source effect and synthesized speech. *Human Communication Research, 30*(2), 182–207.

Lee, M. Y. (2008). Understanding changes in team-related and task-related mental models and their effects on team and individual performance. *Dissertation Abstracts International Section A: Humanities and Social Sciences, 69*(2A), 491.

Leff, D. R., Protess, D. L., & Brooks, S. C. (1986). Crusading journalism: Changing public attitudes and policy-making agendas. *Public Opinion Quarterly, 50*(3), 300–315.

Lefford, A. (1946). The influence of emotional subject matter on logical reasoning. *Journal of General Psychology, 34*, 127–151.

Legge, G. E., & Bigelow, C. A. (2011). Does print size matter for reading? A review of findings from vision science and typography. *Journal of Vision, 11*(5), 1–22.

Leider, J. P., Resnick, B., Kass, N., Sellers, K., Young, J., Bernet, P., & Jarris, P. (2014). Budget-and priority-setting criteria at state health agencies in times of austerity: A mixed-methods study. *American Journal of Public Health, 104*(6), 1092–1099.

Leith, K. P., & Baumeister, R. F. (1996). Why do bad moods increase self-defeating behavior? Emotion, risk tasking, and self-regulation. *Journal of Personality and Social Psychology, 71*(6), 1250–1267.

Lemarié, J., Eyrolle, H., & Cellier, J. M. (2006). Visual signals in text comprehension: How to restore them when oralizing a text via a speech synthesis? *Computers in Human Behavior, 22*(6), 1096–1115.

Lemarié, J., Lorch, R. F., Jr., & Péry-Woodley, M. P. (2012). Understanding how headings influence text processing. *Discours, 10*, 2–22.

Lemerise, E. A., & Dodge, K. A. (1993). The development of anger and hostile interactions. In M. Lewis & J. M. Haviland (Eds.), *Handbook of emotions* (pp. 537–546). New York: Guilford Press.

Lerner, J. S., Goldberg, J. H., & Tetlock, P. E. (1998). Sober second thought: The effects of accountability, anger, and authoritarianism on attributions of responsibility. *Personality and Social Psychology Bulletin, 24*, 563–574.

Lerner, J. S., Gonzalez, R. M., Small, D. A., & Fischhoff, B. (2003). Effects of fear and anger on perceived risks of terrorism: A national field experiment. *Psychological Science, 14*(2), 144–150.

Lerner, J. S., & Keltner, D. (2000). Beyond valence: Toward a model of emotion-specific influences on judgement and choice. *Cognition & Emotion Special Issue: Emotion, Cognition, and Decision Making, 14*(4), 473–493.

Lerner, J. S., & Keltner, D. (2001). Fear, anger, and risk. *Journal of Personality and Social Psychology, 81*(1), 146–159.

Lerner, J. S., Small, D. A., & Loewenstein, G. (2004). Heart strings and purse strings: Carryover effects of emotions on economic transactions. *Psychological Science, 15*(5), 337–341.

Lesgold, A. M., & Resnick, L. (1982). How reading difficulties develop: Perspectives from a longitudinal study. In J. Das, R. Mulcahey, & A. Wall (Eds.), *Theory and research in learning disabilities* (pp. 155–187). New York: Plenum Press.

Levasseur, D. G., & Kanan Sawyer, J. (2006). Pedagogy meets PowerPoint: A research review of the effects of computer-generated slides in the classroom. *The Review of Communication, 6*(1–2), 101–123.

Levenson, R. W. (1994). Human emotion: A functional view. In P. Ekman & R. J. Davidson (Eds.), *The nature of emotion: Fundamental questions* (pp. 123–126). New York: Oxford University Press.

Levenson, R. W. (2003). Blood, sweat, and fears: The autonomic architecture of emotion. In P. Ekman, J. J. Campos, R. J. Davidson, & F. B. M. de Waal (Eds.), *Emotions inside out: 130 years after Darwin's: The expression of the emotions in man and animals* (pp. 348–366). New York: New York University Press.

Leventhal, H., & Singer, R. P. (1966). Affect arousal and positioning of recommendations in persuasive communications. *Journal of Personality and Social Psychology, 4*(2), 137–146.

Levie, W. H. (1973). Pictorial research: An overview. *Viewpoints, 49*(2), 37–45.

Levie, W. H., & Lentz, R. (1982). Effects of text illustrations: A review of research. *Educational Communication & Technology Journal, 30*(4), 195–232.

Levin, I. P. (1987). Associative effects of information framing. *Bulletin of the Psychonomic Society, 25*(2), 85–86.

Levin, I. P., Schnittjer, S. K., & Thee, S. L. (1988). Information framing effects in social and personal decisions. *Journal of Experimental Social Psychology, 24*(6), 520–529.

Levin, J. R., Anglin, G. J., & Carney, R. N. (1987). On empirically validating functions of pictures in prose. In D. M. Willows & H. A. Houghton (Eds.), *The psychology of illustration: Basic research* (Vol. 1, pp. 51–85). New York: Springer-Verlag.

Levine, J. M., Resnick, L. B., & Higgins, E. T. (1993). Social foundations of cognition. *Annual Review of Psychology, 44*, 585–612.

Levine, J. M., & Smith, E. R. (2013). Group cognition: Collective information search and distribution. In D. E. Carlston (Ed.), *The Oxford handbook of social cognition* (pp. 616–633). New York, NY: Oxford University Press.

Levine, L. R., Bluni, T. D., & Hochman, S. H. (1998). Attire and charitable behavior. *Psychological Reports, 83*(1), 15–18.

Levine, S. P. (1998). Implicit self-presentational goals and nonverbal behavior. *Dissertation Abstracts International: Section B: The Sciences and Engineering, 59*(10B), 5621.

Levinson, W., Roter, D. L., Mullooly, J. P., Dull, V. T., & Frankel, R. M. (1997). Physician-patient communication: The relationship with malpractice claims among primary care physicians and surgeons. *Journal of the American Medical Association, 277*(7), 553–559.

Lewandowsky, S., & Spence, I. (1989). Discriminating strata in scatterplots. *Journal of the American Statistical Association, 84,* 682–688.

Lewick, R., & Bunker, B. B. (1996). Developing and maintaining trust in work relationships. In R. M. Kramer & T. R. Tyler (Eds.), *Trust in organizations: Frontiers of theory and reach* (pp. 114–139). Thousand Oaks, CA: Sage.

Lewis, K. M. (2000). When leaders display emotion: How followers respond to negative emotional expression of male and female leaders. *Journal of Organizational Behavior, 21,* 221–234.

Lewis, M. (1999). The role of the self in cognition and emotion. In T. Dalgleish & M. J. Power (Eds.), *Handbook of cognition and emotion* (pp. 125–142). New York: John Wiley & Sons Ltd.

Li, H., & Sakamoto, Y. (2014). Social impacts in social media: An examination of perceived truthfulness and sharing of information. *Computers in Human Behavior, 41,* 278–287.

Libby, R. (1976). Man versus model of man: Some conflicting evidence. *Organizational Behavior & Human Performance, 16*(1), 1–12.

Libby, R., & Frederick, D. M. (1989, February). *Expertise and the ability to explain audit findings* (Technical Report No. 21) Ann Arbor, MI: University of Michigan, Cognitive Science and Machine Intelligence Laboratory.

Liberman, A. M., Cooper, F. S., Shankweiler, D. P., & Studdert-Kennedy, M. (1967). Perception of the speech code. *Psychological Review, 74*(6), 431–461.

Liberman, V., Samuels, S. M., & Ross, L. (2004). The name of the game: Predictive power of reputations versus situational labels in determining prisoner's dilemma game moves. *Personality and Social Psychology Bulletin, 30*(9), 1175–1185.

Libkuman, T. M., Stabler, C. L., & Otani, H. (2004). Arousal, valence, and memory for detail. *Memory, 12*(2), 237–247.

Lichtenstein, S., Fischhoff, B., & Phillips, L. D. (1982). Calibration of probabilities: The state of the art to 1980. In D. Kahneman, P. Slovic, & A. Tversky (Eds.), *Judgment under uncertainty: Heuristics and biases* (pp. 306–334). New York: Cambridge University Press.

Lichtenstein, S., & Slovic, P. (1971). Reversals of preference between bids and choices in gambling decisions. *Journal of Experimental Psychology, 89*(1), 46–55.

Lieberman, M. D. (2007). Social cognitive neuroscience: A review of core processes. *Annual Review of Psychology, 58,* 259–289.

Lieberman, M. D., Gaunt, R., Gilbert, D. T., & Trope, Y. (2002). Reflection and reflexion: A social cognitive neuroscience approach to attributional inference. In M. P. Zanna (Ed.), *Advances in experimental social psychology* (Vol. 34, pp. 199–249). San Diego, CA: Academic Press.

Lim, B. C., & Klein, K. J. (2006). Team mental models and team performance: A field study of the effects of team mental model similarity and accuracy. *Journal of Organizational Behavior, 27*(4), 403–418.

Lindemann, P. G., & Markman, A. B. (1996, July). Alignability and attribute importance in choice. In Garrison W. Cottrell (Ed.), *Proceedings of the 18th annual conference of the cognitive science society* (pp. 358–363). San Diego, CA: Lawrence Erlbaum Associates.

Lingle, J. H., Geva, N., Ostrom, T. M., Leippe, M. R., & Baumgardner, M. H. (1979). Thematic effects of person judgments on impression organization. *Journal of Personality and Social Psychology, 37*(5), 674–687.

Lipp, A., Nourse, H. O., Bostrom, R. P., & Watson, H. J. (1992). The evolution of questions in successive versions of an expert system for real estate disposition. In T. W. Lauer, E. Peacock, & A. C. Graesser (Eds.), *Questions and information systems* (pp. 63–84). Hillsdale, NJ: Lawrence Erlbaum Associates.

Lipscomb, T. J., Shelley, K., & Root, T. (2010). Selection criteria for choosing mental health service providers: A pilot study. *Health Marketing Quarterly, 27*(4), 321–333.

Lipshitz, R., & Shulimovitz, N. (2007). Intuition and emotion in bank loan officers' credit decisions. *Journal of Cognitive Engineering and Decision Making, 1*(2), 212–233.

Littlepage, G., Robison, W., & Reddington, K. (1997). Effects of task experience and group experience on group performance, member ability, and recognition of expertise. *Organizational Behavior and Human Decision Processes, 69*(2), 133–147.

Liversedge, S. P., Rayner, K., White, S. J., Vergilino-Perez, D., Findlay, J. M., & Kentridge, R. W. (2004). Eye movements when reading disappearing text: Is there a gap effect in reading? *Vision Research, 44*(10), 1013–1024.

Livi, S., Kenny, D. A., Albright, L., & Pierro, A. (2008). A social relations analysis of leadership. *Leadership Quarterly, 19*(2), 235–248.

Locksley, A., Borgida, E., Brekke, N., & Hepburn, C. (1980). Sex stereotypes and social judgment. *Journal of Personality and Social Psychology, 39*(5), 821–831.

Locksley, A., Hepburn, C., & Ortiz, V. (1982). Social stereotypes and judgments of individuals: An instance of the base-rate fallacy. *Journal of Experimental Social Psychology, 18*(1), 23–42.

Loewenstein, G. (1987). Anticipation and the valuation of delayed consumption. *Economic Journal, 97*(387), 666–684.

Loewenstein, G. (1996). Out of control: Visceral influences on behavior. *Organizational Behavior and Human Decision Processes, 65*(3), 272–292.

Loewenstein, G., & Lerner, J. S. (2003). The role of affect in decision making. In R. J. Davidson, K. R. Scherer, & H. H. Goldsmith (Eds.), *Handbook of affective sciences* (pp. 619–642). New York: Oxford University Press.

Loewenstein, G., & Mather, J. (1990). Dynamic processes in risk perception. *Journal of Risk and Uncertainty, 3*, 155–175.

Loewenstein, G., Weber, E. U., Hsee, C. K., & Welch, E. (2001). Risk as feelings. *Psychological Bulletin, 127*(2), 267–286.

Loewenstein, J., Thompson, L., & Gentner, D. (1999). Analogical encoding facilitates knowledge transfer in negotiation. *Psychonomic Bulletin and Review, 6*(4), 586–597.

Loftus, E. F. (1979). *Eyewitness testimony.* Cambridge, MA: Harvard University Press.

Loftus, E. F., & Burns, T. E. (1982). Mental shock can produce retrograde amnesia. *Memory & Cognition, 10*(4), 318–323.

Loftus, E. F., Loftus, G. R., & Messo, J. (1987). Some facts about "weapon focus". *Law and Human Behavior, 11*(1), 55–62.

London, M. (2002). *Leadership development: Paths to self-insight and professional growth.* Mahwah, NJ: Lawrence Erlbaum.

Long, D. L., & Baynes, K. (2002). Discourse representation in the two cerebral hemispheres. *Journal of Cognitive Neuroscience, 14*(2), 228–242.

Longenecker, C. O., & Fink, L. S. (2008). Key criteria in twenty-first century management promotional decisions. *Career Development International, 13*(3), 241–251.

Lorch, R. F., Jr. (1985). Effects on recall of signals to text organization. *Bulletin of the Psychonomic Society, 23*(4), 374–376.

Lorch, R. F., Jr. (1989). Text-signaling devices and their effects on reading and memory processes. *Educational Psychology Review, 1*(3), 209–234.

Lorch, R. F., Jr., & Chen, A. H. (1986). Effects of number signals on reading and recall. *Journal of Educational Psychology, 78*(4), 263–270.

Lorch, R. F., Jr., Chen, H. T., & Lemarié, J. (2012). Communicating headings and preview sentences in text and speech. *Journal of Experimental Psychology: Applied, 18*(3), 265–276.

Lorch, R. F., Jr., & Lorch, E. P. (1995). Effects of organizational signals on text-processing strategies. *Journal of Educational Psychology, 87*(4), 537–544.

Lorch, R. F., Jr., Lorch, E. P., Ritchey, K., McGovern, L., & Coleman, D. (2001). Effects of headings on text summarization. *Contemporary Educational Psychology, 26*(2), 171–191.

Lord, C. G., Ross, L., & Lepper, M. R. (1979). Biased assimilation and attitude polarization: The effects of prior theories on subsequently considered evidence. *Journal of Personality and Social Psychology, 37*(11), 2098–2109.

Lord, R. G. (1985). Accuracy in behavioral measurement: An alternative definition based on raters' cognitive schema and signal detection theory. *Journal of Applied Psychology, 70*(1), 66–71.

Lord, R. G., Brown, D. J., Harvey, J. L., & Hall, R. J. (2001). Contextual constraints on prototype generation and their multilevel consequences for leadership perceptions. *The Leadership Quarterly, 12*(3), 311–338.

Lord, R. G., de Vader, C. L., & Alliger, G. M. (1986). A meta-analysis of the relation between personality traits and leadership perceptions: An application of validity generalization procedures. *Journal of Applied Psychology, 71*(3), 402–410.

Lord, R. G., Foti, R. J., & de Vader, C. L. (1984). A test of leadership categorization theory: Internal structure, information processing, and leadership perceptions. *Organizational Behavior & Human Performance, 34*(3), 343–378.

Lord, R. G., Foti, R. J., & Phillips, J. S. (1982). A theory of leadership categorization. In H. G. Hunt, U. Sekaran, & C. Schriescheim (Eds.), *Leadership: Beyond establishment views* (pp. 104–121). Carbondale, IL: Southern Illinois University Press.

Lord, R. G., & Hall, R. (2003). Identity, leadership categorization, and leadership schema. In D. van Knippenberg & M. A. Hogg (Eds.), *Leadership and power: Identity processes in groups and organizations* (pp. 49–64). Thousand Oaks, CA: Sage.

Lord, R. G., & Maher, K. J. (1991). *Leadership and information processing: Linking perceptions and performance.* Cambridge, MA: Unwin Hyman.

Lowenstein, J., Thompson, L., & Gentner, D. (2003). Analogical encoding facilitates transfer in negotiation. *Psychonomic Bulletin and Review, 6*, 586–597.

Lowrey, T. M. (1998). The effects of syntactic complexity on advertising persuasiveness. *Journal of Consumer Psychology, 7*(2), 187–206.

Loyd, D. L., Phillips, K. W., Whitson, J., & Thomas-Hunt, M. C. (2010). Expertise in your midst: How congruence between status and speech style affects reactions to unique knowledge. *Group Processes & Intergroup Relations, 13*(3), 379–395.

Luce, M. F. (1998). Choosing to avoid: Coping with negatively emotion-laden consumer decisions. *Journal of Consumer Research, 24*(4), 409–433.

Luce, M. F., Bettman J. R., & Payne J. W. (1997). Choice processing in emotionally difficult decisions. *Journal of Experimental Psychology: Learning, Memory, and Cognition, 23*(2), 384–405.

Luce, M. F., Bettman, J. R., & Payne, J. W. (2000). Minimizing negative emotion as a decision goal: Investigating emotional trade-off difficulty. In S. Ratneshwar, D. G. Mick, & C. Huffman (Eds.), *The why of consumption: Contemporary perspectives on consumer motives, goals, and desires* (pp. 59–80). London and New York: Routledge.

Lüdtke, J., Friedrich, C. K., De Filippis, M., & Kaup, B. (2008). Event-related potential correlates of negation in a sentence–picture verification paradigm. *Journal of Cognitive Neuroscience, 20*(8), 1355–1370.

Luiten, J., Ames, W., & Ackerson, G. (1980). A meta-analysis of the effects of advance organizers on learning and retention. *American Educational Research Journal, 17*(2), 211–218.

Lulofs, R. S. (1991). *Persuasion: Contexts, people, and messages.* Scottsdale, AZ: Gorsuch-Scarisbrick.

Lundqvist, D., & Öhman, A. (2005). Caught by the evil eye: Nonconscious information processing, emotion, and attention to facial stimuli. In L. F. Barrett, P. M. Niedenthal, & P. Winkielman (Eds.), *Emotion and consciousness* (pp. 97–122). New York: Guilford Press.

Lussier, D. A., & Olshavsky, R. W. (1979). Task complexity and contingent processing in brand choice. *Journal of Consumer Research, 6*(2), 154–165.

Lutz, R. I., MacKenzie, S. B., & Belch, G. F. (1983). Attitude toward the ad as a mediator of advertising effectiveness: Determinants and consequences. *Advances in Consumer Research, 10*(1), 532–539.

Lynch, J. G., Marmorstein, H., & Weigold, M. F. (1988). Choices from sets including remembered brands: Use of recalled attributes and prior overall evaluations. *Journal of Consumer Research, 15*(2), 169–184.

Lyons, M. J., Akamatsu, S., Kamachi, M., & Gyoba, J. (1998). Coding facial expressions with Gabor wavelets. In *Proceedings, third IEEE international conference on automatic face and gesture recognition* (pp. 200–205). Washington, DC: IEEE Computer Society.

Macan, T. H., & Dipboye, R. L. (1988). The effects of interviewers' initial impressions on information gathering. *Organizational Behavior and Human Decision Processes, 42*(3), 364–387.

Macan, T. H., & Dipboye, R. L. (1990). The relationship of interviewers' preinterview impressions to selection and recruitment outcomes. *Personnel Psychology, 43*(4), 745–768.

Macan, T. H., & Dipboye, R. L. (1994). The effects of the application on processing of information from the employment interview. *Journal of Applied Social Psychology, 24*(14), 1291–1314.

Macdonald-Ross, M. (1978). Graphics in texts. In L. S. Shulman (Ed.), *Review of research in education* (Vol. 5, pp. 49–85). Itasca, IL: F. E. Peacock Publishers.

MacGregor, D., & Slovic, P. (1986). Graphic representation of judgmental information. *Human-Computer Interaction, 2*(3), 179–200.

MacGregor, L. J., Corley, M., & Donaldson, D. I. (2009). Not all disfluencies are are equal: The effects of disfluent repetitions on language comprehension. *Brain and Language, 111*(1), 36–45.

MacGregor, L. J., Corley, M., & Donaldson, D. I. (2010). Listening to the sound of silence: Disfluent silent pauses in speech have consequences for listeners. *Neuropsychologia, 48*(14), 3982–3992.

MacInnis, D. J., Rao, A. G., & Weiss, A. M. (2002). Assessing when increased media weight of real-world advertisements helps sales. *Journal of Marketing Research, 39*(4), 391–407.

Mack, D., & Rainey, D. (1990). Female applicants' grooming and personnel selection. *Journal of Social Behavior and Personality, 5*(5), 399–407.

Mackey, M. A., & Metz, M. (2009). Ease of reading of mandatory information on Canadian food product labels. *International Journal of Consumer Studies, 33*(4), 369–381.

Mackintosh, B., & Mathews, A. (2003). Don't look now: Attentional avoidance of emotionally valenced cues. *Cognition & Emotion, 17*(4), 623–646.

MacLeod, C., & Rutherford, E. M. (1992). Anxiety and the selective processing of emotional information: Mediating roles of awareness, trait and state variables, and personal relevance of stimulus materials. *Behaviour Research and Therapy, 30*(5), 479–491.

MacMillan, I. C., Siegal, R., & Narasimha, P. N. S. (1985). Criteria used by venture capitalists to evaluate new venture proposals. *Journal of Business Venturing, 1*(1), 119–128.

MacMillan, J., Entin, E. E., & Serfaty, D. (2004). Communication overhead: The hidden cost of team cognition. In E. Salas & S. M. Fiore (Eds.), *Team cognition: Understanding the factors that drive process and performance* (pp. 61–82). Washington, DC: American Psychological Association.

Macrae, C. N., & Martin, D. (2007). A boy primed Sue: Feature-based processing and person construal. *European Journal of Social Psychology*, *37*(5), 793–805.

Maddux, J. E., & Rogers, R. W. (1980). Effects of source expertness, physical attractiveness, and supporting arguments on persuasion: A case of brains over beauty. *Journal of Personality and Social Psychology*, *39*(2), 235–244.

Mader, F. H. (1988). The influence of multi stop decision making on store choice (Doctoral dissertation, University of Georgia, 1988). *Dissertation Abstracts International*, *49*(11A), 3430.

Magnusdottir, S., Fillmore, P., den Ouden, D. B., Hjaltason, H., Rorden, C., Kjartansson, O., Bonilha, L., & Fridriksson, J. (2013). Damage to left anterior temporal cortex predicts impairment of complex syntactic processing: A lesion-symptom mapping study. *Human Brain Mapping*, *34*(10), 2715–2723.

Maheswaran, D., & Sternthal, B. (1990). The effects of knowledge, motivation, and type of message on ad processing and product judgments. *Journal of Consumer Research*, *17*(1), 66–73.

Maier, S. F., & Watkins, L. R. (1998). Cytokines for psychologists: Implications of bidirectional immune-to-brain communication for understanding behavior, mood, and cognition. *Psychological Review*, *105*(1), 83–107.

Maines, L. A., & McDaniel, L. S. (2000). Effects of comprehensive-income characteristics on nonprofessional investors' judgments: The role of financial-statement presentation format. *The Accounting Review*, *75*(2), 79–207.

Malhotra, N. K. (1982). Information load and consumer decision making. *Journal of Consumer Research*, *8*(4), 419–430.

Malhotra, N., & Krosnick, J. A. (2007). Retrospective and prospective performance assessments during the 2004 election campaign: Tests of mediation and news media priming. *Political Behavior*, *29*(2), 249–278.

Malt, B. C., Ross, B. H., & Murphy, G. L. (1995). Predicting features for members of natural categories when categorization is uncertain. *Journal of Experimental Psychology: Learning, Memory, and Cognition*, *21*, 646–661.

Mandel, N., & Johnson, E. J. (2002). When web pages influence choice: Effects of visual primes on experts and novices. *Journal of Consumer Research*, *29*(2), 235–245.

Manelis, L., & Yekovich, F. R. (1976). Repetitions of propositional arguments in sentences. *Journal of Verbal Learning & Verbal Behavior*, *15*(3), 301–312.

Manis, M., Dovalina, I., Avis, N. E., & Cardoze, S. (1980). Base rates can affect individual predictions. *Journal of Personality and Social Psychology*, *38*(2), 231–248.

Mannes, A. E., Larrick, R. P., & Soll, J. B. (2012). The social psychology of the wisdom of crowds. In J. I. Krueger (Ed.), *Social judgment and decision making* (pp. 227–242). New York, NY: Psychology Press.

Mantonakis, A. (2012). A brief pause between a tagline and brand increases brand name recognition and preference. *Applied Cognitive Psychology*, *26*(1), 61–69.

Manusov, V. (1993). It depends on your perspective: Effects of stance and beliefs about intent on person perception. *Western Journal of Communication*, *57*(1), 27–41.

Marconi, D., Manenti, R., Catricala, E., Della Rosa, P. A., Siri, S., & Cappa, S. F. (2013). The neural substrates of inferential and referential semantic processing. *Cortex*, *49*(8), 2055–2066.

Maritan, C. A. (2001). Capital investment as investing in organizational capabilities: An empirically grounded process model. *Academy of Management Journal*, *44*(3), 513–531.

Markman, A. B. (1999). *Knowledge representation*. Mahwah, NJ: Erlbaum.

Markman, A. B., & Medin, D. L. (1995). Similarity and alignment in choice. *Organizational Behavior and Human Decision Processes*, *63*(2), 117–130.

Markman, A. B., & Moreau, C. P. (2001). Analogy and analogical comparison in choice. In D. Gentner, K. J. Holyoak, & B. N. Kokinov (Eds.), *The analogical mind: Perspectives from cognitive science* (pp. 363–399). Cambridge, MA: The MIT Press.

Marks, L. J., & Olson, J. C. (1981). Toward a cognitive structure conceptualization of product familiarity. *Advances in Consumer Research*, *8*, 145–150.

Marks, M. A., Zaccaro, S. J., & Mathieu, J. E. (2000). Performance implications of leader briefings and team-interaction training for team adaptation to novel environments. *Journal of Applied Psychology*, *85*(6), 971–986.

Markus, D. W. (1983). The budgeting process: Decision makers' perceptions of constraints (Doctoral dissertation, Northwestern University, 1983). *Dissertation Abstracts International*, *44*(9A), 2642.

Markus, H., & Smith, J. (1981). The influence of self-schemas on the perception of others. In N. Cantor & J. F. Kihlstrom (Eds.), *Personality, cognition, and social interaction* (pp. 233–262). Hillsdale, NJ: Erlbaum.

Markus, H., & Zajonc, R. B. (1985). The cognitive perspective in social psychology. In G. Lindzey & E. Aronson (Eds.), *The handbook of social psychology* (3rd ed., Vol. 1, pp. 137–230). New York: Knopf.

Marshall, S. P. (1995). *Schemas in problem solving*. Cambridge, UK: Cambridge University Press.

Marslen-Wilson, W. D. (1987). Parallel processing in spoken word recognition. *Cognition*, *25*, 71–102.

Martin, D. S. (1978). Person perception and real-life electoral behaviour. *Australian Journal of Psychology*, *30*(3), 255–262.

Martin, D., & Macrae, C. N. (2007). A face with a cue: Exploring the inevitability of person categorization. *European Journal of Social Psychology, 37*(5), 806–816.

Martin, J. (1982). Stories and scripts in organizational settings. In A. M. Hastorf & A. M. Isen (Eds.), *Cognitive social psychology* (pp. 255–306). New York: Elsevier/North-Holland.

Martin, J., & Powers, M. E. (1979, September). *If case examples provide no proof, why underutilize statistical information?* Paper presented at the American Psychological Association, New York.

Martin, J., & Powers, M. E. (1980, May). *Skepticism and the true believer: The effects of case and/or baserate information on belief and commitment.* Paper presented at the Western Psychological Association meetings, Honolulu, HI.

Martin, J. R. (1985). Process and text: Two aspects of semiosis. In J. Benson & W. Greaves (Eds.), *Systemic perspectives on discourse* (Vol. I: Selected Theorectical Papers from the 9th International Systemic Workshop, pp. 248–274). Norwood, NJ: Ablex.

Martin, L. L., Abend, T., Sedikides, C., & Green, J. D. (1997). How would it feel if...? Mood as input to a role fulfillment evaluation process. *Journal of Personality and Social Psychology, 73*(2), 242–253.

Martin, S. L. (1987). An attributional analysis of differences in rating type in a performance evaluation context: A use of verbal protocol analysis (Doctoral dissertation, The Ohio State University, 1987). *Dissertation Abstracts International, 49*(2B), 562.

Martire, K. A., Kemp, R. I., Watkins, I., Sayle, M. A., & Newell, B. R. (2013). The expression and interpretation of uncertain forensic science evidence: Verbal equivalence, evidence strength, and the weak evidence effect. *Law and Human Behavior, 37*(3), 197–207.

Mascolo, M. F., & Fischer, K. W. (1995). Developmental transformations in appraisals for pride, shame, and guilt. In J. P. Tangney & K. W. Fischer (Eds.), *Self-conscious emotions: The psychology of shame, guilt, embarrassment, and pride* (pp. 64–113). New York: Guilford Press.

Mason, C., & Stark, M. (2004). What do investors look for in a business plan? A comparison of the investment criteria of bankers, venture capitalists and business angels. *International Small Business Journal, 22*(3), 227–248.

Mason, C. M., & Griffin, M. A. (2003). Identifying group task satisfaction at work. *Small Group Research, 34*(4), 413–442.

Mason, L., Pluchino, P., Tornatora, M. C., & Ariasi, N. (2013). An eye-tracking study of learning from science text with concrete and abstract illustrations. *The Journal of Experimental Education, 81*(3), 356–384.

Mason, M. F., Tatkow, E. P., & Macrae, C. N. (2005). The look of love gaze shifts and person perception. *Psychological Science, 16*(3), 236–239.

Mason, R. A., & Just, M. A. (2006). Neuroimaging contributions to the understanding of discourse processes. In M. J. Traxler & M. A. Gernsbacher (Eds.), *Handbook of psycholinguistics* (2nd ed., pp. 765–800). London: Elsevier Inc.

Massad, C. M., Hubbard, M., & Newtson, D. (1979). Selective perception of events. *Journal of Experimental Social Psychology, 15*(6), 513–532.

Massaro, D. W., & Friedman, D. (1990). Models of integration given multiple sources of information. *Psychological Review, 97*(2), 225–252.

Mast, M. S. (2002). Dominance as expressed and inferred through speaking time: A meta-analysis. *Human Communication Research, 28*(3), 420–450.

Mast, M. S., & Hall, J. A. (2004). Who is the boss and who is not? Accuracy of judging status. *Journal of Nonverbal Behavior, 28*(3), 145–165.

Masters, R. D., & Sullivan, D. G. (1993). Nonverbal behavior and leadership: Emotion and cognition in political information processing. In S. Iyengar & W. J. McGuire (Eds.), *Explorations in political psychology* (pp. 150–182). Durham, NC: Duke University Press.

Mathews, A., & Klug, F. (1993). Emotionality and interference with color-naming in anxiety. *Behaviour Research and Therapy, 31*(1), 57–62.

Mathieu, J. E., Heffner, T. S., Goodwin, G. F., Cannon-Bowers, J. A., & Salas, E. (2005). Scaling the quality of teammates' mental models: Equifinality and normative comparisons. *Journal of Organizational Behavior, 26*(1), 37–56.

Matsumoto, D., Yoo, S. H., & Fontaine, J. (2008). Mapping expressive differences around the world the relationship between emotional display rules and individualism versus collectivism. *Journal of Cross-Cultural Psychology, 39*(1), 55–74.

Matthews, A. M., Lord, R. G., & Walker, J. B. (1990). *The development of leadership perceptions in children.* Unpublished manuscript, University of Akron, Akron, OH.

Matthews, G. R., & Antes, J. R. (1992). Visual attention and depression: Cognitive biases in the eye fixations of the dysphoric and the non-depressed. *Cognitive Therapy and Research, 16*(3), 359–371.

Matthews, H. L., Wilson, D. T., & Monoky, J. F., Jr. (1972). Bargaining behavior in a buyer-seller dyad. *Journal of Marketing Research, 9*(1), 103–105.

Maule, J., & Villejoubert, G. (2007). What lies beneath: Reframing framing effects. *Thinking & Reasoning, 13*(1), 25–44.

Maurer, T. J., & Lord, R. G. (1988). *August IP variables in leadership perception: Is cognitive demand a moderator?* Paper presented at the annual conference of the American Psychological Association (Div. 14), Atlanta, Georgia.

Mauro, R., Sato, K., & Tucker, J. (1992). The role of appraisal in human emotions: A cross-cultural study. *Journal of Personality and Social Psychology, 62*(2), 301–317.

Mautone, P. D., & Mayer, R. E. (2001). Signaling as a cognitive guide in multimedia learning. *Journal of Educational Psychology, 93*(2), 377–389.

May, E. R. (1973). *"Lessons" of the past.* New York: Oxford University Press.

Mayer, J. D., Gaschke, Y. N., Braverman, D. L., & Evans, T. W. (1992). Mood-congruent judgment is a general effect. *Journal of Personality and Social Psychology, 63*(1), 119–132.

Mayer, J. D., & Hanson, E. (1995). Mood-congruent judgment over time. *Personality and Social Psychology Bulletin, 21*(3), 237–244.

Mayer, R. E. (2009). *Multimedia learning.* Cambridge: Cambridge University Press.

Mayer, R. E., & Gallini, J. K. (1990). When is an illustration worth ten thousand words? *Journal of Educational Psychology, 82*(4), 715–726.

Mayer, R. E., & Sims, V. K. (1994). For whom is a picture worth a thousand words? Extensions of a dual-coding theory of multimedia learning. *Journal of Educational Psychology, 86*(3), 389–401.

Mazzella, R., & Feingold, A. (1994). The effects of physical attractiveness, race, socioeconomic status, and gender of defendants and victims on judgments of mock jurors: A meta-analysis. *Journal of Applied Social Psychology, 24*(5), 1315–1344.

McAndrew, F. T. (1986). A cross-cultural study of recognition thresholds for facial expressions of emotion. *Journal of Cross-Cultural Psychology, 17*(2), 211–224.

McArthur, L. Z. (1981). What grabs you? The role of attention in impression formation and causal attribution. In E. T. Higgins, C. P. Herman, & M. P. Zanna (Eds.), *Social cognition: The Ontario symposium* (Vol. 1, pp. 201–246). Hillsdale, NJ: Lawrence Erlbaum Associates.

McArthur, L. Z., & Ginsberg, E. (1981). Causal attribution to salient stimuli: An investigation of visual fixation mediators. *Personality and Social Psychology Bulletin, 7*(4), 547–553.

McArthur, L. Z., & Post, D. L. (1977). Figural emphasis and person perception. *Journal of Experimental Social Psychology, 13*(6), 520–535.

McCandliss, B. D., Cohen, L., & Dehaene, S. (2003). The visual word form area: Expertise for reading in the fusiform gyrus. *Trends in Cognitive Sciences, 7*(7), 293–299.

McCarthy, G., Puce, A., Gore, J. C., & Allison, T. (1997). Face-specific processing in the human fusiform gyrus. *Journal of Cognitive Neuroscience, 9*(5), 604–609.

McCombs, M., & Mauro, J. (1977). Predicting newspaper readership from content characteristics. *Journalism Quarterly, 54*(1), 3–49.

McCoy, M. L. (1997). Jurors' reasoning skills and verdict decisions: The effect of jury deliberations (Doctoral dissertation, University of Wyoming, 1997). *Dissertation Abstracts International, 59*(1B), 436.

McCroskey, J. C., & Mehrley, R. S. (1969). The effects of disorganization and nonfluency on attitude change and source credibility. *Speech Monographs, 36*, 13–21.

McDaniel, M. A., & Einstein, G. O. (1989). Material-appropriate processing: A contextualist approach to reading and studying strategies. *Educational Psychology Review, 1*(2), 113–145.

McDonald, S. A. (2006). Parafoveal preview benefit in reading is only obtained from the saccade goal. *Vision Research, 46*(26), 4416–4424.

McGlone, M. S., & Tofighbakhsh, J. (2000). Birds of a feather flock conjointly (?): Rhyme as reason in aphorisms. *Psychological Science, 11*(5), 424–428.

McGovern, T. V., Jones, B. W., & Morris, S. E. (1979). Comparison of professional versus student ratings of job interviewee behavior. *Journal of Counseling Psychology, 26*(2), 176–179.

McGovern, T. V., & Tinsley, H. E. (1978). Interviewer evaluations of interviewee nonverbal behavior. *Journal of Vocational Behavior, 13*(2), 163–171.

McGraw, K. M., & Steenbergen, M. R. (1995). Pictures in the head: Memory representations of political candidates. In M. Lodge & K. M. McGraw (Eds.), *Political judgment: Structure and process* (pp. 15–41). Ann Arbor, MI: The University of Michigan Press.

McGuire, W. J. (1985). Attitudes and attitude change. In G. Lindsey & E. Aronson (Eds.), *Handbook of social psychology* (3rd ed., Vol. 2, pp. 233–346). New York: Random House.

McHugo, G. J., Lanzetta, J. T., Sullivan, D. G., Masters, R. D., & Englis, B. G. (1985). Emotional reactions to the expressive displays of a political leader. *Journal of Personality and Social Psychology, 49*(6), 1513–1529.

McIntyre, R. M., & Salas, E. (1995). Measuring and managing for team performance: Emerging principles from complex environments. In R. A. Guzzo & E. Salas (Eds.), *Team effectiveness and decision making in organizations* (pp. 9–45). San Francisco: Jossey-Bass.

McKeithen, K. B., Reitman, J. S., Rueter, H. H., & Hirtle, S. C. (1981). Knowledge organization and skill differences in computer programmers. *Cognitive Psychology, 13*(3), 307–325.

McKinnon, L. M., & Tedesco, J. C. (1999). The influence of medium and media commentary on presidential debate effects. In L. L. Kaid & D. G. Bystrom (Eds.), *The electronic election: Perspectives on the 1996 campaign communication* (pp. 191–206). Mahwah, NJ: Lawrence Erlbaum.

McKinnon, L. M., Tedesco, J. C., & Kaid, L. L. (1993). The third 1992 presidential debate: Channel and commentary effects. *Argumentation and Advocacy, 30*, 106–118.

McLaughlin, G. H. (1966). Comparing styles of presenting technical information. *Ergonomics, 9*(3), 257–259.

McNeil, B. J., Pauker, S. G., Cox, H. C., Jr., & Tversky, A. (1982). On the elicitation of preferences for alternative therapies. *New England Journal of Medicine, 306*, 1259–1262.

McQueen, J. M., Cutler, A., Briscoe, T., & Norris, D. (1995). Models of continuous speech recognition and the contents of the vocabulary. *Language and Cognitive Processes, 10*(3–4), 309–331.

Medvec, V. H., Madey, S. F., & Gilovich, T. (1995). When less is more: Counterfactual thinking and satisfaction among Olympic medalists. *Journal of Personality and Social Psychology, 69*(4), 603–610.

Meehl, P. E. (1954). *Clinical versus statistical prediction: A theoretical analysis and a review of the evidence.* Minneapolis, MN: University of Minnesota Press.

Meeren, H. K., van Heijnsbergen, C. C., & de Gelder, B. (2005). Rapid perceptual integration of facial expression and emotional body language. *Proceedings of the National Academy of Sciences of the United States of America, 102*(45), 16518–16523.

Mehl, M. R., Gosling, S. D., & Pennebaker, J. W. (2006). Personality in its natural habitat: Manifestations and implicit folk theories of personality in daily life. *Journal of Personality and Social Psychology, 90*(5), 862–877.

Mehrabian, A., & Ferris, S. R. (1967). Inference of attitudes from nonverbal communication in two channels. *Journal of Consulting Psychology, 31*(3), 248–252.

Melchers, K. G., Klehe, U. C., Richter, G. M., Kleinmann, M., König, C. J., & Lievens, F. (2009). I know what you want to know: The impact of interviewees' ability to identify criteria on interview performance and construct-related validity. *Human Performance, 22*(4), 355–374.

Melone, N. P. (1987). Expertise in corporate acquisitions : An investigation of the influence of specialized knowledge on strategic decision making (Doctoral dissertation, University of Minnesota, 1987). *Dissertation Abstracts International, 48*(9A), 2388.

Melone, N. P. (1994). Reasoning in the executive suite: The influence of role/experience-based expertise on decision processes of corporate executives. *Organization Science, 5*(3), 438–455.

Menenti, L., Petersson, K. M., Scheeringa, R., & Hagoort, P. (2009). When elephants fly: Differential sensitivity of right and left inferior frontal gyri to discourse and world knowledge. *Journal of Cognitive Neuroscience, 21*(12), 2358–2368.

Menne, J., Klingensmith, J., & Nord, D. (1969). Use of taped lectures to replace class attendance. *AV Communication Review, 17*, 47–51.

Meseguer, E., Carreiras, M., & Clifton, C. (2002). Overt reanalysis strategies and eye movements during the reading of mild garden path sentences. *Memory & Cognition, 30*(4), 551–561.

Mesmer-Magnus, J. R., & DeChurch, L. A. (2009). Information sharing and team performance: A meta-analysis. *Journal of Applied Psychology, 94*(2), 535.

Messick, D. M., & Sentis, K. P. (1985). Estimating social and nonsocial utility functions from ordinal data. *European Journal of Social Psychology, 15*(4), 389–399.

Messner, M., Reinhard, M. A., & Sporer, S. L. (2008). Compliance through direct persuasive appeals: The moderating role of communicator's attractiveness in interpersonal persuasion. *Social Influence, 3*(2), 67–83.

Metalis, S. A., & Hess, E. H. (1982). Pupillary response/semantic differential scale relationships. *Journal of Research in Personality, 16*(2), 201–216.

Metcalfe, J., & Mischel, W. (1999). A hot/cool-system analysis of delay of gratification: Dynamics of willpower. *Psychological Review, 106*(1), 3–19.

Metha, P., & Clark, M. S. (1994). Toward understanding emotions in intimate relationships. In A. I. Weber & J. H. Harvey (Eds.), *Perspectives on close relationships* (pp. 88–109). Boston: Allyn & Bacon.

Meyer, B. J., & McConkie, G. W. (1973). What is recalled after hearing a passage? *Journal of Educational Psychology, 65*(1), 109–117.

Meyer, W. U., Reisenzein, R., & Schützwohl, A. (1997). Toward a process analysis of emotions: The case of surprise. *Motivation and Emotion, 21*(3), 251–274.

Meyerowitz, B., & Chaiken, S. (1987). The effect of message framing on breast self-examination attitudes, intentions, and behavior. *Journal of Personality and Social Psychology, 52*(3), 500–510.

Meyers-Levy, J., & Peracchio, L. A. (1992). Getting an angle in advertising: The effect of camera angle on product evaluations. *Journal of Marketing Research, 29*(4), 454–461.

Meyvis, T., & Janiszewski, C. (2002). Consumers' beliefs about product benefits: The effect of obviously irrelevant product information. *Journal of Consumer Research, 28*(4), 618–635.

Michotte, A. (1963). *The perception of causality*. Oxford, UK: Basic Books.

Middlewood, B. L., & Gasper, K. (2014). Making information matter: Symmetrically appealing layouts promote issue relevance, which facilitates action and attention to argument quality. *Journal of Experimental Social Psychology, 53*, 100–106.

Mikulecky, L. (1981). *Job literacy: The relationship between school preparation and workplace actuality*. Bloomington, IN: Indiana University.

Miller, C. A., Wu, P., & Ott, T. (2012). Politeness in teams: Implications for directive compliance behavior and associated attitudes. *Journal of Cognitive Engineering and Decision Making, 6*(2), 214–242.

Miller, C. C., & Cardinal, L. B. (1994). Strategic planning and firm performance: A synthesis of more than two decades of research. *Academy of Management Journal, 37*(6), 1649–1665.

Miller, G. A. (1956). The magical number seven, plus or minus two: Some limits on our capacity for processing information. *Psychological Review, 63*(2), 81–97.

Miller, J. L. (1981). Effects of speaking rate on segmental distinctions. In P. D. Eimas & J. L. Miller (Eds.), *Perspectives on the study of speech* (pp. 39–74). Hillsdale, NJ: Erlbaum.

Miller, K. I., Stiff, J. B., & Ellis, B. H. (1988). Communication and empathy as precursors to burnout among human service workers. *Communication Monographs, 55*(3), 250–265.

Miller, N., Maruyama, G., Beaber, R. J., & Valone, K. (1976). Speed of speech and persuasion. *Journal of Personality and Social Psychology, 34*(4), 615–624.

Mills, J., & Harvey, J. (1972). Opinion change as a function of when information about the communicator is received and whether he is attractive or expert. *Journal of Personality and Social Psychology, 21*(1), 52–55.

Milosavljevic, M., Navalpakkam, V., Koch, C., & Rangel, A. (2012). Relative visual saliency differences induce sizable bias in consumer choice. *Journal of Consumer Psychology, 22*(1), 67–74.

Milroy, R., & Poulton, E. C. (1978). Labelling graphs for improved reading speed. *Ergonomics, 21*(1), 55–61.

Miniard, P. W., Bhatla, S., Lord, K. R., Dickson, P. R., & Unnava, H. R. (1991). Picture-based persuasion processes and the moderating role of involvement. *Journal of Consumer Research, 18*(1), 92–107.

Minsky, M. A. (1975). A framework for the representation of knowledge. In P. Winston (Ed.), *The psychology of computer vision* (pp. 211–277). New York: McGraw-Hill.

Mintz, A., Geva, N., Redd, S. B., & Carnes, A. (1997). The effect of dynamic and static choice sets on political decision making: An analysis of using the decision board platform. *American Political Science Review, 91*(3), 553–566.

Mio, J. S., Riggio, R. E., Levin, S., & Reese, R. (2005). Presidential leadership and charisma: The effects of metaphor. *The Leadership Quarterly, 16*(2), 287–294.

Mischel, W., Cantor, N., & Feldman, S. (1996). Principles of self-regulation: The nature of willpower and self-control. In E. T. Higgins & A. W. Kruglanski (Eds.), *Social psychology: Handbook of basic principles* (pp. 329–360). New York: Guilford Press.

Mitchell, A. A. (1981). The dimensions of advertising involvement. *Advances in Consumer Research, 8*, 25–30.

Mitchell, A. A., & Olson, J. C. (1981). Are product attribute beliefs the only mediator of advertising effects on brand attitude? *Journal of Marketing Research, 18*(3), 318–332.

Mogg, K., Bradley, B. P., Field, M., & De Houwer, J. (2003). Eye movements to smoking-related pictures in smokers: Relationship between attentional biases and implicit and explicit measures of stimulus valence. *Addiction, 98*(6), 825–836.

Mohammed, S., & Dumville, B. C. (2001). Team mental models in a team knowledge framework: Expanding theory and measurement across disciplinary boundaries. *Journal of Organizational Behavior, 22*(2), 89–106.

Mojzisch, A., & Schulz-Hardt, S. (2005). Information sampling in group decision making: Sampling biases and their consequences. In K. Fiedler & P. Juslin (Eds.), *Information sampling and adaptive cognition* (pp. 299–326). Cambridge, UK: Cambridge University Press.

Mojzisch, A., Schulz-Hardt, S., Kerschreiter, R., Brodbeck, F. C., & Frey, D. (2004). *Social validation as an explanation for the dominance of shared information in group decisions: A critical test and extension*. Working paper, Dresden University of Technology.

Monahan, J. L., Murphy, S. T., & Zajonc, R. B. (2000). Subliminal mere exposure: Specific, general, and diffuse effects. *Psychological Science, 11*(6), 462–466.

Monat, A. (1976). Temporal uncertainty, anticipation time, and cognitive coping under threat. *Journal of Human Stress, 2*(2), 32–43.

Mondak, J. J. (1993). Source cues and policy approval: The cognitive dynamics of public support for the Reagan agenda. *American Journal of Political Science, 37*(1), 186–212.

Mongeau, P. A. (1998). Another look at fear-arousing persuasive appeals. In M. Allen & R. W. Preiss (Eds.), *Persuasion: Advances through meta-analysis* (pp. 53–68). Cresskill, NJ: Hampton Press.

Montepare, J., Koff, E., Zaitchik, D., & Albert, M. (1999). The use of body movements and gestures as cues to emotions in younger and older adults. *Journal of Nonverbal Behavior, 23*(2), 133–152.

Montepare, J. M., & Dobish, H. (2003). The contribution of emotion perceptions and their overgeneralizations to trait impressions. *Journal of Nonverbal Behavior, 27*(4), 237–254.

Montepare, J. M., & Zebrowitz-McArthur, L. (1987). Perceptions of adults with childlike voices in two cultures. *Journal of Experimental Social Psychology, 23*(4), 331–349.

Montepare, J. M., & Zebrowitz-McArthur, L. (1988). Impressions of people created by age-related qualities of their gaits. *Journal of Personality and Social Psychology, 55*(4), 547–556.

Monti, M., Boero, R., Berg, N., Gigerenzer, G., & Martignon, L. (2012). How do common investors behave? Information search and portfolio choice among bank customers and university students. *Mind & Society, 11*(2), 203–233.

Montier, J. (2002). *Behavioural finance: Insights into irrational minds and markets.* Hoboken: Wiley.

Moog, C. (1991). *Are they selling her lips? Advertising and identity.* New York: Morrow & Co.

Moore, D. L., & Hutchinson, J. W. (1983). The effects of ad affect on advertising effectiveness. *Advances in Consumer Research, 10*, 526–531.

Moray, N. (1959). Attention in dichotic listening: Affective cues and the influence of instructions. *The Quarterly Journal of Experimental Psychology, 11*, 56–60.

Moreau, C. P., Markman, A. B., & Lehmann, D. R. (2001). What is it? Categorization flexibility and consumers' responses to really new products. *Journal of Consumer Research, 27*(4), 489–498.

Moreno, R., & Ortegano-Layne, L. (2008). Do classroom exemplars promote the application of principles in teacher education? A comparison of videos, animations, and narratives. *Educational Technology Research and Development, 56*(4), 449–465.

Moreno, R., & Valdez, A. (2007). Immediate and delayed effects of using a classroom case exemplar in teacher education: The role of presentation format. *Journal of Educational Psychology, 99*(1), 194–206.

Morris, C. D., Stein, B. S., & Bransford, J. D. (1979). Prerequisites for the utilization of knowledge in the recall of prose passages. *Journal of Experimental Psychology: Human Learning and Memory, 5*(3), 253–261.

Morwitz, V. G., & Fitzsimons, G. J. (2004). The mere-measurement effect: Why does measuring intentions change actual behavior? *Journal of Consumer Psychology, 14*(1–2), 64–74.

Morwitz, V. G., Johnson, E., & Schmittlein, D. (1993). Does measuring intent change behavior. *Journal of Consumer Research, 20*(1), 46–61.

Moscovici, S. (1980). Toward a theory of conversion behavior. *Advances in Experimental Social Psychology, 13*, 209–239.

Moskowitz, D. S. (1982). Coherence and cross-situational generality in personality: A new analysis of old problems. *Journal of Personality and Social Psychology, 43*(4), 754–768.

Moskowitz, D., & Stroh, P. (1996). Expectation-driven assessments of political candidates. *Political Psychology, 17*(4), 695–712.

Motes, W. H., Hilton, C. B., & Fielden, J. S. (1992). Language, sentence, and structural variations in print advertising. *Journal of Advertising Research, 32*, 63–77.

Motowidlo, S. J., & Burnett, J. R. (1995). Aural and visual sources of validity in structured employment interviews. *Organizational Behavior and Human Decision Processes, 61*(3), 239–249.

Moulton, L. (2007). Divining value with relational proxies: How moneylenders balance risk and trust in the quest for good borrowers. *Sociological Forum, 22*(3), 300–330.

Moy, J. W., & Lam, K. F. (2004). Selection criteria and the impact of personality on getting hired. *Personnel Review, 33*(5), 521–535.

Mueller, U., & Mazur, A. (1996). Facial dominance of West Point cadets as a predictor of later military rank. *Social Forces, 74*(3), 823–850.

Mulilis, J. P., & Lippa, R. (1990). Behavioral change in earthquake preparedness due to negative threat appeals: A test of protection motivation theory. *Journal of Applied Social Psychology, 20*(8, Pt. 1), 619–638.

Mullen, B., Johnson, C., & Salas, E. (1991). Productivity loss in brainstorming groups: A meta-analytic integration. *Basic and Applied Social Psychology, 12*(1), 3–23.

Mulvey, M. S., Olson, J. C., Celsi, R. L., & Walker, B. A. (1994). Exploring the relationship between means-end knowledge and involvement. *Advances in Consumer Research, 21*, 51–57.

Mumford, M. D., Marks, M. A., Connelly, M. S., Zaccaro, S. J., & Reiter-Palmon, R. (2000). Development of leadership skills: Experience and timing. *Leadership Quarterly, 11*, 87–114.

Munhall, K. G., Jones, J. A., Callan, D. E., Kuratate, T., & Vatikiotis-Bateson, E. (2004). Visual prosody and speech intelligibility head movement improves auditory speech perception. *Psychological Science, 15*(2), 133–137.

Murase, T., Carter, D. R., DeChurch, L. A., & Marks, M. A. (2014). Mind the gap: The role of leadership in multiteam system collective cognition. *The Leadership Quarterly, 25*(5), 972–986.

Murphy, N. A., Hall, J. A., & Colvin, C. R. (2003). Accurate intelligence assessments in social interactions: Mediators and gender effects. *Journal of Personality, 71*(3), 465–493.

Mussweiler, T., & Englich, B. (2005). Subliminal anchoring: Judgmental consequences and underlying mechanisms. *Organizational Behavior and Human Decision Processes, 98*(2), 133–143.

Mussweiler, T., & Strack, F. (2000). The use of category and exemplar knowledge in the solution of anchoring tasks. *Journal of Personality and Social Psychology, 78*(6), 1038–1052.

Muthukrishnan, A. V., & Ramaswami, S. (1999). Contextual effects on the revision of evaluative judgments: An extension of the omission-detection framework. *Journal of Consumer Research, 26*(1), 70–84.

Myers, B., & Greene, E. (2004). The prejudicial nature of victim impact statements: Implications for capital sentencing policy. *Psychology, Public Policy, and Law, 10*(4), 492–515.

Myers, J. L., Pezdek, K., & Coulson, D. (1973). Effect of prose organization upon free recall. *Journal of Educational Psychology, 65*(3), 313–320.

Nabi, R. L. (1998). The effect of disgust-eliciting visuals on attitudes toward animal experimentation. *Communication Quarterly, 46*, 472–484.

Nabi, R. L. (2002). Anger, fear, uncertainty, and attitudes: A test of the cognitive-functional model. *Communication Monographs, 69*(3), 204–216.

Nabi, R. L. (2003). Exploring the framing effects of emotion: Do discrete emotions differentially influence information accessibility, information seeking, and policy preference? *Communication Research, 30*(2), 224–247.

Nagy, G. (1975). *Female dating strategies as a function of physical attractiveness and other social characteristics of males* (Unpublished thesis). Kansas State University, Manhattan, KS.

Nagy, G. (1981). How are personnel selections made? An analysis of decision strategies in a simulated personnel selection task (Doctoral dissertation, Kansas State University, 1981). *Dissertation Abstracts International, 42*(7B), 3022.

Narang, R. (2011). Examining the role of various psychographic characteristics in apparel store selection: A study on Indian youth. *Young Consumers, 12*(2), 133–144.

Naumann, S. E., & Bennett, N. (2000). A case for procedural justice climate: Development and test of a multilevel model. *Academy of Management Journal, 43*(5), 881–889.

Navarro-Martinez, D., Salisbury, L. C., Lemon, K. N., Stewart, N., Matthews, W. J., & Harris, A. J. (2011). Minimum required payment and supplemental information disclosure effects on consumer debt repayment decisions. *Journal of Marketing Research, 48*(SPL), S60–S77.

Neale, M. A., Huber, V. L., & Northcraft, G. B. (1987). The framing of negotiations: Contextual versus task frames. *Organizational Behavior and Human Decision Processes, 39*(2), 228–241.

Nearey, T. M. (1989). Static, dynamic, and relational properties in vowel perception. *Journal of the Acoustical Society of America, 85*(5), 2088–2113.

Nedungadi, P. (1990). Recall and consumer consideration sets: Influencing choice without altering brand evaluations. *Journal of Consumer Research, 17*(3), 263–276.

Neisser, U. (1976). *Cognition and reality: Principles and implications of cognitive psychology.* New York: W. H. Freeman/Times Books/Henry Holt & Co.

Nelson, D. L., Wheeler, J., & Engel, J. (1970). Stimulus meaningfulness and similarity, recall direction and rate of recall test. *Psychonomic Science, 20*(6), 346–347.

Nelson, K. (1980, September). *Characteristics of children's scripts for familiar events.* Paper presented at the meeting of the American Psychological Association, Montreal, Canada.

Nelson, T. O., & Narens, L. (1990). Metamemory: A theorectical framework and new findings. In G. Bower (Ed.), *The psychology of learning and motivation* (Vol. 26, pp. 125–141). New York: Academic Press.

Nemeth, C., & Rogers, J. (1996). Dissent and the search for information. *British Journal of Social Psychology, 35*(1), 67–76.

Nemeth, R. J. (2002). The impact of gruesome evidence on mock juror decision making: The role of evidence characteristics and emotional response (Doctoral dissertation, Louisiana State University, 2002). *Dissertation Abstracts International, 63*(11B), 5546.

Nemiro, J., Beyerlein, M., Bradley, L., & Beyerlein, S. (2008). The challenges of virtual teaming. In J. Nemiro, M. M. Beyerlein, L. Bradley, & S. Beyerlein (Eds.), *The handbook of high-performance virtual teams: A toolkit for collaborating across boundaries* (pp. 1–27). San Francisco, CA: Jossey-Bass.

Nesbit, J. C., & Adescope, O. O. (2006). Learning with concept and knowledge maps: A meta-analysis. *Review of Educational Research, 76*, 413–448.

Nesdale, A. R., & Dharmalingam, S. (1986). Category salience, stereotyping and person memory. *Australian Journal of Psychology, 38*(2), 145–151.

Nespor, M., & Vogel, I. (1983). Prosodic structure above the word. In A. Cutler & D. R. Ladd (Eds.), *Prosody: Models and measurements* (pp. 123–140). Heidelberg: Springer.

Neuberg, S. L., & Fiske, S. T. (1987). Motivational influences on impression formation: Outcome dependency, accuracy-driven attention, and individuating processes. *Journal of Personality and Social Psychology, 53*(3), 431–444.

Neuman, R., Just, M., & Crigler, A. (1992). *Common knowledge: News and the construction of political meaning.* Chicago: University of Chicago Press.

Neumann, N., Lotze, M., & Eickhoff, S. B. (2016). Cognitive expertise: An ALE meta-analysis. *Human Brain Mapping, 37*(1), 262–272.

Neumann, R., & Strack, F. (2000). Mood contagion: The automatic transfer of mood between persons. *Journal of Personality and Social Psychology, 79*(2), 211–223.

Newby-Clark, I. R., Ross, M., Buehler, R., Koehler, D. J., & Griffin, D. (2000). People focus on optimistic and disregard pessimistic scenarios while predicting their task completion times. *Journal of Experimental Psychology: Applied, 6*(3), 171–182.

Newcombe, N., & Arnkoff, D. B. (1979). Effects of speech style and sex of speaker on person perception. *Journal of Personality and Social Psychology, 37*(8), 1293–1303.

Newell, A., & Simon, H. A. (1972). *Human problem solving.* Englewood Cliffs, NJ: Prentice-Hall.

Newell, B. R., & Shanks, D. R. (2007). Recognising what you like: Examining the relation between the mere-exposure effect and recognition. *European Journal of Cognitive Psychology, 19*(1), 103–118.

Newman, B. (2003). Integrity and presidential approval, 1980–2000. *Public Opinion Quarterly, 67*(3), 335–367.

Newman, B. I., & Perloff, R. M. (2004). Political marketing: Theory, research, applications. In L. L. Kaid (Ed.), *Handbook of political communication research* (pp. 17–43). Mahwah, NJ: Lawrence Erlbaum Associates.

Newspaper Advertising Bureau (1964). *A study of the opportunity for exposure to national newspaper advertising.* New York: Author.

Newspaper Advertising Bureau (1987). *An eye camera study of ads.* New York: Author.

Ngeru, J. (2013). Multi-criteria decision analysis framework in the selection of an Enterprise Integration (EI) approach that best satisfies organizational requirements (Doctoral dissertation, Morgan State University, 2013). *Dissertation Abstracts International: Section B, 73*(11B)(E).

Nicholas, S. K. (1983). A video observational study of the writing process of college students in a non-academic situation (Doctoral dissertation, Oakland University, 1983). *Dissertation Abstracts International, 44*(3A), 684.

Nicholson, G., & Newton, C. (2010). The role of the board of directors: Perceptions of managerial elites. *Journal of Management & Organization, 16*(2), 204–218.

Nickerson, C. (1999). The use of English in electronic mail in a multinational corporation. In F. Bargiela-Chiappini & C. Nickerson (Eds.), *Writing business: Genres, media and discourses* (pp. 35–56). Harlow, UK: Longman.

Nickerson, R. S. (1968). On long-term recognition memory for pictorial material. *Psychonomic Science, 11*(2), 58.

Nickles, K. R. (1995). Judgment-based and reasoning-based stopping rules in decision making under uncertainty (Doctoral dissertation, University of Minnesota, 1995). *Dissertation Abstracts International, 56*(3A), 1005.

Nicosia, G. E. (1988). College students' listening comprehension strategies in a lecture situation (Doctoral dissertation, New York University, 1988). *Dissertation Abstracts International, 49*(5A), 0998.

Niedenthal, P. M. (2008). Emotion concepts. In M. Lewis, J. M. Haviland-Jones, & L. Feldman Barrett (Eds.), *Handbook of emotions* (Vol. 3, pp. 587–600). New York, NY: Guilford Press.

Niedenthal, P. M., Halberstadt, J. B., & Innes-Ker, Å. H. (1999). Emotional response categorization. *Psychological Review, 106*(2), 337–361.

Niedenthal, P. M., Halberstadt, J. B., Margolin, J., & Innes-Ker, Å. H. (2000). Emotional state and the detection of change in facial expression of emotion. *European Journal of Social Psychology, 30*(2), 211–222.

Niedenthal, P. M., & Kitayama, S. (Eds.). (1994). *The heart's eye: Emotional influences in perception and attention.* San Diego, CA: Academic Press.

Niedenthal, P. M., & Setterlund, M. B. (1994). Emotion congruence in perception. *Personality and Social Psychology Bulletin, 20*(4), 401–411.

Niedenthal, P. M., Setterlund, M. B., & Jones, D. E. (1994). Emotional organization of perceptual memory. In P. M. Niedenthal & S. Kitayama (Eds.), *The heart's eye: Emotional influences in perception and attention* (pp. 87–113). San Diego, CA: Academic Press.

Nisbett, R. E., Borgida, E., Crandall, R., & Reed, H. (1982). Popular induction: Information is not necessarily informative. In D. Kahneman, P. Slovic, & A. Tversky (Eds.), *Judgments under uncertainty: Heuristics and biases* (pp. 101–116). New York: Cambridge University Press.

Nisbett, R. E., & Ross, L. (1980). *Human inference: Strategies and shortcomings of social judgment.* Englewood Cliffs, NJ: Prentice-Hall.

Nisbett, R. E., Zukier, H., & Lemley, R. E. (1981). The dilution effect: Nondiagnostic information weakens the implications of diagnostic information. *Cognitive Psychology, 13*(2), 248–277.

Nodine, C. F., & Kundel, H. L. (1987). Perception and display in diagnostic imaging. *RadioGraphs, 7*, 1241–1250.

Nodine, C. F., Locher, P. J., & Krupinski, E. A. (1993). The role of formal art training on perception and aesthetic judgment of art compositions. *Leonardo, 26*, 219–227.

Nolen-Hoeksema, S., & Morrow, J. (1993). Effects of rumination and distraction on naturally occurring depressed mood. *Cognition & Emotion*, 7(6), 561–570.

Nolen-Hoeksema, S., Morrow, J., & Fredrickson, B. L. (1993). Response styles and the duration of episodes of depressed mood. *Journal of Abnormal Psychology*, 102(1), 20–28.

Norman, R. (1976). When what is said is important: A comparison of expert and attractive sources. *Journal of Experimental Social Psychology*, 12(3), 294–300.

North, A. C., Hargreaves, D. J., & McKendrick, J. (1997). In-store music affects product choice. *Nature*, 390(6656), 132.

North, A. C., Hargreaves, D. J., & McKendrick, J. (1999). Research reports: The influence of in-store music on wine selections. *Journal of Applied Psychology*, 84(2), 271–276.

Northcraft, G. B., & Neale, M. A. (1987). Experts, amateurs, and real estate: An anchoring-and-adjustment perspective on property pricing decisions. *Organizational Behavior and Human Decision*, 39(1), 84–97.

Norwick, R., & Epley, N. (2003, February). *Experiential determinants of confidence*. Poster presented at the Society for Personality and Social Psychology, Los Angeles, CA.

Novemsky, N., Dhar, R., Schwarz, N., & Simonson, I. (2007). Preference fluency in choice. *Journal of Marketing Research*, 44(3), 347–356.

Novick, L. R., & Holyoak, K. J. (1991). Mathematical problem solving by analogy. *Journal of Experimental Psychology: Learning, Memory, and Cognition*, 17(3), 398–415.

Nowlis, S. M., Kahn, B. E., & Dhar, R. (2002). Coping with ambivalence: The effect of removing a neutral option on consumer attitude and preference judgments. *Journal of Consumer Research*, 29(3), 319–334.

Nunes, J. C., & Boatwright, P. (2004). Incidental prices and their effect on willingness to pay. *Journal of Marketing Research*, 41(4), 457–466.

Nunes, J. C., Ordanini, A., & Valsesia, F. (2015). The power of repetition: Repetitive lyrics in a song increase processing fluency and drive market success. *Journal of Consumer Psychology*, 25(2), 187–199.

Nygaard, L. C. (2005). Perceptual integration of linguistic and nonlinguistic properties of speech. In D. Pisoni & R. Remez (Eds.), *Handbook of speech perception* (pp. 390–414). Oxford, UK: Wiley-Blackwell.

Nygren, T. E., Isen, A. M., Taylor, P. J., & Dulin, J. (1996). The influence of positive affect on the decision rule in risk situations: Focus on outcome (and especially avoidance of loss) rather than probability. *Organizational Behavior and Human Decision Processes*, 66(1), 59–72.

Oakes, P., & Turner, J. C. (1986). Distinctiveness and the salience of social category memberships: Is there an automatic perceptual bias towards novelty? *European Journal of Social Psychology*, 16(4), 325–344.

Oatley, K., & Jenkins, J. M. (1996). *Understanding emotions*. Malden, MA: Blackwell Publishing.

Oberlander, J., & Gill, A. J. (2006). Language with character: A stratified corpus comparison of individual differences in e-mail communication. *Discourse Processes*, 42(3), 239–270.

O'Brien, E. J., Raney, G. E., Albrecht, J., & Rayner, K. (1997). Processes involved in the resolution of explicit anaphors. *Discourse Processes*, 23, 1–24.

Ochsner, K. N. (2000). Are affective events richly recollected or simply familiar? The experience and process of recognizing feelings past. *Journal of Experimental Psychology: General*, 129(2), 242–261.

Ochsner, K. N., & Gross, J. J. (2005). The cognitive control of emotion. *Trends in Cognitive Sciences*, 9(5), 242–249.

Ochsner, K. N., & Sanchez, H. (2001). *The relation between the regulation and recollection of affective experience*. Unpublished manuscript. Department of Psychology, Stanford University, Stanford, CA.

Offermann, L. R., Kennedy, J. K., & Wirtz, P. W. (1994). Implicit leadership theories: Content, structure, and generalizability. *Leadership Quarterly*, 5(1), 43–58.

Ohbuchi, K. I., Kameda, M., & Agarie, N. (1989). Apology as aggression control: Its role in mediating appraisal of and response to harm. *Journal of Personality and Social Psychology*, 56(2), 219–227.

Ohlsson, S., & Hemmerich, J. (1999). Articulating an explanation schema: A preliminary model and supporting data. In M. Hahn & S. Stones (Eds.), *Proceedings of the Twenty First Annual Conference of the Cognitive Science Society* (pp. 490–495). Mahwah, NJ: Erlbaum.

Ohlsson, S., & Lehtinen, E. (1997). Abstraction and the acquisition of complex ideas. *International Journal of Educational Research*, 27, 37–48.

Öhman, A. (1979). The orienting response, attention, and learning: An information-processing perspective. In H. D. Kimmel, E. H. van Gist, & J. F. Orlebeke (Eds.), *The orienting reflex in humans* (pp. 443–472). Hillsdale, NJ: Lawrence Erlbaum Associates.

Öhman, A., & Dimberg, U. (1978). Facial expressions as conditioned stimuli for electrodermal responses: A case of "preparedness"? *Journal of Personality and Social Psychology*, 36(11), 1251–1258.

Öhman, A., Esteves, F., & Soares, J. J. F. (1995). Preparedness and preattentive associative learning: Electrodermal conditioning to masked stimuli. *Journal of Psychophysiology*, 9(2), 99–108.

Öhman, A., Flykt, A., & Esteves, F. (2001). Emotion drives attention: Detecting the snake in the grass. *Journal of Experimental Psychology: General*, 130(3), 466–478.

Öhman, A., Hamm, A., & Hugdahl, K. (2000). Cognition and the autonomic nervous system: Orienting, anticipation, and conditioning. In J. T. Cacioppo, L. G. Tassinary, & G. G. Berntson (Eds.), *Handbook of psychophysiology* (2nd ed., pp. 533–575). New York: Cambridge University Press.

Öhman, A., & Wiens, S. (2003). On the automaticity of autonomic responses in emotion: An evolutionary perspective. In R. J. Davidson, K. R. Scherer, & H. H. Goldsmith (Eds.), *Handbook of affective sciences* (pp. 256–275). New York: Oxford University Press.

Ohst, A., Fondu, B. M., Glogger, I., Nückles, M., & Renkl, A. (2014). Preparing learners with partly incorrect intuitive prior knowledge for learning. *Frontiers in Psychology, 5*, 664.

Okada, R., Okuda, T., Nakano, N., Nishimatsu, K., Fukushima, H., Onoda, M., Otsuki, T., Ishii, K., Murakamic, T., & Kato, A. (2013). Brain areas associated with sentence processing: A functional MRI study and a lesion study. *Journal of Neurolinguistics, 26*(4), 470–478.

Okhuysen, G. A., & Eisenhardt, K. M. (2002). Integrating knowledge in groups: How formal interventions enable flexibility. *Organization Science, 13*(4), 370–386.

Oliver, E., & Griffitt, W. (1976). Emotional arousal and "objective" judgment. *Bulletin of the Psychonomic Society, 8*(5), 399–400.

Olsen, R. A. (2002). Professional investors as naturalistic decision makers: Evidence and market implications. *The Journal of Psychology and Financial Markets, 3*(3), 161–167.

Olshavsky, R. W., & Acito, F. (1980). The impact of data collection procedure on choice rule. *Advances in Consumer Research, 7*, 729–732.

Olson, D. R., & Filby, N. (1972). On the comprehension of active and passive sentences. *Cognitive Psychology, 3*(3), 361–381.

Olson, I. R., & Marshuetz, C. (2005). Facial attractiveness is appraised in a glance. *Emotion, 5*(4), 498–502.

Onken, J., Hastie, R., & Revelle, W. (1985). Individual differences in the use of simplification strategies in a complex decision-making task. *Journal of Experimental Psychology: Human Perception and Performance, 11*(1), 14–27.

Oppenheimer, D. M. (2004). Spontaneous discounting of availability in frequency judgment tasks. *Psychological Science, 15*(2), 100–105.

Oppenheimer, D. M. (2006). Consequences of erudite vernacular utilized irrespective of necessity: Problems with using long words needlessly. *Applied Cognitive Psychology, 20*(2), 139–156.

Orasanu, J., & Salas, E. (1993). Team decision making in complex environments. In G. A. Klein, J. Orasanu, R. Calderwood, & C. E. Zsambok (Eds.), *Decision making in action: Models and methods* (pp. 327–345). Westport, CT: Ablex Publishing.

Ordonez, L. D. (1994). Expectations in consumer decision-making: A model of reference price formation (Doctoral dissertation, University of California, Berkeley, 1994). *Dissertation Abstracts International, 56*(5B), 2911.

O'Reilly, J. X., Schüffelgen, U., Cuell, S. F., Behrens, T. J., Mars, R. B., & Rushworth, M. S. (2013). Dissociable effects of surprise and model update in parietal and anterior cingulate cortex. *PNAS Proceedings of the National Academy of Sciences of the United States of America, 110*(38), E3660–E3669.

Oreopoulos, P., & Petronijevic, U. (2013). *Making college worth it: A review of research on the returns to higher education* (No. w19053). Cambridge, MA: National Bureau of Economic Research.

Ortony, A., Clore, G. L., & Collins, A. (1988). *The cognitive structure of emotions.* New York: Cambridge University Press.

O'Shaughnessy, J. (1987). *Why people buy.* Oxford: Oxford University Press.

Ostroff, C., & Ilgen, D. R. (1992). Cognitive categories of raters and rating accuracy. *Journal of Business and Psychology, 7*(1), 3–26.

O'Sullivan, C. S., Chen, A., Mohapatra, S., Sigelman, L., & Lewis, E. (1988). Voting in ignorance: The politics of smooth-sounding names. *Journal of Applied Social Psychology, 18*(13), 1094–1106.

Otake, T., & Cutler, A. (Eds.). (1996). *Phonological structure and language processing: Cross-linguistic studies.* Berlin: Mouton.

Otani, A. (2015, January 5). These are the skills you need if you want to be headhunted. *Bloomberg Businessweek.* Retrieved December 31, 2015 from http://www.bloomberg.com/news/articles/2015–01–05/the-job-skills-that-recruiters-wish-you-had.

Ottati, V. C., & Isbell, L. M. (1996). Effects on mood during exposure to target information on subsequently reported judgments: An on-line model of misattribution and correction. *Journal of Personality and Social Psychology, 71*(1), 39–53.

Otto, A. L., Penrod, S. D., & Dexter, H. R. (1994). The biasing impact of pretrial publicity on juror judgments. *Law and Human Behavior, 18*(4), 453–469.

Overby, J. W., Gardial, S. F., & Woodruff, R. B. (2004). French versus American consumers' attachment of value to a product in a common consumption context: A cross-national comparison. *Journal of the Academy of Marketing Science, 32*(4), 437–460.

Ow, T. T., & Morris, J. G. (2010). An experimental study of executive decision-making with implications for decision support. *Journal of Organizational Computing and Electronic Commerce, 20*(4), 370–397.

Ozcelik, E., Karakus, T., Kursun, E., & Cagiltay, K. (2009). An eye-tracking study of how color coding affects multimedia learning. *Computers & Education, 53*(2), 445–453.

Pace, K. M., Fediuk, T. A., & Botero, I. C. (2010). The acceptance of responsibility and expressions of regret in organizational apologies after a transgression. *Corporate Communications: An International Journal, 15*(4), 410–427.

Paek, S. N. (1997). A cognitive model for selecting business appraisal methods (Doctoral dissertation, University of Nebraska–Lincoln, 1997). *Dissertation Abstracts International, 58*(6A), 2283.

Paese, P. W., Bieser, M., & Tubbs, M. E. (1993). Framing effects and choice shifts in group decision making. *Organizational Behavior and Human Decision Processes, 56*(1), 149–165.

Pallak, S. R. (1983). Salience of a communicator's physical attractiveness and persuasion: A heuristic versus systematic processing interpretation. *Social Cognition, 2*(2), 158–170.

Pallak, S. R., Murroni, E., & Koch, J. (1983). Communicator attractiveness and expertise, emotional versus rational appeals, and persuasion: A heuristic versus systematic processing interpretation. *Social Cognition, 2*(2), 122–141.

Palmer, J., & Faivre, J. P. (1973). The information processing theory of consumer behavior. *European Research, 1*, 231–240.

Palmer, S. E. (1975). The effects of contextual scenes on the identification of objects. *Memory & Cognition, 3*(5), 519–526.

Pan, B., Zhang, L., & Law, R. (2013). The complex matter of online hotel choice. *Cornell Hospitality Quarterly, 54*(1), 74–83.

Pan, Z., & Kosicki, G. M. (2001). Framing as a strategic action in public deliberation. In S. D. Reese, O. H. Gandy, & A. E. Grant (Eds.), *Framing public life: Perspectives on media and our understanding of the social world* (pp. 35–65). Mahwah, NJ: Lawrence Erlbaum Associates.

Park, C. W., & Lessig, V. P. (1981). Familiarity and its impact on consumer decision biases and heuristics. *Journal of Consumer Research, 8*(2), 223–230.

Park, C. W., & Young, S. M. (1986). Consumer response to television commercials: The impact of involvement and background music on brand attitude formation. *Journal of Marketing Research, 23*(1), 11–24.

Park, S., & Lim, J. (2007). Promoting positive emotion in multimedia learning using visual illustrations. *Journal of Educational Multimedia and Hypermedia, 16*(2), 141–162.

Parker, L. D. (2008). Boardroom operational and financial control: An insider view. *British Journal of Management, 19*(1), 65–88.

Parks, C. D., & Cowlin, R. A. (1996). Acceptance of uncommon information into group discussion when that information is or is not demonstrable. *Organizational Behavior and Human Decision Processes, 66*(3), 307–315.

Parrill, F. (2008). Subjects in the hands of speakers: An experimental study of syntactic subject and speech-gesture integration. *Cognitive Linguistics, 19*(2), 283–299.

Parsons, C. K., & Liden, R. C. (1984). Interviewer perceptions of applicant qualifications: A multivariate field study of demographic characteristics and nonverbal cues. *Journal of Applied Psychology, 69*(4), 557–568.

Parton, S. R., Siltanen, S. A., Hosman, L. A., & Langenderfer, J. (2002). Employment interview outcomes and speech style effects. *Journal of Language and Social Psychology, 21*(2), 144–161.

Pascual, A., Guéguen, N., Pujos, S., & Felonneau, M. L. (2013). Foot-in-the-door and problematic requests: A field experiment. *Social Influence, 8*(1), 46–53.

Paterson, D. G., & Tinker, M. A. (1942). Influence of line width on eye movements for six-point type. *Journal of Educational Psychology, 33*(7), 552–555.

Patterson, M. L., Churchill, M. E., Burger, G. K., & Powell, J. L. (1992). Verbal and nonverbal modality effects on impressions of political candidates: Analysis from the 1984 presidential debates. *Communication Monographs, 59*(3), 231–242.

Patterson, M. L., & Ritts, V. (1997). Social and communicative anxiety: A review and meta-analysis. In B. R. Burleson & A. W. Kunkel (Eds.), *Communication yearbook* (Vol. 20, pp. 263–303). Thousand Oaks, CA: Sage.

Patterson, P. G., & Spreng, R. A. (1997). Modeling the relationship between perceived value, satisfaction and repurchase intentions in a business-to-business, services context: An empirical examination. *International Journal of Service Industry Management, 8*(5), 415–432.

Payne, J. W. (1976). Task complexity and contingent processing in decision making: An information search and protocol analysis. *Organizational Behavior & Human Performance, 16*(2), 366–387.

Payne, J. W., & Bettman, J. R. (2004). Walking with the scarecrow: The information-processing approach to decision research. In D. J. Koehler & N. Harvey (Eds.), *Blackwell handbook of judgment and decision making* (pp. 110–132). Oxford, UK: Blackwell Publishing.

Payne, J. W., Bettman, J. R., & Johnson, E. J. (1988). Adaptive strategy selection in decision making. *Journal of Experimental Psychology: Learning, Memory, and Cognition, 14*(3), 534–552.

Payne, J. W., Bettman, J. R., & Johnson, E. J. (1993). *The adaptive decision maker.* New York: Cambridge University Press.

Payne, J. W., & Braunstein, M. L. (1978). Risky choice: An examination of information acquisition behavior. *Memory & Cognition, 6*(5), 554–561.

Pechmann, C. (1996). Do consumers overgeneralize one-sided comparative price claims, and are more stringent regulations needed? *Journal of Marketing Research, 33*(2), 150–162.

Peebles, D., & Cheng, P. C. H. (2003). Modeling the effect of task and graphical representation on response latency in a graph reading task. *Human Factors: The Journal of the Human Factors and Ergonomics Society, 45*(1), 28–46.

Peeck, J. (1987). The role of illustrations in processing and remembering illustrated text. In D. M. Willows & H. A. Houghton (Eds.), *The psychology of illustration: Basic research* (Vol. 1, pp. 115–151). New York: Springer-Verlag.

Peelen, M. V., Atkinson, A. P., Andersson, F., & Vuilleumier, P. (2007). Emotional modulation of body-selective visual areas. *Social Cognitive and Affective Neuroscience, 2*(4), 274–283.

Pelham, B. W., & Neter, E. (1995). The effect of motivation of judgment depends on the difficulty of the judgment. *Journal of Personality and Social Psychology, 68*(4), 581–594.

Pell, M. D. (2005). Prosody-face interactions in emotional processing as revealed by the facial affect decision task. *Journal of Nonverbal Behavior, 29*(4), 193–215.

Pendergrast, M. (1993). *For God, country and Coca-Cola.* New York, NY: Macmillan.

Pennebaker, J. W., & King, L. A. (1999). Linguistic styles: Language use as an individual difference. *Journal of Personality and Social Psychology, 77*(6), 1296–1312.

Pennington, D. C. (1982). Witnesses and their testimony: Effects of ordering on juror verdicts. *Journal of Applied Social Psychology, 12*(4), 318–333.

Pennington, D. C. (2000). *Social cognition.* New York, NY: Psychology Press.

Pennington, N., & Hastie, R. (1992). Explaining the evidence: Tests of the story model for juror decision making. *Journal of Personality and Social Psychology, 62*(2), 189–206.

Penrod, S., & Otto, A. L. (1992, September). *Pretrial publicity and juror decision making: Assessing the magnitude and source of prejudicial effects.* Paper presented at the Third European Conference on Law and Psychology, Oxford, UK.

Perkins, W. S., & Reynolds, T. J. (1988). The explanatory power of values in preference judgments: Validation of the means-end perspective. *Advances in Consumer Research, 15*, 122–126.

Perl, S., & Young, R. O. (2015, June). *A cognitive study of incident handling expertise.* Presented at the Annual Forum of Incident Response and Security Teams (FIRST) Conference, Berlin, Germany.

Perlmutter, J., & Royer, J. M. (1973). Organization of prose materials: Stimulus, storage, and retrieval. *Canadian Journal of Psychology/Revue Canadienne de Psychologie, 27*(2), 200–209.

Perry, V. G., & Lee, J. D. (2012). Shopping for a home vs. a loan: The role of cognitive resource depletion. *International Journal of Consumer Studies, 36*(5), 580–587.

Peskin, J. (1998). Constructing meaning when reading poetry: An expert-novice study. *Cognition and Instruction, 16*(3), 235–263.

Peters, L. H., & Terborg, J. R. (1975). The effects of temporal placement of unfavorable information and of attitude similarity on personnel selection decisions. *Organizational Behavior and Human Performance, 13*(2), 279–293.

Peterson, E. B., Thomsen, S., Lindsay, G., & John, K. (2010). Adolescents' attention to traditional and graphic tobacco warning labels: An eye-tracking approach. *Journal of Drug Education, 40*(3), 227–244.

Peterson, K. (1984). An investigation of consumer patronage/shopping decision-making behavior using an information processing approach (Doctoral dissertation, The University of Wisconsin—Madison, 1984). *Dissertation Abstracts International, 45.*

Petrova, P. K., & Cialdini, R. B. (2005). Fluency of consumption imagery and the backfire effects of imagery appeals. *Journal of Consumer Research, 32*(3), 442–452.

Petty, R. E., Brinol, P., Tormala, A. L., & Wegener, D. (2007). The role of metacognition in social judgment. In A. W. Kruglanski & E. T. Higgins (Eds.), *Social psychology: Handbook of basic principles* (2nd ed., pp. 254–284). New York: The Guilford Press.

Petty, R. E., & Cacioppo, J. T. (1980). Effects of issue involvement on attitudes in an advertising context. In G. Gorn & M. Goldberg (Eds.), *Proceedings of the division 23 program* (pp. 75–79). Montreal, Canada: Division 23 of the American Psychological Association (09A), 2921.

Petty, R. E., & Cacioppo, J. T. (1984). The effects of involvement on responses to argument quantity and quality: Central and peripheral routes to persuasion. *Journal of Personality and Social Psychology, 46*(1), 69–81.

Petty, R. E., & Cacioppo, J. T. (1986). *Communication and persuasion: Central and peripheral routes to attitude change.* New York: Springer-Verlag.

Petty, R. E., Cacioppo, J. T., & Kasmer, J. A. (1988). The role of affect in the elaboration likelihood model of persuasion. In L. Donohew, H. E. Sypher & E. T. Higgins (Eds.), *Communication, social cognition, and affect* (pp. 117–146). Hillsdale, NJ: Lawrence Erlbaum Associates.

Petty, R. E., Cacioppo, J. T., & Schumann, D. (1983). Central & peripheral routes to advertising effectiveness: The moderating role of involvement. *Journal of Consumer Research, 10*(2), 135–146.

Petty, R. E., DeSteno, D., & Rucker, D. D. (2001). The role of affect in attitude change. In J. P. Forgas (Ed.), *Handbook of affect and social cognition* (pp. 212–233). Mahwah, NJ: Lawrence Erlbaum Associates.

Petty, R. E., Gleicher, F., & Baker, S. M. (1991). Multiple roles for affect in persuasion. In J. P. Forgas (Ed), *Emotion and social judgments* (pp. 181–200). Elmsford, NY: Pergamon Press.

Pezdek, K., & Evans, G. W. (1979). Visual and verbal memory for objects and their spatial locations. *Journal of Experimental Psychology: Human Learning and Memory, 5*(4), 360–373.

Pfeffer, J. (1981). *Power in organizations* (Vol. 33). Marshfield, MA: Pitman.

Pfeffer, M. G. (1987). Venture capital investment and protocol analysis (Doctoral dissertation, University of North Texas, 1987). *Dissertation Abstracts International, 49*(01A), 112.

Pfeiffer, B. E. (2008). Omission detection and inferential adjustment (Doctoral dissertation, University of Cincinnati, 2008). *Dissertation Abstracts International, 69*(08A), 3232.

Pfeiffer, J., Meißner, M., Brandstätter, E., Riedl, R., Decker, R., & Rothlauf, F. (2014). On the influence of context-based complexity on information search patterns: An individual perspective. *Journal of Neuroscience, Psychology, and Economics, 7*(2), 103–124.

Pham, M. T. (1998). Representativeness, relevance, and the use of feelings in decision making. *Journal of Consumer Research, 25*(2), 144–159.

Pham, M. T., Cohen, J. B., Pracejus, J. W., & Hughes, G. D. (2001). Affect monitoring and the primacy of feelings in judgment. *Journal of Consumer Research, 28*(2), 167–188.

Pham, M. T., & Muthukrishnan, A. V. (2002). Search and alignment in judgment revision: Implications for brand positioning. *Journal of Marketing Research, 39*(1), 18–30.

Phillips, A. P., & Dipboye, R. L. (1989). Correlational tests of predictions from a process model of the interview. *Journal of Applied Psychology, 74*(1), 41–52.

Phillips, J. S., & Lord, R. G. (1981). Causal attributions and perceptions of leadership. *Organizational Behavior and Human Performance, 28*, 143–163.

Phillips, J. S., & Lord, R. G. (1982). Schematic information processing and perceptions of leadership in problem-solving groups. *Journal of Applied Psychology, 67*(4), 486–492.

Pichert, J. W., & Anderson, R. C. (1977). Taking different perspectives on a story. *Journal of Educational Psychology, 69*(4), 309–315.

Pierro, A., Mannetti, L., Erb, H. P., Spiegel, S., & Kruglanski, A. W. (2005). Informational length and order of presentation as determinants of persuasion. *Journal of Experimental Social Psychology, 41*(5), 458–469.

Pierro, A., Mannetti, L., Kruglanski, A. W., & Sleeth-Keppler, D. (2004). Relevance override: On the reduced impact of "cues" under high motivation conditions of persuasion studies. *Journal of Personality and Social Psychology, 86*(2), 251–264.

Pieters, R., Warlop, L., & Wedel, M. (2002). Breaking through the clutter: Benefits of advertisement originality and familiarity for brand attention and memory. *Management Science, 48*(6), 765–781.

Pilkonis, P. A. (1977). The behavioral consequences of shyness. *Journal of Personality, 45*(4), 596–611.

Pincus, T. H. (1986). A crisis parachute: Helping stock prices have a soft landing. *The Journal of Business Strategy, 6*(4), 32–38.

Pinelli, T. E., Glassman, M., & Cordle, V. M. (1982). *Survey of reader preferences concerning the format of NASA technical reports* (NASA TM-No 84502). Washington, DC: National Aeronautics and Space Administration.

Pinker, S. (1990). A theory of graph comprehension. In R. Freedle (Ed.), *Artificial intelligence and the future of testing* (pp. 73–126). Hillsdale, NJ: Lawrence Erlbaum Associates.

Pizzagalli, D., Regard, M., & Lehmann, D. (1999). Rapid emotional face processing in the human right and left brain hemispheres: An ERP study. *Neuroreport: For Rapid Communication of Neuroscience Research, 10*(13), 2691–2698.

Pizzi, G., Scarpi, D., & Marzocchi, G. L. (2014). Showing a tree to sell the forest: The impact of attribute-and alternative-based information presentation on consumers' choices. *Journal of Economic Psychology, 42*, 41–51.

Platow, M. J., van Knippenberg, D., Haslam, S. A., van Knippenberg, B., & Spears, R. (2001). *A special gift we bestow on you for being representative of us: Considering leader charisma from a self-categorization perspective.* Unpublished manuscript, La Trobe University, Melbourne Victoria, Australia.

Platt, M., & Plassmann, H. (2014). Multistage valuation signals and common neural currencies. In P. W. Glimcher & E. Fehr (Eds.), *Neuroeconomics: Decision making and the brain* (2nd ed., pp. 237–258). New Yok, NY: Academic Press.

Pliske, R. M., Crandall, B., & Klein, G. (2004). Competence in weather forecasting. In J. Shanteau, P. Johnson & K. Smith (Eds.), *Psychological investigations of competence in decision making* (pp. 40–70). Cambridge: Cambridge University Press.

Plumm, K. M., Borhart, H., & Weatherly, J. N. (2012). Choose your words wisely: Delay discounting of differently titled social policy issues. *Behavior and Social Issues, 21*, 26–48.

Plummer, J. T. (1985, February). *Brand personality: A strategic concept for multinational advertising.* Paper presented at the Marketing Educators' Conference (pp. 1–31). New York, NY: Young & Rubicam.

Plutchik, R. (1980). *Emotion: A psychoevolutionary synthesis.* New York: Harper & Row.

Polansky, S. H. (1987). An information-processing analysis of the effects of product class knowledge on newspaper consumer behavior (Doctoral dissertation, The University of North Carolina at Chapel Hill, 1987). *Dissertation Abstracts International, 48*(07a), 1572.

Pollatsek, A., Raney, G. E., LaGasse, L., & Rayner, K. (1993). The use of information below fixation in reading and in visual search. *Canadian Journal of Psychology, 47*(2), 179–200.

Pollatsek, A., & Rayner, K. (1990). Eye movements and lexical access in reading. In D. A. Balota, G. B. Flores d'Arcais & K. Rayner (Eds.), *Comprehension processes in reading* (pp. 143–163). Hillsdale, NJ: Lawrence Erlbaum Associates.

Pollick, F. E., Paterson, H. M., Bruderlin, A., & Sanford, A. J., (2001). Perceiving affect from arm movement. *Cognition, 82*(2), B51–B61.

Popham, W. J. (1961). Tape recorded lectures in the college classroom. *Audiovisual Communication Review, 9*(2), 109–118.

Popkin, S., Gonnan, J. W., Phillips, C., & Smith, J. A. (1976). What have you done for me lately? Toward an investment theory of voting. *The American Political Science Review, 70*, 779–805.

Posner, M. I., & Rothbart, M. K. (2007). Research on attention networks as a model for the integration of psychological science. *Annual Review of Psychology, 58*, 1–23.

Postmes, T., Spears, R., & Cihangir, S. (2001). Quality of decision making and group norms. *Journal of Personality and Social Psychology, 80*(6), 918–930.

Potter, M. C., & Levy, E. I. (1969). Recognition memory for a rapid sequence of pictures. *Journal of Experimental Psychology, 81*(1), 10–15.

Potter, R. E., & Beach, L. R. (1998). Imperfect information in prechoice screening of options. In L. R. Beach (Ed.), *Image theory: Theoretical and empirical foundations* (pp. 73–86). Mahwah, NJ: Lawrence Erlbaum Associates.

Poulton, E. C. (1955). Letter differentiation and rate of comprehension of reading. *Journal of Applied Psychology, 49*, 358–362.

Poulton, E. C. (1967). Skimming (scanning) news items printed in 8-point and 9-point letters. *Ergonomics, 10*(6), 713–716.

Poulton, E. C., & Brown, C. H. (1968). Rate of comprehension of an existing teleprinter output and of possible alternatives. *Journal of Applied Psychology, 52*(1, Pt. 1), 16–21.

Pratkanis, A. R., & Gliner, M. D. (2004). And when shall a little child lead them? Evidence for an altercasting theory of source credibility. *Current Psychology, 23*(4), 279–304.

Preckel, D., & Schüpbach, H. (2005). Zusammenhänge zwischen rezeptiver selbstdarstellungskompetenz und leistung im assessment center. *Zeitschrift für Personalpsychologie, 4*(4), 151–158.

Preston, A. R., & Eichenbaum, H. (2013). Interplay of hippocampus and prefrontal cortex in memory. *Current Biology, 23*(17), R764–R773.

Preston, L. E., & Sapienza, H. J. (1991). Stakeholder management and corporate performance. *Journal of Behavioral Economics, 19*(4), 361–375.

Price, P. C., & Stone, E. R. (2004). Intuitive evaluation of likelihood judgment producers: Evidence for a confidence heuristic. *Journal of Behavioral Decision Making, 17*(1), 39–57.

Price, R. (1972). *Droodles.* Los Angeles: Price/Stern/Sloan.

Price, V., & Zaller, J. (1993). Who gets the news? Alternative measures of news reception and their implications for research. *Public Opinion Quarterly, 57*, 133–164.

Prostko, A. L. (2014). Effects of social and non-social interpretations of complex images on human eye movement and brain activation (Doctoral dissertation, West Virginia University, 2014). *Dissertation Abstracts International: Section B, 74*(7-B)(E).

Pryor, J. B., & Kriss, M. (1977). The cognitive dynamics of salience in the attribution process. *Journal of Personality and Social Psychology, 35*(1), 49–55.

Puffer, S. M., & Weintrop, J. B. (1991). Corporate performance and CEO turnover: The role of performance expectations. *Administrative Science Quarterly, 36*(1), 1–19.

Purnell, T., Idsardi, W., & Baugh, J. (1999). Perceptual and phonetic experiments on American English dialect identification. *Journal of Language and Social Psychology, 18*(1), 10–30.

Pyszczynski, T. A., & Wrightsman, L. S. (1981). The effects of opening statements on mock jurors' verdicts in a simulated criminal trial. *Journal of Applied Social Psychology, 11*(4), 301–313.

Qiu, J., Li, H., Chen, A., & Zhang, Q. (2008). The neural basis of analogical reasoning: An event-related potential study. *Neuropsychologia, 46*(12), 3006–3013.

Quattrone, G. A., & Tversky, A. (1988). Contrasting rational and psychological analyses of political choice. *American Political Science Review, 82*, 719–736.

Quigley, B. M., & Tedeschi, J. T. (1996). Mediating effects of blame attributions on feelings of anger. *Personality and Social Psychology Bulletin, 22*(12), 1280–1288.

Quigley, N. R., Tesluk, P. E., Locke, E. A., & Bartol, K. M. (2007). A multilevel investigation of the motivational mechanisms underlying knowledge sharing and performance. *Organization Science, 18*(1), 71–88.

Quirk, S. W., & Strauss, M. E. (2001). Visual exploration of emotion eliciting images by patients with schizophrenia. *Journal of Nervous and Mental Disease, 189*(11), 757–765.

Race, D. S., Tsapkini, K., Crinion, J., Newhart, M., Davis, C., Gomez, Y., . . . & Faria, A. V. (2013). An area essential for linking word meanings to word forms: Evidence from primary progressive aphasia. *Brain and Language, 127*(2), 167–176.

Rachlinski, J. J., Guthrie, C., & Wistrich, A. J. (2006). Inside the bankruptcy judge's mind. *Boston University Law Review, 86*, 1227–1265.

Raghubir, P., & Menon, G. (1998). AIDS and me, never the twain shall meet: The effects of information accessibility on judgments of risk and advertising effectiveness. *Journal of Consumer Research, 25*(1), 52–63.

Raghubir, P., & Valenzuela, A. (2006). Center-of-inattention: Position biases in decision-making. *Organizational Behavior and Human Decision Processes, 99*(1), 66–80.

Raghunathan, R. (2000). What do you do when you are angry, anxious or blue? Motivational influence of negative affective states on consumer decision-making (Doctoral dissertation, New York University, 2000). *Dissertation Abstracts International, 61*(09A), 3664.

Raghunathan, R., & Pham, M. T. (1999). All negative moods are not equal: Motivational influences of anxiety and sadness on decision making. *Organizational Behavior and Human Decision Processes, 79*(1), 56–77.

Raghunathan, R., Pham, M. T., & Corfman, K. P. (2006). Informational properties of anxiety and sadness, and displaced coping. *Journal of Consumer Research, 32*(4), 596–601.

Ramachandran, V. S., & Hirstein, W. (1999). The science of art: A neurological theory of aesthetic experience. *Journal of Consciousness Studies, 6*(6–7), 15–51.

Ramanathan, S., & McGill, A. L. (2007). Consuming with others: Social influences on moment-to-moment and retrospective evaluations of an experience. *Journal of Consumer Research, 34*(4), 506–524.

Ramsey, R. (1966). Personality and speech. *Journal of Personality and Social Psychology, 4*, 116–118.

Randall, K. R., Resick, C. J., & DeChurch, L. A. (2011). Building team adaptive capacity: The roles of sensegiving and team composition. *Journal of Applied Psychology, 96*(3), 525–540.

Randel, J. M., Pugh, H. L., & Reed, S. K. (1996). Differences in expert and novice situation awareness in naturalistic decision making. *International Journal of Human-Computer Studies, 45*(5), 579–597.

Ranyard, R., Charlton, J. P., & Williamson, J. (2001). The role of internal reference prices in consumers' willingness to pay judgments: Thaler's beer pricing task revisited. *Acta Psychologica, 106*(3), 265–283.

Ranyard, R., & Williamson, J. (2005). Conversation-based process tracing methods for naturalistic decision making: Information search and verbal analysis. In H. Montgomery, R. Lipshitz & B. Brehmer (Eds.), *How professionals make decisions* (pp. 305–317). Mahwah, NJ: Lawrence Erlbaum Associates.

Rapp, D. N., & Kendeou, P. (2009). Noticing and revising discrepancies as texts unfold. *Discourse Processes, 46*(1), 1–24.

Rasmussen, K. G. (1984). Nonverbal behavior, verbal behavior, resumé credentials, and selection interview outcomes. *Journal of Applied Psychology, 69*(4), 551–556.

Ratcliff, G., & Newcombe, F. (1982). Object recognition: Some deductions from the clinical evidence. In A. W. Ellis (Ed.), *Normality and pathology in cognitive functions* (pp. 147–171). London: Academic Press.

Ratner, N. B., & Gleason, J. B. (1993). An introduction to psycholinguistics: What do language users know? In J. B. Gleason & N. B. Ratner (Eds.), *Psycholingulstics* (pp. 1–40). Fort Worth, TX: Harcourt Brace.

Ratneshwar, S., & Chaiken, S. (1991). Comprehension's role in persuasion: The case of its moderating effect on the persuasive impact of source cues. *Journal of Consumer Research, 18*(1), 52–62.

Rayner, K. (1998). Eye movements in reading and information processing: 20 years of research. *Psychological Bulletin, 124*(3), 372–422.

Rayner, K., & Duffy, S. A. (1986). Lexical complexity and fixation times in reading: Effects of word frequency, verb complexity, and lexical ambiguity. *Memory and Cognition, 14*(3), 191–201.

Rayner, K., & Frazier, L. (1987). Parsing temporarily ambiguous complements. *The Quarterly Journal of Experimental Psychology A: Human Experimental Psychology, 39*(4, Pt. A), 657–673.

Rayner, K., Kambe, G., & Duffy, S. A. (2000). Clause wrap-up effects on eye movements during reading. *Quarterly Journal of Experimental Psychology, 53A*(4), 1061–1080.

Rayner, K., Reichle, E. D., Stroud, M. J., Williams, C. C., & Pollatsek, A. (2006). The effect of word frequency, word predictability, and font difficulty on the eye movements of young and elderly readers. *Psychology and Aging, 21*(3), 448–465.

Rayner, K., & Well, A. D. (1996). Effects of contextual constraint on eye movements in reading: A further examination. *Psychonomic Bulletin & Review, 3*(4), 504–509.

Raza, S. M., & Carpenter, B. N. (1987). A model of hiring decisions in real employment interviews. *Journal of Applied Psychology, 72*(4), 596–603.

Read, D., Frederick, S., Orsel, B., & Rahman, J. (2005). Four score and seven years from now: The date/delay effect in temporal discounting. *Management Science, 51*(9), 1326–1335.

Read, S. J., Cesa, I. L., Jones, D. K., & Collins, N. L. (1990). When is the federal budget like a baby? Metaphor in political rhetoric. *Metaphor & Symbolic Activity, 5*(3), 125–149.

Reb, J., & Cropanzano, R. (2007). Evaluating dynamic performance: The influence of salient Gestalt characteristics on performance ratings. *Journal of Applied Psychology, 92*(2), 490–499.

Reber, R., & Schwarz, N. (1999). Effects of perceptual fluency on judgments of truth. *Consciousness and Cognition: An International Journal, 8*(3), 338–342.

Reber, R., Schwarz, N., & Winkielman, P. (2004). Processing fluency and aesthetic pleasure: Is beauty in the perceiver's processing experience? *Personality and Social Psychology Review, 8*(4), 364–382.

Reber, R., Winkielman, P., & Schwarz, N. (1998). Effects of perceptual fluency on affective judgments. *Psychological Science, 9*(1), 45–48.

Rebollar, R., Lidón, I., Martín, J., & Puebla, M. (2015). The identification of viewing patterns of chocolate snack packages using eye-tracking techniques. *Food Quality and Preference, 39*, 251–258.

Redelmeier, D. A., & Shafir, E. (1995). Medical decision making in situations that offer multiple alternatives. *Journal of the American Medical Association, 273*, 302–305.

Redish, J. C. (1980). Readability. In D. Felker (Ed.), *Document design: A review of the relevant research* (pp. 69–93). Washington, DC: American Institutes for Research.

Redish, J. C. (1993). Understanding readers. In C. M. Barnum & S. Carliner (Eds.), *Techniques for technical communicators* (pp. 14–41). New York: Macmillan.

Reeder, G. D., & Brewer, M. B. (1979). A schematic model of dispositional attribution in interpersonal perception. *Psychological Review, 86*(1), 61–79.

Reeves, B., Detenber, B., & Steuer, J. (1993, May). *New televisions: The effects of big pictures and big sound on viewer responses to the screen.* Paper presented to the Information Systems Division of the International Communication Association, Chicago.

Rehe, R. F. (1974). *Typography: How to make it legible.* Carmel, IN: Design Research International.

Reicher, G. M. (1969). Perceptual recognition as a function of meaningfulness of stimulus material. *Journal of Experimental Psychology, 81*(2), 275–280.

Reid, J. C., Kardash, C. M., Robinson, R. D., & Scholes, R. (1994). Comprehension in patient literature: The importance of text and reader characteristics. *Health Communication Special Issue: Communicating With Patients About Their Medications, 6*(4), 327–335.

Reilly, B. A., & Doherty, M. E. (1989). A note on the assessment of self-insight in judgment research. *Organizational Behavior and Human Decision Processes, 44*(1), 123–131.

Reingen, P. H., & Kernan, J. B. (1993). Social perception and interpersonal influence: Some consequences of the physical attractiveness stereotype in a personal selling setting. *Journal of Consumer Psychology, 2*(1), 25–38.

Reingold, E., & Rayner, K. (2006). Examining the word identification stages identified by the E-Z reader model. *Psychological Science, 17*(9), 742–746.

Reisberg, D., Mclean, J., & Goldfield, A. (1987). Easy to hear but hard to understand: A lip-reading advantage with intact auditory stimuli. In B. Dodd & R. Campbell (Eds.), *Hearing by eye: The psychology of lip-reading* (pp. 97–114). New York, NY: Lawrence Erlbaum.

Reisenzein, R. (2000). The subjective experience of surprise. In H. Bless & J. P. Forgas (Eds.), *The message within: The role of subjective experience in social cognition and behavior* (pp. 262–282). Philadelphia: Psychology Press.

Rentsch, J. R., & Hall, R. J. (1994). Members of great teams think alike: A model of team effectiveness and schema similarity among team members. In M. M. Beyerlein & D. A. Johnson (Eds.), *Advances in interdisciplinary studies of work teams: Theories of self-managing work teams* (Vol. 1, pp. 223–261). Greenwich, CT: Elsevier Science/JAI Press.

Rentsch, J. R., & Klimoski, R. J. (2001). Why do 'great minds' think alike?: Antecedents of team member schema agreement. *Journal of Organizational Behavior, 22*(2), 107–120.

Rentsch, J. R., Small, E. E., & Hanges, P. J. (2008). Cognitions in organizations and teams: What is the meaning of cognitive similarity? In D. B. Smith (Ed.), *The people make the place: Dynamic linkages between individuals and organizations.* (pp. 127–155). New York, NY: Lawrence Erlbaum Associates.

Reyes, R. M., Thompson, W. C., & Bower, G. H. (1980). Judgmental biases resulting from differing availabilities of arguments. *Journal of Personality and Social Psychology, 39*(1), 2–12.

Rhee, J. W., & Cappella, J. N. (1997). The role of political sophistication in learning from news: Measuring schema development. *Communication Research, 24*, 197–233.

Rhodes, G., Halberstadt, J., & Brajkovich, G. (2001). Generalization of mere exposure effects to averaged composite faces. *Social Cognition, 19*(1), 57–70.

Rholes, W. S., Jones, M., & Wade, C. (1988). Children's understanding of personal dispositions and its relationship to behavior. *Journal of Experimental Child Psychology, 45*(1), 1–17.

Richins, M. L. (1994). Special possessions and the expression of material values. *Journal of Consumer Research, 21*(3), 522–533.

Rickards, E. C., & August, G. J. (1975). Generative underlining strategies in prose recall. *Journal of Educational Psychology, 67*(6), 860–865.

Ricketts, M., Shanteau, J., McSpadden, B., & Fernandez-Medina, K. M. (2010). Using stories to battle unintentional injuries: Narratives in safety and health communication. *Social Science & Medicine, 70*(9), 1441–1449.

Riess, M., Rosenfeld, P., Melburg, V., & Tedeschi, J. T. (1981). Self-serving attributions: Biased private perceptions and distorted public descriptions. *Journal of Personality and Social Psychology, 41*(2), 224–231.

Rietzschel, E. F., Nijstad, B. A., & Stroebe, W. (2006). Productivity is not enough: A comparison of interactive and nominal brainstorming groups on idea generation and selection. *Journal of Experimental Social Psychology, 42*(2), 244–251.

Ritchey, K., Schuster, J., & Allen, J. (2008). How the relationship between text and headings influences readers' memory. *Contemporary Educational Psychology, 33*(4), 859–874.

Ritchhart, R., & Perkins, D. N. (2005). Learning to think: The challenges of teaching thinking. In K. J. Holyoak & R. G. Morrison (Eds.), *The Cambridge handbook of thinking and reasoning* (pp. 775–802). Cambridge, UK: Cambridge University Press.

Ritov, I. (1996). Anchoring in simulated competitive market negotiation. *Organizational Behavior and Human Decision Processes, 67*(1), 16–25.

Robberson, M. R., & Rogers, R. W. (1988). Beyond fear appeals: Negative and positive persuasive appeals to health and self-esteem. *Journal of Applied Social Psychology, 18*(3, Pt. 1), 277–287.

Roberson, Q. M., Collins, C. J., & Oreg, S. (2005). The effects of recruitment message specificity on applicant attraction to organizations. *Journal of Business and Psychology, 19*(3), 319–339.

Robertson, D. W. (2006). A comparison of three group decision-making strategies and their effects on the group decision-making process. *Dissertation Abstracts International Section A: Humanities and Social Sciences, 66*(10-A), 3722.

Robey, D., Khoo, H. M., & Powers, C. (2000). Situated learning in cross-functional virtual teams. *Technical Communication, 47*(1), 51–66.

Robinson, D. O., Abbamonte, M., & Evans, S. H. (1971). Why serifs are important: The perception of small print. *Visible Language, 4*, 353–359.

Robinson, J. S. (1969). Familiar patterns are no easier to see than novel ones. *American Journal of Psychology, 82*(4), 513–522.

Robinson, R. B., Jr. (1985). Emerging strategies in the venture capital industry. *Journal of Business Venturing, 2*(1), 53–77.

Robinson, W. P. (1979). Speech markers and social class. In K. R. Scherer & H. Giles (Eds.), *Social markers in speech* (pp. 211–249). Cambridge, UK: Cambridge University Press.

Rock, I. (1977, June). *Form perception as process of description.* Presented at the 10th Symposium of the Center for Visual Science, Rochester, NY.

Rodd, J. M., Vitello, S., Woollams, A. M., & Adank, P. (2015). Localising semantic and syntactic processing in spoken and written language comprehension: An activation likelihood estimation meta-analysis. *Brain and Language, 141*, 89–102.

Rodin, M. J. (1987). Who is memorable to whom: A study of cognitive disregard. *Social Cognition, 5*(2), 144–165.

Roese, N. J., & Sherman, J. W. (2007). Expectancy. In A. W. Kruglanski & E. T. Higgins (Eds.), *Social psychology: Handbook of basic principles* (2nd ed., pp. 91–115). New York: The Guilford Press.

Rogers, W. T. (1978). The contribution of kinesic illustrators toward the comprehension of verbal behavior within utterances. *Human Communication Research, 5*(1), 54–62.

Rohrman, N. L. (1970). More on the recall of nominalizations. *Journal of Verbal Learning & Verbal Behavior, 9*(5), 534–536.

Roiser, J. P., de Martino, B., Tan, G. C., Kumaran, D., Seymour, B., Wood, N. W., & Dolan, R. J. (2009). A genetically mediated bias in decision making driven by failure of amygdala control. *The Journal of Neuroscience, 29*(18), 5985–5991.

Rojon, C., McDowall, A., & Saunders, M. N. (2015). The relationships between traditional selection assessments and workplace performance criteria specificity: A comparative meta-analysis. *Human Performance, 28*(1), 1–25.

Rokeach, M. (1973). *The nature of human values.* New York: Free Press.

Rook, D. W. (1987). The buying impulse. *Journal of Consumer Research, 14*(2), 189–199.

Rook, D. W., & Fisher, R. J. (1995). Trait and normative aspects of impulsive buying behavior. *Journal of Consumer Research, 22*(3), 305–313.

Roozen, I. (2013). The impact of emotional appeal and the media context on the effectiveness of commercials for not-for-profit and for-profit brands. *Journal of Marketing Communications, 19*(3), 198–214.

Roseman, I. J. (1984). Cognitive determinants of emotion: A structural theory. *Review of Personality & Social Psychology*, *5*, 11–36.

Roseman, I. J. (1994, July). *The discrete emotions form a coherent set: A theory of emotional responses*. Paper presented at the Sixth Annual Convention of the American Psychological Society, Washington, DC.

Roseman, I. J. (1996). Why these appraisals? Anchoring appraisal models to research on emotional behavior and related response systems. In N. H. Frijda (Ed.), *Proceedings of the ninth international conference of the international society for research on emotions* (pp. 106–110). Toronto, Canada: International Society for Research on Emotions.

Roseman, I. J. (2001). A model of appraisal in emotion system: Integrating theory, research, and applications. In K. R. Scherer, A. Schorr & T. Johnstone (Eds.), *Appraisal processes in emotion: Theory, methods, research* (pp. 68–91). New York: Oxford University Press.

Roseman, I. J., Dhawan, N., Rettek, S. I., Naidu, R. K., & Thapa, K. (1995). Cultural differences and cross-cultural similarities in appraisals and emotional responses. *Journal of Cross-Cultural Psychology*, *26*(1), 23–48.

Rosen, D. L., & Olshavsky, R. W. (1987). A protocol analysis of brand choice strategies involving recommendations. *Journal of Consumer Research*, *14*(3), 440–444.

Rosenberg, A., & Hirschberg, J. (2009). Charisma perception from text and speech. *Speech Communication*, *51*(7), 640–655.

Rosenberg, E. L. (1998). Levels of analysis and the organization of affect. *Review of General Psychology Special Issue: New Directions in Research in Emotion*, *2*(3), 247–270.

Rosenblum, L. D. (2008). Speech perception as a multimodal phenomenon. *Current Directions in Psychological Science*, *17*(6), 405–409.

Ross, B. H., & Kennedy, P. T. (1990). Generalizing from the use of earlier examples in problem solving. *Journal of Experimental Psychology: Learning, Memory, and Cognition*, *16*(1), 42–55.

Ross, M., & Conway, M. (1986). Remembering one's own past: The construction of personal histories. In R. M. Sorrentino & E. T. Higgins (Eds.), *Handbook of motivation and cognition: Foundations of social behavior* (pp. 122–144). New York: Guilford Press.

Ross, M., & Sicoly, F. (1979). Egocentric biases in availability and attribution. *Journal of Personality and Social Psychology*, *37*(3), 322–336.

Rosselli, F., Skelly, J. J., & Mackie, D. M. (1995). Processing rational and emotional messages: The cognitive and affective mediation of persuasion. *Journal of Experimental Social Psychology*, *31*(2), 163–190.

Rossiter, J. R., & Percy, L. (1978). Visual imaging ability as a mediator of advertising response. *Advances in Consumer Research*, *5*(1), 621–629.

Rossiter, J. R., & Percy, L. (1980). Attitude change through visual imagery in advertising. *Journal of Advertising*, *9*(2), 10–17.

Rossiter, J. R., Percy, L., & Donovan, R. J. (1991). A better advertising planning grid. *Journal of Advertising Research*, *28*(1), 11–21.

Roth, W. T., Breivik, G., Jorgensen, P. E., & Hofmann, S. (1996). Activation in novice and expert parachutists while jumping. *Psychophysiology*, *33*(1), 63–72.

Rothbart, M., Fulero, S., Jensen, C., Howard, J., & Birrel, B. (1978). From individual to group impressions: Availability heuristics in stereotype formation. *Journal of Experimental Social Psychology*, *14*(3), 237–255.

Rothman, A. J., Haddock, G., & Schwarz, N. (2001). How many partners is too many? Shaping perceptions of vulnerability. *Journal of Applied Social Psychology*, *31*(10), 2195–2214.

Rotliman, A., & Schwarz, N. (1998). Constructing perceptions of vulnerability: Personal relevance and the use of experiential information in health judgments. *Personality and Social Psychology Bulletin*, *28*(10), 1053–1064.

Roozen, I. (2013). The impact of emotional appeal and the media context on the effectiveness of commercials for not-for-profit and for-profit brands. *Journal of Marketing Communications*, *19*(3), 198–214.

Rottenstreich, Y., & Hsee, C. K. (2001). Money, kisses, and electric shocks: On the affective psychology of risk. *Psychological Science*, *12*(3), 185–190.

Rouet, J. F., Favart, M., Britt, M. A., & Perfetti, C. A. (1997). Studying and using multiple documents in history: Effects of discipline expertise. *Cognition and Instruction*, *15*(1), 85–106.

Rouse, W. B., Cannon-Bowers, J. A., & Salas, E. (1992). The role of mental models in team performance in complex systems. *IEEE Transactions on Systems, Man, & Cybernetics*, *22*(6), 1296–1308.

Rouse, W. B., & Morris, N. M. (1986). On looking into the black box: Prospects and limits in the search for mental models. *Psychological Bulletin*, *100*(3), 349–363.

Roy, J. P., & Oliver, C. (2009). International joint venture partner selection: The role of the host-country legal environment. *Journal of International Business Studies*, *40*(5), 779–801.

Rozin, P., Fischler, C., & Shields-Argelès, C. (2009). Additivity dominance: Additives are more potent and more often lexicalized across languages than are "subtractives". *Judgment and Decision Making*, *4*(5), 475–478.

Ruck, H. W. (1980). A cross-company study of decision policies of manager resume evaluations (Doctoral dissertation, Stevens Institute of Technology, 1980). *Dissertation Abstracts International*, *41*(08B), 3222.

Rudebeck, P. H., Bannerman, D. M., & Rushworth, M. F. S. (2008). The contribution of distinct subregions of the ventromedial frontal cortex to emotion, social behavior, and decision making. *Cognitive, Affective, & Behavioral Neuroscience, 8*(4), 485–497.

Rugg, D., & Cantril, H. (1944). The wording of questions. In H. Cantril (Ed.), *Gauging public opinion* (pp. 23–50). Princeton, NJ: Princeton University Press.

Rule, N. O., & Ambady, N. (2008). The face of success inferences from chief executive officers' appearance predict company profits. *Psychological Science, 19*(2), 109–111.

Rumelhart, D. E., & Ortony, A. (1976). The representation of knowledge in memory. In R. C. Anderson, R. J. Spiro, & W. E. Montague (Eds.), *Semantic factors in cognition* (pp. 99–136). Hillsdale, NJ: Erlbaum.

Ruscher, J. B., & Fiske, S. T. (1990). Interpersonal competition can cause individuating processes. *Journal of Personality and Social Psychology, 58*(5), 832–843.

Rush, M. C., & Russell, J. E. (1988). Leader prototypes and prototype-contingent consensus in leader behavior descriptions. *Journal of Experimental Social Psychology, 24*(1), 88–104.

Russo, J. E. (1971). The multi-alternative choice process as tracked by recording eye fixations (Doctoral dissertation, University of Michigan, 1971). *Dissertation Abstracts International, 32*(03B), 1882.

Russo, J. E. (1977). The value of unit price information. *Journal of Marketing Research, 14*(2), 193–201.

Russo, J. E. (2015). The predecisional distortion of information. In E. A. Wilhelms & V. F. Reyna (Eds.), *Neuroeconomics, judgment, and decision making* (pp. 91–110). New York, NY: Psychology Press.

Russo, J. E., Carlson, K. A., & Meloy, M. G. (2006). Choosing an inferior alternative. *Psychological Science, 17*(10), 899–904.

Russo, J. E., & Dosher, B. A. (1980). *Cognitive effort and strategy selection in binary choice.* Chicago, IL: Center for Decision Research, Graduate School of Business, University of Chicago.

Russo, J. E., & Dosher, B. A. (1983). Strategies for multiattribute binay choice. *Journal of Experimental Psychology: Learning, Memory, and Cognition, 9*(4), 676–696.

Russo, J. E., Krieser, G., & Miyashita, S. (1975). An effective display of unit price information. *Journal of Marketing, 39*, 11–19.

Russo, J. E., Medvec, V. H., & Meloy, M. G. (1996). The distortion of information during decisions. *Organizational Behavior and Human Decision Processes, 66*(1), 102–110.

Russo, J. E., & Rosen, L. D. (1975). An eye fixation analysis of multialternative choice. *Memory & Cognition, 3*(3), 267–276.

Russo, J. E., Staelin, R., Nolan, C. A., Russell, G. J., & Metcalf, B. L. (1986). Nutrition information in the supermarket. *Journal of Consumer Research, 13*(1), 48–70.

Russo, J. E., & Yong, K. (2011). The distortion of information to support an emerging evaluation of risk. *Journal of Econometrics, 162*(1), 132–139.

Ryan, C. (1991). *Prime time activism: Media strategies for grass roots organizing.* Boston: South End Press.

Saad, G., & Russo, J. E. (1996). Stopping criteria in sequential choice. *Organizational Behavior and Human Decision Processes, 67*(3), 258–270.

Saaty, T. L. (1980). *The analytic hierarchy process.* New York: McGraw-Hill.

Sachs, J. S. (1967). Recognition of semantic, syntactic and lexical changes in sentences. *Psychonomic Bulletin, 1*(2), 17–18.

Sadoski, M., Goetz, E. T., & Avila, E. (1995). Concreteness effects in text recall: Dual coding or context availability? *Reading Research Quarterly, 30*(2), 278–288.

Sadoski, M., & Paivio, A. (2001). *Imagery and text: A dual coding theory of reading and writing.* Mahwah, NJ: Erlbaum.

Safire, W. (2004). *Lend me your ears: Great speeches in history.* New York: Norton.

Sainfort, F. C., Gustafson, D. H., Bosworth, K., & Hawkins, R. P. (1990). Decision support systems effectiveness: Conceptual framework and empirical evaluation. *Organizational Behavior and Human Decision Processes, 45*(2), 232–252.

Sakai, K. L., Noguchi, Y., Takeuchi, T., & Watanabe, E. (2002). Selective priming of syntactic processing by event-related transcranial magnetic stimulation of Broca's area. *Neuron, 35*(6), 1177–1182.

Salcedo, R. N., Reed, H., Evans, J. F., & Kong, A. C. (1972). A broader look at legibility. *Journalism Quarterly, 49*, 285–289.

Salvadori, L., van Swol, L. M., & Sniezek, J. A. (2001). Information sampling and confidence within groups and judge advisor systems. *Communication Research, 28*(6), 737–771.

Sambharya, R. B. (2011). Security analysts' earnings forecasts as a measure of firm performance: An empirical exploration of its domain. *Management Decision, 49*(7), 1160–1181.

Samuels, S. J., Tennyson, R., Sax, M., Patricia, M., Schermer, N., & Hajovy, H. (1988). Adults' use of text structure in the recall of a scientific journal article. *The Journal of Educational Research, 81*(3), 171–174.

Samuelson, W., & Zeckhauser, R. (1988). Status quo bias in decision making. *Journal of Risk and Uncertainty, 1*, 7–59.

Sanbonmatsu, D. M., Kardes, F. R., & Herr, P. M. (1992). The role of prior knowledge and missing information in multiattribute evaluation. *Organizational Behavior and Human Decision Processes, 51*(1), 76–91.

Sanbonmatsu, D. M., Kardes, F. R., Houghton, D. C., Ho, E. A., & Posavac, S. S. (2003). Overestimating the importance of the given information in multiattribute consumer judgment. *Journal of Consumer Psychology, 13*(3), 289–300.

Sanbonmatsu, D. M., Kardes, F. R., Posavac, S. S., & Houghton, D. C. (1997). Contextual influences on judgment based on limited information. *Organizational Behavior and Human Decision Processes, 69*(3), 251–264.

Sanchez, R. P., Lorch, E. P., & Lorch, R. F., Jr. (2001). Effects of headings on text processing strategies. *Contemporary Educational Psychology, 26*(3), 418–428.

Sandberg, W. R., Schweiger, D. M., & Hofer, C. W. (1988). The use of verbal protocols in determining venture capitalists' decision processes. *Entrepreneurship Theory and Practice, 13*(2), 8–20.

Sande, G. N., Ellard, J. H., & Ross, M. (1986). Effect of arbitrarily assigned status labels on self-perceptions and social perceptions: The mere position effect. *Journal of Personality and Social Psychology, 50*(4), 684–689.

Sanford, A. J., Sanford, A. J., Molle, J., & Emmott, C. (2006). Shallow processing and attention capture in written and spoken discourse. *Discourse Processes, 42*(2), 109–130.

Sankoff, D., Thibault, P., & Berube, H. (1978). Semantic field variability. In D. Sankoff (Ed.), *Linguistic variation: Models and methods* (pp. 23–44). New York: Academic Press.

Sanna, L. J., & Schwarz, N. (2004). Integrating temporal biases: The interplay of focal thoughts and accessibility experiences. *Psychological Science, 15*(7), 474–481.

Sanocki, T. (1987). Visual knowledge underlying letter perception: Font-specific, schematic tuning. *Journal of Experimental Psychology: Human Perception and Performance, 13*(2), 267–278.

Sanocki, T., & Dyson, M. C. (2012). Letter processing and font information during reading: Beyond distinctiveness, where vision meets design. *Attention, Perception, & Psychophysics, 74*(1), 132–145.

Sargis, E. G., & Larson, J. R., Jr. (2002). Informational centrality and member participation during group decision making. *Group Processes & Intergroup Relations, 5*(4), 333–347.

Sasaki, T., Becker, D. V., Janssen, M. A., & Neel, R. (2011). Does greater product information actually inform consumer decisions? The relationship between product information quantity and diversity of consumer decisions. *Journal of Economic Psychology, 32*(3), 391–398.

Sato, W., Kochiyama, T., Yoshikawa, S., & Matsumura, M. (2001). Emotional processing boosts early visual processing of the face: ERP recording and its decomposition by independent component analysis. *NeuroReport, 12*(4), 709–714.

Saunders, D. M., Vidmar, N., & Hewitt, E. C. (1983). Eyewitness testimony and the discrediting effect. In S. M. A. Lloyd-Bostock & B. R. Clifford (Eds.), *Evaluating witness evidence* (pp. 57–78). New York: Wiley.

Sauter, D. A., & Scott, S. K. (2007). More than one kind of happiness: Can we recognize vocal expressions of different positive states? *Motivation and Emotion, 31*(3), 192–199.

Savin, H. B., & Perchonock, E. (1965). Grammatical structure and the immediate recall of English sentences. *Journal of Verbal Learning and Verbal Behavior, 4*(5), 348–353.

Sawyer, J. (1966). Measurement and prediction, clinical and statistical. *Psychological Bulletin, 66*(3), 178–200.

Scannell, L., & Gifford, R. (2013). Personally relevant climate change the role of place attachment and local versus global message framing in engagement. *Environment and Behavior, 45*(1), 60–85.

Scarborough, D. L., Gerard, L., & Cortese, C. (1979). Accessing lexical memory: The transfer of word repetition effects across task and modality. *Memory & Cognition, 7*(1), 3–12.

Schallert, D. L. (1976). Improving memory for prose: The relationship between depth of processing and context. *Journal of Verbal Learning & Verbal Behavior, 15*(6), 621–632.

Schank, R. C. (1975). *Conceptual information processing.* Amsterdam: North-Holland.

Schank, R. C., & Abelson, R. P. (1977). *Scripts, plans, goals and understanding: An inquiry into human knowledge structures.* Oxford, UK: Lawrence Erlbaum.

Scheflen, A. (1964). The significance of posture in communication systems. *Psychiatry, 27,* 316–331.

Scheibehenne, B., Greifeneder, R., & Todd, P. M. (2010). Can there ever be too many options? A meta-analytic review of choice overload. *Journal of Consumer Research, 37*(3), 409–425.

Schelling, T. C. (1984). *Choice and consequence.* Cambridge, MA: Harvard University Press.

Scherer, K. R. (1974). Acoustic concomitants of emotional dimensions: Judging affects from synthesized tone sequences. In S. Weitz (Ed.), *Nonverbal communication* (pp. 105–111). New York: Oxford University Press.

Scherer, K. R. (1978). Personality inference from voice quality: The loud voice of extroversion. *European Journal of Social Psychology, 8*(4), 467–487.

Scherer, K. R. (1979a). Personality markers in speech. In K. R. Scherer & H. Giles (Eds.), *Social markers in speech* (pp. 58–79). Cambridge, MA: Cambridge University Press.

Scherer, K. R. (1979b). Voice and speech correlates of perceived social influence. In H. Giles & R. St. Clair (Eds.), *The social psychology of language* (pp. 88–120). London: Blackwell.

Scherer, K. R. (1982). Emotion as a process: Function, origin and regulation. *Social Science Information, 21*(4–5), 555–570.

Scherer, K. R. (1984). Emotion as a multicomponent process: A model and some cross-cultural data. *Review of Personality & Social Psychology, 5*, 37–63.

Scherer, K. R. (1986). Vocal affect expression: A review and a model for future research. *Psychological Bulletin, 99*(2), 143–165.

Scherer, K. R. (1987). Toward a dynamic theory of emotion: The component process model of affective states. *Geneva Studies in Emotion and Communication, 1*(1), 1–98.

Scherer, K. R. (1999). On the sequential nature of appraisal processes: Indirect evidence from a recognition task. *Cognition and Emotion, 13*(6), 763–793.

Scherer, K. R., Banse, R., & Wallbott, H. G. (2001). Emotion inferences from vocal expression correlate across languages and cultures. *Journal of Cross-Cultural Psychology, 32*(1), 76–92.

Scherer, K. R., Johnstone, T., & Klasmeyer, G. (2003). Vocal expression of emotion. In R. J. Davidson, K. R. Scherer, & H. H. Goldsmith (Eds.), *Handbook of affective sciences* (pp. 433–456). New York: Oxford University Press.

Scherer, K. R., & Oshinsky, J. (1977). Cue utilization in emotion attribution from auditory stimuli. *Motivation and Emotion, 1*(4), 331–346.

Scherer, K. R., & Scherer, U. (1981). Speech behavior and personality. In J. Darby (Ed.), *Speech evaluation in psychiatry* (pp. 115–135). New York: Grune & Stratton.

Schippers, M. C., Den Hartog, D. N., Koopman, P. L., & van Knippenberg, D. (2008). The role of transformational leadership in enhancing team reflexivity. *Human Relations, 61*(11), 1593–1616.

Schirmer, A., & Kotz, S. A. (2003). ERP evidence for a sex-specific Stroop effect in emotional speech. *Journal of Cognitive Neuroscience, 15*(8), 1135–1148.

Schirmer, A., Striano, T., & Friederici, A. D. (2005). Sex differences in the preattentive processing of vocal emotional expressions. *Neuroreport: For Rapid Communication of Neuroscience Research, 16*(6), 635–639.

Schittekatte, M. (1996). Facilitating information exchange in small decision-making groups. *European Journal of Social Psychology, 26*(4), 537–556.

Schittekatte, M., & Van Hiel, A. (1996). Effects of partially shared information and awareness of unshared information on information sampling. *Small Group Research, 27*(3), 431–449.

Schkade, D. A., & Kleinmuntz, D. N. (1994). Information displays and choice processes: Differential effects of organization, form, and sequence. *Organizational Behavior and Human Decision Processes, 57*(3), 319–337.

Schkade, D. A., & Payne, J. W. (1994). How people respond to contingent valuation questions: A verbal protocol analysis of willingness to pay for an environmental regulation. *Journal of Environmental Economics and Management, 26*(1), 88–109.

Schmitt, N. (1976). Social and situational determinants of interview decisions: Implications for the employment interview. *Personnel Psychology, 29*(1), 79–101.

Schmitt, N., & Coyle, B. W. (1976). Applicant decisions in the employment interview. *Journal of Applied Psychology, 61*(2), 184–192.

Schneider, S. L., & Shanteau, J. (2003). Introduction: Where to decision making? In S. Schneider & J. Shanteau (Eds.), *Emerging perspectives on judgment and decision research* (pp. 1–10). Cambridge, UK: Cambridge University Press.

Schneider, T. R., Salovey, P., Apanovirch, A. M., Pizarro, J., McCarthy, D., Zullo, J., & Rothman, A. J. (2001a). The effects of message framing and ethnic targeting on mammography use among low-income women. *Health Psychology, 20*(4), 256–266.

Schneider, T. R., Salovey, P., Pallonen, U., Mundorf, N., Smith, N. F., & Steward, W. (2001b). Visual and auditory message framing effects on tobacco smoking. *Journal of Applied Social Psychology, 31*(4), 667–682.

Schneirla, T. C. (1959). An evolutionary and developmental theory of biphasic processes underlying approach and withdrawal. In M. R. Jones (Ed.), *Nebraska symposium on motivation* (pp. 1–42). Lincoln, NE: University of Nebraska Press.

Schnotz, W., & Baadte, C. (2015). Surface and deep structures in graphics comprehension. *Memory & Cognition, 43*(4), 605–618.

Schnotz, W., & Bannert, M. (2003). Construction and interference in learning from multiple representation. *Learning and Instruction, 13*(2), 141–156.

Scholten, L., Van Knippenberg, D., Nijstad, B. A., & De Dreu, C. K. (2007). Motivated information processing and group decision-making: Effects of process accountability on information processing and decision quality. *Journal of Experimental Social Psychology, 43*(4), 539–552.

Schriver, K. A. (1992). Teaching writers to anticipate readers' needs: A classroom-evaluated pedagogy. *Written Communication, 9*(2), 179–208.

Schriver, K. A. (1997). *Dynamics in document design: Creating text for readers.* New York: Wiley.

Schriver, K. A. (2000). Readability formulas in the new millennium: What's the use? *ACM Journal of Computer Documentation (JCD), 24*(3), 138–140.

Schriver, K. A., Hayes, J. R., & Steffy Cronin, A. (1996). *"Just say no to drugs" and other unwelcome advice: Explorin creation and interpretation of drug education literature* (Final Rep.). Berkeley, CA, and Pittsburgh, PA:

University of Califorina at Berkeley and Carnegie Mellon University, National Center for the Study of Writing and Literacy.

Schuh, A. J. (1978). Contrast effect in the interview. *Bulletin of the Psychonomic Society*, *11*(3), 195–196.

Schul, Y., Mayo, R., & Burnstein, E. (2004). Encoding under trust and distrust: The spontaneous activation of incongruent cognitions. *Journal of Personality and Social Psychology*, *86*(5), 668–679.

Schulz-Hardt, S., Brodbeck, F. C., Mojzisch, A., Kerschreiter, R., & Frey, D. (2006). Group decision making in hidden profile situations: Dissent as a facilitator for decision quality. *Journal of Personality and Social Psychology*, *91*(6), 1080–1093.

Schulz-Hardt, S., Frey, D., Luthgens, C., & Moscovici, S. (2000). Biased information search in group decision making. *Journal of Personality and Social Psychology*, *78*(4), 655–669.

Schulz-Hardt, S., Jochims, M., & Frey, D. (2002). Productive conflict in group decision making: Genuine and contrived dissent as strategies to counteract biased information seeking. *Organizational Behavior and Human Decision Processes*, *88*(2), 563–586.

Schum, D. A., & Martin, A. W. (1993). Formal and empirical research on cascaded inference in jurisprudence. In R. Hastie (Ed.), *Inside the juror: The psychology of juror decision making* (pp. 136–174). New York, NY: Cambridge University Press.

Schupp, H. T., Junghöfer, M., Weike, A. I., & Hamm, A. O. (2003). Emotional facilitation of sensory processing in the visual cortex. *Psychological Science*, *14*(1), 7–13.

Schutz, H. G. (1961). An evaluation of methods for presentation of graphic multiple trends: Experiment III. *Human Factors*, *3*(2), 108–119.

Schwartz, C. E., Wright, C. I., Shin, L. M., Kagan, J., Whalen, P. J., McMullin, K. G., & Rauch, S. L. (2003). Differential amygdalar response to novel versus newly familiar neutral faces: A functional MRI probe developed for studying inhibited temperament. *Biological Psychiatry*, *53*(10), 854–862.

Schwartz, D., Sparkman, J. P., & Deese, J. (1970). The process of understanding and judgments of comprehensibility. *Journal of Verbal Learning & Verbal Behavior*, *9*(1), 87–93.

Schwarz, N. (1990). Feelings as information: Informational and motivational functions of affective states. In E. T. Higgins & R. M. Sorrentino (Eds.), *Handbook of motivation and cognition: Foundations of social behavior* (Vol. 2, pp. 527–561). New York: Guilford Press.

Schwarz, N. (2004). Meta-cognitive experiences in consumer judgment and decision making. *Journal of Consumer Psychology*, *14*(4), 332–348.

Schwarz, N., & Bless, H. (1991). Happy and mindless, but sad and smart? The impact of affective states on analytic reasoning. In J. P. Forgas (Ed.), *Emotion and social judgments* (pp. 55–71). Elmsford, NY: Pergamon Press.

Schwarz, N., & Clore, G. L. (1983). Mood, misattribution, and judgments of well-being: Informative and directive functions of affective states. *Journal of Personality and Social Psychology*, *45*(3), 513–523.

Schwarz, N., & Clore, G. L. (1996). Feelings and phenomenal experiences. In A. W. Kruglanski & E. T. Higgins (Eds.), *Social psychology: Handbook of basic principles* (2nd ed., pp. 385–407). New York, NY: Guilford Press.

Schwarz, N., & Clore, G. L. (2003). Mood as information: 20 years later. *Psychological Inquiry*, *14*(3–4), 296–303.

Schwarz, N., & Vaughn, L. A. (2002). The availability heuristic revisited: Ease of recall and content of recall as distinct sources of information. In T. Gilovich, D. Griffin & D. Kahneman (Eds.), *Heuristics and biases: The psychology of intuitive judgment* (pp. 103–119). New York: Cambridge University Press.

Schweitzer, M. (1994). Disentangling status quo and omission effects: An experimental analysis. *Organizational Behavior and Human Decision Processes*, *58*(3), 457–476.

Schwenk, C. R. (1984). Cognitive simplification process in strategic decision making. *Strategic Management Journal*, *5*(2), 111–128.

Sebastian, A., Jung, P., Neuhoff, J., Wibral, M., Fox, P. T., Lieb, K., . . . & Mobascher, A. (2015). Dissociable attentional and inhibitory networks of dorsal and ventral areas of the right inferior frontal cortex: A combined task-specific and coordinate-based meta-analytic fMRI study. *Brain Structure & Function*, 1–7, doi:10.1007/s00429-015-0994-y.

Sedivy, J., Tanehaus, M., Spivey-Knowlton, M., Eberhard, K., & Carlson, G. (1995). Using intonationally marked presuppositional information in on-line language processing: Evidence from eye movements to a visual model. In J. D. Moore & J. F. Lehman (Eds.), *Proceedings of the seventeenth annual conference of the cognitive science society* (pp. 375–380). Hillsdale, NJ: Erlbaum.

Seggre, I. (1983). Attribution of guilt as a function of ethnic accent and type of crime. *Journal of Multilingual and Multicultural Development*, *4*, 197–206.

Segrin, C. (1993). The effects of nonverbal behavior on outcomes of compliance gaining attempts. *Communication Studies*, *44*, 169–187.

Selling, T. I. (1982). Cognitive processes in information system choice (Doctoral dissertation, The Ohio State University, 1982). *Dissertation Abstracts International*, *43*(08A), 2713.

Sentis, K., & Markus, H. (1986). Brand personality and self. In J. C. Olson & K. Sentis (Eds.), *Advertising and consumer psychology* (Vol. 3, pp. 132–148). New York: Praeger.

Sereno, S. C., O'Donnell, P., & Rayner, K. (2006). Eye movements and lexical ambiguity resolution: Investigating the subordinate bias effect. *Journal of Experimental Psychology: Human Perception and Performance, 32*(2), 335–350.

Serfaty, D., MacMillan, J., Entin, E. E., & Entin, E. B. (1997). The decision making expertise of battle commanders. In C. E. Zsambok & G. Klein (Eds.), *Naturalistic decision making* (pp. 233–246). Mahwah, NJ: Lawrence Erlbaum Associates.

Service, E. (2009). From auditory traces to language learning: Behavioural and neurophysiological evidence. In A. C. Thorn & M. A. Page (Eds.), *Interactions between short-term and long-term memory in the verbal domain* (pp. 277–299). New York, NY: Psychology Press.

Sessa, V. I. (2001). Executive promotion and selection. In M. London (Ed.), *How people evaluate others in organizations* (pp. 91–110). Hillsdale, NJ: Lawrence Erlbaum Associates.

Sessa, V. I., Kaiser, R., Taylor, J. K., & Campbell, R. J. (1998). *Executive selection: A research report on what works and what doesn't* (Rep. No. 179). Greensboro, NC: Center for Creative Leadership.

Seyranian, V. (2014). Social identity framing communication strategies for mobilizing social change. *The Leadership Quarterly, 25*(3), 468–486.

Seyranian, V., & Bligh, M. C. (2008). Presidential charismatic leadership: Exploring the rhetoric of social change. *The Leadership Quarterly, 19*(1), 54–76.

Shafir, E. (1993). Choosing versus rejecting: Why some options are both better and worse than others. *Memory & Cognition, 21*(4), 546–556.

Shafir, E., Simonson, I., & Tversky, A. (1993). Reason-based choice. *Cognition Special Issue: Reasoning and Decision Making, 49*(1–2), 11–36.

Shah, D. V., Domke, D., & Wackman, D. B. (1996). "To thine own self be true": Values, framing, and voter decision-making strategies. *Communication Research, 23*(5), 509–560.

Shah, D. V., Domke, D., & Wackman, D. B. (2001). The effects of value-framing on political judgment and reasoning. In S. D. Reese, O. H. Gandy & A. E. Grant (Eds.), *Framing public life: Perspectives on media and our understanding of the social world* (pp. 227–243). Mahwah, NJ: Lawrence Erlbaum Associates.

Shah, P. (1995). Cognitive processes in graph comprehension (Doctoral dissertation, Carnegie Mellon University, 1995). *Dissertation Abstracts International, 57*(03B), 2191.

Shah, P., & Hoeffner, J. (2002). Review of graph comprehension research: Implications for instruction. *Educational Psychology Review, 14,* 47–69.

Shah, P., Mayer, R. E., & Hegarty, M. (1999). Graphs as aids to knowledge construction: Signaling techniques for guiding the process of graph comprehension. *Journal of Educational Psychology, 91*(4), 690–702.

Shamir, B. (1991). Meaning, self and motivation in organizations. *Organization Studies, 12*(3), 405–424.

Shamir, B., Arthur, M. B., & House, R. J. (1994). The rhetoric of charismatic leadership: A theoretical extension, a case study, and implications for research. *The Leadership Quarterly, 5*(1), 25–42.

Shamir, B., House, R., & Arthur, M. B. (1993). The motivational effects of charismatic leadership: A self-concept based theory. *Organization Science, 4*(4), 577–594.

Shanteau, J. (1988). Psychological characteristics and strategies of expert decision makers. *Acta Psychologica, 68*(1–3), 203–215.

Shanteau, J. (1989). Cognitive heuristics and biases in behavioral auditing: Review, comments, and observations. *Accounting Organizations and Society, 14*(1–2), 165–177.

Shanteau, J. (1992). Competence in experts: The role of task characteristics. *Organizational Behavior and Human Decision Processes Special Issue: Experts and Expert Systems, 53*(2), 252–266.

Shanteau, J., & Edwards, W. (2014). Decision making by experts: Influence of five key psychologists. In E. A. Wilhelms & V. F. Reyna (Eds.), *Neuroeconomics, judgment, and decision making* (pp. 3–26). New York, NY: Psychology Press.

Shapiro, J. G. (1968). Variability in the communication of affect. *Journal of Social Psychology, 76*(2), 181–188.

Shapiro, S., & Spence, M. T. (2002). Factors affecting encoding, retrieval, and alignment of sensory attributes in a memory-based brand choice task. *Journal of Consumer Research, 28*(4), 603–617.

Shattuck, L. G. (1995). Communication of intent in distributed supervisory control systems (Doctoral dissertation. The Ohio State University, 1995). *Dissertation Abstracts International, 56*(09B), 5209.

Shaver, K. G. (1975). *An introduction to attribution processes.* Cambridge, MA: Winthrop Publishing.

Shaver, K. G. (1985). *The attribution of blame: Causality, responsibility, and blame-worthiness.* New York: Springer-Verlag.

Shaver, K. G., & Drown, D. (1986). On causality, responsibility, and self-blame: A theoretical note. *Journal of Personality and Social Psychology, 50*(4), 697–702.

Shaver, P., Hazan, C., & Bradshaw, D. (1988). Love as attachment. In R. J. Sternberg & M. L. Barnes (Eds.), *The psychology of love* (pp. 68–99). New Haven, CT: Yale University Press.

Shaw, E. A. (1972). Commonality of applicant stereotypes among recruiters. *Personnel Psychology, 25*(3), 421–432.

Shea, N., Krug, K., & Tobler, P. N. (2008). Conceptual representations in goal-directed decision making. *Cognitive, Affective, and Behavioral Neuroscience, 8*(4), 418–428.

Sheffey, S., Tindale, R. S., & Scott, L. A. (1989). *Information sharing and group decision making*. Paper presented at the Midwestern Psychological Association Annual Convention, Chicago, IL.

Shefrin, H., & Statman, M. (1995). Making sense of beta, size, and book-to-market. *Journal of Portfolio Management, 21*(2), 26–34.

Sheldon, K. M., & Elliot, A. J. (1999). Goal striving, need satisfaction, and longitudinal well-being: The self-concordance model. *Journal of Personality and Social Psychology, 76*(3), 482–497.

Sheluga, D. A., & Jacoby, J. (1978). Do comparative claims encourage comparison shopping? In J. Leigh & C. R. Martin (Eds.), *Current issues and research in advertising* (pp. 23–37). Ann Arbor, MI: University of Michigan Press.

Shen, H., Jiang, Y., & Adaval, R. (2010). Contrast and assimilation effects of processing fluency. *Journal of Consumer Research, 36*(5), 876–889.

Shepard, R. N. (1967). Recognition memory for words, sentences, and pictures. *Journal of Verbal Learning & Verbal Behavior, 6*(1), 156–163.

Sherblom, J., & Van Rheenen, D. D. (1984). Spoken language indices of uncertainty. *Human Communication Research, 11*(2), 221–230.

Sherer, M., & Rogers, R. W. (1984). The role of vivid information in fear appeals and attitude change. *Journal of Research in Personality, 18*(3), 321–334.

Sherman, M. A. (1976). Adjectival negation and the comprehension of multiply negated sentences. *Journal of Verbal Learning & Verbal Behavior, 15*(2), 143–157.

Sherman, S. J. (1980). On the self-erasing nature of errors of prediction. *Journal of Personality and Social Psychology, 39*(2), 211–221.

Sherman, S. J., Cialdini, R. B., Schwartzman, D. F., & Reynolds, K. D. (1985). Imagining can heighten or lower the perceived likelihood of contracting a disease: The mediating effect of ease of imagery. *Personality and Social Psychology Bulletin, 11*(1), 118–127.

Shi, S. W., Wedel, M., & Pieters, F. (. (2013). Information acquisition during online decision making: A model-based exploration using eye-tracking data. *Management Science, 59*(5), 1009–1026.

Shieh, K. K., & Lai, Y. K. (2008). Effects of ambient illumination, luminance contrast, and stimulus type on subjective preference of VDT target and background color combinations. *Perceptual and Motor Skills, 107*(2), 336–352.

Shimko, K. L. (1994). Metaphors and foreign policy decision making. *Political Psychology, 15*(4), 655–671.

Shimojo, S., Simion, C., Shimojo, E., & Scheier, C. (2003). Gaze bias both reflects and influences preference. *Nature Neuroscience, 6*(12), 1317–1322.

Shleifer, A. (2000). *Inefficient markets: An introduction to behavioral finance*. New York: Oxford University Press.

Shrum, L. J., Wyer, R. S., Jr., & O'Guinn, T. C. (1998). The effects of television consumption on social perceptions: The use of priming procedures to investigate psychological processes. *Journal of Consumer Research, 24*(4), 447–458.

Siess, T. F., & Jackson, D. N. (1970). Vocational interests and personality: An empirical integration. *Journal of Counseling Psychology, 17*(1), 27–35.

Sigall, H., & Ostrove, N. (1975). Beautiful but dangerous: Effects of offender attractiveness and nature of the crime on juridic judgment. *Journal of Personality and Social Psychology, 31*(3), 410–414.

Sigelman, L., & Sigelman, C. K. (1981). Presidential leadership of public opinion: From 'benevolent leader' to kiss of death? *Experimental Study of Politics, 7*(3), 1–22.

Siguaw, J. A., Mattila, A., & Austin, J. R. (1999). The brand-personality scale. *The Cornell Hotel and Restaurant Administration Quarterly, 40*(3), 48–55.

Sikora, S., Miall, D. S., & Kuiken, D. (1998). *Enactment versus interpretation: A phenomenological study of readers' responses to Coleridge's "The rime of the ancient mariner"*. Paper presented at the Sixth Biennial Conference of the International Society for the Empirical Study of Literature, Utrecht, The Netherlands.

Silvera, D. H., Kardes, F. R., Harvey, N., Cronley, M. L., & Houghton, D. C. (2005). Contextual influences on omission neglect in the fault tree paradigm. *Journal of Consumer Psychology, 15*(2), 117–126.

Simkin, D. K., & Hastie, R. (1986). An information processing analysis of graph perception. *Journal of the American Statistical Association, 82*, 454–465.

Simon, H. A. (1955). A behavioral model of rational choice. *Quarterly Journal of Economics, 69*, 99–118.

Simon, H. A. (1956). Rational choice and the structure of the environment. *Psychological Review, 63*(2), 129–138.

Simon, H. A. (1967). Motivational and emotional controls of cognition. *Psychological Review, 74*(1), 29–39.

Simon, H. A., & Hayes, J. R. (1976). The understanding process: Problem isomorphs. *Cognitive Psychology, 8*(2), 165–190.

Simons, T., Hope-Pelled, L., & Smith, K. A. (1999). Making use of difference: Diversity, debate, and decision comprehensiveness in top management teams. *Academy of Management Journal, 42*(6), 662–673.

Simonson, I., Huber, J., & Payne, J. (1988). The relationship between prior brand knowledge and information acquisition order. *Journal of Consumer Research, 14*(4), 566–578.

Sinclair, R. C., Soldat, A. S., & Mark, M. M. (1998). Affective cues and processing strategy: Color-coded examination forms influence performance. *Teaching of Psychology, 25*(2), 130–132.

Singer, J. A., & Salovey, P. (1996). Motivated memory: Self-defining memories, goals, and affect regulation. In L. L. Martin & A. Tesser (Eds.), *Striving and feeling: Interactions among goals, affect, and self-regulation* (pp. 229–250). Hillsdale, NJ: Lawrence Erlbaum Associates.

Sisodia, R., Sheth, J., & Wolfe, D. B. (2007). *Firms of endeavor: The pursuit of purpose and profit.* Upper Saddle River, NJ: FT Press.

Sivacek, J., & Crano, W. D. (1982). Vested interest as a moderator of attitude-behavior consistency. *Journal of Personality and Social Psychology, 43*(2), 210–221.

Sjöberg, L. (1980). Volitional problems in carrying through a difficult decision. *Acta Psychologica, 45*(1–3), 123–132.

Sjödin, H., & Törn, F. (2006). When communication challenges brand associations: A framework for understanding consumer responses to brand image incongruity. *Journal of Consumer Behaviour, 5*(1), 32–42.

Sjogren, D., & Timpson, W. (1979). Frameworks for comprehending discourse: A replication study. *American Educational Research Journal, 16*(4), 341–346.

Skilbeck, C., Tulips, J., & Ley, P. (1977). The effects of fear arousal, fear position, fear exposure, and sidedness on compliance with dietary instructions. *European Journal of Social Psychology, 7*(2), 221–239.

Skowronski, J. J., & Carlston, D. E. (1987). Social judgment and social memory: The role of cue diagnosticity in negativity, positivity, and extremity biases. *Journal of Personality and Social Psychology, 52*(4), 689–699.

Skowronski, J. J., & Carlston, D. E. (1989). Negativity and extremity biases in impression formation: A review of explanations. *Psychological Bulletin, 105*(1), 131–142.

Skurnik, I., Yoon, C., Park, D. C., & Schwarz, N. (2005). How warnings about false claims become recommendations. *Journal of Consumer Research, 31*(4), 713–724.

Slaughter, J. E., & Greguras, G. J. (2009). Initial attraction to organizations: The influence of trait inferences. *International Journal of Selection and Assessment, 17*(1), 1–18.

Slaughter, J. E., Zickar, M. J., Highhouse, S., & Mohr, D. C. (2004). Personality trait inferences about organizations: Development of a measure and assessment of construct validity. *Journal of Applied Psychology, 89*(1), 85.

Slife, B. D., Weiss, J., & Bell, T. (1985). Separability of metacognition and cognition: Problem solving in learning disabled and regular students. *Journal of Educational Psychology, 77*(4), 437–445.

Slobin, D. I. (1966). Grammatical transformations and sentence comprehension in childhood and adulthood. *Journal of Verbal Learning and Verbal Behavior, 5*(3), 219–277.

Slovic, P. (1972). *From Shakespeare to Simon: Speculations—and some evidence—about man's ability to process information.* ORI research monograph, 12. Eugene, OR: Oregon Research Institute.

Slovic, P. (1975). Choice between equally valued alternatives. *Journal of Experimental Psychology: Human Perception and Performance, 1*(3), 280–287.

Slovic, P., Finucane, M., Peters, E., & MacGregor, D. G. (2002). Rational actors or rational fools: Implications of the affect heuristic for behavioral economics. *The Journal of Socio-Economics, 31*(4), 329–342.

Slovic, P., Fischhoff, B., & Lichtenstein, S. (1982). Facts versus fears: Understanding perceived risk. In D. Kahneman, P. Slovic & A. Tversky (Eds.), *Judgment under uncertainty: Heuristics and biases* (pp. 463–489). New York: Cambridge University Press.

Slovic, P., & Lichtenstein, S. (1971). Comparison of Bayesian and regression approaches to the study of information processing in judgment. *Organizational Behavior & Human Performance, 6*(6), 649–744.

Slovic, P., & MacPhillamy, D. (1974). Dimensional commensurability and cue utilization in comparative judgment. *Organizational Behavior & Human Performance, 11*(2), 172–194.

Smeesters, D., Warlop, L., Vanden Abeele, P., & Ratneshwar, S. (1999). *Exploring the recycling dilemma: Consumer motivation and experiences in mandatory garbage recycling programs.* Research report no. 9924. Belgium: Department of Applied Economics, Catholic University of Leuven.

Smith, C. A. (1989). Dimensions of appraisal and physiological response in emotion. *Journal of Personality and Social Psychology, 56*(3), 339–353.

Smith, C. A., & Ellsworth, P. C. (1985). Patterns of cognitive appraisal in emotion. *Journal of Personality and Social Psychology, 48*(4), 813–838.

Smith, C. A., & Ellsworth, P. C. (1987). Patterns of appraisal and emotion related to taking an exam. *Journal of Personality and Social Psychology, 52*(3), 475–488.

Smith, C. A., & Kirby, L. D. (2000). Consequences require antecedents: Toward a process model of emotion elicitation. In J. P. Forgas (Ed.), *Feeling and thinking: The role of affect in social cognition* (pp. 83–106). New York: Cambridge University Press.

Smith, C. A., & Kirby, L. D. (2001). Toward delivering on the promise of appraisal theory. In K. R. Scherer, A. Schorr & T. Johnstone (Eds.), *Appraisal processes in emotion: Theory, methods, research* (pp. 121–138). New York: Oxford University Press.

Smith, C. A., & Lazarus, R. S. (1990). Emotion and adaptation. In L. A. Pervin (Ed.), *Handbook of personality: Thoery and research* (pp. 609–637). New York: Guilford Press.

Smith, C. A., & Pope, L. K. (1992). Appraisal and emotion: The interactional contributions of dispositional and situational factors. In M. S. Clark (Ed.), *Emotion and social behavior* (pp. 32–62). Thousand Oaks, CA: Sage.

Smith, C. M., Tindale, R. S., & Steiner, L. (1998). Investment decisions by individuals and groups in "sunk cost" situations: The potential impact of shared representations. *Group Processes & Intergroup Relations, 1*(2), 175–189.

Smith, D., Stenner, A. J., Horabin, I., & Smith, M. (1989). *The Lexile scale in theory and practice: Final report.* Washington, DC: MetaMetrics. (ERIC document reproduction service number ED 307 577).

Smith, D. M., Neuberg, S. L., Judice, T. N., & Biesanz, J. C. (1997). Target complicity in the confirmation and disconfirmation of erroneous perceiver expectations: Immediate and longer term implications. *Journal of Personality and Social Psychology, 73*(5), 974–991.

Smith, E. (1998a). Mental representations and memory. In D. Gilbert, S. Fiske & G. Lindzey (Eds.), *The handbook of social psychology* (4th ed., pp. 391–445). New York: McGraw-Hill.

Smith, E. E., & Swinney, D. A. (1992). The role of schemas in reading text: A real-time examination. *Discourse Processes, 15*(3), 303–316.

Smith, G. E. (1996). Framing in advertising and the moderating impact of consumer education. *Journal of Advertising Research, 36*(5), 49–64.

Smith, G. W. (1998b). The political impact of name sounds. *Communication Monographs, 65*(2), 154–172.

Smith, J. F., & Kida, T. (1991). Heuristics and biases: Expertise and task realism in auditing. *Psychological Bulletin, 109*(3), 472–489.

Smith, J. M., & McCombs. E. (1971). The graphics of prose. *Visible Language, 4*(Autumn), 365–369.

Smith, P., & Waterman, M. (2003). Processing bias for aggression words in forensic and nonforensic samples. *Cognition & Emotion, 17*(5), 681–701.

Smith, P., & Waterman, M. (2004). Processing bias for sexual material: The emotional Stroop and sexual offenders. *Sexual Abuse: A Journal of Research and Treatment, 16*(2), 163–171.

Smith, P. M. (1979). Sex markers in speech. In K. R. Scherer & H. Giles (Eds.), *Social markers in speech* (pp. 109–146). Cambridge, UK: Cambridge University Press.

Smith, P. M. (1980). Judging masculine and feminine social identities from content-controlled speech. In H. Giles, W. P. Robinson & P. M. Smith (Eds.), *Language: Social psychological perspectives* (pp. 121–126). Oxford, UK: Pergamon.

Smith, S. M., & Shaffer, D. R. (1995). Speed of speech and persuasion: Evidence for multiple effects. *Personality and Social Psychology Bulletin, 21*(10), 1051–1060.

Smith, S. M., & Shaffer, D. R. (2000). Vividness can undermine or enhance message processing: The moderating role of vividness congruency. *Personality and Social Psychology Bulletin, 26*(7), 769–779.

Smith, S. W. (1986). A social-cognitive approach to the nature of input processes in reception of nonverbal messages (Doctoral dissertation, University of Southern California, 1986). *Dissertation Abstracts International, 47*(07A), 2372.

Smither, J. W., & Reilly, S. P. (2001). Coaching in organizations. In M. London (Ed.), *How people evaluate others in organizations* (pp. 221–252). Mahwah, NJ: Lawrence Erlbaum.

Smith-Jackson, T. L., & Wogalter, M. S. (2007). Application of a mental models approach to MSDS design. *Theoretical Issues in Ergonomics Science, 8*(4), 303–319.

Smith-Jentsch, K. A., Campbell, G. E., Milanovich, D. M., & Reynolds, A. M. (2001). Measuring teamwork mental models to support training needs assessment, development, and evaluation: Two empirical studies. *Journal of Organizational Behavior, 22*(2), 179–194.

Smotas, P. E. (1996). An analysis of budget decision criteria and selected demographic factors of school business officials of Connecticut school districts (Doctoral dissertation, The University of Connecticut, 1996). *Dissertation Abstracts International, 58*(02A), 388.

Sniderman, P. M., Brody, R. A., & Tetlock, P. E. (1991). *Reasoning and choice: Explorations in political psychology.* New York: Cambridge University Press.

Sniderman, P. M., & Theriault, S. M. (2004). The structure of political argument and the logic of issue framing. In W. E. Saris & P. M. Sniderman (Eds.), *Studies in public opinion: Attitudes, nonattitudes, measurement error and change.* Princeton, NJ: Princeton University Press.

Sniezek, J. A., & Buckley, T. (1995). Cueing and cognitive conflict in judge-advisor decision making. *Organizational Behavior and Human Decision Processes, 62*(2), 159–174.

Sniezek, J. A., & Henry, R. A. (1989). Accuracy and confidence in group judgment. *Organizational Behavior and Human Decision Processes, 43*(1), 1–28.

Snow, D. A., & Benford, R. D. (1988). Ideology, frame resonance, and participant mobilization. In B. Klandermans, H. Kriesi & S. Tarrow (Eds.), *From structure to action: Comparing social movement research across countries* (pp. 197–217). Greenwich, CT: JAI Press.

Soelberg, P. O. (1967). Unprogrammed decision making. *Industrial Management Review, 8*(2), 19–29.

Soldat, A. S., Sinclair, R. C., & Mark, M. M. (1997). Color as an environmental processing cue: External affective cues can directly affect processing strategy without affecting mood. *Social Cognition, 15*(1), 55–71.

Solomon, H., Zener-Solomon, L., Arnone, M., Maur, B., Reda, R., & Roth, E. (1981). Anonymity and helping. *The Journal of Social Psychology, 113*(1), 37–43.

Solomon, J., Knapp, P., Raynor, D. K., & Atkin, K. (2013). Worlds apart? An exploration of prescribing and medicine-taking decisions by patients, GPs and local policy makers. *Health Policy, 112*(3), 264–272.

Solt, M., & Statman, M. (1989). Good companies, bad stocks. *Journal of Portfolio Management, 15*(4), 39–44.

Sommer, R. (1961). Leadership and group geography. *Sociometry, 24*, 99–110.

Sommers, M. S., Greeno, D. W., & Boag, D. (1989). The role of nonverbal communication in service provision and representation. *Service Industries Journal, 9*(4), 162–173.

Sonmez, M., & Moorhouse, A. (2010). Purchasing professional services: Which decision criteria? *Management Decision, 48*(2), 189–206.

Sopory, P., & Dillard, J. P. (2002). The persuasive effects of metaphor: A meta-analysis. *Human Communication Research, 28*(3), 382–419.

Sotirovic, M. (2001). Media use and perceptions of welfare. *Journal of Communication, 51*(4), 750–774.

Sparks, J. R., & Areni, C. S. (2002). The effects of sales presentation quality and initial perceptions on persuasion: A multiple role perspective. *Journal of Business Research, 55*(6), 517–528.

Sparks, J. R., Areni, C. S., & Cox, K. C. (1998). An investigation of the effects of language style and communication modality on persuasion. *Communication Monographs, 65*(2), 108–125.

Spence, I. (1990). Visual psychophysics of simple graphical elements. *Journal of Experimental Psychology: Human Perception and Performance, 16*(4), 683–692.

Spencer, H., Reynolds, L., & Coe, B. (1974). Typographic coding in lists and bibliographies. *Applied Ergonomics, 5*(3), 136–141.

Spilich, G. J., Vesonder, G. T., Chiesi, H. L., & Voss, J. F. (1979). Text processing of domain-related information for individuals with high and low domain knowledge. *Journal of Verbal Learning & Verbal Behavior, 18*(3), 275–290.

Spiro, R. J. (1977). Remembering information from text: The "state of schema" approach. In R. C. Anderson, R. J. Spiro & W. E. Montague (Eds.), *Schooling and the acquisition of knowledge* (pp. 137–165). Hillsdale, NJ: Erlbaum.

Spyridakis, J. H. (1989a). Signaling effects: Part I. *Journal of Technical Writing and Communication, 19*(1), 227–239.

Spyridakis, J. H. (1989b). Signaling effects: Part II. *Journal of Technical Writing and Communication, 19*(4), 395–415.

Sroufe, L. A. (1995). *Emotional development: The organization of emotional life in the early years.* Cambridge, UK: Cambridge University Press.

Srull, T. K. (1983). Organizational and retrieval processes in person memory: An examination of processing objectives, presentation format, and the possible role of self-generated retrieval cues. *Journal of Personality and Social Psychology, 44*(6), 1157–1170.

Srull, T. K. (1990). Individual responses to advertising: Mood and its effects from an information processing perspective. In S. J. Agres, J. A. Edell & T. M. Dubitsky (Eds.), *Emotion in advertising: Theoretical and practical explorations* (pp. 35–51). New York: Quorum Books.

Srull, T. K., & Wyer, R. S. (1979). The role of category accessibility in the interpretation of information about persons: Some determinants and implications. *Journal of Personality and Social Psychology, 37*(10), 1660–1672.

Stafinski, T., Menon, D., Philippon, D. J., & McCabe, C. (2011). Health technology funding decision-making processes around the world. *Pharmacoeconomics, 29*(6), 475–495.

Standing, L. (1973). Learning 10,000 pictures. *The Quarterly Journal of Experimental Psychology, 25*(2), 207–222.

Stanners, R. F., Jastrzembski, J. E., & Westbrook, A. (1975). Frequency and visual quality in a word-nonword classification task. *Journal of Verbal Learning & Verbal Behavior, 14*(3), 259–264.

Stasser, G., & Birchmeier, Z. (2003). Group creativity and collective choice. In P. B. Paulus & B. A. Nijstad (Eds.), *Group creativity: Innovation through collaboration* (pp. 85–109). New York: Oxford University Press.

Stasser, G., & Dietz-Uhler, B. (2002). Collective choice, judgment, and problem solving. In M. A. Hogg & S. Tindale (Eds.), *Blackwell handbook of social psychology: Group processes* (Vol. 3, pp. 31–55). Hoboken, NJ: Wiley-Blackwell.

Stasser, G., Stella, N., Hanna, C., & Colella, A. (1984). The majority effect in jury deliberations: Number of supporters versus number of supporting arguments. *Law & Psychology Review, 8*, 115–127.

Stasser, G., & Stewart, D. (1992). Discovery of hidden profiles by decision-making groups: Solving a problem versus making a judgment. *Journal of Personality and Social Psychology, 63*(3), 426–434.

Stasser, G., Stewart, D. D., & Wittenbaum, G. M. (1995). Expert roles and information exchange during discussion: The importance of knowing who knows what. *Journal of Experimental Social Psychology, 31*(3), 244–265.

Stasser, G., Taylor, L. A., & Hanna, C. (1989). Information sampling in structured and unstructured discussions of three-and six-person groups. *Journal of Personality and Social Psychology, 57*(1), 67.

Stasser, G., & Titus, W. (1985). Pooling of unshared information in group decision making: Biased information sampling during discussion. *Journal of Personality and Social Psychology, 48*(6), 1467–1478.

Stasser, G., & Vaughan, S. I. (1996). Models of participation during face-to-face unstructured discussion. In E. H. Witte & J. H. Davis (Eds.), *Understanding group behavior, Vol. 1: Consensual action by small groups* (pp. 165–192). Hillsdale, NJ: Lawrence Erlbaum.

Statman, M., & Fisher, K. (1998). *The DJIA crossed 652,230 (in 1998).* Working paper. Santa Clara, CA: Santa Clara University.

Staw, B. (1981). The escalation of commitment to a course of action. *Academy of Management Review, 6*(4), 577–587.

Stayman, D. M., & Aaker, D. A. (1987). *Repetition and affective response: Differences in specific feeling responses and the mediating role of attitude toward the ad.* Working paper. Austin: University of Texas.

Stayman, D. M., & Aaker, D. A. (1989). *The role of believability in the elicitation and effect of feeling responses to advertising.* Working paper. Austin: University of Texas.

Stein, S. K. (1999). Uncovering listening strategies: Protocol analysis as a means to investigate student listening in the basic communication course (Doctoral dissertation, University of Maryland at College Park, 1999). *Dissertation Abstracts International, 61*(01A), 28.

Stephan, C. W., & Stephan, W. G. (1986). Habla Ingles? The effects of language translation on simulated juror decisions. *Journal of Applied Social Psychology, 16*(7), 577–589.

Sternberg, R. J. (1999). *Cognitive psychology* (2nd ed.). New York: Harcourt Brace College Publishers.

Sternberg, S. (1966). High-speed scanning in human memory. *Science, 153*(3736), 652–654.

Stevens, W. D., Kahn, I., Wig, G. S., & Schacter, D. L. (2012). Hemispheric asymmetry of visual scene processing in the human brain: Evidence from repetition priming and intrinsic activity. *Cerebral Cortex, 22*(8), 1935–1949.

Stewart, D. D., & Stasser, G. (1995). Expert role assignment and information sampling during collective recall and decision making. *Journal of Personality and Social Psychology, 69*(4), 619–628.

Stewart, D. D., & Stasser, G. (1998). The sampling of critical, unshared information in decision-making groups: The role of an informed minority. *European Journal of Social Psychology, 28*(1), 95–113.

Stewart, N. (2009). The cost of anchoring on credit-card minimum repayments. *Psychological Science, 20*(1), 39–41.

Sticht, T. G. (1977). Comprehending reading at work. In M. A. Just & P. A. Carpenter (Eds.), *Cognitive processes in comprehension* (pp. 221–246). Hillsdale, NJ: Lawrence Erlbaum.

Sticht, T. G., Armijo, L., Weitzman, R., Koffman, N., Roberson, K., Chang, F., & Moracco, J. (1986). *Progress report.* Monterey, CA: U.S. Naval Postgraduate School.

Sticht, T. G., Fox, L. C., Hauke, R. N., & Welty-Sapf, D. (1977). *The role of reading in the Navy.* (NPRDC-TR-77-40). San Diego, CA: Navy Personnel Research and Development Center, September 1977, NTIS No. ADA044228.

Stiff, J. B., Dillard, J. P., Somera, L., Kim, H., & Sleight, C. (1988). Empathy, communication, and prosocial behavior. *Communication Monographs, 55*(2), 198–213.

Stiles, P. (2001). The impact of the board on strategy: An empirical examination. *Journal of Management Studies, 38*(5), 627–650.

Stillwell, W. G., Barron, F. H., & Edwards, W. (1983). Evaluating credit applications: A validation of multiattribute utility weight elicitation techniques. *Organizational Behavior & Human Performance, 32*(1), 87–108.

St. James, W. D. (2009). Relationships between airline employee morale, motivation, and leadership (Doctoral dissertation, University of Phoenix, 2009). *Dissertation Abstracts International: Section A, 69*, 4796.

Stokes, A. F., Kemper, K., & Kite, K. (1997). Aeronautical decision making, cue recognition, and expertise under time pressure. In C. E. Zsambok & G. Klein (Eds.), *Naturalistic decision making* (pp. 183–196). Mahwah, NJ: Erlbaum.

Stolz, W. S. (1967). A study of the ability to decode grammatically novel sentences. *Journal of Verbal Learning & Verbal Behavior, 6*(6), 867–873.

Stone, D. N., & Schkade, D. A. (1991). Numeric and linguistic information representation in multiattribute choice. *Organizational Behavior and Human Decision Processes, 49*(1), 42–59.

Stone, E. R., Yates, J. F., & Parker, A. M. (1997). Effects of numerical and graphical displays on professed risk-taking behavior. *Journal of Experimental Psychology: Applied, 3*(4), 243–256.

Stormark, K. M., Nordby, H., & Hugdahl, K. (1995). Attentional shifts to emotionally charged cues: Behavioural and ERP data. *Cognition & Emotion, 9*(5), 507–523.

Strange, B. A., Hurleman, R., & Dolan, R. J. (2003). An emotion-induced retrograde amnesia in humans is amygdala- and beta-adrenergic-dependent. *Proceedings of the National Academy of Sciences, USA, 100*(3), 13626–13631.

Strasser, A. A., Tang, K. Z., Romer, D., Jepson, C., & Cappella, J. N. (2012). Graphic warning labels in cigarette advertisements: Recall and viewing patterns. *American Journal of Preventive Medicine, 43*(1), 41–47.

Strater, L. D., Jones, D. G., & Endsley, M. R. (2001). *Analysis of infantry situation awareness training requirements.* (No. SATech 01–15). Marietta, GA: SA Technologies.

Stratman, J., & Young, R. O. (1986, April). *An analysis of novice managers' performances in board meetings.* Annual Conference of the Management Communication Association, Durham, NC.

Strelnikov, K., Massida, Z., Rouger, J., Belin, P., & Barone, P. (2011). Effects of vocoding and intelligibility on the cerebral response to speech. *BMC Neuroscience, 12*(1), 122.

Strong, E. K., Jr. (1926). Value of white space in advertising. *Journal of Applied Psychology, 10*(1), 107–116.

Sturt, P. (2003). The time course of the application of binding constraints in reference resolution. *Journal of Memory and Language, 48*(3), 542–562.

Sturt, P., Keller, F., & Dubey, A. (2010). Syntactic priming in comprehension: Parallelism effects with and without coordination. *Journal of Memory and Language, 62*(4), 333–351.

Sturt, P., & Lombardo, V. (2005). Processing coordinated structures: Incrementality and connectedness. *Cognitive Science, 29*(2), 291–305.

Sugimori, E., Mitchell, K. J., Raye, C. L., Greene, E. J., & Johnson, M. K. (2014). Brain mechanisms underlying reality monitoring for heard and imagined words. *Psychological Science, 25*(2), 403–413.

Sulin, R. A., & Dooling, D. J. (1974). Intrusion of a thematic idea in retention of prose. *Journal of Experimental Psychology, 103*(2), 255–262.

Sullins, E. S. (1991). Emotional contagion revisited: Effects of social comparison and expressive style on mood convergence. *Personality and Social Psychology Bulletin, 17*(2), 166–174.

Sullivan, B. N., Haunschild, P., & Page, K. (2007). Organizations non gratae? The impact of unethical corporate acts on interorganizational networks. *Organization Science, 18*(1), 55–70.

Sullivan, D. G., & Masters, R. D. (1988). Happy warriors': Leaders' facial displays, viewers' emotions, and political support. *American Journal of Political Science, 32*, 345–368.

Sullivan, D. G., Masters, R. D., Lanzetta, J. T., Englis, B. G., & McHugo, G. J. (1984). *The effect of President Reagan's facial displays on observers' attitudes, impressions, and feelings about him.* Paper presented at the 1984 Annual Meeting of the American Political Science Association, Washington, DC.

Sulsky, L. M., & Kline, T. J. (2007). Understanding frame-of-reference training success: A social learning theory perspective. *International Journal of Training and Development, 11*(2), 121–131.

Sundström, G. A. (1987). Information search and decision making: The effects of information displays. *Acta Psychologica, 65*(2), 165–179.

Surber, J. R., & Schroeder, M. (2007). Effect of prior domain knowledge and headings on processing of informative text. *Contemporary Educational Psychology, 32*(3), 485–498.

Surowiecki, J. (2004). *The wisdom of crowds: Why the many are smarter than the few and how collective wisdom shapes business, economies, societies and nations little.* New York, NY: Doubleday.

Svenson, O. (1974). *A note on think aloud protocols obtained during the choice of a home.* (Report No. 421). Stockholm: Psychology Lab, University of Stockholm.

Svenson, O. (1979). Process descriptions of decision making. *Organizational Behavior and Human Performance, 23*(1), 86–112.

Svenson, O. (2003). Values, affect, and processes in human decision making: A differentiation and consolidation perspective. In S. L. Schneider & J. Shanteau (Eds.), *In emerging perspectives on judgment and decision research* (pp. 287–326). Cambridge, UK: Cambridge University Press.

Svenson, O., & Edland, A. (1987). Change of preferences under time pressure: Choices and judgements. *Scandinavian Journal of Psychology, 28*(4), 322–330.

Swales, J. (1990). *Genre analysis: English in academic and research settings.* New York: Cambridge University Press.

Swaney, J. H., Janik, C. J., Bond, S. J., & Hayes, J. R. (1991). Editing for comprehension: Improving the process through reading protocols. In E. R. Steinberg (Ed.), *Plain language: Principles and practice* (pp. 173–203). Detroit, MI: Wayne State University Press. (Original article published in 1981 as Document Design Project Tech. Rep. No. 14, Pittsburgh, PA: Carnegie Mellon University).

Swanson, H. L. (1990). Influence of metacognitive knowledge and aptitude on problem solving. *Journal of Educational Psychology, 82*(2), 306–314.

Swarts, H., Flower, L., & Hayes, J. R. (1980). *How headings in documents can mislead readers.* (Document Design Project Tech. Rep. No. 9). Pittsburgh, PA: Carnegie Mellon University, Communications Design Center.

Sweller, J., Chandler, P., Tierney, P., & Cooper, M. (1990). Cognitive load as a factor in the structuring of technical material. *Journal of Experimental Psychology: General, 119*(2), 176–192.

Swinney, D. A. (1979). Lexical access during sentence comprehension: (Re)consideration of context effects. *Journal of Verbal Learning & Verbal Behavior, 18*(6), 645–659.

Sy, T. (2010). What do you think of followers? Examining the content, structure, and consequences of implicit followership theories. *Organizational Behavior and Human Decision Processes, 113*(2), 73–84.

Symes, B. A., & Stewart, J. B. (1999). The relationship between metacognition and vocational indecision. *Canadian Journal of Counselling, 33*(3), 195–211.

Szpunar, K. K., Schellenberg, E. G., & Pliner, P. (2004). Liking and memory for musical stimuli as a function of exposure. *Journal of Experimental Psychology: Learning, Memory, and Cognition, 30*(2), 370–381.

Taber-Thomas, B. C. (2012). A model of the neural basis of predecisional processes: The fronto-limbic information acquisition network (Doctoral dissertation, University of Iowa, 2012). *Dissertation Abstracts International: Section B, 73*, 2717.

Taggart, B. M. (1993). An analysis of budget decision criteria and selected demographic factors of chief fiscal officers in higher education (Doctoral dissertation, The University of Connecticut, 1993). *Dissertation Abstracts International, 54*(10A), 3674.

Tait, A. R., Voepel-Lewis, T., Zikmund-Fisher, B. J., & Fagerlin, A. (2010). The effect of format on parents' understanding of the risks and benefits of clinical research: A comparison between text, tables, and graphics. *Journal of Health Communication, 15*(5), 487–501.

Talsma, D., Senkowski, D., Soto-Faraco, S., & Woldorff, M. G. (2010). The multifaceted interplay between attention and multisensory integration. *Trends in Cognitive Sciences, 14*(9), 400–410.

Tankard, J., Hendrickson, L., Silberman, J., Bliss, K., & Ghanem, S. (1991, August). *Media frames: Approaches to conceptualization and measurement.* Paper presented to the Association for Education in Journalism and Mass Communication, Boston.

Tankard, J. W. (2001). The empirical approach to the study of media framing. In S. D. Reese, O. H. Gandy, & A. E. Grant (Eds.), *Framing public life: Perspectives on media and our understanding of the social world* (pp. 95–106). Mahwah, NJ: Lawrence Erlbaum Associates.

Tannen, D. (1984). *Conversational style: Analyzing talk among friends.* Norwood, NJ: Ablex.

Tanner, R. J., Ferraro, R., Chartrand, T. L., Bettman, J. R., & van Baaren, R. (2008). Of chameleons and consumption: The impact of mimicry on choice and preferences. *Journal of Consumer Research, 34*(6), 754–766.

Tanofsky, R., Shepps, R. R., & O'Neill, P. J. (1969). Pattern analysis of biographical predictors of success as an insurance salesman. *Journal of Applied Psychology, 53*(2, Pt. 1), 136–139.

Tartter, V. C. (1980). Happy talk: Perceptual and acoustic effects of smiling on speech. *Perception and Psychophysics, 27*, 24–27.

Taylor, C. D. (1934). The relative legibility of black and white print. *Journal of Educational Psychology, 25*(8), 561–578.

Taylor, H., Fieldman, G., & Lahlou, S. (2005). The impact of a threatening e-mail reprimand on the recipient's blood pressure. *Journal of Managerial Psychology, 20*(1), 43–50.

Taylor, J. G., & Fragopanagos, N. F. (2005). The interaction of attention and emotion. *Neural Networks, 18*(4), 353–369.

Taylor, S. E. (1981). A categorization approach to stereotyping. In D. L. Hamilton (Ed.), *Cognitive processes in stereotyping and intergroup behavior* (pp. 88–114). Hillsdale: Lawrence Erlbaum Associates.

Taylor, S. E., & Fiske, S. T. (1975). Point of view and perceptions of causality. *Journal of Personality and Social Psychology, 32*(3), 439–445.

Taylor, S. E., & Fiske, S. T. (1978). Salience, attention, and attribution: Top of the head phenomena. In L. Berkowitz (Ed.), *Advances in experimental social psychology* (Vol. 11, pp. 249–288). New York: Academic Press.

Teigen, K. H. (1985). The novel and the familiar: Sources of interest in verbal information. *Current Psychology, 4*(3), 224–238.

Teigen, K. H. (1987). Intrinsic interest and the novelty-familiarity interaction. *Scandinavian Journal of Psychology, 28*(3), 199–210.

Tessler, R., & Sushelsky, L. (1978). Effects of eye contact and social status on the perception of a job applicant in an employment interviewing situation. *Journal of Vocational Behavior, 13*(3), 338–347.

Tetlock, P. (2005). *Expert political judgment: How good is it? How can we know?* Princeton, NJ: Princeton University Press.

Tetlock, P. E., Lerner, J. S., & Boettger, R. (1996). The dilution effect: Judgmental bias, conversational convention. or a bit of both? *European Journal of Social Psychology, 26*, 915–934.

Tews, M. J., Stafford, K., & Zhu, J. (2009). Beauty revisited: The impact of attractiveness, ability, and personality in the assessment of employment suitability. *International Journal of Selection and Assessment, 17*(1), 92–100.

Thakerar, J. N., & Giles, H. (1981). They are—so they spoke: Noncontent speech stereotypes. *Language & Communication, 1*(2–3), 255–261.

Tharanathan, A., Bullemer, P., Laberge, J., Reising, D. V., & Mclain, R. (2012). Impact of functional and schematic overview displays on console operators' situation awareness. *Journal of Cognitive Engineering and Decision Making, 6*(2), 141–164.

Thibadeau, R., Just, M. A., & Carpenter, P. A. (1982). A model of the time course and content of reading. *Cognitive Science, 6*, 157–203.

Thomas, J. P., & McFadyen, R. G. (1995). The confidence heuristic: A game-theoretic analysis. *Journal of Economic Psychology, 16*(1), 97–113.

Thomas-Hunt, M. C., Ogden, T. Y., & Neale, M. A. (2003). Who's really sharing? Effects of social and expert status on knowledge exchange within groups. *Management Science, 49*(4), 464–477.

Thomason, S. J., Weeks, M., Bernardin, H. J., & Kane, J. (2011). The differential focus of supervisors and peers in evaluations of managerial potential. *International Journal of Selection and Assessment, 19*(1), 82–97.

Thorndyke, P. W. (1977). Cognitive structures in comprehension and memory of narrative discourse. *Cognitive Psychology, 9*(1), 77–110.

Thorsteinson, T. J., Breier, J., Atwell, A., Hamilton, C., & Privette, M. (2008). Anchoring effects on performance judgments. *Organizational Behavior and Human Decision Processes, 107*(1), 29–40.

Tiedens, L. Z., & Fragale, A. R. (2003). Power moves: Complementarity in dominant and submissive nonverbal behavior. *Journal of Personality and Social Psychology, 84*(3), 558–568.

Tiedens, L. Z., & Linton, S. (2001). Judgment under emotional certainty and uncertainty: The effects of specific emotions on information processing. *Journal of Personality and Social Psychology, 81*(6), 973–988.

Timmermans, D., & Vlek, C. (1996). Effects on decision quality of supporting multi-attribute evaluation in groups. *Organizational Behavior and Human Decision Processes, 68*(2), 158–170.

Tindale, R. S. (1993). Decision errors made by individuals and groups. In N. J. Castellan (Ed.), *Individual and group decision making: Current issues* (pp. 109–124). Hillsdale, NJ: Lawrence Erlbaum Associates.

Tindale, R. S., & Davis, J. H. (1985). Individual and group reward allocation decisions in two situational contexts: Effects of relative need and performance. *Journal of Personality and Social Psychology, 48*(5), 1148–1161.

Tindale, R. S., Heath, L., Edwards, J., Posavac, E. J., Bryant, F. B., Suarez-Balcazar, Y., . . . & Myers, J. (1998). *Theory and research on small groups.* New York: Plenum Press.

Tindale, R. S., Kameda, T., & Hinsz, V. (2003). Group decision making: Review and integration. In M. A. Hogg & J. Cooper (Eds.), *Sage handbook of social psychology* (pp. 381–403). London: Sage.

Tindale, R. S., & Sheffey, S. (2002). Shared information, cognitive load, and group memory. *Group Processes & Intergroup Relations, 5*(1), 5–18.

Tindale, R. S., Sheffey, S., & Scott, L. A. (1993). Framing and group decision-making: Do cognitive changes parallel preference changes? *Organizational Behavior and Human Decision Processes, 55*(3), 470–485.

Tindale, R. S., Smith, C. M., Thomas, L. S., Filkins, J., & Sheffey, S. (1996). Shared representations and asymmetric social influence processes in small groups. In E. H. Witte & J. H. Davis (Eds.), *Understanding group behavior: Consensual action by small groups* (Vol. 1, pp. 81–103). Hillsdale, NJ: Lawrence Erlbaum Associates.

Tinker, M. A. (1963). *Legibility of print.* Ames, IA: Iowa State University Press.

Tinker, M. A. (1965). *Bases for effective reading.* Minneapolis, MN: University of Minnesota Press.

Tinker, M. A., & Paterson, D. G. (1928). Influence of type form on speed of reading. *Journal Of Applied Psychology, 12*(4), 359–368.

Todd, P., & Benbasat, I. (1991). An experimental investigation of the impact of computer based decision aids on decision making strategies. *Information Systems Research, 2*(2), 87–115.

Todorov, A., Mandisodza, A. N., Goren, A., & Hall, C. C. (2005). Inferences of competence from faces predict election outcomes. *Science, 308*(5728), 1623–1626.

Todorov, A., & Uleman, J. S. (2003). The efficiency of binding spontaneous trait inferences to actors' faces. *Journal of Experimental Social Psychology, 39*(6), 549–562.

Tolley, B. S., & Bogart, L. (1994). How readers process newspaper advertising. In E. M. Clark, T. C. Brock & D. W. Stewart (Eds.), *Attention, attitude, and affect in response to advertising* (pp. 69–77). Hillsdale, NJ: Lawrence Erlbaum Associates.

Tomkins, S. S. (1962). *Affect, imagery, consciousness: Vol. I. The positive affects.* New York: Springer Publishing Co.

Tormala, Z. L., Petty, R. E., & Brinol, P. (2002). Ease of retrieval effects in persuasion: The roles of elaboration and thought-confidence. *Personality and Social Psychology Bulletin, 28*(12), 1700–1712.

Tosi, H. (1971). Organizaton stress as a moderator of the relationship between influence and role response. *Academy of Management Journal, 14*, 7–20.

Totterdell, P. (2000). Catching moods and hitting runs: Mood linkage and subjective performance in professional sport teams. *Journal of Applied Psychology, 85*(6), 848–859.

Totterdell, P., Kellett, S., Teuchmann, K., & Briner, R. B. (1998). Evidence of mood linkage in work groups. *Journal of Personality and Social Psychology, 74*(6), 1504–1515.

Tourangeau, R., & Rasinski, K. A. (1988). Cognitive processes underlying context effects in attitude measurement. *Psychological Bulletin, 103*(3), 299–314.

Townsend, C., & Kahn, B. E. (2014). The "visual preference heuristic": The influence of visual versus verbal depiction on assortment processing, perceived variety, and choice overload. *Journal of Consumer Research, 40*(5), 993–1015.

Townsend, M. A. (1980). Schema activation in memory for prose. *Journal of Reading Behavior, 12*(1), 49–53.

Tracy, J. L., & Robins, R. W. (2008). The automaticity of emotion recognition. *Emotion, 8*(1), 81–95.

Treisman, A. M., & Davies, A. (1973). Divided attention to ear and eye. In S. Kornblum (Ed.), *Attention and performance IV* (pp. 101–117). London: Academic Press.

Treisman, A. M., & Geffen, G. (1967). Selective attention: Perception or response? *The Quarterly Journal of Experimental Psychology, 19*(1), 1–17.

Trollip, S. R., & Sales, G. (1986). Readability of computer-generated fill-justified text. *Human Factors, 28*(2), 159–163.

Trönnberg, C. C., & Hemlin, S. (2014). Lending decision making in banks: A critical incident study of loan officers. *European Management Journal, 32*(2), 362–372.

Trope, Y. (1986). Identification and inferential processes in dispositional attribution. *Psychological Review, 93*(3), 239–257.

Troutman, C. M., & Shanteau, J. (1976). Do consumers evaluate products by adding or averaging attribute information? *Journal of Consumer Research, 3*(2), 101–106.

Tsai, M. H., & Young, M. J. (2010). Anger, fear, and escalation of commitment. *Cognition and Emotion, 24*(6), 962–973.

Tsai, W., Yang, C., Leu, J., Lee, Y., & Yang, C. (2013). An integrated group decision making support model for corporate financing decisions. *Group Decision and Negotiation, 22*(6), 1103–1127.

Tsay, C. J. (2013). Sight over sound in the judgment of music performance. *Proceedings of the National Academy of Sciences, 110*(36), 14580–14585.

Tsay, C. J. (2014). The vision heuristic: Judging music ensembles by sight alone. *Organizational Behavior and Human Decision Processes, 124*(1), 24–33.

Tse, D., Langston, R. F., Kakeyama, M., Bethus, I., Spooner, P. A., Wood, E. R., . . . & Morris, R. G. (2007). Schemas and memory consolidation. *Science, 316*(5821), 76–82.

Tse, D., Takeuchi, T., Kakeyama, M., Kajii, Y., Okuno, H., Tohyama, C., . . . & Morris, R. G. (2011). Schema-dependent gene activation and memory encoding in neocortex. *Science, 333*(6044), 891–895.

Tumulty, K. (1990, September 3). Abortion polls yield contradictory results. *Austin American Statesman*, p. A29.

Turner, E. A., & Rommetveit, R. (1968). Focus of attention in recall of active and passive sentences. *Journal of Verbal Learning & Verbal Behavior, 7*(2), 543–548.

Tversky, A. (1969). Intransitivity of preferences. *Psychological Review, 76*(1), 31–48.

Tversky, A. (1972). Elimination by aspects: A theory of choice. *Psychological Review, 79*(4), 281–299.

Tversky, A., & Kahneman, D. (1971). Belief in the law of small numbers. *Psychological Bulletin, 76*(2), 105–110.

Tversky, A., & Kahneman, D. (1973). Availability: A heuristic for judging frequency and probability. *Cognitive Psychology, 5*(2), 207–232.

Tversky, A., & Kahneman, D. (1974). Judgment under uncertainty: Heuristics and biases. *Science, 185*(4157), 1124–1131.

Tversky, A., & Kahneman, D. (1980). Causal schemata in judgments under uncertainty. In M. Fishbein (Ed.), *Progress in social psychology* (pp. 49–72). Hillsdale, NJ: Erlbaum.

Tversky, A., & Kahneman, D. (1981). The framing of decisions and the psychology of choice. *Science, 211*(4481), 453–458.

Tversky, A., & Kahneman, D. (1983). Extensional versus intuitive reasoning: The conjunction fallacy in probability judgment. *Psychological Review, 90*(4), 293–315.

Tversky, A., & Kahneman, D. (1988). Rational choice and the framing of decisions. In D. E. Bell, H. Raiffa & A. Tversky (Eds.), *Decision making: Descriptive, normative, and prescriptive interactions* (pp. 167–192). New York: Cambridge University Press.

Tversky, A., & Sattath, S. (1979). Preference trees. *Psychological Review, 86*(6), 542–573.

Tversky, A., & Shafir, E. (1992). Choice under conflict: The dynamics of deferred decision. *Psychological Science, 3*(6), 358–361.

Tyebjee, T. T., & Bruno, A. V. (1984). A model of venture capitalist investment activity. *Management Science, 30*(9), 1051–1066.

Tyler, L. K., Wright, P., Randall, B., Marslen-Wilson, W. D., & Stamatakis, E. A. (2010). Reorganization of syntactic processing following left-hemisphere brain damage: Does right-hemisphere activity preserve function? *Brain, 133*(11), 3396–3408.

Uggerslev, K. L., Fassina, N. E., & Kraichy, D. (2012). Recruiting through the stages: A meta-analytic test of predictors of applicant attraction at different stages of the recruiting process. *Personnel Psychology, 65*(3), 597–660.

Uhlmann, E. L., & Cohen, G. L. (2005). Constructed criteria redefining merit to justify discrimination. *Psychological Science, 16*(6), 474–480.

Uleman, J. S. (1999). Spontaneous versus intentional inferences in impression formation. In S. Chaiken & Y. Trope (Eds.), *Dual-process theories in social psychology* (pp. 141–160). New York: Guilford Press.

Uleman, J. S., Newman, L. S., & Moskowitz, G. B. (1996). People as flexible interpreters: Evidence and issues from spontaneous trait inference. In M. P. Zanna (Ed.), *Advances in experimental social psychology* (Vol. 28, pp. 179–211). San Diego, CA: Academic Press.

Underwood, G., & Foulsham, T. (2006). Visual saliency and semantic incongruency influence eye movements when inspecting pictures. *The Quarterly Journal of Experimental Psychology, 59*(11), 1931–1949.

Urgesi, C., Moro, V., Candid, M., & Aglioti, S. M. (2006). Mapping implied body actions in the human motor system. *The Journal of Neuroscience, 26*(30), 7942–7949.

van Baaren, R. B., Holland, R. W., Kawakami, K., & van Knippenberg, A. (2004). Mimicry and prosocial behavior. *Psychological Science, 15,* 71–74.

van Baaren, R. B., Holland, R. W., Steenaert, B., & van Knippenberg, A. (2003). Mimicry for money: Behavioral consequences of imitation. *Journal of Experimental Social Psychology, 39,* 393–398.

van Bezooijen, R., Otto, S. A., & Heenan, T. A. (1983). Recognition of vocal expressions of emotion: A three-nation study to identify universal characteristics. *Journal of Cross-Cultural Psychology, 14*(4), 387–406.

VanBoven, L., Loewenstein, G., Welch, E., & Dunning, D. (2001). *The illusion of courage: Underestimating social risk aversion in self and others.* Working paper. Pittsburgh, PA: Department of Social and Decision Sciences, Carnegie Mellon.

Van den Oetelaar, S., Tellegen, S., & Wober, M. (1997). Affective response to reading: A comparison of reading in the United Kingdom and the Netherlands. In S. Totosy de Zepetnek & I. Sywenky (Eds.), *The systemic and empirical approach to literature and culture as theory and application* (pp. 505–513). Siegen: LUMIS.

Van den Stock, J., Righart, R., & De Gelder, B. (2007). Body expressions influence recognition of emotions in the face and voice. *Emotion, 7*(3), 487–494.

van Doorn, E. A., van Kleef, G. A., & van der Pligt, J. (2015). How emotional expressions shape prosocial behavior: Interpersonal effects of anger and disappointment on compliance with requests. *Motivation and Emotion, 39*(1), 128–141.

Van Dyne, L., & Saavedra, R. (1996). A naturalistic minority influence experiment: Effects on divergent thinking, conflict and originality in work-groups. *British Journal of Social Psychology, 35*(1), 151–167.

van Ginkel, W. P., & van Knippenberg, D. (2009). Knowledge about the distribution of information and group decision making: When and why does it work? *Organizational Behavior and Human Decision Processes, 108*(2), 218–229.

van Kesteren, M. T., Fernández, G., Norris, D. G., & Hermans, E. J. (2010). Persistent schema-dependent hippocampal-neocortical connectivity during memory encoding and postencoding rest in humans. *Proceedings of the National Academy of Sciences, 107*(16), 7550–7555.

van Kesteren, M. T., Rijpkema, M., Ruiter, D. J., Morris, R. G., & Fernández, G. (2014). Building on prior knowledge: Schema-dependent encoding processes relate to academic performance. *Journal of Cognitive Neuroscience, 26*(10), 2250–2261.

van Knippenberg, D., Lossie, N., & Wilke, H. (1994). In-group prototypicality and persuasion: Determinants of heuristic and systematic message processing. *British Journal of Social Psychology, 33,* 289–300.

van Leeuwen, E., van Dijk, W., & Kaynak, Ü. (2013). Of saints and sinners: How appeals to collective pride and guilt affect outgroup helping. *Group Processes & Intergroup Relations, 16*(6), 781–796.

van Leeuwen, M. L., & Neil Macrae, C. (2004). Is beautiful always good? Implicit benefits of facial attractiveness. *Social Cognition, 22*(6), 637–649.

Van Orden, G. C. (1987). A rows is a rose: Spelling, sound, and reading. *Memory & Cognition, 15*(3), 181–198.

van Raaij, W. F. (1976). *Direct monitoring of consumer information processing by eye movement recorder.* Unpublished paper, Tilburg University, Tilburg, Netherlands.

Van Rooy, L., Hendriks, B., Van Meurs, F., & Korzilius, H. (2006). Job advertisements in the Dutch mental health care sector: Preferences of potential applicants. In S. Carliner, J. P. Verckens & C. De Waile (Eds.), *Information and document design: Varieties on recent research* (pp. 61–84). The Netherlands: John Benjamins.

Van Swol, L. M. (2007). Perceived importance of information: The effects of mentioning information, shared information bias, ownership bias, reiteration, and confirmation bias. *Group Processes & Intergroup Relations, 10*(2), 239–256.

Van Swol, L. M., Savadori, L., & Sniezek, J. A. (2003). Factors that may affect the difficulty of uncovering hidden profiles. *Group Processes & Intergroup Relations, 6*(3), 285–304.

Van Swol, L. M., & Seinfeld, E. (2006). Differences between minority, majority, and unanimous group members in the communication of information. *Human Communication Research, 32*(2), 178–197.

Van Swol, L. M., & Sniezek, J. A. (2002). *Trust me, I'm and expert: Trust and confidence and acceptance of expert advice.* Paper presented at the 8th Conference on Behavioral Decision Research in Management (BDRM), Chicago.

Van Winter, J. A. (2007). The impact of selected cultural dimensions on international services vendor selection criteria: An exploratory investigation (Doctoral dissertation, George Washington University, 2008). *Dissertation Abstracts International: Section A, 69,* 299.

Van Zant, A. B., & Moore, D. A. (2015). Leaders' use of moral justifications increases policy support. *Psychological Science, 26*(6), 934–943.

van't Wout, M., Chang, L. J., & Sanfey, A. G. (2010). The influence of emotion regulation on social interactive decision-making. *Emotion, 10*(6), 815–821.

Vaughan, S. I. (1999). Information sharing and cognitive centrality: Patterns in small decision-making groups of executives. *Dissertation Abstracts International: Section B: The Sciences and Engineering, 60*(4-B), 1919.

Vauras, M., Hyönä, J., & Niemi, P. (1992). Comprehending coherent and incoherent texts: Evidence from eye movement patterns and recall performance. *Journal of Research in Reading, 15*(1), 39–54.

Velmans, M. (1991). Is human information processing conscious? *Behavioral and Brain Sciences*, *14*(4), 651–726.

Vendetti, M. S., Wu, A., Rowshanshad, E., Knowlton, B. J., & Holyoak, K. J. (2014). When reasoning modifies memory: Schematic assimilation triggered by analogical mapping. *Journal of Experimental Psychology: Learning, Memory, and Cognition*, *40*(4), 1172–1180.

Verplanken, B. W., & Weenig, M. W. H. (1993). Graphical energy labels and consumers' decisions about home appliances: A process tracing approach. *Journal of Economic Psychology*, *14*(4), 739–752.

Viscusi, W. K., Magat, W. A., & Huber, J. (1986). Informational regulation of consumer health risks: An empirical evaluation of hazard warnings. *The RAND Journal of Economics*, *17*(3), 351–365.

Viskontas, I. V., Quiroga, R. Q., & Fried, I. (2009). Human medial temporal lobe neurons respond preferentially to personally relevant images. *Proceedings of the National Academy of Sciences*, *106*(50), 21329–21334.

Vlaev, I., Chater, N., & Stewart, N. (2007). Financial prospect relativity: Context effects in financial decision-making under risk. *Journal of Behavioral Decision Making*, *20*(3), 273–304.

von Hippel, W., Jonides, I., Hilton, J. L., & Narayan, S. (1993). Inhibitory effect of schematic processing on perceptual encoding. *Journal of Personality and Social Psychology*, *64*(6), 921–935.

Von Winterfeldt, D., & Edwards, W. (1973). *Evaluation of complex stimuli using multi-attribute utility procedures.* Ann Arbor, MI: Technical Report, Engineering Psychology Laboratory, University of Michigan.

Von Winterfeldt, D., & Edwards, W. (1986). *Decision analysis and behavioral research.* Cambridge, UK: Cambridge University Press.

Voss, J. F., Greene, T. R., Post, T. A., & Penner, B. C. (1983). Problem solving skill in the social sciences. In G. H. Bower (Ed.), *The psychology of learning and motivation: Advances in research theory* (Vol. 17, pp. 165–213). New York: Academic Press.

Voss, J. F., Kennet, J., Wiley, J., & Schooler, T. Y. (1992). Experts at debate: The use of metaphor in the U.S. Senate debate on the Gulf crisis. *Metaphor & Symbolic Activity Special Issue: Expertise and Metaphor*, 7(3–4), 197–214.

Vuilleumier, P., Armony, J. L., Clarke, K., Husain, M., Driver, J., & Dolan, R. J. (2002). Neural response to emotional faces with and without awareness: Event-related fMRI in a parietal patient with visual extinction and spatial neglect. *Neuropsychologia*, *40*(12), 2156–2166.

Vuilleumier, P., & Pourtois, G. (2007). Distributed and interactive brain mechanisms during emotion face perception: Evidence from functional neuroimaging. *Neuropsychologia*, *45*(1), 174–194.

Vyas, N. M. (1981). Observation of industrial purchasing decisions on supplier choices for long-term contracts in naturalistic settings (Doctoral dissertation, University of South Carolina, 1981). *Dissertation Abstracts International*, *42*(05A), 2275.

Vytal, K., & Hamann, S. (2010). Neuroimaging support for discrete neural correlates of basic emotions: A voxel-based meta-analysis. *Journal of Cognitive Neuroscience*, *22*(12), 2864–2885.

Wade, K. J., & Kinicki, A. J. (1997). Subjective applicant qualifications and interpersonal attraction as mediators within a process model of interview selection decisions. *Journal of Vocational Behavior*, *50*(1), 23–40.

Wagenaar, W. A., Keren, G., & Lichtenstein, S. (1988). Islanders and hostages: Deep and surface structures of decision problems. *Acta Psychologica*, *67*, 175–189.

Wakefield, D. S. (1961). A test to determine the relative effectiveness of different styles, colors, and return order solicitation methods in sales letters (Doctoral dissertation, The University of Tennessee, 1961). *Dissertation Abstracts International*, *22*(10), 3453.

Wakslak, C. J., Smith, P. K., & Han, A. (2014). Using abstract language signals power. *Journal of Personality and Social Psychology*, *107*(1), 41–55.

Walker, B. A., Celsi, R. L., & Olson, J. C. (1986). Exploring the structural characteristics of consumers' knowledge. *Advances in Consumer Research*, *14*(1), 17–21.

Walker, B. A., & Olson, J. C. (1997). The activated self in consumer behavior: A cognitive structure perspective. In R. W. Belk (Ed.), *Research in consumer behavior* (pp. 135–171). Greenwich, CT: JAI Press.

Walker, B. A, Swasy, J. L., & Rethans, A. J. (1985). The impact of comparative advertising research. *Advances in Consumer Research*, *13*, 121–125.

Walker, H. J., Feild, H. S., Giles, W. F., Armenakis, A. A., & Bernerth, J. B. (2009). Displaying employee testimonials on recruitment web sites: Effects of communication media, employee race, and job seeker race on organizational attraction and information credibility. *Journal of Applied Psychology*, *94*(5), 1354–1364.

Walker, H. J., Feild, H. S., Giles, W. F., & Bernerth, J. B. (2008). The interactive effects of job advertisement characteristics and applicant experience on reactions to recruitment messages. *Journal of Occupational and Organizational Psychology*, *81*(4), 619–638.

Walker, O. C., Churchill, G. A., & Ford, N. M. (1975). Organizational determinants of the industrial salesman's role conflict and ambiguity. *Journal of Marketing*, *39*(1), 32–39.

Walker, P. (2008). Font tuning: A review and new experimental evidence. *Visual Cognition*, *16*(8), 1022–1058.

Wallace, J. F., & Newman, J. P. (1997). Neuroticism and the attentional mediation of dysregulatory psychopathology. *Cognitive Therapy and Research*, *21*(2), 135–156.

Wallace, J. F., Newman, J. P., & Bachorowski, J. A. (1991). Failures of response modulation: Impulsive behavior in anxious and impulsive individuals. *Journal of Research in Personality, 25*(1), 23–44.

Wallbott, H. G. (1998). Bodily expression of emotion. *European Journal of Social Psychology, 28*(6), 879–896.

Wallbott, H. G., & Scherer, K. R. (1986a). Cues and channels in emotion recognition. *Journal of Personality and Social Psychology, 51*(4), 690–699.

Wallbott, H. G., & Scherer, K. R. (1986b). How universal and specific is emotional experience? Evidence from 27 countries on five continents. *Social Science Information, 25*(4), 763–795.

Wallentin, M., Michaelsen, J. L. D., Rynne, I., & Nielsen, R. H. (2014). Lateralized task shift effects in Broca's and Wernicke's regions and in visual word form area are selective for conceptual content and reflect trial history. *NeuroImage, 101,* 276–288.

Waller, M. J., Gupta, N., & Giambatista, R. C. (2004). Effects of adaptive behaviors and shared mental models on control crew performance. *Management Science, 50*(11), 1534–1544.

Waller, W. S., & Zimbelman, M. F. (2003). A cognitive footprint in archival data: Generalizing the dilution effect from laboratory to field settings. *Organizational Behavior and Human Decision Processes, 91*(2), 254–268.

Wallsten, T. S. (1980). Processes and models to describe choice and inference. In T. S. Wallsten (Ed.), *Cognitive processes in choice and decision behavior* (pp. 215–237). Hillsdale, NJ: Erlbaum.

Wallsten, T. S. (1990). The costs and benefits of vague information. In R. Hogarth (Ed.), *Insights in decision making: A tribute to Hillel J. Einhorn* (pp. 28–43). Chicago, IL: University of Chicago Press.

Wallsten, T. S., & Barton, C. (1982). Processing probabilistic multidimensional information for decisions. *Journal of Experimental Psychology: Learning, Memory, and Cognition, 8*(5), 361–384.

Walsh, J. P. (1995). Managerial and organizational cognition: Notes from a trip down memory lane. *Organization Science, 6*(3), 280–321.

Walsh, J. P., Henderson, C. M., & Deighton, J. (1988, p. 207). Negotiated belief structures and decision performance: An empirical investigation. *Organizational Behavior and Human Decision Processes, 42*(2), 194–216.

Walton, D. N. (1992). *The place of emotion in argument.* University Park, PA: Pennsylvania State University Press.

Wang, S. H., Tse, D., & Morris, R. G. (2012). Anterior cingulate cortex in schema assimilation and expression. *Learning & Memory, 19*(8), 315–318.

Wänke, M., & Bless, H. (2000). The effects of subjective ease of retrieval on attitudinal judgments: The moderating role of processing motivation. In H. Bless & J. P. Forgas (Eds.), *The message within: The role of subjective experience in social cognition and behavior* (pp. 143–161). New York, NY: Psychology Press.

Wanner, H. E. (1968). On remembering, forgetting, and understanding sentences: A study of the deep structure hypothesis (Doctoral dissertation, Harvard University, 1968). *American Doctoral Dissertations, X1968,* 0158.

Warren, J., Kuhn, D., & Weinstock, M. (2010). How do jurors argue with one another? *Judgment and Decision Making, 5*(1), 64–71.

Warren, R. E., Warren, N. T., Green, J. P., & Bresnick, J. H. (1978). Multiple semantic encoding of homophones and homographs in contexts biasing dominant or subordinate meanings. *Memory & Cognition, 6*(4), 364–371.

Watson, D. (1989). Strangers' ratings of the five robust personality factors: Evidence of a surprising convergence with self-report. *Journal of Personality and Social Psychology, 57*(1), 120–128.

Weaver, K., Garcia, S. M., & Schwarz, N. (2012). The presenter's paradox. *Journal of Consumer Research, 39*(3), 445–460.

Weber, E. U., Siebenmorgen, N., & Weber, M. (2005). Communicating asset risk: How name recognition and the format of historic volatility information affect risk perception and investment decisions. *Risk Analysis, 25*(3), 597–609.

Webster, E. D. (Ed.). (1964). *Decision-making in the employment interview.* Montreal, Canada: McGill University.

Wegener, D. T., Petty, R. E., & Klein, D. J. (1994). Effects of mood on high elaboration attitude change: The mediating role of likelihood judgments. *European Journal of Social Psychology Special Issue: Affect in Social Judgments and Cognition, 24*(1), 25–43.

Wegener, D. T., Petty, R. E., & Smith, S. M. (1995). Positive mood can increase or decrease message scrutiny: The hedonic contingency view of mood and message processing. *Journal of Personality and Social Psychology, 69*(1), 5–15.

Wehrle, T., Kaiser, S., Schmidt, S., & Scherer, K. R. (2000). Studying the dynamics of emotional expression using synthesized facial muscle movements. *Journal of Personality and Social Psychology, 78*(1), 105–119.

Weick, M., & Guinote, A. (2008). When subjective experiences matter: Power increases reliance on the ease of retrieval. *Journal of Personality and Social Psychology, 94*(6), 956–970.

Weigert, A. J. (1991). *Mixed emotions: Certain steps toward understanding ambivalence.* New York: State University of New York Press.

Weinstein, N. D., Lyon, J. E., Sandman, P. M., & Cuite, C. L. (1998). Experimental evidence for stages of health behavior change: The precaution adoption process model applied to home radon testing. *Health Psychology, 17*(5), 445–453.

Weisbuch, M., Mackie, D. M., & Garcia-Marques, T. (2003). Prior source exposure and persuasion: Further evidence for misattributional processes. *Personality and Social Psychology Bulletin, 29*(6), 691–700.

Weiss, H. M., & Adler, S. (1981). Cognitive complexity and the structure of implicit leadership theories. *Journal of Applied Psychology, 66*(1), 69–78.

Weitz, B. A. (1978). Relationship between salesperson performance and understanding of customer decision making. *Journal of Marketing Research, 15*(4), 501–516.

Weldon, D. E., & Malpass, R. S. (1981). Effects of attitudinal, cognitive, and situational variables on recall of biased communications. *Journal of Personality and Social Psychology, 40*(1), 39–52.

Welles, G. (1986). We're in the habit of impulsive buying. *USA Today*, May 21, p. 1.

Wells, G. L., & Petty, R. E. (1980). The effects of overt head movements on persuasion: Compatibility and incompatibility of responses. *Basic and Applied Social Psychology, 1*(3), 219–230.

Wells, W. A. (1974). Venture capital decision-making (Doctoral dissertation, Carnegie Mellon University, 1974). *Dissertation Abstracts International, 35*(12A), 7475.

Werth, L., & Strack, F. (2003). An inferential approach to the knew-it-all-along effect. *Memory, 11*(4–5), 411–419.

Westen, D. (2007). *The political brain: The role of emotion in deciding the fate of the nation.* New York: Public Affairs.

Westendorp, P. (1995, June). *Testing pictures, texts, and animations for procedural instructions.* Paper presented at the Conference on Verbal Communications in Professional Settings, Utrecht, Netherlands.

Westphal, J. D., & Bednar, M. K. (2005). Pluralistic ignorance in corporate boards and firms' strategic persistence in response to low firm performance. *Administrative Science Quarterly, 50*(2), 262–298.

Whalen, D. H., & Blanchard, F. A. (1982). Effects of photographic evidence on mock juror judgement. *Journal of Applied Social Psychology, 12*(1), 30–41.

Wheeler, D. D. (1970). Processes in word recognition. *Cognitive Psychology, 1*, 59–85.

Wheildon, C. (1995). *Type and layout.* Berkeley, CA: Strathmoor Press.

Whiskey, E., & Taylor, D. (2005). Evaluation of an antipsychotic information sheet for patients. *International Journal of Psychiatry in Clinical Practice, 9*(4), 264–270.

White, G. L., & Maltzman, I. (1978). Pupillary activity while listening to verbal passages. *Journal of Research in Personality, 12*(3), 361–369.

White, M. (1996). Anger recognition is independent of spatial attention. *New Zealand Journal of Psychology, 25*(1), 30–35.

White, P. A. (1988). Causal processing: Origins and development. *Psychological Bulletin, 104*(1), 36–52.

White, S. J., & Liversedge, S. P. (2006). Linguistic and nonlinguistic influences on the eyes' landing positions during reading. *The Quarterly Journal of Experimental Psychology, 59*(4), 760–782.

White, V., Webster, B., & Wakefield, M. (2008). Do graphic health warning labels have an impact on adolescents' smoking-related beliefs and behaviours? *Addiction, 103*(9), 1562–1571.

Whitmore, R. C. (2014). The use of heuristics by senior executives when selecting senior-level executive direct reports (Doctoral dissertation, Fielding Graduate University, 2014). *Dissertation Abstracts International: Section A, 74*(11-A)(E).

Whittler, T. E. (1994). Eliciting consumer choice heuristics: Sales representatives' persuasion strategies. *Journal of Personal Selling & Sales Management, 14*(4), 41–53.

Whittlesea, B. W. (1997). Production, evaluation, and preservation of experiences: Constructive processing in remembering and performance tasks. In D. L. Medin (Ed.), *The psychology of learning and motivation: Advances in research and theory* (Vol. 37, pp. 211–264). San Diego, CA: Academic Press.

Whittlesea, B. W., Jacoby, L. L., & Girard, K. (1990). Illusions of immediate memory: Evidence of an attributional basis for feelings of familiarity and perceptual quality. *Journal of Memory and Language, 29*(6), 716–732.

Whittlesea, B. W., & Williams, L. D. (2001). The discrepancy-attribution hypothesis: II. Expectation, uncertainty, surprise and feelings of familiarity. *Journal of Experimental Psychology: Learning, Memory and Cognition, 27*(1), 14–33.

Whyte, G., & Sebenius, J. K. (1997). The effect of multiple anchors on anchoring in individual and group judgment. *Organizational Behavior and Human Decision Processes, 69*(1), 75–85.

Wiener, Y., & Schneiderman, M. L. (1974). Use of job information as a criterion in employment decisions of interviewers. *Journal of Applied Psychology, 59*(6), 699–704.

Wiethoff, S., Wildgruber, D., Kreifelts, B., Becker, H., Herbert, C., Grodd, W., & Ethofer, T. (2008). Cerebral processing of emotional prosody—influence of acoustic parameters and arousal. *Neuroimage, 39*(2), 885–893.

Wigboldus, D. H., Dijksterhuis, A., & Van Knippenberg, A. (2003). When stereotypes get in the way: Stereotypes obstruct stereotype-inconsistent trait inferences. *Journal of Personality and Social Psychology, 84*(3), 470–484.

Wiggins, A. H. (1967). Effects of three typographical variables on speed of reading. *Journal of Typographic Research, 1*, 5–18.

Wildgruber, D., Ethofer, T., Grandjean, D., & Kreifelts, B. (2009). A cerebral network model of speech prosody comprehension. *International Journal of Speech-Language Pathology, 11*(4), 277–281.

Will, K. E., Decina, L. E., Maple, E. L., & Perkins, A. M. (2015). Examining the relative effectiveness of different message framing strategies for child passenger safety: Recommendations for increased comprehension and compliance. *Accident Analysis & Prevention, 79*, 170–181.

Willer, R. (2004). The effects of government-issued terror warnings on presidential approval ratings. *Current Research in Social Psychology, 10*(1), 1–12.

Williams, J. M. (1990). Women's preferences for and satisfaction with the convenience services offered by a department store (Doctoral dissertation, Texas Woman's University, 1990). *Dissertation Abstracts International, 51*(06B), 2848.

Williams, L. M., Brammer, M. J., Skerrett, D., Lagopolous, J., Rennie, C., Kozek, K., . . . & Gordon, E. (2000). The neural correlates of orienting: An integration of fMRI and skin conductance orienting. *Neuroreport, 11*(13), 3011–3015.

Williams, T. R., & Spyridakis, J. H. (1992). Visual discriminability of headings in text. *Professional Communication, IEEE Transactions on, 35*(2), 64–70.

Willis, J., & Todorov, A. (2006). First impressions making up your mind after a 100-ms exposure to a face. *Psychological Science, 17*(7), 592–598.

Wilson, M. G., Northcraft, G. B., & Neale, M. A. (1989a). Information competition and vividness effects in on-line judgments. *Organizational Behavior and Human Decision Processes, 44*(1), 132–139.

Wilson, R. A., & Keil, F. C. (Eds.). (1999). *The MIT encyclopedia of the cognitive sciences.* Cambridge, MA: The MIT Press.

Wilson, T. D., & Brekke, N. (1994). Mental contamination and mental correction: Unwanted influences on judgments and evaluations. *Psychological Bulletin, 116*(1), 117–142.

Wilson, T. D., Kraft, D., & Dunn, D. S. (1989b). The disruptive effects of explaining attitudes: The moderating effect of knowledge about the attitude object. *Journal of Experimental Social Psychology, 25*(5), 379–400.

Wilson, T. D., Lisle, D. J., Schooler, J. W., Hodges, S. D., Klaaren, K. J., & LaFleur, S. J. (1993). Introspecting about reasons can reduce post-choice satisfaction. *Personality and Social Psychology Bulletin, 19*(3), 331–339.

Wilson, T. D., & Schooler, J. W. (1991). Thinking too much: Introspection can reduce the quality of preferences and decisions. *Journal of Personality and Social Psychology, 60*(2), 181–192.

Windschitl, P. D., & Weber, E. U. (1999). The interpretation of "likely" depends on the context, but "70%" is 70%—right?: The influence of associative processes on perceived certainty. *Journal of Experimental Psychology: Learning, Memory, and Cognition, 25*(6), 1514–1533.

Wingenfeld, K., Mensebach, C., Driessen, M., Bullig, R., Hartje, W., & Beblo, T. (2006). Attention bias towards personally relevant stimuli: The individual emotional Stroop task. *Psychological Reports, 99*(3), 781–793.

Winkielman, P., Berridge, K. C., & Wilbarger, J. L. (2005). Unconscious affective reactions to masked happy versus angry faces influence consumption behavior and judgments of value. *Personality and Social Psychology Bulletin, 31*(1), 121–135.

Winkielman, P., & Cacioppo, J. T. (2001). Mind at ease puts a smile on the face: Psychophysiological evidence that processing facilitation elicits positive affect. *Journal of Personality and Social Psychology, 81*(6), 989–1000.

Winkielman, P., & Fazendeiro, T. A. (2003). *The role of conceptual fluency in preference and memory.* Unpublished manuscript.

Winkielman, P., Halberstadt, J., Fazendeiro, T., & Catty, S. (2006). Prototypes are attractive because they are easy on the mind. *Psychological Science, 17*(9), 799–806.

Winkielman, P., Schwarz, N., Fazendeiro, T., & Reber, R. (2003a). The hedonic marking of processing fluency: Implications for evaluative judgment. In J. Musch & K. C. Klauer (Eds.), *The psychology of evaluation: Affective processes in cognition and emotion* (pp. 189–217). Mahwah, NJ: Erlbaum.

Winkielman, P., Schwarz, N., Reber, R., & Fazendeiro, T. A. (2003b). Cognitive and affective consequences of visual fluency: When seeing is easy on the mind. In L. M. Scott & R. Batra (Eds.), *Persuasive imagery: A consumer response perspective* (pp. 75–89). Mahwah, NJ: Lawrence Erlbaum Associates.

Winn, A. R. (1984). A cognitive social information processing approach to leadership perceptions (Doctoral dissertation, University of South Carolina, 1984). *Dissertation Abstracts International, 46*(02A), 0464.

Winn, W. (1991). Learning from maps and diagrams. *Educational Psychology Review, 3*(3), 211–247.

Winquist, J. R., & Franz, T. M. (2008). Does the Stepladder Technique improve group decision making? A series of failed replications. *Group Dynamics: Theory, Research, and Practice, 12*(4), 255–267.

Winter, L., & Uleman, J. S. (1984). When are social judgments made? Evidence for the spontaneousness of trait inferences. *Journal of Personality and Social Psychology, 47*(2), 237–252.

Winter, P. A. (1996). Applicant evaluations of formal position advertisements: The influence of sex, job message content, and information order. *Journal of Personnel Evaluation in Education, 10*, 105–116.

Wish, M., D'Andrade, R. G., & Goodnow, J. E. (1980). Dimensions of interpersonal communication: Correspondences between structures for speech acts and bipolar scales. *Journal of Personality and Social Psychology, 39*(5), 848–860.

Witherspoon, D., & Allan, L. G. (1985). The effect of a prior presentation on temporal judgments in a perceptual identification task. *Memory & Cognition, 13*(2), 101–111.

Witte, K., & Allen, M. (1996, November). *When do scare tactics work? A meta-analysis of fear appeals.* Paper presented at the Annual Meeting of the Speech Communication Association, San Diego, California.

Witte, K., & Allen, M. (2000). A meta-analysis of fear appeals: Implications for effective public health campaigns. *Health Education & Behavior, 27*(5), 591–615.

Witte, K., & Allen, M. (2000). A meta-analysis of fear appeals: Implications for effective public health campaigns. *Health Education and Behavior, 27*(5), 591–615.

Wittenbaum, G. M., & Bowman, J. M. (2004). A social validation explanation for mutual enhancement. *Journal of Experimental Social Psychology, 40*(2), 169–184.

Wittenbaum, G. M., Hubbell, A. P., & Zuckerman, C. (1999). Mutual enhancement: Toward an understanding of the collective preference for shared information. *Journal of Personality and Social Psychology, 77*(5), 967–978.

Woehr, D. J. (1994). Understanding frame-of-reference training: The impact of training on the recall of performance information. *Journal of Applied Psychology, 79*(4), 525–534.

Wofford, J. C., Goodwin, V. L., & Whittington, J. L. (1998). A field study of a cognitive approach to understanding transformational and transactional leadership. *Leadership Quarterly, 9*, 55–84.

Wogalter, M. S., Barlow, T., & Murphy, S. A. (1995). Compliance to owner's manual warnings: Influence of familiarity and the placement of a supplemental directive. *Ergonomics, 38*(6), 1081–1091.

Wogalter, M. S., Godfrey, S. S., Fontenelle, G. A., Desaulniers, D. R., Rothstein, P. R., & Laughery, K. R. (1987). Effectiveness of warnings. *Human Factors: The Journal of the Human Factors and Ergonomics Society, 29*(5), 599–612.

Wogalter, M. S., Sojourner, R. J., & Brelsford, J. W. (1997). Comprehension and retention of safety pictorials. *Ergonomics, 40*(5), 531–542.

Wolford, G., & Morrison, F. (1980). Processing of unattended visual information. *Memory & Cognition, 8*(6), 521–527.

Wong, B., Cronin-Golomb, A., & Neargarder, S. (2005). Patterns of visual scanning as predictors of emotion identification in normal aging. *Neuropsychology, 19*(6), 739–749.

Wong, E. (2001, April 5), A stinging office memo boomerangs; Chief executive is criticized after upbraiding workers by e-mail. *New York Times,* p. C1.

Wong, K. F. E., & Kwong, J. Y. (2005). Comparing two tiny giants or two huge dwarfs? Preference reversals owing to number size framing. *Organizational Behavior and Human Decision Processes, 98*(1), 54–65.

Wood, J. V., Taylor, S. E., & Lichtman, R. R. (1985a). Social comparison in adjustment to breast cancer. *Journal of Personality and Social Psychology, 49*(5), 1169–1183.

Wood, W., & Kallgren, C. A. (1988). Communicator attributes and persuasion: Recipients' access to attitude-relevant information in memory. *Personality and Social Psychology Bulletin, 14*(1), 172–182.

Wood, W., Kallgren, C. A., & Preisler, R. M. (1985b). Access to attitude-relevant information in memory as a determinant of persuasion: The role of message attributes. *Journal of Experimental Social Psychology, 21*(1), 73–85.

Woodall, W. G., & Burgoon, J. K. (1983). Talking fast and changing attitudes: A critique and clarification. *Journal of Nonverbal Behavior, 8*(2), 126–142.

Woodall, W. G., & Folger, J. P. (1981). Encoding specificity and nonverbal cue context: An expansion of episodic memory research. *Communication Monographs, 48*(1), 39–53.

Woodall, W. G., & Folger, J. P. (1985). Nonverbal cue context and episodic memory: On the availability and endurance of nonverbal behaviors as retrieval cues. *Communication Monographs, 52*(4), 319–333.

Woodburn, J. L. (2014). A case study analysis of middle school principals' teacher selection criteria (Doctoral dissertation, University of Maryland, College Park, 2014). *Dissertation Abstracts International: Section A, 74,* (8-A)(E).

Woodside, A. G., & Davenport, W. J. (1974). The effect of salesmen similarity and expertise on consumer purchasing behavior. *Journal of Marketing Research, 11*(2), 198–202.

Woolgar, A., Williams, M. A., & Rich, A. N. (2015). Attention enhances multi-voxel representation of novel objects in frontal, parietal and visual cortices. *NeuroImage, 109,* 429–437.

Woolley, A. W., Gerbasi, M. E., Chabris, C. F., Kosslyn, S. M., & Hackman, J. R. (2008). Bringing in the experts: How team composition and collaborative planning jointly shape analytic effectiveness. *Small Group Research, 39*(3), 352–371.

Workman, J. E., Johnson, K. K., & Hadeler, B. (1993). The influence of clothing on students' interpretative and extended inferences about a teaching assistant. *College Student Journal, 27*(1), 119–128.

Worth, L. T., & Mackie, D. M. (1987). Cognitive mediation of positive affect in persuasion. *Social Cognition, 5*(1), 76–94.

Wright, D. B., & Hall, M. (2007). How a "reasonable doubt" instruction affects decisions of guilt. *Basic and Applied Social Psychology, 29*(1), 91–98.

Wright, P. (1968). Reading to learn. *Chemistry in Britain, 4,* 445–450.

Wright, P. (1974). *The use of phased, noncompensatory strategies in decisions between multi-attribute products.* (Research Paper 223). Stanford, CA: Graduate School of Business, Stanford University.

Wright, P. (1975). Consumer choice strategies: Simplifying vs. optimizing. *Journal of Marketing Research, 12*(1), 60–67.

Wright, P. (1977). Decision making as a factor in the ease of using numerical tables. *Ergonomics, 20*(1), 91–96.

Wright, P., Creighton, P., & Threlfall, S. M. (1982). Some factors determining when instructions will be read. *Ergonomics, 25*(3), 225–237.

Wright, P., & Reid, F. (1973). Written information: Some alternatives to prose for expressing the outcomes of complex contingencies. *Journal of Applied Psychology, 57*(2), 160–166.

Wright, P., & Rip, P. D. (1980). Product class advertising effects on first-time buyers' decision strategies. *Journal of Consumer Research, 7*(2), 176–188.

Wright, W. F. (1979). Properties of judgment models in a financial setting. *Organizational Behavior & Human Performance, 23*(1), 73–85.

Wright, W. F., & Bower, G. H. (1992). Mood effects on subjective probability assessment. *Organizational Behavior and Human Decision Processes, 52*(2), 276–291.

Wyer, R. S., & Carlston, D. E. (1979). *Social cognition, inference, and attribution.* Hillsdale, NJ: Lawrence Erlbaum Associates.

Wyer, R. S., Clore, G. L., & Isbell, L. M. (1999). Affect and information processing. In M. P. Zanna (Ed.), *Advances in experimental social psychology* (Vol. 31, pp. 1–77). San Diego, CA: Academic Press.

Yadav, M. S. (1994). How buyers evaluate product bundles: A model of anchoring and adjustment. *Journal of Consumer Research, 21*(2), 342–353.

Yalch, R. F., & Elmore-Yalch, R. (1984). The effect of numbers on the route to persuasion. *Journal of Consumer Research, 11*(1), 522–527.

Yamani, Y., & McCarley, J. S. (2010). Visual search asymmetries within color-coded and intensity-coded displays. *Journal of Experimental Psychology: Applied, 16*(2), 124–132.

Yammarino, F. J., & Bass, B. M. (1990). Long-term forecasting of transformational leadership and its effects among naval officers. In K. E. Clark & M. B. Clark (Eds.), *Measures of leadership* (pp. 151–170). West Orange, NJ: Leadership Library of America.

Yarbus, A. L. (1967). *Eye movements and vision.* Translated from Russian by Basil Haigh. New York: Plenum Press.

Yarlas, A. S. (1999). Learning as a predictor of interest: The knowledge-schema theory of cognitive interest (Doctoral dissertation, University of California, 1999). *Dissertation Abstracts International: Section B, 59,* 5130.

Yates, J. F., Jagacinski, C. M., & Faber, M. D. (1978). Evaluation of partially described multiattribute options. *Organizational Behavior & Human Performance, 21*(2), 240–251.

Yates, J. F., Price, P. C., Lee, J. W., & Ramirez, J. (1996). Good probabilistic forecasters: The "consumer's" perspective. *International Journal of Forecasting, 12,* 41–56.

Yates, J. F., Veinott, E. S., & Patalano, A. L. (2003). Hard decisions, bad decisions: On decision quality and decision aiding. In S. L. Schneider & J. Shanteau (Eds.), *Emerging perspectives on judgment and decision research* (pp. 13–63). Cambridge, UK: Cambridge University Press.

Yeh, M., & Wickens, C. D. (2001). Attentional filtering in the design of electronic map displays: A comparison of color coding, intensity coding, and decluttering techniques. *Human Factors: The Journal of the Human Factors and Ergonomics Society, 43*(4), 543–562.

Yekovich, F. R., & Walker, C. H. (1978). Identifying and using referents in sentence comprehension. *Journal of Verbal Learning & Verbal Behavior, 17*(3), 265–277.

Yeung, C. W., & Wyer, R. S. (2004). Affect, appraisal, and consumer judgment. *Journal of Consumer Research, 31*(2), 412–424.

Yi, Y. J. (1990). The effects of contextual priming in print advertisements. *Journal of Consumer Research, 17*(2), 215–222.

Young, D. M., & Beier, E. G. (1977). The role of applicant nonverbal communication in the employment interview. *Journal of Employment Counseling, 14*(4), 154–165.

Young, G. R., II, Price, K. H., & Claybrook, C. (2001). Small group predictions on an uncertain outcome: The effect of nondiagnostic information. *Theory and Decision, 50*(2), 149–167.

Young, M. J., Tiedens, L. Z., Jung, H., & Tsai, M. H. (2011). Mad enough to see the other side: Anger and the search for disconfirming information. *Cognition and Emotion, 25*(1), 10–21.

Young, R. O. (1989). Cognitive processes in argumentation: An exploratory study of management consulting expertise (Doctoral dissertation, Carnegie Mellon University, 1989). *Dissertation Abstracts International, 50*(08B), 3764.

Young, S. L., & Wogalter, M. S. (1990). Comprehension and memory of instruction manual warnings: Conspicuous print and pictorial icons. *Human Factors: The Journal of the Human Factors and Ergonomics Society, 32*(6), 637–649.

Young, T. J., & French, L. A. (1998). Heights of US presidents: A trend analysis for 1948–1996. *Perceptual and Motor Skills, 87*(1), 321–322.

Yuce, P., & Highhouse, S. (1998). Effects of attribute set size and pay ambiguity on reactions to "help wanted" advertisements. *Journal of Organizational Behavior, 19*(4), 337–352.

Yukl, G. A., & Falbe, C. M. (1990). Influence tactics and objectives in upward, downward, and lateral influence attempts. *Journal of Applied Psychology, 75*(2), 132–140.

Yukl, G. A., & Tracey, J. B. (1992). Consequences of influence tactics used with subordinates, peers, and the boss. *Journal of Applied Psychology, 77*, 525–535.

Zaccaro, Stephen J. (2001). *The nature of executive leadership: A conceptual and empirical analysis of success.* Washington, DC: American Psychological Association.

Zacharakis, A. L., & Meyer, G. D. (1998). A lack of insight: Do venture capitalists really understand their own decision process? *Journal of Business Benturing, 13*(1), 57–76.

Zacharakis, A. L., & Meyer, G. D. (2000). The potential of actuarial decision models: Can they improve the venture capital investment decision? *Journal of Business Venturing, 15*(4), 323–346.

Zadny, J., & Gerard, H. B. (1974). Attributed intentions and informational selectivity. *Journal of Experimental Social Psychology, 10*(1), 34–52.

Zahn-Waxler, C., Radke-Yarrow, M., Wagner, E., & Chapman, M. (1992). Development of concern for others. *Developmental Psychology, 28*(1), 126–136.

Zajonc, R. B. (1968). Attitudinal effects of mere exposure. *Journal of Personality and Social Psychology, 9*(2, Pt. 2), 1–27.

Zebel, S., Zimmermann, A., Tendayi Viki, G., & Doosje, B. (2008). Dehumanization and guilt as distinct but related predictors of support for reparation policies. *Political Psychology, 29*(2), 193–219.

Zeelenberg, M., & Pieters, R. (1999). Comparing service delivery to what might have been: Behavioral responses to regret and disappointment. *Journal of Service Research, 2*, 86–97.

Zhang, J. (1997). The nature of external representations in problem solving. *Cognitive Science, 21*(2), 179–217.

Zhang, J., & Norman, D. A. (1994). Representations in distributed cognitive tasks. *Cognitive Science, 18*(1), 87–122.

Zhang, S., Kardes, F. R., & Cronley, M. L. (2002). Comparative advertising: Effects of structural alignability on target brand evaluations. *Journal of Consumer Psychology, 12*(4), 303–311.

Zhuang, J., Tyler, L. K., Randall, B., Stamatakis, E. A., & Marslen-Wilson, W. D. (2014). Optimally efficient neural systems for processing spoken language. *Cerebral Cortex, 24*(4), 908–918.

Ziebarth, G. E. (2012). Information search and selection of heuristics in multi-attribute choice tasks (Doctoral dissertation, University of South Dakota, 2012). *Dissertation Abstracts International: Section B, 72*, 7078.

Zillmann, D. (2002). Exemplification theory of media influence. In J. Bryant & D. Zillmann (Eds.), *Media effects: Advances in theory and research* (pp. 19–42). Mahwah, NJ: Lawrence Erlbaum.

Zillmann, D., Gibson, R., Sundar, S. S., & Perkins, J. W. (1996). Effects of exemplification in news reports on the perception of social issues. *Journalism & Mass Communication Quarterly, 73*, 427–444.

Zuber, J. A., Crott, H. W., & Werner, J. (1992). Choice shift and group polarization: An analysis of the status of arguments and social decision schemes. *Journal of Personality and Social Psychology, 62*(1), 50–61.

Zuckerman, M., DePaulo, B. M., & Rosenthal, R. (1981). Verbal and nonverbal communication of deception. In L. Berkowitz (Ed.), *Advances in experimental social psychology* (Vol. 14, pp. 1–59). New York: Academic Press.

Zwaan, R. A., & Brown, C. M. (1996). The influence of language proficiency and comprehension skill on situation-model construction. *Discourse Processes, 21*(3), 289–327.

FIGURE CREDITS

1.1 "Decision makers spontaneously create decision matrices," © Oxford University Press. Journal of Consumer Research, 21(1), 83–99; Coupey, E. (1994). Restructuring: Constructive processing of information displays in consumer choice; Figure 2. Sample coding from a subject's notes, page 91.

3.6 "A reader's eye-fixation pattern reading an online newspaper," © UPA. Journal of Usability Studies, 4(4), 147–165; Gibbs, W. J, and Bernas, R. S. (2009). Visual Attention in Newspaper versus TV-Oriented News Websites; Figure 5. Eye path trace of most central fixation sequence for NYT, page 158.

3.8 "A viewer's eye-fixation pattern interpreting a line graph," Journal of Experimental Psychology: Applied, 4(2), 75-100; Carpenter, P. A., and Shah, P. (1998). A model of the perceptual and conceptual processes in graph comprehension; Figure 5. A diagram of the number of transitions between regions from a prototypical trial, page 86.

4.3 "How easy are these drawings to comprehend without captions?" © Springer. Memory & Cognition, 3(2), 216–220; Bower, G. H., Karlin, M. B., and Dueck, A. (1975). Comprehension and memory for pictures; Figure 1. Droodles of experiment 1, page 217.

6.2 "Audiences scan facial expressions to infer emotions," Third IEEE International Conference on Automatic Face and Gesture Recognition, 200–205; Lyons, M. J., Akamatsu, S., Kamachi, M., and Gyoba, J. (1998). Coding Facial Expressions with Gabor Wavelets; Figure 4. Examples of images from the facial expression database, page 203.

7.3 "High-speed photography captures the sequence of emotional appraisal," Proceedings of the Xth Conference of the International Society for Research on Emotions, 82–86; Kaiser, S., Wehrle, T., & Schmidt, S. (1998). Emotional episodes, facial expressions, and reported feelings in human-computer interactions; Figure 1. Game situation: The unexpected and sudden appearance of an unknown enemy that roars like a lion, page 84. Figure 2. Game situation: Start of a new game level that is much faster than before, page 84. Figure 5. Game situation: At the end of level 9, message from AMIGO that he will disappear, page 86.

There are instances where we have been unable to trace or contact the copyright holder. If notified the publisher will be pleased to rectify any errors or omissions at the earliest opportunity.

INDEX

Note: page numbers in *italics* indicate figures and tables.